READINGS
IN
MISSIONARY
ANTHROPOLOGY
II

The William Carey Library Series on Applied Cultural Anthropology

William A. Smalley, Editor

READINGS IN MISSIONARY ANTHROPOLOGY II

enlarged 1978 edition

edited by
William A. Smalley

William Carey Library

533 HERMOSA STREET • SOUTH PASADENA, CALIF. 91030

Library of Congress Cataloging in Publication Data

Smalley, William Allen, comp.
    Readings in missionary anthropology II.

    (William Carey Library series on applied cultural
anthropology)
    Articles originally published in Practical
anthropology.
    Includes bibliographical references.
    1. Missions--Addresses, essays, lectures.
I. Practical anthropology. II. Title.
BV2070.S55 1978   266'.001   78-6009
ISBN 0-87808-731-1

Published by the William Carey Library
533 Hermosa Street
South Pasadena, California 91030
Telephone (213) 798-0819

In accord with some of the most recent thinking in the academic
press, the William Carey Library is pleased to present this
scholarly book which has been prepared from an author-edited
and author-prepared camera ready copy.

PRINTED IN THE UNITED STATES OF AMERICA

CONTENTS

Authors and Order of Publication
Preface
Introduction: Mission and Anthropology, *Paul G. Hiebert*

CULTURAL SYSTEMS AND MANIFESTATIONS

Part I: Religion and World View

Part II: Social Structure

Part III: Sex and Marriage

Part IV: Myth

Part V: Church

CULTURAL PROCESSES

Part VI: Change and Conversion

Part VII: Communication

Part VIII: Missionary Agents

Part IX: Anthropology as Culture Learning

AUTHORS AND ORDER OF PUBLICATION

The original date and issue of publication of each of the papers in this volume is listed here by authors. After the date appears the volume and number of *Practical Anthropology* in which the article was first published. If it was reprinted in the earlier edition of *Readings in Missionary Anthropology* (RIMA), that fact, and the page where it starts, is indicated in brackets. The title of each paper is followed by the page number where it is found in this volume.

x   AUTHORS AND ORDER OF PUBLICATION

PREFACE

The insights of the social sciences, and particularly of cultural anthropology, have made a strong impact on Christian missionary understanding, clarifying problems in the development of churches, and contributing to the effective communication of the gospel. During a twenty-year period beginning in 1953, much of the discussion of such questions as these was centered in a small periodical, *Practical Anthropology* (PA).

In 1967 a volume entitled *Readings in Missionary Anthropology* was published to keep available the articles of missionary concern from the early years of PA. They were in demand for classes in anthropology and missions, for missionary orientation, and by individuals concerned about culture and Christianity, culture and the communication of the gospel, and other related matters.

The demand for this volume has continued through the years, but as new material continued to be published in PA there has been need both to prune the less valuable, more dated material from the volume, and to add later material. Now the revision has been made, and the results appear in two companion volumes: *Culture and Human Values: Christian Intervention in Anthropological Perspective* (selections from the writings of Jacob A. Loewen), and this present enlarged edition of *Readings in Missionary Anthropology II* (both published by William Carey Library).

Readings in Missionary Anthropology II is organized differently from its predecessor. Paul G. Hiebert has written a new introductory article for the volume, to set it in perspective. The study of cultural anthropology and its potential contribution to Christian mission continues to change, and Hiebert surveys the situation as it has developed, and as it is now.

Then the volume is divided into two major sections, each with several subsections. "Cultural systems and manifestations" includes articles on religion, social structure, sex and marriage, myth, and church. "Cultural processes" includes articles on general themes like change and conversion, communication, missionary agents, and anthropology as culture learning. There is, of course, considerable overlap from one category to another. The decision as to where to put an article was sometimes somewhat arbitrary. The categories do, however, reflect to a considerable degree some of the areas where the social sciences have a great deal to say to the church.

The companion volume of articles by Jacob A. Loewen was published separately because there was too much to try to get into one book and because they deserve to be in a volume of their own. A few of Loewen's articles which did not fit the range of topics in his *Culture and Human Values* are included here, however.

In keeping with the nature of this volume, which is to make previously published material available to students and missionaries at as little cost as possible, the previously published contents have not been corrected or reset, but are reproduced in their original form. This means that out-of-date information about authors is still there (and repetitively so when the author has more than one article in the book), editorial introductions are not always still appropriate, and typographical errors have not been corrected. Also, frequent references to articles in PA remain in their original form even though the article may be included in this book. To help you find such articles within the volume, there is a list of authors, with their articles in the order of original publication, after the table of contents.

But the discussion of twenty years reflected here is usually surprisingly relevant for anyone engaged in cross-cultural communication today. Each person who leaves the cultural isolation of his own community has to learn for himself the significance of cultural interrelatedness, to respect the cultural heritage of the community into which he is moving, and how communication takes place across cultural differences. The writers in this book have a lot to say to such people.

William A. Smalley

INTRODUCTION:
MISSION AND ANTHROPOLOGY

Paul G. Hiebert

The Christmas pageant was over — or so I thought. The angels, dressed in pure white, had announced Christ's birth to Mary and Joseph. Their faces were brown and their message in Telugu, for we were in South India. The shepherds had staggered on stage, half drunk, herding the smaller children who were on all fours like sheep. Not quite what I was reared to expect, but something I could explain in terms of cultural differences, because unlike Palestinian shepherds who were known for their sobriety and piety, Indian shepherds are known for their drink and dance. But the message was not lost, for at the sight of the angels the shepherds fell to the ground, frightened sober.

The wisemen and Herod had appeared on stage in regal splendor. South Indians are masters at drama which they use extensively for religious communication in the village. A preacher may attract a few dozen listeners for an hour, but the vivid enactment of a story always attracts large crowds late into the night.

Now we sat crosslegged and crowded, as the shepherds, wisemen and angels gathered with Mary and Joseph around the manger. Suddenly, out jumped Santa Claus! With a merry song and dance, he began to give out presents to Jesus and the others. He was the hero of the pageant. And I sat stunned.

What had "gone wrong?" A case of syncretism, I first thought — a mixture of Hindu and Christian ideas that one might expect in new converts. The older missionaries had warned that if drama were allowed into the church it would bring in Hindu beliefs. But no, Santa was a western idea, brought by Westerners along with the story of Christ's birth. What had happened?

Here some anthropological insights can come to our aid. Recent studies in cognition show us how people formulate their basic concepts, and how they organize these into larger systems of thought. In this case it is clear that Americans have a great many ideas associated with Christmas, but that they divide these into two distinct conceptual domains — into two different Christmases. In one, the sacred one, they place Jesus, Mary, Joseph, angels, wisemen and shepherds. In the other they place Santa, reindeer, Christmas trees, stockings and presents. Nor do they mix the two. Rudolph, the red nosed reindeer does not belong in the same picture, or on the same stage, with angels and wisemen. Missionaries had introduced the Indians to the basic concepts of Christmas, but the separation of these into two different cognitive domains had been lost in the communication.

Ironically, the Indian world view that treats all human experiences as part of a single integrated domain is closer in many ways to the world view of the early Christians than is our own with its sharp division between the sacred and the secular. I began to wonder whether, in fact, we should not bring Santa and Christmas trees and science and "secular" occupations into the same picture with Christ. Theologically, had we not gone astray by confining Christianity to a few limited domains of our lives?

But cognitive theory raises an even more subtle question about the message communicated by the pageant. How did the villagers really perceive it? What did such words as "God", "Jesus" and "incarnation" mean to them?

To answer this we need to know how Indians organize their conceptual world. In their world view there is only one kind of life, whether it is in gods, people, animals or plants. The only difference between them is one of degree. Gods have more life than people, and people have more than animals and plants. Gods are part of creation. They die and are reborn as people or animals, just as these are reborn as gods. And gods appear frequently on earth as incarnations to help humans defeat the forces of evil (Figure 1).

FIGURE 1
Indian and Western Concepts of "Life"

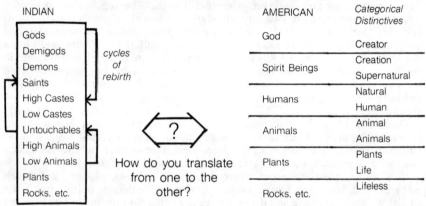

The concept of God in the Bible is quite different from this. He is infinite, eternal and the creator. All other forms of life are categorically different. They are finite, temporal and creation. To worship any of them is idolatry and sacrilegious. In this view, "incarnation" does not mean God lowering Himself to join others like Himself, like a rich man joining the poor. It means God crossed the categorical difference between Himself and humans — a difference of kind, not degree — to become something He was not before, a human.

But how in a pageant can you convey the Biblical concept of "God" and "incarnation" so that they would be understood by an Indian villager? All of the Telugu words for "God" carry the Hindu connotation of gods as part of creation. There is no word in the language that communicates the concept of God as the Christians use the term. Should one then use the English word "God", or, better yet, the Greek word "Theos"? But these are meaningless sounds to a South Indian villager. Or should one use one of the Telugu words for God in spite of the fact that the villager will reinterpret the message in terms of his own world view? How can you communicate across cultures without a loss of meaning?

Mission Anthropology

It is to answer questions such as these that some mission scholars have turned to anthropology and the other social sciences. In doing so, they do not deny the religious nature of the Biblical message, or the spiritual nature of human beings. But they recognize that people are also human: their bodies subject to physical and biological processes, their minds and spirits to psychological and sociocultural processes. And the social sciences are the study of these processes. So long as mission involves human beings, these scholars contend, an understanding of the social sciences can help us to build a more effective ministry.

Linguistics

There are a number of areas in which anthropology has helped us to understand the mission process. Two of the first to emerge were linguistics and communication.

Early anthropologists developed an interest in communication particularly in language, because they were often faced with learning exotic languages in order to study other cultures. For the most part, these languages lacked written forms, grammars, dictionaries and teachers to give instruction. The methods that had been developed by the classical linguists for written languages were, therefore, of little help. Anthropological linguists developed techniques which enabled them to learn languages quickly and accurately without the assistance of language schools. Out of their work developed some of the emphases of modern linguistics, which is the study of the basic nature and structures of human languages.

Missionaries faced the same problems of language, and a number of missionary linguists played and continue to play an important part in the development of linguistic and translation theory. H. A. Gleason taught linguistics to missionaries at the Kennedy School of Missions, when it was still in operation. Kenneth L. Pike and his colleagues of the Summer Institute of Linguistics/Wycliffe Bible Translators did a great deal of pioneering work in linguistics structures. Each summer they also hold a number of intensive courses in university campuses in different countries, teaching prospective translators how to analyze a language in preparation for making accurate Bible translations.

Eugene A. Nida and the American Bible Society (later within the framework of the United Bible Societies) put together a team of highly qualified experts who have done significant work in translation theory, and who serve as technical consultants to national Bible societies involved in translation around the world. Nida and William A. Smalley also pioneered a second type of program, one aimed at teaching missionaries how to learn new languages. Under the sponsorship of a group of mission boards, first they, then Donald N. Larson have operated the Toronto Institute of Linguistics, a program in which candidates are taught methods for learning a language rapidly and accurately even in regions where language training schools do not exist or are inadequate. Since then similar programs have been developed in a number of schools interested in preparing people for overseas ministries.

Communications

At first anthropological linguists treated languages as autonomous structures, independent of the rest of culture. Later they became increasingly interested in the problem of the relationship of language to culture. It became obvious to them that culture would be impossible without language and that language is molded by the culture of which it is a part.

On one level, the relationship between these two raised questions about how communication takes place. What happens in the communication process? What media other than language do people use? Which forms of communication are most effective in transmitting particular types of messages? And how is communication affected by its sociocultural contexts? A number of mission scholars such as Nida (1960), and, more recently Donald Smith (of Daystar Communications Institute, Nairobi) have applied communication theory to the mission process with considerable success.

On another level, the relationship of language to culture raises the question of cognition. To what extent is thought molded and confined by the words of a language and the conceptual categories implicit within them? And how can language help us discover how people perceive their worlds? As we saw in the Christmas drama, how we form our concepts and organize them into larger domains profoundly affects the message we convey.

Anthropologists in cognition, such as Dell Hymes, John Gumperz, James Spradley and Stephen Tyler (see Spradley 1972) have developed a new field in anthropology, sometimes refered to as "ethnoscience", for the study of cognitive systems. Its importance to christian mission and all cross-cultural communication is obvious, for communication is not measured by what is said, but by what the listener understands. So far little has been done to apply ethnoscientific theory and methods to missionary communication, although an encouraging beginning has been made by Charles Kraft of the School of World Mission, Fuller Theological Seminary (Pasadena).

Cultural Differences

Another early concern mission strategists faced was the set of problems that arose out of human variation. Missionaries had to face the question of religious differences — how do you relate to non-Christian religions? Were they totally evil, and, therefore, to be wiped out? Did they contain partial truths on which the missionary could build? The question led to extensive discussions (see Kraemer 1956 and Neill 1961).

But missionaries, like anthropologists, were also confronted with other cultural differences. People in other societies built different types of houses, spoke different languages, organized different kinds of families, had different concepts of right and wrong, and believed in different values.

Such cultural variance raised and still raises experiential problems. People who move into a new culture face culture shock. Misunderstandings arise in their relationships with nationals. And they face the difficult task of learning how to live in a new society. Considerable attention has been given by mission anthropologists to these problems.

Cultural variance also raises some knotty philosophical and theological questions. It appears that all cultures "do the job" — that is, they provide for orderly, meaningful human life. How then can we judge one to be better than another? What criteria can we use to compare and evaluate customs? And what right do we have to try to change other people?

For a time many anthropologists took a position of cultural relativism and held that all cultures and customs are equally good. But relativism raised equally difficult questions. Are, in fact, all customs equally good? For example, is magic as effective as modern medicine in curing diseases? Should we not help people if they desire it or if it is to their benefit? Are there no absolutes, no biological, psychological, social or moral principles underlying all human life, no truth? To deny these is to deny meaning to human life itself. Today, few anthropologists take a completely relativist position with regard to cultural variance, but there is little consensus on what the criteria for evaluation shall be.

Missionaries, too, have had to face cultural variance. Many of them wanted to make people Christians, but does this also mean wearing clothes, using western medicine, having one wife, giving up segregation based on caste or race, and giving up headhunting? If not, where does one draw the line between Christianity and western culture?

The relationship of the Christian message to cultures is complex. On the one hand, the message must always be expressed in cultural terms — in a language, cultural symbols and behavioral practices that will, in part, mold the message. On the other, Christianity claims that its message is universal and transcends any one culture.

The theological question raised by cultural variance goes further. The Bible itself took place in a cultural context. How do we determine what is the universal message to be proclaimed to all people everywhere, and what part was addressed to the people and culture of that day? To say all parts apply equally to everyone is to evade the question. Few, if any, modern Christians put adulterers to death (Lev. 20:10), or stone blasphemers (Lev. 24:14). Not many practice the holy kiss (I The. 5:26), require women to pray with their heads covered (I Cor. 11:13), lend money freely without expecting its return (Luke 6:35), or refuse to participate in war.

Finally, cultural differences raise basic epistemological questions of missionaries and anthropologists alike. How do we relate to those who believe differently than we, but who also claim to have found the truth? As anthropologists pointed out, we must avoid an uncritical ethnocentrism — the tendency we have of automatically assuming our own beliefs and customs are right and of using them to judge other people and cultures to be wrong. To do so only blocks understanding and communication, and in the end each only stands up and declares himself right. Communication takes place chiefly in a context of understanding and trust.

But how do we relate to people if a fundamental difference between us persists? Can we still accept them as persons and maintain relationships with them? How we answer the epistemological question of variance will profoundly affect how we relate to others.

Culture

The discovery of fundamental differences between cultures led to an awareness of culture itself. As anthropologists began to study individual cultures, they found that these are not made up of odd assortments of customs. Rather, cultures are larger systems in which the parts are integrated in varying degrees to the whole, and to each other. Moreover, the parts serve important functions. In other words, they meet important needs in the lives of the people and in the maintenance of the society.

Scholars have pointed out that the holistic view of culture has some important implications for missions. For one, if cultures are integrated, changes in one area of culture often lead to significant changes in other areas of the culture. For example, if people convert to Christianity, it may affect their economic, social and/or political systems. Nor can we always predict just what these changes will be. The missionary, therefore, must be aware of negative side-effects and deal with them, and he must be concerned with all dimensions of the peoples' lives, or in making them Christians he may destroy their society and bring about their extinction.

A second implication springs from the concept of function. If the missionary eliminates or changes a custom, he should see to it that the essential functions served by that custom are met by some other means, or serious cultural disruptions can result. For example, the suppression of headhunting in New Guinea created serious psychological problems for the men because they could not become adult males in their society without taking a head. Consequently Christian men often had to live their whole lives as "boys".

The third implication of viewing culture as an integrated system is that of indigenization. In order for an idea to become a vital part of a culture, it must be integrated into the systems of that culture. Not only must it be translated into the local language, but also it must find its expression in the practices and thought patterns of the culture. As Kraemer put it (Haglund 1972:49), the Gospel must not be brought as a potted plant dependent on the foreign soil of another culture, it must be brought as a seed that is planted and raised in native soil. Only then will it lose its foreignness.

But the process of assimilating a new set of beliefs carries with it the danger of syncretism in which the literal form of the message is translated into local terms, but the meaning of the message is lost. For example, in the pageant referred to at the outset, the use of the form "shepherds" led to the loss of the original meaning "pious common folk." Some might argue that it would have been better to use "farmers" since in South India these convey more closely the meaning found in the shepherds of the Christmas narrative. The danger in indigenizing the message is that its meaning will be lost in a mixture of old religious ideas in the forms of the new religion.

Social Structure

The concept of social structure developed by the sociologists and the British school of social anthropologists opened an important new door for the analysis of the mission process. This is the study of how people structure their interactions. Without this structuring social order would be impossible, and life would turn into anarchy.

Social structures have been analyzed on a number of levels. At the lowest level one can study how individuals relate to each other. For instance, how does a missionary relate to the people among whom he works, to the national converts, to other missionaries, to his home constituency, to his board and to his family? Jacob A. Loewen (1975), and William A. Smalley and William D. Reyburn (see articles in this volume) have used role theory to provide us important insights on the relationships a missionary has. More recently, some work has also been done on how converts learn new Christian roles, and on leadership roles in nonwestern churches, but a great deal of work remains to be done at this level.

Social organization can also be studied in terms of groups and group dynamics. For example, how should missionary groups relate to national churches — should the missionaries be members of these churches, or should they retain their ties to their sending churches? How should churches be organized, and how do cliques, friendship networks and kinship ties affect their operation?

So far little has been done to study mission organizations, mission-church relationships or church operations in terms of group theory. One of the critical questions facing modern missions is how to structure postcolonial relationships between sending churches and newly organized churches in which the integrity and autonomy of both are preserved. In part this may be a theological issue, but in part it is a matter of intergroup structure, for contemporary development programs, governments and businesses face many of the same problems on the international scene.

Then again, social organization can be studied at the level of a society as a whole. These types of analysis are valuable in planning broad mission strategy as Nida (1960), McGavran (1955) and others have shown. Some of the questions raised at this level are: Should missions concentrate on the cities rather than villages or tribes, on regions of high response rather than on all areas equally, on the elite and upper classes rather than on the poor and marginal people? How should one respond when whole tribes turn to Christianity at the same time? And how do social structures such as class and caste hierarchies affect the growth of the church?

Recently there has been a growing interest in the structure and dynamics of human interaction below the level of roles. Anthropologists such as Max Gluckman (1963) and Fred Bailey (1973) have looked at the strategies people use in their relationships, and students in the new field of Transactional Analysis[1] have looked at attitudinal states within a role relationship. Neither of these approaches has been applied to missions, even though the prospect looks promising. Both of them deal with human emotions and aspirations as well as social structure and therefore provide a bridge between the insights provided by anthropology and those provided by psychology.

Another branch of structuralism, namely French structuralism[2], raises some important theological questions, but seems on the surface of it to be less useful for missions.

Religion

Many anthropologists have focused on particular areas of culture. Economic anthropologists began by analyzing economic institutions but have turned to the study of how individuals and societies create and use resources. These may be property, money and material goods, or they may be time and effort. Although missions use such resources and their use generates a great deal of debate on the field, little has been done to apply theories of comparative economics to the mission scene.

Political anthropologists began with political institutions and have now broadened their interest to the uses of power (force, knowledge, wealth etc.) and of politics power (leadership, and decision making). With the exception of some studies on leadership, modern mission strategists have, for the most part, given far too little attention to power and politics. Costas (1974) and other third world leaders are pointing out the critical nature of this issue on the international mission scene, and a few scholars such as John Yoder (1972) are beginning to examine the New Testament in political terms. But these discussions will have to be broadened to include a cross-cultural analysis of political systems and how they operate. Otherwise the judgments passed will be used on western political biases. Work is also needed on the uses of power within mission organizations themselves to make us aware of how this dimension affects the operation of mission programs.

Anthropological studies in the area of religion and magic have had a more obvious relevance to mission. It is not surprising, therefore, that mission scholars have drawn on and contributed to theory in this area. In the anthropology of religion the question of the ultimate truthfulness of a religion is not raised. That is a question to be answered by theology, philosophy and comparative religions. What is asked is how religions function, and how they relate to other areas of a culture.

Some anthropologists have turned to the study of world views — the basic existential and normative assumptions people make about their worlds. What do they perceive to be the nature of reality, and what do they consider to be right and wrong? For example, behind the Christmas story lies a view of reality that assumes not only the uniqueness of human life and its eternal existence, but also a linear view of time in which human beings live but one life and then face a judgment. The human goal is heaven in which the individual is fulfilled. But the Hindu world view assumes that time, like the seasons, repeats itself endlessly, that human beings die and are reborn innumerable times, and that the goal of life is to merge back into the source of life and lose its individuality. The Westerner, influenced by Christianity, believes in progress, and points to modern technological developments as evidence that this is taking place. The traditional Indian sees modern technology as a sign of the increasing depersonalization of life, and therefore a sign of the loss of true values and the decline of civilization.

The basic assumptions a culture makes about reality are often so taken for granted that they are not made explicit by its members. But it is upon these assumptions that people build their concepts of the universe and their social orders. To understand people, we must understand their world views. Only then can we communicate with a minimum loss of meaning.

Other anthropologists such as Turner (1967) have focused on the nature of religious rituals and symbols, and the place these have in the lives of people. Protestants in their rebellion against ritualism have often overlooked its importance in the maintenance of faith and the transmission of religious beliefs. Too often missionaries have been guilty of destroying a people's traditional symbols and rituals without providing them with meaningful substitutes. This is particularly critical in the case of nonliterates for whom rituals are not only the reaffirmations of their faith, but also the encyclopedias preserving their religious knowledge. As John

Carman points out (Luke and Carman 1968), deprived of rituals, dramas and dance, nonliterate Christians are often left only with a lyrical theology rooted in the hymns they know by heart.

Culture Change

Planned change is central to the missionary task. Yet it is only in recent decades that anthropologists have begun to analyze how such change takes place. Early anthropologists were concerned primarily with the broad evolution of culture and with the diffusion of ideas around the world — approaches that raised theological questions but had little to say to missionaries in their work. Structural-functional approaches tended to view cultures as static. Change was seen as essentially harmful. Today, however, anthropologists and mission scholars are studying the nature of both planned and unplanned change.

One approach of interest to missionaries is revitalization theory. This is the study of the rise and growth of the nativistic and messianic cults that make up one of the most widespread religious phenomena of our day. Over six thousand have been reported in Africa alone. Thousands of cargo cults and prophetic movements have risen in New Guinea and Oceania, and hundreds of new religions have appeared in Japan and the Philippines since the Second World War. Some of these are attempts to return to old religious traditions in a search for identity and stability in the midst of the confusion created by rapid culture change. A great many of them, however, are attempts to adapt Christianity to the local cultures, and the results range from orthodox churches to bizarre syncretistic cults. To date most missions have refused to work with them, despite their requests for Biblical instruction and assistance. But they constitute some of the most rapidly growing segments of indigenous Christianity around the world.

Thorough studies of revitalization movements have been made by scholars such as Wallace (1956), studies that have important significance for mission strategists. However, with the exception of some surveys of these movements, not much has been done in mission or church circles to deal with them. These movements may easily become one of the greatest missed opportunities for missions in our day.

Other studies have been concerned with conversion and individual responses to religious change. What leads a person to convert, and what changes do conversion effect in the beliefs and practices of an individual? Here, again, some have been afraid to view religious experiences such as conversion in terms of natural processes. To do so does not deny their spiritual importance. But, as Thomas Acquinas expressed in his famous dictum, "Grace does not suppress nature." To this Paul Tournier adds (1963:10), ". . . man belongs to nature by the will of God, and no spiritual experience, no matter how profound it may be, frees him from his natural state." A better understanding of the processes of conversion would undoubtedly be of value to missionaries.

A third area in the study of change, and the one on which missionaries have drawn most heavily, is that of planned change — the study of how changes can be introduced most easily and with least negative side-effects into a society. H. G. Barnett (1953), Ward Goodenough (1963) and others in the field of applied anthropology have written extensively on innovation and the acceptance of new ideas, and on resistance to new ideas and ways it can be avoided. Applied anthropologists have produced a wide range of materials that has been used in training programs for those going into international programs, such as the Peace Corps, development programs, diplomatic service and missions.

Related to the study of change is that of socialization — the study of how children are raised and taught their culture. Students of socialization in the anthropological field of Culture and Personality have analyzed the importance of child rearing practices in maintaining a culture's beliefs and practices. Now they are becoming aware that extensive changes can occur in a culture through changes in the socialization process. Both maintenance and change are important to missionaries and other agents of planned change, for they are interested not only in introducing change, but also in transmitting the new ideas to subsequent generations. Some attention has been given to this in the establishment of schools but the greatest amount of socialization occurs in the home prior to school age. A failure to develop an adequate socialization process in the home generally leads to the "second generation" problem; the fact that second, third and fourth generation Christians, or for that matter, members of any movement, are only nominal believers and often leave the organization.

Recent Developments

A number of new areas of interest have arisen in anthropology in the past decade. Most of these have yet to be examined for their possible contribution to missions. Cultural ecology looks at the relationship between a culture and its environment, expressive anthropology is the study of the arts and music, and mathematical anthropology is an attempt to understand human beings in terms of cybernetics and mathematical models. These are probably less important for missions than the rapidly expanding studies of complex and urban societies. So far missions have been most successful in tribal and peasant societies. But with the rapid urbanization of the world, missionaries will need to find ways of reaching people in the turmoil of the modern city.

Past and Present

The relationship between Christian mission and anthropology in the past century has been one of ambivalence. On the one hand they shared a common interest in people around the world, and anthropologists often sought the assistance of missionaries who had lived for long periods on the field. On the other hand, they have often been suspicious of each other's activities. It may surprise us, therefore, that anthropology in Britain had its origins in the broad Christian humanitarian movement of the nineteenth century, of which the missionary movement was a part. After slavery was abolished (1807-1833), those concerned with social reform turned their attention to questions of the welfare of the native peoples in the colonies. In 1834 a split occurred on how to protect the rights of the natives. One faction, including most of the missionaries, wanted to grant them immediately the full "privileges" of western civilization. The other wanted to study them before "raising and protecting them" (Reining 1970:3-11). Unfortunately, thereafter the missionaries and reformers too often pursued programs of planned change without perceiving the cultural contexts in which this change took place, while the anthropologists too often proceeded to study the people with little thought to how this knowledge could benefit the people.

But we must avoid stereotyping an age. A reading of old field minutes shows that many of the missionaries of the late nineteenth and early twentieth century were deeply sensitive to the cultures and viewpoints of the people among whom they worked. A number of them — R. H. Codrington of Melanesia, M. Leenhardt of New Caledonia, H. Junod and E. Smith of Africa, the Wisers in India and Father W. Schmidt and the Vienna School of Anthropology, to name only a few — made significant contributions to anthropological knowledge and theory. Many others studied the ethnographic materials of their fields.

Since the Second World War there has been a growing interaction between missions and anthropology. This has been on a much broader scale than just the interest in linguistics that characterized the period between the world wars. Some church-related colleges such as Wheaton had already introduced anthropology courses into their curricula earlier, and journals like the *Anthropological Quarterly* (Catholic) and the *International Review of Missions* (mainly Protestant) had carried a few articles on broader topics of anthropology and missions. But the real impetus in bringing anthropological awareness to missions came largely through the work of Eugene Nida and the members of the American Bible Society translations team.

Nida drew from his work in cross-cultural translations but broadened his interest to cover the whole range of sociocultural anthropology. For a number of years he lectured widely in schools and churches throughout the country. In the process he wrote *Customs and Cultures* (1954), and *Message and Mission* (1960), two pioneering works that have contributed a great deal to the current interest in mission anthropology.

A second major impetus came through *Practical Anthropology,* a journal edited by members of the translation team and other interested colleagues. This served as a forum for anthropological studies of the mission process from 1953 to 1973. The quality of the articles published in the journal is reflected in the fact that they found acceptance in departments of anthropology on university campuses, and that the first edition of *Readings in Missionary Anthropology,* selected reprints from this journal, found wide use in mission circles and has gone through several reprintings.

In the past few years anthropology has found its place in many schools and institutes training people for overseas service. On the other side, there is a widespread movement among anthropologists towards applied anthropology and active involvement in international development. The issuing of a second and much enlarged edition of *Readings in Missionary Anthropology* is therefore most welcome, for it provides in a single volume much of the creative thinking from a very formative period in mission anthropology.

NOTES

1. Transactional Analysis as a field was developed by Eric Berne who wrote *Games People Play* (1964), and *What do You Say After You Say Hello?* (1972). Other leaders in the field have been Thomas Harris *(I'm OK — You're OK,* 1973) and Claude Steiner *(Scripts People Live,* 1975). Currently there is a rapid development within the field including training programs, a journal, and extensive research.
2. The leading in this area today is Claude Levi-Strauss whose work on myths raises important questions regarding the nature of the human mind and its knowledge.

BIBLIOGRAPHY
Bailey, F. G. ed.
    1973 Debate and Compromise: the Politics of Innovation. Oxford: Blackwell.
Barnett, H. G.
    1953 Innovation: the Basis of Culture Change. New York: McGraw-Hill.
Costas, O. E.
    1974 The Church and its Mission: A Shattering Critique from the Third World. Wheaton, Ill.: Tyndale House.
Goodenough, W. H.
    1963 Cooperation in Change: An Anthropological Approach to Community Development. New York: Russell Sage Foundation.
Gluckman, Max
    1963 Order and Rebellion in Tribal Africa. London: Cohen West.

Haglund, Åke
   1972 Contact and Conflict: Studies in Contemporary Religious Attitudes among Chinese Peoples. Berlingska, Boktryikeriet: C.W.K. Gleerups Bokförlag.
Kraemer, H.
   1956 Religion and the Christian Faith. London: Lutterworth.
Loewen, J. A.
   1975 Culture and Human Values: Christian Intervention in Anthropological Perspective. South Pasadena: William Carey Library.
Luke, P. and J. B. Carman
   1968 Village Christians in Hindu Culture. London: Lutterworth.
McGavran, D. A.
   1955 The Bridges of God: A Study in the Strategy of Missions. New York: Friendship Press.
Neill, S.
   1961 Christian Faith and Other Faiths. London: Oxford University Press.
Nida, E. A.
   1954 Customs and Cultures. South Pasadena: William Carey Library.
   1960 Message and Mission. South Pasadena: William Carey Library.
Reining, C. C.
   1970 A lost period of applied anthropology. In J. A. Clifton, ed. Applied Anthropology. Boston: Houghton Mifflin.
Spradley, J.
   1972 Culture and Cognition. San Francisco: Chandler.
Tournier, P.
   1963 The Seasons of Life. Translated by John S. Gilmour. London: SCM Press.
Turner, V.
   1967 The Forest of Symbols: Aspects of Ndembu Ritual. Ithica: Cornell University Press.
Wallace, A. F. C.
   1956 Revitalization movements. American Anthropologist. 58:264-281.
Yoder, J. H.
   1972 The Politics of Jesus. Grand Rapids, Mich.: William B. Eerdmans.

PART I

Cultural Systems and Manifestations:

Religion and World View

Eugene A. Nida

Religion: Communication with the Supernatural

The many and extremely varied forms of practice and belief which are classified as "religion" have long defied the attempts of anthropologists to find a common core or common denominator which would provide a basis for an all-inclusive definition of religious phenomena. In this article Nida discusses many of the varied forms of religious practice as communication[1] with the supernatural, as the sending or receiving of a "message" to or from the non-earthly or non-human sphere. He feels that such communication is basic to non-personalized religious practice like magic, and that it is implicit in a concept of non-personalized religious power (mana) as well as in more obviously communicative religious forms like prayer. The significance of the theory is discussed in relation to Christianity as well as to other religious forms.

Traditional Views of Religion

Many attempts have been made to explain the origin of religion and to provide some unifying approach to this most complex and difficult aspect of human culture.[2] Perhaps the most sig-

[1] It should be noted that in this article "communication" is used in an extension of the general sense given it in information theory (cybernetics). It has to do with the sending and receiving of "messages," ranging from the conversation of people around a dinner table to the intricate electronic system of a guided missile. There is a large and usually very technical literature on the field. One readily obtainable and relatively nontechnical book which discusses the implications of the theory for human behavior is Norbert Wiener's *The Human Use of Human Beings: Cybernetics and Society* (Garden City: 1954). This is a Doubleday Anchor Book (paperback), costing $.75. Other basic books include Colin Cherry, *On Human Communication*, New York: John Wiley and Sons, Inc., 1957, and F. H. George, *Automation, Cybernetics, and Society*, New York: Philosophical Library, 1959.

[2] An excellent summary of different orientations toward religion is contained in J. Milton

nificant of these approaches to the study of religion are (1) the dream-to-soul view, espoused by early evolutionists, (2) the "devolutionary" concept of corrupted primitive monotheism, so ardently advocated by Father Wilhelm Schmidt and his followers, (3) religion as social action and interaction, formulated by Emile Durkheim, (4) the functional view of religion as utilitarian adjustment to the unknown, a position which has appealed to a wide range of investigators, from Bronislaw Malinowski to Wilson D. Wallis, and is particularly congenial in the company of American pragmatists,

Yinger, "The Influence of Anthropology on Sociological Theories of Religion," *American Anthropologist*, Vol. 60, pp. 487-96 (1958). I am indebted to Mr. Linwood Barney, of St. Paul Bible College, and Bethel Seminary, St. Paul, Minnesota, for several significant suggestions leading to the viewpoint expressed in this paper. In addition, William L. Wonderly and William A. Smalley have made a number of highly important comments which have been incorporated into this analysis.

and (5) religion as the outworking of psychiatric phenomena, in which people project into the supernatural realm such conflicts as guilt, dependence, hostility, or emotional attachment.[3]

Each of these viewpoints has brought certain fresh and valued insights to the problem of religion in culture. Edward B. Tylor's view of the importance of dreams in the development of concepts about the soul is useful in attempting to understand certain features of some primitive religions in which people believe that during dreams the soul does commit real deeds, for which the person in question is morally responsible and socially guilty. However, this view of religious phenomena is exceedingly limited in scope and provides no sure base for explaining the origin of religion itself.

It is quite understandable that in opposition to the unvalidated (and unprovable) contentions of the early evolutionary school, Andrew Lang should have reacted with an almost contrary view — that religion may have been corrupted rather than progressively more highly developed. Father Schmidt took up this challenge and proceeded to work out the

implications of such a position with a massive collection of data, but with unfortunate theoretical principles, for he insisted upon certain arbitrary characteristics of so-called original cultures (of which some contemporary primitive peoples are supposed to be more or less unchanged representatives). Schmidt's views have been widely endorsed by Roman Catholic scholars, and by some Protestant missionaries (of whom the most conspicuous example was Samuel Zwemer[4]), but despite the superficial attractiveness of this position for one who holds to a traditional interpretation of the Old Testament, there is very little in Schmidt's position which can be said to be fully provable as regards any attempt to reconstruct the history of religion.

The explanation of religion as the expression of the social conscience, whether as reenactment of real or imagined history in rite and ceremony or as supernaturally enforced sanctions for socially recognized norms of behavior, has much to recommend it. Certainly earlier investigators had placed so much emphasis upon religion as a purely personal response to the supernatural that they had overlooked the role of religion in the life of the community. Nevertheless, such a view of religion has not only failed to explain why religion arose, but also has not done justice to the anti-social aspects of religion, such as the use of black magic.

Religion as a functional response to the unknown has appealed strongly to pragmatically minded Americans, for it is easy to describe material culture as an adjustment to the physical environment, social culture as an adjustment to fellow

---

[3] More extended discussions of these various points of view about religion may be found in chapters on religion in several of the introductory textbooks on anthropology, as well as in such books as the following: William A. Lessa and Evon Z. Vogt, Reader in Comparative Religion, Evanston, Ill.: Row, Peterson and Co., 1958; Robert H. Lowie, Primitive Religion, New York: Liveright Publishing Co., 1948; Robert H. Lowie, The History of Ethnological Theory, New York: Farrar and Rinehart, 1937. A brief popular introduction to some of the kinds of religious phenomena referred to in this article will be found in Eugene A. Nida and William A. Smalley, Introducing Animism, New York: Friendship Press, 1959.

[4] Samuel Zwemer, The Origin of Religion: Evolution or Revelation. New York: Loizeaux, 1945. (Currently out of print.)

humans, and religion as an adjustment to the supernatural. Moreover, anthropologists saw (or attempted to see, depending upon their degree of sympathy for this viewpoint) certain measures of functional utility in everything that was done. Even black magic has been "excused" by some as a way of alleviating outward feelings of hostility and witch-hunting has been judged as a kind of group emotional catharsis. What has made this position somewhat suspect has been the way in which its proponents have always seemed to find positive functioning in all aspects of religious beliefs and practices. The position has been taken that there would be little reason for retaining such characteristics if they were not positive and seemingly beneficial to the culture in question. However, though obvious dysfunction in the material and social areas of life has been recognized, there has been a tendency to defend all kinds of religious practices as functionally valid. Of course, much of this orientation on the part of investigators can be attributed to a reaction against the traditional attitude of people who saw nothing good in pagan religions and hence condemned everything. Nevertheless, the mistake of defending any and all forms of indigenous belief is equally unreasonable. Moreover, even though one may be able to produce evidence that certain religious practices apparently contribute some benefits to the believers (e.g. providing a sense of security in the midst of trouble), this fact in itself does not explain the genesis of such beliefs, nor can it possibly explain some of the antisocial, harmful practices which persist for long periods of time.

Psychiatrists have, of course, had a field day with indigenous myths, for in these they have recognized certain fascinating "group dreams," projections of the personality, sublimations of intense desires, supernaturally imposed sanctions which justify certain otherwise "inhuman" actions. Few persons any longer take seriously certain of the early attempts by Freud to reconstruct the entire history of culture and religion on the basis of an Oedipus conflict in an early primeval horde in which the sons ganged up on their father, killed him, committed incest with their mothers, and then, overcome by feelings of remorse, instituted sacrifice to the "deified" father. However, though these early crude attempts are easily brushed aside as being anthropological fairy tales (professional myths), nevertheless psychiatrists and psychologists have made penetrating observations on such matters as scapegoatism, the messianic complex, nativistic revivals and the relationship of myths to thwarted desires.

Unanswered Problems

However, despite the remarkable contributions made by each of these orientations toward religion, there have been some fundamental failures. In the first place, there has been no satisfactory explanation of the origin of religion. We should not, however, be surprised, for reconstructing history is a precarious undertaking. Perhaps anthropologists specializing in religion will eventually be as content to leave unanswered the origin of religion as are historical linguists forced to admit that one cannot reconstruct the origin of language. But even if we set aside the matter of historical origin, these basic orientations toward religion (all of which are essentially genetic in viewpoint) still fail to take into account a number of essential matters: (1) the relationship of magic to religion,

(2) the extravagant overdevelopment of religion in circumstances which utilitarian considerations can scarcely justify, (3) the serious malfunction and dysfunction of some religious beliefs and practices, and (4) the lack of any essential similarity of practice or characteristic which ties religious phenomena together as a single whole. There is still no functionally valid definition of religion which seems to be diagnostic of the many essential characteristics of such phenomena.

It is interesting that field workers have generally found little difficulty in combining magic and worship together under religion, and yet theorists have seemed to see utterly different orientations. In the one case man is demanding or coercing the supernatural, and in the other imploring. Such attitudes seem so essentially contradictory, that many students of religion have tried to insist that they were quite distinct, that the magician is the primitive scientist and that only the worshiper is essentially religious. Nevertheless, field observers have quite generally rejected this kind of dichotomy, for they have felt that magic is a very vital part of religious practice — inseparably combined with the total view of the supernatural, though just how such views of magical coercion could be combined with pious supplication have seemed remote and dubious.

The numerous views of religion which have been advanced have served to explain various isolated phenomena with remarkable insight, but they have seemed to leave religion as an assemblage of disconnected features, including crystal balls, ordeals, peyote worship, secret passwords, puberty rites, death chants, exotic ceremonies, and hideous masks. No one theme has seemed to be sufficient to unify such a wide variety of objects and events into any meaningful whole — especially is this true in instances in which people have elaborated religion out of all proportion to the rest of life or have kept holding on to practices which are grossly injurious and even openly denounced by leaders of the society.

Part of the difficulty in finding an integrating key to the analysis of religious phenomena seems to lie in the failure of some scholars to distinguish three separate levels of religious experience: (1) practices, (2) beliefs, and (3) the general behavior consequences of such religious practices and beliefs. For the most part specialists in the "higher religions" have focused their attention primarily upon the systems of belief, since the comparisons have usually been worked out in terms of the corresponding or contrasting "theologies." Not enough attention, however, has been paid to the differences between ideal and real beliefs (those religious conceptions which one is supposed to have as a member of a particular society and those which he does in fact possess, as evidenced by his behavior). Furthermore, even among field anthropologists insufficient study has been dedicated to the actual functioning of religious practices in terms of their relationship to the concepts of people's communication to and from the supernatural. It is at this point that the distinctive role of communication, in its wider cybernetic context of communication and control, seems to provide some highly instructive insights, and will be developed here.

Religious Practices as Communicative Events

The view that religious practices can be best understood as essentially a communicative function seems to possess distinct advantages, not only for the insight which it provides for individual features of religion, but also for the over-all synthesis of its highly divergent characteristics. When we view religious practices as a species of communication we can readily combine magic with prayer, group ritual with lonely vigils, and passwords with catechisms. Moreover, we are in a position to explain the fact of emotional involvement, which has always attracted the attention of investigators and which has been the decisive factor in distinguishing between speculation about God as being philosophy, and prayer to God as being religion.

In the point of view toward communication which is being used as the basis of discussion here, a source, a receptor, and a message are necessary. The message is carried in symbolic form. That is, it is encoded (put into symbols) by the source, and decoded by the receptor. The code, or the system of symbols may be language, art, gesture, or an enormous variety of other possibilities. In machines it often consists of electric impulses.

If we view certain religious phenomena as consisting essentially of source-message-receiver relationship, in which a person may be either the source or the recipient of the message, either to or from the non-earthly and non-human sphere (in other words the supernatural), we have all the basic ingredients of religious practice. Of course, there are highly elaborate means by which messages are encoded for the supernatural, and even more exotic ways in which such messages are decoded, but religion can and should be described primarily in terms of a communicative phenomenon.

It must not be thought that this thesis of religious practices as communication must rest necessarily upon the assumption that there is a supernatural which can and does communicate. The reality of such a supernatural source of communication is not an integral part of the viewpoint, for the communication may be explained in various ways (hysteria, group hypnosis, split personality, wishful thinking, etc.). However, in so far as there is a valid revelation of God to man (and I hold this position), then religion as communication provides a fundamental framework for any concepts of revelation or communion, as well as for other types of communication which will be discussed.

A view of the practice of religion as being essentially communication may seem at first to be improbable, and hence, before taking up various of these aspects of religion one by one, perhaps we need to consider briefly two extremes, namely, the magician and the mystic, two religionists who seem to have little or nothing in common. The magician seeks only to control the supernatural and the mystic wishes only to be utterly controlled by the supernatural. However, there is an essential relationship, for both are involved in what is primarily communication. The magician, for example, is in communication with non-personal supernatural forces, not in the sense that he is imploring them to accept his petition, but in the sense that he has a direct line of control upon supernatural power. He communicates with this power by means of magical formulae (word and actions) and thus impels a response. In the same way that an electrical technician can by remote control (i.e., by communication) determine the action of some unseen machine (which is cued automatically to respond to certain stimuli) at some distance, so the magician regards himself as having some direct, though remote, control over unseen forces, which are obliged to act as directed. This communication system will not work, of course, if some other magic power is interfering with his control (in electronic terms, if the message has been jammed or a more powerful transmitter has gotten its contrary message through).

The mystic on the other hand is not primarily a sender of messages, though he believes in prayer to a personal supernatural being. His primary concern is to be spoken to by God. Thus he is first and foremost a receiver of messages, not the source. Furthermore, he does not always expect, or want, verbal messages (though the voice of his God is very important). What is even more important is a sense of the presence of the deity, where communication may be accomplished not only by the ears, but even more by sight, feeling (tactile and internal), smell, and taste. To be possessed by one's god is to be identified completely with him, and thus to have all the senses "deified." This is the mystic's ecstasy, but it is nevertheless communication, in the most intense degree.

A further word of caution is necessary before we examine some of the principal features of the communicative acts — namely, the distinction which is necessary between the message, techniques of transmission of the message, and the processes of encoding and decoding. The simplest form of such communication is to be found in spontaneous prayer, for the worshiper merely encodes a message in linguistic form, as he would to any friend (though often using certain forms regarded as specially appropriate for addressing deity) and speaks them, with the confidence that the supernatural can hear, and hence decode and respond to the message. However, in other cases the message may need to be communicated in some highly formalized manner (for instance in Latin, as a language having greater religious prestige), and hence some specialist must be introduced, who in turn must be paid for his services. Moreover, it may seem necessary to back up such a prayer produced through a priest by some more obvious form (a visual message), and hence a candle is lighted or incense is burned. The candle communicates its message by its light, and the incense communicates through its aroma.

When a message comes from the supernatural to man, the processes of transmission and decoding are even more complicated and usually more highly trained persons seem to be required, for these individuals must be highly suggestive, often capable of hysterical trances, or addicted to significant communications (though not always intelligible ones) under the influence of various drugs. In many instances the message which gets through to the receiver may seem relatively unimportant, but what is important is the fact of the communicative process, for the god has spoken, be it ever so ambiguous or irrelevant.

Sending Messages

Since the sending of messages in religion is technologically less complicated for a man than the receiving of such messages, it is perhaps best to begin with this aspect of religious communication. There are two different goals toward which the message may be projected. It may be directed not only to a personal supernatural being, as in prayer, but also to a non-personal supernatural force, as in magic. In the first instance a personal being is able to decide how, when, and if the request is to be dealt with; in the second case, the magic formulae are regarded as having more or less automatic control upon the supernatural forces, and they can fail only if some other magic communication overrules.

In order to make prayer fully efficacious, it is often felt necessary for such communications to be highly ritualized in special intonational or incantational forms or in particular forms of language, often with archaic words or ancient pronunciations. Prayers with fixed rhetorical forms or metrical patterns are sometimes thought to be more powerful, for they are regarded as having been "sanctified by time," and hence, if they have been effective in the past, they are more likely to be acceptable to the supernatural in the present. So that prayer may be as appealing as possible, some people think that it should be accompanied by gifts, offerings, sacrifices, and suffering, in order to convince the spirit being that the worshiper is worthy of help, sincere in his motivations, and thankful for past benefits. Such gifts are often given to the deity, and then either enjoyed by the priest (as the representative of the deity) or even by the worshipers (as when a gift of food is presented to the deity for him to devour the spiritual substance, while the worshipers feast on what is left). However, some gifts can only be successfully transmitted to the supernatural world if they are "killed," even as a person cannot go to the realm of the supernatural until death. Accordingly, animals are sacrificed, jars are broken, and vestments are torn. One special means of transmitting an object to the supernatural is through smoke — hence the holocaust.

In some aspects of transmitting offerings to the supernatural world, we can discern a certain type of symbiotic relationship between the worshiper and his deity, for not only do such gifts communicate something as to the state and motivation of the worshiper, they are thought to be essential in "feeding the god," thus enabling him to protect and benefit his devotee. However, the essential basis for such transmission of the "spiritual essence" of offerings is communication, as taken in its larger cybernetic sense, for what the spirit consumes is not the physical substance, but the symbolic form, and it is this element in religion which is transportable by the processes of spiritual communication.

At times, in the midst of a sending operation, the worshiper wishes to ascertain whether the message has been received. Hence, one finds that Buddhist worshipers in Indonesia, during the process of feeding a stone statue and intoning prayers, throw down little bamboo sticks and by marking the way in which they fall, these persons may know whether the prayer is reaching the deity and is being favorably acted upon.

As we noted above, magic is essentially a sending operation, but it is not dependent upon the whim of the deity to act upon. Magic has a coercive property and cannot be shortcircuited by another being, except as that person uses some counter magic. In other words, magic is a type of communication which does not involve an intelligence at the other end, but an automatic response, wholly predictable in terms of the type and power of the message. In contagious magic there is an obvious feature of transmission, for the piece of dirt, particle of left-over food, hair, nail paring, or piece of cloth (all of which have been in touch with the object to be affected) are regarded as still having an essential relationship. Accordingly, these are a means of transmitting harmful or helpful "messages." In sympathetic magic the problem is more complex, but it is based on an essential factor in the primitive's view of the ontogony of things — namely, that similar objects are capable of affecting each other, though separated both as to distance and time (sympathetic magic may anticipate the event). Charms, whether based on contagious or sympathetic magic, operate on these same principles (but see below).

Receiving Messages

Though in general we often think of religion as being man's communication with the supernatural, in matter of fact, what counts most in religion is the communication from the supernatural to man, and as in the case of sending messages, communication may be from a personal being (a spirit, ancestor, or god) or from a non-personal power, as in astrology, drawing of lots, or ordeals.

Communication from a personal power takes place in a multitude of ways. In the first place, and most obviously, when the devotee of a god becomes possessed and hence utters the words of the deity. Glossalalia (speaking in tongues) is a not uncommon feature of many religions and as such it is one of the highly regarded means of divine communication.

Messages from the deity may be uttered by persons who undergo hysterical experiences, collapse into trances, or are otherwise "beyond themselves." At the same time, however, what they say may not be a direct voice of the god, but a description of a vision, which they have seen during an ecstatic experience. Such a person may also feel touched or ridden or possessed by the god, in the sense of totality of communion.

A further way in which the supernatural speaks to people is through the recorded messages of the past, i.e. through the study of ancient documents embodying the revelation of the deity in former ages.

In general, however, the supernatural does not communicate with people in such dramatic ways. Rather, there are more prosaic means and the supernatural source is usually a non-personal power, e.g. casting of lots, examining of roasted shoulder blades, inspection of the entrails of animals, noting the effects of poison, judging the results of ordeals of boiling oil, hot iron, or sharp knives, reading of palms, examining horoscopes, and spinning fortune wheels.

The non-personal power which is responsible for communication in many religions, and which, on the analogy of electricity, may itself be communicated, is usually described as mana, or an equivalent.

Reenactment of the Sending and Receiving Processes

One type of religious observance has been omitted from the previous lists because it is not simply a matter of direct sending or receiving of messages. It consists in the ceremonial reenactment of communication or revelation, which in itself is not only a kind of message from the supernatural, but which in turn communicates to the supernatural evidence of the fidelity of the worshipers and their dependence upon continued benefits. The great ceremonials of various religions, whether representing purely supernatural activities (e.g. the deeds of the Greek gods on Olympus), cosmological events (including the origin of man and culture), or historical happenings (e.g. deliverance or victory made possible by the gods), are all means of communication, in the sense that they are techniques by which men communicate the memory of the supernatural event to men *and* to the gods. It is this last factor which is most important, for the gods are supposed not only to take pleasure in such reenactments, but to demand such ceremonies as a price for their continued help. Moreover, in many instances it is thought that the deities themselves, though unseen, are participating in the rites. At times an actor becomes completely possessed by the deity which he is portraying, and thus the communication from the deity is direct.

As illustrative of such ritual remembrances or reenactments of communication, there are, of course, the Jewish Passover (which celebrates God's communicative entrance into history to rescue his people) and the Protestant form of Christian Communion, which reproduces symbolic elements of the covenant meal as a means of remembering the significance of Christ's death. The eucharist of the Roman Catholic Church is likewise a reenactment, but with two added factors, namely, the death of Jesus Christ is symbolically "reproduced" and the wafer and wine become not merely symbols of something else, but the material form of Christ is so communicated to these elements that their nature is supposedly altered.

Though in this review of the sending, receiving, and reenactment functions of religion viewed essentially as communication it may have seemed that everything is entirely too simple, nevertheless there are basic features which help to elucidate otherwise often confusing and apparently contradictory phenomena. A few of these areas of religious communication need to be examined.

Socio-Religious Activities

In the study of socio-religious activities, one of the basic problems confronted by any analyst of religion is to try to determine where religion leaves off and social phenomena begin, particularly in such complex events as puberty rites. Of course, no hard and fast rules can be formulated; but if religion is viewed primarily as communication to and from the supernatural, we do have a means of evaluating some of the distinctive features of such rites. For example, all explanations of the myths about the gods, all enactments which involve communication from deities or about divinely ordered happenings, and all ordeals which make a young person capable of receiving or sending such messages are religion. However, the knowledge of skills, events, or actions which are necessary for him to be accepted merely as an adult member of the tribe, and not as a devotee of the god, are purely social. There is, however, a measure of overlapping, for where the social and religious grouping is identical, then what is learned in order to make the youth a *communicant* of the deity or proficient in magic, also serves to identify him as a member of the social group. In such an instance the religious experience is the determinant of the social grouping.

One instructive problem may be presented by the rite of circumcision. In some instances such a rite is necessary if one is to be received by the deity, that is to say, if one is to be acceptable as a communicant. In other instances the rite seems only to mark social acceptance and to be a symbol of age-grading and sexual maturity. Accordingly, in the first type of situation circumcision is a religious rite, for it is an indispensable part of making a person capable of communicating to or receiving communication from the supernatural. In the latter instance it is purely a matter of acceptance with the human grouping and is primarily unrelated to divine matters. On the other hand, such circumcision for social acceptance may be ordered by the gods. Are we then to regard it as religion?

Our answer is both yes and no. If there are supernatural sanctions affecting a particular type of behavior, such actions must be treated under the third category (noted above), namely, the general behavioral consequences of religious practices and beliefs. On the other hand, merely because a particular matter of conduct is demanded or prohibited by the supernatural (whether by the specific dictate of a god or as means of avoiding contact with too much mana) does not mean that it is in the first category of what we call "religious practices" and which for the most part constitutes the core of religion. It is a derivative feature and not central to the major communicative function of religion. An illustrative distinction in this regard is supplied by the differences in Protestant and Roman Catholic views of marriage. In Protestantism marriage is normally blessed by the church (i.e. certain communications take place as a part of the ceremony), but marriage is not a sacrament, as in the Roman Catholic Church, for it is not a means of communicating grace. Similarly, in most Protestant denominations ordination involves many communicative features, but it is likewise not usually regarded as a sacrament, whereby a person receives a particular supernatural *charisma*, which makes it possible for him in turn to communicate grace to others.

Severe controversies have sometimes arisen over the problem of socio-religious activities. For example, in Japan before and during World War II the Christian community was divided over the issue of state Shintoism. Some claimed that such observances for the dead in Shinto shrines was nothing more than respect for the war dead, and as such it constituted a quite legitimate act of national loyalty (regarded by some persons as being nothing more religious than our saluting the flag). Others, however, insisted that Shintoism involved prayers to and for the dead, and that such was not merely a patriotic ritual but a "pagan" act. Placing this controversy in the context of religion as communication would not have resolved the problem, for the political pressures at the time were almost overwhelming. However, it would have provided a basis for more rational discussion of the differences of opinion, and would have helped define what are the social and what are the religious aspects of such "mixed events."

The Shaman, the Priest, and the Prophet

In this view of religion as communication we can appreciate somewhat more fully the roles of shaman, priest, and prophet. The shaman is one who is in very close personal touch with the supernatural, both sending and receiving messages, whether directly by possession or indirectly through ordeals or divining instruments. The priest, on the other hand, is primarily the one who communicates to the deity on behalf of the people. He is their representative, but at the same time he may communicate to the people on particular occasions of general import, such as auguries of the flight of birds or ordeals as to guilt or innocence. The prophet is concerned principally with communicating from the deity, and he may engage in highly ecstatic forms of pronouncement or deliver sermons with moralistic content as a representative of the supernatural, often calling the people back to earlier communications.

By virtue of the very nature of the communication process in which shamans, priests, and prophets are engaged, it is understandable why the shaman should be restricted to the highly personal type of response, for his very individualism of approach and psychologically "marginal" character limits his range of activity, unless by virtue of extreme shrewdness or unusual events he becomes elevated to greater preeminence. The priest, as an intermediary between the people and the deity, is essentially a conservative, for as the funnel of communication to the deity, it is usually important to him to control things as they are. The prophet, on the other hand, must say something new if anyone is to pay any attention to him. Thus he speaks for change, and very frequently puts himself in opposition to the priest. The history of many religions can be most effectively written on the basis of the conflict between the priestly and prophetic traditions.

Charms and Good Luck

Some investigators of religious practices have been at a loss to explain the relationship of charms and good luck to the larger areas of religious beliefs and practices. Admittedly, these elements are marginal, but they are, nevertheless, matters of communication. A charm, for example, communicates a degree of immunity to the person who possesses or wears it. This communication is not, of course, a verbal message. It is the same kind of control which is a part of magic — an invisible power to direct and control, but nonetheless a fully legitimate feature of communication, in the sense of cybernetics.

The fact that a man has a streak of good luck is similarly a kind of religious phenomenon, for though the luck itself may not be identifiable with any objective charm or amulet, nevertheless, it is a power, regarded by many peoples as just as real as physical strength, for it communicates to anyone who possesses it the capacity for such activities as always to choose the right horse, to throw the dice in the best way, or to receive the best hand at cards. It is communication on a magical level.

Contradictory Beliefs

One of the puzzles for students of religion is the fact that so often people hold quite contradictory beliefs as part of the selfsame religious system. These opposing concepts often include differences as to how the earth was made, who first created man, who brought fire and pottery, and how evil men are punished. What is more difficult to understand is that there may exist within the same society different cults, each promulgating quite different views of the world. Moreover, many people may regard themselves as full members of two or more of these quite different systems of belief. Part of the explanation of these phenomena may be found in the view of religion as communication.

In the first place, people are quite

accustomed to receiving several different explanations for the same event from different people, and giving a measure of credence to all the versions. What is more, if there is no way of deciding which variant is really true (and one cannot reconstruct the cosmogony of the world), people often conclude that there is no advantage in throwing away any idea which might have some truth in it. Actually, people's credence in any story is usually based upon their estimate of the character of the persons from whom they have received the account. Since, moreover, one does not usually believe any one person absolutely and disbelieve another with a corresponding absolute rejection, different accounts of the same event are held in a kind of sympathetic isolation, reflecting the various degrees of respect or emotional attachment which one may have for the different sources of the information.

The same thing exists with regard to religious beliefs. Many Japanese, for example, tend to believe jointly in Shintoism, Buddhism, and ancient indigenous practices (such as making gifts along watercourses at the time when the spirits of the dead are supposed to return). Such beliefs are instilled in Japanese people at different times during their lives and usually by different persons, and since the sources of these beliefs were not antagonistic, why should the believer think that such divergent beliefs could not be subscribed to all at the same time? This may mean, of course, that the person actually does not hold any of the beliefs too strongly or that some of these beliefs, to which he overtly subscribes are only "ideal beliefs" and not the real ones which govern his behavior. We must not presume, however, that differences be-

tween ideal and real beliefs necessarily involve conscious hypocrisy — they may be only part of the unresolved anomalies and tensions which by a process of neat compartmentalization people in all societies carry about in "unresolved equilibrium."

On the other hand, when the sources of religious information are in open and declared opposition, people generally feel that such beliefs are antithetical and hence cannot be held simultaneously. Protestant and Catholic views of the church are of this kind. However, even when the sources of information about religious beliefs are opposed to one another, people often hold contradictory beliefs because of the contexts in which they have learned them. For example, many a genuine "convert" to Christianity in Africa continues to have quite a departmentalized mind as regards native religious lore and Christian doctrines. The first he applies to the "black man's world" and the latter to the "white man's civilization," so that ordeals by poison do not seem to be antithetical to Christianity, for he has never actually seen them in conflict within his own experience, even though he may know that the missionary does not approve of the witch doctor. However, he has never seen so-called Christian and pagan methods operating in the same area of life, namely, in determining guilt for witchcraft or in exorcizing evil spirits.

We must thus not accuse people of stupidity in holding contradictory views; we must only realize that these religious beliefs, as the result of communication, have been "conditioned as to their positions of occurrence," either because of the sources or the situations of communication.

The Relationship of Beliefs to Religious Practices

It is often denied that a mere set of beliefs about the supernatural constitutes religion. Rather, it is said that one must perform certain religious acts, e.g. pray or participate in ceremonies. Our problem is primarily to investigate the nature of these beliefs. If the individual involved believes that his views about the supernatural were actually communicated by the supernatural (that they are not merely the elaborations of men), then it may be said that he has a religion, for though the communication may be quite indirect (as through other human beings), nevertheless, it is in a genuine sense a communication from the supernatural. He may not necessarily reciprocate by sending any communication to the supernatural (in the forms of prayer or ritual), but he will inevitably be guided in many of his actions by the beliefs which he regards as having supernatural origin. On the other hand, a person who has ideas about God, which he regards as derived purely from men's reasonings about the unknown, must be regarded as having a philosophy rather than a religion. If God is thought to be essentially a construct of human reasoning, whether as the result of the flights of fancy or as a necessity imposed by investigations of the universe, one can only conclude that such an approach is philosophical.

The Relationship of Holy Objects to Communication

In our emphasis upon religion as communicating it is easy to overlook the significance of the various so-called "holy" objects. In terms of communication they fall into seven classes: (1) paraphernalia of the communicators, such as robes, vestments, censers, incense, staffs, chains, stools, and whips, (2) objects which are directly involved in the communication, like entrails of animals, tea leaves, crystal balls, benge poison, grains of corn, (3) objects which may be used to induce communication by the human source, including tobacco, hashish (marihuana), mushrooms, peyote, alcohol, (4) objects in which communicable but nondiscriminating supernatural power exists (charms and amulets), such as rabbit's foot, beads, lion's claw, hippo hide, (5) objects in which a communicating power exists (fetishes and idols), (6) objects which make communication more efficacious (by providing proofs of sincerity, earnestness, thankfulness, etc.) or which may be themselves communicated in symbolic essence, like offerings, sacrifices, holocausts, and (7) objects which resemble or symbolize a communicating supernatural power — namely, images and signs. In speaking of charms and amulets as having nondiscriminating, communicable power, we mean that such charms cannot decide when, how, or whom to protect or harm. Their power is nondiscriminating, but it is communicable to the object to which it is assigned or attached. In speaking of the power in fetishes and idols as being "communicating" we also imply discrimination, for the power must be induced to communicate, in much the same manner as a god.

The Preservation of Religious Systems despite their Dysfunction

There is no doubt about the fact that many societies maintain religious systems despite their dysfunction, that is, positive harm in many areas of life, e.g. antisocial consequences of black magic and secret societies, harmful effects of scarification, deformities, and mutilations, and excessive expenditures required to satisfy the dictates of the supernatural. To what can we attribute this apparent disregard for the negative values in such actions? How can such practices be validated when so much obvious harm ensues? Of course, there is a great deal of difference between the individual and the collective conscience in such matters. Black magic generally appears to the man who performs it as being a positive good, at least for himself, and scarification and mutilation provide certain distinctions for those who undergo such experiences. Moreover, lavish expenditures often provide a basis for the acquisition of prestige. Nevertheless, even primitive peoples are not fools, and they can evaluate such actions in terms of their total effects, though it is true, of course, that few people tend to be self-investigative or self-evaluating when it comes to traditional practices. Despite this fact it would seem that such practices would have long since disappeared (even as they are doing in many areas) if it were not for some continuing factors which seemed to validate their religious significance. Possibly the importance of a communication religious practice holds at least a partial answer to the problem. For example, the employment of black magic is not to be judged merely in terms of its social consequences (otherwise it would be nothing more nor less than crime), but as a means of communication with the supernatural. This adds to the actual deed a sinister and mysterious attraction for the participants and provides such an action with a kind of self-validating reality. This communication with the unseen forces, this power to manipulate

objects and persons beyond one's apparent control — this provides magic with its *raison d'être* and gives it a value quite apart from the social consequences of the deed. Mutilation, which may make a person a more acceptable communicant with his god, or excessive expenditures which guarantee effective communication, must be judged not in their personal or social context but as parts of a communicative process, where they seem entirely justified. Our difficulty as outsiders is that we judge such actions in terms of quite a different frame of reference. We seen only social harm, economic loss, and personal disability. The indigenous participants see, however, that all these "dysfunctions" (as we have labeled them) are really essential religious functions for they have communicative relevance.

We must not hesitate to admit that in seeing in religion a dominant role for communication we do not at the same time presume to chart the origin of religion, though it would not be difficult to assume the circumstances in which communication with the unknown or supernatural might have been inaugurated. However, the point is that once we assume even a beginning of such communication, the rest of the process seems to follow, for one type of communication leads readily to another, and ceremonialism, as the reenactment of communication, would be an expected development. Another advantage in this thesis of the central significance of communication in religion is that we can understand more fully the important role which language plays in religious activity, for if religion is centrally concerned with symbolic communication and language is symbolic activity *par excellence*, the extensive use of language in religion is inevitable.

The adoption of the principle of communication as a dominant element in religion may also provide us with a means of typing various religious systems in the most functionally significant way, as to whether cultures emphasize one or another type of communication, such as sending as over against receiving. For example, traditional American Protestantism may be characterized as "individual sending" (the emphasis upon individual, personalized prayers) but "channelized receiving" with verbal techniques used almost exclusively. In Roman Catholicism channelizing sending is either through the priest or by memorized prayers and receiving is strictly controlled, except for "acceptable visions." In Roman Catholicism reenactment is, however, highly institutionalized, to the point of not only commemorating the death of Christ, but, as noted above, mystically reproducing the death in the sacrifice of the eucharist. West Africa religion is very much a receiving religion, including dreams, visions, ecstasy, tongues, ordeals, and divination, and sending is predominantly to non-personal powers through mechanical control (magic). Melanesian religion is primarily a sending religion, with control communication combined with a reenactment communication.

Certain Theological Implications for Christianity

It is impossible here to indicate the entire range of theological implications of such a view of communication as a focal element in religions.[5] However, there are some particularly relevant elements which must be touched on, for

they are of utmost importance to any missionary undertaking.

Uniquely in Christianity, God communicates not mere concepts about himself (as, for example, in Islam), but he communicates himself in the person of his Son, in whom the Word became flesh. Moreover, it is God who takes the initiative in communication, and through the incarnation, both by word and by life, communicates to men. Man in turn communicates with God, preeminently through prayer, but in the relationship of sons to a Father, who reserves the right to decide what is good for his children. We may even say that in the incarnation God "encoded" his infinite qualities in the limitations of human language and human form, and by means of his acts within history showed us what he is like. If, however, we were ever to understand this communication, it had to be adjusted to our finite categories of thought and reinterpreted on the basis of human patterns of behavior. In prayer, on the other hand, we encode messages to an infinite God, but we know not how to pray as we ought, but the Spirit makes intercession for us "with groanings which cannot be uttered." That is to say, our prayers, encoded within the limitations of our own speech and based on our faulty knowledge, are decoded by God in terms of his infinite wisdom and answered on the basis of his divine providence.

The fundamental objective of missionary work is to put people in communicative touch with God, whereby the Spirit of God may have access to the human heart and communicate his divine grace. All of the explanations about religious faith may be regarded as more or less the "grammar" of religion, in contrast with the actual use of the "language" of

[5] These are to be treated in a forthcoming book *Communication and Christian Faith*, to be published by Harper and Bros. in 1960.

religion, namely, communication with God, which is the reality of our fellowship and communion. Moreover, the missionary must not limit his presentation of this great "communicative truth" to merely the historical event of the incarnation which took place some two thousand years ago. God communicates with men today by his Spirit, on the basis of the unique redemptive and reconciliatory event of history — the cross. Our faith is thus not merely in a historically grounded revelation but in a contemporary communication by the Holy Spirit, without which we would all be "dead in our trespasses and sins."

It is not without significance that in almost all "revival movements" it is this emphasis upon the communicative acts of the Holy Spirit which provides not only the spark of religious fervor but the continuing religious dynamic. There is absolutely no doubt but that for the missionary the most essential element is the contemporary communicative act whereby God, as historically revealed in Jesus Christ, reveals himself now to men and women. This is the fact which changes an intellectual encounter with the claims of Christianity into a religious experience of "receiving Jesus Christ."

Eugene A. Nida

New Religions for Old :
A Study of Culture Change

Culture change is of great interest to anthropologists, but none has developed a satisfactory model to explain it. The existence of various approaches to the study of religion points to the multidimensional nature of religion. In order to account for deletion, addition, substitution, and coalescence in religious change, the author proposes the use of models from economics and linguistics (the latter will be handled in the next issue). Economics models provide useful insights through the concepts of value and cost. For experience shows that in religion as in the market place, lowering the price of a "commodity" can also lower its value and therefore its desirability. It is shown also that values are based upon the total worldview of a society. They must also be related to the felt needs of people rather than to artificially ascribed needs. Finally, the author discusses the relevance of the concepts of "unlimited desire" in the face of "limited resources".

ONLY twenty-four years ago the Enga people of the Baiyer River Valley in the highlands of eastern New Guinea were still living in fortified villages along the sharp ridges of steep mountains, afraid to move into the lush plains for fear of head-hunting enemies, with whom they were constantly at war to seek revenge for earlier killings. But now there are in this same region primary and secondary schools, an excellent hospital, a coffee and lumber cooperative, and a number of churches (at least 25 percent of the population regard themselves as Christians). Some of the young people have gone off to study in the university and their parents take great pride in their postal savings accounts and in the cars and trucks which they have bought, usually by the pooling of resources throughout an extended family. Of course, not all the old ways of life have been given up. In fact, the Christians have incorporated a "graveyard cult" into their faith in Jesus. But there has been a radical change from the old to the new—with almost unbelievable rapidity and with remarkable thoroughness, considering the cultural millenia through which the Enga people of the Baiyer River Valley have passed in less than a single generation.

Present-Day Interest in Culture Change

Interest in and concern for culture change are no longer peripheral interests of anthropologists. While such developments were often treated in the past as merely some phase of "applied anthropology," matters of rapid culture change are being regarded as central to the very nature of anthropological investigation.[1] The basic studies by H. G. Barnett,[2] Margaret Mead,[3] Robert Redfield,[4] Allan Holmberg[5] and George Foster[6] have done much to focus new light on the prob-

lems and techniques of culture change; while the research and writing of Vittorio Lanternari,[7] Louis Luzbetak,[8] David B. Barrett,[9] Eugene A. Nida,[10] and Jacob Loewen and William D. Reyburn (in numerous articles in *Practical Anthropology*) have highlighted change in religion.

Nevertheless, despite all the research and writing in this field, it is interesting to note that in terms of overall insight into the basic motivations for religious change, we are at present not much further advanced than we were with Redfield[11] whose book on the *Primitive World and Its Transformations* emphasized the strong cohesive motivations which exist in "peasant society," or with Barnett,[12] whose penetrating analysis of the factors of setting, incentives, roles of participants, and the processes for acceptance or rejection of culture change has helped materially to understand more fully what we observe in culture change. Holmberg[13] has aided

[1] A number of recent articles in the *American Anthropologist* illustrate interest in culture change, e.g. Theodore Graves, "Acculturation, Access and Alcohol in a Tri-ethnic Community," Vol. 69 (1967), pp. 306-321; Fredrik Barth, "On the Study of Social Change," Vol. 69 (1967), pp. 661-669; Henry Rosenfeld, "Change, Barriers to Change, and Contradictions in the Arab Village Family," Vol. 70 (1968), pp. 732-752; Irwin Press, "Ambiguity and Innovation: Implications for the Genesis of a Culture Broker," Vol. 71 (1969), pp. 205-217.

[2] H.G. Barnett, *Innovation: The Basis of Cultural Change* (New York: McGraw-Hill Book Co., 1953).

[3] Margaret Mead, *Cultural Patterns and Technical Change* (New York: New American Library of World Literature, 1955); *New Lives for Old: Cultural Transformation, Manus, 1928-1953* (New York: William Morrow, 1956).

[4] Robert Redfield, *The Primitive World and Its Transformations* (Ithaca, N.Y.: Cornell University Press, 1957).

[5] Allan R. Holmberg, "Changing Community Attitudes and Values in Peru: A Case Study in Guided Change," in R.N. Adams, *et al.*, eds., *Social Change in Latin America Today* (New York: Harper and Row for Council on Foreign Relations, 1960).

[6] George M. Foster, *Traditional Cultures and the Impact of Technological Change* (New York: Harper and Row, 1962).

[7] Vittorio Lanternari, *Religions of the Oppressed: A Study of Modern Messianic Cults* (New York: Alfred A. Knopf, 1963).

[8] Louis J. Luzbetak, *The Church and Cultures* (Techny, Ill.: Divine Word Publications, 1963).

[9] David B. Barrett, *Schism and Renewal in Africa: An Analysis of Six Thousand Contemporary Religious Movements* (Nairobi: Oxford University Press, 1968).

[10] Eugene A. Nida, *Religion Across Cultures* (New York: Harper and Row, 1968); *Communication of the Gospel in Latin America* (Cuernavaca, Mex.: Centro Intercultural de Documentacion, 1969).

[11] Robert Redfield, *op. cit.*

[12] H.G. Barnett, *op. cit.*

[13] Allan R. Holmberg, *op. cit.*

our understanding of the role of traditional values, and Foster[14] has provided important insight in developing the concept of "the limited good" and how it influences the acceptance or rejection of change. But there are still enormous questions. The interaction of people is far more complex than we had ever imagined. Moreover, even when we can describe what has happened, we are often at a loss to explain the dynamics of the change, especially since religious beliefs often seem quite senseless. Frequently the followers of a particular religion appear to be holding quite incompatible sets of beliefs, without being in the least disturbed by the inconsistencies and contradictions. The very motivations which people have for engaging in one or another religious practice may be entirely contradictory. This seemingly anomalous character of religion needs to be explored and understood if we are to comprehend something of its real structure and functioning. Moreover, without an appreciation of certain of these fundamental factors relating to the nature of religious beliefs and practices we can never properly understand the changes which constantly take place in any religious system.

When we are dealing with religious change in Christianity, we must quite naturally try to face up to still other factors: the role of the Holy Spirit, the supernatural involvement in conversion, the nature of repentance, and the function of the "community of faith."

---

[14] George M. Foster, *op. cit.*

If we are to understand the nature of change in religion, we do not need more information so much as more insight. We possess numerous records of culture change which, even though spotty and sometimes inaccurate, nevertheless provide a wealth of background data. What is much more important is the finding of some new models which may provide the basis for fresh insights or perspectives, with which we can view the phenomena of culture change from more realistic and dynamic standpoints.

Traditional Approaches to Religion

Traditionally religion has been studied from a number of perspectives. The history of religions has shed great light on what has happened through the centuries to the "world religions," but we are not much closer to understanding just *why* it happened. A societal approach to religion can help us understand better how religion functions in human organization and how important a determinant it is in human behavior, but religion is far more than a means of social expression or of group solidarity. A philosophical approach to religion is useful in understanding the relation between religious beliefs and so-called "truth values," but for the most part religionists seem to have very little concern with the ultimate truth of what they believe. Faith seems to be self-validating. Functionalism emphasizes the utilitarian values of religion: how religion serves to maintain the status quo, helps people relate to the world around them, and provides the "supernatural power" to get along or to get ahead; but religions sometimes turn out to be malfunctioning. Why do people choose to maintain a religious system which seems so obviously a barrier to the realization of their goals? A psychiatric approach to religion has introduced some interesting viewpoints, but has promised far more than it has been able to deliver. Treating religion as a system of communication[15] can also suggest interesting and relevant elements in religion, but it is certainly far from being the whole story.

The very fact that religion can be approached from so many different standpoints should, however, teach us something very significant about religion itself. Despite traditional approaches to religion, which have often classified it as one of the cultural capstones—a kind of overarching worldview of the supernatural—religion is essentially not this at all. Rather, it constitutes a componential feature of all the basic motivations, thus providing "meaning with supernatural sanctions." If we describe the basic positive motivations for life as consisting of satisfaction of thirst, hunger, sex, belonging (loving and being loved), physical activity, mental activity, and esthetic activity[16] we may say that for all peoples there is also the all-pervading component of "desire for meaning." When this meaning takes on a supernatural character and provides a mechanism by which people may establish communicative links with the supernatural, this is religion. Moreover, this is the universal phenomenon found in cultures throughout the world, except where the so-called scientific approach has succeeded in eliminating religious beliefs from some sector of the population by substituting some competing ideological system, which claims equal ultimacy and a similar kind of "transcendence" demanding a corresponding "faith."

The Nature of Change in Religion

Change in religion may be described as consisting primarily of four processes: deletion, addition, substitution, and coalescence.[17] If, for example, people give up headhunting (whether voluntarily or by force) as a form of socioreligious behavior, one can describe this change as a deletion of an element or feature. Of course, the fundamental attitudes concerning retaliation may not have changed, but at least one of the outward manifestations of such retaliation has been eliminated for the time being. It is also possible to add religious features. In fact, addition is seemingly a very common process. In most of Africa the practice of conquered tribes has simply been to add the spirits and the taboos of the conquerors, in the same way as newly converted Christians have often adopted such practices as Western marriage ceremonies (with white gown, flowers, and bridesmaids) as an essential element in the sacramentalizing of marriage. In many societies marriage is primarily a social contract, until a Western form of marriage (as

15 Eugene A. Nida, *Communication of the Gospel.*

16 Eugene A. Nida, *Religion Across Cultures.*

17 H.G. Barnett, *op. cit.*

advocated, or enforced, by some missionaries) brings a distinctive religious dimension to marriage.

More often than not change in religion means some form of substitution, that is, a combination of addition and deletion. Something is added, which takes the place of an already existing feature. For example, confidence in the Holy Spirit may supplant the fear of evil spirits. However, more often than not the result of new religious elements or features is coalescence, rather than mere addition or substitution. The new is added, but in the process it is so reinterpreted and restructured as to render it almost unrecognizable. For example, in the village of Tetelcingo, Mexico, an ancient Aztec fertility ritual was combined with beliefs in Jesus Christ and the Virgin Mary, so that each year the images of the Christ and the Virgin were placed in a box one night, and nine months later a doll was christened as the "god of the year."

If, however, we are to understand processes of addition, deletion, substitution, and coalescence (or syncretism), we must do more than describe what has taken place. We must be in a position to explain, at least in part, certain of the structures into which such changes fit and which influence so fundamentally the nature of the changes themselves. Culture change, and especially in the case of religion, involves primarily two systems: (1) a system of values, which determines the choices which people make in addition, deletion, substitution, and coalescence, and (2) a system for the learning of new values, that is, for internalizing the new values and making them a part of one's culture.

That religion is a system of values seems in many ways to be merely a truism. The ethical "dos and don'ts" of religion certainly involve values, whether implicit or explicit. Ritual performances are most certainly related to such valued processes and states as propitiation, the protective presence of the spirits, and a sense of wellbeing and belonging. Even the myths, which constitute explanations of this world or instructions as to how to get to the next, are filled with values. But for the person concerned with culture change, the fundamental question is how one can learn new values. What are the mechanisms by which newly offered values will be appropriated and internalized, with the least amount of distortion or perversion as the result of coalescence with seemingly incompatible values of the indigenous system?

Insight from Relevant Models

If we are to understand the nature of values, especially as these are related to fundamental motivations and if we are to appreciate the problems involved in learning new values, then perhaps two of the most important areas from which to choose relevant models are economics and linguistics. Models of economics have special relevance since they are so obviously associated with values and competing choices. Linguistic models offer special advantages since these are related so closely to the internalization of symbolic systems, whether by largely unconscious processes as in the case of first-language learning, or by seemingly conscious ones as in the case of second-language learning.[18] In fact, it is quite amazing to see the extent to which the problems of acculturation in religion parallel problems in language assimilation. In a sense this parallelism should not be surprising, for both language and religion consist of sets of symbols organized into highly complex structures and having both denotative and connotative significance.

One must, however, recognize the danger in the use of models, for as Turbayne[19] has so effectively pointed out, models are only extended metaphors. Such models are, therefore, not descriptions of precisely what takes place, but are structures which permit us to attain somewhat greater insight into the nature of the complex relations which we must explore. The models may be said to provide a basis for constructing relevant hypotheses, which may serve as perspectives—or even as grids or lattices—through which we may view phenomena and by means of which we may be able to understand more clearly some of the processes which we observe.

---

[18] One may argue that in second-language learning the conscious processes are really pre-learning, in that they relate more to the struggle to reduce contamination and to develop awareness when habits are already established.

[19] Colin M. Turbayne, *The Myth of Metaphor* (New Haven, Conn.: Yale University Press, 1962).

Economics Models

Certain economics models are of special usefulness in the study of values since economics is so closely related to problems of values and costs, especially when the latter are usually "weighed" in terms of choices between alternatives. Perhaps one of the most important economics models is the one which describes the relation between cost and value, understood in this context as the subjective value, that is, the value assigned to an object by the person who pays the cost. According to this model, within certain limits the higher the cost greater the value. Similarly, the lower the cost the less the value. When Toni Permanents were first put on the market in the United states, they were priced at twenty-five cents, which provided even then a considerable markup. But women were simply not interested in purchasing something for their hair which seemed too cheap. When later the price was advanced to $1.00, the demand increased immediately, since the increased cost seemed to augment the value. A similar situation exists with respect to the "bride price" in Africa. A woman for whom a very low bride price has been paid usually ranks low in social prestige. She is simply not regarded as having much value. On the other hand, a woman for whom a high bride price has been paid tends to have a high social rating. The same relationship between cost and value may be noted in religious experience. The story of the young pastor who said to one of his elderly saintly parishioners, "I'd give everything for your faith," and who received the reply, "That is precisely what it cost," illustrates very well the intimate relations between cost and value in religion. Perhaps a low value is put on religion in the West because it generally costs so little. For those who suffered "dungeon and sword" for their faith, religion was the most precious possession of their lives—in fact, it was worth more than life. For those who are the spiritual descendants of such heroes of faith, religion may have become merely a pleasant tradition, but for many of their children religion has become a blame nuisance. It is not without significance that those groups which make large demands of their followers are precisely those which tend to grow most rapidly and to retain their adherents most firmly. Note, for example, the demands made by such groups as Jehovah's Witnesses, Seventh-Day Adventists, and the Iglesia na Cristo (in the Philippines).

Of course, when the price of faith is extremely high, e.g. in cases of intense persecution (the Spanish Inquisition) or systematic discrimination (in antireligious totalitarian states), there may be a rapid falling off in the number of persons willing to pay the price. But there are always a few who are willing "to go and sell all that they have in order to buy the pearl of great price." However, when the price is too low, there seems to be an even greater loss—not so much in the numbers of adherents but in the quality of adherence. It simply seems incomprehensible to people that Christ can be preached as the most important value in life, while the demands of discipleship are described as being little more than "joining the club." If the claims of Christianity are true, then it cannot, and should not, be cheap. But if Christian faith is primarily advertised so as to appeal to the bargain-hunter in religion, then it obviously cannot be genuine or true.

Lowering the Price

One principle of economics involves the lowering of the price in order to increase distribution. Apparently, some persons have more or less unconsciously applied the same principle to the presentation of Christian faith. In order to make it more popular, they feel that they must reduce the price, or at least lower the down payment. But the price (or cost) of an article can usually be lowered only in two ways, either by introducing inferior ingredients or by mass production.

Lowering the price of Christianity by the introduction of inferior ingredients may be said to involve such procedures as claiming that it is really not necessary to experience any repentance to become a Christian. Moreover, no fundamental change in behavior is demanded, and little or no mention is made of sacrifice or service. Rather, Christianity is offered as a "new suit of clothes" or a new set of "Jesus taboos." Even ancestor worship can be "accommodated" and in fact theologically justified by some as "honoring your father and mother so that you may live long upon the earth." In contrast with this tendency to lower the price of Christianity, Maoist Communism insists upon a high price for acceptance within the system: first, the denouncing of all former loyalties and, second, some outstanding sacrifice for the cause.

The price may also be lowered by mass production, which in the case of Christianity means a kind of "mass message"—simplistic answers to unasked questions. Christian faith is, for instance, reduced to a "six-point program for getting to heaven"—six verses of Scripture which are to be accepted in a particular order as one sure entrance into the Kingdom. Others would even reduce Christianity to four points. Such a system of providing all the answers while asking no questions can be fatal to faith; but almost equally disastrous is the tendency to ask all the questions, while providing no answers. On the other hand, some propagandists of Christianity have almost ceased to ask questions or to provide answers. They would rather strive to "create a mood," which can lead to presumed "emotional sincerity." This is excellent for creating an aura of religion, but it is so largely form without content—"the form of godliness, without the power thereof."

In the production of the "mass message" considerable use is made of the mass media, but these two must be clearly distinguished. While the mass media involve a communication directed to the masses, the mass message is simply a depersonalized panacea, which fails to recognize people as people and treats them largely as statistics. Such mass production of the message denies fundamental differences in people's backgrounds and problems and ends up in institutionalizing faith

as a popular technique for getting something from God, rather than a personal encounter with Jesus Christ and a decision to take up one's cross as a follower of the Crucified. In contrast with the approach of Jesus, whose conversations with such persons as Nicodemus, the woman of Samaria, and the rich young man were so intensely personal and varied, proponents of the mass message would seek to standardize the techniques and the content of the communication. The result of such a procedure is usually to produce the "lowest common denominator," in other words, to see how little can one believe or how little can one do and still be regarded as a follower of the Christ. The introduction of inferior ingredients and the mass production of the message can be disastrous to real faith.

A System of Values

Though values are often described in terms of particular persons and actions, they can only be accurately described and understood in terms of the systems or structures of which they constitute integral parts. These value systems must be recognized as cultural universals. No person or society exists without them. In fact, all human experience seems to be stored within the memory with some sort of "value tag," as Miller, Galanter, and Pribram have so effectively pointed out in *Plans and the Structure of Behavior*.[20] The existence of values is a universal,

[20] George Miller, Eugene Galanter, and Karl H. Pribram, *Plans and the Structure of Behavior* (New York: Holt, Rinehart and Winston, 1960).

even when the specific values seem to the outsider to be contradictory, as for example when the Pacaas Novas of South America eat the body of a dead relative as a way of showing the individual great honor. In the Philippines local farmers almost always sell their rice immediately after harvest, even though the price may be very much depressed. In fact, they could much more advantageously wait a few months and sell at a much increased price. However, the pressures of indigent relatives are almost unbearable if one has plenty of rice on hand, but if the rice has been sold, one is much more likely to be able to escape the demands of such poor dependents.

In order to understand such seemingly contradictory values, one must always view them within the context of the total stuctures of which they are only parts. In fact, it is only within such structured systems of various grades and classes of values that the different values make sense. One must recognize, however, that the dominant values differ radically from one culture to another. For New Guineans one of the high values is the possession of material objects. For most African cultures, status, as determined by the number and quality of persons who are dependent upon, or obligated to, an individual, is a dominant value; while in the Western world personal achievement, whether as a movie actor or as a business magnate, is rated as extremely important.

Such values, however, come in systems or structured clusters of values. For many African societies there are two very important values: (1) the possession of "life force" and (2) interpersonal loyalties. This life force expresses itself in a number of ways: physical strength and health, sexual potency, material possessions, the size of one's extended family, ability to command, and retention in the memory of one's descendants. Similarly, interpersonal loyalties mean that friendships are far more important than institutions. Accordingly, if one knows the family and clan connections of different candidates and the electors, the results of an election can be readily predicted, since failure to vote according to such a system of loyalties is generally unthinkable. These two important values in African life help to explain why certain types of behavior are regarded as so "bad" or "sinful." For example, loss of self-control in the presence of peers or superiors is much worse than committing adultery, and stinginess is regarded in some African societies as being one of the worst of sins, next to sorcery. In fact, among the Venda of the Northern Transvaal, stinginess is something for which there is simply no means of atonement.

If one is to understand the value system of any society, this can only be done in terms of the total worldview, of which the value system constitutes a part. In many African cultures ultimate reality, or causation, is of two types: material and spiritual. This means, for example, that if a man has been killed by a lion, there have been two forces at work: the material force, which is the lion as the agent of the killing, and also the spiritual force, controlled by someone who has so manipulated the spiritual powers as to cause the victim to be present at the spot where he could be fatally attacked by the lion. The control of such forces must involve religious techniques, which are essential for all kinds of welfare: sufficient crops, luck in gambling, winning a lawsuit, and guaranteeing fertility of women and animals. Such control of spiritual forces would, however, not be so necessary if it were not for the widely prevailing concept of the "limited good" – the fact that there is supposed to be just so much good in the universe and that if one obtains proportionately more than others, it can only be done at others' expense. Those who have more of this life force are supposed to be able to capture more of the good for themselves. Nevertheless, one who gets more than is due his status is most surely employing foul means and therefore he must be whittled down to size. In fact, in many societies it is perfectly all right for the foreigner to prosper, even at the expense of the local population, since he is seemingly not governed by the same laws relating to the supply of "good," but if a local person seems to be too prosperous he may very well have the source of his wealth destroyed, even by members of his own family or clan.

Values are thus not isolated entities, which can be easily maneuvered and restructured. They are all part of a subtly and complexly structured system, in which all the parts neatly blend and dovetail. Moreover, values

can only be judged adequately in terms of the fulfillment of needs, as recognized within the system. It is for this reason that an amplification of the concept of values is necessary before considering some of the broader implications of cost and value as related to need.

Value and Need

To speak only of cost and value is to miss one of the most important factors, namely, need. Costs may fluctuate radically and rapidly depending upon availability, but needs tend to be far more stable. However, in discussing values as related to needs, one may judge values from at least two standpoints: subjective (the value attached to something by the possessor or the one who has paid the price) and objective (the value presumably attached to something by the society). Some economists would like to recognize also a theoretical third type of value–the true worth of something; but only God could determine this value.

In the discussion of need, however, we are faced with the entire range of human reactions and responses. A car, for example, fulfills a physical need for transportation. It may also fulfill a social need for acceptance within a particular set of society, and it may equally be looked upon as satisfying a psychological need, for status or for a feeling of power. It is most interesting how in the United States advertising of cars has concentrated primarily upon the social need for status and the psychological need for power, rather than upon any intrinsic value of the machine itself or the convenience of transportation.

In the case of institutionalized Christianity, where in general the cost has been lowered, with a corresponding lowering in implied value, there is nevertheless a strong tendency to "sell people" on their need for religion. But this has not been easy. One can scarcely appeal to the need for the church because of physical want, since the government has taken over most of the social services for the poor and the sick. Similarly, appeals based upon social needs tend to be somewhat fictitious, for many churches are relatively narrow in the spectrum of persons whom they really accept. On the other hand, this selectivity can provide people with a feeling of class belonging. However, many churches have become highly impersonal and institutionalized, and in some ways much less creative and active, than service clubs and special interest groups. Even when the church claims to be meeting psychological needs there are some serious questions, for many churches seem to be far less realistic in the approach to psychological problems than such groups as Alcoholics Anonymous and Weight Watchers. The old-fashioned Methodist "class meetings" served a very valid function, but in the more sophisticated society of our own day there is little or nothing in the church to take their place. In the final analysis, many people are rejecting institutional Christianity because they do not feel that the cost of the church is commensurate with the needs that are fulfilled. When one realizes that the total value of church properties in the United States, both Protestant and Roman Catholic, amounts to a total of at least $79,500,000,000[21] or more than $500 for each statistical Christian in the country, one wonders just how many of these persons would rather have the $500 and let the church disappear.

It is important to recognize, however, that in this reaction against institutional forms of Christianity, there is, nevertheless, a continuing and greatly increased interest in the Bible. Sales of Scriptures have increased enormously, both in the United States and throughout the world, during the last six years.[22] Moreover, there is a great increase in the number of lay groups meeting to read and study the Bible together. This rejection of the Western forms of Christianity, while retaining loyalty to the Bible, is especially conspicuous in many of the separatist movements in Africa and Asia. People seem to feel at home with the Scriptures, but are alienated from the forms of Christendom with which they have become acquainted.

"Limited Resources" and "Unlimited Desire"

Present-day economic theory is based upon the premise of limited re-

21 Martin A. Larson, *Church Wealth and Business Income* (New York: Philosophical Library, 1965).

22 The United Bible Societies have experienced an increase throughout the world of more than 300 percent during the last six years, from approximately 50 million copies (Bibles, New Testaments, portions, and selections) to almost 175 million in 1969.

sources and unlimited desire, and the resulting need of people to make the resources cover the greatest number of desires. This premise fits man's economic life admirably, but there is a basic problem involved when the same set of concepts is applied to Christianity. In the first place, people have a very "limited desire" for God. In fact, most people regard God as an intruder on man's own domain. The man who is wholly dedicated to God is thought to have lost himself. In a sense, this is quite true, but Jesus would point out that just such a man has found his true self (Luke 9.24). On the whole, however, most persons would rather negotiate with supernatural powers so as to keep them in their places and so as to obtain as many benefits as possible, while keeping such forces well within a defined sphere of influence. An Ecuadorian Quechua Indian does not hesitate to whip his saint if the benefits are not in proportion to the offerings, while more sophisticated Christians in America think that they can get God on their side if only they contribute ten percent of their income to the church. In such "deals with deity" most religionists seek their own advantage. In Asia they buy temple money, so that with a minimal expenditure they can build quite a large fire. In Africa, many people dedicate the essence of the food to the spirits, while they content themselves with consuming the substance, and in any of a thousand ways people attempt through symbolic actions to wring concessions from the Almighty.

People seem to have no difficulty in having an unlimited desire for false or substitute gods, for example, wealth, personal achievement, power, fame, status, or even ethnic and national greatness. But all of these are only subtle (or even not too subtle) extensions of one's own ego. In the ultimate analysis, however, these false gods do not seem to satisfy, for man knows the idolatrous nature of his own creations. However, just as idols of plaster and wood tend to satisfy most people, since most people prefer not to think about ultimate values and reality, so false gods appear to be enough for most men and women. Such gods serve very effectively to insulate people from God himself.

Though in a real sense most people have a strictly limited desire for God, the spiritual resources which God makes available to man are entirely unlimited, quite in contrast with economic resources. The offer of God is one of grace—in a sense, something for nothing. But rather than being good news, this act of grace goes counter to man's pride and self-image. If man must face God, he wants to do so on the basis of his own merits, so that he can have some claims upon divine favor. Accordingly, the idea of a covenant made by God to be accepted by people seems utterly contrary to his "economic theory." The fact that God claims that man can only be radically changed by love appears to be hollow and weak. And the idea that God should proceed from seeming weakness—that is, that he should have gained the victory through the Cross—is unthinkable. Accordingly, man has consistently tended to apply to Christianity his own economics models. Hence, grace has been treated not as an activity of God but as a substance, something which according to Medieval theology could be earned or even purchased.

In reality, then, true Christianity simply does not fit this economics model. What has happened is that Christianity has been shoved onto this Procrustean bed, and what has not fit such a marketplace faith has been discarded as invalid. The economics models do, therefore, have a validity when applied to Christendom. In fact, the analogies are so close that one is almost compelled to think that they are applicable to true Christian faith. But in reality institutional Christendom is perhaps as far removed from true faith in Jesus Christ as one could imagine, since in order to survive it has had to wear such a clever disguise and to conform so closely to the "ways of the world." Such fundamental contrasts as do exist between true faith and institutional adherence are perhaps in no way better highlighted than in these applications of economics models to religious behavior.

In the next issue, we will consider the applicability of linguistic models to religious change.

Eugene A. Nida

Linguistic Models for Religious Behavior

In the last issue, the author discussed the applicability of models from economics to religious change. There are also parallels between religion and language: both employ symbols and arrangements of symbols, and both can be analyzed in terms of deep structures, kernel structures, and surface structures. Various kinds of problems can be viewed as arising from discrepancies between these levels, of the failure of one or the other to function properly. Examples of such discrepancy include racial and social discrimination in churches, and the failure of many young people to internalize the deep structure of their religion (which is shown by their casual abandonment of religion under adverse influences). Finally, comparisons are made between learning a first religion and a first language, and learning a second religion and a second language. These insights are then applied to the problem of communicating a new religion.

THE structural parallelism between language and religion is rather striking, for both employ symbols, and arrangements of symbols, as the essential means of communicating distinctive messages. For language the symbols are primarily the words, and the arrangements consist of the grammatical constructions. For religion there are likewise symbols, for example, offerings, altars, fetish bundles, signs (such as the cross, fish), and consecrated substances, e. g. water (for baptism), wine (for holy communion), and oil (for consecrating or healing). Religious communication also requires rather precise arrangements of such symbols if they are to be significant. For example, in Christian baptism the specific arrangement of the water, spoken words, and the officiating priest or minister, are essential. In religious communication the meaning is generally not to be found in the isolated symbol itself, but in the combined sets of symbols. That is to say, even as in language, the distinctive meanings are not to be found in the isolated units (the words), but in the combinations(the sentences). Hence, for baptism the primary significance is not in the individual elements (whether objects or actions), but in the total combination, since the combination is always to some extent different from the sum total of the parts. Christian baptism, for example, has as its basic meaning "initiation into the faith," whether as a believer or as an infant being symbolically initiated into the "family of God." But it is not possible to add up the different meanings of the individual units which comprise this ritual and to come up with this meaning. In this sense, therefore, religious communication differs from most language communication in that for the latter most combinations of words are endocentric in meaning, that is to say, the meaning of the whole can be predicted from the parts. Idioms, on the other hand, are exocentric, in that the meaning of the whole is different from the sum total of the parts. One could, therefore, say that for religion, as for most types of symbolic behavior, the distinctive combinations of symbolic actions and objects are essentially exocentric, that is to say, they are idiomatic expressions.

There are, however, two very important aspects of the meaning of religious symbols which must be carefully noted. In the first place, such symbols are essentially arbitrary in the sense that they very often depend upon accidents of history. The cross in Christianity is such an arbitrary symbol, arising as it does from the manner in which Jesus was executed. In the southern part of Mexico the sign of the cross was a preconquest fertility symbol. In the second place, one must reckon with the actual value of the symbol as understood by the people in question, rather than assume that some historically relevant value still persists. In the English language, for example, *good-bye* actually comes from *God be with you*, but practically no present-day speaker of English is aware of this fact. Similarly, the rooster on the spires of churches is historically related to sex symbolization, but for many modern Christian worshipers, if they have any special "religious" awareness of such an object, it is usually only a reminder of Peter's denial.

Levels of Structure

Not only does the analogy of language and religion show significant parallels in the areas of symbols and arrangements, but there are also fascinating parallels on the different levels of structure. Generative–transformational grammar has highlighted three important levels of language: (1) the deep structures, where such fundamental features as time, space, agency, instrument, object, and event are structured, (2) the kernel structures, those one-clause basic structures which arrange the elements of the deep structure into basic subject-predicate structures and out of which the elaborate surface structures may be formed by transformations, either single (e.g. transforming actives to passives, statements to questions, positives to negatives), or complex (i.e. combining kernel clauses into more extended structures; e.g. *Just as Bill arrived, he saw Dick leave* consists of three kernels: *Bill arrived, he saw,* and *Dick leaves*), and (3) the surface structures, which are the forms of language as actually used by speakers.[1]

Religion, likewise, may be described in terms of these three structural levels. There are the deep structures in religion, those fundamental universal features of religion and their primary characteristics: (1) supernatural powers (whether personal or impersonal—the latter play an important role in magic), and (2) communication techniques, from people to the supernatural powers (e.g. prayers, sacrifices, votive offerings), and from the supernaturals to people (e.g. dreams, visions, oracles, portents, prophecy). These two fundamental aspects of religion are always carried out by people who possess certain quite specific attitudes toward their involvement (parallel to mode in language), and within the context of time and space.

In this deep structure of religion one should perhaps also place certain potentialities of the basic elements. For example, God, as a supernatural power in some religions, is quite removed from people and his attention can only be obtained through great effort. In biblical Christianity, though not in the ordinary form of Christianity practiced by most Christians, God is always near at hand. In fact, he is ready to answer prayer even before man asks, and it is he who always takes the initiative in seeking out man. This means that God is not the object of propitiation in the New Testament: sins may be expiated, but God is not propitiated, since he is already on man's side.

The kernel level of structures in religion may be regarded as the simplest possible combination of such elements and characteristics of the elements in the deep structure, e.g. (1) man prays to God for healing, (2) God communicates a vision to a prophet, (3) man performs magic to kill an enemy, and (4) the flight of a dove signals death in a Venda village. In each of these instances there is a single participation of the basic elements from the deep structure. In (3) the use of magic implies supernatural impersonal powers, and in (4) the dove is believed by the Venda to be a special emissary from the world of the spirits. In every instance, therefore, there is the explicit or implicit participation of the supernatural powers and a communication which takes place. The result is a change or notification of change.

The actual surface structure of religion is usually far more complex than these simple kernel structures. Worship, for example, involves a number of features: singing, offering, prayer, exhortation, all with highly involved ritual patterns and subject to an almost endless variety of transfor-

---

[1] In the initial developments in generative-transformational grammar considerable emphasis was placed upon the role of the so-called "kernel structures." Later, attention was focused upon the "deep structure," with even a denial of the relevance of the kernel level. On the other hand, some transformationalists questioned the validity of the deep structure, at least in the manner in which some persons had formulated it. However, a number of transformationalists have continued to employ the kernel level, especially in the exposition of transformational concepts, and there is strong evidence to believe that the original insights which led to a recognition of this level are in many ways fully justified.

mations. For example, in the usual Protestant service the tendency is to have singing, prayer, reading of the Scriptures, offering, sermon, and benediction, with various adaptations depending upon whether there is a choir or not, or whether communion is to be celebrated on the Sunday in question. In the indigenous Protestant services in Ixmiquilpan, Mexico, a worship service begins with a period of prayer, followed by an hour or more of singing. Then comes the reading of the Scriptures and the sermon, followed by Holy Communion and an offering. In all such surface-structure expressions of religious life the time and space setting are very important. For many Protestants the appropriate time of worship is 11-12 on Sunday morning. For Roman Catholics it is usually somewhat earlier. For traditional churches the only place where worship can legitimately take place is in some church building or specially consecrated place. For more and more "modern Christians" there is a tendency to worship in homes and halls. The mode (or mood) of the worshiper is also important, for the intensity and quality of expectancy and involvement are crucial and universal elements.

The rite of Christian baptism may be used to illustrate certain relations between the deep, kernel, and surface structures and to show how within Christendom different types of transformations have given rise to what might be called "dialects." In the deep structure is to be found the basic significance of this rite, namely, the commitment of a person to the re-ligious system or, in other words, initiation into the community of faith. In many religious systems there is no such rite as baptism since such commitment is taken for granted in view of the person's membership in the community.

The kernel structure includes such basic features as (1) the desire or willingness of the person or of his parents that he or she be baptized, (2) a specially designated person to perform the rite (usually someone who is "ordained"), (3) the water to be in contact with the person being baptized, and (4) the appropriate verbal formula. On the level of the surface structure, however, there are a number of "dialectal" differences, e.g. the amount of water may vary from a few drops to forty gallons or more. (There is one group of Baptists known as "forty-gallon Baptists," since they insist that less than forty gallons invalidates the rite of baptism.) Though there may be some exceptions in the designation of persons who may perform baptism, in general there are quite strict rules within specific denominations as to just who may perform the rite. There are great differences as to persons who may receive the rite, e.g. infants, small children, believing adults, etc. How many times the person is immersed, the variety of verbal formulation employed, the places where such a baptism may be performed, are all features which undergo radical transformations within the development of different Christian groups.

Though it should be quite evident that there are these significant analogies between language structure and the patterns of religious behavior, it would be quite wrong to push such analogies too far. Most religious activity is structurally much more complex than language. For example, on the surface level there may be a number of activities going on at the same time, all intricately related. Language, however, is primarily linear in surface structure, that is to say, one cannot pronounce two words at the same time, but each word must follow in some linear order. Nevertheless, despite these and other ways in which the parallelism between language and religious behavior are not exact, there are a number of features of both language and religion which are sufficiently similar as to warrant some further exploration of these relations.

Surface and Deep Structures in Religion

In legalistic religious systems the focus of attention is almost always on the surface structures rather than on the deep structures. That is to say, people are primarily interested in the forms of religious expression rather than in the significance of such activity. This is what Jesus condemned in the behavior of the Pharisees, who insisted upon cleansing pots but were largely unconcerned about clean hearts and lives. Of course, when legalists are called to task for such neglect of the significance of their behavior, they will almost always argue that they are truly concerned with the deep structure, for example, personal holiness, the glory of God, etc. But in general they are largely unconcerned about the deep structures, for in reality their behavior is so far removed from any-

thing which can be justified by an appeal to deep structure that they almost instinctively content themselves with outward performance.

Quite frequently one finds that group identity in a religious system depends primarily upon the surface structure. The use of the right words, the proper form of crossing one's self, the automatic genuflection before a saint or altar, all signal to others that the person is a part of a particular system. In fact, strangers are often readily accepted by a religious group if only they can exhibit the proper outward signs, even though their deep structures may be radically different. If a preacher uses such terms as *the blood, saved by grace, in the heavenlies, baptism of the Holy Spirit* he will be almost automatically accepted by certain groups of Christians, even though he may actually differ radically from them in his theological outlook. In contrast, a person who uses such terms as *dialogue, kerygma, confrontation, existential,* and *agape* will be classified as belonging to quite another constituency, regardless of what he may actually be saying by the use of such terms.

A number of the acute problems involving so-called "loss of faith" are quite directly related to the relation between surface and deep structures. A young person who has been brought up with a conservative Christian orientation may discover that the surface structures of biblical teachings and of secular instruction simply do not match. For example, a literal interpretation of the Genesis account seems to him to be entirely at variance with findings of paleontology. Having never been told anything about the deep structure of the Genesis account he simply assumes that, since there are radical differences in the surface structures of the two accounts, the deep structures must be equally at variance. Moreover, since the surface structure of the paleontological evidence is growing constantly and being confirmed by numerous investigators in many different areas of the world, the student concludes that this must have higher priority than any literalist interpretation of the Genesis account.

A more serious problem, however, is the failure of the surface structure to fit the presumed deep structure. In the deep structure of Christianity there is the fundamental doctrine of the dignity and equality of all mankind, but in actual practice many Christian churches engage in widespread racial and social discrimination. The socioeconomic stratification of the various Protestant denominations is a pointed reminder of the manner in which the surface structure of church organization and membership denies the much proclaimed deep structure about man's unity. The issue is sometimes neatly bypassed by those who talk only of "every man's equality before God," thus nicely avoiding the issue of every man's equality in relation to other men.

Another deep structure concept of biblical Christianity is the doctrine of sin, which is basically rebellion against God, and merely manifests itself in different forms. Therefore, there are no fundamentally distinct degrees of sin, but only diverse manners in which sin shows itself. For example, the lists of sins in the Pauline Epistles imply no classification of sins into big and little, mortal and venal, gross and inconsequential. But in the surface-structure behavior of most Christians there is an implied classification of sins, which becomes only too well manifested in the favorite topics of gossip or in the ways in which certain churches discipline their members for various categories of sin.

Perhaps the most serious problem relating to the surface and deep structures of religion is the failure of the deep structure to be properly internalized by the younger generation. In general, young people tend to accept the surface forms of religious expression for what they really are and this means that often the content of the deep structure is quite hollow. But in other instances, young people simply parrot what they hear and as a result have little or no idea as to the real significance of such activity. They hear such phrases as *prince of the power of the air* and *eternally begotten of the Father*, and they learn to mouth the utterances, but have no concept of what is actually involved. Moreover, they accept such translations as "the righteousness of God is revealed from faith to faith" (Romans 1.17) with the same wrong interpretations as their elders have attached to this literal translation. In many instances, therefore, the "faith" that young people are thought to lose when they go off to college (and become intellectually weaned) is not their own faith at all—it is merely the faith of their elders. What they have lost is interest in the form, since they have actually not had any faith based upon deep structures.

When there is a discrepancy between deep and surface structures in religious behavior one often encounters a tendency to estheticize the forms so as to make them attractive, even though the deep-structure content may be almost totally lacking. The esthetic elaboration of the surface structure creates its own satisfaction and people are thus not so likely to be worried about the discrepancies between the surface and the deep structures. Moreover, the estheticized surface structure aims primarily to create a mood, rather than to produce a conviction or action. In the creation of a mood the esthetically pleasing surface forms seem to justify themselves. At the same time, however, this tendency can become so elaborate as to disguise almost totally the original significance of the activity. People become so enthralled with the processions, the candles, the ringing of the bells, the chants, and the swinging of the incense pots that they soon lose track—perhaps conveniently and purposely—of what is being communicated.

Learning a First Language and a First Religion

Normally a first language and a first religion, especially in a homogeneous society, are learned almost completely in an automatic fashion. The deep structures are internalized from observing the surface structures. A great deal of thought and research has been dedicated to the problems of internalization of the language system

and still we do not know just what processes are involved, but evidently there exists in the mental equipment of each human being a capacity to deduce the patterns from hearing the countless occurrences of various words and phrases in different structural combinations. Within a relatively few years each normal child is able to understand combinations of expressions which are quite new to him and to make up sentences which he has never heard before. That is to say, the structure (including the patterns and the way in which they function) becomes internalized. Moreover, this is done without any formal study of grammar. It is normally only after a child learns a language reasonably well that he is subjected to the discipline of grammar, which is only the overt formulation of the rules governing what he has already learned to manipulate.

More or less the same procedure seems to take place in the case of religion. The child observes religious behavior, or lack of it, from those around him—and especially from his parents. From them he internalizes the attitudes of dependence upon powers greater than himself, establishes a pattern of communication with such powers, and often develops a considerable fear of seemingly irresponsible responses from such powers. Only later is he likely to be subjected to a study of his religion—the overt formulation of the rules (often spoken of as theology) governing his relations to the supernatural. But in the same manner that one may speak a language quite correctly without having studied grammar, so one can also participate in a religious system without having been exposed to the theology of it. Conversely, of course, one can study the grammar of a second language without being able to speak the language, and can master the theology of a religion without being in the least religious.

The Introduction of Change into a Language or a Religion

In speaking of change in any cultural system we usually mention such isolated processes as addition, deletion, substitution, and coalescence[2] but these processes may not actually result in any significant change in the system as such. In fact, many changes which take place in a language do not affect the system in the least. They are only peripheral extensions or alternations in already-existing structures. For example, the English language has admitted an enormous amount of vocabulary from foreign sources, to the point where well over 50 percent of the standard vocabulary is non-Anglo-Saxon. Furthermore, new vocabulary may be constantly formed, e.g. *miniskirts, midiskirts, maxiskirts,* and now *miniconferences, miniseminars,* and *minidepartment.* These new forms do not, however, represent any essential changes in the linguistic structure of of English—the potentiality for such formations has existed in English for a long time. Similarly, one does not really introduce a change in the religious system of a Congolese tribe just by emphasizing the Fifth Commandment, requiring one to "honor one's

[2] See Eugene A. Nida, "New Religions for Old," PA Vol. 18, No. 6 (Nov.-Dec. 1971), pp. 241-253.

father and mother." This is precisely what many Congolese have believed for centuries and why some accept this Fifth Commandment as confirmation of their practice of directing offerings and prayers to the ancestors.

In a language one may encounter certain shifts of form, e.g. in the accepted pronunciation of such words as *creek, roof,* and *route,* but the shift in the acceptance of one or another of such forms is not really a change in the language system. Nothing in the deep structure is in any way affected. Similarly, a change in the mode of baptism is basically not a change in the Christian system. Even those churches, e.g. the Friends and the Salvation Army, who reject the formal rite of baptism entirely, have not appreciably altered the system, for they are equally insistent upon the baptism of the Holy Spirit, or the "spiritual baptism," for which the outward form is only a confirming sign and not the spiritual reality. Similarly the Jivaros of Ecuador may be forced to give up head shrinking, but if this in no way affects their beliefs about the spirits of the dead or changes their values about military prowess, there is essentially no change in the system, since nothing in the deep structure is actually affected.

The introduction of biblical Christianity into any situation does, however, demand certain very radical changes, not so much in the surface structure, though this will inevitably happen eventually, but in the deep structure. For example, in biblical Christianity service to God is not to be regarded as a way of winning God's favor—as it is in all other religious systems—but as the response of the person to God's love. Such service is neither to win God's goodwill nor to make converts. The true Christian serves out of a sense of indebtedness to God for what Christ has done in providing not only a new way of life but an abundant one. Similarly, Christian holiness is not to be considered as "separateness" from other people, but total dedication to God for the service of mankind. As a result, all the artificially imposed barriers to human relations must be broken in the process of service. This is precisely what Jesus did when he touched lepers, ate with tax collectors, conversed with a woman (rabbis were not supposed to talk with women), and healed on the Sabbath day. Furthermore, biblical Christianity is dedicated to the winning of the world through love which leads to suffering. This is not the "if-I-were-God" complex, which makes a man act more like a devil than God. This is not a totalitarian system for forcing men to conform, but a means of transforming them by love. Moreover, it is an expression of love which comes from a position of weakness—at least as the world regards weakness. Paul's declaration that "when I am weak, then am I strong" (2 Corinthians 12.10) applies most meaningfully to true Christian faith. Christian love is not sympathy, which comes from a superior position, but empathy, which comes from true identification by learning to suffer with others. These and other equally radical changes which the introduction of Christianity entails must inevitably involve one in the process of "second-religion learning"—a process which is surprisingly similar to second-language learning.

The Learning of a Second Language and of a Second Religion as an Adult

A second language is generally only learned adequately by three processes: (1) exposure and contact, i.e. hearing, (2) involvement, i.e. speaking, and (3) explanation, i.e. learning about the language. Rather than talking only about hearing and speaking, it seems better to describe the relevant processes in terms of exposure, contact, and involvement, since in this way we can highlight the learning of a second language in the real atmosphere of life situations rather than in the largely artificial context of the classroom. It is important to note, however, that for second-language learning, as an adult, it is usually essential that there be some form of explanation. Having internalized one linguistic system in a completely automatic manner, the adult tends to learn a second language almost completely on the model of the first, with the result that there are often serious distortions, due to the influence of the first language. In general, only careful explanation can rid one of the heavy imposition of the first language upon the second. The proper recognition of the various factors in second-language learning has resulted in much more effective courses and programs in teaching and learning second languages.

Unfortunately, however, those responsible for teaching second religions have not exhibited the same sensitivity to the problems of learning. Generally, they begin with theological explanations, that is, overt formulations of the deep structures, and they rarely show the one-to-one correspondence between such deep structures and the surface structures. One of the reasons for this is that too often the correspondence is either so remote or so contradictory, that the less said the better. Some of those responsible for second-religion teaching assume that the second religion can be assimilated by watching others perform. Religious professionals simply take over the responsibility for all the strictly religious activity and the layman is relegated to the role of the onlooker. Under such circumstances, however, it is very rare that the actions ever become internalized. They are almost always reinterpreted by the layman in terms of his first religion

Some of the most effective teachers of second religions are the leaders in the so-called "indigenous Christian movements." These churches are outside the traditional confessional structures, but they are the churches which are growing much more rapidly than those which have been sponsored by missionary activity. One of the most effective "teaching" programs is carried out under the leadership of Venancio Hernandez in Ixmiquilpan, Mexico, where there is now a Christian community of some 3,000 persons in more than twenty towns and villages, located in one of the most poverty-stricken and fanatical areas of the country. For the training of new believers there is no "course of study." Rather, these people are invited to come to a community such as exists on the outskirts

of Ixmiquilpan, where the Christians built their own town, put in sewer and light systems, and developed a number of home industries. There the new converts simply live with other Christians, observing what they do, participating in the religious services, and sharing in the cooperative programs. They learn to worship, pray, serve, and give of themselves, since in this living context they have been able to internalize the new values. Venancio Hernandez does not even have a Bible school for the training of preachers. In contrast with most mission-sponsored programs, he arranges to have all the leaders of the various congregations come in each month for a period of two to three days, during which time the men pray together, talk over their problems, discuss what they will be preaching in the various churches during the coming month, and decide on how they and their churches can most effectively serve the community and extend their outreach to other areas, where interest in this work of the Spirit of God continues to grow.

A program for the development of leadership is based essentially on an apprenticeship system. In reality this type of training is not very different from what Jesus employed in the training of his disciples. There is no better system than demonstration and doing—seeing and imitating. This is one of the aspects of genius in Venancio Hernandez. At one time, for example, he was quite concerned that some people were spending too much to buy water containers when they could just as easily employ goats bladders, which had been used in the region for centuries. However, rather than preach to the people about what they should do, Venancio himself procured a goat's bladder, properly cured it, and then quite naturally, but very pointedly, used it often in his own home and carried it with him when he traveled by foot to distant villages. Under such circumstances the people were not slow to catch on.

One of the significant features of many indigenous movements in the world is the emphasis upon the full participation of each person, in proportion to his training and capacities. In the Interdenominational Church in the barrio of Portales, Mexico City, each member of the congregation has a task to perform. The leadership of this church, with more than 8,000 members in one of the poorer parts of Mexico City, is in the hands of five laymen, who form a joint pastorate and provide the church with outstanding spiritual guidance and equally fine organizational direction. Whether in the continuous series of services held at various times during each Sunday or in the program for providing women with sewing machines to use at the church during the week or in the project for having one member located in each square block within a mile radius of the church and responsible to know all the persons in that block and to offer the help of the church (whether for physical assistance, getting a job, or spiritual needs), each person related to this church feels that God needs him. Rather than preaching exclusively that man needs God, these Christians in the Portales church are equally convinced that God needs them. It is this deep conviction which adds dignity to their limited lives and purpose to their sometimes meager existence, since they too are able to participate in the plans and purposes of God and to share in the task of redemption.

Multilingualism and Multiple Religions

A person who speaks two or more languages normally experiences little or no difficulty in keeping them apart, though of course there are certain situations in which there is a tendency for interference. Such interference is especially prominent in the case of a first language affecting a second language learned after one has become an adult. Rarely if ever does one escape from the "foreign accent," which so conspicuously marks the second-language speaker as nonnative. In a sense, this same situation exists in the case of persons with multiple religious backgrounds. Almost always the first religion tends to exert its influence, even after one has for all practical purposes abandoned it and seemingly committed himself wholly to the second. Of course, one can speak several languages without feeling any special conflict between the languages. They can all be accepted as being equally valid ways of communicating. But for religions this is generally not true, since religions have a way of demanding exclusive adherence. Of course, in places where syncretization has been more or less institutionalized, one can be, for example, a Taoist, a Buddhist, and a Confucianist all at the same time, at least in terms of the surface structures and for the purposes of entirely different types of deep structures. For example, in the Orient Confucianism has traditionally served well the functions of social structure, whether national or familial, while Taoism has performed the function of guaranteeing health and long life, and Buddhism has promised to help one escape from the wheel of existence into the Nirvana of complete bliss. Where the deep structures of religions are for the common people thus neatly compartmentalized, they can exist in a sort of symbiosis which would appear to be utterly inconsistent, since their respective total deep structures are quite competitive and contrary.

Many Christians, however, experience a considerable degree of religious symbiosis. Many Africans think that Christianity is especially potent for ulcers, but that only the indigenous medicine man can provide the religiously potent cures for a headache. Normally, however such syncretistic practices do not represent a partnership of religions in which religions are regarded as more or less of the same status and simply relevant for different activities and diverse human problems. Rather, they are structured in hierarchical sets, in which one religion is regarded as dominating another. One religion may be culturally more acceptable, at least on an overt level, while the other may be regarded as culturally inferior. Under such circumstances Christianity is often a kind of superficial veneer religion. Christian forms are adopted for the surface structure, for this lends prestige to the religious program, but the deep structure may remain quite unaffected. For example, in the Valley of Otavalo, Ecuador, an annual drunken festival has been traditionally carried out in honor of John the Baptist. But when people are seriously questioned concerning the nature of such a rite, they will admit that in fact they are drinking in honor of the gods of the volcanoes which encircle the valley.

Even when a person has adopted a new religion, including its deep structure, there are likely to be circumstances in which the "accent" from the former religion will still manifest itself. Such a carry-over of older patterns should really not discourage one, if such forms are primarily surface, rather than deep, structures. Such practices have been widespread in traditional Christianity, e.g. Christmas trees, yule logs, gifts, and candles. The danger, however, is that some of the surface structures may be internalized in such a form as to radically distort biblical Christianity. For example, there is an increasing tendency to regard God as only an indulgent Santa Claus figure, the "old man upstairs" who passes out goodies to those who are good.

From the standpoint of language, the most pathetic person is the one who has largely forgotten his first language and has not sufficiently mastered a second language so as to be able to communicate effectively. In the field of religion there are similar individuals, who have only bits and pieces of systems and no integrating structure. One West African possessed as the symbols of his "chaotic faith" a copy of the Latin mass, a book on

Rosicrucianism, the *Baptist Leader*, and a fetish bundle which he carefully placed above the door of his urban shanty. The assembly of different religious forms can perhaps be best described as simply a case of multiple insurance policies. Suspecting that no one system would meet all his needs, a man determines to combine as many as necessary, with the hope that in one way or another he would be protected, either from malevolent spirits or from the heartless competition of his detribalized existence.

Communicating a New Faith

In the final analysis, preachers, missionaries, and teachers are primarily interested in what can, and should, be done to effect change, rather than in analyzing the patterns of change and the structures which are involved. They would like to have a program of change described in terms of such features as cultural crises, innovators, catalysts, reactionaries, and settings. Then by the proper manipulation of such factors they would like to assume that change could be fully effected. What they want is some "sure-fire" method which would specify all the elements, tell one precisely what to do, and then guarantee the results as being proportionate to the energy expended. Frankly, however, this cannot be done. Culture change is entirely too complex a phenomenon to be able to describe it by means of a few "rules." There are just too many variables. Moreover, in the case of Christianity one must of necessity reckon not merely with the actions of men but also with the activity of the Spirit of God. As has been so neatly said, real spiritual changes are not worked up but come down. That is to say, their origin is not so much in man's contrivance as in God's providing.

One of the interesting developments of recent years which illustrates well this basic problem is to be found in the Moluccas, where a number of Christian leaders have given extensive and serious concern to the problems of the church. They have had various committees and commissions studying their difficulties, have brought in outside consultants, have tried to "engineer" (in the appropriate sense of the word) a spiritual revival, but nothing has happened. Apparently everything has been done except what is essential, that degree of spiritual openness to the convicting and renewing work of the Spirit of God, without which no real spiritual progress can take place.

But how are people to learn of the changes which they must make? Seemingly, there is no answer other than what the church has experienced throughout its history, namely, by being able to imitate the behavior of truly God-filled men and women, from whom one can learn the "how" and the "why" of faith. The plans and purposes of God have consistently called for the combination of Word and witness, of the Bible and the Church—of the new faith carried by men and women of faith, from whom one could learn the new language of faith. Perhaps what is needed after all is not a new set of techniques for introducing and sustaining culture change, but a new type of dedicated Christian who is willing and able to love and to suffer. This is certainly what happened in Congo during the Jeunesse Movement, when scores of people were martyred for their faith and hundreds more risked their lives to proclaim the only truly revolutionary proclamation: the message of God's love and transforming power through Jesus Christ. As a result, many of the churches in Congo have almost doubled in numbers, for people have found reality in crisis. Something rather similar has occurred in Indonesia, where during the anti-Communist reactions, following the downfall of Sukarno, somewhat more than 300,000 persons were killed. With very few exceptions, however, Christians completely refused to participate in such killings and abstained from using such events as a cloak for settling personal grievances. Furthermore, many Christians ministered to the needs of both Communists and anti-communists alike—often at the risk of their own lives. One result has been that within the last three years an estimated 350,000 persons, mostly of Muslim background, have become Christians.

It is quite unlikely that the world will ever be impressed by the learning or the organizational abilities of Christians. But from the beginning of the church the world has been genuinely amazed to see how certain selfless disciples of the Crucified have taken up their own cross and followed the Galilean, often to their own Golgotha. In the day of the mass man one must not forget the influence of the spirit-filled individual, without whom no truly significant development in religious change can really be effected. The ultimate need is, therefore, not so much for refined techniques, though these have their place, but for transformed men and women, who may be used as the catalysts of change in religion, as prophets in a day when God seems to have ceased to speak, as servant in a time when most people want to be lords, and as guides in a world where men have been blinded by their own success. Only in this way can people learn true values and develop an awareness of the deep structures of their faith.

Eugene A. Nida

Mariology in Latin America

WITHIN the last few years, there has been a marked increase of interest in Mariology within the Roman Catholic Church. This increased focus of attention upon Mary has found expression in the establishment of many shrines, wide publicity of alleged miracles, numerous books and articles on the significance of Mary for the modern world, and intense promotion of the Virgin of Fatima as the protectress of Christendom against Communism. The recent promulgation of the doctrine of the assumption of the Virgin has augmented Mary's theological status, and the much-discussed doctrine of Mary as coredemptrix with Jesus Christ seems to be gaining in influence within the Roman Church.

For the most part, this development in Mariology has been discussed by Protestants primarily in terms of the theological implications of the ever-increasing centrality of Mary within the Roman system. In large measure, however, Protestants have failed to see this development in terms of the broader cultural implications. In order to understand and more fully appreciate what is happening within the Roman Church, we need to view this extraordinary emphasis upon Mary in the light of the anthropological background involved.

Dying Christ and Living Mary

In trying to understand the reasons for the focusing of attention upon Mary, some persons have readily seen that this is an almost inevitable result of making Christ less and less attractive to the people. Rather than portraying Christ as a victorious "culture hero" (if we may be permitted to speak in purely anthropological terms), Christ is the defeated, dying victim. Such a Christ produces feelings of pity and compassion, but he does not inspire with confidence and hope. Christ on the cross reminds the sinner of his sins, but this symbol does not suffice to make the average person want to identify himself with the suffering Savior.[1] Contemplation of the dying Christ does elicit strong emotional feelings, but they tend to drain one of nervous energy. Accordingly, they do not result in a feeling of well-being or confidence.

On the other hand, in contrast with the dying Christ there is the symbol of the radiantly beautiful Mary, the benevolent person who is always accessible and always giving. It is Mary who has compassion for the multitude, and it is the contemplation of this symbol which brings reassurance and a sense of hope and well-being. As the mediatrix between the worshiper and Christ, or God, she becomes the

[1]Masochistic individuals are of course the exceptions to this general scheme, and it is not without significance that a number of the more rigorous orders of the Roman Church have been characterized by masochistic rites centering in identification with the crucified Christ.

Reprinted from Vol. 4, No. 3 (1957), pp. 69-82.

giver of life, the source of health, and the means of power. It is not strange, therefore, that the center of worship in the Roman church should shift from Christ to Mary, for people prefer to identify themselves with a living Mary rather than with a dying Christ.

The Mass and Fertility Rites

This contrast between death and life has been further accentuated in the Roman development of the mass, which in its early New Testament form reflected the covenant meal of the Old Testament. However, during the first few centuries it became in many aspects almost totally assimilated to the fertility cult rites of the mystic religions. Whether as reflecting the rites of Eleusis, Isis, or Osiris, or those which centered in the cult of Astarte, the same dominant principle prevailed — the dying god-son raised to life through the principle of female productivity. As the mass developed, it became no longer a commemorative feast, but a miraculous re-enactment of the shedding of blood. The worshiper was not just reminded of the fact that Christ died and rose again, but that he was constantly dying for the people, and they partook of his very body and blood, whether directly or in the person of the priest. This symbol served only to reinforce their equation of Christ with death, and not with life. The emotional unattractiveness of this procedure left a spiritual and psychological void which was filled by the symbol of the Virgin — readily borrowed from the pagan mystery religions and taken over with very little adaptation into the practices of the Church, though with a certain measure of theological polishing.

The Latin Culture Context

The fact that the symbol of the suffering, dying Christ was gradually replaced by the loving, living Mary is, however, by no means all of the story, particularly in the case of Latin America. There the developments have an even deeper significance as far as their relationship to the cultural themes are concerned. In the Ibero-American culture (excluding the Indian elements) the Church and the society seem to fit like a glove on a hand, and quite understandably so, for in a sense the glove and the hand "grew up together." The Latin culture has, of course, been in a large measure the product of the teaching of the Church, and in turn the Church has adapted itself to the special Latin characteristics. Any attempt to discover the order of priority (the old problem of the chicken and the egg) is a relatively fruitless undertaking, for such adjustments always come as successive waves of give and take. However, within the contemporary life of Latin America there are certain important observations which can be made concerning the reciprocal re-enforcement of the related institutions, and it is this phase of the cultural pattern which we need to note briefly.

Female Orientation

There are three underlying factors which must be understood if we are to appreciate the close relationship between the Roman church and Latin American society. In the first place, Latin American culture is female-oriented. By this we do not mean to imply that this orientation is the only or even the dominant one, but in contrast with other cultures which in this area of life may be described as sex-oriented, certainly Latin American culture shows a dominant tendency toward female orientation. In our own U.S.A. society, as well as in the culture of ancient Greece, the dominant element seems to be more a matter of sex itself than of interest in the female. These differences may be noted in such characteristics as (1) less homosexuality than in our own culture, (2) more overt attention paid to sex characteristics of females, and (3) greater concentration of interest in eliciting female response than in simply gratifying sexual drives. Furthermore, the greater distinctiveness in male and female roles tends to re-enforce the female-oriented nature of Latin society.

The Mother Role

In the second place, in Latin American society the mother is the emotional center of the family. The father is more or less expected to have extramarital relations, whether with prostitutes or mistresses. In fact, in some regions of Latin America the number and quality of one's mistresses is a more decisive factor in gaining prestige than the number of cars one owns. Since the father is expected to have divided loyalties and to possess other emotional attachments, it is not difficult to understand why children should feel greater emotional attachment to the mother, even though they may continue to have a deep respect for their father. In saying that the father is expected to engage in extramarital affairs, we do not imply that all men do, for some are very faithful to their families, especially some in the middle and lower income groups. However, though some fathers may not be unfaithful, there is nevertheless the general attitude that if such men should become unfaithful, it is not to be too severely condemned. Furthermore, the wives in such circumstances are supposed to be more or less tolerant toward such affairs and to accept the fact of competition with equanimity.

A more or less natural consequence of the mother's role as bestower of benefits from the time the children are quite small is that she continues to function in this same way, though in a somewhat different form. Rather than being the direct source of help, she becomes the intercessor of the children with the less approachable father. In fact, fathers are supposed to be somewhat standoffish and mothers are supposed to be more indulgent. Of course, there are numerous exceptions to these roles, but this is the general pattern. Even though in a particular community this pattern may not be the statistically dominant one, it is, nevertheless, regarded by most Latins as being the way Latin life is organized. Hence, the "myth" (or the reality) of the more distant father and the interceding mother becomes a cultural framework in which the concept of an exacting God and a benevolent Mary can have meaning.

Women in the Church

In the third place, there is a very well-defined relationship of re-enforcement between the status of women and the position of the Church. The status of the wife in an outwardly monogamist society is maintained by the Church by denying the validity of divorce. In fact, in some countries of Latin America the Roman Church has had such influence upon the governments that there is no possible way for a person to obtain a legal divorce. The Church, accordingly, confirms and maintains the wife's status by legally preventing or by placing severe obstacles in the way of any other female's threatening the position of the wife. At the same time, the mores of the society permit almost wholesale competition for the romantic affection of the husband, but by threat of excommunication against divorcees (though not against mistresses or adulterers) status is maintained, even though in the actual role of women there is often a wide discrepancy between real and ideal roles and behavior.

It is, accordingly, quite understandable that the wife and mother should be concerned with the re-enforcing of the authority of an institution, such as the Church, which does so much to protect her status. As the faithful, interceding mother, she identifies herself with the Virgin and finds her confidence in the strength of the one institution which maintains her status and which seems to defend her role.

Since there is also a rather well-defined pattern of indulgence of mothers towards sons, it is not difficult to see how in this aspect as well the people assume that the most effective way of reaching the somewhat formidable Christ is through the indulgent, benevolent mother. Accordingly, not only do women find in Mary a cultural type with which they may identify themselves, but many men, whether consciously or unconsciously, tend to transfer their feelings of dependence upon their mother to worship of the Virgin Mother.

All this means that loyalty to the Virgin is not the result primarily of instruction by the Church itself, but of a kind of unconscious reflex of the underlying emotional patterns in Latin life. This is perhaps the principal reason why the Roman Church continues to be so strong, despite the strong liberal and intellectual movements in Latin America. Time and again, the Jesuits have been forced out of various countries, and in many areas

there are strong anticlerical movements, but despite such anti-Church attitudes there seems to be a continued devotion to the Virgin as an unconscious symbol of the life of the people. It is not without significance that for each of the countries or principal regions in Latin America there is some patron Virgin. Individual areas may also have their patron saints, but the overruling focus of emotional attachment is to the Virgin. This promotion of the Virgin as the patron of the nation is a natural outgrowth of the role of the benevolent mother on the lower level of the family unit.

Male-oriented Cultures

In contrast with the centrality of Mary in Latin America, it is interesting to note the differences in the Greek Orthodox Church, as well as such other Eastern Churches as the Coptic, Armenian, and Ethiopic. Though the Eastern as well as the Roman Churches had a very similar early history as regards certain aspects of the mass and the recognition of Mary as "Mother of God" (a significant feature of the Athanasian and Arian controversy), nevertheless the Eastern Church has not made Mary the center of adoration to the extent that the Roman Church has done, especially in Ibero-American culture. Part of this disparity may be attributed to the fact that the Eastern Church rejected the use of images and sensuous art forms. The icons, relics, and mosaics were not particularly well adapted to emphasizing a female sex element. On the other hand, the Eastern Churches are studded with frescoes and murals, but these are predominantly of masculine persons: Biblical heroes, early saints, and Jesus Christ. However, despite the difference in the art forms and objects, one basic reason for this diversity between the Eastern Churches and the Roman ones is to be found — the fact that in the area of the Eastern Churches society is much less female-centered. In this feature there has no doubt been some influence from Islamic culture during the last thousand years or so. But one must also recognize the fact that the culture of the Eastern Mediterranean, even before the rise of Islam, was essentially male-oriented. Important broad patterns of life have had a significant influence in molding the Churches of both the East and the West.

Theology and Emotions

The most frequent criticism leveled against the Protestants is that they do not "believe in" the Virgin. The arguments used by Roman Catholics do not betray any special theological concern for the Virgin. It is only that they cannot understand what seems to be gross lack of respect, gratitude, and filial loyalty. For the average Latin Roman Catholic the Virgin is not primarily the historical personage who lived in Nazareth, gave birth to Jesus Christ, and nurtured him to manhood; the Virgin is the symbolic projection of a series of emotional attitudes formed within the very first years of a child's life. Emotional attachment to the Virgin is thus acquired as one of the deepest and earliest psychological experiences. For the most part, this attitude toward the Virgin is without overt reasoning, though it may be formulated in memorized doctrines and expressed in overt acts of prayer. The fact that Virgin adoration is largely implicit within the cultural framework greatly increases its hold upon the person, for any rejection of the Virgin is tied up with rejection of mother, home, and family love.

To a great extent, Protestant missionaries in Latin America have failed to understand fully the place of the "Virgin-symbol" in the lives of Roman Catholics. They have tried to employ theological arguments against what they have denounced as "Mariolatry." However, for the most part, Roman Catholics have been entirely unmoved by such theological arguments. The reason for this is that they learned to believe in the Virgin not from theological arguments but because of family relationships. Even though admitting the validity of arguments based upon historical revelations in the Scriptures, Roman Catholics find themselves emotionally unable to consider rejecting the Virgin. In fact, they often insist that they know God (even as revealed in the Scriptures) would not want them to do so, for they have never distinguished between filial loyalty and the religious symbol of the Virgin.

The Living Christ

If, however, the break from the Virgin-symbol is so difficult for Roman Catholics, how are we to explain what has happened for so many tens of thousands (about five million in all) who are Protestants in Latin America? There are, of course, a number of more or less overt "anthropological" reasons for people turning from Catholicism to Protestantism: (1) reaction to the authoritarianism of the Church, (2) special educational advantages offered by Protestant missions, (3) personal resentment against the behavior of persons who were identified with the Roman Church, and (4) a sense of frustration which ends up in a nonconformist defiance of the status quo and all it stands for. To this list may be added a number of other minor overt reasons for people becoming Protestants. However, there is another reason which is far more important than any of these "trigger" causes. This is the substitution of the symbol of the victorious, living Christ for the defeated, dying one.

One of the effective ways in which this new symbol has been communicated is through the Scriptures. Time after time, Roman Catholics have commented when they read the Scriptures that they "did not realize that Christ lived." They had thought of him only as dying. The fact that his life was filled so full of service and identification of himself with people and that, though he suffered, he rose from the dead and ascended to glory, seems to be an almost incomprehensible revelation.

Furthermore, in the message of the Scriptures Roman Catholics discover that it was God who identified himself with man in Christ (God is no longer screened off by the ever-present Virgin) and that it was Christ who identified himself wholly with man. It is this identification of Christ with man (he was one like us) which finally reaches through to men and women. Furthermore, Roman Catholics learn that this Christ who lived also lives today and by his Spirit walks with men. Here is the fullness of fellowship and the certainty of penetrating through the veil of uncertainty which always shrouds the well-meaning but sometimes thwarted efforts of the kindhearted Virgin-symbol.

It is not without significance that, for the most part, individual Roman Catholics do not become Protestants over night. In fact, during the process of learning about the living Christ, they often go back time and again to praying to the Virgin, and in times of severe family crisis they feel an almost irresistible urge to seek refuge in prayers and candles to the Virgin. When they do make a final break (sometimes after a number of years), they do so only when the symbol (and the reality) of the Christ as living intercessor has been completely substituted for the earlier symbol of the interceding Mother.

It is just as well that Protestant missionaries recognize the fact that the symbol of the Lord Christ cannot hope to be as popular as that of the benevolent Mother, if by "popular" we mean that which has the greatest appeal to man's sinful nature. In the first place, the Virgin-symbol involves a physical attractiveness with sex appeal (whether admitted overtly or not — but whoever saw an image of a homely Virgin?) and an emotional identification with mother-love. On the other hand, the symbol of the Lord Christ, though it may have some of the popular appeal of the culture hero, can never become simply a Davy Crockett. As God himself, Christ always possesses for man that "otherness" which mystified even his closest disciples. He was one with them, and yet they recognized that he was utterly different. This mystery of the incarnation never escaped them and continues both to mystify and to inspire the believer's deepest thoughts and his highest aspirations.

Celibacy of the Priesthood

In the conversion of a person from Catholicism to Protestantism there is an important shift or orientation from female to male symbolism, with a much-decreased concentration upon the sex element, for it is much easier to identify oneself with the sex element in the more earthly Mother than to symbolize the sex relationship with the more distant Christ.

On the other hand, the celibacy of Roman Catholic priests would seem to deny this sex element, but in reality it only confirms the sex factor. In his function as the earthly representative of Jesus Christ, the Pope and the priesthood which receive their sanction through him must be symbolically identified with Christ. However, in order to be intimately associated with the Virgin-Mother symbol, they must be *symbolically* incapable of sex relations. Otherwise, there would be danger of "spiritual incest." On the other hand, the Protestant minister has no such attitudes toward the Virgin-symbol, and in his status of prophet, rather than primarily as priest, he identifies himself with the people, in order to bring them to God. The Roman priest, however, is primarily a priest, identified with the bestower of benefits (i.e. the Virgin-Mother) and transmitter of blessings to the people.

The close relationship between celibacy of the priesthood and the Virgin-symbol may be seen by comparing further the practices of the Eastern and Roman Churches. Asceticism began in the East as the result, it would appear, of predominantly Syrian influences, in which celibacy of priests in numerous pagan cults was regarded as an essential requisite for attendance upon the goddesses of fertility. (In a number of these religious cults castration was the symbol of identification with the goddess.) However, though celibacy began in the Eastern churches and was widespread during early centuries, it is not now regarded as a requisite for the priesthood, even though it may be encouraged in some of the orders and for certain higher posts in the ecclesiastical hierarchy. On the other hand, though celibacy was relatively slow in coming to the Western churches, it is now obligatory in the Roman Church, for the very reason that only in this way can the priest (whether consciously or unconsciously) attain full identification with both Christ and the Virgin-Mother without the guilt of incest.[2] In the male-oriented culture of the East, where the Virgin is not the dominant symbol, celibacy is not so essential, and hence not obligatory.

Symbols

Perhaps one of the most difficult tasks for the Protestant missionary in Latin America is to realize the nature and importance of symbols, whether verbal or visual. This does not mean that the Protestant does not possess a number of symbols; he does. But for the most part his symbols are primarily words and verbal descriptions of people and events. When the Protestant thinks of Saint Peter, a whole series of images immediately come to the surface of his thinking. They include the denial at the trial, the three questions posed by Jesus after the resurrection, Peter cutting off Malchus' ear, etc. For the average Roman Catholic in Latin America, Saint Peter means a statue in a particular church, a patron saint of a nearby town, a statue before which he prays in times of sickness in the family, a personage in heaven who intercedes with Mary, who in turn goes to Christ. If a Roman Catholic happens to have read the Bible, he may have some mental images similar to those of the

---

[2] It is quite true that these explanations involve several important features of Freudian psychology, but they are by no means dependent solely upon an acceptance or rejection of Freudian theories. These fundamental psychological relationships are recognized in one form or another by practically all psychoanalysts.

Protestant, but for the most part, even if the Protestant and the Catholic use the same words "Saint Peter," they are very likely to be talking about entirely different things.

A number of Protestant symbols are words which stand for important beliefs (many of which the average Protestant cannot explain). These words symbolize important experiences in his life and doctrine which he believes are indispensable to faith: repentance, conversion, redemption, blessing, Holy Spirit, justification, sanctification, the dying Savior, the blood, the cross, the open tomb, saints, confession, prayer, faith, hope, assurance, etc. For the Roman Catholic a number of these words are associated with specific objects (or images) which he can see or rites in which he overtly participates: the blood (the wine at communion or red paint on the crucifix), the dying Savior (the crucifix), the cross, saints (heavenly intercessors and images within the home and at church), prayers (it is not without interest that the Catholic "says prayers" or "recites," but the Protestant "prays"), faith (as a list of doctrines), confession (to the priest), etc. However, for a number of word symbols which the average Protestant possesses there is often no corresponding object or mental image for the Catholic. For the most part, Roman Catholicism has objectified its symbols in attractive or awesome objects or in impressive rites. On the other hand, the Protestant emphasizes much more the abstract or historical value of the word symbols.

Protestant Symbolization for Catholics

If, however, a missionary is going to communicate effectively with people of Roman Catholic background, he must try to bridge the psychological gap which exists between the two systems by choosing word symbols which will help the Roman Catholic to understand the Protestant beliefs. Accordingly, rather than use words which may carry little or no meaning (or which may only define more or less abstract doctrines prior to their being explained at length), he needs to employ figures which will approximate in some measure the degree of objective symbolization which is so common to Roman Catholics. One of these symbols, and a very important one in communicating with Roman Catholics, is that of the rent veil. By means of this symbol one can indicate the significance of the Mediator of the new relationship with God. The symbol of the covenant meal, consecrated by the death of the One who offered himself, can help explain the Biblical meaning of the communion. The symbol of the Risen Lord can help to transform the crucifix and give assurance that death is swallowed up in victory.

One of the reasons for the spectacular success of the Pentecostal churches of Chile is in their rich use of verbal symbols which help to create for their people the vivid impressions of Biblical events and characters, with whom the people in their dramatic times of united prayer and demonstrations identify themselves psychologically. In the relatively unattractive, stern atmosphere of Protestant churches of Latin America some attempt should be made to find compensatory verbal substitutes by which the symbolism becomes as meaningful as possible and the group fellowship as emotionally rewarding as the corresponding sense of beauty and pageantry in the Roman Catholic edifices and rites.

For the missionary one of the most essential elements is adequate understanding of the underlying factors influencing behavior. Without this knowledge we are sometimes immobilized, not knowing what to say nor where to turn. Our understanding of the fundamental concepts of Latin American life is still very rudimentary, but we must make every effort to understand and to appreciate the basic nature of any society, if we are to have any appreciable success in communicating to such people the full meaning of Christ as Savior and Lord.

William L. Wonderly and Eugene A. Nida

Cultural Differences and the Communication of Christian Values

The study of a people's values, the ideas and emotions which form their outlook on life and motivate their behavior, is of fundamental importance to an understanding of that people. Nothing is more basic to a relevant Christian witness than insight into value systems. But the study of values is not easy because these implicit and unanalyzed assumptions which guide people can only be inferred from language and other behavior, never directly observed. Only recently have anthropologists been sharpening the necessary tools for deepened understanding in this area of culture. In the article below the authors take some of the developing insights concerning the study of values, and apply them to the Latin American scene. Readers in other parts of the world will gain many ideas to help them begin formulating their own understanding of the value systems around them.

THE terms "value" and "value orientation" are used by anthropologists and others to refer to any conception of the good or the desirable which influences the action or thinking of people. Such conceptions may be overtly recognized and taught, or may be unexpressed and implicit. They may be characteristic either of an individual or of a group. In the present study we are concerned primarily with values held by people as members of their society and culture, and with the implication of these cultural values for the communication of Christian value concepts.

The missionary who works among the Indians of Latin America is faced with an almost unbelievably complicated task in the communication of Christian concepts or values to the Indian. To begin with, the specifically Christian values, which may be thought of as supercultural as distinct from cultural,[1] were originally developed through God's revelation of himself to people of Hebrew and Greek culture, who however did not begin in a vacuum but already had their own set of culturally determined values in the light of which the new values had to be interpreted and taught. This gave us our Bible and our early Judeo-Christian tradition, which of course contains both cultural and supercultural values. This in turn has been mediated to the North

[1] This distinction was first discussed at length by Smalley in "A Christian View of Anthropology," by William A. Smalley and Marie Fetzer (Chapter 5 of *Modern Science and the Christian Faith.* Wheaton, Ill.: Van Kampen Press, 1948-1950).

American missionary in terms of the value system of his own western European (mostly Anglo-Saxon) culture, which has both cultural and specifically Christian elements and in the light of which the Christian values with their background of Hebrew and Greek cultural values have been interpreted to him.

In the next stage of the process, the missionary has to communicate these values to members of an Indian culture who already have their own culturally established set of values but who are at the same time dominated by the surrounding mestizo or Ladino culture, which has still another set of values! It is small wonder that there are so many cases of work begun among Indians in which missionaries have not succeeded in adequately relating the essential supercultural values of Christianity to the background of cultural values of the Indian; and where this has not been done it is hardly surprising to see the work deteriorate or even disappear within a generation or two.

The Study of Values

People today are increasingly recognizing the fact that every human experience and activity involves a value concept. This ancient Biblical truth about the heart of man is confirmed not only by religious experience as such, but by contemporary existentialist philosophy, behaviorist psychology, and *gestalt* psychology. For anthropology, value studies have become increasingly more important within the past decade or so, as anthropologists have given recognition to the fact that the values people hold determine their motives for action and therefore constitute much of the dynamic for their society.

However, these values are not just personal values or preferences, but are culturally conditioned and determined. What a person thinks is good, and how he behaves as a result of his value judgments, depends not merely upon his personal idiosyncrasies but in large part upon the ideas he has received from his contemporaries in his particular society; and these value concepts differ widely from one culture to another.

There are different ways by which the values in different cultures can be discovered and presented. One way is by general impressions gained by a person who lives in and participates as a member of a society, whether his own or another. The novelist who is sensitive to the values of a culture communicates these in his writings, as for example Ernest Hemingway in *The Old Man and the Sea*,[2] Mariano Azuela in *Los de Abajo*[3] (Mexico), Carlos Fuentes in *La región mas transparente*[4] (Mexico), Jesús Lara in *Yanakuna*[5] (Bolivia), etc. Every missionary should consider it his obligation and privilege to read as much material of this type as possible which has to do with the area and people with whom he works, in order to gain an acquaintance with their values as interpreted by national writers themselves.

A second way to study a people's values, related to the above, is through a literary approach. A study is made of folk literature and other texts that have been created by the people themselves, with a view to analyzing the recurring themes and extracting basic value con-

[2] New York: Charles Scribner's Sons, 1952.
[3] Mexico: Fondo de Cultura Económica, 1960 (paperback edition); English edition, *The Underdogs*, Signet, 1963 (paperback).
[4] Mexico: Fondo de Cultura Económica, 1958; English edition, *Where the Air is Clear*, McDowell Obolensky, Inc., New York, 1960.
[5] Cochabamba: Editorial los Amigos del Libro, 1952.

cepts from those that appear in legends, folk tales, etc. Some of this was done at the Guatemala Conference on Indian Work in 1959, in the shape of an analysis of themes recurring in the Popol Vuj.

Psychologists have developed projective testing techniques such as the Rorschach and TAT tests for studying personality characteristics, and these tests (and adaptations of them) have been used by several anthropologists to study similar characteristics on the level of culturally conditioned value orientations.[6]

Still another approach is that of the sociologist, who prepares a description of a society or of a segment of society. An example of this type of work in the United States is the now classic work of Lynd and Lynd, Middletown: A Study in Modern American Culture.[7] Whyte's The Organization Man[8] is a popular sociological treatment of a segment of North American society, and Riesman's The Lonely Crowd[9] is a semi-popular analysis of this type. Oscar Lewis, whose work has been basically in anthropology, has followed more of a sociological ap-

proach in his Five Families,[10] which presents a specialized type of case studies which reveal a great deal about the values in Mexican proletarian society. His The Children of Sánchez[11] uses an autobiographic technique in which the subjects of his study relate their own life histories in a way which brings out still more of their value concepts. Ricardo Pozas used a somewhat similar technique in his presentation of the autobiography of Juan Pérez Jolote.[12] a Tzotzil Indian of Mexico.

The approach of the anthropologist is similar in many ways to that of the sociologist, but differs in that it is largely cross-cultural; i.e. the anthropologist takes a broad perspective of different cultures and their value concepts, and in analyzing these values he tries to arrive at broad generalizations in a given society which are such as to make it possible to compare it with other societies. He looks not merely for human values in general, but for ways in which these values are culturally defined and how they are emphasized in different cultures. He wants to know how a people's values are interrelated within the culture, in order to arrive at an analysis or multidimensional configuration of values which will reveal their significance in terms of the culture. Significant work of this nature has been done by Ruth Benedict, Clyde Kluckhohn, Margaret Mead, and others. B. N. Colby has recently contributed some helpful techniques for this type of value studies.

6 Recent volumes of American Anthropologist have carried numerous articles which discuss the use of this approach. Among such articles we may mention: Jules Henry and others, "Symposium: Projective Testing in Ethnography" (Vol. 57, pp. 245-70, 1955); Louise Spindler and George Spindler, "Male and Female Adaptations in Culture Change" (Vol. 60, pp. 217-33, 1958); Cyril J. Adcock and James E. Ritchie, "Intercultural Use of Rorschach" (Vol. 60, pp. 881-92, 1958); Walter Goldschmidt and Robert B. Edgerton, "A Picture Technique for the Study of Values" (Vol. 63, pp. 26-47, 1961).

7 New York: Harcourt, Brace, 1929, paperback, 1956.

8 New York: Simon and Schuster, 1956; paperback, Doubleday, n.d.

9 New Haven: Yale Univ. Press, 1950; paperback, Doubleday, n.d.

10 New York: Basic Books, 1959; reviewed by William L. Wonderly in "Urbanization: The Challenge of Latin America in Transition," PA, Vol. 7, No. 4, pp. 205-09 (July-Aug. 1960).

11 New York: Random House, 1961.

12 Mexico: Fondo de Cultura Económica, 1961; English edition, Juan the Chamula, Univ. of California Press.

Sets of Contrasting Values

One of the most fruitful approaches to value studies has been to delineate sets of values which have been found to be significant, and to set up a limited number of contrasting pairs or dimensions somewhat on the analogy of "distinctive features" in linguistics. This was done by Clyde Kluckhohn,[13] who proposed an initial list of thirteen contrasting pairs or binary categories. These have been recently revised and expanded by Colby[14] into sixteen binary categories. The purpose of this approach is, for a given culture, to arrive at a set of primary or distinctive categories in terms of which may be given a configuration or profile of the value system as a whole. In our present study we shall not attempt any such comprehensive approach, but shall consider certain pairs of contrasting attitudes and values which are observable and whose relevance for the task of the missionary is more or less apparent. Some of these pairs are primary in the sense just mentioned, while others are perhaps secondary in the sense that they could be described in terms of other distinctive or primary values.

Some pairs of contrasting values in which individuals and societies differ may be mentioned by way of example; the first seven of these we shall treat in some detail below: (1) Concern for near future vs. concern for distant future. (2) Concept of universe as systematized vs. concept of universe as non-systematized. (3) Emphasis on permanence vs. emphasis on change. (4) Individual-oriented vs. group-oriented. (5) Self-oriented vs. other-oriented. (6) Authoritarianism vs. democracy. (7) Frankness vs. reserve. (8) Aggressiveness (or dominance) vs. dependence. (9) Active attitude vs. acceptant (or passive) attitude.

For each of these pairs, an individual in a given situation may manifest one or other of the contrasting attitudes. These contrasting attitudes or values always remain in tension with each other; this leads to a process of compensation or "relief" on the part of the individual. For example, a person who is dominant and aggressive all day at the office may compensate for this by being dependent at home or in other situations. Or one who is extremely individualistic in certain aspects of life may show special concern for the group in other phases of his activity.

What has just been said for individual persons is also true for persons in a society; i.e. a society may show certain values as predominant, with compensation in certain areas. More accurately, the individuals in any society show a culturally conditioned tendency toward certain values, with people of one society and culture differing from people of another. This is what makes one people different from another, and leads to "national character" or group personality.

However, there are wide individual variations of value concepts within any culture. In fact, the variations within a single culture are often greater than the variation between the averages of two cultures taken as wholes. This is to be expected, and is just as true in the biological realm as in the cultural; for example, there is greater variation in

13 Clyde K. M. Kluckhohn, "Toward a Comparison of Value-Emphases in Different Cultures." In *The State of the Social Sciences*, pp. 116-32 (Chicago: Univ. of Chicago Press, 1956).

14 Benjamin N. Colby, in a privately mimeographed *Manual for the Use of the Clyde Kluckhohn Culture-Value Categories* (1961).

physical features within the negro race than there is between the average physical features of negroes and the average for whites. Thus we shall expect to find wider variation of value concepts among Frenchmen than we would find between the average for Frenchmen and the average for Hindus. That is to say, what we have in common as human beings is much greater than what we have gotten as a result of cultural diversity. This fact, of course, makes it difficult to make statements of value concepts which are valid for a whole culture, since we know only certain people who belong to the culture. It is therefore important to base our study on as representative a sample as possible, in order to gain a valid perspective.

Concern for Immediate vs. Distant Future

Some people show keen interest in and concern for the distant future, including old age and the after life, while others are concerned primarily for the present and the immediate future.

The Indian of Guatemala or Mexico tends to be interested primarily in the present and immediate future. He will carefully keep seed corn for the coming year, and do everything possible to keep possession of his land for use from year to year; but essentially his economy is a "stuff and starve" economy. At fiestas, Indians consume quantities of food only to starve later. Once, when a missionary translator of the Bible had some Chol Indians at a translation center and went to the nearby city to do his weekly shopping for them, he discovered next day that they had gorged themselves on the bag of oranges rather than planning how to make them last for a week.

The Indian sees no reason to save money in order to build capital for future use. After the harvest, he may sell his grain for money, only to buy later for his needs at higher prices. If he works for wages, he is likely to buy more clothes than he can use, rather than save for later needs. He often puts a low premium on education for his children, since the focus of attention is upon the here and now, when they are needed in the fields, rather than upon the distant future.

In contrast, the North American is concerned with life insurance, college education funds and retirement pensions, enacts laws for old-age benefits, amasses capital for long-range commercial operations, buys government bonds which must be held over a period of years before even a reasonable rate of interest is realized, and in general shows an interest in a considerably more distant point in the future than does the Indian. His merchandising is based on volume sales with low profits per unit and with an emphasis on building good will ("the customer is always right"). On the other hand — and perhaps this is a compensation — his foreign policy seems often to be based on day-to-day exigencies and to reflect little serious long-range planning.

The Ladino or mestizo in Latin America probably lies somewhere between these extremes. He builds up a certain amount of capital for the future, but not so much in terms of large long-range commercial operations (due in part to his individualism; see below). His merchandising philosophy is that of large profits on small volume, often without a serious attempt to build customer good-will for the future. To get him to buy government bonds or start savings accounts, he is given the incentive of periodic drawings in which he may be the lucky winner of a larger amount than he invested; and one of the most popular types of "investment" is, of course, the lottery ticket, which gives this incentive without any security whatever.

In the realm of religion, most pagan faiths do not emphasize concern for the distant future. They present the place of the dead as a murky and ill-defined place, in which the living need not have any special interest. In Roman Catholic Christianity, there is more interest in the distant future, but in the somewhat negative terms of escape from purgatory — something which can be gained through money and ritual, but not through good deeds. And since all alike must spend at least some time in purgatory, there is little reason for concerning oneself about the more distant heaven or hell.

But the Indian, in his religion of folk catholicism, is very much concerned about placating the spirits here and now, preserving the balance of nature through offerings and rain ceremonies, and healing of diseases that he believes are caused by spirits or through sorcery. Thus his religion, like the other aspects of his life, is basically oriented to the present and the immediate future. It is for this reason that the Chol Indians have responded so much more to the gospel when presented in terms of its immediate spiritual benefits than when in terms of future bliss or suffering.[15] The "manifold gospel of the grace of God" is ample enough for people with either of these orientations.

---

15 John Beekman, "A Culturally Relevant Witness," PA, Vol. 4, No. 3, pp. 83-88 (May-June 1957).

Opposing World Views: Systematic vs. Unsystematic Universe

Both the North American and the Latin insist upon a view of a closed or tidy universe in which everything fits without contradiction. This concept dates at least as far back as Aristotle, and it was under the influence of Aristotelian logic and philosophy that there developed the major doctrines of the Roman Catholic Church in the Middle Ages and our systematic theology of today. Our Western concepts of a tidy universe have led to emphasis upon symmetry in art, music, philosophy, and theology. It is noteworthy that this was not an especially prominent concept in the Hebrew value system, and even in the New Testament with its Greek influence we find very little of the systematization characteristic of later Christian developments. The Bible makes no attempt to reconcile its paradoxical teachings of divine sovereignty vs. human freedom, predestination vs. human responsibility, security of the believer vs. warnings against falling, etc.; the "need" for reconciling such concepts within a single system developed only with the later formulation of theology under classical influence.

It should be noted that in modern science there are points at which our theories and even our mathematical formulae are not free from apparent contradictions. This is especially true when dealing with the relativity theory, the quantum theory of light and radiation, and related fields. If in this most exacting of all fields it is impossible for us to maintain a concept of an entirely consistent universe it should not seem strange if other peoples refrain from insisting on logical consistency in their philosophy and religion.

The Indian of Middle America has never been especially interested in a tidy or systematic universe. His art forms show more movement than symmetry. He cannot tell you which spirits are more or less powerful than others — it has never occurred to him that this should be a problem for concern. He is not bothered by what to the Western mind are logical contradictions, although with modern education now being brought to him in Western form he is faced with conflicts between the two points of view. The pre-conquest religions regularly adopted the gods of conquerors or conquered, without attempting to reconcile their different attributes; and present-day folk catholicism is a further manifestation of this same tendency. No one worries much about whether it is logical to recite the Lord's Prayer in connection with rituals to placate the spirits, or whether it makes sense to use pagan ceremonies to invoke the name of a Christian saint in order to get rain.

In the Indian's response to Protestant Christianity, he has taken certain aspects of its teaching but has not really adopted it as a system. He sees no need of a logical system. He can accept Protestant doctrines (which we try to teach him systematically in the Bible schools) without seeing any basic conflict with certain aspects of his own religion. This was the case with the Maya Christians reported by Redfield,[16] who abandoned the orthodox or semi-orthodox Catholic part of their ritual (because the missionaries knew about this and told them) but continued to practice the pagan ceremonies of child dedication and the pagan rain ceremonies. With this type of addition or syncretism, which accords perfectly well with the Indian's view of a not-necessarily-systematic universe, it is easy for him later, especially in times of stress, to backslide into paganism. This is what happened after much of the early Roman Catholic missionary work, leading to today's Christo-paganism or folk catholicism. It has also happened after some of the more recent Protestant work in Latin America, in which Indians have turned away from Protestantism after years of careful instruction in what the missionaries thought were the fundamentals of the faith but which turned out to be not nearly so relevant to the concerns of the Indian as had been supposed.

The missionary, whose cultural background has prepared him to notice and abhor logical inconsistencies (except for the ones he has been taught not to notice), often assumes that the Indian reader of the Scriptures will draw "logical" conclusions of the same type that were presented in the books on doctrine and theology which he himself studied. One missionary reported to us his amazement and disgust at the fact that after trying to teach the fifth chapter of Romans to a group of Indian believers, they failed utterly to follow Paul's argument which proves justification by faith by the fact that Abraham was reckoned righteous before, not after he was circumcised. The same missionary, on another occasion, discovered that one of the same group, a believer of some fifteen years' standing, was secretly keeping deer bones in a bag for use in some indigenous rite with which the missionary was not acquainted and which he had therefore never had occasion to discuss with the believers. He proudly reported to us how he had tongue-lashed the Indian believer for not having realized that such prac-

16 Robert Redfield, A Village that Chose Progress: Chan Kom Revisited (Chicago: Univ. of Chicago Press, 1950).

tices were just naturally inconsistent with Christianity.

This situation has a good analogy in Japan, where Shinto and Buddhism, which are mutually antagonistic religions, are both held by most Japanese, and where many people, especially among the young, adopt Christianity as still another religion only to return to their traditional religions in their later years. Both in Japan and in Middle America, the missionary all too frequently assumes that converts who adopt Christianity are bound by its logic as a system and have therefore repudiated all concepts which are in contradiction with it. This logical assumption is possible for the Western missionary only because he thinks in terms of a systematic universe and imagines that other people must also think in these terms.

Concepts of Permanence vs. Change

Different cultures place different values on change; this may be treated under (1) changes in technology, (2) changes in ideas, and (3) changes in space or location.

1. With regard to *technology*, the Indian readily adopts such peripheral things as flashlights, bicycles, corn mills, buses, radios, and movies, especially when these make life easier without drastically changing the old patterns. However, he never becomes enamored of new technologies for their own sake, as people in the United States do. He has little interest in what makes machines work, and although Indians may frequently become good mechanics or factory workers, their interest in the technology involved is utilitarian rather than theoretical or for prestige.

The Indian, while accepting these new things in areas which are peripheral to his culture, does not normally use or develop techniques that are in direct conflict with already established values of the culture. Use of commercial fertilizers, for example, may be thought of as incompatible with the beliefs about agriculture, and deep plowing may be rejected in the fear that it will hurt the earth and make it angry and unproductive. Development of springs and water supply may be resisted, not because people do not want good water but because they are afraid of offending the guardian spirits of the water sources. In such areas as these, where new technologies come into conflict with already existing values and technologies, it is essential for the cultural missionary to exercise special concern in teaching the why and wherefore of the proposed change if it is to be successfully introduced.

Similarly, Indians are often quite ready to use modern medicines, but not as an outright substitute for native medicines. North Americans, with their concept of a tidy and systematic universe, prefer to keep within a given system of medicine; witness the perpetual conflict between the M.D. and the osteopath, for example. But the Indian, for whom the universe is not a closed system, does not hesitate to use modern medicine alongside native medicine, and modern means of diagnosis alongside magical means of diagnosis.

In contrast with the Indian, whose interest in new technologies is utilitarian, the Ladino or mestizo is very much interested in the acquisition of new objects and gadgets for their own sake. True, he is less interested than is the North American, but as a participant in Western culture in general he is more interested in them than is the Indian. New technologies bring to the Ladino new expressions of old values; possession of new objects brings prestige, and a prestige culture is developed which is geared to TV and fine automobiles, whereas it was earlier geared to the possession of land and peons. The basic values remain, but with a different manifestation.

2. With regard to *changes in ideas,* the Indian is not necessarily as conservative as is sometimes thought; but just as in the realm of technology, the ideas which are accepted are such as can be taken on without bringing in new values. Both Roman Catholic and Protestant ideas of religion are accepted without difficulty, but in such a way as to produce a minimum of change in the basic values that are already held. The over-all concepts of relationship to nature, to the land, and to the spirits remain the same, even when Christian ideas are superimposed on the old ones. The outward form changes, and this change involves a change in many of the ideas that are peripheral to their system; but since the Indian does not worry about a tidy universe he can accept these changes and still keep intact his basic concepts and values.

For the Ladino, on the other hand, who shares Western ideas of a systematic universe, new ideas do bring in new values. This is perhaps one reason why the mestizo or Ladino members of a community are often the last to accept Protestant ideas — they tend to realize the conflict between these and their old values more than the Indians do. The implication of this difference for evangelism is something that should be further studied.

3. With regard to *changes in space or physical location,* there is a marked difference in outlook between Indian and Ladino. Since the focus of the Indian is on the land, he prefers not to move to new locations. He may go away to work for periods of time, but the focus of his interest is always his home, where he wants to go if he gets sick and where he always plans to return eventually.

But the Ladino has no such attachment to the land. If he changes from lower- to middle-class status, this almost always involves a change in physical location — often in terms of leaving the village and moving to the city. Or he may move to the city in order to find educational opportunities for his children (compare his concern with the future as discussed above). Moving means progress, and thus mobility comes to have value in itself.

This concept of mobility becomes even more exaggerated in the United States, where an up-and-coming executive feels he must move to suburbia and join the social rat race there, looking forward all the while to an opportunity to acquire a still more prestigeful residence whenever his position in the Organization enables him to do so.

Individual vs. Group Orientation

In the dimension of individual vs. group orientation, there are significant differences between the Indian culture on the one hand and the Latin and North American cultures on the other. There are further differences between the Latin and North American cultures, but these are related more to the contrasts of self-orientation vs. other-orientation and of authoritative vs. democratic structure and will be discussed more fully below under these points.

The Indian is group-oriented in contrast to the person in the individual-oriented Latin and North American cultures. In an Indian community it is not considered good for an individual to stand out from the rest, either through breaking with traditional ways, getting new and educated ideas, or attaining too much wealth. Land tenure is traditionally in the hands of the community, with no provision for the individual to develop large property holdings. One of the functions of the fiesta system among Indians is to operate as a leveling process. If a person gets too rich, or before he does, he is expected to spend his money on a fiesta, thus redistributing his wealth and remaining near the general economic level of the community. The economic system of the Indian community thus provides safeguards against extreme differences of wealth, and at the same time has the disadvantage (in terms of the dominant culture) of hindering the development of capital for larger economic operations.

This leveling process does not operate in Protestant Indian communities, at least not in terms of the fiesta system, which has been repudiated by the converts; but there is a strong compensation which appears in group activities of the Indian churches, which show much more group solidarity than do the mestizo or Ladino churches. In the Otomí Indian church in Ixmiquilpan, Mexico, this group activity has included not only cooperation in worship and evangelistic activities, but the development of group projects of community work, building of schools and churches, and more recently of cooperative farming. This type of development preserves the basic value of emphasis upon the group in the midst of the new emphasis on the individual responsibility of the Christian.

Whereas the Indian cultures are community-oriented, the Latin culture tends to be family-oriented. Spanish-speaking people in Mexico, for example, preserve much closer ties with their extended family of relatives than do the people of the United States, and probably more than do the Indians of Latin America. In the United States the orientation is neither toward the family nor toward the community; at this point the North American is more individualistic than the Latin. The North American takes responsibility only for his nuclear or immediate family, with the result that death or divorce often leaves the children to suffer without any adequate provision. In Latin society, a child is thought of as belonging to the extended family and when in such a situation he generally becomes the responsibility of the extended family to care for. In the Indian society, a child belongs to the community and in situations of need becomes the community's concern. The North American finds security in the impersonal factors of wealth, insurance, and organization (including government agencies), thus compensating for his individualism at this point; the Latin seeks for security more through his individual efforts, at the same time having his extended family to fall back on and also to help; the Indian finds security in his relationship to the community which takes priority over him as an individual.

Other manifestations of the individual orientation in the Latin culture include the emphasis on personalism, or the identification of an ideal or a cause with the person of its leader, the insistence upon doing things as individuals rather than as part of an impersonalized system of mass-production, the prevalence of small business enterprises even where larger corporations would be more efficient, and the development of *machismo* or the "cult of masculinity" so characteristic of some parts of Latin America.

Self-oriented vs.
Other-oriented
(vs. Reciprocal-oriented)

Latins and North Americans are both individual-oriented, but in different ways. The difference between the two kinds of individualism may best be discussed in terms of the self vs. other dimension of orientation. Gillin has described the difference in the following terms:

The Latin American notion of the value of the individual differs radically from that current in the North American culture. To put it as succinctly as possible, each person is valuable because of a unique inner quality or worth he possesses. The United States credo, on the other hand, holds (at least ideally) that the individual merits respect because he has the right to be considered "just as good as the next person," or at least because he has the right to "an equal chance" or opportunity with other persons. In other words, in the United States the average individual is seen in terms of his equality with others — equality, either of right or opportunity. In Latin American culture, however, the individual is valued precisely because he is not exactly "like" anyone else. He is special and unique.[17]

This uniqueness of the individual is something which is to be insisted upon by the individual himself, leading to the

concepts of personal honor and *dignidad de la persona,* which tend to be focused primarily upon oneself rather than upon others. If a North American is challenged as to his rights, the typical response is, "This is a free country, isn't it?" (meaning, "Everyone here has his rights, and therefore I have mine as derived from this general principle"); but the response heard from a door-to-door peddler in Mexico City of "I am a Mexican, and I have a right to sell where I please" would seem to typify the Latin American concept that one's own rights are primary and that the rights of others are the ones that are derived. That is, in a self-oriented culture the other man (and especially the lower man) has rights primarily because he has been given them, not because all men are thought of as naturally having equal rights.

Self-orientation vs. other-orientation is not to be interpreted as meaning necessarily that some people are selfish and others are not, since in the other-oriented culture it is just as easy to focus upon others with a view to "using" them to one's own interest. This is the danger in the "other-directed" orientation which Riesman describes as developing in urban North America, the implications of which were discussed by Herberg[18] in relation to the communication of the gospel.

A further manifestation, however, of the self-oriented culture does come closer to the attitude of selfishness. This is the lack of concern for "the common good," in which, for example, a person does not feel it his duty to protect life and limb by posting a warning sign at an excavation in the street, and the motorist cannot

---

17 John Gillin, "Ethos Components in Modern Latin American Culture," *American Anthropologist,* Vol. 57, No. 3, pp. 488-500 (1955).

18 Will Herberg, "The Christian Witness in an Emerging 'Other-Directed' Culture," PA, Vol. 5, No. 5-6, pp. 211-15 (Sept.-Dec. 1958).

sue the city for negligence if he drives into it. Rather, it is said that "*el golpe avisa* (the bump will let you know)," and the individual accepts his own risk in such situations. Another example of this difference in orientation is seen in the fact that in the United States people are often appealed to for keeping the parks and rest rooms clean by reminding them to think of the next person who uses them, whereas in Latin America the appeal frequently made is "*demuestre su cultura* (show your culture) by leaving the place clean." Of course North Americans are by no means impeccable in their concern for the common good either; when New York's subways were on strike the stream of people coming up from the closed gates passed on the stairway the stream going down to find them closed, without anyone telling the latter that there was no use to continue down the steps.

The contrast of self-orientation vs. other-orientation would appear to be culturally relevant primarily in societies which are individual-oriented. In the Indian society, which is group-oriented, we seem to have an intermediate type of orientation which is reciprocal, rather than toward self or others. Dyadic or reciprocal relationships[19] are highly developed, including gift exchange, exchange of work, hospitality and guest friendship, and so on, in which no one gets very far ahead of the other and reciprocity is maintained. A person is expected to give up his rights in proportion as others give up their rights for him. This is seen in the leveling processes

alluded to above, and in the obligation to share with others as emphasized in a number of Indian societies.[20]

This reciprocal orientation extends into the religious concepts of the Indian. The pre-conquest religions of Middle America placed man in a reciprocal or symbiotic relationship with the gods, in which the latter received nourishment and help from men and in turn provided men with rain and corn harvests.[21] Among the Quichua of Ecuador, the Virgin is sometimes whipped if she does not produce rain, since when men have done their part she is expected to do hers. Foster[22] describes the dyadic contracts of people in Michoacán as being made with supernatural beings as well as with fellow-humans.

The Hebrew culture of the Old Testament tended toward a reciprocal orientation, as may be seen especially in the covenant relationships that were emphasized not only in the Bible but in the affairs of the other nations of the period.[23] In these, the emphasis was upon mutual responsibility between conqueror and conquered, between ruler and subject, and this dyadic relationship was extended to

19 See George M. Foster, "The Dyadic Contract: a Model for the Social Structure of a Mexican Peasant Village," *American Anthropologist*, Vol. 63, No. 6, pp. 1173-92 (Dec. 1961).

20 This has been reported especially for the Toba of Argentina. See William D. Reyburn, *The Toba Indians of the Argentine Chaco* (Elkhart, Ind.: Mennonite Board of Missions and Charities, 1954).

21 William Madsen, *Christo-Paganism: A Study of Mexican Religious Syncretism* (New Orleans: Middle American Research Institute, Tulane Univ., 1957; preprinted from Publication 19, pp. 105-80). Reviewed by William L. Wonderly in "Pagan and Christian Concepts in a Mexican Indian Culture," PA, Vol. 5, No. 5-6, pp. 197-202 (Sept.-Dec. 1958).

22 Foster, op. cit.

23 See G. E. Mendenhall, "Covenant," in *The Interpreter's Dictionary of the Bible*, Vol. 1 (A-D), pp. 714-23 (New York: Abingdon Press, 1962).

apply to the covenant between God and men.

In this dimension of self-oriented vs. other-oriented, with the intermediate aspect of reciprocal orientation, we are very close to something which bears upon a distinctly Christian value, and to which we might well turn our attention in seeking for ways to make the gospel more relevant in the particular cultural situation. This should be important in relation to developing a Christian interest in the common good in Latin American society; and in the North American "other-directed" society it should be related to the development of love and concern for others as a guide for action rather than just using the approval or disapproval of others as a guide. In the reciprocal-oriented Indian society it is possible to emphasize, as the Toba Indians do, the sharing aspect of God's redemptive work for men, as well as to guide in a Christian direction the reciprocal relationships that already exist among the people. At the same time it may be necessary to correct the belief that God is interested in man for what man can do for him, while at the same time giving perhaps more emphasis to the Old Testament concepts of the reciprocal covenant type of divine-human relationships than has been done among Christians with Western cultural backgrounds.

Authoritarianism vs. Democracy

In the dimension of authoritarian vs. democratic orientation, we first consider the contrast between the democratic North American system and the authoritarian Latin system; the Indian orientation is then seen to be democratic but different from the North American type of democracy.

Organizational structure in the United States, especially in recent times, tends toward an emphasis on teamwork and committee action, with a premium placed on the ability to work as a member of a team without forcing one's own ideas upon anyone. In such a team the lines of authority are left somewhat vague so as to permit each member to exercise his initiative and to maintain at least a fiction of being autonomous, even when everyone knows who the "big boss" really is. This is a correlate of the rise of the "other-directed" urban society which Riesman has discussed and in which people get their direction not from tradition or from inner conviction but from the responses of other people and do not like to be under direct authority.

In contrast, organizational structure in the Latin situation is authoritarian and hierarchically structured. This is a natural development from the earlier feudal system, and is also in line with the authority structure of the Roman Catholic Church (whose development was of course not unrelated to the feudal background). This does not mean that Latin people cannot work together in group enterprises, but it does mean that in order to do so there must be a structured authority with well-defined rules and lines of direction. This is very different from the North American concept of teamwork, as anyone can tell who has watched a Latin American committee or governing church body set up their agenda and rules of procedure. One religious organization whose headquarters organization in the United States is set up on the teamwork principle tried to organize along the same lines one of its field offices which was directed in part by Latin Americans, endeavoring to form a "team" of Latin Americans and

North Americans in which lines of authority were purposely left as vague as in the home office. The result was a series of tensions, with the Latin members of the "team" unable to understand why the lines of authority were not better defined and the people in the home office just as unable to see why they should be. One of the new members of the "team," a Latin American, was surprised to learn that a letter he had written to headquarters to find out whether he was to consider one of the North American members as his boss was interpreted at headquarters as insinuating that the latter was trying to dominate the situation.

Both the North American and the Indian societies are democratic in contrast with the Latin society; but the former has a more highly structured type of democracy than the latter. In the United States, even a small committee generally considers itself obliged to conduct its business according to Roberts' *Rules of Order,* even though some of its provisions are often explicitly waived to facilitate teamwork. In contrast, decisions in the Indian society are reached in a more informal and unstructured manner, such that the outsider can seldom tell how the decision was really made or who made it. This is, of course, in line with the group-oriented character of the Indian community, in which no individual should stand out any more than necessary. It would also seem to be in line with the reciprocal character of the Indian culture, which is neither self-oriented nor other-oriented.

An authoritarian orientation may lead to different organizational structures, depending in part upon the orientation of the culture with respect to the dimensions of individual vs. group, and self vs.

other vs. reciprocal. In the historical encounter of the Latin culture (which was individual- and self-oriented) with the Indian cultures (which were group- and reciprocal-oriented), there developed the *cacique* system in which the leader in a still group-oriented society dominates the people but is not considered dependent on them nor responsible to them. The people in such a situation probably tend to identify with the chief or *cacique,* and to the degree to which they do, there results a tendency toward self-orientation within the group-oriented society. This probably leads in turn to a new individual-orientation in the society, since self-orientation is not compatible with group-orientation.[24]

A different organizational structure developed in the Hebrew culture, which was group-oriented and reciprocal-oriented. Here there developed the covenant relation between leader and people, in which the leader might be the one to lay down the rules but where the rules were defined in terms of mutual responsibilities of and benefits to both parties.

Frankness vs. Reserve

North Americans take pride in being frank and open. When a person objects to something, it is felt that "there's no use beating it around the bush" but that the objection should be made in a straightforward fashion. "The truth may hurt" but, ideally at least, it is to be told regardless of consequences. People are

---

[24] We suggest this as a hypothesis worth investigating in connection with the acculturation process in which Indians become mestizos and come to partake of the culture of the nation. As a hypothesis, it needs documentation before it can be presented as a definite historical process.

supposed to be able to both give and take a considerable amount of "straight-from-the-shoulder" talk. The missionary all too often carries this type of outspokenness with him to Latin America, thinks that if the brethren in the church are really Christian they should take his criticisms just as a similar group in the United States would, and finds himself offending.

The Mexican writer Octavio Paz[25] discusses at length the Latin American attitude of reserve as applied to the Mexican. According to Paz, the Mexican is surrounded by a series of protective devices which guarantee his inward privacy, and it is a mark of honor, especially for the male, not to "break open" and expose himself to the view of others. These protective devices include rituals of courtesy (which the North American visitor often tries to bypass), indirection, and formality in both behavior and dress. They also include reserve in telling where one is going or what one is doing, thinking or planning; by contrast, the North American often seeks to show friendliness and inspire confidence by telling everything, or at least by giving the impression of telling everything. Among North Americans this sort of frankness is used to disarm the other person and invite him to be equally frank. When used toward the Mexican, however, it often has the effect more of giving an impression of weakness than of inspiring confidence.

Paz relates this reserve of the Mexican to a feeling of insecurity: "Hermeticism is one of the several recourses of our suspicion and distrust. It shows that we instinctively regard the world around us

to be dangerous.... Our relationships with other men are always tinged with suspicion. Every time a Mexican confides in a friend or acquaintance, every time he opens himself up, it is an abdication. He dreads that the person in whom he has confided will scorn him. Therefore confidences result in dishonor, and they are as dangerous for the person to whom they are made as they are for the person who makes them"[26] He then proceeds to relate this attitude to the attitude of *machismo* or cult of masculine prowess about which so many Mexican writers have spoken, and which Aramoni[27] identifies as an expression of insecurity of the man in reference to the woman.

Continuing his discussion of the Mexican attitude of reserve, Paz connects it with the phenomenon of lying and pretense. He says, "We tell lies for the mere pleasure of it, like all imaginative peoples, but we also tell lies to hide ourselves and to protect ourselves from intruders. Lying plays a decisive role in our daily lives, our politics, our love affairs and our friendships, and since we attempt to deceive ourselves as well as others, our lies are brilliant and fertile, not like the gross inventions of other peoples. Lying is a tragic game in which we risk a part of our very selves. Hence it is pointless to denounce it."[28] It would thus seem that when a person tells a lie or a half-truth (sometimes even when the whole truth would be to his immediate advan-

---

25 Octavio Paz, *El laberinto de la soledad.* Mexico: Fondo de Cultura Económica, 1959; English edition, *The Labyrinth of Solitude.* New York: Grove Press, 1961.

26 Paz, op. cit., p. 27 (p. 30 of English edition).

27 Aniceto Aramoni, *Psicoanálisis de la dinámica de un pueblo,* especially chapter 8 (Mexico: Universidad Nacional Autónoma de México, 1961).

28 Paz, op. cit., p. 36 (p. 40 of English edition).

tage), it is due to the attitude of reserve which seeks to keep something, some secret, that the speaker can consider his very own and which he has not surrendered to anyone. A missionary who had worked in an orphanage in Mexico once said, "If a boy steals six marbles, he may be made to confess to stealing four, but never six!" He refuses to "break open" completely.

However, such an attitude of reserve is naturally not maintained continually. There are times and situations when compensation takes place, when the person does "break open" and communicates frankly with others. This is especially true at fiestas, and Paz considers this to be one of the important functions of the many fiestas in Latin America — religious and patriotic celebrations, national, local, or on the family level.

In the above paragraphs we have discussed the attitude of reserve in terms of Mexico rather than of Latin America in general, partly because of its having been presented so effectively by Mexican writers. Whether the phenomenon is characteristic of Indian culture or of Latin culture is a bit difficult to say, since its development has been discussed in terms of the mestizo population of Mexico. Sociologists in Colombia have used the term *malicia indigena* to refer to a certain type of reserve which they associate with Indians, and in countries where there is no significant Indian or mestizo population this reserve is probably less in evidence than in the others. Paz[29] would seem to think of it as inherently neither Indian nor Latin, but a result of fears and suspicions developed by both Indians and mestizos during the colonial period.

How much difference there is in this respect between Indians and Latins in a country like Guatemala or Bolivia, where there are more Indians but less race and cultural mixture than in Mexico, is something that should be investigated.

The implications of this contrast of frankness vs. reserve are important for the missionary's approach. Just how frank should we be in "spelling out" people's sins and faults? How open shall we expect them to be in confession to one another? Certainly there are legitimate cultural differences — yet how far can one yield to these differences without compromising the basic requirements of the gospel? And if on the other hand we do not yield enough, within such limits as are legitimate, are we erecting human barriers to keep people out of the kingdom of God?

Apart from this problem, there is the problem of finding ways to make the gospel relevant to people's specific needs when these are not made known as frankly as they sometimes are among North Americans. How to penetrate the protective shell of reserve and apply the gospel where it is most needed? Here is needed an emphasis on love — a love which will break down the suspicions and distrust between man and man and produce a Christian fellowship in which mutual confidence and bearing one another's burdens will not be considered an act of weakness. To the extent that attitudes of reserve are the result of feelings of insecurity and distrust, the church should endeavor to work toward the development of frankness — not by encouraging people to violate their privacy and imitate North American frankness, but by removing causes for mutual suspicion and developing a spirit of fellowship.

[29] Ibid., p. 38 (p. 43 of English edition).

It is significant that the worship services of Pentecostal groups among the lower socio-economic classes frequently take the form, not of reserve and solemnity, but of freedom and a fiesta spirit. The people are sometimes reminded specifically that their worship is to take the form of a fiesta of joy and gladness. For these groups, in contrast to our more traditional denominations, church becomes a place where the needed compensation for the reserve attitude can take place; as a result, not only do people thereby avoid having to engage in less wholesome activities to get such compensation, but an atmosphere is created in which the church fellowship becomes the place where people expect to "open up" in the presence of one another. Thus there develops a basis for Christian fellowship and mutual confidence that probably cannot be adequately developed for these socio-economic groups through our more traditional forms of worship.

Some Research Questions

The following questions are intended to suggest some lines of investigation and subjects for discussion relating to the value concepts discussed above. Like our article, the questions are addressed to the Latin America situation. Many additional or parallel questions will suggest themselves to the reader in Latin America and elsewhere.

What tensions exist within the Indian community, or between Indians and Ladinos in the same community, resulting from differences in concern for the immediate future vs. the distant future?

What benefits does the non-evangelical Indian expect from his religion in the here and now? In the hereafter?

What response is given by the Indian people to gospel appeals based on heaven, hell, and future judgment? Have other aspects of the gospel, equally Biblical but relating to the here and now, been observed to exert an equal or greater appeal? What further aspects of the gospel should be explored and emphasized that have not been exploited to date?

What pagan elements are preserved in folk catholicism in the Indian group, which are in apparent conflict with the teachings of the Roman Catholic Church? Which inconsistencies of this type have given greatest trouble to the Maryknoll Fathers in Guatemala, in getting their teaching across to the Indians?

What inconsistencies, from our systematic point of view, have been observed in the beliefs and practices of evangelical Indians? Are supposedly mature Christians ever observed to revert to practices which the missionary had presumed would have been eradicated (perhaps even without the missionary's having preached against them explicitly)? What practices? Have cases of backsliding been related to these inconsistencies?

If by Christo-paganism we mean a syncretism of Roman Catholicism with paganism, what symptoms may be observed of a further syncretism, viz. between evangelical Christianity and Christo-paganism?

What ideas in Protestant Christianity can be accepted, at least superficially, without seriously changing basic cultural values? Which ideas of Christianity are most likely to run into conflict with these basic values?

What is the attitude of Indian believers toward the land they cultivate? Toward belief in spirits? Toward the relationships between the supernatural and the phenomena of nature (rain, etc.)? To what extent do these attitudes correspond to those held by non-believers?

Do Indian churches show more group solidarity than do Ladino churches? If so, in what ways?

Does church life tend to center around the personality of a leader (pastor or other), or is there a true group spirit? How do Indian churches differ from Ladino churches in this regard?

Does the phenomenon of *machismo* appear among the Indians as much as among Ladinos? Some observers have found that young men who engage in group sports activities tend not to express themselves as *machistas* to the same degree as others; is this true in the community where you work?

What shapes do the reciprocal relationships between persons take in the Indian church group? How do these differ from those between non-evangelicals, or between evangelicals and non-evangelicals? In what ways, if any, do these relationships need to be "converted" to make them more Christian?

Do Indian believers think of their relationship to God as reciprocal, in the sense that God needs what they give to him and that they can thereby put him under obligation to help them? How does this differ from Biblical concepts?

Do people in the local community tend to identify with (or put themselves on the side of) the constituted authority, or with the dissenter who defies authority?

In secular matters, do people expect to be told authoritatively what to do, or do they demand to know why? Does this carry over into religious matters and matters of church organization?

Do the organizational structures of the local evangelical church and its relationship with the mission or denominational organization fit the pattern of local authority structure? At what points does the church organization differ from the local pattern in such a way as to cause conflicts?

What kind of answer does the Indian tend to give when asked what he is doing or where he is going? What kind of answer does the Ladino give? What kind of answer does the missionary give?

Is there a difference in degree of "openness" and willingness to confide, on the part of Indians as distinct from Ladinos? Which tend to be more "transparent" in their dealings with others?

Do people confess their sins openly when they accept the gospel? Do Christians confess their faults to one another? Is there any difference between Indians and Ladinos in this respect?

Do Christians tend to be more "open" than non-Christians, in the sense of willingness to confide in one another?

Does the church provide occasions at which Christians can "open up" in a fiesta spirit in the presence of one another? In what ways might the church in your area provide for more of such compensation?

William D. Reyburn

Motivations for Christianity: An African Conversation

How does a missionary anthropologist get information? Does the fact that he is associated with a mission cripple his ability to get at the facts? Whatever may be his disadvantages, the missionary anthropologist must always work with the people in their own language, and he must have an abiding desire to identify himself with the people he serves. His anthropological advantage is that of securing his data from the normal situations of native life rather than from informant interviews only. He is different from his colleagues in that he must be free to question things which other missionaries take for granted. He must be ready to offer explanations of a people's response and interpretation of Christianity as he ferrets these out through investigation.

Such study may be accomplished in a number of ways. The brief account that is given below is intended to provide a small example of the missionary anthropologist's work at his laboratory, attempting to find the answer to a problem which has come to his attention. In this case the question concerns the high motivation which exists among the Kaka of the Camerouns for being "written in the church."

The Problem Appears

"We were written in the mission because we are afraid of our own power,"

Reprinted from Vol. 5, No. 1 (1958), pp. 27-32.

exclaimed an African village chief to me recently. On a previous occasion I had noted that the mission had "written" the names of 164 adults in the Kaka village of Lolo in the subdivision of Batouri, French Cameroun. However, only a handful of women and fewer men ever attended the services regularly.

I tried talking with the local catechist to find out the motivation for "being written," but without success. His reasons were not comprehensive and did not accord with some of the major aspects of Kaka culture. His replies that the women liked to go to church on Sunday and that the men wanted to drink wine were insufficient. I determined to investigate, and what I found out proved the catechist wrong, both in his replies and in his ministry.

Lolo is one of those villages where Christianity in the missionary view has been almost totally unsuccessful. It is a village of some four hundred souls where the leading men must have several wives to be accorded status. On the one hand, Lolo is quite primitive. They scarify their children's bodies, perform circumcision rites and chip their teeth, practice numerous taboos related to birth, death, and the hunt. Their economy is divided between hunting and gardening. Their food is almost exclusively manioc flour which they boil into a gelatinous mush and eat with their hands.

On the other score, Lolo is quite modern. It boasts a Christian church with a paid catechist, a French school (first and second grades) subsidized by the government, and a year-round automobile road which cuts through the heart of the village. Tuesday and Wednesday, as regularly as clockwork, a four-engine plane drones through the clouds high over Lolo. The weekly G-string is covered on Sunday by a flowery print dress, a flowing Hausa robe, or occasionally a tattered European overcoat. A small bus is available several days a week for the eighty-kilometer bounce to the regional center at Batouri. In spite of all this, the power of a dead panther is vastly more significant in the Lolo way of thinking than the airplanes which fly overhead.

Where to Begin?

The problem I wanted to investigate was not complex, but how I would approach it would determine largely the kind of information I would obtain. I could choose to sit at the catechist's house and invite informants to come and visit with me, or I could go into Lolo and live with the people and seek the answers to my problem from the normal conversations of the day and in more subtle ways than asking direct questions. I chose the latter. Taking my regular assistant, a Kaka tribesman who knew many of the men in the village, we moved in with no food and as little gear as we could possibly get by with. It took two weeks to convince the people that a white man could really want to live like the people. Their constant remarks were, "The other tribes don't like our food and say we are dirty. We are so surprised that a white man eats with us, and we thank you." During this two weeks, I did not push for answers

to questions but merely listened to others talk and only talked when I was addressed.

Later our talks often ran well into the night as I was riddled with questions about the strange world of the whites. I even had to attempt to explain about Sputnik, and that in a language that has no words for *rounds, gravity,* or *space.* I wondered often why in all of their incessant questioning they never seemed to want to inquire about the mission. I thought this was perhaps because I was connected with the mission and they did not want to bring up a subject which they were tired of hearing about from the catechist.

The Natural Occasion Ripens

Finally one night, as a group of village elders and I were sitting in the chief's courtyard, the old chief puffed slowly on his clay pipe, blew a gust of smoke against his hand, handed the pipe to the man beside him, and turning to me said, "White man Kaka, what is your name?" I told him my first name. "No," he exclaimed, "that's your pagan name. What is your mission name?" Fortunately my middle name is also good in French, so I told him, and he sighed, "Aha, we will call you Davidi now."

At last it began to look like they were going to start talking toward my subject. I asked him in turn if he had a "mission name." "No," he blurted, "I can't have a mission name." "Why?" I asked. "Look around you," he exclaimed, pointing to six thatched-roof kitchens in his enclosure. "The mission refuses us because we have wives."

I thought to myself, "Shall I unload a long discourse on polygamy as I view it, or shall I see what develops here?"

I sat quietly. There was a long silent pause. The stars were twinkling brightly in the cool night sky. I did not want to lose the thread of this conversation, as I was determined to find out what I was after only by avoiding the traditional informant kind of artificial situation. I went back to the question of "mission" names. "Mboundjeliko, do you have a mission name?" I asked a bearded man wearing a Hausa covering. "Yes, God knows me," was his reply. "Would God know a Kaka name?" he asked, looking at his colleagues. A low grunt of "No" drifted across the courtyard from some of the chief's wives who were listening at a distance. Now they were beginning to expose their thinking, as I wanted.

I thought I'd better probe a bit while they were thinking about this. "All right," I said, "suppose you have got a mission name and now God knows you, is that all God is good for? If God knows your mission name, Satan must know it too." Their faces turned toward me. "God can read, can't he?" asked one man. "Yes, I should think so," I replied. "Can Satan read?" two men asked as they rocked forth toward me. "Why not? Even children learn to read." Then again silence fell over us. "Who is stronger, God or Satan?" asked the chief. "God is, of course," I replied. A sigh of relief arose from the men. Turning to the chief, I asked, "Tell me, what do you care about the strength of Satan? Are you a child that you should cry because of Satan?"

The Pay Load Arrives

The chief stood up and pointed a long bony finger at me and said, "We all cry because of lémbo that Satan puts in us." I knew that lémbo was a supernatural power which enters a human and causes him to kill and perform sorcery. The individual may be treated by a shaman and be cured. Sorcerers are people who are possessed by lémbo but will not submit to exorcism and have their lémbo removed. At last they had touched on the vital source that was underlying their motivation for being written in the mission. "Tell me," I said, "are you afraid of lémbo?" The chief replied, "Yes. All men are afraid of the power of lémbo. With lémbo you kill people without wanting to do so; you never touch them, but it is your lémbo inside of you that has killed them. The mission taught us that God would punish killers. We are all killers and we fear God's punishment. We believe that God can stop our lémbo from growing inside of us. Our lémbo will stay small and quiet. God will read the names and know whose lémbo to arrest."

"But," I objected, "how should that affect you men? Most of you are polygamists and the mission won't write your names." "Oh," he laughed, "we have sent our first wives. This is to show our good heart to God. Would God forget a man who has given him his first wife? The mission will accept only one wife, so we all have put our first wives into God's hands and she will work for us and take care of us in heaven."

I looked about me, and every man in the group was nodding his head in assent to the chief's words. Some of the men started to get up to go home. "Wait," I said, "one more question. What about your lémbo? If you are not written in the mission. . . ." The chief cut me short this time. "No, I'm not written, but I have told others to get their names written. Less chance of me getting killed by their lémbo that way." "That's the way it is," added the group of village elders as they arose and began to depart into the night. I stood up, stretched, called out, "Sleep well," and picked my way through sleeping goats and sheep until I reached my shack. With the aid of my flashlight, I wrote up my notes for this night's interview.

Questions

1. Why had the local catechist, the one literate man in Lolo, been ,unable to provide an answer to the questions concerned? Was he not aware that the people of Lolo were living under considerable stress created by witchcraft assumptions? Yes, he was very much aware of it, but missionaries had always relegated witchcraft to the trash can and the trained catechist's training and contact with missionaries had taught him to be naive about the most dynamic forces in his own life. His education was formed in the categories of the missionaries' experience only, and this had imposed upon him a sophisticated atmosphere which was irrelevant to the task of presenting the gospel in Lolo.

2. If the Kaka belief in witchcraft and its understanding of the male and female roles had been made an integral part of the catechist's training, would the preaching in Lolo be as irrelevant as it is presently? There can be no doubt of the matter. The catechists are trained by the mission to play hide and seek with their own beliefs. They themselves have been successful in their learning of the missionary teaching only by accepting an additional set of assumptions. There is no evidence that they have replaced earlier ones. The people of Lolo must interpret the teaching within their own categories of cultural thought. Had the catechist dealt with the gospel in the light of the people's belief in *lémbo* and in terms of the male and female relations, the function of the church and their relation to God would have been both intelligible and true. As it is, they have been left to interpret it blindly. His teaching left completely untouched the areas of their thinking which were to them the ones related to the subjects which the catechist spoke on, viz. man and his religious world.

3. Is it possible to merely announce the "good news" in the language of the people? Definitely not. Announcing new ideas concerning man and his religious thoughts must compete with the preexisting understanding that is already formed in his life. He must associate ideas, interpret, select, and discard in the light of his comprehension and preexisting belief. It is the task of missionary anthropologists to point up this problem in communication and suggest concrete ways for more effective communication.

William D. Reyburn

The Spiritual, the Material, and the Western Reaction in Africa

"My father, an African tribal chief, had six wives and three children. Two were boys and one was a girl. Then one of my mothers gave birth to a son whose hair and skin were very light in color. He was not an albino, but a light colored baby. From the day of his birth it was generally believed in the village that his life was delicately hanging in a balance. He was a weak baby and did not have a loud cry. My father and his brothers all feared for the child's precarious life and sought out which taboos must be kept in order to protect the child's life. The one day an old uncle came to my father and said that he had dreamed that someone killed a goat in my father's house. He added that no one in the family should kill a goat or shed any blood before the new baby should be old enough to walk. The child became sick after several weeks and was taken to a mission hospital. His stool was black and formed like a goat's. Another uncle, a catechist, searched through the Bible trying to find something to do for the child. Then one day an animal was killed in the forest by one member of the family. At the very instant the animal was killed the baby screamed and died."

The above account was related, not by a pagan African with no knowledge of Christianity or civilization, but by a highly educated Christian. Another example cited to me by a college graduate in Africa:

"Mr. —, a well trained gentleman whom you know, was told by his sick wife before she died that if he should remarry after her death she would reappear to him and tell him the name of the girl he should marry. Mr. —'s wife died, as you know, and within a few days Mr. — was sitting alone in his house when suddenly his wife appeared to him and announced in a clear voice the name of the girl she wanted her husband to marry. Mr. — went immediately and made the arrangements and married this girl."

Recently while lecturing to classes of Cameroun college students on the relation of African pagan religious beliefs to Christianity and Islam, I asked them to write out for me at least one mysterious incident which had happened in their lives, and which they felt was totally without rational explanation. These college students had no trouble filling up pages with accounts of personal encounters with the world of mysterious events such as the two cited above.

Integration of the Pagan View

The pagan view of life expressed in most of Africa south of the Sahara does not make a rigid distinction between the religious and the secular life as found in European society. It goes without saying that the pagan African does not make medicine and throw it into the forest expecting to return tomorrow to find a garden growing. His secular world exists in the sense that he reckons with nature with his iron tools in so far as he can. He sharpens his cutlass and hacks down the forest and plants his seeds and does everything he knows to cooperate with nature in the production of his food. In the hunt he uses his highly trained sense of perception in studying animal tracks and moves in to the kill according to the movements of the wind in order to take his prey by surprise. The integration of the religious and the secular is expressed in the way in which the religious feeling for things is carried out in social life and exists to give social relations a sense of the holy. The intrusion of the West into the African's socio-religious life has created a tendency to separate the two into several distinct spheres into what is often called the secularization of African life.

This secularization of African life or the separation of religious sanctions and values from other aspects of tribal life has been partially produced from contact with colonization and Christianity. This subject is an entire study in itself and we can but indicate the nature of it by giving a few examples. These may be taken from the area of law and authority, economic, as well as from many other phases of life. However, we will part with the view that this secularization is as complete as some are inclined to think.

Prior to the arrival of the German military conquest of what is now the Cameroun, many tribes held adultery to be a very serious offense. Adultery was conceived as a violation of family or clan rights of ownership and was punishable by death or by declaration of war on the family or clan of the guilty man. In this way adultery was not thought of as an act between two individuals, but between two large family groups, clans or villages, depending upon the nature of the social relations involved. If the guilty man were apprehended he was killed outright, or if he succeeded in escaping some other member of his family was killed. This blood vengeance is expressed in Kaka by a commonly heard proverb: "The chimpanzee goes up one tree and comes down another." The man who commits the crime is not always the one who will pay. In addition to this offense being considered a group affair, there was the further belief that such a sin produced an impurity in the village and in the family which had to be removed by religious ritual. This consisted mainly in a rite requiring the sprinkling of chicken blood on the house of the offended party and ritual bathing to remove the personal impurity.

Into this picture came the French colonial machine which simply codified adultery along with many other offenses. Cases of adultery along with dozens of other infractions of the law were placed into the hands of the tribunal. There a fixed penalty in the form of imprisonment or fine was levied and the entire matter was soon removed from the area of the religious and stuffed into the world of economics. The matter was righted in the sight of authorities by paying the fine or spending the time in jail. Since only the guilty party could be sentenced under the law, only one man was required (or allowed) to go to jail. This had the further consequence of conceiving the adulterous act as being entirely personal and no longer the offense between two socially stable groups. However, even though the act of adultery was placed upon a private and individual basis, there was not, and perhaps still is not, produced a personal and individual sense of guilt. Money to pay the fine was and is secured from the clan or family group and the individual is fortified in the sense of a collective act which tends to remove any one individual from blame. Since most any offense can now be arranged by the payment of a fine, the need for righting of the wrong has a material rather than a spiritual dimension. This partial substitution of the material for the spiritual and the individual for the group is a basic process which underlies most of the developing commercial centers of West Africa.

The hunt in the Cameroun is another example of this materialization of religious experience. Under more primitive conditions in the open savanna or jungles, the hunter with his crude implements such as bows, spears and traps hunted the ferocious elephant, gorilla, bush cow and lion with a very real sense of potential failure. All of his hunt was prepared and carried out with the very precise execution of rites and ceremonies. With the gradual introduction of effective and accurate firearms and the obvious superiority of these over local methods, there was a tendency to replace the spiritual concern in the hunt for a material concern for the possession of the firearm and ammunition. However, it is here that

one must be careful not to despiritualize the materialism. *There was little reason to seek the aid of spiritual forces if these forces were obviously already contained in the magical firearm.*

It is just at this point that we must inquire briefly into the nature of what is referred to in French areas as *"le matérialisme des noirs."*

African Materialism

Is the desire for the material, wealth and its rewards, really a mechanical materialism as understood by many writers who see Africa shifting from pagan magic and sorcery into a crass materialism devoid of ethical, moral and spiritual values? Or is there not a conception of the material as containing the spiritual? When I once was told by a group of African school boys that the white man possessed *lémbo* (magic power) because of his inventions, I asked them how they could know whether it were *lémbo* or not. They answered that it is not something which you know in itself. Instead you see the things which *lémbo* can provide for its owner. This is expressed in the words of one writer as: "Ye shall know them by their fruits" (Matt. 7: 16). Regardless of what name is attached to it, the African is concerned that the fruits of his power or being show their presence and guarantee their force by bringing to him material rewards. The lack of such rewards is a poor man, lacking in spirit and therefore in goods.

The manifestation of the material witnessing to the abiding presence of one's *force* plays its role in the social world also. The man who is poor has few friends. This is expressed in another Kaka proverb which says: "The birds roost long in the trees with the leaves." That is, a man whose material possessions witness to the quantity of his personal force, his quantity of life, attracts many others who, basking in his presence, hope that his power will be transferred to them.

Again, the possession of the material transfers a person's status in his group. Upper mobility depends upon the presence of power. If one has no such power he cannot be granted authority over others. If he has such possessions it is generally held that his power will grant him the ability to lead and to decide tribal questions.

Our discussion to this point has brought us to say that the meaning of the materialism of modern Africa has many aspects to it and that the African even in his *search to acquire* is perhaps not primarily moved by the possession of the object as an end in itself as often is the case with Europeans. He is rather attempting to prove to himself and to his world that the presence of *spiritual forces* are at his service and that he stands in good with these. The thick façade of the material is then merely covering this desire to let himself know that all is spiritually well.

Under these conditions Christianity often becomes, not the spiritual reality underlying his behavior, but rather a manifestation that the spiritual reality exists.

The Spiritual Reality

What then is this spiritual reality? We have referred to it here as a force or power. It is best expressed in African languages with the word *life*. In many of the languages of the Cameroun the Christian terms for "salvation" and "to be saved" are "life" and "to live." Now if life or something similar to it is the essence of this spiritual existence, it is most clearly characterized by its relation to time and space which reveal many aspects in African behavior. Life as conceived in the western world is a series of timed events which come and go, and to all things there is a point of beginning and of ending. Time in this view is a sense of experience as running down and ending. Life in the African view does not have these fixed points of beginning and ending. The past is not historically conceived and does not flow out from a starting point. The end of life on this world is not the end because of the very real spirit world which continues to ever exist. Life is not that span which adds up to the time units counted between birth and death. The constant appearances of the dead to the living both among Christians and pagans reflect the fact that life is not a dwindling to zero, but a change in space without reference to time. A careful study of this concept of life and time could throw light on many bewildering practical aspects of African life. One should not be deceived by the possession of the ubiquitous wrist watch in Africa. Counting time units in a day and a concept of time are two different things. To the African there is simply no sense in the statement that "life is a race with time."

Christianity proclaims a view of life which is eternal, and it is this which the African grasps and makes of it an authoritarian expression of his own belief. In saying this it should be emphasized that I do not refer to "African" and "Africans" as individuals or even as groups of tribes or nations, but am rather equating the word African with the view of life and time as I have described it. Of course Christianity also conflicts with many of his beliefs and practices. However, it is precisely here that we return to the original point of our discussion, the relation of African religious beliefs to Christianity.

Western Christian Reaction

The problem is great due to the fact that African beliefs are a bewildering variety and Christianity, like Islam, has a complicated set of expressions. However, we are concerned here only with certain implications of the African view of life described above and the reaction to it by Christian missionaries. This greatly simplifies the problem and makes it possible to come to a few conclusions.

Missions in Africa were often founded upon the principle. that the lost heathen had nothing in his life and that his religious mind was totally void of any revelation. He was a *tabla rasa* on to which religion was to be engraved for the first time. All his beliefs fell into the missionary's category of the superstitious. Fetishism, magic, sorcery and the more underlying religious beliefs for their existence were too often discounted. The European or American missionary who approached his work in Africa with this attitude did so partly because his own history had proved for him that, given enough scientific knowledge and rational thought, all nonrational phenomena could be disposed of as simply superstition or the work of Satan. It did not require much time for the African Christians to become aware that their own world of mysterious phenomena was discounted by the missionary as devilish or not valid at all.

The consequences of this attitude on the part of the western Christian churches caused the African spirit world to go underground. The official position of the church was merely to deny the African reality or to hand out church discipline to the member who delved in this realm. Since missionaries preferred to deny their reality rather than work with the African in appreciation of these phenomena, the African has in many areas of Africa held his Christian faith in one hand and his belief in the mysterious world of his pre-Christian days in the other.

I have never talked confidentially with an African Christian who would deny that the dead appear to the living and affect them in their plans and activities in this life. However, these same Christians are quick to admit that those things are never mentioned in church and that they are not supposed to occur, according to the church.

The attitude of the western missionary toward the African spirit phenomena struck the African at the same time as the invasion of the European secular and material world. The acceptance of clothes, tables, and a wide assortment of European merchandise helped conceal the spiritual gap that existed between the African and the western missionary. The African became aware that the real separation could be covered over by adaptation through the material means made available to him by European industrialization. However, this meeting of two worlds on the material plane has not been a true meeting at all. The underlying orientation for the African view is essentially spiritual, and the grasp for the material has not been entirely what it appears to be on the surface.

This is the nature of a conflict in African Christianity. The conflict is not the fault of the African church but rather the closed attitude with which it was approached by the western church missionaries. This attitude was formed largely out of our secular western world and not out of a true attempt to understand Biblically the nature and validity of the African's "superstitions."

The task which lay before Christian missions in Africa at the beginning still remains largely the same. However, at this time the problem is even more complex, due to the fact that so many social and religious changes have been produced. The African Christian tends to withdraw from the western missionary and to maintain his beliefs in isolation. It is not that the African is any less a Christian believer for this. It is rather that he does not wish to share with outsiders that which brings on ridicule and misbelief.

If the churches of the West are to prepare and work with African Christianity in the face of Islamic advance, there must be an entire rethinking of the deeper reality of nonrational phenomena. Beside this formidable task, all the other problems of Christianity in Africa are of secondary importance. The Western churches and Western cultures are not producing a satisfactory interpretation of religious phenomena. Unless they do, the result for Christianity in Africa is going to be felt soon. A great hope lies in the developing theological education in Africa, provided the lines of inquiry are formulated by African thought open to discussion and sensitive to Christian truth.

William D. Reyburn

Christianity and
Ritual Communication

One of the basic problems confronting the Christian church and African society involves the expressive ritual communication found in each. Western Christians have confronted Africa with a variety of Christian rituals which have often become overlaid by theological and doctrinal verbalizations. African cultures have traditionally placed great emphasis upon ritual, and their people comprehend ritual as the language of religion. Christianity creates confusion for the African in that Christian ritual seems to have become submerged in verbal substitutes which are incapable of communicating to the mythic and psychic dimensions of life. An awareness of the need for mythic and psychic interpretations as well as theological ones should open the way for a deeper confrontation of the Christian faith with African life. This kind of approach sheds new light on a number of controversial issues.

IT HAPPENED on Saturday afternoon. A Kaka tribesman living a half day's journey away arrived in Ndem, the place where I was staying. There had been trouble and he came to represent his clan's side of an argument. The men of Ndem gathered one by one and assembled in the men's house. The speeches began and I listened as the case of the violated virgin was examined and reexamined with micro-scopic realism. A settlement was arrived at just before dark. Money and goods would be passed over to the plaintiff, but the animosity defiling human relationships had to be dispelled. The past must be swallowed, consumed, and thrown off. Eventually women appeared in the club house with the leg of a sheep well cooked for the ritual. The stranger and his ad-versaries washed their hands in water poured from a special bowl. Taking the cooked sheep bone in their hands the men pulled it apart. They exchanged pieces

and bit off some meat, then exchanged pieces again and continued to eat. The ritual eating of *sataka* began. They ate until the meat was gone. It was now Saturday night. Tomorrow would be Communion Sunday in Ndem.

Again it was Saturday afternoon. I stood on a river bank beneath a grove of overhanging raffia palms. Into the stream came an old medicine man bedecked with the charms and tools of his profession. A lean muscular tribesman holding his hands over his eyes hesitatingly ap-proached the old man, then stopped. His naked body was covered with ashes. The old man stepped close to him and rubbed bark powder on the young man's shoul-ders. Taking a small leather pouch from his belt the medicine priest sprinkled bits of powder on the youth's head. On his tongue he placed a small piece of dried leaf. Then the priest commanded the younger man to kneel. Taking a gourd

83

he scooped up water from the flowing stream and slowly poured it on the kneeling man's head and shoulders. Unintelligible words were uttered as he continued to pour. He washed him until his body glistened in the sunlight. The priest then washed himself and threw the pouring gourd into the current where it was rapidly carried away into the silent murmur of the flowing waters.

Why this ritual washing? The young hunter had killed a panther, totem of his mother's clan. Defilement had come upon him and had to be removed through washing. The impurity, the danger, was dissolved. New life was guaranteed. A new birth in harmony with the ancestors and nature was established. It was now Saturday night. Tomorrow would be Baptism Sunday.

Still again it was Saturday night. In the village of Bo a large kerosene lamp hung from the roof pole inside the chief's compound. Twenty puberty-age girls wearing a leaf *cache-sexe* were performing a dance which by comparison would relegate the twist to the feeble gyrations of an octogenarian. Drums beating in a dozen varying rhythms provided the tempo for the churning pulsations of the dancing girls. In the middle of the circle an old professional dancer with a stick in her hand moved about and gave special instruction. to the young novices. This elderly female who had been the queen of the village dance troupe was to be retired that night. A new, younger dancer was about to take her place. The time was crucial. Rebirth was imminent. The new crop was ripe. The new moon stood high in the night sky. The old was passing or gone, the new cycle was beginning. Just as human beings and nature pass through their cycle of life, age, death,

and rebirth, these villagers were gearing their dance activities to the cyclic march of the universe. As day began to dawn the old dance queen was symbolically buried and the new queen was born to lead the initiates in their first public appearance. It was now Sunday and we went to church.

Some Disquieting Questions

Yes, go to church we do. But I am frequently led to ask myself some disquieting questions as I compare Christianity and these non-Christian practices described above.

Missionaries are readily prone to feel and to see the differences between Christian ritual and non-Christian ceremonies. These differences are often real but is it not possible that many non-Christian practices in the form of magic, ritual, ceremony share in some essential and fundamental way with those practiced in Christianity? Without attempting to dilute the distinctiveness of the Christian faith, is it not likely that the Christian missionary and his pagan contemporary are bound by deep psychic and mythic ties which pass for the most part unrecognized? Furthermore, if both the unconverted pagan and the Christian missionary become conscious of dwelling in the same household of creation, is it unthinkable that each will see the other as a fellow human being? Is it too much to ask if a genuine encounter of Christian faith and non-Christian faith could not also take place?

I have seldom experienced a rite or ceremony among a pagan people without being aware of an ambivalent attitude. The thought surges forth saying, "How strange! How incredible! Can they really believe this?" This feeling barely rises into thought when the mood turns and poses the question from the opposite direction, "How familiar this all is! Who could doubt that this is necessary? Is this not also a reflection of my own psychic self?" Probably every missionary as well as any anthropologist who has lived closely to a tribal people and participated intimately in their daily activities has asked himself sooner or later this question, "Where really do these people differ from myself?" They struggle with the problem of getting a living. They express their joy, their anger, their sorrow. They encounter events in life that are tragic as well as humorous. In spite of the outward differences of expression, underneath human beings are everywhere uniquely human.

Of course, differences exist and they are the things that are conspicuous. These differences provide the material for the reports, the romantic tales, the theories for divergent behavior. When sufficiently exaggerated they give birth to racism, attitudes of inferiority and superiority, and excuses for pitting man against man. These differences, it is true, show the great variability of human adjustment and have a value in themselves which when lost often leave their traces in unexpected ways.

By shifting our attention to the common characteristics of peoples we soon find ourselves involved in a humanity which will allow for little ethnocentrism. When we see ourselves as participants in a universal scheme of humanity we tend to lose the snobbery which might tempt us to consider ourselves as a special species of humanity. This mental exercise would be worth the effort even if the ultimate truth in it is not clearly demonstrable. This is particularly true for missionaries.

Many missionaries today are still granted social and economic status not accorded the majority among whom they work. In many areas we are accorded special privilege due to national background, education, money, and material possessions. To emphasize such differences tends to lead us in the wrong direction and away from participation in the common core of humanity.

This common humanity refers not to the presence of certain universal characteristics such as man's need for food, sex, and shelter, but to the psychic symbolization of experience. Mythic and psychic phenomena are the shared property of mankind. Symbolization is the means by which man is able to conceive ideas as well as bring his experiences into the realm of emotion and dream. A universality of myths prompts us to recognize a common fundamental psychology among men. Just as men are one physiologically, they are most certainly united by a common psychology.

This is more a statement of conviction than a demonstrable proposition. However, the evidence which has been adduced over the past fifty years in the fields of psychology and anthropology grants this conviction a great deal of support that it did not have at an earlier period. Differing outward manifestations of these universal myths and psychic experiences should not lead us to suppose that the differences are basic. Quite the contrary, each cultural variation points in its own peculiar way to something more basically and fundamentally shared.

Exclusivist Christianity may object to becoming party to a mere universal humanity. Probably any good missionary will think twice before he will equate the Kaka ritual washing described above with Christian baptism. The missionary is right. These things are not to be equated as some might be tempted to do, but our questions cause us to inquire if there is not some underlying relation between the two, and further if Kaka ritual washing and Christian baptism are not subject to similar psychic interpretations. We would like to ask if the Kaka ritual eating of *sataka* and the eucharist are not fundamentally related in a psychic sense and if the cultural practice of *sataka* eating does not provide an interpretive source for the Lord's Supper. It would also be instructive to know if the mythic import of the dance initiation described above is not also related to a similar theme in the Christian experience of rebirth and the "becoming" a Christian.

Mythic and Psychic Interpretations

These questions could all be answered from the exclusive position of mythology and psychology. The result, however, would be very one-sided. This attempt to give an isolated answer to these questions would be as biased as exclusivist Christianity which grants only theological possibilities for the interpretation of Christian experience. As Hugh Kerr has pointed out, there is always a need for theological interpretation, but "however else Christianity may and should be interpreted, it can and should also be interpreted mythologically and psychologically."[1]

The psychic possibility for the interpretation of Kaka *sataka* as well as the Lord's Supper arises from the fact that ritual is a form of symbolic behavior.

[1] Hugh T. Kerr, "The Christ-Life as Mythic and Psychic Symbol," *The Princeton Seminary Bulletin*, April 1962.

Symbolization is an essential function of the human mind. Ritual, which is the language of religion, is a form of symbolization and communication in which the direct intent found in ordinary communication is replaced by a concern for expressive communication. Religious rituals aim at relating humanity to ultimate concerns. Magic, in contrast, tends to strive for utilitarian ends. Ritual symbolizes man's awareness of that which lies beyond man and reflects at the same time that deepest dimension of the soul of man. *Sataka* points beyond itself to the concern for the ongoing of proper human relations. In a similar way the Lord's Supper points to the event of salvation. These would appear at first to be rather unrelated. However, each in its own way symbolically affirms a vital relationship between two persons. *Sataka* relates men to men and the Lord's Supper renews awareness ("Do this in remembrance") of believers to their risen Lord. The actual human participation in these events converges in oral ingestion. Consequently while we readily admit that both of these acts has a different referent, we must also admit that both aim at relating and renewing of personalities through eating. As soon as we have said this, the two acts have struck a common chord in the psychic domain of their respective participants.

Eating is a nearly universal symbolic form of establishing covenant relations. It is one of the most effective means for dispelling ill feelings between people. The giving of food is a form of sacrifice which aims at adjusting human relations. In *sataka* eating, inter-group aggression is dispelled because the animal upon which the antagonism has been projected is killed. The slain sheep becomes the substitutionary object representing psychologically the past. The past must be swallowed. Eating of *sataka* then is a symbolic ritual in which the enmity between people is removed by swallowing it in the form of a slain sheep. When the eating ritual of *sataka* has been completed the aggression of the group is consumed literally and symbolically.

It is to be regretted that this higher form of symbolic transformation is not culturally practiced in modern societies. In modern society aggressions which are not removed are very often the object of oral ingestion. The result of these unresolved antagonisms is that people eat themselves into pathological obesity or develop a good case of stomach ulcers. Well known, of course, is the practice of going on an occasional binge, which is another form of swallowing. The Kaka are able to project their animosity onto one concrete piece of meat and then swallow it once and for all.

It is probably true that in the Lord's Supper more than anywhere else the individual Christian feels the act of forgiveness and the renewal of relationship to his risen Savior. The fact of eating opens up the individual to psychic depths which very often are only exercised in non-religious areas of his daily experience. Whatever may be his conscious awareness of the psychic value of the Lord's Supper, there is in some deep area a feeling which he has at no other time. The Lord's Supper is likewise a ritual like *sataka* which places the believer squarely before the fact of death. According to Jung, the Christian eucharist provides an opportunity in which the Christian comes to grips with the reality of death. In *sataka* the establishment of a live and life-giving covenant is made possible

through the death of the sheep. The Kaka pass through the stages of threat of death (animosity and war) to death to life. The eucharist enables the believer in a similar way to pass from the merit of death into death (the death of his Lord) and then into rebirth, which is again the resurrection. This cycle of events which is a universal principle must find some means of symbolic expression. For the Kaka it is in part found in the symbolic transformation of mythic and psychic necessities by means of the *sataka* ritual. For the Christian the same mythic and psychic urges find their ritual transformation in the eucharist.

Thus far I have referred only to psychic and mythic experience in the parallels of Kaka and Christian ritual. There are other factors which are also important. These refer to the cultural aspects which are the patterned forms of expression. Food in Kaka society has a value which is not familiar to modern societies. Food and the acquisition of it are concerns which border on the ultimate. The lack of food is a threat to existence and to all of life. Food then is a highly prized element in life which may be used as a highest form of gift and sacrifice. The eating of *sataka* symbolizes the value placed on food. The very practice of *sataka* eating among the Kaka provides them with a conscious, conceptual model for the Lord's Supper. The thoughts, beliefs, and forms of *sataka* cannot readily be disassociated from the eucharist. Because of the fact that *sataka* as a cultural manifestation is known and practiced, the parallels between these two rituals become apparent. While the outward parallels between *sataka* and the Lord's Supper do influence the superficial understanding of the latter, it is the deeper mythic and psychic strings of the human heart which are played upon and convey to the individual the significance of the Lord's Supper. Theological interpretations may be valid and necessary, but they may still remain only the lyrics of a more harmonious symphony of the soul.

Sataka like the eucharist is a communal act. Neither may be taken in isolation. *Sataka* reconciles men to men. The eucharist calls believers to remember the events of salvation. The fact that *sataka* is a ritual which requires the preparation of the *group* is significantly related to the manner in which preparation of the Lord's Supper takes place. This very vital point will come in for discussion later on.

There is a further aspect of these symbolic rituals which may be little understood. Do the Kaka really and literally believe the meat to be a sheep? They call the meat *sataka* which is an Arabic word meaning alms. It has been borrowed from Fulani via the Gbaya with the meaning of sacrifice and with the ritual meaning of sacrificed sheep eaten on this particular occasion. The transfer of meaning from alms to sacrifice reflects the concept of the two parties. The Fulani were on the receiving end and called the sheep-giving "alms." The Gbaya and Kaka on the giving end and understood the word to mean "sacrifice." They sacrificed the sheep to the politically dominant Fulani. If one asks whether or not that piece of meat eaten at the moment of the *sataka* ritual is the meat of a slain sheep, the reply can be yes or no. The question is really foolish and comes only from a non-participant. The person existentially involved in the ritual is faced with no necessity of defining whether or not it is sheep meat or some other animal, or sacrifice, or wood. The meaning of *sataka* is a ritual

meaning which does not confront the necessity of definitions. Its purpose is felt and not rationalized. Its behavior is expressive and not pragmatic. Its meaning is whatever the meaning of the ritual of *sataka* gives it for the persons engaged in the ritual.

We turn now to a familiar argument: Is the bread and wine really the flesh and blood of Christ? It is significant that this question apparently was never a source of controversy during the first centuries. Christ defined it during the very act of the Lord's Supper and the believers apparently knew what he meant. It is probably true that only as the religious ritual loses its expressive meaning and becomes conventional that one is forced to decide whether the bread is really flesh and the wine really blood. Music, drama, or any other form of art is either meaningful to the receiver or else it forces him to seek a meaning. The fact that we ask what an art form means is a confession that we feel that the form is supposed to communicate meaning to us. Meaningful religious ritual does not ask those literalist questions. Only the loss of the significance of religious ritual prompts us to define what we are doing, how we are doing it, and to what purpose. The total substitution of theological questions and theories for the mythic and psychic necessities of life gives rise to the loss of meaningful religious symbolism.

In *sataka* and the Lord's Supper the vital conce᛬ ı is the dynamic appeal to a deep layer of personal existence which, if untouched, makes of the ritual a dead, meaningless, and monstrous rite which has an aura of magic and is therefore to the modern mind repulsive. The best reply to the entire question of religious ritual was made by the thousand East African

Christians who refused to drink the goat's blood required in Mau Mau initiation. Their reply: "We cannot drink this goat's blood for we have drunk the blood of Christ." These Christians knew in the depths of the human soul at the tragic moment of death that they had drunk the blood of Christ. Aside from that moment of crisis there was no real definition. All consequences of faith hung upon this moment of giving expression to past experience which had gone undefined.

Baptism and Exorcism

Turning now from the underlying mythic and psychic aspects of *sataka* and the eucharist, we will examine briefly Kaka ritual washing and initiation with baptism and "becoming" a Christian. We start with that interesting business about washing away defilement in the middle of a river. The case cited above in which a man had killed a panther is only one of many reasons which would require *sembo* washing. Any breaking of taboo results in defilement which must be ritually cleansed. Underlying taboo is a feeling for the sacred. It must not be thought, as some Bible translators have done, that the absence of a word for *holy* automatically means that the concept *holy* is lacking. African traditional religions have been expressed in what is in many areas becoming the forgotten language of ritual. The expressive symbolism of ritual is not to be equated with pragmatic communication. Religious ritual is a means of coming to grips with cosmic concerns whether in primitive rite or in a Christian church. This does not mean that awareness of such concern is always without repulsive displays of human bestiality. Such concern may well find outlets in

ritual which are more a display of hate and cruelty than anything else.

Kaka ritual washing aims at restoring the contaminated individual to wholesome participation in the community as well as in nature. In the strictest sense the purpose is that of exorcism and healing. The Kaka do not recognize or readily express healing as an instantaneous act. Healing is a process with a time dimension and is accompanied by various agencies. The chief of these, aside from the medicine priest, is water.

Psychological literature abounds with evidence that water has been and is a symbol deeply fixed in the human mind as having to do with the unconscious as well as with cleansing, death, and burial. Jung considers water as the most common and universal archetype of the unconscious. Water has to do with the mystery of life; it is a symbol for the deep unfathomable levels of existence. The widely diffused flood stories may well have their origins in the common symbolization among mankind of man's ruthless existence and struggle with nature which plunge him constantly into depths of despair and unfathomable mysteries.

The washing with water in apostolic days may have carried sometimes a meaning similar to that of Kaka *sembo* washing. Alan Richardson, speaking of apostolic baptism, says: "Baptism accomplished not merely the washing away of sin and of all stain and filth of heathendom (cf. John 13: 8-10, Acts 22: 16, 1 Cor. 6: 11, Eph. 5: 26, Titus 3: 5, Heb. 10: 22; cf. Psa. 51: 2, 7, 10; Isa. 1: 16, Jer. 4: 14) but also the driving out of unclean spirits which were in man."[2] There is, to be

---

2 Alan Richardson, *An Introduction to the Theology of the New Testament* (New York: Harper and Brothers, 1958, p. 337 ff.).

sure, a great area of Christian theological meaning in baptism which is lacking in Kaka *sembo* washing. However, the common characteristics of washing away defilement, baptismal exorcism, may be present in both. The main difference is that the old water ritual in Christianity takes on a new action referent, the dying and rising with Christ. Baptism may have been considered in the apostolic church as the continuance of the healing ministry of Jesus. In the current prophet movements among the Bayanzi in the Congo, baptism is the antidote to witchcraft. People confessing witchcraft are baptized in rivers for the purpose of exorcising the evil spirits in them. Prophets claim that God has sent them to "clean up the country." Confession in these Congo prophet movements plays an important role in baptismal exorcism. Modern prophets among the Bayanzi are not diviners who are able to divine the presence of witchcraft. They appear rather to be exorcists. Consequently confession replaces divination and becomes a public spectacle. People under the pressure of the mass movement feel constrained to confess something for the sake of conformity. Even the Larousse Dictionary can be found burning among the more traditional fetishes which are gathered and burned in mass meetings.

Among more modern societies it has been suggested on various occasions that man's concern for physical cleanliness, his preoccupation with bathroom fixtures, reflect more a deep surging concern to purify his inner life than merely to wash his not-very-dirty skin. Guilt is universally present and man will always seek conscious means for removing it.

The Bible is concerned with the matter of healing and it is little surprise to Africans to read that Christ required the leper to go to the priest to make an offering for *cleansing*, or that spittle (a common symbol of forgiveness and blessing in Africa) was used in the healing of the blind man in Bethsaida. Naaman's seven dips in the waters of the Jordan is another example cited frequently by Africans of the use of water in healing.

In spite of the creeds and doctrines which may be elaborated to explain baptism, the crucial fact for faith is not these Biblical-doctrinal-theological statements of the head but the interiorizing of these rituals into personal experience. It is the live encounter between Christ and the Christian that makes the healing washing of baptismal exorcism real and dynamic for life. Where there is a cultural parallel to baptism such as *sembo* washing, the psychic interpretation and self-appropriation are already active forces in the individual's life. These should and can have a strong interiorizing and existential meaning where the catechumen is not forced through doctrinal and theological abstraction to replace them.

The one need not exclude the other but the tendency of missionary instruction is often to ignore any connection, thereby driving a wedge into the convert's psychic life in which pagan ritual and Christian ritual are seen to be totally unrelated. It is precisely for this reason that the new convert often possesses a smattering of head Christianity on Sunday and a heart full of "non-Christian" feeling the rest of the week.

There is again a relation between initiation in a society such as the Kaka and rebirth. African groups as described in the dance scene earlier are preparing for an initiation. This initiation is a ceremony which is tied up with the psychic and physical maturation of the members of the group. In a climactic experience they are surrounded by the symbols of ritual with which they associate themselves. In a group experience they break forth upon the scene of life as mature and responsible beings, vividly aware that they have become incorporated into and made psychologically an integral and functional part of their world. Circumcision rites in a similar way place the individual into the living stream of psychic and mythic rebirth whereby the mythic interpretation of life is realized in the initiation ritual. In circumcision and other rites of passage there is often the vivid destruction of a part of the initiate's vital organs, but in conformity with the symbolic transformation in the meaning of ritual there arises a new and transformed area of existence. Real life is spun into motion and harmony with the deeper feeling for the meaning of ritual. Rather than elaborate these parallels I will now focus the discussion upon some practical implications for Christian missions.

Christian Ritual and Contradictions

There are two striking points which force their attention upon us. The first is the contradiction which arises between sataka and the Lord's Supper. In spite of the fact that each has a different referent and no Kaka Christian would equate sataka with the Lord's Supper, sataka is the ritual which is rooted in the feeling domain of Kaka experience. This is true for both Christians and non-Christians. Sataka like the Lord's Supper is a communal act. I have tried to imagine how two antagonistic Kaka villages would achieve reconciliation if a missionary were to sit in a hut and call in each of the contestants of a dispute one by one to listen to his case. After hearing each individual story he would pronounce a decision and then announce that all will now eat sataka. I can imagine that no feast would be more void of meaning and empty of expression than this. Oddly enough the Lord's Supper is handled in just about this fashion. A community of believers appear one by one before a judge who determines their worth and they are accepted or rejected entirely as individuals. They appear at the Lord's Supper with the aura of individuals justified, like a school boy who has passed his examination, and they eat the Lord's Supper totally divorced from a broken and reconciling community of believers. The disheartening consequences are predetermined by the pathetic procedure.

Very often the chance for ritual to communicate the depths of its message to the community is lessened due to the fact that the elements that are eaten are foreign to the normal food and drink of the people — carbonated orange juice from a bottling factory four hundred kilometers away taken with bread baked in a white man's oven and sold only in the city. Such elements as these offered in sataka would be a mockery of the ritual. Since the foods used are not symbolically meaningful to ritual, it is not surprising that each individual member comes to the Lord's Supper with his individual spoon. The spoons become the symbolization of the individualization of the communion and the elements reinforce the foreignness of the Lord's Supper.

Much more penetrating is a contradiction which would appear to challenge the Westernized structure of Christianity in Africa today. This is the contradiction between Christian ritual and what Christians say about these rituals. If a rite of baptism is consistently practiced in one invariable form and those who practice it claim that the form is not important, how do we manage to explain that the form of the ritual is so unchangeable? The very reason this procedure creates a problem, not only in Africa but in other areas of the world as well, is because the converts understand much better than ourselves the meaning of ritual and magic. The form of ritual or magic has a value in itself. Imitative magic is the expression of a particular form or pattern of forms and gestures to bring about a desired result. The form of ritual is the language which expresses the symbolic message to the receiver. A ritual which would vary greatly in its structure would be a scrambled language which would not be understood. In this connection we are probably touching upon the significant reason for the varying interpretations of Christian ritual from the fourth century on. There apparently developed a variety of ritual forms in the fourth and fifth centuries so that the language of ritual had to be replaced by regular verbal communication and hence the proliferation of doctrines, councils, and creeds. Within the small face-to-face community where religious ritual is largely fixed in its expressive language, there is no attempt or need to bolster it with verbal explanation.

If it is true, as I am here maintaining, that the backgrounds of African and other non-modern societies equip their members to appreciate and understand ritual, then the Christian ritual will present its form to these people in a more focused way than to Western Christians. This does not mean that they will deduce from Christian ritual a Biblically acceptable doctrine nor that they will under stand Christianity. It means merely that they will attach themselves to the form of ritual and place on this a meaning which has an inherent value of its own. This is evident in primitive man's appreciation of certain expressive forms of art, music, and drama. This latter point will reenter our discussion in a moment.

The dilemma for Christian missions is found in our faithful practice of ritual and our faithful denial that the language of ritual — the gestures, the movements, the symbols — is significant. The Presbyterian who practices very rigidly baptism by sprinkling and who maintains that this form of baptism is not the essential meaning in the rite, is saying the truth. But the fact that his ritual language consistently speaks one language and his verbal language speaks another leaves the African very often perplexed. A glance at most books of church order shows how ritual language is designed. Speaking of the communion table, for instance, we read:

> The table, at the communion time, having a fair white linen cloth upon it, shall stand in the body of the church, or in the chancel. And the priest standing at the north side of the table shall say the Lord's Prayer, with the Collect following, the people kneeling.

Or again, for adult baptism in this order of worship:

> And standing there, the Priest shall ask, whether any of the persons here presented be baptized, or no. If they shall answer no, then shall the Priest say ... then the people standing, the Priest shall say ... Then shall the Priest say ... then shall the Priest say ... then shall the Priest take each person to be baptized by the right

hand and placing him conveniently by the font shall ask . . .[3]

Then the congregation standing, the minister, laying his hand upon the head of each kneeling before him shall say . . .[4]

The Service shall begin with a Psalm or Hymn of approach to the God of all grace, then shall the minister say, Let us pray . . . then shall follow the confession and prayer of pardon; the people saying the words of the confession with the minister . . . . Here shall follow a Prayer for Grace contained in this book . . after which, where it is customary, the Lord's Prayer may be said by the Minister and People together. Then shall one or more Psalms be sung or said with this conclusion. . . .[5]

The tendency of Christianity in Africa is to teach Africans to follow white missionaries in the abandonment of the meaning of ritual, or more accurately the substitution of verbal communication for expressive ritual communication. This procedure is characteristic not only of religious Christianity but is seen in nearly every Afro-European contact. Modern society with its mass media of communication, institutionalized education, and government administration is pieced together and made to function on the basis of verbal (and written) symbols. So preponderant is this force in mass industrialized and secularized life that the alternative of ritual communication would seem ridiculous. In the small society in which education and the highly significant crises of life were confronted in ritual and ceremony, each person was raised with a sensitive awareness to receive the messages contained in such language. Modern Westernized life is forcing Africa to give up in a large part a great ritual life and to replace it by conventional communication. The church too often is among the other secular institutions which reflect the same Western outlook.[6]

The church does, however, practice a certain amount of ritual in spite of the contradiction which surrounds it. However, the preponderance of verbal explanation, sermon, teaching, and expounding succeeds in relegating Christian ritual to a very secondary position. Christianity becomes another subject for learning along with literacy, arithmetic, and science. The catechism is the textbook and again the discouraging results are born of the procedure.

There is still another phase of this problem which requires attention. Durkheim and others have proposed that God is the creation of society and that the object of worship in religion is society itself. They have correctly observed that there is one body of religious belief in the tribe. The rituals and ceremonies are the common lot of any group which considers itself an ethnic entity. Christianity with its multitudinous shapes and forms presents this small society with a dizzying array of rituals within denominations. There is a moral efficacy in the unity of non-Christian ritual which is lost in the maze of denominational variations.

[3] *The Book of Common Prayer* (Dublin: 1960).
[4] *The Book of Common Worship* (Philadelphia: 1946).
[5] *The Book of Common Order* (Toronto: 1932).

[6] I am indebted to Reverend Paul Fueter, former Secretary of the Christian Council of Kenya, for helpful discussion concerning the contradictory nature of Christian ritual in Africa. E. A. Nida and R. Bratcher of the American Bible Society have provided helpful criticisms by correspondence.

It is little wonder that the African must switch from ritual meaning to verbal behavior. It is only in the mouthing of meanings that there is a semblance of Christian unity. The heart is left standing quietly and passively at the side sighing, No! There can be little question that the Roman church has great strength at this vital point.

New Light on Old Problems

If it is true, as I have attempted to show, that Christian and non-Christian rituals share in the mythic and psychic interiorizing of experience and if it is true that African cultures have traditionally prepared people psychologically to encode and decode ritual symbolism, and further if it is true that Westerners have lost to a considerable degree this dimension of symbolic transformation, then certain controversial developments in Africa come under a new light which illuminates some formerly obscured issues.

I begin with the subject of drama. The mass was developed in the Christian church as a drama. It is the summing up in symbolic form of the salvation story. It was developed by and presented to a people whose life was ritually oriented. For such people the eucharist was a drama, the unfolding of a story whose symbolic form was a penetrating insight communicated through ritual. For such people the great and vital forces of life are conceived as a world drama, a gripping story in which man was caught up as a participant.

Drama is not only a telescoping of significant events to be remembered, but is also the vehicle by means of which a people can steer themselves psychologically into motion and harmony with these concepts and events. Drama like a proverb summarizes a great thought or event. Where drama is a vital part of a people's way of life they conceive themselves as the participants in life and not its spectators. Into the cosmic as well as the routine of life they project themselves as a vital element. The world and nature may be ruthless, but man has a place in it all which he will not relinquish. Being drama conscious means being personalized. The real world about is not an impersonal one consisting of atoms and molecules but of personalized objects which in legend and story are humanized in the human-object encounter. It is in legends that the strikingly ridiculous humanizations take place. Among the Kaka the snake marries the egg and their children deceive their parents. The monkey, the chameleon, and the manioc plant go on a hunt together. The thin veil separating a world of dream fantasy and reality is torn away in such humanizing projections.

Underlying this mode of conception is a particular way of symbolizing experience and coping with the universe. In spite of Western Christianity's interpretation and presentation, African Christians are ever ready to reach through our verbal fortifications of doctrine and grasp at a significant *whole* by means of drama. They refuse to be locked up within the dry walls of wordy summaries of the Christian faith and so break forth into drama which orders personal existence to participate in the events of the Christian faith. Much of the outstanding thought of existentialists such as Tillich and Bultmann is realized in this way among many African Christians. The self-appropriation of the event of the cross is accomplished by psychologically participating in the cross. Unfortunately, some missionaries are so insensitive to the deeper strivings contained in drama that they discourage its function in the Christian church. It is also the case in some areas that the African's attachment to verbal symbols has become a necessary means of conforming to missionary practice and thereby making a psychological adaption to a foreign religion. Such groups are usually exceedingly Westernized with little sense of African values or are exceedingly passive in their Christian experience.

What has been said about drama can also be stated about music and art. However, each of these aspects of symbolic life is made up of its own forms and would require separate handling. The case of drama is sufficient here to illustrate the art phase of this problem.

A second area of observation is the African reinterpretation of the Christian church as a vehicle for adaptation to social and political change. In the first place I would make clear that conversion to the Christian gospel leads to personal change. Where people change, societies also change. The man who is spending his money in a wasted moral life cannot continue to do so after conversion to Christ. His former financial squandering is transformed into concern for more permanent values and his children often become educated. In one generation there may be a radical upward social and economic swing resulting from conversion.

Our problem is not focused on this area of social change. The argument here is rather that the forces of Westernization, as described above, pit themselves against the mythic and psychic attitudes of Africa and force the African ritual orientation to retreat into the background. The Christian church then shares the flavor of other secular institutions. The historical development of colonialization and Christianity, the integral confusing and confused tie-up between school and church have contributed to the creation of this attitude. On the one hand this situation is nearly inevitable. On the other hand the Christian church has not made sufficiently clear its tension with these secular institutions and has not always sought to communicate its distinctive message in an intelligible fashion. This is all the more significant when we realize that the African will tend to grasp them in a wholistic manner. Consequently the church has the burden to struggle to win the most effective means to make its unique message heard.

The answer to this challenge is contained in the dynamic and revolutionary message of the Bible. This message has to make clear the differences between itself and non-Christian thought in ways intelligible to Africa. This means a confrontation of the Biblical message not construed out of the forms and abstractions and inhibitions of Western thought, but within the categories of African concepts and symbols. When we do this we return to our original suggestion that we and the African are cut from the same psychological piece of cloth, and here we discover a new and vital communion and communication. In so far as we share a common psychic dimension of life we can together achieve a common interpretation of great areas of life. This cannot be done where we tend to repress into semi-conciousness many of the symbols of our psychic existence while Africans display these same symbols as a natural and open part of life.

Turning now to a third area, one observes that the mission indigenized churches in Africa are strong for theological education but not especially active in evangelization. I would propose two major reasons for this. First, the evangelist has been taught to verbalize a message which he perhaps feels in his bones should be better communicated through non-verbal symbols. He may have no idea how. Then, the Western replacement of religious ritual by verbal symbols necessitates an adjustment to the concepts and feeling underlying verbal doctrinal explanations. There are no doubt social and historical reasons to add to these, but our framework is ritual symbolism and the switch to verbal symbolism. It would take us too far afield to discuss the role of the native language in this process. However, it is important to observe the different symbolic character of sermons preached by African pastors trained in the vernacular and those trained in a European language.

The contradiction between Christian ritual and what is said about Christian ritual tends to leave the evangelist without a solid footing. His sermons consequently are often vague verbalizations about important Biblical characters whom he attempts to bring to personalized life or about Biblical events which he attempts to describe. In case neither of these appeals to him he may reveal his own aggressiveness or insecurity by vociferously elaborating some Christian taboo. It often matters little in any case because the congregation really came to sing anyway. They refuse to relinquish their participation in the drama even if it is nothing more than a cut and dried church service. This is not an attempt to generalize the Christian church in Africa, but it is typical of many churches I have seen in West and Equatorial Africa.

Theological education has been and most likely will continue to be dominated by a European language and cast into molds of European thought. An African seminary professor recently returned from Germany was asked to prepare a short article for college students on choosing a vocation. He replied to the faculty committee that he was afraid he would deal with the subject too abstractly for these students. I wonder if he would preach an interesting and intelligible sermon for his mother, or for mine.

It has often been repeated that where there is a proliferation of vernaculars theological education can only be carried on in a European tongue. I doubt now that this is the African's reason. The African wants and needs such education if he is going to accomplish individually the radical transformation of symbolization from an attitude of religious ritual to an attitude of verbalization of religion. His choice has been made and his future sermons will be almost predictably laid out in Western format unless this education receives a new and vital reorientation.

Dynamic diffusion of the Christian faith does not depend upon a hierarchy of church leaders, important as these are. It rests upon the movement of the Holy Spirit within a context of communication which is characterized by spontaneity in form and expression. Theological reflection does not launch such movements, it only tracks them.

Prophet Movement

By prophet movement I refer to the kind briefly described above among the Bayanzi of the Congo. The prophet is an individual who may have received a vision or dream and has been commissioned to proclaim a certain message. He is most likely a personalized symbol which represents a major concern of the local society. In the case of the Bayanzi this concern is life. The threat of life is witchcraft. Witchcraft takes away life. A society plagued by unknown and unknowable witches is in danger of its life. A diviner may be able to keep witchcraft under control by exposing a victim from time to time. However, since no one really knows whether or not he has witchcraft and since a prophet is a baptismal exorcist, all can play safe and be exorcised for the safekeeping of the tribe as well as for the preservation of their own skins.

Prophet movements are doubtless a response to a vast array of challenges. The one considered here is paramount, however, as it has far-reaching implications for Christianity. I refer to the chasm between Western and African ritual symbolism and response. Whatever else 'prophetic' movements are, they are an open declaration that the white man's way of expressing religious values and rituals is not meaningfully felt by Africans. They also reveal the fact that the a major threat to conscious African life, witchcraft, is not adequately dealt with in traditional Western Christianity. Underlying both of these criticisms is the

failure to interiorize the ritual of Christian baptism. The Christian ritual has not had a healing function; or if it had, it was later replaced by verbal denial, rather than being bolstered by a satisfactory doctrinal support. It is further significant that Roman Catholic objects of devotion have been discarded in prophetic movement "clean-ups." This is an indication that objects such as rosaries have been interpreted as magic. The African's required removal of these as an aspect of confession, making baptismal exorcism efficacious, points up the cleavage within the two approaches. This fact also suggests that confession and Christian baptism must be clearly psychologically linked in order for the believer to grasp the significance of the ritual washing of baptism. Such confession must also be related to a Christian (and, at the same time, meaningful) view of sin. Awareness of sin again takes us back to a proper concept of God and man, and it is precisely here that our Western teaching shatters the wholeness of African conceptualization while awkwardly trying to pry God loose from man and nature. These things must be separated and each given its Biblical position; but again if an atomized view of man, God, and nature theatens to form, a prophet will rise to piece the cosmological puzzle back together again.

William D. Reyburn

The Message of
the Old Testament
and the African Church

This is the introductory article in a series which will take up in detail the relationship between the Old Testament and contemporary Africa (south of the Sahara), in relation to the communication of the gospel, and to the life and thinking of Christians. The plan is to present on the one hand the great connection between African life and that of ancient Israel, and on the other the disjunction between the two. One might use an analogy to compare modern Western life with that of the Old Testament: it is like looking out of the rear window of a moving car and seeing a hill recede in the background. When one looks at the Old Testament from the vantage point of African cultures, however, it is like two trains which are traveling in the same direction and suddenly converge upon each other. They click along the rails in close proximity for a time and then swerve apart to lose sight of each other, only to reappear again abruptly, side by side, before separating and reconverging again and again.

ONE of the most subtle and pervasive tensions in the Christian African scene is the relation of the Old Testament to the life of the African church. Missionaries have traditionally battled with this matter in a variety of ways. Some have refused to translate the Old Testament, feeling that the embryonic life of the new Christian community would be endan- gered, finding in the Old Testament Scriptures sanction for pagan ways of life. This refusal to admit the Old Testament as a part of the church's Scripture has reflected the wishful Western thinking that Greek thought provides the background for the understanding of the Christian message. So thoroughly entrenched is this misconception in many

98

missionary-established churches that a cultural transformation to the Western mold is felt to be a necessary prerequisite for an adequate understanding of Christian faith and practice.

The desire to diminish the importance of the Hebrew background of the Christian message often creates a lack of appreciation and understanding of much of African culture which stands in close formal relation to it. The Old Testament and not Plato or Aristotle underlie the New Testament message. African life and thought share in many ways the cultural life of ancient Israel. It will be part of our task in these articles to demonstrate this. If the cultural relationship even in a formal sense exists, we must ask what this can have to do with the Christian message in an African community.

If the events of God at work in the life of Israel appear very close to the African's personal life and far removed from the life of the Westerner, then the African stands in a somewhat different relation to the Old Testament than does the modern Westerner. At least he is aware of it in a different manner. If the Old Testament is said to seem strangely foreign and largely "irrelevant" to Christians living in modern industrial cities, what does the African, who lives closer to the culture and life of ancient Israel, feel about its message for him?

Missionaries often operate on the assumption that the New Testament Christian life grows out of Greek thinking. If the African church also accepts this idea, what are some of its implications for the African church? If the African church can rediscover the Old Testament basis for the New Testament message, what will this mean to the African church, to the churches of the West, and to the

church as a whole? These are some of the questions and problems for which we must seek answers.

The problems of the Old Testament have been discussed from many points of view through the past century by biblical scholars. Many of the results of such studies will be taken for granted throughout these articles. Some are only incidentally related to our purposes while others which deal specifically with the cultural life of Israel will be referred to repeatedly.[1] For the African materials I have attempted to draw on sources ranging from the Islamic tribes of the Niger across to the Nilotic peoples of the Sudan and Ethiopia and then south to the tip of South Africa. While it has been desirable to gather this information from as wide a geographical area as possible,

---

[1] For those interested in pursuing these lines of investigation, the following works are offered as a minimum reference list. G. E. Phillips, The Old Testament in the World Church (London: Lutterworth Press, 1942); Johs. Pedersen, Israel: Its Life and Culture, 2 vols. (London: Oxford University Press, 1959); N. H. Snaith, The Distinctive Ideas of the Old Testament (London: Epworth Press, 1960); C. Tresmontant, Essai sur la pensée hébraïque (Paris: Les Editions du Cerf, 1956); T. Boman, Das hebräische Denken im Vergleich mit dem griechischen (Göttingen: Van den Hoeck & Ruprecht, 1959); L. Koehler, Theologie des Alten Testaments (Tübingen: J. C. B. Mohr (Paul Siebeck), 1947); L. Koehler, Der hebräische Mensch (Tübingen: J. C. B. Mohr (Paul Siebeck), 1953); G. von Rad, Theologie des Alten Testaments (München: Chr. Kaiser Verlag, 1957); G. E. Wright, The Old Testament Against Its Environment (London: S. C. M. Press, 1950). Also of great value are many of the Hebrew word analyses in Kittel's Theologisches Wörterbuch zum Neuen Testament (Stuttgart, Germany: Verlag Von W. Kohlhammer, 1933-1959).

there are nevertheless serious blind spots in the available ethnographic materials on Africa, and this becomes especially evident as one seeks more than superficial descriptive accounts. In addition to the literature I must also draw upon my own work and observations done largely among the peoples of the Cameroun.

The Levirate Marriage

The parallels between African life and the culture of ancient Israel are often striking. These range from deep-seated aspects of social organization to subtle forms of thought and behavior. The African reader of the Old Testament is acutely aware of this fact. For example, the levirate marriage common in much of Africa finds a close parallel in ancient Israel. True, there are differences in detail, but the African villager is prepared to find variations around common themes even in a neighboring tribe. The procedure to be followed in reestablishing the paternal line through the remarriage to the dead brother's widow in Deuteronomy 25 is an example.

If brothers dwell together, and one of them dies and has no son, the wife of the dead shall not be married outside the family to a stranger; her husband's brother shall go in to her, and take her as his wife, and perform the duty of a husband's brother to her. And the first son whom she bears shall succeed to the name of his brother who is dead, that his name may not be blotted out of Israel. And if the man does not wish to take his brother's wife, then his brother's wife shall go up to the gate to the elders, and say, "My husband's brother refuses to perpetuate his brother's name in Israel; he will not perform the duty of a husband's brother to me." Then the elders of his city shall call him, and speak to him; and if he persists, saying, "I do not wish to take her," then his brother's wife shall go up to him in the presence of the elders, and pull his sandal off his foot, and spit in his face; and she shall answer and say, "So shall it be done to the man who does not build up his brother's house." And the name of his house shall be called in Israel, The house of him that had his sandal pulled off (Deut. 25: 5-10).[2]

In the Gate

Members of an African village, like the ancient Israelites, are constantly in the process of adjusting the affairs of its members. For the Israelites the law was sacred and the keeping of it meant peace. In a somewhat different framework but still analogous, the African community members are oriented around the legal assembly. In the village of the Old Testament this important assembly met in the "gate of the city" where all major events of village life were discussed and decided. Likewise in West African villages today the men's club house or so-called "palaver house" is the equivalent of the Old Testament gate of the city.

And Boaz went up to the gate and sat down there; and behold the next of kin, of whom Boaz had spoken, came by. So Boaz said, "Turn aside, friend; sit down here"; and he took ten men of the elders of the city, and said, "Sit down here," so they sat down. Then he said to the next of kin, "Naomi, who has come back from the country of Moab, is

---

[2] All Scripture quotations are from the Revised Standard Version, and are used by permission of the Division of Christian Education of the National Council of the Churches of Christ in the U.S.A.

selling the parcel of land which belonged to our kinsman Elimelech. So I thought I would tell you of it, and say, Buy it in the presence of those sitting here, and in the presence of the elders of my people. If you will redeem it, redeem it; but if you will not, tell me, that I may know, for there is no one besides you to redeem it, and I come after you." And he said, "I will redeem it" (Ruth 4: 1-4).

Since the "gate of the city" was the one entrance to the city, it was the place where everyone had to pass. The Old Testament prophets warned men that righteousness should dwell in the gates. Many a missionary has participated in the discussions that abound in the African "gate" and has witnessed in the Christian villages the desire for righteousness to govern the frequent discussions carried on in the "gate of the village." The manner of discussion and argument and the basis for legal thinking will come in for discussion when these matters are taken up in detail.

The Transformation of God

That the African feels close to parts of the Old Testament is a natural conclusion from the examples given above. This does not mean that the Old Testament presents a cultural picture so similar that the average African reader is merely visualizing the life of a tribal group on the other side of the mountain. There are many problems for the African reader and one of these is the historical nature of the Old Testament account. As the narrative moves away from the explanatory stories of the early chapters of Genesis and becomes involved in the unfolding of historical acts, the tradition-minded African is not prepared to fully

grasp the fact of this as an historical development. Yet, while it is true that the traditional African does not live with a conceptualization of history as history, he does have the advantage of living in a world of very real flesh and blood people where individual concrete acts are more meaningful than abstract principles. Hence the historical essence of the Old Testament is not lost to the African reader, but it is preserved even as it was for the Israelites who lived it as concrete individual episodes which are interpreted as God's intervention in man's daily practical affairs.

The Old Testament is considered here as indispensable in the building process in which a people's idea of God must undergo a transformation. When one communicates the Christian gospel to a people who conceptualize God in the symbol of the spider, there is obviously a great gap between the spider God and the Jahweh of the Old Testament.[3] The spider God of the Kaka is an impersonal cosmological force silently busying itself weaving its web upon which the stars delicately hang in the heavens. Just as a fly caught in a spider's web may occasionally free itself and dart forth, so a star may be seen to become dislodged from the constraining web and fall across the heavens and disappear. The Old Testament provides a vital bridge from an impersonal force, a spider, to the personalized God of Israel. This is made possible due to the fact that the Jahweh of the Old Testament is concerned with the people of Israel and the smallest details of their lives.

---

[3] See William D. Reyburn, "The Transformation of God and the onversion of Man," PRACTICAL ANTHROPOLOGY, Supplement 1960, pp. 16-20 (reprinted from Vol. 4, No. 5).

Old Testament stories such as that of Hagar and Ishmael are an example. I have had the experience of relating this story to old Kaka women who, hearing it for the first time, were admittedly surprised that Sarai, who became jealous of Hagar's fertility, behaved in a true Kaka fashion. "We didn't know there were black people in God's book" is an occasional response. This is quite understandable to these women listeners as most of them were also in polygamous marriages and knew well that the first wife, called by them "woman of the house," often became jealous if a second wife bore children and "woman of the house" retained her authority but not the affection of the husband. When Abram sees that Sarai as "woman of the house" is contemptuous of "lesser wife" Hagar, he allows Sarai to exercise her authority.

It is precisely at this point of female vengeance in the Old Testament narrative that the cosmological force in Kaka life is said to turn away from its exclusive detachment and to become involved with this poor woman and her suffering. For the first time to these ears, the Kaka God is said to speak and addresses his simple question "Where are you going?" to this castoff pregnant girl who wanders through the sunbaked grass country. "I am fleeing from 'woman of the house,'" replies Hagar. Then the Deity speaks again, "Go back to 'woman of the house' and put yourself in her hands. I will make your children and grandchildren so many you won't be able to count them." He says that Hagar will give birth to a son "and

you will call him 'may God hear' because God has heard (Hebrew shāma‘) your affliction."

This story, when presented in all of the wealth of detail which belongs to it in terms of ancient Israel's culture and language, brings to the Kaka listener a radically new concept of the Deity. The God which was an "It" now becomes a "Thou" who seeks out a suffering human, a second-class woman, and hears her affliction. They address each other, and she names her child as a witness to the fact that the Deity hears. Hearing, speaking, helping, advising, were never activities of Kaka Ndjambie, the cosmic spider.

It is not sufficient to make abstract statements and claims about a Christian God in the communication of the gospel in this situation. In such stories as these there is first a recognizable cultural stage upon which play the real live actors so well known in African villages. In some such way as this the creation of the new relation in the pagan heart takes place. The transformation of God and the conversion of man begins then with the change of the I-It relation to the I-Thou reality.

In the articles which will follow in this series, we shall examine in some detail the nature of the cultural relationship of ancient Israel to certain phases of contemporary African life and will attempt to point out how the message of the gospel builds upon the Old Testament life and culture. The implications for the Christian message and the African church will then be examined.

William D. Reyburn

Sickness, Sin, and the Curse: The Old Testament and the African Church

This is the second article[1] in a series which will take up in detail the relationship between the Old Testament and contemporary Africa (south of the Sahara) in relation to the communication of the gospel and to the life and thinking of Christians. Here the parallel between the Old Testament concept of the relation between sickness, sin, and curse, on the one hand, and the very similar present-day African concept is discussed. The next article in this series will continue this line of thought, examining the role of guilt and sin in African societies in the light of the Old Testament message, and will go on to the examination of the relation of these ideas to the communication of the Christian message.

Sin and Sickness

A missionary had been preaching to his attentive listeners on the subject of sin, trying to impress upon them that they were sinners. After several months he was greatly disturbed that no one had shown any inclination to admit as true what he had claimed. Finally he asked them directly, "Are you or are you not sinners?" The reply came back in unanimous chorus, "No, we are well, not sick."

This concept whereby a man relates his strong self or soul to health and a weakened soul to sickness is not only very ancient but also very widespread among the cultures of the world. A man's soul is held to be capable of increasing in power through good behavior, special rites and sacrifices, and by abiding by the rules of society. On the other hand, he is exposed to dissolution or weakening of soul through failure to conform to what is considered correct living or through the evil acts perpetrated against his soul by evil doers. Sickness, then, is the result of evil doing, be it one's own failure to measure up or the curses of one's enemies or others seeking to destroy him. Health is considered evidence of one's power of soul to ward off evil influences or of one's personal integrity and living in the community.

The culture of ancient Israel as revealed in the Old Testament partakes in this attitude in one form or another in ways similar to such disparate peoples as the American Indians and the African tribes. Missionaries who are continually perplexed by this association of sin with sickness and righteousness with health

[1] The first article appeared in PRACTICAL ANTHROPOLOGY, Vol. 7, No. 4 (July-August 1960), pp. 152-156.

will find in the study of the Old Testament a considerable contribution to the analysis of this phenomenon as seen in the life of early Israel and will also find certain valuable insights and approaches to the New Testament message of salvation based upon this particular view of man's soul, his sin, the curse and sickness.

Sin and Covenant

Sin in the life of ancient Israel cannot be understood apart from the notion of the covenant relation. This does not mean an isolated relation between Yahweh and an individual but an interdependent relation of men who must live together. The term community in its sociological sense expresses this idea well. Any form of behavior which threatens the natural carrying on of life in the community is considered a sinful deed. Yahweh is the creator of life and giver of community. Any offense which breaks this community is therefore also an offense against Yahweh. Man dwells in a community or covenant relation with man on the horizontal plane and with God on the vertical, but this community is a totality and not two levels of living divorced from each other. It is in his total community relation that one sins against his fellow man and therefore against his God.

The violations of community living can be listed and dealt with as possessing very specific content. Had Joseph lain with the wife of his master in Egypt as she invited him to do, he would have violated the covenant relation between himself and his master. Therefore he can say, "How then can I do this great wickedness, and sin (Hebrew *chata*) against God?" (Gen. 39: 9). It is Yahweh who has given the relation between the two men. By the same token, "You shall

not hate your brother in your heart, but you shall reason with your neighbor, lest you bear sin (*chet*) because of him. You shall not take vengeance or bear any grudge against the son of your own people, but you shall love your neighbor as yourself: I am the Lord" (Lev. 19: 17-18).

The violation of community is displayed in the selling of Joseph into Egypt. "And Reuben answered them, 'Did I not tell you not to sin (*chata*) against the lad? But you would not listen. So now there comes a reckoning for his blood' " (Gen. 42: 22). Again the disrupting of community interdependence is spoken against as a violation of sexual relations with a neighbor's wife (Deut. 22: 24). Incest, homosexuality, and bestiality are of the same kind of rupture of the biological and sociological togetherness which is considered by Israel to be the natural and proper conduct of life (Lev. 20: 10-21). Even the failure to pay the poor workman on the day his wages are due is a failure to remain in the necessary community relation with the poor man and considered a sin to Israel (Deut. 24: 15). Failure to behave generously in the seventh year of release, or forgiving of debts, would be an act of stinginess and counted as a sin (Deut. 15: 9-11). All of these sins are acts whereby a man fails to maintain the covenant or community between men where life must be lived in a tolerable face-to-face relationship. Behind such living in society stands the creator of Israel's community against whom man sins when he violates his neighbor.

Cultic violation is another cause of estrangement. These transgressions likewise require the extermination of the offender:

If any man of the house of Israel kills an ox or a lamb or a goat in the camp, or kills it outside the camp, and does not bring it to the door of the tent of meeting, to offer it as a gift to the Lord before the tabernacle of the Lord, bloodguilt shall be imputed to that man; he has shed blood; and that man shall be cut off from among his people (Lev. 17: 3-4).[2]

A further aspect of the violation of covenant behavior is its effect upon the whole community. The one who commits sin does so against the group and the many are affected. Therefore the sinner is removed from the community in violent and total fashion. Burning and stoning are the common means. Not only the individual himself but perhaps even his contaminated possessions are destroyed. The presence of such a violator of the community is a sore in the kinship organism which threatens to spread and rob the entire group of health and blessing.

When one compares the life of most any primitive people with that of ancient Israel, there are numerous striking similarities.[3] Witchcraft, incest, and murder are looked upon as sins among nearly all African peoples. They are, as in ancient Israel, viewed within the context of men who live together. The Tiv of Nigeria hold that to kill another Tiv (or a dog) is a most serious offense. However, the killing of a non-Tiv is a

matter of quite a different nature. Witchcraft is widely believed to be capable of being used against members of one's own clan. Incest can be committed against anyone who stands in a particular biological relation or a specifically defined kinship relation. It is easily seen that violations against one's own group constitute the greatest guilt for the individual and the greatest threat to the community. It is from the local community that one draws life and is blessed with whatever blessing is available. It is no exaggeration, therefore, to say that all people sin against their covenant relation with others. The distinctiveness of Israel's covenant relation is twofold: It is held to be initiated by Yahweh and it becomes interpreted in later history as a universal covenant. I refer simply to the covenant relation, not the specific content of it in its historical development.

Sin, the Curse, and the Soul

Having discussed sin as the violation of the Israelite community of men which has its existence in the covenant relationship with God and which results in estrangement to both the community and God, we may now ask how it was believed to affect the soul.

In a word, sin results in sickness or loss of vitality in the soul.

O Lord, rebuke me not in thy anger, nor chasten me in thy wrath. Be gracious to me, O Lord, for I am languishing; O Lord, heal me, for my bones are troubled. My soul also is sorely troubled. But thou, O Lord — how long? Turn, O Lord, save my life; deliver me for the sake of thy steadfast love. For in death there is no remembrance of thee; in Sheol who can give thee praise? I am weary with my moaning; every night I

---

[2] All Scripture quotations are from the Revised Standard Version and are used by permission of the Division of Christian Education of the National Council of the Churches of Christ in the U.S.A.

[3] See Sir James George Frazer, Folk-Lore in the Old Testament: Studies in Comparative Religion, Legend and Law (New York: Tudor Publishing Co.).

flood my bed with tears; I drench my couch with my weeping. My eye wastes away because of grief, it grows weak because of all my foes (Psalm 6: 1-7).

Or again, the suffering due to sin is considered by the psalmist as arrows sunk into his flesh, his strength is gone and misery is his lot.

O Lord, rebuke me not in thy anger, nor chasten me in thy wrath! For thy arrows have sunk into me, and thy hand has come down on me. There is no soundness in my flesh because of thy indignation; there is no health in my bones because of my sin. For my iniquities have gone over my head; they weigh like a burden too heavy for me. My wounds grow foul and fester because of my foolishness. I am utterly bowed down and prostrate; all the day I go about mourning. For my loins are filled with burning, and there is no soundness in my flesh. I am utterly spent and crushed; I groan because of the tumult of my heart (Psalm 38: 1-8).

Furthermore, his relation to the men of his community is severed. "My friends and companions stand aloof from my plague, and my kinsmen stand afar off" (Psalm 38: 11). This aspect of the sickness reproduces its own kind. Having sinned or being cursed by others, he falls sick and his sickness separates him from his kinsmen and his neighbors who see him as a danger to their own healthy and blessed existence. The classical expression of this pitiful plight is that of Job:

He has put my brethren far from me, and my acquaintances are wholly estranged from me. My kinsfolk and my close friends have failed me; the guests in my house have forgotten me; my maidservants count me as a stranger; I have become an alien in their eyes. I call to my servant, but he gives me no answer; I must beseech him with my mouth. I am repulsive to my wife, loathsome to the sons of my own mother. Even young children despise me; when I rise they talk against me. All my intimate friends abhor me, and those whom I loved have turned against me. My bones cleave to my skin and to my flesh, and I have escaped by the skin of my teeth. Have pity on me, have pity on me, O you my friends, for the hand of God has touched me! Why do you, like God, pursue me? Why are you not satisfied with my flesh? (Job 19: 13-22).

For missionaries who work in Africa, the parallel between these laments and the sick, suffering tribesman are so striking as to obviate explanation. On several occasions in Africa I have gone to visit a sick friend and have found him wrapped in a dirty sheet and huddled by a dying fire in an open space where his only friend is a scrawny dog lying beside the ashes of the tiny fire. Perhaps a faithful wife is the only one who remains within earshot while all others are keeping a safe distance. There he sits. His face is fallen, his eyelids half closed. His whole body is bent with pain. The question in his mind, like that of the ancient Israelites, is "What have I done?" or "Who is doing this thing to me?" The visitor hesitates to speak, fearing that his words will be of no more comfort than the admonitions of Job's friends. Like the psalmist, the African tribesman sits thinking of his enemies who might have brought this calamity upon him.

They close their hearts to pity; with their mouths they speak arrogantly. They track me down; now they surround me; they set their eyes to cast me to the ground. They are like a lion eager to tear, as a young lion lurking in ambush (Psalm 17: 10-12).

The sick African tribesman, like the sick psalmist, is seized by a suspecting state of mind.

Be gracious to me, O Lord, for I am in distress; my eye is wasted from grief, my soul and my body also. For my life is spent with sorrow, and my years with sighing; my strength fails because of my misery, and my bones waste away. I am the scorn of all my adversaries, a horror to my neighbors, an object of dread to my acquaintances; those who see me in the street flee from me. I have passed out of mind like one who is dead; I have become like a broken vessel. Yea, I hear the whispering of many — terror on every side! — as they scheme together against me, as they plot to take my life. (Psalm 31: 9-13).

If his misery does not arise within him, then it has originated in the evil curse of others who are bent on destroying him. "Give me not up to the will of my adversaries; for false witnesses have risen against me, and they breathe out violence" (Psalm 27: 12).

Especially fearful is the activity of evil which takes place at night when the souls of witches go forth to do their evil deeds. "For lo, the wicked bend the bow, they have fitted their arrow to the string, to shoot in the dark at the upright in heart" (Psalm 11: 2). And again, "He plots mischief while on his bed; he sets himself in a way that is not good; he spurns not evil" (Psalm 36: 4).

Like the suffering tribesman, the afflicted psalmist pleads that the curse of the wicked might return upon the curser.

Let their own table before them become a snare; let their sacrificial feasts be a trap. Let their eyes be darkened, so that they cannot see; and make their loins tremble continually. Pour out thy indignation upon them, and let thy burning anger overtake them. May their camp be a desolation, let no one dwell in their tents. For they persecute him whom thou hast smitten, and him whom thou hast wounded, they afflict still more. Add to them punishment upon punishment; may they have no acquittal from thee. Let them be blotted out of the book of the living; let them not be enrolled among the righteous. But I am afflicted and in pain; let thy salvation, O God, set me on high! (Psalm 69: 22-29).

Only through total destruction of the enemy, whose powerful curse has seized the soul of the sufferer and caused great pain and sickness, will the sick one be renewed and strengthened.

Totality of the Curse

The most characteristic aspect of the African curse is the total loss of power and possessions which should result to the accursed. A Kaka father who wishes to curse his disobedient son will go to the center of the village and in a loud voice call out the name of his son. "You are no longer my son. You shall not dwell among your fathers and your ancestors. You will wander about looking for friends and you will find none. May everything which your hand touches come to naught. May you beget no sons and any wealth you find in this world, may you lose it. May your body be sick and your soul without strength. May you go without sleep and may the food you eat cause you to vomit and in the end may the vultures eat your body." Perhaps even stronger is the curse of the psalmist:

Appoint a wicked man against him; let an accuser bring him to trial. When he is tried, let him come forth guilty; let his prayer be counted as sin! May his days be few; may another seize his goods! May his children be fatherless, and his wife a widow! May his children wander about and beg; may they be driven out of the ruins they inhabit! May the creditor seize all that he has; may strangers plunder the fruits of his toil! Let there be none to extend kindness to him, nor any to pity his fatherless children! May his posterity be cut off; may his name be blotted out in the second generation! May the iniquity of his fathers be remembered before the Lord, and let not the sin of his mother be blotted out! Let them be before the Lord continually; and may his memory be cut off from the earth! (Psalm 109: 6-15).

Sin and the curse in the Old Testament are very similar. In either case the suffering which follows involves the weakened soul which has been attacked and devitalized. From such loss of strength sickness, misery, and unhappiness are the consequences. Often separation from one's community takes place when the sickness threatens to engulf the would-be-healthy community. The offense against the community is the specific sin. The violation of the covenant holding between men is also a sin against the creator and covenant giver, Yahweh.

In African societies likewise it is difficult to understand the list of proscribed activities unless these are seen as breaches of a covenant relation in which men are expected to live in some sort of regulated community. Among the Mende of Sierra Leone illicit sexual behavior requires confession, particularly if a child delivery is difficult and slow. By confessing this violation, the delivery is supposed to be eased. Likewise, among the same people, there are violations against ancestors who constitute an important dimension in the community. When such violations occur, a sacrifice must be performed in order to reestablish a wholesome community. Where secret societies are the guardians of certain laws and customs, a violation against such a society's domain will require confession to the society. The Mende, the Kaka, and the Bulu would view the act of sitting on the bed of one's mother-in-law as a violation of an unwritten covenant relation between mother-in-law and son-in-law. Such a violation requires the giving of a gift to the offended mother-in-law in order to remove the offense. Failure to reestablish the proper relationship will often result in sickness to the offender and perhaps to the entire community. The blessing which flows naturally from good relations and peace is the opposite of the sin and curses which produce sickness. Among the patrilineal Tallensi a son who pursues his own ends against his father's wishes often ends in failure and sickness. He must then seek his father's forgiveness and blessing in order that he may be restored to a healthy role in his family relations.

Kosuke Koyama

Aristotelian Pepper and Buddhist Salt

An open letter to Dr. Daniel McGilvary (1828-1911), a pioneer missionary who served Christ for over half a century in northern Thailand.

Dear Dr. McGilvary,

THIS is my sixth year in northern Thailand. About one tenth of the length of your ministry! Your old teakwood mission house still stands by the Ping River, overlooking your town, Chiengmai. The residence of one of the Chiengmai princes, a house which you frequented, is now occupied by the American Consulate. My letter to you is in the nature of an inquiry. I want to known the whereabouts of my ministry in the context of the history of the church in northern Thailand. To what kind of spiritual and theological heritage am I heir? This question is of immediate concern for me, for how can I make my witness meaningful to my neighbors if I fail to understand where they are and where I am in the continuing story of the church here? And whenever I undertake the study of the church's past in northern Thailand, you stand, the intriguing pioneer missionary, whose immense spiritual and intellectual influence upon the Thai is still visi-

Kosuke Koyama is a missionary sent by the United Church of Christ in Japan to the Church of Christ in Thailand. He has been a professor at Thailand Theological Seminary since 1961.

ble in churches spread around the countryside, stamped with the color of your own Christian piety. So I have sought to study your message.

The Pioneer message

I have read your book, *A Half Century Among the Siamese and the Lao*[1] with intense interest and eagerness. At certain points in your book you give some clues to the contents of your message:

Why do we worship Jehovah-Jesus? Because he is our sovereign Lord. The Buddha groaned under his own load of guilt, and was oppressed by the sad and universal consequences of sin among men. The Christ challenged his enemies to convince him of sin, and his enemies to this day have confessed that they find no sin in him. Buddhists believe that Buddha reached Nirvana after having himself passed through every form of being in the universe—having been in turn every animal in the seas, on the earth, and in the air. He did this by an inexorable law that

[1] Daniel McGilvary, *A Half Century Among the Siamese and the Lao* (New York: Fleming H. Revell, 1912).

109

he and every other being is subject to, and cannot evade. Our Jehovah-Jesus, as our Scriptures teach, is the only self-existent being in the universe, and himself the cause of all other beings. An infinite Spirit and invisible, he manifested himself to the world by descending from heaven, becoming man, taking on our nature in unison with his own holy nature, but with no taint of sin. He did this out of infinite love and pity for our race after it had sinned. He saw there was no other able to save, and he became our Savior.[2]

The sacred books of the Princess teach that there is no creator. Everything, as the Siamese say, *"pen eng"* comes to be of itself. All this complicated universe became what it is by a fortuitous concurrence of atoms, which atoms themselves had no creator. We come as honest seekers for truth. We look around, above, beneath. Everything seems to imply the contrivance of mind.[3]

We pressed home the thought, new to them, that there must be a maker of the world and of all creatures in it. We told them the old, old story of the infinite love of God, our Father, and of Christ, his Son, who suffered and died to save us, and of pardon freely promised to all who believe in Him. This is the final argument that wins these people.[4]

---

2 Ibid., p. 181f.

3 Ibid., p. 182.

4 Ibid., p. 328.

And then, before that motley crowd, drinking with them their native tea from an earthen teapot, the men seated close around, or reclining as they smoke their pipes, the women and children walking about or sitting on the ground — we tell of God, the great Spirit, the creator and Father of all—the Bible, his message to men — the incarnation, life, and death of Christ, and redemption through his blood.[5]

Then our religion was explained in its two leading ideas—rejection of the spirit-cult and acceptance of Jesus for the pardon of sin and the life eternal. Questions were asked and answered.[6]

These accounts, although brief and written for the English-speaking reader, allow me to feel the contents of the message you preached and the kind of theological avenue you traveled when you proclaimed Christ to the Thai. I have become, then, curious to know whether your audience understood your preaching or not, if you will pardon me for asking. In my ministry here today I am forced to see how thoroughly strange and unrealistic—how "western"— is the Christian vocabulary to the ears of my Thai neighbors!

How did you explain the thoughts such as: "Buddha groaned under his own load of *guilt*," "Our Jehovah Jesus is the only *self-existent being* in the universe," "He did this out of *infinite love* and pity for our race after it had *sinned*," "Everything

---

5 Ibid., p. 342.

6 Ibid., p. 344.

seems to imply the *contrivance of mind*," "Suffered and *died to save us*," "The *incarnation*, life, and death of Christ and *redemption through his blood*," and "*eternal life*." I am asking you this as an evangelist, as you yourself were. These ideas, indeed, constitute the revolutionary Christian good news. But they seem too strange and unfamiliar a cake for the Thai to eat.

My observation is that upon accepting the gospel the Thai season the Christian ingredients — whether they be "infinite love," "sin," "incarnation," "redemption through his blood," or "eternal life"—with their own Buddhist salt. The dish thus produced has, inevitably, a strange "ambiguous" taste for me. But it is not ambiguous for the Thai. So far as they are concerned, the taste has been well "adjusted" to their liking. This ambiguous taste puzzles me.

Then, too, I have discovered that the seasoning takes place in the Thai kitchen, not in the broad living room into which missionaries have access. When I peep into the kitchen of their theology, I realize that the seasoning is done quite unconsciously, unintentionally, and semi-automatically. This discovery has helped me to see the nature of the area of theological haziness in the traditional evangelism and church life of northern Thailand.

Let me illustrate what I mean by the ambiguous taste. The Christian message is based on the "infinite love" of God, as you say, (although it seems to me that "jealous love" may be a more exciting and provocative expression to use in Buddhist

Thailand). According to ingrained Buddhist Thai thinking and the practical interpretation of life dictated by it, the word "love" *(khwam-rak)* denotes man's attachment to things, persons, or super-natural beings. Attachment produces sorrow and trouble. Detachment creates tranquility, honesty, and genuine happiness.

One of my students told me that the idea of *good* in Thai culture can be portrayed as clothing washed, neatly ironed and place in the closed, undisturbed drawer. Don't wear it! If you wear the clothing, it will get dirty! The clothing must stay "detached" from the dirty world.

Several times, both at university campus and rural meetings, I have encountered violent objection to Jesus' censure of the servant who hid his one talent and returned it to the master when he came. What is wrong about this "honest" servant who kept what was entrusted to him in the "tranquil drawer?" Jesus' blame is unreasonable and outrageous! The sense of commitment to a "tranquil drawer" (non-involvement) is there in the groundwork of Thai psychology.

Now when God is said to be love, this is a strange message indeed! How can the quality of "attachment" be given to God? So asks Thai culture. God had better remain alone, nirvanic, transcendent. He ought not to become a man in Jesus Christ— an incarnate God — a God of attachment.

In the Thai theological kitchen, instead of going deeper into the understanding of the Christian theology of attachment, a blurring of the sharp edge of this theology of attachment takes place. The original taste of the love of God is salted by the spirit of detachment and becomes something not quite strong and meaningful enough to substantiate the basis of the Christian Gospel, the covenant relationship (involvement, attachment) between God and man. The love of God is there, but it is blurred.

It is like a two hundred volt electric bulb operating on the strength of a hundred volts. I call this dimness a state of "chronic Asokanization of the Gospel."[7] In the Thai Christian church, syncretism chiefly takes the form of unintentional chronic Asokanization of the gospel, which is perhaps more insidious than open syncretism. An Asokanized Christ is a "dim" Christ, tamed by culture.

Aristotelian Pepper

I am interested, in this context, in your sentence, "We come as honest seekers for truth. We look around, above, beneath. Everything seems to imply the contrivance of mind." You seem to be pursuing, if I am not mistaken, the traditional "cosmological proof" of the existence of God. The remarkable design one discerns in the universe compels one to acknowledge that this universe is not self-explanatory but must be explained in reference to Someone beyond it.

[7] Asoka was a great Buddhist king in India. He died in 323 B.C. after having been instrumental in strengthening and spreading Buddhism widely, contributing eventually to its strong pervasiveness in Thailand today.

The crucial point, which the users of this argument often overlook, is the question of what kind of mind it is that exists behind the universe. Is it a good mind or a bad mind? A redemptive mind or a destructive mind? A "nirvanic" mind or a "history-concerned" mind? Isn't it true that if one speaks of orderliness in the universe, another can speak of disorderliness (accident, confusion in the universe with the same vigor. It has been made clear to me in my rural ministry here that this important question of the cosmological argument — what kind of mind — i met by heightened challenge if in my congregation there is one perso who is born crippled or made blin by accident. People say to me tha there may certainly be a mind behin the universe, but if that mind ca produce such cruel irregularities a the crippled and the blind, it mus be capricious and erratic! Wher then, I ask myself, is the distinctio between the God understood throug recognition of design in the univers and the varieties of spirits my neigł bors worship?

My Thai friends and I may con to an agreement, although not withou much difficulty, that "in the begin ning was the Word."[8] But it is nc self-evident what kind of word th is even when "we come as hone seekers for truth." Honest seeke may find some objective religiou truth, but the God of revelation is hidden God even to the most hone seekers.[9]

Gradually I have come to see th

[8] John 1:1.
[9] John 1:13 and Matthew 16:17.

the medicine of the argument based on the universe, which has been widely prescribed in Thailand both for beginners at the levels of pre-evangelization and evangelism proper, and for Christians at the nurturing level, has proved to be a paralyzing tranquilizer. And it has, in reality, obstructed my parishioners' way to the presence of the "undomesticated God" of the Bible, as Luther called Him. This argument can be useful at the level of pre-evangelization, but it produces unwanted effects when it is incorporated into the substance of the Christian message. Somewhere in the history of the church here this uncritical incorporation must have taken place.

I must confess to you that one uneasy look cast on me by a leper while I was happily discoursing on this "proof" for the existence of God in a leper colony outside of Chiengmai made me take a critical attitude toward this time-honored argument. The Christ theorized under the influence of the over-anxious rationality of the West is as "dim" as the Asokanized Christ, although the color of the lights may differ from each other.

Sometimes I notice that one theology of a blurred Christ asks questions of another theology of a blurred Christ. In this traffic of questions and answers, one is not brought to an immediate contact with the gospel of Christ. In short, I see a double dimness of the gospel here, a mixed flavor of the gospel seasoned by Aristotelian pepper and Buddhist salt.

Christ in culture

I admit that what I have written here is oversimplified. And the problems I raise would involve many thorny theological, historical, and cultural questions which would defy any easy schematic handling. Yet a persistent question comes to me every day: "Where is the sharp edge of the love of Christ in our churches in northern Thailand? From what source did the blurring of Christ come?" I believe that this "doubly blurred" situation, caused by the two distinctive blurring agents of West and East, may have done some service in the past, but is today, in reality, a disservice.

Theological movements are rather like the sputniks which are being sent up around the world nowadays. If they survive the hazards of launching, they get into orbit and continue to describe more or less eccentric paths for longer or shorter periods until eventually they burn out. They serve their purpose if they obtain the limited results expected of them, and each one makes a fresh contribution. [10]

The trouble with Thailand is that the old double-stage logical sputniks of Aristotelian pepper and Buddhist salt refuse to be burned out. As soon as I say this, however, a chain of questions come to my mind.

I ask myself, "Why have we been so incompetent in understanding the development of the 'kitchen theology?' Why have we been so unprepared to present a Christ who can be 'bright' in the kitchen? Or is

10 John Macquarrie, *The Scope of Demythologizing* (London: S. C. M. Press, Ltd., 1960), p. 56.

the 'dim' Christ better adjusted than the 'bright' Christ to the Thai? Is Christ supposed to be seasoned by those elements in order to become an intelligible Christ to the Thai? Is it possible to have an 'unseasoned, raw' Christ? Isn't it true that the incarnation of the Son of God means his 'in-cultureation?' Wasn't he a Palestinian Jew? Doesn't this mean that imagining an 'unseasoned, raw' Christ is as absurd and impossible as a 'de-Hebraized' Yahweh? Does this then mean that one must not simply reject the 'pepper and salt' of any culture, but attempt to see

what kind of pepper and salt is seasoning Christ and try to present a 'bright' Christ in *cooperation* with the pepper and salt? If so, what should I do with Thailand's Aristotelian pepper and Buddhist salt?

This problem of Christ and culture in contemporary Thailand is the center of my theological concern. Would you help me in this?

Sincerely yours,

KOSUKE KOYAMA

Chiengmai, Thailand.

Michael A. Wright

Some Observations on Thai Animism

IN the religion of the Thai[1] we find both classical Buddhism (together with the folk developments which have taken place within Buddhism) and animism. Buddhism and animism are intimately fused in the Thai heart.

Classical Buddhism is an intellectual persuasion. As such it requires an intellectual turn of mind in its adherents. Such a turn of mind is no more common in Thailand than anywhere else in the world. How, then, has Buddhism survived? From India it was driven out by the immense vitality of Indian theism, though it left its mark. In China it became a popular religion, finding its basis not in intellectual principles, but in the aspirations of mankind. In Thailand it has remained, along with Indian literature and art, a potted specimen.

---

[1] In this article I cannot pretend to prove my statements. The very nature of Thai religion precludes the quotation of authoritative sources, and no statement is universally valid. One often hears someone say that the Thai believe this or that, but anyone who really knows the Thai also knows that some Thai believe a thing all the time, more believe it some of the time, and most do not believe anything of the sort.

The Thai have never reduced their own beliefs to a historical, tangible, documented system. They have not yet taken on a wholly analysable, conscious form. Religion is felt, not reasoned. I have therefore not tried to reason too much about it, but have tried to enter into the Thai spirit, speaking for it like a medium, for it is yet inarticulate.

Yet it is by no means a fossil; it survives grafted onto another system. As a result, Buddhism is disguised as a folk religion in Thailand. The Thai may both petition the Buddha as a divinity, and subscribe to the Buddha's apparent atheism when threatened by the demands which the existence of God would make on them. Being a weak occidental, I propose to divide and conquer, to consider animism alone in this article, a thing which no Thai would feel was right.

Animism

The Thai often speak of their animistic practices as "Brahmanism." In fact, Brahmanism has had no deep influence on them whatsoever. They admire Indian mythology and know

Michael A. Wright was raised a Roman Catholic. He became involved with the Buddhist Society of London, and went to Thailand in 1959, where he became a Buddhist monk and studied Buddhism. He travelled widely throughout Thailand, immersing himself in everything Thai. In 1961 he left the monkhood and regained his faith. In his own words, he found God through the pursuit of Nirvana, by discovering what God is not. He has stayed on in Thailand helping in Roman Catholic programs. He plans now to take a degree in anthropology at the School of Oriental and African Studies, London. 232/25 Soi Saint Louis 3, Yannawa, Bangkok, Thailand.

of the Hindu gods much as we in the West know the gods of Greece and Rome. The animism of which I speak is truly their own, and therefore vital and potent. Although Thai animism may have close parallels in Indian village cults, it is from the Thai heart.

The content of animism varies from culture to culture, yet there are certain constants. Animism is a method for the integration of man with himself and with nature. To achieve this integration the devotee seeks a source of power. The animist acknowledges an ideal state, and that he is estranged from that state, and that his beliefs and practices will lead to a return to wholeness. The concept of "wholeness" varies from good hunting or success in love to union with the supernatural. Our investigation will aim at revealing in what forms these elements are prevalent among the Thai.

Sources of power and wholeness

One all-important word in Thai is phra'. It is said to come from the Sanscrit vara (Latin verum), meaning 'excellent,' but it has taken on a purely Thai flavor, and cannot be connected with Indian thought. What do the Thai mean when they use phra' as a noun? The king is phra', so are Buddhist monks, images and amulets.

The Buddha is called phra'. At this point we can forget the historical Buddha and all his moral and rational claims to holiness. Here he is spirit, Lord, magical, a swirling source of power: witness images of the Buddha and paintings by the young Thai artists of today.

The spiritual Buddha (to distinguish him from the historical Buddha) complicates things immensely. He seems to have no place in the rest of the Thai animistic picture. I fail to find any relationship between him and the local spirits. He is worshipped like the spirits.

I have often seen shoddy little productions of popular plays being given in temples. Before the stage is a table with the usual paraphernalia of worship: a pig's head, whiskey, a chair with a parasol over it.

"Who are the offerings for?"

"For the Great Father."

"Which Great Father?"

"Our Great Father, the phra' (image) that presides in the chapel."

I doubt if the spiritual Buddha is considered as existing apart from his images. He does not "come down" to reside in a statue; instead, he is induced, perhaps even created, in the ceremony of consecration. He is power rather than person.

The king's claim to being phra' is also very difficult for someone not a Thai to understand. His title is no mere honor; he is undoubtedly looked on as being superhuman, supernatural. There is a story of King Chulalongkorn[2] going aboard a ship which promptly developed a list because of the weight of his glory. The Thai idea goes much farther than the European "divine right." The king's right is his own, not like the Chinese "mandate of heaven." Nor is the concept an Indian one. That the king

2 One of the greatest and most beloved kings of Thai history, an enlightened and progressive monarch.

s an incarnation of the Hindu god Vishnu is simply a flattering piece of propaganda borrowed from abroad. It neither comes from the Thai heart, nor touches it.

Local spirits of the land have no material qualities but can become sensible through the mediumship of the human unconscious. Their job is to guard and to rule their various pieces of land. But guard against what? And who set them to guard? The Thai do not presume to ask these questions. Any simple Thai will tell you that they are immortal. It would seem that they are truly personal, not mere personifications of the land, because they can come and go. They were there before men came. Indeed, it can be said that man holds and uses the land on lease as it were from the original spirit owner. The name for them, "lord (or owner) of the place," suggests that they are first of all "owners" and only then rulers or guardians. In fact, according to Thai thought, we can say that man borrows the very ground he walks on. The world was not ours from the beginning.

Are the local spirits one or many? The Thai language does not show. The fact that they do not have individual names suggests that they are uncountable. Most spirits and ghosts in Thailand have names, but the local spirits, never. Even though a Thai may have a most intimate relationship with the spirit of the land he owns, he does not give him a personal name.

How is it that they have so many shrines? Sell half your land, and a new shrine will be put up. To the

same spirit? To a new one? As a branch office of the old? No one can say. "They" or "he" would seem to be uncountable, like Christ in the sacrament, indefinitely divisible, yet always completely there. "He" or "they" have no lord, but rule in "his" or "their" own right, almost Elohim,[3] the Person behind nature.

Thai skilled artisans and traditional performers have ceremonies when they pay their respects to their teachers, and behind the immediate teachers, to the spirit masters of their profession. These spirit masters worshipped by boxers, swordsmen, bronze-casters, and artists in general, are an important source of integration for the Thai. The approbation of the spirit master makes the drummer a drummer. Should he offend his master, he would lose his art.

The masters are not only a heirarchy of teacher's teachers going back into the dim past, but are original "owners" of the art, and giver or withholder of success in it. Their power descends from master to pupil. The human, historical teachers share in the spirit power of the original master, thus suggesting that the Thai animist does not distinguish completely between the material and the spiritual.[4]

---

3 Elohim is one of the Hebrew names for God in the Old Testament.

4 The fact that matter and spirit are so easily identified in the Thai mind suggests that Thai would have little difficulty in believing that Christ is God, but that they cannot easily accept God as pure spirit, unless he is presented in Hebrew terms as the *person* in the *powers* of nature. As power and person overlap in the Thai mind, so do matter and spirit. Even we admit that our classical distinction between them is a matter of convenience.

Amulets which have been "enlivened" are said to be *phra'*, or to have *phra'* in them, thus giving the wearer a sort of communion. While he wears the amulet he has *phra'* with him. The *phra'* may leave the amulet if it is treated with disrespect, though the *phra'* does not go somewhere else. When he urinates the amulet wearer must remove the amulet. To commit a robbery, however, he must wear it in order to insure safety and success. The *phra'* is concerned that the devotee observe taboo, but is not the least interested in what we, and the historical Buddha too, would call morality. Again we find ourselves dealing with a natural power, not a moral person.[5]

Man and his estrangement

The Buddha taught that there was no unchanging soul, no existential person in man. The most soul-like

Has the missionary the right to demand to the non-Christian, "Distinguish!"? If he does this he creates a materialist, for he is killing the spark of natural religion, unless, as usually happens, he manages to plug the convert into the circuit of European natural religion. But what a cruel and unnecessary demand this is to make on a Thai! Under those terms, if he converts he must become in the most essential sense a Westerner. Though you give him a "native" liturgy and a church with a curving roof, he has lost his birth-right.

[5] Person and power are very perfectly identified in the animist mind. To see personality in the forces of nature and to judge a person by his power no longer comes easily to an occidental. Our long history of being influenced by rational philosophies has made it our nature to distinguish at all costs, to distinguish even things which may profitably and legitimately be identified. I think that here the animists have a psychic advantage over us; they are heir to a calm concept of wholeness which we may only attain by much struggle.

thing the Buddha recognised was the *winyaan* (Thai pronunciation). This word to the Buddha meant the 'knowing' which results from contact between sense organ and sense object. It cannot be understood as a "knower."

When the Thai says *winyaan*, however, he definitely has a spirit "person" in mind. At death the *winyaan* leaves the body, floats out, suggesting a person rather than a power, in fact a conventional, materially conceived ghost which haunts a picture of the deceased, his house and the graveyard, before "going to heaven."

The Thai officially believe in reincarnation, but that is a sophistication, a borrowing from abroad. The fact that the soul is finally liberated only at cremation instead of at death shows how strongly the spirit is bound up with the physical being of a person in Thai opinion. Thai death and funeral customs demand more study. Offerings and obeisance are made before the coffin. Despite what the sophisticated say about this being merely an "in memoriam," the simple Thai undoubtedly feels that he is honoring a more or less non-material "presence."

A more difficult word is *khwan*. The *khwan* can be missing from the body even when a person is still alive, although it does not seem to go elsewhere; it does not "haunt" like a *winyaan*, or like the common spirits. In the absence of his *khwan* the person becomes sick, lethargic, unlucky, mad, or severely frightened.

The *khwan* does not seem to be a separable soul, inhabiting a body, but is intimately bound up with a person's qualities as a man, his completeness, his dignity. One can have more or less khwan. An accident or an insult, such as an assault on the head, damages the *khwan*. The *khwan* suffers, and even leaves the body when taboos are broken, just as *phra'* will leave an amulet if it is not respected. This is not to say that it "floats out" substantially; rather it fades or lessens. *Khwan* can be brought back or increased by honor, by gifts, by ceremony, and by making up for wrong done.

A further understanding of the nature of the *khwan* may be had by realizing that it is a characteristic of inanimate objects as well. Both *phra'* and *khwan* are to be found in useful objects, musical instruments, tools, etc. They make a thing be what it is. A drum cannot be beaten until life has been breathed into it, and once it has come alive it must be treated with the deepest respect or that "life" will leave the drum and bring misfortune, even madness to the one who has mistreated it. Perhaps the *khwan* is little more than a personification of the article because before the thing was made it did not exist and when the thing breaks the *khwan* is no longer there.

The *khwan* in a human being does not "live" in the body and float out at death as the *winyaan* does. It is not an entity, but a quality.

Sin

"Why should I have a religion?"
"To put right what is wrong."
"Well, what is wrong with me?"

A Thai normally feels dis-ease only very faintly. Whether this is due to lack of introspection or whether he really is so well integrated that sin does him little psychological harm, is difficult to say. This subject needs careful attention by a truly qualified person because the situation here is so utterly different from that in the West.

The Thai do feel guilt, but in what situations, and how do they act on it? We feel that our individual faults are related to something much bigger than the immediate facts of a case, to an original sin, to a total wrongness.

The Thai see their sins in a much narrower context. Buddhism, whose great interest is *malum poenae*, has never demanded that they face *malum culpae*. Any wrong that a man may commit is his own private misfortune, and has no bearing on the universe at large nor is it against a righteous God.

Classical Buddhist morality is a borrowing and has little to do with the question: witness the killing of animals. An Indian Buddhist who killed a bird would find it hanging around his neck like an albatross, even though it were only a sparrow; A Thai can shoot a whole flock without a qualm.

It is my observation that the Thai are even more subject than we are to feelings of disappointment, futility, anguish. When material and social consolations fail them they have little to fall back on. Despite their apparent resilience, they are easily subject to neurosis.

Thailand is a shame society, not a guilt society. It can be grouped with Japan, where public disgrace is deeply felt, while guilt is not particularly in evidence. This contrasts with India, where a hidden wrong causes an agony of conscience. Shame needs its audience; guilt is its own witness.

Sacrifice

In Thailand we may see all kinds of offerings made to various *phra'*: flowers, incense-sticks, gold, food, etc. But we see no sacrifice in the sense of ritual killing, the blood of a victim flowing on the altar. We may suppose that the Thai ancestors made such sacrifices before the coming of Buddhism. I have heard of animal sacrifices performed in the northeastern part of the country, but have never witnessed one.

The pig's head does not count, nor do ducks and chickens because they are killed and cooked before they are offered. It is not their life which is offered, but their food value. Coconuts are not smashed before the images as they are in India, but are opened and stuck with a straw to the greater convenience of the *phra'* concerned.

However, I think I have found one real sacrifice — a human sacrifice at that — acted out in symbol at the very heart of Buddhism. This is the Buddhist ordination ceremony.

The text of the ordination ceremony shows that it was intended to be no more than an inquiry into the character and motives of the postulant, and an invitation to the brethren either to accept or reject him. By various additions and by the attitude they take to unchanged parts of the ritual, the Thai reveal that in ordaining a new monk they are doing much more than going through a length of ecclesiastical red tape.

First of all, the postulant is given a ceremony for increasing his *khwan* before the ordination. The name for this ceremony implies "to make amends." Make amends for what? Similar attentions were paid to those who were about to be slaughtered to become ghostly "gate guardians" in the classical Ayudhya period of Thai history.

Immediately before the ordination the postulant is caught by old ladies who paint him all over with saffron, like an animal victim chosen for sacrifice. This is a "laying apart." On the way to, and three times around, the ordination hall he is accompanied by dancers and musicians. These are said to be symbolic of the godlings who accompanied Gotama (the Buddha) on his journey of renunciation. But why is the dancing purposely undignified and often even indecent? At another ceremony the prettiest girls are organized to dance in order; but at an ordination the oldest people, usually toothless old crones, and young men, dress up in ridiculous costumes to leap and cavort around the postulant.

At a stone in front of the hall a candle, flowers and incense sticks are placed in the postulant's hands as they are placed in the hands of the dead, and of criminals about to be executed. This may be rationalized as being symbolic of his being "dead" to the passions, but there is something very un Siamese about a statement like that. The postulant prostrates three times before the stone and leaves the candle burning at its foot. He does not step into the ordination hall, but is pushed, pulled, and half carried.

Thereafter there seems to be no more hint of a sacrifice; but to show that a "death" has taken place the new monk is no longer considered a man; he is a *phra'*. I once heard a new monk use honorific language in speaking to an old woman. She replied, "Oh don't, your holiness! You're a *phra'* now, a human being no longer." Her words were beyond a manner of speech. In her eyes he had become something quite different from what he had been before, apart from his fellow men.

Buddhist monks in Thailand preserve their celibacy to an admirable, an incredible degree. I am prepared to vouch for this. As anyone knows who has attempted celibacy, mere moral advice, "Thou shalt be chaste," is no help at all. Only a psychic motion of immense depth can preserve one in so hard a state. If not psychic power, then psychic damage.

There is no reason for supposing that Thai Buddhist monks are mentally sick; witness those who return to the lay state after several years with perfect resilience. This strength does not flow to the Thai from classical Buddhism; in Ceylonese temples scandal is the order of the day. The celibacy of Thai Buddhist monks

could be called heroic if it did not seem to come so easily. Their celibacy can only lead us to admit the vast strength that animism still has even in the hearts of the sophisticated. The monks know themselves to be more than men, not in moralistic or rational terms, but in magical terms.

Amulets and images have already been mentioned as providing a sort of communion. A Thai looks upon his amulet as something more than a Roman Catholic's miraculous medal, and something less than a consecrated host. When it has been enlivened, the amulet is *phra'* in a material thing, or a material *phra'*, with a lack of distinction between matter and spirit. The *phra'* does not "reside" in the amulet like a pea in a pod; the *phra'* is identified with the clay or metal.

Another form of communion, more intimate than that with the amulet, is to be had from the monks. Since his ritual death at ordination the monk is no longer man but *phra'* among men, an Emmanuel.[4] "*Phra'*-the-Father" is as intangible for the Thai animist as God the Father was before the incarnation. His sons, born from the sacrificial death of ordination, are with us in the flesh. They are a tangible presence of the Power behind the power of nature. This explains why offerings to monks are looked upon as being so much more meritorious than charity performed for the poor. When food has been offered to the hand of a monk it has been offered to God.

[4] A Hebrew title meaning "God with us," and applied in the Bible to Jesus Christ.

PART II

Cultural Systems and Manifestations:

Social Structure

Paul Abrecht and William A. Smalley

The Moral Implications of Social Structure

It has not been often that the editor of PRACTICAL ANTHROPOLOGY *has received a letter raising serious objection to any of the many viewpoints which have been expressed in the pages of the magazine. We welcome such letters, of course, as they draw attention to weaknesses of presentation, faulty logic, wrong data, unwarranted conclusions, and many other possible problems with material published in PA. We did receive one such letter from the Rev. Paul Abrecht of the Department on Church and Society, Division of Studies of the World Council of Churches in Geneva. Since it was in reference to something I had written, I am taking this opportunity of printing the letter along with an explanation of my earlier statement.*

The Letter From Mr. Abrecht

With much of Mr. Smalley's interesting statement on "Planting the Church in a Disintegrating Society" (PRACTICAL ANTHROPOLOGY, September-December 1958) I can agree. However, I would like to take issue with some of his remarks on page 232. He writes:

There is nothing intrinsically moral or right and wrong about social structure as such. The many different social structures as found today in the world are simply many different ways of organizing group behavior into useful channels and of making life more valuable to the participants in the society. The missionary's role in relation to this as in relation to other cultural matters is to let history take its course and to concern himself with more important issues.

There is, I agree, no "Christian" structure of society; all social structures stand under the judgment of God. But from the Christian point of view, might it not be argued that some social structures are definitely bad? How to go about changing

them is another question. Would not Mr. Smalley agree that the Christian has a responsibility today to work for change in the structure of racially segregated communities in the U.S.A.? And suppose a Christian convert in a colonial society complains of the injustice of the political setup. Is it not within the missionary's responsibility to help him understand his responsibility — as a Christian — in working for change in the political structure? Or suppose that a woman living in a polygamous society has become a Christian and begins to understand the meaning of the monogamous family ethic developed in the New Testament. Is she not to be encouraged to think out the meaning of responsible change in the structure of family life?

Mr. Smalley reacts very rightly against missionaries who have attempted to promote change or resist it in a tactless way in the past. But in reacting to this he goes to the other extreme adopting a positivistic attitude of ethical neutrality to structures. It is true that later in this

125

message Mr. Smalley qualifies his statement by declaring that the missionary may point to "possible avenues of change." But the suspicion remains that Mr. Smalley believes social structures are really outside our Christian concern.

Toward the end of his statement Mr. Smalley says in regard to the problems of illegitimate birth and extramarital sex behavior, "They too will not be remedied by any direct action upon them as such, but only through a restructuring of the whole value system of the people involved." Who is to do this restructuring of the value system? The government administrator? The lawyer? The anthropologist? May not the Christian community itself have a role in such "restructuring"?

The Christian, I believe, is concerned with the whole of life including the moral basis for the structures of society. In the change or reform of such structures the Christian has the duty to work for responsible human relations. Mr. Smalley's view would seem to deny the obligation of the church to express its concern for man in all his social relationships. At least his way of stating his position might give rise to that suspicion.

Form and Meaning

In replying to Mr. Abrecht's well-taken comments, I would first like to point out a distinction in my own thinking which I obviously did not make clear in my earlier article under discussion. It is the difference between a structure, and the meaning of that structure. To take a clear-cut case from language, many different structures can convey roughly equivalent meaning, and the same structure can carry different meanings. To illustrate with two languages which are rather alike in structure, as languages in the world go, "He read it to me" and "Il me l'a lu" (literally "He me it has read") are pretty much the same, meaning-wise, but very different structurally. They belong to entirely different language systems, involve different kinds of grammatical agreement, consist of different sounds, etc. On the other hand, "He is in the dog house" (to use a hackneyed example) has two entirely unrelated meanings for the same English sentence.

To say that language structure and meaning are different is not to say that they can ever be divorced from each other. But they are different, and the ability to keep this difference in mind is of great importance to the linguist who works with a variety of languages in an analytical way. It can make his understanding of both form and meaning clearer as it separates out the variables which are found from language to language. An extreme case of the confusion of form and meaning in language is the situation where the actual phonetic form of the name of God becomes sacred, as it did among the ancient Jews, where to utter the name of Yahweh was sacrilege. Less extreme examples of this kind of confusion of linguistic form and meaning may be found in many churches today.

It seems to me that it is important to keep this kind of distinction in mind for other kinds of cultural behavior as well as for language. Let's take one of Mr. Abrecht's questions as an example: "Racially segregated communities in the U.S.A." carries a charged meaning to almost any American. But is it the structural fact of segregation of race which is bad, or is it the tremendous variety of meaning overtones which such segregation happens in this cases to imply: "second-class citizens," unequal opportunity, contempt, suppression, congenital inferiority, etc.? The simple formal, structural fact of segregation in itself is not evil. French- and English-speaking Canadians live relatively segregated lives. So do the various ethnic groups of Switzerland and Belgium. Why is the segregation of Negroes and Whites in U.S.A. communities evil but the segregation between millions of African Negroes and American Whites (or Negroes) not bad? It surely is not the Atlantic Ocean which makes the one immoral and the other amoral. The meaning underlying the two forms of segregation is entirely different.

To us, slavery is "bad." It was a burning issue at one time in American history until we eliminated it to replace it with other evils. The Biblically oriented Christian, however, would have a hard time justifying the idea that the structure, the institution of slavery, is universally bad. St. Paul was certainly not bothered about it. It was not one of the issues that Jesus made anything of. The "badness" of slavery is related to new meanings which have been read into it since New Testament times, meanings of the degradation of the individual, deprivation of spirit, destruction of human dignity and independence, to name only some.

Restructuring Comes from Within

If it is granted that there is a distinction between structure and its meaning, what is the practical relationship between them when it comes to culture change? Structures which acquire unfavorable meaning often have to be changed. In language we see clear examples of this. A word like "damn" (and many much more vulgar words) in English has nothing wrong with it so far as its structure is concerned. The sequence of sounds is no better or worse than any other sequence of sounds. "Nice" people are careful about

the use of it, however, and some children will in fun use the homophonous word "dam" because of the association of the sound of the two words. The meaning makes it relatively taboo. The illustration could be made stronger if it were not that some other words are so more decidedly taboo that I do not even feel comfortable in using them as an illustration.

In similar manner, as the meaning of slavery in the Western world gradually changed because of new ideas about human dignity and justice, the form of slavery became intolerable. An internal restructuring of values resulted in the elimination of those social structures which seemed to reflect outgrown attitudes. But here lies a very interesting fact about human culture. Such a change in values results in change in social structure only in those social relationships which at the time symbolize the repudiated meaning. Slavery was abolished, but it was to be another generation before issues of colonialism would be called into question. The same changes in values concerning human beings eventually found a new symbol to fight against in the structure of colonialism. I doubt that the men who worked so energetically for the freedom of the American slaves would have seen colonialism as being a related issue at all. At that time colonialism meant Christianizing the heathen, medical facilities for the sick, philanthropy for the underprivileged, education and enlightenment for darkened minds.

In other words, a change in values, new ideas, a sharpened sensitivity will produce structural change, but it will produce it only in those structures which *seem to the participants* to be symbolic of the "badness." The new values, the new sense of right and wrong, the new feeling against injustice, may well be due to stimulation from outside the culture. I suppose that it usually is. Any significant change, however, comes only from within the culture. It is only as people in a particular society begin to attach new meanings to old forms (or old meanings of badness become intensified to the point where the form becomes intolerable) that change in structure which has any significance takes place.

The new meanings which bring about changes in habits of behavior are not necessarily what the outsider would expect. There is, for example, an ancient custom among some of the mountain tribes of Vietnam, in which the upper incisors of adolescent children are sawed or hacked out as a beauty measure, and as a symbol of growing up. Missionaries have long opposed the custom as being unhygienic (because of resulting infections), cruel, and evidence of heathen superstition and degradation. The custom has been disappearing, until now it is rather rare except in remote areas, but I am sure it is not disappearing primarily for the missionaries' reasons. There are certainly some cases of Christians who have been taught and believe that this is an unchristian type of behavior, but they believe this ritually, without emotional conviction. The real reasons for the change are probably simply that the mutilation symbolizes cultural "backwardness," and that there are more and more people who want their children to look more like the neighboring Vietnamese and even the Westerners living there. What was once a beauty mark has become a symbol or mark of lack of cultural progress and development. There is certainly not the same horrified meaning of savagery and badness which the outsider feels about the custom. This change, then, has little or no significance in terms of Christian ethics, humanity, mercy, or anything of the kind. It is much more a matter of keeping up with a new set of Joneses.

Mr. Abrecht's question about the Christian convert in a colonial society who complains of the injustice of the political setup is a case in point. Is it, or is it not the missionary's responsibility to help him understand his responsibility, as a Christian, in working for change in the political structure? Put in those terms, terms of helping a man understand his responsibilities, there can be only an affirmative answer. But it is precisely here that the rub comes. The missionary in this situation may assume that the man's responsibility is to work for culture change. But is that necessarily so? Biblically, the themes of resignation to one's social lot are as strong as the denunciations of social injustice. What is the man's responsibility in working for change in political structure? This is something the alien missionary can never really know. The missionary's role here as always must be primarily that of leading the convert to an ever-deepening understanding of God, of His revelation in Jesus Christ, and of the relationship of responsible obedience and fellowship which God seeks in His people. He must encourage and stimulate the Christians to seek that cultural expression which will best reflect within the meanings of their cultural habits ·these new values which they are gradually coming to understand. He must help them see in the Scriptures some of God's history of dealing with men in an enormous variety of cultural circumstances, and to seek from the Holy Spirit that intimate personal guidance which God seeks to give His church in all times and cultures. If, as in so many places in the dwindling colonial world today, such new values focus upon a meaning of overwhelming "badness"' in the colonial political structure, certainly that will come within the sphere of change, in one way or another. But the restructuring comes from within. It is in a sense the by-product. Responsible allegiance to God within any human cultural framework will show up in culture change, sometimes enormous change. It is, however, the allegiance, not the change, which is ultimately significant, and which it is the missionary's role to foster.

Sometimes culture change can be enforced on such a large scale that it becomes permanent. Headhunting, scarification, polygamy, or human sacrifice have been eliminated from several cultures by the police-reinforced diligence of an alien administration. I am not necessarily opposed to all such activity on the part of administrators, but it is very clear that resulting change has no moral value whatsoever. The meanings expressed by these cultural forms are preserved in some other way, and as long as the same meanings are preserved nothing of moral value has been accomplished.

Some individuals may have been saved from suffering or death, and from a Western viewpoint this is of enormous value, but within the local culture it may have no significance whatsoever. It is only when a sense of respect for the personality of other individuals, for their physical welfare, and above all, for them as actual or potential brothers in Christ, gets reflected in a change of behavior toward reducing suffering and death within the culture that such change has moral significance.

The Role of the Church

Who is to do this restructuring of the value system? The government? No. It cannot. Neither can the lawyer, the anthropologist, or the missionary. No alien can, although new ideas, stimulus for change, awareness of new horizons, alternative forms of behavior, may all well come from these outside sources.

It is precisely the community itself, including the Christian community, which has the principal though generally quite unconscious role in the change of values and habits. For the Christian community there is yet another force, and that is God in culture, the Holy Spirit dwelling within the children of God. It is interesting, though, that God seems more willing to work through the existing forms of culture than many of His more intellectual followers want to admit.

The missionary, no matter how complete his identification with the local community, remains an alien. I have discussed his role in culture change elsewhere.[1] If he honestly and perceptively faces up to the issue of leading men to God, to total commitment to Christ, to an awareness of Christian life in culture, *their* cultures, stimulating them to find the structures which will best express their new faith, he has fulfilled his role. He may then well "let history take its course" because he has "concerned himself with more important issues."

[1] William A. Smalley, "The Missionary and Culture Change," PRACTICAL ANTHROPOLOGY, Vol. 4, No. 6 (Nov.-Dec., 1957), pp. 231-237. See also, William A. Smalley, "Cultural Implications of an Indigenous Church," PRACTICAL ANTHROPOLOGY, Vol. 5, No. 2 (March-April, 1958), pp. 51-65, and in this volume.

Donald N. Larson

Church, Plaza, and Marketplace

How hard it is to see the many factors at work in the shaping of our religious beliefs! In all sincerity we seem to assume that it is possible to isolate "pure Biblical beliefs," and to transplant them into the brains of others. Failing to see how his own beliefs have been influenced, the missionary may try to carry on without realizing social and economic factors at work on the hearts and minds of the people whose beliefs he is attempting to alter. Or even worse, he may deny that they have any relevance at all to his work, that there is a close-knit relationship between church, plaza, and marketplace.

THE missionary who approaches his work with a wholistic view of culture is on the alert to uncover and understand the ways in which religious beliefs are related to other aspects of culture. As this picture emerges, he begins to see more clearly the relationship between his own beliefs and the general character of his own culture. A red shirt is just red when it is seen among blue, white, yellow, or brown shirts; but when viewed among pink, dubonnet, vermilion, or old rose shirts, its own true and unique character is seen more clearly. Its color did not change; what changed was the viewpoint of the observer. So it is with cultures. Our own is never seen so clearly as when it is contrasted with another.

The missionary's message may take on new forms after a second look at his own

culture. When he sees how his own culture has shaped his religious beliefs, he may begin to realize that they aren't as "purely Biblical" as he had assumed. Now, the Bible become a judge of his beliefs; before, it was only a confirmation of them. He approaches the missionary task with a different set of questions. How are the people prepared to accept Biblical ideas? Which of them will be in open conflict with the culture? Which will not?

The Philippine Vendor

A comic strip in the *Manila Times* features "Hugo, the Sidewalk Vendor." Roddy Ragodon, the cartoonist, does a masterful job at portraying the Filipino's struggle for social acceptance and economic security. For example, in one of his cartoons Hugo is portrayed as a rebel against the traditional conduct of lowland Filipinos. The center of interest in the first frame is Hugo. He is standing behind his baskets of oranges, which he is selling to passersby. Lying on the oranges is a sign: "1.80 pesos per kilo." On his

For the past two years Donald N. Larson has been director of the Interchurch Language School in the Philippines. He has accepted a position with the Translations Department of the American Bible Society, 450 Park Ave., New York 22, N. Y., U. S. A.

left and on his right are two other vendors, both selling oranges, and both selling
them for the same price, "1.80 pesos per
kilo." There are no customers. The three
faces wear a forlorn look.

Now we glance at the second frame.
With his back to the reader, Hugo is
seen down on one knee, changing the
sign on his oranges. His fellow vendors
watching him. In their faces is a mixture
of disbelief and anger, for Hugo is lowering his price to "1.78 pesos per kilo"!
And then in the third frame, as you
might anticipate, there is Hugo being
mobbed by customers. His two friends,
representing the traditionalists in Filipino
society, are looking daggers at Hugo. For
them — not a sale!

This cartoon depicts the norms of buying and selling in the typical Philippine
street scene. Peddlers of a given item
tend to set up their stalls near each other,
with uniform quality and price. But we
must probe this situation more deeply.
What was your reaction, for example,
when you read the description of Hugo's
circumstances? The interpretation and
evaluation of the Americans seem to be
quite uniform. They praise Hugo for his
ingenuity, for his wisdom in seeing that
profit is a matter of volume, not simply
percentage of mark-up. They praise the
customers for their frugality. They remark about the dullness and stupidity,
the lack of resourcefulness of Hugo's
friends.

But how does the Filipino react to the
cartoon? It is in his reaction that some
of the basic differences between Filipino
and American attitudes begin to reveal
themselves. Showing the cartoon to Filipino friends over a period of several days,
I asked them to explain it to me, to
comment on it, to tell me how it made

them feel. The reaction was uniform, and
uniformly different from that of the
Americans. In every case Hugo turned
out to be the villain. His fellow vendors
were the victims of a despicable, shameless creature. Those who patronized such
a person were not much better. There
was only one way to correct such a situation: Hugo should put back his price
where it was.

One of my young Filipino friends,
when he was a boy living in a rural area,
sold religious medals and pictures with
a gang of kids his own age. They would
buy certain pictures for 15 centavos, and
it was customary by unwritten agreement
to sell them for 20 centavos. One day
my friend began to sell his for 25 centavos
and did a thriving business. His friends
became angry. He faced a crossroads:
profit or loss. He could continue to make
material profit only at the expense of
losing his friends. He was forced to
return his price to the norm. There was
no physical force, no verbal agreements;
there was simply an understanding. The
Tagalogs have a proverb which makes
the point crystal clear: *Ano ba ang
kuwarta? Madaling hanapin ang kuwarta.
Mahirap hanapin ang pakikisama* 'Money,
what's that? Money is easy to find, but
to find smooth interpersonal relations is
really difficult.'

What lies behind the very different
reactions to this cartoon? It is to be
found, of course, in the ways our respective cultures have shaped our thinking
and our attitudes. Filipinos living in the
lowland areas of the Philippines are said
to be driven by three principal values.[1]

---

[1] Fr. Frank J. Lynch, *Understanding the
Philippines and America: A Study of Cultural
Themes* (Ateneo de Manila: Institute of Phil-
ippine Culture, 1962).

Valued most highly is social acceptance. To be accepted by one's fellow men is the primary goal toward which the Filipino strives. Next, although subordinate, are the drives toward economic security and social mobility.

Getting back to the cartoon, the emotional ties between the vendors are stronger than the economic ties which bind buyer to seller. Hugo is without shame; he is more interested in himself, and in the money that he is making, than in his relationship with other vendors. His sense of economic security is strong enough to cause him to break the rules by which his behavior is socially acceptable. Furthermore, Hugo is ignoring traditional beliefs: success cannot be earned, good is limited.

Hugo has set his sights on becoming a success, he is plotting his way toward economic security, he is out to grab whatever good he can get. Behaving in this manner, he shocks his fellow men. They say: "Doesn't he know that success is deserved, not earned? Well, he'll have his day, but we'll have ours. Yeah, look what he's got, but he's just plain lucky. What's he done to deserve it? There's only so much good to go around, and he'll be making the gods angry by plotting to get more than his share. If he stores up that extra profit and doesn't share it, he might live to regret it. They'll get even with him." In this commentary a great tale is told: the profit-making motive is in open conflict with the traditional beliefs of the Filipino.

American Reaction

The American gropes for an explanation of this situation which he feels is most unusual. Coming from a land of gas wars, discount houses, and trading stamps, he is puzzled by this apparent lack of business sense. Tradesmen, shopkeepers, and vendors have little formal organization, yet there are unwritten agreements which control prices. The one who "bucks the system" is ostracized.

An American in Hugo's situation would decide whether or not he could make a profit on such-and-such a margin. If he fails, his fellow men will ridicule him. If he succeeds, he'll receive praise for careful management, shrewd investment, and willingness to take risks. But Hugo is ignored and condemned. His closest friends may attempt to reason with him. If they fail, for the sake of their own reputations they may have to abandon Hugo also. They will urge him to put back his price. They will try to convince him that he is making enough without trying for more.

The American believes that success comes through hard work and self-sacrifice. He believes that there is plenty of good around for anyone who just uses his capacities to find it. If he wants something worth while, he is willing to fight alone, even competing at great odds. He looks at the cartoon, and he either fails to see a problem in it, passes it off as irrelevant, or is further convinced concerning the woeful lack of ambition among Filipinos. Not until he sees and evaluates the Filipino's own reaction to it does he begin to see these practices in relation to the total, coherent system of beliefs and values. He must reckon with the fact that Hugo is not the hero of the traditional Filipino.

Still within the buying-selling matrix, but in a different set of circumstances, the American is often upset by the problem of making purchases. He hears about "fixed prices," "last prices," "first prices," and "first sales." He is badly confused by the whole business. He stops at a stall in the market to buy bananas. The vendor asks a certain price, and he pays it, but behind him comes a Filipino who inquires the price from the same vendor. It is thirty percent lower. They haggle, and the Filipino walks off with the same number of bananas at a fraction of the cost. "Don't they have any standards?" he mutters to himself, fully expecting that the law of supply and demand regulates costs and prices. He fails to see the social implications in bargaining routines. He simply wants the most for his money. He is uninterested in cultivating the friendship of the shopkeeper.

Among Filipinos there are important social considerations in bargaining. It is a means by which total strangers come to have a personal relationship with one another. Where there is a buying-selling situation which might conceivably be developed into a long-term relationship, bargaining serves as an ice-breaker. If the relationship continues and deepens, the vendor and the consumer may reach a *suki* relationship. At this point, without verbal agreement, the consumer informally reveals his intention to give his business to the vendor, and the vendor informally shows that the consumer will get the best price without the haggling preliminaries. They may never learn each other's names! But the consumer who is bold enough to ask for a *tawad* 'consideration,' and the vendor who has enough foresight and willingness to take a risk, pave the way to a deeper and deeper interdependence. The emotional factors serve to cement the economic ties.

It is no surprise to find that Filipinos do not like to bargain with Americans. They seem to know instinctively that the buying-selling contacts never develop along Filipino lines. The Filipino does not have enough interest in the American's problems to give him a good deal; he knows that the American has considerably more money in his pocket at any moment than 90 out of 100 Filipinos. The American needs no consideration. The vendor saves it for a Filipino, for he needs it, and he might return steady business for it. Bargaining between Filipinos and Americans does not produce emotional ties which would undergird the economic security of the vendor. Without such emotional ties, the Filipino, whether buyer or seller, sees little reason for bargaining.

How is the discussion so far related to the problems of church, plaza, and marketplace? A steadily growing number of missionaries join those who believe that culture is an integrated network of human behavior, an intertwining of religious, social, economic, political, and esthetic matters. They will attempt to connect up the economic factors which we have discussed with religious beliefs. For these readers, and for others who might need persuasion, let us go on to account for the Filipino's resistance to the missionary in terms of the relationship between economic and social influences on his religious beliefs.

Competition vs. Social Acceptance

The Western missionary brings with him certain attitudes which strongly support competition and profit. In his congregation he will capitalize on the competitive instinct. He will sponsor contests, give rewards, compile statistics, submit reports. He'll challenge a fellow pastor at the other end of the country to a race for new members. He is an expert at measuring his work in quantitative terms. He meets resistance on the mission field from the day of his arrival. Not in negativism, just in do-nothing-ism and care-nothing-ism. People just don't get enthusiastic about his ideas, plans, goals, and gimmicks. They're in favor of them, but very willing to accept the status quo if it can be done without hurting the missionary's feelings. The missionary can fight error, but he's helpless in the battle against apathy. He finds in the Filipino a master at the art of leveling out extremes in behavior.

The missionary counters this resistance in typical Western fashion. How else? He rewards activity and punishes everything else, and of course he uses typical forms of reward and punishment. In meting out this judgment, something which his own countrymen understand and encourage, he creates misunderstandings between Filipinos, alienating winners from the losers and everyone else. The winner may have won the missionary's contest, but he will not find satisfaction for long in it! He will give it up for his social acceptance. Of course, some indigent persons will often find social acceptance by the missionary as a functional substitute for the loss of status with their own people.

In this hypothetical situation are implied three common oversights. When one believes in competition and profit, it is natural to assume that everybody believes in it until one meets people who obviously do not. The first oversight is to overlook one's own beliefs, which may not even be recognized as beliefs! It may be these unformulated beliefs more than the theological formulations that set off the resistance of the national. The second oversight is to ignore the fact that beliefs can be taught without being learned. The missionary may simply be engaged in "belief-plating," laying his own beliefs over the top of those which pre-exist in the national. The third oversight is to assume a permanent acceptance of new beliefs from a premature manifestation of certain outward behavior, considered by the missionary to be a sign of belief. The national may have only learned to imitate the behavior which the missionary expects without sharing the belief which produces it. Beliefs don't come and go, but are tied up with every aspect of life.

What is offered, then, by way of an approach to the problem of beliefs? There are four stages in the solution. First of all, there must be a thorough-going attempt to analyze and understand the traditional beliefs of the national within the framework of his own culture. Then there must be comparison and contrast of these beliefs with those which the missionary intends to impart. This comparison and contrast will reveal hierarchies of difficulty, some sense of periphery and margin, some appraisal of familiarity or lack of it. In the third place, the results of this analysis must serve as a prelude to the discovery of an over-all approach to evangelism which will anticipate the nature and degree of disruption. It must also have durable qualities and be helpful in preparing the way for innovations. Finally, there is the implementation of the approach together with a thoughtful appraisal of success and failure, not to stimulate reprisals but to stimulate further refinement of the approach.

It is not surprising that the strength of Protestantism in the Philippines is found in a small, relatively powerless but rising middle class. These rebels against the traditions, who can afford to give up one kind of social acceptance for another, who have gained a measure of economic security, are most receptive to the beliefs of Protestant missionaries. They are the fighters, the Hugos. But while the missionaries rally a small army of middle-classers, they leave almost untouched the vast majority of Filipinos who cling tenaciously to traditional beliefs.

Independence vs. Economic Security

Consider, in the second place, the problems of the missionary's belief in a "personalized faith" as it is related to the Filipino's goal of economic security. The missionary calls upon the Filipino to make a clean break with the past, to stand on his own two feet, not to leave the question of his peace with God to be decided by another. His rugged, individualized gospel calls for a kind of independence which the Filipino has never exercised. In fact, there are strong sanctions against such individualized behavior. Such persons who break away are often considered ungrateful to the parents who have raised them, unmindful of friends who have helped them. The families and friends who are left do not understand why the allegiance to these new beliefs requires a person to ignore debts of gratitude, manifestations of reciprocal generosity. "Is God telling him to leave those who have raised him, and at the same time telling us that the family which prays together stays together?"

The missionary may assume that family structures in the Philippines exert the same kind of influences over the individual member as he experiences in his own family. However, let us consider Narcissa, who is the oldest and only girl of four children. During the war her father was killed by the Japanese. She and her three younger brothers worked long and hard to help their mother to make a living. For months they drifted from place to place, hiding in hills and caves, until they were finally rescued by American occupation troops. They started over again to build a new life.

After a time Narcissa married, and mother took the three brothers to another island to live with relatives. When Narcissa's first baby was due, she sent for her mother. After a time, mother returned to her home with the relatives. Back and forth for two more pregancies. Today Narcissa, her husband, and their three children live in Manila. Narcissa's mother is a regular member of the family, operating a small general store during the day. While the salary of Narcissa's husband goes entirely into the education of the three children, a costly thing in the Philippines, the income from the store supports the family.

But now the trouble starts! Narcissa's teen-age brother comes to live with them. He contributes nothing to the family treasury, getting his room and board free. He neither works nor studies. He plays and loafs. A few months ago Narcissa's mother-in-law informed them that she was coming to Manila with a twenty-year-old daughter and a twenty-year-old nephew to live with them. Today the daughter works regularly, and contributes not one cent to the family treasury; the nephew goes to school, rooms and boards with the family for nothing; the mother-in-law hangs around the house without contributing a cent to the maintenance of herself, her daughter, and her nephew.

They are completely dependent on the others.

This situation continues simply because Narcissa recognizes her duty as a daughter-in-law and a wife to care for the other three. The family structure is so stable and tenacious that things are arranged in such a way that ten people live on $150 per month, in a two-bedroom apartment. Some of the members are Roman Catholic, the rest are Protestant. There are three generations represented, and there are members of three different nuclear families living under one roof. Add all of this to the fact that one half of the group speaks one language, while the other half speaks a different one. A measure of bilingualism in Narcissa and her husband paves the way, rough as it is, for communication between the various members.

Consider the many pulls on Narcissa. How necessary she is to the security of the family. Consider what is involved in her making a complete break with the past. The Filipino lives close to the soil, much closer than any modern missionary has ever done. An extra pair of hands, an extra income in the family treasury, is vital to survival; it doesn't go into a savings account or stocks and bonds, it buys fish and rice. Few missionaries ever faced such a problem. Like a little bird, he was thrown out of the nest to peddle newspapers, to empty garbage, to sell magazines, all for the purpose of achieving some degree of independence by the time he was a teen-ager. Individualized behavior was the norm for him and he found great satisfaction in his independence, however small.

How he misunderstands the Filipino! He thinks he sees signs that the Filipino "is making a break," but then they disappear. There is a break, but it is only partial and not for long. The missionary demands a degree of separation that forces the Filipino to abandon his two most valuable treasures, social acceptance and economic security. Belonging to the missionary's congregation entails a further drain on his economic resources. How hard he finds it to contribute to the congregation, to the church, a rather impersonalized institution, when all through his life he has been taught to express his generosity to his own family, to those specific individuals who have reared him.

Nature of Resistance

Of course, the missionary's message poses no great threat to those Filipinos who are ready to abandon their traditions, either by virtue of new forms of social acceptance or greater economic security. For the masses, however, accepting the missionary's beliefs is seen as a threat to the mainstays of life. As long as the missionary lacks an understanding of the resistance of the Filipino, and fails to find adequate compensation for it, he excuses himself in various ways, continues to employ the same approach, or makes one experiment after another until he finds followers. Were he able to understand the nature of the resistance in relation to the totality of the Filipino's traditional beliefs, he might see the need for modifying his approach. He must view the national as he is prior to contact with the new beliefs. He must capitalize on already existing forces and patterns to accomplish his objectives most efficiently.

Hugo has the makings of a "believer." He has wandered far enough away from traditional beliefs to feel the need for replacing them with new ones. He has upended the traditional scale, putting more emphasis on his own economic security than on his social acceptance. He wants to move up the social ladder. He is surviving attempts by his fellow men to level out his extreme behavior. As his values are being reshaped, he is open to new ideas. The social equilibrium which once held him fast has been broken. He is ripe for contact with the missionary. But how about the vendors and the consumers? Suppose they are confronted with the same new ideas, while still tightly held by the forces from which Hugo is breaking away. They will react differently to the missionary's beliefs. Will he know this? Will he care? Will he compensate for it?

Whether the missionary likes it or not, believes it or not, the cohesive forces of culture make it impossible for nationals to accept his beliefs in a vacuum. The cross-cultural tensions, perhaps too long discounted in missions, or attributed to the national's "hardness of heart," must be understood today in a new relation. Beliefs do not exist in a vacuum; they are part and parcel of the total culture. At specific points of difference the missionary who wishes to impart features of his own culture to those of another may expect to encounter special difficulties. However, when he is able to anticipate the nature and extent of these problems, he is in an improved position, theoretically speaking, over the missionary who does not anticipate them; for it is he who will prepare "programed innovation," compensating for the difficulties by giving them special cross-cultural attention. This is the beginning — even the preliminary — to successful missionary activity.

The Westerner has been imitated around the world. In a ramshackle airline terminal on a lonely spot in Mindanao a two-year-old girl did the "twist" for us a few months ago. On a small island of Luzon there are less than two dozen automobiles, but there are metal signs advertising a world-famous soft drink on what seems to be every other stall in the market. The missionary achieves a great sense of importance as he sees himself imitated. Back in a remote corner of a cane field fifty people meet for a devotional service in a bamboo chapel. They read their mimeographed hymnals by the light of a single kerosene lamp. Regular as clockwork, they sing the first verse, the second verse, and the last verse of hymns. Why? The missionary comes from a background in which the middle verses of a hymn are usually neglected.

Nida[2] distinguishes three different aspects of religion: belief, practice, and ritual. Nationals may be quick to imitate ritual and practice. Note, for example, the form of church bulletins, the orders of worship, the worn pages in Bibles and hymnals, the methods of receiving offerings, taking in new members, getting rid of old ones. The missionary may be just as quick to interpret this imitation as the real thing, a sign of successful work. Belief, however, cannot be imitated; it is only shared. The recitations of creeds, or of passages from the Bible, are rituals which may not necessarily point to the beliefs of the participant. The missionary who wishes to share his beliefs may have to work without Western types of evidence of success for a long time. It is only in his understanding of the national's beliefs, and how they are interwoven in all of life, that he can hope to find the way to share his own with them.

[2] Eugene A. Nida, *Message and Mission* (New York: Harper and Bros., 1960).

Harriet R. Reynolds

The Filipino Family
in its Cultural Setting

There is no unit of social structure more important in determining behavior, outlook, values, and the general tone of life in a society than the family, however that is defined in the particular case. Family structure is a stable part of society, but it can and does change. With these changes may come modern values of individual freedom, privacy, elevation of the status of women and of youth, but the losses may be as great or greater. Gone may be the security of belonging to an established, closely knit group, the understanding of one's place and role in society, sanctions for morality, and religious roots. In this paper the author outlines some of the patterns of family structure which are nearly universal in the Philippines, and pictures some of the changes taking place with their implications for the church.

SINCE World War II Roman Catholic and Protestant churches in the Philippines have had a growing interest and concern in working with and through the family. They have recognized it as the basic structural unit and the most powerful institution in Filipino society. However, the family has usually been defined in terms of the American background of the missionaries, the strongly Spanish-influenced family of the city-reared leaders, or the present-day family of the barrio people. Very often ideals have been proposed and goals set with reference to the present and the hoped-for future. The past, especially the distant past, has had little or no consideration.

During the same years, there has been an increasing awareness of the need for all of those who are associated with social institutions, including religious organizations, to understand more of the background and the development of the cultural milieu, and to become aware of the social processes affecting groups and individuals of that society.[1]

Harriet R. Reynolds is a missionary of the United Church of Christ in the Philippines, and has been in Vigan, Ilocos Sur, since 1952. She and her husband are also working on research and writing their Ph.D. thesis on the Chinese in the Ilocos Provinces.

[1] Indicative of this interest has been the holding of a Religious Acculturation Conference for three days each Christmas vacation from 1957 to 1961. Participants have included missionaries and others from Roman Catholic, Anglican, and Evangelical churches. Filipino family life has also been studied by the East Asia Christian Family Life Seminar-Conference, Manila, the Christian Family Life Workshop of the Philippines with headquarters at 1743 Taft Avenue, Manila, the Christian Family Movement of the Roman Catholic Church, and in the Institutes sponsored by the various Protestant churches with the help of the Department of Home and Family Life of the Philippine Federation of Christian Churches.

This paper is an attempt to recognize both the importance of the family approach of the church and the need for greater understanding of how the Filipino family operates. It will try to do two things: (1) use a depth perspective in a brief analysis of the Filipino kinship system with comments on the developments that have been and are taking place, and (2) indicate some points at which church leaders can find opportunities for promoting Christian growth of individuals and churches through families, and openings for Christian service with and to members of families.

With more than 150 language and dialect groups,[2] such varied cultural types as pagan, Moslem, and Christian, and such extremes of setting as isolated mountain valleys and a great population center like Manila, can we say there is a Filipino family, or are there only Filipino families?

Anthropologists generally agree that there is a family structure which may be designated as Filipino which is found throughout the archipelago.[3] Fox says, "There are many fundamental similarities in the social organization of the eight major Christian groups," which, he goes on to explain, make up more than 90 per cent of the total Philippine population.[4] Research by others on the mountain peoples, including that of the research team in Apayao during April and May 1961, of which the writer was privileged to be a member, show that in these minority groups, basic structure and main details of social usages may also be included in the generalization.[5]

The fundamental characteristics of the Filipino family can be traced back to pre-Spanish times. Historical developments, population movements, invasion, and colonization have brought modifications and elaborations, but these have not erased the early structural form. The Spanish-type, American-type, and Oriental-type Filipino families that exist today are sub-familial types in which the general framework is still evident to a greater or lesser degree.

Probably in the remote mountain regions, where the Spaniards were not able to impose their rule and the Americans entered comparatively recently, the form most like that of the earliest Filipino family is found today. It has not yet been possible to determine which Filipino group is nearest the early pattern for it is certain that all have undergone some significant changes.

Characteristics of the Filipino Family

The Filipino family is a part of the Indo-Malayan cultural area, but it must be remembered that it is not the only family type found in the Malayan region of Southeast Asia. As in all known ancient and modern societies, Philippine societies have *nuclear family units* (also called primary families or elementary

[2] Harold C. Conklin, "Outline Gazetteer of Native Philippine Ethnic and Linguistic Groups" (Chicago: Philippine Studies Program, 1952), p. 13.

[3] Cf. A. L. Kroeber, "Kinship in the Philippines," *Anthropological Papers of the Museum of Natural History*, Vol. XIX, Part III, 1919, pp. 69-84; Fred Eggan, "Social Structure of the Sagada Igorots" in *Social Structure in Southeast Asia*, edited by George P. Murdock (London: 1961).

[4] Robert Fox, "The Filipino Family in Perspective" in *Saturday Parade Magazine of The Evening News* (Manila: Oct. 15, 1960).

[5] See writings by R. F. Barton, Otley H. Beyer, Fay Cooper-Cole, Fred Eggan, Robert Fox, E. A. Jenks, Felix Kessing, and others.

families) each of which has a certain degree of autonomy. These are composed of father, mother, and unmarried children (the Civil Code speaks of "unemancipated children").[6] However, in the Philippines, the autonomy of nuclear units is limited as regards residence, authority, and obligation, for they are usually closely linked to the larger family.

This linkage occurs within the traditional *bilocal extended family* "which unites the nuclear family of a married couple with those of some but not all of their sons, [and/or] of some but not all of their daughters, and of some but not all of their grandchildren of either sex."[7] (In other words, a group consisting of more than one nuclear family in various combinations.) In the past not all families had two complete nuclear units in the same household, nor was this either the group "ideal" or the actual practice among all the peoples, but the pattern of one or more married children living with or near the home of either or both of the sets of parents has been sufficiently accepted and followed to be characteristic.

Since residence practices are the first family pattern to show change and lead to further change, this form, which allows for a considerable degree of flexibility, is important. When couples marry, it has been usual for them to live in or near the home of the man's parents. But there are many cases when, because of the preeminence of the bride's family, the failure of the husband to complete the dowry payments and the consequent work obligation to the wife's family, or other reasons, the two go to live in the

place of the wife's family. In the past, relatively few nuclear families lived neolocally (in a separate home located away from the family of either the husband or the wife).

At the present time a young couple may live with the husband's or wife's parents for a year or several years, then move to their own home, usually, but not always, near one of the parental homes. Even when they live separately, a nuclear family will frequently have one, two, or several relatives living in the household either permanently or for shorter periods.

Under the impact of professional ambition, educational opportunity, high cost of living, and the developing cash economy, the number of neolocal family residence units is increasing. This is bringing problems such as emotional conflicts between generations over location, difficulties in caring for the children and for meeting the needs of other dependents, and strains in fulfilling the customary family obligations in support and hospitality. It, of course, also brings opportunities such as encouragement to individual initiative and advancement, mobility in terms of location and type of vocation, acceptance of new patterns of family living and child care, simpler entertaining, and less complex family living arrangements, with more privacy.

The Filipino family is *bilateral* in that children are related equally to members of their father's and their mother's families. The active kinship group is known as *personal kindred*. Here, also, flexibility is possible, and an individual may be closer to one set of relatives than to the other due to proximity, prestige-rating, or compatibility. The family is bilineal, for it traces descent and passes on inheritance through the line of both the father and

6 *Civil Code of the Philippines* (Bureau of of Printing, Philippines, 1957), p. 67.

7 George P. Murdock, *Social Structure* (New York: MacMillan, 1949), p. 35.

the mother. Because the kinship group increases in number very rapidly and becomes cumbersome, relation depth and obligation is usually considered only as far as third cousins (descendants of the great-great-grandparents), with a practical range of only four or five generations. However, the Ifugao and some other groups are genealogical experts and trace their ancestry back many generations. On the other hand, many Isnegs could not tell the names of all four grandparents. The behavior of individuals within the kinship system is clearly defined as to generation, relative age, and degree of collaterality (distance of relationship), and the practices regarding reciprocal duties and privileges are carefully followed.

Authority has been centered in the parents who have traditionally had complete control over their unmarried children. The father is recognized as the head of the family, but the mother shares responsibility, is usually consulted about family matters, and may own property. Generation and relative age affect the general authority structure, to the extent of there being a provision in the Civil Code, "Grandparents shall be consulted by all members of the family on all important family questions."[8] Children are expected to be respectful and obedient in all instances to those older than themselves, especially to parents, and in cases when one or the other must give way, the welfare of the parents is to be placed before that of the children.

Most of the language groups have kinship terminologies which provide descriptive terms for each relationship with the same term being used for the corresponding member of both parents' fami-

lies. But, in usage, the terms for father and mother and for the grandparents are often applied to their siblings as well, and possibly as terms of respect to other elderly people. Sibling terms may be extended to cousins. The degree distinctions of these relationships are noted in behavior — the merging of terms seems more related to respect and emotional closeness than to an identity of expected behavior.

When an individual marries, his spouse and the parents and siblings of the spouse become a part of his kinship group. Thus, there is a strong, closely interwoven complex of relationships which binds together fairly large and sometimes widely distributed groups on the basis of kinship, but there is no evidence of clans now or at any time in the past. The traditional unit of identification other than the family has been the village, which varies in complexity of social organization among the various language groups. Even if some of the family lives in another location for many years, the family village is still considered "home."[9]

Courtship and Marriage

The Philippines has courtship and marriage patterns which traditionally and at present are quite varied. Traditionally the attitudes toward premarital contact of young men and women have been relatively permissive, but this changed under Spanish influence. Invariably, sanctions have been more restrictive for the

---

[8] Op. cit., p. 66.

[9] Mr. Corpuz, a retired municipal treasury employee, who has raised fifteen children in the larger town, still considers his "home" as the small municipality of San Isidro, ten kilometers away. In the last election, he was chosen municipal councilor of San Isidro. Many Manila residents consider "home" to be a provincial barrio.

female than for the male, but generally less rigid than in many societies. These do not so much reflect moral judgment as the fact that in some groups virginity calls for a higher dowry to be given for the girl. In most groups there is some kind of dowry given by the man's family to that of the girl. This may be Chinese jars and beads in the mountain areas, or land, animals, money, clothing, or other property in either highland or lowland areas. Sometimes in the lowlands professional success and a lavish wedding paid for by the groom's family suffices, but in other cases those who have been educated are expected to pay a higher dowry price.

There are groups, however, which place highest value on the assurance that children will be produced. Among these, marriage may not be negotiated in some cases until impregnation has occurred. Exceptions are often made in marriages for the wealthier girls, for whom parents almost always arrange a marriage which will serve to keep property and other wealth under family control. In the Philippines as a whole, arranged marriages (sometimes in infancy or before, sometimes during adolescence or even for older unmarried individuals) have been common, and various uses made of go-betweens, usually members of the family. Marriage has been considered to be a contact between families rather than an agreement between two individuals. However, young people themselves have often had a good deal to say about the selection of a mate. Where the parents have not been willing to heed the desires of their children, elopement has often occurred. In most cases parental forgiveness follows, if not immediately, after dowry payments or after the birth of the first child.

In cases of premarital pregnancy, social pressure is applied to force marriage. If the young man is not willing to marry the girl, his family is expected to pay a heavy fine. Formerly such matters were readily handled by family groups; now because young people have wider contacts and family authority is less absolute, new tensions and problems are arising in such situations.

Among lowland groups, the veneer of Spanish culture and the strong influence of the Roman Catholic Church have produced a rigid chaperonage of unmarried girls. So strong has it been that a girl who is inadvertently or intentionally placed in the company of a man unchaperoned is expected to be compromised, and the opportunity for seduction may be made as strong a basis for demanding marriage as pregnancy itself would be.[10] At present a good deal is said about girls being expected to remain virgins, but in families closely related to the Church, and even among young people who have entered Church vocations, premarital pregnancy often occurs. While it is not "socially approved," when it occurs there usually seems to be no lasting stigma.[11]

Girls in areas not so penetrated by

---

[10] In the neighborhood of our home in the Ilocos region, a neighbor lad had taken his girl friend to the movies. When he took her home, her mother said: "She cannot return here after being out at night with you. Take her to your house." He did this. He explained that they could not be married until the next year, for one of the girl's sisters had been married in the current year. One January morning before we had risen, he knocked at our door to invite us to his wedding breakfast — right away. The couple had just been married by the local priest.

[11] Sometimes members of the family of a young man will encourage relations before marriage to make sure that the girl will marry into their family.

Spanish culture, are not considered so helpless that they cannot defend their honor if they wish, and they are not expected to become pregnant until they are ready to be married.

It can be easily seen that both the traditional and the Spanish-era patterns have laid a foundation for frustrations and problems as the Church has tried to insist on sexual relations within the marriage relationship only. The situation has been intensified by the introduction of coeducation, close association in many vocational and recreational activities, and the emphasis on romantic love in modern magazines and movies.

Traditionally the Filipino family practiced both monogamy and polygyny. Monogamy is now the national legal form, and, so far as is known, has been the form practiced by the majority of families throughout history. There are fairly numerous instances of polygyny as approved practice in some minority groups now, and concubinage, known in the Philippines as "the querida system," and extra-legal marriage in a common-law arrangement seem to be increasing. The fact that divorce is not legal, and legal separation is given only for adultery and attempted murder, does not mean that there are no family problems such as lead to divorce in other countries and have made divorce rather common and relatively easy in areas in the Philippines not strongly influenced by the Roman Catholic Church. The Civil Code, which prohibits divorce, has given special consideration to provision for children born out of wedlock. A question may be raised as to the wisdom of enacting rigid laws which express an imposed ideal, such as do the parts of the Civil Code dealing with the family, then having to balance the strictness of one statute by laxness of another as a stop-gap measure. Church people might well promote serious discussion of national laws regarding the family and exert influence toward having them brought into line with social needs.

Ceremonial Kinship

The Filipinos have a strong and impressive *compadre* system based on ceremonial relationships which developed within the Roman Catholic Church. These were intended to be mainly spiritual, but since they imply social privilege and obligations similar to some of those of relatives, they have become a ritual co-parenthood which brings into use many kinship concepts and terms. As a part of the social system, the ceremonial kinship has come to include many of the other aspects of society which among other peoples would be dealt with through less personal, associational relationships, an approach which is still unfamiliar to and uncomfortable for many Filipinos.

Originally the Roman Catholic Church provided for godparents at baptism, a sponsor at confirmation, and legal witnesses at marriage. Even with these, the ritual kinship ties of a family with several children sometimes extended to most of the village. However, now the breadth of the system is tremendous. The writer was one of forty sponsors at a wedding recently. The mayor of a provincial capital town invited more than two hundred to be sponsors at the baptism of his infant son. Asking persons of property, prestige, and influence to serve as godparents or sponsors has become a means of social climbing, securing or repaying votes or political patronage, and of "sharing the wealth" of those who will give gifts or contribute toward an elaborate feast. Many Protestant families have adopted

the customs of inviting sponsors and recognizing ceremonial relationships.

Ceremonial kinship is now an integral
part of the Filipino family which has its
roots in the fairly recent rather than in the
distant past. Its connection with social
obligation, hospitality, and the prestige
structure lends importance to its inclusion
in consideration of matters relating to
the family.

The Filipino Family and the Social System

Under the traditional social organization, the community was relatively
homogeneous, isolated, and family-centered. This type sociologists have called the
gemienschaft (or, in Tagalog, *damay*),
characterized by face-to-face relationships
and the direct, personal kind of contacts
between its members.[12] This is in contrast
to *gesellschaft* with its organized, impersonal relations which is developing at
the present time. All institutions were in
the past an extension of kinship relations
or their counterpart. If an actual kinsman
was not the employer or head of the
household in which work was done, then
some form of the feudal lord-serf or
landlord-sharecropper or master-servant
arrangement was followed. The spirit of
paternalism became characteristic, not only
of the family, but of the Church, the
private school, the economic system, and
the functioning units of government. The
"father" figure (who might really be the
mother or the mother and father) headed
the sub-system; others were responsible
to him as authority, owed respect, gifts,
share of crop or wage income, and subli-

mated their interests to his. In turn, he
"cared" for them, and they acquired
status because they were within his kinship, compadre, or other influence group.

The economic system has depended very
heavily on the family. In the barrios it
is the main productive unit; in business
concerns, factories, companies, and even
in private schools, there is usually a family
hierarchy in control. One of the very
real problems in securing the efficiency
and degree of service necessary for financial success in some Filipino businesses
has been the conflict of these standards
and their enforcement with kinship obligations. Families exert pressure on churches in the matter of the selection of a
pastor or deaconess, or refuse to let a
Christian leader be assigned to another
locality if he still has dowry obligations to
fulfill. The vocation of a young person
has been chosen not so much on the basis
of his interests and abilities as by the
criteria of what the family wants and
expects him to do to bring honor and
financial gain to them. Most Christian
families want one child to become a
priest or a pastor; one or more is expected to stay at home, possibly forgoing
educational advantages, to remain with
the parents. If one is in a position to
employ others, his first obligation has been
to hire members of his own family.

Who is to be the leader in social or
political enterprises has been largely
decided by family factors: wealth, size
of family, and prestige of the kinship
group. In the field of government the
concept of democratic precedure based on
equality of opportunity and responsibility
for those of equal ability has not been
in keeping with the stratification growing
out of strong family patterns based on

---

[12] Chester L. Hunt, Richard W. Coller, So-
corro C. Espiritu, John I. de Young, Severine
F. Corpus, *Sociology in the Philippine Setting*
(Manila: 1954), chapter 4.

generation, age, and reciprocal obligation.[13]

Religiously, the family has had a central place, and, as is characteristic, kinship forms and religious beliefs and practices are generally resistant to social change. Those interested in change will be wise to study carefully the relationship of family patterns and religious beliefs and practices of both the past and present. In the Roman Catholic families the ceremonials have been family-centered, the home had a shrine, the role of the Church in the life cycle events of baptism of children, marriage, and death were rigidly prescribed and fitted into the family schedule along with other feast and fast days. The Church tended to support rather than challenge the authoritarian role of the older members of the family on the one hand, and, on the other hand, often ignored the areas where tensions were apt to develop, so long as one influential member, often the mother, saw that religious forms were carried out, and Church obligations met. Fox speaks of the typical Filipino family as folk-Catholic.[14] The same term has been used in Central and South America to imply that the present religious beliefs have been added to, imposed upon, and mixed with the traditional and largely family-centered beliefs and practices of pre-Christian origin. Instead of being a faith that replaces the previous religion in beliefs, concepts, and loyalties, it has accommodated itself to it, and the people have tried to make place for two sets of patterns that are somewhat in conflict in principle.

We can see that Protestantism has also done a certain amount of accommodating. Instead of a "new birth" with its new spirit and fresh commitment we find that sometimes pagan fears and superstitions have remained, and on top has been brushed a thin coating of superficial Christian beliefs and ceremonials to produce a folk-Protestantism.

At the present time among both Roman Catholics and Protestants some are trying to find means of correcting this situation. Also, there are very commendable efforts being made to express the essence of the Christian faith in ideas, liturgical music, family festivals, buildings, and other forms which are truly Filipino and lend themselves to Christian use.

A Society in Transition

This is a time of transition from a largely rural society to a more urbanized social system in the Philippines. It is a time of movement with a great deal of instability of individuals and within society in general. Urban standards and ideas are increasing, but the vast majority of Filipinos are still rural in locale and in orientation. More than 75 per cent of the people still live in the rural areas, and the city population includes many typically rural families and individuals. The young people and adults who go back to their rural localities after education in the cities, and those who hope to act as innovators in their capacities as teachers, pastors, rural extension leaders, and community development workers, find in most cases a resistant rather than a receptive response when they attempt to introduce change, and are often frustrated. Those in the city doing social work, and in politics, education, and religious

---

[13] Mary R. Hollnsteiner, "Reciprocity in the Lowland Philippines" (Ateneo de Manila University, Quezon City, 1961).

[14] Robert B. Fox, "The Filipino Family in Perspective" in *Saturday Parade Magazine* of *The Evening News* (Manila: Oct. 15, 1960).

vocations find that many of the people with whom they work are confused, bewildered, and bitter about the conditions of city life. A good many newcomers to the urban areas have changed their addresses but not their mental and social orientation.

A transitional society is often plagued by a condition which has been spoken of as "normlessness," but is really a confusion of norms which causes the society and the individual to vacillate between more than one set of goals and standards.[15] This seems to be the condition of the Philippines now. A few random questions will illustrate the difficulty of making some decisions. When one is asked about a matter does he answer according to the bare facts of the case, what he thinks the questioner wants to hear, or in a way to show the person or persons about whom he is speaking in the very best light as he sees it? If one signs a contract or makes a verbal agreement, does he expect to adhere to it, or is it to be automatically canceled if his father becomes ill or a compadre needs his help to complete some job within a certain time limit? If a family cannot give a big marriage celebration without going into debt, will it borrow money to meet the necessary social obligations for such a wedding, will the couple delay the marriage, or will they slip away and be quietly married with a minimum of expense?[16]

[15] Ruben Santos-Cuyugan, "Social-Cultural Change and the Filipino Family" in *Science Review* (Manila: March 1961).

[16] In the latter case the couple might be as resourceful as one reporting in a conference discussion: "We planned a traditional wedding and feast, but set the date in the rainy season. We invited all our relatives and others to whom we were obligated, but we were pretty sure the weather would cooperate to keep the

In many of these and other situations we can see that there is no completely right or wrong choice. There may be a traditional Filipino way, or there may be one that is typically American. Which is "Christian"? The need of the times seems to be for the people concerned to think and to help each other think through the best possible alternatives for the present time, which will in many cases be something new, a fresh solution for a new problem situation. In searching for new answers let us not forget that some of these may arise out of some of the Filipino heritage of the past. Among some sub-groups such as the Tingguian and the Isneg, one finds democratic procedures which the nation as a whole could adopt with profit. In the basic culture and at the present time women have been given some share in the authority structure and opportunities that have prepared them to assume a more responsible place in making new adjustments than can be done readily in some other societies. The Filipino kinship system is comparatively flexible in structure and behavior patterns and of a type more amenable to change than are some others, and the absence of a firmly entrenched and uniform hereditary class system reaching back into antiquity leaves the whole social system more open to change.

Changes and Some Effects on the Family

The changes most affecting the family may be summarized as follows: (1) There is increased mobility and productiveness with the development of a higher standard of living for more of the population. (2) From the ascribed status of Spanish times and the present, movement is toward

crowd to be fed sufficiently small to fit what we could afford."

more democratic society with greater recognition of individual ability and achievement within the social framework. (3) individuals and couples and the nuclear families are having more participation in making choices and carrying responsibility within the family. (4) The family now shares many of its functions with other institutions so that it has a more specialized function, and there is growing emphasis on associational rather than family-dominated relationships.

In the society as a whole there is movement toward differentiation and specialization in contrast to the relative simplicity of organization and the wide use of unskilled labor in the earlier times. This has brought tensions within the family as old patterns are no longer applicable or are challenged, and new techniques have not been fully developed.

One of the most difficult steps in meeting the new day is to encourage family members themselves to accept the fact of change. It is not a matter of choice as to many who cling to old customs and traditions with blind tenacity seem to think. The war, the influence of other countries, the coming of opportunity for more democratic government have all played their parts, but they have been factors in an on-going process which is present in all dynamic groups. The Philippines has been moving as have Europe, the United States, and Japan, and as all of Southeast Asia must move. When societies open their doors to other influences, when families give up their self-sufficiency and isolation, the coming of other changes is inevitable. The question to be asked today is: "How can we understand and use the changes for the satisfaction and happiness of members of the society; and how, to some extent at least, can we help to direct change?"

There have been both gains and losses for the family and its members. The family now, particularly in urban areas, usually cannot provide the individual his job, protect him from outside pressures, support him at all costs in political matters, and propel him into a more or less established set of religious patterns as it did in the past. On the other hand, the family has great significance as the basic institution which brings him into being, cares for him, gives him a personality as an individual, and socializes him so he may be able to adjust to his larger society. The home continues to serve as the center for emotional satisfaction, moral guidance, and psychological security. Instead of being the center of a tightly interlocking network of relationships as it has been traditionally, it is now becoming the balance mechanism which should serve to bring equilibrium in the whole social organization and help individuals absorb the stresses and strains produced in the less personalized parts of everyday living.

Psychologist Mrs. Estefania Aldaba-Lim speaks of the changes taking place from a more personal point of view:

The younger generation, especially in the urban communities, is eager for change — sometimes at great sacrifice to the family. Where this desire conflicts with the still-tradition-bound and authoritarian-structured Filipino family, mental stress, irresponsibility amounting even to delinquency, and insecurity on the part of both the older and younger generation, results.

She continues, regarding the handling of this situation:

Our concern, therefore, is how to prepare parents and children to live in a changing community without disturbing their integrity and mercilessly leaving them prey to the hazards of change.... It has been demonstrated that change is safest when people choose progress them-selves and when they move together — grandparents, parents, children — as a total community into the new way of life.[17]

The changes within the family cannot be judged just as good or bad in them-selves, but must be considered as they conflict or harmonize with the rest of the social structure. Under any social system, kinship is one aspect only; it is integrated, for better or for worse, with all other parts. It will do no good to look at the changes in the family only and try to deal with them in iso-lation, although it is necessary to note and try to analyze them. There must be an attempt to try to understand the place of each change in its relation to the whole social system. In this way it is possible to evaluate the way in which the family is or should be changing to maintain its own place and contribute to the well-being of its members in the whole Filipino society and culture.

The Churches and the Family

This brief and incomplete review of the traditional Filipino family and the changes that have occurred and are in the process of taking place seems to point to four definite matters about which churches and church leaders may well be concerned:

1. The Filipino family needs help in re-orienting its value system to meet the more complex social situation. The churches should be well-grounded in

[17] Estefania Aldaba-Lim, "Cultural Change and the Filipino Family" in *Saturday Parade Magazine* of *The Evening News* (Manila: Oct. 15, 1960). She refers especially to planned rapid change described in the books by Marga-ret Mead, *Coming of Age in Samoa* (1928) and *New Lives for Old* (1956).

theology and Christian ethics and be able to interpret these to their members and prospective members in terms of God-man and man-man relationships, so that families can find in the church resources for selecting and implementing values and norms for setting their own standards and patterning behavior. They also need the strength that comes from belief in God as well as through worship and fellowship in the Christian community

2. The family is still a dominant factor in the orientation of Filipino society. The churches, to do effective work, should recognize this and work with the home in a manner befitting its importance. The churches, in spite of lip-service to the place of the family in society, have placed main emphasis on individual initiative and most of their evangelistic work has been aimed either at individuals or at masses of people. Their educational work has taken people out of the family into compounds, schools, and dormitories rather than making first emphasis on education within the family where all members can participate and the family be encouraged to make changes together (This is not a call to abandon the indi-vidual and mass approaches, but to realize the need to undergird them with programs in the home and for the family in the churches, to bring commitment and build character.) Christian families can help through efforts to enlist parents in the Christian education of their children, and by finding ways by which both family and church can more effectively guide young people in selecting their partners, planning their marriages, and setting up their homes.

3. The churches should go forward in the processes of analysis and planning The leaders should keep abreast of social change — if possible, move ahead of it —

o that families may be given guidance
o strengthen their homes, and the indi-
idual members helped to enable them to
1eet the points of strain and tension
vhich they face. Also, there should be
·rovision within the "family of Chris-
ians" for purposeful development of
acilities for giving aid in ministering to
pecial needs and in helping to solve
roblems. The churches should also en-
ourage their members to understand and
se the facilities provided through psy-
hology, sociology, anthropology, and
xial work.

4. Churches and church leaders can
xtend their efforts to encourage and,
vhere possible, participate in study proj-
cts which will gather information, de-
elop techniques, train leaders, and
romote evaluation relative to matters
nportant to family and church.[18]

"We Ifugao must do what our ancestors have told us," is the expression which
one tribal group has used "since time
immemorial" to determine right or wrong,
good or bad, obligatory and essential —
"the hundred-handed norm which is
invested with unchallenged power and
authority."[19] Today, the Filipino should
surely get acquainted with all that his
ancestors have to teach him about the
family. He should then be alert to
the scientific information and techniques
which present-day experience in the Philippines and resources from other countries
have to offer him. Then, in the light of
the value system which the church should
help to formulate, rapid social change
can be dealt with in ways to secure the
greatest possible amount of successful
adjustment and satisfaction, with the least
possible disruption and strain for families
and their members.

[18] Two examples of such studies are: (1)
he work of a sub-committee of the Faith
1d Order Committee of the Department of
hristian Education of the United Church
f Christ in the Philippines, on "Problems
f Christian Marriage as Related to Church
Iembership and Leadership," which involves
se studies and analysis, and theological inter-
retation in the light of the Filipino cultural
tting. The final report is to be given to
lministrators of churches and conferences for
e in guiding decisions regarding practical

field problems. (2) Three missionary couples
of the United Church were granted two
months' time from regular assignment to become members of a team of eight which has
done research and writing on cultural change
among the Isneg in Apayao, Mountain Province, Philippines.

[19] Francis Lambrecht, in *Proceedings of the
Religious Acculturation Conference* (Baguio:
1961).

Eugene A. Nida

The Relationship of Social Structure to the Problems of Evangelism in Latin America

For many years those concerned with the problems of evangelism in Latin America have been keenly aware of some of the significant correlations between differences of social structure and the response of the people to the gospel. For one thing, relatively few people from the upper classes and not too many from the middle class ever become associated with evangelical churches. This has meant that the membership of most of the Protestant churches has come from the upper brackets of the lower class. The leadership within the churches has seemed to come primarily from the families of independent tradesmen and merchants, e.g. carpenters, shoemakers, blacksmiths, and shopkeepers. It would appear as though the gospel had an attraction for just those groups which had much to gain, e.g. education for their children, a sense of importance (as co-laborers with God in the Kingdom of Heaven), and recompense for having been so largely excluded from the upper brackets of Latin American society. Conversely, these same people had very little to lose by becoming Protestants, for they were not so likely to lose their jobs, were not dependent upon some one person for their social and economic security (as in the case of the day

laborer or peon), and had never been cultivated to any great extent by the Roman church, which has concentrated most of its attention upon the elite classes.

The phenomenal growth of the Pentecostal movement among the people of Latin America has also served to highlight the relationship of social classes to the communication of the gospel, for not only is the Pentecostal movement as large as all the other denominations put together but it has had success not only among the lower classes, from which its membership is largely drawn, but also among some of the upper classes.

Furthermore, missionaries have been quick to note that it is ever so much easier to begin work in new towns or recently built communities than in areas where people have lived for a long time. All of these facts have served to focus our attention upon the possibilities of understanding more adequately some of the fundamental problems of social structure in Latin America and their bearing upon the task of evangelism.

Acute Problems in Evangelism

On almost every hand the average missionary faces certain acute problems in evangelism, and a number of these seem to be directly related to factors in social structure. For example, not infrequently

Reprinted from Vol. 5, No. 3 (1958), pp. 101-123.

there are churches which have flourished and grown for a period of five to ten years, only to be followed by twenty years of almost complete stagnation. Such churches seem to have reached a particular group within a community, and then to have stopped growing. In some instances, a few persons are won to the gospel in the initial attempts to start a new church, but their very presence within the church seems to prevent the entrance of others. In other churches the social standing of the members rises rapidly through improved education, greater ambition, and the indirect results of a higher sense of responsibility — characteristics which lead to greater financial rewards. However, the tendency is for such churches to lose touch with the very classes from which most of the members originally came.

A particularly difficult problem exists in Protestant churches in which there is a class cleavage within the church. In one church in Cuba there is a morning congregation composed primarily of upper middle class young people, many of whom have a university education. The evening congregation consists of older people from the lower middle class and upper lower class. The rivalry between such groups in all phases of the church life is pathetic, for it hampers the potential ministry of such a group and serves to rob the people of a true sense of fellowship.

The differences of response between people in small rural communities and those in the cities has always called for certain adaptations in missionary approach but the basic problems become increasingly more acute as churches in the urban centers assume responsibility for work in rural areas. So often they fail completely to establish a really vital work in which the rural people feel anything more than a

kind of "poor country cousin" relationship to the city congregation. This distinction of class levels becomes even more difficult in a divided society, that is to say, one made up of a Spanish and Indian constituency. The Indians are usually left out, not because of any desire on the part of the Spanish-speaking people to thrust them aside, but simply because they do not understand the means by which they may effectively develop and promote a vigorous Indian constituency.

The Role of Schools

In the early years of Protestant missionary work in Latin America the establishment of schools, both primary and secondary, was supposed to be a major factor in overcoming certain of the major difficulties inherent in the social structure of Latin America as it was related to the development of the Evangelical church. These schools were not only supposed to educate the children of Evangelicals, but were calculated to create among the non-Evangelicals a favorable attitude toward the Evangelical cause. Some schools have largely fulfilled this purpose, but a number have singularly failed. By an essentially secular viewpoint these schools have educated certain people away from the Evangelical community, and have often failed to bring into the Evangelical group those from the outside who might have special talents or abilities. The so-called neutralist view of many so-called Evangelical schools is well illustrated by the recent boast of a principal of one of the largest mission schools of Latin America, who insisted that during the last eleven years of the school's existence not one student had been converted.

In view of the numerous problems posed by various factors in the social structure of Latin society, we cannot help but ask ourselves such questions as, What is the basic class structure of these societies? What explains the acceptance of the gospel by one group and not by others? What are the forces and techniques of social change? How do people change their class status within Latin American society? What bearing has the proclamation of the gospel on such changes? What should be our basic strategy in approaching Latin society?

The Structure of Latin American Society

The structure of society in Latin America is highly complex and differs considerably from area to area. However, despite the possibility of a certain amount of error resulting from oversimplification, we can describe certain essential characteristics of Latin American society by means of a type of inverted diamond diagram:[1]

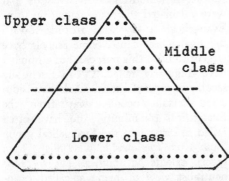

Figure A

Figure A symbolizes what are probably the major characteristics of most societies in Latin America, in which the narrow point represents the elite, the central

portion the middle class, and the base portion the lower class. The upper class is divisible generally into two classes of elite: (1) the old families, representing the traditional aristocracy, and (2) the *nouveaux riches,* who have only recently acquired wealth and prestige. Some very rich people in the lower upper class may be accepted into the upper upper class, if they have some special influence or political power, but in general the two layers of elite are rather well defined.

The middle class is similarly divided between (1) the upper middle class, consisting of successful but not so wealthy professionals such as doctors, lawyers, professors, politicians, engineers, and businessmen, and (2) the lower middle class, consisting of the white-collared workers, e.g. clerks, bookkeepers, small businessmen, schoolteachers, and preachers.

The lower class is divided between (1) the upper lower class, made up of less prosperous tradesmen, factory workers, independent small farmers, domestic workers, and day laborers, and (2) the lower lower class, consisting of the extremely poor seasonal workers, indigent sharecroppers, and the habitually unemployed.

We must not assume that diagram A reflects accurately the actual proportion of the respective population, for the relative size of the various classes differs greatly in the various countries. We do not have the necessary statistics in order to produce a thoroughly accurate picture of the various societies, but we can approximate something of the diversity in types in the diagrams in Figure B, designed to portray Haitian, Cuban, and Peruvian societies.

There are several significant features of the diagram in figure B. Diagram 1 has a definite constriction between the

---

[1] See Eugene A. Nida, "The Roman Catholic, Communist, and Protestant Approach to Social Structure," in this volume.

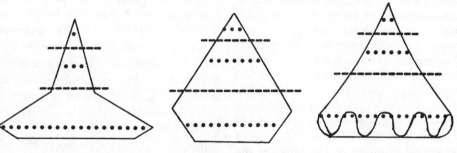

1. Haitian Society   2. Cuban Society   3. Peruvian Society

Figure B

class one elite and the class two elite, a distinction which is fully recognized by the Haitians themselves and a boundary which is as difficult to pass over as any in the social structure. The Haitian middle class is also quite restricted, and the lower class is largest at the lowest level.

In Cuban society the middle class is not only relatively large, but the transition from the lower class and into the upper class is not so pronounced as in the case of Haiti. Moreover, the number of people who are indigent is not as great as in Haiti, hence the narrower base.

In the case of Peruvian society the middle class is proportionately less than in Cuban society, with a gradual transition from the upper lower class, but the society bulges in the lower portions of the upper lower class. In diagram III, however, there is an additional feature, namely, the wavy solid line which marks the division between the predominantly Indian population (classified roughly on the basis of habitual use of an Indian language and the wearing of Indian type clothing) and the Spanish-speaking people. It should be noted that the Indian population is the lowest in the social structure, as far as general prestige is concerned,

but some members of this class reach up into the upper lower class. However, if they are to go up very far, they must adopt the classificatory symbols of the dominant group, namely, the Spanish language and the "Western" dress.

In the case of Peruvian society it would be more accurate to diagram the relationships between the two co-existing subcultures as follows:

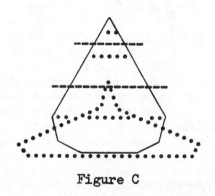

Figure C

In this structure an individual may possess a double status. For example, he may be in the elite within the Indian society, but only in the upper lower class or lower middle class of the non-

Indian society. However, it would be a serious mistake to assume that the social role of Indians within the Indian community can be determined by any general classification of the Indian within the composite national structure.

This same principle of the multiple classification may apply to any subculture or dependent social group. For example, in a small rural area the local "elite" may only rate as upper middle class in the society of the nearby town and as lower middle class in the still more inclusive structure of the nation.

Bases of Class Structure

From our description of the constituencies of the respective classes one could presume that wealth would be the primary criterion of class membership. There is no denying the importance of money, but it is certainly not the only factor, nor even the principal one, at least not for certain divisions. For example, some members of the first-class elite (the upper upper class) are often less wealthy than many persons in the second-class elite (the lower upper class). In fact, the so-called "aristocracy" often prides itself on being a class set apart by blood (i.e. the so-called bluebloods) who spurn the criterion of money as a culturally inferior basis of ascertaining "human worth." The position of the Roman Catholic clergy also contradicts the criterion of wealth, for priests from relatively low classes are accepted in the upper brackets despite their lack of personal wealth, but they are usually never admitted into the highest class, unless a papal appointment to the hierarchy overrides local class lines (something which rarely happens). Persons with exceptional talents, e.g. artists, singers, and dancers, or those with gifted intellects, e.g. writers, professors, and orators, may be admitted to a class which for the most part consists of considerably more wealthy members.

Class membership is thus not simply a matter of wealthy or family lineage or special talents. It includes all of these plus political influence, leadership ability, and the favor of influential friends.

In speaking about such classes we tend to give the impression that they are perfectly obvious to everyone, including the members of the society in question. However, these class distinctions are not fully evident, for people do not wear labels. Nevertheless, people are quite conscious of the class to which they belong (something which is much less true in the life of the United States, where the classes are less well defined and where people are supposed to deny the existence of classes and most people insist that they belong to the middle class). The classes in Latin America can, however, be delineated without too much trouble by determining those groups which (1) participate together in social functions, (2) tend to intermarry, and (3) recognize their essential identity of outlook and mutual interests. Furthermore, each class is aware that those "above" have greater prestige and those "below" have less. Accordingly, all classes, except the top, want to climb up in the scale of prestige.

What we have described as the different social classes are essentially prestige classes. There is no inherent reason why certain groups should be granted more prestige than others (other societies in the world have quite different prestige systems), but the Latin American societies do possess their typical structure, and with this we must reckon.

In describing classes as lower and higher, we only have reference to the built-in prestige factor. Certainly such terms as "higher" and "lower" must not be interpreted as representing any moral evaluation (though that is what many members of the upper classes would like to have others think). If we were to judge the social classes on the basis of such criteria as honesty, reliability, sense of responsibility to family, hospitality, and willingness to sacrifice for the sake of the community, it is quite likely that the upper lower class and the lower middle class would come out on top, with some notable examples of these virtues in the other classes, but not as predominant features. Accordingly, our isolation of classes and their scaling from high to low is based essentially on one principle, namely, the degree of prestige which the members of a society associate with the respective classes.

In speaking of prestige as a determinant of classes we recognize that the pattern is not one of absolute grades and fixed boundaries. That is to say, the classes of Latin American society are not castes, as in India. Rather, they are somewhat fluid groupings of people who associate together in various ways and who recognize in some measure the equality of their status. Prestige, therefore, is a polar element easily recognizable in the extremes, but less obvious in the central zones. Moreover, within the six classes, which constitute the major divisions recognizable in Latin life, there are numerous minor scales of prestige.

Orientation of Classes

The orientation of most members of all but the highest class is upward. That is to say, most people want to have more prestige. A number of people in the lowest classes have seemed to be largely resigned to their prestige status, but within the last few years the development of leftist labor movements in Latin America has resulted in a widespread concern for upward drive among the lowest class.

Most members of the highest class are relatively content with their lot. Their only concern seems to be the preservation of the status quo. Hence, they are skeptical of any radical changes and unwilling to make room for many competitors in the highest class. In fact, any major assault on their class of top elite by the "newly rich" is usually resisted vigorously with all the snobbishness of which this snobbish class is capable.

The pressures for change of class status are strongest in the rising elements of the middle class, but liberal political ideas have also induced major segments of the lower class to believe that what they would like, namely, more prestige and a greater share in the material rewards, are not only desirable but attainable, and if not by their own efforts then by means of political revolution. The creative minority within the proletariate is thoroughly convinced of this fact and hence is ready to rally the masses behind almost any leader who will promise them a higher status and more things.

On the other hand, while this upward-reaching group in the lower classes is intent on changing the status quo for them and their supporters by any and all means, the top classes are intent on preserving the social structure and the rewards which it provides. In most countries the intensity of the conflict is directly proportional to the degree of separation and the strength of the intervening barriers.

Techniques of Mobility

Though we often speak as though political events were the dominant factors in the change of class membership, this is essentially a false assumption. A change of political parties may slightly modify the rules by which persons may change social status — e.g. giving preference to those of liberal or conservative orientation, as the case may be — but for the most part it takes a thoroughgoing revolution to break open the social structure. Even the Mexican revolution, the most drastic in Latin American history, did not completely overturn the social structure. What it did accomplish was to remove some of the first-class elite and to remove the caste restrictions on the lowest classes. It ultimately had a profound effect upon Mexican society in that it released social pressures bent on upward mobility, but it was far from being a Communist-style revolution in which the higher classes are liquidated or reduced to lower-class status and the revolutionary leadership takes over the place of the elite and erects a high wall of isolation between the party leadership and all the rest of the classes. What is more, the Communist social structure functions so as to draw its leadership, not from the immediately inferior middle class of professionals, but from exceptional persons in the lower class, who are not likely to favor competition from the potentially "dangerous" professionals.

For a woman, the surest means of raising one's status is to marry into a family with higher social rank, for the husband's social position is largely the determining factor in a wife's status. If a man marries "above himself," he may or may not make the grade. This will depend upon personal charm, money, and, in the case of the first-class elite, primarily the determination of his father-in-law to give him social status.

In many segments of Latin society the parents' obtaining for their children a *compadre* 'godfather' or *comadre* 'godmother' of a higher status than themselves is a means of going up in social rank. This is only a kind of indirect benefit, but it does serve to enhance the prestige and tie the social unit together.

Obtaining a *padrino* is an even more important method of advancing in social standing. A *padrino* is a person who agrees to help someone in business, often guarantees loans, protects him against abuse by other elite, seeks opportunities for the advancement of his "client," and introduces him to a higher social group than the person enjoys at the time. In return the "client" always supports the *padrino's* political ambitions, will carry out any favors he is asked to do, and if the *padrino* should ever have need, the "client" is supposed to help to the limits of his resources. This is, of course, a carryover from feudal times, but it is a very important contemporary feature of Latin American life, and though it exists on a strictly informal basis (that is to say, there are no legal contracts binding the two parties), the social institution lies at the very heart of Latin life.

A number of other techniques in upward mobility have already been mentioned in other connections, namely, the acquisition of wealth, distinction in artistic performance, brilliance of intellectual endowments, and unusual leadership ability.

Orientation of the Roman Catholic Church Toward Latin American Society

In view of the fact that the Roman

Catholic Church is a strictly authoritarian institution with a completely pyramidal structure (after all, the Roman church and Latin society both arose from the hierarchical structure of Roman society), it is not surprising that the Roman Catholic Church has concentrated its attention on the cultivation of the elite. Not only are all the benefits of the church open to such people, but the church obtains practically all its leadership (from bishops on up) from the elite and in turn provides the elite with the best possible education in the Roman Catholic tradition. Whether the masses remain illiterate or not is not the primary concern of the church. What does count is the identification of interests and viewpoints with the ruling minority.

On the other hand, the Protestants have directed their appeal to the masses, not only because they were the most numerous, but because they were the most concerned with change and responded to the hope of a better chance.

The Protestant appeal to the masses has seemed to many Roman Catholics as being nothing but a veiled form of Communism, for Communist agents likewise appeal to the lower classes and hold out promises of a better life. Any further comparison between Protestantism and Communism immediately shows the profound differences, but there is enough superficial similarity to convince the less-informed or the already prejudiced that they must "repudiate the Communist and Protestant propaganda," as Roman Catholic publicists have repeatedly declared.

Justification of the Protestant Approach

Some persons have questioned whether Protestant missionaries did right in appealing primarily to the lower classes. Certain individuals have contended that a concentrated "attack" on the leadership of Latin America would have ultimately resulted in greater gains. However, it is extremely doubtful that this would have been the case, even if the personnel capable of such an appeal to the upper classes had been available. All that we can judge from the results of Protestant work in the light of the structure of Latin society seems to confirm the view that early missionaries acted in accordance with sound sociological principles, even though at the time they did not analyze the problems nor define the goals in these terms.

The sociological principles which seem to amply justify the course of Protestant missions in Latin America are three:

1. *The future always rests with the masses.* This is particularly true in contemporary society in which the vestiges of feudalism are rapidly crumbling in the assault of the so-called "mass man."

2. *The creative minority* (to use Toynbee's phrase) *which is reshaping Latin life has its origin primarily in the upper lower class and the lower middle class,* the very groups to which Protestantism has directed its approach.

3. *The only way to raise the masses is to become identified with them.* The Biblical principle of the leaven in the lump is the only means of altering in any substantial way the condition of the masses. Even if the elite were won to Protestantism, there would be no guarantee that these persons, whose social position depends upon preserving the *status quo,* would feel any constraint to change the condition of the lower classes, except in some superficial manner of urging a change of ecclesiastical loyalty on the part of the lower class "subjects."

Theological Justification

Despite what seems to be an evident sociological justification for our Protestant strategy, we also need to ask ourselves as to whether there has been a corresponding theological basis, or has our historic approach been essentially opportunistic? The answer to this question seems to be quite clear. We do have a theological justification, for in fundamental essence this approach to the masses reflects the divine principle underlying the incarnation, namely, (1) humbling of oneself in order to identify, and (2) giving leadership to others by participation and the challenge to "follow me."

The Face-to-Face and the Urban Societies

Though the general principle of appeal to the masses is fully justified, it is quite evident that in working out the implications of this principle there are wide differences of practice and response between small face-to-face communities and large urban agglomerations. What works in an urban situation often fails miserably in a small town, and conversely what appeals to rural people falls on deaf ears when directed to an urban audience. What, then, are the basic differences in the social structures and the effective means of communicating to these diverse constituencies?

A face-to-face society is just what it implies, namely, one in which all the members are known to each other, and everybody knows all about everyone else. What is more, in such a group most people are related, either through blood or marriage, and if not in this way, then through the godparents and *padrino* systems. Such a face-to-face society func-

tions in many ways like an extended family and as such tends to (1) make collective decisions, (2) have considerable inner cohesion, (3) present a unified front against intrusion, (4) be conservative in orientation, and (5) be centralized in its control, in the pattern of the family.

If, in approaching one of these face-to-face communities, it is possible to win over the leadership, one can soon gain access to the entire group. That is to say, the community follows the lead of the "ruling" family or group of elders, even as members of a family tend to follow the direction of the father or other strong personality. On the other hand, if one succeeds only in isolating some of the disgruntled members of such a community and in making them the "leaders" of the newly formed Protestant church, it is very likely that one will never be able to penetrate very deeply into the community structure. Such a "church" will always be a kind of appendage to the social structure, isolated from its essential life and a haven only for the community outcasts.

Many missionaries have felt that the best approach to a face-to-face society is to preach the good news to the entire group and to challenge the community to accept the gospel as a group. This procedure does not overlook the necessity of individuals making personal commitments, but it proceeds on the basis that a group which is accustomed to making group decisions should be confronted as a social unit. Some German missionaries have been singularly successful in this approach in some of the face-to-face communities in Indonesia. Dr. Alcibiades Iglesias, who has carried on a remarkable work among his own San Blas people in Panama, has adopted a somewhat similar approach. He has not isolated the Christians nor himself from the community, but has related the message of the gospel to the entire life of the community. A very similar approach has been employed by the Baptists of the eastern part of Cuba, who have sought to minister to all the needs of an entire community and to make the gospel relevant to all without attempting to isolate or estrange individuals within the community life.

On the other hand, it must be recognized that in Latin America the likelihood of an entire community accepting the gospel as a unit is not very great. This means that any Evangelical church will be made up of people who are more likely than not to be a minority in a community. As a minority they will be subjected to all kinds of severe social pressures depending largely upon (1) the extent to which the church group is composed of those who are already regarded as community outcasts (hence the importance of not formally organizing a church until it contains at least some of the responsible members of the community, who are not subject to the same patterns of rejection), and (2) the degree of pressure which the Roman Catholic clergy can arouse concerning this "intrusion" into the community life.

Compensation for Social Pressures

When social pressures are brought against a newly established Evangelical church, there must be some types of compensation or the entire church structure is likely to collapse. These people need to experience a kind of fellowship which is even more satisfying than what they have known in the community as a whole. If people can be taught the meaning of their new fellowship in Christ Jesus and what the "new community of the saints" can and should mean, they can be brought into a type of fellowship which will be not only satisfying but creative. The difficulty is, however, that too often this out-group feeling within the Protestant communion is largely defensive rather than creative; and though it does protect the members, it is largely ineffective in reaching out for others.

One of the very important ways of compensating for the loss of a feeling of social security within the immediate face-to-face community is to relate the small Protestant community to a larger fellowship of other believers in the country. This is done by attendance at rallies, conventions, and official meetings of various church associations, so that they may realize that they are a part of a large, growing body of believers. In Peru one missionary discovered that it was of immense importance to have such meetings in towns which had newly established churches. If the small, struggling church could be the host to a relatively large group of people, who by their dress and behavior exhibited obviously higher social status than was regularly attributed to such Protestant groups, the impact upon the community would be of great importance in the evangelistic efforts of the church in question.

The approach to the urban community is by no means as restricted as that involving the face-to-face society. The urban community is made up largely of people who are dislocated from their former face-to-face communities. They are more independent, more easily attracted into new movements, and more anxious to find means of personal profit and advancement. In the largely impersonal atmosphere of the city, where one fights with one's neighbors but does not know them, the Protestant church has a very special ministry, for it can help to create an effective, mutually beneficial social group in the midst of the impersonal environment and thus meet peoples' basic need for fellowship.

This aspect of personal fellowship in the midst of an impersonal society is one of the keys to the unusual success of the Pentecostal churches in Latin America, which, in addition to a number of other extremely significant appeals to the Latin temperament (factors which are beyond the scope of this article), have succeeded in large measure in making people of all classes, and especially the very lowest, to feel that they belong, are needed, and must make their own distinctive contribution within the community of believers which recognizes them as an integral part. This sense of belonging, of social security, and of being "indispensable" has resulted in the Pentecostal group's far outdistancing so many of the denominations which have depended more upon trained leadership, foreign funds, and an emphasis upon what the church could do for the people, rather than what the people must do for the church. In other words, the Pentecostal churches have succeeded in large measure in creating a face-to-face, living fellowship in the midst of a competing, impersonal agglomeration of people.

Problems of a Divided Society

Within a face-to-face society there may be an almost insuperable barrier which excludes one group from any vital social contacts with the other. In Latin America this situation exists in those communities which contain both Indians and Latins. Except for some of the strictly primitive groups (as in Amazonia and a few other marginal areas), the Indians of Latin America are a part of the larger social unit. The culture is basically a folk culture, and the Indians stand in a dependency relationship. The whites are dependent upon the Indians for some simple artifacts and for work and raw products from their small farms. The Indians are dependent upon the whites for legal rights, guarantee and possession of their farms, rudimentary education, and all sorts of manufactured articles. There is an almost complete symbiosis, but with the white community being largely parasitic upon the labors of the Indians.

This type of arrangement, involving dependency and exploitation, almost inevitably produces severe strains of feeling, deep suspicion, and outright antagonism. One would think that in view of this situation the Protestant missionary could make a strong appeal to the Indian to "throw off the shackles" and to separate himself from the religious system which is identified with the upper class. However, this is not so easy, for the Indian knows full well that this economic and social security depends very largely upon his keeping in good with his *patroncitos* 'landlords' or 'sponsors,' or *palancas* as they are called in Ecuador.

Some missions have attempted to minister exclusively to Indians and peons and have discovered that unless they actually controlled the land, as in the case of the Canadian Baptist mission in Guatajata, Bolivia, they had little or no success. In fact, some of the people whom they helped the most seemed most intent upon proving their continued identity with the upper class by spending large sums of money on liquor with which to entertain the *patroncitos*. Wherever missions have experienced any appreciable success in working in such divided societies it has been found that in some measure they either acted as the *patrón* (as in the case of the Canadian Baptist mission in Guatajata, Bolivia), or there were some Evangelicals in the Latin society who would act as *padrinos* for the Evangelical population. This means that the presentation of the gospel must be directed at the entire society, so that within the newly formed Protestant group there may be some who may fulfill the vital function of the "upper class."

Means of Communication

Without doubt, one of the most difficult aspects of evangelism in Latin America is to discover those means by which the communication of the gospel may be made in a relevant and socially acceptable manner. This does not mean that the Good News must be distorted in order to accommodate it to men's ideas. Rather, it must be presented in such a context as to make it really "Good News," not just foreign propaganda.

One Protestant missionary working in an Indian community of Ecuador discovered that the people were not at all interested in the beliefs of the Protestants, but they were very anxious to know about the Catholic doctrines. Accordingly, he offered to tell them about the various Roman Catholic beliefs and in a series of evening meetings in his own home he explained to them, without attempting to criticize or argue, the various doctrines of the Roman church. He used a Roman Catholic catechism and employed a Roman Catholic copy of the Scriptures. After several evenings of teaching and discussion, some of the group insisted that he tell them what the Protestants believed. At their invitation, he then explained, in

the same objective and meaningful way, what he as a Protestant believed. In the very community where other missionaries had been singularly unsuccessful in presenting the gospel this missionary was able to communicate effectively, because he spoke to their need and in a context which was relevant to their understanding at the time.

A missionary in West Africa made it a regular practice in his earlier days of itinerant evangelism to stop in villages for several days and in the evenings to inquire of the elders as to their belief in God. He never tried to explain his own faith until asked to do so by the leaders, who invariably inquired of him after he had spent long hours in learning from them. The missionary's purpose was not, however, just to elicit curiosity. He was convinced that in order to tell the people about God he had first to learn what they knew about God, or otherwise he might fail utterly to make his message relevant.

One outstanding missionary in Peru has made it a practice never to enter a village to evangelize the people except at the express invitation of some person within the village. His Quechua helpers often enter new villages in order to establish important first contacts, but the missionary has become convinced that if he is not to thwart the ultimate effectiveness of his ministry, he must enter a village as a guest of a member of the community, who will not only guarantee his safety during his stay but will be an important means of inviting others to hear the Good News, brought by the "foreigner."

There is a considerable tendency for missionaries to "barge ahead" irrespective of the local situation. One way in which this is done is through the free distribution of Scriptures and other Christian literature. Such materials seem to be so cheap and people appear to be so ready to accept whatever is offered free that missionaries are deceived as to the ultimate effectiveness of their endeavors. In the first place, a high percentage of such literature is never read, and not infrequently the people react to the gospel as being nothing more than cheap propaganda. What is even worse, the distributor loses the priceless opportunity to communicate to the people in a context which they can fully understand, namely, the necessity for the bookseller to convince people of the desirability of his product. In the process of selling, whether or not the person buys, the bookseller has the chance of witnessing to the truth and effectiveness of the Good News. He also has a chance to challenge the prospective customer to study this for himself and to accept it. However, the man who is distributing free literature is immediately classed as a propagandist, a job for which he must be well paid, and his own testimony is relatively valueless.

The necessity of communicating within a meaningful context may sometimes lead to amazing methods. One agriculturalist working with the YMCA in Mexico· discovered that in the area in which he had set out to help the people, everyone was suspicious of his efforts and refused to listen to his advice. Accordingly, the agriculturalist proceeded to introduce improved varieties of vegetables, grains, and fruits, and employed new methods of putting humus back into the soil by the generous use of compost made from abundant organic material in the area. So the villagers would not "misinterpret" his efforts, he put up a high fence around his gardens and ostensibly attempted to protect his choice products. The inevitable result was that the people stole his products in order to sell in the nearby markets. This method of teaching might seem unnecessarily "indirect," but it was effective for it was fully meaningful within the context of these people's lives.

The importance of communicating by identification has been so emphasized that some missionaries have wrongly exaggerated its significance to the point of thinking that identification consisted primarily in imitation, largely of an external type. This has led some missionaries purposely to dress poorly and to live in ostensibly humble quarters. The people, however, have detected the false ring in this type of superficial imitation and have reckoned it as a kind of cheap paternalism, which in fact it is. The identification which is required is not imitation, but full participation as a member of the society. In order to participate effectively one must not deny his own cultural heritage — something which cannot be done even if one wished to do so — but to employ this background for the benefit of the total constituency.

Some missionaries have assumed that "natives can best reach natives" (as they have so often framed the principle). In a sense this is quite true, but at the same time it is a general experience of missionaries that Latin American converts often refuse to work among people of the very class from which they themselves have come or among those who are in the immediate class below them, especially if these classes are both rather low on the social scale. This should not be too hard to understand, for any convert who has advanced in the social structure as the result of hard work and diligent application often feels quite insecure in his new social position. To return immediately to work among people representing the very class from which he has raised himself would seem to endanger his status. Furthermore, a great deal of the education which he probably has received in mission schools has prepared him for a middle class social position and in a sense he has been "de-classified" as far as his original status was concerned. He no longer really feels at home.

But even those who have not been educated up and out of a class are often reluctant to minister to people immediately beneath them, for it would seem to imply that they are lowering their own status and hence endangering their prestige position within the society. On the other hand, such persons are often quite willing to work among those considerably below their own status, for then they do not feel that there is any danger of being mistaken for a member of such an inferior class. In a sense this explains why it is somewhat easier to get missionaries from the United States to work in areas in which nationals of the respective countries are reluctant to serve. The missionary runs no risk of losing status. In fact, among the in-group of which he is a part in the United States his very going to such "benighted heathen" enhances his prestige, but this is not the case with so-called "national workers."

The sensitivity of national workers to these problems of class within their own society must be fully recognized if one is to understand their special problems and some of the reasons which dictate what appears to be such strange behavior. In one instance, for example, an Indian from southern Mexico went off to study in a Bible school in Guatemala. Upon his return he began preaching in Spanish, which he did with considerable skill, but

of course his audience understood little if anything of what he was saying. This continued for about three weeks, after which time this young Indian pastor shifted to the Indian language and has continued to use it ever since. The ability to use Spanish was an essential symbol of his new status, and once this was adequately confirmed, he could then safely afford to identify himself with the Indian constituency.

This principle of security in social position helps to explain why it is sometimes easier to get university students to undertake work in some slum area than to get people who have just emerged from the slums to return to them in order to minister. This also explains why one Negro pastor in Cuba found it difficult to work among his own people, for they preferred to have a white minister, for this gave their church more prestige. On the other hand, a well-educated constituency of whites was quite willing to accept this brilliant Negro, for the prestige of this group would not be endangered.

Backsliding and Class Identification

One of the apparently puzzling phenomena in the experience of some evident converts is the almost pathetic concern for reinstatement which characterizes those who turn from Protestantism and go back into their former socio-religious grouping. Time and again missionaries have mentioned how incredible it was that certain outstanding people who seemed to show every promise of developing into outstanding leaders within the Protestant movement would go "so far back into sin," once they dissociated themselves from the Evangelical constituency. In fact, such persons often become far more addicted to their favorite vices than they ever were before coming in contact with the gospel. It would seem that the more conspicuous has been their testimony the more severe is their backsliding.

The sociological explanation for this is the fact that such persons feel constrained to do all they can to be accepted again in the constituency of which they were formerly a part. To do this they must completely violate the mores associated with the Protestant element in order to prove to their non-Protestant friends that they no longer belong to the Protestant group. A somewhat similar reaction occurs, of course, with the new convert to Protestantism. In order to be accepted within the Evangelical community, he often symbolizes his break with the past by strong denunciation of his former friends, publicized breaking or burning of images, unnecessarily harsh denunciation of the Roman Catholic Church, and even unwarranted disrespect for the religious sentiments of conscientious people.

The Work of the Holy Spirit

From what has been said up to this point some readers might conclude that we have little or no regard for the role of the Holy Spirit in the program of evangelism. Quite to the contrary, the more one studies the methods and procedures of foreign missions the more one becomes convinced of the function of the Spirit of God in transforming the lives of people. However, it does seem quite evident that God's Spirit works with and not contrary to the basic need of human beings, as exemplified in certain aspects of social structure. A study of the human elements in the divine-human drama of God's role in human history does not deny God's part; it only helps one to appreciate better the way God has chosen to work within the context of human life by the principle of incarnation, rather than from outside by a continued series of supernatural interventions.

Those who fully appreciate the living reality of the incarnational element in our Christian faith take seriously the meaning of revelation by word and by life ("the Word became flesh"). On the basis of this the fundamental procedure of missions may be developed in terms of identification ("He humbled himself") and participation ("He was tempted in all points"). Herein lies the key to effective witness, sacrificial ministry, and vital growth for the churches in Latin America.

Eugene A. Nida

The Roman Catholic, Communist, and Protestant Approach to Social Structure

EVEN the most casual observer of what is going on in the world today recognizes that there is something essentially different in the approach which Roman Catholicism, Communism, and Protestantism make to social structure. In country after country, one finds the Roman Catholic hierarchy concentrating on the elite, drawing its principal leadership from this class, and seeing that important members of the class feel no lack of education or spiritual assistance. At the same time, Roman Catholicism has a wide appeal to the impoverished masses, while among the middle classes there is often a strong anticlerical sentiment.

On the other hand, Communism talks of a classless society and yet has succeeded in creating the most class-conscious structure known in the Western world (almost equivalent to the caste system of India). The Communist leadership itself constitutes a special elite, which is drawn principally from the proletariat — a dictatorship by representatives of the proletariat.

Protestants, however, have their strength not in the elite classes nor in the lower classes, but primarily in the middle classes, and especially in those segments which are on the upward move in the socio-economic scale.

Do these differences in Roman Catholic, Communist, and Protestant "societies" reflect simply an accidental development? Or are they the result of well-thought-out plans of social organization? Or are such developments an inevitable reflection of other fundamental features of these rather diverse ideologies? The answers to these questions can only be found in an analysis of the structure of society and certain significant features of social control and movement.

Diagrammatic Representation of Social Structure

As a means of visualizing something of the nature of social structure (though with obvious oversimplification and hence skewing of the data), we may diagram a typical social structure as follows:

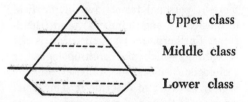

Upper class

Middle class

Lower class

In this diagram the various classes are schematically arranged as higher, middle, and lower, with a subdivisional distinction within each class, thus giving us a traditional six-class structure (which may or may not be true of particular societies, but which is typical of a number of soci-

Reprinted from Vol. 4, No. 6 (1957), pp. 209-219.

eties). Rather than being a strict pyramid (as is usually taught by Communist propaganda), most structures tend to be a kind of inverted diamond, since the indigent population is actually less numerous in most societies than other segments of the lower class, such as factory laborers, unskilled day laborers, and tenant farmers. The middle class is generally divided between the independent tradesmen and small merchants in the lower middle class and the semiprofessional persons, clerks and lower-bracket white collar workers in the upper middle class. The upper class is divided usually between the "older families," constituting the first-class elite, and many of the leaders in business and the professional world. However, in many instances some members of the "old families aristocracy" are not as wealthy or as politically influential as many members of the second-class elite (or the lower upper class).

Class structure is not to be considered simply a classification of earning power or occupation. It involves such additional factors as family lineage, education, personal attractiveness, basic attitudes (such as attitudes toward the chances of success, value of hard work, saving of money, desirability of education, and sex mores), personal talents (as in the field of music, art, entertainment), and friendships. Furthermore, class structure is not something which the anthropologist or sociologist decides to "impose" on the society in order to describe it. The social structure is there and recognized in covert or overt forms by the people. Although in some societies many persons tend to deny its existence (something which is true of a number of communities in the United States), the behavior of people within such societies reveals a set of

human relationships which are based upon such class structuring.

Because of the wide differences in types of social structures, it would scarcely be fair not to emphasize such diversities by comparing certain widely varying structures. For this we may take the following diagrams, based on an impressionistic view of the structures of the U.S.A. and of India:

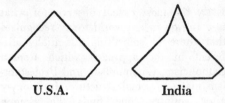

U.S.A.   India

The Roman Catholic Approach to Social Structure

Without exception, the Roman Catholic approach to the social structure is through the elite, who are provided with good schools, considerable personal attention, and from which group the leadership of the Church comes. There are, of course, many priests drawn from the lower classes, but with very rare exceptions any member of the priesthood having a rank of bishop or higher is drawn from the elite, and, if possible, from the first-class elite — the aristocracy. Moreover, the Church exerts its control on the society by means of the elite, who generally dominate the political and economic life of the people. This means that the Roman Catholic clergy are almost without exception on the side of the conservative political party.

It is quite understandable that the Roman Catholic Church should approach the social structure in this way, for the Church itself is a strictly pyramidal structure with very overt ranking of authority. In a sense the Church is a kind of institution apart from the society and regarded as being above the society, for the laity are not really members of the Church, only adherents. Accordingly, the Roman Church, which has never relinquished its claim to complete temporal as well as spiritual authority, proceeds to exercise whatever control it can by means of the same type of hierarchical attitude toward the social structure as is contained within its own organization.

Historically, the Roman Catholic Church is the carry-over of the authoritarian structure of ancient Roman society, and its present structure was more or less "frozen" during the Renaissance, when society was completely controlled by the first-class elite. There have been some notable attempts to introduce certain changes in such structuring, and in a sense the equalitarian character of certain of the Catholic orders (not, of course, the Jesuits) fulfills this function, but these orders have not gained control of the papacy. Most recently there was a very significant attempt to bring the Church closer to the people by instituting the role of "worker-priests" in France. However, the authorities of the Church abandoned this scheme entirely when they discovered that the priests were themselves becoming "too sympathetic" with the workers. Had such a movement continued, it would have undermined the authoritarian structure, based upon a definite class consciousness, which identified itself with the elite, not with the workers.

In the almost exclusive identification of the Roman Church with the position and interests of the elite there lie the seeds of greatly diminished power and influence, for the future is with the masses. The general repudiation of the Roman Church by the masses in Europe, the rise of strong anticlerical movements, especially among the middle classes, and the indifference of the average man to the doctrines of the Church, in favor of the new cult of "scientism," poses a real threat to the Roman Church.

On the other hand, in countries in which the Roman Church is the exclusive dictator of the school system or where the elite have almost complete control of the masses, the lower classes continue to have a strong allegiance to the Church. In the elaborate and attractive ritual the people participate vicariously in a pageantry provided by the elite and characteristic of their opulence. The Church provides the only evident hope of any changed status in the next life. Furthermore, the dependency relation to the Church in spiritual matters is only a symbolic continuation of economic and social dependency upon the elite. In these circumstances, however, the middle classes are often anticlerical, for they recognize in the Roman Church their principal obstacle to breaking into the elite position. Accordingly, politicians, who arise primarily from the upward-moving segments of the middle class, cultivate the masses by means of liberal political doctrines and thus lay the groundwork for taking over governments from the conservatives. When, however, as has happened several times in Latin America, the amoral attitudes of certain liberal leaders (as reflected in their evident concern for purely personal gain) leave the masses disillusioned, they are then amenable to overtures from the conservatives, who promise law and order, even at the expense of freedom.

The Communist Approach to Social Structure

The Communists are authoritarian and totalitarian, even as the Roman Catholics are, but their approach to social structure is very different, even though in the end they create a strictly pyramidal structure with highly centralized controls. In the first place, the first- and second-class elite (the upper class) must be liquidated by killing (in which case the property may be expropriated) or brainwashing. The first process is employed primarily with the rich, and the second is used on intellectual groups. Once these two classes of elite have been eliminated, the party can superimpose upon the society a new ruling clique, a new elite. This new elite, however, is not drawn from members of the former elite, except in rare instances. It is drawn, rather, from members of the lower class or from certain disillusioned persons of the middle class (especially members of rejected minority groups) who have tried to break through into the upper class but have been prevented from doing so, despite their evident personal capacities. This is a reason why in a number of countries of western Europe and the United States there is such a high percentage of Jews in the Communist movement, and why in the United States Communism has had such a wide appeal to certain intellectuals in the Negro population.

The purposeful and planned discrimination against representatives of the upper middle classes or former upper classes is evident in eastern Germany, where the sons of professors are often rejected for advanced studies, despite their high qualifications, in favor of the sons of tradesmen or day laborers who may actually be somewhat inferior in intellectual ability. By plucking a person out of a lower class and thrusting him into the elite in such a way that the person is completely dependent upon party loyalty for every advance in status or advantage in living, the Communist leadership knows full well that it can produce a much more loyal servant of the state. Such a person is not so likely to want to push into the first-class elite, but will be more content with second-class elite status. His viewpoints are likely to be more amoral with regard to party loyalty than if he felt that he had a right to certain prerogatives. As a "representative" of the lower classes he can more satisfactorily live the fiction of the "dictatorship of the proletariat."

The Communist emphasis upon creating a big social gap between the elite leadership and the rest of the populace helps to provide a distance which can better justify the doctrine of "infallibility," which the Communists have been entirely too clever to formulate as a creed (in contrast with the Roman Catholics), but which constitutes an implicit doctrine. This is evidenced in the fact that the people are never provided with more than one slate of officials to approve. In other words, the State knows best, in the finest paternalistic and Tsarist fashion. By providing a large gap between the governing elite and the masses the party is able to place a higher "price tag" on membership (the price of unquestioned loyalty), and not only will men do anything to get in, but they will perform any type of function in order to stay in.

On the other hand, the social structure of Communism contains the seeds of crisis, for what is to happen with the second and third generation of Communists? Human nature being what it is, is there not a possibility that the elite class will want to perpetuate itself as an aristocracy, in which case the Soviet social structure will then be frozen into a kind of caste system? Even at present the Soviet system is not a dictatorship of the proletariat, but a dictatorship of men of whom the majority arose out of the proletariat. But there is every likelihood that within two or three generations there will be a dictatorship of an aristocracy which in times past arose out of the proletariat, and there will be only a propagandistic touch with the masses. There is no doubt but what such a fiction may be maintained for some time, especially in an age where controls of power and communication can be so centralized. However, the dictatorship of the proletariat will only be a fiction, even as "the classless society" is also a fiction.

The Protestant Approach to Social Structure

On the whole, Protestants have not purposely avoided any class, but have infiltrated all classes, as reflected in churches which range from Episcopal to Pentecostal. It is quite true that during the Reformation the decisions of princes were of great importance in the political struggle, but the real strength of the Protestant movement existed in the rapidly growing merchant classes, not primarily among the ruling classes. It can still be said that the major strength of Protestantism exists in the lower middle and upper lower classes.

By concentration on doctrines involving personal salvation, moral integrity, thrift, financial responsibility, hard work, and the elimination of personal vices, Protestantism has not only attracted people who are interested in personal improvement, but has started many people on the upward "climb" in the social structure, since precisely these virtues are important in the individualistic, profit-motive society of the West. The

Methodist movement in England, for example, began primarily among the lower classes, but within a short time the descendants of these people were predominantly middle-class people, and now there is a sizable group of British Methodists who are members of the lower upper class.

In this upward movement of Protestant groups there has always been the tendency of the group to lose effective contact with the class out of which it has come. Accordingly, Methodism, which "outgrew" its appeal to the lower classes, indirectly fostered a Nazarene revival, and the Nazarenes and similar groups, who tended to move away from the lower classes, made room for Pentecostals, whose principal appeal is directed primarily to such classes.

Protestantism does not have a particularly strong appeal to the very wealthy, for in general it demands too high a standard of stewardship of money and too great a sense of responsibility for social ills. Furthermore, since salvation cannot be purchased by money, there is no guarantee of special favors for the rich. (There are, of course, some unfortunate exceptions in which Protestantism falls far short of its historical and Biblical basis.)

Protestantism is far more racially prejudiced and class conscious than Roman Catholicism. The principal reason for this is the fact that in Protestantism the laity are "members" of the church (not just "adherents," in contrast with the ordained who alone constitute the Church, as far as Roman Catholicism is concerned), and hence they have a greater sense of congregational participation and oneness. This type of in-group consciousness leads to greater class awareness and the tendency to segregation, following the patterns of the social structure.

On the whole, the Roman Catholic Church has a greater appeal than does the Protestant to the very poor. It is less bothered by problems of class consciousness and prejudice, which arise from the congregational character of the Protestant movement. It also provides elaborate, beautiful ritual in which the poor may participate and thus identify themselves with something immeasurably higher than their own humble status. The poor remain attached to the Church in the same dependent relationship which they have toward the elite on whom they are socially and economically dependent, and the Church may provide a sense of status and well-being, even in the worst of circumstances, for it is the one claim which such persons have for "pie in the sky by and by." Furthermore, in order to attain these ultimate goals the Roman Church does not make the same demands upon the lower classes for personal initiative, responsibility, and ambition — factors which are noticeably lacking in members of this class.

The ideal Protestant approach to society is the incarnational one, in which those of any one class are willing to reach down and, in identification with those who have not found the way, introduce them to "the Way, the Truth, and the Life" in Christ Jesus. This is the way of the *kenosis* (the "emptying") of prerogatives in order that men beneath may be reached and raised up. However, except for the foreign mission enterprise, it is not usually the case that members of a church have such a ministry of reaching down as Christ did, but they reach out to those of the same social class. In fact, those who reach down (who dare to preach

in the streets and without official sanction, as Wesley did) are often ostracized from the original constituency and excluded. They accordingly form a new denomination, with a distinctive message for and appeal to a particular social segment. Since Protestantism not only directly and indirectly fosters such movements, but refuses to censure such departures as heresies (as is the case with parallel departures from Roman Catholicism), it is inevitable that Protestantism will continue to produce a series of different denominations. Actually, however, this capacity to reach new and different segments within the social structure and to bring into leadership (often quite unintentionally) persons of ability within the diverse social groupings is the genius of Protestantism. If, on the other hand, in pursuance of the ideal of a united Protestantism this belief in the priesthood of the believer is denied to the point of crushing such new and creative movements (a kind of totalitarian ecumenicity), Protestantism will have sown the seeds of its own destruction. It could only be successful in such a pursuit of conformity by becoming a completely totalitarian organization. However, those whose ecumenical thinking is most realistic within the Protestant movement recognize that the high-priestly prayer of our Lord (John 17) does not mean organizational identity as much as spiritual unity. In the age of the mass man one must not be deceived into thinking that only in organizational identity is there strength, for masked beneath an outward unity may be smoldering antagonisms, while within a group of freely cooperating entities there may be the greatest capacity for the fullest expression of latent human creativity.

Eugene A. Nida and William L. Wonderly

Selection, Preparation, and Function of Leaders in Indian Fields

To what extent has the choice and preparation of evangelical leaders in the Indian fields of Latin America followed patterns that are compatible with the existing ways in which the Indian society has selected and prepared its own leaders? How does the function of evangelical leaders compare with that of other leaders in the society? Failure to ask these questions has led to many problems and, no doubt, failures in the development of a lasting leadership structure in some of the Indian churches.[1]

THE PURPOSE of the present essay is to endeavor to stimulate a study which can contribute to the improvement of the systems at present used in selecting and preparing leaders for the Protestant churches in Indian areas of Latin America in general, and especially of Mexico and Central America, and to the discovery of better ways of assigning responsibilities to people in these churches.

The organization and structure of civil and religious authority in the Indian communities of Middle America derives from pre-Columbian times and, in its traditional form, is something which has resulted from a combination of the patterns of Indian government and the forms of government brought over from Europe. Protestant missionary work among the Indians of this area, on the other hand, has been developed with the use of patterns of authority derived in large degree from the ecclesiastical government of the churches and missions that have been responsible for this work, with relatively little adaptation to Indian patterns.

Lack of understanding of how Indian communities operate has inevitably led to certain mistakes in dealing with Indian churches and Indian communities, on the part of both missionaries and national leaders in the evangelical churches. The tendency to give ecclesiastical authority to younger people, in a society which has always required that the younger men be subject to the authority of the

Most of the present article was written for use as a study document in preparation for the May 1962 *Conferencia Pro-Obra Indígena* (Conference on Indian Work) in Guatemala, which was attended by missionaries and Indian leaders from that country and from Mexico and at which Dr. Wonderly was present as special lecturer.

[1] A multilithed Spanish version of this paper was used in connection with the conference on Indian work held in Guatemala, and can be obtained by writing to William L. Wonderly, Apdo. 1373, México 1, D. F., Mexico.

171

older, is an example of this which has
resulted in many conflicts. There is also
a tendency to depend too much upon
bilingual persons, many of whom are to
some extent marginal to their own culture and society and who therefore are
not in a position to effectively carry out
their leadership responsibilities. Many of
these lack the necessary support and
approval of their people and an adequate
understanding of the organization and
leadership patterns of their own community.

Another example is the tendency to
appoint and give responsibility to certain
people without taking into account the
structure of authority which already
exists in the community, as regards leading families, factions organized about
these families,[2] etc. This type of error
has been committed partly as the natural
result of having insisted upon the use
of an election process which the Indians
do not use in their local affairs and with
which they are not familiar.

Existing Systems of Authority among Indian Groups

As a basis for understanding the
function of leaders, it is important to
take into account the characteristics of the
following authority systems in the Indian
communities: (1) The traditional system
of civil-religious authority (the so-called
"ladder system"), (2) the traditional
orthodox system which is used by the
Catholic Church, (3) the system used
at present by the missions in the Catholic
Church (e.g. the Maryknoll Fathers),

(4) the system of civil authority in the
constitutional government, and (5) the
system of authority used by the Protestant churches. These different systems
coexist, with various degrees of conflict,
in most Indian areas.

Tradition civil-religious system. This
system of political-religious authority is
characteristic of the Indian communities
of Middle America and has been studied
in considerable detail from the anthropological point of view.[3] It is sometimes
called the civil-religious hierarchy or
"ladder system" because of its typical
form in which an individual climbs from
one step to another, first with a lower
civil position, then a religious one, then
a higher civil responsibility, and so on
in zigzag form till he reaches the higher
positions in the community and finally,
if he shows sufficient capacity, becomes
one of the *principales* or ex-mayors who,
like the Hebrew Sanhedrin, represent the
highest authority in the society. This is
the system which really represents the
chief and most effective authority within
the traditional Christo-pagan society, or
that represented by "folk Catholicism."
It presents certain characteristics which
are very important if we are to understand the function of leaders among the
Indian groups.

This "ladder" structure presents a

---

2 For an example of the contribution of
this toward the decadence of the Protestant
work in a Mayan village, see Robert Redfield,
*A Village that Chose Progress: Chan Kom
Revisited* (Chicago: University of Chicago
Press, 1950).

3 See Gonzalo Aguirre Beltrán, *Formas de
Gobierno Indígena* (México: Imprenta Uni-
versitaria, 1953); Fernando Cámara, "Religious and Political Organization," in *Heritage
of Conqest: The Ethnology of Middle America*
(Glencoe, Ill.: The Free Press, 1952); Pedro
Carrasco, "The Civil-Religious Hierarchy in
Mesoamerican Communities," in *American Anthropologist,* Vol. 63, No. 3 (June 1961)
pp. 483-97; Harry S. McArthur, *La Estruc-
tura Político-Religiosa de Aguacatán* (pape.
presented to Fourth Interamerican Indianis
Congress, Guatemala, 1959).

minute gradation; no one can reach a position of authority without having first passed through the lower positions and demonstrated his aptitude in them. There is also a well-defined relation between the civil and religious aspects, such that each individual must serve the community in both of these in his process of climbing the ladder.

Sooner or later, almost all adult men in the community participate in one aspect or another of this system. Besides, the ex-officials have great prestige and continue to exercise, throughout their life, a powerful authority. It is a very efficient system, and one in which everyone has opportunity and also an obligation to participate. Decisions reached within this system may not appear to the Western observer to be very "democratic," but actually they are the most satisfactory type of decision for the Indian community, because they are made by men who have risen through the required steps and who are therefore considered as the legitimate representatives of their community.

Another important aspect of this graded structure is that it is based upon an apprenticeship system. The participants are not prepared by means of formal study, but begin as apprentices with a simple responsibility and climb from one position to another, preparing themselves in this way by means of the experience gained. This also guarantees that the positions of greater responsibility shall be occupied only by older men, who have previously gone through the lower positions. Naturally, those who do not have sufficient aptitude for exercising authority tend to be eliminated before they get to the higher positions.

Traditional system of orthodox Catholicism. Although the traditional system just described includes one aspect of the re-ligious authority in the community, there is another aspect which is not subject to it. The priest and his immediate associates do not participate in the "ladder system." They form rather a part of the hierarchical system of the Roman Catholic Church, with the priest at the top as far as the local situation is concerned (under the bishop, who lives elsewhere), and under him the catechists and also the cantors and sacristans. Depending upon the local situation, the sacristans and the cantors may also form part of the traditional civil-religious system or they may play a dual role, alternating between the two systems. A cantor may function as a member of the traditional system and at the same time, since he knows how to read and write, he can participate in the Catholic system in the orthodox sense.

This system differs from the traditional system in that it is headed by a person who has final authority (subject to the bishop, of course, but not to his inferiors), and made up of persons who have been appointed by the higher authority. On the other hand, it is similar to the traditional system in that it has a certain gradation of authority, and also in that it is to a certain degree an apprenticeship system. However, in sharp contrast with the traditional system, the apprentice never gets to the top, or to the position of highest authority, in this way. The top is reached only by those who take formal studies and who become ordained by others who already occupy the higher positions; and even for the lower positions such as that of cantor, it is important to have a certain amount of formal study.

Present-day Catholic system. In the missions established by the Maryknoll Fathers and similar groups, the system is essentially the same in its structure as that of traditional orthodox Catholicism, but with a change in personnel. Persons have been eliminated who in the older system were in too close contact with the traditional or pagan system, or who actually participated in both systems, as was the case in many Indian communities. There has thereby resulted a break between the two systems, so that it is no longer possible for the same person to play a dual role, serving simultaneously or alternately in the two as before.

System of civil authority in the constitutional government. The system of civil government, under the authority of the constitution, is theoretically modeled after a democratic pattern in which every citizen has equal right and vote. But this ideal has not yet been attained in practice, especially in the Indian areas. The tendency is rather that of placing in positions of civil authority persons who have been named by the higher authority or the official party, and whose appointment is later confirmed publicly by the formality of an election. The officials who have been appointed in this way designate in turn other persons for the lower positions, and certain of these are also confirmed by the formality of election. There is no system of apprenticeship as in the other cases mentioned above. The important factors to attain the positions of authority are formal education and political influence; the experience gained from having climbed up the lower steps does not have the same importance as it does in the traditional system, nor is it considered necessary that a person have any certain age in order to occupy a given position.

This leads to a state of tension between the indigenous civil-religious authority and the constitutional authority. The secretary of the *municipio,* regardless of the support that he may have from the people, has greater power than the Indian mayor in the external relations of the *municipio* (i.e. with the departmental or federal government), due to his formal education. He is the one who controls the degree of intervention or help which the government from outside may exercise in the Indian community. If the Indian mayor wishes to show his power, his only way of doing so is to deny to the constitutional authority the cooperation of the local people. His own lack of education and of knowledge of the national language do not leave him with any way to exercise a positive initiative.

Protestant system. The Protestant denominations have different systems of church government, some more adaptable to the Indian situation than others; but we may point out certain general characteristics which these systems tend to have in common, in comparison with the other systems that have been mentioned.

The Protestant organizations show certain features of similarity with the civil constitutional system, in contrast with the traditional civil-religious system. The leaders are appointed, in many of the cases, by the mission or by the higher authority in the church, and may then be confirmed by the formality of an election. In these cases, and also when there is an election which is more than a mere formality, it is a matter of the more important positions; there are other positions which, as in the civil system, are occupied by persons named directly by the higher authority.

The Protestant system of the denominations is analogous to that of the Roman Catholic Church in various aspects. There are certain persons who are designated by the mission and paid by it. Although there is a certain degree of apprenticeship at the lower levels, no one can arrive at a top position without having had formal study, usually in some place distant from his native village. Another similarity is that one cannot normally attain a position of authority in the mission (as distinct from the national church) without having been born in the country where the headquarters of the mission is.

Authority in these organizations depends principally upon outside control, as is demonstrated by the power vacuum which is left whenever a mission tries to "nationalize" or "integrate" the work in the country. Usually it takes several years to create a structure of authority within the national church group in these cases of integration, in which the mission gives the authority into national hands.

The Protestant type of church organization in the Indian communities shows very little similarity to the traditional pattern of civil-religious authority in these communities.

On the other hand, there are some Protestant movements, which have grown up largely from the grass roots in the different countries, which do show a marked similarity to the indigenous patterns. These groups have a system of apprenticeship and of informal education, with degrees of authority that correspond to maturity and which can be attained only by having come up through the lower positions. In these Pentecostal groups there are very few people under forty years of age who have positions of authority in the church. Those who lack sufficient leadership ability tend to be eliminated before they attain positions of greater responsibility, and those who do attain these positions enter them with the necessary practical experience and prestige which enable them to exercise

leadership in a situation that places a high premium on these qualities. These Pentecostal movements in Latin America already include as many followers as do all of the other Protestant denominations combined and they are continuing to grow rapidly.[4]

Apprenticeship vs. Formal Education

The Indian system of apprenticeship always implies a method of informal education. That is, for a person to climb up the steps from apprentice to the higher positions, he must learn by experience, under the direction of those with whom he is working. He must also demonstrate his aptitude and perform well his lower responsibilities, before he is permitted to assume higher ones. This is an almost universal system among aboriginal peoples for education in general, and it is also the system that was used in the civilized world until not many centuries ago. The peripatetic (i.e. ambulatory) schools of the Greek philosophers, and the example of Jesus Christ himself with his disciples or apprentices, are examples of this method of apprenticeship and informal education.

One the other hand, if a person is to be catapulted upward to a higher position without passing through the intermediate steps, he must do so by means of formal education, in a system which permits this kind advancement. This is the modern system, in which a person learns in school and then goes out to carry responsibilities which in earlier times would not have been possible except through

---

[4] For a fuller discussion of these groups in relation to their cultural setting, see Eugene A. Nida, "The Indigenous Churches in Latin America," PA, Vol. 8, No. 3 (May-June 1961), pp. 97-105.

slow ascent by the apprenticeship system.

At present, the Indian groups of the Americas are in a stage of change and transition, in which are found stronger or weaker survivals of the apprenticeship system together with elements of the newer system of formal education. Besides, the ethos or value system of the Indian society, which originally led to its system of authority, presents conflicts with the present-day values of the Ladino society and its authority structure. This coexistence of two value systems and two authority structures inevitably produces conflicts.

Age vs. Youth

The resulting conflict in the society is a struggle between age on the one hand and formal preparation on the other. In modern society, the young men who complete their studies are given authority which in former times was given only to the elders. The degree of authority that is exercised is no longer related to the age of the person who exercises it. This is happening in all aspects of life: politics, social life, and the churches. And, in the latter, the disparity of age has produced many problems, conflicts, and divisions.

In a country such as the United States, the tension between young and old is not so pronounced, since a person is recognized for his abilities more than for his age. But in Latin America there is a much stronger tension between the elders and the young men. This is due to various factors. For one thing, tradition has always given greater importance to the older men in these countries than in those of the North, where there has been more of a break with tradition and where the prestige has been given to the pioneer and scientist.

In addition, the changes going on at present in Latin America are so rapid that they have left a greater inequality between the younger men and their elders. While the latter frequently remain illiterate, their sons acquire knowledge of modern science and of many other things which prepare them for activities that their fathers cannot engage in. And the older men, adhering to the tradition of the *paterfamilias* who rules with a strong hand, tend to tighten the reins and show a certain lack of confidence in a world whose advance they are unable to detain. Still another factor is the emphasis upon male dominance or *machismo*, which contributes to these conflicts by placing the mature men in competition with the younger ones for the attention of the young women, to a greater degree than in societies where the men observe greater marital fidelity. So that, from many points of view, this struggle between age and youth is accentuated in Latin America; and in the transitional Indian areas the conflict is even more acute than in the mestizo communities due to the stronger Indian tradition in favor of the authority of the elders.

Conflicting Value Systems

But this is not only a conflict between traditions as such; it also implies a conflict between two value systems, or two concepts of what is good and what is correct. The structure of real authority (as opposed to theoretical authority) is based, in the last analysis, upon the values held by people. This aspect of culture has barely begun to be studied during the past decade by anthropologists, but it promises to reveal much about the essential characteristics of different societies and the differences between cultural groups that need to be taken into account both in the communication of the message and in the organization and structure of authority.

There are a number of different dimensions of contrast which can be described in relation to these values.[5] At least two of these dimensions would seem to be of special importance in relation to authority structure. One is that of focus upon the *individual* vs. the *group*. Another is the focus upon the *good and rights of oneself* vs. the *good and rights of others*.

These differences may be diagramed in the following form:

First dimension	individual	group

Second dimension	good and rights of self	good and rights of others

As may be seen in the diagrams to follow, these two value dimensions tend to be combined so as to produce three different patterns in (1) U.S. society, (2) Ladino or mestizo society, and (3) Indian society. In U.S. society there tend to be combined a focus upon the individual and a sense of the good and rights of others. The Ladino or mestizo society has in common with that of the U.S. a focus upon the individual, but combined with a sense of the good and rights of oneself. (Benito Juárez had to remind his own people that "respect for the rights of others is peace.") But the Indian societies differ from both that of the U.S. and that of the Ladino, in having an emphasis upon the group; this emphasis should probably be considered as being combined with a sense of the good and rights of oneself (or at least of the local group in contrast with other groups).[6] These differences may be represented graphically in the following form:

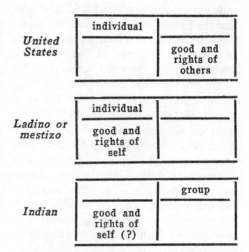

This difference between the U.S. society and the Ladino society no doubt constitutes part of the difficulty which has been encountered in establishing a true democracy in the Latin countries; it also produces problems whenever there is an attempt to introduce a democratic system into the church government of the Protes-

---

[5] See Clyde K. M. Kluckhohn, "Toward a Comparison of Value-Emphases in Different Cultures," in *The State of the Social Sciences* (Chicago: University of Chicago Press, 1956). More recently Benjamin N. Colby, at the Laboratory of Social Relations, Harvard University, has prepared a *Manual for the Use of the Clyde Kluckhohn Culture-Value Categories* which, when published, promises to be an especially useful tool in this field.

[6] This particular concept is subject to further definition and correction, inasmuch as the category of "self" is treated by Colby specifically as referring to the individual rather than to the group of which he is member. But there would seem to be need for differentiating at some level the concept of the good and rights of one's own group from that of the good and rights of other groups or of individuals outside one's own group.

tant groups. The difference which has been mentioned between the Ladino and Indian societies causes difficulty whenever there is an attempt to adapt to the Indian situation the authority structure that is used among the Ladinos or mestizos, especially when such a structure, as in the case of Protestant church government, is based upon U.S. norms. Note that as regards the two dimensions indicated, the Ladino has one factor (focus upon the individual) in common with U.S. society, and the Ladino and Indian societies probably have one factor (focus upon the rights of oneself) in common; but U.S. and Indian societies have no common factor as regards these two dimensions (although there are of course other dimensions in which they do have factors in common).

In the light of all this, when a decision must be made in an Indian community (such as naming a leader or deciding upon a particular action), the local people see no particular point in consulting each individual by means of his vote, and to do so could even have ill effects if a minority of individuals were to express themselves as opposed to the decision that is finally taken. What is more important is that the decision reflect (or at least appear to reflect) the unanimous opinion of the community; and this is achieved by delegating to the respected elders the responsibility of deciding on behalf of the group.

Besides, in a community which emphasizes the life of the group and the good of its own circle, it is considered much more important to name as leaders persons who have already demonstrated in their own community their aptitude and willingness to serve the group, than to name persons whose preparation has been mostly theoretical and by means of formal studies made in distant places.

Nominal Leaders vs. Real Leaders

Another factor, recently called to our attention by MacCoby and Modiano,[7] is that of nominal vs. real leadership. In their studies of children's activities in a mestizo village south of Mexico City they discovered that the boys who are real leaders tend to refuse positions of nominal or overt leadership. Rather, in the organization of boys' clubs a non-leader was usually chosen as head, and the real leaders would exercise their leadership from behind the scenes. Similarly, in adult life the men of this village who are the real leaders refuse to be named as overt leaders in the local political structure, saying they will be looked upon as corrupt if they do. The men who do accept positions of nominal leadership often turn out to be of the most ineffective type, and the real leaders tell them how to run things, or manage to work around them and get things done. (Among girls and women of the same village, however, the real leaders do accept positions of leadership.)

A similar phenomenon was noted some years ago when one of the authors of this article had the opportunity of observing, over a period of time, the development of a Ladino-Indian church in a rural community of Chiapas, Mexico. This church was completely indigenous in its origin, and before coming into contact with missionaries was organized along practical lines devised by the local group itself. During at least part of the time of observation, the man to whom the

---

[7] Michael MacCoby and Nancy Modiano, "Children's Games in Rural Mexico"; a paper presented and discussed at the 35th International Congress of Americanists, Mexico, 1962.

SELECTION OF LEADERS IN INDIAN FIELDS

entire group looked as leader and counselor was not the main leader in the overt
or nominal sense, yet continued to be
the spiritual leader year after year and
the one to whom the nominal leaders
constantly turned for guidance.

This raises a question which should be
investigated more fully, and whose implications for Christian leadership should be
explored more carefully. Certainly the
pattern of community life in Middle
American Indian societies (in contrast
with those with heavy Spanish influence)
tends to be such as to reward the person
who lives inconspicuously and to discourage the one who stands out as different from the rest. One therefore wonders
to what extent the most "available" church
leaders in some situations may or may
not be the ones best qualified for the
task. On the other hand, the question
may also be raised as to the cases of real
leaders who, willing and able to work
behind the scenes, have been promoted
(?) to overt leadership by ordination or
other recognition through the influence of
well-meaning missionaries who felt that
God-given leadership should be recognized
in such overt ways. Actually the real
leadership of such men may have been
more effectively recognized by the church,
albeit on a covert level, prior to their
being assigned an overt position. It would
probably not be hard to find numerous
cases of such natural leaders, who might
otherwise have continued effectively behind the scenes, being rendered ineffective
as a result of a type of official recognition
that is both foreign to their culture and
unnecessary to their exercise of real leadership.

We may well question the advisability
both of the outside ecclesiastical leader
(missionary or national) exercising too
much influence in the choice of the overt

leaders, and also of his introducing into
the Indian church categories of overt
leadership (via ordination or otherwise)
that are too unlike those already operative in the society or for which the
local church does not feel a need. The
introduction of such may actually place
the real leaders in nominal positions that
will reduce their total effectiveness. The
above-mentioned church in Chiapas, on
its own initiative, later become a part
of a national church organization — a
step which was probably necessary and
advisable from many points of view. But
when this local church, nearly all of
whose members had until then felt personally responsible to evangelize the neighboring ranches and villages, found itself
organized along the new (to them) lines
of the national church, with a new category of elders, they now assumed that
these should be responsible for the
evangelizing by virtue of their nominal
position in the church, and the members
in general ceased to feel responsible. Other
factors were no doubt present as well,
but the intrusion of a pattern of overt
leadership different from the traditional
pattern was probably one of the causes
of decadence.

Leadership in a Society in Transition

It should be emphasized that most of
the Indian communities are no longer
tribal groups living in isolation from the
rest of the world. The very presence of
authority systems other than the traditional one is evidence of this. Today,
with highways, schools, and mass communication media, the process of transition is accelerating. This means that,
although the traditional apprenticeship
patterns need to be taken into account
more seriously than has been done, it is

necessary also to consider the contemporary trends toward recognition of leadership via formal education.

The traditional pattern needs to be taken into account in order for the leaders to be recognized by the older generation and in the community structure as a whole, which is still traditionally oriented. The more modern pattern must be kept in mind, not only to satisfy the demands of the younger men for leadership, but also because today's leaders must point the way for their younger brethren who are advancing into a world where formal education and more youthful leadership are being recognized and who must learn to cope with the problems of Western culture.

This is part of the church's dilemma in Indian work in Latin America today: how to prepare leaders (whether Indian or mestizo) who on the one hand can appreciate the Indian cultural background, guide their people in terms of it, and be recognized as leaders in the society; and who on the other hand can prepare the newer generation in the Indian church to effectively participate in the national life to which they aspire, to relate themselves to the fellowship of the church on the national level, and to withstand the social and moral pressures brought upon them through their increasing and inevitable contacts with the world at large.[8]

Questions to be Investigated

We now give a number of questions which may be asked regarding a given local situation, and whose purpose is to suggest lines of investigation and themes of discussion. These should be considered not so much a questionnaire to fill out as a series of subjects to be investigated.

What is the particular form of the five systems of authority described, in the Indian community in question?

To what extent is the structure of authority in the local Protestant church similar to that of the local traditional civil-religious system? To that of the Catholic systems? To that of the civil constitutional system? (This should be studied both in regard to the local internal relations and also the external relations with the authority outside the community.)

Do you know of concrete cases of conflicts that have resulted from imposition of an authority from outside, either in the church or in a social or political matters?

When a person is to be named for some particular responsibility in the Indian community, how is that person chosen? Who makes the choice?

If some project is to be carried out in the community, how is the decision made? Is there a popular vote, or is it decided by the elders? Does there remain a minority who are opposed to the project? If so, do they continue to express their opposition after the decision is made?

At what age are the men considered to be adult members of the community? In the case of young men who leave their community before this age and later return, how are they looked upon by the community? Are they recognized as full members of the society, or do they remain somewhat marginal to it? What role do they play in the authority structure after returning?

Is there in the community a division

---

8 For more on this aspect of the problem, see William L. Wonderly, "Indian Work and Church-Mission Integration," PA, Vol. 8, No. 5 (Sept.-Oct. 1961), pp. 193-99.

in two parts or factions, dominated by two important and competing families and including other families in a satellite relationship to them? If so, to which division or divisions do the leaders in the local Protestant church belong? How were these leaders chosen?

What kind of churches are there in the community: Ladino and Indian completely separated? Indian congregation with Ladino pastor? Mixed congregation with two pastors? Which arrangement do you consider would be best for this community? Why?

Who exercises the real authority (not necessarily the position of theoretical authority) in the local Protestant church? If the pastor is a Ladino who lives outside the community, what is his real function in relation to the direction of the work? If it is a mixed congregation, which of the two groups exercises the real authority? Are there conflicts resulting from this?

Who really has the spiritual power in the local church: the Ladino pastor, some Indian brother, or some other person or persons?

What opportunities are there in the local church for a person to assume progressively greater degrees of responsibility and authority as he demonstrates his abilities in lesser positions? Is there an apprenticeship system? What recognition is given to persons who show leadership ability and spiritual discernment within the Indian congregation?

What relation do the elders of the local church have with the outside church groups (presbytery, conference, etc.) or with the mission?

When the missionary ceases to assume formal authority, how much authority does he retain in practice?

How many times a year does the local church have baptisms and the Lord's Supper? If they are not observed with sufficient frequency, is this due to lack of visits from an outside pastor?

Does the church have degrees of ordination (e.g. local preachers, elders with full ordination, elders ordained to administer the sacraments in their local church only, etc.)?

If the Ladino or mestizo pastor is the one who administers the sacraments, who then explains their significance to the Indians? Is this explanation satisfactory, in terms of what the sacraments mean in relation to the problems of the Indian believer? Which requires greater spiritual discernment: the administering of the sacraments, or preaching and teaching? Who has actually succeeded in giving the most significant teaching in the local Indian church?

Do you believe that mestizo or Ladino pastors should be prepared for ministering to Indian churches? If so, what special preparation should they have which the pastor in other rural churches or in city churches does not have, in order to relate their message and their role of authority to the Indian situation?

In the preparation of Indian pastors for Indian churches, what special preparation should be given which is not given to other pastors? Should they receive their preparation in the Indian language, in Spanish, or part in one and part in the other? Should the preparation be given in the Indian area, or outside? If they take formal study outside their community (or in a boarding institution within their area), at what age should they do so in order that they may upon returning function as full members of their own society?

James Emery

The Preparation of Leaders in a Ladino-Indian Church

Faced with the problem of setting up a single program to train leaders for a church whose constituency includes peasant Indians, Spanish-speaking urban dwellers, and intermediate transitional stages, James Emery has made an analysis of the differing leadership patterns at different levels. He has drawn up a project of a type of seminary preparation which would combine the Indian apprenticeship system with the modern system of formal education. The same problem faces other denominational churches in Latin America and it is hoped that the author's approach and the pilot project he outlines may serve as a stimulus for other efforts.

THE Presbyterian Church has been working in Guatemala for eighty years, yet one problem which remains to be solved is that of developing the leadership needed within its churches. This same problem is shared by the Latin American countries of Ecuador, Peru, Bolivia, and (to a lesser extent) Mexico and other countries with an Indian population. It is created in Guatemala by the fact that more than half the population consists of Indians speaking their own languages and a minority of Spanish-speaking Ladinos with their own culture. The first step toward a solution is to understand to some degree the cultural relationships arising out of this range of population and then to use this knowledge in setting up leadership training projects.

Within the field in which we work

James Emery, as a fraternal worker of the United Presbyterian Church, is in charge of the Presbyterian Seminary of Guatemala. This paper is an outline of the discussion at the *Conferencia Pro-Obra Indígena* held in Guatemala in May 1962. Hartford Seminary Foundation, 55 Elizabeth St., Hartford 5, Conn.

there is a whole series of gradations from communities that are almost completely Indian to those that are almost entirely Spanish. Figure 1 indicates this relation. Of course, whenever the dominant culture, such as that of the Ladinos, finds itself a small minority, even it must cede to some extent to the majority. Thus in the Indian communities there are always a few Ladinos speaking the Indian language (while protesting that they do not understand it), because all business is carried on in it. The reverse situation holds for areas such as the capital city, where Spanish is the language and modern Western culture is dominant. Where there is a more nearly equal proportion (near the center of the chart in figure 1), there are many conflicts. This is the area of rapid acculturation where different values are being contested, and it is in this type of situation the Presbyterian churches are located. Since the highlands are predominantly Indian, it is in the coffee and agricultural area of the coast that this process is most rapid, and even violent. Many Indians go to this area as seasonal

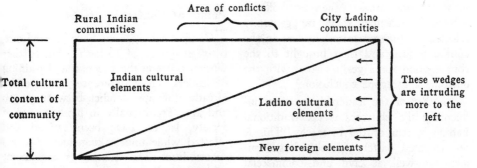

Figure 1. Cultural gradations in Guatemalan communities

agricultural laborers, never to return to their old habitat. Also, the land reform movement in opening up homesteads has drawn away the landless surplus population of the highlands.

While the Indian is coming into contact with Spanish culture, the country as a whole is involved in cultural borrowing from the United States and Europe. In addition, the rapid industrialization of the country leads to further change, and thus the Indian in contact with the Ladino culture is not facing a stable situation. This change is accelerating with the extension of rural schools and available secondary educational opportunities. The needs of modern industry for mechanics and drivers, and the introduction of modern equipment are forcing change in order to move into opening opportunities. Possibly the most important influence is the building of all-weather roads into areas which hitherto have been severely limited in outside contacts. That this influence will increase and produce a synthesis which is neither Ladino or Indian is highly probable.

Traditional Leadership Patterns

These aspects of material culture are of course the first to change and the most superficial. Attitudes, thought patterns, and customs are much more persistent. It is with these that we must deal in any leadership training program. The most obvious of the patterns which will affect our work is that of the role of the traditional leadership. The leadership patterns among the highland Indians have been analyzed by a number of persons and it is clear that while the traditional system is not conventionally democratic, it is representative. It is a group leadership system in which the group by a process of consensus comes to a conclusion, and the chosen representative, possibly the most revered of the elders, announces it. These elders are not self-chosen, but arrive at their place of leadership by a process of training in successive responsibilities.

This pattern of leadership development is still in use in a rudimentary form in many partly Indian or rural Ladino areas. Even in communities where the various titles and the specific process of moving up the ladder are not known, the idea of group decision is still the important form. This has been noted when there has been an attempt to initiate the usual North American forms of church govern-

ment in rural areas. When new officers
are to be elected, they are generally
selected by the recognized leaders in the
church group, and then brought to the
congregation for a yes/no vote, with the
outcome a foregone conclusion.[1]

Another of the leadership patterns influencing the churches is the traditional
Ladino system of the hierarchy. This is
the accepted pattern for church government as well as civil and commercial
enterprises. It is clearly becoming more
dominant in many parts of the country
as there is increased contact between the
cultures.

A further type of leadership pattern is
that of the Protestant churches of the
United States which through the missionary has influenced the local situation. This
influence is most strongly felt among the
leaders of the church who have learned
the system and feel it is the only one.
Many do not understand that possible
variations of it may exist even within
the same tradition in the United States.

Of limited, though growing influence,
is the so-called New Testament leadership
pattern. In this type the heads of households are selected as elders and these men
(who generally do not leave their ordinary
occupations, but become leaders without
remuneration from the congregation)
carry the load of teaching, preaching,
pastoral care, and administration. It is
significant that this pattern already seems
to exist to a great extent in the rural
areas, both among Ladinos and Indians.

---

[1] Fortunately, the Presbyterian church government is, with slight modification, quite
similar to the government of the rural Ladino
and Indian cultures. If the elders function as
elders and govern in the prescribed way with
decisions made in conference and not by one
person, then the two should be very compatible.

Points of Conflict

Conflict exists, as we have pointed out,
between systems of leadership, but further
tension arises in the selection and training
of leaders. These differences increase the
already unhappy conflict between youth
and age. Traditionally in most sectors of
society, leaders have been trained and
selected while undertaking successive responsibilities. The training is concurrent
with the job and selection is indicated
as the person either advances to the next
stage or else is dropped. This takes place
in the Indian culture in ways previously
mentioned. The same thing happens,
however, in other areas of the culture
and is the procedure in most trades. A
person learns by working at the side of
a master carpenter for a number of years;
if his work is good, the training will
continue; if not, the apprenticeship ends.
In other areas of community life certain
people will have a reputation for clear
judgment and a kind heart and will be
consulted by other members of the community regarding sickness, marriage, or
property problems. If this person's advice
is not good or his motives doubted, the
people will turn to someone else next
time. The selection is thus informal, but
effective.

But the modern world, through education, accelerates this method of slow advancement and natural selection. By going
to school it is possible to begin at a higher
place, and from there the traditional system in a moderated form takes over. This
new possibility produces problems and
conflicts in many ways. For instance, a
man who has been a competent accountant
for years may find himself pitted against
a young graduate with a degree but no
ability. The young man gets the job because he is authorized by the government

to sign official documents, while the older man is not. The same process occurs in the churches if a young man fresh from seminary or Bible school steps in as pastor of a congregation originally built up by a layman. The natural leader is the resident layman, while the new pastor is a transient. If a conflict arises, as frequently happens, clearly the pastor must leave. If by some chance — or rules of the governing ecclesiastical body — the pastor is confirmed, then a division occurs and a second church will be formed of most of the members and with the elder as leader again. This conflict between the traditional growth in leadership and the modern short-cut-to-success-through-education is one of the most serious.

There are other differences between the cultures which must be considered. Within the Indian and rural Ladino cultures, everybody is expected to participate in the activities of the community and the church. In the cities there is much less compulsion and more freedom of choice. The excessively rigid control of each individual's activities in a rural area forces a person to cooperate and to take responsibility. A person from the more open and permissive urban society going to a rural area is often resentful over what he considers intrusions upon his rights. This may prevent an urban person from obtaining a leadership position with the closed community.

In the rural areas there is no rigid division of labor. The carpenter or storekeeper also plants corn and cares for his own land and animals. Life is viewed as a unity and all its activities are coherent. Thus, lacking a professional class, the leader will handle many different activities. He must be able to advise on marriage, death, property transfer, or sickness. His wife, who also influences to a great extent his position as leader, may be the local midwife. He is expected to exert leadership in varied aspects of the group life. In the cities, on the contrary, the doctor cares for the sick, the lawyer advises on property matters, the mason builds houses, and the pastor is fully involved in church activities. This contrast in specialization produces many points of conflict and needs to be considered in any training program.

Leadership for Different Types of Churches

Since there are already churches in existence in Guatemala, their very presence indicates that some leadership has been trained in the past. A consideration of what has been done and the resulting type of church should help in future planning.

There are generally three types of churches in the field, as indicated in the three diagrams of figure 2. The first is very similar to those in the United States. These are located in the cities and the larger towns. There is a full-time paid pastor, and a session (consistorio) of elders drawn from the area. These elders probably do not have any specific leadership functions among the people of the congregation in affairs which do not involve the church. The pastor does most of the preaching, teaching, and pastoral care. The elders may be active in these fields, but are definitely subordinate to the pastor. This requires relatively high training for the pastor, with sufficient secular educational background to put him on a basis of equality with the more highly educated members of the church. Of about 16 Presbyterian churches of this type in Guatemala, 12 have pastors and one has a part-time pastor. Most of these pastors are seminary graduates.

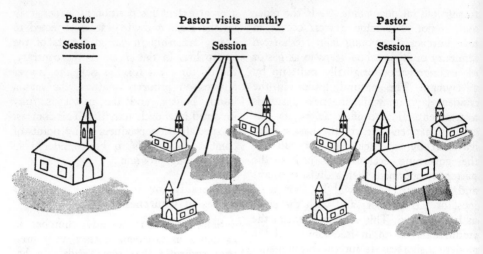

Figure 2. Three types of churches.

The second type of church is the purely rural one with a number of congregations scattered over a large area (20 to 25 square miles), each with a central meeting point. At each of these points there may or may not be a strong congregation. In each of these congregations there is a leader who represents the group on the church board and directs the activities of the local group. Of about 34 churches of this type only two have full-time pastors completely supported by the congregations. There are two others which have a full-time unordained paid worker. Some six others have pastors or workers, but these are supported with foreign funds.

The third type of church is an intermediate one and has a strong central group in a small city or large town, from which are drawn some of the officers, others coming from the surrounding rural areas with congregations as described above. Of 21 churches of this type, six

have full-time pastors, four half-time pastors, and two have full-time unordained workers.

It is clear that churches in a type of society accustomed to a professional approach to occupations will have more full-time pastors. In communities with no rigid division of labor, there tend to be fewer professional pastors. Undoubtedly other factors are at work here, such as unwillingness of trained men to go to rural areas and lower salary scales. These, however, are concomitant cultural factors. The problem remains the same, to provide adequate leadership for all parts of the church.

The various presbyteries in Guatemala each have the control of their own candidates for the ministry, with power to ordain them and to set requirements within certain broad constitutional lines. But even these constitutional requirements can be set aside by a three-fourths vote of a presbytery. Consequently, the presbyseries have for many years each had their own training program, different in each presbytery, and at times changing within the presbytery itself in succeeding years. Among the students under the care of any one presbytery, there are usually a rather large number who study only the courses provided by the presbytery and do not go to seminary. There is no specified educational requirement for entrance into the ministry. Most of the students are over 25 year old and relatively mature. Most are married. A few others may meet the requirements for entrance into seminary: four years of primary school and two of secondary, plus a recommendation. These students are often immature, with very little concept of what they are undertaking. The people who most need the training are not those who traditionally attend the seminary, but those of the larger group who are more mature, and with experience. These, however, cannot attend seminary for economic reasons, even if they could meet the academic requirements.

Another problem which has found no easy solution, is that of training students of a wide cultural and educational spectrum in the same institution. A few have had some university training, while others have never even completed primary school. Cultural backgrounds differ as well. There is the university level student, the middle class Ladino of the city, the rural Ladino, the progressive Quiché Indian, the student from the more retarded Mam Indian community. It is impossible effectively to reach any group of such broad range in the same classroom. How can it be done at all within the same system? In most countries it is accomplished by the stratified levels of training programs found in the different denominations.

Need for a New Approach

That the past training programs have been inadequate is clear from the fact that almost half the seminary graduates have left the pastorate and many are no longer connected with the church in any capacity. Relatively few have finished the presbytery course, partly due to the lack of continued supervision as well as the frequently changed curriculum.

There are certain other elements which should be incorporated in any system of leadership development if it is to produce the results desired. The curriculum should challenge the students to remain informed and interested even after leaving school. They need to learn personal discipline of a high degree, if they are to persevere with their training. With the limited personnel available for the teaching task, it must be used as efficiently as possible and the program needs to be capable of becoming self-sustaining once it is under way. Otherwise the number of candidates who can be trained will be limited and this will severely curtail future possibilities. There must be a large number studying at any one time in order to train adequate leadership for the whole field.

Furthermore, the selection of the students must be made on the basis of experience as well as the clearest possible evidence of a call and a sincere desire to serve the Lord. The winnowing should be done before effort and money have been expended, not afterward. At present only two types of people can attend the usual seminary: those with money (and therefore leisure), or those who have not as yet assumed any responsibilities (and for this very reason may be those who will never accept any). Thus it is desirable that those who enter training should be those who have proved themselves to have a record of competence in practical, concrete responsibilities. A man's work and position within his community are a good guide on this point.

The course should be such that the students will derive sufficient breadth of viewpoint and sympathy to be able to see the values and weaknesses of each group within the country's culture. A person who views the Indian as a cultureless animal will not succeed in a church in which most of the believers are Indians. Likewise a person from a closely knit and conservative rural area needs to learn to appreciate and understand his brethren in the more permissive city churches.

A Project for Leadership Training

What type of program then will meet the needs of these conditions? Certain lines seem clear. It cannot be done alone with an institutional program which requires students to leave their family and livelihood for three years. Some other solution must be sought. We have projected an extension department, relating it directly to each of the presbyteries of the church, and working closely with other institutions of the church, such as the Indian Bible institutes, the Lake Amatitlán Conference Center, and the University Student Center. The courses can be adapted to each academic level, with the educational backgrounds of the students controlling the rate at which they advance. Though all students will be chosen for competence, those of good academic background can advance rapidly and those with limited educational opportunities can proceed more slowly. The program can thus be useful to a greater variety of people than could possibly be taught together in a single classroom.

The course would begin with a one- or two-week institute to introduce the basic subject matter. The students would then return home, taking the lessons with them to study and sending in the written assignments for correction. It is hoped that it will be possible for each student to make monthly visits to the seminary campus, as well as receiving visits from the seminary faculty members or other qualified persons to observe and advise him in his local church situation. These counseling sessions would provide directional guides for the student, and enable the seminary and presbytery to make a more adequate assessment of the quality of work and capacity for leadership of the person. At the end of the year there would be another period for review at the seminary and then final examinations. The grading would be based not only on the examination, but also on the assignments completed during the year.

It is expected that at this time the student will be encouraged to learn a basic trade as well. Believing that man is intended to benefit his fellow man as well as provide for himself, we want students to enter into occupations not only adequate to support themselves but also helpful for the community of believers and society in general. If it is clear that he has the capacity to be faithful on the level of concrete love and good works, he will have passed a crucial test for entering the spiritual ministry.

The courses to be provided are concentrated on the following areas:

Inductive Bible study. This gives the student confidence in handling the basic tool with which he has to work throughout his life. Not only will he learn to think for himself and dig meaning out of the Bible, but he will acquire the capacity to do the same with other literature. The need to be specific and write out answers to questions in a clear and logical way disciplines his mind to formulate answers for other problems as well. It is helpful in preparation of sermons, lessons, or instructive articles.

Historical study. We feel that a thorough grasp of the history of the church and the movements within it, is essential to an understanding of the church and the problems confronting this generation. After an outline study of history, the origin, causes, and results of such movements as the Reformation, the Wesleyan revivals, and the modern missionary movement will be studied in detail. Other lessons will deal with the sects and non-religious movements of this century on the same basis.

The cultural matrix of Guatemala. To assist the students to understand the situation in which they find themselves today, we plan to teach the basic, practical aspects of psychology and anthropology — the latter being especially geared to the problems of the present Ladino-Indian relationship in Guatemala. They will study the church as it is, in the light of what it should be. From this base the courses will branch into the communication of the gospel in available media, from personal counseling to radio and films. Some of these methods requiring equipment and group participation will be taught in short institutes.

Vocational training. Realizing that not all pastors will be fully supported, we plan to stimulate work in vocations which will provide a living while the person works in the church, as mentioned above. Much of this will be done by directing the person to places where he can receive vocational training, and then encouraging him to persevere. By having a vocation he will sink deeper roots and have a more lasting influence in his community. An honest, integrated, well-disciplined life earns the respect of others. Maturity and experience gained in business and industry are of particular value to the minister, for many people often feel he does not understand their problems or responsibilities. He should be able to introduce new ideas and practices for the community much as an agricultural extension agent does. This should be done in the fields of agriculture, health, education, and possibly small industry. To this end we plan to teach some agriculture, simple medicine, and hygiene. These will be of direct benefit to the community.

We feel that this type of program will solve the majority of problems presented for consideration. The need for financial support is reduced to the minimum. Once set up, the course can carry on with a modicum of highly trained supervision and so could be handled in the absence of foreign personnel. It will give the student experience of several kinds while securing formal education, and leadership is developed on more than one cultural level. Thus the student need not lose his roots in the local community, and have to struggle to find his place later. He will learn to appreciate the history and culture of others and be better able to deal with the variety of problems to be faced at national church assemblies. The program has enough flexibility to provide for the fast and the slow, the highly trained or poorly trained student. We hope that this plan, modified if needed by future experience, will prove of service in the church.

Benjamin N. Colby

Indian Attitudes Towards Education and Inter-Ethnic Contact in Mexico

In an earlier article in PRACTICAL ANTHROPOLOGY, *the author discussed the significance of values, attitude, and social relationship for the part which they play in influencing social change, centering the discussion on resistance of Indians to girls' learning Spanish and learning to read. Now, in the present article, Dr. Colby presents more data on Indian attitudes toward education and toward contact with Ladinos. No educational system operates in a vacuum. Inevitably the community in which it operates abounds in a complex of attitudes toward it, attitudes which will militate strongly for or against the goals of the educators. This article presents one brief case in point.[1]*

THIS study concerns an area in the southern Mexican highlands where two distinct cultures, one Indian, the other Hispanic, participate in a mutually dependent way in the same social system. The rural Indians supply labor for the urban, hispanicized Mexicans, who occupy the upper prestige positions in the society and who look down on manual labor as socially degrading. The hub of this particular social system is the town of San Cristóbal de las Casas, lying at an altitude of 7000 feet in the rugged central plateau of the state of Chiapas. The town has some 20,000 inhabitants who are locally

referred to as Ladinos. The distinction is cultural rather than racial. Ladinos contain varying degrees of Indian and white racial characteristics but are of essentially hispanic culture.

In the mountainous hinterland surrounding San Cristóbal are some 125,000 Tsotsil and Tseltal Indians. These Indians depend on the Ladinos for certain religious services, for political administration.

Benjamin N. Colby is a research associate of the Department of Social Relations, Harvard University. A previous acticle based upon his research in Chiapas, Mexico, entitled "Social Relations and Directed Culture Change Among the Zinacantan," appeared in PRACTICAL ANTHROPOLOGY, Vol. 7, No. 6 (Nov.-Dec. 1960).

[1] This study is part of the Harvard Mexican Culture Change Project directed by Prof Evon Z. Vogt and supported by the National Institute of Mental Health. Part of the results reported here appear in more detail in a doctoral dissertation written with the aid of a Social Science Research Council fellowship The help of the following people is gratefully acknowledged: John Baroco, Frans Blom, Julie de la Fuente, Domingo de la Torre P., Rober Laughlin, Frank Miller, Fidencio Montes S. Jorge Rodríguez G., Mariano Trujillo R. Artemio Utrilla, Pierre van den Berghe, Leo poldo Velasco R., Alfonso Villa R., Evor Vogt.

for wage work or land rental, and for the marketing of agricultural produce. But their cultural values are, for the most part, independent of Ladino culture.[2]

In one Indian group, the Zinacantans, about 24 per cent of the adult males are able to speak Spanish. A smaller proportion of Zinacantan women can speak it. Other Tsotsil and Tseltal groups have even lower indices of bilingualism. Indians learn Spanish, according to their own statements, by working on plantations, by doing highway construction, or by acting as servants during childhood and early adolescence in Ladino homes, or by learning it in school.

The Ladinos depend on the Indians for produce, labor, and for the purchase of manufactured goods such as hardware, clothing, cloth, "patent medicines," candles, fireworks, and alcohol. Those that deal frequently with Indians have sufficient command of the Tsotsil and Tseltal languages to barter with monolinguals. But the percentage of truly bilingual Ladinos is extremely small.

The paternalistic and abusive treatment of the Indians by the Ladinos has caused tension and anxiety among the Indians. Though usually suppressed, it is discoverable in the folk tales, in intimate conversations, and in psychological data, and sometimes breaks into violence. Particularly oppressive Ladinos have been killed on occasion and several rebellions have broken out, the last one as late as 1935. In general, relations with Ladinos are sometimes charged with feelings of ambivalence and suppressed emotionality. These feelings

extend to questions of knowing Spanish and of knowing how to read and write because such attributes are so closely associated with Ladino identity. By further extension, ambivalence and emotionality normally associated with Ladino contact sometimes exist in attitudes about school attendance.

Opportunities for Education

Since the implementation of the principles of the Mexican revolution during the past twenty-five years, opportunities for limited education have been available to some Indians. Recent work of the federal Indian agency, the Instituto Nacional Indigenista, has increased these opportunities substantially.

In spite of these new opportunities, the major obstacles to the government program exist in the Indians themselves. Among the Huistan and Zinacantan Indians, economic necessity keeps many children from the schools. The families that do send their children to school do not understand the importance of steady attendance and have little knowledge of the requirements of learning. Learning to read or to speak Spanish is sometimes approached magically. Special liquids and pills are sold in San Cristóbal pharmacies that are supposed to make one bilingual or literate. In addition to this magical approach towards learning, certain esoteric powers are sometimes associated with literacy itself. In the Huistan town of Chilil, some Indians fear their few Indian companions who are literate. Other individuals may keep a notebook and pencil in their houses without knowing how to use them, because of the special powers associated with them. However, it is also true that more enlightened Indians may

---

[2] For an excellent description of ethnic relations in Mexico see Julio de la Fuente, "Ethnic and Communal Relations," *Heritage of Conquest,* edited by Sol Tax (Glencoe, Ill.: The Free Press, 1952).

keep notebooks in which literate friends record certain debts and obligations for them.[3]

Usually, reading and speaking Spanish are viewed as desirable goals. In some cases Spanish can be so highly valued that Indians will devalue the need for reading in their own language. This varies from one individual to the next. Others value their own language more highly than Spanish. In the Huistan area, the women are expected to stop speaking Spanish (if they have previously learned how) when they get married, or perhaps sooner, for it is not proper for a woman of marriageable age to speak Spanish. The explicit reason is that women are not expected to know Spanish because they have to remain in the home weaving, tending sheep, or doing other household duties and they do not travel to distant places (except perhaps for marketing) where Spanish would have to be used. The implicit reason, inferred from the association with marriage, concerns the possibilities of Ladino-Indian sexual relations. This will be discussed later.

Motivation to learn Spanish and to learn to read appears to be stronger among those young men in families owning very little land. They know they will not inherit land enough for a living and they may have to move to new places where Spanish is more important. School attendance in Chilil in the Huistan area is slightly higher among the poorer families.

The results to be reported in this study

concern the Zinacantan Indians — a group of perhaps 8000 individuals living in mountain valleys adjacent to San Cristóbal.

Method of Investigation

An oral interview consisting of questions and answers in Tsotsil was administered by a bilingual literate Ladino and a bilingual literate Zinacantan. The procedure was to go from house to house in three hamlets or *parajes* in the *municipio* of Zinacantan and interview the heads of families by reading Tsotil questions from a printed interview form. Thirteen out of the forty-five questions were open-ended questions, which were filled in by the interviewing team in Tsotsil for precision of communication. The remaining questions were yes-no, good-bad, or multiple-choice questions.

The questions were translated into Tsotsil by two members of the interviewing team and Lore M. Colby, who has been making a linguistic study of Tsotsil. They were retranslated and tested for accuracy of meaning and connotation with the aid of other bilingual Indians. These questions were subsequently tested in the field and revised a number of times before the final form was printed. A few of the questions were reciprocal to those of a Ladino questionnaire administered in San Cristóbal.[4]

The interviewing team had been under training for interviewing and for linguistic work by the author and his wife for six months before the final version of the questionnaire was ready. The author accompanied the team during the trial runs until the details of interviewing were

---

[3] The uses of literate skills are a mystery to some Indians. Others conceive of rather limited and unusual possibilities. One man explained that he wished he knew how to read so that when he was in the strange town of Tuxtla Gutiérrez (the state capital some sixty miles away, where he has been twice in this life) he could read the street signs and not get lost.

[4] P. van den Berghe and B. N. Colby, "Ladino-Indian Relations in the Highlands of Chiapas, Mexico," *American Anthropologist,* forthcoming.

ufficiently worked out. After this time he team worked alone until ninety-one interview forms had been collected.

The exigencies of the field situation made a randomized sampling procedure, or any other type of rigorous procedure, impossible. We do not have precise information on the response rate but it was

TABLE 1
"What things do Ladinos do that we don't do?"

Abilities and activities:	Frequency
Reads, writes	30
Makes or drives car	12
Knows how to make money or where to find his meals	3
Speaks Spanish	1
Plays the marimba	1
Roles:	
Carpenter	15
Mason	14
Merchant	10
Blacksmith	6
Teacher	4
Highway construction foreman	3
Doctor	3
Lawyer	3
Barber	3
Engineer	2
Shoemaker	2
Weaver	2
Pharmacist	1
Judge	1
President	1
Manufacture the following objects:	
Houses	4
Tile	3
Shoes	2
Cloth	2
Chairs	2
Book or paper	2
Untranslatable	4

Others (one reply for each): airplanes, bread, chicle, cookies, oil, sugar, silk, pok (Indian neckerchief), lamps, highways, hats, bricks, hardware, Coca-Cola, thread, comb, baskets, sheet metal, mirror

high. The Indian member of the team was himself a Zinacantan and he took the initiative in asking the questions, while the Ladino member wrote down the answers. Because Zinacantan culture is characterized by an elaborate etiquette, the Zinacantan member of the team proved to be indispensable for his particularly tactful approach in compliance with the requirements of this etiquette.

Except for a forty-year-old widow and thirteen students, the remaining seventy respondents were men ranging in age from twenty to ninety with a median age of thirty-five, a mean age of thirty-nine, and a modal age of thirty. The thirteen students ranged in age from nine to fifteen. Three of them were girls and ten were boys. Including all respondents, forty-three were from the village of Nachij, twenty-seven from Paste', and twenty-one from Chainatic. All of the students stated that they spoke Spanish and knew how to read, while only fifteen in the remainder of the sample said they knew Spanish, and only five claimed they knew how to read.

Ladino-Indian Relationships

One of the first things we wanted to find out was how the Indians viewed the differences between themselves and the Ladinos.

When asked the question, "What things do Ladinos do that we do not do?" the most frequent answer given cited the Ladinos' ability to read and write. Out of 150 answers to this question, thirty of them concerned literacy. The remaining answers had to do with occupational roles: building, artisan, professional, and selling roles in that order, or with the making of objects such as houses, shoes, tiles, clothes, books, paper, and articles often used by Indians (Table 1).

In the reciprocal question, "What things do we do that Ladinos don't do?" all but one of the responses were about agricultural activities (Table 2).

From these answers it is obvious that the Zinacantans look on themselves as a rural, corn-raising people, while they regard Ladinos as literate persons engaged in professional or skilled manual or artisan trades and as the providers of manufactured goods.[5]

The following question series explored the positive or negative evaluation by Indians of Ladinos: "Do you know any Ladinos that are very bad?" "If so, why are they bad?" "Do you know any Ladinos that are very good?" "If so, why are they good?" Ten respondents reported that they knew good Ladinos, but did not know bad ones. Seven reported the reverse, that they knew bad Ladinos but not good ones, and sixteen reported knowing both good and bad Ladinos. Fifty-eight said they knew neither good nor bad Ladinos; one had no answer. Thus 64 per cent knew neither good nor bad Ladinos, while 32 per cent knew good, bad, or both.

One reason for Ladinos being good was given seven times. It was that "he is good if he speaks, talks, or converses well." The remaining reasons were given only once: "They teach us to understand or help us to communicate." "They are good if they offer their friendship." "Because God made him good." "Because if he is

---

[5] While the ability to read and write was the most dominant characteristic in defining Ladinos, most of the respondents in answer to another question thought that only about half the Ladinos knew how to read, though as many as twenty-seven believed that all Ladinos could read.

TABLE 2
"What do we do that Ladinos don't do?"

Agricultural activities:	Frequency
Raise corn, including the following activities: clear ground, burn, hoe and weed, harvest	65
Use hoe or machete	4
Go to hot country (i.e., to raise corn)	2
Plant beans	1
Other activities:	
Weave palm (for hats)	1

bad he will be punished by the devil." "Because according to God we are the same." "He is good if he doesn't beat me."

Reasons why Ladinos are not good were even more varied. Two received three replies each: "They don't speak to us," and "They beat us, kill us." The remainder had one each: "Because God made them bad." "They are angry when we do not understand them." "Because they don't know (our?) God." "They do not speak clearly." "They speak with a hard heart." "They feel superior because they read." "They envy us."

In comparing the replies to these two questions, it becomes immediately evident that the major reason for liking or disliking Ladinos has to do with communica-

TABLE 3
"Is it good or bad for girls to learn Spanish?"

Answer	Frequency
Good	49
Bad	26
Good and bad	9
No answers	7
	—
	91

to read?"
TABLE 4
"Is it good or bad for girls to learn

Answer	Frequency
Good	41
Bad	29
Good and bad	10
No answer	11
	91

tion. Next in importance, especially in the reasons for disliking Ladinos, are aggressive acts or attitudes towards the Indians.

Indian children of all ages, up through adolescence, will sometimes work for Ladino families in San Cristóbal. As much as 43 per cent of the adult males in the sample had worked in Ladino homes at one time or another. However, most of them worked for around three weeks (the median), with the range all the way from

TABLE 5
Positive reasons given for girls learning Spanish

Answer	Frequency
To be smart (one man said: to be smarter than we are)	12
For communication with Ladinos (3 answers specified female Ladinos)	8
Good for work (a job) One specified working in a Ladino house, another in San Cristóbal, and another said it was good in order to understand the directions of the Ladino woman employer)	5
Good for buying or selling (good for counting)	4
Can become a teacher	2
For traveling	1
For finding food	1
Good, if they want to learn it	1

one week to four years. Eighty-six per cent of them worked no longer than a month at the most. Not many answers were given for leaving work, but the majority of them stated that they had to work on their own cornfields, or that they did not like the work, or had enough of it. Two said that the work was too hard, one that there was not enough pay, one that there was some trouble over an animal, and one had an accident. A succinct answer was, "God wanted it (that I quit), I had to burn my corn-field, I ate very little."

An examination of the amount of traveling done to Tuxtla Gutiérrez (capital of Chiapas, about sixty miles from San Cristóbal), and the amount of Spanish-speaking ability and the association of these two variables with the ages of our respondents show that important generational changes are presently in process. Not including students (who all spoke Spanish), over one-fourth of the people under thirty-five knew Spanish, while less than one-tenth of the people thirty-five or older knew Spanish. Younger people tend to do more traveling than older people. Close to a third of those who have been to Tuxtla Gutiérrez six times or more speak Spanish, compared with slightly over one-tenth who have been in Tuxtla Gutiérrez less than six times. Thus traveling and knowledge of Spanish are associated with each other and with the younger generation among the Zinacantans. The reasons for this must be primarily the improvement of roads and transportation in the area.

Another association, though slight, is that of the wearing of Ladino clothes with the ability to speak Spanish. Sixty per cent of the Indians knowing Spanish occasionally wore Ladino clothes, while only 35 per cent of non-Spanish speaking Indians occasionally wore Ladino clothes.

Education of Girls

One of the major problems besetting the government educational program was the reluctance of Indians to send girls to school. This was approached directly with the following questions: "Is it good or bad for girls to learn Spanish?" and "Is it good or bad for girls to learn to read?" and "Why?" The results are summarized in Tables 3 and 4.

For both questions the majority of answers were favorable. However, the answers to the literacy question were more negative or slightly more uncertain than the answers to learning Spanish. Positive reasons given for girls learning Spanish are classified in Table 5. The negative reasons given for this question are in Table 6. Out of the twenty reasons, only three had to do with the idea of school interfering with activities around the house. All the other reasons showed a concern with ethnic identity, marrying Ladinos (which involves ethnic identity), or not being proper wives to Indian husbands.

Thus we are led to the conclusion that in the case of women learning Spanish, negative reasons do not tend to be economic ones so much as psycho-social ones concerning sex status and relations within and between cultures.

Positive reasons given for girls learning to read are recorded in Table 7. Negative reasons for girls learning to read are in Table 8. The pattern again is a fairly clear one. The positive answers are overwhelmingly in favor of a girl becoming a teacher, with being smart, or making money, or working in San Cristóbal following in second place.

TABLE 6
Negative reasons given for girls learning Spanish

Answer	Frequency
She will boss, mistreat us men, not be afraid of, not obey her husband	7
She will (in effect) no longer be Zinacantan or will not associate with her (Indian) companions	4
She should not speak to or marry Ladinos (speak to, 1; marry, 3)	4
She should make tortillas or herd sheep	3
We don't think or feel like Ladinos	2

The negative reasons seem split between concern with the division of labor and ethnic identity (five each); marriage and becoming too forward or rebellious, perhaps "spilling over" from the answers in Question No. 39, where these reasons had major representation.

Perhaps the most important single ques-

TABLE 7
Positive reasons given for girls learning to read

Answer	Frequency
To become a teacher	18
To be smart	4
To make money, see how to work, work in San Cristóbal	4
For buying and selling	1
To be a store owner	1
She can do what she wants to (meaning either that she can learn to read if she wants to without interference, or it might mean that once she can read, she is free to do whatever she wants to)	2
She can learn to sew	1
She can be like the Ladinos	1
She feels good if she understands Spanish (referring to the previous question)	1
She can become a secretary	1

tion for educators to ask is whether Indian attitudes toward Ladinos are significantly related to their acceptance or rejection of education. We predicted that rejection of Ladinos would correlate with rejection of schooling for girls. To test this it was first necessary to decide on a measure of acceptance and rejection of Ladinos. A scale was derived by combining two questions: "Would you accept a Ladino for a neighbor?" and "How often do you visit Ladino friends in San Cristóbal?" The subjects were placed into three categories: high acceptance,

TABLE 8
Negative reasons for girls learning to read

Answer	Frequency
She should make tortillas, tend sheep, carry wood, has other duties already	5
She will no longer like her Indian friends	3
We are different from the Ladinos	2
She should not marry a Ladino	1
She will become too forward	1

medium acceptance, and low acceptance.[6] Those Indians visiting Ladino friends two to three times a month or more and who also hypothetically accept a Ladino neighbor were placed in the high acceptance category. Those Indians who visited Ladinos less than twice a month or not at all, and who also rejected a hypothetical Ladino neighbor, were placed in the low acceptance category. The remaing ones were placed in the medium category.

Then a measure of acceptance of education was needed. The best one available was a combination of the questions: "Is it good for girls to learn Spanish?" and "Is it good for them to learn to read?" Unfortunately, we had no questions asking about boys' learning Spanish or reading. This was originally intended, but the entire interview form was so long that many questions had to be omitted in the main study when it was found that respondents grew tired of answering any interview that lasted over forty-five minutes. Thus, in using this measure, the results might be good only for girls, but it is the closest approximation possible.

The index for this second variable was composed as follows: Negative: Those respondents who answered negatively to both the Spanish and the literacy question, or answered negatively to one, and did not answer the other. Medium: Those respondents who answered positively to one and negatively to the other, or those who gave no answer to either one. Positive: Those respondents who answered positively to both Spanish and literacy for girls or who answered positively for one, but gave no answer for the other.

The results indicate the prediction to be true.[7] Thus there is not only a definite link between the attitude of Zinacantan Indians toward Ladinos and toward schooling (for girls), but we have successfully predicted the direction, or rather, the nature of the link: Those Indians that tend to accept Ladinos, also are in favor of schooling for Indian girls, while those Indians that tend to reject Ladinos have

---

6 It is possible that a negative answer to question one, not accepting a Ladino for a neighbor, is a good measure of fear of Ladinos as well as of Ladino rejection. However, this could not be demonstrated without further testing in the field.

7 Using the chi-square test of significance, we found that the level of significance is .05 with $x^2=9.494$, which means, in effect, that in making the assertion that a relationship exists, there is a 95 per cent probability of being correct.

a negative attitude towards schooling for Indian girls.

Finding such relationship to exist does not, of course, preclude other relationships. It has already been pointed out, for instance, that economics is a crucial factor. Perhaps the most important factor of all is the personality of the teacher. This is difficult to study objectively, but experience in Chiapas has shown that there is no equal to genuine interest and enthusiasm on the part of the teacher unless it be the ability to learn from the students and the community and to listen to what they have to say. Success in teaching Indians comes from undistorted two-way communication between the teacher and the community.

William A. Smalley

The Gospel and
the Cultures of Laos

IN northern Laos, which lies on the southern border of China between North Vietnam and Burma, three different ethnic groups have been particularly subject to missionary effort. There are other ethnic groups in the country as well, local tribes and migrant minority populations like the Chinese, Indians, and Pakistanese, but their contact with the gospel in North Laos has been more sporadic, and missionary work with them less systematic. The three groups which have had intensive evangelization present a very important problem in missionary anthropology, for in spite of the fact that in many cases the same individual missionaries work among the three groups, that some of the same mission stations serve them all, and that the same mission policies apply, the differences in the response of the three groups to the Christian message are striking. And what is more, some of the usual assumptions about missionary work do not apply, at least on the surface. The only one of the three groups which has the Scriptures in its language is the least responsive. The one with the shortest contact with missionaries is the most responsive. The best results have been achieved in the cases where the misionaries did not know the language, where they used interpreters, or where preaching was in a language foreign to the listeners.

Reprinted from Vol. 3, No. 3 (1956), pp. 47-57.

As Christians we feel that God does inject himself into history and perform what we call "miracles." As anthropologists we are also aware that there are cultural reasons (complex though they may be) for differences between peoples. We want to study those cultural problems whether we consider them to be instruments of God's dealing with men or whether we consider them independent of or contrary to God's purpose for man. Although the problem of these three groups plagued me throughout my term as a missionary in Laos, I could not give detailed, systematic attention to it. There are some observations of a more general nature which can be made about them, and perhaps that will help to point up something of the magnitude of the problem of presenting the gospel to peoples of all cultures in such a way that it is relevant to the problems of each.

Culture A: The Lao

The *Lao* are the politically predominant people of Laos. They are of a general Thai pattern, and differ little in speech or culture from those Thai (Siamese) who live across the Mekong River or any other part of their mutual political border. The Lao live principally in the river valleys and cultivate both irrigated rice (in the general manner familiar for East Asia) and non-irrigated mountain rice by a slash-and-burn technique. Lao communities are loosely structured politically and socially, but there is a deep-lying consist-

199

ency to their patterns. Centuries of influence from other cultures have resulted in a thoroughly syncretic pattern with historical roots in India and China as well as in Southeast Asia. But whatever the roots, it is thoroughly Lao now.

The Lao are devout Buddhists, but they are great fish and meat eaters, and they see no inconsistency there. Rituals stemming from the local animism are intermingled with rituals from India with no embarrassment. The resulting religious culture is a most fundamental part of Lao life, and most men spent a part of their boyhood in a monastery or pagoda where they were students or apprentice priests.

More modern influences from the West are not so fully assimilated. Western artifacts (flashlights, lamps, watches, cigarette lighters, some clothing, etc.) which fill a Lao need are assimilated and are to be found everywhere. (The Lao need for watches is often a desire for jewelry, not for telling time.) Western forms of government, business, education have been adopted by only a small segment of the population, the elite in the cities. Chinese people and Indians do most of the business; until the present independence, Vietnamese office workers were often imported by the French because the Lao were so uninterested in government employment; education is traditionally in the hands of the Buddhist monks, but government schools are increasingly more important.

Christianity has made no impact whatsoever on the Lao, and this goes for Catholicism as well as Protestant Christianity. The handful of Lao converts consists almost entirely of marginal people — someone whose mother was Vietnamese, or someone who has been rejected

by the Laos as being possessed by a *Phi Poop*, a spirit which is declared to enter some individuals and control them. (Some of these cases of *Phi Poop* are obviously pathological. In other cases the accused is the victim of witch-hunting. But in any event he is usually driven out of his community and is cut off from normal social intercourse.)

The Lao temperament shows very little anxiety, very little stress. Westerners consider the Lao improvident. When Point-Four aid was trying to set up a pilot program on the use of fertilizer, Lao farmers were much impressed with the yield of adequately fertilized crops. Orders for fertilizer were below expectations, however. The Lao had estimated how much acreage it would take to produce the same amount of fertilized rice as they had previously produced without more than haphazard fertilization, and were reducing their area under cultivation to produce the same crop rather than increase their yield. From the standpoint of their lack of anxiety, they are the closest to the old stereotype of the idyllic simple life of the "primitive" of any group I have seen. The Lao are, of course, by no means "primitive." Their culture level is more that of a folk culture.

Culture B: The Khmu

In contrast to the Lao, the Khmu are a minority group of mountain-dwelling people with no political importance. Their culture is more that of a tribal "primitive" culture although they have learned a great deal from the Lao. They are not Buddhists. They are poorer than the Lao, and have traditionally been considered slaves of the latter. They put up little resistance, although the Lao take every possible advantage of them.

Whereas the Lao show a high degree of internal integration in their culture, the Khmu show signs of deterioration and disintegration. The gongs and jars of tremendous value which are characteristic of tribal peoples in southeast Asia and which are remembered as a part of Khmu culture of the past, are virtually gone. In all af southeast Asia these gongs and jars are a focal point of interest in the culture. They are symbols of prestige and wealth. The fact they have disappeared among the Khmu, and that apparently nothing has replaced them, is certainly of significance.

I cannot state for certain the causes of the deterioration of Khmu culture. I suspect that generations of pressure and domination by the Lao is a factor. Some of the results, however, are very obvious. There is less zest for life among the Khmu than among other peoples of similar culture in the area. Their general attitudes is one of resignation, of apathy. They have a collective feeling of inferiority to the Lao and to the West. These remarks are possibly more true of the Khmu in the western than in the eastern part of the country.

The first Khmu converts to Christianity were made a generation ago by the same missionaries who were itinerating among the Lao. Through the years, particularly since the last war, the number of Khmu converts has grown appreciably. They were reached through the Loatian language and through their own student preachers who preached in Khmu but studied in Lao. Latest figures are not available to me, but an estimate of two thousand Khmu Christians is probably a safe one.

The tradition of the mission in the area has been strongly paternalistic, and the Christian Khmu have accepted that paternalism with real gratitude. They look on both God and the missionary as powerful protection aginst an unfair and capricious world of the Lao, sickness, and even the elements. Some of the missionaries have been disturbed over the fact that Khmu Christians were so dependent on the mission, and have made changes to enforce more independence and self-reliance on the church in the more superficial respects of finance and internal government. These changes have been a real source of anxiety to the Khmu. The big problem remains: how to present the gospel to the Khmu in a way that will be relevant to their need for security in their dying culture, and yet build for a "responsible Christianity"[1] among them.

Culture C: The Meo

The third ethnic group to be mentioned here is a relative newcomer to Laos. The Meo (called Miao in China and Thailand) are moving by the thousands out of south China into northern Vietnam and Laos, and on into Thailand. In contrast to the easy-going Lao, and the apathetic Khmu, the Meo are vigorous, aggressive, and purposeful. New things which they meet through culture contact they meet with amusement, wonder, and delight. I have repeatedly observed both Meo and Khmu people as they come in contact with a sample of the West — a missionary home, the missionary plane, a missionary and his air mattress, clothes, etc., or missionary children. The Khmu stand at respect-

[1] On "responsible Christianity" see William D. Reyburn, *The Toba Indians of the Argentine Chaco* (Mennonite Board of Missions and Charities, 1711 Prairie St., Elkhart, Indiana; 1954), p. 58.

ful distance and look. The Meo exclaim and laugh, poke and ask questions and make comments, their faces beaming with delight.

The Meo women do excellent needlework, which is lavished on their costume. The folklore is rich, though material culture in most other things than clothing is poorer than that of the Lao and just as poor as that of the Khmu. Many Meo have wealth through opium growing, and many would rather buy their rice than grow it. As a rule several people in a village are addicted to opium smoking.

There are signs that Meo culture is undergoing transition, and in a state of stress. For one thing, they have changed within just a few years from being an exclusive group, one which avoided contact with other peoples, one which stayed on its mountain peaks and never came into the valleys where the Lao are, to a people which, though it does not like the valleys, moves freely through them, trades freely in Lao towns, and has even taken an important commercial place in the town of Xieng Khouang.

The biggest sign of change in the Meo, however, is in relation to its response to Christianity. For years the Christian witness made no impression on the Meo. Then, suddenly, in the space of a month in 1949 about a thousand converts were made. Today there are several thousand Meo Christians. Furthermore, occasionally "prophets" declare themselves to be Jesus. So far none of these splinter movements has become widespread, but they are symptomatic of the fact that the Meo are undergoing a period of cultural reformulation which was triggered and given its particular form by the Christian gospel.

The Meo revival is discussed by Barney

elsewhere in this book. In reference to the subject of this paper, however, there are some observations which should be made. The relation between the mission and Meo Christians has never been as paternalistic as in the Khmu case. This is partly because of the good sense of some missionaries who disliked the paternalistic role, but it is also due to the fact that the Meo do not feel so strongly the need for such complete supervision. When given half a chance, they take the initiative.

Once they are Christians, the Meo are vigorous, aggressive witnesses. The missionaries (their communication problem compounded by the distances and the ruggedness of the mountain trails) can never quite keep up with the new converts. It is not unusual for a whole village of 50 to 100 people, or the major portion of a village, to "enter Jesus" at the same time and send a messenger to the missionary to ask, "What do we do next?"

"Revitalization" of Culture

Wallace[2] has spoken of five stages which comprise the cycle of a "revitalization process" in culture — that is, the stages in a culture transformation which is not of the slow, "normal" chain-reaction type in which new element A is introduced and is gradually assimilated, causing changes in C and D, which in turn affect E and F and G, but rather a culture transformation which affects a whole system or an important part of a cultural system rather suddenly and rather completely. Some of the different types of such "revitalization processes" are "nativistic movements,"

---

[2] Anthony F. C. Wallace, "Revitalization Movements," *American Anthropologist* 58.264-275.

"reform movements," "cargo cult," "religious revival," "messianic movement," "utopian community," "sect formation," "mass movement," "social movement," "revolution," etc.[3]

Wallace's five stages are: (1) Steady State, (2) Period of Individual Stress, (3) Period of Cultural Distortion, (4) Period of Revitalization, and (5) New Steady State. The Lao are clearly in a steady state. Needs are satisfied by present patterns on the whole. Stresses are not severe. Innovations have not produced bad dislocations. Potentially a danger point will be the growth of a city such as Vientiane. The stresses between an essentially rural culture and an urban development may cause trouble but they are at present met without serious difficulty.

The Khmu, it seems to me, represent a period of cultural distortion, in terms of Wallace's formulation. The distortion is of long standing, I believe, and it is manifested now in what he characterizes as "disillusionment with the mazeway [traditional patterns of reaction as perceived by the individual member of the society] and apathy towards problems of adaptation." This is a different way from which other peoples will react to distortion. In some groups it may mean violence, in others a disregard for traditional mores, in others irresponsibility. To the Khmu it means an uneasy resignation. There is no sign of the beginning of a period of revitalization among the Khmu. Some individual Khmu have been assimilated to Lao life. Khmu villages nearest the Lao centers have adapted somewhat to Lao patterns. Christians have sought escape through dependency on a mission and on God.

Whether present developments among the Meo represent completely a period of cultural distortion, or whether there may be in the Christian movement something of a revitalization tendency, would be an evaluation which someone who knows the situation better than I would have to make. It seems to me that there are signs of both. The sudden and widespread acceptance of Christianity certainly has produced disparities with former habits, and presents inconsistencies. As Barney's article on the Meo points out, however, in a large percentage of cases, these conflicts have been settled on the basis of what the individual Christians felt the Christian reaction should be. This was, in many cases, influenced by the direct and indirect teaching of missionaries and their students.

Wallace maintains that a period of revitalization almost always begins with a particular prophet or leader from whom the major ideas of the new reformulation stem. There is no such figure in the Meo Christian community. As offshoots of it some have started up (often calling themselves Jesus, as was remarked above), but they have been abortive. I am not convinced that revitalization of such a community could not occur in a Christian context without such a local prophet.[4]

The Meo movement could easily develop nativistic tendencies as happened with the Karen of Burma, so many of whom are Christians. Meo Christians do feel a sense of solidarity. They want their language in written form but the Lao government has been opposed to such a development. The Meo have revolted before. They have an increasing self-consciousness.

---

3 Ibid., p. 264.

4 Reyburn, op. cit., p. 46.

That, sketchily and imperfectly, is the picture of three cultures among whom one mission is working, usually through one language (Lao) and interpreters. The Scriptures and some (very little) Christian literature exist in Lao. The translation of the Bible is poor, and is in the process of revision.

The Church and the Cultures of Laos

Because of these vastly different pictures, the problems which remain for church and mission working together are vastly different in the three cases. In the Lao case the problem is still one of basic communication. Apparently the gospel has never been made to seem relevant to the Lao. I feel deeply that a careful study should be made of the communication of the gospel in relation to the Lao culture in the way that the Reyburns have been pioneering in South America and Africa.[5] How can the Good News be made to seem good — to be something that people will really *want* — in this culture which does not, on the whole, see other needs than those met by its normal experience? Here the problem is not primarily one of language mastery. The missionaries are no worse than the average, and some are much better than the average, for missionary language learning. The communication problems here are cultural ones. They are doubtless the same problems as the ones which face Christianity in Thailand, where the people are much the same, and where results in terms of response to the gospel have been meager.

---

[5] Ibid. See also the articles by Dr. and Mrs. Reyburn in this issue and othe s of PRACTICAL ANTHROPOLOGY.

For the Khmu a part of the problem is to encourage them to find the security they need in God without an unhealthy dependency on the mission. A few individual Khmu (but not the Christian Khmu community as a whole) have found a new purpose in life in their Christian faith. We would like to see a revitalization of Khmu culture, centered in a faith in Christ as Lord. There is danger that the mission might fight any such revitalization, because inevitably it would not take the form which missionaries unthinkingly would feel it should take. A vital Khmu Christianity, rooted in Khmu culture, cannot be anything but strikingly different from imported American Christianity in its form, although its dedication to its Lord may be just as significant, if not more so, than ours.

The great problem of missionary anthropology among the Khmu, then, is to so understand the Khmu that the mission can adapt to, cooperate with, and stimulate Khmu forms of growth. Of course the Khmu need the Scriptures in their own language. Of course they need missionary teaching in their tongue. But the Khmu language is not enough. Christianity, if it is to become truly significant among the Khmu must find a significant place in Khmu life. Perhaps the terms "self-support" and "self-government" should not be used with the Khmu, for they promote stress and anxiety, but some Khmu way must be found to divert the Khmu dependency on the mission.

For the Meo a major part of the problem is to guide tactfully, and to provide the bases for greater growth in non-autocratic teaching, the development of literacy and literature, the encouragement of Meo forms of worship, and of a Meo Christian culture. One tremendous problem is the training of Meo leadership in a way that will be compatible with Meo leadership patterns, but still be strongly oriented Biblically and in the broader Christian tradition.

As God injects himself into human history — in the Incarnation, in the revelation of the Bible, in the redemption of any individual — he uses human culture as his means of revelation, and human beings respond to him in their own cultural manner. As cultures differ, responses differ, and a man is no more at home in a culture form which does not meet his needs than he is in a language which is foreign to him. Christian anthropology can do much to help the missionary watch the Khmu or the Meo, or even the Lao, respond to redemption in his own way, to worship God in his own way, to participate in the church in his own way, and watch them with sympathy, understanding, and encouragement.

This article is not an example of such an "understanding." It is merely a statement of some of the more obvious problems in one particular situation. Understanding of this kind is not arrived at without careful, perceptive, and sympathetic study of each of the cultural situations involved — the particular missionary culture, and the particular cultures in which the church is being planted.

Joseph E. and Barbara Grimes

Individualism and the Huichol Church

THE Huichol Indians who inhabit the southern Sierra Madre Occidental in the states of Nayarit and Jalisco, Mexico, are markedly individualistic. This means that the Huichol manifest a type of behavior which has wide cultural limits of acceptable variation, and consequent to the wide range of variation a low predictability of specific actions. Some of the more obvious elements of the individualistic complex as they occur in Huichol culture have their effect on practices of the Christian community. These features will be taken up one by one; their cultural manifestation will be discussed first; then their effect on the Huichol church.

Individualism should not be interpreted as implying full freedom from cultural restraint. As in all cultures, there are important limits to Huichol individualism. The kinship group, for example, is one of the factors which limit individual action. In theory the kinship group consists of all people who have any common ancestor up to the fifth ascending generation. In practice, however, only people who know of some common ancestor consider themselves of the same kinship group. Customarily, only people belonging to the

same kinship group marry each other or settle on the same ranch.

Age is a second limiting factor. Most civil and religious leaders are over forty years of age. Younger men show reticence to tell stories or sing in the presence of their elders, though if they are performing and an older person joins the group they do not stop performing on his account. Older relatives frequently command the services of younger relatives.

Correlate to both kinship group and age limiting factors is the structure of the immediate family. Children live with their parents until they marry. A man then lives with his father-in-law's family after marriage unless he is an eldest son, in which case he eventually moves back to his father's. A son prefers not to move very far away from his father as long as his father is alive. These three factors in the culture tend to limit individual action.

Freedom of Movement

In residence pattern the Huichols consider themselves free to move wherever they like within a wide area, subject, of course, to the restrictions already mentioned. Partly because of the poor soil and the necessity for changing maize fields each year, and partly by inclination, some families move as often as once every two or three years. In 1941 there were eleven Huichol families living at the ranch, La Piedra Gorda. In 1954 there

Reprinted from Vol. 1, No. 8 (1954), pp. 127-134. Joseph and Barbara Grimes are missionary linguistics and Bible translators with the Wycliffe Bible Translators among the Huichol Indians of Mexico. Dr. Grimes has the Ph.D. degree from Cornell University.

was only one family on the ranch, and all of the families living there in 1941 had moved elsewhere. Most moved to another ranch after two or three intermediate steps made independently. The father of one of the Christians moved three times during 1953. On one ranch the Huichol families each year moved farther up the mountain on which the ranch is situated. They considered themselves as living on the same ranch as formerly though one family of Huichols which remained at the foot of the mountain lived closer to the ranch where the authors lived than it did to some of the families on its own ranch.

Until 1954 the Huichol Christians showed no tendency to group themselves apart into a Christian community, but retained this pattern of freedom of movement. However, two of the Christians made plans to build their houses together on the same ranch in 1954, although they were not related to each other in such a way that they normally would have done so. Due to subsequent developments they were not able to carry out their plan. In this case it seemed that their relationship in Christ took precedence over their relationship — or rather lack of it — in the kinship group.

Visiting between persons or families is frequent and, especially near harvest time, is sporadically accompanied by gifts of food brought by the person visiting, though there is no rigid custom regarding exchange of gifts. Visits normally last less than a day. However, a person who feels inclined to prolong his visit may stay for several days. One family came to visit the authors for medical treatment and stayed for approximately two months. They built themselves a shelter and helped with the work of other families on the ranch. Other visitors stayed for two and three days. None gave indication of how long he planned to stay or when he planned to leave until he was ready to go.

Through this pattern of visiting the gospel has been carried to other areas within the tribe. Whenever the oldest believer has time or feels inclined, he goes on a visit to a town two days by trail from his ranch. There he stays with his relatives, plays records in Huichol made by Gospel Recordings, Inc., reads portions of the Scriptures, and discusses the gospel at length with his relatives and other visitors. He also witnesses to visitors who come to his ranch. There is no way of predicting who will come to visit, or when they will arrive or leave, but the irregular visiting pattern has been the main channel of evangelization within the culture.

Story-Telling Patterns

Story telling is fairly well developed in Huichol culture. Individualism in story telling takes the form of unpredictability of repetition. Stories are never told the same way twice. There is an over-all pattern of folk-tale structure which involves the use of paragraph introducing morphemes and the narrative mode. Actions are frequently repeated by five characters in sequence, instead of three as in European tales. However, innovations are made on the spur of the moment, with the result that the exact words used are never predictable. At times even the identity of principal characters is changed between tellings of the story, as when different species of grasshoppers are substituted for each other or the wolf in one telling becomes a coyote in the next. When the Gospel of Mark and the Epistles of John were translated into

Huichol and made available to the Christians, it was at first expected that the Christians should memorize portions of Scripture as part of their instruction. However, due to the influence of individualism in the story-telling pattern, such attempts failed; a verse was never repeated the same way twice. Synonyms were introduced in the repetition for words in the original; equivalent grammatical constructions of various kinds were substituted (for example, substitution of the narrative mode for the affirmative and vice versa); the order of words was changed. These changes were not of the same order as corrections of the accuracy or style of the translation, though such corrections, happily, came to light in the process as well. They were the same type of changes as occurred between different tellings of the same story and seemed to be made purely for variety.

After several attempts to introduce Scripture memorization it was found that those who regularly read the Scriptures, especially the Epistles of John, were perfectly familiar with the content of these portions. In the songs they composed the Scripture text appeared, though of course not in the same form in which the translation had been cast. The oldest believer, who was trying to improve his facility in writing, made up writing exercises for himself without reference to the Scripture text. However, they contained such a high proportion of quotations and allusions that it was evident that he had, in effect, rethought and reuttered the Scripture message in detail. So, no further effort was made to promote the verbatim recitation of Scripture passages, and emphasis was put on the verse-by-verse understanding and exposition of passages, usually a paragraph or more at a time.

Singing

Songs for amusement or dancing are sung to the accompaniment of violin or guitar or both. Some people are recognized as more proficient than others in composing songs, which they make up on occasion to commemorate or lampoon something or often merely to provide amusement.

Songs are not sung the same way twice. However, as distinct from stories, the words remain relatively unchanged from singing to singing, through one singer's version of a song frequently differs from that of another singer. The characteristic treatment of songs is the rearrangement of lines in a verse. A quatrain may be sung one time *abab, aab, abcd, cdaa, dcdd*, with instrumental interludes between stanzas as marked by commas. The next time the same song may be sung *abcd, abcc, aacc, a, ddccdd, cd, ad*, etc. Songs of more complex structure or more lines are varied in analogous ways. Only one person sings at a time. He may or may not play an instrument or dance as he sings; or he may do both.

The three older Christians have all composed songs about the gospel. The first believer, 54 years old, has composed several. His wife composed one which was sung only a few times. His son composed two, one of which is sung frequently. The other was sung only a few times. These songs are of the same form as those used for amusement and are accompanied on instruments but are expressions of Christian truth or portions of Scripture set to music. Their Huichol character is attested by the observation that most unbelievers in the area also know the songs, and that one song was even learned and used for side amusement in a Huichol ceremony in another area.

When the first believer heard his son's song, he made extensive additions and modifications of the words. Probably because of the factors of age and family relationship, the son now sings more or less his father's version of his own song.

The only Western song which was introduced into the Christian hymnody is "Jesus Loves Me." Not much attention was paid to the song, and not much emphasis was put on it. However, the oldest believer's four - year - old granddaugther picked it up, changed the rhythm and the tune to Huichol patterns, and sang it while playing. It is not sung at gatherings of Christians.

An attempt was made to encourage congregational singing as practiced in most Christian communities. It was expected that congregational singing would help unify the Christians and encourage others to join them as it has elsewhere. However, after a few tries, the uniform response of the Christians was unenthusiastic, and they continued with their pattern of having one person sing to the accompaniment of instruments. One difficulty with congregational singing was that with no set form for the order of lines in a stanza and much repetition no one knew how anyone else was going to sing the same song. As a result the basic Huichol pattern of one singer at a time has been retained in all gatherings of Christians. Sometimes one person continues on with the singing of a song when a previous singer stops.

In summary, the Christian Huichol community has retained regular Huichol patterns in regard to visiting, learning the Scriptures, and singing. The restrictions of the kinship group on the dwelling pattern have shown signs of reshaping to include the Christian community. The restrictions of age and immediate family relationship have given a place of prominence and respect to the older members of the Christian community, but have been modified in that younger members have shown no hesitation to pray in public in the presence of their elders, or to help in the instrumental accompaniment of songs.

Huichol Culture Change

The rate of acculturation of the Huichol tribe has in general been extremely slow. Certain features of the culture have tended to limit the incursion of features from other cultures. One such factor is the kinship organization and the concomitant endogamy within the kinship group. Marriages outside the kinship group are rare enough; marriages with non-Huichols are extremely rare though Huichols occasionally marry members of the neighboring Cora tribe.

Another feature is the integration of religious, social, and civic organization to provide maximum participation and coverage of all areas of life, with a resultant high stability. Roman Catholicism, to the degree in which it has been accepted, has been regarded as an accretion added to the basic Huichol framework — in effect, a few more deities to be added to the list — so that a certain amount of Catholic forms are observable in the culture. Catholic influence is, however, superficial, and the Huichols apparently do not feel that it is inimical to cultural integrity.

Evangelical Christianity, on the other hand, has among its implications for the Huichols the destruction of the integrity of their religion. Pressure has been brought to bear on the Christians from time to time for this reason. However, paradoxical as it may seem, the older Christians are respected members of the culture. Their advice is sought on personal and civic matters. Some pressure on the younger ones continues.

It is not easy to understand why the strong acculturative influence of evangelical Christianity, with its destructive implications for a significant portion of the activity carried on within the culture, should be at all tolerated by a people noted for their successful resistance of Western influence over a long period of time. One reason so little resistance has been met may lie in the type of tolerance demanded by a complex of permitted individualistic behavior in diverse areas of cultural activity. After a period of initial disapproval, members of the culture have observed that the Christians continue to participate fully in the social and civic activity of the group. Coupled

with this is the recognition, heard from many sources, that the Huichol religion does not completely fulfill its aims of providing health for people and livestock and insuring good crop yields. The Christian are not yet fully instructed in the Scriptures, but their experience points toward an eventual integration and completeness of their Christian lives, which in the thinking of the non-Christians may be regarded as a satisfactory and permissible substitute for the abandoned religion. Because of the retention of social and civic ties, the life of the Christian community remains firmly rooted within the Huichol culture. The gospel has been propagated within the culture rather than from outside the culture in that the missionaries have concentrated their work on a few who have told the gospel message to many more. Therefore, it is possible that Christianity may be accepted as a valid substitute within the culture for the Huichol religion, rather than as a destructive influence from outside the culture.

Charles V. Turner

The Sinasina "Big Man" Complex: A Central Culture Theme

There is no more fundamental problem in inter-cultural relationship, be it in the missionary sphere or any other, than the differences people have in basic outlook and motivation. The problem is highlighted in this article in a useful way, which is none the less enlightening for being over-simplified. One caution may be in order: Most societies probably have more than one extremely important cultural theme. These sometimes reinforce each other and sometimes exist in tension. The search for the integrating, dynamic factor in a culture is not easy, but it may be most rewarding.

AFTER finishing my first term as a missionary in New Guinea, I was sailing back to the United States on a large ship. The time at sea gave me a chance to reflect on the years just finished in New Guinea.

I had sought to learn the Sinasina language and understand something of Sinasina culture. As I began to think about the many features of Sinasina culture that I had witnessed, I wondered what the mainspring was in this culture. There were many times when I had felt like a fish out of water because I could not understand why the Sinasina did certain things to me.

Charles V. Turner is a missionary linguist with the New Tribes Mission, Kundiawa Post Office, Territory of New Guinea. His most recent article in PA was "Culture Change and the Sinasina Church," Vol. 13, No. 3 (May-June 1966), pp. 103-106.

For example, not long after I had obtained a piece of ground and built a house, I decided that my wife and I would spend a few nights at Molgime village. As we were gathering things together, Wisunga, the owner of the ground we had obtained, asked where I was going. When I told him we were going to stay at Molgime for a while he became very angry. He yelled at me in a nasty way, and said that I could not go to Molgime. Later he calmed down when I told him that these people needed to hear God's talk too. I dismissed the incident as interclan jealousy, but yet I wondered what had caused such a rage of anger in Wisunga. I did not understand then that it was not inter-clan jealousy, but that I had delivered a blow to the very core of Sinasina culture.

Now as we sailed along and I was able to reflect on the many features of Sinasina culture, I began to see a central theme to it all. Wisunga was a short man, and all his life he had been struggling against this disadvantage. Sinasina people look on short men as unable to become a *yobal kun* (usually a tall, handsome, well-dressed, wealthy, powerful man). These men are also called *yal ore engwa* 'a man who does big' or 'a big man.' Wisunga, like every other male in the tribe, wanted desperately to be a "big man." By controlling the new missionary to some degree, he had gained another rung or two up the ladder toward becoming a "big man." But when the missionary showed interest in other villages and other competing "big men," this was dissipating his gathering strength as an emerging man of power.

Central culture themes

I would like to try to illustrate the concept of central culture themes in this article. Others have used the terms "world view" or "patterns of culture."[1] The term is not important, but the concept of a culture as a system with a central dynamic theme is important.

Eugene A. Nida says, "The features of a culture which tend to give it a distinctive quality, or ethos, are far more likely to be nonmaterial than material."[2] I will call the distinctive quality of a culture its central culture theme. I will define the central culture theme as a set of relationships

between culture features which unites these features into a system.

For example, we may study a culture and begin to recognize recurring culture features. We see a kind of dance take place. We see a ceremony. We notice a means of exchange, and what is considered valuable. We see men become angry and fight. But we do not see how all these things are related in a system. We do not understand the dynamic which is producing these culture features.

This was the case when Wisunga became angry at me. I did not know why. I needed to look for the nonmaterial system of relationships between the culture features that I was seeing. This would lead to an understanding of the dynamic which was producing these various culture features.

The Trobriand Islands

Bronislaw Malinowski described the central culture theme of the Trobriand Islanders at the time of his visit to them.[3] Most Trobriand Island people live on the island of Kiriwina, about thirty miles long and six miles wide, just off the southeast extremity of New Guinea.

Trobriand technology centered around the *kula* exchange, a vast inter-island and intertribal trading complex. The framework of the *kula* trading cycle involved the exchange of white shell arm bands called *mwali* for necklaces of red shell called *soulava*. The exchange within the tribe

---

1 Ruth Benedict. *Patterns of Culture* (New York: Penguin Books, 1946)

2 Eugene A. Nida, *Customs and Cultures* (New York: Harper Brothers, 1954), p. 42.

3 Bronislaw Malinowski, *Argonauts of the Western Pacific* (New York: E. P. Dutton and Co., 1953).

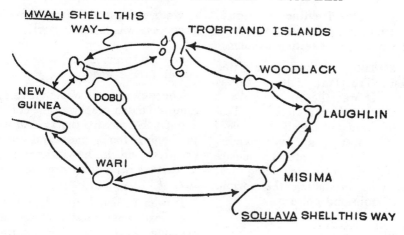

Figure 1.

ind between islands always followed ι pattern. *Mwali* shells from Tro-riand went counterclockwise, and *oulava* from Dobu went clockwise ιround the trading ring, as may be ιeen in Figure 1. The exchange of he shells was in itself only symbolic. Jnder cover of the elaborate *kula* ex-·hange ceremony a utilitarian trade ·f raw materials and handicrafts took ιlace.

Trading was carried on with greatest ·unning and intrigue in order to gain he advantage over a trading partner. ·anoe building was highly developed ·ecause of its necessity in inter-ɩland travel. Yam raising was a ·redominant culture feature because he abundance produced could open he way to better trading advantage ɩ the *kula*. Raw materials for handi-raɩts were not obtainable locally. ɩhis made much of the local techno-ɔgy further dependent upon success ɩ the *kula* exchange.

Trobriand religion was bound up ɩ the success or failure of the *kula*. ʌt the onset of a trading voyage and at its return a great deal of magical rite and ceremony was performed to insure the success of the trading ven-ture. Sorcery was also used to the advantage of the trader over his trad-ing partner.

Trobriand social life was a result of success or failure in the *kula* ex-change. To succeed in the *kula* meant gaining a position of wealth and prominence.

A religious reverence was given to certain *kula* shells. These shells had gone around and around the *kula* cycle and had taken on tremendous importance. The person who was at a given time in possession of one of these shells was afforded great pres-tige and social elevation. It also meant that he was a man of wealth. Wealth led to the privilege of poly-gyny. This in turn made possible the role of a chief or a man of au-thority.

Trobriand ambitions, thinking, de-sires, emotions and vanities were all very much bound up with the *kula*. Magic, elaborate ceremony, overseas travel, pleasure, feasting, intrigue, and prestige, all went into the *kula* to make it a very exciting system.

It is evident that the *kula* ring tied the basic Trobriand culture values together. It was the central culture theme which gave distinction to Trobriand life and united all features of the culture around an ever moving cycle of trading intrigue. The desire to succeed in the *kula* exchange was the dynamic producing the various parts of Trobriand culture.

The Jivaro

The Jivaro Indians live at the foothills of the Andean Mountains in Ecuador, South America.[4] Here, at the headwaters of the Amazon basin the tropical rain forest begins.

Among the Jivaro as described by Karsten, the *tsantsa*, or shrunken head ceremony, was the central culture theme which gave cohesion to all culture features. The *tsantsa* theme was a cycle of blood revenge. Instead of uniting groups together in aggressive trade relations like the Trobriand *kula* exchange, the Jivaro shrunken head ceremony splintered groups into enemy camps. Fighting between these groups was continuous and serious.

After a Jivaro took an enemy head he prepared it with great care. The shrinking process took hours of delicate work. On coming to the village with the head, the owner was given

a victory feast. Before that feast great care was taken to perform many rites and ceremonies to purify the victorious warrior and ward off the power in the head.

The victory feast was elaborate, and required much preparation. This feast opened the way for the *tsantsa* owner to honor, fame, material wealth, prestige and to new victories over enemies with a long and prosperous life.

It was believed that the head of the dead enemy was thirsting for revenge. This danger was neutralized and then redirected by elaborate rite and ceremony. The power of the head was thereby controlled to become a fetish charged with great power. This power could then be used by the victor to his own advantage.

The soul of a murdered Indian required that his relatives avenge his death. If they failed to fulfill this sacred duty, the anger of the dead man's vengeful spirit would turn against them. This requirement for revenge of a relative's death was instilled in a child from his earliest years. It became his highest ambition in life. He longed to avenge a death, take a head, and be celebrated as a great warrior. If he was successful in this it led to every cultural benefit. In the success of the head-shrinking complex a man's social position was elevated, and he gained material wealth as well.

It is evident that the *tsantsa* cycle of revenge was the basic Jivaro culture value. It is the central culture theme which gave distinction to Jivaro life and united all culture features

4 Rafael Karsten, *Blood Revenge, War, and Victory Feasts Among the Jivaro Indians of Eastern Ecuador* (Washington D.C.: Smithsonian Institute, Bureau of American Ethnology, Bulletin 79, 1923).

around an ever-moving cycle of revenge. All facets of Jivaro life pointed to it.

The Sinasina

The Sinasina is a tribe of 24,000 people living in the Chimbu District of the Eastern Highlands of New Guinea. They live in a valley about seven miles square, at about 6,000 feet elevation.

One of the features of Sinasina culture which one notices first is a near obsession with fertility. Sinasina religious life is bound up in the pig ceremonial. The main objective is to make pigs, plants and people fertile.

The ceremony is centered around a small circular fence about six feet in diameter. Formerly every clan had such a circular fence, which was used to work sorcery on enemies as well as to produce fertility. The English translation of a text about the circular fence goes like this:

The story of making the circular fence. The past generations and also the present generations do like this: They said, "Let us make a circular fence".

So they sharpened the ends of fence stakes and stuck them in a circle. Then they said, "Let us kill and cook pigs, for it is almost time for the pig ceremonial." Then they picked sweet potato vines, and dug up some sweet potatoes. They took the vines and the sweet potatoes and buried them inside the circular fence. Then they killed pigs [by clubbing them on the head, and then cutting the jugular vein.][5]

As the pig bled freely they took it to the circular fence and put it on top of the buried vines and sweet potatoes. The blood ran over the vines and sweet potatoes. Then they took the vines and planted a new garden. They took the sweet potatoes and fed them to the remaining pigs [literally, the 'seed pigs.']

When they gave the sweet potatoes to the "seed" pigs, they multiplied to become plentiful. So they took the geluwa boards off their heads, and placed them inside the circular fence. So they accomplished the appeasement of the spirits of the pigs they had just killed.

The geluwa boards referred to in the text are three to four feet tall. They are worn on the head, and at the end of the pig ceremonial they are placed inside the circular fence to please the spirits of dead relatives and the spirits of the recently slain pigs. Thus the spirits of relatives cause the clan to be fertile. The spirits of the dead pigs cause the pigs to be fertile.

The geluwa boards are shaped as in Figure 2. They are always beautifully painted with various geometrical designs containing the diamond shape as the basic motif. This diamond shape is a fertility symbol which is also carved on fences and houses,

Figure 2.

[5] At the last pig ceremonial which I saw I estimated close to one thousand pigs killed.

painted on bark cloth, and tattooed on the faces of the majority of the young men and women. Animals and human beings are supposed to see it and to be excited sexually.

After many years of missionization, the fertility feature in Sinasina culture is still very strong. Instead of the *geluwa* board a cross is now placed inside the circular fence. Instead of the blood of pigs, the priest sprinkles holy water over the sweet potatoes and vines.

In our own work, not long after Wisunga (mentioned earlier as the man who wanted to be a "big man") had become one of the elders in his village, he brought some sweet potatoes and coffee beans into the church.[6] He then took a pig, killed it and placed the bleeding pig on top of the sweet potatoes and coffee beans at the front of the church. Milan, the other elder there had strongly objected, but Wisunga had gone ahead.

Recently we could not understand why some villages did not want to build church buildings. Finally they said that they could not because their pig herds were small. I could not see what this had to do with church building until they told me that after building a church they always killed pigs and performed the fertility rite on the sweet potatoes. They had few pigs, so they could not build a church and kill pigs just now.

The fact that the Chimbu area is the most heavily populated area in all of the Territory of Papua and New

---

6 Coffee is the only cash crop.

Guinea indicates a successful pursuit of fertility. Closely related to this fertility is the desire which people have for plenty. There is always more vegetable food than people can eat. Every man strives to gain so many objects of wealth that he can count it as nothing. At the nut festival food is collected all week long and piled in great mounds of sweet potatoes, pandanus nuts, sugar cane, bananas, etc. A great display of food is the big thing. It shows that certain clans are prospering and that certain "big men" are growing in power.

Sinasina ceremonies

In addition to the pig ceremony, there are two other main ceremonies in Sinasina life. These are the wedding and the nut festival. At all three ceremonies there is elaborate decorating of the body with paint, feathers, shells, etc. There are always great mounds of food on these occasions. At the wedding each pig is announced after being killed. The speaker, a "big man," announces the owner of each pig. At a nut festival each bundle of pandanus nuts, of sugar cane, and other food, is announced as it is brought into the village. The "big man" announces who brought it and from what village it has come. At a wedding the food is piled in separate mounds and again the "big man" calls out loudly, announcing who is to get which mound of food.

At these ceremonial occasions there is always a great deal of arguing. People argue about whose pigs are to be killed, and how many. There is a bedlam of arguments, screams and wailing as the pigs begin to be killed.

Almost everyone has his say, and then one of the men gains the floor by shouting everyone else down. With reluctance the other men shut up and the "big man" presents his arguments for or against killing more pigs. If his arguments are valid, and appraised so by the majority of the people, then the argument ceases and the activities proceed.

Since weddings are very common, and nut festivals occur each year, and big ceremonials are often being held by some clan or other, this makes for some very exciting times. It affords men opportunity to display their oratorical abilities and to press up the ladder of prestige and wealth. It is possible, by skillful argument, to gain more wealth in giving a bride than one would pay in receiving one. If a man succeeds as a persuasive orator in these ceremonies, his prestige grows along with wealth and privileges. He is an emerging "big man."

During a wedding or the settling of a dispute there is much bitter wrangling. Superficially, there does not seem to be a leader. Yet there is always the man in the midst who is held as a leader, although he is always under constant scrutiny for a crack in his armor of leadership. "Big men" rise and fall as every male strives for dominance.

The "big man" complex has been noted in other parts of New Guinea also. Berndt notes it in his work on the Fore people to the east. He says, "Change [in the Fore] is seen in terms of variation in behavior, a widening or narrowing range of choices, alterations in role, and differing means employed to achieve what are in one sense the same ends as before: the struggle and jockeying for power and prestige..."[7]

Again Marie Reay writes of the "big man" complex among the Kuma people to the west. She says, "It seems that nearly every man has the opportunity of becoming some sort of leader, of moving into some kind of ascendency over others. It is no exaggeration to say that more than half the Kuma become leaders at some time."[8]

When we sought out men for leadership in the church they were immediately anxious to be leaders. This meant still another avenue open for self-aggrandizement. By standing before a group of people (meetings) and being the only speaker (sermons), one had the opportunity to emerge as a "big man." But when we tried to institute plurality of leadership in the churches we hit a rattlesnake's nest. Each leader was continually trying to down the other and emerge as the one "big man" in the church.

It is a generally accepted fact that women are supposed to yield to a "big man" when he makes sexual advances, and many do. This is a "big man's" right. Leadership is looked upon as a position of privilege, not a position of service to others. Service is only a necessary evil that one puts up with in order to bolster one's own self-aggrandizement.

The "big man" complex is the central culture theme in Sinasina life

---

[7] Ronald M. Berndt, *Excess and Restraint* (Chicago: University of Chicago Press, 1962), p. vi.

[8] Marie Reay, *The Kuma* (Melbourne: Melbourne University Press, 1959), p. 116.

because all other features of the culture revolve around this one dynamic desire. Men are occupied with fertility because fertility brings plentifulness. With plenty of pigs and food comes wealth and prestige. An owner of pigs controls many things. His pigs are needed to buy wives, for no woman can be bought without payment in pigs. In order to have plenty of pigs and gardens he wants more than one wife who can bear many children, raise many pigs, and care for several gardens.

In the proportion that a man can supply food and pigs for a feast, in the same proportion can he have some say in the distribution of the food. As he gains more and more say in affairs, he more and more emerges as a "big man." So he is caught in an ever entangling web of hard work, intrigue, arguing and aggression in order to be a "big man." He must obtain so many pigs and objects of wealth (shells, money, etc.) that he can look on it as nothing, and give it away freely. Not really freely, but to maintain his position. Each item he gives must be returned in a later exchange.

Need to understand central themes

As we are able to discover a culture's central theme we will be able to understand something of the dynamic which is producing the various culture features. As we begin to understand something of a people's central theme, we can have a sense of empathy with the people among whom we live. We can appreciate their way of life and understand some of the complications in which they live and which have a bearing on their response to us and our message. With some understanding of the whole of a culture complex with its central dynamic theme we can help people who live out that culture gain insight into the possibility of changes which can be made in keeping with obedience to Christ.

With an understanding of the people we can more readily make God's Word seem relevant to their own felt needs. We no longer shoot in the dark at what we see as needs, but speak to the needs of which people are conscious. This leads to a grass roots witness that effects the whole of a people's life. It gets to the root of a people's life, not merely to the outward fruit.

Barry Irwin

The Liability Complex among the Chimbu Peoples of New Guinea

The basic concept of liability governs every facet of life in Chimbu (New Guinea) society. It reveals itself in major events such as marriage settlements, blood feuds, and house-building, as well as in ordinary community life, including daily meals. Once a gift has been given, the recipient has liability resting upon him until he fulfills his obligations to the giver. The foreigner who has received a "gift" of "free" services may incur the hostility of the giver if he fails to reciprocate later. This philosophy also affects Chimbu attitudes towards Christianity. When a clan feels it has paid enough for Christ's grace by attending church services and communion, it returns to its former way of life again.

The Chimbu include some thirty different tribes loosely gathered in larger groupings as Kuman, Dom, Chuave, (Elimbari) Sina Sina, Gumine, and Salt. They number around 150,000 people, who speak a variety of languages and dialects all of which are related grammatically. Their culture with minor variations is one culture.

Barry Irwin is a member of the Summer Institute of Linguistics. For the past nine years he has been working among the Salt-Yui people of the Chimbu District of Papua New Guinea. Mr. Irwin is a graduate of Sydney Teachers College and at present is studying with the University of Queensland. He has taught linguistics at S.I.L. summer sessions on many occasions. His address is Box 52, Ukarumpa, E.H.D., Papua New Guinea.

Contact with Western culture ranges from over 30 years in the Kuman to less than 10 years in the Salt.

In this culture the basic concept which governs religious practices and beliefs, behavior in the society, and attitudes to foreigners is one of *pring pangwo*. (This phrase, which means 'the existence of liability,' occurs in all the languages with slight phonemic variations. The spelling here is from the Yui language of the Salt grouping.) This concept of *pring pangwo* covers such a range of concepts in English as guilt responsibility, liability, obligation, vendetta, and respect. No being, human or otherwise, is outside the sphere of this controlling force. Every action depends upon the fulfilling of one's obligations and the creation of a sufficient amount of liability in others, thus ensuring firstly,

219

that one is freed of any indebtedness, and secondly, that one has built up an ample amount of indebtedness towards oneself, so that others are in one's debt.

There are many and various ways in which this governing concept reveals itself. It is almost impossible to gain any true idea of its existence simply by a casual acquaintance with the culture or by questioning informants, as there is no conscious formulation of its extent in people's minds. After living in a village situation for nine years and participating in as much of corporate village life as possible, I have only begun to sense its influence.

Within the sub-clan the influence is noticed in major events such as marriage settlements, blood feuds, and house-building. It is also felt within the family in meals, and in joint ownership of ground, pigs, property, and wages. During the wedding settlement which may take a whole generation, the sub-clan has its share of responsibility in ensuring that it provides enough pigs and food to keep liability existing in the minds of the other party. It is imperative that the clan not be outdone in its efforts.

A whole clan is morally responsible to support any one of the clan in trouble regardless of the rightness or wrongness of an action. (A clan numbers around 500 people.) Failure to do so incurs liability. Should one clansman be killed then of course every other clansman is "guilty" until he *mong pring pai tongwo* 'repays the obligation.' He is under obligation until he avenges the killing, and the other

party are liable until they have paid with a "life for a life." Both the negative and positive aspects of this complex are seen here.

The vicious circle can be seen in community life within the sub-clan. Every meal is a social occasion. One family will provide the food for a number of other families, thus building up liability and ensuring a "free" meal at some later date.

Other examples of the practical outworking of *pring pangwo* philosophy also exhibit this never-ending cycle of liability.

At one marriage feast the bride price of $140 was paid to the father of the bridegroom's clan. Five pigs of various sizes and four fowls were also handed over. This was a simple action. The father then proceeded to distribute the money, pigs, and fowls both to clansmen and others. Firstly he began by paying off his own obligations. This involved much debate as it was necessary to satisfy everybody that he had indeed fulfilled his obligations. In one case argument lasted for days just discussing the size of the pig and its value to pay off the *pring pangwo* which existed. As soon as the recipient took the pig the *pring pangwo* 'died.' After doing this paying off, the father of the bride used the remainder to create some liability towards himself and provide in a sense an insurance against future catastrophe. The author received two dollars as a gift with all the implications that at a later time he would repay this when it was needed.

An awful tension resulted from one missionary's declaring that bride prices were non-Christian as they were not mentioned in the Bible. The case under consideration occurred in the following manner: the missionary encouraged the young man and his betrothed to elope after he had married them in a church ceremony. The bride's father demanded payment from the bridegroom's clan. The bridegroom's clan began to "stand on the Bible" for the first time in their life. Eventually the government intervened and the couple had to return and go through the customary functions of *pring pangwo*. One sad result was the mental derangement of the bridegroom's father as he had lost face tremendously over the whole issue.

Another example of the effects of this liability complex has been described by Turner.[1]

'Nothing is given for nothing' is a translation of the expression *yamoro tongwo paikungwo*. Interpreted, this means that once a gift is given the recipient has *pring pangwo* resting upon him until he fulfills his obligations.

How does this affect the foreigner? Or more especially, how does this affect the *yal nol* 'red man' (European, white man)? When I first entered the village in 1963, I was given a piece of ground for house-building and, amongst other things, a fowl. In my ignorance I accepted these gifts as spontaneous expressions of goodwill. In 1967 I rebuilt my house. I contracted with thirty village men to build but omitted the owner of the ground. Quite suddenly the owner be-

[1] Charles V. Turner, ''The Sinasina 'Big Man' Complex: A Central Cultural Theme,'' PA, Vol. 15, No. 1 (Jan.-Feb. 1968), pp. 16-23.

came obnoxious in his behavior towards me. He brought up the subject of the ground which he had "freely given" and demanded that I employ him. In a rare moment of insight I paid him some money "for nothing" and immediately his attitude changed. The liability was finished as far as he was concerned. Seeing this result, I remembered the fowl "given freely" four years earlier and called the owner of the fowl and gave him money "for nothing." The owner hugged me and said, *"Pring pai ni tomga para wai sungwi,"* which freely translated means 'Your liability towards me is finished' (literally, the liability resting I gave to you is finished).

In confrontation with Christianity the Chimbu react with typical *pring pangwo* philosophy. "Christ died for our sins" is interpreted as meaning that Christ took all my *pring pangwo*. This initially gives a tremendous sense of relief until the full weight of one's indebtedness to Christ is realized. Then the Chimbu begin to "pay off" Christ by attending church services regularly and assisting the mission to whom they are affiliated as much as possible. No demand is too great. But a time comes when each clan feels it has paid enough for Christ's grace and church attendance drops off and there is a gradual decline in following the particular mission's rules for Christians. It is not so much a return to paganism as a completion of obligations. Of the missions in the area only one has succeeded in combating this philosophy with any success. By taking much of the pagan life and beliefs and transforming them into Christian religious practices, this church has kept its adherents from fulfilling their obligation—that is, the obligations are always growing as is normal in the culture. Other missions have condemned this as compromise and as a result have great initial responses but after five years or so things seem to return to the pre-Christian culture. In talking to one such convert who had ceased going to church I was told, "I am still a member of the church but I have *mong pring pai tomgi* (I have returned the liability); now I can get back to living my own life." After doing what it necessary, the Chimbu often regard further participation in mission activities as in fact putting the mission in one's debt.

Included in the convert's "repayment" was the attendance at five communion services and the paying of ten cents at each one. This payment of ten cents is interpreted as a gift to God (or the mission) to cover the cost of absolution for the sins committed in the period since last communion. In a practical interpretation I was told that if someone steals twenty dollars during the interval between communions, then the ten cents paid and sin confessed is sufficient to gain absolution for the theft. In contrast to this, an adherent of another mission, while condemning this procedure, stated that he would get his own forgiveness by prayer and voluntary exercises of self-condemnation but would not pay back the twenty dollars.

The depth of this liability complex needs to be realised if Christianity is to be a long-term proposition.

The government has managed thus far to keep ahead in the vicious circle by paying for everything done by the people (such as bridge-building) and by freely conducting courts. This has beneficial results except when the judgment of the court is the gaoling of an offender rather than the payment of satisfaction to the grieved party.

It is interesting to note the attitude that a clan has to a "big man" in its midst. All missionaries, Europeans, government officials, and the like are automatically "big men." This puts a large burden on them. Because they have been given many material things they are expected to share these things with everyone else. In one sense this is inconsistent with the liability concept. The very sharing creates *pring pangwo*. Yet after observing the return of relatives from money-earning expeditions to the towns and seeing the wailing for joy by the clansmen followed by an appointed time for the distribution of the goods brought back by the clansman, I noticed one significant fact. The relatives of the traveller had in fact built up obligations in his absence by looking after his pigs, wives, and garden. Therefore, payment was due to them. Should one of the enterprising men of the clan set up a trade store, he is usually doomed to financial failure. The reason is that he is forever giving his store articles away as payment of his obligations or as an insurance against future calamity—he is building up his status as a "big man."

Most "big men" are not so much those who have, but those who had and gave it away. By subtle means, such as helping the "big man," the Chimbu justifies his demand for a share in his goods.

There is no word in the language equivalent to "thank you." No gift is accepted with any sincere expression of joy. The one who gives is the one who should be thankful, because he is either paying a debt or creating a debt. The recipient is getting his due or being put into the giver's debt. If anyone requests something from someone else, the person who receives the request is morally bound to give. He loses face if he doesn't and is liable to be given the name *bina yal* 'fringe of society man.' This he is loath to do and so he may protest half-heartedly but he always gives. Christ's words on giving in the Sermon on the Mount are accepted, even though in the wrong spirit, because they naturally fit the culture.

The idea of repentance as a change in attitude cannot co-exist with a philosophy such as *pring pangwo*. As examples I can cite the numerous cases of Christian leaders from all missions in the area committing adultery. In discussions with them I have found that they only "act" repentance if the missionary demands it; otherwise they consider that if due payment is made to the offended parties then the matter should "die." Hardly any of them has expressed any sincere sorrow for his sin. Usually they lose their mission jobs once they are found out and this is considered sufficient penance. The *pring pangwo* has "died." However, the sin was not against God or a moral law, but against the mission—a kind of letting the team down.

An incident in which the author was involved further illustrates this liability complex: a boy drowned while chasing a fellow from another tribe who had stolen his shirt. This boy was the nephew (through a sister) of one of the clansmen with whom I live. My reaction was that this clan would join the nephew's clan in a fight against the clan of the offending boy who stole the shirt. This did not happen. My clan attacked the clan of the nephew, destroying crops and taking away pigs and fowls. A week later they went to the clan to arrange a settlement. They took $96 to pay for the damage they had caused and brought back $220 paid to them by the dead nephew's clan. This latter payment covered the *pring pangwo* or debt the dead nephew's clan had incurred by allowing the boy to die. It also included *breng sungwo* 'head payment' for the boy born into the clan. This nephew was on loan (unpaid for) to his father's clan as his mother had borne him and she was a sister to my clansmen.

Death duties are also paid. There is tremendous care and respect for the aged, dying, and recently dead. Should this respect in food, kind, or wailing be not given, the spirit of the dead person will return and extract *pring pangwo* payment by annoyance or even death.

The author, through ignorance of the full implications of this complex, has committed untold blunders. I have sensed my failures more especially when something has been stolen from me. More often than not, the thief has some grudge against me. He considers I owe him something for services rendered and not completely paid for. It is for this reason that I do not believe the Chimbu are thieves by nature. The odd case of thieving without cause is judged very severely by the village elders. Recently a ten-year-old girl stole a mandarin from one of my trees and shared it with another girl. The village elders fined the girl, through her father, $2.00, and the one who had eaten part of it $1.00. I considered this excessive and offered $1.50 back to the father. The village elders were most upset by this offer and I then incurred liability towards them for rejecting their judgment. The outcome was that I now owe them $1.00

and so does the father for accepting my offer. (One mandarin now is worth $5.00!)

As *pring pangwo* is so comprehensive, it is imperative for anyone communicating the gospel to the Chimbu to be aware of how easily his statements become part of this complex by interpretation. Any communication other than in the vernacular is particularly prone to misunderstanding.

Much more study is needed by the missions to ensure that Christianity deals with this central theme.

PART III

Cultural Systems and Manifestations:

Sex and Marriage

Walter A. Trobisch

Congregational Responsibility for the Christian Individual

The article which follows is not an "answer" to the John R. Davis article above. It was written entirely without reference to Davis' remarks, but it discusses creatively and in detail Trobisch's own approach to the problems which Davis raises. Trobisch has received over two thousand letters from people who have read his books and want his help and advice. There can be no doubt of the significance of the issues he raises to people in many cultures, nor of the insight with which he approaches their problems.

"JESUS took the man aside, away from the crowd...and said to him 'Be opened.' With that his ears were opened, and at the same time the impediment was removed..."[1]

What we need is a message *tailored*

[1] Mark 7:33-35

Walter A. Trobisch, formerly a missionary in the Cameroun, now conducts a Marriage Guidance Service for Africa (Traitteurstr. 60, 68 Mannheim, Germany). Two of his books, *I Loved a Girl*, and *I Love a Young Man* have been translated into about fifty languages around the world, and have been very useful in helping Christians from different backgrounds develop a Christian understanding of marriage. Previous articles in PA include "Attitudes of Some African Youth toward Sex and Marriage," Vol. 9, No. 1 (Jan.- Feb. 1962), pp. 9-14. The present article was delivered as an address to the Lutheran World Federation Third All-Africa Lutheran Conference, Addis Ababa, October 1965. It will be published with other studies in booklet form by Editions Trobisch, 757 Baden-Baden, Langestr. 50, Germany.

for each individual. In a concrete situation, general principles alone are not enough. Let us therefore take three people aside—away from the crowd. Let us try to help them and take responsibility for them as a congregation. All three of them are real persons. Of course, I have changed their names. They come from three different African countries, thousands of miles apart, but I shall not tell you from which countries. They have given me permission to use their cases as an example, so I am not breaking their confidence.

Joseph

Joseph is a teacher at a mission school. He is about 26 years old. I never met him, but we corresponded for almost three years. He wrote me after he had read my booklet *I Loved a Girl :*[2]

Three years ago I married a 15 year-old person. I have ten years of

[2] Walter A. Trobisch, *I Loved a Girl* (London: Lutterworth Press, 1963; New York: Harper and Row, 1965).

227

schooling, my wife only six. God blessed us one year ago with a baby. I purposely did not choose a girl with a higher level of education, for I intended to educate my wife in order that she become exactly as I wanted her to be in her work and cleanliness, in her whole life. But she does not satisfy me any more with her obedience. She does not do what I command her to do. If I insist, we quarrel. I ask you for a solution to save this young marriage.

In order to help Joseph we have to understand his way of thinking. For him, marriage is an alliance with an inferior being. For him, a woman is primarily a garden. Man is then primarily the bearer of the seed of life. Such is their mutual destiny. Their destiny decides their function. Their function defines their relationship. According to this conception the woman can never be as important as the man, any more than the soil can be as important as the seed. By her very nature, she is secondary, auxiliary. This is the root of all discrimination between man and woman that has shaped the history of mankind, not only in Africa, but also in Asia and, until of recently, also in Europe and America. This conception of marriage is not only based on a wrong and inaccurate biology, but it is also not in accordance with the New Testament which conceives of husband and wife as equal partners before God.

My task was to change Joseph's image of marriage. Here is my answer:

Joseph, you have not married a wife. You have married a daughter. You were looking for a maid, obedient to your commandments. She

was 15 when you married her. Now she is 18. In these three years she has developed from a girl to a young woman. In addition she has become a mother. This has changed her personality completely. She wants to be treated as a person. She wants to become your partner . . . It strikes me that your quarreling started after God gave you a baby. How long is the period of lactation in your tribe? Could it be that your quarreling has a deeper reason? It is not God's will for a married couple to abstain from physical union for such a long time.

Joseph's answer came quickly: You are exactly right . . . It is true that we abstain from sex relations for two years after the birth of a child . . . This habit is incorporated in us. Otherwise we are afriad of losing the baby, especially if the mother breastfeeds it and if it is a boy . . . My father - in - law pointed this out to me when our child was born.

The practice of abstaining from sex relations during the period of lactation presupposes a polygamous society. According to the biological conception of marriage, a man can have several gardens to be planted one after the other. A garden can have one proprietor only. Joseph wants to be a Christian. He has been taught by his church that polygamy is sin. But he has been left with this negative message. He has not received any positive advice on how to live with one wife as a partner, nor has he been told how to space his children.

It is interesting that he did not confide his problem to his pastor. Evidently he did not expect any help from him.

Still Joseph looks for a counsellor. He may find him in a doubtful friend, maybe not a Christian, and he may be advised to do things which are poison for his marriage. The method our couple uses for spacing their children—complete abstention—will lead to an estrangement and husband and wife will slowly drift apart.

Let us imagine that Joseph would have tried to solve his problem by taking a second wife. It is evident that refusing him communion as punishment for this action would have been the most inadequate answer to his problem on how to space his children. What is needed in Africa are not church disciplinarians, but marriage counsellors.[3]

In this case had Joseph not gone ahead and simply taken a second wife, but confided his intention to his pastor, explaining his motive, would his pastor have been able to help? Would the pastor have received enough training in this respect at the seminary? When a Christian takes a second wife, it is mostly due to the fact that his congregation has not carried responsibility for him.

It is unkind and merciless if missionaries condemn polygamy as sin, but keep silent to Africans about methods of conception control[4] which they themselves use. It is even more so because a missionary usually has powdered milk at his disposal while an African villager does not.

Let us imagine another possibility. Maybe Joseph did not take a second wife, but secretly had sex relations with an unknown girl, or even the wife of another man. In other words, he had committed adultery. Now, since he wants to be a Christian, his conscience hurts him. What could he have done? Would he have found someone in your congregation to whom he could have gone, confessed his sin and received the absolution? If he had come to you, whether you are a pastor or not, would you have known what to do?

What is needed in Africa are not excommunicators but confessors, able to keep the secret of confession absolute. What kind of training do our pastors receive in this respect? Here is the heart of the congregational responsibility for the individual. The offer of private confession is probably the most helpful contribution the Lutheran Church could make to the African churches as a whole. Martin Luther says: "No one knows what private confession can do for him, except he who has struggled much with the devil. Yes the devil would have slain me long ago, if the confession would not have sustained me."[5]

It is also possible that Joseph would not have dared to confess, but maybe you would have heard about his sin. Then it would have been your duty to go to him. Responsibility for the individual means to take the initiative. Just

---

[3] It is not the purpose of this paper to teach methods of conception control or to explain why certain methods lead to estrangement. The purpose of this paper is only to point out that such teaching belongs to the congregational responsibility for the individual.

[4] The expression "birth control" is misleading. It conceives of birth as the beginning of life. As a result abortions can be justified as a means of birth control. We prefer therefore the expression "conception control," because it recognizes the fecundation of the ovum through the semen as the beginning of life. Every destruction of this new life is murder.

[5] Martin Luther, *Sermons in Lent, 1522,* Weimar Edition, Vol. 10, No. 3, p. 61.

as God has taken the initiative in Jesus Christ and has spoken to us without our inviting him, so we have to take the initiative and talk to our brother, even if he does not ask us. This is "church discipline" according to the New Testament. "Go ye therefore…" not to put him out of the church but to win him back to Jesus Christ.[9] Church discipline means to go and to win, not to wait and to judge.

There is not time to report the case of Joseph in full. The relationship between him and his wife improved after I informed him about other methods of conception control. Later on a new problem arrived. The family moved from the village to town. While living in the village Joseph's wife had fed her family from that which she had grown in her own garden. But in town she did not have a garden. She had to go shopping. Joseph had to give her money, which had rarely happened before.

Here is Joseph's letter:

Tell me how to make up a family budget and how to convince a woman—however idiotic she may be—to keep it. Most of the time my wife buys things which we don't need and then they spoil.

I made up a detailed monthly budget according to Joseph's income and included as one item, " pocket money for each one of you." Joseph wrote:

My wife was very happy about it. After we had divided up the money, she was frank enough to tell me also the criticisms which she had in her heart about my spending habits. She was overwhelmed by joy to see the item, " pocket money for each one of you."

6 Matt. 18 15; 2 Thess. 3:15; 2 Tim. 2:25.

This was, after almost three years of correspondence, the first time that Joseph had reported to me a reaction of his wife. The fact that he had shared my letter with her, that he even listened to her reproaches, but above all the fact that he gave her spending money, shows that his marriage had grown from a patriarchal pattern where the husband-father dominates his wife, into a marriage of partnership. A garden cannot rejoice and talk. One cannot listen to a garden. Joseph's wife had changed from a garden to a person. She had become a wife.

Formerly the course of life was channeled. The individual had to make very few decisions of his own. The road was marked by customs and traditions. This had changed now. The individual has to make up his mind about many things which formerly were decided by the family and the group. But—as the case of Joseph and his wife shows—the individual is not trained to make these decisions. Counselling therefore becomes indispensable. It belongs to the responsibility of the congregation. It is the service which the Christian church must give in a situation of social change.

The work of the counsellor can be compared best of all with "swimming." The time is past when a counsellor could stand on a solid hilltop and give prefabricated rules and commandments to the counsellee. The counsellor has to descend from the hilltop and go into the water. Counsellor and counsellee have to swim together. With this picture of "swimming" in mind, the fact of uncertainty is expressed. At the outset the counsellor may be more in need of advice than his counsellee. But he swims together with him, trying to make out beforehand the whirlpools and the rapids, the islands and the riverbanks. For a limited time, while exploring the situation for clarification and solutions, the counsellor becomes the partner of his counsellee. God is in this situation and the counsellor has to find his will together with the counsellee. Only what the latter is able and willing to accept and put into practice will help him.

The development of Joseph's marriage during the time of our correspondence proves that marriage guidance by letter can be fruitful. It may even be easier to confide the most intimate problems to a complete stranger. Because of the long distances and the lack of trained counsellors, marriage guidance by mail has great promise in Africa, all the more because a personal letter there is highly treasured. It gives the receiver the experience of "being taken aside, away from the crowd," to have his impediment removed.

Marriage guidance is not only a counselling task. It is also a missionary opportunity. Since marriage is part of practical Christian living, the Christian marriage counsellor has the possibility of proclaiming the Gospel to non-Christians along with the advice he gives. Marriage has become *the* problem of life today. People of all confessions, religions, classes and races are interested in it. Every heathen, Muslim or Communist will listen to those who have something useful to say about marriage. As Christians, I believe, we do have something useful to say. But, do we say it? Or is the church in possession of a treasure of knowledge and wisdom, but keeping it locked up instead of handing it out?

Elsie

Elsie is a high school student and the daughter of a "minister of religion" as she calls it. I know her too only by letter. She wrote to me in June 1964 and asked. "How can I meet a Christian boy?" I advised her to attend church. There she could meet boys.

Here is her answer:
The old people in our churches don't want boys to meet girls, not even to talk to them in their presence. Always the Sunday service begins by speaking against boys and girls. This has turned away most of the boys and girls from attending church. The other day the pastor said: "If any boy has written to you a letter, return it to him and tell him never to write to you any letter."

I answered, but for a long time did not hear from Elsie. Later I learned that her school principal had confiscated my letter. I was not on the list of men with whom she was allowed to correspond. So my letter went to her parents, who lived in a small village, hundreds of miles away from her school. It took three months before the permission came and my letter was handed over to Elsie.

Finally she wrote again:
I have met a boy who is not of my tribe. He is a keen Christian and a student in a secondary school. It appears to me as if he would make a good husband according to the direction in your book *I Loved a Girl*. I went home and talked to my parents about him. They said they would not allow me to marry from any other tribe apart from mine. They claim that men from my boyfriend's tribe are going about with other women, even if

they are married. I have tried to tell them that not all men from that tribe are bad, but they insist on my marrying someone from my own tribe. Since we are told that we should honor our parents, I cannot do something which is against their will. To make it worse: I do not live at home. I know very few boys from my own tribe. Seeing that this boy is interested in me, should I disregard my parents' advice?

In my answer I advised Elsie to take her boyfriend home once and present him to her parents, in order that they could meet him as a person. If she is certain about God's will for her marriage, she should obey God more than men.

Elsie's answer, dated January 21, 1965: My parents have become impossible. They cannot approve the choice I have made. They say they have heard rumors that the man I have chosen was misbehaving at college. But ever since I met him, he has never showed me any nonsense, I have decided to remain single for the whole of my life, unless I can marry him.

Marriage between two Christians must be based on mutual trust and confidence. Confidence demands free choice. Free choice demands opportunities where young people can meet in a healthy atmosphere without suspicion. It belongs to the responsibility of the congregation to provide such opportunities. Many marriage problems in Africa have their root in the fact that the couple never had time and opportunity to really meet and get acquainted before marriage.

Many African boys and girls have a list with names of a limited number of persons with whom they correspond. In a society where the meeting of the sexes is still difficult, also for outward reasons, we have to recognize that letter-writing as a means to establish contacts, can be a good one. Instead of intercepting mail, schools should rather teach criteria of how to evaluate a letter and give helpful instructions for answering.

Elsie's case reflects two areas of conflict. There is the conflict between the younger and older generation. Dealing with the parents, uncles and grandparents of the couple involved is probably the thorniest problem of a marriage counsellor in Africa. But it has been overlooked that in a fast-changing society the education of the older generation also belongs to the responsibility of the congregation. The church may also have to speak out on the rules of exogamy (the tradition forcing a young man to find a bride outside a defined group of relatives) or endogamy (reversely, the rule that a bride can only be found within a close core of relatives.)[7]

There is also the conflict between individual freedom and the obligation to tradition and family. Elsie has new possibilities of choice, unknown to her parents. She is caught between making use of this freedom and submission to rules originating from customs not any more relevant to her situation. Again, like Joseph, she is in need of personal counselling in her new freedom.

[7] Once a young African wrote me that he had 11,000 girls ("sisters") in his tribe which he could not marry. Unfortunately he fell in love with one of them.

Her decision, however, to renounce this freedom and the wish of her heart, even against the advice of her counsellors, poses for us the following questions:

If you had been her counsellor, what would you have advised her to do? Assuming that God called Elsie to stay single, would it be possible for her to put this decision into practice? Does our church have a message for single girls? What would be the responsibility of her congregation for her? Is the decision against individual freedom and for submission to tradition always God's will? Where are the limitations of the fourth commandment? What is behind the attitude of her parents? (Her father is a pastor!) How far here is also the "biological" conception of marriage at work? Will they be pleased by her "obedience" or rather be shocked, that their "garden" shall never be planted? What could be done to help her parents to better understand their daughter?

Elsie's case, after all, is an encouraging one. She has character. She proves that one of the oncoming generation of African girls is able to make up her mind by herself, instead of being pushed around and dominated, that she is on her way to mature womanhood. Africa's future will depend upon this growth. There will be no free nations, unless there are free couples. There will be no free couples unless the wife grows into true partnership with her husband. It is the responsibility of the congregation to help towards such growth. It is the solution for Joseph's case as much as for Elsie's and even for our next case.

Omodo

On one of my trips I worshipped in an African church where nobody knew me. After the service I talked to two boys who had also attended.

"How many brothers and sisters do you have?" I asked the first one.

"Three."

"Are they all from the same stomach?"

"Yes, my father is a Christian."

"How about you?" I addressed the other boy.

He hesitated. In his mind he was adding up. I know immediately that he came from a polygamous family.

"We are nine," he finally said.

"Is your father a Christian?"

"No," was the typical answer, "he is a polygamist."

"Are you baptised?"

"Yes, and my brothers and sister too," he added proudly.

"And their mothers?"

"They are all three baptised, but only the first wife takes communion."

"Take me to your father."

The boy led me to a compound with many individual houses. It breathed an atmosphere of cleanliness, order and wealth. Each wife had her own house and her own kitchen. The father, a middle-aged, good-looking man, tall, fat and impressive, received me without embarrassment and with apparent joy. I found Omodo, as we shall call him, a well-educated person, wide awake and intelligent, with a sharp wit and a rare sense of humor. From the outset he made no apologies for being a polygamist, he was proud of it. Let me try to put down here the essential content of our conversation that day which lasted for several hours.

"Welcome to the hut of a poor sinner!" The words were accompanied by good-hearted laughter.

"It looks like a rich sinner," I retorted.

"The saints come very seldom to this place," he said, "they don't want to be contaminated with sin."

"But they are not afraid to receive your wives and children. I just met them in church."

"I know. I give everyone a coin for the collection plate. I guess I finance half of the church's budget. They are glad to take my money, but they don't want me."

I sat in thoughtful silence. After a while he continued, "I feel sorry for the pastor. By refusing to accept all the polygamous men in town as church members he has made his flock poor and they shall always be dependent upon subsidies from America. He has created a church of women whom he tells every Sunday that polygamy is wrong."

"Wasn't your first wife heart-broken when you took a second one?"

Omodo looked at me almost with pity. "It was her happiest day," he said finally.

"Tell me how it happened."

"Well, one day after she had come home from the garden and had fetched wood and water, she was preparing the evening meal, while I sat in front of my house and watched her. Suddenly she turned to me and mocked me. She called me a 'poor man,' because I had only one

wife. She pointed to our neighbor's wife who could care for her children while the other wife prepared the food."

"Poor man," Omodo repeated. "I can take much, but not that. I had to admit that she was right. She needed help. She had already picked out a second wife for me and they get along fine."

I glanced around the courtyard and saw a beautiful young woman, about 19 or 20, come out of one of the huts.

"It was a sacrifice for me," Omodo commented. "Her father demanded a very high bride price."

"Do you mean that the wife, who caused you to become a polygamist is the only one of your family who receives communion?"

"Yes, she told the missionary how hard it was for her to share her love for me with another woman. According to the church my wives are considered sinless because each of them has only one husband. I, the father, am the only sinner in our family. Since the Lord's supper is not given to sinners, I am excluded from it. Do you understand that, pastor?"

I was entirely confused.

"And you see," Omodo continued, "they are all praying for me that I might be saved from sin, but they don't agree from which sin I must be saved."

"What do you mean?"

"Well, the pastor prays that I may not continue to commit the sin of polygamy. My wives pray that I may not commit the sin of divorce. I wonder whose prayers are heard first."

"So your wives are afraid that you become a Christian?"

"They are afraid that I become a church member. Let's put it that way. For me there is a difference. You see they can only have intimate relations with me as long as I do not belong to the church. In the moment I would become a church member their marriage relations with me would become sinful."

"Wouldn't you like to become a church member?"

"Pastor, don't lead me into temptation! How can I become a church member, if it means to disobey Christ? Christ forbade divorce, but not polygamy. The church forbids polygamy but demands divorce. How can I become a church member, if I want to be a Christian? For me there is only one way, to be a Christian without the church."

"Have you ever talked to your pastor about that?"

"He does not dare to talk to me, because he knows as well as I do that some of his elders have a second wife secretly. The only difference between them and me is that I am honest and they are hypocrites."

"Did a missionary ever talk to you?"

"Yes, once. I told him that with the high divorce rate in Europe, they have only a successive form of polygamy while we have a simultaneous polygamy. That did it. He never came back."

I was speechless. Omodo accompanied me back to the village. He evidently enjoyed to be seen with a pastor.

"But tell me, why did you take a third wife?" I asked him.

"I did not take her. I inherited her from my later brother, including her children. Actually my older brother would have been next in line. But he is an elder. He is not allowed to sin by giving security to a widow."

I looked in his eyes. "Do you want to become a Christian?"

"I *am* a Christian." Omodo said without smiling.

As I walked slowly down the path, the verse came to my mind: "You blind guides, straining out a gnat and swallowing a camel."[8]

What does it mean to take responsibility as a congregation for Omodo? I am sorry that I was nót able to see Omodo again, because I had met him while I was on a trip. I just report to you the essence of our conversation because it contains in a nutshell the main attitudes of polygamists toward the church. It is always healthy to see ourselves with the eyes of an outsider.

I asked myself: What would I have done if I were pastor in Omodo's town? Let me share with you my thoughts and then ask for your criticism. They are based on many experiences in dealing with other polygamist families. Maybe you have better ideas than I have. Please, help me to help Omodo.

The trouble with Omodo is that, unlike Joseph or Elsie, he did not ask for help. But that does not mean that he is not in need of help. The fact that he did almost all the talking and hardly gave me a chance, proves his inner insecurity. His sarcasm showed me that deep down in his heart he was afraid of me.

In order to take this fear away I accepted defeat. You will have noticed that I was a defeated person when I left him. If you want to win someone

---

[8] Matt. 23:24.

over, nothing better can happen to you than defeat. In the eyes of the world the cross of Jesus Christ was a defeat. Yet God saved the world by this defeat. In talking with our fellow men we must remember this truth. We can easily win an argument, but lose a person. Our task is not to defend (no, not even the church), but to witness.

Humble acceptance of defeat is often the most convincing testimony we can give for our humble Lord. It is the one thing which the other one does not expect. Counselling is not preaching at a short distance. It is ninety percent listening.

When I have a conversation like this I ask myself first of all, where is the other one right? I think Omodo is right in his criticism of contradictory church policies, which sometimes deny our own doctrines. We have made the church the laughing-stock of a potentially polygamous society. We have often acted according to the statement, "There are three things that last forever: faith, hope and love, but the greatest of them all is church order and discipline."

Some churches demand that a polygamous man separate himself from all his wives, some from all but one. Others demand that he keep the first one; others again allow him to choose. Some allow that his wives stay with him under the condition that he has no intercourse with them.

Some do not even allow polygamists to enter the catechumen class. Others allow them, but do not baptise them. Again others baptise them, but do not give them communion. A few allow them full church membership, but forbid them to hold office.

The most generous solution was to baptize a polygamist only on his death bed. It happened to a Swedish missionary once that such a polygamist did not die but recovered after baptism. The church council decided, "Such things must not happen." They did not specify whether they referred to the recovery of the polygamist or to his baptism.[9] We have made ourselves fools before the world with our policies. Let us admit honestly our helplessness first of all. We are facing a problem here where we just do not know what to do.

Maybe our mistake is that we want to establish a general law for all cases. We want to be like God, knowing what is good and evil and have decided that monogamy is "good" and polygamy "evil" while the word of God clearly does not say so. The Old Testament has no outspoken commandment against polygamy and the New Testament is conspicuously silent about it. Instead of dealing with *polygamy*, the Bible has a message for *polygamists*.

Therefore let us not deal with an abstract problem. Instead let us meet a concrete person. Let us meet Omodo.[10] What would I have done?

First of all I would have gone back to visit him again. Church discipline, as the New Testament understands it, starts with me, not with the other one. If possible, I would have taken my wife along. I would have asked her to tell Omodo what she would think of me if

---

[9] Reported in Gunnar Helander, *Must We Introduce Monogamy?* (Pietermaritzburg, S. Africa, Shuter and Shooter, 1958), p. 20.

[10] Is he a special case? Every one of us is a "special case." There are no two persons exactly alike. Still, if we can help in one case we might find the key to deal with many others.

I let her work all day in the garden, get wood and water, care for the children and prepare the food while I sit idly in the shade all day under the eaves of my hut and watch her work. I think she would have told him that he does not have three wives, but actually he has no wife at all. He is married to three female slaves. Consequently he is not a real husband, but just a married male. Only a real husband makes a wife a real wife.

In the meantime I would have talked to Omodo's first wife and told her precisely the same, that only a real wife makes a husband a real husband. I would have challenged her because she had not demanded enough from her husband. She had behaved like an overburdened slave trying to solve her problem by getting a second slave. Instead she should have asked her husband to help her. She should have behaved like a partner and expected partnership.

She probably would have thought I was joking and not have understood at all. So I would have explained and we would have talked, visit after visit, week after week. Then finally I would have asked her why she ridiculed her husband. I am sure there was something deeper behind it, a concrete humiliation for which she took revenge, a hidden hatred.

At the same time I would have continued to talk to Omodo not telling him anything which I had learned from his wife, but listening to his side of the story. I am sure I would have heard precisely the opposite of what his wife had said. I would have tried to make him understand his wife and to make his wife understand her husband. Then, maybe after months, I would have started to see them both together at the same time, possibly again accompanied by my wife.

The best way to teach marriage of partnership is by example. One day we were discussing it in our "marriage class," a one-year course I taught at Cameroun Christian College. The students were telling me that African women are just not yet mature enough to be treated as equal partners. While we were discussing this, rain was pouring down. We watched through the window of the classroom the wife of the headmaster of our primary schools, who jumped from her bicycle and sought refuge under the roof of the school building. After a little while a car drove up. Out stepped her husband, handed her over the keys, and off she drove with the car, while he followed her on the bicycle getting soaked in the rain. This settled the argument. It is up to the husband to make his wife a partner.

Then one day I would have attacked the case of the second wife. I can imagine her story. She probably was given into marriage with Omodo for a high bride price at a very young age. I would have tried to find out how she felt about her situation. Young and attractive as she was, I cannot imagine that she was so terribly excited by old fat Omodo. It is very likely that she had a young lover alongside. I have found that women in polygamous marriages often live in adultery, because their husbands, staying usually with one wife for a week at a time, are not able to satisfy them.

Solving the problem of the second wife would involve talks with her father and "fathers" and also with the young man she really loves. It would have been a hard battle, but I do not think a hopeless one. It is a question of faith ; I would trust Jesus that he can do a miracle. I would ask some Christians in the congregation who understand the power of prayer to pray when I talk to the father. Every father wants to have a happy daughter. I would try to convince him to pay the bride price back to Omodo or at least a part of it.

The first time I would have suggested to Omodo to let his second wife go, he probably would have thrown me out the front door. So I would have entered again through the back door. I would have tried to tire him out by an unceasing barrage of love.

It is very important that by now a very deep personal contact and friendship is established between Omodo and me, a "partnership in swimming." In this partnership Jesus Christ becomes a reality between us even though his name is not mentioned in every conversation.

One day, I think, he would have admitted that he did not take his second wife just out of unselfish love for his first one, but that he considered his first wife as dark bread when he had appetite for a piece of candy.

Now we could start to talk meaningfully about sin. Not about the sinfulness of polygamy, but about concrete sins *in* his polygamous state.[11] So I would

have talked to Omodo about his selfishness, to his first wife about her hatred, lies and hypocrisy, to the second one about her adultery. In the minute they begin to see how these things separate them from God, it would not have been difficult to make them aware of their need of forgiveness. Then we could have talked about reconciliation with God. This reconciliation would have happened through the absolution. "He has enlisted us in this service of reconciliation."[12]

After the experience of the absolution we would have tried *together* to find the will of God for each person involved. Would the separation of Omodo from his second wife be a divorce? It depends upon whether we consider polygamy also as a form of marriage.[13] I believe we have to. Let us be fair, It is not "permanent adultery" as once a missionary told me. Adultery is never permanent. It is a momentary relationship in secrecy with no responsibility involved. Polygamy is a public state, based on a legally valid contract, involving life-long responsibility and obligations. If polygamy is marriage, separation is divorce.

---

[11] To talk to a polygamist about the sinfulness of polygamy is of as little help as talking to a soldier about the sinfulness of war or to a slave about the sinfulness of slavery. Paul sent the slave Onesimus back to his slave master, while he proclaimed a message incompatible with slavery and which finally caused its downfall. He broke the institution of slavery from *inside*, not from outside. This is a law in God's kingdom which can be called the "law of gradual infiltration." It took centuries until slavery was outlawed. God is very patient. Why are we so impatient?

[12] 2 Cor. 5:18

[13] If we campare marriage with a living organism, husband and wife can be compared with the two essential organs, the head and the heart. In all higher-developed organisms one head corresponds to one heart. Only primitive organisms are just a plurality of cells as for example the *Alga volvox globator*. Parts are relatively independent from the whole. A tapeworm can be cut apart and the parts are still able to live. One could compare polygamy with a primitive organism, which has not yet reached the state in which one head corresponds to one heart. Still a tapeworm is an organism as much as polygamy is marriage.

Our dilemma is that we want monogamy and we do not want divorce. Yet we cannot have one without the other. There are situations in life where we have the choice between two sins and where the next step can only be taken in counting on the forgiveness of our crucified Savior. It is in such situations where Luther gave the advice in all evangelical freedom, "Sin bravely!" being guided by the love to your neighbor and by what is most helpful to him. For me there is no doubt that in Omodo's case the most helpful solution for his second wife would be to marry the man she loves.

The case of Omodo's third wife, whom he had inherited from his late brother, is probably the most difficult one. In Omodo's case it was especially difficult, because she was blind. I would have gathered the elders of the church and explored possibilities on how to support her through congregational help in case she wanted to live independently. The way a congregation treats their widows is the most outstanding test of their willingness and ability to carry responsibility for the individual. One question is still open and I know you are waiting for the answer. When would I have baptized Omodo? I do not know. One cannot answer this question theoretically. I hope you understand that what I have just described is not the work of an afternoon, but of months, maybe years. Under the condition that this work is done, the moment chosen for baptism is not of decisive importance. There are no chronological laws in the process of salvation.

I would not have baptized Omodo before he had an experience of private confession and absolution. But then, some

place along the way, I would have done it, asking God for guidance together with the congregation for the right moment.

We should get away from considering church discipline as a matter of sin and righteousness, but rather put it on the basis of faith and unbelief. Faith is not a nothing and the use of the sacraments is not a nothing. In case it would have taken years to find a solution for Omodo's wives, I would have expected such a solution as fruit of his baptism and not as a condition for it.

In the meantime, while working and praying for a solution, Omodo would have to "sin bravely," sensing his polygamous state more and more as a burden. As his brother in Christ, together with the congregation, I could only act then according to Gal. 6:2: "Bear one another's burden and fulfill the law of Christ."

Would then the walls break and the church be flooded by polygamy? I do not believe so.[14] I think we overestimate ourselves, if we always think we have to keep up the walls, otherwise they will break.[15] The church has been so busy just being church, that it has lost sight of the individual and his need. The statement "God is a God of order" is not to be found in the Bible. 1 Cor. 14:33 reads, "God is not a God of disorder, but of peace."

[14] Polygamy is on the retreat any way for economic reasons. The young generation of Africans longs for a monogamous marriage of partnership.

[15] There is an inherent tendency in every society towards order. Russia, which abandoned marriage laws in 1917, has now introduced the strictest rules in the world—on an atheistic basis.

To help the individual in the name of the God of peace we need both the rules *and* the exceptions.[16] Laws are broken by the situations we face today. The time of timeless principles is past in our rapidly changing society. The counsellor has to give himself into life with its many different situations and happenings and "swim" with his counsellee. God is with them in the water.

Counselling the individual is putting congregational responsibility into practice. In the process of counselling, the unacceptable one is taken aside, away from the crowd, and unconditionally accepted. Therefore in counselling the justification of the sinner becomes a reality.

[16] All churches in Europe forbid remarriage of divorcees. Yet all of them allow exceptions. Why should the African churches not have the same freedom in dealing with polygamy?

William D. Reyburn

Kaka Kinship, Sex, and Adultery

A DETAILED description of Kaka kinship system and the socially regulated behavior that is built into it would require more space than would be justified here. Hence I will attempt to develop only those points in Kaka kinship and social behavior which have a bearing upon sexual mores. It is hoped that a review of these factors will structure for us the context from which the Kaka Christians and non-Christians derive their sexual codes which are so divergent from our own.

In stating these matters I wish to remark that in attempting to understand Kaka sexual values from the kin and social system I am not hereby pleading for the justification of such behavior nor for the defense of the Kaka traditional ways of thinking about such things. Evangelization of an African tribe is very much tied up with sexual behavior. This is as true to state as the remark that frontier evangelization in the western U.S. in the last century was involved in horses, six-guns, agriculture, and law enforcement. The fact that church sessions are swamped with adultery palavers in African communities is sufficient reason to warrant an attempt to understand the foundations of sexual values in African societies.

Reprinted from Vol. 5, No. 1 (1958), p. 1-21. This paper was originally prepared for a mission meeting and was not written with PRACTICAL ANTHROPOLOGY directly in mind. This accounts for its question-and-answer form.

While the data here are drawn from personal investigations among the Kaka of the Eastern Cameroun, it should not be thought that the Bulu and Basa are radically different. In a general way the systems, attitudes, and values are essentially similar. The details will vary. Any missionary can and should investigate these subjects for his own comprehension of his work. In order to assist missionaries who care to follow up these leads among the tribal peoples among whom they work, I have set this paper out in the form of a series of questions and answers.

One should be cautioned on two points, however. First, the questions that I have written are too generally stated to be of value to ask an African. However, within the replies following each question there will be found material which will be suitable for more specific questioning. Also, questions should be addressed to people who are sure where you stand. If the informant feels that you are out to trap him, his replies will be nothing more than a defense for himself. There is no substitute for confidence and close rapport. Christians and non-Christians, young and old, male and female should be questioned. If a missionary has lived with a people for a number of years and suddenly appears to become inquisitive about many aspects of the African's private life, it may be resented and the African will politely sidestep each question. The best informant is one who is convinced that the missionary is respect-

241

fully attempting to *learn* the African way of doing things.

1. What is the largest socially cohesive group to which every Kaka individual belongs?

The clan. Every Kaka person belongs to a patriclan which is made up of all the people who issue from a common legendary male ancestor. Descent is reckoned through the male line only. Hence each person, male or female, belongs to the clan (*mbo*) of his father. The clan is an exogamous group, meaning that no man or woman of the same clan may intermarry. Furthermore, premarital and extramarital sex relations between members of the same clan are considered incestuous and the offenders subject to supernatural punishment. The clan often coincides with the village, but in many cases a clan is large and is spread over a number of villages. It is not infrequent that struggles for clan leadership cause one portion of a clan to split into several subclans. These continue to practice clan exogamy and other clan taboos and rituals. The strength of a clan depends upon its population and wealth. It is the desire of each clan to be the largest dominating force among many clans.

In the clan, be it Bulu, Basa, or Kaka, one regards all the other people in the clan as being related to himself, and he calls them by classificatory kin terms. His real father and father's brothers and other men of his father's generation are all "fathers." His grandfather and grandfather's brothers are all "grandfathers." His cousins are all "brothers" and "sisters," and his nieces and nephews, along with his own offspring, are all "sons and daughters." His mother belongs to a different clan (that of her father) and in that clan he has many "mothers," since he extends this terms to cover all the female members of his mother's clan. Likewise among the Kaka, he calls all the women of his father's mother's clan "mother," and the same for the women of his mother's mother's clan.

2. What is a "family"?

In addition to being a member of a clan, a Kaka individual is born into a specific family group. However, "family" does not mean to an African what Europeans and Americans take it to mean to them. The lack of an equivalent term in the language of the South Cameroun for the European elementary family reflects the fact that the Africans do not conceive of the elementary family as being a valid concept. A Kaka belongs to a residence group (*ddité*, 'a common fireplace'). A lineage group within the clan forms a cluster of residences. There are brothers and their wives and offspring.

Looking at this lineage group from the viewpoint of a child, I see a cluster of houses in which are living my fathers and my brothers and my mothers. Since I am treated the same in any one of them and will be fed and helped or scolded alike at any one of these, there is little point in singling out "my family" as against "your family." Consequently, the residence group of the Kaka is a cooperative, sharing-common-authority residential group where the European idea of "family" is spread over and completely mixed into several elementary families. The residence group is a more personal one than the clan taken as a whole. While a person calls many men "father," he knows which is his real father and the behavior toward him differs from that of more removed "fathers." Likewise, the boys in one residence group have a stronger feeling as "brothers" than they do for all the other "brothers" in the other residence groups of the clan.

To summarize, then, the patriclan is a male descent group. It is like a club in which every child born belongs to his or her father's club. The rules of the club say that girls must go and live where their husbands' fathers' club men are. Also there are strict prohibitions against marriage between members of the same club, or even into the club of your mother or your two grandmothers. One classifies people in his clan roughly into four groups: grandfathers, fathers, brothers and sisters, and offspring.

3. What is the basis for authority in the clan and residence group and how is it structured?

The Kaka conceive of authority as an aspect of the male lineage. The greatest authority is the one who originated the clan. Consequently, each male ancestor receives his authority from his predecessor and passes it down through the lineage. It is because of this that the dead are literally more powerful and respected than the living. The oldest living male, unless he has become too senile to function, is the respected authority of the clan. The outstanding elderly leader of the largest clan in a village is normally the village chief. Wealth and numbers are the criteria for strength in the clan. Among the Kaka it is common for a village to include a half dozen clans. Bulu villages are commonly one clan only. The married women are, of course, outsiders and belong to clans other than their husbands'.

Authority may be transferred at the

will of a chief who does not wish to pass it on to his incapable son. In this case the new chief accepts the members of the expiring chief's clan as his "orphans" and he thereby puts himself under great obligation to those people.

In a village consisting of several clans each has its own clan head man. These individuals form the group of notables who are present for discussion of village affairs with the village chief. A village chief may be much younger than his notables, but his authority rests not in his personality but in his relationship as heir of his father's lineage group. The power and authority in the ruling lineage does not cease unless another lineage becomes stronger and takes over by sheer weight of wealth and numbers.

The lines of respect within the residence group flow from the oldest males (grandfathers) down to fathers and on down to sons and finally to grandsons. A female has authority in the residence group as a paternal aunt. She functions as a "female father" in authority over her brother's children. Women and girls are on the bottom rung of the hierarchy and do not count in the general scheme of things as people with authority. However, a mother who comes from a large clan and residence group may call on the help of her fathers and brothers to assist her in exerting influence in her family.

It should be remarked that the real authority in the Kaka areas is the village chief. The "Chef de Canton" is an administration-linked position created by the whites. The success of the Chef de Canton depends upon his ability to secure the cooperation of the *real* village authorities, the village chiefs. It is still common for a village to put up a straw chief who will receive the abuse and probings of the administration. They value their native authority too much to expose him to the often crude and unwelcomed contacts with administrators engaged in such tasks as recruiting laborers, taking census, and collecting taxes.

4. What are the primary kin relations within the clan and residence group, and what are some of their socially established relations?

In the following discussion we will speak from the point of view of a male "I". Remember that I am of my father's clan. My mother belongs to a different clan.

Grandparents. As a child my relationship to grandparents is the most pleasant and most indulgent experience imaginable. I can get away with anything. If I break their dishes, they think I am the cutest little thing. If I cry, they bounce me on their knees and coo at me, and if I scream to the top of my voice, they merely laugh and howl with me. They will stop anything they are doing to get food for me, and if I have a long, heartbreaking experience to relate, the most tender, sympathizing hearts in all the world are my grandparents'. My paternal grandfather, I later come to learn, is the most feared and respected of all the men in my residence group, but since we have all learned to love him for his indulgence we continue as men to love him for his ability and old age. He will someday be joining the big grandfather in another world, and they will be strong to help our residence group. Someday I shall grow up to have the power of my grandfather.

Fathers. I have lots of fathers: my real father who says he bore me, and his brothers. They are the ones who teach me to hunt and fish and to make my way in the world. They instruct me about women, and they tell me the secrets of our clan. I never question their authority because they are the sons of my grandfather. Someday they will have his power. I have many other fathers. All the men in my clan who are of my father's generation I call "father," and "grandfather" those in the next older generation. These men are like real fathers, but they have their own residence groups and they are not quite so close as my real father and his brothers. Other men I call "father" are the husbands of my father's sisters and of my mother's sisters. You may wonder how I know to call all of these men "father." It is real easy; as a child I heard them all call me "my son." So I know which ones to call "my father."

Mother. Just as I have many "fathers," I also have many "mothers." First, there is my real mother who gave birth to me. Then there are all of her sisters. For all of the men whom I call "father" I likewise call their wives "mother." This includes the many wives of my father. While I call all of them "mother," I know that my heart is always on the side of just one when I hear them argue and fight; that's the one who bore me. My real mother gives me lots of "mothers" because I call all of the women of mother's clan by the term "mother." When I say "mother" to all of these women of many different ages, I don't really mean "mother of my residence group." It is just a way I have of showing respect for all the women of my mother's clan.

Sometime I may see a girl who is very pretty and want to have relations with her, but if I call that girl "mother" I would get sick in my stomach if I should think of her genitals. If I know one of these "mothers" is bathing in the river, there is something in my heart that causes me to turn my head and not see her, or I cross the river at some place where I won't see her. This is true also for all the girls and women in my maternal and paternal grandmother's clans. They all call me "son" and I call them "mother." My fathers have always told us that, if we had sex relations with a "mother," both the mother and the man would die an awful death and no medicine, not even the Christian's God, could prevent it.

Once one of my "fathers" dreamed of sleeping with one of his "mothers." In the morning he awoke with a fever and after he confessed what his spirit had done in the night he became terribly ill and in a few days was dead. My fathers use this story to remind us never to allow our spirits to stray toward "mothers." We hear that white people can marry nearly anyone except sisters and that they don't die. The fathers that come back from the cities tell how our tribe brothers in the cities are beginning to do like the whites. Maybe someday we will start trying the white man's ways in the villages, too. The Christian God may protect us like he does the whites.

Brothers and sisters. Just as I call every woman "mother" who calls me "son," so I call every boy "brother" and every girl "sister" who calls me by those terms. Speaking of people of my own generation, I make a distinction between all those born before and after me. So I am careful to recognize the difference between older and younger brothers and sisters. This is very important for us Kaka people because the wives of all my older brothers are "my wives" also. At least that is how I'm taught to call them. And since I call them "my wives" they call me

"their husband." I can marry them if my older brother dies. However, for my younger brothers I call their wives "sisters-in-law" and can never look forward to marrying or being given one of these "sisters-in-law." All of the children of my generation in my clan are brothers and sisters to me. If I am ever in doubt about whether a certain boy or girl is a brother or sister, I merely stop to ask whether his father is a "father" to me, too. In mother's clan there are no brothers or sisters, however, just "mothers" and "fathers" (except for mother's brothers).

The closest relations I have are with my brothers. I look up with respect to older brothers because they stand closer to my father's authority than I do. I am likewise respected by my younger brothers.

As for my sisters, it is not a question of authority. We have that same feeling for "sisters" that we do for "mothers." For instance, if some boys from another clan are joking with me about a sexual affair and my sister is present, I feel compelled to go and hide in the grass. My sister, too, will get up and leave. If we go to bathe after eight or ten years of age and there is a "sister" bathing, we will pass on and come back after she is gone. If I should be with girls who are not "mothers" or "sisters" and we would see two dogs copulating, the boys will point to it and laugh and try to get the girls in a similar mood. But if I should see such a thing while in the presence of a "mother" or "sister," I would feel embarrassed and would act as though I had never noticed the copulating dogs.

We know that the young white people kiss their sisters, but if such a thought makes you sick at your stomach, it must be best to avoid such close contact with a sister. There are many words in our

language which signal a sexual connotation. When I speak around "mothers"
and "sisters," I talk with guarded lips so
that these words do not offend them and
embarrass me.

Uncles. In a patrilineal society the main
spot open for an uncle is mother's brother.
In Kaka I call mother's brother *koko* and
he calls me *taa.* Our relationship is a
difficult thing for the mind of a white
man to grasp. Here are some of the things
maternal uncle and I do. I can go into
his house and help myself to about anything he has and he doesn't say a word.
If he buys a new bicycle, I will probably
be the first to break it for him, but I
won't have to pay for it. If I am hungry,
I will go catch a chicken or goat belonging
to maternal uncle and carry it off without
saying "Please," "Thank you," "Hello,"
or "Goodbye." We feel that is just the
way maternal uncles are. We children
often say that God made two good people
in the world, grandpa, who is so indulgent,
and maternal uncle, who is so naive.

Another aspect of the maternal uncle
complex is that I call his wife "my wife"
and she, of course, calls me "my husband," just like she calls her husband,
my uncle. This is about like the wives of
my older brothers, but in the case of this
"wife" I can have free sexual access to
her while maternal uncle is alive. If I am
at maternal uncle's house and "my wife"
(maternal uncle's wife) is not too busy,
we get together on uncle's bed. If uncle
comes home while we are engaged, I
merely call out, "It's sister's son," (*taa*),
and he acts as though he doesn't know
what is going on inside. When I have
finished with uncle's good wife, I may
pick up a chicken in the yard and amble
back home. When maternal uncle sells
his tobacco, all of his sister's sons really

become pests, for we go sit down at his
house and joke with him about his wealth.
Finally he goes to my father and gives
him some money. Then we leave him alone
until we hear he has gotten hold of some
more cash. Soon we do it all over again.

However, custom declares that I pay
my uncle in certain cases, too. If I kill
an animal, the whole front quarter belongs to maternal uncle, and if he doesn't
get it there will be trouble afoot. If
maternal uncle kills an animal, sister's
son gets the head. Since there are many
maternal uncles with still more *taa,* who
is the one to get the meat? Every *koko*
has his favorite sisters' sons, and certain
nephews have favorite uncles. However,
the first nephew or uncle to appear may
often be the recipient of the meat. It is
for this reason that we nephews always
make it a point to know what maternal
uncle is up to. If I suffer a wound which
disables me in the slightest, I am obligated
to make a payment to my maternal uncle.
If he is wounded, he must pay the father
of one of his sister's sons, or the nephew
himself if the latter is an adult. If my
child dies, I must pay that child's maternal
uncle for the death. (That is, my wife's
brothers.) I pay also to my maternal uncle
if I am ill, and he pays his sister's son
if he is ill. If I go to prison, I pay him
or if he goes, he pays me. A sister's son
may inherit the wives of his maternal
uncle upon his death. However, the
maternal uncle's younger brothers have
first choice. If there are no younger
brothers, the sisters' sons are the next in
line. (The woman has considerable freedom to choose for herself.)

You may ask why all this reciprocity
between sister's child and maternal uncle.
We Kaka see it like this. First, the marriage relationship surrenders the girl's

productivity to another clan. This girl's brothers do not wish it to be entirely a onesided affair. Hence her brother retains an economic relation with her sister's offspring. While a male from another clan has paid for the productive rights (the dowry), the woman's brothers keep a secondary utilitarian interest in the offspring. Under the Kaka life of the hunt, the meat which a sister's son provides for uncle is considerably more than the older maternal uncle provides for the nephew. Consequently, the death, illness, imprisonment, or other indisposition of a nephew means less meat supply for his maternal uncle. Therefore a financial settlement is felt to be in order.

To make the distinction between maternal uncle's wife (who is not of my mother's clan) and her offspring who are in my mother's clan, it follows that "my wife's" daughter turns out to be "my mother." Likewise, maternal uncle's son is also called koko, and his wife is "my wife," while his daughter is again "my mother." In English this first "mother" would be my first cousin and the second "mother" a second cousin (or first cousin once removed).

Wife. The people whom I call "my wife" (they call me "my husband") are: (1) maternal uncle's wife of wives, (2) the wives of my older brother, and (3) my wife's younger sisters. Maternal uncle's wife is sort of a self-service kind of a neighbor. However, I am not free to have promiscuous relations with my older brothers' wives. I may have relations with my wife's younger sisters, but after these are married this is less frequent. They are potentially "wives" for me, since I may marry one or more of them after I marry the first. For this reason it is advisable to marry an older sister always so that

you can get the younger ones, too, later on. One cannot marry the older sisters of one's wife. If my first wife does not bear children, her family is obligated to provide another "sister" without the additional payment of dowry.

The relation of husband and wives is complex, and we won't discuss it here except as this relation bears upon the sexual code.

Fathers- and mothers-in-law. My father- and mother-in-law represent two highly respected symbols for me. Not only do I pay them for the productivity rights of their daughter, but I will continue throughout their lifetime to pay in cash and kind if I am satisfied with my wife as producer of children and garden stuff. I shall never enter the sleeping quarters of my parents-in-law. This spot I hold to be holy. If I should ever trespass here, I might behold the sex act which brought forth my wife, and this would be against all proper thought and conduct. Because I respect my in-laws, I will not use their names in conversation nor address them as anything other than the respected term ki. If I have a relative with the same name as my in-laws, I will pay at the wedding for the right to speak this name. In this way my in-laws will know that I am not being disrespectful if he or she should overhear me pronouncing his or her name.

Just as I avoid all sexual symbolism with my "mother" and "sister" kin, so I do the same with in-laws. Furthermore, I am not free to joke with them like I do with mother's brother. When I meet an in-law my face is long and sad, reflecting my deepest humility and highest respect. My mother- and father-in-law are not my only such relative. My wife's older sisters are also called ki and merit the same kind of preferential respect.

5. How is the sexual orientation of a Kaka tribesman determined by his kinship system?

Within the kinship system there are two sets of females: those who are considered *sisters* and *mothers* (the incest block), and the *wife* group who are potential spouses (the sex contact block). Consequently, the Kaka makes a fundamental separation between this incest group and the available or potentially available set on the basis of linguistic symbols. The word *nyari* 'wife', which includes maternal uncle's wife or wives, my wife's younger sisters, and my older brothers' wives, signals to me a potential sex contact, and the behavior that follows is according to the expected signal. "Sister" and "mother" are terms which signal "incest, stop, on guard, death to the offender, etc."

The symbolism associated with both these categories builds itself into a full-blown world of symbolic reality that is transformed into real behavior. The result of having linguistic symbols to mark off sexual behavior is very neat and precise as long as the old kin groups remain in contact and as long as outside influences do not intervene. This means merely that a Kaka depends upon language signals to provide for his primary clues as to how he should or should not behave as regards the opposite sex.

6. What does this imply as to non-kinship sexual attitudes?

It implies that one knows how to behave sexually within the kin system. This system reveals that the outer limits (maternal uncle's wife, wives of older brothers, etc.) of the kin group are the starting point for increased sexual interest which

begins by the signal "my wife." Every other female who is not a mother or sister (or grandmother or female father, i.e. father's sister) is a potential spouse, although all of these outside women do not carry the kin term of "my wife." The African has a polar concept of sex (not frigid as an iceberg). At one pole he lumps together the incest block and closes his thought to it. At the other pole is an open accessible female world, all of whom are potential wives. It is into this world he moves with sexual aggression which is as positive at this pole as it is negative at the other.

7. Does the kinship orientation of sexual behavior explain the Kaka sexual attitudes?

It does to a large extent. At least it sets the position from which he views sex, i.e. the incest block vs. the rest of the female world. The one is associated with supernatural punishment, while the other attains to life's greatest good — productivity and continuation of the male lineage, which is his greatest moral obligation to the fathers of the clan.

8. How do premarital sex relations affect extramarital ones?

When a girl reaches puberty or near puberty, the women begin to remind her that her nubile state is given her to produce children. At her first sex contact at puberty the father will be wounded in the hunt or at his garden work. This is a signal for him to inquire as to his daughter's sex relations. If the girl admits having had a contact (there is no punishment or disgrace connected with it, and hence no reason to conceal it), the father will collect a "defloweration" charge from the boy. This means that the girl is now available for dowry payment. If a dowry is paid, the father of the future groom requests that the girl be protected from further sex contacts. If the girl's marriage is not begun at this time, she is free to indulge in sexual promiscuity as often and with as many males as she chooses.

The reason for requesting that a future bride not be allowed promiscuity is that a partial dowry payment has been made, and if the girl becomes pregnant, there will be a struggle over the ownership of the child. During this period of open or hidden promiscuity (hidden somewhat if a partial dowry has been paid) a girl picks up dozens of suitors. These males never relinguish their claims on the girl even after marriage. Consequently, her premarital suitors often continue to seek relations after marriage.

9. What does a Kaka understand in the term adultery?

Sex contacts are defined according to the persons involved. Relations between an individual and maternal uncle's wife are simply "sex relations." This is considered about on the level of paying a social call. Premarital relations, called *bindi,* is an act which young people are expected to indulge in. It is the way in which girls prepare themselves for the ends to which a woman has been born, to produce children. Extramarital relations called *wandja* is a complex of its own with no exact equivalent in Euro-American societies.

Wandja is like a game in which I win a *ko-mbe* 'comrade', much to my delight and to his disgust. If I have sex relations with Mvondo's wife Mata, then I get to call Mata my *wandja* 'mistress', and Mvondo has to call me his *ko-mbe* 'comrade'. It is the desire of most men to be

able to call as many women as possible "mistress" and thus to be called "comrade" by as many men as possible. However, to become a comrade I must pay a "fine" for getting a man's wife as my mistress. Once she is my mistress, she is under obligation to feed me if I am hungry and to take care of me when I pass through her village. I, in turn, am expected to present gifts to my mistress. A woman wants to become a mistress, as she will receive gifts from many men in this way. None of these acts are understood in the same way missionaries take the term adultery. The Kaka concept of incest is much more serious than the Christian idea of adulterous unions. In other words, there simply is no exact equivalent.

10. Can the idea of wandja serve as an equivalent for adultery in the Euro-American sense of the word?

It is true that *wandja* is an offense to the husband of the adulterous female. However, it is not so because the wife has broken the "sacred vows of marriage," nor is it because a man would suspect the paternity of his wife's offspring. The offense is in the thought of having been forced into the comrade relation which gives the adulterous male a position of superior social prestige. Also important is the fact that an adulterous woman implies that her husband is less potent than some other male. This is a bitter bit of ridicule which no Kaka man can easily take. Consequently, his reputation as a sire of offspring is belittled in the eyes of the other village women and his chances of gaining mistresses for himself are crippled. It often results in the man taking his wife and family and moving from the village. A further factor is that of the food relation between a man and his mistress. If a husband's meat from the hunt is going to feed his adulterous comrade, he himself will suffer and such meat will injure his chances in the hunt as well as his medicine for the traps.

11. Who is actually wronged in a wandja relation?

The answer again is the economic one. The rights of ownership for the purpose of production paid via the dowry is the thing which is wronged. No person as such is wronged. If the adulterous wife bears a child, the paternity of the child is never a question. It is ownership that counts. The owner of the child is the one who has paid the dowry. If no dowry has been paid, the offspring belongs to the mother's father's brothers or some other male relative.

12. How important is the woman's attitude in adulterous unions?

Younger and middle-aged women encourage adulterous unions by ridiculing men as impotent if they do not make sexual advances. It is common for a group of women to mock a man and jest with him ridiculing the size of his genitalia. The natural defense of the male is to subdue one of the women and convince her or them that he is equally as potent as the other men of the village.

13. What is the symbolism of sex dreams?

The incestuous dream is often a foreboding of death. There are dozens of other dreams among the Kaka which are interpreted as omens of evil luck and death. However, there is one dream which can issue only in the greatest of all good fortune: *extramarital sex relations*.

14. How do Kaka Christians rate adultery in their moral concept of right and wrong?

First of all, the greatest wrong is incest, the stinginess within the residence group, and then theft. *Wandja* or adultery is a wrong against the dowry, but since it is an act into which two agreeing parties enter, it is not looked upon as harmful to any party on the order in which incest, stinginess, and theft are.

15. Why is there such a moral gulf between incest and wandja?

Simply because incest violates religious values, the sanctity of the clan and residence group, and is punishable by the spirits of the dead, while *wandja* is a misuse of ownership rights which can always be righted by payment in cash or kind. The spirits cannot be satisfied with money payment because they are the supernatural defenders of the holiness of the tribe or clan.

16. How does polygyny figure in the sexual foundations of the Kaka?

First, a man who stands to inherit wives from his older brothers or his maternal uncle is likely to become a polygynist. Polygyny is dominated by economic interests. We discuss three kinds here. (1) Chief polygyny is the possession of plural wives in order to feed and care for the large number of notables who are necessary for handling village affairs. (2) Fonctionnaire polygyny is an institution developed by the French administration by adding to the salary of government employees for each of their children. This is the reflection of the economic bent of polygyny. (3) Ordinary polygyny or village polygyny is the possession of plural wives in order to provide the work force necessary to keep up large gardens, tobacco, coffee, and cocoa farms. Polygyny is the "desired" form of marriage among the Kaka. At Mindourou, the oldest center of Protestant influence in the subdivision of Batouri, one third of the husbands have two or more wives. Fonctionnaire polygyny is doing the greatest moral harm to the Christian efforts of the South Cameroun.

Polygyny should be considered primarily from its economic position. In this way a woman may be thought of as a bond or stock. (1) There is always full return on the cash investment. (2) The woman produces steady dividends in the form of children and labor. (3) If the woman is in default (no children), another will be given in her place. Polygyny is not primarily related to sexual matters. However, some women prefer to be co-wives as they will have less sex contact from the same man in this way.

17. Is the dowry related to sexual values among the Kaka?

The dowry is a financial or economic arrangement between two clans or families in which the one group recompenses the other for the right to claim the offspring born into the marriage. The dowry (or lack of it) secures for the child his right to claim his legal position as a member of his father's or mother's clan. In a patrilineal society he naturally belongs to his father's clan, provided, of course, his father has him through dowry rights of clan possession. Otherwise he is the property (member) of his mother's clan. Hence the dowry establishes clan rights and is not concerned with sex behavior as such.

18. Is there no end in sight for the dowry?

The dowry will last probably as long as the clan does because they are integrally related. The dowry is a woman's pride. If women had independent careers and educational opportunities, they would not feel the need of the dowry. However, the desire of some pastors to do away with the dowry for their children's marriage must assume two basic considerations. (1) That the establishment of clan identity is no longer important and functional. (2) That the girl involved is sufficiently independent and satisfied with her status in the world that other females cannot bring ridicule pressure upon her. The pastors who make these assumptions often fail in the second requirement. The women of the Cameroun do not have economic and social status of sufficient ranking to free themselves from the stigma of "dowrylessness."

19. Christians often have huge families which are the envy of non-Christians. Does this mean they have been given God's special blessing for becoming Christians?

I do not believe that God blesses fourteen or fifteen children on a poor pastor or catechist just because he has become a Christian, especially in view of the fact that the mother may be neurotic with frequent childbirth and the father, living on a small salary, is unable to feed, clothe, and educate the offspring. This problem occurs everywhere throughout the Christian world where people have been accustomed to having free extramarital relations and then become conjugally faithful after becoming Christians. Rather than blaming or crediting God for rewarding a Christian for what he is normally expected to do anyway, one can expect that the faithfulness of man to wife and vice versa prevents the malfunction of organs through venereal infections and allows the wife to become pregnant more readily. Also important is the fact that the husband is more likely to be seeking relations from his own wife during her fertile period, whereas before he may have been indulging in extramarital relations at the time when his wife could have conceived.

20. The transitional life among the Kaka has produced many changes. What is the nature of some of these?

(1) The loss of former moral supporting beliefs. The Kaka, like many other African tribes, have, through European contacts, questioned some of their strongest moral linking beliefs. The idea that incest would result in immediate death is a very rigid belief which snaps when too much pressure is brought to bear on it. The witness of Christianity is often only a one-sided communication in which the new symbols and the new life are readily accepted. Those who are accepting the new life are readily accepted. Those who are accepting the new *cannot* continue to hold on to the old. Consequently, unless there is a filling of the old moral support, the tendency to be a Christian with a crumpled moral life is the result. Many African Christians are capable of the transition to Christianity while others merely find the transition a happy escape from an older order which wore heavy on their conscience. A truly converted African may find no inner weakening; on the contrary, the Christian life is apt to provide him with a renewed spiritual energy which has deep moral ramifications. However, the loss of old moral supports creates new problems for Christian as well as non-Christian. Often the Christian, while having made a successful

adaptation to Christian standards, simply has no precedent or tradition for coping with newly developed situations.

(2) The economic base that is replacing the kin group orientation. Formerly when one's entire universe was the village or clan there were, as indicated here, strong orientations toward the economic and ownership aspects of life. As people have come out of the village and gone into education and work they have carried these orientations with them. The kin group direction is not possible where one is disassociated from that group. The Kaka have learned that the only way to have recognition from the whites has been to simulate as nearly as possible the white man's standard of living. Money is required to do this, a great deal of money. Consequently, many Kaka impress the whites as having an abnormal lust for money and material goods. The payments which are exchanged between *taa* and *koko* continue in force today even where *taa* and *koko* are living separately and engaged in professions. In the village the payments are greater in cash due to the decrease in meat supply and the increased desire for European goods.

21. Can the mission help the African church in such problems as sex and adultery?

In the first place, Christianity among the Kaka (peoples of the Southern Cameroun) must not be envisioned in the Euro-American family setting. The problem for Christianity among the Kaka people is the establishment of a Christian patrilineal society and the Christianization of the residence group and clan. If the only way in which Christianity can be implanted is to supplant the patrilineal clan with some form of European soiety, then Christianity is nothing more han an elaboration of our Western ideas nd forms of life.

The Kaka view of sex, kinship, and dultery is undergoing change. Part of his transition is stimulated by Christian nd part by non-Christian sources. These lements are working directly against each ther. Sexual perversions, prostitution, nd other institutions are making them-lves felt right along with endeavors to aintain standards of conduct which have onstituted the central stream of Christian adition. In this conflicting picture of ultiple stresses, the Kaka are sure only ithin the familiar direction of the resi-ence group and clan. Consequently, a hristianity which does not make itself telligible on familiar grounds runs the ance of becoming irrelevant.

An example of how such relevancy can e established is the ˙case of the African ncept of productivity. The African is iented toward productivity on the basis ˙ what constitutes the *good life*. As long productivity leads to the good, then l things associated with productivity are od. This is in essence how a Kaka ilosopher might state the case. Conse-ently, premarital relations, extramarital lations, extreme sexual indulgence, urality of wives, and many children are l aspects of the good life. The Christian es not and need not give up entirely is African view of the good. However, a Christian he is expected to transform e value and associations of productivity. is transformation does not come simply becoming a church member.

There needs to be a joint effort of Afri-n Christian leaders and missionaries to amine these questions together so that e younger churches may be informed as the biological bases of human pro-

ductivity. However, in so doing it will be necessary for medical missionaries and other whites to remember that the high value which the African places on fertility and productivity arises from a moral obligation to his patrilineal society in which man is expected to maintain the continuation of his lineage. This obliga-tion is to him close to the deepest moral springs of his being. The mechanization of biological facts must be woven into a moral fabric in order that the African will benefit from these facts as he should. Such an exchange should go a long way to assist foreign missionaries to appreciate and sympathetically understand the Afri-can transitional viewpoint as well as to assist the young churches to face this changing life with a satisfactory set of values.

22. Looking at Kaka life from the side of Christianity, what is the major problem?

The conversion of the Kaka concept of God.[1] The Kaka concept of God is that of a spider, *Ndjambie,* who before the coming of Christianity quietly spun the heavens and kept the stars and clouds in their place. Since Christianity, *Ndjambie* has been asked to give up his patient impersonal toiling and to come down and intervene in the lives of men. *Ndjambie* is, according to Christian teach-ing, the God of history who thought ahead, conceived of an idea for many years in advance, worked out a plan and carried it out, and now, having made a huge personal sacrifice, remains intensely interested in man as an individual. This planning ahead for the coming of Christ,

[1] See William D. Reyburn, "The Trans-formation of God and the Conversion of Man," in this volume.

doing it, and being interested in man in a personal dimension does not in any way fit the personality of the unpredictable *Ndjambie*, who never had any plan, never could have brought forth a son, and who, of all things, was never interested in the ethical doings of anybody. *Ndjambie* (the spider) was not and is not predictable. He is part of the whole world, which has no history but which is punished along by accident and the cosmos. If *Ndjambie* had been interested in doing anything for anyone, the people might have felt like asking him for something. No one ever did.

As in the case of most nonliterate peoples, the idea of *Ndjambie* is tied up with the undifferentiated Cosmos. The Cosmos-God is the least personal any concept can become. Consequently, it is not surprising to see that *Ndjambie* is *Fate* and that man is utterly controlled by a cruel, unpredictable, and impersonal fate which is symbolized by *Ndjambie*.

The greatest transformation which can come in the life of any society is the conversion of their God to the personal Christian idea of God. The societal changes which will follow in the wake of such a conversion may be witnessed in the history of the Hebrews, who separated God from nature, or better, whose God through his self-revelation separated himself from the primitive nature idea imbedded in man's thinking.

This task is not accomplished by missionaries speaking and assuming that *Ndjambie* and God are equivalent substitutable symbols. They are not. For most *Ndjambie* in 1957 is not the Christian God, even though the translated Scriptures call him by that name. The missionary who will make a contribution to the Christian transformation of Kaka ideas will first recognize the nonequivalence in our terms and then will make his teaching relevant and instructive to the Kaka world of reality.

William D. Reyburn

Polygamy, Economy, and Christianity in the Eastern Cameroun

Polygamy as a desired form of marriage among the tribes represented in this study appears to be inseparably linked with economic aspects of life as these are developing in the eastern Cameroun today. Motivations for polygamy are a complex set of cultural factors which have not and will not be readily changed. Christianity in its total condemnation of polygamy has failed to discriminate between things which are totally different. The emphasis upon monogamy has often led Africans into a false picture of the monogamous union and a resultant reaction to it. While there are certain immediate and practical steps Christian churches can take concerning polygamy, the church is neither equipped nor is it operating in the real sphere of its message by following these superficial approaches to the problem. The Christian church, particularly Protestant, makes its fatal mistake in attempting to operate with neither a formulated missionary science nor an articulate missionary theology. From the side of missionary science we must learn that the case involved in this area is primarily economic and not primarily isolated polygamy. From the side of missionary theology we need to take the findings of such information and in true Christian identification with the human being involved move with our theology to his inner longings and WITH HIM communicate a gospel that speaks to the roots of his real need and show him that Christ is the ultimate answer to the POWER problem of his heart. When this has been done the transformed individual displays a transformation of symbols in his new relation to the power of the gospel and his regenerate life.

A KAKA tribeswoman, the mother of three children, sat on a low stool with a mortar between her bare legs. Rhythmically she raised her right arm high above her head,

Dr. William D. Reyburn's article on polygamy is based on a talk given in September 1958 in Douala, French Cameroun, at a conference on the social responsibility of the church before the social changes in the Cameroun. The report provoked a vigorous discussion among the delegates and some of their conclusions are incorporated in the article.

then brought a heavy wooden pestle down with a sharp blow, beating the manioc into flour for the evening meal of kamo. Her left hand shot into the mortar to stir around the manioc meal and then was quickly pulled aside as the pestle hammered down again and again. A child sat silently in the dirt beside her tugging gently at a fetish hanging about its neck. Soon the child arose and tried to move in toward a lank breast that was bobbing back and forth on the mother's chest. The woman stopped, took the child and put it to her breast, wiped the sweat from her forehead, and turning to her husband said, "If you had two wives I could go to my mother's tomorrow." Her husband lay stretched out on a mat, appearing to pay no attention to his wife. The woman continued in a louder voice: "Look across the courtyard at Abele. She sits and plays with her children while Kana cooks tonight." Turning toward her husband she picked up a stick and pointed it at him, and with an angry scowl on her face she called out, "Poor man, poor man, who respects a poor man?" The husband arose from his mat, walked to the fire, picked up a live coal between his leathery fingers and dropped it into his pipe. Turning toward his wife he spat, cursed softly, then slowly walked away. The woman sat the child on the ground, picked up her pestle and continued to prepare the evening meal which her husband would eat by himself by the embers of his fire while her half would be for herself and his children to be eaten in the flickering light of her mud floor kitchen.

Motivations for Polygamy

The Kaka woman described above reveals something of the feminine motivation for the polygamous[1] family. She wants more freedom for herself and blames her husband's poverty for not securing this liberty. She often provokes her husband into a polygamous union by employing the ridicule of "poor man." Polygamy is an institution which appears to many modern Africans as something

[1] Because of the popular usage of polygamy to denote plural wives, it is used here in that sense. More exactly, it should be called polygyny. Polygamy actually refers to plural marriage, whether of husband or wife. Polyandry is the technical term for plural husbands.

natural to Africa. As some say, "Polygamy is beautiful; it is a symbol of that which is truly African." Since a very large number of modern Africans were born into polygamous families and have experienced both the rewards and frustrations of westernization, it is not surprising that many Africans feel a strong pull toward the polygamous family as a satisfying security in a world that is changing perhaps too quickly. The gregarious nature of the large polygamous family fits the Kaka[2] personality, which is constantly endeavoring to express itself in interpersonal relationships.

The Desire for Children

Perhaps the most commonly voiced reason given by people of the Cameroun for the continuation of polygamy is the desire to have numerous children. The African looks upon offspring in a way which is often different from European ideas. In the first place the traditional African conceptualizes a marriage union as centered primarily around fertility. This view that all things should produce their kind causes him to conceive of humans as producers of their own kind. He views his life as a gift which he has received from his father, who received it in turn from his father, and so on. The gift of life has been handed down from generation to generation and each one is morally responsible to participate in that continuity. When a man has been given the gift of life from his father he will be most unfaithful to his father, if he fails to pass it on himself. Not only is there a sense of responsibility for reproduction among men, but the woman is likewise prepared to conceive of herself as the property of a man who has paid

[2] The Kaka are the group in the Cameroun with which the author is primarily working.

for her productive rights and she is responsible to produce children as well as gardens. It is little wonder then that many Africans read the accounts of Jacob, his wives and concubines, in the book of Genesis with a greater avidity than they read the Gospels or the Epistles.

Children are a great asset in the African household particularly in the traditional village life. There is a separation of boys and girls which takes place even before puberty in which boys are associated with the male segment of the patriclan (the father's family and line of descent) and girls with the female side. This separation is often a further motivation for children. If a woman has only sons she has no one to associate with her and to identify themselves with her in her work and life. She is therefore anxious to have boys for her husband but also to have girls for herself. Girls are particularly valued in the monogamous marriage where they will for a certain number of years be available to assist the mother in her work. Girls are the source of dowry payment which will increase the father's wealth and give him the opportunity to form a marriage union between his daughter and a friend who may often be of his own age group. It is this friendship pact between men which gives rise so often to the marriage of young productive girls to old senile men. The girl's father is more concerned to prove his long standing friendship to a man of his own age class than to arrange a compatible marriage for his daughter. To the traditional Kaka father his friendships come before the assumed conjugal compatibility of his daughter. He conceptualizes his daughter in terms of *ervice* and not in terms of happy marriage union. It is because of this attitude, which many young African

girls no longer share, that such marriages become extremely pathetic.

Boys are desired particularly because they are the visible continuation of the father's lineage. They will continue to inhabit the paternal village and to continue the family names which have been handed down through the generations. The father of an African household expects his offspring to help him and to provide him with a retinue of servants. The African father who is visibly well serviced by his many offspring is considered as a man of standing and is envied by others who for lack of children are forced to perform many menial tasks for themselves. In African societies such as in the southern French Cameroun, where land is plentiful and every man is an independent cash crop producer, it is impossible to hire workers. Consequently a man who has a large number of children can increase his cash crop production through the labor of his children. The economic aspect of polygamy will be taken up in more detail below.

A modern development of child motivation for polygamy in some African areas, particularly French, is the financial compensation for children. Many men in government service as well as private service are extremely anxious to increase the size of their families in order to receive this financial aid. Since children belong to their fathers and will not be lost due to separation of father and mother, there is often not much restraint in divorce and a turnover of wives is often common.

The high infant mortality rate of children is another factor which increases the pressure of polygamy. Africans are vividly aware that only a portion of the children born to them will live to serve them and to grow up and reproduce themselves. As one man said to me once, "I have eighteen children. Some are bound to die, some will be of no account, and I hope that the few that are left will grow up to be worth something."

Not only is the African man aware of the fact that he will lose children through death but also that he may lose his wife through death or for some other cause, such as interclan disputes. Since a marriage union is not often viewed as being a lifelong association, a man is prone to view the taking of a woman as a temporary arrangement in life. Many Kaka men have said that they would not have much security if married to only one wife. "What would I do if I had only one wife and she died?" It is especially true that a man who has had plural wives and has a large number of children feels it necessary to keep a retinue of mothers for his children.

Sexual Contact

While sexual considerations per se are probably secondary as a motivation for polygamy, Kaka men often express their concern that the death of a wife would leave them deprived of sexual contact. Also a man finds it convenient to have more than one wife for sex contacts when one wife is sick, called to her paternal village, or is having her monthly period.

The literature on the subject of polygamy often cites the long period of abstinence between birth and the weaning of the child as a reason for polygamy. This may have been true at an earlier time, but at least among the Kaka it is presently insufficient reason. Sex relations with a nursing mother are tabooed, but this is primarily to protect the child. If a Kaka man has a sex contact with a nursing woman, he must carefully bathe

himself and put medicine on the eyes of the child. Otherwise his impurity will pass on to the infant and cause it to die. Kaka men do not observe a strenuous abstinence code during the period of lactation and are unable to defend this as a reason for wanting plural wives. Christian Kaka men who do not practice fetish medicine and who do not plan to enter a plural marriage are beginning to have children more frequently than before. They are not entirely free from a sense of shame in doing this.

Failure to have children is perhaps one of the strongest motivations to enter a plural marriage today among the Kaka. If a woman is sterile a man is often compelled to take on a second wife so that he may have offspring. Among some Kaka families it is felt to be an obligation of the father-in-law to provide another daughter when the first has proven sterile. Among many Kaka this involves the husband in no additional dowry payment, but for others the husband is instructed to return the daughter and his money is refunded and it is entirely up to him to find another wife. In many cases in the Kaka tribe men have been able to keep the first wife, who continues to serve her husband, but always with remorse over the fact that she gave him no children. Some monogamous men who have large families in the villages of this study are not as a rule anxious to enter a polygamous union.

On the basis of demographic counts of male and female births as well as marriageable youths, there is in this area no disproportionate female excess in population. Men disappear earlier in the upper age grades leaving a larger group of old women than old men. However there is no population imbalance at the marriageable age level to motivate polygamy. If one counts the number of young males and females living with their fathers, there is always a great excess of sons over daughters. This is due to the fact that daughters are placed in marriage shortly after sexual maturity while sons must wait considerably beyond maturity to amass the money necessary for dowry payment. It is very rare to find a Kaka girl over fourteen in her father's family village, while his unmarried sons may be there at twenty to twenty-five years of age without having been able to take a wife. *Hence it should be underscored here that the two most common reasons for polygamy given by French administrators and missionaries in particular (viz., long sexual abstinence and female population excess) are in this area of no motivational validity whatsoever.*

The Role of the First Wife

The role of women and their attitude toward the family and marriage is a major aspect of monogamy and polygamy. A woman who has more work than she can handle is often anxious that her husband take on another wife. This frees the first wife from much of her burden and gives her free time to take produce to a market, sell it and perhaps spend her money. She will be free to go to her village and visit, to spend more time with her small children and to undertake other tasks in which she finds pleasure. In addition to the freedom that polygamy gives the woman, it creates a special position of authority for the first wife, called *nya toū* in Kaka, which means "woman of the house." It is *nya toū* who directs the other wives and makes the final decisions when problems and arguments arise among the co-wives. Only *nya toū* has direct access to her husband and may call him by his name, and it is she who

receives the orders from the husband. In many Kaka marriages in which the husband is advanced in years, *nya toū* may be an elderly woman managing the polygamous compound made up of co-wives and junior wives who are expected to obey her commands. *Nya toū* plays a very important role in the husband's decision to espouse another woman. *Nya toū* usually talks over with her co-wives the advisability of another wife, and if they are agreed that the presence of the potential wife would disrupt the harmony of the compound, *nya toū* presents these facts to her husband and often makes alternative suggestions to him. If the husband disregards *nya toū*'s advice, he soon finds out that the price of peace means returning the new woman to her family. In the case where a man marries a young girl, it is the responsibility of *nya toū* to take care of the girl like a mother and the husband does not sleep with the girl until *nya toū* advises him. Hence, the attitude of the first wife toward the possibility of co-wives is a very important factor in the creation of the polygamous family. In the villages of this study it was often found that the first wife was not anxious to have co-wives provided that the husband's demands were not too great. Also, if he bought her European goods which represented an equitable share in the cash income and if she had children, she did not feel extremely anxious for the presence of co-wives.

Frequency of Polygamy

In order to investigate the relation of polygamy in the changing economy of the eastern French Cameroun, a survey was made of five villages. The area covered by this survey represents a zone which is sparsely inhabited and consists of some seven relatively small tribes (Kaka, Yengele, Mponpong, Bizom, Ngounabem, Mpomam, Bangando). The distance by road between the two most extreme villages (Gounté and Mbateka Ndjong) is approximately 650 kilometers. The results obtained showed that the detailed study of this problem at Lolo was quite typical of the greater area. A full account of the Lolo study will be prepared at a later time. In order not to burden this paper with statistics I will give only the summary figures for the various villages.

1. *Ngola.* An Mponpong speaking village in the Subdivision of Yokadouma and located twenty kilometers south of Yokadouma on the Yokadouma-Molondou road. Ngola has 58 husbands and 95 wives, making a ratio of 1.6 wives per husband. Thirty-nine percent of the husbands are polygamous, 56 percent of the wives are in polygamous unions.

2. *Mbateka Ndjong.* A Bangando (Gbaya dialect) speaking tribe in the Subdivision of Molondou, located 20 kilometers north of Molondou on the Molondou-Yokadouma road. Mbateka Ndjong has 16 husbands and 22 wives, making a ratio of 1.37 or 1.4 wives per husband. Thirty-one percent of the husbands are polygamous, and 50 percent of the wives.

3. *Mindourou.* A Kaka speaking village in the Subdivision of Batouri, located 40 kilometers south of Batouri. Mindourou is divided into two halves; one is Protestant and the other Catholic. The statistics on this village include only the Protestant half of Mindourou. Mindourou has 35 husbands and 50 wives, making a ratio of 1.4 wives per husband. Thirty-seven percent of the husbands and 56 percent of the wives are in polygamous marriages.

4. *Gounté.* A Kaka speaking village in the Subdivision of Batouri, located 25 kilometers east of Doumé Station. There are 25 husbands and 38 wives, making a ratio of 1.5 wives per husband, with 44 percent of the men and 63 percent of the wives in polygamous unions.

5. *Lolo.* A Kaka village in the Subdivision of Batouri, located 80 kilometers east of Batouri on the Batouri-Gamboula road. Lolo has 56 husbands and 78 wives, making a ratio of 1.4 wives per husband. Forty-three percent of the men and 50 percent of the women are in polygamous unions.

From the foregoing data, the following conclusions may be drawn.

1. The percentage of wives in polygamous marriages is greater than that in monogamous marriages. In Lolo and Mbateka Ndjong they are equally distributed.

2. The percentage of husbands in polygamous marriages is always less than the number of husbands in monogamous unions.

3. The ratio of wives per husband is in all areas less than 2.

4. The overall frequency of polygamy and the ratio of wives to husbands is essentially equivalent throughout the entire area of this study.

Sexual Reproduction at Lolo

It was stated above that one of the major motivations for polygamous unions is to increase the number of children. In the following paragraphs we will examine briefly the sexual productivity in Lolo and then proceed to review these factors in the light of the changing economy.

In order to study the productivity of polygamous and monogamous marriages, it is impossible to arrive at just conclusions without comparing women of similar age groups whose productive activity has been over a similar span of years. In the data given below such a grouping has been done and only the final figures are given. Children here refer only to surviving offspring.

In Lolo 10 percent of the polygamous women have produced no children while nearly half of the monogamous women have produced no children. This statement must be understood in terms of the general age grouping of these women because there are just as many polygamous women in Lolo as monogamous. A detailed explanation will be given under the section on polygamy and the new economy. The polygamous women of Lolo have produced on an average 2.5 children per polygamous mother, while the monogamous women have produced an average of 2 children. On the surface it appears that the comparable age group of polygamous women has many more children than the equivalent group of monogamous women. However in Lolo nearly half of this group of monogamous women have had no children at all. If we remove them from the group, the monogamous women have produced an average of 3 children as compared with 2.5 for the productive polygamous women.

This quantitative view of productivity looked at from the male's position is somewhat different. The average number of children per polygamous male household is 5.3 while the average number per monogamous household is only 2.

It is extremely difficult to provide a quantitative account of this kind of data. In the first place no marriage is conceived in Lolo as being permanently monogamous. Likewise what are today polygamous unions may be tomorrow monogamous and next month will revert again to polygamy. However a qualitative account of child productivity in polygamous and monogamous unions in Lolo helps to show that certain kinds of monogamous unions are tending to produce more children than polygamous unions taken as an average. This is extremely valuable in the light of the fact that selected monogamous unions in Lolo are achieving what 90 percent of the men of Lolo claim can only come through polygamous unions.

It was said above that only 10 percent of the polygamous women have failed to produce children while 50 percent of the monogamous women have had no children. Does this then prove that the polygamous union is more productive? If so, why? The answer to these questions is entirely one of *selection*. The matter may be stated very simply. If a woman has given birth (before marriage or after), she is marked as productive and this in turn increases the price of her dowry. A polygamous man with wealth can afford to pay for a proven producer whereas a poor man with little source of income is doing well to get a low-priced wife who may often be a woman sent away from another marriage for her failure to give birth. If a man has money he can afford to buy the producing wife; if not, he cannot. Consequently we may say that financial position (usually gained through polygamy) makes possible the *choice* of productive wives. When this form of village capitalism was pointed out to a group of anti-capitalist college students, it came to them as quite a shock.

Monogamous marriages that can be compared in terms of time of monogamous union and period of productivity potential fall into two groups: those that bear children and those that do not. A further comparison shows that the 18 child-bearing monogamous unions tend to be stable and with less desire to seek extramarital sex contacts than the other 18 unstable nonproductive monogamous unions.

Venereal Disease

It has long been noticed by Africans and missionaries alike that pastors and catechists have often tended to produce large families. At least one of the reasons for this is the fact that sex relations in these cases are restricted to the husband and wife, thus reducing the possibility for contracting venereal disease. Among the Kaka the wide-spread occurrence of venereal disease may be attributed largely to the wide-spread practice of premarital and extramarital sex relations. It is estimated by one doctor working among the Kaka that nearly half of his women patients are cases involving a venereal infection and resultant sterility.

The spread of venereal disease, which in many cases eventually prohibits conception, is due to two main sets of factors. In the first place is the commonly accepted practice among the Kaka of sharing wives between close friends[3] and the premarital promiscuity practiced by the young. The second set of factors stems more from the economic development. Many young men are unable to secure the money required for dowry payment. Consequently they seek relations with prostitutes and transmit venereal disease. Many wives find that their husbands do not share with them enough of the income from the cash gardens,

[3] See the description of Kaka sexual practices referred to here in William D. Reyburn, "Kaka Kinship, Sex, and Adultery," PRACTICAL ANTHROPOLOGY, Vol. 5, No. 1 (Jan.-Feb. 1958), pp. 1-21, and in this volume.

and so these women seek sexual relations with other men in exchange for money, cloth, or other gifts. These women feel that European goods are necessary to life now and find this as a means of obtaining some of them.

In view of these factors it is exceedingly difficult for a Kaka man to maintain a selfish economic control of his wife and expect her to be faithful to him. It been found in Lolo that the productive monogamous and polygamous marriages cannot indulge in outside sexual contacts if they expect to have large families.

Polygamy and Economy

So far we have only alluded to some of the effects of the desire for money and European goods. It will now be necessary to describe briefly the type of economic development taking place in the eastern Cameroun and to show how this economic activity and polygamy are interrelated.

The economic life of the eastern Cameroun has been retarded, due mainly to its distance from the coast. Before the arrival of European colonizers in the Cameroun in the last quarter of the 19th century, coastal tribes were trafficking in ivory, rubber and slaves, which they secured from interior tribes. These coastal tribes maintained an exclusive contact with Spanish, Portuguese, German and French merchantmen sailing the west coast of Africa. Following the German occupation of the Cameroun it was discovered that the Kaka area contained considerable quantities of native rubber. Before establishing contact with the Kaka, it was necessary for the Germans to cross the hostile Meka tribal area as well as several other smaller tribes who had killed and eaten the few German merchants and officers venturing into this part of the

Cameroun. Punitive expeditions were carried out against various tribes and a communications route established, opening up the southeast Cameroun for rubber exploitation. Rubber and ivory were exchanged for European trade goods from approximately 1906 until the Germans were driven out in 1914. Following this initial period of influx was a period of some fifteen years in which the French attempted to organize its administrative units and did practically nothing to encourage economic development in this area. It was not until about 1935, when the road connecting Batouri in Cameroun and Gamboula in French Equatorial Africa was built, that the economic aspect of this country came again under outside stimulation.

In 1907, at the time of the first rubber exportation from the Kaka country, an average dowry payment was twenty *boukas*, which is a flat hoe-like piece of iron. By 1914 the price was still twenty *boukas*, but also included some European trade goods, especially cloth. In the 1920's the number of *boukas* was about five, but the amount of trade goods was greatly increased and in addition money was included. By 1939 the *boukas* had disappeared entirely and the dowry payment was entirely cash and trade goods.

This change in the dowry payment reflects the way in which the economy of the country was changing. *Soumba* is the term used in Kaka for iron, dowry, wealth and money. From time immemorial the dowry and iron have been synonymous. All wealth was in iron, and iron was used primarily in agriculture, hunting, war and marriage. The iron ceases to be the token of wealth today, but money, also called *soumba*, is used in payment of dowry.

The introduction of cash into the eastern Cameroun has been based upon two principal sources, labor and crops. Labor has always meant working for the administration, merchants or missions, in each case European institutions. Job opportunities have been relatively few. However, the introduction of money crops of cacao, coffee and tobacco have recently become available to all. The opening up of the roads in the eastern Cameroun (and in all other areas) made it possible to market crops in local central markets as well as to transport them off for exportation. Cacao was introduced into the western Cameroun before 1900. However, in the area of this study it was greatly delayed due to the lack of roads and communication and did not get started in the grasslands until in the last fifteen years.

Effect of Changing Economy

Cacao and coffee began to be exported from the forest areas of the eastern Cameroun as early as 1920. However it was not until 1946-50 that the tobacco development began in the forest and grasslands. The result of tobacco production has had a vast effect on nearly every aspect of the life in the area. Throughout the area of this study, social organization, village settlement patterns, daily routines, economic values and a host of other aspects of these cultures have been vastly affected. Some of those factors relevant to polygamy are presented here.

1. Most outstanding is the increased work burden for the woman. The men of this area (if not of Africa in general) do not believe that a man is obliged to work to the same extent as a woman. A man is responsible for numerous details of village and family life which require hours, days and weeks of deliberation which cause him to be absent from his

gardens. However, he expects his wife or wives to spend full time on the job. The result of greatly increasing the woman's work with all of the detailed jobs in the production of coffee, cacao and tobacco has the effect of causing the woman to object to her disproportionate burden. She is therefore, in many cases, obliged to seek help in her tasks through the assistance of a co-wife or wives.

2. The general increase in wealth tends to make those who have money appear richer than those who do not. Consequently the feeling of being "poor," which is opprobrium to the African, is increased. He feels impelled to avoid being left behind while others gain more wealth. Polygamy is a way to keep up and avoid the ridicule of poverty.

3. It is impossible in the area concerned to hire workers. Land is free and available. Every man is in competition and attempts to make gardens as large as his work force will allow. In some cases, extended families or subclans work cooperatively and in this way assist one another in their gardens. However, this form of cooperative labor is not extensive and it is not aimed at increasing everyone's garden but rather to reduce the total amount of heavy labor for the men. A man must depend upon himself, his wives and children to produce his income from his gardens.

4. The increase in cash has meant the increase in dowry price. In the area of this study, the majority of the money that is earned goes into dowries. Trade goods such as clothing, bicycles and sewing machines come next, and education lags far behind. Many young men find that their fathers do not pay them anything when the crop is sold. Hence they are not motivated to remain and continue the work. It is also the case that marriage has become exceedingly unstable due to the increase in available cash and the competition for wives as laborers. Many a father will encourage his daughter to leave her husband so she can go into another marriage where the father will receive a larger dowry. Consequently the father-in-law may blackmail his son-in-law for additional payments. If the son-in-law is unable to pay, the girl is forced by her father to leave her husband and enter another marriage. The original dowry is then repaid and the girl's father has made a handsome profit. With this profit he may be able to buy another wife for himself.

Sex and the Changing Economy

It is a thesis of this paper that the desire for the possession of wealth among the peoples of the eastern Cameroun has caused them to make certain adjustments which are tending toward their own ruin. In early times extramarital sex relations were formally forbidden and to break this law meant death, war or separation of subclans. With the coming of the European administration, particularly the French, all of this has been changed. Former controls have been lifted. It was formerly part of the responsibility of village elders or parents to guard their daughters from too frequent sex contacts. Any infraction of the laws of extramarital sex relations (except in wandja, the exchange of wives between close friends) was dealt with by the most serious punishment, usually death. The French administration, unlike the German, put the political responsibility into the hands of chefs de canton who were backed by French authority. Courts were set up to put into practice French laws. Punishment for sex offenses were adjusted to the levying of a fine. This was new to the Kaka and was entirely removed in his thinking from any moral dimension. The French authorities encouraged people to be married civilly, and when a man committed adultery with a woman having had a civil marriage it was in the eyes of the French an infraction upon a person who was in the process of becoming *evoluée*. Consequently the fine for such a case of adultery is fixed at 3,000 francs while the fine for adultery with a woman married only by traditional arrangement is only 1,500 francs. Since the responsibility for acting against adultery was removed from the hands of the village notables and placed in the courts, there was no longer any fear connected with adultery. In fact, often a man has found that if he can successfully accuse another man of committing adultery with his wife, he can collect the money from the offender and the matter is settled entirely on the basis of a financial agreement outside of court.

The codification of adultery as an offense against the colonial law had the effect of removing the traditional control of adultery. Since the payment of a fine was such a meager punishment and a new means of securing money for the offended party, it actually served to vastly encourage extramarital sexual relations with the result that in recent years the spread of venereal disease has become a front rank social problem among the Kaka, reaching the point of social pathology.

The result of the widespread occurrence of venereal disease has been, as was cited above, a sharp decline in the number of births in Lolo.

It is only fair to point out that it has not been the administration's policy alone which has created this situation. The cultural preparation which had been laid for many millennia before the arrival of the European colonizers has also contributed its part. This orientation among the Kaka as among many other African ethnic groups has been one which viewed the woman primarily in terms of sexual fertility and social inferiority. As long as the Kaka lived within a closed kinship world, his sexual behavior toward all the women with whom he associated was extremely well defined. However the extension of that small world through roads, the cessation of interclan and tribal wars, the opening of schools, and migrations sent him abroad into a new world where his rigid village *structural morality* was insufficient to guard him. Mission schools have often been more of an open temptation to sexual promiscuity for young people than a place where new moral attitudes were instilled. The traditional attitude of the young male has been that of sexual aggression, and the cultural and psychological preparation of young girls has been that of submission as part of the preparation for fertility expected of females.

The Kaka practice of *wandja*, in which two men in close friendship trade wives for sexual purposes, has had certain economic aspects which have come into play in the extension and reinterpretation of this practice. When two men establish the relation of *so* ("friend"), they trade gifts. Each takes turn giving the other a gift, which must be increased with each exchange. The *so* relation has not been primarily concerned with wife exchange but with material gain. The giving of a wife creates a new relation between the two men and their wives, in which the men are now expected to pass gifts to the wives. However, these gifts do not remain the property of the wives but are given to the husbands. Consequently the institutionalized practice of *so* has been extended in recent years in order to gain gifts through the lending of one's wife. This in turn has increased the spread of venereal disease, and when gone unattended for long periods, sterility has been the frustrating result. This in turn has caused the husbands to seek other wives for the production of children. Other practices of this type could be cited; however, the *so* relation is typical of the ways in which certain Kaka practices have undergone extension in practice motivated primarily out of economic considerations.

The Problem Is Economic

It is evident now that polygamy as well as freedom of sexual relation, the spread of venereal disease, the sterility of many women, and associated problems share a common nucleus which is of an economic nature. That is, there is a conceptualization of wealth which is the heart of this problem. Women and children are viewed largely as laborers and producers. Wives produce children and gardens, girl children produce dowry and provide personal service and are valuable for increasing garden income. The cash income from all a man's gardens belongs to him exclusively and he shares as little as possible with his wife or wives. Wives have a great desire to own, and if they do not find that they receive an equitable proportion of the cash income from their labor, they are anxious to seek other means of securing money. This they may do by encouraging and helping the husband to secure other wives. This gives each wife an opportunity to free herself from the close control of her husband, to sell her garden produce in a market town, to find employment, and to have

financially rewarding extramarital sex relations.

It is then in conformity with the facts that the matter of polygamy in the eastern Cameroun today is motivated more out of economic consideration than from anything else. Consequently it is both futile and dangerous for the Christian church to set up ecclesiastical laws against polygamy. What is needed rather is a reorientation of both men and women concerning money and wealth, and in particular a new conceptualization of the African family, in which economic considerations are secondary to other values. Such an attitude should have to begin with the male.

What Is Polygamy and
What Is a Marriage

The mission and church in the Cameroun have at various times attempted to legislate the admittance of polygamous women into the church. In essence the approach has been that the polygamous man is viewed as guilty of polygamy while the wives are innocent. This judgment has been based upon the fact that the man in these societies, because of the dowry, is the instigator of marriage. This is true in principle since the woman has had very limited choice in matters of marriage.

This position is not entirely just, however, since in many cases it is the first wife who provokes the husband into marrying a second wife, a third, and so on. Where only one wife in a polygamous marriage is admitted on the assumption that the man has only one real wife, the first one, there is the problem which often occurs due to the dictatorial power of the first wife over the co-wives. A second or third wife may be one who merits church membership but the first wife becomes a member in spite of the fact she may be unfit. If a man returns his wives in order to be a church member, he normally keeps the one which pleases him and who is fertile. He and his *selected* wife are then eligible for admittance.

It appears that by condemning polygamy per se, Christianity in Africa has done needless harm by a lack of discrimination. The question of a type of marriage union has appeared to be more important than the nature of the family involved in any kind of parental union. In the first place, the Christian church in its absolutist position of monogamy has impressed Africans that monogamy automatically produces a wholesome Christian family. While this has not been the purpose of Christian missions, it has nevertheless been implied.

The various kinds of polygamous unions found throughout Africa do not display the same basis for the foundation of the family. Neither are all polygamous marriages to be simply lumped together without discrimination.

In the French Cameroun today there are polygamous marriages involving chiefs who have upward of thirty wives. These wives are given out for child production and are exchanged quite as freely as merchandise. This is the exception. It is the remnant of the chief-polygamous marriage of the past generation, in which a chief might have a "wife" in nearly every village in his tribe. These wives played a definite political role as well as serving as wives and child producers and economic exchange. In the Cameroun today there are also polygamous marriages in which the family is the center and the relations in the polygamous family are most pleasant. Co-wives treat each other like sisters and all appear to be inter-

ested primarily in the welfare of all the members of the polygamous family group. The husband has a genuine concern for his wives and children and provides for them in a truly benevolent fashion. After one has lived in close contact with such a family, there can be no doubt why some Africans say: "I am proud of the fact that I was raised in a peaceful, compatible polygamous household." It would be extremely false to classify a peaceful, happy polygamous marriage and family with the type of chief-polygamy cited above. Likewise it would be unjust to lump a wrangling, arguing polygamous group of co-wives with either of the two cited above. It is a true and unfortunate fact that the majority of polygamous unions in the area of our study classify themselves as "incompatible marriages," due often to reasons related to the economy. In all five villages there is at least one generally recognized "ideal" polygamous family. It is possible to set up four types of family groups in these villages based upon the general peacefulness and compatibility that exists in the parental union and family group. There are two types of monogamous family and two types of polygamous family: (1) incompatible monogamous, (2) compatible monogamous, (3) incompatible polygamous, and (4) compatible polygamous.

Objections to Polygamy

If we admit that all polygamous unions and families are not made of the same stuff, just as all monogamous-based families are not of the same moral quality, we are brought back to the question: Should some cases of polygamy be admited to the church and others not? This is the question that the ecclesiastical authorities of churches ask themselves and they will continue to legislate the matter. Our purpose here is not to plead for one decision or another but to examine some of the implications of polygamous unions in the light of Christian thought.

The Christian church bases its objection to polygamy upon the Scriptures. However, on the level where these anti-polygamous decisions are made, it is commonly assumed that the New Testament is explicitly clear on the subject. This is not the case. The New Testament is conspicuously unconcerned with the subject. There is ample historical evidence to show that monogamy was the accepted and honored form of marriage among both Jews and Gentiles in the time of Jesus. Geoffrey Parrinder states in his study of polygamy:[4]

> Much of the teaching of Jesus on moral questions seems to have been given in answer to queries brought to him, on matters that were keenly debated at that time: for example, the penalty of stoning for adultery, divorce, the payment of taxes, the greatest law.
>
> Now it is very significant, and a point often overlooked, that there is no record of a question about whether a man might, in any circumstances, take a second wife. If there had been any doubt at all about whether a serious-minded Jew could have several wives, we should very probably have some reference to it in the Gospels or the Epistles. This would certainly have been preserved by the early Christian communities, if the problem had ever arisen in their own moral life. The absence of a negative command against polygamy, in the New Tes-

4 Parrinder, Geoffrey: *The Bible and Polygamy,* S.P.C.K.: London, 1950, p. 43.

tament, is therefore very significant, in exactly the opposite direction to that which is commonly and rashly assumed. It shows that the question no longer arose among the Jewish or Gentile communities to whom the gospel was addressed.

If it can be accepted that the teachings of Jesus and the apostles took place among monogamous people where polygamy was not common enough to be in the minds of the people, we may ask if the New Testament has nothing to say on this subject. The answer, of course, is that the New Testament teaching regarding marriage and the family are fundamental attitudes which are often incompatible with polygamous unions as we know them. Jesus exalted sexual morality, and the permanence of the marriage union (Mark 10: 2-12). Paul exhorted wives to obey their husbands, but also placed a responsibility on the husband to love his wife. The emphasis in the Gospels upon a marriage between two people is a

> . . . quotation from Genesis given in the Gospels, as also in the Epistles, (which) is from the Greek Septuagint translation of the Old Testament. It is even stronger than the original in Genesis, where the words "the twain" did not occur. The Gospel still further reinforces this by adding, "So that they are no more twain, but one flesh."
>
> If, then, a man cannot leave his wife, it is obvious that Jesus would not countenance a man's taking a second wife. This would be sheer adultery. The "one flesh" makes this quite clear. It is not permissible to have two marriage contracts at once, "two flesh." Nor can the unity of man and wife be broken up by the admission of a concubine.

"They are no more two, but one flesh," excludes a third party.[5]

Another serious objection to polygamy which should be presented is suggested in the Golden Rule. Now polygamy is the *ideal* form of marriage in the villages investigated in this study; over 90 percent of the men in Lolo replied that they preferred a polygamous marriage. This means that the majority of men in these areas are monogamous by circumstance and not by choice. In these villages we have shown that only slightly more than one-third of the men presently have plural wives. Between one-half and two-thirds of the men are not being able to realize their ideal. Polygamy as an ideal form of marriage union if conceived as permanent is an *impossibility*. Only under the most rare circumstances would it be possible for every man to have at least two wives. Since ideal polygamy is not practicable and the available women go to the men with the money to pay for them, many young men are therefore driven to seek relations with prostitutes and to be late in marriage, and to spend long frustrating years attempting to amass the necessary wealth to afford a wife. During this process a man is tempted to steal, usually contracts venereal disease, and often becomes quite cynical desiring to have wealth more than anything else. It is only natural that such a person would believe that adequate wealth would purchase all kinds of happiness.

The objection may be raised here that in most societies there are things which cannot be shared equally. The American executive position may be cited as a parallel in our own society. Other things such as driving Cadillacs, owning a suburban home, having a swimming pool,

may be indicated as desired aspects of American life which are wanted by the majority but of nearly impossible realization. We may certainly admit to the truth of this and show the frustrating effects upon our society due to the fact that the *personal failure* is a resultant institution which fills psychopathic wards, amusement escapes, crime and even evangelistic halls. However, the parallel is not complete due to the fact that the marriage union is a universal form basically necessary for the continuation of mankind.

Polygamy as it is today in the eastern Cameroun is an open attempt at female monopoly and is incompatible with the Golden Rule. Any people who idealize and live in expectation of that which is unrealizable and impossible are thereby imposing serious strain on the structure of their society. This is particularly true when it concerns something as expectable as is the marriage union and the family.

We may sum up the past two sections now by saying that polygamy varies and in some cases it is concerned for the family welfare and in others, just as in many cases of monogamy, it has no such concern. We are also safe in saying that there are basic attitudes in the New Testament which are contrary to the principle of polygamous unions when this is an ideal form of marriage for the majority of men. We may go further and question whether or not a Christian conception of marriage partnership would allow the continuation of polygamy. Polygamy dies out where the status of the woman is raised and where the woman becomes highly conscious of her own personality and aware of marriage as a sharing reciprocal relation rather than a servient relationship. It is safe to say that modern Africa cannot make the

5 *Ibid.,* p. 48.

adaptation to the modern world without allowing and favoring the changed status of its women. Consequently, by moving toward an identification with the other countries of the industrialized world, African societies are of necessity moving toward monogamy. Independence for African nations will bring women into positions and responsibilities which they never knew under colonial administrations. These adjustments will unquestionably create conditions unfavorable to "buying wives."

Approach to the Solution

Having described the nature of polygamy in one large area of the Cameroun and having stated that polygamy is an institutionalized form of wealth today, we are now ready to outline how this problem may be faced by the Christian church. In the first place, for the church to preach against polygamy is simply going at the matter backwards. Legislating against it by church councils, while at the same time encouraging the economic build-up of the churches, creates a contradiction which the Africans in the area do not comprehend. The orientation of Christian missions is definitely cast in a financial mold which it brings from its home churches and ecclesiastical heritage, in which self-propagation means often that the local church needs to pay the catechist or pastor and keep books. This is to the missionary a mere step which the indigenes must learn if they are to be a self-supporting church. Actually many native churches would be self-supporting if missionaries had not made such an issue of it and caused it to become a front line aspect of the missionizing movement. European backgrounds with money-conscious values and organizations have in effect often impressed native groups that upon the financial handling of the church depends everything else. Consequently the conceptualization of the church has often been in the natives' mind a kind of primitive bank in which everyone is a member of the board. There is probably nothing in the native churches of the Cameroun today which merits one tenth of the time taken up in budgets and money matters. As one well educated Cameroun pastor put it, "All the work of the church depends upon money, and if we don't make our budget we are weak and unable to work."

The native church in the Cameroun feels a dilemma in that money is felt to be so terribly necessary for the ongoing of the church, but those who can often contribute most (the polygamous men) are excluded from its membership. It is as though General Motors Company were told to increase its total output of automobiles, but also to send its employees on vacation. The African is not entirely responsible for the situation in which he finds himself. Neither is he entirely free from responsibility for it. Christian mission churches are over-concerned with the idea of membership which no doubt helps to assess increase and decrease and provides figures for the home board. A first step in a Christian solution to the problem in the eastern Cameroun would be to reconsider the idea of church membership and to embrace a fellowship of families without consideration for the status of the marriage union. As it is presently, the father of the family is forced to be an outsider. The source of authority is excluded. The family takes on a feeling of separation from the one they really honor, the father. Anywhere in the Cameroun where a person is asked if X is a Christian, the reply is Yes or No; and if Nó the qualification is frequently added that X is a polygamist. The church in the Cameroun is by and large a female church where the man who needs the teaching of the church is felt unwanted. However, there are certain basic attitudes shared by the men which will not be affected by the church as long as the church communicates itself along the artificial lines of "membership." Consequently the church has no choice but to work in reverse and tell women (who have little choice or voice in the matter) that polygamy is wrong.

If the church does not want to re-adjust its lines of communication and prefers to be based upon membership, then the church will have to get out of its narrow confinements and address itself to the males in other ways. It may hold men's institutes, sponsor gatherings for men outside of the church atmosphere, and through the personal contact of its present male constituency attempt to bring about a changed attitude toward money and wealth. Where polygamy is a sign of status, it is sometimes possible to take on a new sign which serves the old purpose. Cement houses in the villages of the Bulu tribe are beginning to receive the recognition formerly granted to polygamists only. Careful financial arrangement may enable male Christians among the Kaka to build such houses and the prestige accorded to the polyg-amist only may be shifted to the owners of cement houses. The church could help by advising Christian men on how to economize and to plan their expenditures.

The status of women must be visibly changed. This is being started through education, but here again we cannot assist present adults by thinking always of people of a generation or two in the future. Christian men and women who have proven that marital fidelity produces more children today than unfaithful po-lygamy or monogamy, will continue to be a strong influence for the cause of Christianity.

Reorientation of Values

Most fundamental of all perhaps is the necessity for Christian village men to conceptualize their wives as partners in a permanent marriage concerned for the welfare of their families. In order to do this, it is absolutely necessary that these men change their attitude toward work. In spite of the fact that they are ridiculed, they must not demand of their wives more than they are willing to do themselves. Here is precisely one of the greatest problems. Christian missions have created the specialized class of African pastors who see themselves as professional men who do not work in gardens if at all possible to avoid it. Seminaries have failed to take into sufficient account the social reality of African life. It may be necessary that the Cameroun seminary student be taught to appreciate a new meaning of physical labor and actually be taught to work with his hands as an integral part of his training. This would mean that his teachers, Europeans and Africans, would also have to participate. Pastoral theology is not enough. If the African pastor conceives of himself as above work, he will be at a loss to bring about any fundamental change in the male attitude toward work.

A great danger for the Christian church which concerns the matter of polygamy is that the church gives the impression that a monogamous marriage is automatically good. The African knows that this is not necessarily so. In fact he knows that monogamous marriages are sometimes completely impractical.

For instance, a village or clan chief with heavy responsibilities and a constant flow of visitors to feed would not be able to perform his expected duties with one wife. If he tried, his wife would soon die of overwork. Polygamy cannot be viewed from European labor class and economic points of view.

There can be no doubt that two factors would automatically lead toward monogamy: male and female equality of rights with mutual respect, and the existence of a complex class system where hired laborers were available. As for the first of these, the Christian church may have a great deal to say. The second matter is a problem of cultural change which fortunately or unfortunately may come eventually. Probably the thing which will have the greatest practical influence in the Cameroun for some years to come will be the fact that many Christian men have taken on a new idea of womanhood and marital fidelity and this has in turn often been rewarded by numerous offspring. These outward signs will change with the time. The Christian message must continue to seek in the African's heart and in identification *with him* the answers to the deeper longings that find their outlets in polygamy. I suggest one of these here because of the fact that Christianity can effectively work in this sphere. I refer to it as "transformed symbolism." The argument is essentially that the African feels a compulsion to represent in tangible form his innermost feelings. That which is purely symbolic to Europeans the African fills with a meaning and action. The Christian sacrament of the communion cannot be equated for the European and African. To the latter the Roman Catholic doctrine of transubstantiation is real and meaningful. The Prot-

estant view is given lip service but is not satisfying to the heart. It would take us too far afield to follow up this discussion in detail. However, it has its outworkings in the matter of marriage and the family, wealth, and polygamy. Children, crops, gardens, and wives are all aspects of the traditional African's compulsion for a visible sign to mark what he believes. They are the tangible living representations which guarantee for him the meaning of life. Life is an aspect of power. All that polygamy ideally produces are vivid signs of the presence of this power. Now we have come to the core of this longing. This deepseated emotion, which silently lies hidden in the heart beckoning and calling, is a desire for power. The possession of force is the possession of being and vice versa. Everything in the African's life partakes in this power and life is conceived as a gamble for the gain or loss of power. One need only listen to the prayers of the African Christian to witness the extent to which this concept of power is the truly motivating aspect of his life. Life needs to be continually reinforced through the addition of power, by the increase of life. All life is lived in a dynamic drive for power, for human vitality. It affirms this life and finds it totally inconsistent with some aspects of the Christian message aimed at renouncing life. All in this life exists to serve man and to affirm his living presence. Is there little wonder, then, that a living compulsion moves the African toward all those outward symbols of such a world outlook? The Christian songs that are choices among the people of this study are ones which affirm this life or look forward to the eternal life which is a blessed continuation of this life. Christ has come "that they might have life, and that they might have it more abundantly."

It is absolutely necessary that Christianity not confuse this existence in power of the African with European ideas of power. This is not power as an idea. It is not just power as a lust for submitting others to one's will. The *ddeti* of the Kaka is a dynamic force in all existence which one must partake of and be a part of in order that life may be guaranteed. This power naturally plays its role now as it mingles with political ideas and nationalism. It was all-important at earlier times in war. It is the nucleus of medicine, of fetishism, of magic. It is the essence of the African's concept of God. It makes even the most stubborn western forms of Christianity take on an African feeling. It is the generating principle behind ancestor worship and kinship bonds, social structure and village life. African Christianity, as it matures, comes back to it and makes it serve its task of revealing the meaning of life.

The insipid nature of much of the African's Christianity stems from the fact that he joins a church and relies upon this association (church contagion) to place him nearer to the source of power. The step which is badly needed in the communication of the gospel to the African is that the presence of this power is realized in submission to the role of the humble servant to be filled with a power for service to others. This means the acceptance of a new and vital aspect of this dynamism which the African hopes for. It means that the tangible symbols of its presence must be seen. It is for this reason that the African believes when he sees and one act speaks more than a thousand words.

Walter Trobisch

Pre-Marital Relations and Christian Marriage in Africa

At least two previous articles in PRACTICAL ANTHROPOLOGY have highlighted the dilemma of the African church in the face of problems of
adultery and premarital intercourse.[1] In the present article, the author
summarizes the findings of an informal inquiry on premarital sexual practice
traditionally practiced by certain groups in the Cameroun. This article
attempts to lay the foundations for a study of the problem by reconstructing the traditional attitudes and motives of people in these African groups
toward this area of behavior, and the implications for the church and the
gospel. In a subsequent issue the present-day attitudes of some modern
African youth will be analyzed.

IT HAS become increasingly evident that
many of the problems facing the growing
African church are primarily related to
social behavior and to the transitional
nature of changing social patterns. I have
had opportunity during the past five years
to observe young Africans, both male and
female, in the setting of a Christian college where it has been possible to initiate
a course for upper-level male students on
the subject of marriage and the family.
In order to draw upon the thinking of
my students and to be consciously aware
of their personal as well as tribal lives, I
have made several investigations. These

do not claim to be finely calculated bits
of social research, but in spite of this,
these findings have considerable value, as
they are being used constantly in the
regular discussions and study of marriage
and the family.

When one attempts to discuss the subject of marriage to a group of young
Africans, it becomes apparent that one
is faced by a host of varying attitudes
toward women, changing values of the
home, and a generally confusing array of
impressions held concerning sexual relations, both premarital as well as marital.
I have, from time to time, asked my
mature male students to write out what
they know about pre-European concepts

Walter Trobisch is a teacher at the
Cameroun Christian College in Libamba.
German born, educated in Europe and
the United States, he is a pastor of the
Evangelical Lutheran Church. An earlier
article by Mr. Trobisch, highly relevant
to the theme of this present one, appeared in PA, Vol. 8, No. 5 (Sept.-Oct.
1961), pp. 200-206, under the title,
"Church Discipline in Africa."

[1] William D. Reyburn, "Kaka Kinship, Sex,
and Adultery," PA, Vol. 5, No. 1 (Jan.-Feb.
1958), pp. 1-21; William D. Reyburn, "Polygamy, Economy, and Christianity in the Eastern Cameroun," PA, Vol. 6, No. 1 (Jan.-Feb.
1959), pp. 1-19; Walter Trobisch, "Church
Discipline in Africa," PA, Vol. 8, No. 5
(Sept.-Oct. 1961), pp. 200-206.

and practices of premarital sex relations. The students participating were asked to inquire of their parents and older village fathers in order to get a more complete and authentic description of the subject. The students, who are between the ages of 17 and 20, numbered 22 in all, and are members of the Bassa, Bulu, and Bamiléké tribes of Camerouns, all of which are northern border Bantu language groups. They are also members of Protestant churches and have been under the influence of mission and government schools for approximately eleven years.

Classification of Pre-Marital Relations

The purpose of this paper is threefold: (a) to summarize the findings gathered by the students, (b) to describe the various attitudes maintained by these young men today, and, finally, (c) to relate certain of these attitudes to a Christian concept of love, marriage, and the family.

It is possible to classify the findings of the students into three categories based upon permissiveness toward premarital relations. Group 1 may be termed non-permissive, Group 2 permissive with tolerance, and Group 3 permissive with encouragement. However, it should be remarked at the outset that two categories of permissiveness are not mutually exclusive. Not only were premarital relations sometimes said to be permitted and not permitted in the same tribe, but this opposition of attitude can be found to exist even within the same household group.

Two students representing the same tribe living in neighboring villages reported diametrically opposed permissiveness toward premarital relations. However, a false conclusion would be drawn if one did not keep in mind that permissiveness is not based here upon an ideal code of sexual behavior, but rather upon a utilitarian value of the sex relation. If premarital protection and subsequent virginity resulted in a higher dowry, and if this were the motivation for the given situation, then, non-permissiveness is said here to arise from utilitarian values. It will be shown that such is often the case.

Non-Permissiveness

Most students were agreed that virginity was an ideal and was functional in the arrangement of marriage. Various tests for virginity were said to be conducted. An egg may be forced into the bride's vagina to determine virginity. Recall that African eggs are very small indeed. If blood was found at the first contact on the wedding night, the groom placed a container filled with water on a table the following day. This act was to signify that his bride was a virgin and hence there was cause for celebration in the village. The public display of the "tokens of virginity" is a well-known practice in Semitic cultures and is referred to in Deuteronomy 22: 15-21. The "tokens" of virginity are subject to considerable manipulation and are of little actual proof of virginity. However, most students in the investigation agreed that virginity was a definite asset in the marriage arrangement. Parents who have protected their daughter through her nubile stage and are certain of her virginity could ask a higher dowry.

As in the Biblical case cited above, the groom's family had the right to demand a return of part of the dowry if the bride's virginity was not well attested in the first sexual contact. Some students believed that a virgin bride would be more fertile than a non-virgin.

Since virginity was of considerable marriage value, these societies formulated various safeguards for the girls. For the most part this task of surveillance was the responsibility of the mother. The mother watched over the girl by day and required her to sleep near by at night. Rigid exclusion of girls from contact with marriagable young men was enforced. Some families carried out a custom called "fattening." This means that some girls were closely guarded and well fed so as to become as fat as possible in preparation for marriage. These girls were kept naked so that their developing bodies and degree of fat could be clearly observed.

Another control which was aimed at discouraging premarital relations was the custom of promising a girl in marriage while the girl was still in infancy or, more rarely, even before her birth. The future husband's family who had already paid an installment on the dowry would bring constant pressure on the girl's family to safeguard the virginity of the betrothed. In some cases a child bride might be taken into the groom's household to live where she would then come under the direct care of the women of his family.

It would sometimes happen that a girl in a non-permissive situation would have clandestine sex relations. The punishment would be extremely severe. She might be exposed to the hot sun, to ants, mutilation of her body, or even removal from the tribe. One student reported that a "fattened virgin" who was caught having premarital relations was burned alive. A more common punishment was the introduction of hot pepper into the girl's vagina. It is interesting to note that in most such cases no punishment was given to the male, although a fine was sometimes required to repay for the misuse of what was considered a "purchased virgin." Physical punishment of the offending male occurred only where a man had relations with a "fattened virgin." This could include torture such as cutting the man's eyelids, ears, marking his back, cutting off a member of the body or even burning him alive.

Permissiveness with Tolerance

Existing along with the custom of the "fattened virgin" in some tribal areas were other practices of premarital relations. It seems from the reports of some students that it was permissible to have relations with girls if no one discovered it. These societies placed a very serious restriction on certain classes of virgins, but placed little or no restrictions on the boys. Hence, when I refer to permissiveness with tolerance as one of the sets of attitudes regarding premarital relations, I refer mainly, but not exclusively, to the males.

One set of rules held for the girls, who were for the most part to be protected, and another set for the boys. The latter were encouraged to prove their potency and to establish their reputation as suitable future husbands. It follows from this split sexual orientation that much of premarital relations in these societies resolved itself into a clever kind of game of cat and mouse.

Permissiveness with Encouragement

Finally, there is at least one reason for which girls were sometimes encouraged to indulge in premarital relations. This was to provide the girl's father with a child who would, of course, become a fully recognized member of the young mother's paternal household. In case a man had paid a partial dowry he might succeed in making his future wife pregnant, pay the remainder of dowry, and then receive full rights to the child. Hence, in order to avoid losing the child to its own biological father, the girl's father might encourage such premarital play with a young man who would have no possible claim to any resulting offspring. Here again we are forced to the conclusion that protection of virgins or the encouragement of promiscuous relations was motivated more from total material gain for the girl's family than for anything else. A man who had paid part of a dowry might encourage a friend to make his future bride pregnant so that he could demand a subsequent decrease in total dowry to be paid to the girl's father.

Illegitimate Children

The students were unanimous in referring to children born outside of the dowry as illegitimate. The Bamiléké students were agreed that an illegitimate child could not inherit from his mother's father. They described the lot of these children as very unfortunate. The child in this case belongs to the biological father, but because of the shame attached, the child's own father may not care for the child. In this connection it should be noted that it is only in the Bamiléké area of this study where one finds a huge mission orphanage crowded with unwanted children. Some of the other tribes described the illegitimate child as "a gift given in a wrong way." However, such a child was still very much a highly valued gift, be it a boy as heir or a girl as future dowry.

Christian Implications

The whole complex of marriage and premarital relations in the earlier society stood exclusively under the measure of material value. Utility justified contradictory behavior. In the area of premarital sin a moral code in the sense of a deduction from a moral principle and for the purpose of realizing ethical standards and values did not exist. Even where chastity was proclaimed and virginity favored, the purpose was not entirely ethical but rather largely commercial.

If missionaries and missionary-trained African pastors argue today with modern African youth that their increasing immorality is not only a falling away from Christian teaching, but also in contrast to their own tribal traditions, they are right to a certain degree, but they overlook the fact usually that the motive behind these traditions was not an ideal of "purity," but of material gain.

The wrong in premarital relations was never "guilt" before a Supreme Being or violation of an ethical law. What led to restriction and interdiction was fear of shame or loss, not fear of "sin."

The conception of "love" as a personal relationship, as the unconditional surrender of one person to another for the benefit of the *other* one's happiness, was unknown in the pagan society. Love in this sense and premarital relations were unrelated. The "fattened" girls were given to the highest bidder. The early engaged girls were not even asked their choice, and the ones permitted premarital sexual experience were not married to the one who fathered their child.

A missionary approach that takes for granted a concept of love and a sense of guilt which actually does not exist in an individual's mind, is condemned to failure. The appeal to responsibility in respect to the offspring out of wedlock will not hit home either, since the illegitimate child is usually considered as a "present," except in the Bamiléké case.

The African native church finds herself in a dilemma. She has to proclaim a moral behavior as Christian which is neither based on psychological experience, nor sanctioned by customs, nor accessible to utilitarian reasoning. Her solution has been to force her believers under an outward law by means of church discipline. The evidence of this is the fact that 95 per cent of all cases of church discipline are for sexual misbehavior. There is a connection between the African abuse of church discipline and the almost entire lack in the normal missionary approach of a positive teaching about marriage.[2]

The teaching of marriage must not start with "do's" and "don'ts," but with a new interpretation of Christian love in respect to the relationship between the sexes. After a one year's course on mar-

riage, the students were asked to make a brief statement of what had impressed them the most. It was interesting that they hardly mentioned what they had learned about sexual behavior and biological facts. But all of them, without exception, mentioned that they had received a new understanding of love. One student, after having been in mission schools for eleven years, said: "Until now, I always thought of love as something cruel." What he meant was, "Until now I thought that love was identical with sexuality, and sexuality had only an egotistical and utilitarian purpose."

Finally, in order to give effective help to the present generation of African youth we have to consider the fact that their thinking and reasoning is not only influenced by their original customs though this is one important factor, but by many other sources which help to form their sexual codes. These will be considered in a subsequent article.[3]

------

2 A more extensive discussion of this problem is to be found in Trobisch, op. cit.

3 Walter Trobisch, "Attitudes of Some African Youth toward Sex and Marriage," to appear in a later issue of PA.

Walter Trobisch

Attitudes of Some African Youth toward Sex and Marriage

In this article the author analyzes the results of an informal survey of the attitudes of his students toward premarital sex relations and marriage. The article is written in the light of two previous articles in PRACTICAL ANTHRO-POLOGY.[1] *Trobisch discusses the need for an African Christian theology of marriage, and for relevant teaching in the light of African assumptions and presuppositions as revealed in this small sample and through his other observations.*

A EUROPEAN one can hardly imagine the degree of confusion in the mind of a young African of the present generation concerning sexual behavior and marriage customs, including premarital relations. The most contradictory influences pile up on him and finally he finds himself lost without orientation in a thick jungle of do's and don'ts, conflicting authorities and allegiances, foreign examples and his own experiences.

There are the customs of his own tribe which still have formed his way of thinking to a great degree. There is the white missionary, most often of pietistic origin, for whom sexuality is almost identical with "sin" and who takes for granted that his own marriage is

the normal Christian marriage. He is prone to believe that motive and content are intelligible and imitable for every African of good will. There is school education on the secondary level where he had to read, for instance, the plays of Molière, which take their humor mostly from situations which his church would label "adultery." In spite of this they are presented to him at a mission school. There is his church, always ready to "discipline" him for action which his own conscience does not condemn and which forces him into hypocrisy, hiding, and false repentance. Sometimes girls are sent away from school because they are

Walter Trobisch is a teacher at the Cameroun Christian College in Libamba. German born, educated in Europe and the United States, he is a pastor of the Evangelical Lutheran Church. He is author of two earlier articles related to this same theme, which have appeared in recent issues of PA.

[1] Walter Trobisch, "Church Discipline in Africa," PA, Vol. 8, No. 5 (Sept.-Oct. 1961), pp. 200-206, and "Pre-Marital Relations and Christian Marriage in Africa," PA, Vol. 8, No. 6 (Nov.-Dec. 1961), pp. 257-261. See also, William D. Reyburn, "Kaka Kinship, Sex, and Adultery," PA, Vol. 5, No. 1 (Jan.-Feb. 1958), pp. 1-21, and "Polygamy, Economy, and Christianity in the Eastern Cameroun," PA, Vol. 6, No. 1 (Jan.-Feb. 1959), pp. 1-19.

pregnant or a classmate is summoned by the village chief because of an adultery palaver. These experiences frighten the young person. On the other hand, there are the polygamous chiefs and political officials. There are the white administrators and traders for whom a native concubine is often a matter of course. There are his own natural desires and the insurmountable problem of the dowery before him, and then, of course, there is that great contribution to society made in Hollywood, U.S.A.

Therefore, when twenty-two unmarried male students of marriageable age report what they think is the general trend of opinion among present-day African youth concerning premarital relations, one has to understand it with some reserve. An influence from one side or the other may cause them to see things in a different light. Also, the fact that all of them have attended mission-directed schools for at least eleven years may have minimized their ability to see things as objectively as the topic would require.

However, just this point was the first surprising observation about their reports; they had great difficulty stating any basic difference between the thinking and practice of Christians and non-Christians in respect to premarital sexual behavior. One exceptional fact was that the Christians were threatened by church discipline and the others were not.

The students were asked to describe the current attitudes of their parents and those of their contemporaries, both male and female. Their reports showed such an astonishing unanimity across tribal lines and geographical regions in what they hold for the general way of thinking today, that I believe their findings have to be taken seriously and can help us to

find a message for this age group and their greatest problem.

Parental Attitudes of Today

The parents, the boys thought, would in general today discourage and forbid sexual relations to their children, both boys and girls, before marriage. Their reasons are, as in the earlier days, mainly utilitarian.[2] They fear a palaver with the other family involved. The girl who is still a virgin can be married more easily and brings a larger dowery. Today a pregnant daughter clouds the authority which the parents seek to maintain.

These reasons weigh even heavier today through the influence of modern civilization. The palaver may not be just a private feud between two families; it may involve a public trial. The dowery has increased considerably and is a mighty economic and social factor. To have to write on the birth certificate of the offspring "father unknown" augments the shame. This fact was mentioned many times. What formerly was clan shame now becomes public and national shame.

An important factor today is the increasing knowledge of medical facts. That sexual diseases may be easily acquired by such relations and that they may cause sterility is evidently considered by parents as a very serious argument against premarital relations. Some included that the "law of the church" would be important for Christian parents.

They all thought that their own Christian parents would discourage premarital relations. Just how well they succeed and how well they even want to succeed deep in their hearts is another question. There is still the one fear which surpasses all

2 Walter Trobisch, "Pre-Marital Relations and Christian Marriage in Africa," op. cit

others in every African heart, the fear of impotence. Parents may prefer to put up with a palaver and pay a fine, or even accept church discipline rather than carry doubts in their hearts as to their son's virility. Being impotent is the greatest possible shame that can fall on an African and his family. The impotent man is called a woman. Parents do not feel capable of giving their sons guidance. As soon as their boys reach a certain age, the parents close their eyes and hope that all will come out as well as possible.

None of these boys claimed to have received any sex education from their parents. This they pick up from age-mates and older brothers, and that in a very casual and general way. Some accused their parents of deception and lying. One student, son of a catechist, wrote, "My parents always tried to discourage me and show me the bad side of it. My older friends, on the contrary, tried to encourage me and cause me to practice what they told me. That's the way I acquired knowledge of the bad and the good side of the sex act."

Male Youth Attitudes of Today

In general, these boys think today that premarital sexual relations are not only useful, but indispensable. There are believed to be greater advantages gained through premarital relations than bad consequences to be suffered. The reasons they gave can be divided into two groups, physical and psychological.

Physical reasons given include the following: The sexual desire "never leaves one." The sex organs must be exercised in order to avoid underdevelopment and atrophy. "Because these organs exist, they have to function."

All the boys feared ejaculation during sleep. They interpreted it as a sort of a punishment by their own nature for not having used their sex organs enough. Many lived under the impression that to practice continence would cause the semen to accumulate in their stomachs and result in sickness. Some thought that the work of having to wash their bedding with expensive soap is enough reason to seek intercourse. This factor indicates a certain fear of semen.

The girl should be tested for suitability before marriage. There is a common fear of the "wife with water." This fear was always mentioned, though none of them had experienced it personally. They claim that there are women who discharge at the moment of penetration an abnormal amount of fluid which makes intercourse impossible. Therefore, a girl has to be tried before marriage is even considered.

The papers gave the impression that premature orgasm and ejaculation is a very common evil in the African marriage. It is interpreted as a form of impotence. The theory is that the ability to avoid it can only be acquired by repeated intercourse before marriage.

Psychological reasons included the theory of learning by doing. "Before you go hunting, you have to sharpen your spear" (an African proverb). Some claimed that the instruction in natural sciences and experiments in physics and chemistry have strengthened this argument and have awakened the "taste for experimenting." Curiosity combined with the fear of shame of "not knowing" was strong.

A major motive was to avoid being mocked by other boys and also girls. "What do you think you are? Do you want to be holier than all of us? You are just a coward." If a girl would suggest to a boy that he may be impotent, the boy has virtually no other way of proving to her the contrary than by having intercourse with her. Many African boys have confided to me in private conversation that this was what finally made them give in. The challenge of the female was greater than their own sexual desire.

Prestige is important. Proof of masculine courage and superiority is necessary. The boy exercised his masculine authority by seeing a girl underneath and himself on top of her.

As reasons which could possibly restrict an African boy today from premarital relations, the students mentioned in the first place the fear of venereal diseases. They also mentioned the desire of keeping an eventual offspring themselves and not having to give it to the girl's family, as the case is when she becomes pregnant before dowery payment and marriage. Finally, they also thought that some might realize the contradiction of wanting an untouched girl as their wife, but at the same time of wanting to have as many girls as possible before marriage. One student wrote, "What young man is able to know while he is spoiling the bride of another whether his own bride does not suffer the same fate?"

When asked whether the commandment, "You shall not commit adultery," could motivate restriction at least for Christians, the boys stated that it was generally thought that this did not apply to premarital relations. "An unmarried girl belongs to no one, so nobody can be wronged." "It is only possible to commit adultery with an engaged girl or a married woman."

What then would distinguish a Christian youth from a non-Christian? A non-Christian would argue, "She had bad luck, if she got pregnant. But that is her problem. Why should I feel bad about it? I have not obliged her to accept. She has conceded to satisfy me because she also found pleasure in it. Now she has to take the consequences." A Christian youth in such a case, however, would "have pity on her and express that by secret gifts." He would "counsel her to accept her fate and not to complain too much."

Female Youth Attitudes of Today

What follows here has to be taken with considerable reservation since these are the opinions of boys expressing what they believe girls today think. Naturally, the boys were divided on the subject, probably according to individual experience. Some thought that the main reason for female opposition to sex relations is the desire to appear "young," for after having given birth they would be counted as "old." Others thought just the contrary. They would then be recognized as "women." However, most of the boys had the impression that the girls would be more on the side of their parents. They observed that non-educated girls would be more opposed to sex contacts than educated ones. In general all girls were believed to be opposed. As reasons they mentioned the fear of punishment by their parents, the fear of pain when the hymen is ruptured, the fear of pregnancy and of having to care alone for their child, and the smaller chance of marriage. For Christian girls in school the fear of being sent away from a mission-directed school and thus lose their education would be an additional factor. Girls would, however, consider becoming pregnant in order to force parents to permit them to marry the ones they prefer rather than the men their parents prefer simply because they make the highest bids. Just as the boys are afraid of impotence, the girls are afraid of sterility. To be rid of this anxiety may be the one comfort a girl has if she becomes pregnant before marriage, but it did not appear to be a major motive to seek intercourse.

Premarital Intercourse and Christian Morality

The contribution of Christianity to the premarital sex problem is seen by the African youth as a matter of law. Instead of meeting Christ as their personal Redeemer, they meet the church as a spying, judging, and punishing authority. One wrote: "Abstention from premarital relations has been imposed as a custom by the church. That proves that religion works sufficiently in my tribe."

To exclude a boy or a girl from the Lord's Supper because of premarital relations is the most irrelevant treatment of the problem that is conceivable.[3] It produces only hypocrites. About a Christian school in Africa one can say with Bonhoeffer:

It may be that Christians, notwithstanding corporate worship, common prayer, and all their fellowship in service, may be still left to their loneliness. The final breakthrough to fellowship does not occur, because though they have fellowship with one another as believers and as devout people, they do not have fellowship as the undevout, as sinners. The pious fellowship permits no one to be a sinner. So everybody must conceal his sin from himself and from the fellowship. We dare not

be sinners. Many Christians are unthinkably horrified when a real sinner is suddenly discovered among the righteous. So we remain alone with our sin, living in lies and hypocrisy.[4]

Vague and general pious statements such as "Submit everything to Jesus and he will make you happy" will be of little help either. If we really want to help, we have to meet the African on his own level. If he thinks in utilitarian categories, all right, let us argue with utilitarian arguments! The task would be to show that premarital relations are not useful in establishing a happy marriage.

To show this we would, first of all, have to do away with false conceptions such as the myth of the "wife with water" and of the hymen as a proof of virginity, the fear that abstention could cause sickness, the wrong interpretation of nocturnal ejaculations, etc. Concrete and sober instruction concerning biological facts has to be given. I was surprised that eighteen- and nineteen-year-old students had not been taught in their biology courses (French system) the most simple facts of how fertilization takes place.

The following arguments as to the uselessness of premarital relations have been well received according to my experience:

1. One cannot try marriage by having sexual intercourse just as one cannot try death by sleeping very hard. In the same way one cannot try to parachute by merely jumping out of a tree.

2. What has to be "learned by doing" is not the satisfaction of your desire but the mastering of it, otherwise your marriage will be unhappy.

---

[3] Walter Trobisch, "Church Discipline in Africa," op. cit.

[4] Dietrich Bonhoeffer, *Life Together* (New York: Harper and Brothers, 1954).

3. A boy becomes effeminate by giving in to every desire, but masculine by resisting. If he has learned to resist, he is a man; if not he is a "dishrag" (most insulting term a girl can use in reference to a boy). A good girl wants a *man*.

4. A boy will never get sick because of abstention, but he can easily do damage to himself physically and psychologically by indulging in premarital relations.

5. Intercourse in situations where one is in a hurry and afraid of discovery will help to acquire the habit of premature ejaculations, rather than the contrary. There is a truth in the theory of "learning by doing" but only with one's own wife. "To enrich oneself too quickly will often impoverish" (another African proverb).

6. If a boy is afraid of mockery and insult, he should think of Jesus, who has been mocked and insulted for him. Christ is the only one who can make him a man.

7. By having premarital relations he does irreparable damage to himself and to the girl. In the little booklet *Avant le Mariage,* edited by the Reformed church of Switzerland, there are two phrases which hit home the most: "The girl receives an indelible imprint from the first man to whom she gives herself. She will not be able to detach her thoughts from him, even if she hates him when she later marries the one she loves." And, "Sexual adventures before marriage can awaken in the young man a polygamous instinct, a taste for change, which will endanger his future marriage in advance." Also the phrase of Benjamin Franklin has made many Africans think: "Marriage without love leads to love without marriage."

It has to be shown that "love" and "sexuality" are not identical, but that sexuality is only a part of love, which has a psychological and spiritual side. The great difficulty is that love as a psychological experience is almost unknown in Africa. How to "teach" this is for me as yet an unanswered question.

Premarital medical check-ups should be encouraged. Here the African runs into difficulty due to lack of confidence in the doctors. "Our African doctors would not tell us in case they found something wrong with our organs for fear of palaver with our family."

Theology of Marriage

We need a new theology of marriage, which points out that children are not the only purpose of marriage, but that the fellowship between husband and wife is a fulfillment in itself. Furthermore, instead of basing our argument on the commandment, "You shall not commit adultery," which to the African is indeed disputable as far as premarital relations are concerned, we should rather base it on two others. The first is: "You shall not steal." To my surprise the Africans listened very well when I pointed out to them that as long as a girl does not belong to any man she belongs to God. One student expressed his idea about Christian marriage this way: "On the marriage day the man receives his wife from God's hand as Adam received Eve in the garden where they lived alone. In knowing your wife before marriage you are like a child stealing from its father." Several other students expressed the same idea.

The other relevant commandment is: "You shall love your neighbor as yourself." Since both the girl and the boy are hurt by premarital intercourse, this commandment is transgressed. But this again shows that all our teaching about marriage in Africa depends upon a new interpretation of Christian love.

PART IV

Cultural Systems and Manifestations:

Myth

Jacob A. Loewen

Myth and Mission: Should a Missionary Study Tribal Myths?

A missionary and the translations consultant were checking the translation of the Gospel of Mark into an Amerindian language which had experienced considerable exposure to English. Without doubt the word tepʌlʌ, which was being used to identify the devil of the Scriptures, was a loanword from English. The phonological changes were readily explainable, but the question remained: Why had an English word been borrowed? Most animistic cultures have rather well-developed spirit worlds and thus also a variety of terms to denominate spirit beings—one or more of which usually can be used to identify the devil of the Scriptures. The missionary who had not previously recognized tepʌlʌ as a loanword was even more puzzled than the translations consultant. When they tried to investigate the borrowing with a number of Indian informants, their puzzlement soon became frustration, for informant after informant took refuge behind statements such as: "I do not know about the pagan past;" or "I know little about the olden days, and since I'm a Christian now, I don't think it is fit to talk about those things." In desperation the translations consultant finally enlisted the help of an informant who had been excommunicated from the church, but no sooner did the conversation approach the subject of the spirit world, this man too became defensive. To head off a premature closing of the door to information, the consultant quickly began to tell him about the spirit world of Chaco Lengua who distinguish some seventeen different kinds of spirits. He became so engrossed in telling about Lengua spirits that he failed to notice a grandmother and her three-year-old granddaughter had entered the room. They had quietly taken a seat on the floor by the door and were waiting for the lady of the house to appear. The consultant was telling the man that the Lengua say: "Never pull out the hair on your toes because it serves as the receptor through which you become aware of the presence of evil spirits. When the hair on your toes stands up stiff, you know that evil spirits are near." He concluded his narrative with the question: "Have you ever heard anyone say something like this before?" The informant was again debating whether or not he should plead ignorance, when the grandmother by the door spoke up vehemently: "That's exactly what I've been telling my granddaughter: 'Don't pull out the hair on your toes. If you do, coral snake will take your soul and you will become insane.'"

287

No sooner had she said this, than she realized what she had done. She had revealed some of her "pagan" beliefs to a foreigner. To correct her slip, she got up, walked into the middle of the room, shook her finger at the consultant and said: "I'm not going to talk to you anymore. I'm a Christian!" Then she stomped out of the room.

The Gospel of "Hard" Words

Eventually, however, it was possible to establish sufficient rapport with a number of the tribal believers so that they began to speak quite freely about the past and present beliefs and practices. Among other things they told the following myth:

[1][1] One day while god and the people were walking through the forest, a poisonous snake suddenly bit god in the hand. It was a very poisonous snake, so all the people expected him to swell up at once and die. However god told them: "Don't be afraid. I will not die. This happened so that I could teach you how to cure illness when you get sick once I am gone." Then he spoke some "hard" words and blew *taleng* 'magic' on his hand, and at once he was completely restored. Then he taught "hard" words to the people so that they also would be able to cure.

During the discussion that followed, a leading believer confided that it was wonderful to be a Christian.

Christianity gave one so many "hard" words with which to heal or to inflict hurt.[2] "If you have an enemy," he said, "you just need to kneel behind him in a prayer meeting, mutter some of the bad, "hard" words and blow on him, and at once he will become ill and die. Or if you have a friend who is ailing, you mutter some of the good, "hard" words, and at once the person will recover."

Later during a discussion of the *imawari*, the much feared 'mountain people' or 'mountain demons' who steal human beings when they wander too far away from their village, the consultant expressed fascination and wondered where they might come from. One of the church people asked him whether he didn't know about the children of Ishmael. The consultant admitted that he knew about Ishmael but he did not know how the latter was related to the mountain people — "since his father had never taught him that." The believer then explained: "Abraham had two kinds of descendents: the children of Isaac who are today's believers, and the children of Ishmael who are the mountain people who try to harm and kill the believers."

This fragmentary account of a mission situation in which the mission-

---

[1] All myths and myth fragments will be numbered in square brackets for future cross reference.

[2] They distinguish two kinds of "hard" words: those used for curing and those for doing harm. Examples of English words that have become "bad, hard" words are: *wikik* 'wicked,' *tepʌlʌ* 'devil,' *kismasi* 'Christmas,' and *tutechang* 'temptation,' etc.; "good, hard" words from English are: *epong* 'heaven,' *chisek kulaik* 'Jesus Christ,' *soichi* 'church,' *katʌ* 'God, *patele* 'priest, etc.

aries had always preached through interpreters illustrates some of the serious problems that can result when a mission program proceeds without knowledge of tribal mythology. Obviously the interpreters had converted into "hard" words much of the technical religious vocabulary which they did not understand. The missionary preacher, however, thought the people were getting God's "pure" Word. The reason for national hesitance to talk about the tribal past had come, of course, from the many sermons that had been preached against pagan beliefs and practices. The believers had thus been forced into a splitlevel existence. On one level, in the missionary's presence, they denied and disowned everything about their pagan past. On another level, however, behind the missionary's back, they believed and practised a good number of their tribal myth-based rituals. In fact, the many new good and bad "hard" words that resulted from the interpreted sermons, actually confirmed some of their pre-Christian beliefs so that people believed, feared, and practised them all the more fervently.

What may be even more disturbing is that the above example is not unique—there are others like it. Such situations render mute testimony to the negative attitude that missionaries from medieval Roman Catholics to modern evangelicals—have had toward mythology. They have usually regarded all mythology as evil, or at least as superstitious nonsense; for this reason they either tried to actively stamp it out as pagan belief, or they

ignored it as fables. But whether ignored or persecuted, these beliefs have continued to flourish and have remained a serious obstacle to Christian development.

Christo-paganism

This phenomenon of the persistence of traditional mythic concepts and values is not unique to the so-called "primitive" animistic societies. It is very evident in folk religion in general.[3] We see relics of it in American Christianity in such superstitions as fear of broken mirrors, black cats, or walking under ladders. For Latin America studies like the one made by William Madsen have shown that underneath the universal Catholic super-structure—which itself is an amalgam of aboriginal and Catholic beliefs — there is a "firm foundation" of pre-Catholic myths and beliefs.[4] This substratum of myths is so firmly entrenched that evangelical missionaries have complained it is easier for conversion to deal with the "Catholic" than with the "tribal" substratum.

Because of the general unfavorable attitude toward aboriginal mythology,

3 For a fuller discussion of this topic see: Eugene A. Nida, *Religion across Cultures* (New York: Harper and Row, Publishers, 1968).

4 William L. Wonderly, "Pagan and Christian Concepts in Mexican Indian Culture," *Practical Anthropology*, Vol. 5, No. 5-6 (Sept.-Dec. 1958), pp. 197-202; William Madsen, *Christo-Paganism: A Study of Mexican Religious Syncretism* (New Orleans: Middle American Research Institute, Tulane University, 1957, pre-printed from publication No. 19), pp. 105-180, and Eugene A. Nida, "Christo-paganism," *Practical Anthropology*, Vol. 8, No. 1 (Jan.-Feb. 1961), pp. 1-15.

very few missionaries have taken pains to study it. Those who felt it was nothing but a pack of lies, reasoned that to study it was only a waste of time and all that was really needed was to teach the people God's truth. Others, while more sensitive to national feelings about native beliefs, opined that if they did take them seriously and inquired about mythology and beliefs, they would by the very fact of asking about it lend tacit approval on its content. Since they felt that such approval was incongruous with their missionary purpose, they were obliged to disregard them. Thus when a national did venture to speak about his tribal myths, his remarks were either slapped down as heresy or ignored as fables.

There have, however, been a few brave souls who felt that they must know what the people believed and who therefore collected mythological materials. The author has met several missionaries in recent years who have made extensive collections of tribal lore, but even some of these people were frustated—now that I have it, what good is it? How can it help me in my missionary assigment?

Purpose of this Study

This study of mythology and missions proposes:

(1) To strengthen the awareness that ignorance of a people's myths and values is dangerous for a missionary and his work — what you don't know can hurt both you and the indigenous church you are trying to build. This has already in part been illustrated in the preceding paragraphs.

(2) To illustrate the nature, content, and form of mythological materials.

(3) To demonstrate the far-reaching influence of myth in the life of tribal societies.

(4) To explore the dynamics of myth preservation and change.

(5) To show some examples of analytical interpretation of mythological materials.

(6) To suggest a range of application that a knowledge of myth offers to the sensitive missionary.

Points 2-6 will each be explored in a separate paper.

The Structure And Content of Myths

Every society has an inventory of lore which it transmits from one generation to the next. This lore takes several forms. There are laws, proverbs, legends, folktales, and myths. Myths are distinguished from other types of tales in that they deal with ultimate realities, spiritual powers, and supernatural events that took place in primordial, sacred time.

A distinguished German theologian has defined myth as "the expression of the unobservable realities in terms of observable phenomena."[5] John Greenway calls myth "sublimated reality."[6] Stith Thompson defines myth as a "tale laid out in a world supposed to have preceded the present order. It tells of sacred beings and of semidivine heroes and of the origins of all things usually through the agency of the sacred beings. Myths are intimately connected with the religious beliefs and practices of the people."[7]

Edmund R. Leach insists that every myth system recognizes a sequence of paired opposites, such as human/superhuman, mortal/immortal, male/female, legitimate/illegitimate, good/bad, etc.[8]

In contrast to myths, folktales tend to deal with the "natural" exploits of people and animals in ordinary, profane time. Folktales are usually concerned with personal morality. Legends also take place in profane time, but they tend to be more concerned with group morality.[9]

It is, of course, possible that a folktale may contain mythic elements, especially a mythic ending. The Waunana of Colombia have an extensive series of folktales describing the exploits and encounters of *Guatin*[10] and Tiger. Tiger is a big, stupid brute that generally gets mauled by the superior intelligence of little *Guatin*. Here now follows the final scene of this folktale series:

[2] One day *Guatin* decided: I'm going to go to the world above; so he went to the headwaters of the river where the notched pole ladder that leads up above is located. The ladder itself was guarded by a scissor-like machine. *Guatin* said to himself: "Having been able to cheat everyone in this world, surely I can cheat this machine too. I will go up." Then he approached the machine from an angle, took a quick leap, but the machine caught him right in the middle and cut him in half. His head proceeded to the upper world, but his tail end remained in ·this world. Then *Guatin* said: "Because I was cut in half by this machine, no Indian will be able to pass from this world to the upper world without first dying."

In this way a long series of animal stories suddenly ends with a mythic pronouncement about the mortality of man.

5 H.W. Bartsch, *Kergyma and Myth* quoted in John Middleton, editor, *Myth and Cosmos: Readings in mythlogy and Symbolism* (Garden City ; The Natural History Press for American Museum of Natural History American Sourcebooks in Anthropology, 1967), p, 1.

6 Melville Jacobs, compiler, and John Greenway, editor, *The Anthropologist Looks at Myth* (Austin : The University of Texas Press for American Folklore Society, 1966), p.x.

7 Stith Thompson, *The Folktale* (New York: The Dryden Press, 1951), p, 9 ; also Mircea Eliade, *Myth and Reality* (New York : Harper and Row, Publishers, 1963), pp. 8-9.

8 Edmund R. Leach, "Genesis as Myth," in Middleton, *op. cit.*, p. 4.

9 Cf. Philip Freund, *Myths of Creation* (New York : Washington Square Press, Inc., 1965), p. 36.

10 The *Guatin* is a capybara, the largest South American rodent, that inhabits the borders of lakes and rivers. It is edible and is one of the most common hunting prizes in Waunana territory.

The Structure of myths

Most myths have relatively simple structures whose basic element is the motif, which Stith Thompson defines as "the smallest element in a tale that has a power to persist in tradition,"[11] Such motifs usually fall into three classes.

The first type includes the actors in the tale—gods, supernatural creatures, unusual animals or even conventionalized human characters.[12]

A second motif type deals with the backgrounds or settings of the action—unusual customs, magical objects, strange beliefs, etc.

The third kind involves individual incidents or events. This latter group makes up by far the greater majority of all motifs.[13]

We can illustrate these motif types on the basis of myth 4 dealing with the leg-born twins. The *actors* are the twins, the old woman caretaker, the sun, etc. The *background settings* involve the inside of the monster's belly, the underworld, the ladder at the headwaters which link the worlds etc. Some of the *event motifs* include the unnatural birth of the twins, the death of the person giving birth to the twins, the origin of blood-sucking insects, etc.

Motifs are usually very durable elements in tribal lore. The plot and certain parts of their content

may undergo revision with changing circumstances, but the motifs themselves remain relatively constant.

Myths generally have only a minimum plot. Some myths have only a single event motif. In others a series of event motifs are strung together in more or less serial fashion The same myth told by a different raconteur may differ in arrangement or in the length of the sequence, but the motifs and the incidents themselves remain relatively unchanged. Individual motifs, especially events, may even "float," i.e they may become attached to several different tales, and as a result the same event will be attributed to several characters.

The most frequent form of myth presentation is of course narrative prose,[14] but it may also include songs (such as the Australian Wuradilagu Song Cycle of Northeastern Arnhem Land),[15] dramatic reenactment (such as the periodic travels of Australian tribes over the trails used by mythological ancestors during which even the actions and the gestures of the ancients are repeated),[16] and graphic art (e.g. the rock paintings which depict the events of creation and which must be periodically renewed).[17]

Myths and mythological materials

11 Thompson, *op. cit.*, p. 415.

12 Eliade suggests that in the U.S.A. comic strip heroes represent a modern version of mythological heroes. They also exert a tremendous influence on the reading public See: Eliade, Myth . . . *op. cit.*, pp. 184-185.

13 Thompson, *op. cit.*, 415-416.

14 Eliade, *op. cit.*, p- 192 suggests that the novel also employs a seemingly historical time with all the freedoms of an imaginary world.

15 William A. Lessa, "The Discoverer-of-the-Sun," in Jacobs and Greenway, *op. cit.*, pp. 195-199.

16 Mircea Eliade, *The Sacred and the Profance.* Torchbooks edition (New York: Harper and Row, Publishers, 1961), p- 86.

17 Eliade, *Myth . . . op. cit.*, p. 43,

in general are often characterized by special linguistic styles including distinctive introductory or concluding expressions, special intonations, archaic linguistic forms, and standardized hearer responses.[18] In Northern Lengua there is even a special tense marker used for events that took place in myth age.

The Content of myths

The content of myths is usually consistent with reality as the people understand it. Myths need not be "logical" in their arrangement nor consistent with each other. Thus, for example, in the story of the Waunana twin culture heroes (myth 4) who are born from the leg of a man, one of the twins is killed while disposing of a giant water creature that was hindering traffic on the San Juan River. However, in the next episode the "killed" twin reappears. When this inconsistency was pointed out to the informants, they generally just shrugged their shoulders and said: "I don't know, but that is how the story is told."

Another important feature of myth content is the fact that certain themes seem to recur in so many parts of the world. The motifs and the detailed treatment of the plot remain distinct, but the theme as such can be present in many cultures. Such universal or near universal themes include creation, the flood, the destruction of the world, the after-life of the soul, etc. Many of these recurrences are of course based on the fact that both the physical universe and the human psychic needs and responses are more or less universally similar. [19] We will now try to illustrate some of the major themes of mythology.

The Origin, Shape, Function, and Destiny of the Universe

Most peoples, even those who are preliterate, make some attempt to account for the origin of the world. Sometimes they exhibit detailed descriptions not of the original creation itself, but of the cataclysms that have modified the nature and topography of the world. When the Chulupi of the Paraguayan Chaco were asked about the origin of the world, they said: "We do not know where this world comes from, but we know that this present earth used to be the sky, and the sky of today used to be the earth." Myth 3 contains the account of their exchange of position:

[3] One day the earth which was standing on a root-like, giant tree trunk, said to the sky, "There are so many animals and people living here and they are continually defecating. I am sick and tired of this nasty smell. I do not want to be the earth any longer." Then the sky answered: "Smell does not bother me at all. If you want to, let us change places." So they decided to change. At first they did not

18 John Greenway, *Literature among the Primitives* (Hatboro, Pennsylvania: Folklore Associates, 1964), pp. 24-25.

19 For more detail on the common human element as a basis of recurring myth themes, see: Clyde Kluckhohn, "The Current Themes in Myth and Mythmaking," in Henry A. Murray, *Myth and Mythmaking* (New York: George Braziller, 1960), p. 49.

know how to make the exchange. Finally the earth suggested that it ought to be easier to let go on top and come down than to climb up. So the sky let go and hit the earth with such a wallop that the latter was tipped upside down, lifted off its root and thrown into the sky. Then the former sky settled upon the root of the earth and became the earth. But when the former earth "arrived in the sky," it was unable to hang on because it wasn't the sky. So pillars had to be built on the edge of the new earth to hold up the new sky; however, the new sky was very heavy and bent the edge of the new earth downward. That is why the edge of the earth slopes downward at the horizon.

The Waunana of Colombia see their world as three-tiered. There is the underworld which is both lower and older, and the sky-world which is both higher and future, i.e. the world-to-come, and in between is the world of here and now. The interaction between these levels is illustrated in the myth of the leg-born twins.

[4] One day a man went out hunting. While he was far away from his home all the (what seemed like) animals of the forest came and copulated with the calf of his leg. The deer came, the *guatin* came, the wild pig came, the tapir came, the partridge came, the toucan came, the turkey came, they all came and copulated with the calf of his leg. When he got home his leg

began to swell. It hurt very much. For two weeks the leg continued to swell. The man could not sleep anymore After two weeks the leg burst open and the man died. However twin boys were born from the calf of the burst-open leg.

An old woman decided to take care of the twins. They grew very rapidly. By the time they were several months old, they were already young men. The twins liked menstrual blood. As long as they were small, the women thought it was funny; but when the twins grew up, the women became embarrassed.

One day the twins asked: "Who killed our father?" The women did not want to tell them the truth, so they lied: "The moon killed your father.[20] So the twins decided to go to the sky-world to tear down the moon. They planted a bamboo pole which grew until it reached the moon. Then one of them put on palm fiber insulation and climbed up. When he got to the top of the pole he found that it was little too short — he could only reach the moon with one hand. He grabbed the moon and pulled, but was able to tear off only one piece which we today see as a dark spot on the moon's face. Before he could grab the moon again, Woodpecker came from the

[20] A series of such lying answers are the basis for the exploits of the twins. Among those blamed are a water monster, *he*, the poisonous snakes, the moon, etc.

headwaters and cut off the pole. The twin fell down, but since he had palm fiber on his arms, he floated like a bird until he landed on the beach where the sun goes down. In the afternoon the sun came by and offered to take him to the underworld. So he grabbed the sun's waist-string as the latter dived into the ocean and went along to the underworld. He came to a village. The people were eating. But in *ʔaʔārmia*, the underworld, people only smell their food. They have no anal openings. When the people saw the twin defecate, they wanted to have anuses too. So he began to "open" them. Their insides just ran out and they died. When the sun came back he scolded the twin and said: "You are killing all the people here. I will take you along again." So he went with the sun to the headwaters of the river. When they had climbed to the top, the sun left him and went on to the sky-world, and the twin back to his village.

While he was gone his twin brother was sitting by the fire asking for menstrual blood. Since he was alone, the women decided to kill him. So they poured a pot of boiling corn mush over him. He at once turned to stone. In order to eliminate the evidence of their deed, the women took axes and tried to chop him up. All the chips that flew off became blood-sucking insects and bats that today suck people's blood

and make them sick.

In an earlier translation of the Ten Commandments a missionary, who was not aware of the three-tiered structure of the universe, followed the informant's suggestion and prefaced the translation with a myth formula: "when this world was not." By introducing the Ten Commandments with this statement, their validity was placed in the myth age; in this way their applicability to the current generation was tacitly denied.

The Origin, Behavior, and Destiny of Man

Even more universal are the accounts of the origin of people, usually the local tribe. Often there are detailed accounts of the development of tribal behavior as it was first taught by the deity or some god-like culture hero. The Waunana of Colombia described the origin of men as follows:

[5] At the beginning of this world god, *Ewandama*, was living with his son near the ocean. There still were no people. One day the son begged his father for playmates, so *Ewandama* sent him to make some dolls. First the son cut some dolls out of black palm wood. It was very hard and so he had made only two when he cut his finger and came back crying. His father said: "Make them from something else." So the son went back next day and carved more dolls from lightweight balsa wood. But again, after making only two, he cut his finger and came back crying. Once more the father

sent him away saying: "Make them from something else." On the third day he made them from mud. Soon he had the whole beach covered with mud dolls. This time the son came to *Ewandama* and said: "I am still unhappy because I cannot play with them They are not people. They do not talk. They do not play with me." Then *Ewandama* told his son to go to sleep. When he awoke next morning all the dolls had become alive. The two black dolls became the ancestors of the black magic spirits, the two white dolls became the ancestors of white magic spirits, all the mud dolls became Waunana. But, alas, they were all women. Thus *Ewandama* had to remodel half of them to make men.

The Lengua of the Paraguayan Chaco exhibit both interesting similarities and striking differences in their version of the origin of man.

[6] When Beetle (when used generically it seems to refer to a personified spirit power like god) began to make things, he first made some giant creatures who were like people. Then one day he decided to make real people from mud. He made two mud dolls and put them side by side near a lagoon to dry. But he put them too close to each other so they dried together. They became people, but they were like Siamese twins until the latter screamed to Beetle saying: "It is not fair that we are linked together and cannot defend ourselves against these giants. So Beetle separated them. But the "small" men were still unable to defend themselves. Then Beetle took away the bodies of the giant creatures. Having lost their bodies, they became -*quilyicjama* 'evil spirits.' However, since they lost their bodies because of the people, the evil spirits are perpetually angry with men and are forever trying to steal their bodies and to make them sick.

Relationships between God and Men, Men and Spirits, Men and Men

Another very common theme of mythology is the description of a primitive, glorious, and happy state in which God or the gods and men lived together in perfect harmony. Then something tragic happened. Usually the deity became angry, withdrew from the world, and left men to their fate. Very frequently the evil-spirit world or a trickster played an important role in bringing about the estrangement. The withdrawal of the deity, however, did not leave men entirely to the whims of the evil-spirit world, because either he or a cultural hero tried to teach men how to live right. The Waunana speak of this glorious past as follows:

[7] *Ewandama* lived with the people. Everybody was happy. *Ewandama* had a big coat with which he travelled across the ocean to bring many good things to the people. He always provided them with food. Whenever they lacked anything, they only needed to tell him and he would

say: "Children, go to sleep."
Next morning when they awoke,
the food they had asked for would
be ready to cut and eat. One
day while *Ewandama* was away
on a trip, *Dosiata*, the trickster
or devil, came and offered to sell
the Waunana some axes. He
showed them how delightful it
is to chop down trees, and he
added: "If you buy them, you can
have your own plantains, bananas, and other food and you will
not have to wait for *Ewandama*
to provide it for you." The
Waunana were so intrigued by
the prospect of raising their own
food, and they liked to cut down
trees with the axes, so they
bought them. When *Ewandama*
returned and saw what had happened, he was angry with them
and said: "Your buying axes
shows that you no longer trust
me. Since you do not want me,
I will leave you." So he left
them and went into the upper
world. Since then the people
belong to *Dosiata*.

Often mythology also tries to account for the presence of other people.
The Waunana describe the origin of
other races as follows:

[8] One day the Waunana began
to hear noises undergound. They
decided to dig in order to find
out what the noise was and from
where it came. They dug a very
deep hole. It was so deep that
only the longest bamboo pole
could reach the bottom. They
cut notches in the pole and put
it into the hole. Via this notched

pole ladder some white and some
black creatures crawled out. They
became the white men and the
negroes respectively.

In a surprisingly large number of
societies the culture hero makes his
appearance as one of two brothers—
usually twins (see myth 4 on the
Waunana twins). One of them is
good, the other is evil, thus providing
a rationale for the origin of good and
evil. This is the case with the
Shiriana in Brazil in whose mythology
such a pair of miraculously born twins
plays an important role:

[9] One day Tiger ate Woman.
Woman was pregnant. Tiger ate
everything except the placenta.
The placenta fell into the water
so that he could not eat it. An
old woman kept looking after the
placenta so that it would not dry.
Finally twins were born. Their
names were *Omam* and *Joao*.
When the twins grew up, one of
them was good, the other one
was evil. *Omam* was good and
he did many good things for the
people. He cleared the world of
monsters that harrassed men and
he provided men with many
fruits and foods. He also taught
people the art of right living.
But *Joao* forever made trouble.
He damaged the work of Omam
and made the evil *hekura* spirits
that today molest men.

Illness, Health, and Healing

Most mythologies include a description of the origin of disease which
is frequently supplemented by an
account of the supernatural institu-

tion of appropriate curing procedures. Possibly the most well-known myth on the origin of disease and evil in the Western world is that of Pandora's box which Zeus gave to her for safe-keeping. However, Pandora's curiosity overpowered her, so she opened the forbidden box and let out every kind of evil which today afflicts mankind.

The Lengua of Paraguay account for disease and death in terms of the struggle by the evil spirit—*quilyicjama* to appropriate human bodies in revenge for the loss of their own. (See myth 6)

Myth 1 serves as an example of the beliefs of a people who base their healing ceremony on instructions received from the creator deity. In contrast to this the Waunana attribute their curing ceremony to evil spirit origin:

[10] Before *Ewandama* left the people he said: "After I am gone you will get sick. But I will return and will teach you how to make people well." The people waited and waited. *Ewandama* did not come. Then one day *Dosīāta* arrived and asked what the people were waiting for. They told him they were waiting for *Ewandama* to teach them how to make people well. *Dosīāta* then told them: "Why, I know a very nice little ceremony which you will like. You take eight gourd dishes, put them down in two sets of four, pour liquor into them, then you drink and I drink, and we make an agreement. You give me your

hand and I give you my hand. If you do this, then I will give you power to make people well. The people watched and were intrigued by *Dosīāta's* ceremony so that they gave him their hand as a seal of their agreement. That is why all the people belong to *Dosīāta* today.

Cosmic Events

Very frequently mythologies deal extensively with such cosmic phenomena as earthquakes, lightning, thunder, rain, frost, eclipses, and other catastrophies. Both the Lengua and the Chulupi of the Paraguayan Chaco "know" that rain is brought by myth-age birds. These birds are not real; they are the "souls of the birds" from myth-age when human beings, animals, and birds all were like people:

[11] By the sea of the north there live the souls of the birds of the myth-age. Their task is to bring rain to the Chaco. Periodically they fill up their gourds, tuck them under their wings, and wend their way toward the Chaco—a two day journey—and they deposit the water as rain. These bird-souls do not want to be seen by men, therefore they always hide behind clouds. That is why it only rains when there are clouds in the sky. Sometimes all the birds hide behind one cloud. That is why it rains from others. Among these bird-souls are some that have angry "innermosts." Some people say they have fire in their "innermost." Others say they have red-hot

stones. Sometimes these angry birds throw these red-hot stones or the fire at the ground. White people call this lightning. Once they begin throwing this fire, the birds yell to each other. White people call this thunder.

The preceding examples of myth content are by no means exhaustive, they merely illustrate a few of the more universal themes. In addition to these very widespread general themes, each culture develops additional specific myths to authorize and support its unique inventory of beliefs and practises. Since cultures vary, myth inventories also vary greatly.

The Function of myth in Society

A myth can be succinctly described as a conceptual statement about man, his society and his universe. In general such statements are symbolic, but this fact makes it all the more important that we understand the reality which these statements symbolize.[21]

Eliade summarizes the function of a society's mythology as follows:... myth, as experienced by archaic societies, (1) constitutes the History of the acts of the Supernaturals; (2) that this History is considered to be absolutely *true* (because it is concerned with realities) and *sacred* (because it is the work of the Supernaturals); (3) that myth is always related to a "creation," it tells how something came into existence, or how a pattern of behavior, an institution, a manner of working were established; this is why myths constitute the paradigms for all significant human acts; (4) that by knowing the myth one knows the "origin" of things and hence can control and manipulate them at will; this is not an "external," "abstract" knowledge but a knowledge that one "experiences" ritually, either by ceremonially recounting the myth or by performing the ritual for which it is the justification; (5) that in one way or another one "lives" the myth, in the sense that one is seized by the sacred, exalting power of the events recollected or re-enacted.[22]

We will now detail these and other functions and document them with myth examples.

Explanatory Function

Life brings many strange and contradictory experiences, and some of the "quirks of fate" or "caprices of nature" can have a very unsettling effect on the human psyche unless they can be "explained" or given ultimate meaning. Sooner or later man asks fundamental questions like: Where did I come from? Why am I here? Does my existence have any meaning? Does it all end with death?

21 Middleton, *op. cit.*, p. x.

22 Eliade, Myth.., *op. cit.*, pp. 18-19.

Man wants answers to these and other questions, and according to Eliade the answers are found in a society's mythology. In fact, Eliade states that for a tribal man the world "speaks" and he understands its symbolic language. For him the world is no mass of opaque objects thrown together, but a living cosmos, an articulated and a meaningful whole. To him the world is transparent, "alive and looking at him." The animal bagged in a hunt has not been caught accidentally—it let itself be caught because it "knew" that the man was hungry. For the animist every rock, tree, and river transmits information.[23]

This explanatory function covers the full range of human experience. Note the following explanations of physical phenomena in the universe.

The horizon. The explanatory function of myth is quite obvious in the Chulupi account of the changed position of the earth and sky (myth 3). First this exchange explains the phenomenon of the descending horizon. The heavy, new sky (the former earth) resting on pillars on the edge of the "lighter," new earth (the former sky) causes the latter to bend downward. It also explains the origin of clouds which represent the "smoke" emanating from the pillars under the weight of the new sky.

Drought. The Lengua myth of the origin of rain (myth 11) also provides an explanation for the absence of rain:

[12] Sometimes the bird-souls become tired or they fall asleep. Then it does not rain. This condition is relatively simple to solve.

23 *Ibid.*, pp. 141-143.

It merely requires that the shaman awaken the birds. Once awakened, they immediately pick up their rain-bearing function. At other times, however, enemy-*quilyicjama* have laid siege to the bird-souls and prevent them from carrying out their rain-bearing function. In this case the shaman must charm the *quilyicjama* and remove them in order that the birds can again bring rain.

Moon phases. A Chulupi myth accounts for the phenomenon of moon phases:

[13] The moon had a daughter whom he loved very much, but she had no husband. One day a young man appeared and became the husband of the moon's daughter. But the girl was too shy to sleep with him, especially since her father's face made so much light at night. In order to provide enough "darkness" and privacy for the newlyweds, the moon turned himself on edge. He continues to do so now every month in memory of the first night which his daughter spent together with her husband.

Earthquakes. The Waunana explain the phenomenon of earthquakes on the basis of the following myth:

[14] A girl was experiencing her first menses. The family built a special hut for her to go into seclusion. But the girl disobeyed. Her father warned her, but she would not listen. Thereupon the bed upon which the girl was lying began to sink. Her father got under the house and propped up

the floor with heavy poles, but to no avail. Finally the whole house with the father and daughter sank into the ground until they reached the middle of the earth. Every time the girl now wants to turn over, she produces an earthquake. Her father is sitting beside her reminding her that it was all her fault and that she should lie still and not hurt the people on the earth.

Delirium. An Empera myth, describing a shaman's encounter with and his eventual escape from a mountain demon by means of four magic puzzles, has been recorded in an earlier issue of PA. For the Empera this myth provides the authentic account of the origin of delirium, which is seen as the demon's revenge for the mental chaos the puzzles, made by the escaping shaman, produced for him.[24]

Man alienated from deity. The Waunana myth (myth 10) concerning the origin of the curing ceremony tells how *Dosīāta* tricked the people into making an agreement with him. This made *Ewandama* angry and so he withdrew from man. Being a benevolent diety, however, he offered to give man eternal youth, Man's failure to respond to *Ewandama's* call explains his mortality.

[15] When *Ewandama* returned, he found that the people were already busily curing *Dosīāta's* way. He was deeply grieved and

[24] Jacob A. Loewen, "A Choco Miraculous Escape Tale, "*America Iudigena,* Vol. 20, No. 3 (July 1960), pp. 208-215; also in "The Choco and their Spirit World," PA, Vol. 11, No. 3 (May-June 1964), pp. 101-102.

said: "His way will not always keep you alive. I wanted to teach you how to keep people alive always. I will give you one more chance. I will go back to the sky-world. From there I will call you. If you answer me, then you will get the power to moult. Every time your body gets old, then you will shed your old body like a snake sheds its skin. You will become young again." Then *Ewandama* left. The people wanted to become young again. They were determined to stay awake in order to listen for *Ewandama's* call. Since *Dosīāta* had taught them how to make liquor for the curing ceremony, they decided to make some so that they could drink a little to keep awake. But they drank and drank, and finally all of them became drunk. Thus when *Ewandama* called, no people answered; only the cockroach, the snake and the shrimp responded. That is why all three of them moult and shed their skin and become young again. But people die.

End of the world. A Cherokee myth explains that this world will not always be, for it is growing old and worn out. One day, therefore, all the people will die. and the "cords" that hold the earth in place will break. and it will sink into the ocean.[25]

Integrating Function

Myths tend to provide a comprehensive framework into which the universe and its parts, man and all his

[25] Eliade, Myth... *op, cit.,* p. 59.

experiences, and natural and supernatural events are all organized into
an integrated whole.[26] This framework, of course, is multi-dimensional
and the component items are organized
into hierarchical structures with corresponding higher and lower values.
The three tiered world of the Waunana described in myth 4 is an
attempt to locate the Waunana in
both time and space.

Such a comprehensive framework
also functions to provide a means
of evaluating, classifying, and relating
all of life's new experiences. The
hierarchical arrangement within the
worldview provides a reference system
by means of which new experience
can be compared and consequently
given both meaning and value. When
the Argentine Toba saw a picture
of an elephant for the first time,
they at once compared it with the
mythological, female spirit being,
qasoxonaxa, whose shape is variously
described as a mountain, a huge bear,
a bull, or some other large animal.

Such an ideological framework can
be said to function like a pair of
ground, colored glasses which color
everything that man sees and which
exert pressure to adjust all new experience or new truth to "shapes"
that can be readily accomodated within the existing worldview system.

This, of course, is one of the bases
for syncretism and restructuring. On
the other hand, it is also possible
that new truth can cause basic modification of the existing framework.
Thus when an Empera Indian, Aureliano, discovered the globe shape of
the earth during his visit to the
United States, his view of the physical universe underwent a radical
change. He considered this modification so basic that he asked the
missionary to bring a globe to the
tribe on his next visit, since "the
people will not be able to understand
the gospel if they do not know what
the world is really like."[27] In a way
Aureliano was right, for it is a successful integration of man's concept
of the universe and of his experience
that makes it possible for him to
function successfully in society. This
applies both to the individual and to
the society as a whole. A social
group can function smoothly only
when all its members operate within
a coherent and relatively similar
framework of values.[28]

The integrating function of myth
is closely linked to a society's ethnocentric orientation, i.e. each society
puts itself and its way of life in the
center of the universe. Thus the
Waunana consider themselves the
creation of *Ewandama*, but white
people and Negroes are creatures
"that crawled out of a hole in the

---

26 The integrating function has fascinated
many scholars. See: Bronislav Malinowski,
*Magic, Science and Religion and other Es-
says* (Garden City: Doubleday and Company,
Inc., 1948), p. 101; Felix M. Keesing, *Cultural
Anthropology. The Science of Custom* (New
York: Rinehart & Company, Inc., 1958), p. 366:
also Mark Schorer. "The Necessity of Myths"
in Murray, *op. cit.*, p. 355.

27 Jacob A. Loewen, "A Choco Indian in
Hillsboro, Kansas, "PA, Vol. 9, No. 3 (May-
June 1962). pp. 129-133.

28 Greenway in Jacobs and Greenway, *op.
cit.*, p. x suggests that Christianity had "to
invent" the evangelists Mathew, Mark, etc.,
in order to "rescue it from the chaos of individual interpretation."

ground." Again, the divinely-taught Waunana folkways are good and right, while those of other people are wrong, bad, or, at least queer.

The need for integration. A society's feeling of need for integration is visually and ritually demonstrated in the Navajo sand - painting curing ceremony. The Navajo assumption concerning illness is that the patient is out of harmony either with his fellows or with the universe. In order to restore the person to health, he has to be reintegrated into the system. The sand-painting ceremony consists of drawing a miniature universe by means of colored sand. Into this "universe" the shaman places the heavenly bodies, the earth, Navajoland, various mythic reference points, and finally also the sick person and his household. Once successful integration is achieved, the sick individual is restored to health.[29]

Such myth - based integration of life is very obvious among Australian tribes. During their annual totemic *intuchiuna* cermony each Aranda clan re-enacts the events of dream time *alcheringa* of their particular clan ancestor. They stop at countless places where the ancestor stopped and repeat the same acts and gestures he performed.[30] In this way not only are time and history integrated, but the whole of temporal life is anchored in sacred time. The mythic sanction is so pervasive that even residence

(health can only be guaranteed if a man continues to live on his traditional ancestral soil) and reproductive capacity (their women can only conceive when they frequent the water holes in which the souls of their ancestors reside),[31] indeed, even the very designs and decorations of their artifacts are covered by it.

Dynamic integration. Such an integration should, of course, not be viewed as static. There is constant reformulation, reassessment and re-evaluation going on within parts of the total structure. However, since the parts most deeply anchored in myth often lie outside of the realms of verifiable science, the person's "understanding" of events may not necessarily be realistic nor consistent with empirical reality. Since, however, this conceptual framework does provide order, reason, and form, especially in those areas of human experience which would otherwise be disordered and bewildering, we can affirm that change in the basic structure is usually very slow.[32]

Validating Function

Every society has its rules of behaviour. Generally these rules, mores, taboos, and even attitudes find their validation in mythology.[33] We have already alluded to the fact that some of the most extensive validation of behavior by means of myth occurs

29 Clyde Kluckhohn and Dorothea Leighton, "The Religious World of the Navaho," in Walter Goldschmidt, *Exploring the Ways of Mankind* (New York: Holt, Rinehart and Winston, Inc., 1960), pp. 508-520, reprinted from *The Navaho* (Cambridge, Massachussetts: Harvard University Press, 1939),

30 Eliade *The Sacred ... op. cit.,* p. 86.

31 A.P. Elkin, *The Australian Aborigines.* Anchor Books Edition (New York; Doubleday and Company Inc., 1964). p. 21

32 Alfred G. Smith, *Communication and Culture: Reading in the Codes of Human Interaction* (New York: Holt, Rinehart and Winston, 1966), p. 368,

33 Greenway, *op. cit.,* pp. 251-253.

among Australian aborigines.[34] Such
mythological validation of the status
quo can convince men to undergo
all sorts of privations. Max Weber
has convincingly argued that myth-
based beliefs concerning the trans-
migration of souls undergirds the
caste system in India; and even
though the untouchables are much
more numerous than the controlling
castes; the former submit to the
domination of the latter because they
accept the system as supernaturally
validated.[35]

Another such "rule"–the obligation
to undergo a puberty ceremony–was
already alluded to in the Waunana
myth on the origin of earthquakes
(myth 14). Thus if a girl does not
submit to the puberty ritual, she is
a danger not only to herself, but to
the whole society.

Incest is forbidden. Most societies
prohibit incest, and they tend to
validate this prohibition with a myth.
The Waunana myth that follows can
be considered quit typical:

[16] A brother and sister went
to the forest to get some firewood.
While they were alone in the
forest the brother said to the
sister: "Let us lie together." At
first the sister objected. Finally
she agreed. While they were
cohabiting, a thunderstorm arose.
Lightning struck the two and
turned them into stone. Then
came a great flood to "cleanse"
the world of this wickedness.

Myth: a model for ritual. Myths

34 Elkin, *op. cit.*, p. 21.
35 Ernst Topitch, "World Interpretation and
Self-Interpretation," in Murry, *op. cit.*, p. 107.

usually underlie ritual. This is true
in a double sense: first of all, by
providing an authentic explanation
for the ritual; and secondly, in providing logical models for ritual behavior. Both phenomena can be seen
in the puberty ceremony of several
Chaco tribes in which the pubescent
girl is dragged over the dancing area
till she faints.

[17] When the people first appeared on the earth, they were
only men. In fact, all the animals and birds were like men.
These males were living beside
a waterhole in perfect peace.
One day they began to realize
that their dried and smoked
surplus meat was being stolen,
so they decided to find the cul-
prit. As the first sentry they
chose lizard. Lizard, however,
became so excited when he saw
what happened, and his tongue
was so thin that when he came
to tell the men what he had seen,
all he could say was "brr brr brr."
The men decided to set hum-
mingbird to watch. Humming-
bird was small and could hide
easily. He watched and here is
what he reported: "About ten
o'clock in the morning the water in the lagoon became rough.
Out of the middle of the lagoon
there came some women. They
came to the water's edge and
said: 'I'm going to eat my
lover's meat.' So they each ran
to one of the men's beds and
began to eat meat." When hum-
mingbird reported this to the
men, they decided: "Let's catch
the women. Then we'll have

wives. The one who runs fastest can catch the prettiest one...." Pigeon slept with his wife that very night. Next morning the men noticed that he was very sad. They asked him why he was sad. "I am sad because I am a man no longer. That woman has teeth in her vagina, and they bit off my male member." Then all the men became very sad. They sat and thought for many days. Finally they knew the answer. They would dance the women until they fainted. Then the teeth would fall out. So the men arranged for a great dance. When the woman fainted, the teeth fell out and they became fit wives.

This myth underlies the puberty ceremony and thus provides both a valid reason and the model for the ceremony—girls must be made to dance until they faint, then they will be decontaminated and become fit wives and mothers.

Why myths validate beliefs. This validating function of myths is reinforced from several sources. First of all, supernatural beings of superior authority figure as the authors or originators of the rules of behavior. Next, the myth usually is rendered as "real" history. Even though the date and the place are remote, the events are considered to be historical. Finally, there is the actual experience of living people. This can involve everyday experience interpreted in the light of the myth, or it can be testimony about corroborating events witnessed by some member of the group.[36] The author has personally observed that almost invariably after a myth has been told, some person or persons listening will relate an experience to point out the current functional validity of the myth. This provides "up-to-date and factual" evidence to support the myth both in content and function.

The validating function of myth has two additional facets that are of vital import to missions. The first is that prophets of major social or group movements generally "receive revelations" that coincide in substance with traditional mythology. This truth is of crucial importance for the missionary's message. Should he not be conscious of the values that are supported by myth, he can easily create obstacles for his message by overemphasizing truths that conflict with the existing value system.[37]

The other side of this coin is that once a society loses faith in the validity of its value system, individual behavior will become unpredictable and cooperation increasingly more difficult. A.P. Elkin likens such a group to a "ship without a compass or anchor."[38] Such a group is headed for social disintegration and usually also severe depopulation. By the same token, the church can func-

---

[36] Such testimonial reinforcement of beliefs has also been reported for the Berens River Salteaux in A. Irving Hallowell, *Culture and Experience* (Philadelphia: University of Pennsylvania Press, 1955), p. 151.

[37] Vittorio Lanternari, *The Religions of the Oppressed ; A Study of Messianic Cults.* Mentor Books (New York : The American Library, 1965), p. 240.

[38] Elkin, *op. cit.*, p. 31.

tion only if the believing group achieves some degree of new integration in their system of beliefs and behavior norms.

Sanctioning Function

If myth provides the charter for life and existence, it stands to reason that it will play a very important function in social control. As long as a given charter is in force, i.e. is believed and is acted upon by the people, it is the ultimate source of authority. However, as Wesley Culshaw has already shown, it can fall into disuse; and when myth no longer is considerd "reality," rituals will lapse and the control of myth over behavior is broken.[39] However, while it is in force, this exerts strong social pressure. In many societies it has kept slaves and outcastes "content with their lot" at the bottom of the social order.[40] For the Australian aborigine, myth determines his residence in a given ancestral territory, and at the same time makes war to possess other people's territory irrelevant — who would want to take someone else's territory and live cut off from his own "life root?"

Where a myth exacts of a person some sacrificial or dangerous exploit, such as a solitary fast under difficult conditions to meet the guardian spirit, it also assures the aspirant not only of supernatural favor on his exploit, but provides him with a "true, historical" account of the mythic hero's

accomplishment, thereby proving that the required exploit is feasible.[41] The degree of influence which myth exerts on behavior is related to its value. The higher its social value, the greater its influence on behavior. The Guarani of the South American Matto Grosso offer us a striking example of the power of myth to influence behavior. Being warned by a myth that the world was ripe for destruction and that all men who lived outside of the "land without sin,' would be destroyed, the Guarani set out to seek this earthly paradise. The result was a series of migrations that lasted for more than a century.[42]

Clyde Kluckhohn suggests that it is a tribe's myths and rituals which, in the absence of a codified system of laws and an authoritarian chief, help a face-to-face society to present a unified front to the many disintegrating influences that attack every social group.[43]

Sometimes, of course, a behavior pattern will continue even though the current generation is ignorant of the actual mythic base of the behavior in question. This seems to be the case among Philippine tribes people who still prepare "food without salt" which they then recook with salt for actual consumption. This behavior pattern, of course, is based on the myth about the culture hero, *Maka-andog*, who refused baptism with holy (salt) water. The unsalted food is essentially an offering to pre-hispanic spirits now called *ingkantos* (from Spanish *encanto* 'charm') whose power can be enjoyed

---

[39] Wesley J. Culsaaw, *Tribal Heritage: A Study of the Santals* (London: Lutterworth Press, 1950), p. 64.

[40] Topitch, *op. cit.*, p. 167.

[41] Eliade, *Myth ... op. cit.*, p. 141.

[42] *Ibid.*, p. 57.

[43] Kluckhohn and Leighton, *op. cit.*,, p. 517.

only by those who refrain from using salt.[44] Even though the practice is still almost universal, few people know the reason for the two-step food preparation.

Personal testimony reinforces sanction. If one wonders why the individual subscribes to such a code, the answer probably lies in the social setting. Man looks to his fellows for support and approval. Even the rebel will seldom dare defy those mythic injunctions which his fellows firmly believe. In fact, it is from the testimonials of his fellows that a man learns to respect and to fear such supernatural myth-based sanctions.

One night the author listened to a conversation in which several skeptical youths asked about a certain mythological monster that supposedly resided in a waterhole they were to pass next day. They were obviously tempted to experiment and to find out whether the monster actually existed. But as the evening wore on, the other people present told experience after experience of persons who had seen the monster and of the destruction of those who had dared to irritate it. In fact, one man recounted how in his grandfather's time a whole family had been wiped out because some unbelieving rascal threw his spear into the waterhole. When they passed the waterhole next day, the rebel youths gave it wide berth. When the author asked whether it wouldn't be interesting to try and raise the monster, they told him emphatically that he could go alone–they weren't having any part in such an experiment.

Myth and socialization. A further aspect of the infuence of myth on behavior can be seen in socialization practices. It is through the myths and tales, which parents and peers tell the child, that he absorbs the values and ideals of the culture. Should a child question a specific command or prohibition, his parents and socializers will automatically take recourse to citing mythic injunctions as the basis for the respective commands. As long as elders and peers have no doubt about the validity of the sanction, the socializee himself will seldom be tempted to doubt it.[45]

Renewal Function of Myth and Ritual

There is little question that the tremendous interest in the beginnings of things relates to the belief that the first time something happened, its fullest power was manifested–be this in creation itself or the first time a given ritual was performed. In fact, since man usually experiences time as divided into seasons and his very life is a cycle of new beginnings–birth, marriage, death, etc.; he is therefore concerned that every new beginning have the prerequisite power content. When he experiences crop failure, catastrophes, illness, etc., he assumes that the "good" power has somehow run down. This is why myth and ritual often seek to renew the strength to its original

---

44 Donn V. Hart and Hariett C. Hart, " 'Maka-andog :' A Reconstructed Myth from Eastern Samar, Philippines," in Jacobs and Greenway, *op. cit.*, pp. 84-108.

45 For more detail on the importance of the socializer's conviction see: Jacob A. Loewen, "Socialization and Conversion in the Ongoing Church," to be published in PA.

fullness, or to re-establish the original condition.

Re-enacting creative events. Many societies have annual ceremonies to assure the renewal of their socioeconomic structure   This usually involves a re-enacting of the original creative acts. Thus among the Californian tribes the mortals annually perform the rituals of creation, thereby making the world just as it was in the days when the Immortals first created it.[46] The Maidu and the Pomo renew the world not only to insure good crops, but also to initiate their youths into the pristine strength of original creation.[47] In India such re-creation was not an annual event, but was a part of the installation service of each new regent, the *rajasuya.*[48]

Others, though they do not actually re-create, still "renew" the creation. Thus even though the Australian myths consist of long, monotonous narratives of the wanderings of mythical ancestors and of totemic animals, the repetitions of these are considered absolutely essential to insure the fertility of plants, animals, and people.[49]

In New Guinea the myth-telling season coincides with the early (November - December) growth season. At dusk after all have eaten their fill, people gather to listen to the tales of how the earth and its inhabitants began. The retelling of the creation myths at this specific time will insure both rapid crop growth and human fertility.[50]

In a similar vein Australian aborigines periodically repaint the rock paintings presumably prepared by the ancestors at the time of creation so as to restore the world to its pristine powers.[51]

Renewal of health. The principle of renewal also lies at the base of many magical healing practices. Erland Nordenskiöld has already pointed out that in order to insure the full power of magical curing rites or even prepared remedies, one must know and repeat their origin.[52] Many curing ceremonies actually represent a going back to the creative beginnings when "everything was good." If the patient is transported back into this "good beginning," he will be healed. Eliade cites the case of the Bhils of India who in their curing ceremony "create" a miniature universe around the patient very much like the one described earlier for the Navajo. The curer first of all purifies the room in which the patient lies, and then draws a miniature universe by means of corn flour. At the very center of this space he puts the creative deities and their residence. In this way the patient is immersed in the primordial fullness of life and the primitive creative

---

46 Eliade, *Myth* ... *op. cit.,* p. 45.
47 *Ibid.,* p. 46.
48 *Ibid.,* p. 39.
49 *Ibid.,* p. 14.

50 Catherine H. Berendt, "The Ghost Husband: Society and the Individual in New Guinea Myth," in Jacobs and Greenway, *op. cit.,* p. 246.
51 Eliade, *Myth* ... *op. cit.,* p. 43.
52 Erland Norbenskiold, "La conception de lâme chez les Indiens Cuna de I 'Isthme de Panama," *Journal des Americanistees,* N.S., Vol. 24, 1934, p. 14, quoted in Eliade, *Myth* ... *op. cit.,* p. 16,

forces are brought to bear upon him.[53]

Myth Helps Man Transcend his Limitations

Man as a finite and individual creature has desires for and finds fulfillment in going beyond himself. Myth and ritual afford him one of the major vehicles to meet this need. Jerome S. Bruner has already pointed out that through myth man can share his inner experience with others. Like drama and the novel, myth serves as a "window" to permit others to "see" what another man's "inner eye" sees and his soul "feels." By externalizing this inner experience in myth and ritual man can participate in the lives of others and can experience the satisfaction of having others use him and his experience as a model.[54]

Discharging negative impulses. Even at best man finds within himself aggressive and otherwise negative impulses. Herein too, myth serves as a transcending vehicle. In the first place, man can sublimate such tendencies in myth-based ritual under ceremonial conditions so as not to endanger his status in society or the unity of his group. Again, myths—especially witchcraft myths—provide a means of projecting one's hostilities on culturally accepted culprits and to have these act them out. For other less creative individuals myth provides a vehicle for vicariously participating in the expression of negative impulses without accruing personal guilt.

Experiencing the divine. Myths also help man transcend the mundane and human. They awaken in man the awareness of a world beyond, be it the sphere of the gods or of his ancestors. In fact, they function as a link between time-bound, earthly existence and the unlimited "beyond." Since myths tell man what "really" happened in creation or in the beginning, man transcends his finite limitations and "knows eternal truth"

In those cases where myth telling is considered a re-enactment of original creation or as a means of stimulating the creative forces of the universe, man actually participates with the "Immortals" in the creative processes that began and maintain the world. Joseph Campbell goes a step further and says that when a man puts on the mask of a "supernatural" to participate in the re-enactment of some mythlogical, creative event, the actor becomes a part of the reality which the mask represents. Thus "he does not merely represent god: he *is* the god" (italics mine).[55] Participation of this type can be a deeply moving experience, and it is this depth participation that suggests a reason why myths are so firmly rooted in man's belief system that they will survive all kinds of attempt to root them out—having once experienced deity, why should he settle for anything less? In fact, anything less will seem like a vulgar attempt to prevent him from actualizing what he is or can be.

---

53 Eliade, *Ibid.*, pp. 24-25.
54 Jerome S. Bruner, "Myth and Identity," in Murray, *op. cit.*, p. 286.

55 Joseph Campbell, "The Historical Development of Myth," in Murray, *op. cit.*, pp. 33-34.

Myth as Vehicle to Preserve and to Transmit Truth

If a society wants to survive in time, it must transmit to the next generation the body of its accumulated knowledge. Myths have been a favorite vehicle of most preliterate societies for the preservation and the transmission of truth and knowledge as they see it.

First, the narrative form of myth provides not only a useful medium for instruction, but also many hours of meaningful entertainment—not only for the young who are being initiated, but also for the elders who have actually heard them repeated many times. Each repetition serves to fix the values and patterns more firmly in the hearer's consciousness, and in that sense functions as a preservative of the "truth."

Myths, as we have earlier established, are also re-enacted, or they provide the immediate basis for ritual behavior. This means that myths are transmitted not only by oral com-munication, but by the ritual behavior which symbolizes or re-enacts them. People not only hear the "truth," they act it out. Eliade reports M. Hocart's description of the enthroning of a new Fiji king. The ceremony is called "the creation of the world," "fashioning the land," or "creating the earth," for the accession of a new sovereign involves the symbolical repetition of the entire mythological cosmogony.[59]

Finally, myths provide the ready answers to the questions that arise in life, especially for the endless queries of children who want to know the why's and wherefore's of things. Parents need only to remind the child of specific motifs of myths which validly describe behavior. Thus a child's quest for knowledge and understanding of the universe around it is generally answered by the body of lore which the society transmits. In fact, myths and proverbs are two of the important vehicles in child training.

---

[56] Eliade, *Myth ... op. cit.*, p. 39.

The Dynamics of Myth - Changing and Mythmaking

Everyone who has participated in an aboriginal setting in which myths were shared with the younger generation, will have been struck by the reverent attitude with which these tales were told and listened to. Usually the attitude is one of awe and utmost respect, if not sanctity. Eliade concludes that the reason for this is that in reciting or listening to a myth, one establishes contact with the "sacred" and with "reality," and in so doing the person transcends his profane, human condition. In other words, he rises above the temporal and the dull self-sufficiency of everyday life and participates in the eternal realm of the supernatural.[57]

Resistance to Change

So deeply engrained is this respect for myth that even conversion brings about little change in a person's attitude toward it. David Wirsche tells of a recent experience with the Choco church in Panama: The evening began like many others with the people sitting around and chatting about the day's activities. Suddenly someone asked a question. This started off the host, Aureliano, in telling "stories which the ancients used to tell." On several occasions he stopped and said: "Our fathers said it this way, but we now know that it is this way;" however, he went on and told the story in the old way just the same   After a while he became so involved in his tales that he began to act them out before a rapt audience. The sequence grew longer and longer. Finally, well past midnight he asked what time it was. When he learned how late the hour was, he abruptly announced: "Now let us pray." He prayed and then everyone went to bed.[58]

If conversion appears to be inadequate for eliminating faith in mythology, then force seems to be an even less effective means. Mission history is replete with attempts to eradicate myths along with other forms of "pagan" superstition. But myths are

[57] Mircea Eliade, *Images and Symbols: Studies in Religious Symbolism* (London: Harvill Press, 1960), p. 59.

[58] Personal communication from David Wirsche who since 1959 has been spending his summers in short-term service with the Choco in Panama.

not easily destroyed or changed by external pressure. If they are prohibited publicly, they usually go underground. Once myths have to go underground, orthodoxy, i.e. the preservation of the myth in its original unadulterated form, acquires a previously unknown importance. In fact, overt prohibition usually tends to greatly increase the overall value of myth, for in addition to its traditional, supernatural value, it now becomes the group's symbol of passive resistance to oppression. The Waunana of Colombia were subjected to severe pressures by the state church to forsake their "superstitious beliefs' and to be baptized. They submitted to the external ritual, but they clung all the more tenaciously to their mythology. This was the reason why they were so secretive about myths during our early missionary experience.

The persistence of indigenous beliefs under persecution is not an exclusively missionary phenomenon. Melville J. Herskovitz has also highlighted it in his writings on the belief systems of New World Negroes. He asserts that the suffering of slavery not only caused the Negro slaves to cling more doggedly to their traditional beliefs, but it also tended to exert pressure to reduce the system to a consistent hard core of essentials, which once achieved, was capable of defying both time and inquisition. The reduction not only involved the loss of certain non-essentials of a given tribal belief system, it also included the sacrifice of certain tribal distinctives so that ultimately only that core of myths and beliefs persisted which was common to West African tribes in general.[59]

Even though the preceding paragraphs have stressed the stability of myths, it is important to recognize that they do undergo a variety of changes. We can subdivide such changes into at least four categories: unconscious adjustment, obsolescence and disuse, conscious adjustment, and the development of new myths.

Unconscious Adjustment

Inasmuch as myths are an integral part of a people's oral tradition, they also manifest many of the characteristics of oral law which is unconsciously adjusted to changing circumstances, because it is the *spirit* of the law that counts, and not its precise wording. Yet unlike oral law which usually will be invoked only on the occasion when an actual case is being tried, myths are repeated much more frequently, for they often are the common means of entertainment after the day's work is done. On the one hand such constant repetition keeps the details clearly fixed in people's minds, and in that sense serves as a preservative against change. On the other hand, however, frequent retellings with some individual liberty in content or arrangement can also play an important role in gradual myth

59 Melville J. Herskovitz, "African Gods and Catholic Saints in New World Religious Belief," in William A. Lessa and Evon Z. Vogt, *Reader in Comparative Religion: An Anthropological Approach*, second edition (New York: Harper & Row, Publishers, 1965), pp. 541-547, reprinted from *American Anthropologist* 39:635-643.

readjustment.

Obsolescence

Since no culture ever achieves absolute homeostasis, i. e. remains completely constant without any change, it stands to reason that changes in the overt and behavioral aspects of a culture will cause parts of its ideal worldview based on mythology to become incongruent. In fact, we can predict: the greater the exposure to other cultures, new ideas, or different circumstances, the greater the pressure toward change in the observable aspects of culture; and by the same token, the greater the changes in behavior, economics, etc., the more irrelevant certain aspects of the old myth-sanctioned ideology will become.

Because the Waunana ancients failed to heed some of the lessons that *Ewandama* taught them in regard to sex and family life, child birth became fraught with complications. For this reason family members live in fear when a woman is giving birth to a child. To prevent this fear from permanently impairing their lives, a Waunana myth prescribed that men above the age of puberty must bathe in the river immediately after the delivery of the child in order to wash away the fear and to keep their hands from trembling when they hunt. During one particularly difficult birth the missionary doctor was asked to assist. We accompanied the nurse and the doctor who after some tense moments safely delivered the baby. When all the men and boys jumped into the river, the host remained seated beside us and said: "I am getting civilized. I am not afraid of childbirth anymore. So I do not need to go and wash away my fear." Should such a feeling spread, both the myth and the ritual will become obsolete.

William Lessa describes how German and Japanese influence on Ulithi undermined native confidence in the myth and ritual of giving a woman's skirt to the sea spirit in order to assure successful fishing. As a result both the myth and the oracles connected with this ritual are gradually being forgotten.[60]

Another example of myth obsolescence has been reported from the Manus Islanders who under the unifying leadership of Paliau, the prophet of the new religion, threw all the Sir ghost skulls into the sea as an expression of their liberation from an obsolete oppressive system of beliefs.[61]

Conscious Adjustment

Over and above such gradual and often unconscious adjustments, there also are mechanisms of conscious readjustment. Of these we highlight two: inspiration and group concensus.

Inspiration can be viewed as change based on individual effort over against consensus which involves the group as a whole. Prophets and other

[60] William A. Lessa, "The Decreasing Power of Myth on Ulithi," in William A. Lessa and Evon Z. Vogt, *Reader in Comparative Religion* (New York: Harper and Row, Publishers, 1965), pp. 180-185.

[61] Margard Mead, *New Lives for Old : Cultural Transformation — Manus*, 1928-1953 (New York: William Morrow, 1956).

leading individuals who experience some crisis encounter with supernatural forces are the most likely agents of myth change through new inspiration. When such individuals modify an existing myth or introduce a new one (new myths usually arise by inspiration), they will always justify the departure from tradition on the basis of the new insight of which they have become custodians. Such new inspiration may range from the dream of the Toba evangelist, who saw the Blessed Virgin and received command to instruct all his people to wear a certain medallion as a protection against the spirit forces that cause illness and that should anyone become ill he could be cured by the smoke from burning pages of the Bible, to Joseph Smith who received the complete *Book of Mormon* from the hands of the archangel. If a group accepts such a prophet's leadership, it will also accept his "vision," or vice versa.

Change by group consensus usually is much more conservative and for that reason also more common. Even though here too, some individual raises the question of change or adjustment, it is crucial to recognize that such an innovator does not function as an individual, but rather as a "loudspeaker" for a change that is being generally accepted by the audience. The myth is told in its orthodox form, but during the discussion which follows, possible changes are weighed. As the message of the myth is related to life, the participants recount experiences which either bear out its validity or point out some incongruity.[62] If there is incongruity the discussion will often continue until the group finds a consensus on how the story *ought* to be told in the light of the current circumstances. Even though such consensus should never be considered a formal agreement, it usually permits the recognized raconteur to incorporate this change in the next rendition of the myth.

The process of adjustment on the basis of consensus can be seen in the following episode in which an elderly Waunana shaman told the myth of the flood. (See myth 16.) We first present the version as actually told by the shaman.

[8] No sooner had the two committed incest, than thunder crashed, lightning flashed, and a terrible downpour, called the "mother of waters," began. It soon covered the whole earth, and all the houses, people, and animals were swept downriver to their destruction. Only several little children who were floating downriver in a *sāū* 'gourd dish' were saved when *Ewandama* lassoed them and pulled them to the top of the high mountain on which he was standing.

When the author, who had been listening to the rendition of the myth, expressed surprise that five children could fit into a *sāū*, a rather lengthy and emotionally charged discussion resulted. One man affirmed a very old man had said that the children actually floated in a *hapdam*. (The

Waunana word *hapdam* literally means 'little canoe,' but it also is used as the name for a large wooden bowl in the shape of a canoe in which corn in usually soaked before cooking.) Several of the people present supported his explanation either by expressing their belief in it or by testifying that they, too, had heard the myth told that way. The episode was concluded when the raconteur turned to the author and categorically stated: "It wasn't a *sāū*, really, it was a *hapdam*."

Change in folktales. It has been very instructive to observe the difference in attitude toward folktales over against myths among the Waunana. As already stated earlier, they were very secretive about myths during our early mission experience. Only after we had become well accepted in the culture, were we permitted to participate in myth-telling sessions. This reticence did not extend to folktales, for they were telling them to us long before we were able to appreciate them linguistically. What attracted our attention, however, was the difference in audience reaction toward the changes in folktales as contrasted to changes in myths. Thus when a person telling an animal story innovated and changed some detail quite markedly from the standard, people would shrug their shoulders and say: "Well, that is his story," and leave it at that. But their attitude toward change in myth was quite different. If a raconteur did feel it necessary to propose a change, he would generally do so in terms of a question rather than a declarative statement.

---

62 Hallowell, *op. cit.*, p. 151.

Only if and when the audience indicated their approval through feedback, would he make it a statement of fact. If the proposed change did not meet with audience agreement, the older people, especially, marshaled experiential evidence to prove the validity of the supposed original and pointed out the dire consequences of heterodoxy.

Examples of Adjustment

Reinterpreting old elements in terms of new information. The Waunana offer us a telling example of a modern reinterpretation in their account of the origin of men. Traditionally when *Ewandama's* son (myth 5) made dolls from three kinds of material—black palm wood, white balsa wood, and mud—the black dolls became the black magic spirits, the white dolls became the white magic spirits, and the mud dolls became the Waunana. During one story-telling session the author witnesssed the process of reinterpreting this myth. White men and Negroes were now living near the Waunana, and since the author is a white man was listening to the story, a woman turned to him after the myth had been recited and asked: "Don't you think this story should really say that the black dolls became Negroes, the white dolls became white people, and the mud dolls became the Waunana?" This question precipitated a discussion of the pros and cons of the two possible interpretations. Several years later when the author heard this story retold, the raconteur explained that the black dolls became Negroes and the white

dolls became white people, without any question as to the orthodoxy of this interpretation on the part of the listening audience.

Reclassification or reorganization of traits. Very frequently new information through culture contact necessitates that a part of the original worldview be restructured. Thus with the advent of missionary medicine the Choco had to reorganize classification of disease. According to their mythology all illness was caused by *hai* 'evil spirits,' and the diseases were subdivided according to the kind of spirit and the type of condition under which the *hai* invaded the body. Since, however, many of the diseases responded best to medicine given at the dispensary, a new classification of disease arose: natural diseases, i.e. those which could be treated by dispensary medicine—this included malaria, yaws, worms, etc.— and "spiritual" diseases, i.e. those which were still viewed as being the result of evil spirit action and therefore also in need of a "spirit" remedy.

Adding new elements. Frequently new experiences can be successfully absorbed by reinterpreting a part of the old structure In other cases a new element may simply be added to a myth without any major change or adjustment. For example, in those Choco areas that were exposed to extensive Roman Catholic indoctrination, the Virgin is now appearing as a new character in certain myths. At still other times the new element is broken up into smaller units and the resulting separate items are linked with different elements of the existing structure. This latter result was illustrated in the introduction where the story of Abraham's children was restructured and reinterpreted so as to provide an explanation for the origin of the *imawari* spirits who were now termed the children of Ishmael as opposed to the true children of Abraham who were the people of the tribe.

Substituting something new for the old. Sometimes a complete element can be lifted out and a new one put in its place. This happened when Aureliano discovered that the world had the shape of a globe rather than a series of concentric rings of land and water.[63] John Greenway reports a most fascinating adjustment in mythology from Australia where one clan took possession of territory belonging to another clan. This was an obvious violation of the myth-sanctioned residence pattern, but the invaders solved the dilemma by developing a new series of mythological stories to account for and to justify the anomalous state of affairs.[64]

An old element gets a new name. One of the most common changes in myths due to missionary presence is the introduction of a new name for the tribal deity or culture hero.[65] Missionaries working among the Shiriana in northern Brazil began by using the Portuguese word *Deus* as the name for God. The people at once responded: "We know about whom you are talking. You are

talking about *Omam*. What you call *Deus*, we call *Omam*." One can thus predict that in time *Omam* will also be referred to as *Deus*.

One of the problems of identifying something old by a new name is that the content of the old name usually remains unchanged, i.e. the characteristics originally attributed to *Omam* in the mythology will also be attributed to *Deus*. This has happened repeatedly in Latin American folk Catholicism.[66]

It is also possible, of course, that due to changed beliefs the attributes of the deity rather than the name be changed. Missionaries working among the Maquiritare in Venezuela reported that during more than ten years of missionary work they had always used *Diyo*, an adaptation of the Spanish Dios, for God. Then one day they became aware that when Maquiritare believers witnessed to people who had not previously been exposed to missionary preaching, they used the name of the native culture hero *Wanaari*. Knowing that *Wanaari* was a rather questionable character in Maquiritare mythology, the missionaries had plenty of reason for concern. *Wanaari* had engaged in deceit, immorality, and wickedness of sundry kinds. When the missionary pointed to all the bad things *Wanaari* had done, the elders of the church at once responded: "The bad things that were told about *Wanaari* are lies which the devil invented so that the people should not believe he is God."[67] In this situation the

---

63 Loewen, "A Choco ... *op. cit.*, pp. 129-133.
64 Greenway, *op. cit.*, p. 245
65 Joh. Warneck, *The Living Christ and Dying Heathenism* (Grand Rapids: Baker Book House, 1954), pp. 139-141.

66 Madsen, *op, cit.*, pp. 105-180.
67 Personal communication from Jim Bou, missionary to the Maquiritare with New Tribes Mission.

content of the character attributes of *Diyo* actually replaced a large part of the aboriginal content, but the original name was retained.

New ritual expression. It is also possible for a myth to remain relatively intact while the meaning of the ritual with which the society re-enacts it is changed or reinterpreted. The Toba of the Argentine Chaco offer us a noteworthy example. Their current conversion pattern for young people appears to be a new ritual interpretation of the puberty ceremony. As stated earlier, Chaco puberty rituals, including those of the Toba, required the pubescent girl to faint.[68] This was based on the re-enactment of the myth concerning the vagina dentata of the first women. The puberty ceremony as such has been discontinued since the Toba became Christians, but today the conversion experience of teenagers seems to have largely replaced it. Here is a summary of a missionary observer's report: On Saturday night a group of young people danced until they fainted. The meeting lasted from 6:30 in the evening until well past two o'clock on Sunday morning. At the Sunday morning service the same young people came forward to give themselves to God. One by one they were again seized with the spirit and then they danced ecstatically. When we inquired what this meant, the believers explained that the unconverted young people had been full of bad *gozo* (literally Spanish 'joy,' but here the meaning is 'conviction of sin' or

'consciousness of being evil') and that they had to die to this bad *gozo* so that they could give themselves to God and be filled with good *gozo*.[69] In this case the ritual reinforcing the myth was filled with new content, but the burden of the basic meaning remained intact.

Developing New Mythology

Earlier we cited Greenway's example of an Australian tribe which seized territory belonging to another clan and which then developed a new series of myths to justify the existing state of affairs. We need to underscore, however, that such making of new myths is not a characteristic exclusive to aborigines, but rather a universal human trait. In his novel *The Lord of the Flies*[70] William Golding builds upon this trait of developing metaphysical explanations for the existing situation and of establishing supernatural sanctions for the developing behavior patterns in his realistic description of a group of school boys who develop their own "culture" with both myth and ritual after a plane crash leaves them stranded on an isolated tropical island.

Philip Slater goes even farther and proposes that any group—in therapy, in training, etc.—which finds itself in a situation in which it faces problems without rules, plans, restraints or goals, at once proceeds to develop a "mythology" to help

---

[68] For more detail see: Jacob A. Loewen, "Socialization and Conversion...", *op. cit.*

[69] Personal communication from James Kratz, missionary to the Toba with the Mennonite Board of Missions and Charities.

[70] William Golding, *The Lord of the Flies* (New York: G. P. Putnam's Sons, 1955).

explain away the frightening responsibility and the aloneness that such situations of unprogrammed existence force upon it.[71] Slater feels that one of the first steps in the process of myth-making is the deification of the absent leader as a sort of psychological antidote to the deprivation the group is experiencing.[72] The second step involves seeing in the current

---

71 Philip E. Slater, *Microcosm, Psychological and Religious Evolution in Groups* (New York: John Wiley & Sons, Inc., 1966), pp. 12-13.

72 *Ibid.*, pp. 7-23

frustration some ultimate plan designed by the absent deity—"God is testing us."[73]

Again, Henry Hatfield's study of the Nazi *Weltanschauung* demonstrates how the evolution of national socialism in Germany was accompanied by a parallel development of a supporting mythology complete with motifs, beliefs, archetypes, etc. He calls the resulting philosophical system "one vast hideously effective myth."[74]

---

73 *Ibid.*, p. 16.

74 Henry Hatfield, "The Myth of Naziism," in Murray, *op. cit.*, p. 199.

Myth Analysis

Many missionaries have serious reservations about collecting and working with tribal mythology; even the few who have overcome their inhibitions and have collected myths, have often been frustrated because they did not know how to extract relevant data from the collected materials. While certain features of analysis have already been alluded to in the section on myth function, we here want to analyze several myths in order to illustrate the kinds of information they contain and to show how they can be interpreted.

Three Schools of Myth Interpretation

Anthropologists have recognized at least three orientations in myth analysis: (1) the historical, (2) the psychoanalytic, and (3) the sociocultural.

E. B. Tyler[75] can be considered an early representative of the historical school with was interested in motif and theme distribution. Underlying this approach was the belief that myths represented half - forgotten, actual historical events which had been imaginatively embellished by the people. It was therefore thought that a study of the distribution of motifs and themes could tell the anthropologist something about the actual history of a people. This approach encouraged extensive data collections of which Sir James Frazer's *Golden Bough*[76] is one of the early classic examples.

---

75 E. B. Tylor, *Primitive Culture : Researches into the Development of Mythology, Philosophy, Religion, Language, Art and Custom.* 2 Vols., 2nd edition (London: John Murray, 1873).

76 James Frazer, *The Golden Bough: A Study of Magic and Religion.* 12 Vols., 3rd edition (London: MacMillan and Co., Ltd. 1911-1915).

The psychoanalytic approach is usually attributed to Sigmund Freud,[77] who unlike the historical school, collected little original data but rather used certain selected parts of the mythological material that was already available to support his psychological theories. Freud and his followers see in mythology extensive sexual symbolism, repressed Oedipal and Electra complexes, projected aggressions, and generally externalized wishful thinking.

The third approach has been identified with E. Durkheim,[78] Marcel Mauss[79] and Levi-Strauss[80] who emphasized that myth lays the foundation for interpersonal relationships and the understanding of both individual and group behavior. This school insists that the values of a people, both positive and negative, as well as their behavior patterns will find their origin and support in mythic lore.

The analytical approach followed in this paper will borrow elements from all three of these approaches without subscribing totally to any one system. If they should be ranked, the third possibly provides us with the best insights into group behavior, while the second has application especially on the individual level. The

[77] Sigmund Freud, *Totem and Taboo*. Enlish translation (New York: Moffat, Yard and Co., 1918).

[78] E. Durkheim, The Elementary Forms of Religious Life (London: Glencoe, 1912 [1947]).

[79] H. Hubert and M. Mauss, "Esquisse d'une théorie générale de la magie," *Année Sociologique* 7, 1902.

[80] Claud Levi-Strauss, "The Structural Study of Myth," in *Structural Anthropology* (New York: Basic Books, inc 1963).

historical school has largely been superseded.

It is imperative to underscore that while myths are often told as "history," they should not be treated as *actual* history. Christianity is possibly the only religion that tries to maintain a definite historical basis. However, having said that myth is not actual history, we hasten to emphasize that it is nonetheless "real"—it is non-historical "reality." For this reason consistency in time and events is not an essential feature of myths.

It will be impossible within the space available to analyze in detail all the myths cited in this study. We have selected myths 2, 4, 5 and 7 for more detailed treatment since they exhibit a fairly representative range of myth content. Other myths and motifs will be referred to in the course of the analysis.

Myth Two

The tiger–*guatin* type of conflict episodes is very widespread in oral literature. In other sections of South America the opponents are Tiger and Rabbit, in North America it may be Bear and Coyote, in parts of Africa it may be Lion and Jackal, etc. The basic theme is that "brains can overcome brawn." Tiger is the big bully— the enemy who is forever threatening the smaller *Guatin*, but the latter by his superior intelligence always outsmarts the bully. Psychologically this story has several levels of application in Waunana society. There is no question that they in general identify with *Guatin*, and that he can be said to represent the Indian collectively over against the encroaching Western world. (Incidentally, Tiger speaks Spanish. This is signalled by certain stereotyped Spanish expressions recurring in Tiger's speech)

However, the conflict can also be applied at a lower level to the Indian teenager who must take a wife on a strange river, in a strange home, and live under the domination of his in-laws at least until after his first child has been born. This trying experience was already alluded to in the paper "Aureliano: Profile of a Prophet"[81] Only after a child is born can the young man escape the domination of the in-laws under the ruse that he must go to show the child to his father.

At still a different level this struggle is seen in the tension between the ordinary Indian and the domineering shaman. There is no doubt that the shaman has power over the people and that he is feared by the ordinary Indian, but the wise individual will always find "escapes" even when bullied by a shaman's threats. This is reflected in the fact that almost every household contains someone who is learning shamanistic arts. A full-fledged practitioner must have eight canes, each with a subservient spirit entity. Most adult men had only one or two canes for their own protection; it is only full-fledged practitioners who are considered capable of hurting others.

The headwaters. The headwaters

[81] Jacob A. Leowen, "Aureliano: Profile of a Prophet," PA, Vol. 13, No. 4 (July-Aug. 1966), pp. 97-114.

in Choco symbolism represent the distant, higher ground, the mysterious, unknown world beyond their ordinary habitat. It is often the seat of dangerous spirit powers. (See myth 4 where the individual goes too far from his home and becomes involved with the dangerous spirit powers. This supernatural association is also seen in the fact that the woodpecker comes from the headwaters and does not permit the moon to be destroyed.) In actual fact the Waunana do not control the headwaters either of the San Juan or of the Baudo Rivers, so even historically and geographically these regions represent foreign territory to them. It is at the "unknown" headwaters where the notched pole ladder, which connects both the underworld to this earth and this earth to the sky-world, is located. (See myths 2 and 4.)

In the ten or more episodes of the *Guatin* cycle, the latter's superior intelligence always brings him out on top, but the episode described in myth 2 serves as a strong reminder that such superiority does not extend to the next world. *Guatin* tries to fool the guardian of the next world with his superintelligence, but he is not only foiled, he is killed. This is a solemn warning that human intelligence is not equal to supernatural problems.

Myth Four

A large number of societies have myths of culture heroes. Often they are twins who are miraculously born, and who provide men with life's necessities and clear the world of evils.

The Waunana version begins with a dilemma. Men must hunt and game is most plentiful away from the inhabited regions, but he who ventures too far beyond the realm of the known, enters the realm of the unknown and mysterious spiritual forces. This same motif is also seen in the myth explaining the origin of delirium in which a hunter has an encounter with a mountain demon. That we are not dealing with actual animals in myth 4 is seen in the statement "what seemed like." Inasmuch as each animal species has its individual character, it also has its individual power. The conjoint impregnation by animals of all kinds emphasizes that the total creative power was operative in the birth of the twins. In the case of the Lengua shaman in the Paraguayan Chaco who needs to absorb the power of the universe, the spiritual essence is abstracted from all manner of things and elements—leaves, bones, nails, axes, paper, leather, etc.[82] This myth also implies that men and animals have certain affinities and a certain type of interdependence. Man needs animal resources to survive, but he must never kill more animals than he actually needs or can give away. Spoiled animal flesh will stand as an indictment against man and society, and is almost certain to bring about supernatural punishment. The man who kills needlessly is a threat to his whole society. On the other hand, when man cooperates with the

[82] Jacob A. Loewen, "Mennonites, Chaco Indians, and the Lengua Spirit World," *The Mennonite Quarterly Review* (October 1965), pp. 280-306.

animal world, he makes it a better place to live.

Twins are definitely not considered a normal number of offsprings for human beings. When a woman gives birth to twins, the Waunana at once suspect that she has violated taboos by eating a double-yolked egg, a peanut with three kernels, or a "Siamese" banana. Even where no taboo violation is suspected, twins are nevertheless considered to be a supernatural omen, if not of supernatural origin. The Waunana generally consider them a negative omen, and for that reason they usually dispose of them through neglect. Other groups like the Chaco Indians kill them at birth. The twins in the myth were definitely of supernatural origin. However, they were representatives of the good supernatural that helped man get rid of many of his enemies and thus made the world more hospitable. In the case of the Shiriana twins (myth 9), however, one of them was evil. *Oman* tried to help man, but *Joao* often destroyed the good that *Oman* had done. The theme of the culture hero who makes the world a better place to live is very widespread in preliterate societies, nor is the Western world free from this motif. We also have our inventor heroes who through technology made the world a better place to live. The only difference is that we consider ours to be based on fact, and not on myth.

Virgin birth. Phsychoanalysts find the concept of "virgin" birth, i. e. nonsexual pregnancy, of special interest. It, too, is a very widespread mythological motif. Among North American Pacific coast tribes it is usually Raven, and among Plains Indians it often is Coyote who is ingested in the form of a grain of dust, a piece of ashes, or a small leaf, and who in this way impregnates a woman who then gives birth to him. In the Waunana myth, even though there is sex involved, it is not natural nor human sexuality that provides the basis for the birth of the twins. The emphasis in the Shiriana twin story is slightly different. We are not told how the woman conceived the twins, but pregnant Woman is eaten by Tiger, and only her placenta is saved. Thus the twins are supernaturally born.

The motif of menstrual blood in in this myth emphasizes the nonhuman nature of the twins. In general the Waunana are not nearly as concerned about menstrual blood as many other tribes. For some tribes it is the epitome of negative power. In such cases the society usually demands strict avoidance. Often it is accompanied by severe taboos so that women may not eat meat of wild animals lest the animal spirits be offended by the odor of menstrual blood and thus deprive man of his livelihood. The killing of one twin by the women because he was asking for menstrual blood illustrates some of the ambivalence that man's relationship with the spirit world involves. It is embarrassing for the women to provide menstrual blood, but when they become too embarrassed and kill the twin, they create for themselves and for their society a permanent problem through the blood-sucking creatures that result.

Myth Five

A very important point in this myth is the fact that creative initiative in the universe always comes from the supernatural (God), and never from man. The supernatural creates man, never vice versa.

Another point is the fact that created man is not perfect. This is often accounted for in different ways. In the Waunana myth, for example, it is the son, an intermediate agent, not *Ewandama* himself, who makes human beings, and as a result they turn out imperfect. Had *Ewandama* himself made man, he would have been perfect; but because the intermediate agent made him, the result was something less than perfect.

The wooden dolls who become the spirit forces of magic point out that most animistic societies do not consider materials such as wood and stone to be inert. They contain spirit power. In fact, each Waunana shaman has a series of canes carved out of hardwood in which specific spirits subservient to him reside. The inherent spirit power is already seen in the fact that the son cuts himself when he tries to carve the wooden dolls. This serves as a warning that manipulating spirit power is never child's play. That is why unwisely used spirit power can often harm the very user himself. The author once purchased a long deceased medicine man's outfit of canes which were still lying in the attic of an abandoned house. A shaman relative of the deceased mustered enough courage to bring the canes to the author and take the money. When the author became ill shortly thereafter, however, his informant took him alone and suggested that he get rid of the canes because the spirit forces resident in them were not subservient to him and were making him sick. In fact, he suggested: "If there. is someone you don't like, you had better give them to him."

The later reinterpretation according to which the black dolls became the ancestors of the Negroes and the white dolls those of white men, stresses the awareness that there are differences in people not only in appearance, but also in more basic make-up. Contact with both white men and Negroes certainly confirms this implication that there are physical, cultural and personality differences.

Indian inferiority. The inferiority of the Waunana over against the spirit world (and/or the white and Negro cultures) is already implied in the very materials used in making them Man's inferiority to the spirit world is pointed out again in the fact that making him creative required a special intervention by Ewandama. The spirit world required no such second act. While this myth does not emphasize the point, the Waunana have several other myths that stress the Indian's inferiority to other people, e. g. the myth of the distribution of cattle. When *Ewandama* released domestic animals, the Indian was afraid of them and hid. Only white man and the Negro grabbed them. That's why they today own domestic animals and the Indian does not.

The use of mud stresses man's impermanence—when he dies, his body reverts back to the soil from which it was taken.

Fellowship. The motive for the creation of man was social fellowship. *Ewandama's* son did not like to be alone. He wanted companionship. This social aspect of man's nature is further alluded to in the fact that a whole beach full of individuals was made. It would almost seem as if the social nature of man takes precedence over his sexual nature in the Waunana myth.

It is noteworthy that *Ewandama* works while others sleep. This motif appears in the creation story in that man is made alive during the time the son sleeps. It also appears in myth 7 where *Ewandama* provides food and the other necessities of life while men sleep. The implication, of course, is that night is the time of increased spirit activity. That is why curing séances are held at night, but by the same token the night is much more dangerous to man than daytime. No Waunana would travel at night except in direst necessity, and then only under favorable moon conditions.

Myth Seven

Cultural innovations and new cultural artifacts come from across the distant waters; and even though the myth describes *Ewandama* as bringing these artifacts to men, the development of the plot clearly shows that *Ewandama* is paternalistic and on the side of the *status quo*, while *Dosīāta*, the trickster, is on the side of progress. It is he who sells the axes to the people so that they can control their food supply. It needs to be pointed out, however, that progress is not a pure blessing. This is implied in the fact that it strained the relationship between *Ewandama* and the people. (The classic Western illustration of this motif is the Prometheus story.) While on the one hand, man was partially tricked into the way of progress, since he did not realize the full implications of the acquisition of axes; yet on the other hand, the myth also points out that man does not like to be in a dependent relationship. In fact, one of the ethnocentric points of pride of the Waunana over against others in their area is that they are independent—they are nobody's serfs.

The motif of desiring independence has another application. Every Waunana young man must enter the economic structure of his in-laws' household. Many a young man remains trapped in the situation and thus becomes a satellite to his father-in-law. On several occasions while the author travelled in Waunana territory, young son-in-laws volunteered their service to him in an effort to break the economic hold in which they found themselves. Every young married man yearns for the day when he too can make a deal and thus become independent.

Even on a broader scale man seldom is content to be a mere creature. He too wants to work creatively. The psychoanalyst would undoubtedly see this story as expressing tension between generations and the projection of the younger generation's feelings concerning their elders.

God is kind. Almost universally in South American mythology the deity figure is kind and paternalistic. Basically man does not need to fear him. Even when man wrongs him, he usually withdraws rather than avenges his hurt. In fact, Waunana mythology contains accounts of several attempts of the kind deity to help even in the face of continued rejection by man. (See myths 10 and 15.) Eventually, however, the deity figure withdraws, leaving man to his own resources and largely to the whim of the negative spirit forces. From the psychological point of view such a withdrawal by the deity figure, of course, represents a projection of man's feeling of alienation based on his accumulating guilt.

Genesis 3. On the surface myth 7 looks very similar to the account of the fall of man recorded in Genesis 3. It also starts out with an Edenic condition—man is living in an undisturbed relationship with his creator who provides an easy life with an unlimited food supply. We also have a trickster-devil who invades this paradise with a trick proposition that casts doubt on the creator's basic long-range purpose for man. This is shown in *Ewandama's* later rebuke: You do not trust me anymore; that is why you bought axes from *Desīata.* Again, man's acceptance of the trickster's proposition results in his ejection from paradise. But in spite of all the similarities, the two accounts are separated by a very fundamental difference. In the Genesis account man is faced with a moral decision—he must obey or disobey an express command; this choice is entirely absent from the Waunana version.

The foregoing statements by no means exhaust the symbolic content of the four myths analyzed, but they illustrate something of the kind of information myths carry and also how they can be interpreted in the light of a specific culture.

Myth As An Aid To Missions

We have already stressed the fact that every society has a body of mythic lore in which lie embedded its basic values, ideals, beliefs, and fears. However, even more important than the individual motifs or themes is their overall arrangement, for in this "structure" of beliefs lies crucial information about a people's worldview. Again, it is in terms of this framework that all new information, including the gospel, will be interpreted and evaluated. Therefore, adequate knowledge and proper understanding of myths can provide valuable guidelines as to what will be meaningful, how it can be best presented, and how negative interpretations and associations can be avoided. If a message is not geared for easy and accurate understanding, restructuring and warping are almost inevitable. Such restructuring of the missionary message in terms of traditional myth-supported categories, has been well illustrated by William D. Reyburn who described how Lolo men had their first wives' names entered into mission books in order to get a mission name.[83] This was an insurance against *lembo* 'the negative power that kills.' At the same time it assured them of some kind of reciprocity in the beyond from the deity to whom they had lent a wife here on earth. Similarly Reyburn reports how the Kakas restructured the Christian communion service in terms of their ceremonial *sataka* meal to purify offended individuals.[84]

As a Point of Contact for Missionary Witness

Frequently aboriginal myths can serve as useful points of contact for a missionary's message.

First of all, they can provide convenient topics for beginning conversations. As translations consultant the author is frequently asked to help investigate problems that have arisen in various mission areas. In order to create an atmosphere of confidence and reciprocity in which information will flow freely and questions will be answered honestly without too much hesitation, the author usually begins with a discussion of mythological materials which he has either read in published sources or has learned from the resident missionary. This was the

83 William D. Reyburn, "Motivations for Christianity: An African Conversation," PA,, Vol. 5, No. 1 (Jan.-Feb. 1958), pp. 27-32.

84 William D. Reyburn, "Meaning and Restructuring: A Cultural Process," PA., Vol. 5, No. 2 (Mar.-Apr. 1958), pp. 79-82.

approach used with the Chimane in Bolivia where the author was asked to investigate some problems. The missionary briefed him on the creation myth. The author recounted this myth to an informant and asked whether he would be able to explain some of the details to him. After they had discussed this myth at some length, the situation was ripe for investigating additional problems.[85]

Secondly, a missionary's interest in tribal myths can earn a hearing for the gospel. One missionary in Africa began his evangelism by having the elders of the village instruct him in tribal beliefs. After they had instructed him for a period of time, they usually turned to him and said: "You have listened to what we have said about our beliefs. Why don't you now tell us what you believe?" This invitation provided him with an open door to deliver his message.[86] And, since it now was a solicited message, it also lost the propaganda flavor which all too often colors missionary preaching.

In the third place, since myths are based on motifs or standardized units of experience, these very units themselves will frequently provide excellent starting points for the missionary message. The German expression for points of contact, Anknüpfungspunkte, adds to the idea of contact the notion that motifs

can be pegs of known truth upon which the new message can be meaningfully hung. In the article "Good News for the Waunana"[87] a number of motifs from Waunana mythology were used as anchors for the first message. These known and accepted "facts" helped provide the impact which caused all the Waunana on that river to decide "to give God the hand and to walk on God's road."

As an Aid in Preprogramming the Message

Like food, the missionary message can be prepared for easy digestion, or it can be presented in a strange and rather unpalatable form. The careful preparation of the message for a specific situation is called preprogramming. There is probably no area of aboriginal culture that provides as much crucial information for proper preprogramming of the gospel message as a people's mythology.

In the first place, the missionary wants to deliver his message in terms of categories that will be understood. Here a knowledge of myths and the general framework into which they fit can provide him with many of the basic beliefs and values that will be truly meaningful to the listeners. Furthermore, he not only wants his message to be understood, he also wants to prevent it from being warped and distorted. He can do this only if he prepares it adequately. Veteran missionary

85 Jacob A. Loewen, "Religion, Drives and the Place where it Itches," PA., Vol. 14, No. 2 (Mar.-Apr. 1967), pp. 49-72.

86 E. A. Nida, "The Relationship of Social Structure to the Problems of Evangelism in Latin America," PA., Vol. 5. No. 3 (May-June 1958), p. 119.

87 Jacob A. Loewen, "Good News for the Waunana," PA., Vol. 8, No. 6 (Nov.-Dec. 1961), pp. 275-278.

Hendrik Kraemer has well said that the gospel can be responded to only through "the existing chords."[88] Those who disregard mythology are excluding themselves from valuable material that will make their message both applicable and desirable. Kraemer goes on to say that most Protestant missionaries depend almost exclusively on clarification and exposition to stir the people, forgetting that most people tend to be stirred by "symbols,"[89] and the great repository of a people's symbols is their mythology.[90] Indeed, it can serve as the veritable symbol dictionary for the missionary.

An example of the need for preprogramming the missionary message about Jesus Christ and God's Word has been well illustrated in the paper "Mushroom Rituals Versus Christianity," which demonstrated how tribal beliefs about the hallucinogenic mushroom caused serious problems for Mazateco converts,[91]

The negative effects of an unprogrammed message have already been illustrated in the introduction to this study of mythology. A further example has been reported previously: When the Choco of Panama were exposed to a series of recorded messages without being given the prerequisite context of explanation, they were thrown into a terrible panic thinking that the world was coming to an end.[92]

The missionary also wants to use appropriate vocabulary. Once again, mythology is a recognized source of vocabulary, especially in the area of non-material experience. Furthermore, words must not only explain the concepts of the gospel adequately, they must also carry the proper emotive connotation. Here again, the language of myth is not only highly valued, but actually embodies the kind of solemnity and seriousness that God's message to man demands.

Finally, since the mythology is part of the overall framework of thought of the aboriginal society, an adequate knowledge of this worldview will permit the witness to develop a new comprehensive conceptual frame into which all the parts of his message will properly fit.[93]

[88] Hendrik Kraemer, *From Missionfield to Independent Church. Report on a Decisive Decade in the Growth of Indigenous Churches in Indonesia* (The Hague: Bockencentrum. 1958), p. 106.

[89] *Ibid.*, p, 81.

[90] The symbolic value of myths has already been underscored by Dell Hymes when he says that certain Wishram rituals require only allusions to specific myths. At other times first lines or special quotations are enough to release "their power." This inherent power is also seen in the fact that present day Wishram often refuse to narrate the full myth because they are not certain that they can do so with absolute correctness. See: Dell Hymes, "Two Types of Linguistic Relativity (with Examples from Amerindian Ethnography)" in William Bright, editor, *Sociolinguistics* (The Hague: Mouton & Co., 1966), pp. 149-155.

[91] Eunice Pike and Florence Cowan, "Mushroom Ritual Versus Christianity," PA., Vol. 6, No. 4 (July-Aug. 1959), pp. 145-150.

[92] Jacob A. Loewen, "The Church among the Choco of Panama," PA., Vol. 10, No. 3 (May-June 1963), pp. 97-108.

[93] Jaceb A. Loewen, "Message and Matrix," PA, Vol. 11, No. 2 (Mar.-Apr. 1964), pp. 49-55. This principle has now been applied in a thirteen-lesson beginners Bible course prepared by CELADEC (Comisión Evangélica Latin Americana de Educacion Cristiana), Casilla 3, Concepción, Chile,

Locating Points of Conflict

On the other hand, adequate knowledge of the mythology will also make the missionary aware of the points at which his message conflicts with the existing worldview. For example, the first message to the Waunana used as its thrust the idea that *Ewandama* was concerned about people even after the latter had become alienated from him. The Waunana myth, however, emphatically stated that *Ewandama* was angry with the people because they had bought axes from the trickster, and in his anger he withdrew from them. This discrepancy with the Biblical message was handled as follows: "Your fathers told you that *Ewandama* was so angry with men that he withdrew from the world, but here there seems to be a mistake. Maybe this mistake developed because the story was not written, and was transmitted by word of mouth over many generations and thus got twisted." The message proper was interrupted at this point with a factual account of an event that happened near the missionary's residence. The story had arrived in the Indian community in a very distorted form. Using this illustration of change in an orally transmitted message, the missionary pointed to the Bible saying, "Here is what really happened: God was sad because of what man had done, but he continued to try to help the people. It was not God who went away; it was the people who went away from God because they had bad consciences."

If the discrepancy between the worldview of the people and the message is not dealt with consciously, there is danger that the people will parrot the missionary version, but will actually live according to the older, "authentic" version. This was already demonstrated in the introduction by the case of the believers who in church said that "blowing" was from the devil, but who continued to practice it because in their hearts they knew that it had come from God.

Nativistic group movements. The delivery of a prophetic message based on the established concepts of mythology has already been referred to earlier.[94] It is important that we recognize it is the myth sanction which serves as the basis for the depth penetration and the popular appeal that such messages tend to have in group movements. If we look at preprogramming from the communications point of view, we can predict that a message which meets the inner longings of a people will have greater impact than a message that leaves the hearers unmoved. If one looks at Jesus' ministry from the standpoint of meeting the expectations of the pious Jews, one can readily understand why his ministry had such a tremendous impact—he fulfilled the full range of messianic prophecies.

A preprogrammed form. Missionaries working among the Culina in Peru report that they encountered great reluctance among tribal believers to discuss the Scriptures after they had been read. While searching for ways and means to present the message in a more appealing form, the missionaries noticed that topics which were discussed were usually

94 Lanternari *op. cit.*, p. 240

first introduced as chants. They therefore tried to put the Scriptures to tunes. The first attempts based on Western melodies, however, were not very successful. One day one of the leading individuals in the tribe came and asked whether it would be inappropriate to use the "tiger tune" (i.e. the tune used to relate the myth about the heroic exploits of Tiger) for the message about Satan going around like a roaring lion (I Pet. 5:8). The presentation was an immediate success and occasioned a long and serious discussion about the nature and work of the devil. As a result of this experience the missionaries assigned passages to leading individuals who then selected appropriate tunes for the presentation of these messages at subsequent Bible study sessions.[95]

For Properly Valuating the Message

Very often a missionary delivers the gospel message in terms of his own experience, i.e. in terms of a Western worldview with its own hierarchy of values. If he is not aware of the values of the culture he wants to reach, he is bound to fall back upon his own cultural background for value support. There are many truths which are very important to Westerners, but which seem to have little appeal or application to the tribal mind. Missionaries to the Chols in Mexico report how their early messages were "shrugged off" as irrelevant by the people. When the missionary said: "You have sinned," the

people responded: "So what? We know that we do wrong." When he said: "You will go to hell if you do not repent," they said: "Fine, if it's a place where there's perpetual fire, we want to go there. Here in the mountains where we live it is always too cold." When the missionary said: "You must believe in Jesus Christ if you want to be saved," the people answered: "We don't only believe in him, we already have his image."[96]

In the same vein Dutch missionary Johannes Warneck tells how missionaries to the Dutch East Indies found that their message had little appeal because it represented the theological outlook and concern of the missionary rather than the felt needs of the people.[97] Someone has said that the Western preoccupation with monogamy has often distorted the value of the gospel in areas where polygamy is predominant. What should be good news about Jesus Christ, really becomes the bad new about polygamy.

For Locating Felt Need

Changing circumstances can frequently jeopardize traditional values, especially where such changes create imbalances that tend to produce negative behavior. These points of cultural imbalance or frustration often represent areas of deeply felt need. If in such a situation the gospel is able to alleviate the problems in

---

95 Personal communication from Patsy Adams and Arlene Agnew, missionnaries to the Culina with the Wyc.iffe Bible Translators.

96 Personal communication from missionaries; also see: John Beekman, "A Culturally Relevant Witness," PA, Vol. 4, No. 6 (Nov. - Dec. 1957), pp. 85-88; also "Minimizing Religious Syncretism among the Chols," PA, Vol. 6 No. 6 (Nov.-Dec. 1959), pp. 241-250.

97 Warneck, op. cit., pp. 149-151.

question, it is good news indeed.

The mythology of the Shiriana in Brazil contains obvious references to the ideals of a proper relationship among men and of an ordered sex life. In actual fact, however, social belonging and marriage represent areas of severe frustration. Since the bands are small and there are severe restrictions on marriage to certain blood relatives, many bands do not have an equitable distribution of the sexes for marriage. Under friendly conditions this imbalance of sexes could be solved by exchange between the bands. The actual situation, however, is one of great physical and social distance between the groups so that instead of exchanging women, they are raiding each other to steal them. If a change of heart wrought by the gospel could reduce the enmity and the church could provide the arena for followship, then peaceful contact between groups would not only be possible, but desirable. Under such conditions the old patterns of peaceful exchange of women would again be practical.[98]

A Choco example. That this not only can but actually does happen, has been shown by the Choco church in Panama. Their main social activity used to be the drinking festival. Overtly this was designed as a fellowship activity. In actual practise, however, it had become the arena in which personal enmity was settled by means of poison. The person wanting to eliminate an enemy, put some poison into a container of liquor and sent it to the unsuspecting victim once drink had clouded the latter's

senses and provided the former with enough "courage." This spelt a double dilemma. If a person stayed away from the festival, he would, of course, be suspected of having practiced the sorcery. If he came and drank, he might be eliminated by an unknown enemy. While Aureliano was in the United States in 1960 he suddenly grasped the fact that the church could fill a deeply felt Empera need. It could be the place where the people could gather to fellowship, eat, and drink without the fear of being poisoned. As a result he instituted week-end eating festivals in connection with the church services.[99] In this way the gospel helped to actualize the myth-supported fellowship ideals which were being severely threatened by social disintegration.

As a Source of Information for Problem Solving

In most societies the transition from tribal religion to Christianty will not be accomplished without problems, but often the difficulty can be lessened by wise help. In fact, it is probably true that the problems of transition will be multiplied or aggravated to the degree to which the missionary is ignorant of native mythology. In the mission situation described at the beginning of this series of papers, work was begun through interpreters. This, of course, meant that the preacher was completely oblivious to tribal beliefs. After two decades of mission work, missionaries were becoming increasingly aware that in spite of all their preach-

---

98 Loewen, "Religion..." *op. cit.*, pp. 57-61.

99 Loewen, "The Church..." *op. cit.*, pp. 100-101.

ing against pagan practices, many of these were still being carried on. It was during a discussion of mythology that the missionaries discovered even the believers were still convinced the curing ceremony based on "hard" words was instituted by God rather than by the devil, as missionary preaching insisted.[100]

As an Aid in Translation

As already indicated earlier, myths are a rich source for vocabulary dealing with religious experience. This includes terms both for the nonmaterial universe, as well as the various aspects of ritual experience. In addition, oral literature will provide the missionary with appropriate text material for making grammatical, syntactic, and discourse analyses. It can also provide examples of style: narrative, proverbial, prayer, etc. At other times the motifs of mythology can provide the appropriate linguistic settings in which the translator can elicit vocabulary needed for the translation of the Bible.[101]

Preventing Syncretism and Increasing the Penetration of the Gospel

The mission situation described in the introduction would awaken concern in any missionary's heart. Had the missionaries involved been more aware of native beliefs and mythology, it would seem that many of the problems could have been solved long

before they developed into the current pattern of pernicious syncretism.

Peter Elkin is quoted by Vittorio Lanternari as saying that for the most part the missionary message has had little effect on native life. With a few exceptions the people have preserved their traditional religion in belief, if not in practice.[102] For example, when the German Lutheran missionaries were interned during World War II, the people of Markham Valley in New Guinea at once returned to openly practice their pre-Christian fertility rites saying: "If the missionaries asked us who made our crops grow, we told them it was as they said: God, who lived above, made them come up. But we knew it was not God. It was the magic we had performed that made the yams grow big. Food does not come up on its own, and if we stopped these things we would have nothing. We hid them and knew our gardens would be well.[103]

Obviously, no missionary wants to repeat situations like the preceding. Every missionary wants to present his message in the most relevant and most penetrating manner possible, but he will be able to actualize this desire only when he is thoroughly familiar with his audience's beliefs and values.

Probably one of the most fascinating attempts to minimize syncretism and to maximize the positive communication of the Christian message was performed by missionary-anthropologist Don Jacobs in a seminary in East Africa. His early attempts to

100 For a discussion of techniques of investigation see: Jacob A. Loewen, "Missionaries and Anthropologist Cooperate in Research," PA, Vol. 12, No. 4 (July-Aug. 1965), pp. 158-190.

101 Jacob A. Loewen, "Matrices for Eliciting Translation Vocabulary, "The Bible Translator, Vol. 18, No. 4 (Oct. 1967), pp. 184-191.

102 Lanternari, op. cit., p. 251.

103 Ibid., p. 252.

teach Biblical theology resulted in serious frustration on his part and both overt and covert misinterpretations and syncretism on the part of his students. To circumvent these problems, Jacobs began by spending the entire first semester of his course in a systematic investigation of the traditional myths and beliefs of the various members of his class. This experience not only made Jacobs more aware of the capacity of the "communication channel" through which his second semester theological message would have to pass if he wanted it to be understood, it also provided him with valuable guidelines as to where to begin, what to emphasize and at what points to warn his students about subtle differences. However, it also produced dividends for the African students. The semester of mythological and religious investigation brought into their consciousness many of their determinative, but usually covert, beliefs and values. This overt awareness of their traditional religious heritage not only assisted them in gaining a fuller and clearer understanding of Christianity, it also helped them avoid many of the pitfalls of misinterpretation and syncretism that usually confuse African students of Christianity.

On the other hand, many, and maybe even most, missionaries will find themselves in situations with long histories of syncretism and restructuring. Even here a belated investigation of myths and beliefs can often produce some happy results. A missionary to the Chulupi in the Paraguayan Chaco discovered that one of the converts, a former shaman, had hopelessly syncretized Christian beliefs and practices with his traditional shamanistic concepts and rituals. So warped was his view that the missionary literally felt sick after he had listened to the man "expound" his "new" beliefs for several hours. In his own heart the missionary was convinced that the man hopelessly lost in a Christopagan world. But two days later, much to the missionary's surprise, this former shaman returned and confessed:

"People have been telling me that I am mixing up the Jesus-message with evil-spirit medicine, but I did not believe them. After I told you all those old beliefs the other evening, I suddenly realized that it was true what the people were saying—I was trying to believe in Jesus, but I was also still believing in my old medicine. I want you to tell everybody that I have recognized my wrong and that I am going to change now. When sick people come to me for help now, I will only pray for them, I won't chant or suck like I have been doing."

In this case one brief look into the hidden recesses of traditional myth and belief opened the way for the light of the gospel to bring a man to a fuller realization of the truth.

Don E. McGregor

Learning From Wape Mythology

Don E. McGregor is a New Zealander who has worked among the Wape people of New Guinea since 1957 under Christian Missions in Many Lands. He has done some Bible translation and some cultural studies among the Wape. Lumi, via Wewak, Territory of New Guinea.

IT IS easy to reject all mythology on the grounds that it is devoid of objective historical reality. In doing so a missionary will probably miss some insights very important to his task, for the forces which influence a people's value system and world view and which motivate behavior, to some extent at least, come from their mythology. Myths help fulfill the universal need for identity, security, and destiny.

A people's mythology cannot be separated from their total culture and neatly isolated into a watertight compartment. The fascinating (though fantastic) stories mold thinking and logic, giving reasonable explanations to otherwise inexplicable happenings and situations.

The Wape people number 10,000 and live in the West Sepik District of New Guinea. They have had contact with Europeans since the 1930's and almost all adult males have been away to coastal plantations for at least one two-year term. Like all peoples they have a mythology, which to them is unquestioned history. There may by some historical

base to these legends, albeit in symbolic form.

The purpose of this article is to highlight (1) the part mythology plays in Wape culture, (2) what can be learned about the people from their mythology, and (3) some problems in helping the people themselves work out a satisfactory relationship between the world of their mythology, the world of the Bible, and the scientific world into which they are being orientated.

Discussion of Wape mythology will be based on a particular myth which I recorded on tape in 1964. This paper is an attempt to interpret the material and draw some conclusions.

Details surrounding the telling of the myth are as follows. A New Guinean man named Epli volunteered to tell me a story about his early ancestors, no doubt because I had shown interest in their legends. So one evening I went to his house in a nearby village. Epli has had contact with Europeans since shortly before World War 11, when as a young man he went and worked in some gold fields in another part of the Territory. He is the traditional storyteller of the village, and at the time he related this story was the elected member of the village on the Local Government Council. This position however has now passed to younger hands. Over the years he has received considerable religious instruction from a large mission which has a center adjacent to his village.

He told me the story in the Wape vernacular and I took it down on tape. It runs for 55 minutes. Just a few other villagers were present with us at the time. The narrative appears to consist of a number of myths, put together in logical sequence to make one story. Parts of the story have been rather significantly changed through European influence and it is this which makes it most interesting. It also raises important questions concerning missionary endeavor.

The following translation is a slight abridgment.

Creation

A long time ago Furu was by himself hanging in mid-air with nothing to support him. He shone like the brilliance of the sun. ("The name you people give to the person who made everything is God. We call him Furu," he said to me.)

"Will I just hang here for ever by myself?" he asked himself one day. "Why?" he thought. He decided to make the ground. He 'blessed' it and it appeared. At first he thought he would leave the ground with nothing on it, like a beach by the sea. Later he changed his mind and commanded that plants, trees, and food should grow. He said to himself, "What will I put on the earth now?"

Taking some earth and the branches of a certain kind of tree which has many knots in it, he commenced to form an image. From some *ton* wood he carved the pelvis. This form he laid on top of the ground, covering it with banana leaves. The shining sun eventually split the leaves following which the form underneath began to move.

"What is this?" said Furu as he cleared away the leaves. "I think it must be a man," he said. So the form came to life and Furu called him Oruwa. "It is not good for just this man to be in the very big bush by himself," said Furu. Then in exactly the same way he made another person, Oruwa's sister, whom he called Sikau. ("You people," said Epli looking at me, "say that woman was made out of a man's rib, but we don't.")

This woman Sikau became Oruwa's wife and over a period of time gave birth to three sons, Womau, Fompai, and Tuwou, and finally a girl named Opai.

Some Other People Were Made Differently.

Womau and Fompai worked so hard at making a living for themselves that they decided they needed more people to help them. So they built a very big house like a large *house lotu* (church building). Then they made baskets and hung them around the walls inside the house. Shooting some wild pigs in the bush, they collected their blood, and going inside the large house, poured a little of the blood into each basket, saying alternately to each basket, "brother, sister, brother, sister,"

A large log slit drum was then pulled inside the house after which the door was securely fastened. Not long afterwards Womau and Fompai heard people talking inside. "There," they said, "they are people now." Fearful lest pig's hair grow on their skins, they collected worms and washed the skins of the recently made people with worm's blood. ("They are our ancestors and I think they are your ancestors too," Epli said to me as he glanced in my direction trying to assess my reaction.)

Why We Do not Live on Forever

Womau and Fompai picked shoots off a sago palm and with other ingredients prepared a concoction for the people just made to drink. This would make them live on forever, simply by their shedding their skins at the normal time of death, as snakes do. Another man, Koufai (no one knows where he came from and it is not relevant to ask) warned the people that they would die if they drank the mixture. A small harmless snake said, "No, you should all drink it and you will not die." However the people believed Koufai and so threw the concoction away. Various snakes and animals who found and drank the mixture have lived on forever. If only the people had not believed Koufai, we would all live forever.

God (Epli from here on drops the name Furu and uses God, which is now much more familiar) angry with the people for not drinking the mixture, changed their language that night. Next morning the people could not understand each other for they were speaking several languages. Womau and Fompai dispersed the people, sending each language group to a different area.

Oruwa and Sikau visited several villages, and in one place made more people in the same way as Furu (God) had made them. Finally they went to Manam Island and put the volcano on top of the mountain. There they now remain.

Adventures of Womau and Fompai

Womau and his younger brother Fompai lived on at Maui village. Then when Fompai started imitating Womau in everything he did, Womau was furious. But Fompai would not stop imitating. So one day Womau said he would go away to another area. "I will go with you," said Fompai. So collecting belongings and food they sat in the large slit log drum and moved off down a creek. It floated like a canoe. Entering a river it continued floating downstream for some miles until it got entangled in undergrowth. That night people from a nearby village lit bamboo torches and came fishing in the river. Kuwes, a young unmarried woman, thinking the log drum to be an ordinary log, sat on it, Womau put out his hand and pinched her. She jumped up, turned and saw a man inside the log drum. She sat down again, her heart now lost in love to him. Her parents told her to come fishing but she would not move. She did not want another woman to find her lover. Eventually Womau and Fompai went and lived in this village and Womau married Kuwes. By magical means the two brothers did much to help the villagers. They increased the area of their bush by flattening the mountainous country into rolling plains. They also gave them many magical plants. The people however were often scared out of their wits. After Womau and Fompai had stayed a long time at the village, they one day did something wrong. Womau and his wife Kuwes and Fompai then ran away down to the Sepik villages. There the people spent their time fighting and killing each other. When the two brothers told the people to stop this sort of thing they at first listened. But it wasn't long before they were at each others' throats again. So Womau, Kuwes and Fompai left and visited many areas, finally going to far off European land.

Womau and Kuwes' Mistake

Traveling along the road they came to a junction guarded by a soldier. "You follow that road," said the soldier pointing to it. "No, this is our road," said Fompai and walked straight past the soldier. They came to a European woman. "Where are you going?" she asked. "We are trying to find 'God', our ancestor," they replied. "Where do you come from?" continued the woman. "From New Guinea," they replied. "That is really a long way away," said the woman who went to get her husband, the king of the area. He asked the the same questions and received the

same answers. "God doesn't live here", said the woman. "Did you see a soldier guarding the road junction?" she asked. Womau, Kuwes and Fompai then retraced their steps to the road junction. Along the way 'God' met them and set about to test them. "What do you want to work at?" God asked. "We want some *laplaps* (loincloths) replied the wise and shrewd Fompai. God then gave them each a *laplap* which they wrapped around themselves. Fompai sat, but the other two remained standing because they thought the *laplaps* being so thin would break on sitting. Later Womau and Kuwes took off their *laplaps*.

After a night's sleep, Womau and Fompai set to work splitting a tree and planing the timber into planks. Then getting some sheets of corrugated iron they built a house. 'God' gave them the idea of planting cabbages, onions, and tomatoes to offer to himself. Fompai did this, but not Womau because he preferred to eat taro, yams, and sago. Kuwes chipped and washed sago, for they both liked this kind of food. And she much preferred a string skirt to a *laplap*. Womau and Kuwes then ran away back to new Guinea. (Epli then said to me, "You people say that the reason we are not living properly is because of the 'wrong' of Adam and Eve. But that is not right. It is because of the 'wrong' of Womau and Kuwes. If it hadn't been for them we would all be like you people.")

The younger brother Fompai remained in European land and he has not been heard of since. Womau and Fompai's sister is the mother of the Americans. (During World War II the people became acquainted with American soldiers.)

Bad Treatment back in New Guinea

When back in New Guinea Kuwes gave birth to a son whom they called Kofti. They told everybody to stop fighting and killing each other. "Be like the Europeans I saw," Womau would say. "They don't fight, and further, they work hard. You should do the same. Plant food and offer it to God." His wife spoke in similar strain. But the people would not listen. They accused Womau and Kuwes of lying and telling them *bembo* (cargo cult) talk. We have only one son and it is not good for him to grow up in this atmosphere," said Womau to his wife one day. Later Kuwes became pregnant again, but before their baby was born Womau died. Kuwes gave birth to a daughter but died when the placenta did not come away. Kofti seeing his mother dead called out to the villagers to help him bury her. But they would not come because Womau and Kofti had been far too bossy. Neither would they help Kofti look after his newly born sister. "We don't want to care for the child of a dead woman," they said. So Kofti had the heartless task of burying his mother and looking after his baby sister. He continued reiterating what his parents and been telling the people. But the people still refused to listen.

At night the spirits of the parents would return to the house and look after Kofti and their daughter. The mother would pick up her daughter and give her milk.

Because of the continual fighting, one day Kofti picked up his baby sister and went away to another area. But just as much fighting and killing went on there. So once again he set out, this time for European land to find his uncle Fompai. He carried his sister in a loincloth for she was still small and her skin still red.

A Fight with Satan

After sleeping many nights on the road, Kofti and his younger sister arrived in European land and commenced eating their food. His sister grew up quickly and was soon walking, and not much later was a fully grown woman. One day Kofti climbed a tree to see where he was. Seeing a corrugated iron roof about eight miles away they set out for it. Arriving at the house they learned it belonged to Satan, who was away in the bush. When Satan arrived back at his house he invited Kofti and his sister inside. "Where do you two people come from?" he asked. "Oh, we come from New Guinea," they replied. "Are you ghosts or real people?" he asked. "Real people," they replied. Satan said they could sleep the night and then proceeded to get them some food. He brought them wild *mamis*, wild yams, shoots of bush ferns, *Kumu, palpal*, tulip leaves and other New Guinea foods. He cooked this food and then gave it to them. "Satan doesn't give us good food," they said. "This is the bad food New Guineans eat." When Satan wasn't looking they threw it away, and the two ate a little European food they had brought with them. Then they slept.

Early next morning Satan brought a drum filled with water which he heated for them to wash. While Satan was away getting some more food, Kofti and his sister realized that Satan would throw them into the boiling water and kill them. So they decided they had better get in first and throw Satan in. All this time their parents were with them in the form of dogs. Kofti told his sister that they would tip Satan into the boiling water head first when he came back. The two dogs yelped telling them to be sure not to put his body in just his head. Satan returned. "Is the water boiling yet?" he asked as he went to see for himself. "Yes," they replied, and without further ado, Kofti lifted Satan's legs and tipped him head first into the drum of boiling water. The dogs went into his stomach. Kofti found a bayonet and proceeded to cut Satan into very small pieces, upon which the dogs came out of Satan's stomach. Then the small pieces of Satan's flesh were put into the water and boiled. "Let's go now," said his sister not wanting to be around the place any longer. "No, we will sleep first," replied Kofti. So they slept.

Kofti's Sister Leaves Him

Next morning they left and followed the road until they came to a soldier. The dogs followed. The soldier was hiding from another Satan. "Where have you come from?" asked the soldier. "From New Guinea," they replied. Then Kofti asked the soldier where he could find water to wash. The soldier pointed in the direction of some water whereupon Kofti went to wash. While he was away the soldier and Kofti's sister had sex relations. The dogs barked furiously. Kofti came running back and sternly rebuked his sister. So angry was he that he left his sister with the soldier, and calling the dogs to follow, set off by himself. The soldier and Kofti's sister gave birth to Americans.

Appeasement for Another Satan

Further along the road Kofti came to two naked European women hiding behind the buttress of a large tree. "Where have you come from?" they asked him. "I have come from New Guinea," he replied. "You had better not go further along this road because a Satan lives there. He continually deceives us, makes us sick, kills us, and now everybody has decided that he should be given the the king's daughter to eat so that he will be appeased and leave us all alone. After Satan has eaten her then we can return to our village safely." Kofti slept the night near the women and next morning set out along the road taking no heed of their warnings.

Satan was away in the bush when Kofti arrived at his house. Entering he saw the king's daughter sitting by herself. He promptly pulled the woman out of the house, took a ring off his finger and put it on hers, and sent her back to her village. When she had gone about two hundred yards Satan arrived back. Satan and Kofti talked together. She stood and watched. A soldier hiding in another direction also watched. "Where have you come from?" asked Satan. "From New Guinea," he replied in a friendly tone. "Come," said Satan, "let us shake hands." So the two shook hands. Kofti pulled Satan's hand. Satan also pulled Kofti's hand, and each tried to pull the other's hand off. They pulled and pulled. When Kofti was out of breath, the two dogs went for Satan. The male dog went for Satan's nose and the female for his genitals. They bit and ate and before long Satan fell down dead. Exhausted by the duel, Kofti lay on the ground. When he got his breath back he found a bayonet and cut off Satan's head, upon which the dogs let him go. Kofti then cut Satan's body into very small pieces and cooked it in boiling water.

Soldier Tries to Get the Credit

After seeing the duel to the end, the king's daughter went home to her village. The people were angry with her for returning, but she said that Satan himself had sent her back. The soldier also went home to the village and that night told the people he had something important to say. Word went out over a large area for everyone to come and hear the talk. He saw to it that a special platform on which he could stand was built while talking to the people. Kofti, suspicious of the soldier told the two women to stay where they were while he went and heard what the soldier had to say. Finding a horse he rode it to the village. He

tied up the horse outside the king's property, went to the house and asked the domestic servant for a drink of water for his two dogs. The king's servant got a small plate that cats drink from, and filling it with water put it on the ground for the dogs. Kofti was furious. "Are these bad dogs?" he asked. "Why have you given them a small dirty plate that cats drink out of? Go on, get a good plate that people eat from."

The startled servant went and told the king of the incident. The king came and spoke to Kofti asking him where he came from. "I have come from New Guinea," he replied. Looking intently at Kofti, the king summed him up to be a good man with a lot of knowledge. He therefore instructed the servant to give the man just what he wanted. So the dogs drank from a good plate.

At this moment the soldier commenced talking to everybody as he stood on the specially erected dais. "You people, everyone here today," he cried. "I myself have killed and cut up two Satans who have been continually terrorizing us. They will eat us no more. Now we will live our lives peace." On hearing this the king's daughter went and spoke to her father. "This man is lying. You look at that man with the black skin sitting down there. That is the man who sent me back to you. He is the man who gave me this ring and who killed the Satan," she said. "All right," said the king to his daughter, "You listen to me." He stood, and in a loud voice called out to the soldier. "Are you telling the truth or are you lying?" he asked.

"I think you are lying. It was not you but another man who killed the Satans," he said. The soldier hung his head in shame, for he was then not able to say anything. The king continued. "Go on you people, have a good look at him. Has he got anything to say?" The soldier descended from the dais thoroughly disgraced. Shortly afterwards they all went back to their villages.

Kofti Brings Power to Europeans

Kofti then went back to the two women who were still hiding behind the tree. "Come on," he said to them, "We will go back to the village." "Satan will eat us," they replied. "No he won't," said Kofti, "a soldier has killed him."

As they walked back together the two women asked Kofti to marry them. He refused. When they insisted, he only agreed that they cook food for him, which they did.

At Kofti's request the people in the village built him a house. When Kofti saw that the posts were not put in straight he took them all out. Next morning the people arose to find the house completed and full of decorations, possessions, cloths and goods of all kinds.

The following morning the people again arose to see many new houses in the village, all full of goods. The people said, "We Europeans haven't got many goods, but this man with the black skin has come to live among us and lots of good houses have been built by him, and goods have come his way. Yet no goods have come to us. Why is this? What about us?"

The Europeans kept working away without much reward for their labors. Then one day the king said to his daughter, "You must marry this man." He spoke to Kofti saying he should marry his daughter. "No, I didn't come to marry," he said. "I want to remain single."

The king kept on asking but still the man from New Guinea remained firm. Then the king told his daughter to get up and go and live with the New Guinean, which she did. She cooked his food, lived with him, and the two were married and remained in European land. And so Europeans have possessions, prestige and power.

An Interpretation of the Myth

It is difficult to recognize in this myth much objective historical fact either in symbolic or non-symbolic form. In other Wape myths one often feels there is a thread of truth running through the narratives. But it has to be faced that the people unquestioningly believe this story and on the village level at least, will continue to believe it (or something like it) for many years and generations.

Efforts to prove by scientific means that myths are fantasy and not fact seldom if ever succeed. Endeavoring to expose the falsity of such stories by objective reasoning and empirical means is like trying to determine whether a piece of music is good or bad by a foot rule. Another standard is needed. Such efforts often result in mythology going underground. This makes it very difficult to say the least. We can learn something of the people's worldview or cosmology from such myths. Whether the local worldview originally came from their mythology or vice versa is not known. The two are entirely consistent with each other. The narrative is permeated by spirit magic forces. The events are so fantastic to our scientifically oriented minds that we regard the whole story as fantasy. Not so to the New Guinean, for causality questions do not seem to bother him. Spirit magic power is able to do practically anything. The pragmatic "what" and "how" questions don't concern him nearly as much as the philosophic "who" and "why" propositions: It is expedient that they find satisfactory answers to these questions for only then can their spirits and magic be manipulated for their good.

Also shown in the story is the high estimation the people have of themselves. Of course such ethnocentricity and egocentricity are common to all peoples. With the first people (their direct ancestors) being created on their land the Wape folk believe they are, in our idiom, "the hub of the universe," and even "God's own people." After all, it was one of their culture heroes who, in helping us Europeans, brought us to our present state of prestige, power and plenty.

Another factor in their worldview shown by the myth is the close relationship between living humans and ancestral spirits, the latter knowing all that goes on in the world. Things and animals in the world are thought to be either filled with or potential containers of spirit magic power. For example, Kofti's dead parents looked after their living baby daughter (Kofti's young sister) and later in the form of dogs followed and helped Kofti defeat the Satans. Thus things, birds, animals and the world itself, all have animistic meaning and power.

The myth also shows that death is not thought to be natural in that it was not originally intended by Furu.

The Value System

Closely related to the worldview, or even part of it, is the value system. Spirit magic power is highly valued, for possession of it secures material things which in turn give prestige and social power. The possession of things is proof of having spirit power. Kofti had abundant spirit power and used it to his advantage.

The incident where Fompai refused marriage is understood to show that he was a really strong man— While in many cultures status increases with marriage, and continues to increase with each additional wife, this is not always the case among the Wape. A young man strong enough to refuse marriage is respected, even though the refusal may be more in the realm of "ideal" than "actual" behavior.

Their culture heroes had a certain modesty about them. They liked to play down their power and not blow their own trumpets. Perhaps this was to give a greater element of surprise when others suddenly became aware of their strength.

Fighting, killing, and disobedience are not right. Such acts have bad and lasting consequences. For example one act of refusal to drink the special concoction prepared by Womau and Fompai resulted in all humans dying from that time onwards. It also meant that we speak different languages. Again, the fighting and killing carried on by the Wape people resulted in their culture heroes leaving them to help Europeans. Ever since, Europeans have had everything, leaving the Wape people in a much inferior position.

Functions of the Myth

1. The ethnocentricity of the myth already mentioned fulfills a most important function in helping the people experience their identity, security and destiny. The narrative helps answer such basic and universal questions as "Who are we?" "Where did we come from?" "Where are we going?" "What is the meaning of our existence?" Of course these questions are also asked in the first person singular. Folk societies, or anyone for that matter, can seldom explicitly formulate such questions. But they are there nevertheless.

In comparison with many of the peoples of the Highlands of New Guinea, the Wape people are relatively insecure, and thus this function of the myth is important in the present situation. When a people's cultural heritage (and this includes their mythology) is abandoned instead of being modified and reinterpreted, the vacuum and resulting insecurity can be devastating.

2. The myth plays a unifying role in the culture. The myth (regarded as objective history), and the world

view-value system, in reinforcing and validating each other, integrate the various aspects of their culture into a unified whole.

3. Such mythology is the basis for determining accepted behavior. It is the foundation of the code of ethics. Further, prescribed behavior is enforced by fear of the spirit world and social pressure. For example, the myth shows that the reason why New Guineans do not have the prestige power and goods of Europeans is that they would not obey the injunction to stop fighting and listen to their leaders. Disobedience of the command of Womau and Fompai in not drinking the magical concoction had its unfortunate consequences also. Obedience is stressed in another Wape myth which gives the origin of the moon. A man who found a round shining object in a water hole took it home. From then on he used it at night whenever he needed a light. It was very useful for he no longer needed to light bamboo torches. During the day it was safely kept inside his house up in the roof, and his children were told to never touch it. One day when other children came to the house, the man's children disobeyed. Carefully they took the round shining object down and showed it to their visitors. Suddenly it escaped out of their hands and went up into the top of a tree. When the children climbed the tree it jumped to another tree, and finally went right up into the sky where it now remains.

The retelling of such myths has the effect of making children obedient. The Old Testament stories also are intended to have a salutary effect on our behavior.

4. The myth reveals a very real tension common to many parts of New Guinea. It concerns the great disparity between Europeans and New Guineans in the matter of power, possessions, and prestige. This is brought about through a conflict between their worldview-value system, and the actual situation. Their ethnocentric outlook declares them to be basically superior to any other people, including the white man. They, the important Wape people, should have more spirit power than others as proved by owning an abundance of possessions. Yet Europeans have more than they. So tension arises. This myth, in giving a logical explanation of the present situation, does no violence to either their worldview, value system, culture heroes, or the local setting. Their ethnocentricity is retained in believing that it was their culture heroes who gave the white man his present position. Further, surely the way is still open for them to become like Europeans. It must be. Womau and Fompai won't forget us, will they? So hope is retained in their hearts.

From such mythology it is not difficult to see the logic behind the several cargo cults which have arisen from time to time in this and other parts of the Territory. Myths give logical explanations to the existence of things even though they deal more with the "why" than the "how" of creation and events.

5. Narrators of the myth and the listening audience experience great satisfaction as they participate in reliving the events. No doubt illit-erate societies have a void filled by such participation. We Westerners have our books.

Changes in the Myth

Obviously there have been several changes in the myth over the years. For example, the original account of creation where Furu makes the first man is so similar to the Biblical account that it seem likely to have been inserted into the narrative after the early missionaries arrived. The latter part of the myth which deals with the encounter with the Europeans appears to be of a different order from the first portion. Certainly it is of much later origin, for the white man was not in the area prior to the 1930's. So the latter part of the narrative could not be more than 40 years old at the most. Many Pidgin words for English concepts such as king, soldier, Satan, God, bayonet, corrugated iron, cabbages, onions, etc. are assimilated into the story. Though there are a number of good Wape words for spirits and ghosts which correspond to the concept of Satan yet the word Satan is used.

On the other hand there are parts of the narrative resistant to change. For example, the Biblical account of woman being made from a man's rib is rejected. Sympathetic magic operating on an image of a woman and bringing her to life is to them a more logical explanation of her creation. To them it has more of a ring of truth about it. Although God is taking Furu's place (the name Furu is not known outside Epli's village), culture heroes Womau and Fompai will likely remain for many years.

Their names give emotional feelings of importance and belonging to the Wape folk.

Changes in the myth are still acceptable providing there is no violence done to the worldview, tribal ethnocentricity, culture heroes, or the local setting. Another condition would be that satisfactory answers be given to their tensions and questions. This doesn't really give much latitude.

Whenever I played the taped narrative to a few of the neighboring villages the people without exception listened most attentively. Then they discussed it among themselves. Most had heard the story before, or one of the many versions of it. Culture heroes Womau and Fompai are claimed by many villages. Of course even listening to the myth provided the opportunity for them to participate emotionally in the events. And they were very pleased that I now knew the narrative and yet didn't ridicule them in any way. At one village the men said to me after listening to the tape right through, "Let's sit down together and you put your history with ours, and together we will make one story."

They believe the white man has at least some truth and some secrets capable of releasing powerful spirit magic. Of course I was not able to accede to their request, for I come from a background where truth is regarded as a matter of factual reality and cannot be modified to fit in to local mythology. Even had I been willing to do what they wanted, I would not have known where to start. It seems to me that the peo-

ple themselves are the only ones who can modify their stories.

It is unrealistic to think that the people will one day forget or reject their myths simply because we ignore them. The only situation where this could work is where individuals are taken out of their village and culture, educated in an institution and reoriented into urban life. Such an approach is hardly possible for the majority who have no option but to remain in their villages.

Important Questions Raised

Answers are required to some rather basic questions. What is to be the relationship between the people's mythology and the biblical stories, between the world in which they live and that into which they are emerging? The people need help in finding satisfactory answers. The above realms cannot be kept separate. Even if it were possible for the people to hold two value systems, two histories, and two sets of beliefs side by side without conflict, this would be undesirable. Where unconscious attempts have been made along this line, chiefly in the Western world, hypocrisy abounds. Neither of the two conflicting viewpoints is fully believed, and a dangerous discrepancy emerges between ideal and actual behavior.

It is inevitable that the people by themselves will reach some unified system in which these realms are harmonized. Their understanding of the world and life as a unity is quite remarkable. The danger of course is that the people will interpret Scripture by their mythology, and fit it into their mythology, rejecting or radically twisting parts of the biblical teaching not easily accommodated. Where this sort of thing happens not only is biblical theology damaged, but syncreticism is an ever-present danger.

It is granted that the people have no alternative but to interpret Scripture by their cultural background, but there are some interpretations better than others, and some are wrong. The Bible does not specifically deal with their history for it was written in another land, within another culture. Wape history is not mentioned, and neither do Europeans know Wape history.

Meeting the Situation

It appears to me there are four valid ways the people may deal with their mythology and the situation. They are not mutually exclusive and each has its place. Our role is to in some way suggest these alternatives.

1. There are a few myths which raise no serious conflict with either the biblical accounts or life today. These may be left as they are, at least for the time being. It could be argued that should some of the myths which deal with the origins of things continue to be believed for a while, there will be no real damage done to theology nor likelihood of syncretism, providing it is understood that God is over all.

2. Other myths may be rejected as being historically untrue by the majority of the people. The realization of this will be gradual. There will be no official pronouncement by the village leaders but just a growing awareness of their incredibility. They then become the equivalent of our children's fairy stories.

3. Other myths, as has been already stated, may be modified by the people. Only changes which are consistent with their worldview will be accepted, however. This highlights the necessity of helping the people change their worldview, and this is, as we all know, a slow process. In this regard the missionary should not lag behind nor go ahead. Discussions with the people, giving alternatives and the freedom to choose and reject, the ability to act as a mirror for them, a knowledge of their vernacular and existing worldview are all necessary.

4. The fourth method aims to help the people give a more Christian interpretation to their myths. Like everything else, myths have to be interpreted. Sickness, adversity, health, things and events all have meaning, and each has several possible interpretations. Some are true, others are false, and some better than others. Paul Tournier in his books points out that the meaning of a thing is often more important than the thing itself.

There can only be a satisfactory relationship between the myth and Bible teaching where there is some sort of realization of the true meaning of the myth. It is not so much that the story needs to be changed or rejected as that a more Christian interpretation and meaning must be arrived at.

For example, there is a close relationship, it seems to me, between tribal ethnocentricity (and egocentricity) and God's love and concern for us. When an individual comes into an experience of God's love, he is unaware that he is only one of countless other people all being loved by the same God. God's love makes him important and establishes his identity with God. This may and should be translated into tribal security.

Another example of an interpretation in the right direction would be the relationship between spirit magic power, and God's power which he exercises through individuals when they know him and do his will. Perhaps the reason for the mistakes of even their culture heroes was that they did not do what God wanted them to do. How much more good would they have done had they completely obeyed him.

Of course Womau and Fompai's exhortations against fighting and killing are already in line with New Testament ethics.

An animistic interpretation of the myth would be simply, lust for spirit magic power, prestige, and possessions at other people's expense. Such desires may consume participants like a fire.

Therefore in facing the problems raised by mythology an effort should be made to help the people intrepret the myths more correctly and to find their true meaning. We need not worry too much about the specific acts in the mythology which at first seem so contrary to Christian ideals.

This fourth method seems to me the most important.

Conclusion

In the above four approaches we need to realize two things. Firstly, the revelation of God is progressive. This is true in Scripture, in history, in a culture, and in the life of an individual. Thus the interpretations, meanings and answers people accept may not always correspond with ours. But they may be steps in the right direction, and this is what matters. Far better to make slow progress at the grass roots level than have rapid superficial growth on a temporary basis. I recall what one of the leaders of the area said to me recently, "When we steal from someone else's garden we get sick," he said. "We used to think that it was the spirit that made us sick. But I think we were wrong. It is not the spirits but God." We could not wholly concur with this statement, but it seems to be a step in the right direction. And for that man at that time it was the right answer.

Secondly, truth is communicated through the symbolic vehicle of cultural forms. These are the languages, thought forms, worldviews, value systems, magical beliefs, and even the mythologies of diverse cultures. The Good News of Jesus Christ has been communicated through many of these exterior vehicles. They are not God's revelation but are necessary carriers of his message.

Concepts learned from mythological material can be used to real advantage in telling and making understood the Good News of Jesus Christ. The abundance of illustrative material in the myths can be profitably used for the same purpose. However, it needs to be remembered that these concepts and illustrative material belong to the total culture, and cannot always be lifted out of the immediate context. This has to be continually reckoned with.

When we know more of the local mythology and total culture, the people will more readily come to us with their problems which sometimes they themselves cannot formulate in to words. They will come to us because they trust us and realize that we are aware of what they believe.

Marilyn Bergman Gregerson

Rengao Myths:
A Window on the Culture

IT IS frequently the case in the scientific investigation of complex phenomena that far-reaching insights may be gained by scrutinizing the entire mass of data as it relates to one aspect or feature of the whole. This is especially the case when the focal aspect widely pervades or plays a central role in the entire system under analysis.

It is suggested in this paper that the field worker who is studying the language and culture of a people with a view to effectively communicating the Christian message can fix on no more fruitful entering wedge than the analysis of the myths of that culture.

As the well-known functionalist Malinowski expressed it:

> Studied alive, myth is not symbolic, but a direct expression of its subject matter. It is not an explanation in satisfaction of a scientific interest, but a narrative

Marilyn Bergman Gregerson is, with her husband, a missionary linguist serving in Vietnam with the Summer Institute of Linguistics. She has worked among the Rengao for one and one-half years. She holds an M.A. in anthropology from the University of Minnesota, and is currently chairman of the Anthropology Committee of the Vietnam Branch of S.I.L. Kontum, Vietnam.

resurrection of a primeval reality, told in satisfaction of deep religious wants, moral cravings, social submissions, assertions, even practical requirements. Myth fulfills in primitive culture an indispensable function. It expresses, enhances, and codifies belief; it safeguards and enforces morality; it vouches for the efficiency of ritual and contains practical rules for the guidance of man. Myth is thus a vital ingredient of human civilization; it is not an idle tale, but a hardworked active force; it is not an intellectual explanation or an artistic imagery, but a pragmatic charter of primitive faith and moral wisdom.[1]

The study of myths is especially relevant for the missionary because 1) in general, it is an effective means of getting at the whole spectrum of cultural concerns; 2) in particular, it involves one immediately in the study of the belief system which is of primary relevance in communicating the Gospel.

The Rengao

The Rengao are a Mon-Khmer

[1] Bronislaw Malinowski, "Myth in Primitive Psychology," in *Magic, Science, and Religion* (Glencoe, Ill.: The Free press, 1948), p. 101

348

peaking group inhabiting an area in South Vietnam's central highlands stretching between Kontum City and the Laotian border.

Roman Catholic missions began work among the Rengao many decades ago and now have quite a number of adherents in villages in the Kontum City vicinity. Many of these Rengao apparently did not know some of the origin myths given us by animistic believing Rengao. The Christianized Rengao seem to have adopted the Biblical accounts to a large degree. They do, however, believe in the existence of some of the spirits though they do not sacrifice to them. They do believe in ghosts and sometimes practice sorcery.

During recent years the Rengao have been in a state of rapid culture change due to the war. The young men enter military service which takes them away from the hitherto tightly knit village life and acquaints them with the values and attitudes of the national and foreign cultures. The recent availability of the motorbike has also given the young men greater mobility, thus contributing another factor to the rapid culture change.

Malinowski reported that the Trobriand Islanders had different words for each of the categories: folktales, legends, and myths The Rengao have only one word which we translate "story" with a corresponding lack of sharp distinctions separating these three theoretical types of accounts. The same characters figure in tales that are apparently told only for pleasure as appear in myths that are told to explain origins or support the existing institutions.

A fair amount of prestige accrues to the person who is a good story teller. Such a person is adept at the forceful use of expressive words, words comparable to *clippity-clop* (for horses running) and *zing* (for an arrow's flight) in English. He is also skillful in employing the rhyme formula. This form is constructed by putting two phrases together in such a way that the final word of the preceding phrase rhymes with the initial word of the following phrase and in which the first words of each phrase are somehow semantically parallel.

Explanations of the Physical World

In Rengao mythology, the world, the stars, the moon and the sun were in general brought into existence by Grandfather Thunder (*Bobrok*). Grand-father Thunder now lives in the sky and the sound of thunder is his voice.

According to Rengao cosmogony, there is a world renewal every three thousand years. One informant told us that now 1,969 years have passed since the last world was destroyed by flood. The people living on the earth at that time were swept up by the rising flood and deposited in the sky where they now appear as stars and other heavenly bodies.

The constellation that we call the the Big Dipper is explained in this way: two brothers, Tang and Sit, went to put a bird trap up in a banyan tree. After putting up the trap, the older brother came down down, and then cut the large root supports coming down from the top of the tree. Thus as one looks up in the sky (at the Big Dipper) one can see a banyan tree. At the top of the tree is Sit, who is stuck up there. His older brother would not leave him and is still waiting at the bottom of the tree.

The second highest deity in the Pantheon is Grandmother Pom. She also lives in the sky and when the moon is out she can be seen in the markings on the face of the moon. To the Rengao she appears to be standing under a banyan tree pounding rice.

Various local topographical phenomena are also explained by myths:

Once there were two brother elephants. The older one fought a giant fish and was killed by the fish. The younger brother waited until he was big enough so that his footprints matched his brother's and then he went off to fight the fish. He wounded the fish so badly that the fish died, but he was also mortally wounded and died.

Two large mountains in the area are the remains of the elephants who turned to stone when they died. Some holes in a large rock are the place where the elephants sharpened their tusks before fighting the fish.

The mythological Paul Bunyan-like Tang and his younger brother Sit are said to be responsible for still other local physical features. Some curiously large depressions in stone on either side of the river near one of their villages are explained

as Tang's footprints where he stood straddling the river as he was making dams. Three narrow gorges in the area are the dams which Tang made to catch fish, but which another character, Bogap, broke open. Bogap, a cannibal, opened them because he hoped people would then fall from them and he would be able to eat them.

The soil around Kontum is a rather blackish color and is said to be less fertile than the red soil found further south near Pleiku. This is all a result of an argument long ago between the rich man and Grandmother Pom, in which he accused her of stealing his soil and therefore having better crops than he. She denied it but said she would "give his soil back" if he felt that way. So it was that she took his red soil to make room to "replace" the soil she had "stolen" from him. Then with a sweep of her arm she "returned" his (black) soil to him.

A strange rock formation in a nearby village is said to be the remains of a man who married a rock spirit. They lived in his village for a time and had a child. Then the rock spirit wanted to return to the rocks. In an attempt to follow her, he reached into the stone, but could not further enter. He died there and turned to stone.

As for fire, it is said to have been lost (its initial origin is unknown) and then re-created by Grandmother Pom. She made fire by rubbing a rattan cord and a certain kind of wood together and from it igniting charcoal. The fact that Grandmother

Pom brought fire into existence is perhaps connected with her important role as the spirit who taught man to raise and eat rice, their main food and one that requires fire for cooking.

Trees were created by the spirit Nang Grai who now lives in water. The banyan tree is the most important tree in Rengao mythology. Its origin is as follows:

Nang Grai gave Grandmother Pom the seed of the banyan tree. She planted it in her front yard and some elephants came along and tried to knock it down. They were persuaded not to knock it down completely but had already bent it over, and so it often grows at an angle today. Some birds came along and ate some of the fruit. The spirit in the seeds that they had eaten said to the birds, "If you defecate on the ground, I won't grow, but if you defecate on a tree, I'll grow, and not long after I'll furnish food for you to live." So the birds defecated on a tree and the banyan tree grew there, sending its roots down and using the host tree for its own use until it had finally killed the tree.

Human Origins

The period following creation seems to be a sort of mythological golden age. There is some dispute among the Rengao as to whether or not those who lived in this age were spirits or people. Perhaps they are most accurately viewed as a combination of both, for though they were possessed of human characteristics and engaged in human activities, they were also capable of prodigious supernatural feats.

Grandfather Thunder is always referred to as the original spirit, but Grandmother Pom as well seems to have no origin, and apparently always existed. Grandmother Pom and Grandfather Thunder were not married nor did they have any children by anyone else. Grandmother Pom took a boy named Torit to live with her and treated him as a grandson. Some say that Torit was the child of Sit and Tang's younger sister, Luy. At any rate Grandfather Thunder is credited with having made the first people, though informents were unable to relate an account of how this was done.

Proper chronology of events does not seem to be the focal point in Rengao mythology, and informants have different ideas about when certain events took place. Apparently, however, at the end of the golden age came the great flood, the account which runs as follows:

Grandfather and Grandmother Drum (Hogar) made a big drum and climbed inside of it along with two of each of all of the animals. After they were inside, the water started coming up from the ground and the earth sank down into the water as fire consumed the earth from beneath. Then as the sun shone down, the water dried up. When the earth was dry again, they cut open the drum and came out. Then *God* made the mountains and trees over again just as they had been made before.

In this myth the one who made the mountains and trees over again is not identified as Grandfather Thunder but as the Christian God (Father Spirit). This may be evidence that Grandfather Thunder and God have been syncretized in the thinking of at least some Rengao. Grandfather Drum and Noah have also become so syncretized that now some Catholic Rengao say, "Grandfather Drum is the Rengao word for Noah."

The myth of the flood goes on to say that after Grandfather and Grandmother Drum had had several children they became drunk and their children helped cover up their parent's nakedness but the others just ran away. Those who covered up their parent's nakedness were the ancestors of the Vietnamese, the French and the Americans. Those who ran away were the forebears of the various Montagnard tribes in this area, the Bahnar, Sedang, Jarai, Rengao, Halang, etc. "They didn't cover up their parent's nakedness and that is why we montagnards are so ignorant." Thus the Rengao myth teller explains the disparities with respect to civilization and technology that the "curse of Ham" from the Biblical account (Genesis 9:25) has been appropriated as applying to the Rengao and other tribal groups and substantiates their feeling of cultural inferiority.

The origin of the Rengao people themselves is traced back to two descendants of Grandfather and Grandmother Drum. They are Grandfather Tanung and Grandmother Goat who appear in a myth as the ones who bought their present territory from the Laotians. They had two sons and a daughter. The daughter died of a broken heart over a Laotian prince who jilted her. The Rengao say, "Grandmother Goat raised goats, and that is why we Rengao can only eat goat meat in sacrifice." Whether this constitutes a form of totemism is not yet clear.

Economy and Technology

Grandmother Pom as a type of fertility goddess is concerned with the various activities of plant food production and especially rice. She originally gave people rice, showed them how to plant it and even taught them how to cook it. One myth in particular gives the hearer instruction as to the proper way to raise rice.

Torit and another boy had no father and mother so they tried to sneak rice from other people's rice houses. Then Grandmother Pom appeared to Torit in a dream and told him to clear a small clump of bamboo for a rice field. Then she told him to go plant rice there.

Yang Hri, the rice spirit, whom Grandmother Pom had made, came to the rich man's house. He looked as if he was covered all over with a reddish rash (mountain rice is brown or red). The rich man wouldn't let him in and told him to go down to Torit's little hut. So Yang Hri went down to live with the boys. Then he caused a big rainstorm and went to the rich man's house to see if he would pity him and take him in, but the rich man still wouldn't let him come in. Then Yang Hri went back to live with the boys. They had no tools so he stole tools from the rich man for them. Then Yang Hri told them to get some large bamboo lengths. When they brought them to him, he filled them with rice for storing and some for eating. Then Yang Hri got ready to leave. He said there was no need for rain now so he would go. He told them they should sacrifice. They said they didn't have anything to sacrifice. He told them to cut off the long handles from the axes and hoes and sell them to buy pigs and chickens. They bought a big pig and sacrificed it and got an abundant rice crop. Afterwards Yang Hri appeared in a Dream and told them to build five rice houses. He told them to celebrate the "taking up" of the rice into the rice house by sacrificing a chicken. At that time Yang Hri himself also "Went up" to live with Grandmother Pom until harvest was complete. The boys took the chicken's blood, put it on the bottom of the basket so the soul of the rice would live in the basket, and then went and harvested the rice. They filled all five rice houses from their one little plot of ground. The rich man said, "You've only got a little patch and I've got big fields and lots, of slaves. How could you get so

much?" It was because Yang Hri had called the souls of the rice of the other fields to come to the field of the boys. Then Yang Hri told them to celebrate "the taking down" of the rice for token eating. So the boys sold one house of rice and bought a water buffalo, a goat, and a pig. These they sacrificed as they took some rice down to their hut to cook it. Then Yang Hri and Grandmother Pom descended together in a fury of wind and rain. The boys heard their voices but couldn't see them, so that is why the Rengao sacrifice today according to what Grandmother Pom said.

In present-day practice, Torit is one of the spirits to whom sacrifice is made at planting time. The present ceremonial taking up and taking down of the rice seem to recapitulate the ascending and descending of the spirits in this myth. Though among the Rengao industry is valued and laziness scorned, most important of all is the maintaining of a proper relationship with the spiritual world. In another myth, for example, Grandmother Pom tells Torit, her intermediary with humans, "If they sacrifice a lot, we'll give them a lot of rice, but if they sacrifice just a little, we'll give them just a little rice." Theoretically then, the success of the rice crop is in proportion to the amount of sacrificing that is done.

When Grandmother and Grandfather Drum came out of the drum

after the flood they prepared fields,
then planted rice. After planting
they sacrificed. When the rice was
knee-high they sacrificed again.
When they took the rice up to the
rice house after harvest, they sacrificed again. And finally when
they began taking rice down from
the rice house and over to their own
houses to cook they sacrificed
again. To the present time it is the
practice to sacrifice to the spirits
at these four junctions in the rice
cycle. Catholic Rengao do not sacrifice, but on the same four occasions they kill animals for a feast
and invoke God's blessing. This seems
to have provided a quite natural
functional substitute celebration.

Rengao houses are constructed
on pilings with wooden floors, mud
walls, and thatched roofs. Torit, the
"grandson" of Grandmother Pom,
originally taught people how to make
houses.

The rich man made a house and
used large leaves to make the
roof. Torit also made a house
and used small grass-like leaves
which had been thoroughly dried
for the roof. When the rainstorns
came, the rich man's house was
all torn up, but Torit's house
wasn't disturbed. The rich man
sent his slaves over to check on
Torit's house. They found Torit's
house so cozy and nice that they
just stayed there and warmed
themselves. So Torit taught the
rich man how to thatch roofs
and so it is to this day, because
the spirits and *God* enlightened
Torit.

In the center of each Rengao
village is a communal house, This
house is used for meetings and for
entertaining guests who come to
the village. All of the boys and
young bachelors of the village sleep
in the communal house. The appearance of the communal house
seems to be a real matter of pride
to the villagers, and the taller and
more graceful it is the better. One
myth is told to validate the building of communal houses by the
Rengao,

The rich man located a spot in
the jungle to build a village.
Sit volunteered to make the
communal house. He worked
and worked at it, but it still
wasn't right. He called his wife
to look at it, but it still wasn't
right. So he tore it down. Finally, it was just right. They called
the rich man to come and
celebrate. When he saw the
communal house, he exclaimed
at its beauty. Then they feasted
on buffalo, cow, horse, and goat.
Sit said he was going off to see
if there were any other communal houses as beautiful as
his. He came to the village of
Dun Dang and saw that their
communal house was more beautiful than his for it glittered
like crystal and gold. He guessed
that its beauty was because a
girl lived there. Sure enough,
he found that Dun Dang's sister,
Crystal, lived up inside the roof
peak above the boys of the
village. She was beautiful and
shone as the sun. He went back
to the village to get his younger

brother, Gya, and soldiers to attack the village and take Crystal as a wife for Gya. When they reached the village to attack it, Dun Dang came out and said he wanted Sit to adopt him. So the go-betweens worked out the arrangements and they went through the adoption ceremony. They invited Crystal to come down, but she wouldn't, so Sit and Gya went up and got her and hauled her away to their house. She wouldn't marry Gya, though, because she already had a boyfriend, Jring Kong. Jring attacked them to get Crystal back, but he lost the battle and Gya kept her for his wife.

The heroes of Sit's era are considered to be the original communal house builders. The removal of the girl from the communal house perhaps explains and reinforces the custom that restricts the house to males only.

Personal Attributes

Individual characteristics that are particularly valued as revealed in Rengao myths are beauty, cleverness, bravery, and industry. If someone is really good looking, he has "got it made," regardless of anything else. The following brings out some of the values in personnal attributes:

Bar Hmeng was the youngest of seven brothers. His brothers got mad at him because he was wise and clever and so they put him in a big back basket and hung it out in the jungle. After a while the string rotted and the basket fell down and he was freed. Bar Hmeng walked on until he came to the place where Torit and Grandmother Pom were making a field. Then he stayed there with thém, and Grandmother Pom became really attached to him. It came to the ear of the rich man what people were saying about Grandmother Pom having a boy who was brave, strong, and really handsome. He asked someone to act as go-between to get him for a husband for his daughter. Now his daughter was beautiful beyond words. The two were very well matched. After the go-between business was finished, they had a wedding ceremony. Then the [rich man turned over to the couple all of his wine jars, gongs, slaves, buffalo, cattle, pigs, and chickens. There they continued to have a happy and prosperous existence in a house that was big and beautiful.

Until recent years, the Rengao have had the practice of filing the teeth of the young men and piercing the ears of both the girls and the boys. The reason given is that Gyong, a figure from the golden age, began doing it to make himself more attractive and then everyone else followed his lead. Informants tell us that when the practice was still carried on, no girl would want to marry someone who hadn't had his teeth filed. Everyone said such a person, besides being ugly, was not worthy because he was not brave.

Property and Wealth

"From rags to riches" is the plot for most Rengao stories. Often the hero of the story gains his material wealth by cleverness or trickery, but even more often by marrying a rich man's daughter. The following myth supports the spirit quest as a way to bring riches:

Plon was very poor. One time someone said something embarrassing about his poverty and he went home and cried himself to sleep. While he was sleeping, his spirit said "Oh Plon, one who is poor needs to go see the spirit over yonder." So Plon started out. That night he came to a big bamboo. He chopped some firewood for himself, and the spirit in the bamboo said, "Oh, who is here cutting a log on my front porch?" He said to Plon, "Why did you come here?" Plon said, "I came to ask you for riches." The spirit invited him to come in and served him rice and wine. That spirit told him he couldn't give him riches, but invited him to stay for the night. The next day he went on to a big tree. The tree spirit came out and invited him to eat and drink and stay overnight, but he also could not give him riches. The next day he went on and talked to the little mountain spirit, who was equally hospitable but suggested he go on to the big mountain spirit. The big mountain spirit told him to go to Grandfather Thunder's village. So he went

on to Grandfather Thunder's village. Now Grandfather Thunder, the chief spirit, was very, very rich. Grandfather Thunder already knew why he had come, but he asked him anyway. Plon was afraid to tell him the real reason, so Grandfather Thunder served him wine until he was drunk. Then he told him why he had come. Grandfather Thunder gave him a piece of iron, and four seeds of rice. He told him to make tools out of the iron, and to plant the seeds in the four corners of a rice field. Plon did as he was told and then he made twenty rice houses. The large field had an abundance of grain. At harvest time, the rice crawled right into the rice houses all by itself and filled all twenty rice houses. That year there was a famine and everyone came to Plon to buy rice. He sold the rice and bought buffalo, gongs and wine jars and became exceedingly rich. Then he sacrificed a buffalo to the spirits.

Among the Rengao, each person has a unique alliance with a particular spirit. Thus the spirit to which Plon was personally allied was the one who told him how to begin his search for wealth. Other spirits associated with physical phenomena could not help him, but Grandfather Thunder, the chief spirit, was able to give riches. Contemporary practice is to sacrifice to Grandfather Thunder in order to become rich. Wealth is measured in livestock, wine jars, kettles, and gongs.

In many stories and myths, the hero or heroine is the youngest child in the family. The story teller creates real sympathy for this youngest child who is often mistreated or the victim of fate. In inheritance practice the Rengao pass property down bilateral lines, but have a tendency toward ultimogeniture, that is, the youngest child is favored in the inheritence.

Often the villain of the story is a rich man and the hero is a poor man, but by the end of the story, the poor man usually becomes rich.

Death and Afterlife

The Rengao explain the origin of death with the following myth:

Long ago whenever someone died they would drink the medicine of death and life and come back to life. Then Jway got jealous of them. He said there wouldn't be enough land for everyone. "Where are we going to put the Jarai, the Bahnar, the Sedang, and the Rengao?" he said. So he pulled a trick on them and stole the medicine of death and life. Since then people have died.

People who die what the Rengao term a "bad death" die because one of seven spirits has taken their soul. A spirit named Royang takes the soul of someone who dies of stabbing or shooting. Grai takes the soul of someone who dies from a fall. A woman who dies during pregnancy or at childbirth dies because the bachelor spirit Yin (who plays a stringed instrument to serenade women) wants to marry her and he sends his bird and dog to her in a dream to act as go-betweens. After her dream, Yin takes her soul and she dies. Grandfather Thunder takes the spirit of someone who dies by lightning. If someone doesn't sacrifice enough, Grandmother Pom will send the spirit Potu to that person who will make him hungry. A person who starves to death does so because Potu has taken his soul.

Myak is the spirit who takes the souls of people who then drown. The following myth is told to validate this belief :

One day two brothers paddled a canoe up the river to cut bamboo. After a while they got hungry so they stopped and started a fire to cook their food. The spirit Myak came out of the water and became a human being in order to kill the two brothers. As he came up on the river bank he asked them where they were going. "How about you, where are you going ?" they said. "Oh, I was just floating down the river and I decided to come over and visit you," he answered. Then he noticed that each of the brothers was carrying a knife. Myak said, "How sharp are your knives?" They answered, "Our knives can cut stone and large hard wood trees, but they can't cut a banana tree." Then Myak told them he had to go home. That night after the boys had eaten and he thought they were sleeping, Myak changed himself into a rock that was as big as a house and was about to roll down on top of them when they pulled out their knives and he was afraid they would cut the rock. Then he changed himself into a hard wood tree and was about to fall over on them but they again pulled out their knives and he was afraid they would cut the hard wood. So he changed himself into a whole grove of banana trees since they had said their knives couldn't cut banana trees. He was about to fall over on them when they pulled out their knives and hacked one of the banana trees in two. Myak's blood poured out of the tree and filled the river. Then the boys went home and sacrificed a pig. Soon after that they both died of malaria.

So Myak who appeared by the river and who was slain by the river has come to be associated with all who die of drowning.

Everyone who dies becomes a ghost. The kind of ghost that one becomes depends upon the type of death one experiences. If one dies a "bad death," he will become a "bad ghost." If he dies a natural death, say from some disease, he will become a "good ghost." Portions of three separate accounts show what information can be gained from myths in regard to the nature of ghosts.

(1) Torit and his three friends went hunting. They were able to shoot quite a few animals, so after preparing the meat for drying, they left one of the young men named Splash Water there to watch it. The young man heard the ghost Twing Twih coming down from the mountain. Closer and closer he came. Splash Water was very much afraid. He was there all alone. Now the ghost Twing Twih was really weird, exceedingly tall, and looked just like a bare skeleton. He asked for some meat, but Splash Water wouldn't give him any. Splash Water tried to spear him, but he couldn't pierce him. Twing Twih got mad. He grabbed Splash Water, pulled hair out of his own beard and tied Splash Water up and threw him on an anthill. Then Twing Twih ate up the meat. The next day someone else stayed, and the same thing happened. The following day the third fellow stayed and was treated the same way. Finally it was Torit's turn to stay. When the ghost Twing Twih came Torit graciously fed him the meat as well as some well-cooked sharpened bones. The ghost ate the bones, then drank cold water which hardened the bones again. The bones pierced his stomach and he died. Then Torit ran to the village of Twing Twih and freed the (human) maidens that Twing Twih had captured. They came back with him and became his secondary wives.

(2) Luy was walking through the forest when she met a child ghost who was carrying her

younger brother on her back while her mother was chopping firewood. The ghost asked her for some dried meat and said she would trade some medicine to heal wounds for the dried meat. Luy accused the ghost of lying. The ghost proved the power of the medicine by killing her younger brother and then making him "live" again. So Luy took the medicine and later used it to bring her fatally wounded husband, Jri Dong, back to life.

(3) A couple had only one daughter. When the daughter was approaching womanhood, the mother died of malaria. After a period of mourning the father and daughter went out to make fields. They would work in the daytime and then at night the mother, who felt sorry for her family, would get some ghosts together and help by working in the field also. Finally the mother came to her daughter in a dream and told her what she was doing and invited her to come and visit her near her grave. That night she went out to her mother's grave and saw her mother rising up out of the ground. Then her mother followed her around and talked with her as she collected viands. The mother kept close watch on her daughter so that other ghosts would not bother her.

These myths verify for the Rengao the existence and nature of ghosts. Ghosts are seen to have certain human characteristics: (a) they carry on humanlike activities such as gathering wood and working the rice fields; (b) they have humanlike needs, eg. they can get hungry: (c) they have emotions such as anger and pity; (d) they can die, though what their status would then be is never a focal point. Their superhuman qualities include: (a) some kind of awesome phantom appearance; and (b) miraculous powers.

Conclusion

It has been the aim of this paper to discuss briefly the role of myths as an integral part of Rengao knowledge and action. It has further been observed that mythology, penetrating as it does into so many areas of culture and involving as it must the belief system, can provide an ideal aspect around which the Christian field worker may meaningfully organize his knowledge of a people.

PART V

Cultural Systems and Manifestations:
Church

William A. Smalley

Cultural Implications of an Indigenous Church

OVER the past generation, a large amount of thought concerning the strategy of modern missions has gone into the question of the relation of the new churches (which have resulted from missionary work) to the missionary body and to the society (the non-Christian culture) around them. It is not my purpose here to go into the extensive literature dealing with this subject, but a classic work, often referred to and widely read, is Roland Allen's *Missionary Methods, St. Paul's or Ours?*[1] The burden of a great deal of this discussion has been the well-taken observation that modern missions have all too often resulted in churches which are tied to the supporting home church in the West, protected by the mother denomination, and unable to stand alone in their society. This is an oversimplification, but I am in substantial agreement with a great deal of it. There are some anthropological problems which have not always been faced in such discussions, however, although many writers have at points touched upon them and Roland Allen seems well aware of many of them.

A False Diagnosis

It seems to have become axiomatic in much missionary thinking that a church

which is "self-governing, self-supporting, and self-propagating" is by definition an "indigenous church." It further seems to follow in the thinking of many people that such an indigenous church (and so defined) is the goal of modern missions. There are some very serious reservations which may be made to this point of view, however, and it is a point of view which may be very misleading as it molds policy for the development of a church, if we look at some of its cultural implications.

It seems to me, first of all, that the criteria of "self-governing, self-supporting, and self-propagating" are not necessarily diagnostic of an indigenous movement. The definition of such a movement has to be sought elsewhere, and, although these three "self" elements may be present in such a movement, they are essentially independent variables. The three "selfs" seem to have become catch phrases which can be stamped without any particular understanding on one church or on another. Yet it is evident on an examination of the facts that they are not necessarily relevant at all.

Misinterpretation of Self-government

It may be very easy to have a self-governing church which is not indigenous. Many presently self-governing churches are not. All that is necessary to do is to indoctrinate a few leaders in Western

[1] Roland Allen, *Missionary Methods, St. Paul's or Ours?* (Chicago: Moody Press, 1956).

Reprinted from Vol. 5, No. 2 (1958), pp. 51-65.

patterns of church government, and let them take over. The result will be a church governed in a slavishly foreign manner (although probably modified at points in the direction of local government patterns), but by no stretch of imagination can it be called an indigenous ment patterns), but by no stretch of of mission fields today under the misguided assumption that an "indigenous" church has been founded.

It is further possible for a genuinely indigenous Christian movement to be "governed" to a degree by foreigners. Even in the large-scale Christward movements which have taken place in the world, movements which have been so extensive that the foreign body has had more difficulty in controlling them than what it has had in most of its mission work, the mission body has often exerted its governing influence upon the upper level of the society, at least, where it was related in any way to the movement. This may have been by the direct action of missionaries or by the action of church leaders who were trained in the foreign patterns of government. Although such government may be unfortunate in many cases, it does not in the least detract from the indigenous nature of such a Christward movement on the part of a group of people.

Misapplication of Self-support

It is unlikely that there would be any disagreement with the idea that the Jerusalem church in the first century was an indigenous church. The Jerusalem Christians were so strongly Jewish in their attitudes that they resented the conversion of Gentiles unless they joined the Jewish ritualistic performance of the law. That church, however, in its time of need received gifts from abroad, from Europe — in modern-day terminology, from the West. Paul himself carried some of those gifts to Jerusalem. No one would argue that the receiving of such gifts infringed upon the indigenous nature of the Jewish church.

Neither can one argue, I believe, that the receiving of such gifts by the younger churches today will necessarily infringe upon their indigenous character. This is true in spite of the very real dangers which exist in the subsidy of the younger churches by the mission bodies.

I was in Indo-China as a missionary during some of the years of civil war. Those were days when the whole country was badly upset, when church congregations could be cut off from the mission without more than a few hours notice as the battle line shifted, when groups which had been under mission subsidy could suddenly lose their mission help and be placed in a fearful economic position. Together with most of my colleagues, I felt the tremendous weakness of a missionary program which was based upon the foreign financing of its national workers. In a time of crisis such as that we worked hard to see to it that the church was placed on a footing of self-support.

Self-support is, wherever possible, really the soundest method of church economics. It is healthy for the church and for the mission, but there certainly are situations in which it is not possible, or where it is not advisable, where self-support can make church growth nearly impossible, and in such situations its presence does not necessarily imply the lack of an indigenous church. It is an independent variable within the pattern of the mission and church. All depends on how the problems are handled, and how the temptation to control church life through the manipulation of funds is resisted by the mission body. If foreign funds are handled in an indigenous way, they may still have their dangers, but they do not preclude an indigenous church.

Examples of areas in which the younger churches can usually not be expected to be self-supporting are publication, Bible translation, education, health and medicine, and many other fields entirely outside the range of their economy. These are not indigenous activities, but they are valuable activities for many churches in the modern world. Whether or not such things enter into the life of a church in an "indigenous manner" is entirely dependent upon the way in which the changes take place, not the source of income. If the changes in the younger church society take place as the result of the fulfillment of a strongly felt need, and in a manner planned and executed by them for their own purposes and in their own way, the simple presence of foreign funds in the project does not destroy its indigenous character.

The richness of Western economy makes it possible for many Western church groups not to need to seek for funds elsewhere. However, even in the rich West many groups have to seek for funds from foundations or other institutions. This does not destroy their indigenous character in the least; it is simply a part of the Western economic scene. Such economic possibilities are usually not open to the younger churches except as they seek their help from the mission body. It is the way the funds are administered, the way the decisions are made, and the purposes to which they are put, that are diagnostic of an indigenous

church, not the presence or absence of such foreign funds.

It would be hard to think of any more fiercely or self-consciously independent country than India today, yet it receives large sums from abroad to bolster its economy and to do things which badly need to be done for its people. On the other hand, it would be very easy to find many examples of self-supporting churches in which the basic indigenous character is not present. There is, for example, a church which is advertised by its founding mission as a great indigenous church, where its pastors are completely supported by the local church members, yet the mission behind the scenes pulls the strings and the church does its bidding like the puppets of the "independent" iron curtain countries. This colonial manipulation may even be quite unconscious on the part of the missionaries. If the church makes its own decisions, without outside interference, as to how its funds shall be used, and does so on the basis of economic patterns natural to it in its own cultural setting, this church may be considered indigenous, even if funds are provided by an outside source.

Misunderstanding of Self-propagation

Of the three "selfs," it seems to me that that of self-propagating is the most nearly diagnostic of an indigenous church, but here again the correlation is by no means complete. In a few areas of the world it may be precisely the foreignness of the church which is the source of attraction to unbelievers. There are parts of the world where aspirations of people lead them toward wanting to identify themselves with the strong and powerful West, and where the church provides such an avenue of identification.[2] Self-propagation in such a case may be nothing more than a road to a nonindigenous relationship.

I very strongly suspect that the three "selfs" are really projections of our American value systems into the idealization of the church, that they are in their very nature Western concepts based upon Western ideas of individualism and power. By forcing them on other people we may at times have been making it impossible for a truly indigenous pattern to develop. We have been Westernizing with all our talk about indigenizing.

The Nature of an Indigenous Church

What, then, is an indigenous church? It is a group of believers who live out their life, including their socialized Christian activity, in the patterns of the local society, and for whom any transformation of that society comes out of their felt needs under the guidance of the Holy Spirit and the Scriptures. There are several basic elements in this tentative formulation. For one thing, the church is a *society*. As society it has its patterns of interaction among people. If 'it is an indigenous society, an indigenous church, those patterns of reaction will be based upon such patterns existing in the local society. This is true simply because people learn to react with each other in their normal process of enculturation, of growing up, and those normal habits are carried over into church structure. If other patterns are forced upon a church by missionaries, consciously or unconsciously, such a church will not be an indigenous one.

The presence of the Holy Spirit, however, is another basic factor in the indigenous church, and the presence of the Holy Spirit implies transformation both of individual lives and of society. But, as I have tried to point out in another article on the nature of culture change,[3] such transformation occurs differently in different societies, depending on the meaning which people attach to their behavior and the needs which they feel in their lives. Missionaries generally approve of and strive for culture change which makes people more like themselves in form (and this is true even though they may overlook the meaning of this form). An indigenous church is precisely one in which the changes which take place under the guidance of the Holy Spirit meet the needs and fulfill the meanings of that society and not of any outside group.

Many have said things like this, and such a statement should and could be elaborated considerably to provide a more adequate description of the nature of an indigenous church. Sometimes in our search for an understanding of the nature of the church we turn to the New Testament (as we rightly should) and seek for it there. But it is not in the formal structure and operation of the churches in the New Testament that we find our answer As a matter of fact, the church of Jerusalem was apparently different even in operational matters from the churches in Europe, and it was certainly different in the outlook on the basic cultural issue which were so important to the Jews. In the New Testament we do find the picture of the indigenous church. It is tha of a church in which the Holy Spirit ha

---

2 William D. Reyburn, "Conflicts and Contradictions in African Christianity," in this volume.

3 William A. Smalley, "*The Missionary an Culture Change*," PRACTICAL ANTHROPOLOGY Vol. 4, No. 5 (1957), pp. 231-237.

worked its transformation within the society. And where that society differs from another (as the Greek world is different from the Jewish world) the church resulting is different.

Missionaries Do Not Like It

But having said this much, we would now like to stress some of the implications of an "indigenous church," implications which have often not been realized. One is that missionaries often do not like the product. Often a truly indigenous church is a source of concern and embarrassment to the mission bodies in the area.

An example of this which every reader of PRACTICAL ANTHROPOLOGY should study is that of the Toba Indians as reported by Dr. William D. Reyburn.[4] The mission was disturbed and unhappy about the indigenous church which spread so rapidly among the Toba people because it assumed a form so different from that of the mission group. It was not until they saw something of the nature of the church in the sense in which we are discussing it here and of the working of the Holy Spirit in societies other than their own, that the missionaries not only became reconciled to the indigenous church's existence, but sought to harmonize their program with it, to the strengthening of that church and to the greater glory of God.

There have been indigenous movements which missionaries have approved of. This approval was sometimes due to the unusual insight and perception of the missionaries who saw beyond the limitations

of their own cultural forms and recognized the movement of the Holy Spirit among other people. At other times the general value systems of the new church group so nearly coincided with our own that the result was a church which reflected many of the things that we hold very valuable. Movements in China such as the Jesus Family[5] displayed outstanding personal qualities of frugality, cleanliness, thrift, and other virtues which rate so highly in our own society and which were considered to be the fruits of the Christian movement. These are, however, ideals present in non-Christian Chinese life. A transformed life in such a case resulted in the perfection of such value systems already in existence in the culture. But that was not the case among the Tobas, where the giving away of possessions, the sharing with one's relatives and neighbors, and the joining in of emotional expressions of religion characterized the group because it was in these ways that their values were expressed.

However, as Dr. William D. Reyburn put it some time ago, most of us want to join in the jury as God is making his judgments upon people and cultures, yet we don't even understand the meaning of the trial. We are quick to make our evaluations and quick to decide what course the new church should follow or what course a new Christian individual should take, but we simply are neither competent nor qualified to make such decisions, having little or no real knowledge of the cultural background of the people or individual.

It is our work first of all to see the Bible in its cultural perspective, to see

God dealing with men through different cultural situations. It is our responsibility to see him change in his dealings with men as the cultural history of the Jews changes, to recognize that God has always, everywhere, dealt with men in terms of their culture. It is next our responsibility to take new Christians to the Bible and to help them see in the Bible God interacting with other people, people whose emotions and problems were very similar to their own so far as their fundamental nature is concerned, but also at times very different from their own in the specific objective or working of their forms of life. It is our responsibility to lead them in prayer to find what God would have them do as they study his Word and seek the interpretation and leadership of the Holy Spirit.

It is the missionary's task, if he believes in "the indigenous principle," to preach that God is in Christ Jesus, reconciling the world unto himself. That message is supercultural.[6] It applies to all cultures and all places. The faith it engenders is supercultural, but the medium of its communication and the outworking of its faith in individual lives is not supercultural, it is bound in with the habits and values of every people. It is to deliver that message, the message that turned the world upside down and continues to do so, that the missionary is called.

It is, furthermore, the missionary's responsibility to be a source of cultural alternatives for people to select if they want and need them. The missionary,

with his knowledge of history, his understanding of the Scriptures, and his knowledge of the church in his own land and in other missionary areas, can often suggest to local groups that there are ways out of their dilemma, that there are ways of a better life in Christ than what they are now living. This is certainly a legitimate function of the missionary and this is his role in culture change. But if genuine change is to take place, the decision, the selection, has to be made by the people themselves, and if the church is to be an indigenous one, we can know that the selection will be made in the light of the needs and problems, the values and outlooks, those people have.

It is the church which will have to decide whether boiling water, abstinence from alcohol, the wearing of clothes, and monogamy are the proper expressions of a Christian in that society. It is the church under the leadership of the Holy Spirit which will have to determine the best ways of fostering its own growth, spreading its own witness, and supporting its own formal leadership (if it should have any formal leadership at all).

As we have already suggested the problem of the implications of the indigenous church are as old as the Judaizers of Jerusalem. Those Judaizers saw Greek Christianity through Hebrew eyes. They are like many missionaries in that, if they were content that any Gentile should be converted at all, they saw conversion in the light of filling of a formal mold.

The New Testament, however, clearly repudiated that view and sets up the church as a group of believers within its own society, working a chemical change within the society like salt in a dish, rather than cutting the society to pieces as the Judaizers would. This is not to

---

6 William A. Smalley, "Culture and Superculture," PA, Vol. 2, No. 3 (1955), pp. 58-71; William. A. Smalley and Marie Fetzer, "A Christian View of Anthropology," Modern Science and Christian Faith, (Wheaton, Ill.: Van Kampen Press, 1950).

gainsay the exclusiveness of Christianity. The church is a separate group, but it is separate in spiritual kind, in relationship to God. It is in the indigenous church that the relationship between the Holy Spirit and society comes into being. This is the New Testament church.

The converts of an indigenous movement are not necessarily cleaner than their neighbors, not necessarily more healthy, not necessarily better educated. It is, furthermore, often the moment at which they become cleaner, more healthy, more educated that the barrier begins to grow which makes their indigenous interaction with their neighbors less likely and the growth of the movement begins to taper off. As Dr. McGavran has pointed out in his tremendously significant book *The Bridges of God*,[7] missions have traditionally poured their funds not into the people's movements but into the station churches, into the huge mission compounds, into the churches which are their satellites, rather than into the grass roots growing development of an embarrassing indigenous church.

Not only do many missionaries not like some of the outstanding examples of indigenous church movements, but to an even greater degree their supporting home constituencies are likely not to approve of them. Our cultural values as applied to our churches are so strong that we feel that a corporate structure, a profit motive, individualism, and thrift are *ipso facto* the expressions of Christianity. That God should work his will in any other forms than our own is inconceivable to most of us.

An implication of the indigenous church which I think is very unwelcome to many missionaries is that the missionary can make no cultural decisions for the Christians. By this I do not mean that the missionary does not make value judgments. As an individual he cannot help doing so, nor should he wish not to do so.[8] His value judgments, if they are to be worth while, have to be cross-culturally oriented, but they will be there. Neither do I mean by this that the missionary cannot exercise an important measure of guidance, of suggestion, on the younger church as he fulfills his functions of teaching and preaching and, in many respects, advising.

An Indigenous Church Cannot be "Founded"

The next implication which has often not fully penetrated into the thinking of missionaries who discuss indigenous movements is that it is impossible to "found" an indigenous church. The Biblical figure of planting and harvesting is far more realistic than our American figure based on our American values and expressed in the idea of the "establishment" or "founding" of a church. At one time I had the opportunity to observe the effort of a group of missionaries as they very sincerely were concerned about the "founding" of an indigenous church where up to that time they recognized that the believers were heavily dependent upon the mission for their sustenance. The procedure followed by the mission was to establish a constitutional committee which contained three tribesmen and two missionaries. The mission considered that they were extremely generous in their outlook by putting more tribesmen than missionaries on the committee.

When the committee met, the mission-

---

[7] Donald McGavran, *The Bridges of God* (London: World Dominion Press, 1955).

[8] William D. Reyburn, "The Missionary and the Evaluation of Culture," in this volume.

aries asked the tribesmen what they wanted in their constitution. The tribesmen, of course, did not know what they wanted in their constitution. They had not even known that they wanted a constitution until they had been told so. The missionaries suggested some of the possibilities for a constitution and the tribesmen readily agreed to most or all of them. The result, worked out in good faith by both the missionaries and the tribesmen, was a replica of the denominational constitution of the mission body. To this day no one seems to have sensed the fact a tribal church with a constitution is no more an indigenous church than a tribal church without one, as the existence of a constitution is entirely irrelevant to the relation of the church to God and to surrounding human life.

In any honestly indigenous work a true constitution (if there were any at all) would be one which would describe the structure of the church society in its workings. This does not mean that those culture changes which are needed to move toward a greater church action than is possible in the original local pattern should not take place. A constitution, if it is truly the expression of forward-looking church leaders, may guide the group in that direction, but it will only do so if it is an expression of such internally felt needs or vision.

Some missions have legislated the gradual withdrawal of financial subsidy from younger churches. This is done in order to put the younger church on its "self-supporting" feet. It is a step toward the day when the church will be indigenous, as the mission sees it, but the withdrawal of subsidy by the mission is a foreign act and not in the most remote sense indigenous.

No, indigenous churches cannot be founded. They can only be planted, and the mission is usually surprised at which seeds grow. Often they have the tendency to consider the seeds which do grow in any proliferation to be weeds, a nuisance, a hindrance in their carefully cultivated foreign mission garden, and all the time the carefully cultivated hothouse plants of the mission "founded" church are unable to spread roots and to derive their nurture either from the soil of their own life or from the Word of God in the root-confining pots of the mission organization and culture.

Indigenous Churches Start Apart from Missions

Another implication of the whole idea of an indigenous church is that the great indigenous movements are often not the result of foreign work in any direct way. Sometimes they are the result of the witness of someone who was converted by the efforts of foreign missionaries, but usually it is not the foreign missionary himself whose witness brings about the establishment or beginning of an indigenous movement. Saint Paul was not a foreigner to the Greek world. He was a bi-cultural individual, one who was as much at home in the Greek world as he was in the Hebrew world and whose preaching carried to the Greek world the message which came to him from the Christians of the Hebrew world.

Prophet Harris, who wandered along the west coast of Africa preaching about the men who would come with a Book, was not a foreign missionary. The men from whom the Tobas heard the gospel as it came to them in its pentecostal form were not foreigners. True, they were not Tobas, but they were the poorer-class

Latin-Americans and mixed Spanish-Indian inhabitants of the areas where the Tobas lived. They were very much a part of the cultural picture in which the Tobas found themselves; they were not foreign missionaries. The people's movements in China were usually the result of the energetic faithful work of a Chinese Christian, not the result of foreign missionary evangelism except as he may have been a convert of missionaries.

The Meo movement described by G. Linwood Barney[9] was not brought about through the preaching of a missionary, but through the cooperative work of a Meo shaman who had been converted (under a missionary) and who took another tribesman of the area with whom the Meo were very familiar from village to village, preaching from town to town. Our distance from most other culture is so great, the cultural specialization of the West is so extreme, that there are almost no avenues of approach whereby the work which we do can normally result in anything of an indigenous nature. It is an ironical thing that the West, which is most concerned with the spread of Christianity in the world today, and which. is financially best able to undertake the task of world-wide evangelism, is culturally the least suited for its task because of the way in which it has specialized itself to a point where it is very difficult for it to have an adequate understanding of other peoples.

The New Testament Indigenous Churches

Of many quotations which could have been taken from Roland Allen, the following has been selected to conclude this

9 "The Meo — An Incipient Culture," in this volume.

article. The significant thing, as Allen points out, is that the Apostle Paul did not approve of much of the behavior of either of these churches, but neither did he legislate to either one. He did not even stay around and spoon-feed them. He wrote to Corinth, persuaded, entreated, advised, addressing them always as the "church of God."

The Church began in Jerusalem as a body of Jews who carefully maintained their Jewish tradition and observed the custom of their fathers. The Church in the Four Provinces consisted almost entirely of Gentiles ignorant of that tradition. Consequently, if a Christian from Macedonia or Achaia went up to Judea he must have found himself in a strange atmosphere, in a community as unlike that to which he was accustomed as it is possible to imagine. Circumcision was practiced, Sabbaths were kept, meats avoided as unclean, the Law was the practical rule of every-day life. There was a strictness and a reserve which must have oppressed and dismayed him. Christianity in Jerusalem must have seemed to him a thing of rules hardly distinguishable from pure Judaism. Many of the Christians shrank from a Gentile, or tolerated him only as a sort of proselyte. In the meetings of the Church the prayers were modeled on Jewish patterns and expressed Jewish thought in Jewish speech with which he was not familiar. The only point of real contact was a common devotion to the Person of Jesus, a common recognition of the same Apostles, and a common observance of the same rites of baptism and the Lord's Supper.

On the other hand, when a Christian from Jerusalem went down to Corinth the shock must have been even more severe. The Corinthian in Jerusalem found himself in a society stiff, uncouth, severe, formal, pedantic. The Jewish Christian in Corinth must have thought the Church there given over to unbridled license. Uncircumcised Christians attended the feasts of their pagan friends in heathen temples. Every letter of the ceremonial law was apparently broken every day without rebuke. Even in the meetings of the Church, preachings and prayers were built on a strange system of thought which could hardly be called Christian, and there was a most undignified freedom of conduct. He must have welcomed the presence in the Church of a party led by men from his own city who argued that in dealing with a people like this it was useless to compromise matters: the only possible course was to enforce the observance of the whole Law throughout the whole Church. To omit anything would simply be to admit the thin end of a wedge which would split Christian morals into fragments. If a man wanted to be saved he must keep the law.[10]

Denominationalism is in many cases a result of the development of more or less indigenous churches in various subgroups or social levels of Western society. Usually they start in the lower brackets, fossilizing in their cultural forms as they move up in society and on through time. Until we are willing for the church to have its different manifestations in different cultures as between the Jewish Christians and the various kinds of Greeks, rather than export the denominational patterns rooted in our history and often irrelevant to the rest of the world, we will not have indigenous churches, whether they are "self-governing, self-supporting, and self-propagating" or not. It is not until we are willing to let churches grow also that we have learned to trust the Holy Spirit with society. We are treating him as a small child with a new toy too complicated and dangerous for him to handle. Our paternalism is not only a paternalism toward other peoples it is also a paternalism towards God.

---

10 Op. cit. pp. 166-167.

James E. Bertsche

Kimbanguism: A Challenge to Missionary Statesmanship

ALONG rural waysides and in urban centers, among unlettered country folk and among highly trained city dwellers, in areas dominated by single large tribes and in those characterized by an admixture of many clans, they are increasingly to be found. Benefiting neither from foreign subsidies nor from overseas organization, the movement continues to spread with vigor. While requiring great blocks of donated time and serious financial support from its adherents, the movement is carried along by the spontaneity and enthusiasm of lay support. Demonstrating tremendous dynamic, commanding deep loyalty, and manifesting abundant evidences of its Protestant heritage and orientation, Kimbanguism is a popular religious movement which the Protestant community of Congo dares not ignore and cannot afford to misunderstand.[1]

A Reluctant Messenger

Born sometime in the 1890's in the village of Nkamba of parents belonging to the Bakongo people of the Ngombe clan, Kimbangu Simon early came under the influence of Baptist Missionary Society missionaries at Ngombe Lutete some twelve kilometers away. By approximately 1915,

Kimbangu had attended a mission village school long enough to have become semiliterate and to have acquired baptism.[2]

Following his abbreviated schooling, Simon made his way to Kinshasa and reportedly worked both as a laborer at an oil factory and as house help for a missionary family. In the meantime he was married and had several children, among them three sons who are still living and are well known: Charles Kisolokele, Dialungana Salomon, and Joseph Diangienda.[3]

It seems to have been in late 1919 or early 1920 that Simon began to experience troublesome dreams in which he sensed himself being urged by God to give himself to his service. The more he resisted them the more persistent they became. Finally his personal crisis reached an emotional peak when in a dream he heard a voice saying: "If you will not go, you will die here in Kinshasa." Simon thereupon made his decision to obey his voice of call and returned to Nkamba, his home village.[4]

---

[1] See also Harold W. Fehderau, "Kimbanguism: Prophetic Christianity in Congo," PA, Vol. 9, No. 4 (July-Aug. 1962), pp. 157-178.

[2] E. Andersson, *Messianic Popular Movements in Lower Congo*, Studia Ethnographica Upsaliensia XIV (Uppsala: Almqvist & Wiksells Boktryckeri, 1958), p. 49.

[3] J. Chomé, *La Passion de Simon Kimbangu* (Bruxelles: Présence Africaine, 1959), p. 6.

[4] Andersson, op. cit., p. 50.

A Zealous Preacher

One day, soon after his return to Nkamba, Kimbangu Simon fainted and fell while accompanying his parents on a visit to a neighboring village because of the death of a friend. Returning home ill, he dreamed during the night that he saw a stranger bearing a Bible saying, "Here is a good book. You must study it and preach it." This dream was shortly followed by a second in which he heard himself commanded to go to a nearby village where he would find and heal a sick child by laying his hands upon it. According to Kimbanguist literature, he went, found the child, laid his hands upon it, and after a moment of muscular spasm, the child was completely healed.[5]

In a matter of days, word spread like a prairie fire and the village of Nkamba became the center of increasingly larger crowds of people who came with the ill, the crippled, and even the dead hoping for the reportedly miraculous touch of the new healer. Procedure quickly fell into a pattern. Before any healing was attempted, services were always held, characterized by much group singing of hymns and periodic exhortations by Simon, a portion of Scripture in hand. With free group participation, excitement quickly reached a peak and Simon, himself often trembling in the traditional pattern of the tribal diviner-prophet, would summon the seekers before him. Going from one to the other, he would lay hands and a portion of Scripture on those whom

[5] Chomé, op. cit., pp. 7-10.

James E. Bertsche has been a missionary of the Congo Inland Mission since 1948. He is the author of a pamphlet, *The Profile of a Communist Offensive,* reprinted under the title, "Congo Rebellion," in PA, Vol. 12, No. 5 (Sept.-Oct. 1965), pp. 210-226. B.P. 1, Tshikapa, Republic of Congo.

he deemed worthy of help but would reject those whom he considered to have sinned. Various instructions were given those to whom Simon ministered. Some were sent to the nearby stream Mpumbu to bathe. Some were referred to associates for counsel and prayer. Others were simply told to go, that they were healed and should sin no more.[6]

Kimbangu Simon, during his brief public career (approximately March to May 1921) seemed to see himself and his ministry to be clearly within the framework of the established Protestant community. He was convinced that his was the task to call his people to the Protestant faith as he knew it and interpreted it. Scriptures in hand, his messages were animated, simple, and direct. His standards of personal conduct for his converts were exacting and uncom-

[6] C. A. Gilis, *Kimbangu: Fondateur d'Eglise* (Bruxelles: Librairie Encyclopédique, 1960), p. 33.

A favorite hymn used at the hour of healing was No. 462 in the present edition of *Mikunga mia Kintwadi, The Songs of Fellowship,* a Protestant hymnal of the area. The text runs as follows:

> Zimpasi zingi vava nsi,
> Mayela tweti monanga,
> O Mpeve, wiza, wiza,
> O wiza kutusadisa.
> Many troubles here on earth
> Sickness all the time we see,
> O Spirit, come, come down,
> O come and help us.

promising: no palm wine, no tobacco, no dancing, and monogamous marriage only. While accepting the universal Bakongo belief in malevolent spirit beings, he demanded that all protective fetishes be thrown away and be replaced by a trust in God for protection. For the sick there was his confident claim of power to heal. Despite the accusations of his detractors, Kimbangu was neither anti-white nor antimission in his attitudes or pronouncements. On the contrary, during the brief period that he was the controlling personality of his movement, he urged his followers to attend Protestant services and to secure their own copies of the Scriptures. Mission records from that period testify to an upsurge of church attendance and augmented Bible sales. As far as the government was concerned, Kimbangu urged respect and the payment of taxes.

In brief, while coming in the manner of the tribal diviner-prophet with singing, group excitation, and animated speaking, his message was largely orthodox and seems to have been a sincere effort to bring the Christian faith to bear upon the life, fears, and needs of his people.

An Acclaimed Prophet

But while Kimbangu was busily engaged in trying to deal with the increasing crowds that were deluging him at his village Nkamba, accounts of his messages and activities were rapidly making their way up and down the rail line from one stop to the next. Soon it was not only the village folk of the Thysville area who knew of the preacher-healer at Nkamba but the better educated and better paid people in the centers also began discussing among themselves the person and reported activities of Kimbangu. Who and what was he? A particularly gifted prophet? Could he really heal? A new prophet with unheard of talents? If the answers to all these questions were not immediately clear, there was none the less a ground swell of enthusiasm and support throughout Bakongoland that was new and exciting. And in the heart of more than one of the Bakongo people there stirred the realization that the massive public support so spontaneously offered this suddenly popular figure might just possibly serve more than one set of interests. Sizable gifts began to find their way to Kimbangu at Nkamba and the ranks of his declared followers continued to swell.

The crowds at Nkamba soon reached such size that it became impossible for Simon to even see them all much less minister to them. Such was the public contagion that the rail line had to add extra coaches to handle the traffic. From far and near they came all hoping to benefit from the widely advertized healing powers of the new prophet.

Patterning after the life of Christ, Kimbangu selected twelve helpers whom he consecrated with a ritual whereby he authorized them to preach, to heal, and to install other local leaders. Thus for yet a little while longer Simon was able to maintain some control of the movement. But the time inevitably came, and soon, when the demand for leaders overran this limited supply and a mushroom growth of prophets began, Kimbangu was no longer able to determine the views and attitudes of everyone. Many new trends and practices for which he was not personally responsible began to make their appearance in his name. While Kimbangu was still the well-known head of the movement, he was no longer its effective leader.[7]

A Social Catalyst

The Kimbanguist movement, in the pattern of popular religious movements, did not "just happen" nor can it be explained in terms of Kimbangu Simon alone. For an understanding of the dynamics which gave it such dramatic force and form, one must attempt to probe into the historical and socio-cultural setting in which the movement erupted.

By the time Kimbangu made his appearance in 1921, the Bakongo people had already been in nearly continuous disruptive contact of one kind or another with the European for over 400 years. First there was Diego Cão, the Portuguese explorer who in finding his way into the mouth of the Congo River in 1482 found the surprising Kongo Kingdom and marked the beginning of Portuguese influence and activity in Africa. First were gifts and offers of friendship and trade. But these soon gave way to balder demands as the West Coast of Africa slipped under the murderous shadow of the slave trade. Under its impact, the Kongo Kingdom gradually disintegrated and became but a bitter memory to be carried in the hearts of Bakongo generations to

come. With the passing of the slave trade, the colonial era was ushered in and the Bakongo people found themselves face to face with the white man from Banana to Stanley Pool.

Confronted by the rapids and rocky stretches of the Congo River as it twisted and plunged its way through the Crystal Mountains, the exploring colonizers resorted for transport to a human porterage system by which literally thousands of tons of supplies and equipment were manhandled by brute force on the shoulders and heads of perspiring men through the mountains to Kinshasa. Meanwhile other great squads of men were recruited to gouge a railroad bed through these same mountains and through the heart of Bakongo country at staggering losses of human life. For the Bakongo people, the erosive fear of the slave trade had been replaced by the insistent demands of the exploring traveling, building white man whose cry was continually for more labor For many an ablebodied man th haunting possibility of a trip to a slaver's boat on the coast with a chain about his neck was exchanged for repeated trips upstream with a fifty kilo case on his head.[8]

And upon the heels of the exploring builders came the colonizing adminis trators. Chiefs were sought out, gift offered, pledges proposed, and docu ments drawn up and signed. And by a process but dimly understood, triba authorities found themselves subjec

7 Andersson, op. cit., p. 58. Also Gilis, op. cit., pp. 38-39.

8 R. J. Leveque, Le Congo Belge: so histoire (Bruxelles: Editions du Marais), p. 3 and R. P. Van Wing, "Kimbanguisme vu p un témoin," Zaïre, Vol. XII, No. 6 (1958), 565.

to a white king far away who, it was declared, expected their loyalty and their tributes in return for his help and protection. Traditional tribal authority was curtailed. Restrictive pressures were brought to bear upon various aspects of Bakongo life. Commercial men were introducing new items and values wholesale along with the concepts of contract and a monetary system. There were the missionaries who urged upon the people a belief in one named Jesus who was Nzambi's Son, the Saviour of every man who believed in him. Furthermore there were the missionaries' little grass and stick school houses in which it was declared that killing fevers should be blamed on mosquitoes rather than the spirits and that debilitating dysentery had more to do with unwashed hands than with the malevolent spirits of the night. In brief, cultures were in direct collision and the intra-societal stresses and disorientations which the Bakongo began to feel with increasing sharpness were predictable.

One measure of the growing strain felt in the fabric of Bakongo life in the early 1900's was the spreading obsessive fear of black magic. Undergirded by tribal lore and unwavering belief on the part of all, magic became a handy cultural peg upon which to hang the woes, frustrations, and fears that now were so much a part of Bakongo life. As belief in and fear of magic grew, the greater was the reliance upon the tribal ordeal who in turn named suspects who were to undergo the test of the lethal *nkasa* cup. Withal there was a proliferation of the Bakongo protective fetishes.

This, then, was something of the socio-cultural setting in which Kimbangu made his appearance — one of tension, disorientation, and searching. Did Kimbangu actually heal people? In the absence of documented cases, there is great skepticism on the part of observers. But in the atmosphere of intense belief and complete faith which characterized Kimbangu's meetings, it is entirely possible that some healings, psychosomatic if no other, may have taken place. But healings or not, what is of greatest significance is the passionate desire of the people of that time to believe in the person, the message, and the declared powers of the new prophetic figure among them. While his message and demands cut squarely across the cultural grain of his hearers, the alacrity with which they sought to comply bespeaks loudly the search that was theirs for a stable and meaningful framework of beliefs and values. Bakongo society was in a state of deep restlessness; Kimbangu became a catalyst.

A Pursued Fugitive

But the excitement among the people and the increasing crowds making their way to Mbangu were not going unnoted. Because of his clearly stated devotion to the Protestant community and message, the early attitude of the Protestant missionaries was chiefly one of wary interest. Interestingly enough, the government officials at first also seemed tolerant and rather hesitant to interfere. It was in effect, the Roman Catholic missions supported editorially by the Léopoldville newspaper *L'Avenir Colonial Belge* which first and most persistently raised a cry of alarmed opposition. If the movement initially found most of its followers in the Protestant communities, it was not long until Roman Catholic adepts were also making the trek to Mbangu. Seeking in Kimbangu a powerful if slightly irregular propagandist for the Protestant faith, he was quickly opposed and condemned by Roman Catholic missions.[9]

But as the movement mushroomed beyond the control of Kimbangu and rapidly came under the influence of tribal prophets in the rural areas and politically restive elements in the centers, the government soon came to share the alarm of Roman Catholic missions and began to take restrictive measures, actions which were frenetically seconded and encouraged by L'Avenir.

On June 6, 1921, the territorial agent at Thysville went to Nkamba with twenty-five soldiers. Details concerning the following action are vague but it is clear that the soldiers were met with opposition by Kimbangu's followers, that there was some gunfire, that there were a few casualties, and that Kimbangu escaped into the surrounding bush in the confusion.[10]

During the ensuing three months, Kimbangu lived the life of a fugitive among people who loyally screened him from the efforts of the government to locate him. In the meantime, the leadership of the movement came solidly to rest in other hands and it came very rapidly to take on political

and insurgent overtones. Pamphlets were circulated which spoke of the white man in aggressive terms. Rumors were rampant to the effect that massive strikes were being planned, that taxes were no longer to be paid and that no more fields were to be cultivated.[11]

There are conflicting accounts of Kimbangu's capture. One states that he was taken by surprise by night in a small village upstream from Kinshasa.[12] A second and seemingly more accurate one states that Kimbangu of his own accord returned openly to Mbangu and after some public meetings with his followers awaited the arrest which he knew would soon take place. In any event, September 15, 1921, found the Thysville area under martial law and Kimbangu as well as a considerable number of his followers in custody awaiting trial by a three-man military tribunal.[13]

A Condemned Prisoner

Legal procedures evidently moved at a brisk pace, for by October 3, after a total of seven three-hour sessions, all testimony had been taken, all people interviewed, and severe sentences passed. For Kimbangu himself it was the death sentence. Life imprisonment was decreed for his close associates and various prison terms for those less directly involved.

One member of the tribunal objected to the severity of the sentence and was soon joined by some Protestant missionaries of the area in an

---

9 P. Dufonteny, "A propos du Kimbanguisme," *Congo II*, No. 4 (1924), pp. 380-388.

10 Chomé, op. cit., p. 39 and Andersson, op. cit., p. 64.

11 Van Wing, op. cit., pp. 572-576.

12 Chomé, op. cit., p. 50.

13 Andersson, op. cit., pp. 66-67.

effort to secure a reprieve. It was finally the Belgian King Albert who made the decision to commute Kimbangu's death sentence to life imprisonment.[14]

Kimbangu was then sent to Elizabethville's central prison where he was to spend the rest of his life, first in solitary confinement and, after exemplary behavior, as a member of the kitchen crew. Until his death in 1951 after twenty-six years of imprisonment, he maintained a polite and cooperative attitude vis-à-vis the prison officials and fellow inmates. Throughout his prison life he took active part in religious services. He on no occasion before or after his incarceration gave indication that he saw himself as anything other than a believer whom God called to preach the word of life to his own people.[15]

A Drafted Messiah

The imprisonment of Kimbangu and his closest associates marked the beginning of the official ban of the entire movement. Being now convinced that it was in effect political and subversive in nature, the government set about the task of its suppression. Public meetings and the building of chapels were forbidden. Sympathizers and propagandists of the movement were promptly taken into custody and either imprisoned or deported. It is at this point that Kim-

banguism becomes a classic study of a nativistic movement. Its leaders in prison and the movement itself banned, the faithful turned in the only direction still open to them, that of secretive underground activity. The movement consequently became very diffused and segmented in nature. While still claiming allegiance to Kimbangu, the local groups of adherents meeting in secret and in isolation came more and more to reflect the ideas and predilections of their particular *ngunza* or prophet leader. Students of the movements of this period suggest that a broader and more accurate blanket term would be *Ngunzism* for every group was led by its own *ngunza* or tribal prophet-seer in the typical Bakongo tradition.

There was, for instance, Matswa André and his *Amicale Balali*. A member of the Sundi-Ladi tribe, he was born at Ngoma Tsetse some twenty-five kilometers from Brazzaville. Gathering funds under the guise of aiding fellow countrymen in financial difficulties in Paris, it was soon discovered that those contributing to the fund were also being promised an eventual equality with and supplanting of the white man. Arrested and jailed, his followers spoke of his "way of the Cross" and of his "Calvary."[16]

With the *Amicale Balali* under suspicion, another movement stemmed from it which came to be known as *Nzambi ya Minda* or *Lusambulu lua Bougie*. A prominent feature of this movement was the "sacred wood," a piece of wood some ten centimeters

---

[14] The tribunal member who dissented was a Mr. Dupuis who was the local Commissaire de District Adjoint and served on the tribunal as Ministère Public. The missionaries were Rev. Phillips of the Baptist Missionary Society and Rev. Clark of the American Baptist Foreign Mission Society.

[15] Andersson, op. cit., p. 90, and Van Wing, op. cit., p. 567.

[16] Andersson, op. cit., p. 117 ff.

long and five centimeters in diameter cut from a sapling never touched by a woodman's axe. Such sticks, after elaborate rites, were worn as protection against magic. The movement seemed to achieve rather detailed organization as there were references to priests, bishops, and even a pope. Services were held in which altar-screens, flowers, and candles had a place.[17]

With the arrival of the first representatives of the Salvation Army in 1935, Ngunzist circles were buzzing with excitement. Kimbangu Simon had returned in the form of a white man! The Elizabethville jail had not been able to hold him. As a white man he could not now be prosecuted by the government. He had come to free his people from their oppression. The proof? What more was needed than the bright red letter "S" that was on the collar of the Salvation Army personnel?

Flooded with requests for teachers, the Salvation Army but newly arrived in Congo had to accept elements that had been trained by various missions but whose later involvement in Ngunzist movements they had no way of knowing. Swiftly the groups which flocked to affiliate with them began to profess that here, finally, they had found an effective remedy for the feared malevolent spirits. It soon became apparent that while these groups had taken on some of the external accoutrements of the Army, basically the people remained in the Ngunzist stream of belief and hope.[18]

And there were the *Khakists*. Mpadi Simon, a Mukongo from the Sona Bata area, was first a village teacher, then a village sergeant for the Salvation Army. Apparently a restless, dynamic spirit, he determined in 1939 to establish a "Negro Mission." Picking the village Kisangi, a Kimbanguist stronghold in 1921, he built a "temple," established himself as "pope," installed an old area chief as "king," decreed that no one would be permitted more than three wives and that khaki cloth was to be the approved form of clothing. His loyalty to Kimbangu Simon was unswerving. Quickly pursued by the State, he began a legendary five years of fox and hare existence which led him from Angola to French Moyen Congo. Before he was finally captured in 1944, he had ample occasion to meet Ngunzist leaders from far and near, contacts which undoubtedly served the double purpose of some consolidation of thought and practice as well as the renewal of loyalty to the imprisoned Kimbangu.[19]

But if there were surface differences from one group to another, there were also some basic similarities which when viewed in their entirety bring to light a basic pattern of emphases and practices for the period in which all largely shared.

For one thing there was a gradually hardening hostility toward the white man, missionaries included. While it was the government agent and the Roman Catholic missionary who were most aggressive in combatting the Ngunzists, the Protestants had by

17 Ibid., p. 125.
18 Ibid., p. 128 ff.

19 Ibid., p. 138 ff.

this time also signaled their disfavor by repudiating the movement as any legitimate expression of the Protestant faith.

Underground tactics developed. Denied all public expression of their faith, leaders were forced to turn to other means of maintaining group interest and loyalty. Given the passively sympathetic attitude of the general population toward them as against the passively negative attitude toward the white man, it was possible for the Ngunzists to lead a certain dual existence. While on the one hand they entered wholeheartedly into the authorized religious gatherings conducted by mission teachers, their alternate religious life was a secret one revolving about secret nocturnal meetings in forest clearings or along streams where they felt safe from betrayal and thus free to give full expression to their emotions.

Development of Legend

A body of legend emerged. Kimbangu's success during three months in evading capture gave rise to numerous legendary accounts of his supernatural powers. As time passed and Kimbangu's prison term stretched on and on, the legendary accounts tended to turn from what he had done to what he would do in the future.

A strong syncretistic trend became apparent. While Kimbangu's position had been very near that of orthodox Christianity, the movement was later characterized by a sharp nativistic shift toward the incorporation of tribal practices and values. Notable features of this trend were less emphasis upon Christ and more upon national heroes and upon Kimbangu as a coming messianic figure; less emphasis upon a strict moral code of personal conduct and the reappearance of the dance; a new accent upon ancestor worship, upon polygyny, upon identification of malevolent spirits, and upon spirit possession.

A body of regulations and taboos was developed. Kimbangu had early imposed upon his followers proscriptions against polygyny, dancing, and protective fetishes. Before his imprisonment, others were added against the use of alcohol, tobacco, and hemp. As other leaders assumed control of the movement, they began to draw up their own sets of regulations. Typical of these were prescribed types or cuts of clothing, opposition to the payment of taxes, a particular day in the week set aside in memory of Kimbangu's suffering, and the careful maintenance of burial grounds and paths leading to them. Sleeping in the nude was forbidden as was any physical contact with a prophet. Some groups refused to eat pork. Others let their little fingernails grow explaining that anyone really possessed of the spirit was capable of flight and the nails were useful in clinging to a support in case of difficulty.

A complex of distinctive Ngunzist practices emerged. Among the activities that came to be the earmarks of Ngunzism, group singing was important. Kimbangu himself seemed to need a context of spirited group singing in which to perform his acts of healing. While he used Protestant hymns almost exclusively, a great deal of improvisation and original composition followed, much of which gave excellent insight into the mind and heart of the Ngunzist.[20]

"Nkongo Day" was observed by many Ngunzists as a day of rest and mourning in memory of Kimbangu's suffering. Wednesdays and Saturdays

---

[20] Following is a sample text of a Ngunzist song from Musana in the French Congo in 1930:

Jesus shall come to judge the world.
Many shall fly when he shows himself.

(Refrain)
In heaven witnesses, on earth witnesses.
All that the Lord has done, God knows.

Father Abraham, send me Lazarus,
That he may moisten the tongue that is drying up.

The virgins are about to be lost on account of evil passions.
Lord, pardon them that they may be saved.

The youths are about to be lost on account of adultery.
Lord, pardon them that they may be saved.

The young are about to be lost on account of disobedience.
Lord, pardon them that they may be saved.

Others think, Verily, we are not saved.
Lord, pardon them that they may be saved.

The members of the congregation are about to be lost on account of temptations.
Lord, pardon them that they may be saved.

The teachers think, We cannot wait.
Lord, pardon them that they may be saved.

The Whites are about to be lost on account of the earning of money.
Lord, pardon them that they may be saved.

The chiefs are about to be lost on account of their money.
Lord, pardon them that they may be saved.

The police are about to be lost on account of collecting of taxes.
Lord, pardon them that they may be saved.
(Andersson, op. cit., pp. 275-276 ff.)

were usually reserved for Ngunzist meetings.

It was the need for extreme secrecy which led to meetings in secluded spots at night. Hidden in forest clearings or distant ravines, Ngunzists and their sympathizers were able to give full ecstatic expression to their religious emotions without fear of being heard or apprehended. Some of the features of these nocturnal reunions were dancing in a state of extreme excitation, talking in strange tongues, public confession of sins, faith healing, fire walking, and frequentation of burial grounds.

As time passed and Simon remained in prison, it became increasingly popular for Ngunzists to make a trip to his home village for the purposes of prayer and bathing in the Mpumbu. Water from the stream was at times bottled and sent to the distant ill.

During the years of oppression, the Ngunzist movements offered an umbrella under which restless spirits of mixed motivations and interests together found common ground. But the most persistent and possibly the most significant feature of this period was the deeply emotional messianic emphasis. Banned and driven underground as a movement, harried and deported as individuals, Kimbangu the preacher, the healer, the evangelist, and prophet, now became Kimbangu the messiah. Under the pressures of frustrations, thwarted ambitions, and blighted dreams, followers cast Simon in the role of one who would break through his prison walls and would return as a triumphant messianic leader to drive out the white man, restore his people in their land and set up his kingdom — the ancient Bakongo Kingdom of which he would be the royal head.

An Enduring Symbol

By the mid 1950's, reprieve for the Ngunzists was indeed on the way though in a form they neither foresaw nor well understood. The same legal statutes were still in force and the movement was just as subject to prosecution as ever. But the winds of freedom were blowing across Africa and the colonial powers were already bowing to them. Quick to sense subtle change taking place, the Ngunzist leaders moved from the defensive to the offensive. The resultant resurgence of the movement in the mid-fifties presented many facets.

The village Mbangu had been the traditional stronghold of Ngunzist influence from 1921 on. However, realization gradually came that Léopoldville offered definite advantages over rural Mbangu as a center of control and direction. The better trained, better informed, better paid faithful were there. It was a center of communication and influence. In accepting this shift, it meant that the locus of control was moving from a rural setting steeped in tribal culture to an urban extra-tribal setting. It meant a transfer of reins of authority from hands of largely illiterate leaders close to the Bakongo tribal traditions to the hands of much better educated men whose lives were shaped by the concerns of the salaried Westernized people and the influences of the multilingual and multitribal communities in and out of which they moved daily. With the move of the locus of

control to Léopoldville in 1954, the first problem was one of bringing together the widely scattered and divergent Ngunzists groups in some sort of affiliation. While declaring a basic loyalty to Kimbangu as titular head of their group, still local loyalties and group emphases were strong. Neutral grounds were needed upon which to meet and this was shrewdly provided by the organization of cells called *kintwadi* or fellowship groups. In these circles, gradual indoctrination by Kimbangu's followers was achieved, and they proved to be the means of gradually bringing together the many splinter groups. Power and authority began to be centralized in Kimbangu's own family.

In tracing the emergence of the family in places of prestige and authority, one immediately encounters the man Emmanuel Bamba. Described by one observer as the first Congolese intellectual who genuinely revived Simon Kimbangu's teaching,[21] he was apparently the first person to take the initiative of establishing uniform contact with Kimbangu's immediate family and his followers. It was he who brought Joseph Diangienda, Kimbangu's third son, for a visit to Mbangu as early as 1948. Though arrested in 1951, Emmanuel had already given direction to developments which by 1954 found Diangienda Joseph serving as a sort of executive secretary for the movement.[22] By 1956 there was a "Kimbanguist Church

---

21 "Le Kimbanguisme," C.A. (Centre de Recherche et d'Information Socio-Politiques (CRISP), Léopoldville), Vol. 1, No. 47 (1960), p. 9.

22 Ibid., p. 10.

Council."[23] In 1958 a published constitution listed four legal representatives, Kimbangu's wife and his three sons. But in 1959 at the occasion of the dedication of a new temple at Kintsasa Bibubu in French territory north of Nkamba, Joseph Diangienda emerged as the formally recognized legal and spiritual authority of the movement.[24]

Although practically speaking the movement leaders enjoyed much greater freedom, legally they stood banned and discredited as before. Only by official recognition could they remove their stigma, achieve equal status with other faiths, and qualify for some educational subsidies for the primary schools they began to organize just before 1960.

The year 1955 saw an orderly Kimbanguist demonstration in Ndjili, a Léopoldville suburb. In 1956 a memorandum was addressed to the United Nations protesting tneir situation and asking intervention so that the ancient Kongo Kingdom might be restored under the rule of Kimbangu Simon.[25] In 1957 a protest was addressed to Belgian Prime Minister Van Acker, which erupted in the Belgian press.[26] Such representations were not without effect for by 1957 all deportations in Congo had ceased. It had become only a matter of time,

and in August 1961 the Kimbanguist movement was incorporated.[27]

The single most important move made to focus attention on the Kimbanguist "New Jerusalem," as they came to call it, was the transfer of Kimbangu's remains to a small mausoleum in stone built in his home village on the former site of his own house. It is stated that a larger edifice is planned for the future.

While the old line prophetic emphasis remains strong and commands a large following particularly in rural areas, the leaders in Léopoldville have brought a wide range of groups and personalities together into an organization which is now legally recognized as "Church of Christ on Earth by the Prophet Kimbangu Simon" or, in abbreviated form, the EJCSK. This group, while demonstrating a utilitarian elasticity in doctrinal matters, has maintained a steady pressure in the direction of organization and centralized authority as well as toward an organized and stratified leadership.

While during the period of ban and deportation political and spiritual needs and protests came to be greatly mingled, political freedom brought the opportunity to engage in political activity per se. With the formation of "L'Alliance des Bakongo," the church leaders soon began to insist that the church's concerns were purely religious and that they welcomed into their fellowship all tribes and races.[28]

Thus on the threshold of the 1960's Kimbangu fulfilled yet another role

23 Gilis, op. cit., p. 94.

24 P. Raymaekers, "L'Eglise de Jésus-Christ sur la terre par le prophète Simon Kimbangu: contribution à l'étude des mouvements messianiques dans le Bas-Kongo," Zaïre, Vol. XIII, No. 7 (1959, pp. 717-718. Also see Moniteur Congolais, No. 19 (August 23, 1961).

25 Van Wing, op. cit., p. 615.

26 CRISP, op. cit., p. 10.

27 Moniteur Congolais (August 23, 1961).

28 Article 7 of the official statutes of the church, published in the Moniteur Congolais of August 23, 1961.

in the history of this popular movement, that of serving as a rallying symbol for a depressed and scattered following.

A Denominational Founder?

What, then, is this movement that has not only survived long years of ban, prison, and deportation but has surged into new prominence? What is the nature of these beliefs and practices which have such dynamic appeal for the African of this day? What is this new church which so proudly carries the name of Kimbangu Simon? There are no quick or simple answers, for Kimbanguism is, in reality, many things. But in an effort to arrive at a partial evaluation let us look at present day Kimbanguism from the viewpoints of organization, beliefs, message, methods, attitudes, and appeal.

In terms of structure and organization, as outlined in its literature, the Kimbanguist church resembles closely the Protestant background out of which it has come. In addition to pastors and catechists, provision is also made for what are termed "Wise Men of the Church." These are chosen by pastors from among themselves and serve as a council with which the legal representative, the legal and religious head of the church, can confer. Regions of activity are defined and each has its head within the framework of an overall organization.[29]

At the local village level, the pattern is again similar to that of Protestant programs with a catechist type lay leader taking responsibility for the shepherding of the flock, which in the

[29] Raymaekers, op. cit., pp. 724-725.

process is not a little influenced by the personality, emphases, and gifts of its leader.

Viewed from the standpoint of formally stated beliefs, here again the Protestant roots of the movement are obvious. At least four catechetical booklets have been published by church leaders. While the earlier ones had largely to do with Kimbangu Simon himself and ascribed to him a wide range of attributes and powers, the latter one has taken the form of a systematic statement of doctrine which is almost identical to the sort used by the Protestant missions both in format and content.

As a matter of fact, as long as one stays with questions which are matters of simple historic record and direct derivation from Protestant creed and practice, there is considerable uniformity and orthodoxy. It is when one probes into Kimbanguist claims regarding the origins of their movement, the person and function of Kimbangu, and the traditional Bantu religious beliefs, that one finds a tremendous range of contradictory statements and conflicting pronouncements. It could scarcely be otherwise for the movement leadership has demonstrated tremendous elasticity and tolerance in its attitude toward the divergent beliefs and practices of the various affiliating groups. The primary concern has been to find those who share a common loyalty to and belief in Kimbangu and to bring them into a common fellowship that has emerged in the form of a church named after him. Doctrinal divergences have been viewed as of secondary importance and will, presumably, be dealt with when and if they pose a problem.

Thus it is that there are some who see Kimbangu as someone closely akin to a divine savior.[30] But there are others who insist with vehemence that while Kimbangu was truly a prophet raised of God to call his own people to repentance, they must look to Christ for redemption as did Simon himself.[31]

In brief, Kimbanguism seems to accept uncritically the body of Protestant belief on the one hand and much of tribal religious beliefs on the other. Thus far there seems to be small concern about the problems that would seem to be inherent in such a position.

The Message

In an effort to determine the Kimbanguist message, one encounters the same problem that is faced with regards to Kimbanguist dogma. There are, on the one hand, the official pronouncements and there is, on the other hand, what is actually preached and taught by the local leaders. On the basis of published statements, the Kimbanguist message to the faithful might be summarized somewhat as follows: As a people we were suffering because of the evil of the government and the people of this world. But as God heard the cries of the Israelites and gave them Moses, so he heard our cries and gave us Kimbangu. He was God's prophet chosen from among us to lead us. Our prophet was received with great joy but joy turned to sorrow for Kimbangu and his believers were imprisoned and deported. But again our supplications were heard by

God. Now there has appeared the EJCSK. We already have many leaders and many followers but our strength is being taxed to the limit. Let us respect and honor the law and orders of the church. Let us eliminate all laziness, all shame, all vanity, all jealousy, and all dispute among us. Let us be of a single mind and purpose. We have a leader who was sent by Christ. If we persevere in spite of all difficulty and persecution, we will receive eternal joy. There are many signs about us. Great things are ahead for the faithful.[32]

In actuality, of course, Kimbanguist preaching in any given setting goes beyond such generalities and deals in the specific terms of its local situations and cultural values. Given the great freedom of Kimbanguist leaders, it is inevitable that the Kimbanguist message in any given time and place should be greatly colored by the preacher's views, community problems, and the relations of a particular group with the established Protestant community.

It is most interesting to note that as early as 1960 the young Kimbanguist church was attempting to formulate its views with regard to social, political, and economic problems "in Congo, in Africa, and in the world."[33] On political issues, it is stated that while the church does not deem it useful to express an opinion as to the political system a country ought to have, it does spurn the system which deprives the citizen of funda-

---

30 Ibid., pp. 737-738.

31 Gilis, op. cit., p. 105.

32 Raymaekers, op. cit., pp. 722-724.

33 A mimeographed paper put out by Kimbanguist leaders that carries no date but was likely written in 1960 or later.

mental liberties. It further condemns any ideology which denies the existence of God or which is based on tribalism, regionalism, or racism.

As regards social relations, it condemns all controversies, including those of a confessional nature, and sees no reason why all faiths which are founded on the doctrine of Christ cannot adopt "parallel paths."

In these same pronouncements, economic issues are treated in the following terms: The church is opposed to all spoiling of private property; it holds that the interests of both capital and labor must be taken into account and that it is the duty of richer countries to help the countries "which are the least endowed."

On social issues, it is stated that the workman has the right to a salary which enables him to provide for his essential needs; that the government has the duty to inaugurate free medical care and free education for its citizens; that every citizen has the right to a decent home at a low price; and that with regard to food stuffs the government must adopt "a policy of abundance."[34]

On reviewing these positions taken by the church, one is impressed by two things. The leadership of the young church has at least an awareness if not a full grasp of the problems of a world larger than that known by their fathers. Also, the paternalistic colonial regime under which the church leaders have grown to adulthood has drastically conditioned their thinking and has predisposed them toward a socialistic concept of government.

As for the emphases found in Kimbanguism, one of the first that strikes the observer is that of a strict standard of personal conduct. Adherence to the Mosaic code is expected. Furthermore, it is demanded that respect be shown those in authority, that all fetishes be abandoned, that taxes be paid promptly, and that personal faults and sins be regularly confessed in public. Forbidden in the established Kimbanguist tradition are tobacco, hemp, alcoholic drinks, bathing or sleeping in the nude, and the eating of pork and monkey.[35]

There is also emphasis upon a theme of fraternity among men. With the easing of legal bans upon the movement, it was early insisted that Kimbanguists bore no one ill will and that they welcomed any and everyone into their fellowship. In a statement issued by the church leadership, it is urged upon its members to show love and charity by imitating Christ, to demonstrate a horror of evil and a love for good, to practice moral purity, and to pursue "every religious practice which favors respect and harmony among men and nations, which is the essential foundation of true peace and harmony in the world."[36]

While there are surely exceptions, observers testify to the generally friendly and open attitudes shown by

---

[34] A mimeographed paper entitled "L'Eglise du Christ sur la terre par le prophète Simon Kimbangu face aux problèmes politiques, economiques, sociaux tels qu'ils se posent au Congo, en Afrique et dans le monde." The paper is signed by J. Diangienda, "Le chef Suprême du Kimbanguisme"; Représentation Légale, Léopoldville.

[35] Raymaekers, op. cit., p. 695.

[36] Article 4 of the church's published statutes, appearing in the Moniteur Congolais, No. 19 (August 23, 1961).

leaders and their followers toward others and particularly those within the Protestant community.

There are further the typical Kimbanguist emphases upon frequent meetings characterized by much group singing and prayer. There is emphasis on the baptism of the Spirit which leads at times to esoteric rituals in secluded places and emphasis upon combatting witchcraft and the trial by ordeal by the power and protection of the Spirit in the Kimbanguist pattern.

Methods Employed

In viewing Kimbanguism from the standpoint of methods used, one sees immediately that there is clever use made of effective propaganda. The church leadership distributes material regularly in French, Kikongo, and Lingala pointed at explaining Kimbanguist aims and views. Kimbanguist leaders have had regular radio time on the Léopoldville station during which religious programs are aired which bear striking resemblance to other Protestant programs. In areas where the movement is strong, efforts have been made to maintain rural dispensaries and primary schools. School work has been facilitated by the acquirement of legal recognition and the consequent access to subsidy funds for educational purposes. For teaching staffs and materials, they rely heavily upon traditional Protestant sources.

Though not in a belligerent tone, there is none the less continually kept before the public the idea that Kimbanguism is truly African in every sense of the word. If only by impli-cation the thought is all the same clear that other Congo churches are non-African.

Lay participation and lay responsibility are heavily underlined. The ordinary worshiper has ample opportunity for self-expression in their services and it is constantly impressed upon him that as a follower of Kimbangu he is responsible to make personal contributions to the cause in whatever manner possible.

There is a tendency to cluster believers together in their own rural villages or, if in urban centers, in their own neighborhoods. These communities tend to follow a detailed schedule of weekly activities, including worship and prayer services, choir rehearsals, and separate meetings for women and men. Kimbanguist services resemble closely the Protestant pattern with emphasis on choral singing and preaching. Outsiders and visitors are generally welcomed to these services and are treated as appreciated guests. There is less accurate information concerning the meetings reportedly held in private for purposes of baptism, healing, and instruction.

In the matter of ordinances, apparently the only one formally observed is that of baptism, which in Kimbanguist teaching is the baptism of the Holy Spirit. It appears to be the general pattern to require that a person be first baptized by an established Protestant church which, in their interpretation, is a baptism with water only. It then remains for the convert to be baptized with the Spirit at the hands of a Kimbanguist leader. There seems to be no practice of

Holy Communion as an ordinance though there is some emphasis upon the fellowship of shared food.

In Kimbanguist literature it is repeatedly stated that the church bears rancor toward none, that it has no political interests or ambitions, and that it welcomes one and all into its fellowship. Here once again one has the problem of attempting to balance the formally declared position of the church with its actual activity and conduct. In their relations with missionaries, the declared position seems to be borne out in daily activity. While there have been specific instances of encountered hostility, by and large attitudes have been open and friendly. Church leaders and followers alike consistently declare their Protestant roots.

Attitudes toward the African community, however, seem to be considerably more aggressive. Traditional beliefs and practices which do not lie within the Kimbanguist framework are dismissed with disdain. Pressure is typically brought to bear upon clan elders who in turn exercise large social authority over those under their jurisdiction, sometimes overriding in the process the personal preferences of other individuals involved.[37]

It is perhaps at the point of its declared nonpolitical nature that there is reason for the closest scrutiny. There was, for instance, the formal effort that was made soon after independence to have Kimbanguism legally declared as the new nation's state religion.[38] There was the occasion

of the reunion of Abako representatives about the casket of Kimbangu's remains as they were being returned to Mbangu.[39] There have been the occasional areas of unrest where Kimbanguist groups have been accused of involvement.

In all of this, however, it must be remembered that during the thirty-five year ban, the attitudes of the Ngunzists arose out of an intricately interwoven matrix of political protest, social revolt, and spiritual searching. It would indeed be expecting much to ask that all of these motivations be brusquely sorted out and abandoned. Before passing judgment, we would be wise to attempt first to trace carefully the watershed of genuine Kimbanguist intention in this regard.

Kimbanguism's Appeal

Any missionary who has come into more than the most casual contact with Kimbanguism has soon found some questions tumbling about in his mind. What makes this movement "go"? Wherein lies its dynamic? What is there about it that appeals so tremendously to today's Congolese? Without pretending to isolate the appeal, at least parts of the answer are clear. In a heady atmosphere of political independence and the reassertion of old cultural values, there is the appeal of an African personality and an African church. Against a background of missionary-established churches and programs which reflect a sober and reserved approach to the expression of religious faith, there is the appeal of the emotive "everybody

[37] Raymaekers, op. cit., p. 695.

[38] Chester Jump, Field Secretary of the ABFMS, 1963; a personal letter.

[39] Gilis, op. cit., p. 73.

pitch in" atmosphere of the popular movement.

As African society and culture struggle to adjust to the encroachments of an outside world and seek to find place and purpose in the new scene, there is for many an African the appeal of a movement in which he can feel himself not on the periphery but in the main stream of events — known, recognized, and value. In the midst of a society which reflects its internal strains and uncertainties by the resurgence of ancient beliefs in witchcraft and black magic, there is the appeal of a religious faith which speaks to their fears and says, "Of course there are spirits and trial by ordeal but we can protect you from them."

Having as a result of seventy-five years of missionary effort become familiar with the terminology and ideology of the Christian faith, there is the appeal of a movement which applies known religious concepts to everyday problems in culturally relevant terms.

So then, to return to our original question, what is it that carries Kimbangu Simon's name at the masthead? A popular movement with religious trappings that cover essentially secular and political interests? A nativistic movement that embodies a protest against foreign influences and spearheads a revival of old cultural patterns and values? A sect characterized by such syncretism that it cannot rightfully take its place in the framework of orthodox Christianity? A dynamic new expression of the Christian faith which attempts to bring the gospel to bear in a meaningful manner upon the life and problems of today's African?

Or, to put the question otherwise, what is essentially the nature, form, and content of Kimbanguism? It would by this time seem clear that Kimbanguism is primarily a religious movement and that those who identify themselves with it do so essentially because of spiritual needs and concerns. But it is at the points of form and content that it seems still too early to attempt evaluation. As the Congo itself continues on its weary way of violent flux, so Kimbanguism also continues in a state of great fluidity. Within the stream of the movement there are two clearly discernable currents. The one with its Léopoldville based leadership strives to structure the movement as a church with all the implied hierarchy and organization. The other, which is village based, leans strongly toward the pattern of loosely knit, highly autonomous local groups exercising great freedom under their local leaders and giving, in the process, freer expression to their feelings in activities familiar to their culture. Which current will eventually prevail? Will both continue to flow strongly under the force of Kimbangu's name? Or will there eventually be a split? Only the passage of time can tell us this.

And what about its content? Where does Kimbanguism actually fall in terms of the established Protestant community? Crucial, here, are two issues. The first, obviously, is that of the persons and ministries of Jesus Christ and Kimbangu Simon. What will Kimbanguism finally decide concerning each of these two and what in their creed will the relationship between the two be? If, as we very much hope, the belief will come to be that Jesus Christ is Lord and Savior and Kimbangu an earnest and dedicated messenger and interpreter of the gospel to his own people, Kimbanguism's place on Christianity's scene will be much easier to determine. But if, as some of its proponents currently insist, Kimbangu is indeed declared to be the African's savior and Christ is relegated to a status of a co-savior or no savior at all, Kimbanguism will of its own initiative take itself outside the framework of the Christian faith.

A second basic issue is that of its syncretism. To what degree will cultural beliefs and practices finally be incorporated in Kimbanguism? Will they be of such a range and nature as to make the movement irreconcilable with the Christian faith? This is another question that only time can answer for us. But in the meantime let the warning be sounded that he who attempts to draw lines of demarcation between what is "Christian" and what is "pagan" assigns himself a heavy task indeed. As a matter of fact, some of the lines that have been traditionally drawn for years by missionaries may upon closer scrutiny be found to have been hastily, unwisely, and subjectively drawn. At what points, for instance, does the profoundly rooted Bantu belief in malevolent spirit beings actually collide with the Christian faith? The missionary pattern has generally been to brush aside such beliefs as superstition, as evidence of spiritual and intellectual immaturity. But the African has continued believing, and often fearing, while the missionary has for the most part ignored the whole business. We would do well, rather, to come to honest grips with this problem and attempt to see what the gospel has to say to the point of this and many other very real needs and fears. Dismissing them with an amused smile has been a poor answer in the past and will be an even poorer one in the future.

Could it perhaps be that Kimbangu Simon will eventually and posthumously be established as the unknowing founder of a new Protestant denomination? This must surely be accepted as a possibility. And in the light of the veneration and honor we typically accord the John Wesleys, the John Calvins, and the Menno Simons of our own religious traditions, why should something like this strike us as being strange or undesirable?

A Challenge to Missionary Statesmanship

Springing from Protestant roots, nurtured on Protestant traditions, using Protestant Scriptures and hymns, thriving in long established Protestant areas, Kimbanguism is not something which will disappear if ignored, weaken if criticized, or change if scorned. It is a religious movement which has deep roots both in Congo Protestant tradition and missionary endeavor. It has been shaped both negatively and positively by missions and missionaries. It is a movement with which we have both historic and spiritual links. It is an inescapable part of today's Congo scene. It constitutes a many-faceted challenge which we must honestly face.

Against a background of a partially subsidized and largely institutionalized mission program, there is the challenge of Kimbanguism's dynamic grass roots lay movement. Spreading along arteries of communication, across tribal lines and language barriers, its shock troops have been its enthusiastic, unsalaried laymen. Without the benefit of Western style programing, multiple committees, and financing schemes, the movement continues its growth carried along by the infectious excitement of ordinary people who are of the opinion that they have found something worth sharing. We must admit that Kimbanguism has succeeded in recapturing something of the same dynamic that carried the New Testament church with such irresistible force through its first precarious years, the dynamic of a cause from which every participant derives valued benefits and for which he feels personal responsibility. By comparison with the effervescence of this lay movement, the average mission-established church program must appear quite routine and unexciting indeed to the Kimbanguist.

There is in Kimbanguism the challenge of its forthright acceptance of the fears and problems and beliefs of the common African as they are and the attempt to bring solace and help to bear upon them. No time is spent in trying to disprove or discredit African beliefs. Effort is rather made to help the African face the realities and circumstances of his life and to triumph over his fears. We, as missionaries, may have for too long taken the easy path of superficial acquaintance with the African mind and soul. It has been easy to equate our concept of what African beliefs ought to be with what they actually are. Much more serious effort must be made to plumb the wellsprings of African motivation, belief, and need. Until we have an accurate understanding of African fears, how can we hope to bring to bear a gospel which is designed to cast out fear? If nothing else, Kimbanguism's success indicates that it speaks a language that is understood and addresses itself to problems that matter a great deal to the average African.

There is the challenge of Kimbanguism's syncretism. What happens when a religious faith whose precepts and practices have been shaped in a Western world of nuclear families and insular living, private enterprise and furious competition, formal contract and technical sophistication, is introduced into a society of extended families and face-to-face living, communal endeavor and shared resources, clan loyalties and humbler scientific achievements? If this faith is to be more than a rootless transplant, there must be adaptation of the gospel to the realities of the African scene and an orientation of practice that says something in an African context. Here too it has been easy to bring to Africa "lock, stock, and barrel" the views and practices of our own spiritual traditions. The time is upon us to take the more difficult path of creative, exploratory, and meaningful Christian living in the context of an African setting.

There is the challenge of a practiced

faith. There is something deeply disquieting about the repeated testimony of newly won followers of Kimbanguism. Upon being questioned they will typically declare that the teaching and exhortation of mission-established churches and of Kimbanguism are essentially the same. But, they go on to add, Kimbanguists do what the established churches say people ought to do! As the older established churches tend to settle into the accepted patterns of institution and tradition, it is dangerously easy to substitute passive intellectual assent to the claims of the Christian faith for the active practice of this faith in terms of transformed daily life.

Finally, there is the challenge of Kimbanguism's allegiance to its Protestant roots and heritage in spite of long years of harassment, scorn, and abuse. That the leadership and laity generally find it within themselves not only to acknowledge freely their Protestant origins but to extend a hand of friendship is in itself witness to a striking spirit of Christian fraternity. This is a gesture we dare not ignore. Whatever irritation, excesses, irregularities, or extremes there may be in given places and specific instances, we owe it to ourselves and to them to make every effort to maintain meaningful dialogue between us.

It would be tragic if, because of a lack of comprehension and charity on our part or because of a failure to establish meaningful communication, we would finally, as a Protestant community, come to alienate this movement. Rather may it be that through mutually beneficial contacts and the disciplining ministry of the Spirit of Christ in both our camps, Kimbanguism may come to take a rightful place within the Protestant community where it can make a rich contribution to the Body of Jesus Christ our Lord.

Kenneth I. Brown

Worshiping with the African Church of the Lord (Aladura)

No ONE can study the full religious scene in tropical Africa without long and serious attention to the increasing number of independent church groups. Some of these are break-aways from the mission churches; and some are break-aways from break-aways, in a chain reaction. Others were originally African with a continuum of African leadership. Roughly defined, the African independent church is a Christian-based group having no organizational ties to a non-African church or mission body.

If one asks why, the reasons for the existence of these groups are numerous and often local. In the case of the defections from the historic churches, dissatisfaction with Western leadership rather than doctrinal differences most likely brought the break. A second reason may have been the hunger for African cultural expression within the experience of worship, especially if the white leadership was demanding Western patterns and Western ways as a test of Christian loyalty.

Kenneth I. Brown retired as Executive Director of the Danforth Foundation in 1961, after which he made two prolonged trips to Africa. His special interests include the African independent churches, African education, and cultural changes, about which he has written books and articles. 718 Audubon Drive, St. Louis, Missouri, 63105.

For many of the churches springing initially from African leadership the intent has been to interpret Christian faith and practice in ways that were harmonious with African thought and habits. Many of these churches, although by no means all, accept polygamy as a cultural practice, although it is now generally agreed that polygamy was not a dominant motive for the organization of these churches, as was once believed. Fundamentally the African independent churches came as an expression of creative and ambitious African leadership, burning with desire to establish an African Christianity, as opposed to the Western Christianity of many of the mission churches. The generous response of the African people appears convincing that many were willing to seek the assurance that they could be both African and Christian, holding to their traditional customs while serving the Lord as African Christians. Many of these independent churches are held within tribal or national bounds. No one of them has succeeded in establishing itself throughout all the nations of tropical Africa. A few, however, have spread beyond national boundaries to cover recognized regions.

Within West Africa, for example, there is a group of independent churches commonly grouped together for classification as *Aladura*. *Aladura* is a Yoruba word, built upon *adura* 'prayer.' The full word stands for "one who prays" or "a prayer group." The Aladura churches correspond to those termed "Zionist" in other areas. The descriptive terms, "prophet-healing" is sometimes used to reflect two of their major emphases, prophecy and faith-healing. Within the Aladura grouping are commonly included the Apostolic Church, the Christ Apostolic Church, the Cherubim and Seraphim Society, and the Church of the Lord (Aladura).

Professor H. W. Turner, Lecturer in the Crowther School of Religion, University of Nigeria, Nsukka, has made a definitive study of the history and doctrines of this fourth group, the Church of the Lord (Aladura). Portions of his thesis will soon be available in print. It was my interest in Professor Turner's work that urged me, during a visit to Africa in 1964, to visit as many member churches of this organization as possible and to participate in as many of the services, rites, and ceremonies as the leaders might be willing to permit me. My interest and my participation increased with their abounding friendliness and rich welcome. I visited their gatherings and talked with their leaders in Sierra Leone, Liberia, Ghana, and Nigeria, the four West African countries where there are branches. My wife and I were received most cordially by the primate and founder of the church, Dr. J. O. Oshitelu, and his staff, at their Ogere Headquarters, near Shagamu, Western Nigeria. And in Monrovia, for the fortnight when the local church under

the leadership of Apostle S. O. Oduwole, Administrator for Liberia, played host to the thirteenth annual (Liberian) Conference of the Church of the Lord (Aladura), I was privileged to see the church in full and vigorous action.

Special Ceremonies

It was in 1961 that I first met Apostle Oduwole[1] and visited his new church structure, not yet completed. His friendly welcome, his ready answers to my numerous questions, and his gracious invitation to participate in a river baptismal service the church was celebrating[2] served to feed my curiosity which moved to genuine interest in the Church of the Lord. During the months of my return to the U.S.A., the apostle and I corresponded, and when it came time to

[1] *The Liberian Star*, April 8, 1965, with the headline "Brutal Murder of a Prophet," reports the assassination of Apostle S. O. Oduwole on April 7, 1965, allegedly by Walter Sayjreh, a Liberian. The report reads that Sayjreh came to the headquarters of the church, asking for prayers on his behalf to be said with him, by the apostle. As they knelt by the apostle's bed, Sayjreh, according to the account, "pulled out a foot-long axe from under his shirt and started dismembering" Mr. Oduwole who died shortly after his arrival at the Government General Hospital. *The Daily Listener* for April 24, 1965 (like *The Star* published in Monrovia), uses for its headline, "Sayjreh Pleads Insanity" and reports that Sayjreh believed that he had been promised full healing for an illness he was suffering, within a fortnight of his first visit; instead his condition worsened. No word has been received of the appointment of Apostle Oduwole's successor.

[2] Kenneth I. Brown, "Aladura Baptism," *The Hibbert Journal* (January 1964), pp. 64-67.

prepare our itinerary for the 1964 African visit, I sought his counsel. His reply was somewhat overwhelming. Not only did he promise that during the fortnight of the national conference I might "participate in all the special ceremonies of the church," but he also listed those services: the regular Sunday morning services of worship and thanksgiving, the churching of babies, the semi-weekly service of faith healing, a mass baptism (at the 1961 service there had been only two candidates), a late evening communion fellowship of the Lord's Supper, a circumcision, ordination and anointing, the spiritual exercise of rolling on the mercy ground, and possibly a naming ceremony for a child born to one of his parishioners.

Except for the naming ceremony, the promises of the apostle were amply fulfilled. I attended all the services and was cordially welcomed. The African child by tradition receives his formal name at a family gathering, given a specified number of "purification days" after his birth — eight for the male, fourteen for the female. It so happened that the Monrovia church did not celebrate a naming ceremony during the days of our visit. Compensating for it was the service of churching the apostle's twins and the Old Testament rite of "slaughter for thanksgiving." Throughout the fortnight there were many hours of happy conversations with the apostle and his wardens, the fine young group of disciples, young men in training for the church's ministry, and also some of the visiting delegates from the eighteen branches outside Monro-

via. The door of welcome was opened wide, and I entered gladly.

During the days in Monrovia I was studying the work of this important independent church within the African religious scene. I was determined to maintain, as fully as I could, my objectivity of judgment, but also to avoid any hostile criticism. I came as a friendly witness, not as judge. As far as I was able, I tried to see the activities of the Church of the Lord (Aladura) through African eyes. So often when their customs of worship or action differ from Western ways, there are sound African reasons. If I allowed myself to judge difference only on the evidence of Western reasons, I would have failed to see truth as the African sees truth. I was eager to hold my mind open to differences, with ability to view them objectively; and a willingness to accept such differences as integral aspects of the African cultural pattern, worthy in the eyes of the African, as the Western pattern is to us.

When the African invitation came to me, I participated with gladness in their rites and ceremonies. I preached upon their invitation in the Monrovia church, removing both my shoes (as is their custom upon entering their sanctuary) and my socks (the African seldom wears socks) and entered their high pulpit in my bare feet. I prayed with them. I accepted their prophecies foretelling what was to come to my wife and to me. I was honored when they invited me to be anointed a cross bearer and I rolled with a young disciple friend on their mercy ground.

Sunday Morning
Worship Service

The new Monrovia structure for the Church of the Lord (Aladura) is of yellow stucco, conventionally rectangular in shape, with a square front tower which will some day support a steeple. The large, open nave is approached through the front vestibule or the side doors. Short steps lead up to the choir, where a ponderous reading pedestal stands, and beyond, the railing dividing the altar enclosure from the choir. In large features of construction, the impression is Western. In smaller features, such as the angular golden figure supporting the desk for the Bible, the carving and lighting of the altar, the impression is African. The nave together with the rear balcony must seat, when crowded, close to a thousand persons. Both Sundays that we attended the morning worship service, about three hundred chairs had been put on the floor between two columns of pillars, generously spaced and with a ten foot aisle for separation. The men sat on the left, the women on the right, from the position where my wife and I were assigned at the back of the choir. Everything was scrupulously clean and in good order for the sacred occasion, a condition which does not always pertain in the African church.

The service, scheduled to start at ten o'clock, suffered a short delay, but by ten-twenty the processional hymn was sounding on the wheezy reed organ which is soon to be replaced by an electric organ. We who were to have parts in the order of worship gathered in the anteroom, waiting for the voice of prayer. Those of us with shoes or sandals slipped them off; most of the Africans were barefooted. Typed programs of the service were distributed, calling for twenty-four specific items of worship. The mood of the little group was vibrantly expectant, worshipful, matching that of any similar group in any similar anteroom that Sunday morning throughout the Christian world.

The young disciples, minister-apprentices in training, in their white prayer robes were prepared to lead the procession, followed by the conference visitors in garments of many bright colors, each carrying his "rod of Moses," an iron instrument betokening authority and power to heal. Apostle Oduwole was wearing a saffron gown with a broad red sash; around his neck hung his rosary and ecclesiastical cross. His hand bore the sacred rod. The women choir members were in red, wearing mortar boards; the men wore white surplices over red cassocks.

As we marched singing to our places, I noticed that the seats in the nave were completely filled. The number of men appeared to equal the number of women, all wearing white prayer gowns. Many of them were spotlessly clean and fresh; a few were in rags and less than white. In the far vestibule, there was a tier of bleacher seats, comfortably filled; but uncomfortable seating, I should judge, for the long service. Later my query brought the information that this section is reserved "behind the tent" for menstruating women or women unchurched following childbirth, and also for men and women without the prescribed white covering.

Three of the first four program items were hymns. The African independent church is a singing church. In variety and volume and in glorious harmony, their singing surpasses that of the historic churches. And always, it comes *con amore*. There are few hymn books to provide the words, for the congregation is largely an illiterate group. The African repertory of hymns is amazingly wide to the visiting American and if African memory falters, there is always someone lining out the hymn after the manner of our own colonial days. Charles Campbell, an attractive, capable young disciple, lined the processional hymn, skillfully thrusting the words for the next musical phrase into the moment of musical pause in such fashion that the singing continued in strict, although slow rhythm. The order of service for the morning called for seven hymns, and always all verses, sometimes mounting to ten or twelve, were sung. On several occasions I have heard a hymn immediately repeated, again with the entire series of verses, and the verve and the gusto never diminished with the repetition. There is an indefatigability about the African church singing.

The quality of their church music is difficult to describe. The voices sit widely on a note, not centering cleanly but spilling over to the fringes of the note. There is an organ fullness and richness to them. In a quartet of Western voices, one can distinguish the four threads beautifully blending into a common weaving. With African choral music, among untrained congregational singers, it is more like great handfuls of differing notes, not always in strict harmony, yet melding together like a tremendous organ chord that is neither quite major nor definitely minor. Rather than being one apart, listening to music, I felt myself surrounded by music, embraced and cherished by music, and, in moments of intense delight, literally swallowed by music. Many of the melodies were adaptations of Western hymns. Others were beloved folktunes from African lore. A few seemed to be relatively new hymns, which one imagined may have come from a night singing group in the glow of a swinging lantern, rather than the self-conscious creation of an individual. Much of the emotional strength of the Sunday services of the African independent churches comes through their gift of music, tender hands for offering the presence of God to the rejoicing, worshiping man.

The Beat of the Drum

One cannot do justice, however, to the music of the African church without special tribute to the drum. The African drum, so completely a part of indigenous culture, is fully accepted in most, although not all, of the independent churches, and also within a few of the historic churches. Occasionally one meets with the cymbal or the tambourine, infrequently the huge bass viol, and many cleverly improvised rhythm beaters. But the drum is master, and the mighty pounding beat with its colorful syncopation and intricate variations, undergirds the gusty congregational singing and creates a world of fire as well as of music.

Four different types of drum had part in the service of the Church of the Lord (Aladura): the great bass drum provided its heavy marching pace; the snare drum contributed its more fanciful rumbles; the secoul (a rectangular drum held vertically and hit with a stick) which offered its own individual sound; and the tembley, held between one's knees, like a cello, and played delicately with one's fingers and the heel of the palm. The insistent, pacing, unrelenting rhythm beat in my brain long after the service had finished.

Two hymns, a long period of spoken "adoration" based on the fifty-first Psalm led by the apostle, a "victory" hymn — four items of the twenty-four, and I noted mentally that an hour of time had sped since the prayer in the anteroom. The total service continued for five hours. I thought of the American Christian, free to criticize his pastor if the benediction follows the prelude by more than fifty-nine minutes — with one minute of grace. Later I asked a church member what was the average length of the Sunday morning service. With African distaste for the specific, he answered, "Maybe four, maybe five, sometimes six hours. I have known longer, when the Spirit moves."

During our times together, our two Sundays in Monrovia, I was not aware of any restlessness or uneasy movement on the part of either adults or children. African children are beautifully disciplined to sit quietly in formal adult gatherings, and should any young one be in a disturbing mood, it is the pleasure and duty of the community, as well as the parent, to rebuke and chastise. Occasionally an adult would slumber. Occasionally also, an adult would leave for natural reasons, only to return in a short time. At no time was I conscious of holes in the congregation.

The long, sustained adoration at the beginning was in part the apostle speaking and in part antiphonal, with many responses from the choir and congregation: "Holy, Holy, Holy: Praise the Lord; Hallelujah," shouted many times, always in repetitive groups of the sacred number three or seven, and infrequently, the multiple of twenty-one.

The Scripture reading brought us from the first chapter of the First Book of Samuel the story of Hannah, presenting the infant Samuel before the Lord. Were we not that day to see the apostle and his wife, "spiritual mother of the church" present their newborn babes before the Eternal One, even as Hannah? Then a well sung *Te Deum,* offered with full Western harmony; a second lesson from Luke, all reverently and enthusiastically offered and received. Another hymn, the Creed, the announcement of the river baptism that evening, the conference plans for the week, and then the "assessment." Young leaders with pad and pencil passed through the congregation, row by row, asking each member for his self-assessment. How much could he, how much should he give the church that week? It was a substitute for the biblical tithe, and appeared to work satisfactorily.

The Aladura service is one of reverent hilarity. In African eyes reverence is not uncompanionable with boisterous joy, if one will squeeze from the word "hilarity" all connotation of profanity. "Make a joyful noise unto the Lord," the Psalmist commanded, and the African Christian in the independent church is doing just that with his handclapping, his eager and fantastically speedy drumming, and his ready responses: "God be praised," "Thank you Jesus," "Serve the Lord with gladness," and the ever present, "Hallelujah." In hearty conscience they make their joyful noise. Gladness, noisy shouted gladness, is the heart mood of many of the worship moments. It was, moreover, a service of personal involvement and much individual participation "even as the Spirit moves," — and the Spirit, like the worshiper, seemed to be in frequent movement on that Sunday morning.

The Aladura churches, like the American Pentecostal churches, put great emphasis upon the work of the Holy Spirit, and its outward manifestations within the experience of "possession." These manifestations include violent shaking, trembling, foaming at the mouth and dripping saliva, waving of the arms with crying and dancing. I have seen them all at various times in the African independent churches, the violence decreasing with the increase of education and cultural refinement. In illiterate Africa, as opposed to metropolitan Africa, there is an easy release of inhibition, an emotional freedom that one never finds in the services of the historic churches.

I discovered, however, a noticeable difference in the response of men from the response of women, to the experience of possession. The men were always more restrained, less open to obsessive emotional hunger. From time to time, women both young and old, under possession, would twirl in the wide aisles, tossing their arms high and sometimes hopping over and over on one foot. During the months in Africa I saw very few men in such moments, and indeed, I felt there was on their part occasional embarrassment as they seemed purposely to avoid watching a possessed woman.

But I shall give a totally false impression if I suggest continued pandemonium throughout the hours. For much of the service the congregation was as restrained and as attentive with their calls of praise as the early American Methodist camp meeting, shouting "Hallelujah" and "Amen." There were times, when unsuppressed emotional expression was invited, with the ministers and officials participating; and the invitation was always accepted with alacrity. There pertained a curious sensitivity to their own pattern of response, subtly led by the elders. I have seen times when a woman might continue her dancing in the aisle when time had come for the Scripture reading. Everything was held in suspense. If the awesome silence did not restrain her, a woman cross-bearer would put her arms around the dancer and lead her gently to an empty seat. It was always done without obvious rebuke.

In a questioning period with one of the wardens I said, "You count these women, possessed, to be especially blessed of God and under the impulse of the Holy Spirit?" His answer was an emphatic "Yes, we do." "But," I continued, "why do you restrain them at times within the service?" His answer was given smilingly, "We believe in possession but in moderation." While checking my notes I wrote a query to one of the Aladura officials, "Why do I never see the ministers of the church in ecstatic movement or speech?" His answer was, "The fiery Spirit, or the Holy Spirit, which you see on the women, is on everyone. The apostle, ministers, men, are all in the Spirit. The men control and suppress the power. That is why some of the men prophesy without shaking."

The Cross-bearers

During our first Sunday service at the Monrovia church, three women were anointed and charged as "cross-bearers" — an official title given a group of lay members who are dedicated to the service of the church. They were given hand-sized wooden crosses which they are expected to carry with them whenever on church missions, sometimes sticking them in their broad belts, sometimes carrying them in their hands.

The following Sunday the order of service called for ordination and anointing. A follower was anointed a disciple, having expressed his determination the previous week to train for the ministry. After giving satisfactory answers to the apostle's catechismal questions, he was anointed with oil three times and given the hand cross and a palm branch as symbols of spiritual victory. Three church leaders were advanced to the post of elder, with authority to preach and assist the apostle. About eight men and women, all Africans except myself, were anointed cross-bearers. For the higher orders of the church, there were no candidates; had their been some, the ceremony would have been more elaborate, with specific designation of authority and, for an evangelist, the gifts of a hand bell and a Bible.

It is recorded in the church book that the text of my sermon that morning was taken from John 13: 34-35. I began in the African fashion of calling "Hallelujah," three times and after each call the congregational response came in a hearty "Hallelujah." I had patterned my sermon to include at frequent intervals a series of Bible texts. It is an African custom and always there is valiant competition to be the first to locate and to read aloud the verse called for. One young drummer of drum-like girth wanted so eagerly to read, but each time another voice rose before he was ready, usually that of a bright young woman nearby with agile fingers to scoop the pages. My delight was great when for the last text he responded first and his booming voice rang out exultantly.

Churching of the Twins

The churching of the twins followed the sermon. Preparations began the previous noon when a male sheep without blemish had been slaughtered "at the door of the tabernacle of the congregation before the Lord . . . on the side of the altar northward," according to the prescription of the first chapter of Leviticus.

As we gathered with the small group of attendants, we noted two sheep tethered at the rear of the church headquarters. A hole had been dug to receive the blood of the animal that it might return without defilement to the good earth. One of the wardens presided, reading first the instructions from Leviticus and then the Eighth Psalm. The prayer that followed came to us as though directly from the pages of the Old Testament:

If the ram be killed for oneself, then, O Lord, bless this ram; if for another, Lord, bless the giver. . . .

All the power of death against me, all sickness and trouble, let them go into this ram. Death, trouble, and sickness in my family, let them go into this ram. All power of death and sickness and trouble against the church, let them go into this ram. . . .

Bless this ram for peace and for joy, to me and my family and this church.

An attendant tied the legs of the animal and held him so that the throat rested above the hole. The jackknife provided proved too dull for the occasion and a Gillette razor blade was located. The blood from the slashed throat poured forth into the earth. In like manner a second sheep was brought as an offering, one for each of the babies.[3]

My wife and I slipped away at this point. Later, we were told that the bodies of the animals were singed and severed into the traditional parts: the right rear quarters plus the heart for the apostle; the neck to the presiding warden; the head and legs to the

young disciples. The remainder was carefully cooked into a tasty stew and served over rice from a huge container to all the Sunday congregation who lingered.

At the Sunday churching, Warden Fyneah presided, calling to the altar the apostle and his wife. They came bearing proudly their two lovely twins, Peter and Patience Edith, in spotless white. During the earlier hours of the service, the children had been sleeping cuddled in their snow white blankets on the floor or wriggling noiselessly on the broad laps of their mother and her companion. There were nursing bottles of milk and pacifiers handy and once when a whimper came, Mrs. Oduwole opened her lace *buba* and gave her ample breast to the baby. The formal ceremony of the churching is scheduled for thirty-three days after birth (sixty-six for the girl),[4] when the mother has been cleansed and purified from the defilement of birth. It is a service wherein the children are formally received by the welcoming congregation. This was Africa, but it was also the ancient land of the Israelites. A long ago past was being enacted in a contemporary African Christian church.

Before the reading of the 116th Psalm, the apostle and his wife gave thanks for the twins, praising God for his goodness. Then Warden Fyneah took the twins, one at a time, carrying them tenderly to the altar for presentation to God, with three loud hallelujahs and appropriate response. The giving of gifts brought

---

[3] According to Apostle Oduwole, the Church of the Lord always uses sheep, never goats, for their offerings. "The sheep is slaughtered not as sacrifice but as an offering of thanksgiving. We believe only in the sacrifice of the Lamb of God, Jesus Christ."

[4] Leviticus 12: 1-7.

palm leaves, signs of victory, for each child, and two bottles of holy water and seven palm leaves for the parents, all with loud shouts and the three hallelujahs and the congregational loud echoes. The constitutional generosity of the African is continually reflected in his church services.

The twins were lifted high in the air in glad thanksgiving and the people sang their gleeful "Blessed be the name of the Lord." Then, as one of the disciples commented later, "the fire broke forth." The apostle led the church in a series of twenty-one resounding handclaps of exultancy. The apostle jumped in his joy seven times and danced his way down the choir into the broad aisle where he was joined by the church officials, the disciples, and the people. Their joy was hilarious, unrestrained. The drums blared like trumpets with their fantastically long rolls. The fire burned furiously, but it was the fire of the Spirit.

The ability of the African to move quickly and easily between extremes of emotion is impressive. One is reminded of American youth conferences where the same rapid travel from hilarity of praise to solemn intercessory prayer, from almost rowdy fellowship to hushed emotion, is easily accomplished.

Thanksgiving

From the noisy acclaim of the churching, we moved without break to the solemnity of what the program called, "Special Vows and Thanksgiving," followed by "General Thanksgiving and Divine Revelations and Holy Interpretation." Throughout our African journeys I was greatly impressed by the continuing emphasis upon public thanksgiving common in most of the independent churches but especially stressed in the Church of the Lord (Aladura). It far exceeds anything I have observed in the historic churches, either African or Western. The African Christian lives in a consciousness of the relevant, daily presence of God. Unlike the Western man who explains good and bad fortune as the result of scientific causation (either understood or concealed within the inexplicableness of chance), the African sees the good things of life as direct gifts from God. Or, if he still lingers within the assumptions of his primitive religion, he acknowledges them as gifts from God or the lesser deities, or from the powerful ancestors who are looked upon as creatures of power but with semi-divine status (something like the Catholic saint). If God has given, God must be thanked — thanked with words of gratitude and praise, thanked with gifts to his church, thanked with actions of gladness. Every independent church service I have attended found abundant time for vocal and contributory thanksgiving.

In recognition of the opening of the annual conference, the thanksgiving service welcomed the eighteen branches of the Liberian Church of the Lord (Aladura). Each of them came forward to kneel at the rail, to pour forth their thanks, and to leave their gifts. Then individuals came by designated groups, or sometimes alone, to tell their thanks and to give. Everyone, I think, came forward at least once, and some several times, kneeling or prostrating themselves before the altar rail, a spokesman telling their thanks, reporting their special pleas, and recording their fresh vows of faithfulness. Each time the apostle or the warden made individual recognition and the plate was passed for their thank offering. Routine though it may have become with tradition, it appeared to be a section of the service to which the African heart responded in wholeness.

On one occasion, with special jubilation from all, a woman of years was assisted to the railing. The apostle announced that a week before she had been carried there on a stretcher, a victim of crushing paralysis. Now the healing hand of God had separated her from her affliction and she was on her way to full healing. The friends and the worshipers shouted their praise to the healing God, and her worn and wrinkled hand left a crumpling of American greenbacks, for Liberia uses our currency.

On the second Sunday, as the faithful were coming forward, I noted with special interest a very beautiful young Liberian woman walking very stately as she carried a lovely baby on her arm. As she came closer to where I was sitting in the choir, I saw she was leading a ram by a rope, straight down the aisle, up and through the choir to the altar rail. The apostle and the young woman spoke together. For five years she had borne no children, burdened by the disgrace of barrenness, than which there is none greater for the African woman. She had prayed to the Lord many times. She had vowed a ram in exchange for a child and

the Lord had accepted the bargain. Here was the child, blooming, healthy, and lovely; here was the ram. The congregation shouted its joy.

The final items of the twenty-four were the closing hymn, prayer, the benediction, and the recessional. The hour on my watch showed three. I marvelled at my own body restraint and my lack of hunger. The group in the rear was still crowding the uncomfortable bleachers and I saw no change in the size of either the male or the female sections.

It was evident that this long, unhasteful service was deeply attuned to the wishes and perhaps the needs. of the African friends. Although very occasionally on the long, long prayers, a faulting brother or sister might need to be restored to wakefulness, their attentiveness was beyond question. When the apostle preached, there was once when he broke his sermon with the traditional hallelujah, expecting a full response. The voices came feebly and he cried, "Are you all asleep? Hallelujah!" and with a roar like the movement of the ocean came the response, "Hallelujah! Hallelujah! Hallelujah!" Even in departure there was no haste. The men and women moved slowly toward the house next door where women were ready with the stewed meat of yesterday's sheep served with small hills of rice and savory sauces.

Night Baptism

In the program of the national conference of the Church of the Lord (Aladura), the first Sunday night had been set aside for the services of baptism. The site commonly used is the Mesurado River, flowing through the capital city. Like many of the African independent churches, including those of Anglican origin, baptism is by immersion, sometimes once, more often three times. There is preference for an outdoor service. Tradition reports that in the early apostolic days baptism was administered in running water and the African churches are minutely obedient to Scripture and tradition. The new structure of the Church of the Lord in Monrovia contains no indoor baptistery. Liberian weather is not a matter to be reckoned with.

Darkness had fallen that Sunday evening when the faithful began their three-mile trek from the temple to the water site. Up through the congested, noisy, neon-lighted heart of the city the procession marched; then down the hill to the long-spanned Mesurado Bridge, following the main highway until they came to Clara Town and the by-pass which led to a quiet spot on the bank of the river, their destination. It was a spot in total darkness except for the faint, far gleam of lights from traffic on the bridge and a few bright spots from the opposite bank.

Using a taxi from American laziness, I had arrived at the site at the hour announced for the evening service — only to have to wait. But the waiting brought its own delight of quiet and peace and an invitation for reflection. An hour passed, and a church leader and a woman member arrived. Later, Bibi, one of the baptismal candidates came. Bibi was an appealing young Liberian, country born, who at twenty-three had come to the city to find work. From lack of early opportunity or perhaps lack of that interior drive which sometimes, in Africa as in America, creates its own opportunity, he had had no schooling whatever and possessed scant familiarity with English. He appeared to understand my simple sentences as we talked, but his replies were fragmentary and halting, and sometimes unintelligible. He spoke what I judged to be a mixture of tribal vernacular and strangely contorted English. It was evident that the coming event held deep significance for him. I longed to know the full nature of that significance, but Bibi was unable to share that with me and I with my own handicaps could not peer into his mind. Between us there came a clasping of spiritual hands, but the warmth of outreach never rose to the level of easy words.

About two hours after the scheduled time, Bibi and I heard voices singing and the steady beat of drums becoming louder as the procession moved down the highway. There were about fifty or sixty in the group with a fringe of children coming, I judge, from the neighborhood. Children everywhere like parades. The beloved African rhythm pounded steadily; the voices rose and fell, all in a high mood of joy. As they neared the river, the temper became more violent; the tempo quickened, the rhythms multiplied, doubling upon themselves, and there was a glowing frenzy of anticipation. The group members were in white, wearing the simple prayer gown I had seen at the morning-service. It made an admirable baptismal gown for the candidates.

Warden Fyneah was in charge, substituting for the apostle. An evangelist, serving as assistant to the warden, drew in the sand of the river bank the holy circle of containment, symbolizing the oneness of the church. Candles were set and lighted, both within the circle and in a row along the water edge. The singing group surrounded the circle while one of the leaders read the Scripture and led in loud prayer, with the ready group responses of "Hallelujah," "Praise the Lord," "Thank you Jesus." Someone spoke in strident tones of the demands of Deity upon the human condition. Between and behind the drum beat, the collective voice rose in praise.

One of the disciples waded into the river to plant the white cross in the water at the site of baptism. The warden consecrated the water with prayer. Another disciple formed the candidates into two files: twelve young men and nine women, some young, some old. The warden and his assistant took their places in the waist-deep water by the cross and one by one the file of men advanced to them. The candles with their scanty light flickered. No one had thought to bring flashlights. Except where dark faces stood directly over a candle, one could not be recognized by facial features. Only the white robes of the two ministers and the candidates in the river, and the splash of sudden immersion marked the site of baptism.

The candidate knelt in the water as the warden addressed him, "State your faith and confess your sins." The candidate made his reply. The warden admonished, "If God forgives you, will you leave all your sins? Promise 'yes.' " If the candidate equivocated or became evasive, the minister compelled him to direct answer, "Say yes or no." There were none that night who refused to make a full affirmative reply.

Then with intended violence (for in the eyes of the Aladura churches the second birth, like the first, comes with violence and pain) the warden plunged the candidate backward, deep under the night waters until he was swept by buoyancy and suddenness from his kneeling position, and found himself horizontal. With the first immersion the warden intoned "I baptize you in the name of the Father," and from the bank came the group singing, resting on the heady drum beat; then the second time, "I baptize you in the name of the Son," and the voices and the drum throb continued; for the third time, "I baptize you in the name of the Holy Ghost." The candidate was then brought to his knees in the water and knelt there while the warden, his hands on the bent head cried, "God will forgive you your sins and will pour forth his Spirit upon you." Blessed with the blessing of God, the man who had come confessing him rose, erect.

That it was a high moment of life, even a high moment of religious life, none of us present could doubt. The baptized left the site of the cross in exultation, with the step of a sprightly dance — joy within, emotion fulfilled, a sense of belonging, of assured belonging. This, I believe, was certain; and what else? That must have depended on the individual heart. I prayed especially for young Bibi when his turn came; he without ability to write or to read; coming from a condition cabined, cribbed, confined, and yet so eager, so expectant, so certain.

The men coming from the water gathered on the bank, waiting for the others to join them. The file of women advanced. But here there was a difference. Their high spirits brought wild waving of arms. At the immersion of the first woman, perhaps because of fright or emotional seizure, the candidate was possessed by the Spirit. She thrashed about in the river, beating her arms against her body and shouting against the noisy music from the bank. The warden persevered with the aid of his assistant, and she and others following were put beneath the water three times, often with some difficulty, and then assisted from the water by the young men in their wet robes who came forward to help. After several hymns, which the group sang with a heart devotion, and prayer, the little procession formed again to find its way back to the city and its homes.

This service was in stark contrast to the semi-private ceremony I had participated in at the same site in 1961. Then the apostle, for my benefit, had arranged a worship service of great beauty on the sandy bank, and the rite of baptism for two candidates. The mood at that time had been restrained; here it was pentecostal. For a Western observer the earlier service had been filled with spiritual insight; tonight the observer caught a taste of African life, the throbbing

of an African heartbeat. Even on the edge of this great, national metropolis, heavy with Western influence and under a veneer of sophistication, the genuine Africa was speaking and singing, confessing its evils and believing in the promised righteousness as the drums beat steadily.

Holy Communion

The sacrament of holy communion was appointed for the evening of the last Sunday of our visit to Monrovia. "Why evening?" I asked, and Apostle Oduwole, surprise registered on his face, answered, "Why, the last supper of Jesus was held at night. Of course it is set for the even hour. In America, do you not ... ?" I confess to some uncertainly of mind as I faced the sacred occasion. How could the boisterous drum, the ecstatic dance, the unpredictable acts of the possessed be fitted into the solemnity of heart and mind so important for the partaker at the holy feast. But my fears were ill founded, my anxiety unworthy.

The service began at nine o'clock and ended a half hour before midnight. The apostle, the wardens, the disciples, and the church members were all in their simple white prayer gowns. There were no drums, no choir, no high jubilation such as had marked both Sunday worship services. It was a celebration in the root sense of "to solemnize," marked by simplicity and utter reverence. It was, I suspect, to accentuate this solemnity that the tempo of the singing and of the entire service was hesitantly slow.

The early part of the service included the regular items of their worship service: hymns, adoration, prayers, and praise. This was followed by a roll call of the church members and the inspection — a checking on the eligibility of those present to partake of the communion, cared for by the apostle himself. No one is invited to attend this service as an observer. If he comes, it is as a Christian intending to participate in the celebration. The apostle moved among the people, row by row, questioning, scrutinizing, judging. "The Spirit of the Lord allows me to see into the hearts of people and if I find any not right with God, unworthy, evil in intent, it is revealed to me and I ask him to leave." When later I asked how many he had had to remove at this inspection he happily answered, "None." Later, however, during the act of cleansing, I had seen him linger for several minutes, talking with a man who later rose and left the church. "Why?" I asked in our conversation the next day. The apostle answered, "He was not eligible. He was not ready to commune. It was only last Sunday that he was baptized and normally I expect not less than three months between baptism and the first communion. Before communion he must have teaching." I did not press further and do not know whether this pattern is one of the apostle's designing or common practice throughout the church. Although communion is stated to be held regularly, often at an interval of three months, I judge that it is held rather infrequently. None of the church leaders whom I questioned throughout West Africa spoke of it as coming at specific times of the year. They regard it as a major mystery within the church which must never be secularized.

After the inspection, the handbell was rung and the items of the normal service — hymns, prayer, Scripture reading — followed. A unique feature of the preparation to receive the sacrament is the ceremony of cleansing. I had first participated in this ceremony in the Church of the Lord (Aladura) in Freetown, Sierra Leone. There, after consecrating the water and the palms, the young Prophet Adofo had passed through the congregation. Each member knelt as the prophet shook water from a hyssop branch three times on each bowed head. Then he blessed the kneeling one and gave him a piece of palm. In many African churches the palm leaf is the symbol of spiritual victory, even as the water is the symbol of purification. Later he explained that in the Sierra Leone church the rite of cleansing comes on the first Sunday of each month.

In Monrovia, Apostle Oduwole consecrated the bowl of water and the palm fronds. Then passing through his group of clergy, he sprinkled water over the head and shoulders as they knelt, and immediately every worshiper prostrated himself in supplication. The apostle, assisted by the prophets, went through the congregation, cleansing and blessing.

Whereas the movement of the service to this point had been sluggish according to Western standards, when we came to the supper itself, it was cared for with reverent dispatch. The familiar Gospel words setting forth the first supper were read. The hymns were those familiar to Western ears, apparently beloved by all. The apostle served the bread and the wine first to the two wardens, the clergy and the young disciples as they knelt at the altar rail. Then the wardens moved to the high altar to assist the apostle as the members of the congregation moved forward to partake.

It appeared to be a service patterned by and entirely acceptable to the African Christians, and at the same time it duplicated in outline and mood of spirit the Episcopal form, beloved in the West. The bread was the African bread, hand torn in fairly large pieces. The wine, I judge, was a native beverage, served from a tray in individual cups. As soon as each group had been served, they were dismissed with prayer. When the last group had departed from the rail, the recessional hymn sounded, "Where He Leads Me I Will Follow."

The Clinic of Faith Healing

One item of doctrine, foremost in the life of the Church of the Lord (Aladura), as it is in many of the African independent churches, is a complete trust in the power of God, especially the power to heal. Sometimes it is called "divine healing," sometimes "faith healing." The terms seem roughly synonymous: the Lord of power responding to the call of human faith, or human faith summoning divine power to its need.

The calendar of the Monrovia church called for such services two mornings each week, with additional clinics in times of special need. The clinic I attended was on a Tuesday morning. The healing seekers gathered in one of the open rooms on the first floor of the church's headquarters next to the sanctuary. All chairs and benches had been removed. We sat on the floor, the African with more apparent comfort than I. At one end of the room was a table with a white cloth covering, a seven-branched candlestick and other candleholders with partially burned candles.

On the floor beneath the table were standing fifty or more open bottles of water. During the first hour of the clinic at least thirty more were added as each attendant brought a bottle, sometimes with a name tag. The Church of the Lord (Aladura) places heavy stress upon water as a symbol, also upon holy water, meaning water which has been consecrated for healing and for blessing. In later conversation Apostle Oduwole reported that after a clinic service, those in attendance would carry their bottles of blessed water back to their homes.

The clinic started at nine in the morning and continued until past two o'clock, with the group lingering on so persistently that I never saw all of them leave. I absented myself during the lunch hour, but no one else left, probably because this was Shrove Tuesday, when they were expected to observe the ordinary fast, abstinence from all food until after sunset.

An acting apostle of strange appearance but infinite kindness presided. Although short of stature and slender in build, he had the most thunderous and also the most delicate handclap I have ever heard. Shifting from beating the heel of the palm against heel, to variations of heel against fingers, or fingers against fingers, he made a variety of rhythms within a variety of loudnesses which fascinated me. Attentive to detail, sensitive to the needs of the people, he offered effective and apparently wholly acceptable leadership. When he led us in song, his throaty, hoarsely resonant voice shifted between singing and shouting with cries that were rather terrifying.

The acting apostle began in the customary manner of lighting three candles in the large candlesticks. An assistant came through the group with an incense pot made from a perforated tin can, swinging it vigorously. The apostle followed with hyssop, to sprinkle the water of cleansing upon the group as each prostrated himself to receive it.

At the beginning of the clinic service there were about twenty-five women present (young or middle-aged rather than elderly), and six or eight young men, most of them in their early twenties and of athletic appearance. We sang a hymn, kneeling, "Spirit Divine, Attend our Prayer," our leader directing both by voice and with an accordion. We prostrated ourselves as he read a familiar psalm, the group crying "Amen" at each metric pause. Then prayer by a young prophet and by others — an outpouring of emotion, of heart desire, of inner urging, coming at times in words which I found unintelligible and at times in wordless crying or a plaintive whining. "Adjuba," the prophet cried, using a vernacular name for the Deity. Again and again,

"Adjuba, Adjuba," and we responded, "Adjuba." The prayers were often antiphonal with the worshipers responding to his words with cries of "Thank you, Jesus," "Hallelujah," "God be merciful," "Adjuba." All of this was to a vigorous accompaniment of handclapping, but without drums.

The succession of prayers with responses, of familiar and beloved hymns, and familiar chants must have proved effective in opening the hungry hearts to the waiting Spirit. The mood was that of eager expectancy, of happy anticipation. From time to time a woman would moan or rise and dance under possession.

A friendly young disciple had chosen to sit by me so that he might help me to understand the service. I asked him to name for me some of the hymns, so often sung in vernacular, with constant repetition of a single phrase. He listed:

There be no one like Jesus to me,
No matter how sinful I be.

Jesus, you know, you know, you know
Our worry . . . our trouble . . . our trials.

Jesus never fails.
The people of the world will let you down,
But Jesus never fails.

I know,
Jesus loves me everywhere I go.

The music at the healing clinic was not pleasing as song, as it had been in the Sunday worship. Here it was less music as music, but rather a vocal release from hurt, from need and suppression.

Suddenly the apostle stopped the singing and waited with infinite patience for the three possessed women and one in the act of prophesying to sink into quietness. His reading of the One Hundred Fiftieth Psalm was appropriate with its admonition to praise the Lord with all the instruments and dance of man's being. At each pause the group responded with a loud "Amen." Then, "I never disappointed one day since I joined the army of the Lord; I never disappointed one day," sung softly, *con amore*.

To rest my aching limbs, for we had been standing now for an hour or more, I spread myself on the floor and studied the notebook belonging to my disciple neighbor. It was open at the order for clinic service. The first item was the lighting of the candles and the ringing of the handbell seven times. The items that followed duplicated the order of worship of Sunday with the hymns, adoration, prayers, dreams and visions, and holy interpretation and prophecies. How binding this listing was I do not know, for our presiding officer had not followed it exactly, preferring, I judge, to "play it by ear" — and by Spirit.

It is significant that the actual anointing of the sick came only after three or more hours of prayer and chanting, but prayer and chanting which surrounded and embraced the theme of healing and the importance of faith. During these early hours, I had seen women with their wooden crosses — cross-bearers — gathering around a kneeling woman to pray with her and to bless her. The power to heal, the Church of the Lord believes, is not a monopoly of the apostles or the prophets, but a spiritual strength which lies in other consecrated hands.

Anointing of the Sick

The anointing of the sick came as the climax to this careful and lengthy preparation. It was somewhat less dramatic than I had anticipated. In no case was it a striving for a charismatic healing, but rather a laying before the Holy One a human condition in which by faith his help was sought. The sick came forward in groups, separated by ages and condition and sex. By this time the small room and the adjoining room were crowded, a group numbering as many as seventy. Probably two-thirds of them on the fringe had been standing for several hours.

Twenty-one children formed the first group to push their way forward through the crowded room. The cross-bearers made the sign of the cross in holy oil on their foreheads and the leaders blessed them, touching gently each bowed head. "Now the big bellies," the young prophet called, and four pregnant women came forward to kneel in prayer. Then the barren women, more than twenty of them, some gaily dressed and attractive. They knelt for the anointing oil, and in each case there were prayers and the hands of the prophet in blessing. Someone called for a hymn, and with a throbbing of voices (for there was an outreach of eager faith and hoping desire that could not be ignored), they sang, "Remember me, remember me, remember me, O Lord." One felt the pronoun was always in the first person and very close to home.

Some in the room continued to clap and sing and dance quietly while the cross-bearers anointed the kneeling sisters, plagued by the greatest unhappiness an African woman can support (the unhappiness of being without child), and the prophet blessed them. The barren women extended their open hands for a blessing, and this time the prophet sprinkled them with holy water.

The fourth group was the general group of women who were ill with various diseases. They left singing, "Jesus never fails." Then came the men, some twelve of them, moving forward to ask for healing prayers. Two handsome young Africans, powerfully built, attracted my admiration. I had noted them earlier as they were participating fully throughout the hours of the service. When the clinic had been dismissed, I asked one of them what his particular ailment was. His reply was surprising and yet threw light on the entire procedure: "I'm not ill. Do I look it? I came seeking an added blessing from the Lord."

The last group was the cross-bearers, with time for individual prophecy as some of the women spoke their assured hopes for their needy friends or confirmed their faith in the new health that the power of the Spirit could bring. They too were blessed by the prophet.

The service ritual in my disciple friend's notebook called for closing hymns, closing prayers, and the benediction. In weariness I moved to leave before the clinic had formally ended, but one of the kindly young giants put out his hand to stop me. "Better not leave now. One of the women has asked that you pray for them, each one, and bless them with your hand on each head. Better stay." I was grateful for his kindly suggestion for I had not understood.

In time the apostle called upon me and bade them make a path through their ranks as they knelt. It was a traumatic experience as I moved among them, opening my heart and my lips to seek and to bring to them the assurance of God's love, God's forgiveness, God's grace and power for all their needs, by touch, word, and love. When I had finished with a general prayer, several of the women prophesied relating their visions: "I saw a circle of angels in the room as we prayed." "There was bright light in the room." "I heard voices other than the single voice."

The apostle pronounced the benediction, but they lingered on. I moved to speak to the leader who had presided so graciously and to the young African who had spared me the embarrassment of unintended rudeness. There had been no visible miracles of healing, and yet there was no obvious disappointment. They would wait, believing in the power of their God to give his healing in his own good time.

Circumcision

In indigenous African culture, circumcision for the boy stands as the threshold to manhood. In the older days and still current in the African rural areas, at puberty the boy and his age group enter the bush school for their training in the customs, the history, and the mores of the tribe and then undergo circumcision as the symbol of their readiness to accept adult responsibilities. An uncircumcized man is less than human. Female circumcision (clitoridectomy), common in the past, has steadily decreased and is now generally practiced only by the more primitive tribes.

In the Church of the Lord (Alalura) male circumcision commonly takes place shortly after birth or in connection with the naming ceremony; sometimes later within the years of childhood or at puberty. The surgery, in the eyes of the church, may be performed in a hospital by a trained physician, or by the apostle or a qualified official of the church. It is, however, the definite expectation that by the time the male seeks baptism for church membership (commonly between the age of twelve and eighteen), he shall have been circumcized. I asked Apostle Oduwole and other leaders of the Church of the Lord whether circumcision would be required of an adult seeking membership, who for some strange reason might not have undergone the surgery. Their answers were halting and vague, for the reason, I suspect, that they had never encountered such an animal. If an uncircumcized European came seeking membership, they would recommend circumcision, I believe, but not require it.

When the apostle wrote me, naming circumcision as one of the rites of the church to which I would be admitted, it was my expectation that I should be present at a religious ceremony. At least in Liberia at the present time (and also in Sierra Leone, I am told), this is not the case. There was no prayer, no Scripture reading, no devotional atmosphere.

A young boy of three had, through his parents, come seeking circumcision and the apostle was accepting his responsibility. An operating table, covered with a rubber sheet, was set up on the upper porch of the church headquarters. Charles Campbell and another young disciple assisted, this being for them a learning experience. Some day, within their ministry, they might be required to perform the operation. The boy, an active, eager youngster, accepted the situation cheerfully, although fear hovered near the surface of his cheer. The apostle and the young men were protectingly kind to him as he mounted the table and stretched out on his back, although I assume that he had not been prepared in advance for what was to follow. In the tribal initiations the boys received the surgery while standing erect, the initiates in a row, their hands clasped behind their heads. I have heard of some tribes where the patient is stretched in a sitting position on a chair where he is held in place by the hands of his elders. The apostle was following the common mode of the hospital.

Remembering that the Church of the Lord takes a strong position against all medicines, both Western and African, I was surprised to see the apostle carefully sterilize a syringe and needle, with which he administered novacaine deep into the foreskin and the penis while the disciples gripped the boy to the table. The surgery was done rapidly. The unsterilized knife proved too dull and a Gillette razor blade became a successful substitute. (The attention to hygiene was African rather than

Western.) The total foreskin was removed with five or six swift strokes of the blade and then a moment for careful trimming. There was no finger of skin left hanging as is the custom in some African tribes. Apostle Oduwole dripped carbolic acid on the wound and then made an anointment of oil for healing — "holy oil," Campbell called it. As soon as the surgery was completed, the boy's struggle lessened and his cries diminished to a whine. The apostle skillfully bandaged the penis with sterilized gauze and helped the boy to his feet for a picture. Later the apostle commented to me that he is frequently called upon to perform circumcision on small boys, infrequently for boys at puberty, practically never for adults. I asked him about the use of the local anesthetic, in an anti-medicine church. "Ah, but we do not regard the anesthetic as medicine; I use it only to reduce pain in circumcision. To reduce pain is good. It is the will of God."

As I have traveled among the independent churches of Africa which ban all medicines, African and Western, I have sensed a diminution of hostility to Western medicine. The questions are rising: Perhaps God does not choose to use African medicines for his own ends of healing, but can he, perhaps does he, not use Western medicine, supplemented by faith, to achieve the bodily wholeness which is the Christian's goal?

"The church does not count circumcision surgery as contrary to its stand on medicine?" I asked the apostle.

"Definitely not, for circumcision is required by the Old Testament. More-over it is a nationally accepted custom among Africans."

"But are there other situations where surgery is deemed necessary and wise even by your own church? What if an African is suffering from a ruptured appendix. Would you sanction surgery?"

"We have never had that situation."

"But have you ever recommended surgery to any of your seriously ill members?"

The apostle was thoughtful. "I remember one who was operated on for hernia and the church did not disapprove. Perhaps, someday, in very serious cases we might accept surgery."

I felt that the apostle's answer indicated a breach in the wall of opposition to Western surgery and medicines, which in time might open wider while still banning African juju, witchcraft, and sorcery. Later, in Lagos, I met the Rev. Dr. S. O. Adejuwom King, Apostle of the Pentecostal Church of Christ, a breakaway group from the Church of the Lord (Aladura). Apostle King stressed that one of the differences between his church and the Church of the Lord is in the use of Western medicines. "I advocate the use of Western medicine for it is God's intelligence, God expressing himself to care in the way we understand. In Nigeria and all over the world, we have seen the great work done by the hospital."

I suspect that the Church of the Lord, along with other African independent churches, will move gradually, under the impact of Western science, to augment their present emphasis on faith healing with the medicines and surgery of the West.

Rolling on the Mercy Ground

My young Liberian friend, Charles Campbell, had invited me to roll. "I do not know how," I replied, wondering if my eagerness to participate in all the rites and ceremonies of the Church of the Lord (Aladura) should extend this far. "I teach you," Charles replied. "Teach me as you would an African friend," I said. I think he took me at my word.

I had been told by the young Prophet Adofo at the Freetown (Sierra Leone) Church of the Lord that their Mercy Ground was on the sands of the ocean. "You roll under the consecrated sun," he said. But at that time I had not known the significance of the rite and had not asked to visit the site. Later at the Kumasi (Ghana) Church, I saw their Mercy Ground carefully encircled with whitewashed stones. The Mercy Ground on the premises of the church in Monrovia is a rectangular section of sandy soil, about nine by fourteen feet, surrounded by a wall seven feet high. At one end is a wooden cross. There were two crosses the night I rolled.

Charles and I agreed to meet that evening at nine. The hour was unfortunately chosen, for it proved to be the time when the long business session of the general conference was dismissed and immediately a dozen women crowded the enclosure to jump and clap and shout and pray. All were Africans, for my wife and I were the only non-Africans I saw at any of the church's services during our fortnight visit.

Charles and I attempted to pray quietly together in an empty corner, but a stout-bosomed prophetess sought to take us over. We fled. Still determined, we waited until after eleven when the women left. I confess that my dominant motive was curiosity; for the young disciple it was ardent hunger for spiritual strength. "I must, I must roll tonight. I must get the power of the Spirit. I'm empty! I'm like a barren woman within me. The power is gone from me. It will return if I roll."

Someone has generalized that for the young African Christian the guide word is "power," for the young American Christian it is "meaning." That night Charles's search was definitely for spiritual power. "Rolling is a spiritual exercise," he said. "We plan to do it, we disciples, and the church members, three times a day — morning, noon, and night. And power always comes."

Knowing the allegiance of the African independent churches to scriptural texts to validate their actions, I questioned him. His reply came quickly, "Did not David roll? Does not the Bible say that David rolled naked before the Lord?" Frankly, I didn't know. No such verse came to my mind, nor have I been able to locate any in a concordance; but for Charles this was unimpeachable authorization.[5]

---

[5] Later I questioned an official of the Monrovia church on the scriptural justification of rolling. He offered two biblical references (2 Samuel 12: 16 and Ezra 10: 1) but neither seems pertinent to the African custom. Micah

"Naked?" I was responding to his quotation.

"Only when it is very late at night and one is alone. Tonight we wear shorts and a shirt." Earlier he had suggested this garb, saying it was hard to roll in long trousers.

Outside the Mercy Ground, I stripped to swimming trunks and a sport shirt. Charles was wearing blue denim shorts and a faded shirt. He lighted a fresh candle at the foot of the cross and we knelt to pray. Very quietly one of the elder prophets attending the conference entered, choosing a square of ground apart from us, where he quietly, persistently rolled over and over, back and forth, repeating in a scarcely audible voice his fervent prayers. It was for him obviously a sincere act of devotion; perhaps, as Charles had said, "a great spiritual exercise." So quietly did he leave and so absorbed was I in our own exercise, I did not notice the moment when he left.

The next forty or fifty minutes brought an experience I have never successfully analyzed; doubt followed doubt, question followed question, and yet there were moments of exaltation. That it meant something quite different to African Charles than to

---

1: 10 comes nearest: "In the house of Aphrah roll thyself in the dust." During a visit to the Nima Temple of the Church of the Lord in New Town-Accra (Ghana), Prophet Samuel Krow praised the exercise of rolling as a manifestation of humility, an expression of intense desire, an act of mortification. "Does not the child roll on the ground," he asked, "when seeking gifts from his father? The act of rolling lightens the body, opens the spirit to inspiration; therefore we roll on the Mercy Ground."

American me was probably inevitable. Whether my non-African cultural background, my inexperience, or my years would forever bar my full entrance into the mood and experience, I do not know. I record what took place.

Possession by the Spirit

Charles had me kneel before him and with his hands variously on my head, clasping my neck, or spread wide on my shoulders, he prayed fervently, ecstatically, words pouring out, "The power, the power, of the power of the Holy Spirit. Give us the power. O God, O God, O God, send down thy power on this seeking brother to prepare him for thy work that he may preach and heal in the power of the Spirit." Over and over they came, words that seemed to be pleading for an idea.

Earlier he had said, "We shall light the candle and then we shall pray. Then you will jump and clap and shout, maybe three times, maybe seven times, maybe twenty-one times. All sacred numbers." He bade me jump twenty-one times and I jumped twenty-one times, reveling in long forsaken exercise, although my leg muscles screeched their discomfort. He bade me clap and I jumped again and clapped twenty-one times, turning myself as I jumped in a kind of ballet figure. I stopped, panting.

"Pray now." We prostrated ourselves before the cross and touched our foreheads to the sand. We both prayed with our own words in all sincerity, for the experience of the power of the Holy Spirit, although I was troubled by doubts that power would normally come through the activities we had engaged in. Charles, perhaps fortunately, entertained no such doubt as he lay by my side, fervent in prayer.

Charles had me kneel before him and this time, almost in a cherished state of possession, or at least of unrestrained emotion, he worked my head and my body back and forth in circles and in spirals. I gave myself freely to his leading, wondering if a proxy for a religious chiropractor had me in his hands. Meanwhile he was praying with words that came tumbling over each other, "The cross, the cross, the cross, the Spirit, the Spirit, the power, the power, the power."

I felt myself growing dazed and a little dizzy but never unaware nor uncritical of the situation in which I was involved. For a moment I wished I could put the reaching for rational analysis aside and give myself totally to the fervor, the ecstasy which were so patently his.

Then again we jumped and clapped and shouted, and then we rolled. It was exactly as the word implies. With hands clasped to protect my face, I rolled over and over from one wall to the other and back, again and again. At first the physical sensations were uppermost in my mind — the feel of the warm sand, the motion of turning, the encircling; but these quickly diminished and finally disappeared, and in their place came a kind of neutral vacuum. I had no compelling inner delight; I felt no buoyancy of fresh power. I rolled until I was out of breath and lay panting.

Charles favored me with the compliment, "Good, good," and then,

"Now I roll." I sat against the fence and watched. With his youth and experience, he was as agile as a gazelle and as graceful as an impala. Perhaps it was for five, ten, perhaps fifteen minutes that he rolled. I lost all sense of time. He was racing from wall to wall, his young body whirling and whirling, over and over, back and forth. All of the time he was spewing his words between ejaculations of breath, "The power, oh the power, oh the power; the power is coming to me. The power is coming, is coming. Mine the power, the power." He lay still, panting heavily. "It is enough, enough."

Then, speaking to me, he said, "Kneel down." I knelt before him and again he prayed in blessing, pressing his hands strongly upon my head, uttering again and again the key words of his spiritual vocabulary. That it meant much to him I shall never doubt. As for myself, I do not know. I am certain, however, that it was enriching to be in the presence of a dedicated young African who undeniably and fervently believed that his path was leading him into mystic union with the Spirit of the everlasting God. In retrospect my memory is of an hour, physically exhilarating, enjoyable because of its novelty, undeniably interesting, and with clear spiritual overtones; but quite removed from the realm of high spiritual significance. I never achieved that delight in spiritual exercise so uppermost in Charles's mind. I never once put credence into the concept that this is the open road by which all may achieve oneness with the Holy Spirit. The idea of the Spirit of the true and holy God using these avenues for his approach to his seeking creature man was never within my bounds of my faith. And yet, in the past men have believed otherwise; in the present, men do believe otherwise, including my friend Charles. I would share religious experience; indeed I would make serious attempt to share such religion experience with all honest men. And so I rolled one night at midnight on the African Mercy Ground.

Promises Fulfilled

Our days in Monrovia were coming to a close. Apostle Oduwole had fulfilled his promises except for the naming ceremony, and for that there could be no blame. The fellowship with the entire church had been warm and friendly. The experience of complete acceptance was unforgettable.

"For your last night in Monrovia, a reception," the apostle had said. "The church will have a reception for you and your lady." We eagerly accepted, now knowing what an African reception might entail. But last days and nights have a way, when one is moving on a tight and crowded schedule, of accumulating more appointments than the hours can digest.

In the late afternoon of that last day we attended a garden party at the beautiful estate of Dr. Charles Sherman, Minister of the Treasury, as well as retiring President of the President's Advisory Council of the International Y.M.C.A., then meeting in Liberia. We were prepared to leave in ample time but the cry was raised, "President and Mrs. Tubman have arrived." Protocol in Liberia, as in

the U.S.A., irrevocably demands that no one shall leave a social engagement at which the President is present, until he and his party have taken their departure. Our situation was further entangled by a dinner engagement following the church reception.

Therefore, for good reason we were late to the reception, finding ourselves upon arrival in the midst of their evening "Lenten Service of Praise and Prayer" — words at the top of the typed program given us. We slipped into our accustomed places at the back of the choir, aware of the many friendly glances coming our way. The apostle, knowing our predicament, with sensitive kindness, broke the continuity of the program as soon as it was permissible, to move to the item, "Presentation."

Mr. Maximilian J. Tagoe, an official of the church, rose to read an address of farewell, extravagant words of appreciation for our small contributions to the members — extravagant for they had given us far more than we had given them. The sincere friendship of the statement, however, moved us.

The apostle, knowing the document was a matter of three typed pages, suggested that the reader skip to the final page. When he had finished we were presented with gifts. There is no people more hospitable or more generous than the African. My wife was given a beautiful Liberian dress, with swirling skirtcloth and an exquisite lace *buba*, or waist, and a colorful headdress to be tied in butterfly fashion. For me they had a white prayer robe with embroidered shawl collar and a blue waist sash similar to the borrowed ones I had worn for their ecclesiastical gatherings.

The African joy seemed to match our joy, ours expressed in faltering words of gratitude and theirs in shouts and hand claps, dancing and singing. Reluctantly and with glowing hearts we slipped away, knowing we dared not interrupt further their period of worship and regetting that we could not touch each hand in the congregation, exchanging the African embrace of the thumb with its unspoken prayer that God will bless our friendship. So often since that fortnight in Monrovia our spirits have reached back to the yellow stucco church on Centre Street to the neighboring church headquarters with its inclusive fellowship — the ebullient apostle, the kindly wardens, the cheery disciples, and the Aladura friends.

The deeply cherished image which is mine of the religious life of the Church of the Lord (Aladura) in Liberia, is that of an earnest, enthusiastic, dedicated group of seeking African Christians — Christian with a faith centered in the Bible, although often looking at the verse rather than the book and sometimes stalling in the Old Testament at the price of deeper insight into the New; and African, loving the best in their own centuries-joyful before the Lord. They have old culture and joyful as David was not found their way as yet into ecumenical Christianity, and for that matter many Western Christians are lagging along that highway. But in their white prayer gowns or their Western dress, they are African Christians, seeking afresh the countenance of God and the ways of the Spirit, as they peer through African eyes. The promise, "Seek and ye shall find." was not given first to Western Christians, and never was it given to Western Christians alone.

Kenneth I. Brown

Forms of Baptism in the African Independent Churches of Tropical Africa

The sacrament of baptism is accepted as one of the great symbolic ceremonies by both the Western and the African churches. Within the African Independent Churches baptism is joyously received, deeply beloved, enhanced for their members by the respect for water and the rites of cleansing inherited from their traditional African faiths. Complete immersion is the generally accepted form.

Among the African Independent Churches (AICs), baptism is usually by immersion, three times in the names of the Trinity, and in running water. Within this generalization, however, there is infinite variety.

Since many of these churches are breakaways from non-immersionist churches, the insistence on complete immersion may appear strange. Of the two sacraments of the Protestant mission churches, holy communion and baptism, communion, or the Lord's Supper, is without precedent within the African traditional religions, except for possible distant relation to the custom, still practiced among some tribes, of the rite of blood covenant. Some of the independent churches reject the Christian tradition of communion entirely, and even when it is adopted, it is frequently reserved for special occasions.

Baptism, on the other hand, is the generally recognized gateway through which the new Christian is expected to pass in his desire for "salvation" and/or church membership; consequently the service of baptism is held with

Kenneth I. Brown, Ph.D., is the retired Executive Director of the Danforth Foundation. Previous to this appointment, Dr. Brown served as president of Hiram College and Denison University. Since his retirement he has made five extended trips to Tropical Africa, giving special attention to the work of the African Independent Churches. Because of long interest in the forms and the theology of Christian baptism, he has studied with care their baptismal patterns. He writes from the experiences of attending many of their baptismal services and from his endeavor to see this beloved sacramental ceremony of African church life through African eyes. Orient, N.Y., 11957. U.S.A. An earlier article was "Worshiping with the Church of the Lord (Aladura)," PA, Vol. 13, No. 2 (March-April 1966), pp. 59-84.

reasonable frequency, in almost all the independent churches. It may fairly be assumed that its popular acceptance is due in part to the large place that water has in African thought and especially in the traditional rituals of cleansing.

The use of water, with sprinkling or complete immersion, has long been common among the Africans for cleansing, for healing, and for ceremonial occasions. "Blessed water," for body-washing, sprinkling or drinking, has traditionally been an African custom, useful for medicinal purposes, for the driving out of evil spirits in cases of witchcraft, and in seeking for the power of revenge. Some of the tribes of Ghana use a form of sprinkling in their naming ceremonies whereby the infant is believed to be brought out of the spirit-world of the womb into the full life of human beings. Water is poured upon the thatch of the house, so arranged that it will fall upon the infant, and thereby bring cleansing. The He-he tribe of South Africa is said to immerse in a running stream the girls who have undergone female circumcision. In the Krobo tribe of Ghana, where female circumcision is not used, there is a public ceremony of immersion in a stream, called a "washing away ceremony," whereby the girl passes from girlhood to womanhood.

Among the African Independent Churches, tradition, reinforced by Scriptural examples if not by textual command, is strong that baptism shall be out of doors, and in running water. Practically none of these have indoor baptistries, or desire them.

The custom of triune immersion comes from the deep respect of both clergy and laity of the AICs for the concept of the Trinity, wherein the Holy Spirit is strongly emphasized, and also for holy numbers: three, seven and their multiples. In the Church of the Lord (Aladura) when a member jumps in religious exultation or prepares himself for "rolling on the mercy ground," he must jump twenty-one times. The African Apostolic Faith Church in Zion, an independent group in Durban, South Africa, baptizes with seven immersions, "three times for baptism and four times for the first cleansing."

"It is unthinkable," as one bishop explained, "that baptism should be other than threefold and by immersion. Do you Westerners not read Matthew 28:19 '...baptizing them in the name of the Father *and* of the Son *and* of the Holy Spirit'?" Some African ministers follow this textually, repeating before each immersion the name of the first, second or third person of the Trinity, whereas others use the full formula at the beginning.

Forms of Baptism by Immersion

The two most common forms of baptism by immersion are, first, the Western or horizontal, whereby the candidate is laid backward from a standing position; and second, the African or vertical form, in which the baptizer brings the candidate into chest-deep water, where he presses upon the head and shoulder, the candidate's knees bending, until he has lowered himself with the water closing over his head. The African puts heavy insistence upon *complete* immersion.

The Divine Healer's Church (formerly the Lord is There Temple) uses the common Western form. I have attended three of their services: two at the mother church in Accra, Ghana, the headquarters of Brother and Sister Lawson, founders and senior ministers of the Church; and another in Kumasi at one of their branches.

The custom of the Mother Church is to hold a revival-service each Saturday night, lasting from nine o'clock until two or three, Sunday morning. Baptism for the new converts of the revival is offered shortly after dawn in the nearby Atlantic Ocean.

The church members, largely women with Sister Lawson, arrange themselves along the beach. Those seeking baptism are lined up at the water's edge, where attendants take them out to the baptizing ministers, working in pairs, knee-deep in the water.

The candidate takes his position between the two baptizers. Behind them the ocean rumbles and roars, but the two ministers seem little concerned whether they lower the seeker into an oncoming wave or into the swirling water between the surf's curls. For obvious safety it is necessary that there be two men, each with one hand on the candidate's neck or back, the other clasped tightly upon his arm. The senior baptizer shouting against the wind cries, first naming the candidate, "I baptize you in the name of Jesus Christ," repeating it three times. Then, they plunge the man or woman backward into the ocean water, raising the person for a moment of

breathing, while the senior minister puts both hands upon his head for a word ot prayer and a blessing. The attendant assists the candidate to dry land and another takes his place from the waiting line.

It is an impressive service, not strictly formal but informality seemed appropriate. What it may have meant to the believers, I have no way of knowing; apparently it satisfied a hunger or a fear in their hearts.

The second most common form of baptism among the AICs is the vertical immersion, in contrast to the horizontal form used in the Western churches. Here the baptizer, usually with one hand on the candidate's head and the other resting on the shoulder, presses downward until the water has covered the head. To be performed easily, it is necessary that the water be chest-high on both the baptizer and the baptized.

It was at a service of the Free Nazareth Baptist Church, a sabbatarian independent church outside of Pietermaritzburg, Natal, that I saw this method used with grace and skill. The Free Baptist church is a former Isaiah Shemba church, which broke away some fifty years ago on the grounds, as given me by the pastor, the Reverend Jeremiah Malinga, of too much dancing and too much stress on wearing heavy animal skins.

The church sits perched on one of the Thousand Hills. The baptismal service was to be held in a small river in the valley. The procession of church members and the visitors started down the green slope led by Pastor Malinga and his Assistant, Elphas Madonda, a youngish, muscular fellow, his handsome face serious, furrowed with deep lines. Pastor Madonda, serving as the baptizing minister, was wearing a white church robe tied with a black cord, when he made his way over the bottom of the stream, to a place opposite the seated group. His initial task was to bless the water: first a prayer, earnest and in volume, that the Lord would consecrate the waters of the stream as the waters of baptism, waters to cleanse those who had sinned. Then with a sweeping gesture of his arms, he blessed the narrow river and declared it to be "holy water."

One by one the candidates were helped to take their place, facing Madonda. One question was asked, "Are you a Christian?" And when the answer "Yes" was given, Madonda raised his hand high in blessing and proclaimed, "In the Lord, our Father, and in Jesus Christ, his Son, and under the Holy Spirit, I baptize you." His handling of each person was easy, unhasty, and deeply sensitive. Gently he pressed upon the candidate's head and shoulder until with bending knees the person dropped downward, the water rising first to the neck, then the mouth and nostrils, and as Madonda quickened the action, covered his head. With speed, Madonda raised him to a standing position. With both hands on the wet head, he prayed a personal prayer and benediction. The form of vertical baptism with a single immersion, simple, leisurely, carefully planned, had a quiet dignity to which the friends on the bank responded with reverence.

The Christ Apostolic Church of West Africa baptizes with the candidate sitting on the floor of the stream, lowering him backward until his full body rests at the bottom of the water. My acquaintance with this church came through my attendance at their Cathedral in Ibadan, where the late Olubadan, or King of Ibadan, was member and president; and with the Prophet J.T. Durojaiye, who gave me his friendship; his church is in the more crowded section of the University-city. The prophet is a forceful leader, a man with a deeply etched, crag-like face, strong with the strength of time and suffering, although in years he is not old. His smile has a radiant strength, greater perhaps because he never seems to use it unless there is valid occasion. Limited in what the book-bound West calls education, his spoken words as I have heard them in his prayers are clothed in flame and hurled with the vibrations of Thus-Saith-the-Lord.

It took some persuasion to get his invitation to observe one of his baptismal services, and when he agreed it was with the condition that I be with them for their hour of preparation of the candidate, as well as the water baptism. I have never attended any training session for baptism where the information was so carefully and systematically presented, always with Bible references.

Young Pastor Idowu, whom I had heard in eloquent preaching, was in charge, the prophet sitting by quietly. Idowu followed through from the early history of Christian baptism, the baptism of Jesus, to the meaning of the sacrament, its symbolism, and the renewal of life which it could bring. The one male candidate was told exactly what the procedures would be, what would be expected of him, and especially the mood of heart and searching of mind that he was expected to bring to the service. The Pastor continued speaking quietly, gently: "In preparing you for baptism, I prepare you both for baptism by water and baptism by the Holy Spirit. They are one, although they may not come at the same time."

The prophet spoke the final word: "The Holy Ghost is God's gift. You must stand ready to receive it. It may come at once, or on your way home. It may come during the night when you will be surprised to hear yourself speaking with tongues. It may not come for months or longer. But the Lord has promised that in your baptism He will plant the Holy Spirit in your heart; you can receive the seed and you can help it to grow."

The small group of men in which they graciously included me, started the ride to the river. Night darkness had come and the traffic was heavy. The men sang as their church bus bounced its way over the rough and crowded street. The driver turned onto a less crowded lane, and parked near a gas station. Below we could hear the noise of running water.

The immersion followed in the pattern that Pastor Idowu had described. The prophet took his place knee-deep in the river. He consecrated the spot for the baptism with scriptural passages and prayer. With the extension of his arms he called for the presence of the Spirit, and with the tinkling of the prophet's bell he announced the divine Presence.

The candidate took his place in front of the prophet, seating himself on the sandy bottom of the shallow river, his two legs together, his arms stretched forward, palm to palm below the water surface. The prophet asked the candidate's name. Then the question: "Do you believe in God and His son Jesus Christ? Do you believe that Jesus came to redeem the world from sin?" The Prophet's voice was gentle, never rising to the crescendo of his church prayers. From the bank Pastor Idowu and the interpreter (for my benefit) responded with the familiar "Aa-mein." When the candidate had answered, the prophet continued, "Upon this confession of your faith in Christ as the Son of God I baptize you," using the familiar formula. He placed his right hand on the man's clasped palms, his left behind his neck, and lowered the candidate until the water covered his face and hands in one complete immersion.

In kindness the group agreed to drop me at the University Club, singing as we drove through the night streets, the mood of service deeply upon all of us. The singing in stirring male harmony included a spiritual I had known from an American camp, little dreaming I should ever hear it in Africa: "Hallelu, hallelu, hallelu, hallelu, praise ye the Lord." We sang it over and over, they in Yoruba and I in English.

We laughed in the darkness as we parked, one white face and seven black faces, but for that, like God, no one cared. They had allowed me to be with them for one of their most sacred moments. They had given me one of the richest gifts Africa has to offer the Western man, the gift of acceptance.

We shook our fists in the air—in the vocabulary of the Christ Apostolic Church, "Glory, Glory, Praise God." We raised our hands high shaking them vigorously: "Hallelujah, Hallelujah!" As the prophet breathed a quiet benediction, we raised our arms, cupping our hands to receive that which the Lord might will to give. The prophet prayed: "Give, O Lord, to us, unworthy ones, that which is in thy loving care to give."

I have long felt in the Western baptismal services for which I have been responsible that all in attendance should properly participate in the expression of renewal and dedication that we expect to find in the candidate. It was so that night, I believe, for all of us. For myself, I felt renewed within, revived, somehow freshly clean, ready for time and circumstance as they stalked ahead in the darkness.

The prophet's parting word: "I saw a tongue of flame tonight, back there above the water, hovering over the spot where we all were … I think it was a sign."

Bishop Samson Sibanda, leader of the Zion Apostolic Church of Rhodesia, uses a variation of the horizontal baptism, akin to that which Prophet Durojaiye follows, the difference being that the candidate kneels in the river instead of sitting on the river bottom. The bishop gently lays him backward until the immersion is complete; then while he is still kneeling, places his hands on the candidate's head and blesses him, after the third immersion.

One of the few receptions for new members I have seen in Africa was conducted by Bishop Sibanda's church. The new members sat on the floor of the church building, within a circle of church members, who danced around them, praising God and offering the new members, as they danced, the right hand of fellowship.

Infant Baptism

Without statistical certainty I question the frequency of infant immersion within the AICs. The Russian Orthodox Church has long had the custom of baptizing babies by complete immersion. I witnessed such a service in the Moscow Cathedral, where a large font, filled with water, parhaps eight inches deep at the center, was used. The baby was handed naked to the priest by the parents; he carefully laid the crying infant below the face of the water, returning him to godparents who wrapped him in his new christening robe. The practice, however, is extremely rare among the independent groups.

I have witnessed only two such services within the AICs, where infant immersion was practiced not by church polity but under parental pressures. One of the Nigerian branches of the large Cherubim and Seraphim Church had announced its service of baptism, under the ministry of Apostle Sholagbade Shodipo. The place was a small stream in the heart of the teeming city of Ibadan; the time, afternoon rather than their customary evening hour, for they were eager for pictures.

It was a carefully planned service, conducted with reasonable dignity, except for the handling of the babies. The apostle and his assistants carried their metal staffs, and wore their church robes and shirred Lenten headdresses, with the white train covering the neck. There were eighteen candidates, half of them adults, men and women; three or four preadolescent childen and about six babies less than a year old. The form of the baptism was Western, with threefold immersion.

The mothers of the babies queued up on the bank, the infants in their arms. When the adults and the boys and girls had been cared for—one of the young women with a violent case of "possession"—the baptizer turned to the waiting women. The first mother stripped the loose gown from the baby and passed him, hanging by his small forearm, down the line of assistants to the baptizer in the water. Quickly, placing his large hand over the face, he plunged the baby beneath the water three times, then passed the human flesh, screaming lustily, dangling by the wrist like an over-ripe apple from a tree branch, back through the line to the mother.

It was a sadistic performance, in Western eyes, which may have left some sort of psychic bruise on the baby.

Later I reached for an explanation: "I thought you baptized only adults. This afternoon six infants."

The apostle groped for an answer. "But what can I do? I not approve. The mothers insist. They afraid baby die and go to hell. They say, if I don't they find church that will. So...!" So...!

Baptism by Combination of Forms

It is rare to find an African Independent Church offering a new member his choice of form of baptism; personally I know of no such situation. Rare but nevertheless practiced, is the custom of combining the traditional forms of immersion with effusion or sprinkling.

The Nomiya Luo Church, with headquarters in East Africa, requires baptism by effusion *and* complete immersion. The service was first described to me by Assistant Archbishop Gideon Charles Owalo, son of the founder of the church, John Owalo, and also by General Secretary Solomon O. Oiro, of the Nomiya Luo branches in Nairobi. "The pastor of the Nomiya Luo Church, wearing his white robe, stands in the river, not far from the shore. The candidates in line wait at the water's edge, each wearing a white robe which is taken off before he enters the water, leaving him in his white shirt and shorts; for a woman, a white dress. A new name is given to the candidate by the godfather, on the bank. He approaches the pastor, who scoops up a handful of water and pours it over the candidate's head, saying, 'I baptize you [using the new name], in the name of God the Almighty,' and then with prayers makes the sign of the cross upon the forehead. The candidate goes out into the deeper water, where he has been instructed to immerse himself completely, returning to don his white robe and to kneel in private prayer."

The form is the combination of effusion and self-immersion; the baptismal formula unique, coming from this church's insistence upon the monotheism of Christianity, in reply to the Muslim critic who so often cries "polytheism" in response to the Christian trinitarianism. Believing that Jesus and the Holy Spirit are less than God the Father, it is no oversight, but conviction that causes the Nomiya Luo Church to omit all reference to the second and third Persons in the baptismal formula.

Three small neighbor churches, practicing baptism by sprinkling, but also requiring immersion in the nearby Atlantic, also deserve inclusion.

It was in the suburbs of Accra that I came upon the little Bethel Church, a small independent group, pastored by Prophet George K. Amoah, a former Methodist minister. He was a vigorous young man, doing carpentry work, which he willingly left to answer my questions about his church and the necessary "steps for membership."

"First I require them to memorize the Apostles' Creed. Then, we have baptism in the church. I ask them questions from the Catechism. I say, 'Do you believe in Jesus Christ as God's Son and your Savior?' And when they have answered, then, second, I sprinkle them on the head with water." Here is the influence of his Methodist training. "The third step is baptism in the ocean, only we call this 'Confirmation.'" Here is indigenous Africa calling for threefold immersion, which the pastor performs with the aid of his deacons. "In the water I ask them to give me their confession and then I say, 'Do you solemnly forsake all these sins you have just mentioned? And will you promise never to repeat them again?' Then I pray for God's forgiveness of their sins, and the spiritual power to keep them away from sin, and I baptize them three times, as we do in Ghana." The second baptism with the emphasis on confession resembles a fairly common form of African cleansing. "When they have passed through these three steps, I say, 'You are now *confirmed* as a full member, entitled to take communion, the fourth step.' That is why we call this third step in the ocean, his confirmation."

Within sight of the Bethel Church is the Holy Temple, a small structure, whose people were ministered to by Pastor Ezekiel Moibrown. Pastor Moibrown told me that his was a breakaway church from the small Bethel Church. Pastor Amoah confirmed this, reporting that Moibrown wanted "to win souls and preach on his own; and this," concluded Amoah, "is all right by me." The doctrines and practices of both churches are presumably identical. Moibrown, like Amoah, has the two forms of baptism, one of which he calls confirmation.

A short distance from both minichurches is the Church of the Saviour, pastored by Robert O. Lamptey, an impressive young leader who, on our way to see his church, told us he had founded it in 1960, and already by 1966, had sixty members. The church is a substantial hall, without benches, but with altar, drums, and usual African paraphernalia. Lamptey has taught his group to follow Amoah's plan of dual baptism, with full confession of sin before the sea immersion. Also, at this time the candidates for membership are required to prove their knowledge of the Apostles' Creed, the Lord's Prayer, the 23rd Psalm, and the Ten Commandments.

One wonders on what grounds the Ghanaian makes his choice among the three groups. Ecumenism is still an unknown among the independent churches, and the multiplication of churches, whether new groups with new leadership or new branches of their own church, is welcomed with no apparent fear of evil rivalry.

No Baptism, Dry Baptism, and Miscellaneous Forms

Traditionally baptism implies water. The seasonal droughts so common in areas of Tropical Africa are often in conflict with the AIC members' eagerness for frequent services of baptism. But when the dry season is prolonged, the leaders have no choice but to postpone for the waiting converts the desired spiritual experience.

I have heard stories of extreme efforts to find water, even a little, before the complete drought settles upon the land. One story is of a church using the meager remnants of a small pool, some six inches deep at its maximum point. Six or eight strong men lay the candidate, man or woman, stretched horizontally on their forearms, and as the "I baptize thee" is pronounced lave the exposed head and parts with such water as may be available. Surely with efforts of such extremities, the deity must recognize the fullness of their intent. And the human observer knows how much the ritual means to the African heart.

Some AICs, however, like the American Quakers, entirely omit baptism in any form from their church practices. Very often this may be due to the lingering influence of the mother church from which they have broken. The Salvation Army, registered as a church in certain sections of Tropical Africa, does not administer baptism. The Marching Army of God, a breakaway from the Salvation Army and an AIC, continues the omission.

There is in East Africa a large group of Holy Spirit Churches, whose members are known as "Aroti," or "the Turban People," from their custom of covering the head with a white turban. The Aroti put major emphasis upon prophecy and upon the physical presence and the activities of the Holy Spirit. Their prophets claim that they have seen the visible attendance of the Spirit during their prayer periods. These churches do not practice either the sacrament of holy communion, inasmuch as bread and wine are forbidden their members, or baptism, believing that the Johannine tradition of water baptism has been superseded by Bible command, with the baptism of the Holy Spirit. It is their claim that only as persons join their group is it possible for a human being to receive this experience, wherein he may have a new name, given him by their prophet through the Spirit's inspiration.

The Holy Apostles at Aiyetoro, a water-isolated community on the ocean front some one hundred miles southeast from Lagos, Nigeria, call themselves a religious community. They practice no form of communion and when asked regarding their procedure of baptism, replied, "Our work is our baptism." They hold their "chapel service" irregularly, at the call of the oba or king. The chapel I attended came at 6:15 at the beginning of the day. Their music was stirring; the service resembled an ethical culture gathering, with concern with the daily life of their people. It is doubtful, however, if the Holy Apostles would desire to be recognized as a Christian church, or to have fellowship with the AICs.

In my many visits to African Independent Churches, I have found only one, the African Israel Church Nineveh, of Kenya, which practices "dry baptism," according to an official of the Nairobi branch. This is a service without water, essentially a ritual of confirmation with catechumenical questions and answers, including the promise of full obedience to the Israel Church. Then the church official lays his dry hands upon the head of each new believer and pronounces the words, "I baptize thee in the name of the Father and of the Son and of the Holy Spirit." There is no nearby unused font.

The variety of forms and procedures of baptism within the AICs is great, as the pages of this study have suggested. The most unusual form coming to my knowledge is that employed by the Gospel Sabbath Church of Zambia, popularly called "The Basket Weavers." All of the members in this community are basket weavers; their work is sold on the streets of the nearby towns. On the day of our visit, the men and the women, as well as the children in the groups around us, were all working on baskets of intricate design and varying sizes. An elder of the church, an old man with a fuzzy beard, whittling on the base of a large basket, agreed to answer my questions. Their holy day like the Jewish Sabbath is from Friday sundown through Saturday. "Might we attend your worship service?" "No, only members." "Your teachings?" "...No dancing, no beer drinking, no smoking, no eating of pork, no eating of any animal flesh we have not killed." They apply the name "Christian" to themselves and use both Testaments. "Holy communion?" "We have no such service." "Baptism?" "Yes, the new believer kneels, and the head of the church pours over his head water mixed with the blood of a dove." There is Biblical authority for the participation of the dove in the service of water baptism, but in this case, surely the centuries and the practice of the Basket Weavers have radically altered the role of the dove within that participation.

Meaning and Symbolism of Baptism

Among the AICs there is near unity upon the importance of baptism; there are very few churches which do not practice it in some form. There is, however, no common understanding or united agreement on the significance of the service. Moreover, that division of thought increases as one moves from the unsophisticated and usually illiterate church of the bush, to the the more privileged church, culturally and educationally, of the city. In addition, for those churches which have broken from historic mission churches or the Western sects, common in Tropical Africa, the theological influence of the original group makes for some further division of understanding.

No one, I believe, can know the AICs, participate in their services, share in their worship, and fellowship with their people, without a conviction that for them all, baptism is a major highly emotional experience not easily translated into words. The service is always a serious moment, but with a seriousness entwined with that exuberant joy they make a part of all their worship, a joy both for the new member and for the welcoming church. Often the members encompass the ordinance with their "soul" music, and their shouts of "Hallelujah" and "Praise the Lord," fervid and resounding.

Many of these churches expect water baptism to be accompanied by the baptism of the Holy Spirit, and the candidates, coming up from the water, may be in a state of "possession," crying loudly, with ecstatic movements. This is welcomed especially by the rural groups who accept it as abiding evidence of the presence of the Holy Spirit.

There is sound evidence that for the large majority of adults who seek baptism within the AICs, and come to it outside of group pressures, the decision is witness to two major desires. First, the eagerness to belong to the human, group fellowship of the church, with all the heart-delight that such participation brings. And second, the desire for some kind of religious experience within the Christian climate, sometimes cataclysmic, but far more often nominal, which will provide a wider pathway into the spirit world. The two are not unrelated.

The African is a group-minded man. "A person is born potentially a member of a tribe. Even so, nearly always he has to undergo a period of initiation and perhaps even be marked as such by physical means such as circumcision or scarification."[1] He thinks of himself fundamentally as a group man, not as an individual, as the Western man conceives himself. The African sees himself first as a family man, a clan man, a tribesman (in other words, a member of the various groups which may claim his loyalty), and for many, as a Christian. This experience of belonging is for him a major source of his security and assured satisfaction and protection.

Baptism becomes, therefore, an initiation into this final group, enlarging his sense of security with one more "belonging" to a human fellowship under God, rather than the Western mystical concept of incorporation into the ethereal Body of Christ.

Moreover, for many baptismal candidates immersion may be the fuller acquaintance with and the sense of belonging within the world of spirit. Basic in African thought of the supernatural, the concept of spirit is central. Spirit may be conceived sometimes as energy or force, sometimes, especially in cases of the ancestral or

---

1 Noel Q. King, "Reflections on Baptism in Parts of Tropical Africa," *Dini na Mila*, No. 2 (Sept. 1965), page 1.

ju-ju spirits, as person. The concept is thoroughly African that this world of spirit is closely impinging upon our daily living, responsible for the blessings and the sufferings that come; and that we may enter into it more completely by means of various ceremonies and rituals. "Water especially is recognized as an abode and agency of spirit"[2]

The candidate has probably heard the words that came to Jesus during his baptism: "Thou art my beloved son in whom I am well pleased." It is not difficult for the African to identify himself with the company of the Spirit-High God speaking such works, with the Spirit-Jesus, and especially with the Holy Spirit in active presence. For the African members of the AICs, and often of the rural mission churches, the Holy Spirit is distinctly nearer at hand and vastly more companionable than either the God-Father or the Christ-Son.

Baptism, then, carries for many the choice of a dramatic way to secure from the Holy Spirit a blessing within the temporal needs. And when water baptism is taught as concurrent with the baptism of the Holy Spirit, the African enters enthusiastically this new "belonging" within the spirit world, to which his traditional tribal religion has introduced him and given reality to mystery.

It would appear that less than major emphasis is given to baptism as a threshold to church membership. Indeed membership itself as understood within many of the AICs is a far less important factor than in the mission

2 *Ibid.*, page 2.

church. For example the great Divine Healer's Church keeps no statistical record of membership although its lists of baptisms with names and dates are complete. But baptism without request for membership is not unknown among the AICs. If there is a threshold of church membership within the AICs, it is rather the experience of healing. Probably (and again one speaks without statistics) the large majority of AIC members have come into membership through the door of physical or psychiatric healing, and it is healing which is first spoken of, not conversion or confession in baptism, as the threshold of the church. This may account for the infrequency of the careful preparation in church background and teaching, for baptism; the ready postponement in some churches of baptism for many months, during which the person is counted a "member" although often without right to hold office; and also the infrequency of a formal welcoming service, for the baptized persons into church membership.

Like the historic mission churches, the AICs stress the symbolism of death, burial and resurrection, in the act of immersion. Many pastors justify the violence of their baptisms by the fact that they are reenacting death and birth with its pain and violence of labor.

Pastor Idowu of the Christ Apostolic Church, Ibadan, in his careful instruction reminded his candidate that St. Paul pointed out that baptism symbolizes Jesus' death, burial and resurrection. "When you hold your breath as the water covers your face, think of yourself as a dead man, a corpse without life. Then when you are raised, it will be as the reborn man, the new man who comes from the watery grave." From an African tongue so full of faith, the simple suggestion must have held deep meaning.

Two common forms of African burial are the horizontal, taken from the colonial powers, and the foetal position. Immersion backwards, sometimes in shallow water so that the body lies on the watery bottom, reenacts the first. The foetal burial finds the corpse in a sitting position, with hands clasped around the knees and the head resting on the hands. For the thoughtful African of the bush, baptism vertical, wherein the candidate is pushed downward, his knees bending until he is in an approximate sitting position, must have made St. Paul's symbolism of death considerably more meaningful.

The symbolism of cleansing, tying in as it does with the cleansing ritual of the traditional African religions, probably makes a stronger and more relevant impact upon the African mind than St. Paul's threefold analogy with Christ's death, burial and resurrection. If baptism for the AIC African is witness to his putting aside all evil doing, a purging of the accumulation of sin within a life time, the reality of the cleansing is not alone symbol but event.

Baptism is never, to my knowledge, an appendage to or a minor item within a major church service. It is always a religious occasion of sufficient importance to stand alone. Not infrequently it lacks the dignity and the refinements which Western pastors attempt to bring to the sacrament.

"Crude," "uncouth," "unlovely" are words sometimes spoken in derision, but the criticism comes from Western lips. Such services within the AICs must be judged by African standards, set within African meaning, and understanding, and acceptability. Baptism is not administered for the comfort of the baptized but for the enlightenment and the symbolic instruction of the occasion. To the African, if not to the Western Christian, there is no loss of dignity when the members greet the newly baptized while still in their wet garments; or when the minister covers a delicate face with his giant palm and closes the nostrils between his thumb and forefinger. This is Africa.

Uniformly, I dare say, baptisms are occasions of solemn joy, held in happy memory both by the baptized and by those participating as observers. There is a brave note of originality within them, and an absence of boring routine.

To the picture-mind of the African the occasion of baptism in African fashion is more impressive, more memorable than the Western service to the word-mind of the West. The African sees in it the role of initiation as the threshold of a great "belonging." Vaguely historical to the African, it is the great symbol of Christ's death, burial and resurrection; still more relevant to him, it is an act of cleansing, a longed-for cleanness which is fresh beginning. And in that symbol of the new beginning, do you not have the essence of resurrection and the new man? "I want to be a clean Christian," one freshly baptized convert cried as he came from the water.

Moreover, it is impressive to note the commingling of their own African culture with the Christian sacrament and its connotation: the memories of their own traditional uses of water, sacred water, beyond that of mere cleansing; their response to the sacred numbers of three and seven; the sense of the corporate, corporate fellowship, corporate joy, corporate outreach to the good gifts of the Spirit; and their assurance of a lasting partnership with the spirit world.

Baptism for the African in the African Independent Churches, I believe, is more fully expressive of that African spiritual outreach, more relevant as a bond between his traditional faith and the substance of the Christian gospel which he is attempting to place within his own cultural experience, than is Christian baptism with its connotations of Western culture to the average Western man.

As increasingly African thinkers, theologians and men and women in the street, *shamba* or farm, take over their own thinking...they will know how much of the best values of their traditional cultures can be kept alive by such fundamental Christian rites as baptism and how in the modern world baptism may become a means of conveying that knowledge of "belonging" and being someone which is so often otherwise lacking. They may also contribute to the outside a new understanding of the meaning of Christian baptism which hitherto had escaped other Christians. It is not easy to see in detail at this stage how their work will shape, but undoubtedly the African grasp of the dwelling together of many in one corporate whole to present to the world one "personality," and the African awareness of the Spirit, His reality and power, will play a large part."[3]

With this prophecy and with this profound hope, I take my stand.

---

[3] *Ibid.*, p. 4.

K. A. Dickson

Christian and African Traditional Ceremonies

The author points out some areas of discrepancy between the traditional African naming ceremony for children and the traditional marriage on the the one hand, and the Christian analogs (infant baptism and marriage ceremony) on the other. He rejects the suggestion that the former be simply adopted unmodified by the Christian church, but suggests adjustments in the Christian ceremonies to take into consideration worthwhile values from the traditional ceremonies and to make the ceremonies more meaningful to participants.

IN THE last few years a great deal of interest has been shown in the church's task in Africa. Several works on the history of the church in this continent h ve been published, and generally the interest of African Christians has been awakened in the story of the growth of the church. This awakening has resulted in a desire to ensure among the Christians of Africa a clearer understanding of the fundamentals of the Christian faith, stripped of its cultural wrappings.

One of the areas which have attracted some attention is Christian worship, within the context of the relevance of received forms in Africa. There are several elements in worship, and these, with some plausibility, may be reduced to three: the actual liturgical orders of service which characterize a worshiping community; the various external media embodied in the liturgical forms or orders of service, such as music; and the personal inward

feeling of being in the presence of God. Much has been said about music and dance, and indeed a certain amount of innovation has already been carried out.

Our concern here is with the orders of service which bring the faithful together in worship. In a land where traditional life cannot be described as the Plotinian flight of the alone to the alone, it is important that the church's corporate acts should be such as to help its members achieve that corporateness which underlies society's very integrity. Hence our study of

K. A. Dickson is senior lecturer in the Department for the Study of Religions at the University of Ghana (P. O. Box 66, Legon, Ghana). He attended the University College of the Gold Coast (1952) and obtained a B.D. with first class honors from the University of London. He was editor of *Akan Religion and Christian Faith* (Accra: Ghana Universities Press, 1965).

434

the significance of the infant baptism and solemnization of matrimony orders.

The Naming Ceremony and Infant Baptism

Usually, before the child is presented for baptism, a traditional family ceremony with the child as the central figure is performed; this is the naming ceremony. When at a Ghana Christian Council Conference held in 1955 the subject of infant ceremonies was discussed, the suggestion was made that the church might consider merging the two ceremonies, the traditional naming ceremony and the Christian rite of infant baptism. Several speakers made the point that the naming ceremony had important features which the infant baptismal order could profitably take account of. If exactly nothing has been done in Ghana since 1955 to implement, no matter how tentatively, the suggestions made at the Conference, it is because it has been wondered, on the one hand, how such an amalgamation might be meaningfully brought about, and, on the other, whether such an amalgamation is indeed desirable.

A recent experience illustrates the doubts in people's minds regarding the advisability of making the baptismal order take account of the traditional naming ceremony. The present writer was invited to baptize the child of a friend, a Methodist layman and church leader. This friend asked almost apologetically whether there would be any objection to the naming rites, which had been arranged to be performed after the baptism, being carried out. In response we expressed our preference for making the naming rites part of the baptismal ceremony. This friend did not quite know whether to take us seriously or not.

In West Africa, whether among the Fon of Dahomey, or the Ashanti of Ghana, or the Yoruba of Nigeria, there is some importance attached to a particular day in the life of the child—the day on which the child is named. The ceremony differs from people to people in some details, but there are certain common characteristics, and it is upon these that the discussion here is based. In essence the new child does not really belong to the family until the day set by tradition, when the child's continued existence would be deemed to indicate that he had really come to stay. This day is usually the eighth day, though the Igbos of eastern Nigeria do not have the naming rites till the twenty-fourth day. Hence on the eighth (or twenty-fourth) day, if the child still lives, it is assumed that the ghost-mother, who is in the spirit world, has relinquished her right to the child; the understanding seems to be that if the child's stay were meant to be temporary, he would have died before that day.

On that day, then, the child acquires a place in the family which becomes richer with the addition of a new member. Not insignificant is the Ashanti custom of the mother addressing the eight-day-old baby: "I thank you for not having caused my death"[1]

The child is now addressable—he has acquired a full personality of his

---

[1] Rattray, *Religion and Art in Ashanti*, second impression (London: Oxford University Press, 1954) p. 62.

own. Of course, by the naming-day, the child would have already acquired a day-name; for example, among the Akan of Ghana a child automatically earns the name that goes with the day on which he is born. Evidently, there is nothing personal about such a day-name, seeing that in the same family there could be more than one person bearing the same day-name. It is the special ceremony, at which a personal name is given to the child (the name that distinguishes the child from others) which is being studied here.

At the naming ceremony the officiant is usually the child's father, the paternal grandfather, or any member (especially male) of the father's family. In these days, any respected person, whether he belongs to the father's family or not, may be invited to officiate. Before the occasion the father, or at the father's invitation the paternal grandfather, would have selected a suitable name.

In the following brief description of the ceremony the paternal grandfather plays the role of the officiant. On the eighth day (among the Akan of Ghana) the father presents gifts to the child: an assortment of articles of food, toilet materials, and often a gold ring. There is a gathering of members of the wider family and some friends. The paternal grandfather takes the child in his arms and invites the father to name the child. The father announces the name (often the name of the paternal grandfather). The officiant then puts the ring on the child's finger, saying: "With this ring your father names you (so-and-so) after (so-and-so)." Following this the officiant takes two containers

and pours into one water and into the other liquor. He dips his finger first into the liquor and moistens the child's lips or lets a drop or two drip into his mouth, saying as he does this: "So-and-so (the child's name), when you say it is wine, then it should be wine [3 times]"; then the officiant goes through the same process with the water, saying this time: "So-and-so (the child's name), when you say it is water then it should be water [3 times]". The meaning of this is that the child's yea should be yea, and his nay nay; that is, he should be truthful.

This over, addresses are made by various members of the gathering, reminding those present that the child has been named after someone of note so that he is not to be maltreated in any way. The parents may also be exhorted to pay particular attention to the child's upbringing. Then when refreshments have been served and gifts from various people presented to the child, the rites come to an end.

At a subsequent date, the child's parents, if Christian, will take the child to the church for baptism. It is to be noted that generally at the indigenous naming ceremony the child is given African names, while at baptism he receives so-called Christian names, which are often more Anglo-Saxon than biblical.

The adoption of indigenous customs for use in Christian worship and practice may proceed along one of two lines: the custom may be imported wholesale and given a place in the church; or, the cognate church practice may be modified in such a way as to reflect the spirit of the indigenous practice; the latter, of course, would involve a modification of the indigenous custom itself. The first method is easy of accomplishment, but evidently fraught with difficulties; the church would not be in a hurry to import wholesale customs which involved immoral practices and had polytheistic presuppositions. It is true that the church would have no really valid objections to the Akan traditional naming ceremony in its entirety; however, the question whether a Christian purpose would be served by adopting it in its entirety without adaptation must be honestly faced. On the whole, we would feel that such a procedure might turn out to be unwise.

Our own preference is for modifying the naming custom to serve a Christian purpose. Here also there seem to be two possible approaches. A paper titled "The Naming of an Akan Christian Child: The Indigenous Custom Modified" was recently circulated by A. C. Denteh (Research Fellow, Institute of African Studies, University of Ghana). In this paper Denteh suggests the institution in the church of a naming ceremony, to be followed, if necessary, by baptism. As worked out by Denteh this Christian naming ceremony would involve the following:

1. Introductory speech by officiating member; and the announcing of father's gifts to child
2. A hymn (optional)
3. The actual naming, with the application of drops of wine and water on the child's tongue and ending with the words: "So-and-so (child's name), I now charge you to grow to the full measure and stature of your.... after whom you have been named; grow to take the place of the illustrious ones of the family, and may the Lord grant you his grace."
4. Officiating member hands over child to mother, charging her to bring him up in the right way.
5. Open speeches to the family, and gifts (if any)
6. Response by parents or their representatives
7. Closing: prayer and benediction (Note: "If the minister is present and is prepared beforehand, baptism can follow immediately, after he has dedicated and hallowed the place.")

Denteh's order follows closely the order of the traditional naming ceremony, and would therefore have much meaning for the assembled. It may be wondered, however, whether it is necessary to institute *The Naming of an Akan Christian Child* as a church order, particularly since the Christian baptismal service which might follow (see above) is in effect a naming ceremony. A more profitable proposition might be to design a baptismal service which would take over the essentials of the traditional naming ceremony. Such a baptismal order might have the following elements:

1. Opening by the head of family, indicating *inter alia* that the minister has been invited by the family to baptize the child, who is joining not only an earthly family but also the family of God. (Participation by the head of the family or paternal grandfather

side by side with the minister of religion would be a powerful symbol of the involvement of the family into which the new child is being initiated.)

2. Minister or priest reads relevant passages from Scripture, asking the assembled to affirm their faith in the Trinity.

3. Prayer by minister or one of the assembled, asking especially for God's blessing on the family and those who have the care of the child.

4. Naming: The paternal grandfather receives child from father, announces the name selected indicating the one after whom it is being named. He then dips his middle and forefingers into a bowl of wine, lets a drop or two drip on to the child's tongue saying, "So-and-so (the child's name), when you say it is wine then it should be wine." He repeats the performance with water.

5. Minister receives child, baptizes him with water (from the same glass used by the chief officiant), calling out his name clearly. Then he says, calling upon the assembled, "This child has been named after X who is/was the child's .... (relation). He has been named after an elder and therefore deserves every respect. He is now a member, not only of the family of ..... (name elder after whom named) but also of God. As God's son, he shares in all the privileges

that have been granted us as Christians. The Lord bless him ...."

6. Prayer: by minister for child, parents and family

7. Benediction.

At the risk of repeating myself, there is need for taking into account two considerations: the order should be meaningful to the general membership of the church; also it should seek to bind us to the foundations of the church. We tend to be concerned about the latter without taking any account of the former.

Solemnization of Matrimony

The order of service for the solemnization of matrimony poses a problem that is well worth investigating. We shall here attempt an investigation by first taking a look at two of the features of this order. [2]

Reference is made over and over again in this order to the fact that the man and the woman are the principal, almost the *only*, characters in the drama. Apart from the officiating minister the only other actor referred to specifically is the prospective bride's father (or "friend") who "giveth away this woman to be married to this man," and whose only line is "I do"; otherwise the prospective bride and bridegroom have the stage all to themselves. They are the two who "make their vows" before God; each promises the other "to have and to hold from

---

[2] We are here drawing upon the order authorized "for use in the Methodist Church by the Conference at Newcastle-on-Tyne, July 1936"—this is still the authorized order in the Methodist Church in many parts of Africa.

this day forward, for better, for worse..."

Secondly, "causes for which matrimony was ordained" are spelled out. These are two: "for mutual society, help, and comfort, that the one ought to have of the other, both in prosperity and adversity"; and "that children might be brought up in the knowledge and love of God, and to the praise of His holy name." These "causes," incidentally, emphasize the fact of the prospective bride and bridegroom being the only actors in the drama, not only of the service, but also of life.

Our evaluation of this order is mainly from the point of view of matrilineal societies. The importance attached to the two principal actors being made into one is negated by the fact that in a matrilineal society the son does not inherit. In no sense do the children issuing from such a marriage belong equally to the couple—they belong to the mother. There is an Akan (Ghana) proverb which goes: "If a man is living with his wife and children in a lonely cottage somewhere, the man is the stranger." And another, "No matter how closely a child resembles his father, he belongs to his mother's family." Since the children do not belong to the father's clan, they (sons and daughters) cannot possibly be his heirs. The legitimate heirs are his maternal uncle, his brother, etc.[3] Admittedly the true heirs are supposed to provide for the needs of the children;[4] nevertheless, the two principal

actors do not become one in the fullest possible sense in the eyes of the two families from which the pair have come.

The reference to the two families brings up a related matter which detracts from the seriousness of the order's emphasis on the pair as the principal actors. It is a well-known fact that in African societies marriage involves the coming together of two families. Inter-family consultations end, either in the rejection by one or the other of the two families of the marriage proposal, or in their agreement to bring the couple together in marriage. The Christian order does not at any point refer to the families of the couple; the role of the families in a ceremony which is sufficient to make the couple a microcosm of the coming together of the two families should be given recognition in the Christian order of service. This is all the more important since before the Christian service of matrimony the couple would have already entered into a legitimate conjugal union through the performance of traditional rites. In the eyes of the families the two would be man and wife following the traditional rites.[5]

A more delicate issue might be raised in connection with the "causes for which matrimony was ordained." In African life and thought, the importance attached to the bearing of children is made evident in prayers on behalf of brides-to-be; perpetuating

[3] See R. S. Rattray, *Ashanti*, second impression (London: Oxford University Press, 1965) pp. 41-42.

[4] This is often neglected, though the courts of law would back the children's claim to maintenance by the father's family.

[5] On this subject of marriage see S.G. Williamson's comments in his *Akan Religion and the Christian Faith* (Ghana Universities Press, 1965), pp. 77ff.

the family is uppermost in the minds of the families whose son and daughter are coming together in marriage. The Christian order refers, it is true, to the bringing up of children, but this is clearly secondary to the first cause: "mutual society, help, and comfort." Hence, while childlessness is viewed as a disgrace in Africa, and is a legitimate ground for divorce in the traditional set-up, the church would prescribe in this situation "mutual society, help, and comfort that the one ought to have of the other, both in prosperity and adversity," and would therefore deeply frown upon the traditional expedients often adopted in such situations: if it is the woman who is barren, the man is encouraged by his family to have children by another woman; if the fault is the man's, the girl's family may take away their daughter and give her away to someone else who might (hopefully) have children by her. Such expedients are not by any means confined to non-Christian families.

In view of the above it is necessary for the church to devise a new order for the solemnization of matrimony. Such an order should take cognizance of certain elements in the traditional custom:

1. The pair would usually have already been married by the time they presented themselves "to be joined" by the minister. The question arises whether the church should not view traditional marriage with more seriousness than she has hitherto done. In the nineteenth century Thomas Birch Freeman, a Methodist missionary to the then Gold Coast, reacted to a charge of condoning immorality (for considering couples married according to traditional custom as properly married) by saying in effect that he did not see why he should not consider such marriages as valid. Of course, it is not in all cases that traditional marriage customs are performed; one immediately thinks of mixed marriages involving an African and a Westerner. However, where the marriage involves two people from the same type of African society, there is no reason why the Christian order should not take into account the marriage which the pair had already contracted.

2. Reference should be made in the order to the contracting families and the responsibility they bear for the success of the marriage. When the families are made aware of their responsibilities they would have been by implication brought closer to the children that issue out of the marriage—the traditional concern for cohesion would have been accentuated. It is this cohesion that would make a man's "people" have concern for his children when he is no more in the living.

3. As in the service of infant baptism, so here also a role might be found for a paterfamilias; the uniting families would agree on someone (from a third family) to act on their behalf.

4. In view of (1) and (2) above, the Christian marriage order would be given mainly to emphasizing the need to have God in the home, etc.; in other words, it would not be quite as meaningful as the minister would like for the pair to repeat: "I do solemnly declare that I know not of any lawful impediment why I..... may not be married to....."

5. There is no reason why the order should not feature a prayer asking for children; whether we like it or not, this is usually uppermost in the minds of the families concerned. This, of course, would not make it any easier for the childless couple. While the expedients adopted in the traditional set-up cannot but cause pain and should therefore be frowned upon, yet it may be asked whether the church has an effective word for the childless couple. We do not pretend to know what word would be best in this situation. Or is it that marriage is for "mutual society, help, and comfort.....?"

It was T. S. Garrett who wrote as follows on the basis of his experience in India:

What, we must ask, is the evangelistic value of our present ways of worship? To say that the normal worship of the church is for the instructed Christians and that it does not matter if a Hindu thinks it strange or foreign is not enough. The new convert, when he comes to church for the first time, will inevitably find some things strange and new to him; but in the main he ought to feel that the service in which he is taking part is something which could soon belong to him and to which he could soon belong. Can this be said of many of our Christian services?[6]

---

[6] T. S. Garrett *Christian Worship: An Introductory Outline* (London: Oxford University Press), p. 177.

Harold W. Turner

Pagan Features in West African Independent Churches

WITHIN the last fifty years there has been a widespread independent and indigenous religious development in most of the areas of Africa south of the Sahara where Christian missions have been establishing churches. The extent and variety of these religious groups presents a bewildering phenomenon to church leaders and missionaries, and they have often been lumped together under derogatory labels such as "separatists" or "sects" and dismissed as unfortunate reversions to traditional paganisms or as dangerous syncretisms of pagan and Christian elements.

It is true that there is a great range of belief and practice in these indigenous groups. In West Africa, to which the following remarks primarily apply, we can identify "healing homes" which are often both commercial and pagan in nature, eccentric or charlatan prophets who exploit a

Harold W. Turner is Senior Lecturer in the Department of Religion of the University of Nigeria, Nsukka, Nigeria. Previous articles in PA include "The Litany of an Independent West African Church," Vol. 7, No. 6 (Nov.-Dec. 1960), pp. 256-262, and "Searching and Syncretism: A West African Documentation," Vol. 8, No. 3 (May-June 1961), pp. 106-110.

personal following, occult and spiritualist groups mixing African and imported forms of paganism, Judaistic bodies which are African forms of Jehovah's Witnesses, revivals of the worship of traditional gods, and a wide range of prophet-healing groups claiming to be spiritual Christian churches. These latter are Christian at least in intention and the increasing willingness to describe them as independent African Christian churches is to be welcomed. How far they are also Christian in practice and to what extent they represent an uneasy syncretism with traditional pagan elements is the question to which this article is addressed.

Any evaluation of the independent churches must begin by recognizing certain ways in which many of them have made a radical departure from pagan worship, for we shall probably exaggerate whatever pagan features do undoubtedly exist, unless we see these latter against the basically Christian nature of most independent churches.

Their main achievement seems to consist of a radical breakthrough, from pagan idolatry and worship of a number of divinities, to worship of the one true, living, loving, and all-powerful God of the Christian Scriptures. This is the African equivalent of the rejection of paganism and idolatry made by Israel in the earlier Old Testament period and is fundamental to all other development. The history of Israel shows that the battle for rejection of idolatry and the recognition of the one and only God lasted some six hundred or more years, from the Exodus to the Babylonian Exile. It is widely recognized that this battle has not yet been won in the older churches in West Africa, even where they are now into their second century of existence. We are satisfied that there has been a more complete breakthrough, in some of the independent churches of *aladura* or prophet-healing type, for a much higher proportion of members.

This is more than the kind of breakaway from past beliefs strikingly manifest in the destruction of fetish objects and medicines, but not necessarily accompanied by conversion to a Christian confidence. In many of the prophet-healing churches there is a most impressive and convincing breakthrough into dependence on faith in and prayer to the one living God of the Bible and this provides the basis for their healing practices.

Faith Healing Replaces Magic

These practices represent a rejection of traditional methods of healing involving native practitioners, with magic and idolatry intermingled in the treatments. The great majority of members make no use of magico-pagan treatments. In place of these there is the innocuous use of holy water, oil, or sand as a physical agent

for the divine healing power, together with fasting as a spiritual discipline, and all set in a context of prayer. Most of this treatment can find biblical support, and the appropriate texts are commonly quoted.

At the same time there is the danger that the holy water etc. can become a new magical power acting apart from God, and that the sacramental use of wine and bread in the Lord's Supper and of water in Christian baptism will be replaced by a different sacramental use of water and these other elements in new rites of African devising. Some in these churches undoubtedly fall into these dangers and so drift back towards paganism, but we must remember that a magical interpretation of the Christian sacraments is a constant menace in Christian history and is not peculiar to these new churches.

As another Christian achievement, we may mention the collective and active nature of worship in the independent churches and the signs of Christian joy in these people of God. Unlike so much of the worship in the older churches, there is a minimum of passive listening to a minister and of watching him do most things for the congregation. There is a total response in voice and action, through clapping, dancing, choruses, ejaculations, individual spontaneous prayers, and public thanksgivings. A warm community life undergirds this active corporate worship, and there is a great emphasis on the need for loving one another — perhaps all the greater because of the tensions and quarrels that do occur.

As a Christian achievement, this

presents a striking contrast to pagan worship, which is essentially individual; in the main, individuals bring their own problems, sacrifices, petitions, or thank offerings to the priest at the shrine of the god. It is true that pagan worship has its communal occasions, its festivals for the whole community, but it does not demand the regular assembly of the people of the god. This is why pagan shrines and temples do not provide a house of meeting for a whole congregation — but only a shrine for the god and a place for the priests. On occasion large groups of worshipers can gather round in the open, but they are not essential for the regular service of the god.

Christian worship, on the other hand, is congregational, the regular assembly of God's holy people, and this aspect of Christian worship is often more evident in these independent churches than in some of the older churches.

Not unconnected with the corporate nature of these fellowships is the considerable degree of pastoral care which many of them offer their members. This again is a distinctively Christian feature that is not characteristic of paganism, where the individual goes to the shrine or to the priest, but is not sought out by the latter under the impulse of a gospel of love and fellowship. Some African prophets are assiduous in proclamation of their message and in bringing the spiritual power of their church (as they would put it) to individuals in need. In this they are assisted by the fact that they often minister to fairly small groups, and live among their members with very much the same style of life. This is a notable Christian achievement when compared with the widely acknowledged lack of a pastoral ministry in the older churches, which is an important factor in the drift of their spiritually needy members towards the independent groups.

At the same time there is another kind of ministry found among the independents, that of the "practitioner" who is consulted by "clients" in need of personal help and who sometimes operates on a semicommercial basis. Even this ministry has pastoral possibilities, for large numbers do go to these leaders with spiritual reputations, but it is obviously more impersonal and open to abuse; and is a development that leads in a pagan rather than in a clearly Christian direction.

Pagan Tendencies

After this brief recognition of some of the Christian achievements which exceed those of the older churches in West Africa, we are in a better position to comment on certain pagan tendencies characteristic of many independent churches.

All over Africa independent churches have adopted adult baptism by immersion, even though infant baptism by affusion is the normal practice in most of the older churches from which their leaders and members have taken their departure. This almost universal change deserves a study it has not received. Here we are concerned only with its relation to paganism, and at first sight the change seems to reduce the possibility of a magical interpretation which so easily attaches to infant baptism. Unfortunately there are some signs that adult baptism is used as an effective ritual for the treatment of personal problems, such as sickness, and so rebaptism can occur as often as necessary. This amounts to a transference of baptism to the realms of magic and of pagan purification rites, where it is regarded as efficacious for particular human needs and detached from all Christian significance.

Adult baptism is also used as a rite of admission into a particular independent group, rather than as the sign and means of incorporation into the one people of God under the one Christ as head. Therefore those who transfer from one independent group to another, sometimes many times, are found being rebaptized on each occasion in order to become members. It is then no longer the Christian sacrament, but an entry ceremony for a religious society. Most older churches — both Roman Catholic and Protestant — do not rebaptize those who transfer from one church to another, but the reason for this has not been appreciated by the independent churches.

The Lord's Supper is usually neglected among the independents. Some have discarded it altogether, others celebrate it very infrequently and without understanding or as a special rite for an inner circle of more sanctified members. All these practices can be paralleled in the older churches, and there is a pagan implication in some of them. There is, however, no very open and specific paganizing of this sacrament in the independent churches, probably because the death of Christ and the atonement figure very little in the life and thought of most of them. The stress is more likely to be on the resurrection and on the life of joy and power awaiting the faithful, and these themes have not been discovered in the Lord's Supper.

There is no doubt that these churches, which welcome the description "spiritual churches," rest upon their claims to have received the power of the Holy Spirit to meet human needs. This in itself may help the older churches to realize their poverty at this point. It is, however, plain that dealings with the Spirit are not sufficiently related to and tested by the Christ of the Scriptures, and that too often what is implied is a new direct revelation from God through the "spirit" by means of dreams and visions, ecstasy and possession, or through men of special charismatic spiritual powers who are regarded as powerful prophets.

Christian history, however, and the modern Pentecostal churches in many parts of the world, should teach us not to dismiss these phenomena as necessarily pagan. If set in a context of Christian teaching in a stable Christian community, they can serve to illumine and release men for a more effective and Spirit-filled Christian life. On the other hand, if divorced from the Christ of the Scriptures, they can readily assume pagan forms.

It is possible for these experiences to become the vehicle for other spirits, evil and lying spirits which degrade men, destroying character and responsibility instead of developing the strength and beauty of Christ which the Holy Spirit of God seeks to create. This may be evident in an alleged revelation bidding the taking of another man's wife or encouraging a semiliterate man of limited talents in his unrealistic ambitions of personal advancement to power and greatness.

Others may seek these spirit-revelations for the pagan purpose of divination, for information extracted from the spirit-world to serve our human purposes. Here consultation of prophets has degenerated to the level of fortune-telling, often semi-commercialized and quite divorced from a pastoral context within which it could be redeemed.

Emphasis on the Spirit means, therefore, that many of the independent churches are in a dangerous position, especially among their illiterate members who cannot read the Scriptures. While they sometimes exhibit the power of the Holy Spirit vividly applied to the human situation in conversions, healings, and other examples of faith, they also demonstrate how readily the spirit of paganism can infiltrate into their Christian intentions and practices.

Occultism

One example of this is so widespread as to merit special 'mention. In many churches a secondary or subordinate cult of angels is to be found. A hierarchy of named angels is approached for help through prayers and the use of candles, much as candles might be lit for the saints who are invoked in some forms of Latin Christianity. Sometimes the names of the angels and their associated signs are drawn from imported occult literature, such as the *Sixth and Seventh Books of Moses,* and an elaborate ritual from

similar sources is employed. While these practices may commence with the idea of guardian angels found in the Scriptures, they quickly assume a form and an importance that is akin to pagan cults of spirits or divinities.

The occult element in the above practices is also seen in the use of mystic words of power revealed by the spirit or in the appearance of wholly new scripts and "spirit-languages," of which there are several examples in West African independent churches. All of these are misguided but impressive attempts to secure a more effective and powerful revelation than has been given us in Jesus Christ as witnessed to in the Scriptures.

At the same time, if one probes deeply enough, it is possible to discover many signs that independents themselves are aware of the dangers of an undisciplined spiritual church. Those longer established, or with better leaders, tend to recognize that the spirits must be tested, and may name certain prophets among them as specially gifted in distinguishing the spirits. Rules are made to prevent members from demanding revelations from prophets at any time or recounting their own unchecked revelations, their dreams and visions, in the midst of public worship. Sometimes moral and biblical rules for distinguishing true prophets from false are provided, and the exposure of false prophets has occurred on some occasions.

The people of Israel and the members of the early Christian church have already trod this path, and it is most moving to see biblical history being repeated in Africa. Many of these churches are endeavoring to fulfill their intention of being truly Christian and are doing so not through pressures and demands for orthodoxy from the older churches but under what we must recognize as the authentic leading of the Holy Spirit of God in their midst. Indeed, this capacity for self-criticism and internal reformation is one of the essential marks of a genuine Christian church, and it is not lacking in some of the West African churches we are considering. The growth of various means of testing and controlling pneumatic phenomena is far more significant than the excesses which continue to dominate the image of the independents in the minds of the older churches.

Despite the highly evangelical language often used in these churches, especially in gospel hymns and choruses borrowed from Western sources, there is little understanding of an evangelical gospel based on the work of Christ for our salvation. This is, of course, a continually repeated situation in Christian history and infects the older churches also to a large extent. Among the independents it tends to appear in certain characteristic forms, such as reliance on a routine of prayers, fastings, food, and other taboos, rituals connected with thanksgiving after childbirth, recital of specific psalms for particular needs, water purification rites, etc. Some of these practices pass over, as we have noted above, into the realm of magic. All of them are capable of interpretation in a pagan way, and the greater the emphasis placed on such practices the greater the danger of their being regarded in themselves as the effective means of salvation and of spiritual

power. The impressive spiritual disciplines of these churches are thus liable to be of an ambiguous nature when subjected to close inspection. For example, the almost universal rejection of tobacco may be due to the belief that the smell of smoke drives away the benevolent angels — a sentiment that could be harmless enough but which is scarcely calculated to strengthen an evangelical faith.

In general we may describe the outlook of the independent churches as moralistic and legalistic in its understanding of Christianity. This would probably be confirmed by an analysis of their use of the Scriptures in their preaching. In one case it was clearly shown that the favorite books were Proverbs and Ecclesiastes in the Old Testament and the Epistle of James in the New Testament. These books are especially open to a moralistic, legalistic use divorced from the gospel. On the other hand, and despite the pagan tendencies of all emphasis on human effort and righteousness, it would be wrong to label this outlook as no more than paganism. It is still a moralistic, unevangelical form — not of paganism or of Islam or of any other religion — but of Christianity, and in spite of various pagan elements these are still properly called Christian churches.

Conclusion

Some writers have emphasized the survival of pagan features from African traditional religions in the life and worship of these independent churches, especially in the practice of divination through revelations, in ecstatic worship and spirit possession, and in purification procedures. It is true that externally Christianized forms of such fundamentally pagan practices can be discovered and that this amounts to a religious syncretism that is always at the expense of the Christian element in the mixed form. It is our conviction, however, that this syncretistic element, like the messianic outlook in African independents, has been much exaggerated. This is partly due to the fact that investigators assumed that these independent groups must be a mixture of traditional African and Christian religious elements, and so found what they set out to discover.

We are much more impressed by the sharp break from African animism and polytheism, and from reliance on traditional magic and medicine, as well as by the small attention given to ancestral spirits. The distinctive and characteristic phenomenon in these independent churches is the prophet-leader. Both the prophet and his revelations of warning and divine judgment are cast much more in an Old Testament mold than in any to be found in African traditional religion, and most investigators (but by no means all) agree that prophecy as found in these movements is at bottom a post-Christian development which would not have occurred without the biblical model and stimulus.

These radical departures from the traditional religions of Africa are so fundamental to the independent church movement that they probably explain why many of the pagan tendencies which do exist in these churches are not specifically African. Our remarks above have suggested that they are very often similar to the distortions and corrosions of genuine 'Christianity that have occurred throughout Christian history and that will probably continue to do so, not only in Asia and Africa but also in Europe and the Americas.

A striking example of this has already been alluded to — the importation of Western and Asian occultism, spiritualism, and literature of the "new thought" kind, into West Africa. This may present a threat to the independent and to the older churches that is just as serious as the survival of African religious practices in syncretistic guise. Indeed, rank-and-file members of the older churches, who have not made the radical breakthrough found in many independents, may be even less able to resist this imported paganism, which benefits from the prestige of the West or of the ancient civilizations of Asia.

The whole question of pagan features in the life of the independent churches in Africa is, therefore, not nearly so simple as many have assumed, and the dangers and defects of this kind are neither to be derived entirely from African religions, nor located solely in the independent churches.

Yoshiro Ishida

Mukyokai: Indigenous Movement in Japan

An indigenous church by definition will never be made in the image of the Western churches. When indigenous expression of Christianity is to be found it often varies from Western churches so much in its structure and outlook that Westerners find it hard to understand, and it is almost invariably a subject of considerable controversy and of strong differences of opinion. In this article we have a discussion of one important group in Japan, treating it primarily from the standpoint of its theology, but discussing some aspects of its social structure as well. PRACTICAL ANTHROPOLOGY *would be glad for additional treatments of this movement, particularly dealing with the social structure of the groups and group meetings, and the teacher-discipline relationship. Even a group which denies that it is a group has a group structure (perhaps a very loose one) when it has meetings and a sense of group identity as this one does.*

IN JAPAN there is a unique Christian group under the name of *Mukyokai*. Fully aware of the concept of indigenousness they advocate a "Japanese Christianity" through what they call "Reformation." This they compare to the reformation of Luther, which according to them, however, was an "arrested movement." This *Mukyokai* movement began to develop after the death of its advocate, Kanzo Uchimura (1861-1930),[1] who was an outstanding teacher of Christianity, yet did not associate himself or his adherents with any church. He had a deep

conviction, in Latourette's phrase, "to give to Christianity a peculiarly Japanese dress, to divorce it from dependence on the churches of the West, and to erase the denominational differences which had

---

[1] Kanzo Uchimura studied at Sapporo Agricultural College (the Sapporo Band) in 1877, where he came under the influence of Puritan ideals established there by W. S. Clark, who had returned to the United States shortly before Uchimura's arrival. In such a spirit he was baptized in 1878. He studied in the United States at Amherst College and also at Hartford Theological Seminary from 1884 to 1888. It should also be noted that he was influenced by the Quakers during his stay in America. His stay in America had important significance for his future work in both a positive and a negative sense. Cf. John F. Howes, *Uchimura Kanzo (1861-1930): A Biographical Sketch* (New York: Columbia University, 1953), and Raymond P. Jennings, *Jesus, Japan and Kanzo Uchimura, A Brief Study of the Non-Church Movement and its Appropriateness to Japan* (Tokyo: Kyobun Kwan, 1958), pp. 10-59.

Yoshiro Ishida is General Secretary of the Tokyo Student Center of the Japan Evangelical Lutheran Church. His article is taken from his thesis *A Study on the Anthropological Issues of the Christian Kerygma in Japan*, presented at Chicago Lutheran Theological Seminary for the S.T.M. 1-1 Sadoharacho, Ichigaya, Shinjuku-ku, Tokyo, Japan.

arisen in the Occident and through which Christianity had come to Japan."[2]

Mukyokai is generally understood as the "non-church movement" or "church-less Christianity." The literal translation of the word is "churchless church." According to Uchimura, Mukyokai is based on a "we-need-no-church principle."[3]

If you say Mukyokai you think of no government, no party, or such. Something destructive. But it is never anything like that. Mukyokai is a church without a church. . . . The mu in mukyokai should be read nai 'no', but is does not mean mu or mushi 'non' or 'reject'. People without money, people without parents, people without houses are pitiful people, aren't they?[4]

Masao Sekine, one of the distinguished theologians in Mukyokai, defines it as follows:

Mukyokai Shugi is not a mere ism and the mu is not a mere negation; it is a greater or more positive affir-

mation of the church than that of the churches themselves.[5]

The Character of Mukyokai

As Michelson mentions, a definition of Mukyokai is difficult to determine, "for the very connotation of structure and norm required in a definition is alien to the spirit of Non-church."[6] Emil Brunner, after his stay in Japan, called it "Utschimura Kreis,"[7] taking the originator's name. In fact there are a variety of definitions, yet all of them infer some form of denial of ecclesiasticism as it has appeared in Western Christianity. This movement, thus, is characterized mostly as an exclusive, anti-movement against the churches, particularly in their Westernized institutional form.[8] Supporters of Mukyokai point out that it is a fundamental mistake to believe that the churches are indispensable for the salvation of the soul. One of the present leaders of Mukyokai, Toshio Suzuki, says, "The worldliness and apathy of the churches must be attacked severely."[9]

Followers of Mukyokai do without any definite form of group.[10] The group has developed into a series of Sunday meetings under a sensei (a teacher or a leader), but they have no further intention than to get together upon the conviction that "only those who have no church have the very best church."[11] As seen so often

---

[2] Kenneth Scott Latourette, The Great Century A.D. 1800-A.D. 1914 in North Africa and Asia (Vol. 6 of The History of the Expansion of Christianity) (New York: Harper and Brothers, 1944), p. 407.

[3] Uchimura announced the principle of Mukyokai for the first time in a pamphlet under the same title in 1901 (Cf. Kanzo Uchimura, Uchimura Kanzo Zenshu 'The Collected Writings of Kanzo Uchimura' [Tokyo: Iwanami Shoten, 1933], Vol. 9, p. 210). What Uchimura saw in the struggling churches of Japan gave him the feeling that "the odium of Christianity is in its churches" (ibid., Vol. 15, p. 544). He says also: "There is happiness outside of the church. In the church there is competition and jealousy. The church is not the place where one who loves the freedom of God can long abide" (Kanzo Uchimura, Uchimura Kanzo Chosakushu 'Selected Works of Kanzo Uchimura' [Tokyo: Iwanami Shoten, 1953-1955], Vol. 5, p. 139).

[4] Uchimura, Complete Works, Vol. 9, p. 210 f.

[5] Quoted from Jennings, op. cit., p. 55.

[6] Carl Michelson, Japanese Contributions to Christian Theology (Philadelphia: the Westminster Press, 1960), p. 18.

[7] Quoted from Toshio Suzuki, "The Non-Church Group," in The Japan Christian Quarterly, Vol. 18, No. 2, p. 136.

[8] Cf. Jennings, ibid., p. 53.

[9] Toshio Suzuki, op. cit.

[10] Since they scorn statistics, membership is not known exactly, but it is estimated to have 50,000 to 70,000 followers.

[11] Uchimura, op. cit., Vol. 9, p. 213.

in other groups in Japanese society, the *sensei-deshi* relationship, or 'a master-his followers' relationship, forms the backbone of this movement.

By means of their monthly tract or correspondence, the followers get together around their teacher regularly in addition to the Sunday meetings.[12] Some teachers travel very widely. A *sensei* and his followers are, therefore, very closely connected, but they are free in the matter of faith, and they have no common confession nor regular form of worship. The main content of the meetings is Bible study, often using texts in the original biblical language,[13] and prayer. Their teachers are not ordained and not paid.[14] Every one of them is a layman, and it is also possible to become a teacher after studying the Bible under a certain *sensei* for some years.

From the above description of *Mukyokai* we can agree with such an observation as follows:

> Phenomenologically, the movement Uchimura initiated would fall somewhere between Quakerism and Anabaptism. Like the Quakers, though not entirely for the same reason, *Mukyokai* rejects clergy, hierarchy and sacraments. Like the Anabaptists, it is Bible-centered rather than dependent on the "inner light."...

Membership is less formal than in either Anabaptism or Quakerism.... Like Anabaptism and Quakerism, *Mukyokai* lays great stress on its "lay" character.[15]

According to this group the church should always be accepted as a spiritual reality in Christ and not an empirical institution. Their rejection of any kind of institutional church contains, however, not only negative aspects but also positive ones. Without seeing the latter ones, merely describing their rejection of the churches in a negative sense may point out a certain characteristic of this group but does not touch the real heart of the movement, which is attracting a wide range of people in Japan.

Theological Emphases

One of these positive aspects can be mentioned as a strong emphasis on a cross-centered faith. Uchimura writes:

> Christianity is essentially the religion of the Cross. It is not simply the religion of Christ but the religion of Christ *crucified*.... The Cross is not merely a symbol of Christianity; it is its center, the corner-stone upon which the whole structure rests. Sins forgiven and annihilated on the Cross, blessings promised and bestowed upon the Cross — indeed, no Cross, no Christianity.... It is desirable that we should call Christianity by a new name. I propose Crucifixianity as such; and when it too shall have been abused and vulgarized by new theologians, I will coin another.[16]

His followers do not regard the churches as the chosen instrument necessary for the salvation of souls, but believe that

---

[12] For example, Prof. Tadao Yanaihara in Tokyo and Mr. Kokichi Kurosaki in Osaka have an audience of 100 to 300 every Sunday. This figure shows a big meeting in Japan compared to the average attendance (around 50) of a local church.

[13] It should be acknowledged that in the field of Bible study in Japan the pioneering works and substantial contributions have been made from the *Mukyokai* group. Cf. Suzuki, op. cit., p. 140.

[14] Cf. John F. Howes, *Uchimura Kanzo (1861-1930), A Biographical Sketch* (M.A. Thesis, Columbia University, 1953), p. 188 f.

[15] Paul Peachey, "Mukyokai-Shugi" in *Mennonite Quarterly Review* (January 1960), p. 1.

[16] Uchimura, op. cit., p. 377

Christianity, as distinct from the churches, is a vital and relevant force, and that God gives immediate experiences of his will to the hearts of those who know him through the Bible. This saving will of God which is revealed in the Bible centers in and culminates in his redeeming deed on the cross of Jesus. This cross is the center and pivot of *Mukyokai*, "apart from which the *Mukyokai* principle is of no import. It is cross-centric *a fortiori*."[17]

Naturally "justification by faith" is part of their faith. But in this group it is elaborated as follows:

Looking up at the cross is enough for us to be justified, sanctified, and glorified; any religious experiences and meritorious works, any clerical intermediary and holy sacraments are of no use to be saved.... *Sola fide*, therefore, is a more reasonable watch-word for *Mukyokai* than for Luther-ans.[18]

On this point they differentiate their movement as "Re-reformation" from that of Luther's, since the latter could not abandon the institutional church and thus his became an "arrested movement."[19]

The movement lays great stress on the authority of the Bible. Like the *Collegia Pietatis*, originated by Philip Jakob Spener in Germany or the Methodist Society founded by John Wesley in England in the eighteenth century, Kanzo Uchimura in *Mukyokai* urged the necessity for a deeper acquaintance with the Bible accompanied by a cross-centered faith.

Indigenous Nature

Another positive aspect is the advocacy of *Japanese* Christianity. This advocacy

of nationalism in *Mukyokai*, just as in the case of the Methodism of the Wesley-an revival, has been attracting many Japanese.

An idea that non-Christian Japan is less God's than Christian England or America is entirely false.... And when I speak of God in this con-nection, I do not merely mean the Ruler of the Universe and Mankind. I mean the God of Luther and Calvin, of Dante and Milton, the Father of our Lord Jesus.[20]

But at the same time the concept of *Japanese* Christianity has been the focus of severe criticism. Uchimura himself once explained it in order to avoid misunder-standings on this point:

Japanese Christianity is not a Chris-tianity peculiar to Japanese. It is Christianity received by Japanese directly from God without any foreign intermediary; no more, no less. In this sense, there is German Christianity, English Christianity; and in this sense there will be, and already is, Japanese Christianity.... The spirit of Japan inspired by the Almighty is Japanese Christianity. It is free, independent, and productive, as true Christianity always is.[21]

It is undeniable that *Mukyokai* is very patriotic and trying to be indigenous to the Japanese nation. Thus it has occu-pied a peculiar position among Christian churches in Japan, especially reflecting the early stage of the Protestant history when the reaction to Christianity was positive and negative depending largely on cultural reasons. *Mukyokai's* claim is quite legitimate:

Since the Meiji Era, the leaders of Japan have introduced Western civi-

17 Suzuki, op. cit., p. 138.
18 Ibid.
19 Cf. Tadao Yanaihara's lecture, quoted in Peachey, op. cit.

20 *Japan Christian Intelligencer*, Vol. 2, No. 1, pp. 3-4, quoted from Jennings, op. cit., p 57 f.
21 Quoted from Suzuki, op. cit., p 139.

lization with all their might, except for Christianity. They imitated the outside of it, and not without success in this respect. But her new civilization has been like a body without a soul. . . . If Japanese society is not to return to the former primitive, feudalistic state, it cannot but accept the Christian faith and live up to it, to modernize and rationalize everyday life. So thinks the Mukyokai group.[22]

We do not hesitate to recognize the significance of this group as an indigenous expression of Christianity in one of the mission countries "at a time when indigenous expressions are still more often a desideratum than an actuality."[23] Truly, the members of this group are consciously and positively aware of their special task in Japan.

Relationships to Churches

Mukyokai is certainly peculiar not only to Christian church history in Japan but also, probably, to church history in other countries. It is a fact that most of the ministers and foreign missionaries look upon Mukyokai as exclusive, hostile, or even negative to church activities and deem it detrimental to the Christian proclamation of the gospel. It is also true, however, that some appreciate this movement and are trying to find its appropriate meaning to the church in Japan.[24]

We have to ask, then, how much Mukyokai is actually contributing to the indigenousness of Christianity, in view of the issues coming out of the confrontation of the Christian Kerygma with the unique Japanese thought-pattern.

It is clear that the Mukyokai movement intends to cut the church away from its traditional form and thus, they believe, the Mukyokai group will be regarded as the "third and independent group alongside Roman Catholicism and Protestantism, and as the true and final form of Christianity."[25] They raised a valid point in saying: "If the church is found from beyond history, then in every moment Christians must maintain the attitude that makes it possible for the church to be born anew in their time."[26] As long as they base their advocacy of "Japanese Christianity" on this foundation, the point is valid. But serious objection must be raised if the church is trying to be indigenous at the expense of adopting entirely foreign elements into Christianity. If we remember the unique thought-response of the Japanese, we have to require of them a thologically more profound confrontation of the Christian gospel.

Concerning "Japanese Christianity" the followers of Mukyokai even go on to say: "Only Christianity not borrowed from other people, but received directly from

22 Suzuki, ibid., p. 141.

23 Peachey, op. cit., p. 1

24 Cf. Jennings, op. cit., pp. 62-81. Also Charles W. Iglehart, Cross and Crisis in Japan (New York: Friendship Press, 1957), p. 52 f.; Emil Brunner, The Misunderstanding of the Church (Philadelphia: The Westminster Press, 1953), p. 131, and Brunner's comment in The Japan Christian Quarterly, Vol. 21, p. 16 f. As Iglehart mentions, Prof. Brunner openly says that he admires the inner vitality of this genuine Christian fellowship, but he seems to

emphasize the church as fellowship at the expense of institutional forms. On this point, cf. H. Richard Niebuhr, The Purpose of the Church and Its Ministry, Reflections on the Aims of Theological Education (New York: Harper and Bros., 1956), p. 21 f.

25 Masao Sekine, Mukyokai Shugi to Seisho 'Non Church and Bible' (Shizuoka: Sanichi Shoten, 1950), p. 49.

26 Masao Sekine, Mukyokai Kirisutokyo 'Christianity of the Non-Church' (Tokyo: Kobundo, 1949), p. 39 f.

God by the Japanese themselves, can save them."[27] But, what is the theological implication of this emphasis on "by the Japanese themselves"? This question is raised by the other aspect of their determined advocacy of "Japanese Christianity." They claim that the Christian church is the great all-inclusive fellowship of those who bear witness to the reality of God in their lives, and in this way they assert a direct and unbroken continuity from the Japanese religious tradition as such to Christianity. In fact, Uchimura even pictured Paul as a samurai.[28] The same question is further raised by the fact that the way of preserving their group has been reflecting the group-structure typical and traditional in Japan: feudalistic loyalty between sensei and his followers, a paternalistic relationship by means of visible and direct connection, and fellowship around such a respected person. This aspect of the structure of Mukyokai becomes fatal because its followers lack the right and positive understanding of the human dimension of ecclesiastical affairs.

As for the human dimension of the church, if it is seriously considered, many Japanese Christians are believed to be ready to agree with Mukyokai. The reason why they are still out of the Mukyokai group seems to come, in most cases, not from the positive understanding of the human dimension of the church but from their effort to ignore the problems arising from the human dimension. The problems in this respect are very often treated negatively or passively as an unavoidable limitation in this world. Consequently, it is understood to be the best thing to keep the church away as much as possible from all elements reflecting this human dimension. This is exactly what Mukyokai thinks.

A man is not saved by law, institution, or tradition, but is born again by faith in Christ. In other words, we must worship God not by institution or tradition but in spirit and truth. Therefore we need neither receive baptism, nor be a member of the church, nor attend communion service in order to receive the salvation of Christ. Even though we receive baptism or communion, we need not have it done by a qualified person confirmed by the church but anyone can do it.[29]

Fatal Limitations

The mistake of Mukyokai is not because they believe that "man is not saved by law, institution, or tradition" — this is certainly what evangelical Protestantism believes — but because they cannot accept "law," "institution," or "tradition" as anything else but "worldliness" or "human product." Their attitude toward the human dimension of the church is not only negative but a complete negation as the prefix, mu, denotes. Mukyokai believes that it needs the ecclesia but only as "the whole centering around Christ in spiritual faith." The followers have to recognize, however, that the ecclesia cannot exist in this world unless it takes a visible form, and this visible form must have some organization, management, and office, which are necessary and indispensable not only for good order, but in order that Christians can be and act as the body of Christ.

What the church possesses is not immunity from sin and error but the abiding presence of him who is the

(Continued on page 43)

---

[27] Suzuki, op. cit., p. 142.

[28] Cf. Jennings, op. cit., p. 58.

[29] Yanaihara, quoted from Peachey, op. cit.

way, the truth, and the life. It is promised, not safety, but victory.[30]

On this point we cannot but recognize the fatal limitation of *Mukyokai's* theological approach.

It is true that the *Mukyokai* movement has so many appropriate insights applicable to Christian evangelism in the unique situation of Japan, that if *Mukyokai* had not come into being, another similar movement would have. It is also true that, as Iglehart points out, of all the branches of Christianity during World War II, *Mukyokai* was the most independent.[31] We should say, however, that the advance of indigenous Christianity by way of *Mukyokai* faces severe limitations. These limitations make *Mukyokai* essentially an exclusive movement, in spite of elements of profound appropriateness to Japan.

---

[30] T. W. Manson, *The Church's Ministry* (Philadelphia: The Westminster Press, 1948), p. 80.

[31] Cf. Iglehart, op. cit., p. 52 f.

Delbert Rice

Local Church Government among the iKalahan

Traditionally, decisions among the iKalahan (North Luzon, Philippines) are made by the entire community in open conference. Elders, chosen for maturity, civic-mindedness, activity, memory, good public relations, cooperativeness, and dependability, formulate community decisions and assist in settling disputes. Mutual moral support is strong, and community disapproval and removal of support is a powerful means of social control. When the United Church of Christ in the Philippines came on the scene (1954), it brought its own Western-type Book of Government. *But the prescribed representative structures were rejected by the iKalahan in favor of open congregational meetings; church officers are task oriented and do not exercise much authority. Congregational nurture, as distinct from making decisions, is the province of specialists, which is in accord with tradition. Means of social control are also being evolved along traditional lines.*

THE iKalahan people reside on the precipitous slopes and in the valleys at the southern end of the Cordillera Mountains of North Luzon, Philippines. They are one of several ancient ethnic groups in North Luzon who are frequently grouped together under the

Delbert Rice is Director of Evangelism for the Kalahan Mission, United Church of Christ in the Philippines (Imugan, Santa Fe, Nueva Vizcaya, Philippines, A-711). Previous articles in PA include "Evangelism and Decision-Making Processes," Vol. 16, No. 6 (Nov.-Dec. 1969), pp. 264-273; and "Developing an Indigenous Hymnody," Vol. 18, No. 3 (May-June 1971), pp. 97-113.

general title, "Igorot." Although there is no accurate census of their numbers, there are probably about 20,000 of them, the majority of whom live in Nueva Vizcaya. There are other groups, however, living in Benguet, Ifugao, Pangasinan, and Nueva Ecija Provinces. Few of the majority peoples of the Philippines are even aware of their existence as a separate ethnic group.

Their basic agriculture is swidden ("slash and burn") farming on the mountain slopes. They plant dry-land rice, camote, ginger and broom straw in these plots, but they also make terraces and plant wet-land rice. Pigs and chickens are their primary livestock but goats, cows, and horses are also important. Dogs are used for hunting some of the time but much of the hunting is accomplished by various kinds of traps. The hunting in these present days, however, is infrequent because there are few wild animals left in their mountains. Each family has its own residence and there are seldom more than five or six houses in a given area.[1]

The iKalahan culture is community centered as contrasted with the neighboring lowland peoples who have a family-centered culture. The tribal unity is strong in spite of acculturation forces from the neighboring Ilocano people.[2]

Community Government

Government among the iKalahan people centers in the community elders. These elders are usually male but they can be female. No election is held by which an individual is set apart as an elder but any resident in any community can tell you exactly the names of all of the elders in all of the nearby communities including his own. They hold office by ascription or by community agreement. Actual decisions are made by community consensus but it is the elders who call the conference *(tongtongan)* at which decisions are made; and it is again one

of the elders who will finally verbalize the decision when the consensus has been achieved.

The qualifications for the office of an elder are as follows:

1. Maturity—usually over 40 years old.
2. Civic mindedness—they must show interest in community welfare.
3. Activity—must attend most of the conferences and take part in deliberations.
4. Memory—must be able to remember the decisions of previous conferences.
5. Good public relations—companionable.
6. Dependability.
7. Cooperativeness and obedience to the community mores.

There seems to be no strict financial prerequisite but it is understood that a person who does not make a fairly good living for his family is not careful or intelligent enough to be considered as an elder.

The seventh point mentioned above is well illustrated by the life of a young man who, although born in the Kalahan mountains of iKalahan parents, was taken by another family in the lowlands when he was quite young. He was educated by them in the lowlands and took their name. After finishing college, he began his career as a public school teacher and soon returned to his original home community in the mountains where he married a mountain girl. He began to take an active part in the community life and considered himself to be a leader by virtue of his education. In spite of his activity, however, he was never

---

[1] Delbert Rice, "Developing Indigenous Church Music in the iKalahan Society," *Silliman Journal*, Vol. 16, No. 4 (4th Quarter 1969), pp. 341-342.

[2] Delbert Rice, "Evangelism and Decision-Making Processes," PA, Vol. 16, No. 6 (Nov.-Dec. 1969), pp. 269-270.

accepted as an elder and was seldom called to conferences because he, himself, refused either to request or accept direction from the elders in his own life and his own problems.

By contrast, another individual who is not an iKalahan recently entered the community from a distant area. This person, however, has both requested and accepted the guidance of the elders in conference in his personal as well as in public matters and, as a result, is now frequently called to serve with the other elders in many conferences.

Elders may also be removed from their position. They will be removed if they have damaged their own reputations by flagrant violation of local mores (adultery, for instance, or excessive drunkenness) or lack of ability in handling the work of an elder. There is nothing overt done in order to remove an elder, but when a conference is held, he is no longer called.

It should also be mentioned at this point that the iKalahan community is the basic decision-making unit in the society. Even matters such as engagements or marriages, family disputes or farm practices are made the subject of conferences. All conferences are public and are noted for the openness and frankness of the discussions held. No conference is valid, however, unless the elders, or at least the majority of them, are present. It is the elders who will finally decide that a consensus has been reached and who will express that consensus to the group. If one of the elders is unable to attend the conference, the ones present will discuss his absence. If they feel certain that he will accept their verdict and that he and his family are not directly involved in the dispute, they will probably continue with the meeting, If, however, they know that he is personally involved or some relative is personally involved and his presence is personally important, they will simply postpone the conference until he can be there. No one's rights are ignored.[3]

The elders maintain the peace and welfare of the community by quickly instigating a settlement whenever a dispute or a crime occurs. An elder also serves as a powerful model through his own personal life and conduct. He exercises a very positive influence on the community in that way.

Social Climate and Social Control

The iKalahan community is a very supportive unit. In the very frank and open discussions held during a conference, it is easy to see the genuine concern which people have for the welfare of the other people. Even when the conference is held to settle a crime, the emphasis is upon the restoration of the "criminal" to the society and not upon retribution or punishment.[4]

This climate of *support* is demonstrated in individual personalities within the society also. The writer has given a thematic apperception type of psychometric test to several individ-

3 Delbert Rice, "Evangelism and Decision-Making Processes," *op. cit.*

4 Delbert Rice, "Punishment for Crime," *Silliman Journal*, Vol 17, No. 2 (2nd Quarter, 1970), pp. 170-194.

uals within the society[5] and, although the results are not yet complete, the writer has been struck by the fact that in nearly every case where an iKalahan sees some type of violence or danger, he also sees some person who will intervene to save the endangered person or settle the dispute. Many pictures which, to Western eyes, suggest violence, suggest only comfort or encouragement to the iKalahan.

A psychologist viewing such a culture would immediately recognize that the strongest tool for social control within the culture would be the threat of withdrawal of support from a given individual. This is probably true in the iKalahan culture but the writer, in spite of long involvement in the culture, can not recall having ever witnessed such a threat. Perhaps it is more covert that overt. The more common technique used in social control is the mere expression of public disapproval. At the present it is common for someone to mention to a friend of the violator that what the person is doing is not good. The message is quickly passed on and the problem is solved.

Public disapproval in the past, however, was most often expressed through music. The writer has been collecting iKalahan songs and chants for several years. Fully 80 percent of them are poetic and picturesque expressions of disapproval of some action of another individual or group. They are phrased in such a way that no person can take offense but they bring across the point

in a devastating way to people who understand the innuendos and technique.[6]

Religious History

Politically, these people were not brought under the control of Spain. In 1789 the Spanish Friar Antolin could still say that these people constituted an "independent republic."[7] The Roman Catholic religion brought to the Philippines by the Spanish Government made no important contacts with these people. They have continued in the animistic religious practices which they inherited from their ancestors. Most of their ceremonies are in relationship to death memorials or sicknesses. Sicknesses are usually interpreted as the result of the displeasure of a spirit of the forest or of the netherworld although many illnesses are supposedly caused by the displeasure of some ancestor of the sick person. A celebration is usually held at which time animals are killed and certain myths are recited. The ancestors and/or spirits are invited to join the festivities and stop bothering the sick person. In a few days time the person is expected to recover, and frequently he does.

The Evangelical Christian message first came to the iKalahan area in the years shortly before World War II, but it was sporadic and no firm work was established. In 1954 workers of

---

[5] Cora DuBois, The People of Alor (New York: Harper and Row, 1944).

[6] Rice, "Developing Indigenous Music," op. cit.

[7] Fransisco Antolin, "Notices of the Pagan Igorots in 1789," ed. and tr. by William Henry Scott, Asian Folklore Studies, Vol. 29 (1970), p. 194.

the United Church of Christ in the Philippines came into the mountains from Pangasinan province. They made their contacts in Nozo and began working their way up the mountains toward the east. The work took on the character of a lay movement shortly after its beginning although there were no strong charismatic leaders such as are characteristic of many lay movements. At the present time the congregation in Imugan has become self-supporting and there are six other congregations which are organized and self-governing. Of these six, the one in Kayapa Centro is pastored by a young man supported by Philippine Mission funds. One other is pastored part-time by the writer (a fraternal worker from the United States). Another is pastored by a lay worker. One is pastored by by a lay leader in cooperation with the fraternal worker and the other two receive regular visits from the fraternal worker, the Imugan pastor or one of the elders or young people from Imugan.

Church Government in History

Before beginning the study of church government in the iKalahan churches, it is important that the background of church goverment be analyzed historically, even though such an analysis be brief.

The Christian workers who made the contacts in 1954, being members of the United Church of Christ in the Philippines, naturally brought with them their own *Book of Government* and their own customs and techniques. The style of church goverment which

they brought had been developed out of the various governmental styles of the denominations which established the United Church in 1948. The highest governing body is the General Assembly which is composed of voting delegates sent by the various annual conferences scattered throughout the nation. The annual conferences are similarly composed of delegates chosen by election in each local church. Local churches are governed by a church council which is also composed of members elected to represent the total membership of the congregation. Ordinarily, a business meeting of the total membership is conducted only once a year in order to elect the officials. All other congregational business is conducted by the council of representatives.

That type of church government is, of course, directly inherited from the United States, whose political life is organized around the principle of "representative" democratic practices and would tend readily toward that type of organization in the church.

Spanish Influence. There is, of course, some amount of Spanish influence in the lowland Philippine cultures which were represented when the Constitution of the United Church was adopted in 1948. Spanish influence tends toward a more autocratic centralized government with the gathering of powers into the control of one or a few individuals. Spanish culture, as such, has had very little influence in the mountains but it has had definite, though perhaps unconscious, influence upon the membership and government of the United Church of Christ in the Philippines. The Roman Catholic influence in the Philippines is, of course, Spanish and the centralization in that church is in the hands of the clergy. There is some tendency towards this type of control within the United Church of Christ, but it is balanced by the representative lay influences inherited from the United States and Protestant circles which have a more direct influence upon the government of the church as such.

Jewish Influence. Both of these tendencies, the American and the Spanish, have developed over a period of many centuries within Europe and come from both the Romanized and Hellenized branches of the Christian church of the very early centuries. The early Jewish culture, in which the Christian church first found root, was patriarchial, governed by freedom-loving Jewish elders. These men were imbued with a love for independent thinking and the sometimes conflicting love for tradition and the wisdom of the fathers.

Most of the churches of the first century seem to have been governed by a group of elders, one of whom was sometimes either designated or described as a ruling elder. This custom was undoubtedly influenced by the organization of the synagogue.[8] There was little tendency toward centralization until the church came into intense contact with Roman culture. The concept of representation was an even

<hr/>

8 Albert Henry Neuman, *A Manual of Church History* (Philadelphia: American Baptist Publication Society, 1933), pp. 125-135.

later concept to enter church government.

Congregational Administration with the iKalahan

During the first years following the organization of the Kalahan church some of the early workers made somewhat of an attempt to follow the *Book of Government.* Their efforts were not notably successful, however, since such an organization did not seem to function the way it was assumed to function.

Since the cultural decision-making technique calls for complete community involvement, the iKalahan people did not accept the idea of being "represented" by anyone else. The mutual trust exhibited between the various people in the community and between the members of the church is noteworthy, but it is not in their culture to act as representatives for each other in making decisions; and therefore, the concept is difficult if not impossible to apply. At the present time, therefore, no attempt is made to apply such a concept. The congregation is governed by a meeting at which all members are present.

The congregations also maintain the cultural technique of "government by ascribed elders" in the way that it determines a quorum. In Western societies a quorum is usually determined by pure percentage (e.g. 51%, 67% or 75%). The iKalahan people determine a quorum by whether or not the elders are present. The elders of the church are nearly identical with the elders of the community with the addition of a few who are somewhat younger but are outstanding in their Christian commitment. If the individuals whom they recognize as elders are not present, the meeting cannot continue as a decision-making body although it will probably discuss matters and clarify various options.

Church Officers are Task Oriented

The congregations have, however, elected chairmen, treasurers, secretaries and a few persons whom they designate as officers. In this way they have satisfied the denominational regulations, but when the actual functions of these persons are examined, it is observed that their positions are definitely "task oriented". The officers do not have any stronger function concerning governing or administration than any of the rest of the membership and generally they refuse to exercise any such governing functions. The treasurer has the specific task of holding the money and keeping the records. The chairman leads the meetings and calls work crews together when a task has been set.

There are very few of these functioning officers who are ever reelected to their post. It must be reiterated that this is not because of lack of trust but rather because the office is not considered to be either an honor or a position of leadership but rather it is considered to be a *task* and they wish to share the tasks and not overburden any one person by asking him to serve for longer than one year.

It has also been observed that there is a great deal of concern for each individual in the choices that are made. Such phrases as "He will be helped..." or "He will learn from this task..." are heard when election to office is being discussed.

This is observed as well in other special tasks such as the organization of a work crew to plant ginger on the church lot or the organization of a group of adults to present a drama at Christmastime. Certain individuals with ability are requested to lead in those activities if they are not already overburdened with personal or community responsibilities and if the congregation feels that the individual will be helped in his personal growth by accepting such a task.

Congregational Care among the iKalahan. The problem of pastoral care differs from the concept of congregational administration in the minds of the iKalahan people. Government, to them, belongs to the entire community but pastoral care requires some specialized knowledge and training. It may be that the ancient office of *mabaki* in their animistic religion has had an influence in this matter, for it was his function to know by heart the many myths and chants which must be recited on special occasions as well as all of the rituals which should be used for each ceremony. He did not have any special function in the government, however, unless he happened to be an ascribed elder also. Of the four *mabaki* known to the writer two are also elders and two are not.

The comparison between the Christian pastor and the non-Christian *mabaki* breaks down very quickly, however, because the primary qualification which they seem to place upon a pastor is the ability to explain things clearly. The *mabaki* did not explain anything, and it was not necessary for the people to understand the chants for the ceremony to be efficacious. As a matter of fact, the writer has never noticed anyone trying to listen to the chants except another visiting *mabaki*.

The people do recognize, however, the need for special abilities and knowledge and hence, they do not desire to rotate the tasks of preaching, teaching and pastoring as much as they do the task of governing. They have recognized that certain of their elders and certain others who have taken special training have ability to pastor and by this recognition these individuals become, in essence, community pastors. They may be either male or female, but they must possess the following qualifications:

1. Ability to explain the Bible and the Christian life.
2. Willingness to accept responsibility to teach and preach (these two are frequently synonymous).
3. An honorable personal life.
4. An amiable personality.

The financial support of the pastor depends upon whether or not he is from the community and already self-supporting. If he is a local person and already self-supporting, he will not receive additional support from the local church except for transportation expenses or study expenses. If he or she is from outside the community and serving in the pastoral work full-time, he will be supported full-time from local funds. Both of these patterns and variations of them exist already in the area.

Christian Social Climate and Social Control. Since the iKalahan people already have a strongly supportive social climate, it is important that the climate be continued. If such a climate were to be damaged or destroyed, it would be a very great disservice to the people and the Christian gospel. Many of the techniques of social control, however, were conducted during the celebrations which were very closely related to their pre-Christian religion. Since the frequency of the celebrations has been drastically curtailed because of the entrance of the Gospel, there has been some interference with the function of social control in the society.

An attempt is being made at the present time by many of the Christians in the area to determine the proper functional replacement for the old celebrations. Progress is being made in this matter, but the task is far from complete. The problem is to try to find the proper balance by which the social functions of recreation, interpersonal involvement and influence can be accomplished without continuing the non-Christian elements of prayers to the spirits. It is also important to realize that the heavy expenses of some of the old ceremonies such as the *padit* (a prestige feast sometimes lasting for ten days) have become dysfunctional due to the present need for educating the youth and taking part in the economic life of the nation.

Some of the musical culture, in fact most of it, has already been incorporated into the regular church services, and in that way some of the elements of social control have already been brought over into that meeting. The chants are now used for greetings, farewells and other similar special occasions, however, and are not often used for their former purposes of giving advice or making criticism of improper behavior. The practice has not stopped but the writer personally feels that there is a partial vacuum in this area which needs to be filled.

A recent experience indicates one possible technique for filling this vacuum. Excessive drinking at celebrations was well known to previous generations but the culture had adequate facilities for keeping it under control so that it did not disrupt individual lives or the community welfare. Recently, however, the ready availability of bottled liquor from the lowlands and the stress of acculturation with the lowland cultures has caused drunkenness to be a problem to most of the iKalahan communities. In response to this problem, two of the young people, with the writer, took a clue from two verses in Proverbs 23 and, utilizing an appropriate tune, wrote a Kalahan song in the old style. The tune is one generally used by the iKalahan people for any humorous but pointed story or comment.[9] The results were surprising to many but were readily accepted. The children

9 Rice, "Developing Indigenous Church Music...," op. cit.

learned it immediately and began singing it in church and also in their homes or on the streets or trails. From there it has been feeding back to the places where it can accomplish its intended purpose of exercising social control. The words are as follows:

Hay mata ambalanga,
Way hogat, agto amta.
Kamanhakit ni olo
Tep lingayoy naitlo,
Kadnengto bakalanto;
Igototoy gaitto.
Maokong idan halaw,
Hi-gaday mabalaw.
The eyes are red,
There is a wound, he does not know it.
The head is aching
Because unhappiness has been put in.
He fights his closest friends;
He murmurs against his companions.
They have their arms around the wine jug.
They are to be criticized.

Very likely other similar songs will soon develop and continue to exercise the same power of social control in the new Christian life style of the iKalahan people.

Summary and Conclusions

Although the evangelists did not plan to do it, the church government in the iKalahan society has continued to follow the style and techniques of the community government already well established within the culture. The fact that this is also true within the United States and other cultures seems to indicate that church government generally is more strongly influenced by theology. This is probably as it should be.

The church government in the iKalahan church shows a strong similarity to the church government in the early church as it was established in the Jewish society. The reason for this similarity is rather obvious when it is observed that the actual cultural organization of the West Asian Jews was very similar to the present cultural organization of the Southeast Asian iKalahan.

The iKalahan churches have paid lip-service to the governmental pattern of the denomination by using the official titles indicated in the *Book of Government* to designate some of the chosen officers, but at the same time they have changed the function of those officers and the attitude toward them in order to be more consistent with their own concept of government. They have also altered their definition of a quorum to suit their own concept of government by the majority under the guidance of the elders.   This is not a hypocritical action on their part nor is it deceitful. It is an essential adjustment which they have made in order to accomplish two important tasks: first, to develop and experience a truly functioning

government for their own church within their own society; and second, to allow that local congregational government to interact smoothly with the church government of the larger body on the national level. The wisdom of these adjustments should be self-evident.

What has been done by the iKalahan people regarding their church government is indicative of what can and should be done by other societies when, as Christians, they join together in the common life of faith. First: following the basic patterns of control and influence which are already built into their own culture and personalities, they must plan the proper government for their local church. Second: for the sake of the larger fellowship with other Christians, they should make such necessary adjustments to enable the communication and fellowship to be as broad as possible. Third: provide as quickly as possible the functional replacements for any components of their culture which are found to be truly incompatible with the Christian gospel.

It is educational to study the techniques of church government which have been used in other cultures and other generations, but it is not often helpful to attempt to follow them.

G. Linwood Barney

The Meo —
an Incipient Church

OF THE 45,000 Meo in the area around Xieng Khouang Province, in Laos (Indochina), about 4,500 have become professing Christians since May 1950. During this same period, about 1,500 Khmu, a neighboring group of different culture, have also accepted Christianity. They had heard of it, but never in a ·comprehensive manner. How has Christianity· spread as an innovation in Meo culture?

The Meo people of Xieng Khouang represent part of the great numbers who have drifted southward from China, where they are known as Miao, into· Northern Indochina and Thailand. Roux, who has followed their development for four decades, feels that the trail of their "slash and burn" clearings and other changes that they have wrought in the land would indicate that they first entered Laos and Vietnam about 120 to 140 years ago.[1] According to my informants, their ancestors first entered Xieng Khouang Province about a century ago. They located, as is their custom, in the highlands and on mountain ridges, where the elevation

---

[1] Roux, Henri: "Quelques Minorités Ethniques du Nord-Indochine," *France-Asie*, No. 92-93, p. 388.

Reprinted from Vol. 4, No. 2 (1957), pp. 31-50. Rev. G. Linwood Barney, a former missionary in Laos under the Christian and Missionary Alliance, is studying for the Ph.D. in Anthropology from the University of Minnesota and is teaching Missions at Bethel Seminary and St. Paul Bible College in St. Paul, Minnesota.

runs from 4,000 to 8,000 feet. The Meo still reflect their influence from China by many loan words from Chinese.

A Protestant mission had been in operation in North Laos for about fifteen years when the first missionaries entered Xieng Khouang in 1940. The ministry of these new missionaries was abruptly interrupted by World War II. At this initial entry, little or no contact was made with the general Meo population, which was seldom to be seen in town (a Lao community). It was not until late 1949 that a young missionary couple again took up residence in Xieng Khouang and began a study of the Lao language, the language of the culturally dominant group and of the government of Laos. Catholic missionaries also had some contact with the Meo, with little if any response.

Xieng Khouang town, with a population of about 1,500, is the administrative center for the province and serves as the home of Tubi, the highest Meo official in all Laos. Tubi is appointed by the federal government to be representative for the Meo population of Laos to the Laotian government.

We will use May 1950 as the time of initial contact between the Meo and Christianity. As background for understanding its entry among them, we give a description of the cultural setting at the time of contact, but limit the description to those factors which are relevant to the introduction of Christianity. An account of the early dissemination of Christianity will follow. In this connection we shall see the early beginnings of church development until the time of the evacuation of the missionaries because of Viet Minh (Communist) war action in 1953. Next, the church as it existed after eighteen months of Communist occupation is described and its further development during the next twelve months is indicated. Finally, this data will be interpreted in the light of anthropological theory, with a projection of developments into the future.

Meo Culture at the Time of Contact: May 1950

Rice is the basic food staple for the Meo, although corn is grown and used when necessary. The Meo are the only people in the whole Xieng Khouang area to grind corn in rotating stone corn mills. They are famous for their horses, which are usually somewhat larger than the typical horse in Southeast Asia. They are proud of these animals, care for them fondly, train them well, and produce a beast of burden whose sure-footedness and stamina on the steep rugged trails is amazing. Cattle, goats, pigs, chickens, and dogs make up the remainder of the livestock common in a Meo village.

A village may number from one large household (I visited one with thirty-five members) to a village with as many as forty households. Usually a household consists of the conjugal family with occasional additional elderly members or a married son who remains temporarily until his own house is built.

Clan members do not marry within the clan, and usually several clans will be represented in one village. Polygyny is practiced, usually as the result of adding

the widow of a deceased brother. One case of polygyny was observed in which a man had married sisters. Wealthier men, like Tubi, may have several wives, but the "big wife" is considered most important and accompanies him at public functions. Trial marriage, a normal practice, is carried on with a semblance of disapproval by the girl's parents. Marriage is contracted through intermediaries but is not actualized until the young man has earned and paid the agreed bride-price. Thus girls may get married soon after puberty, but men are often eighteen to twenty years old before they have sufficient funds to meet the contract price.

Every Meo household has an opium poppy field. This provides the cash income. French administrators declared that an estimated sixty to seventy percent of the Meo adult male population had been addicted to the opium habit. The women seldom use it except in severe illness and suffering. Boys may be introduced to it, but their frequent use of it is frowned upon until after marriage.

The village chief is the most powerful political figure in a village and, although not commonly a dictator, he is highly respected; when he gives an explicit command it is obeyed. His house is usually large enough to accommodate the entire village when a meeting is called.

The shaman, who probably holds status below that of the chief, is considered necessary in any Meo village. Indeed, many villages have any number of them. Their duties take much of their time, and they are reimbursed considerably. The shaman and the chief seem to operate in different phases of life and thus have little cause for conflict. The shaman is expected to serve the people. Some of his functions are: (1) protecting the newborn child from evil spirits by placing fetish bands on his neck and limbs; (2) performing rituals at funeral and marriage ceremonies and reciting long dirges at the former; (3) securing protection for a rice field at planting time; (4) securing protection for trail and hunting expeditions; and (5) performing extensive rituals for the sick, including the sacrificing of a chicken or some animal offered by the family of the sick person.

The Meo culture is rich in a folklore which is handed down in couplet form and may be recited for days. The folklore and present day practices reflect their deep belief in a spirit world. They believe in a supreme deity, Fua-Tai, who created everything but who has become uninterested in mankind. The Meo are left at the mercy of the spirits who make constant demands on them for offerings and sacrifices. They even set up the specifications for the home, requiring them to be made of hand-hewn boards erected in vertical position. Board shingles form the roof. A central part of the house contains an altar for the spirits.

Another factor which has bearing on the subject of this paper is the relationship between the Meo and another tribal people, the Khmu. The latter live in the foothills and have adopted much of the Lao culture, but are animistic much like the Meo. Their relationship with the Meo is one of mutual respect with no marked friendship or hostility.

Patterns of Culture Change

In the ten years that had passed since the brief stay of missionaries in Xieng Khouang before World War II and the re-entry of new missionaries in 1949, circumstances had changed. Trends of culture change were evident among the Meo.

Reasons are only speculative. Perhaps newer generations were breaking from older traditions due to the migrations. Perhaps Japanese control had given temporary equal status to Meo and Lao alike. Perhaps the personality characteristics of the Meo, their aggressiveness, alertness, inquisitiveness, etc., built up until internal combustion revealed itself in an external manner.

Today the Meo descend in large numbers upon the market. They have little produce to trade, but they make their purchases with opium and silver. (Seldom will the Meo offer or accept any form of paper currency.) The Meo who, ten years before, were seldom seen in town now not only attend market but occasionally take up residence near town and obtain employment there. Many Meo youth, with Tubi's encouragement, have enrolled in the town school, where they can acquire the equivalent of an eighth-grade education. Few actually remain in school for more than a couple of years, but some have completed this schooling and are now in attendance in the *lycée* at Vientiane, and one Meo, a Christian, is in college in Saigon.

Meanwhile, in some Meo villages, education is considered a real attainment and some Laotian teachers have been paid wages above that of the Laotian school to open school in the Meo villages for the local youth. Such schools are rather unorganized, but they have helped toward some literacy in the Lao language. Mission records show that approximately three or four per cent of the Meo are literate. This percentage would increase with closer proximity to town. Learning Lao is considered by the Meo as a necessary evil in order to gain prestige and advancement. (Many are now obtaining semiofficial positions with the government.) Already the Lao, who have dominated the economic and political scene, sense the rising tide of the Meo society. Regardless of what may have triggered these new developments in the Meo culture, they must be considered along with the more static cultural traits described above as part of the over-all setting into which Christianity was introduced. Certain elements were conducive to its acceptance, while others were in direct opposition to it.

Introduction of Christianity

In May of 1950 the missionary family residing in Xieng Khouang left to attend a conference of missionaries in Vietnam. A young Khmu tribesman from the province of Luang Prabang came to the mission station to watch the property and also to let the local population realize that the missionary had left only temporarily. This young man, Nai Kheng, went about town telling of his Christian faith. One who listened intently was Po Si, an old Meo shaman who lived close to town. He stated that a female shaman had prophesied two years before that in two years someone would come to tell them about the true God, Fua-Tai. Po Si was convinced that Nai Kheng was telling him about the same God and became a professing Christian. He took Nai Kheng to his own village, where the chief led his entire group in expressing faith in Fua-Tai-Yesu, as Jesus came to be called in Meo. Kheng was then taken to the village of the female shaman who had made the prediction mentioned above. After listening to Nai Kheng's message, she stated firmly that she was convinced that this was the one of whom she had spoken,

and she led her village in placing faith in Fua-Tai-Yesu.

With this, other villages in the area sent for Nai Kheng, who traveled almost constantly relating the simple events of Christ's life and the means of salvation through faith in him. After being delayed weeks by a typhoon, the missionary returned and was amazed to find nearly 1,000 Meo tribespeople who had announced their faith in Christ.

The missionary then accompanied Nai Kheng and Po Si to the villages of the new Christians where, by request of some and consent of others, he removed and destroyed all fetishes from their bodies, homes, fields, etc. This became an expected ritual on the part of any new convert. The Christians refer very frequently to their freedom from the spirits, explaining that the evil spirit, Tlan, is more powerful than man but less powerful than Fua-Tai, who through his Son, Yesu, has again become intensely interested in man and thus liberates him from the power and effects of the evil spirits. This faith in Fua-Tai-Yesu is very real, as is evidenced by the manner in which the Meo, with no exhortation from the missionary, travel widely in the area telling others about their newly found faith.

At this time another missionary fluent in the Lao language came to Xieng Khouang to teach in a hastily formed catechist Bible school. (No missionary spoke Meo; all communication was carried on through interpreters.) The first session was attended by about thirty-five students. Every village having Christians sent at least one representative who could understand Lao and who was respected by the members of the village. Some of these individuals had attended one to six years in the public school.

Church services were conducted in Xieng Khouang at one o'clock every Sunday afternoon and were attended by 200 to 300 people. A temporary structure of bamboo and thatch was erected for these services.

Beginning Linguistic Analysis

In 1951 my family and I arrived in Kieng Khouang to undertake reduction of the Meo language to writing. I used a monolingual approach as I knew no Lao and therefore had no intermediary language. Gradually I learned not only the language but many of the underlying facets of the Meo culture. In early 1952 the other missionaries left for furlough and I was left in charge of the work. Sharing the responsibility was Pastor Sali, an ordained Lao clergyman (actually he was of Lao and Vietnamese descent), who quickly picked up a practical knowledge of Meo and was a great help in ministering to the church. All missionary-national communication was carried on in Meo. Only the Bible school, now taught by Sali, continued in Lao, and this because of a ruling by the federal government.

Almost exclusive use of the Meo language broke down barriers and brought to light Meo practices which were in contradiction to American Christianity and some which seemed to oppose the Judeo - Christian tradition everywhere. However, the main concern at this stage was to establish the Meo in the Christian faith, which in its essential element is a God-man relationship apart from cultural factors of any particular society.

Just prior to my arrival in Xieng Khouang, another event of considerable importance took place. Tubi, the Meo leader, became intensely interested in Christianity and attended the services regularly with his family. He called the missionary and the catechists to his home and stated his intention of having a Christian home. He did not want to go on record as having become a Christian himself because of the Buddhist government but his entire family, including his several wives and all the children, expressed their faith, and Tubi requested that all fetishes be destroyed. His principal wife has been a faithful adherent and supporter of the local church and was in the first group to be baptized. This led to even greater receptiveness among the Meo population and was directly responsible for the conversion of a Meo district chief Sai Pao, who was responsible for many villages and has himself been instrumental in guiding a large number of those under him into the Christian faith.

Like the expanding ripples caused by a stone thrown into water, the dissemination of Christianity began to spread out from Xieng Khouang and continues today. By March of 1953, about 2,000 Meo and 1,000 Khmu had become Christians. One could travel about four days from Xieng Khouang before he reached the periphery of the movement.

At this juncture, the Viet Minh Communists struck from across the border. Xieng Khouang was one of the first places to fall into Red hands. No time was allowed for preparing the Meo for the sudden forced departure of the missionaries and Sali. Left behind were fourteen catechists who had had training for about two years and six others who had received training for six months. It must be noted that there were also several strong lay Christian leaders who were very earnest in their Christian conduct and witness.

Upon my departure, I was greatly disturbed about the future of this young church, fearing that it was not too well established, wondering whether I should have pushed the Meo into a system of Christian ethics, and questioning the real stability of the faith of the Meo.

Before moving to a description of the situation eighteen months later, when missionaries could again make residence in Xieng Khouang, I should like to recount three personal experiences which illustrate developments in the thinking of the Meo. Each of these situations arose spontaneously, although one might legitimately ask, "Did these concepts arise within these individuals, or did they result from their associations with the missionaries?" It would be nice to think that the former was the case.

The Marriage Ceremony

Tua Pao, a twenty-year-old catechist, was engaged to be married. He had paid the bride-price and approached me as to the manner in which he should get married, since he did not wish to follow the traditional form completely. After discussion, elements of the Meo culture which were not related to the spirits were retained and a simple Christian ritual was added to produce an over-all ceremony which the Meo have followed with enthusiasm. In substance the entire procedure includes the usual overtures to the girl's parents by an intermediary of the young man, an agreed amount of bride-price, reciprocal feasts by both families, and then the brief ceremony at the bride's home when neck bands are exchanged and a local pastor or catechist asks God's seal of blessing on this new home. Then the couple go to live in the young man's village. Tua Pao's wedding was the first Christian Meo wedding, but many others have followed.

Trial Marriage

Ntrua, an informant sixteen years old, raised the question of trial marriage. He had been a Christian for two years. Now he was approaching the age when young men practiced trial marriage. The Meo parents offer only a semblance of disapproval when the young man spends the night with their daughter. Actually she is allowed to sleep on a platform apart from the rest of the family and the young male intruder is expected to come and go surreptitiously between the time that family retires and arises. This may continue for some time until the young couple decides that it does or does not want to become recognized by the community as husband and wife. If they do not want to continue, then each looks elsewhere for another partner. Apparently the Meo have frowned upon a repeated change of partners, considering this to be immoral and not for the real purpose of securing a wife. Ntrua questioned the practice in either form for the Christian. I discussed the problem with him without making any ruling. Ntrua drew his own conclusion that he could better follow Christ by not following this practice. He became quite influential in encouraging other youths to do the same.

Opium as a Source of Income

A Meo tribesman of about forty years of age, who had achieved wealth according to Meo standards, approached me. He had enough rice fields to keep his household but had been very successful in the production of opium. He was not addicted to it himself, but stated that he felt it was improper for a Christian to use opium and therefore questioned whether he should even grow it. He stated that the opium hindered the Meo from working the way he should, eventually making him a "murky" thinker, and kept him in a state of poverty. I discussed other possibilities for cash income. Finally, of his own volition, the man turned to raising market produce instead of opium and reported that he was doing well.

Other cases could be related, but these brief accounts give some indication of the alert Meo mind, his intense persuasion of the Christian faith, and perhaps some of the reasons for the content in the next section of this paper.

After the Occupation

On our return, it seemed that everyone had some experience to relate in which his faith had proven effective during the difficult and meager days of the occupation. Space does not permit giving these accounts. Except for two abbreviated contacts, the Christians had been separated from the missionaries during this entire period of eighteen months. Perhaps a little comparison will give a quick glimpse of what transpired.

In March of 1953, there were about 2,000 Christian Meo living in fifty-six scattered villages which were located from an hour to four days' travel from Xieng Khouang. Ten villages had chapels. Catechists were supported, the mission and the Christians sharing equally. Most of the Christians came to the missionary for advice and counsel. In September 1954, the Meo Christians numbered between 3,000 and 3,500 and seventy-three villages had Christians. They extended to six days' travel from Xieng Khouang. The

church had continued without mission funds. There was a matured Christian concept among many of the Christians, as was evidenced by their ability to make decisions concerning the interpretation of Christianity in their own conduct. The catechists were often sought out for counsel. Some of the catechists had not been too effective as leaders but others had developed splendidly. We were deeply impressed by the strides made by the Christians of Xieng Khouang.

The movement continues. Later reports number the Meo Christians over 4,000. These live in some ninety-six villages, with forty-two villages professing to be one hundred per cent Christian.

Organizational developments have also appeared. Lay leaders are selected from each village by the Christians in that village. Generally, these men have the combined qualities of being typically Meo so as to be respected by the Meo population and also meet what the Meo understand to be the Scriptural requirements of a deacon. The Meo are very ethnocentric and have grown to assume Christianity is as much Meo as it is American. Often a village has not expressed an interest in Christianity until its members are convinced that it is not just Western culture.

The school for catechists is taught by a missionary and by Sali, with forty catechists attending. A new development has been short-term schools conducted for the deacons and slanted to help them in discharging effectively their spiritual responsibilities. Special conferences at Christmas and Easter are attended by groups numbering 1,200 to 1,800. A national church organization has been formed with an executive board consisting of Sali as president, a catechist as secretary, a group of laymen as keepers of the treasury, and representatives from the Lao, Meo, and Khmu ethnic groups. The missionary is adviser.

Along with this progress there remain factors which present and will continue to present problems for some time. Some of these have developed from mission programs; others have been a natural development caused by the contact of Meo culture with Christianity; still others are the fault of neither, but the result of extraneous circumstances.

As natural result of the culture contact there are such issues as follow: (1) the used and production of opium; (2) the practice of polygamy, by choice and by inheritance; (3) the practice of trial marriage; and (4) misconceptions and misinterpretations occurring most commonly at the periphery of the Christian community. For example, at one time a Meo trinity developed with three men representing God as Father, Son, and Holy Spirit. They had quite a following until Holy Spirit died in trying to fly, as a dove, from a high elevation.

Some problems have arisen as a result of mission administration. The time element here has not always been made clear in mission reports, and much improvement has been made, as will be indicated in the next section. Included among these problems are those arising from the following procedures: (1) despite eighteen months of self-support, the mission again became engaged in giving a subsidy to the catechists; (2) the mission has contributed largely to the planning and erection of a permanent church building in Xieng Khouang, and likewise of school buildings; (3) the curriculum and teaching in the Bible school is under mission domination; (4) the church constitution began to be formulated by a committee consisting of three missionaries and only two nationals, both Lao; (5) allocations and assignments of catechists have been made by the missionaries; (6) the missionaries have performed most of the church ordinances; (7) the missionary handled all funds, both mission and local offerings; and (8) the Christians have had the concept that somehow the missionary had greater influence with God than did the catechists.

The constant threat of renewal of Communist aggression and the soaring inflational trend are further factors that create new problems and add to some of those just listed.

Analysis and Evaluation

Despite many mistakes by commission and omission on the part of the missionaries, I do not feel presumptuous in concluding that Christianity has been well received by the Meo and that the process of acculturation has been much more than a superficial one. A cynic might add, "And this in spite of missionaries."

I should like to attempt an analysis of the data which has been given above in light of conclusions and principles that anthropologists have postulated in other studies of culture contact.

First, in reference to the introduction of Christianity to the Meo, the missionary is an indirect factor. Nai Kheng, a Khmu, might be considered the innovator in that he was the carrier. However, more important is the fact that Po Si, a well-known shaman, became the first convert and in a very real sense was the innovator. It was Po Si who arranged for Nai Kheng to visit the Meo villages and accompanied him on these visits, giving personal testimony to the reality of his newly found faith and urging the Meo to give audience to this Khmu catechist. Following this pattern, in village after village, it has been the chiefs and shamans who have led their people in an acceptance of Christianity. This was given further support by Tubi, the Meo leader, and very active support by Sai Pao, the district chief. Though Po Si was the innovator in the first instance, one might say that there have been many innovators in different villages and districts, and nearly always a prominent person has been the initiator. Christianity has benefited from the prestige derived from these respected individuals. "With respect to prestige, the relation between the innovator and his innovations is a reciprocal one. The fact that he introduced it reflects some glory on him, but the new thing becomes associated with him in the minds of the group and gains or loses its potentialities for conferring prestige upon those who accept it later according to what his status may be."[2]

The acceptance of Christianity throughout the Meo population bears out Linton's further comment in this connection, that a new innovation will filter down in a culture from those of high status to those of a lower status, but seldom does it climb from a low status group to a high status group.[3]

A second factor which is very important in this study is the manner in which the innovation was introduced. Nai Kheng was himself a young convert. He recounted only his faith in Christ, the procedure for attaining this faith, and finally could give, in simple story form, some of the episodes from the life of Christ. He knew little or nothing of ecclesiasticism. Therefore his message did what the missionary's usually does not. It dealt with matters which point more directly to Christian faith without the cultural trappings inherent in the missionary's presentation. It seems that Nai Kheng unwittingly established a pattern which the misionary followed and by which Christianity spread rapidly in Xieng Khouang. Emile Cailliet asserts, "...We should realize that no Christian approach to culture is safe which does not begin by disengaging Christian truth from the cultural forms in which it has been embedded."[4]

A third factor closely related to the one just mentioned is the splendid rapport between the missionary and the Meo in the Xieng Khouang area. There was a marked hesitancy on the part of the missionaries to pressurize the Christians to abandon all their practices, since the former were not sure of the significance of the practices to the Meo themselves. If contact with Christianity resulted in some conflict with the Meo culture, it became apparent to the Meo himself and he struggled with the problem, as in the three cases studied above.

The new objects . . . moral standards and religious beliefs must be introduced through native authority and acceptance, so that natives themselves can work out the consequent changes or cultural and social adjustments. They alone can do this, and it takes time, experience, and experiment.

Of course, this may seem frustrat-

[2] Linton, Ralph: *Acculturation in Seven American Indian Tribes*. D. Appleton Century Co., New York, 1940. p. 473.

[3] Ibid., p. 474.

[4] Cailliet, Emile: *The Christian Approach to Culture*. D. Appleton Century Co., New York, 1940. p. 15.

ing to the efficient administrator or zealous missionary, but the development of a people in culture has no meaning apart from their continuing as a people with an integrated social and cultural system. A people cannot be preserved by authority, and no people is willing to be "preserved." A people lives from within or dies without.[5]

It seems possible ... to support the following generalization: people resist changes that threaten basic securities; they resist proposed changes they do not understand; they resist being forced to change.[6]

The first strong action by the missionary in the destruction of the fetishes met with the approval of the Christians and the function of these items was substituted for through Christian practices, often nothing more than simple prayer. Thus there appeared to be little conflict within the culture as a result of taking away the fetishes and the cessation of the shaman's practices. There is only one case known to me in which a village reverted to its powerful drum fetish. This village was located at the periphery of the Christian movement and perhaps had not received sufficient teaching and thereby as clear an understanding of Christian faith.

Some of the problems which are given above in three classifications have been greatly reduced or solved in very recent months. Allocations and assignments of catechists are now made by the executive committee of the recently formed national church. Rites are now performed by Sali and licensed Meo catechists. Baptism and communion are extended to those who are approved by local church committees in conference with the catechist responsible for the group. Delegation of authority to the catechists has resulted in the Christians' placing more confidence in them and going to them for counsel where they would probably have gone to the missionary.

Mission funds are handled by the missionary and are generally used for mission expense, while church funds are handled and administered by the national church. Other measures in progress include a three-year program whereby a third of the subsidy to the catechists will be removed each year and will be replaced by local church support. Thus by 1958 the church should be self-supporting.

Inflation has made the cutting of the subsidy difficult, but it has had its benefits. It has prevented the erection of a rather elaborate church in Xieng Khouang, although the structure will still not seem natural to the tribespeople. One questions whether they themselves would even have the technology for repairs.

Thus far, polygamy, the use of opium, and trial marriage have been considered difficult problems which will have to be handled within the society in time and as their faith takes on clearer manifestation within the framework of the Meo culture. I believe these problems can be worked out if the missionary does not insist on enforcing the attitudes of his own culture toward these items.

Bride-price, frowned upon by many missionaries, has not been considered evil by the missionaries in Xieng Khouang, since it is a cultural trait which gives a measure of solidarity to the Meo marriage. It functions as a proof of the young

---

5 Elkin, A. P.: *Social Anthropology in Melanesia.* Oxford University Press, London, 1953. p. 148.

6 Spicer, Edward H.: *Human Problems in Technological Change.* Russell Sage Foundation, New York, 1952. p. 18.

man's worth and his esteem for the girl. At the same time, it serves to discourage divorce, which would necessitate a financial adjustment. Bride-price to the Meo does not mean female slavery or a purchase of a piece of property. Hence it should be retained because of its function in giving stability to the family and thus to the culture.

Missionaries commonly refer to the concept of an "indigenous church" as though it were some magical formula consisting of three ingredients: self-support, self-government, and self-propagation.

In Xieng Khouang self-propagation has developed naturally. Self-support was practically established during the Communist occupation but was partially undermined by the new mission subsidy. It is now being reintroduced with difficulty, by the three-year plan. The committee of three missionaries and two nationals working on the constitution has been dissolved, but self-government is far from a reality. There needs to be a definite program put into action whereby the nationals will be given experience in administration of church and school in order that they may be adequately prepared to take over an ever-increasing amount of the administrative responsibilities.

I had opportunity to observe missionary work in other parts of Laos, in Vietnam, and in Thailand. There are certain principles which I believe should be basic in missionary work. There is not space to draw comparisons from other areas, although such would be most helpful in giving more support to these principles. I have seen groups who have been Christian for twenty years but are not as rooted in local culture as the church in Xieng Khouang. Other groups are completely in operation without missionary supervision. Thus drawing on personal observation and the wealth of anthropological material available, I would make the following summary statement.

The missionary's goal should be: (1) to present Christianity apart from the implications of the missionary's own culture, since he recognizes the latter to be entirely relative and not essential to the establishment of a God-man relationship for the individual who is the recipient of Christian faith; (2) not to be satisfied with the threefold standard traditionally used to indicate an indigenous church, but to be satisfied only as essential Christian faith takes root deep in a culture and the resulting Christian society makes outward manifestation and takes organizational form within the framework of the local culture; and (3) to become, thereby, dispensable to the continuance of the local church and yet be in such a place of rapport with the local church that he shall be welcomed as a guide and stimulus in the growth of the church.

To accomplish this the missionary must be convinced that the nationals — the Meo for the sake of illustration — are not to become American church puppets but rather strong Christians although still Meo. He must be convinced that the Meo can be one hundred per cent Meo and still one hundred per cent Christian.[7]

I would propose that any culture, any society, and any member within a society may become Christian without losing the majority of its distinctive characteristics.

---

[7] Diasuke Kitagawa expresses this concept in his paper: "Racial and Cultural Relations in the Ministry to American Indians." National Council, New York, 1954.

The missionary introduces Christianity. Given time, its real essence will find its level in the depths of a culture, and when it has been accepted wholeheartedly on the level of basic values, acculturation will be possible and the necessary changes will be made from within. "A basic reformation of personality takes place in the acculturation process only when people and values of the dominant culture are successfully attained."[8]

Efforts on the part of a missionary to bring about conformity to his denominational background or even traditional American concepts will bring about, at best, a superficial church which will fade away should the missionary leave and which will not be likely to grow or spread beyond the area which the missionary himself is able to reach.

Christianity, as an innovation in any culture, will cause changes, but when properly introduced and cultivated it will produce a Christian ethic within the configuration of the pre-existing culture without having caused a disintegration of that culture.

With my people, it is not so much what you say as how you say it, and who does the saying.

To my people, one "let us do" is worth more than a thousand "you must do's." Africa is a child, but our paternalists fail to observe that this child is growing. They also forget that in many instances it is more important to work *with* than to work for.[9]

The African clergyman and scholar who uttered those words re-echoes the thoughts of national Christians on most any mission field in the world.

---

[8] Spindler, George, and Goldschmidt, Walter: "Experimental Design in the Study of Cultural Change," *American Anthropologist,* Vol. 58, p. 80.

[9] Smith, Edwin W.: *Aggrey in Africa.* A study in black and white. Doubleday, Doran and Co., Inc., New York, 1929. p. 2.

PART VI

Cultural Processes: Change and Conversion

William D. Reyburn

The Transformation of God and the Conversion of Man

THE major obstacle to the effective communication of the Christian message of God's redeeming love looms up in the receiver's notion of God. The universal question which should be posited by Christian missions is, *Can a man be converted to Christianity without the transformation of his idea of God to conform to a Christian concept of God?*

In order to throw some light on this question a discussion of these matters will be given within the framework of two disparate folk cultures, the peasant Quechua Indians of the Ecuadorean Andes and the hunting Kaka tribe of the southeastern French Cameroun. These two societies provide a widely divergent cultural base from which to view this problem.

The notion of God as held by any group of people is one of the most vital keys they can offer the missionary as an insight into the depths of their human feelings about a score of subjects other than the purely religious. In fact, the missionary who will know his people will have to first know their God. How a people symbolize the supernatural, and the way they think and feel toward their God or gods is not only a clue to the stuff of which the society is made, but also an indication of what in Christianity will be immediately relevant. It shows also what will undergo radical reinterpreta-

tion to fit the existing scheme of things, and what will have to be rejected as unintelligible (although it is possible to embody paradoxes and contradictions and to make little or no attempt to have things logically consistent). What a society or any individual will think about man is not determined so much by his method of studying man (as historian, anthropologist, or biologist) but by what he assumes man to be. Likewise, what a society thinks about man's relation to God and vice versa is not set by the manner of approaching God, but by what it assumes man and God to be.

The two societies dealt with here assume similar yet quite different things about God. These in turn are reflected in basically different human orientations which give life's purpose (or lack of it) different ends. Knowledge of a man's view of God is not immediately given by simply asking for it but is gotten at rather through his practices, attitudes, values, institution, systems of beliefs, and relations to other human beings.

It is no exaggeration to say that man creates God in his own image. This creation of God in the image of the people likewise affects and determines much of the way in which man creates his culture. The two things are interdependent. Christianity's claim to withstand this charge is contained in the view of God which originates from a self-disclosing God who reveals himself to man.

Reprinted from Vol. 4, No. 5 (1957), pp. 185-194.

481

In order to catch a comparative view of God, we will first give Christian conceptions of God with their counterparts seen from Kaka and Quechua concepts. This may be done best by separating the Christian set into (1) God as God, and (2) God as Redeemer. The confusion of these two aspects of God in the minds of the Kaka and Quechua creates a barrier to understanding Christianity.

God as God

Christian: God is perfect.

Kaka: God is a spider, Ndjambie. His character is impersonal, thus perfection or lack of it cannot be one of his attributes.

Quechua: God is Father, Taita Dios, who is as personal as Taita may decide to be. He is not granted a state of perfection. He is only reckoned as good or bad according to his acts.

Christian: God is one and infinite.

Kaka and Quechua: Ndjambie and Taita Dios are not infinite but submerged in an infinite cosmos. Therefore they are not the creator even though called that. Not being truly creator, Ndjambie and Taita Dios are not infinite.

Christian: God is lawgiver and judge.

Kaka: Ndjambie is not connected with enforcing supernatural sanctions, such as punishment for incest. The "law" is given through the ancestors whose spirits enforce its sanctions.

Quechua: Taita Dios is judge without being lawgiver; therefore his judgment is capricious.

Christian: Since God is perfect and the lawgiver, humans are dependent morally.

Kaka: No such dependence follows.

Quechua: Dependence is entirely on a material level since Taita Dios is unrelated to perfection.

Christian: God is the creator and author of cosmological order.

Kaka and Quechua: Such order as exists is unquestioned and indifferently ascribed to Ndjambie and Taita Dios.

Christian: Individual feeling of responsibility on part of man to God; man therefore acknowledges himself as sinful.

Kaka and Quechua: Ndjambie and Taita Dios are responsible to man; no feeling for the converse. Therefore, man is not a sinner before Ndjambie and Taita Dios, nor responsible to them.

Christian: Anthropomorphizes in God the essence of the highest moral and spiritual values.

Kaka: The highest moral and spiritual values are held to be in the spirits of the dead who attained to socially approved status in this life.

Quechua: The highest moral value is one which is sanctioned by the group and the Quechua seeks in no way to universalize it.

Christian: God is personal, the Father of man.

Kaka: Ndjambie is totally impersonal, a spider.

Quechua: Taita Dios ("Father God") may be cajoled into being personal, but his impersonality shares in the impersonality of volcano peaks which are codivinities with Taita Dios. These are also called Taita. The fatherhood of volcanoes comes about through the marriage union of these mountains which gave origin to man (Quechua man).

Christian: God is eternal and man's relation to God is an eternal one.

Kaka: Ndjambie is eternal but remains so independent of man.

Quechua: Life and Taita Dios are viewed as static without reference to eternity.

Christian: God is omniscient but loving and caring for man.

Kaka: Ndjambie neither knows nor cares about human beings. His job is to help keep the cosmos regulated.

Quechua: Taita Dios knows only what the saints or the Virgin may care to pass on to him. These may be cajoled through fiesta rites.

Christian: God is unchangeable.

Kaka and Quechua: Ndjambie and Taita Dios are egocentric and can and do look after their own interests first. They are not attributed any persistent unchanging personality qualities. While Taita Dios is quite durable and static he is characterized by whimsical moods.

Christian: God is the embodiment of all truth.

Kaka and Quechua: The existence of universal truth is not posited.

Christian: God is just, holy and good independently of man.

Kaka: None of these qualities are attributed to Ndjambie.

Quechua: Taita Dios is good if he accords the request of his petitioners. Otherwise he is bad or angry, getting revenge on man.

God as Redeemer

This second view of God, *the Christian revelation*, does not come ordinarily to such people as the Kaka and Quechua after they have cleared the ground for a redemptive God, but at the very outset. The confusions which result are directly or indirectly responsible for the general syncretistic conceptualizations of God one finds on the mission fields.

Christian: Man stands guilty before God as a sinful creature.

Kaka and Quechua: Man is simply an unfortunate die tossed by fate.

Christian: God is moved through loving compassion to deliver man from his sinful state.

Kaka: Ndjambie has no care and man is not sinful. Men simply do bad deeds.

Quechua: Taita Dios can be placated for his wrath and provoked to help man in his unfortunate conditions. Man is not a sinner but does wrongs such as stealing.

Christian: God initiates a plan to bring man unto himself motivated through love. Such a plan becomes a part of human history. God the lawgiver and judge receives in himself his own penalty because of his love for man.

Kaka: Ndjambie has had no plan because he has had no concern for man as man. History to which Christianity refers its revelation does not exist. The personalized dealing of the Christian God can in no way fit impersonal Ndjambie.

Quechua: Taita Dios in the Roman Catholic notion is admitted to have made a plan of salvation. However, the purpose for this plan remains an anomaly for the Quechua since after four hundred years of indoctrination he still does not make the assumptions about man's conditions which would prompt Taita Dios to reveal himself.

Christian: God is the self-disclosing God of revelation unfolding in history and witnessed to in Scripture.

Kaka and Quechua: The non-present world is not historical but mythological. The witness of a written record for Ndjambie would presuppose that the Bible Ndjambie begins with the contact with the literate white population. For the Quechua the written record of Taita Dios is denied by the local parish priest, which strengthens and confirms the Quechua hold on a syncretized Taita and Dios.

Religious Views Revealed in Culture

If we keep these religious assumptions in mind and trace through some of the aspects of these cultures we will see readily how these unvoiced statements of faith provide a key note for behavior. Some examples follow.

1. "God" is not infinite to the Kaka and Quechua and is not in control of the universe. He is enmeshed in the cosmos in such a way that he is totally lacking in concern for man as such. This lack of concern for man flows on through to man's lack of concern for man.

2. Ndjambie and Taita Dios are totally removed from ethical considerations because they have no attributes of perfection. Among the Kaka the idea of God the Judge is also lacking. Consequently behavior is curbed by the fear of being caught by another man. What is expedient is right. Ends justify means.

3. Men do not assume that they are guilty sinners before Ndjambie and Taita Dios. Hence they are not responsible before these gods. This freedom from responsibility before Ndjambie and Taita Dios allows a freedom from responsibility on the human level also. The Kaka and Quechua do not make assumptions about their gods which would allow them to be morally dependent upon these gods. It is much safer to be independent of these capricious divinities than to trust one's lot to their whims.

4. The core of ethical behavior for the Quechua and Kaka does not arise from feelings about the perfection and moral attributes of Ndjambie and Taita Dios. Ethical considerations are based upon the idealized behavior of the ingroup. However, the ethical relations of one's kin or social group are of such deep value that they are held to be sacred. Among the Kaka the violation of such proper behavior can result in supernatural punishment. Since these punishments are not forthcoming for "unethical" behavior outside of one's own group, there is a double standard of ethics fully consistent with the dichotomy of the sacred society and the indifferent and impersonal Ndjambie. Man does not compare his ethical or moral self with a holy, righteous Ndjambie but with the accepted standards of behavior for his ingroup, a heritage from the ancestors.

5. Ndjambie and Taita Dios are unrelated to "truth." Therefore, there is no search for truth with respect for the truth. One is more interested in establishing a point of view favorable to the support of the ego.

6. A major orientation in both societies is that of being controlled by fate. Ndjambie and Taita Dios are not the creative Will, they are not infinite. They do not have personal concern and love for man in his plight. They are whimsical, changeable, impersonal and show no concern nor love for man. A major difference between the Kaka and the Quechua is that the latter assume one can solicit through Catholic fiestas the aid of Taita Dios through his mother (the Virgin). The Kaka, because Ndjambie is too far removed to be concerned, rely upon magic, mainly in the form of medicines. If the medicines fail, the Kaka appeals through the sorcerer to spirits in nature or the spirits of the dead. The Quechua may pray for help from the spirits of the volcanoes. In both cases, i failure results one has completed the circle of fate and is ready to start again The Quechua's subservience makes him a ready pawn of fate but basically th two meet at the same point.

Translator's Dilemma

When the translator writes Ndjambie or Taita Dios in the context of the Christian Scriptures, is he really translating? There is no better native term in these two cultures and a foreign word would be lacking entirely in the few equivalences which do exist. On the other hand, Ndjambie and Taita Dios, in spite of the fact that converts use them, are not on their face value equivalent to the Christian God. However, it is precisely the convert who is attempting to fit to his god concepts for which he has derived little or no feeling from his culture. The Biblical Ndjambie who cared for man, worked out a plan, carried it out at a certain point in history and plans ahead for the future is hardly recognizable to the average Kaka tribesman. His Ndjambie shares with the tribe the lack of concern for men outside of the clan. The thinking forward to carry out a plan and then actually doing it is contrary to the ideal of Kaka effort which makes no plan ahead of today because no one knows what might happen tomorrow. Because of this he does not recognize his relation to any such farsighted Biblical Ndjambie.

The comparative assumptions about God as God are quite different between a Christian concept and the Kaka and Quechua notions. There are some similarities, however. When we move to a comparison of notions of God as Redeemer, the disparities between the Christian on one hand and the Kaka and Quechua on the other become immense.

Conclusion

Christian missions compound confusions with their ubiquitous catechisms which begin by parading past a multitude of unknown Bible characters from Genesis through Revelation in order to show the learner who God is. These names, usually adaptations from a colonial language, fully convince the would-be convert that the white man's God is not only a trinity but a pantheon of immense proportions. These catechisms assume the convert's religious mind is an empty basin to be filled for the first time in his life. This procedure not only defeats the purpose of catechising but leaves the learner with a fragmented confusion of his own god and little or no idea of the Christian God. The result of this can hardly be called Christianizing. It could be more properly called "detheizing." Such a process leads naturally among many complacent nonliterate people to a general apathetic "Christian" life. Essentially this is what has happened to millions of the inhabitants of Andean South America and is one of the great moral blights in history.

A conceptual transformation of God as God is necessary before man can understand and grasp the idea of God as Redeemer. People are known to have thrown over their gods. The Hawaiians are an example. People everywhere in history have been putting away old gods for new. However, such a total renunciation comes from a motivation to do so completely. It does not follow that such a transition means an automatic preparation to accept a radically different notion of God. The task for Christian missions is to so deal with man's religious ideas that the Christian notion of God prepares a man to accept the Redeemer notion of God. Merely renouncing a pagan god or belief system does not in any way in itself mean that the renouncing individual is thereby prepared to grasp in faith the idea and spiritual reality of the Christian God of loving redemption.

Charles H. Kraft

Christian Conversion
or Cultural Conversion?

THE Christian God is represented in the Bible and Christian doctrine as desirous of communicating himself to men.[1] We observe from the Biblical record that this communication has taken into account the cultures in which men are wrapped. We gain the impression that God views the cultures of men as channels usable for interaction between himself and men.

God saw fit to reveal himself to the Hebrew people in terms of the Hebrew language and culture. The New Testament shows the same God beginning to reveal himself to the Greco-Roman world in terms of first century Greco-Roman language and culture. By analogy, then, we may assume that it is God's will, not

[1] I want to acknowledge my debt to and dependence upon the ideas and personal stimulation of Drs. Nida, Smalley, and Reyburn of the American Bible Society. So much of their thinking has (however imperfectly) become a part of my own that I find it quite impossible to properly identify the source of much of what I have to say. I will not, therefore, endeavor to provide extensive footnoting to their writings.

Charles H. Kraft, formerly a missionary linguist in Nigeria, is now a graduate student at the Hartford Seminary Foundation, 55 Elizabeth St., Hartford, Conn. He is author of "Correspondence Courses in Anthropology," PA, Vol. 8, No. 4 (July-Aug. 1961), pp. 168-175. The present paper was read to the Society for the Scientific Study of Religion in New York, October 1962.

simply accident, that the revelation of himself to 20th-century Americans be in terms of 20th-century American language and culture. And, on the basis of this assumption, we witness to the fact that God wishes to communicate with man, and recommend response to God in terms of 20th-century American life.

At the risk, then, of the considerable oversimplification implicit in any attempt to represent God's approach to man diagramatically, we may say that the following diagram pictures something of the nature of God's desire in communicating to man:

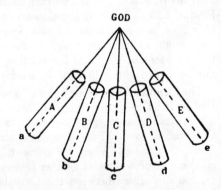

DIAGRAM 1. God desires to communicate with a given man through the channel of the culture in which that man is immersed. Cylinders A, B, C, D, E represent specific cultures of men. Points a, b, c, d, e represent individuals within these cultures. Direct broken lines pass from God to individuals a-e through cultures A-E to represent the possibility of direct communication by God to e.g. individual a in terms of his own language and culture A. Culture A is the channel used by God to reach individual a. Culture B is the channel used by God to reach individual b, etc.

The tops of the above culture cylinders might be considered to represent specific cultures at their highest, most generalized level where each culture is most similar to every other culture (i.e. at a level where such statements can be made as "every culture has language, religion, family, etc."). The bottoms of the cylinders, then, would represent cultures as they are actually worked out in the human context — where they are most dissimilar from each other. Statements made to describe cultures at this level would describe the particular type of language, religion, or family found in the culture under consideration. It is on the latter, lower level — where there is a maximum of diversity between cultures — that men live and that cross-cultural communication takes place.

Peter and Cornelius

God's revelation came to Peter in terms of Hebrew (Aramaic) culture. Peter was a Jew and, though a Christian, understood Christianity in the Hebrew cultural context and continued to live according to Hebrew patterns,[2] though, at times, making certain adaptations.[3] God's revelation had come to Peter and he had responded to it thus:

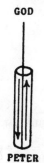

GOD

PETER

DIAGRAM 2. God had made contact with Peter as a member of the Hebrew culture of his day, evoking Peter's response in terms of the same culture. The arrows indicate that communication takes place in both directions between Peter and God, but all within a single cultural framework.

But it was Peter's task[4] to carry the revelation which he received in Hebrew dress and to which he responded in Hebrew terms, to Cornelius, a Roman, a member of another culture. Diagramatically, Peter's problem might be represented as follows:

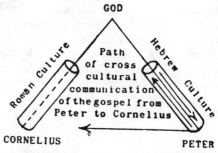

DIAGRAM 3. Peter, having established contact with God from within his own culture, seeks to communicate to Cornelius, wrapped in another culture, concerning his experience with God. For Cornelius, Roman culture is as yet but a potential vehicle of God's communication.

Peter could easily assume that only Hebrew culture was a suitable vehicle of God's communication and only a Hebrew type of response acceptable to God. To Peter, Roman culture and Roman people were alike unacceptable to God.

But God communicated to Peter (in a Hebrew way by commanding him in a vision to kill and eat animals which Peter considered unclean) the fact that at least one Roman person (hitherto regarded as "unclean" by Peter) was acceptable to God. Peter testifies to his new-found discovery saying, "I can now see that God is no respecter of persons, but that in every nation the man who reverences him and does what is right is acceptable to him!"[5]

The record goes on to indicate that a considerable number of Cornelius' "rela-

---

[2] Acts 10: 15.
[3] Galatians 2: 11-14.

[4] Acts 10.
[5] Acts 10: 34, Phillips Translation.

tions and intimate friends" responded to the message delivered by Peter and received from God the confirmation that they had been accepted by him, without the necessity of their first becoming Jews. That is, they received God's Holy Spirit into their lives and were baptized into the Christian fellowship without reference to matters of Hebrew custom — and this in spite of the fact that Cornelius (and, presumably, many of his friends) are identified as "God-fearers"[6] and thus might well have been expected to become proselytes to Judaism.

A diagram of Cornelius' situation as a Christian would thus look like this:

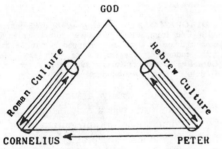

DIAGRAM 4. Peter, in contact with God within Hebrew culture, has communicated the possibility and terms of such contact with God to Cornelius across cultural boundaries. Cornelius, upon hearing the message, responds to God (not merely to Peter), whereupon contact is established between God and Cornelius without the necessity of a change of cultural allegiance on the part of the latter.

This is not to imply that the conversion of Cornelius, minus the necessity of prior allegiance to Judaism, means that his approach to God was therefore completely divested of all trace of Hebrew cultural elements. On the contrary, we must assume that Cornelius' response to and subsequent practice of Christianity embodied considerable assimilation of Hebrew Chris-

_____
6 Acts 10: 2.

tian practice into his Roman Christian life. In this incident the influence of Hebrew culture on Christianity was not being removed (this must forever remain), but the necessity for each convert in embracing Christianity, to embrace likewise the culture in which Christianity was born.

However, it was necessary for Peter to experience the events recorded in Acts 10 to bring him to the correct view of conversion. Previously he (in common with, apparently, nearly all the Christian leaders except Paul) had assumed that conversion to Christianity implied conversion to Judaism, the Hebrew approach to God. God had made contact with Peter through this approach, and in terms of this God had accepted Peter's response. Rather naturally, the apostles regarded the culture into which God had come personally in Jesus Christ both as a particularly well-suited vehicle of God's self-manifestation, and (wrongly) as prescribing the only proper forms of human response to God.

Perhaps it was to be expected that they would assume man's response to God must retrace the path along which the revelation had come. Diagramatically, their assumption would look thus:

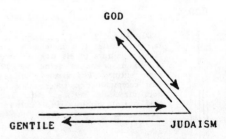

DIAGRAM 5. God's revelation has come first to the Jew and only thence, through Judaism, to Gentiles (following the outside arrows). Conversion of Gentiles involves, therefore, first a conversion along the horizontal line to Judaism, then a response to God in terms of the same culture

in which his revelation is couched. In other words, a Gentile must first become a Jew to become a Christian.

The Position of the Early Church

God, in Acts 10, leads Peter to re-pudiate this view of the nature of Christian conversion. In Acts 15 a gathering of the apostles and elders, provoked by some rather determined Judaizers,[7] came to the same decision. The apostolic church thus came to the position that Gentiles need not be required to become Jews to become Christians. Their official position may, therefore, be diagramed as follows:

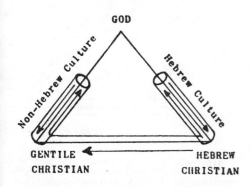

DIAGRAM 6. Though the communication of the gospel takes place cross-culturally from Hebrew Christian to Gentile (along the base of the triangle), the Gentile Christian establishes direct communication with God and God with him, employing his own culture as the channel rather

[7] W. D. Davies, in his *Christian Origins and Judaism* (London: Darton, Longman and Todd, 1962), says: "The New Testament would not seem to present us with a single fixed pattern of Church order which we are to regard as normative . . . , it is constantly evolving by adapting itself to ever-changing conditions that it may properly fulfil the . . . tasks committed to it" (p. 229). "Any Church order, therefore, which presumes to impose terms upon the sovereign freedom of Christ, which limits His activity to certain prescribed channels, episcopal or other, is a denial of His sovereignty" (p. 225).

than the (Hebrew) culture which provided the channel for the original revelation. That is, though the intermediate source of the Gentile's knowledge of the true way to God is a culture other than his own, his response to the supracultural God (the expression of his faith) will be in terms of his own Gentile culture. He, or his group of believers as a whole, may, however, retain certain minimal cultural evidences of the fact that Christianity was originally practiced by those of another culture and certain of its institutions (baptism, communion) developed therein (hence the inner arrow from Hebrew to non-Hebrew culture).

Church History

Church history, however, provides illustrations of reversion to the type of presentation of the Christian message represented by Diagram 5, which demands primary allegiance to a particular cultural or sub-cultural approach to God as pre-requisite to being regarded as Christian.

To some groups the idea that one must be converted to a particular philosophy or world-view (particular culture or sub-culture different from one's own) is obligatory if one is to be considered "Christian" by them. Such groups, especially those more inclined toward ex-clusiveness, commonly predicate their own *raison d'être* upon the truth of their particular theological or organizational position as opposed to all others. And, according to our terms of reference, their approach to the matter of conversion can be diagramed as follows:

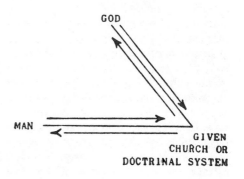

DIAGRAM 7. God reveals himself to man via a given church or doctrinal system and is approachable by man only via the same medium.

This kind of approach takes little cognizance of the possibility of God's using any but a single culture or subculture as a vehicle for his interaction with men. Each such view tends to identify its own approach to God with that of the first century and fails to make allowance for differences of approach based on difference of culture or sub-culture. Such a position may either ignore such differences completely, or consider the cultural factor irrelevant. It will tend to be absolutistic not only with reference to the claims of Christianity as a whole, but also with regard to its own particular cultural norms, and may even revert completely to the attitude of the Judaizers in considering both the type of Christianity espoused and its cultural or sub-cultural milieu as the products of divine-human interaction and, therefore, sacred.

The Present Situation in Missionary Work

Unfortunately, many possessing such inadequate views with regard to culture in general and Western culture in particular, find their way into Christian missionary work. And these attitudes provide a primary hindrance to effective cross-cultural communication of the Christian message, since they generally lead to a definition of "conversion to Christianity" which is concerned primarily with purely cultural issues. That is, this type of attitude toward conversion aims more at promoting Western moral and spiritual ends than at the demonstration of the acceptability of any culture as a vehicle of God's interaction with man. Nor does it take proper cognizance of the fact

that Western culture is but one such vehicle, and neither the original nor the only vehicle usable by God.

Thus much of modern missionary effort is, in effect, promoting an approach to Christianity more akin to that of the first-century Judaizers than to that of Paul and Peter. It has merely substituted Western culture for Hebrew culture as the *sine qua non* for God's acceptance of man.

A diagram of the message presented by such missionaries would, therefore, be the same as diagrams 5 and 7 but with different labels, thus:

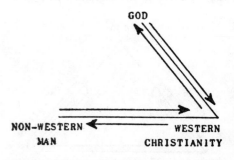

DIAGRAM 8. God's message has been proclaimed to non-Western man through the instrumentality of Western Christianity. The non-Western convert is urged to respond to God by embracing that Western-style Christianity. "Conversion to Christianity" is, therefore, defined as conversion to the particular Western system of Christianity presented. The non-Western man must first become Westernized to become a Christian.

Many Western missionaries fail to recognize the fact that Western culture is but one of many usable by God, even though Christianity has displaced, through long association, all previous religious systems in the West. This latter fact merely means that there are now two Christianities which the missionary must take into account. I will attempt to distinguish between them by spelling one with a small *c* and the other with a capital C.

The christianity of which we are most aware is really the adaptation of Christianity to Western cultural forms. Western christianity is (ideally) God in Christ made relevant to the members of Western culture. Thus it is characterized by familiar forms of worship, music, organization, philosophy (theology), moral standards. This is the religious aspect of the culture of which we are a part.

The christianity of the first century which we see in the New Testament is the same Christianity but adapted to a different culture. Thus, for example, first-century christianity accepted and regulated slavery, 20th-century Western christianity cannot. First-century christianity felt it necessary to speak against haircutting on the part of first-century Christian women. 20th-century Western christianity feels no such compulsion.

Christianity (capital C), on the other hand, is at once more than and less than its cultural manifestations. This Christianity is supracultural, absolute, universally applicable, yet only visible to finite, culture-bound mankind as expressed in culture — seen only dimly and partially, as in reflections.[8] Nevertheless, the glimpses are there — many, including that of God in human form, recorded in the Book, many apparent in the lives of modern-day Christians — glimpses of Reality beyond the cultural "real," glimpses of Truth beyond cultural truths, glimpses of God beyond man's understanding of him. Christianity (capital C) is more than christianity in the same way that God is more than man. It is less to the extent that cultural christianity necessarily accrues to itself non-essential cultural elements (details of organization and prac-

tice), as it is communicated to culture-bound men.

A missionary stands, as it were, committed to attempt to communicate Christianity on the basis of his best understanding of it as seen through the Western cultural christianity of his native land. His allegiance must be to God and to the supracultural Christianity to which he subscribes in spite of his culture-bound understanding of it and of God. His concept of conversion must therefore be conceived in terms of bringing about a relationship between the non-Western individual or group and the supracultural God and Christianity, rather than in purely cultural terms, if it is to square with the missionary's own commitment.

And such commitment to supracultural Christianity implies a like commitment to the conviction that non-Western converts must be allowed to develop their own particular type of cultural christianity — differing as much from Western christianity as their non-Western culture differs from Western culture. The missionary and his fellow Western Christians have demanded just such a right to adapt the supracultural message which came originally in Hebrew dress.

Present Approach in Africa

But a consideration of the present missionary situation leads us to question whether the present approach is actually designed to bring about the desired kind of conversion. In Africa, for example, the most effective means of bringing about conversion to Christianity is through mission schools. Missionaries were early impressed with the lack of education (in the Western sense of the word of formally organized, daily schools) in Africa. Ac-

---

[8] 1 Cor. 13: 12.

cordingly, the establishment and management of schools became one of the major
activities of many missions. As children
attended these schools they were required
to study at least the basic subjects taught
in American (or European) schools —
reading, writing, arithmetic, history
(often European), geography — as well
as Christianity (usually the Bible). In
the process of such schooling it was found
that a majority of the children embraced
the religion of the white man along with
his reading and writing.

A method of conversion as successful
as the mission schools have been — in
some areas, it is said, over 90 percent of
the children in the schools become Christians — is seldom seriously questioned;
especially if other benefits such as literacy,
widened horizons, more adequate preparation to effectively participate in the
modern world are considered important.
Yet hereby missions are allowing a false
understanding of the nature of conversion
to Christianity to be communicated.

Without questioning the many very
desirable cultural benefits which may
assist the emerging Africans to participate
in an increasingly Westernized world, it
is to be expected that the presentation
of Christianity primarily through the
medium of Western schools would lead
to an emphasis on cultural conversion
rather than on true Christian conversion.
We may expect that the religious teaching
provided in the schools will be interpreted
by the students as part and parcel of the
same culture as is the reading, writing,
and arithmetic, and accepted as merely
such. And this appears to be the case for,
in spite of wide-scale indigenization of
mission-started churches, Christianity is
regarded as much "the white man's religion" today as it ever was. Acceptance

as church members thus comes to be
regarded by Africans as a sort of school
diploma, attainable by any one who can
pass the necessary examination, and
signifying a pledge of allegiance to the
white man's way.

Other aspects of Western missionary
activity in Africa often appear to confirm
rather than offset the impression given
by the schools. Hospitals, bent on dis-
placing traditional African medicine and
techniques for handling unseen evil forces,
never require the Western doctors to
understand the African's point of view,
and so strongly support the position of
the schools. The message of the mission
hospitals is that the Christian God en-
dorses only one approach to medicine and
is determined to displace all that is African (without bothering to examine it)
with that which is Western.

Western schools and Western medicine, as promoted by missionary organizations, have provided much of considerable
value in the African context. But the
degree of reliance which many missions
place on these as methods of bringing
about Christian conversion appears unwarranted. Such reliance appears, rather,
to support the contention that Christian
missions seek to be no more than advance
bases for the spread of Western civilization.

Nor have more directly evangelistic
efforts provided the necessary corrective
to the situation, though it must be said
that basic evangelistic work has shown
far more promise as a means of relevant
cross-cultural communication of the Christian message than most other aspects of
missionary work. Evangelistic effort has,
however, too easily encouraged converts
and potential converts to focus primary
attention on cultural issues such as "Chris-

tian" (which always means Western) marriage, "Christian" attitudes toward adultery and other moral issues, and Western patterns of church government or full-time clergy. Many of the attitudes thus encouraged are based, missionaries claim, on the Bible. But too often the impression is given that the Bible can only be interpreted in Western ways.

Nevertheless, when the more personal witness demanded by undisguised evangelistic work is combined with a sincere appreciation of the people and an adequate command of their language, the true message of God is usually communicated. Here, at least in some sense, the missionary or native preacher is less able to demand — more compelled to win — his hearing. On this level it is less possible to merely ignore embarrassing problems of culture. It will be a sad thing, indeed, if the process of indigenization results in a lessening of such face-to-face, person-to-person contact between Western Christian and non-Western potential convert.

Need to Redefine Aims and Revamp Means

In Africa and in many other areas of the world there is need for a redefining of exactly what the aim of missionary endeavor is with regard to conversion. Missions have had and continue to have a major hand in the process of Westernization. They have in most cases exported Western culture at its best and have acted worthily as ambassadors of the culture (including its religious aspect) within which they have developed.

Missions and missionaries claim, however, to be ambassadors of God and of supracultural Christianity (capital C). They claim to be dedicated to bringing about Christian, not merely cultural conversion, on the part of their adherents. Their aim is not to Westernize but to bring about direct interaction between non-Western man and God, without the necessity of allegiance on the part of the convert to the culture of the missionary. Yet their methods appear to detract from rather than to contribute to the success of their aim. The type of conversion encouraged by the primary methods employed appears to be more cultural than Christian.

Perhaps it is not presumptuous to suggest that the present approach needs revamping and that the opportunity for change is still with us. The message of the Judaizers was repudiated by the first-century church. Its 20th-century counterpart must be repudiated by the 20th-century church. The same freedom must be allowed to Africans and other non-Western converts to Christianity to develop non-Western styles of Christianity, as was allowed to our Roman and Greek forebears to develop non-Jewish types. Present missionary practice in Africa and in other non-Western areas of the world does not appear to be allowing such freedom or to be aiming at truly Christian conversion.

I fear that the heresy of the Judaizers is perpetuated every time a Western-originated rule forbids the baptism of a polygamist to whom God has vouchsafed his Spirit. The heresy combatted by God through Peter's vision is allowed to continue unchecked wherever the impression is given that God demands literate membership, paid, Westernized clergy, non-indigenous hymn types and forms of worship, church government according to *Robert's Rules of Order*, or church discipline based on rules which contradict both Biblical principles[9] and indigenous conscience.

The cultural dimension needs to be taken into account in modern missionary endeavor. Missionaries must come to understand and appreciate both the importance of each culture to those born into it and the usability of each as a vehicle of God's interaction with man. They must learn to refrain from regarding Western culture too highly or non-Western culture too lowly. Most of all they must take pains to see to it that the message communicated by the totality of the mission witness (in word and deed) appeals for truly Christian conversion, not merely conversion to a new cultural allegiance — no matter how profitable this might be in terms of other values.

---

[9] Such as those set forth in Matthew 7: 1 and Romans 2: 1 ff. The Nigerians among whom I worked were strong on this point.

Richard L. Schwenk

Some Uses of the Past: Traditions and Social Change

Traditions are strong beliefs which legitimate a social system and a culture. Though it would seem that traditions would invariably hinder creative social change, this is not so. A potential agent of change must understand well and respect the traditions of the people among whom he works, but he need not be paralyzed by them. Some traditions contain within themselves a justification for change. Some can be mobilized for development, some are merely irrelevant, some are inimical to change but can be attacked easily, others are inimical to change but must be handled very carefully.

When a potential agent of change prepares to go to work with people of a different country, he is often briefed about the "dos" and "don'ts" of working in that other culture. The customs and traditions may be explained in some detail, but never really adequately.

The writer remembers being impressed by some general rules that were given in his training prior to going to work in the Philippines and later in Sarawak, such as: "Be sensitive to the needs to the people." "Start where they are." "Teach adaptation, not adoption." "Moderniza-

Richard L. Schwenk is involved in rural development work in Sarawak under the Board of Missions of the United Methodist Church (Box 44, Kapit, Sarawak, East Malaysia). He holds the M.A. from Cornell University, and has also served in the Philippines.

tion, yes, Westernization, no." "Don't go it alone." "Train local leadership." "Work yourself out of a job." "Follow the little customs and the big ones will take care of themselves." "Help people help themselves."

These are still good "rules of thumb" for dealing with a traditional society, but there is need to be more explicit in the light of new insights into the realm of tradition as they relate to social change.

First of all, what is a tradition? Tradition, according to Max Radin is not a mere observed fact like an existing custom, or a story that exhausts its significance in being told; it is an idea *which expresses a value judgment*. A tradition therefore is not the institution but the belief in its value. [Italics added][1]

An example would be a custom which no longer exists but the memory of belief in that custom can exist in the form of tradition. Radin goes on to say:

In fact it is generally when the tradition is no longer a description of actual fact and when it has become somewhat evanescent as a rule of conduct that it has most clearly justified its name and performs its real functions. Nationalism can scarcely be understood except as based in some fashion on a common tradition.[2]

What is a traditional society? Very few strictly traditional societies exist any more; almost all have been influenced by modernization.

A "traditional society" is used here to mean an "ideal type," and also a society in which traditions are the *greatest* social principle influencing its existence and continuance. These societies hold beliefs in various legendary and/or historical happenings that give its members a sense of identity.

The traditions a society holds are the "ultimate legitimator"[3] of the extent and kind of change possible. In traditional societies then, in Dov Weintraub's words:

Tradition serves not only as a symbol of continuity, and of looking at the present in terms of the past, and the future in terms of the present; but also as a guardian of the range of the very creativity and innovation of the society.[4]

While there are few purely traditional societies today, there are even fewer that can claim to be fully modern and devoid of traditions; it is a matter of degree.

What is social change? The writer once told a visiting sociology professor that he was interested in the study of social change. The latter's curt reply was, "So are a lot of other people, but not many know what it is."

Social change is defined as an inevitable process characteristic of all societies and cultures. It is any modification in the modes of thinking or acting in a society. It occurs by the alteration of goals, structures or processes in a social system. Social change means alteration of custom, values, institutions and social behavior.[5]

"Social change" is used in the title of this paper as a general term that may encompass such terms as "development" or "modernization."

Dr. Weintraub has chosen four key words commonly used today in nation-building literature and he removessome of the ambiguity surrounding them; they are "growth," "development,"

[1] Max Radin, "Tradition," in *Encyclopedia of the Social Sciences* (New York: Macmillan, 1934), Vol. 15, pp. 63f.

[2] *Ibid.*

[3] Dov Weintraub, from class handout, "B. Structure and Organization of the Rural Sector," p. 1.

[4] *Ibid.*

[5] S. Stanfeld Sargent and Robert C. Williamson, *Social Psychology* (3rd ed.; New York: Ronald Press, 1966).

"transformation," and "modernization." The first three words are quantitative terms as contrasted to modernization which is a qualitative term. Very simply defined (with much help from Dr. Weintraub's more detailed explanation):

a) Growth is almost synonymous with output in production, and is often used by economists.

b) Development refers to the process of institutional unfolding and differs from "growth" in that it implies change in institutional structures and activities, rather than in output.

c) Transformation is a process in which the changes transcend and re-shape existing values and institutional terms of reference, and which forms new traditions and patterns of behavior.

d) Modernization, by contrast, is a qualitative distinction [perhaps one of the reasons it is often seen in quotes!] or "breakthrough." It is specifically a process of increasing societal (and individual) openness and flexibility, of purposive exposure to and ability to solve problems of growing complexity, and of creation of novel opportunities. Its essential sense, in other words, is a legitimation of or institutionalized potential for a continuous rearrangement of existing commitments, and for an untrammelled flow, exchange and mobilization of all social goods.[6]

Changing Traditional Values

History [tradition] and value are worlds apart, but men are drawn to both, with an emo-

[6] Weintraub, op. cit., p. 4ff.

tional commitment to the first and an intellectual commitment to the second; they need to ask the two incompatible questions, and they yearn to be able to answer "mine" and "true."[7]

The people of developing countries have two common problems to face: the breakdown of traditional values and the impact of Western values. The society in transition must reorient itself in at least three directions:

1. in its relationship to the West,
2. in its relationship to its own past, and
3. in its relationship to the masses of its own people.[8]

As the leaders of the new nations successfully come to grips with these problems, a new ideology or set of values emerges which provides:

(1) a self-definition, (2) a description of the current situation, its background, and what is likely to follow, and (3) various imperatives which are "deduced" from the foregoing. In ideology there is a strong tendency to merge fact and value, to superimpose upon things "as they are" the things "that are desired "[9]

It is always possible to discover values in the past tradition that can

[7] J.R. Levenson, "'History' and 'Value': Tensions of Intellectual Choice in Modern China," in *Studies in Chinese Thought*, edited by Arthur Wright (Chicago: University of Chicago Press), p. 150.

[8] Mary Matossian, "Ideologies of Delayed Industrialization: Some Tensions and Ambiguities," *Economic Development and Cultural Change*, Vol. 6, No. 3 (April 1968), pp. 217-228.

[9] *Ibid.*

be emulated for making a modern nation. For example: In the Philippines there is a tendency to look back at the colonialists as a corrupting influence on values, e.g. the Spanish taught them disdain for manual labor and the habit of being late for appointments, i.e. "Spanish time." The Americans set a bad example in political "wheeling and dealing," "pork barrel," etc. The wars taught the people how to deal on the black market, to fight and to collaborate with the enemy. Some look back 350 years prior to the present "Colonial Hangover" period as being a time of "pristine simplicity and virtue." And who is to say it is not true, for this is one of the uses of tradition. It is part of the rhetoric of nation building and development.

Cyril S. Belshaw offers a comprehensive analysis on the manner in which certain characteristics of values in the social system effect economic growth. He notes that there are usually some elements in a social system that are ready for change. They will likely be the systems of authority and decision taking, the use of available resources and of skills, the distribution system, and the communication network. "To some degree, values and social structure influence the nature of each of these elements, and their ability to perform adequately within the system."[10]

There are three methods of approaching value as outlined by Belshaw:

10 Cyril S. Belshaw, "Social Structure and Cultural Values as Related to Economic Growth," *International Social Science Journal*, Vol. 16, No. 2 (1964), pp. 217 ff.

1) ... there is an empirical relationship between cost, value, and effective demand ... Authorities are concerned with bringing about fundamental changes in value: cost ratios so that new patterns of action emerge. This is what the anthropologist calls cultural change.

2) The ... idea of value is that of cultural change pattern or theme. It may well be that some economists and political figures have made too much of the apparent need for a revolutionary change in traditional mores in order to permit a breakthrough into continued economic growth ... I do not wish to appear to be on their side, for this can be the lazy way of avoiding the attempt to find, within traditional society, the dynamic mainspring of change. But the opposite error is also possible ... the *potentiality of the contribution of the non-conformist is overlooked* [Italics mine].

3) A third method of approaching value is to consider it to be the enduring ethos of a culture, expressed primarily in moral judgments or statements of desirability.[11]

Belshaw argues that it is usually not philosophical systems that inhibit economic growth, for society has the ability to rationalize and change them too. In fact societies do this when

11 *Ibid*.

they manipulate mythology to give new meaning to symbols, to legitimize actions and interests.[12]

A social system then can represent a dynamic structure within which individuals act and organize and meet new situations and get things done. When a social system is exposed to a favorable environment such as would likely foster growth, the adaptability of its values will determine whether there will be change.

It is therefore important for the agent of change, whether he be the party elite or the extension worker, to discover the adaptive forces in the society and use these for *creative* change.

Propositions:

Any integrated social structure can become a basis for economic growth ... The keys to economic growth are to be found, not in the forms or principles of the social structure, but in the specifics of organization, and the nature of the value system.

In the field of values and of social structure there are few barriers to economic growth, and these can usually be clearly identified. The problem is not so much to destroy what might stand in the way, but to build on what is there, and to supplement existing arrangements where necessary.[13]

This is similar to the "rule of thumb" saying "take the people where

they are." It may be compared to Dr. Frank Young's idea of "explication" of what is in the society in nascent forms.[14]

Belshaw goes on to explain:

It is desirable to introduce notions about the way in which values are linked with one another, and particularly to refine ideas about the differences in multiplying effect as between values. Far too frequently, a productive effort is directed towards a specific point in demand which has no further ramifying consequences for the aspects of demand ... There is a multiplication of demand, with an alteration in the value pattern such that people are more prepared to meet new costs, and hence are motivated to further action. There is thus a case for concentrating supply to encourage such changes.

The point is reinforced by the consideration that disequilibria call forth rectifying action and generate change. This applies both in terms of social organization and values.[15]

Hirschman's idea that balanced growth may inhibit both growth and welfare because of not having the proper stress might also be applied here.[16]

---

[14] Frank W. Young, Berkeley A. Spencer and Jan L. Flora, "Differentiation and Solidarity in Agricultural Communities," Cornell International Agricultural Development Reprint 27. Reprinted from *Human Organization*, Vol. 27, No. 4 (Winter, 1968), *passim*.

[15] Belshaw, *op. cit.*

[16] Mentioned by Dr. Dov Weintraub in class lecture.

[12] *Ibid.*

[13] *Ibid.*

Thus it is seen that values are not static but are subject to change when man finds he needs a new paradigm to make different conditions in his environment fit.

Types of Responses to Modernization

Some common types of responses to modernity by traditional societies as suggested by S.N. Eisenstadt are as follows:

In a modernizing traditional society there may be:

1. ... An erosion of old patterns of life with no ideology thus causing disorganization and anomie.

2. A traditionalistic response characterized by:

(a) Resistance to change and its negation;

(b) Attempts to use the processes of change for fortifying the traditional [traditions become "ritualized," e.g. the solidarity becomes stronger among the Ibans when their traditions are threatened to be lost and they put more emphasis on the old sacrificial ceremonies. Author's note].

(c) Militant conservative ideologies and coercive orientations and policies are prevalent.

3. An adaptive response in which a modern practice from another country is indigenized by renaming or reforming to make it their own. [e.g. In Malaysia IR-8 or Miracle Rice was named "Padi Ria" and IR-5 was called "Padi Baghia" which is Malay for "Happy Rice." The latter variety was actually a better rice because it was selected for better grain quality. Mr. Bill Golden of the International Rice Research Institute says that virtually every country has adapted the rice in such a way as to make it its own. Author's note.]

4. A transformative response is forging out and crystallizing of a new viable over-all social framework with its own institutional and symbolic center. [e.g., a new autonomous Methodist Church of Malaysia and Singapore with its own President, Discipline and polity or, the impact of "Miracle Rice" on the farmers' outlook, his using "dapog" seedlings instead of the less complex ordinary method. Author's note].[17]

Some cultural and other responses to modernization by traditional societies are listed by Robert N. Bellah:

1. Traditionalism is a way of defending and preserving identity at any cost.

2. Neo-traditionalism is a way of defending and preserving identity at the least possible cost.

3. Nationalism, especially in its conservative forms, puts

---

17 S. N. Eisenstadt, ''Tradition and Modes of Response to Modernity,'' to be published in papers on China and India by the Center for the Study of Developing Societies, New Delhi, pp. 6-7, *passim.*

emphasis on identity more than modernity.[18]

The difficulty of these three positions, especially the first two, is that they tend to forget about development; as their traditional identities break down they react with paranoiac tendencies.[19] Nationalism, however, appears to be the most effective way thus far for the new nations to achieve the solidarity needed to reach a "take-off" point in development.

The responses to modernity in the traditional models of both Eisenstadt and Bellah are helpful in analyzing a society. It is significant that both are dealing with "anomie" or loss of "identity." The "identity crisis"[20] is a very crucial stage in the growth of an individual and the analogy seems valid when speaking of a new nation. The extent to which the identity crisis is resolved is one of the prime gauges of a society's maturity and modernity.

If a nation's identity crisis is not resolved, and if it does not have a tradition that can provide answers to questions such as: What is our heritage? What is the justification for our existence? What are our goals? Who are we as a people? then it becomes a question if its social change will be significant or worth the turmoil and lack of focus that often results. Ac-

cording to Frank Young's theory these questions would be resolved in a solidarity movement.[21]

Another problem linked with identity is that of the "double standard" or "schizophrenic" society which lives by two different standards. This is especially so in a country that is traditionally dogmatic in its religious norms such as among Moslems. Yusif A. Sayigh claims, however, that this is not a problem:

> The Arabs have proved able to achieve accommodation between traditionalism and open revolt. We can almost call it hypocritical adherence to the cultural heritage, occurring side by side... Tradition is humored while modernization is accepted.[22]

What this means is that the tradition will have to die a slow death for when no one really believes in a religion or culture then by definition the tradition dies. Societies like individuals must eventually come to terms with a dual set of values and just as with identity "one must be singular or be dammed!"

Examples of Tradition and Social Change

Based on the general premise that some tradition can be adapted or transformed to promote social change, the following sections present some examples of how certain traditions fit into

18 Robert Bellah (ed.), *Religion and Progress in Modern Asia* (New York: The Free Press, 1965), pp. 215 and 272.
19 *Ibid.*
20 Erik Erikson uses this to describe a stage in personality growth between about 15 and 30 years. The classic example of analysis is seen in his book, *Young Man Luther: A Study in Psychoanalysis and History* (New York: W. W. Norton and Co., 1958).
21 Frank W. Young, "Reactive Subsystems," *American Sociological Review* (January 1970).
22 Yusif A. Sayigh, "Cultural Problems and the Economic Development of the Arab World," *Religion and Progress in Asia, op. cit.*, pp. 71ff.

the patterns of social change. It is helpful to group traditions into the four types as outlined by Professor Dov Weintraub.[23] All of these are shortened for simplicity's sake and probably a person from one of these countries will readily find exceptions and reject the generalizations made, but the implications are of heuristic value even if not taken as formal typologies.

Traditions Which Can Be Mobilized

First are traditions which can be mobilized for development:

1. The extended family is a mixed blessing; however, some of the positive aspects are mentioned here. These are a combination of factors such as provision for social security, insurance, investment, credit, a labor supply, a babysitting nursery and an old folks' home. The norms are "help one another," not "everyone for himself." The extended family has provided scholarship aid for many Filipinos to go through college and has been the source of entrepreneurship pooling of resources to finance industries or business concerns like Araneta industries, Puyat Steel Mills, Madrigal & Sons, etc. Despite the frequent criticism of some "developers" that the extended family system does not give incentive for achievement and is therefore inefficient in business, it can be argued that there is perhaps a greater mobilization to win family respect for a job well done than from an unrelated business associate. To be called a

"breadwinner" is a status symbol which most family members would like to achieve and there are censures for those who do not do their share of the over-all responsibilities.

Some Western observers have charged that the concept of sharing has been a deterrent to maximizing farm incomes and this is the reason people lack incentive to earn beyond a certain point. The surplus will have to be shared even further. A rural sociologist from the Philippines counters with:

Since we have neither a comprehensive social security and welfare system nor a Sargent Shriver with an anti-poverty program, who else is supposed to take care of the less fortunate? In more ways than one, every American taxpayer is sharing his wealth with a "relative" who might be unemployed, sick, aged, or who belongs to the $3,000 and below bracket. And yet you [Americans] do not wish to earn less simply because Uncle Sam is siphoning away your pennies to Appalachians, or to us.[24]

As long as the extended family dominates a social system it is foolish to fight it when no other institutions can take its place. The kinship system can be used to promote development in a country. Weintraub suggests, "when the object is the individual,

---

[23] Dov Weintraub, "The Concepts Traditional and Modern in Comparative Social Research—An Empirical Evaluation," *Sociologia Ruralis*, Vlo. 9, No. 1 (1969).

[24] Gelia Tagumpay Castillo, "A New Look at Old Concepts in Development: A Minority Report," paper presented at the International Agricultural Development Seminar, January 18, 1967. International Agricultural Development Mimeograph No. 18, Cornell University.

then kinship is a hindrance, but when societal development is our concern, kinship can help."[25] A frequent false assumption Westerners make is to think in terms of individual development rather than that of the society as a whole.

2. In Iban society the *bilik* 'family,' composed of the mother, father, grandparents and children, is the autonomous unit of society. The extended family is not highly institutionalized. All live in a one-room apartment of a longhouse. Their relationship with the rest of the longhouse is one of limited cooperation and obligation. There is competition between the families to get ahead. Inheritance is kept in the *bilik*. A child who marries and follows his partner to a new *bilik* loses any rights and obligation in the former *bilik* as he joins in all the rights and obligations of the new *bilik*. The Ibans are also very individualistic, which leads one to think he is dealing with a nascent form of capitalism.

3. The Ilocanos of the Philippines have a tradition of being frugal and adventuresome. As one Filipina observed, the Ilocanos have a "Protestant Ethic," or a predilection to entrepreneurship. They have competed almost on a par with the much more experienced Chinese businessmen. Their belief that they can save and invest and make something out of nothing is a very strong tradition that they seek to live up to.

4. A societal norm based on shame rather than guilt is strong among the

25 Dov Weintraub, Class notes, Rural Sociology 635, Cornell University, Fall 1969.

Filipinos and Ibans. The Ibans often talk about being ashamed to do something, and to the Ilocanos *mabain* 'shame' seems even a stronger inhibiting factor. This writer once saw a girl crying unconsolably because her older sister said, "*Awan ti bainmo*" ("you are shameless") for some fault or misdemeanor. A street salesman once wanted to overcharge this writer for an item and when asked, "Aren't you ashamed to charge so high?" he brought the price down and his parting words were, "Now I don't have to be ashamed, do I?"

The point about shame as opposed to guilt is that shame is something one experiences in a face-to-face relationship with others, i.e., one feels shame especially when confronted with a fault, while guilt seems to be more deeply embedded in the psyche (e.g., "guilt complex") of a person. Therefore, the guilt remains even when the wrong conduct is not found out. A tradition based on shame would thus, it seems, be more susceptible to change because it does not have the conflict of the psyche or the wrath of the divine associated with it. Professor Weintraub found that the traditional Kurdish group, whose religious culture was based relatively more on shame than guilt, found it consequently easier to secularize than the more autonomous-minded Yemenites.[26]

5. For the Ibans, their capital in the past has been in the form of brass gongs and Chinese ceramic jars and gold jewelry. But as with the extended family structure, when savings banks

26 Weintraub, "The Concepts Traditional and Modern...," *op. cit.*, p. 31.

and other institutions are introduced, more capital will likely be invested there. The inheritance of the Ibans is kept within the *bilik*, thus avoiding both the fractionalization of land and capital needed for economical farming and the inequality of primogeniture. The children share equally as long as they remain in the *bilik*. They are free to go to work in the forests or towns or stay at home and farm. In fact most of the able-bodied men under thirty go off to the army or work on plantations, in lumber, oil industries, etc.

The custom of going on a *bejali* 'journey' is still strong among the young men. In the past it was to go marauding for heads to show their bravery, or to go in search of a fortune which usually was in the form of Chinese jars or brass gongs. Today *bejali* usually means going off to work in the lumber, oil or construction industry of Brunei or Sabah. The treasure brought back these days may be a transistor radio or recorder, sewing machine and other manufactured items. The practice of tatooing as a sign of *bejali* is now much less prevalent.

6. In Iban society there is a high degree of mobility with little obvious class distinction. The Ibans pride themselves at being egalitarian. Women are also given equal status with men. The headman and chief(s) are given only as much respect as they deserve. There is great resentment that anyone should rule over another. Education is now the key to getting ahead.

The method of choosing a leader or making a decision is by consensus through discussion. The headman of the longhouse is respected but not usually a charismatic or strong leader. He is more often the guardian of the tradition and system of taboos. He has become more of a legal institution now that the central government requires each longhouse to register his name as headman. The headman can only lead by a clear mandate of the adult men and women. This often results in inaction as no one can speak for the group, but should they develop more solidarity they could develop rapidly unfettered by a traditional hierarchy of status or caste.

Thus one of the "frozen" assets of the Ibans is their ability to work cooperatively. The "thaw" has not been great but in one longhouse eight families (out of 36) cooperate together on various work projects one day a week. They rotate from one farm to another among the eight families of the labor cooperative, doing such minor development projects as building fish ponds or rice fields. As they slowly give less energy in the direction of shifting, slash-and-burn farming methods and more to intensive agriculture they may serve as a model for other Ibans to follow.

Kevin Le Morvan who has worked with the cooperative movement in Nova Scotia and in Latin America tells of a missionary who devised an ingenious method to bring a very traditional tribe from a barter trade economy into a money economy using a similar kind of labor pool. He started a credit cooperative in which labor was the capital. The labor was directed towards developing their farms, e.g.

they would borrow the labor of a man for ten days and then pay back later with 11 days' (one day for interest) work or an equivalent amount of money. Thus they learned cooperation, channeled their labor towards developing and learned how to use money.

Irrelevant Traditions

Certain traditions are merely irrelevant or unimportant to the main goal of development. By maintaining these relatively minor traditions the people can still keep a sense of identity as a people. Here are some examples:

1. Dress, ornamentation, architecture, songs, legends, proverbs, riddles, certain myths, etc. are encouraged. The oral literature of the Ibans is now being written by the younger educated Ibans to preserve a cherished heritage. The etiological myths and proverbs are especially valuable to give meaning to their past and serve as a corpus for molding new perpectives for the future.

Some of the high school girls are wearing miniskirts (an actual traditional Iban dress called *kain*) and the boys wear shirts, suits, and ties made from Iban handwoven cloth or the Malaysian *batik* cloth. They use brightly colored mats, hats, baskets, beads and even feathers like those used by their ancestors. They hang on to whatever they can that will give them a sense of identity.

2. In the hostels of the schools it is very important that the food be prepared in a way that has some similarity to what they have at home. Rice is the chief sign of wellbeing and a symbol of having eaten a full meal whether or not there is a balanced diet. Without rice, what Westerners would call a meal is considered only a snack. Perhaps one of the reasons U.S. surplus milk, oats and cornmeal were not very well liked was their being just another foreign thing introduced into their lives.[27] Bulger wheat was mixed with the rice, however, and it was actually relished.

3. The use of the mother tongue is also a meaningful way for the students, often far from home, to maintain their identity and fully express themselves. The stress on national language or using proper English in school is needed but the home dialect can carry them through times of difficulty.

Traditions which Hinder Development but Can Be Attacked

A third classification includes traditions that might hinder the process of modernization but can be attacked without upsetting the social system's sense of identity.

1. When the author was teaching in a longhouse about modern rice production and pest control, an old Iban woman was motivated to sing a song she had used many times to chase away the rice pests. This practice is still used in connection with the ceremony, *mali umai* (literally taboo on the farm). Specimens of the rice pests that can be found are collected and placed on a small raft and a pig and/or chicken are sacrificed, the blood is placed on the raft which is then allowed to drift down the river to the sea. The song

[27] The other reasons were that the foods sometimes were mildewed or that the cook did not know how to prepare them in somewhat familiar recipes.

that was sung to our extension team
was in rhyme and very artfully done.
It went something like this:

Go away from my rice farm,
you insects [they were listed one
by one], you rice birds, rats,
monkey, deer and wild pigs and
all other pests. Go down to
Kapit, to Sibu, to the countries
across the seas, to Singapore,
to the Philippines, etc.

The younger Iban Christians displayed somewhat embarrassed amusement. When the author asked her if
she thought it helped to get rid of the
pests she replied, "No, it is only words,
but it is all we know how to do."
This kind of answer was given many
times as we taught about modern agriculture. They said, "We would do it
but we do not have your pesticides,
sprayers or knowledge." The same
idea is expressed to some extent by
those who go to the witch doctor for
healing, i.e. "We would use modern
medicine if it was readily available."
The witch doctor near our clinic would
come for treatment from the nurse
occasionally!

A longhouse headman said the
reason we do not have enough rice in
the country "is because we do not observe the traditions and taboos." Also
mentioned were helicopters, planes,
bombs, and war as causes of a poor
crop. But at the end of the discussion
someone said, "Each generation has
its own problems and answers. There
is now a new era that needs the help
you in agriculture can give." It gave
one faith in the dynamics of the group
discussion to see the people finally

coming up with a very concise analysis
of the situation. More important was
their ability to change tradition before
our very eyes, to accommodate development.

2. Rice, according to Iban etiological myths, was received from the
gods in the form of one grain which
possessed a soul. Care must be taken
not to offend the rice spirit or soul
lest it flee. Because of this belief
several taboos are quite rigorously
practised. The most easily observed
taboos are seen in the method used to
harvest and thresh their rice. It is
taboo to use a knife to cut the rice
stems. Instead a small hand cutter is
used to cut one particle of rice at a
time. In threshing, only the hands
or feet can be used to gently separate
the grains from the straw. Flailing
is taboo.

As strong as the taboo is, it was
interesting how quickly they were
willing to use a larger cutting tool to
harvest and then to use flails or small
machines to thresh the rice. The rationale used was this: "Since this new
rice (IR-3, IR-5, C4-63, etc.) comes
from another country it does not have
a soul or any *mali* ('taboo'), so one can
use the more efficient methods and
not cause offense." Their faces would
brighten, for here was a way to reason
out of a tradition that they now sensed
was oppressive but which their mores
up to this time would not allow them
to change.

The paramount chief of the Ibans,
Temenggong Jugah, was asked to
demonstrate a new foot pedal thresher
at an agricultural fair and he said,

"The old tradition of *mali* taboo is foolishness, our people should use these new methods to get ahead."

3. There is also the practice of augury by observing omen birds' calls or flight that could be interpreted to mean the divine will making itself known to man. The older generation of Ibans often would tell how they would hear certain birds and be forced to stay in the longhouse for a day or more to the detriment of their farms. This was the reason most mentioned for their wanting to become Christians. Thus Christianity was the legitimating force that could free them from the bonds of the old tradition.

Along similar lines of Christianity's role as a legitimator, but on a deeper level, is the case of the Iban woman who told the author after a Christian worship service, "I have known for a long time there was a God like you describe but now I know his name." Perhaps a more descriptive term than "legitimator" would be the word "explicator."[28] An explicator unobtrusively makes apparent what is already intuitively known. This fits in with the rule of thumb" stated at the introduction of this paper, "Start where they are," or "help make known what is already present."

Traditions which Hinder Development but are Sensitive

Some casual observers look upon the institution of the Iban longhouse as more a liability than an asset to

modernization, because of the long distance people must travel to their farms, the higher incidence of disease and the difficulty to grow livestock or a garden. But the longhouse has strong institutional and symbolic meaning. Its role as an institution is similar in some aspects to the extended family mentioned above with the strong exception that there is often competition among the families in gathering possessions. They do work cooperatively as in times of crisis, e.g. birth, death, fire and in the traditional ceremonies.

Thus if the longhouse would suddenly dissolve as an institution people would be at a loss to know how to deal with their ritual for the farming cycle. One man gave a more practical reason for helping rebuild a twelve-family longhouse. It was so he would have someone to bury him. The members of this longhouse had dismantled their old longhouse and each family had built a separate house near his rubber garden. Some of these farmers have made good progress towards having surplus fruit, vegetables, chickens, pigs and fish from fish ponds plus the cash crops of rubber and pepper. They will still maintain their individual farm houses and in fact probably live there most of the time, so they can be near their farms. In fact, most Ibans have a small farm hut where they live much of the rice-growing year. But the long-house serves as a center for them to have their ceremonial feasts and to entertain visitors on the common porch (which serves much like a plaza) and finally as a symbol of their prestige. Many Iban communities are rebuilding

---

28 Young, "Intervention Versus Explication Applied Science," *Journal of Home Economics*, 60, No. 4 (April, 1968).

their longhouses with concrete floors downstairs for entertaining visitors, with the family room upstairs. So it seems that the longhouse is a traditional institution that will obstruct or slow down modernization but must be delicately handled for fear that its absence will do more harm than good.

Therefore, traditions play an important role in bringing about sustained and regulated social change that can be assimilated by the system, Traditions understood and used in the right way can help in preventing a degeneracy into either modernism or traditionalism.[29]

On the other hand, Weintraub cautions against three general fallacies in approaching traditions in order to expedite development:

1. The "Pressure Cooker" approach is a warning against the "witch hunt" syndrome, characterizing primarily (but not only) the impatient policy maker, even when he is not under the special pressure of time and circumstance that has characterized settlement in Israel. This pattern conceives of tradition as indiscriminately inimical to development and modernization, and maintains that all traditional elements must be sought out and firmly subordinated to (if not actually eliminated by) the modern agrarian system.

2. The "Pepper Pot" (a stew with a particularly long simmering process) approach to modernization is in contrast to

the "witch hunter." This second type is labelled the "obstacle hound." He is more often than not an anthropologist or a community developer (although sociologists are not immune in this respect) who also views tradition as an obstacle to development, but one to be respected rather than to be swiftly and abruptly removed. Mention is made here not of the intrinsic value of any culture, but of a spirit of total *functional* adoration, approaching each cultural and social system as a balanced, interdependent and fully integrated whole, in which a change of any one item may pull down the whole social fabric.

3. The "Apologetic" approach tries to select the best traditions that will help development. The trouble is that this process is too selective and does not start with the need of the society so much as to reflect the cultural bias of the change agent.[30]

There is a need to analyze how the various kinds of traditions affect the different types of development, as well as how the traditions themselves can be modified or adapted. The problem of these three approaches is that they do not take into consideration the fluidity of some tradition. Using the four major types of traditions and the examples given above allows for greater sensitivity on the part of developers who want to plan within the

---

29 *Ibid.*, p. 35.

30 *Ibid.*, p. 36.

framework of the social system, or if planning is out of the question at least understand the dynamics of changing traditions.

Conclusion

The average Westerner probably looks at change with ambivalence for as he contemplates the conveniences of modernity he looks at the more slowpaced past as the "paradise lost." The tendency is to transfer this attitude to the new nations and contrast the simplicity of traditional societies with the upheaval caused by modernization.

The Western agent of change is apt to be pessimistic about the capacty for traditions to change, often after he has lived a number of years with the developing people and iden- tified with them. If he is sensitive to their customs, taboos, mores, etc. (i.e., the tradition) he becomes an "obstacle hound;" if he is insensitive he could develop a "witch hunter" syndrome; and if he tries to "pick and choose" traditions that fit his bias he also runs into the problem of Westernization.

The point of this paper is that there is not an unbridgeable chasm between traditions and modernity, that it is possible to build on certain traditions, mobilize some, set aside or modify others, while being careful not to alter certain ones. This philosophy should help make the agent of change more realistic, successful and meaningfully sensitive as he seeks to promote development by making use of the past.

William D. Reyburn

The Missionary and Cultural Diffusion

I

Two Gbaya workmen at Batouri, French Camerouns, had a prolonged and vociferous argument which they finally brought to the missionary to arbitrate. Their stories revealed only that the first man accused the second of stealing his money and the second in turn accused the first of killing his dog. In the missionary's view of the matter it was a question of determining the "truth" of the stealing and the killing. Since the missionary was unable to prove or disprove either story, he refused to listen to further discussion of the case.

The two disputants were at a loss to understand why the white man with his marvelous machines and wealth had no means of discovering the person who was at fault. Consequently the two went to a native medicine doctor who performed a series of magical rites to determine if the man accused of dog killing had the power to kill the dog. The missionary had not bothered to ask how the dog was killed. The native doctor knew that the recognized process was by turning oneself into a snake and biting the dog. The accused dog slayer underwent the rites of the native doctor who "proved" beyond a doubt that the man did not possess the power to transform his body into

Reprinted from Vol. 5, Nos. 3, 4, 5 (1958), pp. 139-146, 185-189, 216-221.

a snake. The logical conclusion was that he was not guilty. Therefore his accuser was forced by the local African authorities to pay the accused a sum of money plus two goats.

The Problem of Two Contrasting Views

The argument which is presented here is essentially that the modern missionary's inherited view of the universe is an inseparable part of his own ethos (the distinctive point of view of his culture) with which he comes to terms with Christianity. His thinking and action are cast in a framework which is for him necessary and meaningful but which appears to the folk societies quite often as meaningless. There is therefore an inevitable confusion which arises in these two ways of thinking. The missionary will not forsake his view for what appears to him as superstition, and the folk can only partake in the modern missionary's point of view as they are brought into a systematic contact with it. This usually means formalized education.

It is often remarked in anthropological writings and in the pages of PA that life in the primitive world is viewed as a whole synthesis in which all of life partakes in the religious feeling of things. Whether we agree to this proposition or not depends largely upon the way in which we define the religious. However, there can be little dispute with the observation that the folk societies do not divide the rational and nonrational into separate spheres in the way modern societies do.

Some anthropologists such as the late Lévy-Bruhl attempted unsuccessfully to tell us that primitive man has his own kind of psychology and logic, and that in these lay the essential differences between the folk and modern societies. Anyone who has lived in a folk culture is certainly tempted to make such statements. However, this position fails to see that a set of propositions about any matter can be exceedingly logical and at the same time very untrue. The people of the folk societies differ from moderns in that they have a different ontological perspective, a different sense of the nature of existence. That is, there exists a unity of life in which things are, regardless of their nature, interrelated. Whereas modern man assumes a uniform order of nature which operates within its own fixed laws, the folk man assumes an interrelatedness between man and nature. Therefore man's spiritual activities can effect changes in the natural world simply because they both share in the same metaphysic. In central Africa a parasitic vine growing on a tree is viewed as an indication that the tree has a supernatural power which causes the vine to grow on that particular tree. By the same token, if a man is able to secure material wealth, it is because he partakes in the same endowment as the tree which attracts the vine.

Modern man inherited from Greek culture a way of viewing the world in which uniform order is assumed and sought out. What is not scientific is usually admitted and there is little attempt to placate, cajole, and appeal to nature. Rather, modern man controls nature in so far as he can by employing natural laws to do so. Moderns are the heirs of two vast changes in cultural history. The first is the separation of God from the rest of nature which the Hebrews gave us, and the second is the Greek gift of separating out order in nature as immanent without any reference to God or the gods.[1] These two historical developments, in which the folk societies do not share, serve to drive the deepest imaginable wedge between the thought of a twentieth century missionary and the people of his folk congregation.

A simple illustration is the case of the bush fire hunts in Africa. At the end of a strenuous day's hunt behind leaping walls of flaming grass fires the hunter may wearily trudge home with nothing in his hands but his smoke-stained spears. To the missionary it is obviously the case that the animals escaped or that there were none in the area. To the African there is a reason that goes deeper. Something went wrong with the procedure which is carefully executed in order to assure the kill. The procedure is partly in taboos kept by the women. If a woman has been talking noisily in her compound instead of sitting quietly in the house, she is at fault and will be punished. Perhaps a careless wife has swept the floor of her house. She has thereby caused the animals for miles away to flee. This is due to no lack of logic but rather to the assumption that spirits of dead animals must not be aroused during the hunt. The relatedness is vividly assumed to exist.

_____

[1] See Robert Redfield: *The Primitive World and Its Transformation*, Cornell University Press, 1956.

Confusion over the Missionary's Viewpoint

The missionary's dichotomy of natural and supernatural strikes the folk Christians and non-Christians as an unintelligible confusion. The folk man is in no intellectual position to see this problem nor to appreciate it. He does not have at his disposal the means of knowing how the missionary divides up the universe. Consequently as the missionary flits back and forth in his conversation between his worlds of the religious and natural, the mind of the folk man gets lost in the switches. The missionary doctor may carefully explain microbes to an ailing native and allow him to see them dashing about under the microscope. When the missionary has done that and then from a bottle of medicine he destroys the whole bunch and says, "You see, just take your medicine and you'll be all right," the native is most likely posing other questions to himself. "Admitted that there are such little animals. Where did they come from and why did they come to me and not to someone else? Who put them in me? Who is trying to kill me with these microbes?"

Missionaries discourse on a wide range of subjects, assuming too often that their listeners share in their view of the universe. The villagers at Lolo were intensely interested in the fact that Europeans can make so many iron instruments. However, one of their questions which they continually repeated was, "How does the European blacksmith protect himself?" I always answered this in terms of mechanical protection of the body while smelting, pouring, pounding, etc. But my listeners always appeared dissatisfied with these replies.

Finally I asked how the local blacksmiths did it, and they revealed that they were speaking in terms of protection against the supernatural power contained in the heated metal. Since I did not share their presupposition about the nature of hot metal, I could never give an intelligible reply. When I replied at last that they retire at sixty-five so as not to die on the job they were satisfied that the European blacksmith has sense enough to realize he is dealing with supernatural forces which can harm him. However, the fact that the European blacksmith's family practices no taboos again threw the whole subject into confusion for them.

I use these illustrations to point out the fact that the missionary carries Western culture with him and communicates it whether he wants to or not. This is so even if the communication of Western thought forms comes across as nonsense and confusion to the native. The missionary who disavows being a carrier of Western culture is denying himself the very structure of his thought into which he cradles his presentation of the gospel and life.

The ordered view of the universe means that faith to believe must be placed in something which is not beneath that order but over and above it. The modern Christian, like the Psalmist, in whose debt he must remain — "Oh Lord, thou hast searched me, and known me" (Ps. 139) — places his faith in a transcendant God. He combines a Hebrew view of God and a Greek view of the universe. The modern man does not sacrifice the ordered feeling for the universe when he finds faith to believe. He views his faith as finding its locus in the source of order.

The folk man has no need to express his faith in a God which transcends an ordered universe. He rather finds faith to believe based on considerations quite unrelated to the universe. In the folk view God tends to be part of the cosmos and enmeshed in it. Belief in the Christian God (often to the missionary's dismay) does not separate scientific order from metaphysical reality. It is largely because of this fact that folk Christians often tend to equate God with fate and are at a loss to move against what fate has brought upon them. Among the folk Christians God replaces the former medium for placating and petitioning nature. On one hunt in which I participated I knew the Christians had of their own accord left off the making of medicines in preparation for the hunt. The chief, a non-Christian, also knew this and was very careful to make sure that the Christians petitioned their God before the hunt. These men felt that prayer was automatically needed in place of the medicines. When the hunt was unsuccessful, none of the Christians felt free to punish their wives for breaking taboos, but they were exceedingly wroth with God, who appeared to have failed them, so they questioned in turn their relation to God and decided that they had not paid their mission pledges as regularly as they should. I attempted to present another alternative to them, but as soon as they saw that I was approaching the hunt failure from a secular point of view (it had rained to the east and the animals were moving that way), they refused to be sympathetic with my reasoning. Their reply: "Sometimes we almost think that God doesn't have a stomach like a man."

Two Views of Man

A second source of the modern missionary's ethos is his view of man which is historical and abstract. Here again the missionary soon becomes vividly aware that his folk parishoners have a nonhistorical and nonabstracted view of man. We may more properly call the folk man's view as mythological rather than nonhistorical. His origins are set out for him in terms of myths which he seldom reflects upon until they become nonfunctional in the process of passing them along to his offspring. Parents of another generation do not feel much rewarded in attempting to tell their children local folk tales while the latter have one eye in a mathematics or history book.

In the folk world the historicity of Christianity is felt as unnecessary. It is not part of the local myth and the distinctiveness of Christianity as an historical event is not realized in the local church. This fact reduces the historical Jesus to the kinship son. The importance of Christ lies in the kin relationship of son which shares with the feeling for family, clan, and village relationships. Here again the folk man is a kin man. He is built into blood and marriage ties which replace the modern man's feeling for historical ties. Modern man's feeling runs in depth to other generations and other historical epochs, while the folk man is really related in space here and now.

Modern man and therefore the modern missonary speaks and thinks in terms of nations, united nations, one world, space, and the universe. Consequently he can if he wishes take a very abstracted view of man. The folk man is seldom if ever conscious of belonging to a worldwide mass of humanity. He is more properly a very well identified member of a certain well identified family within a known clan or village and his belongingness seldom extends beyond these confines. Consequently man as an abstract is not a popular idea with him. He has little feeling for such an impersonalized human idea.

The results of the abstracting of man from men gives the modern a peculiar position from which to see the good and the bad in man. This is especially true in our tradition in which we separate out the evil nature of man and emphasize certain characteristics such as overeating or sexual excess as contrary to the ascetic qualities which Christianity has emphasized in both its personalized and abstract view of man. The folk man does not tend to carry out such an abstraction, and consequently there is little place for the ascetic emphasis. One of the greatest confusions for missions in modern Africa today is the fact that the missionary living in plenty and comfort stresses in his teaching the ascetic aspects of the Christian life. In a relative way he is practicing some aspects of the modern industrial society's idea of the lightly ascetic life. However, the folk man in Africa is neither interested nor prepared intellectually or emotionally to appreciate what value asceticism might have for the Christian life. The African tends rather to view Christianity (depending upon other conditions) as a means for achieving the fruits of modern living, as a part of the new education.

Finally, it is worth mentioning that the modern missionary is culturally prepared to be conscious of contradictions while the folk man tends to embody contradictions without bothering his head about it. Just as has been the case with European Christianity in the seventeenth and eighteenth centuries, when kings and princes bounced the populations back and forth between Catholicism and Protestant-ism, the folk masses can contain conflicting ideologies without being aware of the contradictions. The citizens of Heidelberg, Germany, found that they could switch back and forth between the dictates of Rome and Luther apparently without being in the least disturbed ideologically. They simply didn't care. Great portions of folk Christianity do not find it contradictory to give lip service to the tenets of the Christian faith and at the same time adhere to pagan practices and presuppositions. It is exceedingly common for the missionary to recoil emotionally when a trusted convert turns up describing in vivid detail how spirits from the spring chased a man into the forest and nearly killed him.

Conclusion

The contact of modern missionaries with the folk world introduces the latter to the presuppositions of a modern age. However, these assumptions are such a subtle force within the ethos of the missionary that they seldom come in for discussion. When a missionary learns the language of a tribesman and speaks with him, his point of contact is the language, but often not the thought concealed in the meanings which the words have for the folk man. The missionary's view of the world is quite ordered. The physical and the metaphysical are rather well separated. The folk man operates upon the assumption that the two are integrally related and interacting. The modern partakes in a recorded history, the folk man in an unrecorded mythological past. It is impossible for a twentieth century missionary to live a single day in his workaday routine without exposing the assumptions upon which his thought forms are based. Whether it be his preaching, his teaching, or his silent living, he does so within the framework of ideas which are strange and largely unknown to the folk world. It is because of this that the missionary, no matter how he may endeavor to hide his Western material culture, can never hide his long ontological inheritance.

II

Impedimenta Americana

"We are here only to present the gospel, not American or Western civilization," remarked a missionary in Africa recently. At the very moment these words were pronounced this individual was sitting in a large brick house covered with a metal roof with rain gutters which carried the water to a cement cistern. A radio was broadcasting in French the news of developments in Algeria. A neatly set table under electric lights was being prepared for the eating of wild buffalo shot in the early morning by a Remington semiautomatic rifle. A polished pickup truck sat in the garage nearby. Children's tricycles and toys lay scattered about on the veranda. Stacks of books, newspapers, and magazines in several European and African languages were neatly arranged against the living room walls. Two évolués Africans sat in comfortable leather chairs awaiting dinner, listening to the news, and occasionally asking about buying certain household articles when the missionary went on furlough.

The truth of the matter is that the missionary in Africa seldom opens a barrel from home that he does not introduce some gadget of Western civilization à la twentieth century. There was a time when it was difficult to diffuse these luxuries. Today, however, in the French Camerouns at least, it has become standard practice for the missionary eventually to sell his goods (from kitchen utensils to trucks) to the African who has the cash, i.e. the évolué class of Africans who are mainly government employees, private planters, or shop owners.

The introduction of education, largely the work of missions at first, provided the groundwork for the existence of the government employee group. The awakening caused by education aroused the desire for European goods. The introduction of cash crops by missions and government agencies means cash incomes. Cash incomes mean (in this area) acquisition of goods and further education, which in turn make it easier for the upper-class African to acquire European goods and ways and be acceptable to the white population. So great is the value of material culture in our own society that the missionary traveling in the bush will often go a long distance out of his way just to spend the night with an African who can provide a gas-lamp-lighted room with supper on a table and a metal bed to sleep on. Often such a person is sought out and admired by the European, who often prefers to overlook any lack of personal integrity in the individual.

A New Status to Maintain

Mission activity, with its schools and institutions, almost inevitably creates a social ranking in the local society. In certain parts of Africa today the mission hospitals have created a class of moderately wealthy doctors and nurses, and the schools have created the class of teachers. Industrial schools turn out artisans such as carpenters and masons. The church creates a new social status in the role of the pastors, the elders, and the catechists. These new roles are those which adapt themselves most effectively to European ways and serve as the bilingual link between European and African. They are the object of the mission's efforts and the channel through which the mission diffuses spiritual, technical, and gross material culture. This class is granted in African society a high position by the *non évolués*, and consequently there is a certain amount of pressure exerted to maintain upper status. In some cases this attempt to maintain a gap between upper and lower is costly and in the eyes of the European ludicrous. I have been invited to eat dinner with *évolués* Africans who sit about supressing miserable hunger pains in order not to eat before nine in the evening. This is a way of indicating to me that they are doing things as in French society. But more important is that they are communicating social status to the local Africans.

A postparturent mother at the Batouri mission hospital, the wife of an *évolué*, sat feeding her newborn babe from a baby bottle while her breasts painfully dripped with milk. She was willing to endure the physical pain in order to maintain her social distance from the common village women who would never dare take the privilege of bottle feeding.

The two cases cited above are to these Africans signs of status which they have appropriated from Western culture, having seen it in missionaries and other Europeans.

Another slightly similar case is that of a man in the village of Lolo who was an excellent hunter and tracker until he got hold of an overcoat. Now when we hunt together he insists on wearing this huge moth-eaten overcoat which inhibits his movements, wears him out, and gets tangled in the under brush. If he hunts by himself or with his brothers, he leaves the coat behind, but when I am there he feels the coat is absolutely necessary. The fact that I tell him repeatedly that I do not have an overcoat makes no impression on him, possibly because he sees that I have shoes and he does not.

The European Social and Ideological Link

The missionary is not there to carry European or American culture, but he inevitably feels a pull toward his European neighbors. I have experienced this gravitation tendency in Quechua Indian villages in the high Andes of Ecuador and in the tropical forests of West Africa. After spending days with Quechua people, it was always a refreshing experience to deviate off the trail and pass the night with a Spanish-speaking rancher whose world of thought was so much closer to my own than the Indians'. In the Camerouns I have spent a few weeks among the Kaka people without seeing another European. Finally when I encounter a French administrator or tobacco planter and we sit down to discuss the news of the day or talk about Africa, there is a common tie in our cultural background which makes the visit extremely enjoyable. One is struck by the ease with which interpersonal relations are established. To my mind, it is much more satisfying to hear a French administrator say, "I will pass by the village at six o'clock and pick you up," than to accustom myself to the Kaka statement, "I will arrive when the sun is about so." When the Frenchman fails to arrive on time, he has the expected excuse, but my Kaka friend has no excuse to offer and leaves me wondering.

The common cultural bond with the European is very obvious to the African and tends to form an association and identification of missionary with administration, whether the missionary cares for it or not. In one Cameroun village where I was staying a French tobacco inspector heard a missionary was living in the village, so he came to visit me. Upon his arrival, an old woman put her head in the door and said, "Your brother has come." I had never seen the man before.

The Role Is Often Acquired at Birth

The problem we are discussing here is simply that of role identification. It is possible to identify oneself under certain conditions with Africans so that you will be told that your heart is black. This is extremely heartening, especially in view of the political and national events these days. However, the separation is obvious and deep. It stems from birth.

While living in Ecuador in a tiny Quechua village, I asked the men why they called me *patroncito* 'master,' and they replied, "Because you do not work." I immediately went to work with them in all their manual labor, such as planting fields, cultivating, hoeing corn, building a road, and numerous other tasks. After six weeks of hard work, I asked again, "Why do you still call me *patroncito?*" They replied, "Because you go with the white men." I managed to avoid contact with the Spanish-speaking townspeople for a long period. When asked again, they replied, "Because you wear shoes." I put away my shoes and wore homespun fiber sandals like the Indians. This process con-

tinued until I did not see how there was any difference left. Then one day a group of men said, "Now, we will really tell you why you are *patroncito*. You were not born of an Indian mother." I was convinced.

New roles created in a society tend to shift the respect and prestige accorded to older roles. In the Cameroun the teaching of girls has tended to increase their dowry value, which the father receives. In a society where the women are expected to be inferior to the men, a highly educated girl such as those at college level do not wish to marry their college classmates who would be their equals. These young ladies insist on marrying a doctor or wealthy African whose status is unquestionably superior to their own. This comes to educators as quite a frustration. The main problem of concern to these educated girls is not just education, but also status, a factor which makes African life intelligible to them.

Conclusion

It might well be thought that the missionary disrupts culture by disapproving heathen practices and insisting that people wear shoes. My own personal experience is that missionaries do not harp on heathen practices, but they very definitely encourage the wearing of shoes, simply by wearing them themselves. The introduction of education in the forms of schools and churches has wide ramifications which set the machinery rolling for culture change. Even the printing of a book in a folk language is one of many ways in which Christian missionaries begin to feed in information which will accelerate change and make inroads in the old way of life.

The introduction of Christianity in this

century is heavily secularized and institutionalized. The creation of a new class or classes within the old society opens up new channels for the diffusion of Western culture. The process is that of making a copy, an imitation. The copy can only be partial, especially where there are barriers for intimate contact. Strong pressures existing within the local society's values tend to interpret the meaning of the copy and regulate the way this process works.

III

The Christian Predicament

High on the wind-swept slopes of Mount Mojanda in the Ecuadorean Andes a group of Quechua Indians knelt silently in the Roman Catholic church and listened with awe as a Spanish priest chanted mechanically through the early dawn funeral mass. Their stares were fixed upon a huge mural depicting the torments of hell which appeared to blaze and then simmer as flickering candles animated this awesome plight of suffering souls. At the last tinkling of the bell, shrouded figures arose, crossed themselves, pulled their woolen ponchos about them and drifted slowly out into the mist-chilled air of the semi-darkness. Casting a hurried glance over their shoulders at the fiery inferno on the wall, they headed for the graveyard burial, and then moved in a body to the liquor shops to blur their minds to the hellish horror that haunted their sober imaginations.

It was late afternoon before bands of drunken Indians staggered homeward followed by their faithful wives who sat beside fallen husbands and redeemed the time by spinning yarn from a distaff of wool. When a husband awoke and arose to continue on the path the wife got up and followed close behind, never ceasing to spin and twist her yarn. The path wound through eucalyptus trees and century plants past the edge of another sight which caused the staggering Indian to stop, rub his bleary eyes, urinate against a wall and then stumble on down the path. On the wall were the words "Misión Protestante." Here a mechanical demon replaced the medieval flames of the church's devil. Cars, trucks, generators, washing machines, saw mills, tractors, and a score of other devices made a thundersome noise that sent the drunken Indian hurrying toward his hut. Finally, sitting in the darkness of his windowless shack, he breathed freely, feeling that he had escaped the fire of the Roman hell and the machines of the mechanized mission.

The above description serves to indicate something of the impression made by the medieval Spanish Catholic and modern Protestant mission upon the Quechua of the Andes. It illustrates what may justly be termed "the predicament of the Christian mission." Here represented were two contrasting forces attempting in very different ways to make claims about Christianity. The Roman Catholic church in the town of Tabacundo, a mile from the Protestant mission, was nestled into the quiet, pious, reflective, selfish atmosphere of medieval Spanish life. The rhythm of this life was symbolized by the slow pealing of the church bells both day and night. The atmosphere was one of maintaining the status quo. Life was envisaged as unchanging and lived out in terms of centuries. All of this was evident in the ancient architecture of the buildings, the trade of the small craftsmen, and the gossip and small talk on the lips of those who gathered to pass the time of day on the one cobble-stone street of the town.

The Protestant mission was a sharp contrast. Such a contrast, in fact, that it was looked upon by the most liberal of the townspeople as being there to pur-posely threaten the quiet gossipy life of the little town. The mission's attitude was obviously set for gearing life to another pace. Early-rising, hard-working, time-conscious foreign missionaries were busily up to something which could end in no good in the eyes of the villagers. The mechanical aspect of the mission was in the view of the townspeople a mech-anized invasion of their feudal domain. The third side of this peculiar triangle was the Indian who for centuries had adjusted himself to the townsmen and looked upon the bustling mission activity with even more suspicion than did the whites.

It may appear at first unwarranted to place the Protestant mission in this case in the same predicament as the Catholic church of Tabacundo. However, the same process was at work in both. The Catholic church was presenting the Indian with a view of Christianity brought out of the medieval ages in which the pictorial art and the dazzling architecture of that day were the content expression of Chris-tianity. The Protestant mission on the other hand faced the Indian with a technological world which was just as strange and mystifying to him as the former. Each within its own predicament had something to say about Christianity. That they lead to different conclusions is obviously true.

The predicament of the Christian mis-sion referred to here is seen in the diffu-sion of cultural complexes, medieval art and architecture, twentieth century wealth and technology which enter the Quechua's world as part and parcel of the Chris-tian message which may or may not lie deeply encrusted within. The Quechua Indian of the Andes has adjusted his life to the Catholic complex imported from Spain and has maintained a passive rela-tionship to it for centuries. He appears as yet to be frightened by the Protestant innovation.

The Role of Colonial Governments

There are two approaches to the prob-lem of the church, its organization, and its activities which may be seen on many mission fields. One is the missionary direc-tion and participation type in which the missionary sets the pattern for church organization and practice until he has successfully trained local leaders to copy his pattern. This is a form that is com-monly seen and appears to be the "nat-ural" process of missions. The other mis-sion approach is what we may call the *laissez-faire* doctrine in which the mission-ary seeks to make individual converts and teaches them, but does not do so in a "church." Under this approach the folk are obliged to form their own church organization and practices along the lines which seen natural to them. The latter is not entirely "indigenous" because it is missionary stimulated and missionaries are teaching and are available for counsel and advice if this asked for.[2]

Both of these approaches are clearly in contrast in the French and British Cam-

2 Wm. A. Smalley: "Cultural Implications of an Indigenous Church," in this volume.

eroun. In the former the aim has been to create a church entirely along Reformed lines in which the African pastors may often wear robes in the pulpit, well rehearsed choral groups sing the Hallelujah Chorus, and where a European member of the Reformed tradition would be quite at home. A sophisticated atmosphere dominates in the churches in the French Cameroun where there has been considerable education and the availability of cash crops for the acquisition of many aspects of French culture.

The church in reference in the British Cameroun stands in sharp contrast. Here the educated choir singing from the written music score is replaced by native singing with drum beating, hand clapping, and the blowing of native cow horns. The services are conducted along lines which are somewhat spontaneous and outside the direction of missionaries. I am not attempting to say here that one of these is inherently better than the other. The sophisticated people of the French Cameroun would for the most part be shocked (now) to see their northern "British" neighbors at worship in church. Those in British Cameroun would no doubt feel awed by the formality and lack of spontaneity if they witnessed the churches of the French Cameroun.

These two churches exhibit each in its own way a basic difference in French and British colonial policy. The French attitude is that of suppressing native languages and employing the French language from the first year of school. The British usually use the native languages in the first several years of education. The French conceive of the African as potentially Frenchmen while the British look upon the Africans as Africans. The result is that these two colonial points of view greatly influence the kind of mission development that has been possible in British and French territories in Africa.

The influence of colonial patterns on the development of church behavior is at this time deep-seated. This may be illustrated by our experience in getting a song book prepared for the Kaka churches in the French Cameroun. Blind Kaka tribesman "Die-tomorrow" is known throughout the tribe as an ardent troubadour of Christian hymns and one of the most capable drummers in the tribe. After I had watched "Die-tomorrow" beat the drums I asked him to work out words and music to the accompaniment of the drum. He showed no interest but continued to sing the Bulu hymns in Kaka (with American church tunes). More than a hundred of these Kaka-from-Bulu hymns were recorded and a song book prepared. "Die-tomorrow" has consistently rejected the possibility of adapting his words to local music. It is not simply that "Die-tomorrow" is incapable of doing that task. It is rather an awareness that the Christian people would ridicule him for making the people go backwards rather than forwards in their conscious process of becoming more Europeanized. This again illustrates how the church behavior and ritual is affected by the pressure of the colonial power.

The question that naturally arises is whether or not the Africans will feel constrained to continue this European adaptation after full independence is achieved in the French Cameroun.

New Gods for Old

Life in Africa is conceived of in a way which is often closely parallel to Old Testament life and thought. African life is controlled by a consciousness of law very much on the order of the legalism of the Jews. The African is aware of traditional law which embodies an unwritten code of behavior which when violated brings on impurity, and a cleansing from this impurity must follow a specified ritual. Respect of traditions, the status of the elders, polygamy, the dowry, the desire to multiply the race, a feeling for spiritual causation, are but a few of the kinds of similarities between the modern African and ancient Hebrew cultures.

The predicament for the modern missionary is his separation from much of this point of view. The attempt on the part of missions to make Greek-thinking rationalists out of Africans is often met with strong resistance. The African Christian wants and reads the New Testament, but there is a home-like atmosphere in the Old Testament where he finds a bond that it largely absent in the writings of Paul and the other apostles.

The introduction of Christianity inevitably takes one of two paths in laying a foundation for Christian teaching. Old gods are destroyed and new ones substituted for them, or the old gods undergo a remodeling process in which they are shaped up to fit Biblical statements about God. The Bulu *Zambe* was a creator but he created and then left man with no more concern for him. *Zambe's* job was completed in the creation of the physical world. Christianity recalled *Zambe* out of his oblivion to complete the unfinished task of redemption. The Kaka *Ndjambie,* a cognate word, had also the role of creator but remained in the form of the spider as an impersonal force maintaining the creation in the skies, but man and the earth were largely independent of

him. *Ndjambie* has undergone a radical transformation.[3]

The making over of *Zambe* and *Ndjambie* has been possible because they shared something (creation) with the Christian idea of God. In many societies the transformation of God is the selection of one of several available gods who then undergoes the process of being promoted and replaces all lesser gods. In many cases the lesser gods are not, however, forgotten as their function continues in some changed aspect.

It appears to be the case in many primitive and folk cultures that the spirit world here below is of much more concern than some abstract creator or fateful force off in the heavens. The world of the dead, the presence of evil powers, witchcraft and magic are things which to many tribes are here and now, and upset or control the ongoing life of a group. In the cultures of the Cameroun these spirit entities were freely moving things without any organization among themselves.

However, the Christian introduction of the personality and idea of Satan has been grasped much more vividly than have many other infusions of new religious ideas. It was as though the spirit world were waiting for a ruler to whom the erratic behavior of spirits could be subject. Satan has become the reason and excuse for all human frailty. While God was never a personal idea, the introduction of Satan into the realm of the very close personal-spiritual relation has made Satan a great personal force in the lives of church members. Satan entered a realm where people consciously rub shoulders

[3] Wm. D. Reyburn: "The Transformation of God and the Conversion of Man," in this volume.

with spiritual beings. Satan is in the here and now and gets the blame for nearly everything. *Ndjambie,* on the other hand, is in the far away and appears to be still at long range from the Kaka Christian's thought world.

In addition to the God-Satan introduction among the Kaka, the distinction of heaven and hell are received with interesting reactions. Among the Kaka Christians heaven (called Paradise from the Bulu trade language Scriptures) is essentially an extension of this life. However, it is fraught with difficulties because there is "no marriage and giving in marriage."

While preparing a catechism in the Kaka language, we came to the writing of a statement to the effect that those in heaven would *serve* God. In Kaka there is no word to express any difference between hard labor and merely rendering a service. When I suggested the term *ñélo saé,* "to do work," my two assistants threw down their pencils and looked at each other in disgust. "Is that the reward of a good life?" shouted one of the men. We had to seek a better expression.

The Christian Scriptures

The translation of the Scriptures is an excellent example of the way in which missionaries infuse native cultures with strange and different ideas from Biblical cultures. I handed a student of the Mpompong tribe a French Bible and asked him to read the twentieth chapter of Genesis. I watched his face as he silently lipped through the words. He frowned slightly as he read how Abimelech had taken Sarah the "sister" of Abraham but did not "approach her." Then he continued to verse twelve where Abraham said that Sarah was his half

sister. The student stopped, looked at me, and with a stunned expression said, "No, how could he marry his own sister? He would call her 'sister.' How could his family face their shame? If they should have a child it would die." All of this he read into the passage from his own tribal laws governing the relation between children of the same father.

On another occasion I asked a Kaka teacher-catechist to find for me in his Bulu Bible the most difficult to believe passage he could find. He turned immediately to no New Testament miracle, nor to the birth of Christ, but to the 19th chapter of Genesis and with his eyes blinking and bulged he haltingly read the account of Lot and his two daughters who intoxicated their father and conceived children from him. Putting down his Bible he placed his hands on top of his head in a sign of shame and said, "Oh, no, no. Those children would have to be born dead to remove their sin." This was followed by a long series of "Oh, oh, oh, what customs those people had!"

Conclusion

Many missionaries decry the loss of indigenous arts. Instead of taking time to make a drum an African may prefer to buy a phonograph and become a listener of music rather than a creator of drum rhythm.

Missionaries may remark that it is to be regretted that the women do not make the beautiful clay pots as formerly. However, one is prone to forget that by encouraging monogamy and establishing church structures that are operated on money values, one is also affecting native art.

When I asked some Kaka women

recently why they had bought pans instead of making clay pots, they replied that since they had no co-wives to help in their husband's cocoa gardens, they had no time to make and decorate a pot. The cash crop helps pay the cathechist who has to be paid according to the established mission pattern. The women are the laborers in the market crop gardens and there is little time now for anything else.

The African is asked why he has given up the beautiful decorative work on his upright drum. His workmanship appears to the missionary as sloppy and careless. The reason is that the African wants a guitar or other European musical instrument. His native drum has had no functional role in the church so why should he be motivated to elaborate it and express his creative art in its manufacture. In order to acquire the European instrument he needs money. He is thwarted and frustrated in his attempt to secure the necessary money and is often criticized by the Europeans as having allowed himself to love money unduly.

Mission developments that have taken place since the beginning or middle of the last century have grown at the same time with American industrial power and technical specialization. Many American and European missions tend to be a symbol of the wealth and technology which is the goal of those who share a feeling for a mechanized world. The more the missionary has become *homo faber* (the machine-age species of human being) the more he has separated himself from the ways and thinking of most of the world's population.

While talking to a group of Kaka villagers about the gospel, I paused to ascertain if they followed what I had claimed. "Do you grant it so?" I asked. A village elder sitting in the rear spoke up saying, "Why should we say you don't speak straight? Haven't we seen that you can fly through the skies?" What this old man meant was that if a white man can cause an airplane to fly, why should the African villager doubt his word about such a simple matter as God's love.

Here is precisely the predicament of modern Christianity and missions. What is the motive to believe? To what extent is Africa south of the Sahara today filled with Christian churches promoted by a feeling of inferiority rather than a desire to believe? What has been the effect on the Indians of the Andes exposed for centuries to the medieval artistic impressions of hell? Be it the flaming scenes on a church wall or the magic of modern transportation, the folk man is destined to be on the receiving end of this worldwide promotion. The missionary is forced by the nature of the age in which we live to view critically and carefully the process by which we spread *Christianity in cultures*.

Dale W. Kietzman and William A. Smalley

The Missionary's Role
in Culture Change

THAT the missionary has historically been an agent of culture change in non-Western societies, no informed, thinking person would deny. His role of initiating culture change has often been seriously misunderstood, however, in different ways by the missionary himself, his supporters, and his critics. The basic attitude of the missionary on this matter, and fundamental missionary policy in an area with respect to it, will inevitably influence profoundly the successful communication of the gospel and the possible development of an "indigenous" expression of Christianity.

Some critics of the missionary enterprise have grossly exaggerated the missionary's influence in their condemnation of the "rape" of non-Western cultures, with destruction of values, detribalization, apathy, or conflict resulting. There certainly have been some such direct cases of unnecessary and damaging cultural disturbance in missionary history, but for the most part the missionary's part has been very minor relative to the impact

Rewritten to combine the following articles: "The Missionary's Role in Cultural Change," by Dale W. Kietzman, Vol. 1, No. 5 (1954), pp. 71-75, and "The Missionary and Culture Change," by William A. Smalley, Vol. 4, No. 6 (1957), pp. 231-237. Dale W. Kietzman is director of the work of the Wycliffe Bible Translators in Brazil. In addition to his training and field experience as a missionary linguist and Bible translator, he has done graduate study in Anthropology at the University of Chicago.

of Western business, politics, and education, not to speak of the often unsavory influences of motion pictures and printed matter. There have also been some outstanding cases where the gospel and resulting culture change have provided an opportunity for the reintegration of a segment of a culture already in rapid change.[1]

Many supporters of Christian missions, on the other hand, have gauged the success of their whole program in terms of some overt, symbolic types of culture change. These may be anything from monogamy to haircuts, from attendance at church to the disappearance of scarification, but the missionary sees in them signs that his ministry is taking effect. Missions and missionaries which declare that they are not going out to introduce Western culture, but only to preach the gospel, are no different in this respect from those with whom they contrast themselves. It is usually institutionalism (hospitalization, education, agricultural mission, etc.) which they are rejecting by such statements, not really their roles as agents of Westernization. They, too, are thrilled when Ay Blah learns to bathe with Ivory soap, brush his teeth with Ipana, and cut his hair in "civilized" fashion. And if Ta Plooy does not give up his second and third wives or contribute

[1] For a case study of a problem such as this see G. Linwood Barney, "The Meo — An Incipient Church," in this volume.

524

to the church treasury, this is a matter for deep concern, for Ta Plooy obviously is not following the "gospel teaching" which he has been getting.

The Problem

To many a perceptive missionary, sensitive to cultural values, there has been a very real problem, a dilemma, at this point. On the one hand, there is a realization that cultural forms are relative, that the meanings of different kinds of behavior change in time and from society to society, that the Greek Christians were not bound by Jewish ceremonial law, that God did accept as perfectly normal the plural marriages of the patriarchs, that to have uncovered breasts is not immodesty among the hill tribes of Southeast Asia, and many other parts of the world. On the other hand, there is the clear Biblical record that God, through the prophets and the apostles, condemned sin in terms of overt cultural behavior, like that of David arranging for the death of Uriah so that he could marry Bathsheba,[2] or like women talking in church,[3] or like Onan refusing to have sexual intercourse with his dead brother's wife because "the offspring would not be his" (so that God slew him),[4] or like braided hair.[5]

Clearly the preaching of the gospel in New Testament times did "turn the world upside down," and that at least partly in terms of widespread changes in cultural behavior. Culture change has resulted historically from any widespread acceptance of Christ. But what should that change be? Should monogamy result?

Should agricultural methods be changed? Should people put on clothes? Should drinking stop? Should romantic love be substituted for family alliances as a basis for marriage? Should the bride-price be dropped? Should all Christians learn to read? Should churches be built? Should Christians kneel to pray if crouching is their position of reverence and respect? How do we know what culture change is for the best and what is not?

And how can we be sure that a needed culture change will come about? If we feel that reading the Scriptures is necessary for Christian life, do we force Christians to learn to read in order to gain church membership? Such a course of action seems theologically untenable, as well as culturally "loaded" in giving an entirely distorted picture of the meaning of the church; but it has been done, and has been considered essential in some areas. Do we set rules of behavior to which Christians have to conform if they are to remain in good standing? If so, how do we decide what the rules are to be? Are these rules to be imported wholesale from the rules which the missionary observes? If so, which missionary? Are they to be imported wholesale from the Bible? If so, will they include levirate? polygyny? washing of feet? reclining at meals? silence in the churches? How will the choice be made?

The Cultural Orientation of the Missionary

The picture of a culture being reshaped as a necessary accompaniment of gospel preaching, and the unfortunate misarrangements of bygone years, cause many of the present problems on the mission field. They also provide part of the impetus for a scientifically oriented ap-

---

2 2 Samuel 11:2 — 12:23.
3 1 Corinthians 14:34.
4 Genesis 38:7-10.
5 1 Timothy 2:9.

proach to the problem of the conflict between the missionary's message and the native culture. In exploiting this new approach there is the evident possibility of making more adroit the manipulations and changes that are brought about in a culture. The chief advantage of doing so is the avoidance of much adverse popular reaction. This more obvious possibility for missionary anthropology hides its more central application, namely to teach the missionary to remove himself, as an individual, as far as possible from the sphere of conflict between the message and power of the gospel and the individual.

One of the biggest handicaps of missionary work in the present generation is the nationality and color of the missionary. Yet on the whole we have not attacked the problem of making our presentation of Christianity less of the "white man's religion." It seems, rather, that we seek only to make the "white man's religion" a little more palatable and a little less disastrous to the native culture.

With many areas of the world already effectively sealed to the reception of the gospel message, missions are making a pointed effort at correcting methods in order to avoid further misunderstanding. But has the situation really been improved simply by turning over to native leaders some of the previous functions of the missionary? Will those leaders whose minds are inflamed with nationalism be able to see the distinction between a foreign institution manned by foreigners and an institution created and regulated by foreigners, and labeled by them indigenous?

Church policy is a case in point. While no one now seemingly opposes the principle of the indigenous church, with its policies of "self-support, self-propagation, and self-government," is such a church really an indigenous one when the form for it is decided upon by the missionary? Even raising the question of how soon the church is to "become indigenous" betrays the fact that the missionary is considered to be the judge of the fitness of a group of believers to cope with the problems presented by their own culture.

A related problem is that of the preparation of the native leaders for the church. Education is generally considered to be the answer for this problem. Can we say that these men are trained for leadership in an indigenous church when the training is not given in the place and at the time prescribed by the culture, when instruction is by teachers not recognized in the culture, often in a language other than the mother tongue? At the same time, any culturally recognized training, harmless or not, is frequently ruled out of the student's life.

The Motivation for Culture Change

Culture change comes only as an expression of a need felt by individuals within a society. People do not change their behavior unless they feel a need to do so. The need may be trivial, as that for some new excitement or amusement, or it may be profound, as for security in a disintegrating world. Usually it is relatively unconscious. People have not analyzed it or given it a name, but it motivates behavior. Something which no missionary who senses culture change going on around him should ever forget, however, is that the need being satisfied by a change very likely is not the need which the casual observer from our Western culture might see.

Among some of the tribal peoples of Laos and Vietnam, for example, the missionary sees the need for clothing. Many missionaries would feel that people need clothing for reasons of modesty (as in cases where women habitually wear nothing above the waist) or for warmth in the chilly season of the year. The second need is one which is felt by the people themselves to some degree, but it is strongly overshadowed by the other needs which they feel and which will be discussed in a moment. The need for modesty in the use of additional clothing is not felt at all, because people consider themselves adequately dressed from that point of view.

When the missionary barrel arrives and the clothes are given out, or when the missionary gives away an old shirt, or when some individual buys a new piece of clothing, what are the needs which he is meeting? One is the need to look respectable in the sight of outsiders — the need for being accepted by people who have prestige. This is why women will often not wear blouses in the village, but will wear them into town or put them on when the missionary shows up. Thus clothing may be a symbol of acceptance by the missionary, of status and prestige in relation to him. Another is the desire to look well among one's equals, to wear something difficult to obtain, something impossible for one's neighbors to buy.

A case in point is a preacher from one of the tribes of Southeast Asia after he had been given a topcoat out of the missionary barrel. This was the only topcoat in the lot; he was the only tribesman who possessed a topcoat. It never got so cold in the area that a missionary ever wore a topcoat, although a woolen suit was comfortable in the evening for two or three months of the year. On a trip over rather rugged, mountainous jungle, when people in T-shirts and cotton trousers were perspiring profusely because of the heat, our friend with the topcoat was, of course, wearing it. How else would people see him with a topcoat on unless he wore it?

Then there was the woman who wore nothing above the waist but a substantial pink bra . . . .

A man who starts to wash his clothes after his conversion is probably not doing so because of his love for Christ, even though this seems to the missionary to be vindication of the view that cleanliness is next to godliness. What are the needs being expressed in a change from polygamy to monogamy, in church attendance, in church government, in learning to read, in sending children to school? We would be the last to say that the need of man for God is never involved in some of these, in some places, but even then, as in all human situations, motives are mixed.

Clearly, the typical missionary reaction to culture change is to approve of that which makes other peoples more like themselves in *form,* in the outward aspects of behavior, whether the meaning of the behavior is the same or not. It is quite possible to give encouragement to the development of a form which is expressing a meaning, fulfilling a need, which the missionary would seriously deplore.

The Role of the Church in Culture Change

Culture is constantly changing, and what is vital for our purpose, it is constantly changing from within. While a good bit is said and written about acculturation, seldom has the role of the innovator, the nonconformist, the rebel been described. Yet all societies have them, and they have their place in bringing about the constant change that is characteristic of culture. The important thing for the missionary to note is that change is almost always initiated by someone within the cultural community. Even though the idea may have been sparked by contact with another culture, it still must be introduced from within to be accepted. The alternative to this scheme is change forced upon a people through superior might, whether moral or physical. This is the sort of change that missions have often been responsible for, and that resulted in such unfortunate reaction.

The real agent of the Holy Spirit in any society for the changes in the culture of that society is the church, the body of believers (*not* necessarily the organized church of any particular denomination). The church is the salt working through the whole dish. It is that part of the society which has a new relationship to God — yet it reacts in terms of the attitudes and presuppositions of that society. It understands, in an intuitive, unanalyzed way, motives and meanings as the missionary cannot. It must make the decisions.

The Missionary's Part

What, then, can the missionary do about culture change? Is he to be only an evangelist preaching a noncultural gospel without making value judgments? This is an impossibility, even if it were desirable. There cannot be preaching except in cultural terms, and no human being can or should try to escape value judgments.[6]

---

[6] By this statement we are not, of course, condoning the highly ethnocentric preaching and value judgments many missionaries make, nor the mistaken views of culture on which they may be based. See "The Missionary and the Evaluation of Culture," by William D. Reyburn, in this volume.

The missionary cannot legitimately force or enforce any culture change. Nor does he have an adequate basis for advocating specific changes in a culture unless he has a profound knowledge of the culture.

The missionary does, however, have an extremely important function in the tactful, thoughtful, serious presentation of alternate forms of cultural behavior to the Christians in a society. On the basis of his knowledge of history, his understanding of the church elsewhere, and above all, his knowledge of the tremendously varied ways in which God dealt with men, as recorded in the Scriptures, he can make it clear to them that there are alternative ways of behavior to their own, and help them in prayer and study and experiment to select those cultural forms which would be the best expression of their relationship to God in their culture.

The missionary's basic responsibility is to provide the material upon which the native Christian and church can grow "in grace and knowledge" to the point where they can make reliable and Spirit-directed decisions with regard to their own conduct within the existing culture. This involves a complete freedom of access to the Word of God, with such encouragement, instruction and guidance in its use as may be necessary to obtain a healthy and growing Christian community.

The missionary's role in culture change, then, is that of a catalyst and of a source of new ideas, new information. It is the voice of experience, but an experience based on his own culture for the most part and therefore to be used only with care and understanding. Part of the value of anthropological study, of course, is that it gives at least vicarious experience in more than one cultural setting, for by study in this field the missionary can gain awareness of the much wider choice of alternatives than his own culture allows.

It is the church which is the legitimate agency in which the missionary should work. It is the people who must make the decisions based on the new ideas which they have received. It is they who must reinterpret old needs and expressions, examined now in the light of their relationship to God and to their fellow men in Christ Jesus.

Delbert Rice

Evangelism and Decision - Making Processes

THE task cf evangelism is to witness and inform people concerning Christ and his activities so that a person can and will make the decision to trust him as Savior and Lord. An evangelist is any person who feels it necessary to participate in the work of evangelism. Since evangelism is so centrally concerned with the making of a decision, the first questions which any evangelist should ask as he endeavors to perform his function in a particular area with a particular people are: (1) How do these people make decisions? (2) What processes are involved in this culture when individuals or groups make decisions? Probably one of the main reasons why the Christian church is not growing faster than it is, is simply that very few evangelists today bother to ask these questions. (It may be true that there is a small increase in membership in the church today, but in most areas it is less than the in-

crease in population and is therefore not actual growth.)

The ideal evangelistic technique would be for the evangelist to enter into the decision-making processes in the given culture at every possible point in order to influence as many individuals as possible to make the correct decision in depth concerning Christ.

In order to illustrate the application of this principle let us examine two different Philippine cultures to observe how decisions are made. Some aspects of these cultures are in process of change today, it is true, but no culture is ever static. Every culture is fluid. For the sake of illustration it is valuable therefore to examine these cultures to see how decisions are being made and how an evangelist can influence people in them.

Ilocano Decision-Making

One of the largest cultural groups in the Philippines the Ilocanos live primarily in the northern part of Luzon although they are now found throughout all of the islands as families have immigrated to open new homesteads. They are an agricultural people, very industrious, aggressive and thrifty.

Delbert Rice is Director of Evangelism for the Kalahan Mission, United Church of Christ in the Philippines, where he has served for 13 years. He has served as a resident missionary on the staff of the Missionary Orientation Center, Stony Point, New York. Imugan, Santa Fe, Nueva Vizcaya, Philippines, A-711.

530

The small peer group. Ilocano men can be seen gathering at midday under a tree or under a house either resting or engaging in repair work on their farm equipment. Again in early evening they will gather on the street corners or in front of the *sari-sari* stores. Women will gather in small groups while they do their laundry at the river or well or while they bathe their children. Young people similarly gather at convenient times depending upon their schedule. At these times they discuss various plans, ideas, and problems preparatory to making decisions. The decisions might concern planting new crops in the family fields, the marriage of a son or daughter, building a new house, moving to a new area, voting for a particular candidate, a new religion, or matters of faith or theology. (In contrast with the usual pattern in U.S. culture, theological doctrines are discussed very openly in this culture.) These discussions are not formal; they are open and free discussions between peers with each person testing his wisdom and ideas which he has heard against the reaction of his peers. The kind of feedback that a person gets in these discussions has a great deal to do with the ultimate decision which will be made.

The family unit. Every decision influences a family (this is usually the extended family, not the nuclear family). The family as a unit takes part in the making of most all decisions. No individual can take the entire responsibility for a decision upon himself: rather, he must include the other members of the family. This accounts, in large measure, for the custom, frustrating to Westerners and especially medical doctors, of calling home all of the family members whenever an individual becomes sick. The family members cannot help medically, but together they make the decision concerning which physician to employ, etc., so that no one person needs to bear the responsibility. The family may not call a special meeting, but the discussion may take place during the regular times that the family is together; it is generally the family that makes the decision, nevertheless. In cases of very difficult or important decisions, however, they will likely have a time of formal discussion concerning the matter. Each member of the family can express his opinions or ideas although some members are more important than others, or at least carry more authority in their statements. In descending order of importance we usually find the oldest male members, the oldest female member, the older male members, the more highly educated members, and other members of the family.

The personalities of the persons involved and their rank in importance in the family, as well as the importance of the various ideas they express, all provide data by which the family reaches a consensus. This might take place over a long period of time, or it might be developed rapidly, but no decision can be announced until the consensus is reached. The decision will probably be announced by the concerned party or by the father of the family.

The public discussion or debate. Whenever a matter involves more than one family, it seems important to the Ilocanos for the matter to be debated or discussed publicly. The members of the community are usually very active spectators in these debates. Sometimes two or more people will take sides in a matter and debate it vigorously. If there is a new idea to be presented to the community, some individual or group will make the public presentation and the entire community then will take part in the debate over its relative merits or demerits. If an idea can stand up in such a trial, it has a very good chance of finding ultimate acceptance by a large percentage of the population. The data from these discussions and any points drawn from them return to the family units where the ultimate decision is made. The results of these public discussions carry great influence in the decision.

The opinion former. In each community there are one or more persons who, because of their inherent recognized wisdom as demonstrated by their part in community life, have great influence over other people. These people are not generally the elected officers of the community, but in their quiet way they mold public opinion and their advice is sought throughout the community. If they should be convinced of the wisdom of a certain action, their ideas ultimately play a large part in influencing other people toward that same action.

Going against the consensus. As can be readily implied from the communal nature of the decision-making processes among the Ilocanos, the consensus is the essential element. The smallest unit which can make a decision is the family. The group making the decision might be enlarged to include several families or even one or more communities. It must be remembered, however, that every individual involved in that decision was also involved in making that decision. Young and old, men and women, all had opportunity to discuss the decision and take part in it. In a very real way, the communal decision which was reached is the personal decision of every member in the group.

It is possible for an individual to go against the family decision and this does happen occasionally, but it is a very difficult path to take. That individual suffers at least temporary social ostracism. The ostracism could be permanent and complete, depending upon the importance of the decision. Reconciliation can be brought about at a later time through other processes, but at the time of the decision, individuals who do not agree to the decision receive some form of ostracism.

If one or more families in a community decide to go against the consensus of the community, there is also a separation which takes place. The result might be the development of parties which could successfully split the community into two opposing camps. If only one family refuses to go along, they might just be left out of future community activities, or they might just be ignored and re-included at a later time. It is usually not as serious to have this type of schism as to have a schism *within* the family.

Evangelistic Techniques with the Ilocanos.

After recognizing the processes by which Ilocanos reach their important decisions it is appropriate now for the evangelist to study these processes and determine where he can fit into them to influence people to accept Christ as Lord and Savior. He must first recognize that an outsider cannot enter into the family unit to influence the decision on that level. That particular area is closed to him although he might be invited in to dicuss some matters prior to the actual making of the decision.

Parenthetically, it might be helpful to see the relationship of the evangelist to his own family. Within his own family he is a full member and can take part in the family decisions. If his own family has not accepted the Gospel, then his testimony with other families is handicapped and suspicious. The immediate reaction of other families would be to think, "If this Gospel is so good, why could this person not convince his own family? There must be some other bad things which his family knows but which he is not telling us. We had better not believe in this, either."

The evangelist can easily enter into the other levels of decision-making, however, and he should do so. He (or she) can meet with the peer groups insofar as he is accepted by them. He can steer the conversation into a discussion of Christ and the Gospel. He must be willing to discuss all of the ramifications of the Christian faith and do so respectfully in a free and open discussion. He should try to contact as many levels of peers as possible. The evangelist must make every effort to relate himself properly to these groups, also, so that his words will be accepted in that group. Lectures and sermons are not appropriate on this level.

The evangelist can also meet with the opinion former (s). Here it is essential that the evangelist become well acquainted with the community so that he can recognize the true opinion former. He should befriend such a person in respect and do his best to clarify any problems which might arise concerning faith in Jesus Christ. He should also express the need for the persons in the community to accept Christ. He cannot push in this matter because, if he does so, he is immediately suspected of having ulterior motives.

Parenthetically again, it is very important to note that the life that the evangelist lives with the people of the community is the primary evidence which he has to present to the community. The opinion former is generally not as interested in the obtuse theological conflicts which arise as he is in the practical results of a new faith. His decision is usually based on the practical analysis of the type of life which the evangelist lives: i.e., it is helpful to the community, it makes for more peaceful relationships among people, it tends toward social and financial progress, etc. These are very important.

It is also possible, and usually necessary, for the evangelist to enter into the public discussion. On this level the lecture and/or sermon is very helpful, but the presentation dare not end with a sermon. An essential part of the process of influencing decisions is the discussion which must follow. Sometimes it becomes a debate and the evangelist should be prepared to present his answers and his evidences clearly and convincingly. Occasionally a debate gets out of control and sides are drawn up for real verbal battles (sometimes physical battles result) and this must be avoided if at all possible. Under no circumstances should the evangelist himself become hotheaded. Remember, however, that it is not necessary to reject the debate because it sometimes gets out of hand. A jeep can get out of control also and do much damage, and thousands of people are killed yearly in automobile accidents. We still continue to use jeeps in spite of the dangers because they accomplish their task of providing transportation better than our feet. A good public discussion can do much to speed up the process of communication. One technique which we have used quite successfully to encourage free and open discussion while avoiding the heat which is sometimes generated in open debate is to offer to answer from the Bible any and all questions, but to require that the questions be written.

When the evangelist has done all that he can to influence the opinion former and the peer groups and when he has submitted his theology to the test of open discussion (or debate if that is what it turned out to be), he must leave the decision to the family groups and wait patiently until they have had a reasonable opportunity to act. If the evangelist should force a decision at the close of the first public discussion, he would be ignoring the family group which is the usual place where the decision is made.

The next step will be for the evangelist to present a valid opportunity in which the people can actually recognize that a true decision is required. A public affirmation of faith at some public meeting subsequent to the public discussions might be such an opportunity. Joining an existing Christian congregation or a newly organized congregation might be another opportunity which would show the need for a decision. Patience is again essential as the evangelist waits for the family units to declare their decisions.

It is important to note here that since decisions are made by family units, evangelism should be directed toward that same unit as was nearly all of the evangelism in the New Testament. For an evangelist to insist that an individual make a private decision without considering the family unit(s) of which he is a member is to ask the individual to violate his own nature as a member of his own culture. As a member of his family, he will come to a personal decision with his family concerning Christ. He is wilfully and personally involved in that decision. This decision does not violate God's requirement that the person's will be involved nor does it violate his family involvement or responsibilities. He is free to develop spiritually as a Christian Ilocano under the guidance of the Holy Spirit.

Kalahan Decision-Making Processes

These people are an "Igorot" tribe located in the southern end of the Cordillera Mountains of North Luzon in the Philippines. Their agriculture is basically slash-and-burn in the steep mountains. Pigs and chickens are their basic livestock although cows and carabao also are important to them. They are also hunters, using dogs and various kinds of traps as well as firearms, spears and knives. Their lands border on Ilocano lands at several points.

Opinion formers. As with the Ilocanos, there are also opinion formers among the Kalahan people. These individuals are known to everyone in the community but seldom recognized by outsiders. They need hold no official position but can generally be recognized by their being invited to all of the conferences (the conference is described below) or by the frequency with which people visit them for advice. These individuals are respected because of their wisdom. They have usually cared well for their families and their children are of good character and likewise respected. Sometimes they take a very active part in settling disputes. In at least one area the opinion former is a woman who seldom takes an active part in the settling of disputes but, because of her wisdom and her relationship as daughter of the former chief, she influences the persons who do take an active part in community affairs.

The conference. These are meetings called by any member of the tribe with the agreement of one or more of the elders. The elders, although they do play a leading role, do not monopolize the discussions, which are very democratic. Women do not usually take an active part in these conferences, but they may if they desire; and if the subject is something of particular interest to them, they will speak freely and convincingly. It seems that the men take a leading part primarily because the women permit them to do so.

If the conference was called to settle a dispute, every involved person has an opportunity to testify and express his opinions. Some individual elder will usually serve as a master of ceremonies but anyone can cross-examine anyone who speaks as long as he does so properly. The elders and heads of families then speak concerning the problem at hand. They will continue to search for facts or work toward a decision or settlement until a consensus is reached. If fines are levied on some individual, the pressure of public opinion ensures that the fines will be paid. In a recent case of adultery, the guilty man paid some fines to the husband and some to the community in the form of a feast enjoyed by all.

Sometimes an interested party will spend more time trying to build up his side of the case with other individuals before a conference is held, but there seems to be no such process as the peer group process of the Ilocanos. Likewise, although a family unit might become a voting block which is important in developing the consensus during the conference, the actual decision is made by the people attending the conference.

Occasionally a certain family or an individual involved in the dispute or problem will not be able to come at the stated time or perhaps he (they) will boycott the conference. In that case no decision can be reached. The rights of the individuals are highly respected and protected, but the obligations of the individuals in the community are insisted upon also. If, after a period of time, the conference cannot reach a decision, it usually finds some reason to adjourn temporarily. Other people (witnesses or elders) might be called to assist in providing information or wisdom and the conference will be continued at a later time. When a strong consensus is reached, the decision is given. All of the parties involved and all of the members of the community agree that it is the best decision.

Celebrations. The Kalahan people also have frequent celebrations sometimes known as the *Kanyaw*. These are related to ancient pagan rituals, but they are also times of recreation and fellowship which are quite important to the people. At such times the elders enjoy reciting antiphonal poetic chants, usually extemporaneous, in which they discuss various personal or community matters. If the celebration concerns a marriage, for instance, there will be many chants (called *Ba-liw*) expressing good advice and good wishes to the couple. If a funeral is the cause for the gathering, there will be chants about the life of the deceased and about the responsibilities of the survivors. At these times, however, it is possible to open nearly any subject through a chant and in this poetic manner a semi-formal presentation can be made which is listened to carefully and studied by the people present. Most everyone present for the celebration is attentive to the chant. Sometimes the chanting can become a battle of wits between some of the individual elders or a contest to see who can produce the most beautiful chant. At other times no competition is involved, but merely a formalized poetic debate or discussion. Indirect but powerful influence can be brought to bear on the community through this means.

Going against the consensus. If some person or family decides to reject the decision of the conference or if he refuses in advance to accept the authority of the conference, he can do so. He would suffer no physical harm, but he would be very effectively ostracized from taking part in community life and community affairs. Usually such individuals decide to leave the area entirely and permanently. They usually take up residence with the Tagalog merchants along a highway someplace or go to Baguio and enter some type of employment. If one should prosper greatly "outside" (in Baguio or elsewhere) and should decide to come back, he might be accepted somewhat, but this usually would not happen. In general he would be considered as no longer a member of the tribe.

Evangelistic Techniques for the Kalahan

In the light of the decision-making techniques of the Kalahan people, it is obvious that evangelism there must be done on a community basis. Reaching the opinion former (s) is, of course, very important as well as reaching the various elders and other members of the community. It is helpful to get a great deal of individual discussion going before problems or new ideas come up for public discussions or decisions. During all of this preliminary discussion, however, it is clear that the evangelist is not trying to dehumanize a member of the Kalahan tribe by forcing him to leave his tribe and join another. The decision making unit in the Kalahan tribe is the community and so evangelism must be aimed at the community.

Next, the evangelist should use every celebration and every other occasion to present his faith and its implications to the members of the community. When a conference is called for some social purpose, it is usually possible for people to suggest other topics for discussion. Even more appropriately an evangelist can, after listening to the comments made by the elders concerning a particular case, read a section of the Scriptures which has particular importance to the case being discussed, introducing the reading with a statement that "Another elder of the church a long time ago when he came against this kind of a problem said this:..." In this way the entire community realizes the relevance of Christian faith to their present situation and are more inclined to accept it.

Later, after the evangelist has been accepted by the people and after several individuals have expressed a sincere interest, a conference might be called to discuss the decision of becoming Christian. At this time the Christian faith can be discussed in as much detail as the members of the community desire. If, at that meeting the decision seems to be negative, it can be accepted as a tentative decision of "not yet," and the discussion process can continue. When the community is ready, they will reach the affirmative decision to accept Christ as Lord of their lives as Kalahan. This will be a communal decision, but it is also a personal decision of all of the members of the community and should be accepted as such.

Conclusions

In the United States and most of Europe the decision-making unit is the individual. The evangelist should aim his work at convincing the individual of the truth of the Gospel and his need to trust Christ. In Western culture it is valuable to analyze the different motives which cause people to make or alter their decisions. This strong emphasis upon the individual is an adaptation which was made in evangelistic techniques as the Gospel reached into Europe and into modern society. It is just as valid to retain the original family and community emphasis as it is to continue the Western individual emphasis.

Each culture has its own processes for making decisions. Whether it is the family or the individual or the community which makes the decision, decisions are still being made which change the lives of individuals. The most important change which can be made is the change of heart which takes place when a man becomes a Christian. The most effective way for this change to occur is through the cultural processes of decision-making which already exist for every person.

There are two types of defective decisions which can be caused by wrong evangelistic techniques. These types of decisions may handicap both the present and the future of the spread of the Gospel among any particular people.

The surface decision. Many times it can be demonstrated that the surface decision is not a real decision at all. It is merely the response of an individual to certain pressures so that, for the sake of friendship or prestige, he will adopt certain "christian" customs and/or vocabulary while his inner allegiance and motivation remain unchanged. Sometimes the veneer of Christianity will remain intact for several years before it is worn through and the basic nonchristian motivation of the individual is revealed. This is not true evangelism.

The dead-end decision. In some cases an individual in a communal society such as the Ilocano or Kalahan will, under pressure from an individualistic evangelist, make a private decision without going through the usual process of involving others in his decision. Most usually, however, the person who does this is already a misfit or rebel in the community and he is in the process of rejecting his culture or some aspects of it. His individual decision might be a surface decision as mentioned above or it might be deep and genuine. In either case, however, that individual cannot effectively return to his original culture as an evangelist for the simple reason that he has already taken himself out of his culture. He can no longer be an influential part of his own culture and he cannot be effective in it since it is clear to everyone in his culture that he has rejected that culture and them with it.

When, on the other hand, a valid and vital decision has been made to accept Christ as Lord and Savior, it is a necessary and obvious corollary that the new Christian is immediately involved in the process of stimulating more decisions. If new Christians continue to operate within the basic processes of decision-making in the culture, this task is the most natural thing for them to do. Evangelism should progress and mushroom. If evangelistic techniques are forced and unnatural, converts will not be able to utilize them and growth is impossible.

The effective decision is one which enables each individual to grow spiritually and manifest his new faith where he lives. It will also enable him to both live and speak his witness concerning the reality of Jesus Christ. Effective decisions are the aim of all evangelism. It is worthwhile for the church to spend a little effort to learn new techniques in order that decisions might be effective.

Delbert Rice

House Dedication in the Kalahan

The iKalahan people of the Philippines have traditionally had a rich religious involvement in every aspect of their lives. Since the majority of the people of the southern Kalahan area have become Christians within the last decade, they are still trying to work out the problem of maintaining the unity and richness of their community life while they readjust their religious activities to conform to their new faith. The author describes and gives a sample text of a traditional house dedication ceremony, then gives a Christian adaptation which has been successfully adopted by the iKalahan Christians. Much is made of functional equivalence between the two ceremonies.

The People and Their Customs

A large percentage of the Cordillera Mountain Range in the Philippines is forested with the well-known Benguet pine. The southeastern end of the range, however, the area where the Caraballos Ridge joins, is forested primarily with deciduous trees, known in the local language as *kalahan* trees. This area includes much of Nueva Vizcaya, and adjacent portions of Nueva Ecija, Pangasinan, Benguet

Delbert Rice is Director of Evangelism for the Kalahan Mission, United Church of Christ in the Philippines (Imugan, Santa Fe, Nueva Vizcaya, Philippines, A-711). He holds an M.A. in anthropology from Silliman University, and has taught a course there on Faith and Culture. His most recent article in PA was "Church Government among the iKalahan" Vol. 19, No. 2 (March-April 1972), pp. 49-58.

and Ifugao Provinces. The area has come to be known locally as the Kalahan area and the people, in order to distinguish themselves from the other groups of mountain people residing in the pine tree area, are known as the *iKalahan* (people of Kalahan).

The iKalahan have always had a very rich and extensive religious involvement in every aspect of their lives. Specific ceremonies were enjoined for all of the important occasions in their lives. These ceremonies included the entire community and served at least two important functions: first, they were an important means of uniting the members of the community together into a cooperative whole. Second, they were an important means of maintaining the felt unity between the people of the community and the spiritual forces that they knew.

Since the majority of the people of the southern Kalahan area have become Christian within the last decade, they are still trying to work out the problem of maintaining the unity and richness of their community life while they readjust their religious activities to conform to their new faith. These adjustments are slow, but they are taking place. The results of the adjustments made by the iKalahan people may serve to encourage other groups who are engaged in the same struggle.

Naturally, not all of the developments take place simultaneously. The new wedding ceremony was developed in 1968 and has been used many times. It seems to be an effective ceremony which accomplishes the functions which have been assigned to it.[1] In 1970 the pastor and the people were met with the problem of a house dedication. This brief report is a record of their study and planning in developing a new ceremony to fulfill the various functions which a dedication should perform. The process is not yet complete. As the ceremony is used, it will undergo changes, but this is indicative of the process which they have gone through and the direction of the development.

The Pre-Christian House Dedication and Its Function

In times past a dedication ceremony called a *paltik* was conducted for any newly constructed house before anyone was allowed to live in it. At the opening of the ceremony a pig was placed outside the house and held by one of the young men of the community. The religious leader, the *mabaki*, then called together the various spirits including the people's ancestors and asked them to join the celebration of the *paltik*. The pig was then killed by pushing a wooden stake through its heart. The *mabaki* then took the stake, covered with the blood of the pig, and proceeded to mark the foreheads of the members of the family who would live in the house and also various parts of the house. This marking is known as *boyag*, a word known in other Philippine languages for the same act.

During the marking of the parts of the house, the *mabaki* recited a beautifully poetic chant addressed to the various *ginoman* (dreamgiver) spirits asking them to give good dreams (and thereby good fortune) to the members of the household. During the letter part of the chant the house was addressed in the second person using anthropomorphic verbs, e.g., the door should open wide for good things, the windows should blink closed to evil, etc.[2]

During the continuation of the chant some of the young men of the community began to clean and cook the pig. After the close of the chants, the recreation began. Both young and old joined in the dances to the accompaniment of gongs and drum music. The older people took part in the conversational chanting of various

---

[1] D. Rice, "An Indigenous Wedding Ceremony." *Evangelical Missions Quarterly*, Vol. 7, No. 3 (Spring, 1971), pp. 151-153.

[2] The complete text of the main recitation is in the appendix.

ba-liw (antiphonal chants).[3] In the past they have also had contests of singing the various *dayomti* (indigenous songs), but this art was fast dying out until recently when it has been revived somewhat. When the pig and rice were cooked, the people enjoyed the food. The celebration continued all night or stopped after the meal, depending upon the circumstances.

The ceremony, as mentioned above, performed several functions within the culture.

1. Through the recreation and fellowship, it served to strengthen the unity of the community.

2. Through the assistance of every family in the work of the house and the completion of the ceremony, each person had a sense of involvement in the well-being of the householder who is also his neighbor.

3. Through the invitation to the dead ancestors, it served to nourish the feeling of oneness of the living with the dead and, thus, strengthen the sense of continuity of the community.

4. Through the *ba-liw* and *dayomti* the community was enabled to give guidance and advice to various members of the community who were transgressing or apt to transgress community standards of behavior.

5. Through the performance of the *paltik*, the good fortune of the family and its house was supposedly assured.

6. Through the invitation of the spirits, it served to maintain the con-

tractual relationship which the community had with the spirits. This relationship was based upon fear, not love, which is a common characteristic of animistic beliefs; nevertheless, it was definitely contractual and predictable.

The Function of a Christian House Dedication

As the Christian community looks to the task of preparing a Christian ceremony of house dedication, it needs to evaluate the functions which have been accomplished by the pre-Christian ceremony. It needs to decide which functions should be continued as a part of the new Christian ceremony, which functions are contrary in spirit to the Christian faith, and which functions might be adjusted and altered to make them consistent with the new faith. It must also consider whether or not new functions should be added. It needs to evaluate, as well, the various techniques which could be used and choose among them.

The Christian leaders among the iKalahan people evaluated the six functions of the dedication ceremony as follows:

1. Unity of the community: the Christian faith encourages us to maintain a strong community unity and sense of cooperation. It is important that this function continue to be performed by the Christian ceremony.

2. Involvement of the individuals in the welfare of the householder: the Christian gospel also encourages involvement of every Christian with every other on the deepest levels of

---

3D. Rice "Developing an Indigenous Hymnody" PA, Vol. 18, No. 3 (May-June, 1971), pp. 97-113.

human experience. This function should also be performed by the Christian ceremony.

3. Unity of the living with the dead: in this function a conflict arises. The Christians no longer believe that their dead ancestors can return to be involved in the life of the living, but they do feel the sense of continuity between the believers of the past and the believers in the present which has been an important part of the Christian gospel from its beginning (see Hebrews 11). The unity which Christians now feel with their ancestors is through their involvement with Christ and he is the only means by which the living can have fellowship with the dead. Therefore, it is necessary to reorient this function of the house dedication toward strengthening our relationship to Christ and his involvement in our lives.

4. Social control: it is essential to the welfare of the entire community that the techniques of social control be maintained and strengthened. If these techniques are broken down, the entire community will suffer through the rebelliousness and delinquency of many members of the society. This function should be maintained if at all possible.

5. The good fortune of the family and house: this function of the dedication can also be reoriented to make it consistent with a Christian faith. Rather than assurance of good fortune because the family has fulfilled the obligations to the spirits, the Christian ceremony should express the dependence of the family upon God to provide for their needs and to guard their welfare in the full assurance that he will do so.

6. Maintaining the contractual relationship with the spirits: the Christian no longer retains his former contracts with the spirits since he has decided that only God the Creator is worthy of worship and that it is against God's will for Christians to maintain contractual relationship with usurpers of his prerogatives. It is, however, important for the Christians to nourish their contractual relationship with God and the dedication of a house is an excellent opportunity for this to be accomplished.

A Christian House Dedication Ceremony

Having determined the functions which a house dedication ceremony should accomplish, the next step was to examine the techniques which should be used in the dedication. In the pre-Christian ceremony the *boyag* (marking with blood) was employed. This same technique is employed throughout the entire Old Testament beginning with the passover (Exodus 12). It was an important part of the Old Testament practices, but it would have been very difficult for that particular ceremony to have been transferred over into the early Jewish or Greek church because the New Testament Christians were no longer a pastoral peple.

The iKalahan Christians felt that there was nothing in the *boyag* ceremony which was inherently contrary to the Christian faith. They felt also that there was nothing in the *boyag* which made it exclusively pagan. therefore, it was decided to continue to use the *boyag* technique in the dedication ceremony.

The ancient chant addressed to *ginoman* spirits could not be used, of course, but some of the poetic aspects might be borrowed. The involvement of the community could be expressed through singing portions of the ceremony. The contractual relationship of the family and of the community with God would be maintained by the wording of the various parts of the ceremony. It would be almost necessary for the householder to feed the people who came to the dedication since the houses are scattered around the mountains, and it is necessary for the people to eat at least one meal away from home in order to be in attendance. The householder expects to serve this meal, anyway; therefore, the killing of an animal would not be an unnecessary burden within that society.

The ceremony which was finally developed by the poets and leaders of the communities begins with the singing of various Christian *dayomti* and hymns from the regular hymnal. The passover hymn entitled "Boyag" is included, of course. The following *dayomti* will follow the others and form the opening of the dedication ceremony.

DAYOMTIN PALTIK NI ABONG	SONG OF HOUSE DEDICATION
(Dayomtin Kaphedan)	(tune: Kaphedan)

Diyoh ohdongimokami
Diyan naha-nopanmi
Abong akahaadmi
At da-tegimokami,

God look down on us
Here where we are gathered
In the house we have newly finished
And witness our actions,

Tep hiadada tawa
Tan anggan pantaw ida
Idyan boyaganmida
Ngeden Kristo toto-wa.

Because these windows
And the doors
We now mark them
Truly in the name of Christ.

After the people sing the "Dayomtin Paltik", the pastor uses the stick with the blood from the newly killed animal and marks the door of the house saying:

BOYAG NI PANTAW   **MARKING THE DOOR**

Boyagantakan pantaw
Ni ambalangan kohiyaw
At pangotyabka
Di ligat, baoh, nilado;
Nem kalwatika at
Panga-takad halo
Hi-mat, gaya tan amin ni pehed.

I mark you, door,
With red blood
And you should blink closed
To difficulties, curses and illnesses;
But open wide and
Yawn to industriousness,
Enthusiasm, joy and all things good.

After, the people sing the following brief response:

DAYOM NI BOYAG	RESPONSE TO THE MARKING
Diyoh mo ngo bindihyoni	God also bless
Pantaw ngon binoyganmi	The door we mark
Tep hi-gam i kamamohi	For you are all powerful
Kakayngan ni amami.	Our highest Father.

This same response is sung after every *boyag* with the exception of the name of the part of the house which is being marked. The pastor then moves to the window of the new house and marks it saying:

BOYAG NI TAWA	MARKING THE WINDOW
Boyagantakan tawa	I mark you, window,
Kalkabika at padapdaplahka	Close and become a cliff
Di tamoy ni pahol,	To the point of the spear,
Di bongat ni oleg;	To the mouth of the snake;
Nem katakwabika	But open,
At pantakangka	Open wide
Di halahal ni eggew	To the shining of the sun
Ni indawat Diyoh ni mawalawal.	God gave to illuminate.

When the congregation finishes singing the *dayom*, the pastor marks the floor saying:

BOYAG NI DAT-AL	MARKING OF THE FLOOR
Boyagantakan dat-al,	I mark you, floor,
Tapayam i obi, pagey	Hold in your hands the camote, rice
Tan amin ni onhegep	And all that enter
Gayoim iday onkebeb	Cradle those who lay down
At onpehed i ogipda.	And their sleep will be good.

When the congregation finishes the *dayom*, the pastor marks one of the posts, saying:

BOYAG NI TOKOD	MARKING OF THE POSTS
Boyagantakan tokod	I mark you, post
Kambilkayo	Be strong together
Panhinlalakamkayo,	Together hold things straight,
Panhintatadmakkayo	Together hold things up.
At kanegkayo	Get stronger and straighter
Di na-let ni dagemto.	Before the strong wind.

When the congregation has again finished the *dayom*, the pastor marks the fireplace in the kitchen saying:

BOYAG NI DAP-OLAN / MARKING OF HEARTH

BOYAG NI DAP-OLAN	MARKING OF HEARTH
Boyagantakan dap-olan	I mark you, hearth,
Kapanapoyi, kapanogani	Place of fire, place of cooking,
Kad-an idan gambang	Place of the cooking pot,
Kad-an idan balikan.	Place of the serving basket.
Hokokmoy bitil	Roof out the famine,
Ha-nibim iday gawat	Wall out the hungers,
Hay apoy matbel, mangalab	The fire flames, glows
No ha-not pakgeh ni ahokto	As its smoke goes through to go
Ni kaolaw di nangkayang;	above;
Ingahto ngoy kapgeh ni kaladag	So also the prayers
Idan makaabong niyan	Of the householders go through
At hankaatikan	And quickly
Himomang idan Diyoh.	God answers them.

At the end of the *Dayom ni Boyag ni Dap-olan* the householder and his family stand out and sing the following *dayomti* which is an expression of their gratitude and commitment.

DAYOMTIDAN MAKAABONG / SONG OF THE HOUSEHOLDER

DAYOMTIDAN MAKAABONG	SONG OF THE HOUSEHOLDER
Diyoh a wad Kabonyan,	God who is in Heaven,
Ya halamatmin ateng	Here is our great thanks
Mokami namendihyonan	For your blessing to us
Ni hankapamilyaan	Of one family.
Indawatmoy eletmi	You gave us strength
At hiyay inohalmi	And we used it
At hiyay an naha-dan,	That is how the house is now here,
Abongmin naboyagan.	Our marked house.
Amin pankolanganmi	All of our weaknesses
Hi-gam panindalanmi	You are the one to lead us
Tep hi-gam i kamamohi,	Because you are all powerful,
Mahmahmak a Diyohmi.	Our loving God.
At manlapo ngon haya	And now it begins
Ineggew mi ikanta	Everyday our song
Tan ikararagmida	And our prayers
Panaydayawanmika.	Our praise to you.

The pastor then expresses the blessing as follows:

Hi Diyoh paltakantokan, abong;	God blesses you, house;
Handi mabagibagiwanka	You will therefore experience mold
At ondaankan abong.	You will grow old, house.

Hi-gam ngon atep
Hokokmoy odan
Panapitan at ngon hayothot
Baoh, ligat, tan hakit
Onli-li-teng ida at i makaabong.

You also, roof,
Deflect the rain
To the place for criticisms, curses,
difficulties and sicknesses.
The householders will instead be
increasing in health.

The congregation sings one of the prayer responses to close the entire service.

The leaders seem to feel that through this ceremony they have maintained the beauty of the ancient pre-Christian ceremony and all of the functions which are consistent with the Christian faith.[4] The integrity of the Christian faith and of the iKalahan culture have both been maintained, enabling the Christian community to continue to grow into a deeper and more vibrant faith through the experiences of their daily lives.

[4] M. M. Thomas, "Indigenization and the Renaissance of Traditional Culture," *International Review of Missions* (April, 1963).

APPENDIX

The following is the complete transcript with translation of the ancient house dedication *baki* (recitation) performed in the iKalahan society. The text comes from Mr. Inway Oliano of Imugan, Santa Fe, Nueva Vizcaya, an outstanding mabaki.

BOYAG

Hay di ginoman di kabonyan,
Ginoman di da-olan,
Di ginoman di kabonyan tagon
   baboy, tagon manok;
Pagomgomanyo at daddan
   ni makabaley
Niya ni katloto, kalimato
Ay ho linawan manok,
   linawan baboy,
Ihmoyo at daddan di daka
   pakipakpakan..

Ihmoyod pangaboaboloandan
   pakibiyakianda

MARKING

Attention, dreamgiver of heaven,
Dreamgivers of underworld,
Dreamgivers of heaven who
   enliven pigs, enliven chickens,
You (p) should make this
   householder dream
On the third day, fifth day,
So that you will bring down the
   spirits of the chickens and pigs
and even the pigs
   to feed.

Bring down the agreed results of
   their commerce,

Pakibelinandan katloto,
kalimato,
Ay idaka mangaddo ida
kamangaddangyan.

Make them become on the third
day, fifth day,
Rich and
Prestigious.

Mandi pagomgomanyo at
daddan ni makabaley niya
Ni katloto, kalimato
Ay ho baliti mahibeg.
Di pahibegyoda at niti
daddan ni hanpangabongan
Pahibegyoy daka
pakipakpakan daka
pakimegmegmeg.

Now make this householder
dream
On the third day, fifth day
Of the fruitful balete tree.
You (p) should make them
fruitful, also, this
household, and make fruitful
Their pigs and
chickens.

Mandi pagomgomanyo at
daddan ni makabaley
Niya ay ho labeng attan,
ni ag maba-han,
Ay di ag ida at kono daddan
Hanpangabongan, ag mowango
Maba-han i daka pakapakpakan,
Daka pakamegmegmeg.

Now make this householder dream
of the deep pool
Which does not dry up
So that also therefore,
This household will not
And also the pigs and
Chickens will not
Dry up.

Mandi pagomgomanyo at
daddan ni makabaley niya
Ay ho baliti a kamana-da-lay
Di doma-lay ida at daddan
law ni hampangabongan
Makida-lay i binaknang,
kinadangyan.

Now cause this householder
To dream of the spreading
Balete tree.
And then will spread out
the Household to
Spread out their riches
and prestige.

Maihmo at daddan di daka
pakipakpakan daka
pakimegmegmeg.

Bring down, therefore, to them
their pigs to feed
and chickens to feed.

Maihmod panggahagahatanda,
Pakialbatanda, pakibelinanda
ni katloto, kalimato ay
I daka mangaddo, i daka
mangadangyan tep igyan
Ilada ho baboyda i
panhandida, i panboyagda.

Bring down their luck
They will take their turns
On the third day, fifth day
To become rich, wealthy,
Because they took their pig,
They used it as a sacrifice, they
Used its blood as a mark.

Mandi pagomgomanyo at daddan
Hampangabongan niya ay ho
Kitlabong dapdapnahan ni
   lanah ay kaakwa di omakwa
Ida at daddan law ni
   Hanpangabongan,
Makakiakwa ho binaknang
   Kinadangyan.

Now cause this household to
Dream of enduring the slides
   And standing up, again,
So this family will stand up,
   again,
Their riches and
   Prestige
Will stand up, again.

Mandi pagomgomanyo at daddan
Ni makaabong niya ay ho
   potpotod dapdapnahan ni
Alwangay kabalo-ngangaw,
Aydi bomalo-ngangaw ida at
   daddan law ni
   hanpangabongan.
Kamakaibalo-ngangaw i daka
Pakipakpakan daka
   Pakimegmegmeg i daka
Nangaddo i daka mangadangyan

Now cause this householder to
Dream of the river grass
   which though knocked down
   by the flood,
Branches out, again
In the same way, this house-
   hold will branch out, again
Their pigs will branch out
   And their chickens,
And their riches and
   Their prestige.

Mandi boyagantakan, abong,
Pangotyabkan, abong, aga
Papalpalokah ho abong.
Halikoboim at daddan i
Makaabong ni hi-gam.
Pakihalikobom i daka
Pakipakpakan daka
   pakimegmegmeg
Hiyay wada niti ingah niyan
Pakiboyaganmon bokol
   la abong.
Mandi boyagantakan, pantaw.

Now I mark you with blood, house,
Be strong, house
Don't be destroyed, house
Shelter this one who
   made you.
Shelter also their pigs
Their chickens, so that
There will, again, be another
   marking ceremony
In you like this someday, house.
Now I mark you with blood, door.

Kalkabika a pantaw.
Padapdaplahka a pantaw
Aga malwatan di lageb, di
Ginitang, dingga, inolo,
Nilado di kinapkapyan
nan-ayak, namantala,
   nandohi ay ho baoh ni too.
Aga malwatan di tadam ni
Atak, pahol, tadam ni bala,

You are a precipice.
You are closed.
Don't open to fire, backache,
Sickness, headache, illness
Or to any of the types of
   curses which are
   curses of men.
Don't open to the blade of the spear,
   knife or point of the bullet

Bongot ni gayaman,
Bongot ni oleg.
Aga malwatan di pihti,
   balandaw.
Aga malawatan di gilet,
   bigo.
Kalwatanmo at daddan ni
   katloto, kalimato ay ho
Binaknang, kinadangyan.
Kadagwatan ni kakakipakpakan
Kapakimegmegmeg ni
   makapantaw
Tep igyan ila ngo makaabong
Niya ho baboyda a impahandi
Impamboyagda ay nakiboyagka
   A pantaw.

Mouth of the centipede,
Mouth of the snake.
Don't open to pestilence or
   infection.
Don't open to trial by nail
   or to fines.
Open, however. on the third
   day, fifth day,
To riches, prestige.
Multiply the pigs and the chickens
   of the one that made you
Because there is the
   householder
Here who took his pig as a sacrifice
   and used its blood as a mark,
   and you, door, were marked.

John A. Rich

Religious Acculturation in the Philippines

The problem of how far the missionary should go in accommodating the pre-existing beliefs and religious practices of the people among whom he is working is a very sensitive one, and one may not always agree with a given solution, such as that proposed in this article. What is certainly true is that the missionary had better be aware of the kind of automatic accommodation the people will make spontaneously as they seek to understand the new in the light of the old. Whatever the dangers of conscious and deliberate accommodation, it is not certain that they are greater than those which result from ignoring the problem.

THIS paper will consider a case of religious acculturation in a Mansaka community in Davao, Mindanao. To set the situation in its proper context, the historical factors involved will be taken into account. This concerns the belief system of the Catholic Church and the conversion pattern used by the missionaries as well as the traditional animistic belief system of the Philippines.

Origin

The Catholic Church has its roots in the Jewish religion which grew

John A. Rich, MM, is a missionary priest and member of the Maryknoll Fathers, and the Director of the Institute of Language and Culture Research (Box 143, Davao City, Philippines). He holds the M.R.E. from Maryknoll Seminary and the M.A. in anthropology from the University of San Carlos, Philippines.

and developed in the Near East and whose traditions and customs are found in the Talmud and the Old Testament. Jesus Christ, a charismatic leader claiming to be the long awaited Messiah of the Jewish people, began a new sect. In the beginning the belief system hinged on Jewish theology but grew with beliefs about Jesus Christ and his teachings about God his Father, his relations to men, and the relations between men, which are found in the excerpts of the life and sayings of Jesus Christ written in the New Testament.

A system or pattern of conversion was initiated and developed by a man named Paul of Tarsus. Paul was instructed to bring the new sect to the non-Jew. In the Acts of the Apostles, there is an account of the missionary activities of this man who tried to carry out the command of

Jesus to convert "all nations." In his method, Paul did not force the Jewish ritual nor law on the non-Jew. All that was initially required of the non-Jewish converts was to believe in the Savior Jesus Christ and to "abstain from things sacrificed to idols and from blood and from what is strangled and from immorality" (Acts 15:29). In his conversion work he approached religious and/or educated people. In Athens he stood up on the Areopagus to declare to the Greeks, "I found also an altar with this inscription, 'to the unknown God;' what therefore you worship in ignorance, that I proclaim to you" (Acts 17:23).

Paul's policy was to be "all things to all men," that is, an accommodation and adaptation resulting in his being a Jew to the Jews and a Gentile to the Gentiles, as he relates in I Corinthians 9:22. He respected the religious capacities of others, realizing that God had given all men the ability for good, a law written in their hearts (Romans 2:15). His "good news" was expressed in terms already associated with religion in the culture he was dealing with. He respected the cultural values of the people he evangelized (Romans 2:17). Paul expected each community to be able to govern itself (Acts 14:22; 20:17-31), support itself (Gal. 6:6; I Tim. 5:17), and extend itself (I Thess. 1:8; Col. 1:7; 4:12). This meant a development of a stable and permanent local leadership which would be the light and life for limitless expansion (I Tim. 3:2-5).[1]

[1] Joseph Grassi, MM, *A World to Win* (Maryknoll, N.Y.: Maryknoll Publications, 1965), ch. XIII.

With the passage of time and the growth of the new sect, it disassociated from the Jewish religion both in belief system and in ritual. In formalization and institutionalization, rituals and rites were assimilated into the new Church. The belief system became more rigid and theological problems were debated and answered. The belief system was uniform but the rituals varied from place to place. In time, a complete religious system of beliefs emerged along with a hierarchical structure of roles within the Church. A model of conversion was generalized based on the work and writings of Paul of Tarsus.

A model of the Church structure as regards the belief system in a hierarchy began with a triune God; the Father was seen as Creator, Jesus Christ, the Son, was the God-man and Savior, the Holy Spirit was the life of the Church which was the channel of the power system, Sacraments and Blessings, between God and man. Later cults consisting of devotions to the angels, the lesser spirits, to the saints, the Blessed Virgin Mary being the highest, and to the souls of the dead, developed as auxiliary intercessors. The devils or evil spirits could influence men but their direct power was overcome by Jesus Christ. This can be seen in the schema in Fig. 1.

The rites and rituals are concerned with the power level of the Church, that is, the Sacraments and Blessings. Man's contact with the Supreme Being is through Jesus Christ in the sacrifice of the Mass and prayers in the name of Christ but the Church acts as the

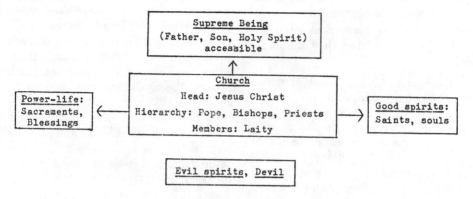

Figure 1

channel and dispenser of the gifts of God. The angels, saints and souls of the good dead are potential mediators and intercessors between God and man.

The model for the missionaries included the following norms:

1) all men were entitled to be God's children and heirs of eternal life;
2) accommodation to the rituals and rites of non-believers was to be fit into the Church's system where possible;
3) worship of other gods was not allowed.

Pre-Spanish Philippines

Before the coming of the Spanish in 1521 with the arrival of Ferdinand Magellan, the religion of the people in the Philippines was basically animistic. The experiences of life made it clear to the people that there existed other forces and powers outside themselves. They believed in personal spiritual forces which had no dependence on human persons or natural objects. They also believed in other forces alive and powerful, that have existence in human and inanimate objects. To these spirits and powers belong the control of the things of nature and the changes of life, and, in many instances, things concerned with the necessities of daily living. Man has to deal with these forces as they become an area which magic and religion enter.

From the writings and reports of the chroniclers, officials and missioners since the arrival of Magellan we have information about the people's animistic system. Among the Tagalogs and Visayans (the two largest dialect groups) there seemed to be some idea of a chief or supreme being who was called *Bathala* by the Tagalogs and *Laon* by the Visayans. He was considered inaccessible and thus the people troubled themselves little about his worship. They were more concerned about the lesser spirits or gods. They made a distinction between good and bad spirits; to the former is attributed all good fortune and to the latter all sorts of evil and death. Both are invoked; the former are served for the good that might be given, the latter that they might not do harm.

Objects and phenomena of nature are likewise venerated and feared; these are called *anitos*. There are *anitos* of cultivation, of the rain, of the sea, of the forest, of the life phases, of the heavens and under the world. Trees, especially the *balete*, are regarded as abodes of the spirits and become objects of veneration and worship. The most prominent of the venerated animals was the crocodile, probably because it was feared. The spirits could have human forms, acting like men, having the same passions. Prayers and sacrifices were offered in the places of veneration and to the *anitos*, since they possess extraordinary power. There was also veneration of the dead ancestors. Anyone who perished in battle or was killed by a crocodile became *diwata*, a guardian spirit. Thus ancestors could become household gods, who protected the family. Health, protection, and aid were sought from the spirits. *Anitos* were invoked in times of need, in sickness, war, or planting. Sacrifices and offerings were aimed at gaining their sympathy or appeasing their anger. Thus offerings could be given for personal intentions, for recovery of the sick, a successful trip, a bountiful harvest, victory in war, an easy childbirth, a happy marriage and the like.

The early Filipino had no clear conception of the final abode of men. When death came they hoped to be taken up among their ancestors and continue to live as they lived upon the earth. Different places were assigned according to the type of death of the person. Warriors and those eaten by crocodiles were received among the gods. Others had to be redeemed by sacrifices. Since the next life was like the present, slaves were sometimes killed and buried with their masters. People held the same rank and position as they had on earth.

At death the body was washed, covered with perfume, and dressed in the best attire. After a few days of mourning the body was buried in a wooden coffin made of one piece carved out of a trunk of a tree. Burial was under the house or in the field.

Moral laws came from their forefathers. The right to make laws was handed down to the chiefs. No mention is made of punishment which would be the result of a sinful life. The one thing to avoid was being poor. Obligations consisted in offerings and sacrifices in time of necessity or time of sickness. Things were called good or bad as they were prescribed or prohibited by law. Theft and insults were punishable, as were murder and adultery. Ordeals were not uncommon. These were undertaken to prove guilt or innocence of a person. Oaths were sworn to the sun and moon.

Evil was that which occasioned temporal loss or damage. It was wrong or bad to cut down certain trees for fear of the *anitos*. Murder was a great crim . Drunkenness was not considered a moral evil. Kidnapping and slavery were common. Usury was very common. Punishment was usually meted out by the person offended or his family who took the law into their hands. Judgment was based on who was poor and who was rich. The poor were obliged to remain in the underworld because no sacrifices or offerings could be made for them to the spirits.

It seemed that the people had no fixed times or places to offer sacrifices and prayers. Sacrifices for those lost at sea were offered on the water. There were no temples or public places of worship. Sacrifices and offerings made to the spirits of the dead were put on the graves of the dead. There were no common feast days. Drinking was part of the ceremonies. Anyone could offer sacrifices but there were certain men or more often women especially chosen for this. The women seemed to outnumber the men, who were mostly effeminate. They prayed and danced to the *anitos*.

Statues were used. These were the places where the spirits came when especially invoked or a sacrifice was offered in their honor. The people believed in magic, sorcery and witch-craft. Certain men and women were called to cure illnesses. A verdict of theirs that someone would die was accepted and the person lost all hope.

Figure 2 gives a schema of the pre-Spanish animistic religion.

Spanish Culture

With the conversion of the Spanish people to the Catholic Church there were traditional rites and rituals absorbed and/or accommodated to the people's likes, temperaments, culture and religious background. Elaborate ceremonies evolved along with stress on the intercessory powers of the saints for the needs of life and protection. The invocation of the saints included hopes for miracles. The souls of the dead needed prayers but could also intercede for men. Jesus Christ was seen in his role as suffering Savior and Conqueror of Sin. The Spanish Church tended to be rigid in form because of the contact and wars with the Moors. Then in the sixteenth century the European Church, in general, was going through the crises of the Reformation where many things in the Church were being questioned. This led to a strong

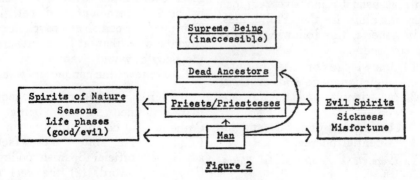

Figure 2

reaction against change and disrespect for Church authority. Anyone questioning the Church was considered a heretic and anything not Catholic was considered to be from the devil. This was also the time when Spain sent out her conquerors and missionaries.

The Spanish friars brought the Church to the Philippines along with the territorial conquest under the king of Spain in the sixteenth century. The Spanish model for conversion was influenced by the experiences encountered in Mexico and South America. The model and content of the belief system for the Philippines was clearly defined according to Church regulations and policy. The requirements for entering the Church according to the Jesuit missionaries were as follows:[2]

(1) knowing the prayers (Our Father, Hail Mary) and belief system (Creed)
(2) knowing the ten commandments (a religiously sanctioned code of social control)
(3) fulfilling the obligation of Sunday Mass and annual confession.

The model for conversion differed a little as used by the five religious orders working in the Philippines. But in general, the following points were stressed:

(1) knowledge of the people, their language and customs;
(2) a friendly and helpful approach;
(3) convincing of chiefs and influential people;

[2] De La Costa, *The Jesuits in the Philippines*, p. 168.

(4) non-Christian images and rites replaced by similar Christian ones;
(5) converts must become good Spanish subjects and cease to be what they formerly were.

On the social level there were factors that influenced the people to accept the religion of the Spanish. One of the values of the people concerns respect for authority and being socially acceptable to others. This is rated high in their social system and anyone in a position of authority is given great respect. It is important to give in to what others want especially if they are in an authority position. It is better to submit to another rather than make a scene or show a spirit of contention and strife. Blind obedience is expected to be given to those in authority, especially in the family. Since the Spanish came as conquerors and could offer the Filipinos many material and social advantages, this fitted into their system and they tried to get along with the Spanish. Smooth interpersonal relationships were something to be aimed at. Benefits were offered to the people in return for their cooperation with the Spanish in both government and religion. This put the Spanish at a psychological advantage so that, at least outwardly, the people would want to go along with whatever the conquerors wanted.

Lynch suggests four definite factors that combined to help bring the Catholic Church into the lives of the Filipinos. He states these factors as: (1) the official Spanish policy of Cross and Sword, (2) the zeal and adaptability of the early missionaries, (3) the traditional religion of the Filipinos was not highly structured and thus gave little opposition, (4) little resistance was shown to the Spanish because of their superior force of arms.[3]

In the application of the conversion model and the belief system of the Church there were certain conformities and discomformities. The obvious abuses concerned the use of military force or strong social pressure to convince the people. The sword was used to demand respect for the person and function of the missionary. Since the people lived mostly in small scattered groups, many had to be induced or forced to live in towns or centers so they could be instructed and guided in the new faith.

There was also a lack of friars to care for the comparatively great numbers of people. Local Spanish officials were used to instruct the people and give them protection in exchange for taxes. But unfortunately many of the officials were poorly instructed or could only stress non-essentials in their instructions. Others just neglected to teach at all. Thus many candidates for entering the Church were sometimes poorly taught. There was an abrupt break with the traditional past in many cases. Idols were burned and Spanish type clothing imposed. The answer to the problem was a Filipino clergy but the Spanish had a racial bias: these "natives" were considered to be unfit and inferior.

Some of the Spanish officials in an effort to help with the Christianization of the people said that baptism was also a cure for the ailments of the body.[4] The people were introduced to the power of the saints and the miracles they performed. Towns were put under the protection of a patron and the fiesta celebrated every year in his or her honor. Holy week was celebrated in order to commemorate the sufferings of Jesus Christ.

Philippine Christianity

All these factors led to the Philippine Christianity. In theory the model of the Catholic belief system was presented but certain levels and relationships were stressed by the Spanish missionaries and conquerors. The Filipinos themselves accepted the doctrines and chose certain levels that corresponded to their traditional practices and beliefs. There was an overstress on the power of the saints to the detriment of Jesus Christ. Miracles were considered to be the normal state of affairs through the invocations and novenas to the saints and souls. The lack of instruction also led to ritual formalism and pomp without the belief system that was supposed to be the basis for it. Jesus Christ was known in his role as the Suffering Savior. Baptism was the essential and in practice often the only sacrament of the seven. Many of the old religious rites and ceremonies of daily living and economic life continued along with the traditional priesthood. tFear and/or respect

---

[3] Frank Lynch, *Area Handbook on the Philippines* (New Haven, Conn.: Human Relations Area Files, Inc.), Vol. II, p. 477.

[4] Jean L. Phelan, *The Hispanization of the Philippines*, (Madison: University of Wisconsin Press, 1958), p. 55.

for the dead continued in the Church's doctrine on the souls in Purgatory where the dead await the cleansing from their sins before entering heaven. Catholicism underwent a process of acculturation and a normative situation evolved. This saw the official Catholicism as a doctrine, ritual, and administrative organization, proposed, approved, or maintained as normative by officially designated authority. Jocano calls this a type of "folk Catholicism" where the official doctrines and practices of the Church have been modified in order to suit local cultural practices.[5] In his study of a remote barrio in Panay he traces the progress of the people from Catholicism to Protestantism and then a reconversion back to Catholicism. He sees the pre-Christian beliefs and religion of the people acculturated into the form of Catholicism that penetrated the barrios. The Catholic saints were accommodated into the belief system of the good environmental spirits, the *engkantu*. The local religious functionaries continued with their rites and rituals to the local environmental spirits. There was no conflict with the parish priest since the barrio was far separated from the town and the priest seldom came except for the barrio fiesta.

There are other instances of the prevalence of animistic and magical practices throughout the Philippines. Frs. Arens, S.V.D. and Madigan, S.J. have given documented data in the area of agriculture. There are rites

connected with the land clearing, planting, and harvest which are a combination of Catholic and animistic formulas and actions. Fr. Frank Lynch, S.J. describes the same kind of "folk" or popular rites that accompany the various liturgical ceremonies and fiestas of the Catholic Church. These are mostly paraliturgical ceremonies including processions, devotions, practices and dances.

On the psychological level, Fr. Jaime Bulatac, S.J. would call such an acculturation "split-level" Christianity, which consists in holding a set of learned formulae in one's mind, which however do not become principles of actual behavior. He describes it as follows:

> At one level he professes allegiance to ideas, attitudes and ways of behaving which are mainly borrowed from the Christian West, at another level he holds convictions which are more properly his "own" ways of living and believing which were handed down from ancestors, which do not always find their way into an explicit philosophical system but nevertheless now and then flow into action.[6]

In order to show more clearly this acculturation Figure 3 gives a structural model of the traditional animism of the Philippines upon which the Catholic structure has been superimposed.

It would be safe to say that the majority of the Filipino people, especially in the rural areas, use a

---

[5] F. Landa Jocano, "Conversion and the Patterning of Christian Experience in Malitbog, Central Panay, Philippines," Eight Annual Baguio Religious Acculturation Conference, 1964.

[6] Jaime Bulatao, "Split-Level Christianity," Eight Annual Baguio Religious Acculturation Conference, 1964.

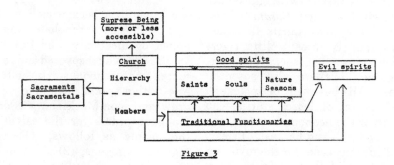

syncretized, acculturated or "folk Catholicism" system. Through reinterpretation and integration the Filipino has combined Roman Catholicism with his pre-Spanish system, especially in the areas that were found compatible with his world view. God, the sacraments and sacramentals, and some devotions to the saints are used through the Church's official ministers. Some sacramentals and saints are also used and invoked personally but with strong emphasis on material needs, daily life and problems. When the spirits are invoked or placated, either personally or through traditional ministers, a magicoreligious system is used. Dead ancestors or souls are placated through the Church with masses and personally through novenas. In the area of sickness, environmental spirits and agriculture there is also made use of personal offerings and services of the quack doctors and traditional priests. These functionaries use a system of magicoreligious rituals which comes partly from the animistic background of the Philippines and partly from the Catholic Church. The animistic system is built mainly on magic, which is manipulation, while the Church system should be a supplication.

The Non-Christian 20th Century

Garvan in his book, *Manobo of Mindanao*,[7] gives data on the pagan tribes who live in the areas of the province of Agusan and upper Davao. In general, these people have a belief in the supernatural which they consult for the ordinary activities of daily life and the phases of the life cycle. According to Garvan their religious system is based on fear of the deities, of evil spirits, of the dead, in other words, all that is unintelligible, unusual or somber. They do not possess a supreme being as understood by the Christians. They have a duality of good and evil spirits. One group of spirits is called *Umli* but these are far removed from the ordinary life of men. They are considered to be favorable but out of touch. A second group are the *Diawata* who dwell in the upper heavens and are beneficial

7Garvan, *The Manobos of Mindanao* (Washington, D.C. : U.S. Government Printing Office, 1931).

to men. Contrasted with these are the evil spirits called *Busau*. Then there is a group of spirits like men who dwell in the forests, cliffs, rivers and mountains. These can be favorable to men but are also potential enemies. All have to be placated. There is a set of lesser spirits who take care of the economic system, the planting, growth and harvest. Priests are used in many cases for the invoking and placating of these spirits. Men or women can become priests by inheritance or some sign of predilection. Trances, fits and unconsciousness are signs of divine intervention. The priests converse with the spirits and detect the evil spirits, the *Tagbusau*, who are the spirits of war. A man becomes a warrior priest when he has killed a certain number of people. This was a very active group in past history.

There were different kinds of religious paraphernalia including gongs, altars, offering stands, images and different rites connected with the life phases. Omens were consulted for certain events, other instances of natural phenomena were considered as ill or good omens. Divination was practiced by a complex set of figures from vines, suspension of a knife, eggs, and the liver, blood, gall and intestines of pigs and chickens. Dreams were also used for divination. Garvan also lists a few of the myths and beliefs including the immortality of the soul, its duality, and a hope of a future life.

Garvan records a religious movement that took place while he was among the Manobo. It lasted for two years, from 1908 to 1910. A certain Meskinan, who became sick with what was diagnosed as cholera, was abandoned by his family and left to die. In three days he recovered and returned to tell that a good spirit had cured him with a special medicine A cult grew and soon Meskinan was deified. He gave orders for the salvation of the people as follows: (1) kill all pigs and chickens, (2) plant no crops, (3) build a good building for religious purposes, (4) each village or group must have a priest who received his power from Meskinan, (5) hold services to pray to Meskinan, have sacred dances and forward offerings to Meskinan. In one month, he said, the world would come to an end. When nothing happened after one month, things were postponed for three months so more people could be saved. He instigated a deity of a new order called *Magbabaya*. Meskinan was the official dispenser of Magbabaya's spirit to all those who could afford to pay for it and thus to perform the ceremonies to save others. Garvan said it was a fraud in which the priests were getting the valuables offered in sacrifices. It was finally discovered because of the various inconsistencies and continual postponements.

Mansakas of Mindanao

The community now under consideration is a group of Mansaka Filipinos who are a dialect community of the Manobo or Mandaya. These people live in the Maragusan Valley of Mindanao which is a six-to seven-hour walk over a muddy, sandy and rocky river trail. They dwell in small groups usually under the authority of a head man or chief. Their staple food is a type of sweet potato called *camote*. Their traditional religion compares with that of the previous structures given above in Figure 2. In some cases the names of the spirits are different but their function or power is the same.

Christian Filipinos have moved into the Mansaka area for the past ten years. The Mansaka came to look up to their Visayan neighbors and began a process of acculturation in order to change their old way of life to conform more to the Visayan pattern and structure. The Mansaka have been trying to imitate the Christians in as many ways as possible. They still have their traditional crops of *camote* and vegetable called *gabi* but they also have been planting some upland rice and corn. They have entered the money economy of the Visayans by planting more rope fiber and working as carriers for the Visayan merchants of the barrio of Maragusan. A government school was opened and the enrolment was half Visayan and half Mansaka. Thus a basic education and closer Christian contacts were had by the Mansaka children. New needs and social contacts have been acquired in this acculturation.

The men have learned the Visayan language from contact with the Christians. The women can understand but cannot speak it since their contacts with outsiders are fewer. Their houses are beginning to look more like the Visayan homes. There are two or three rooms instead of the traditional one room. Tin cups and plates have replaced the old clay pots and dishes.

The women still have their old traditional clothes but the men have changed to Christian type clothing.

The Mansakas became ashamed of their old religious ways and beliefs. The Catholic Visayans keep encouraging them to become baptized. Thus pressure was put on the Mansakas to become completely like the Visayans and the biggest and final step was religious. Many had already removed the wooden idols from their homes. But two strong practices persisted, the sacrifice and idols for the planting season and the idols and sacrifice used for curing serious sickness. The harvest celebrations were integrated into the Visayan fiesta. Finally the Mansakas formally requested baptism through a Visayan go-between and a priest went out to visit them.

The priest went out with the idea of accommodation and adaptation that has been in the foreground of the thinking of recent popes. Pius XII in his *Evangelio Praecones* stated:

The Church from her very beginning down to our own day has followed this policy. When the gospel is accepted by diverse races, it does not crush or repress anything good and honorable and beautiful which they have achieved by their native genius and natural endowments.

Again in a talk on December 6, 1953:

The right to existence, the right to the respect from others, the right to one's own good name, the right to one's own culture and national character...(these) are exigencies of the law of nations dictated by nature itself.

And finally Pope John XXIII states in his *Princeps Pastorum:*

The Church...does not identify herself with any particular culture not even with the accidental culture to which her history is so closely bound.

Fortunately the priest was able to read Garvan's book on the Manobos of Mindanao. From this a general knowledge of the people's way of life and beliefs was gained. In order to update his knowledge the priest had a questionnaire taken on the present state of the Mansakas. One questionnaire was given to a Mansaka from another area who was educated under the Americans and could speak English. Another was given to a catechist who worked among Mansakas peoples. A final one was given to the go-between who requested the priest to come out.

A basic pattern for the instruction of the Mansakas was made up and the go-between became the religious teacher to bring the "good news" to the Mansakas. The points stressed were:

(1) The whole community had to undergo instructions;

(2) There were fifty lessons that covered a period of about six months in order to cover the essentials of Christianity;

(3) Christianity was a perfection of their traditional religion;

(4) Evil spirits would no longer have to be feared since Jesus Christ had conquered all;

(5) Sickness was primarily rooted in poor sanitation and the weakness of the human organism;

(6) Jesus Christ and the sacraments were stressed in their proper roles in contradistinction to the role of the saints and the souls of the dead;

(7) Traditional rites would be replaced or used as part of Catholic ones where possible;

(8) The *baylans* or priests (priestesses in this case) would continue to use their chants but with new prayers and Bible stories.

These points were set up in order to avoid the syncretism of the Catholic beliefs and rites into the traditional religion. The priest had to visit them now and then to make sure the instructions were being followed. The children in the government school were also getting religious instructions according to the government regulations on released time. As was expected, some learned fast while others were slower. Questions were asked during each visit in order to test their progress.

The priest also provided medicines for the common local ailments such as dysentery, headaches, goiter and skin infections. He also purchased colored beads for the women at reasonable prices. The Commission on Cultural Minorities was contacted in order to ask for help and redress on national and local levels.

Finally as time for baptism drew near those with idols still in their homes were asked to turn them in. Each family was then given a crucifix to act as the guardian of the home. The idols they used in their fields before planting also had to be replaced. Each family had to make a wooden cross which was solemnly blessed. These were to be used in place of the former fields idols to invoke God's blessing on the crops. After baptism each person was given a medal, a sign of their commitment to Christ in the Catholic Church.

There seemed to be no change of their social or kinship structure because of the religious change. Parents were encouraged to let their children attend school in order to put off too early marriages of the young girls. Socially the Mansakas felt part of the Visayan community and were mostly accepted as such. The women changed their traditional dress to Visayan or Western style. But they were told that a change of belief or entering the community of the children of God was spiritual and dress as such had nothing to do with it. Many were soon back in their traditional dress.

The Mansakas were requested to build their own chapel for worship. Traditionally the Mansakas had offered sacrifice, usually a chicken, to the spirits over a small table held up by four bamboo poles. The front and back sides of the table top were specially designed wood carving. The new altar in the chapel would be tablelike and set on four poles with carved designs in the front and back. In their homes, the Mansakas used a small four-sided container suspended from the ceiling under which they offered prayers of petition. This became the design of the *baldachin*

which would be placed over the altar.

The people were encouraged to go to the chapel on Sundays just to offer a few prayers together in union with all the Christians all over the world who take time out on Sunday to give honor to Our Father through Jesus Christ.

Conclusion

The process of religious acculturation of this Mansaka community was the climax of an ongoing process of acculturation of the people on many other levels. Old traditions were being lost and replaced through the contact with Visayan Christians. There were no abrupt changes since the community was seven hours away from strong outside influences and the process was over a period of years as the Visayans moved into the area.

Garvan had said that five things were accountable for the success of the Spanish missionaries in the Philippines. These consisted of: (1) the person of the missioner, his condescension and understanding of the ways and beliefs of the people, (2) threats, (3) gifts and awards, (4) the missioner acting as mediator between the government and the non-Christians, and (5) Catholic ceremonial.[8] In the present situation of the Mansaka acculturation, these factors were indeed employed to some extent with the exception of number 2 (threats). But most of the credit lies with the overall acculturation process going on where a new and better way of life was presented to them in the person of

[8]*Ibid*, p. 250.

the Visayans and Catholic Christianity was part of the packet.

An interesting topic for future investigation would be to see the belief system and ritual which the Mansakas finally adopt. Here we have three variables, their traditional animistic religion, the Visayan "Folk Catholicism" and the ideal Catholic belief presented by the priest. Decisions are going to be made by the people and only time will tell which system or what parts of the different systems emerges as predominant and the motivations which influenced their choices.

John C. Messenger, Jr.

The Christian Concept
of Forgiveness
and Anang Morality

This paper examines the major causes underlying the spread of what African elders and Westerners alike regard as immoral behavior among Anang youth in Southeastern Nigeria. The Anang have experienced profound cultural change since World War I, at which time they were finally pacified by the British and the first trading post and Christian mission were established among them. When this change is assessed, it is apparent that most of the forces contributing to immorality among young people in other African societies are also operative in Anang society, namely the breakdown of traditional political, religious, and kinship forms and the adoption of Western values, especially those in the economic realm.[1] This paper treats these common causal factors, but emphasizes one in particular which is important in producing immorality among Anang youth: their acceptance of the Christian concept of forgiveness. Probably this new doctrine is affecting the behavior of other African peoples in a similar manner, but, if so, it has not received adequate attention in acculturation studies.

CERTAIN beliefs embodied in the indigenous Anang religion partially explain why the adoption of a new conception of divine intervention in human affairs has so strongly influenced the conduct of

John C. Messenger, Jr., is Assistant Professor in the Departments of Social Science and Sociology and Anthropology of Michigan State University. He has the Ph.D. in Anthropology from Northwestern University, and in addition to the field work represented in this article he has done general ethnographic research among the Arran Islanders of Western Ireland. He is author of several previous publications on the Anang. The present paper was delivered before the American Anthropological Association in 1958, and is based on research conducted in Nigeria during 1952.

youth. The Anang are monotheistic, the central theme of their religion being the worship of a sky deity, named *abassi*, who rules the universe and mankind. He is assisted by numerous spirits residing on earth in shrines, and by souls of the dead awaiting reincarnation in the underworld. Although he is considered both omniscient and omnipresent, he lacks ultimate omnipotence, for ghosts, witches, and the

[1] For a general account of culture change in Anang society, I refer you to my *Anang Acculturation: A Study of Shifting Cultural Focus*, Ann Arbor, University Microfilms, Pub. No. 23525, 1957, pp. 196-290; also to my "Religious Acculturation Among the Anang-Ibibio," in *Continuity and Change in African Cultures*, ed. by W. Bascom and M. Herskovits, Chicago, University of Chicago Press, 1959.

spirit of evil magic possess powers over which he sometimes exerts no control. The Anang do not know where these malevolent powers originate, so they must be combatted with preventive magic.

Fate as ordained by *abassi* directs the course of each human life, but rather than remaining immutable following assignment at conception, it may be modified within narrow limits through the exercise of free will by the individual. A divinely enunciated moral code embracing every aspect of human behavior forms the basis for evaluating acts transcending fate. Should these acts conform to his code, the deity will alter a person's fate so that future misfortunes are canceled. On the contrary, should the freely perpetrated deeds of an individual transgress against this code, *abassi* will compound predestined misfortunes.

Supernatural retribution takes many forms, from the extreme of causing an object of little value to be misplaced to that of transforming a soul into a ghost at death. The severity of the sanction depends upon the nature of the misdeed and the predilection of the deity. The most favored sanctions, however, are to have a person be found guilty of a crime in court and be subjected to judicial punishment, or to have the oath spirit attack one who has sworn an oath falsely or who has committed one of several other specific crimes.

The recognition of a divine moral code and the ability of *abassi* to punish any divergence from its tenets constitute the most powerful mechanisms of social control. The Anang individual is far more sensitive to external controls, most of which are ultimately religious, than he is to internal ones, and there is little evidence of a well-formed conscience that

evokes feelings of guilt for a socially disapproved act.[2]

Anang Response to Christianity

The foregoing features of Anang religion provide a framework for appraising the impact of Christianity and other aspects of Western culture. The first mission in the region was founded in 1919 by the Wesleyan Methodists. Seven other Christian bodies, two of them African in origin, were installed between 1919 and 1948,[3] and today all maintain churches, some schools, and several hospitals. Most of the denominations have had marked success in gaining converts during recent years, and slightly more than half the people now profess the Christian faith.

The Anang have reacted to religious acculturation differentially according to sex and age groups. Women as a whole have embraced Christianity,[4] whereas

[2] The relationship between internal and external controls in personality and its consequences is discussed in R. Benedict, *The Chrysanthemum and the Sword*, Boston, Houghton Mifflin Co., 1946, pp. 222-227; F. Hsu, "Suppression vs. Repression," *Psychiatry*, Vol. 12, 1949, pp. 223-242; D. Riesman, *The Lonely Crowd*, New Haven, Yale University Press, 1950, pp. 10-31. The Anang culture is a "shame culture" rather than a "guilt culture," "suppression" rather than "repression" is the basic mechanism of socialization, and the Anang personality is predominately "tradition-directed" rather than "inner-directed" or "other-directed."

[3] These are the Kwa Ibo (English interdenominational) established in 1920, the Roman Catholic (Holy Ghost Order) in 1925, the Lutheran (Missouri Synod) in 1936, the African Apostolic (nativist) in 1936, the Christ Army (nativist) in 1940, the Assemblies of God in 1946, and the Seventh Day Adventist in 1948.

[4] The major reason for their acceptance is their belief that the Christian God affords them greater protection in child bearing than does

only boys and young men among the males have done so. Old men are either antagonistic or indifferent toward the encroachment of Christianity and, almost without exception, are attempting to preserve traditional beliefs. Incapable of arresting emergent change, since they no longer possess the political and kinship authority they once did, the old men spend much of their time together extolling the past and criticizing Western innovations. In particular, they remonstrate against the immorality displayed by youth, holding that the assorted political, economic, and social ills which have befallen the Anang during the past three decades have been perpetrated by *abassi,* who is angry with young people for disobeying his moral mandates.

Middle-aged men, on the other hand, have been much more susceptible to conversion, but among those declaring themselves Christian, few are orthodox in their beliefs, according to mission reports.[5] They *abassi.* One of the principal prestige symbols for both men and women is offspring, and prior to the introduction of Western medicine the infant mortality rate was over forty per cent. Women soon learned that care by European-trained midwives and delivery in mission or government hospitals ensured increased success in child bearing. European medical specialists are believed to gain their abilities through manipulation of supernatural power emanating from the Christian God, just as indigenous workers of magic and diviners are thought to control power bestowed by *abassi.* The reduction of infant mortality following the use of Western medical techniques convinced women that God is superior to the traditional deity.

5 Lutheran statistics indicate that although fifty per cent of the Anang and neighboring Ibibio have been converted to Christianity, only an estimated ten per cent are "true believers." See H. Nau, *We Move Into Africa,* St. Louis, Concordia Publishing House, 1945, p. 161. It is my opinion that the author has considerably overestimated the latter percentage.

tend to reinterpret and syncretize Anang and Christian dogmas while preserving many traditional forms of worship. The two nativist denominations are supported almost entirely by men in this age category and by women.

The strongest supporters of Christianity among the Anang are those who were born after religious proselytizing commenced. Many were reared as Christians, and most claim to be Christians whether or not they are members of a denomination. They tend to join missionary churches, mainly because only these can finance well-equipped schools and hospitals. Formal education is highly prized, since it is a prerequisite to positions that bring high income and prestige, such as medicine, law, business, teaching, and the civil service. Young people express admiration for most things European, and the person who adopts Western customs, including religious ones, gains recognition as a result. The nativist denominations are denigrated in the urban centers, as they are financially incapable of sponsoring schools and hospitals, and are severely criticized by missionaries for their pseudoChristian doctrines. Belonging to either of the African churches means "losing face" in the estimation of Westernized Anang youth.

Ignorance of Anang Religion

Young people tend to have only a vague understanding of the indigenous religion. Systematic probing of the religious knowledge of numerous children and young adults revealed that they were either ignorant of or misunderstood such basic Anang beliefs as the role of fate in guiding human affairs, the nature of the nether world, and the functions of numerous shrines and sacred groves. They betrayed an even greater ignorance of sacred rituals. Only in the areas of magic, witchcraft, and oath administration did they reveal extensive knowledge of traditional customs.

One of the important reasons for this ignorance is that teachers in both government and mission schools inculcate Christian doctrines and denounce Anang religion. In government institutions this is done by instructors who, for the most part, have received their education in mission schools. Nigerian law limits formal religious instruction to fifteen minutes each day, but since many of these institutions offer room and board facilities, there is ample time outside the classroom for students to be proselytized. Those children who do not attend schools and express an interest in the indigenous religion are held up to ridicule by friends who are students.

Another reason for the vagueness of religious belief among youth is that many of them leave home at an early age to pursue occupations in urban communities, and thus never receive adequate religious instruction from their parents and other kin. Even when living at home, children spend much of their time away from adults as members of organized gangs, and the adults themselves are frequently absent while engaged in farming, trading, and political activities.

In addition, it has been noted that women have accepted Christianity to a greater degree than their husbands. Most of them object to having their children taught what they consider false beliefs. Family quarrels often center about whether or not younger members should be allowed to attend traditional religious ceremonies, join secret associations having religious functions, or become members of a Christian church.

Finally, with the loss of authority as a result of acculturation, older men are no longer in a position to command the obedience and respect of youth, and thus are unable to impart religious knowledge to them effectively. Indigenous governmental and judicial forms have been abolished in large measure by the British, and new leaders have arisen who serve as models for young people, men who are educated, financially successful, and Christian.

Spread of Immorality

Theft, bribery, fraud, perjury, adultery, murder, and many other infractions of Anang and Western morality are committed on a broad scale by Anang youth, largely in pursuit of wealth and prestige. The spread of immorality is attested by the rapid increase during recent years in offenses tried by Native and Magistrates' Courts and by traditional judicial bodies which, although illegal, continue to meet in a few villages. Prison capacities are overtaxed as well, with youth making up the bulk of the prison population. Village life is disrupted because of the deep schisms between young people and their elders. The latter bitterly resent the adoption of Western customs by the former and are, as indicated above, especially critical of deviations from Anang morality. They place the primary blame for this condition on Christianity, in particular on the concept of God and salvation embodied in Christian dogma.

Protestantism, by preaching an "intellectual" gospel emphasizing salvation through faith, and Roman Catholicism, by introducing the sacrament of confession, have fostered, however unintentionally, the widespread belief among young people that the Christian God forgives all sins. The youth tend to accept Christian morality as expounded by the missionaries, largely because of its similarity to Anang morality, and they understand that it is divinely sanctioned, yet the opinion is widely held that its tenets may be disregarded without fear of spiritual punishment if belief is maintained or if sins are confessed and absolved.

Sermons by Protestant ministers stress the extreme sinfulness of man and the possibility of salvation through faith, seldom urging the practice of good works as a principal means of expressing faith. Lutheran and Methodist missionaries, as far as could be determined, are unaware of the powerful impact of this doctrine on young people, although several Catholic priests who were interviewed recognize, to some extent, what is transpiring and admitted stressing punishment in hell for sinful acts when instructing youth.

Many young persons wear Christian crosses because they believe that this will assure God's forgiveness for an immoral deed, as well as protect them against the machinations of evil spiritual forces. They also believe that the Holy Spirit is especially capable of obtaining the forgiveness of God, and they direct prayers and sacrifices to this being. A favorite song among the youth reveals the attitude of this age group when criticized for misdeeds. It has the following words: "I don't care. I will tell the Holy Spirit. He will tell my Father. All will be well."

Few converted Anang comprehend the nature of the Trinity. Most believe that three distinct entities exist: God, the creator of the universe; Jesus, his human son, who was sent by him to spread the Christian doctrine to the peoples of the world; and the Holy Spirit, whose major tasks are to heal the sick and injured, to foretell future events and to gain from God forgiveness for sins. Seldom were Anang able to explain the significance of Jesus' dying on the cross to atone for the sins of mankind, although most realized that belief in this act must be maintained to ensure salvation. It is not an exaggeration to say that worship of the Holy Spirit dominates the belief system of young Christians, even though God is known to possess ultimate power.

The nativist denominations, whose chief support comes from women, middle-aged men, and youth from rural villages, owe their considerable success to the emphasis they place on the Holy Spirit and salvation through faith and confession. "Evangelists" assigned to each nativist prayer house are able to become possessed by the Holy Spirit and heal and prognosticate, much in the manner of traditional workers of magic and diviners. When foretelling the future, the evangelist speaks in a jargon purported to be the voice of God interjected into his mouth by the Holy Spirit, and only the specialist can translate what he has uttered once the state of possession is terminated. These denominations are known as "spiritualist" ones, and their dogmas are based upon various Biblical verses stressing the nature of the Holy Spirit, healing, prophesying, and speaking in diverse tongues.[6] Christ Army "catechists" instruct their communicants that abassi will forgive all sins so long as belief is held in Christ as Savior and these sins are confessed in a ceremony resembling that of the Catholic Church. Thus this body has incorporated into its doctrine elements of both Protestant and Catholic dogma.

[6] For example, the Christ Army Church bases its legitimacy on the following Biblical excerpts: Joel 2: 28-32, Matthew 10: 1-14, Mark 16: 17, Luke 9: 1-6, Acts, 2: 17, and I Corinthians 12: 4-11.

Whereas *abassi* is conceived in the indigenous religion as one who is largely unforgiving and will punish all misde-meanors, the Christian God is regarded as a forgiving deity. We saw that belief in a divine moral code and the ability of *abassi* to punish any deviations from its strictures are the most potent social control devices in Anang society. The acceptance by youth of the concept of a forgiving deity has greatly reduced the efficacy of supernatural sanctions and has actually fostered immorality. Lacking well-developed internal controls and freed from important external restraints, the Christian can deviate from prescribed ways of behaving with impunity.[7]

Effect of Legal Sanctions

The major regulator of conduct now is the threat of legal punishment for civil and criminal offenses. However, the British-introduced judiciary is viewed with contempt, and the Native Courts, in which most cases are tried, are notoriously corrupt. As a result of missionary influ-ence, oath swearing before indigenous practitioners was discontinued in Native Courts in 1947 and swearing on the Bible substituted. Since young people be-lieve that the Christian God will forgive perjury, and they are no longer forced

[7] It would appear that the nature of the per-sonality controls of a people being converted to Christianity is an important factor explain-ing the success or failure of the proselyting effort. Roman Catholic missionaries are often more successful than their Protestant counter-parts in converting Nigerians because of their willingness to employ strong external religious sanctions, which often involves modifications of Catholic dogma and rituals. This willingness to reinterpret Catholic and traditional religious forms, supplemented by a greater emphasis on ceremonialism and the use of icons, appeals to the Nigerians.

to take the dreaded oath spirit into their bodies, there is no compulsion for them to speak truthfully. This eventuality has slowed judicial procedure, placed undue emphasis on circumstantial evidence, and caused many unfair verdicts. Persons wronged in court usually resort to sorcery in order to obtain redress, and as a result the practice of "black magic" has increased rapidly during the past few years.

Even though accepting Christian doc-trines on a broad scale, most youth maintain indigenous beliefs concerning the power of the evil magic and oath spirits, witches, and ghosts. Despite attempts by most missionaries to discount the reality of these supernatural entities, traditional attitudes persist, or else these beings are collectively regarded as manifestations of the Devil, a view some missionaries sup-port. Young people are fearful of the attacks of sorcerers, ghosts, and witches, and they employ preventive magic as frequently as do their elders to defend themselves. The only success traditional leaders have had in exerting any measure of authority over many recalcitrant youths is by resorting to the use of the oath spirit, who, in addition to castigating those who have sworn oaths falsely, is also able to punish other forms of im-moral conduct.

It is important to note that immorality is more prevalent among young men than among young women. The latter are prone to be less honest in their trading affairs than in the past, and husbands generally claim that their young wives are more quarrelsome and adulterous than their counterparts thirty years ago. The Anang consider women to be more strongly motivated sexually than men, and the problem of adultery on the part of wives, especially those living in large polygynous households, was regarded as a rather serious one before the advent of the British. Many women when interviewed admitted that Anang wives are more adulterous today, but asserted that the Christian God forgives this offense. Most wives refuse to swear an oath when first married that they will not commit adultery, as was customary before the introduction of Christianity.

In conclusion, let it once again be pointed out that acceptance by youth of the Christian doctrine of a forgiving deity is only one among a number of major causes of immorality. The importance of non-religious forces, referred to only briefly and tangentially above, cannot be overemphasized in accounting for this phenomenon, so it is hoped that the accusation of "religious determinism" will not be directed against the paper.

Benjamin N. Colby

Social Relations and Directed Culture Change among the Zinacantan

Why did Zinacantan Indians of Chiapas, Mexico, resist efforts to teach girls to speak Spanish and to learn to read? Since, after a very few years of education, an Indian leaves school and books forever, leaving very little place in adult life for a literate person, what kind of books could fill this vacuum? These and similar problems were the concern of part of the research reflected in this paper, and they are discussed from the standpoint of the social relations which exist both within Zinacantan society, and without, as it faces the LADINO world. Something of the nature of culture change and the communication of social relations between cultures provides the framework for the discussion of these problems in directed culture change.

THE communication of social relations between cultures is the medium of culture change. One culture cannot affect another unless the social relations of its members extend to members of the other. Social relations exist when individuals reciprocally orient their behavior to each other, and some kind of communication, real or imagined, occurs between them.[1] As Max Weber once pointed out, a collision between two cyclists is not a social relation but the discussion which follows is.

Individual Needs and Social Relations

The intensity and extent of social relations are necessary data for the social scientist. More necessary, though, is the categorization of social relations. In order to lead a satisfactory life, the individual needs (1) to fulfill his subsistence needs (food, shelter, etc.), (2) a certain amount of attention or status from others, and (3) affection from others.[2] While sub-

---

[1] The perception and interpretation of a shrug of the shoulder or an unconscious frown are included with conversation as real communication, whether intended or unintended. An imagined communication would be the false perception of communication — the perception and interpretation of a sign which was not, in reality, a sign.

[2] Higher level needs for religion, philosophy, and so on are not included in this analysis. They interrelate with environment, subsistence, status, and affection in so many ways that we would lose ourselves in the attempt to bring them into culture change analysis in its present primitive stage. For a discussion of attention and affection as categories of basic

572

sistence needs, in principle, can be fulfilled without having to enter into social relations, needs of attention and affection require the presence of other people, being, by definition, social needs. Although these latter two social needs are at a higher and more abstract level than subsistence needs, they are no less necessary to the individual.

Applying this categorization to social relations in Chiapas, Mexico, we may say that among the Zinacantan Indians a man may have many relationships with *ladinos* (non-Indian Mexicans, usually of white or mixed Indian and white origins) to fulfill his subsistence needs. He buys and sells in the shops and markets of *ladino* towns and he may even do short periods of wage work for *ladinos*. However, such activities of subsistence exchange do not seem to affect his cultural identity as much as the exchange of relations with *ladinos* on the higher level of attention and affection.

The traditional Zinacantan Indian is married to a Zinacantan woman, has a family in a scattered hamlet or in Zinacantan center, engages in *cargo* activities (special year-long religious offices to care for and honor the saint images in church), and wears Indians clothes. Such a man fulfills the majority of his status and affection needs via other Zinacantan Indians.

If, on the other hand, an Indian begins to wear *ladino* clothes he probably wants *ladino* approval and attention or wants to avoid their discrimination against him. In either the positive or negative

Benjamin N. Colby, a research associate of the Department of Social Relations, Harvard University, spent a year in Chiapas, Mexico, as part of the Harvard Culture Change Project supported by the National Institute of Mental Health. Its purpose was to study the role of bilingualism and education in culture change among the Indians.

aspect of the case, attention from *ladinos* is important to him.

An Indian who avoids his *cargo* responsibilities is rejecting his culture as a source of status. This may mean that he either does not feel a need for status and attention from any social source and hence tends to be a marginal man (in this respect) to both cultures, or he carries out activities in *ladino* society which he believes will bring him status from *ladinos*. The more an Indian seeks *ladinos* instead of other Indians to satisfy his needs of attention and affection, the more he himself will move in the direction of *ladino* culture. In most cases, the Indian approaches *ladino* culture via his needs for attention or status. Only after marriage to a *ladino* does the Indian fulfill his or her major need of affection via *ladino* culture. Once this has occurred, the sequence of acculturation is close to completion, for all three needs (subsistence, attention, and affection) are being fulfilled within the new culture. It only remains for the acculturated Indian to adopt the values, world view, and religion of *ladino* society. Like language, it is difficult to effect such a change without an "accent" or without "value interference," unless the change were begun before puberty. For this reason, it is often necessary for a generation to pass before complete ladinoization has come about, unless the person has spent some

---

human social needs see Schultz, William C., Firo, *A Three-dimensional Theory of Interpersonal Behavior* (New York: Rinehart & Co., 1958).

period of time living with *ladinos* before his teens.[3]

We are less interested, for the moment, in these later changes, than we are in the initial change — or rather at the point at which the Indian rejects his own culture as a source of attention or affection and seeks fulfillment of these needs in *ladino* culture.

The Newly Acculturated Indian

Most Indians changing to *ladinos* move into *ladino* society at the very bottom of the social ladder and hence receive less attention and status than anyone else in *ladino* society. At the same time, by changing into a *ladino,* he has lost the status and attention of his Indian companions. The result is a reduction in status and attention. Unless this is balanced by an increase in the fulfillment of affection or by a very significant increase in his economic or subsistence position, the net result will be loss rather than gain.

The more intuitive and perceptive Indians in Zinacantan probably realize that a loss would result from such a change. When one Zinacanteco was asked if he would like to be a policeman in San Cristóbal, the local *ladino* center, he just laughed and indicated such a job to be beneath his dignity. This particular Indian, incidentally, hardly ever wore *ladino* clothes, yet he had a much clearer understanding of the differences between the *ladino* world and the Zinacantan world than, for instance, many of his companions who frequently wore *ladino*

clothes and tried to identify themselves with *ladinos* when in *ladino* areas.

In sum, an Indian will try to change the objects of his attention and affection needs from Indians to *ladinos* only if he believes that the over-all positive reward for him will be greater than the rewards which he previously received.[4]

Changes in Values

When an Indian moves into the *ladino* orbit, one of the first and most profound changes happens after his discovery that competitive action no longer has a greater negative sanction than it does have a positive one. In Zinacantan society, competition was held down by various leveling forces, the most drastic of which were witchcraft and envy.[5] The Indian newcomer to a *ladino* village finds, on the other hand, that competition is usually rewarded positively instead of negatively.

A more subtle and difficult change for the acculturated Indian to perceive and to adapt to is the shift in the type of authority or power-sanction in his social surroundings. Such an Indian must shift from what Max Weber has called a traditional type of authority structure to a slightly charismatic one. According to Weber, traditional power is based upon a belief in the sanctity of tradition and in the necessity to obey those of the culture that rule by such traditions, while

---

[3] This depends entirely on the local feelings of cultural prejudice. In some areas of Guatemala an almost caste-like situation exists and it takes many generations of living as a *ladino* before a man of Indian origin may be accepted as one.

[4] Many changes occur when young Chamula girls are brought into *ladino* households as servants, due to the economic hardships of their parents. Such girls are thus initially thrust into the *ladino* environment because of subsistence needs. However, the subsequent acculturation that takes place is still due to these higher level needs of attention and affection.

[5] Although witchcraft and envy are also feared in lower-class *ladino* society, it figures more prominently among Zinacantan Indians and competition is vigorously suppressed.

ZINACANTAN AND SAN CRISTOBAL ORIENTATIONS

Zinacantan   *San Cristóbal*

Family Relations

Zinacantan	San Cristóbal
1. Sharp division of labor.	1. Sharp division of labor.
2. Women sexually aggressive.	2. Women sexually passive.
3. Family unity frequently disrupted and aggression often physical.	3. Family unity not frequently disrupted and aggression mostly verbal.
4. Both men and women condemned for adultery.	4. Women condemned, men condoned for adultery.
5. Competition within the nuclear family is not blocked by cultural controls as much as in extra-familial relations and is usually intense.	5. Close ties between male-female siblings, mother-son and father-daughter along with concern for family honor inhibits intense intra-familial competition.
6. Castration complex exists in dream interpretations and in folklore.	6. Ascension complex (the desire to be placed above others, to receive admiration, particularly the admiration of mother for son) rather than castration complex predominant.

Extra-familial Relations

Zinacantan	San Cristóbal
1. Ambivalence, uncertainty and anxiety about relations with others.	1. Relatively little anxiety about social relations.
2. Rigid and intricate pattern of etiquette functions to reduce anxiety about social relations.	2. Etiquette not rigid or complicated and functions more to distinguish social class rather than reduce anxiety about social interaction.
3. Fear of· witchcraft and of envy from others.	3. Fear of witchcraft or envy exists in lower class but not to same extent as among Indians.
4. Open competition avoided.	4. Open competition encouraged.
5. Hierarchy of position in ceremony and of age-deference in etiquette patterns, but hierarchy of command does not exist (with exception of *caciques* and civil authorities) to any large extent. Men are to be influenced and persuaded and harmony is a crucial social goal.	5. Command-and-obey hierarchies pervade the society. There is the desire to dominate or exploit others. Men to be commanded directly.
6. The role is emphasized rather than the man.	6. A man's personal qualities are emphasized rather than the role or office he occupies.
7. Status gained by engaging in ceremonial activity and spending for ceremonial entertainment.	7. Status gained by attention-attracting activities, show, wealth, and by being a *patrón*.
8. No social class distinctions.	8. Class distinctions made.

Zinacantan	*San Cristóbal*

Work and economic orientations

1. Routine work and manual labor highly valued.	1. Routine work and manual labor avoided.
2. Land valued for subsistence.	2. Land ownership valued as a sign of status.
3. Play and idleness censured.	3. Play and idleness sought.

Religious orientations

1. More pluralistic view of religion and universe. Belief in both Catholic and pagan deities including underground earth-owner, mountain and spring gods. Multiple-soul concepts, including one divided into 13 parts and another in the form of an animal with supernatural guardian.	1. More dualistic view of religion and universe. Roman Catholicism of the Spanish variant.
2. Need to maintain health and integrity of soul in the face of an unpredictable supernatural universe and an evil social environment. Bargaining and exchanging with the gods. Curing ceremonies for restoring or keeping harmony with the supernatural forces.	2. Desire for control over social environment and belief in foreordained destiny, changeable only through supplication of God and the saints. Confession and sacraments for restoring personal relationship to God.
3. Water used from sacred springs and streams for curing and prenuptial ceremonies. Holy water blessed by Catholic priest also used in orthodox ceremonies.	3. Water for Catholic ceremonies made holy by priest through ritual rather than sanctity being derived from the specific source. Water has relatively little prominence.
4. Wide adult participation in religion through holding one-year *cargo* offices at four successively higher levels through which all males are encouraged to pass in their lifetime (heavy expenses and a long waiting list are such that most of the men get through only the first or second level).	4. Specialization of religious functions in hands of professional clergy.

charismatic power derives from the submission to the heroism, sanctity, or outstanding merit of a single person's personality. These are ideal types and may overcharacterize this aspect of Indian and *ladino* culture. A closer approximation to the specific Indian-*ladino* situation in Chiapas today may be made in the use of role and personality concepts. In the Indian society more attention is given to the role and less attention to the man performing that role, while in *ladino* society the role or office it not as important as the man in that role or office.

Those Indians having *ladino* friends in San Cristóbal and who visit them with the greatest frequency are precisely those Indians who accept the *ladinos'* structuring of a paternalistic type of behavior toward them.[6] Such Indians by placing themselves in the subordinate position of such a structure have taken the first step from a basically horizontally structured society to a vertical one.[7] The Indian that does not become a *ladino* and remains in his own culture approaches this vertical structure only in his subsistence exchange relations with *ladinos*. In these relations he perceives that he will receive more reward from the *ladino* if he acts in a pattern expected of him by the *ladino* (i.e. paternalistic rather than equalitarian or competitive). However, when the Indian makes the switch from Indian to *ladino* society, he places himself completely in the vertical structure at all times. Furthermore, he articulates with *ladinos* in additional need areas besides the economic or subsistence ones. He begins to choose *ladinos* as objects of attention and affection exchanges and soon afterwards experiences more fundamental value changes.

The change or "passing" of a single Indian into *ladino* culture is an *ex situ* change, a movement away from the norm. It is an important subject of anthropolog-

ical theory. Most studies of Indian-*ladino* relations (relations between Indians and non-Indians) in southern Mexico and Guatemala have been done at the level of individual or *ex situ* value changes rather than on the second, more abstract level of culture or *in situ* value changes. Work at the second level has barely begun and anthropologists are a long way from the elegance and precision we find in comparable linguistic studies. The closest that anthropologists have come to such linguistic elegance is in the recent work of Clyde Kluckhohn,[8] which enables us to make better statements of value inventory. However, it still remains for us to be able to make accurate systemic statements of cultural values which would, among other things, permit us to analyze cultural value change in terms of dia-systems as the linguists are now doing with phonemic systems.

Changes Within the Group

One method we are presently using for the study of *in situ* change is the study of two groupings of individuals: the first group is made up of individuals chosen by the anthropologist that represent all major types of variation in personal behavior, habits, dress, and speech. The second group of individuals examined are those representing extremes of positive and negative reward receipt from other members of the culture — the best and least respected individuals, the best and least liked ones, the ones with the most and least number of *compadres,* and those receiving most and least goods and services. An examination of how

---

[6] B. N. Colby and P. L. van den Berghe, "Ethnic Relations in Southeastern Mexico" (forthcoming).

[7] Dr. Eugene A. Nida (in correspondence) suggests that the contrast between horizontal and vertical power structure is an effect of a rural or folk social structure based on family distinction as opposed to an urban social structure based on class distinction. This is undoubtedly the case in Chiapas, especially since *ladino* and Indian groups exist in semi-feudal and symbiotic relationships with each other. Many of Redfield's criteria for the folk-urban distinction seem to hold for Chiapas also. The most notable exception is in family emphasis. Urban *ladinos* stress family cohesiveness much more than rural Zinacantan Indians, contrary to Redfield's findings in Yucatán.

[8] C. K. M. Kluckhohn, "Toward a Comparison of Value-Emphases in Different Cultures," in L. D. White, (ed.), *The State of the Social Sciences* (Chicago: Univ. of Chicago Press, 1956).

these two groups articulate is a prerequisite for understanding the dynamics
of *in situ* change.

Though there is not yet enough data
from Zinacantan to make a carefully
detailed analysis along this order, part of
the pattern is already clear and we know
that the exchange of attention (status,
respect) is a much more powerful vehicle
for change than the exchange of affection
(patterns of friendship, marriage, ritual
kinship, etc.). Further, economic wealth
as a positive reward has had little force
against rewards of attention such as is
received by holders of religious and civil
offices, *h'iloletik* (curers) and *htotil
me'iletik* (special men with advisory
functions that direct office-holders and
others in carrying out their duties). We
shall discuss this in more detail shortly.

Application to
Practical Problems

Making the distinction between individual value change and cultural value
change is to divide what really is a continuum. Such a working distinction, however, is not only useful for theory, but
for practical problems as well. Our analysis of processes of culture change first
began with the practical study of Indian
attitudes toward the *Instituto Nacional
Indigenista* (INI) program of education,
towards literacy and bilingual ability. To
illustrate one approach to practical problems at the individual level of value
change we shall treat two INI problems
that were relatively simple.

The two problems were (1) the resistance of Indians to girls' learning to
speak Spanish and (2) the resistance of
Indians to girls' learning to read. These
difficulties were approached by over a
hundred structured interviews in the

Tsotsil language given in three areas in
Zinacantan.

We found that the resistance to girls'
learning Spanish centered around two
attitudes. The first was one of cultural
identity. Men felt that a Spanish-speaking Indian girl would no longer be Zinacantan or would no longer associate with
her Zinacantan companions.

The other attitude concerned the male
dominance pattern. Answers in this category were that she would become the
boss or that she would mistreat her husband or would no longer fear or obey
her husband.

The reasons given against a girl's being
able to read polarized also around two
main attitudes, one of them being again
concern with cultural identity; the other
involved the division of labor between
the sexes: the girl should make tortillas,
tend sheep, carry wood, and do her work,
instead of studying to read.

In view of these findings our recommendation for INI is to alter its persuasive
efforts to get girls into school by initially
limiting the attendance of girls to a
briefer period than the boys and by teaching girls to read only in Tsotsil, not in
Spanish. Such a measure would simultaneously take care of the cultural identity
objection and the fear of threats to male
dominance. By spending a shorter period
in school, the objection about the economic division of labor for the sexes
should be weakened also.

Thus both the question and answer
to the problem of female education lie
at the level of individual values and attitudes. When we began to work on
another problem of education, that of
post-school education (perhaps the most
important single problem INI has to face
in Chiapas), it was necessary to seek the

solution at a more general level of analysis. It was necessary to draw upon an understanding of the institutional structure of Zinacantan culture arrived at by traditional methods of anthropological investigation.

The problem was this: After a few years of instruction, an Indian· leaves school and his books forever. His adult life has little use for a literate person. The question is: What kind of book might properly fill this vacuum? What books might be kept in an Indian house and referred to from time to time with real interest and enthusiasm?

Books about modern agricultural methods or modern hygiene are too foreign and impractical for Zinacantan interests. Also, folklore published in Tsotsil or Spanish and read in halting phrases by a young boy is a poor substitute for the animation and color of an older accomplished story-teller.

Capitalizing on a Social Need

Our proposed solution to this problem is to capitalize on the Zinacantan institution of the *totil me'il*. The *totil me'il* is a man especially qualified to provide instruction at crucial times in the life of a Zinacantan Indian. Marriage proceedings, religious ceremonies, and other activities require the advice, direction, and help of the *totil me'il*, who is chosen for his efficiency, capability, intelligence, and wisdom. The Zinacantan Indian always feels the need for a guide or teacher that helps a man in his relations with other members of his culture during critical points in his life. But he has no guide or teacher to help in his relations with *ladinos,* relations which are often characterized by anxiety and uncertainty.

To fill the vacuum in reading practice that occurs after leaving school, it may be possible to introduce a book that acts as a *totil me'il* for certain modern activities to complement the living *totil me'il* for traditional activities. Each student leaving his school might be given such a book to take home to be kept there for consultation during important times, particularly for occasions of culture contact with *ladinos.* Such a book would contain advice on purchasing land and manufactured goods, on buying and selling in remote areas and in recently accessible cities on the highway; opportunities for short periods of wage work, lists of rentable land in the lowlands for growing corn and so on. Once the content of these books were known, they may be wanted even by those people unable to read, who would then seek out a reader.

Current Changes in Indian Values

Shifting from current problems of practical anthropology in Chiapas to results of practical anthropology, we find a recent development in Zinacantan that may be very important, due to its relations with a focal value orientation of the culture. This orientation is the avoidance of competition and unequal power distributions. While in our present work on value-analysis we have not passed the inventory stage, one can still have a fairly good idea as to what values and orientations are basic to a culture, even if one does not understand how they may relate in a system.

In Zinacantan society, strongly competitive actions are kept to a minimum by fear of witchcraft and envy which act as a kind of leveling force, preventing the accumulation of wealth. Another important leveling force is the expenditure of large sums of money for carrying out certain ceremonial roles in which universal participation in expected.

A change in this orientation is occurring rapidly in Zinacantan. In the last two years a proliferation of Indian stores has come about in the *municipio* center and in outlying areas. This has been caused by a chain of events. First the INI organized a cooperative Indian store in Zinacantan center. Then the *cacique* of Zinacantan and several INI Indian employees opened two other stores. As these groups began to operate their stores and successfully withstood the cultural and social pressures against them, men of slightly lesser wealth and prestige were encouraged to-sell Coca-Cola, liquor, cigarettes, etc. in their houses to friends and neighbors. As more people began to do this the leveling forces of social pressure and fear of witchcraft apparently had less effect, and we believe the threshold was reached in just the last six months when the number of stores in the area almost doubled.

Because the individual Zinacantan personality system is strongly competitive to begin with, the removal of cultural sanctions against competition is bound to cause a significant change in the society. The introduction of the INI cooperative store along' with greater legal protection for the Indians against *ladino* reprisal acted as a catalyst for a reaction of components that were already close to the reaction point.

Because we do not have an understanding of the systemic nature of Zinacantan value structure, it is difficult to predict what other value changes might occur along with the increase of competition and an unequal distribution of wealth. We hope to approach such an understanding as more data is processed in the next few months.

Unstressful vs. Traumatic Change

All the forms of culture change discussed here are changes of a gradual and relatively unstressful nature. Some critics of programs aimed at changing individuals in a culture have been impatient with this approach and have demanded a more direct, faster change by bringing direct pressure to bear on the central institutions or beliefs of the culture. Such a change in the focal institutions or values of the culture by outside pressure is more abrupt and *en masse*. It is brought about by manipulation of institutions or by direct assault on the value or belief system. If one were, for example, to seek a change in the status system of Zinacantan, so that Indian models for higher status would have to be shifted to *ladino* ones, certain limiting or expanding manipulations of the system of civil or religious offices could be envisioned which would drastically disrupt the native status system.

Such procedures should be strongly avoided. Stress may appear at unexpected points in the cultural system. For example the cult of talking saints (boxes containing spirits which are made to talk by their charlatanic owners) that is wide spread in Zinacantan now may receive greater impetus and get out of hand Also conceivable is a wider proliferation of curers represented by frustrated *cargo* holders, and so on. Therefore, unless the resulting new system can be predicted beforehand, unforeseen and undesirable results may occur. But more important such activities are subject to serious moral religious, and philosophical reservations. We must maintain the distinctior. of acculturation pressure being brought to bear on individual personalities and acculturation pressure brought to bear on institutions and value systems of a culture, and also whether such changes are elective or forced. Practical programs must continue to bring about their objective via the elective change of individuals in much the way that the educational branch of INI, with the initial help of the Summer Institute of Linguistics, has been doing with such success in Chiapas.

By a close study of these changes as they are happening, at all levels from that of the individual, to the group, to the institutions and values, as well as a study of the context of *in situ* and *ex situ* changes, we hope to get at a better understanding of cultural dynamics in Zinacantan.

Benson Saler

Religious Conversion and Self-Aggrandizement: A Guatemalan Case

"It is ... important to see that the self is in part a ceremonial thing, a sacred object which must be treated with proper ritual care and in turn must be presented in a proper light to others."

ERVING GOFFMAN[1]

THE capacity for self-identification,[2] as Hallowell has pointed out, is a generic human trait, and the realization of that capacity is essential for the operation of all human social orders.[3] Self-identification, of course, is intricately bound up with self-expression in a social context. We may suppose, moreover, that self-expression itself is in significant measure the manifestation of a drive — whether inborn and/or acquired — to affirm the self existentially. Every viable human sociocultural system affords a number of institutionalized ways through which individuals can achieve some gratification of that drive in accordance with the status positions they hold and the roles they play. But human beings are not always content to affirm their selves within the narrow bounds of conventional social proprieties. They may do things and assume social postures, which, in kind or in degree, somehow overstep the range of traditional social approval relative to their group and their own positions within that group. When, in our society, for instance, we observe individuals behaving in certain ways which strike us as exceeding the norms, we may accuse such individuals of self-aggrandizement. Self-aggrandizement denotes the act, or attempted act, of making great or greater the self. The term as voiced in popular parlance, however, carries a pejorative connotation. To accuse a person of-

---

[1] Erving Goffman, "The Nature of Deference and Demeanor," *American Anthropologist*, Vol. 58, 1956, p. 497.

[2] This paper is a revised version of a paper read at the 1962 annual meeting of the Society for the Scientific Study of Religion. The author's field work in Guatemala, 1958-59, was supported by an Organization of American States Fellowship and a research grant from the Department of Anthropology of the University of Pennsylvania.

[3] A. I. Hallowell, "The Self and Its Behavioral Environment," in *Culture and Experience* (Philadelphia: University of Pennsylvania Press, 1955), pp. 75-110.

Benson Saler is Assistant Professor of Anthropology at Brandeis University, Waltham 54, Massachusetts. This paper is a result of a year in Guatemala where he made an ethnographic study of a Quiché group.

self-aggrandizement is to imply that, in the attempt to make himself great or greater, he has expressed himself too strongly relative to our norms. Self-aggrandizement, therefore, is some manifestation of the drive to affirm the self existentially which other people interpret as excessive.

The thesis to be presented here in the form of a case study is that religious conversion may sometimes constitute a therapeutic act of self-aggrandizement. Where an individual with a strong drive to affirm himself existentially cannot achieve adequate gratification of that drive by utilizing traditional sociocultural means, conversion to a new religion in the face of strong social disapproval may be instrumental in achieving the greatest gratification. Moreover, conversion in such cases may represent a psychic economy in that it is a less severe alternative to more autistic[4] attempts to affirm the self.

The Setting

The setting for our study is the village of Santiago El Palmar in the Pacific piedmont of Guatemala. According to the government census of 1950, Santiago El Palmar contained 977 Indians and 113 Ladinos or non-Indians. The great majority of both Indians and Ladinos account themselves to be Roman Catholics. The beliefs and rituals of Palmar Catholicism (especially among the Indians) are not, however, in all respects identical to the beliefs and

---

[4] Webster's *New Collegiate Dictionary* defines autism as "Absorption in phantasy to the exclusion of interest in reality."

rituals officially endorsed by the Bishop of Rome.

In the traditional Indian culture, highest status and attendant prestige tended in most cases to devolve on men of fairly advanced years. The Indian segment of Palmar's population actively supported a series of public offices centered on the Catholic church and the municipal building. These offices collectively constituted the civil-religious hierarchy, a salient institutional aspect of many middle American Indian communities. The highest offices of the hierarchy, those with the greatest prestige, were normally occupied by men who were at least in their forties. In the usual course of events, a man would enter the hierarchy, by way of its lowest offices, when an adolescent. With increased age and family responsibilities, he would ascend to positions of greater community trust and prestige.

None of the offices were salaried. Indeed, office holders were expected to defray out of their own pockets the expenses immediately connected with the proper discharge of their duties. Occupants of the highest offices in the religious branch of the hierarchy would normally bear the heaviest financial burdens, and it was not unusual for individuals holding those offices to spend a hundred dollars or more in "honoring the saints" during the time of their service. Inasmuch as many men could not afford such expenses, high office holding was often effectively restricted to comparatively wealthy members of the community. Because high office holding constituted a public acknowledgement of an individual's worth and esteem in the community, the hierarchy represented, among other things, an institutionalized channel for socially approved self-affirmation. Young men in the lower rungs of the hierarchy were directed to look to eventual occupancy of the highest offices as a manifest and traditional expression and affirmation of their worth as individuals. Occupants of the highest offices were supposed to be men of good character. But in order to reach the highest offices, a man with good character would ordinarily need at least two other things: patience and money.

For individuals who lacked either patience or money, or both, the culture offered certain short-cuts to a gratification of the drive to affirm the self within an approved and traditional social frame of reference. Personal conspicuous consumption — that is, spending money on the adornment of one's person, one's family, and one's house — was not one of these institutionalized short-cuts.[5] But the profession of calendar shaman was such a short-cut.

The calendar shaman is a diviner, curer, and imparter of moral advice who deals with individuals on a client basis. In the idealized Indian view, a person does not voluntarily choose to become a shaman. Rather, he is selected by an other-than-human agency to serve as shaman. Selection is announced through the divination of a practicing shaman, and the selected individual must become a practitioner himself in order to be cured of some

present ill or to avoid some future misfortune. Many people so selected do in fact become shamans after a period of study with a practicing shaman. But of those who, so to speak, graduate as shamans, very few actually practice the profession. Being a successful shaman requires a certain *savoir faire* and self-confidence, and not everyone has a temperament adequate to sustain the role. But for those who do, there are various rewards, not least among them being the respect of clients and the reputation of being a personage of important accomplishments.

Another traditional short-cut to a high degree of self-affirmation, though in a manner that immediately represented self-aggrandizement, was the practice of sorcery. The techniques of sorcery are culturally constituted, but the utilization of those techniques is socially disapproved. That is, the gross content of sorcery rites is part of the traditional culture, yet most Indians react negatively against the actual practice of sorcery. The sorcerer is typically represented to be a person who, because of exaggerated emotions of revenge or envy, or because of some overweening desire to take advantage of others, attempts to harm individuals through the instrumentality of magic. Without enlarging any further on this brief discussion of sorcery, suffice it to say here that sorcery is part of the traditional culture, that it is socially frowned upon, and that it represents what is probably a seldom utilized but extreme form of self-aggrandizement.

Sorcery, shamanism, and the civil-religious hierarchy are among the

---

[5] The traditional Palmar Indian community was characterized by "the cult of poverty" described for other Guatemalan Indian communities in the ethnographic literature.

traditional modes of existential self-affirmation in the local Indian culture. All constitute instruments for making great or greater the self. The practice of sorcery is outside the range of social approval, and anyone who engages in it is clearly engaging in self-aggrandizement. But improper performance of role in shamanism and the civil-religious hierarchy might also connote instances of self-aggrandizement.

Within the last several decades, a new medium of self-expression has been introduced from without the local community: Protestantism. Protestantism has thus far attracted only a handful of adherents. Most Palmar Indians reject the new religion. They dislike the fact that Protestant converts disparage the saints, calling them "idols." They regard the new religion as promoting unsociableness inasmuch as it interdicts smoking, drinking, and dancing — traditional expressions of affability. And they resent assertions of Protestant converts to the effect that Protestants will go to heaven whereas Catholics will not. Furthermore, Protestants make other statements which Catholics interpret as boastful, and Protestants are not always unostentatious in their refusals to accept alcoholic beverages or cigarettes offered them by their Catholic neighbors. Some Catholics, when under the influence of alcohol, occasionally manifest their dislike of Protestants by pouring rum on Protestant heads or blowing cigarette smoke in Protestant faces. The Protestants, Catholic informants have told me, "say they are better, but they are not." Catholics, moreover, often delight in accusing Protestants of secretly smoking and drinking in their homes.

Marcelino

One of the earliest converts to Protestantism in Santiago El Palmar was Marcelino. Marcelino had "served the saints" by holding offices in the lower rungs of the religious branch of the civil-religious hierarchy. It is doubtful, however, as to whether he would have ascended to the most prestigeful offices in the religious branch inasmuch as he was not wealthy. He was, however, a shaman, and, according to what he told me, a highly successful one. But one day he overheard some men discussing him. It was the consensus of these men, from the snatches of their conversation that he was able to overhear, that he was a sorcerer. Marcelino was angered by the accusation. He reasoned that he could not be a sorcerer inasmuch as he had effected a number of cures in his role of shaman, and a shaman who indulges in sorcery is supposed to lose his power to cure. But he continued to brood over the accusation for it disturbed him deeply. He suffered a loss of appetite and general malaise. He concluded that he had enemies who were spreading lies about him, and he was preoccupied with trying to calculate who they might be.

Shortly thereafter, Marcelino encountered an emphatic North American Protestant missionary who informed him that the people of Palmar were worshiping "idols" (the saints). The missionary called upon Marcelino to set an example that would lead others to God, to become a Protestant.

Soon after this encounter with the missionary, Marcelino began to experience vivid dreams. In these dreams, Marcelino learned that Santo Mundo, the earth essence which selects a man to be a shaman, was in reality the devil. In one dream, God placed a crown upon Marcelino's head and told him that he must lead the ignorant people of Palmar to God, even if those same people were to persecute him for attempting to do so.

Following another meeting with the missionary, Marcelino became a Protestant. For several weeks after his conversion, he told me, he was "persecuted" by transforming witches. These evil beings, in the forms of birds, flew over his house, beating their wings and crying out in order to prevent him from sleeping. Inasmuch as the witches are believed to derive their power from a covenant with the devil and to delight in harassing the virtuous, Marcelino interpreted his "persecution" to be a corroboration from an infernal source of his own righteousness.

In addition, Marcelino was the recipient of open scorn and verbal abuse from other Indians. He asserted that several conspired to murder him by direct physical assault — sorcery would be of no avail against a person as close to God as himself. In several long interviews he detailed for me the events of what he called his "martyrdom." Interestingly enough — and I take this to be another example of his strong proclivities to self-affirmation — Marcelino never repudiated the cures he had made when a shaman and a Catholic. In response to my questions, he assured me that the cures were real enough, but that he had accomplished them when he was "ignorant." If a sick person were to come to him today, Marcelino told me, he would not cure the ill person; rather, he would give him a Bible so that he might read, or have read to him, the word of God.

In all of my sessions with Marcelino, he impressed me as being strongly convinced of his own uniqueness, spiritual superiority, and sacred mission. He was, moreover, greatly respected by his fellow Indian Protestants; indeed, they looked to him for leadership. And a North American missionary of my acquaintance spoke of him with admiration and affection. The opinions of Catholic Indians, however, were mixed and decidedly less favorable. Some of my Catholic informants professed to admire him for his resolution and courage; but such admiration, I think, was colored by the fact that Marcelino was then an old man, and the Indians traditionally show a certain deference to the aged. At the same time that they voiced compliments, however, they also intimated that they considered him to be excessively outspoken as to the value of his religion and his own moral and spiritual worth.

Discussion

We could speculate as to what might have become of Marcelino had he not converted to Protestantism. The fact that he had been a practicing shaman suggests a temperament somewhat out of the ordinary. Had his proclivities to self-expression been markedly stronger than those of most other shamans, however, then I doubt that shamanism would have sufficed as a vehicle for their full gratification. As I have pointed out elsewhere, "the calendar shamans rely to a great extent on a structured, abstracted, externalized system by which events are organized and judged," and the shaman typically "experiences an externalized control as if it were given by the environment."[6] Calendar shamanism structures and strictures freedom and fancy; an unusually imaginative and self-assertive individual would probably not find sufficient satisfaction in keeping within its bounds.

Nor do I think that Marcelino would have been able to achieve sufficient satisfaction in the civil-religious hierarchy. The most prestigeful offices, those in the religious branch, were probably closed to him because of his lack of wealth. It is not impossible that Marcelino, fearing that he had enemies who were spreading lies about him, and brooding on the conviction that he was inadequately appreciated despite the cures he had effected, might have withdrawn further into himself or, in his frustration, turned to the dark rites of the sorcerer.

If these were possible courses in his development, then Protestantism was probably a less drastic alternative to them. By identifying himself with the new religion, Marcelino achieved what he regarded to be a spiritual superiority over his fellow Indians. Further, the "persecutions" he endured were gratifying to him in that

they affirmed his status as an existent of social interest. Prior to his conversion, the belief that he had enemies made him despondent. Following his conversion, he did indeed have enemies, but now he openly derived a certain pleasure from that fact. And, finally, the support and admiration he received from missionaries and other converts were of considerable psychological value to him. Instead of withdrawing further into himself, Marcelino developed into a preacher and a religious leader; he became, in brief, an active participant.

Marcelino's worldly self-affirmation is paralleled in the life histories which I recorded for several other Protestant converts in Santiago El Palmar. There was a woman who had been an object of malicious gossip because of her many sexual liaisons; following her conversion, she became — at least for a time — a paragon of virtue. There was a man whose effeminate mannerisms earned him the epithet *mujercito* 'little male woman'; though he remained effeminate after his conversion, he became a preacher whose sermons were highly admired in Protestant circles. In these and similar cases, converts previously out of harmony with their society achieved gratifying status and respect, at least within their own Protestant group.

Conclusion

Protestantism, as presented by the missionaries, idealizes humility before God. It is perhaps ironic that Marcelino, in embracing that religion, was able to achieve an assertion of self so emphatic as to hint at megalomania. Irony aside, however, the introduction

---

6 Benson Saler, "Unsuccessful Practitioners in a Bicultural Guatemalan Community," *Psychoanalysis and the Psychoanalytic Review*, Vol. 49, No. 2, 1962, pp. 108-109.

of Protestantism into El Palmar has opened up a new channel for the existential affirmation of the self. And the missionaries responsible for introducing the new faith have thus performed a socially and psychologically valuable service for at least a few people in that they have afforded frustrated individuals with an alternative to much more autistic kinds of self-expression and self-aggrandizement.

I hope that missionaries will not take it amiss if an anthropologist now addresses himself to some issues which are of theoretical interest to him and of practical importance to them. The major official *raison d'être* for missionary activity in Santiago El Palmar is a "spiritual" concern, a concern for the salvation of souls. Yet Protestant missionizing has thus far made less than thirty-five converts in the village (including Ladinos as well as Indians). One of the reasons for this lack of quantitative success has been the kinds of people who have become converts. In most cases, they have been disaffected individuals, persons somewhat "marginal" to their own society. This fact has not escaped the notice of Catholic Indians.

In situations where individuals of high prestige in their own societies accept missionary tutoring, the task of missionaries is often greatly facilitated. This was evidently the case in Hawaii following the overthrow of the traditional taboo system in 1819. Some of the established Hawaiian leaders, including the influential queen Kaahumanu, played an important role in abolishing taboos. When the missionaries arrived a short time there-

after, a number of powerful chiefs and chieftainesses listened sympathetically to their message and became converts, thereby facilitating the conversion of the populace at large. Blackman has given it as his opinion that the "extreme love and reverence for their chiefs on the part of most Hawaiians was the decisive influence in turning the people to Christianity."[7]

The situation in Santiago El Palmar, however, has been quite different. In that place, Protestantism has attracted individuals who were not highly esteemed by other members of their society and who, in at least several cases, have used the new religion as a prime instrument for self-aggrandizement. The very conversion of such people has probably increased the disenchantment of other villagers with the new faith, thereby making it more difficult for the missionaries to enlarge the number of converts.

From an immediate tactical point of view, we could argue that the missionaries have significantly impeded their own work by having encouraged such people. Yet the missionaries, according to the creed they espouse, are obligated to accept everyone who gives evidence of a sincere desire to learn and to live in accordance with the tenets of the religions which they are charged with introducing. I have reason to believe that the missionaries are aware of the fact that some of their converts

---

[7] William Fremont Blackman, *The Making of Hawaii: A Study in Social Evolution* (Norwood, Mass.: The Macmillan Co., 1899), p. 24.

are a poor advertisement for Protestantism. Insofar as I know, however, the missionaries have consistently chosen to convert all who appear to be sincere in their willingness to embrace the new faith, regardless of the immediate tactical disadvantages that may accrue from doing so. I would suppose that the missionaries have thus kept faith with what they regard as the "spiritual" focus of their calling, despite the fact that low conversion rates may not seem very impressive to the members of sponsoring mission boards.

Yet in the long run this keeping of faith might possibly prove tactically advantageous as well as dogmatically correct. Converts who affirm themselves existentially through the medium of the new religion are likely to undergo not only a "spiritual" transformation but a social and psychological transformation as well. To the extent that they then come to exhibit social qualities which others admire or learn to admire, they may prove to be models which their fellow villagers will eventually seek to imitate.

Marion M. Cowan

A Christian Movement in Mexico

The study of how Christian movements get started in specific cases, how they grow or decline, and the social forces involved is one of the prime purposes of this periodical. Miss Cowan has provided us with an interesting and valuable case study which no reader should overlook simply because it deals with a remote Mexican group. We could well use more such studies from the peasant villages or the cities of Asia, Africa, and other parts of the world.

IN 1955 a Christian movement began among the Tzotzil Indians of Mexico. This paper is an attempt to point out some of the factors which influenced the growth of this movement.

The Huixtán Tzotzil, probably numbering between three and four thousand people, occupy the greater part of the municipality of Huixtán in the state of Chiapas (see Map of Tzotzil Tribe). Huixtán covers an area three to four hours by foot from north to south and four hours by foot from east to west. Huixtec is the most easterly dialect of Tzotzil, and is bounded on the north, east, and south by another language, Tzeltal. Both belong to the Mayan language family and are to some degree mutually intelligible. Customs and dress, although generally similar, differ greatly in detail. Between San Cristóbal de Las Casas and the western border of Huixtán lies a part of the large area of the Chamula Tzotzil, who have a social structure very different from that of the Huixtán Tzotzil.

Four walking hours from the northeast corner of Huixtán lies the region of Corralito where a Christian movement among the Tzeltal had its beginnings in 1949 and continues on today with about two thousand converts. Around 1951 this Tzeltal movement had reached to the northeast border of Huixtán. Tzeltal believers were continually passing through Huixtán on their way to market in Las Casas, four hours west of the western border of Huixtán.

Las Casas, situated on the Pan-American highway, is the market center for Indians of the Tzotzil and Tzeltal tribes who live within a half day's walk to the west of the city, a day's walk to the north of the city, and on the east anywhere up to two or three days' walk. The Indians bring to Las Casas chickens, rope, blankets, and flowers, and return with salt, sandals, hats, bread, thread for weaving their clothes, and marriage gifts.

The Beginning of the Movement

In December of 1955, on the trail about an hour from Las Casas, a Tzeltal

Marion M. Cowan is a missionary nurse, linguist, and translator working with the Wycliffe Bible Translators in Mexico. She has also contributed to published studies of hymn writing for aboriginal languages.

Christian on his way to market met a Huixtec man and his son-in-law. The Huixtec was a friendly person and curious, and since he understood some Tzeltal he asked the man where he was going. As the conversation progressed, the Huixtec offered the Tzeltal a cigarette, but the Tzeltal refused it. The Huixtec was amazed, for it is unusual for an Indian to refuse a gift. The Huixtec was curious to know why the Tzeltal did not smoke, and he explained that it was because he now knew where God was and worshiped him. He added that he no longer went to fiestas in honor of the saint-images in the church because they were not alive anyway; he did not drink liquor or smoke any more because liquor, especially, led to fighting and killing, which God did not want.

The Huixtec was interested and wanted to hear more, but it was late in the afternoon and the Tzeltal was anxious to get to Las Casas before dark. They made an agreement that when the Tzeltal returned the next day, he would give a shout when he got to the bottom of a certain cliff on the trail, and the Huixtec would be waiting for him there. And so they parted.

As the Tzeltal went on into Las Casas, he could hardly contain his excitement. For almost five years he and his fellow Tzeltal Christians had walked through Huixtec territory praying that some Huixtecs also would come to know God. They had told Huixtecs about their new faith in Christ whenever they had had opportunity, but they were usually sneered at and derided with, "Oh, you think you're God now." Once or twice the Huixtecs, known as killers, had threatened them with murder. This Tzeltal was so excited that he hurriedly made his pur-

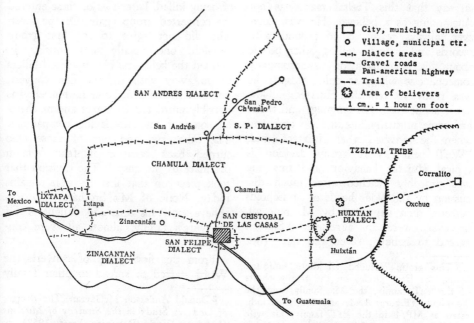

MAP OF TZOTZIL TRIBE, in the State of Chiapas, Mexico

chases, had a few hours' sleep, and by four in the morning was on his way back over the trail.

When the Tzeltal came to the planned place of meeting, he gave the signal and the Huixtec (we will call him M) stepped out of the bushes and took him to his house. M's son-in-law (we will call him N) who had been with him on the trail the day before, was watching from his cornfield near by. He went with them to hear what the Tzeltal had to say.

The night before M had informed his brothers and his wife's relatives of what he had heard, and of the expected visit of the Tzeltal. He urged them to come and listen, too. When the Tzeltal arrived, he found a group gathered which included some of M's brothers and a nephew, all of his own family, and many of his wife's relatives.[1]

Missionary colleagues among the Tzeltal say that this Tzeltal man was not outstanding as a believer. He was, however, always ready to go around with records and victrola, telling other people about his new faith or to accompany someone else who was doing this, so he was ready to tell the Huixtecs all he knew about God. His language and theirs had some mutually intelligible words and when he finished the Huixtecs said, "We'll believe." A group decision is typical Huixtec behavior, and this one was probably reached after much discussion by the older heads of households present, then expressed by M. Not all, however, were in agreement. Sixteen agreed to believe; seven did not. (See Figures 1, 2, and 3.) McGavran explains group decision as follows:

> For the group mind to be formed, many individuals must express agreement. So that we may truly say that *when a group comes to Christ, every member has had a share in the final decision.* Only those who have loved the light (even in a small degree) have participated in the group decision. This truth is made clearer by the realization that in most groups there is a section that do not become Christian. Since each individual is free to move or to stay back, "coming with others" indicates a degree of "following the light."[2]

We believe, then, that in such group conversions it is not "membership in the group" but "participation in following Christ" which is the vital factor.

Of the sixteen who agreed to believe, four soon turned back because of fear of being killed. Later two of these entered the converted group again. Of the seven who did not agree to the first group decision, one openly and consistently derided the believers. He also hired killers to do away with M, the first convert, but God intervened. Later he himself was horribly murdered with axes and machetes by some of his unbelieving companions. The other six, and two of those who turned back because of fear, remain obstinate to the gospel. The division that took place on that first decision remains today. None of M's brothers or sisters believe, only his sons and daughters. Of his wife's family, almost all were converted.

From this first group of converts the Word started to spread to other family

---

[1] This group included all those indicated within the large circles on the family charts of the PeT family, the Ma family, and the To family (Figures 1, 2, and 3). M is indicated as MP/1 in the PeT family, his wife as MMa/2 in the Ma family, and N as NHe/3 in the To family.

[2] Donald Anderson McGavran, *The Bridges of God: A Study in the Strategy of Missions* (London: World Dominion Press, 1957), p. 97.

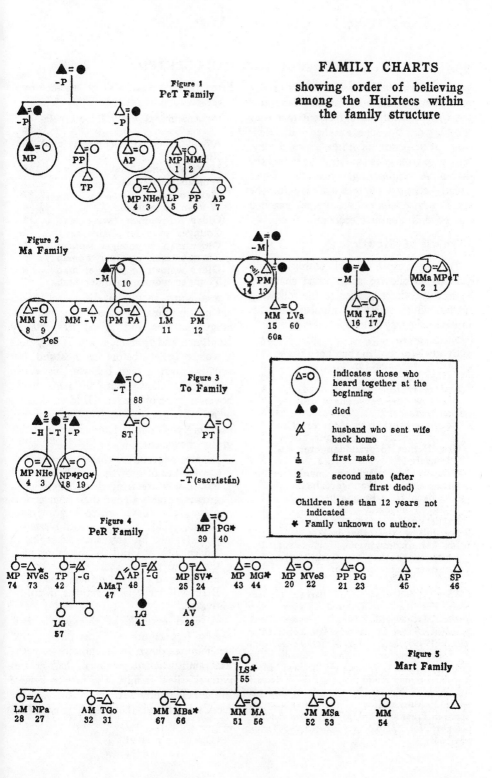

FAMILY CHARTS
showing order of believing
among the Huixtecs within
the family structure

Figure 1
PeT Family

Figure 2
Ma Family

Figure 3
To Family

⬭=◯   indicates those who
      heard together at the
      beginning

▲ ●   died

∅   husband who sent wife
      back home

1/=   first mate

2/=   second mate (after
                  first died)

Children less than 12 years not
indicated
✱ Family unknown to author.

Figure 4
PeR Family

Figure 5
Mart Family

groups nearby within an economic group-ing. The men of these families were tied together by a mutual agreement that they would work for one another with their oxen at the rate of three pesos a day, one peso for each ox and one for the driver. A neighboring cooperative group usually charged ten pesos a day for the same service. Later the gospel reached out beyond this first economic group.

Channels of Growth

As the gospel spread within family groups, it followed some social channels[3] more than others, as seen in the following listing, which gives the number of cases in each category:

Husband to wife	26
Brother-in-law to brother-in-law	9
Father to daughter	8
Father to son	5
Son to mother (father dead)	4
Older brother to younger brother	4
Son to father	3
Younger brother to older brother	3
Older brother to younger sister	3
Grandfather to granddaughter (in household)	3
Neighbor to neighbor (men)	3
Older sister to younger sister	2
Grandson to grandmother	1
Wife to husband	1
Father-in-law to son-in-law	1
Son-in-law to father-in-law	1
Mother to daughter	1
Younger brother to older sister	1
Younger sister to older sister	1

[3] See the following: H. G. Barnett, *Innovation: The Basis of Cultural Change* (New York: McGraw-Hill, 1953); George Peter Murdock, *Social Structure* (New York: Macmillan, 1949); Siegfried F. Nadel, *The Theory of Social Structure* (Glencoe, Illinois: The Free Press, 1957); William A. Smalley, "Making and Keeping Anthropological Field Notes," *PA*, Vol. 7, No. 4 (July-August 1960), pp. 145-152; Mischa Titiev, "The Importance of Space in Primitive Kinship," *American Anthropologist*, Vol. 58, No. 5 (October 1956), pp. 854-865.

From these we can also get these group-ings:

Consanguineal kin ("blood relatives")	39
Affinal kin (relatives by marriage)	38
Non-kin	3
Man to woman	46
Woman to man	1
Man to man	29
Woman to woman	4
Older to younger (same sex)	13
Younger to older (same sex)	5
Older man to younger woman	14
Younger man to older woman	6
Older woman to younger man	0
Younger woman to older man	1

These figures show how the gospel spread among the Huixtecs equally through con-sanguineal ties and affinal ties, mainly from men and from older kin. Rarely does a woman believe before her husband, but usually when a man believes, his whole household follows suit. In some cases, however, part of the household constitutes what McGavran calls "unconverted pockets" which may later come into this group movement:

> People Movements have enormous possibilities of growth.... The group movements are fringed with exterior growing points among their own peoples... also have internal growing points; that is, the unconverted pockets left by any such sweeping movement.... Until the discipling of the entire people, there will be both internal and external growing points. Both will yield large returns if cul-tivated.[4]

A good example of this is the PeR family (see Figure 4). This family lived ten minutes down the mountain from the Ma family. It had previously had no ties with the PeT family. The first to believe in the PeR family were two of the younger men who heard the gospel from N as

[4] Op. cit., pp. 90-91.

SPATIAL MAP OF HUIXTEC BELIEVERS

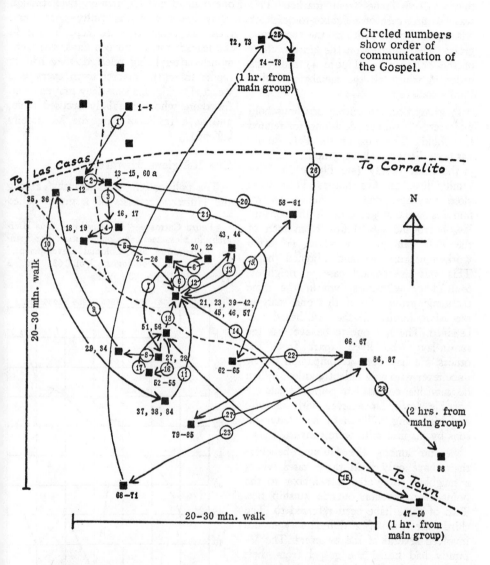

Circled numbers show order of communication of the Gospel.

72, 73

74-78
(1 hr. from main group)

To Las Casas

13-15, 60 a

R-12

35, 36

To Corralito

N

20-30 min. walk

16, 17

18, 19

58-61

43, 44

20, 22

24-26

21, 23, 39-42, 45, 46, 57

51, 56

29, 34

27, 28

52-55

62-65

66, 67

86, 87

(2 hrs. from main group)

37, 38, 84

79-85

88

To Town

68-71

47-50
(1 hr. from main group)

20-30 min. walk

25 houses
88 believers indicated
Numbers correspond to
   family charts
Turned back: 13, 14, 49, 50

Died after believing: 39, 41
Turned back then reconsidered
   when took wife: 15 (or 60a)
Number of believers, June 1961
   82 adults.

they walked home from market. This was the first case of neighbor-to-neighbor witnessing, even within the economic group. The numbers on the kinship chart of the PeR family (Figure 4) show the order in which all the members of that family believed.

A group decision within one household may set off similar decisions in related households. The case of the PeR family has been discussed above. Another example is the Mart family (see Figure 5). This family lived in five houses. Four were close together; one was about twenty minutes' walk away. One of the sons-in-law heard the gospel first from men of the PeR family with whom he often worked because his land adjoined theirs. This was the second case of neighbor-to-neighbor witnessing within the same economic group. From this one man in the Mart family all the rest heard and believed. The last one to believe was the son-in-law who lived apart from the others. He had been a companion of the unbeliever who was violently killed. When he saw his companion come to such a horrible death, he believed with his wife and his young children by her. Later his sons by his first wife were converted also.

So far among the Huixtec believers there have only been three cases where a neighbor stimulated a neighbor to the point of conversion outside kinship ties. Two of these have been referred to. The third case was of a different type and involved several of the believers. The Ve family had heard the gospel from their neighbors, the Go family and also the PeR family, but they were not interested in following. Later, would-be murderers entered their home one night and wounded two of them seriously. The Ve family falsely accused three men of the PeR family, two men of the Mart family, and

one man of the Go family. Even though many knew who the guilty ones were, these six believers were kept in jail in the market town fourteen days. For eight months after being released, they had to report in to the market town every two weeks. During this time they prayed often for those who had falsely accused them, and as a result of this, the Ve family believed.

The Religious Hierarchy

The politico-religious hierarchy[5] among the Huixtecs consists of a group called

[5] Pedro Carrasco, "The Civil-Religious Hierarchy in Mesoamerican Communities: Pre-Spanish Background and Colonial Development," *American Anthropologist*, Vol. 63, No. 3 (June 1961), pp. 483-497.

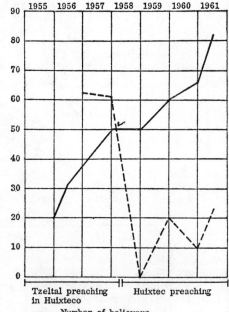

Tzeltal preaching in Huixteco   Huixtec preaching

——— Number of believers
— — Gain per year (per cent)
↙ Missionaries entered Feb. 20, 1958

GROWTH OF HUIXTEC CHURCH

sacristanetic ranging from young boys to old men. To gain status in the community a man may enter his son as a *sacristán* when he is around ten years of age. It is the work of the *sacristanetic* to govern the religious life of the community. They care for the saint-images in the local church and see that fiestas are celebrated regularly in their honor. This group greatly influences the thinking of the elected president of the municipality, always a Huixtec. So far the gospel has not penetrated this pillar of Huixtec social culture but it has reached its borders in that one of N's relatives is in this group. N is the leader of the Huixtec Christians and his cousin is a junior *sacristán* (see Figure 3). This cousin and his father have both heard the gospel through N. It is an encouraging sign that one of the younger brothers in the family, who has been ill most of his life, is no longer treated by native practitioners, but is now sent to us for medical help.

Growth of the Church

The growth of the Huixtec church has not been as spectacular as that among the neighboring Tzeltal, but it has been steady from nineteen at the end of 1955 to eighty-two in June of 1961. The gain in numbers of believers per year and the percentage of gain over each preceding year is shown in the chart entitled "Growth of Huixtec Church." From this chart we might predict a continued growth of at least two or three small groups per year.

Reasons for Growth

The qualities of the first two Huixtec men to hear and believe the gospel seem to be directly connected with the growth of the Huixtec church. Warneck describes such men under "Agencies that clear the way for Christianity":

These men . . . are called to be guides and interpreters of the Christian religion to their heathen countrymen. They are wedges driven into heathenism. . . . The herd requires individual leaders with the courage to break through the tradition and show the multitude that they can become Christians without suffering any harm. The whole odium of the violated tradition will of course fall first on them, and they will seldom escape a martyr's death. But that only strengthens their own faith, and increases their power to draw others after them.[6]

Before hearing the gospel, M had gained ladder status[7] in the community by engaging in ceremonial activity and spending money for ceremonial entertainment.[8] For one year he had taken part in the fiestas for the saint-images. The usual pattern among the Huixtecs is to accept these duties when asked to do them, but M had refused several times before finally consenting. This and the fact that he seldom went to fiestas indicate that he was somewhat of a nonconformist.

He was also an initiator of new ideas. He introduced the making of home-made

[6] Joh. Warneck, *The Living Christ and Dying Heathenism* (Grand Rapids: Baker Book House, 1954), pp. 182-183.

[7] Carrasco, op. cit., specifically p. 483 where he states: "One of the basic features of the traditional Indian peasant communities of Mesoamerica is the civil-religious hierarchy that combines most of the civil and ceremonial offices of the town's organization in a single scale of yearly offices. I will call it the ladder system. All men of the community have to enter into it and all have a chance to climb up to the highest steps and reach the status of elder."

[8] Colby mentions a similar situation among the Zinacantán Tzotzil in his "Social Relations and Directed Culture Change among the Zinacantan," PA, Vol. 7, No. 6 (November-December 1960), pp. 241-250.

liquor into his area. He also initiated several land deals, most of which fell through due to his lack of ability to speak Spanish fluently, or due to the fact that those he interested to join him in the deals were not as solvent financially as he was. He is currently planning to build a house with a galvanized iron roof, and if he succeeds in this he will be the first Huixtec to have one.

He is a hard worker and as a result economically independent. Laziness is strongly censured in his home. He owns three houses, usually has six or more oxen, a horse, and ten or twelve sheep. Any Huixtec does well to own one yoke of oxen and with difficulty buys another pair for his teen-age son. M is in a position to lend money and his services in this respect are constantly sought by unbelievers and believers.

M and his wife were probably between forty and forty-five years of age when they believed. At that time they had had ten children, seven living. Because so many had lived, he was thought to have power to curse the children of others so that they died.

This was the type of man that God used to introduce the gospel to the Huixtecs: one who was looked up to in the community, who did not feel tied down by the traditions of his fathers but could introduce new things and make a success of them.

Leadership

N was the first one of the Huixtec believers to change his behavior and put into practice the new things they were hearing from the Bible. He encouraged the others to do so also and in this way became their leader. He had been living at M's house for almost two years (as part of the marriage agreement) when he heard the gospel along with his father-in-law. He worked for M in the daytime but at night made liquor for a little personal cash.

He was about twenty-two when he heard the gospel. He had been to school as a child and was the only one of the first converts who knew how to read. He could also write a little. He has the ability to teach his own people. He tries to obey the new truth which he is learning himself, and is able to explain it to others. He is compassionate and considerate of those who are weaker in faith.

He takes an active interest in seeing that we learn his language correctly. When he corrects us, he explains the meaning of what we said wrong, then tells us what we should have said. On some occasions without being asked, he has given me a whole conversation in which I was going to take part if I went to visit at a certain home. He told me what I should say on arrival, what they would answer, then how I should reply, what other things they would probably say to me and how I should answer those, etc.

He is precise in translation work. Of the four converts who are helping translate parts of the New Testament into Huixteco, he is the only one who consistently picks up the little shades of meaning which make the difference in whether or not the translation speaks as they speak. Sometimes in the midst of reading the Bible to his people, he has stopped and said to me, "You should put *ta* there" (incompletive aspect needed instead of punctiliar) or "That ought to have *me* there" (an emphatic particle needed with the verb). But even while catching these minute details, he often expresses amazement over the insights he gains from the Bible.

N wants the best not only for himself but also for his fellow Huixtecs and is willing to learn in order to attain this. He who always takes the lead in his home, telling his wife and children what their duties are for each day, is willing to be taught by women missionaries things for his own improvement and the improvement of his people. For instance, he asked that we teach him something about administering medicine so that when we are away he can help his own people. A few months ago when we were not with them, disease was spreading among their chickens. N had heard us say that there was vaccine available in Las Casas and had seen us give injections to both people and animals. So although not having been taught how to give an injection, he bought the vaccine, some alcohol, cotton and a needle, borrowed one of our syringes and saved all his chickens and those of another believer.

In establishing new customs for his people, N shows an awareness of the fact that the gospel fits into his culture. He only institutes changes where the old customs are not consistent with the Bible. For instance, the Huixtec who is an evangelical Christian pays out the same amount of money in marriage gifts as the non-Christian Huixtec, but the Christian buys meat, bread, cane sugar, and cocoa while the non-Christian buys liquor, bread, cane sugar, and cocoa. After having thought through changes that needed to be made in the marriage customs, N and his fellow preachers determined the new customs. They require that before going to ask for a wife for their son, the parents come to be instructed by them in these new customs. They urge the parents to obey the new rules set up on the basis of the Bible and to be finished with those handed down by tradition from their unbelieving forefathers. In this way the new customs are gradually being established among the Christians.

Missionary Influence

On the chart of the growth of the Huixtec church no increase in numbers is reported for the year 1958. It was on February 20 of that year that we entered Huixtec territory and settled down to live among them, two single ladies, the first foreigners to succeed in doing so. Before that time two other attempts had been made by missionary colleagues to enter that area; in both cases they were told to leave.

In 1958 we were able to obtain a letter from the governor of the state which gave us permission to live in Huixtán. As a result there has been no open opposition to our being there. Many rumors, however, were soon spread around on our arrival. For a week after we entered Huixtán, there were high winds which tore the shingles off roofs and blew down trees. We were blamed for bringing the wind. The unconverted people were saying that one of us was a man and that soon the little girls would become pregnant. This story continues to be spread around among the non-Christians. Now it is said that we snatch women for evil purposes. These stories are so believed that on several occasions when non-Christians have come to our house seeking medical help, they have refused to enter and sit down at our invitation. With some their voices have shaken with fear as they talked to us.

On our entrance into Huixtán, we lived in a newly built house belonging to one of the Christian families. They let us have it until the group of them were able to build a house for us. As the regular wooden shingles which they use are becoming difficult to buy, the Christians suggested we put on a galvanized iron roof. When this was done, the story went around among the non-Christians that everyone who entered this new religion had to pay two hundred pesos each to help pay for the roof.

Pilots and planes of the Missionary Aviation Fellowship have been serving missionaries in the state of Chiapas for twelve years. Where the Huixtec Christians live there is no airstrip, but during 1958 the pilot had occasion to drop us two or three messages. The people had never seen any plane come as close to the ground as those did without either landing or crashing against the mountains. They were sure it was miraculous and that if it could drop messages, it could also drop bombs. They also believed that the plane guarded us.

Another incident which shows that they felt the plane had special powers occurred when the six falsely accused Christians were being held in the town jail before being sent up to Las Casas. At that time the pilot came over to drop another note at our house. When he circled over the town to lose altitude, the town police thought that the plane had come on behalf of the prisoners. So they ran to the jail to see if the Christians were still there. They were, of course, and that night at the request of the town police and other town authorities they had ample opportunity to explain their new-found faith in Christ.

In my opinion there was no growth in numbers that year because it took the people that long to become accustomed to the foreign element that had been introduced among them. During that time, however, there was much spiritual growth among the Christians and progress was made in translating the Bible into their language.

Inward Growth

Prior to our entrance into Huixtán in 1958, some of the Huixtec Christians had gone to Corralito and then later to Las Casas to work with us on the translation of the Scriptures into their language. When the Tzeltal Christian witnessed to the Huitxecs in 1955, he had invited them to go down to the Christian Christmas fiesta at Corralito which was soon to take place. Having heard that the evangelicals ate people, the Huixtecs went with considerable fear. But when they saw the thousands of Tzeltal Christians there at the fiesta and were so cordially received by them, the four Huixtec men and one woman were greatly impressed. Even though the languages are somewhat mutually intelligible, our missionary colleagues working at Corralito found that the Huixtecs were not able to understand much of the religious content, so they asked that some of us who were working in other dialects of Tzotzil come in to Corralito to translate for these new Huixtec Christians. During 1956 this was done.

On intermittent visits by the Huixtec Christians the following parts of the Bible were translated: the Ten Commandments, several stories from the Old Testament including the Creation, the Fall, the First Murder, the Fiery Furnace, etc., a short Life of Christ, and a few chosen Scripture verses. Twenty-one hymns were also written. These were all made available in typewritten form to N, and to three Tzeltal Christians who were faithfully walking the eight-hour trail every weekend to visit the Huixtec Christians and teach them more of the Scriptures.

They continued to do this over a period of two years until we were permitted to enter Huixtec territory. Then with our help the Huixtecs took over the teaching of their own people.

On our entrance into Huixtán we saw the need of more translation to be done and during that year a great deal was accomplished with the help of N and P, a member of the PeR family. The following translation was done in first draft: the Sermon on the Mount, the Gospel of John, the book of Acts, a tract about heaven and hell, and miscellaneous Scripture verses. The Life of Christ was revised and twelve more hymns were written and taught to the Christians. While this translation work was going on, the two Christians who worked on the translation during the week taught it to their fellow Christians on Sunday.

During that year also the first Christian funeral and wedding took place, and the first civil marriages were registered in compliance with the law of Mexico. N then had two men from the PeR family helping him teach the Bible on Sundays. These two were the first who had learned to read in our reading classes. That year also they organized the first Christian Christmas fiesta as a substitute for the old type of fiesta. They saw the need of counseling those who were weak in faith and began to do so. And as these three worked with us on the translation of the Bible, using it to help their weaker brethren and to establish Christian customs, they gradually left off more of the old life and beliefs and looked to the Bible for guidance in all they did.

During that year also, a set of three primers was completed and reading classes were held in our house for the Christian men, women, and children. By the end of the year, twenty, including the three who were preaching, could read the Scripture portions we had mimeographed for them. So although 1958 did not show any increase in the number of believers, it was a year of progress: the establishing in the faith of those who had believed up to that time, their being prepared to read the Scriptures for themselves, the establishing of teachers among them, and the transformation of old customs. This all formed a solid base on which the church could grow.

Now after five years the movement continues to grow as relatives of the first believers come to join those they once thought had strayed from the right way. The Christians have outgrown the house they have been using as a church and are now in the process of putting up a church building. This is being financed from their Sunday offerings. Just recently when we were away from them, some of them wrote us letters assuring us of their prayers, asking us to pray for them, telling us the good news that others have believed and that the construction of the church has begun. On Sundays and Wednesdays they gather together to be taught by one of four of their group. This past summer they have been learning about those who lived from David's to Daniel's time and about the work of the apostles in the book of Acts. All those who can read have their own books and follow along as the preachers teach them. These men continue to spend many hours a month teaching the new believers, establishing them in their new faith, and guiding those of the older believers who are weak in faith. This, I believe, keeps the church strong and growing.

John Beekman

Minimizing Religious Syncretism among the Chols

Syncretism is the tendency for new culture patterns to be combined and intermingled with existing patterns when they are adopted into a society. In one sense syncretism is an inevitable characteristic of any profound culture change, because change does not take place in a vacuum, but is developed on, or out from, or in contrast to an existing way of life. In this article John Beekman discusses some of the dangers of syncretism where the resulting behavior is out of keeping with the gospel. He also discusses the "reorientation" of Chol values and practices in the light of the gospel. This reorientation places the gospel in a framework which seems relevant to the Chol people. In a sense it is a syncretism in which pertinent elements in Chol culture are used to point toward the gospel, or are selected for the way in which they highlight the gospel to the Chol mind. At the same time they avoid the kind of mixture which points essentially toward paganism rather than toward Christ.

IN his recent book *Christo-Paganism,* William Madsen gives evidence that the present beliefs of the Aztecs living in San Francisco Tecospa are a result of a syncretistic process which began long before the introduction of Catholicism.[1] Morris Siegel, in his article "Cultural Changes in San Miguel Acatán, Guatemala," says that the religion of the Indians of San Miguel Acatán is a fusion of Indian and Catholic beliefs and practices, which does not resemble the Catholic religion in its orthodox form.[2]

William Reyburn introduces his article "The Spiritual, the Material, and the Western Reaction in Africa"[3] with an account of the death of a baby which was told to him by an African Christian. Apparently this man's beliefs concerning health, sickness, and death still admit elements of paganism.

Juan Comas, an outstanding Mexican anthropologist, in a conference held last year in Peru, made the following observation: "Practically the same thing has happened [in Peru] as with Motolinía and the Franciscan friars who arrived in Mexico in the early years of the conquest. They baptized about five thousand at one time. Theoretically these are Catholics. Actually, however, they practice their Indian religion simultaneously with

---

[1] See William Madsen, *Christo-Paganism: A Study of Mexican Religious Syncretism* (New Orleans: Middle American Research Institute, 1957; preprinted from Publication 19, pp. 105-180), and William L. Wonderly's review article "Pagan and Christian Concepts in a Mexican Indian Culture" (PRACTICAL ANTHROPOLOGY, Vol. 5, Nos. 5 & 6, Sept.-Dec. 1958).

[2] *Phylon, The Atlanta University Review of*

Race and Culture, Vol. 15, No. 2 (1954), pp. 165-176.

[3] PRACTICAL ANTHROPOLOGY, Vol. 6, No. 2 (March-April 1959).

Catholicism. This syncretism means that there is a religious factor and primitive superstitions that have not been eliminated."[4]

Missionaries also give wide testimony to the fact that certain concepts or practices of paganism persist for years among their converts and often are found in second and third generation Christians. These concepts become an integral part of their new religion. What can be done by the missionary to avoid unwarranted degrees of this type of syncretism? What can legitimately be done to at least attempt to reorient these cultural beliefs? What can be done to encourage suitable substitutions which are introduced by a new group of converts?

Since there are many factors which enter into possible answers to these questions, the author, who has had no formal study of anthropology, does not intend to answer these questions even as they relate to the Chols among whom he has worked as a missionary-translator for ten years. Selected field experiences are presented in which a certain recurring pattern may be seen. This may suggest an approach or methodology which may be helpful to others. It is not presumed that this is the complete answer to avoiding unwarranted religious syncretism, but merely a method of communicating religious concepts in such a way as to direct or guide the process of change by which pagan belief is reoriented in terms of Christianity. Many predisposing factors in the culture in general or in the experience of the individual are not dealt with in this paper.

In the first years of his work, among the Chols, the missionary often accom-

[4] Unpublished paper, presented August 20 1958.

John Beekman is a member of the Wycliffe Bible Translators, working among the Chol Indians of Chiapas, Mexico, and one of the translators of the Chol New Testament. He is also Director of the work of this organization in Guatemala. The present is the first of two articles which expand and further develop some of the concepts introduced by the same author in "A Culturally Relevant Witness" which appeared in PRACTICAL ANTHROPOLOGY, Vol. 4, No. 3 (May-June 1957).

---

panied some of the converts in evangelistic trips and noted some of the oft-recurring objections which were raised to the gospel. After there were readers, classes were conducted in the study of the printed portions of the New Testament for groups from different villages. As many as seven different groups were taught independently in the course of each month. Opportunity was given to them to tell of their experiences in witnessing and in strengthening new converts. The problems which had been both seen by the missionary and reported by the Indians were presented to each group who came for Bible study. The discussion was guided for the most part with pertinent questions in the same manner in which the missionary conducted the Bible study classes.[5] Sometimes a conclusion reached by one group would be different from that reached by another. Sometimes that which had been studied from the Old Testament Bible stories or New Testament portions was presented in the course of a discussion as pertinent to a problem.

[5] One visiting missionary after observing the classes made a criticism which later was reported to the writer: "Anybody could do what he does. All he does is sit there letting the Indians explain the passage. He asks questions but doesn't stand up and lecture."

The author recalls a discussion concerning the problem of young girls who were given in common marriage and after a few weeks or more returned to their homes. While the usual reason given was that the fellow and girl did not like each other, it was suspected that the real reason was that the girl did not work hard enough to please the mother-in-law. The missionary, therefore, suggested that perhaps the girl could live at the home of the groom's parents during the day and return to her own home in the evenings. The marriage state would then begin when the girl's father was asked permission to have his daughter live at the boy's home. This suggestion was not accepted. Rather the Chol Christians insisted that in God's sight a couple entered the marriage state as soon as the promised girl began to live at the fellow's home. A recent tendency has been observed of solving the problem by building a separate house for the new couple. This house is built by the groom's father, usually very close to his own. In view of this procedure, it seems fair to say that the Indians themselves arrived at the conclusions as to how to cope with this problem. On the other hand, without the presence of the missionary to note the problems and to focus the attention of the Indians on them, it is doubtful that some of the solutions presented in this paper would have been discovered. In any case, whether the idea originated primarily with the missionary or with an Indian, they were at complete liberty to try it or to ignore it.

The first example which we shall give of actual syncretism among the Chols exists among those who call themselves Catholics. Except for new forms and symbols introduced among the Chols, their beliefs remain basically pagan. For the lack of a better name reference will be made to this group with the phrase, 'followers of the traditional religion.' Those who have been converted from this group to the evangelical faith will be referred to as the 'converts.'

Problems of Syncretism in Easter Observances

The ancient Chols had a feast at corn-planting time which, in part at least, has survived to the present time. Its form may be somewhat modified, but its purpose has probably undergone no change. The Roman Catholic priests apparently tried to substitute the Easter celebration for this, since both occurred at about the same time of year. An image of Christ on the cross was used, and today the Chols follow the practice of covering the image with a black cloth during Holy Week and of removing it on Easter morning to indicate the resurrection. The Chols have accepted this ritual, reinterpreting its significance in the light of their own corn-planting ceremony. With some variations from village to village, the following summary indicates how these new items are reconciled to their purposes. The 'god' is covered so that he will think it is dark and cloudy and remember to send sunshine to dry out the recently felled trees and underbrush so that the fields can be burned. When the cloth is removed, it is to show him the blazing sun in order that he will send rain for the newly planted corn. During this season sacrifices are made in the corners of the fields which have been cut for planting. Fasting is also practiced. The only item which one may drink in any measure is liquor. To encourage the fast the religious leaders explain to the people that eggs eaten at this time are vultures' eggs, black beans are flies, the corn drink is pus, tortillas are dung.

For the converts, on the other hand, the Easter celebrations have become extended love feasts with services from Thursday evening through Sunday; though some villagers attend to their work on Saturday. At these feasts one or two steers are often purchased and cooked in front of the chapel by the women, or each family provides chickens, beans, or other food items much as in American pot-luck suppers except that the food is not brought fully prepared. At first the services included prayers for the crops, but more recently they center almost exclusively around the events of the life of Christ which happened on these days as recorded in Scripture.

This latter development may be due to two causes. The availability of ma-terials relating to the death and resurrec-tion of Christ, along with men who can read and explain these in the services, has contributed to this trend. The second cause originated with the feeling on the part of one or two of the missionaries that such fiestas were an economic bur-den to the Indians and not a proper observance of Easter. A Mexican worker in his visits to the Chol villages, there-fore, discouraged these fiestas which had become a symbol of their very purpose. A feeling of guilt still persists in the minds of some, and as a result communal gatherings of this type in some villages are not as fully attended as before. In view of this some meet this need by holding a family feast, usually of turkey, for the purpose of praying for good crops and protection from falling trees, machete cuts, and snake bites.

These converts had had their beliefs concerning the 'world owner' and the elements of nature reoriented to the beliefs of Christianity. If this had not been so, this prohibition might have resulted in a combination of Christian ideas and the old ceremony with the sacrifices made in the fields. Syncretism could have been produced rather than prevented.

Abortive Attempts at Syncretism

Among the converts in the village of Tumbalá were those who could read and understand some Spanish. In their reading of the Old Testament and from messages which they heard from Spanish-speaking pastors they became acquainted with the sacrifice of animals as a symbol of the sacrifice of Jesus. They also read that the Israelites were to eat no pork. Their own cultural background reminded them of the importance of animal sacri-fices and the central use of blood in the witchcraft ceremonies. These fellows be-came the proponents of the teaching that the blood of pigs is the blood of our Holy Father. It should not be eaten. Therefore when a pig is killed its blood must be caught in a gourd and cere-monially buried behind the house. This practice was short-lived.

Here is another example of what could have become a peculiar character-istic of Christianity among the Chols. A shaman who continued loyal to the traditional religion attempted to synthe-size his ceremony with some of the items connected with Christianity. In a village where more than half of the families had become converts, this enterprising shaman suggested some substitutions in his ceremonies. A shelf was set up, decorated with flowers and satin, on which a Bible was placed. His chants were then directed to the God of the Book and to the land-owning spirit. The convert was permitted to substitute liquor with a soft drink, but was required to provide liquor for the shaman. In questioning some of these believers it became obvious that the reason for the substitutions was very hazy in their thinking. Others felt it removed what God hated in the shaman ceremony, but did not affect its usefulness in regaining health. All still felt that health would be restored when the land-owning spirit had been effectively contacted on their behalf. Even though some items and terms of the Christian faith had been used, the basic pagan idea was unchanged.

Why did these converts accept the modified services of the shaman? Christianity at this point in their experience had been related to only a small part of their basic religious needs. They knew what it meant to be reconciled to the living God, but beyond that Christianity did not yet seem to have any real relevance. Their beliefs as to the cause and cure of sickness had not been changed. The modified ceremony did not seem to them to endanger or overlook the area of their Christian experience and conviction. While some opposed this syncretism, they were unable to explain their stand or to adequately answer the claims of the shaman. When the cultural beliefs concerning sickness were explained in terms of related Christian truths, the shaman received no further calls from the converts.

Up to this point our illustrations refer to actual or aborted attempts at religious syncretism. The following illustrations refer to potential areas of syncretism. This is based on the premise that wherever a group of converts accepts a new idea or practice without a proper understanding of its full significance or meaning, resistance to the new by the followers of the traditional religion tends to result in syncretism. To be sure, other factors limit or provoke this tendency. Some success has been observed among the Chol Indians in eliminating potential areas of syncretism by reorienting cultural beliefs. Five examples follow.

Reorienting Beliefs concerning Shamanism

The shaman with his chants, guitar, violin, and sacrifices to the land-owning spirit is a real temptation to the evangelical convert and fills a very important role for the followers of the traditional religion. In fact, one of the first questions asked by those who are approached with the gospel is what one does in times of sickness. The chants and music are believed necessary to bring the shaman into communion with the land-owning spirit. This they believe is effective only because he is indwelt with seven extra spirits. Others using these same means would not be able to communicate because of spiritual impotence. The animal sacrifice is the basis of success for his plea on behalf of the sick individual. The land-owning spirit desires other spirits and at times imprisons the spirit of a person which he releases in exchange for an animal spirit. The spirit which is acceptable to him is revealed to the shaman usually in audible communications. Often a shaman is accused of having failed to contact the land-owning spirit if a person does not recover after the prescribed sacrifice has been made. Among at least some of the Chol converts the idea that a spirit being could be contacted through music and by addressing him was not refuted; nor the idea that one must be indwelt with a spirit or spirits in order to commune with spirit beings. At the same time, the belief that a sacrifice was necessary in order to receive any benefits from a spirit being was not only considered worth retaining but worth emphasizing. One can see that many of these pagan practices are motivated with ideas that are in at least some measure compatible with Christianity. These beliefs which parallel Christian truth to be sure will need reorientation, but once they are recognized they become an important point of contact for teaching which should be exploited. The compatible ideas are extracted from the details and given emphasis. Then on this hook of mutual belief are hung the fuller truths of Christianity. One convert in speaking to a follower of the traditional religion during a measles epidemic said in part, "You call us 'monkeys' because you think our singing is like their chatter. We want help from God. You do too. You go to the old men to have them recite for you and to the shaman to have him chant. We pray and sing in our homes and in church. Our children get better; yours die."

Hymns, gospel phonograph records, and prayers are explained as the true means of contacting God. The church leaders who have been entrusted with the phonographs also know the hymns and can pray and read from portions of the New Testament. They were the logical ones to be called upon to minister to the sick instead of the shaman. The teaching that by faith in God's Son God gives us his Spirit to live in our hearts was not difficult for them to accept for it was a reorientation and extension of

their belief that the snaman is indwelt. The sacrifice of God's Son (who committed his spirit into God's hands not because he was afraid that the land-owning spirit would imprison it, but to show that God was well pleased with the sacrifice of his Son) could be accepted as a sufficient and better sacrifice, making the sacrifice of animals no longer necessary. In some cases it was necessary to point out that the Old Testament sacrifice of animals and the sacrifice of Christ were not to a spirit-hungry God. The first was a picture of and the latter the actual payment for our sins, so that with nothing written against us God could hear us. Payment for sin as a basis for reconciliation and fellowship was easily understood in view of their experience with ranchers to whom they frequently were heavily indebted.

Concepts of Sin

The subject of sin is so close a corollary to the sacrifice of God's Son and so closely related to the belief in the land-owning spirit and the shaman, that one is never dealt with without the others. It seems pertinent, therefore, to make the following observations.

Making extractions from stories and comments about sin, we can begin with those ideas which correspond to Christianity. Thus we would say that sin is an offense to a spirit-being or to one's fellow man. To the followers of the traditional religion, nothing is sin unless it involves offense. Drunkenness is therefore not a sin unless it ends with a fight. Theft is not sin unless the owner 'hurts in his heart' over what has been stolen and consults the shaman to find out who stole his goods. Converts lost much of their corn through theft perhaps because it was known that they no longer consulted the shaman. Unless the thief was caught, he was quite certain that even though offense had been caused, the convert had no way of avenging himself. (However, since the converts attended services and never worked in their fields on Sunday, and since most of these thefts occurred on Sunday, this may be the major reason for these thefts.) To the follower of the traditional religion, the physical condition of his family is one of the main factors in determining whether he is guilty of offense. If he offends the land-owning spirit, sickness will fall. If he offends his fellow-man, sickness may fall if a spell of black magic is cast on him or a member of his family through the services of the shaman. Health, then, although never explicitly stated as such, is a measure of one's spiritual relation to others and to the land-owning spirit. (The term 'God' as used by the followers of the traditional religion includes the concept of the land-owning spirit, although there is a separate term used to specifically refer to the latter.)

Converts often made the statement to the followers of the traditional religion that Christ died for their sins and they should believe on him. Invariably the answer received to such a statement was: "I don't have any sin." This was a sincere answer although the author was unable to explain it in his early years among the Chols. The Indian did not mean that he had never lied, stolen, or beaten his wife. He meant that since he and his family were well, there was no unappeased offense in his life. The convert, there-fore, developed another set of criteria on which to base his relationship with God. Instead of arguing that he was a sinner and God's Word said so, he pointed to the greater well-being of the converts in general. He compared his shirt and trousers to those worn by the individual to whom he was talking. He compared his shoes to the other's bare feet. He spoke of eating crackers with the family instead of losing money, hat, and machete in drunkenness. He spoke of owning mules and tin-roofed houses instead of carrying firewood on his back and patching up a grass roof. His argu-ment implied that health is not the only criterion of one's relationship to God, and it has been a very effective answer in winning converts. It should be noted that medical work among the Chols is a very effective means of gaining converts. When the followers of the traditional religion come for medicine, it usually indicates that they have tired of the un-availing services of the shaman. They come with a subconscious feeling that all is not right because of sickness in the family. They are ready to listen to culturally related spiritual truths.

House-Dedication Practices

When a new hut is constructed the shaman is generally called upon to dedi-cate it to the land-owning spirit whose property (trees, grass, land) has been used in its construction. In his chants he requests protection from fire, the wind, thieves, and spirit manifestations. The drumming and violin-playing and drinking of liquor lasts from one to three days. The converts, however, dedi-cate their new homes by inviting the church leaders and friends to an evening of refreshments consisting of cookies and soft drinks. Prayer for the occupants of the new home and for the protection of the house, along with singing, charac-terizes the evening's activities.

The desire for protection from the forces of nature and from thieves is legitimate for any people. The purpose of the shaman's ceremony has been carried over into that which was substituted by the converts. Its focal center, however, has been shifted from the land-owning spirit to a more powerful spirit, i.e. the Holy Spirit. Instead of being based on appeasing the land-owning spirit through the medium of the shaman with his extra spirits, it became based on the indwelling Spirit through whom one had guidance and protection from God. The fact that rattling gourds, whistlings in the grass roofs, dirt throwings, etc. were reported as no longer occurring at the homes of converts was convincing evidence of the power of the Holy Spirit.

Use of Liquor

It is interesting to note the efforts made by one of the leaders of the convert group in the Tumbalá church to undermine the religious significance attached to the use of liquor. All the shaman's activities as well as all religious observances require the use of liquor, which the followers of the traditional religion believe to be of divine origin. The old men feel it is necessary in their prayers in order to 'get warm in reciting.' The shaman declares that he cannot offer his chants without liquor. Often when speaking to the cross he may order that 'the bottom of the gourd be poured on the cross' in order to cause the Father to be more communicative and less angry. Week-end drunkenness, apart from religious fiestas, has been a long-standing problem in Spanish-speaking cities. In the Indian village drunkenness is almost exclusively related to religious functions. In appealing to his fellow-converts to

desist from all use of liquor, the above-mentioned leader made reference to Proverbs 20: 1, 2, which reads, "Strong drink is raging. . . . The fear of a king is as of the roaring of a lion," and also Luke 13: 1 which speaks of the Galileans whose blood Pilate had mingled with their sacrifices. These verses became the text for a Sunday sermon. The Indian preacher declared that liquor, which causes us to become ferocious like a lion, originated when the blood of people from Galilee was mixed with the blood of a raging lion. While this fellow's intentions were good and the impressions of his message vivid, his understanding of these verses was quite defective.

A more biblical way was found to meet the objection often raised that liquor is necessary for religious expression. Those who raised such objections were told that it is true that some outside stimulant is necessary to man in order to free his inhibitions. It is impossible to pray right without this, and the true God wants us to have it. Then the teaching of Acts 2, where the Pentecostal experience is clearly explained to be the result of the Spirit rather than liquor, is made relevant here. Again it may be seen that the purpose in the use of liquor, i.e. that an outside stimulant or constraining power is necessary in order to worship God properly, is retained but reoriented. It becomes based on the Spirit rather than on liquor. Thus the religious use of liquor with its accompanying drunkenness is no problem among the converts and can no longer be considered an area of potential syncretism.[6]

6 Would this approach to the emotional experiences connected with the ritual use of mushrooms, as described by Pike and Cowan

Images

When the converts were asked why their church building contained no images, which the followers of the traditional religion call 'God's image,' the first answer used was the conventional one. The theological reply was given by the convert: "God is a Spirit and we cannot see him; however, he is present in our churches." This answer, however, did not seem to entirely satisfy the inquiring follower of the traditional religion. The statement was often made in ridicule: "All your churches have is a phonograph machine on a table. The saloons in Yajalón have the same." The underlying assumption was that a church, to be more than just a building, had to have in it something visible. To be a place of real worship and not just a place of play, it should contain something sacred, something like God. This assumption was not refuted. It was reoriented by showing that the church building does have in it those whom God himself has declared to be in his own image. The answer now given has been more or less along the following lines: "God's book tells us that he made *man* in his own image. The more we obey his commands the more fully do *we* become his image. What you call 'God's image' is something made by man. God tells us what really is his image. It is something *he* made, not what we make. It is ourselves, not a wooden idol. He gives his Spirit to all his children. Nowhere does he say that something which *we* make

in PRACTICAL ANTHROPOLOGY, Vol. 6, No. 4 (July-August 1959), be a fruitful way of showing that the Christian message has an adequate substitute for these chemically-induced 'revelations'? [W.L.W.].

has spirit power. Our churches are full of God's images when a service is held."

Candles

The followers of the traditional religion use candles in all religious functions. Prayers conducted in the Catholic church by the older men and women as those conducted by the shaman are accompanied with the burning of candles. The total disappearance of candles in the religious life of the converts has often become a point of ridicule. "You must have candles and sometimes even incense in order to make real prayers" was the answer normally given by the followers of the traditional religion as to why candles were used. A few reports filtered back to the missionary that some converts resorted to the use of candles in times of critical illness and in funeral wakes. It finally became clear that the use of candles was motivated by the idea that light made one's prayers acceptable. The converts now have an answer to queries as to why they do not use candles. They explain that God likes light and all that it represents. He wants us to have a light when we pray to him, but not a small flickering light made by man. He wants to see a great light which he himself sent down from heaven to shine in our hearts. Jesus said that he himself was the light of the world. This is the light God wants to see in our hearts. Here again is an illustration of reorienting a religious motif after one understands its purpose. Whatever in this purpose is compatible with the gospel becomes an equally acceptable starting point to both parties before proceeding to the new and fuller truth or practices of Christianity.

Perhaps all that should be claimed from the foregoing discussion as a method of avoiding religious syncretism is that it has given converts an intelligent understanding of what their new faith embraces and why they desist from certain practices and have adopted substitutes for others. It has removed what would otherwise be temptations into which they would frequently fall. For at least some of the honest inquirers, this approach has contributed much toward removing their fears and doubts concerning the way of the gospel.

PART VII

Cultural Processes:
Communication

David J. Hesselgrave

Dimensions of Crosscultural Communication

There are at least seven dimensions of crosscultural communication: the worldview, the cognitive process, the linguistic form, the behavioral pattern, the media, the social structure, and the motivational dimension. These are operative at both micro-cultural and macro-cultural levels, and serve as either channels or obstacles to effective crosscultural communication, depending on how they are understood and exploited.

FOR our astronauts those fantastic journeys in which they view our earth from high in the stratosphere and cross over all barriers—ethnic, political, economic, linguistic—with unbelievable ease and velocity are becoming routine. It is ironic however that even in the twentieth century there are numerous areas where their sudden advent from the skies would be considered a mystifying intrusion or even a hostile invasion. The barriers are, after all, very real and challenging.

There is a very real danger that as our technology advances and enables us to cross geographical and national boundaries with singular ease and increasing frequency we forget that cultural barriers are real and formidable. The gap between our technological advances and our communication skills is perhaps one of the most challenging aspects of modern civilization. Western diplomats are beginning to realize that they need much more than a knowledge of their message and a good interpreter or English-speaking national. Missionaries now understand that much more than a microphone and increased volume is involved in penetrating cultural barriers. Many educators have come to the position that crosscultural communication is a *sine qua non* for citizenship in this new world.

Unfortunately, in addition to being a kind of *summum bonum* in education for mission and even survival, intercultural communication is as complex as the sum total of human differences. The word "culture" is one of the most inclusive terms in the English vocabulary. It takes into account linguistic, political, economic, social, psychological, religious, national, racial and other differences. These aspects of culture do not develop in a parallel way, and distinctions based entirely upon Western educational disciplines may or may not be applicable for intercultural communication.

DIMENSIONS OF CROSSCULTURAL COMMUNICATION

E N C O D E R

E N C O D E S

| M | E | S | S | A | G | E | CULTURE X |

MICRO-CULTURE

The Motivational Dimension – Ways of Deciding

The Social Structure – Ways of Interacting

The Media – Ways of Channeling the Message

The Behavioral Pattern – Ways of Acting

The Linguistic Form – Ways of Expressing Ideas

The Cognitive Process – Ways of Thinking

The Worldview – Ways of Perceiving the World

MACRO-CULTURE

| M | E | S | S | A | G | E | CULTURE Y |

D E C O D E D

R E S P O N D E N T

How shall we introduce the problem of talking and listening crossculturally in such a way as to titillate and motivate the student rather than discourage him with a seemingly hopeless task? Initiation by immediate immersion into the voluminous bibliography on linguistic, anthropological, social and other differences would be enough to dishearten all but the most mightily motivated of students. If, as Kenneth Burke says, "You can persuade a man only insofar as you can talk his language by speech, gesture, tonality, order, image, attitude, idea, identifying your ways with his,"[1] where does one begin? If, as Karl Potter suggests, we communicate crossculturally when we perceive the "self-image" of the respondent,[2] how shall we heighten our perception?

At the very real risk of over-simplification, I propose that an introduction to crosscultural communication deal with seven dimensions which seem to be most important and promising. The accompanying diagram will serve to illustrate how these dimensions are at once channels and chasms in communication. Every message is encoded and decoded within the framework of these seven areas—there is no way "between" or "around" them, only "through" them. But cultural differences have the effect of narrowing these channels, both at the "micro-cultural" and "macro-cultural" levels.[3] As messages filter through the cultural grid they are delimited by cultural differences, first at the micro-cultural level and then at the macro-cultural level. A message must be well aimed to hit the mark! We aim well when we grasp the self-understanding of the respondent and address our message to him in terms of his way of viewing the world, his way of thinking, his way of expressing himself in language, his way of acting, the media he utilizes, his way of interacting with his fellows, and his way of deciding future courses of action. At the same time, we must keep in mind that these dimensions interpenetrate and impinge upon one another. They are separable for pragmatic purposes, but combine to form one reality.

Ways of Perceiving the World : the World-view

Robert T. Oliver,[4] in talking about the contribution of the speech profession to internationalism, insists that we think in terms of rhetorics in the plural rather than of rhetoric in the singular as though one rhetoric were

[1] Kenneth Burke, *The Rhetoric of Motives and the Grammar of Motives* (Cleveland: The World Publishing Company, 1962), p. 579.

[2] Karl Potter, "The Self-Image Approach" in *Approaches to Asian Civilizations*, ed. by Wm. Theodore de Bary and Ainslee T. Embree (New York: Columbia University Press, 1964), pp. 273-275.

[3] For want of better terms, "Micro-culture" refers to the numerous sub-cultures which exist within large groupings in which people identify with one another by giving allegiance to the same flag, obeying the same government, speaking the same language, operating with similar values, etc. The latter we have called "macro-culture." Of necessity the terms are imprecise.

[4] Robert T. Oliver, *Culture and Communication* (Springfield, Illinois: Charles C. Thomas, 1962).

universally applicable. From a missionary standpoint it is instructive that he differentiates rhetorics on the basis of worldviews related to religious philosophies. He elaborates Shintoist, Hindu-Buddhistic, Taoist, and Confucian rhetorics as well as the Communist rhetoric. Aristotelian rhetoric fits hand in glove with the classical view of the world, but Oliver is saying that when we speak, for example, to the Chinese portion of the human race, their view of the world is so profoundly different as to necessitate an entirely new rhetoric. Missionaries ministering in many parts of the Orient become aware of the fact that they are engaged, in one sense, in a "whole new ball game"—and an exciting and challenging one at that!

A case in point would be the Buddhist monistic conception of the universe as contrasted with the pluralistic universe of the West. The corollary of the monistic worldview is the doctrine of "no-soul" and the belief that no individual has a separate and independent existence. The consequences of this view tend to ramify throughout the whole of the cognitive, motivational and behavioral pattern. Whereas our western goal is to think independently, be true to oneself, and strive-for individual achievement, the Buddhist would tend to deny the self and merge his individuality with the totality of the universe or its larger expressions.

Oliver makes the very good point that the Buddhist as well as the Westerner can be expected to be self-centered (or selfish) because such is the characteristic of human nature. But an understanding of the Buddhist worldview would indicate that while appeals may be made *from* self-centeredness, they should not be made *to* it. The missionary who takes this orientation seriously will stress (among other things) the fruits of faith as they accrue to family and nation, not just the individual. Obedience to God is not simply to enjoy his favor personally, but to become the vehicle through which others may come to enjoy his favor. It is not individualism per se that is the barb in many a missionary appeal, but Western individualism. The monistic error, once understood, may prove to be a corrective to the extreme individualism of the West. (But we have anticipated ourselves and in the process have demonstrated how the decision-making process grows out of the worldview!)

Not only rhetoricians, but orientalists, anthropologists and others stand ready to help the student with this dimension of communication. For example, Sidney Lewis Gulick distinguishes between static and kinetic worldviews and relates the static view to the Hindu-Buddhistic religious system.[5] Franz Boaz has written extensively on the worldview of the primitive.[6] The student of intercultural communication should be made aware at the outset that his own view of the world—its genesis, goal, values,

5 Sidney Lewis Gulick, *The East and the West* (Rutland, Vermont: Charles E. Tuttle Co., 1963).

6 Franz Boas, *The Mind of Primitive Man* (New York: The Macmillan Co., 1938).

and composition—is shared with members of other cultures only in part, if at all.

Ways of Thinking: the Cognitive Process

About the same time that F.S.C. Northrop contrasted Eastern and Western ways of knowing in his book *The Meeting of East and West*,[7] F.H. Smith elaborated *three* basic cognitive approaches to reality. Edmund Perry reports on the lecture at the University of Manchester (May 2, 1950) where Smith differentiated between the conceptual, psychical (or psychological), and concrete relational ways of thinking or knowing.[8] The *conceptual* corresponds to Northrop's cognition by *postulation;* the *psychical* corresponds to·Northrop's cognition by *intuition;* and the *concrete relational* is a way of thinking in which *"life and reality are seen pictorially in terms of the active emotional relationships present in a concrete situation."*

Being a rather typical product of Western culture, I required years of of living in Japan (and communing with Japanese) to acquire an appreciation for their distrust of truth when it was presented as an inescapable conclusion resting on two or three simply stated premises. Slowly I came to the realization that about the only provision I had made for anything other than Western logical thought patterns was an occasional bow to a "woman's intuition" (and a not too

polite one at that!). The comparatively depreciated value placed on debating points; the "feeling" that attended "right" decisions; the "communicativeness" of a garden or grove—these and many other factors assisted in my "education." Propositional truth lost none of its force, but there developed a greater appreciation for the mysteries and antinomies of Scripture, the appropriateness of treading more softly at times, the desirability of silence when the situation called for it.

To the Western student it may come as a shock to discover that logical concepts are not sacrosanct all over the world. But he will be much better prepared to communicate crossculturally when he realizes the fundamental importance of the "mental experience" and the "living imagery of the objective world" in the cognitive processes of the Indians and Chinese. Northrop and Smith are not saying that we are complete strangers to the ways in which these friends from the East think. Indeed there is a contemporary taste for Indian *gurus* and Zen *koan* in the West! Nor are we saying that the missionary communicator will agree that the "mystery of divine reality eludes the mystery of speech and symbol." But a careful consideration of psychical thinking will enable him to understand why the Indian wants to make his "assault on the citadel of truth" without reliance on concepts or scriptures. And he will be more appreciative of the Japanese concern for proper timing and surroundings (context) for a religious message. In fact, the activities of Old Testament prophets, the parables of

---

[7] F.S.C. Northrop, *The Meeting of East and West* (New York: Macmillan, 1953).

[8] Edmund Perry, *The Gospel in Dispute*, (New York: Doubleday, 1958).

our Lord, and the ministry of the Holy Spirit will become more meaningful.

Ways of Expressing Ideas: the Linguistic Form

The argument concerning the causal relationship between culture and language, and which affects the other to the greater degree, has always seemed somewhat unproductive to me. But language is important from more perspectives than the obvious one. For example, languages tend to reflect that which is important in a given culture. The European languages reflect the primary importance of time in Euro-American culture. A man was, is, or will be sick. Languages which do not require this distinction between past, present, and future by virtue of their grammatical structure may seem strange to us, but at the same time are instructive at that very point of strangeness.

The importance of the kind of information which is being communicated is reflected in the structure of the languages of some non-literate peoples. The language structure may require that the source of the knowledge—personal experience, other evidence, or simply hearsay—be divulged in the communicating of it.

Again non-literates may not speak in abstract terms, avoiding such categories as goodness, truthfulness, or blissfulness apart from the specific individual or circumstances to which they apply. This does not mean that the non-literate is not a philosopher. But it probably indicates that some peoples have a different way of phi-

losophizing and that communication which majors on abstractions will be difficult for them to comprehend.

Somewhat different insights may be gained by reference to the Japanese language. In the words of Douglas Haring (referring to the Japanese language),

A new dimension in student thinking about languages emerges with the discovery that thoughts can be communicated in the absence of familiar categories of gender, number, definite and indefinite articles, and relative words, phrases, or clauses.[9]

A brief introduction to the *honorific forms* of Japanese verb conjugation will serve to demonstrate how verbal forms communicate relative social status. A presentation of *ideographic* writing will help the Western student in his appreciation of the possibilities of non-phonetic systems of writing. Again, the dependence upon *indirect modes* of expression involved in proverbs, riddles, and legends helps explain how people often communicate pointed and even highly personal information with a minimal risk of being offensive.

Again, take the personal questions which cause Westerners to chafe when talking crossculturally. The inquiries into age, destination, personal plans, personality traits of close kin, etc., may seem to be impertinent to Westerners, but when understood as ex-

---

9 de Bary and Embree, eds., *Approaches...*: *Asia via Japan* by Douglas Haring, p. 193.

pressing concern and interest rather than as a "nosey" prying into what we may consider to be private affairs, they become bridges rather than barriers to intercultural communication.

The student who tends to think that language learning is simply a case of finding one-to-one linguistic correlations is in for an exciting experience when he begins to think in terms of that which languages reveal about the people who use them. When he is made aware of the intimate relationship between language and culture, the basic differences between languages, and the importance of linguistic bridges, he will have made a great stride forward in his preparation.

Ways of Acting: the Behavioral Pattern

The uninitiated will add an entirely new dimension to his understanding when he begins to examine just a few examples of the multitudinous behavioral conventions through which peoples of the world communicate. I cannot improve upon Ina Corinne Brown's way of expressing it in her book *Understanding Other Cultures.*

Whether you do or do not open a gift in the presence of the giver; whether you should or should not turn the plate over to look at the maker's symbol on the back; whether you put your coat on quietly or as noisily as possible; whether you carry on a conversation during a meal; whether you walk in front of or behind a seated person; wehhter it is a friendly or an offensive gesture to put your hand on the arm of the person with whom you are talking—these and a thousand other questions are matters of cultural definition. None of them is inherently right or wrong, and none is good or bad manners except as a society defines it so.[10]

An esteemed former professor of mine, Dr. William S. Howell, has asserted that "the Ugly American award is won more often by failing to meet expectations of appropriate behavior than by misusing the local language."[11] He notes, for example, that many North American professors in Lebanon manage to insult their students and fellow faculty without realizing it. The offensive behavior involves the positioning of the foot in such a way that the other person is confronted by the sole of the shoe. This usually happens when the speaker is seated so that in the crossing of his legs the sole of his shoe faces the one with whom he is conversing. It is ironic that in the effort to be informal (to heighten the degree of communication!) the North American professors tend to cross their legs or even put their feet on a desk in such a way that communication is all but impossible. As one indigene put it, "I doubt that any Middle Eastern

10 Ina Corinne Brown, *Understanding Other Cultures* (Englewood Cliffs: Prentice-Hall, Inc., 1963), p. 86.

11 William S. Howell, "The Study of Intercultural Communication in Liberal Education," *Pacific Speech,* Vol 2, No. 4.

student could ever fully accept and trust the professor after he has demonstrated complete contempt for them, whether on purpose or accidentally." His assessment of the situation may be extreme, but it is nevertheless instructive.

It is ironic that the average missionary spends countless hours studying the vocabulary, grammar and syntax of the verbal language of his adopted culture while willy-nilly picking up a limited number of rules of this "silent language." The reason for this may be found in Edward Hall's insight that appropriate nonverbal behavior is learned at the informal, out-of-awareness level.[12] What is learned in this way is seldom brought to the level of awareness, and then pondered and justified. It is simply the "way one ought to act." Therefore the missionary gives it little thought except in the most obvious (and sometimes, embarrassing) circumstances, and the national simply concludes that he has met yet another ignorant foreigner. Cultural shock, after all, is a two-way street. And it occurs primarily because of faulty communication at the nonverbal level.

What is needed is an introduction to nonverbal communication in the classroom as a part of a systematic study of intercultural communication. This preparation will enable the missionary to gradually and meaningfully build an inventory of the local culture once he has arrived on the field. Dr. Howell explains what is involved:

The norms of non-verbal interaction involve kinesics, the purposeful use of the body to transmit meaning; proxemics, the use of space and the physical relationship of those communicating; and paralanguage, vocal elements other than those integral to the spoken words, e.g. quality, volume, etc. Interwoven, they consitute the non-linguistic codes of a culture.[13]

Ways of Channeling Communication: the Media

In time past the emphasis in communication has been upon communicators and respondents, the context in which they encode and decode their messages, and upon the messages themselves—their intent, style, etc. Recently we have been made aware of the fact that the media or channels through which we put the mesage are not neutral.

In a telling article, David Riesman examines the importance of oral tradition as over against written tradition and on this basis poses the question of what might happen in those cases where electronic media break in without warning upon those societies that are still oral.[14]

At a more demonstrable level, Marshall McLuhan insists that we make a colossal mistake in assuming that

---

12 Edward T. Hall, *The Silent Language* (Greenwich, Conn.: Fawcett Publications, Inc., 1966).

13 William S. Howell, *op. cit.*

14 David Riesman, "The Oral and Written Traditions," in *Explorations in Communication*, ed. by Edmund Carpenter and Marshall McLuhan (Boston: Beacon Press, 1960), pp. 109-116.

the very nature of the motion picture does not radically influence what is communicated. The movie as a medium assumes a high level of literacy. The literate follows the eye of the camera and is quite oblivious to the fact that the edge of the screen is "screening" him from much of the action. Not so with the nonliterate. If someone disappears off the side of the film he wants to know why, and where he has gone. This upsetting experience may completely overshadow the intended message!

Or, to take another case in point, imagine the struggle of the Japanese to rebuild their country and homes, and raise their level of living in the aftermath of World War II. I remember an occasion when I went to considerable trouble and not a little expense to secure a Christian film that seemed to have been well received in the American churches. Anticipating a similar (if not more significant) result I scheduled the film for our area. The audience seemed enraptured with the story as it came across via picture and translated narration. I was encouraged. In keen anticipation of getting to the essentials of the Christian faith, I asked for questions after the showing. One after another, inquisitive Japanese asked whether the homes in the movies were typical American homes; how Americans seemingly had so much time for leisure activities; whether all churches had steeples; and numerous other questions in the same vein. To my chagrin, the nature of the medium which had necessitated the inclusion of massive amounts of extraneous detail had in this case almost completely obliterated the Christian message.

If we think of communication as including the *total* "meaning" of the communication act (i.e. impact upon target audiences), or if we think of the "message" as including changes the communication act introduces *à la* McLuhan, then we will be forced to admit that to a large extent the "medium *is* the message."[15] The interplay between cultural factors and the impact of the media then become a fundamental consideration of crosscultural communication.

As for mission, it remains to be seen as to what extent current programs of research in communications will influence thought and practice. Much of this research is in mass communication—a factor which may prejudice the results. As Eugene Nida has noted, the tendency to emphasize the mass approach is already indicative of imbalance, as is the almost exclusive focus upon the spoken sermon as the medium of communication of the gospel.

Here is a dimension of crosscultural communication thet has long been neglected. It represents an exciting challenge to students of mission.

Ways of Interacting: the Social Structure

Men not only have ways of acting which are largely culturally determined according to accepted rules of conduct and meaning, they interact on the basis of where they fit into the social structure of a society or societies.

15 Marshall McLuhan, *Understanding Media* (New York: McGraw Hill, 1964).

Social structure dictates which channels of communication are open and which are closed; who talks to whom and in what way; and what communication and messages will carry most prestige.

Lucian Pye tells of an election campaign in Jahore State, Malaya, involving two Westernized political candidates.[16] One took his message to the people via rallies which attracted large crowds in village after village. Since his reception was so enthusiastic it was assumed by many that he would be overwhelmingly successful on election day. The election, however, was won by his equally Westernized opponent who engaged in little direct campaigning. Why? Because in conducting his campaign the popular candidate had bypassed the opinion leaders in the various areas where he had gone. This omission resulted in distrust and cost him the election. Obviously, success in politics is more than "taking your case to the people" or "competing in the open marketplace of ideas" in a case such as this.

A map of social structure is also a map of communication. Such maps have transcultural similarities and yet are characterized by important differences in every situation. It makes all the difference in the world whether communication takes place in a rural or urban setting; a primitive, transitional or industrialized community; a totalitarian or a democratic state.

One of the most significant contributions to missionary thinking in this area is Eugene Nida's chapter on "Communication and Social Structure" in which he compares Protestant, Catholic and Communist approaches to Latin American culture.[17] But there is a great wealth of materials which illustrate the importance of this dimension for the student of crosscultural communication.

Ways of Deciding: the Motivational Dimension

One reason for talking interculturally is to reach decisions—decisions which grow out of information and suasions and are reflected in changed attitudes and new courses of action. Indeed to a great degree the missionary task can be summed up in Paul's words "Knowing therefore the terror of the Lord, we persuade men." But here again the basis on which men make such decisions varies considerably with the culture. One of the best known attempts at a psychological analysis of culture is that of Ruth Benedict who distinguished between guilt and shame cultures.[18] A more recent study in cultural psychology is that of Francis L.K. Hsu.[19] In a study of China, Japan, Germany and America, Professor Hsu delineates "suppression" and "repression" cultures. "Repression cultures" as represented by Germany

16 Lucian Pye, "Communication Operation in Non-Western Societies," in *Reader in Public Opinion and Communication*, ed. by Bernard Berelson and Morris Janowitz (New York: The Free Press, 2nd ed., 1966), pp. 612-620.

17 Eugene Nida, *Message and Mission* (New York: Harper and Row Pub., 1960), pp. 94-132.

18 Ruth Benedict, *The Chrysanthemum and the Sword* (Boston: Houghton Mifflin, 1946).

19 In *Psychiatry*, Vol. 12, No. 3, pp. 223-242, referred to in Perry, 1958, pp. 101-103.

and America tend to exclude from the individual consciousness those ideas and desires which are taboo. Such cultures are individual-centered and stress internal controls. "Supression cultures" such as Japan and China tend to stress restraint from certain courses of behavior because of the circumstances which appertain. In such cultures external controls are important and the "pattern of life is situation-centered."

Take the case of the American missionary who presses a Chinese for a decision. Once the decision has been made the missionary is elated. Some days (or weeks) later the Chinese "convert" does an about-face and in one way or another gives evidence of a lapse of faith. The response of the missionary is almost automatic. Having been so quickly let down he becomes immersed in the slough of despondency and cries, "That's the way it is with these Chinese (Orientals). They decide for Christ and the next thing you know they have gone back on it. You just can't count on them." It never occurs to him that his "disciple in the rough" may be simply reflecting the philosophy of Confucius (not because he is a Confucianist, but because he is a Chinese) who explained that "The superior man goes through his life without any one preconceived course of action or any taboo. He merely decides for the moment what is the right thing to do." In accord with this philosophy, the Chinese might just as well judge the missionary as foolish for thinking that as circumstances radically change he should be held to a course of action which

seemed right at the moment but subsequently (in other circumstances) proved to be extremely uncomfortable. That which was virtue for one was vice for the other, and vice versa. To point out the problem is not to argue for the correctness of either Confucius or his unsuspecting contemporary "disciple." It is rather to plea for understanding and preparedness.

Conclusion

The above is, of course, only suggestive. There are great vistas to be explored in each of these dimensions for the differences between cultures are immense. Yet, as Edmund Perry suggests, it is all-important that the student be reminded that while cultures are radically different they are not completely so.[20] Ways of perceiving the world, thinking, expressing ideas, acting, channeling communication, interacting, and deciding which are in evidence in other cultures are not entirely absent from our own. In other words, what is primary in another culture is likely to be secondary or tertiary in our culture. This means that we already have *some* understanding of cultural differences and a great part of the educator's task is to bring this understanding to a new level of awareness.

Nothing short of Christian love for the respondents as people for whom Christ died will be sufficient in communicating the Christian Gospel. But an understanding of crosscultural communication is a part of the "second

[20] Perry, 1958, p. 103.

mile" of Christian love. To a degree it enables the missionary to sit where they sit, experience what they experience, feel as they feel. It enables him to control the communication situation rather than be controlled by the situation. It enables him to more effectively consummate communication by modifying his own concerns, expressing his thought, adjusting his behavior, and appealing to motivations that answer to the self-understanding of the respondent. After all, the respondent we are attempting to characterize in this enquiry is the one who *really* exists. To project only our own self-understanding into the skin of the respondent is tantamount to talking to a person who is not really "at home" to the communication.

Eugene A. Nida

Communication of the Gospel to Latin Americans

Without doubt one of the most strategic problems facing Protestant missions and churches in Latin America is that of relevant communication. This does not mean that communication in the past has been totally ineffective. The remarkable increase in the evangelical constituency indicates quite the contrary, for whereas one hundred years ago there was probably not one evangelical to two hundred and fifty Roman Catholics, at present there is an estimated one evangelical to every thirty-nine Roman Catholics. On the other hand, in terms of the expenditure of time, effort, and personnel, communication of the gospel appears to be surprisingly inadequate, seemingly superficial, and apparently indicative of the Protestant church's having reached a plateau of creative involvement in the life of the Latin American community.[1]

THE basic problem of communication was brought home to me some years ago in a conversation with a very devout Roman Catholic professor of philosophy in Ecuador who said, "We are really not at all concerned about Protestant missions in Latin America, for it is so obvious that you do not understand us; therefore, how can you ever convince us?" This is a very valid observation, for how many American missionaries actually have a thorough knowledge of Roman Catholic doctrine as a religious-philosophical system? Of course, all have some knowledge of certain points which are supposed to be vulnerable to attack, but this type of superficial sniping is not very profitable for it neither convinces many unbelievers nor does it really instruct those who need to understand the new and

creative basis of their recently discovered faith in Jesus Christ.

Moreover, relatively few Bible schools and seminaries have courses in the cultural characteristics of Latin life, the major philosophical and religious themes which dominate contemporary thinking, and the fundamental features of Latin social structure. Of course, there is usually some time given to studying the rival sects, but this again is so largely "straining out gnats and swallowing camels." Where are we to find in Spanish and Portuguese some thoroughly scholarly treatments of Existentialism (undoubtedly the dominant philosophical trend in Latin America) written by Latin evangelicals and aimed at a systematic and vital communication with those of Existential orientation? Many missionaries and their Latin associates become so involved in the day-to-day routine of largely traditional forms of communication that they tend to miss the dynamic development in modern life, especially if evangelical maga-

[1] This article was prepared for the Latin American Congress on Evangelical Communications, held at Cali, Columbia, in 1959. The conference was particularly concerned with radio and literature.

627

zines "from home" are not discussing such matters.

As a result, the British-American "spiritual colonies" of evangelical work in Latin America become more and more isolated from the main stream of Latin thought, particularly since so much of what is going on in Latin intellectual life comes from Continental Europe rather than from the United States or Great Britain. Just because Latin countries are buying American cars and refrigerators does not mean that they are importing American ideas.

Contrasts in Protestant and Roman Catholic Orientations toward Life

Perhaps we can never quite understand some of the vital elements in Latin life and their relevance to communication, unless we recognize some of the essential differences between American Protestantism and Latin Roman Catholicism.[2] As Rycroft points out, these are not mere divergencies in doctrinal positions, but fundamental contrasts in "world view." Of the many which we might mention, the following are perhaps the most relevant for our purposes of study in communication:

Authoritarianism. In the Latin system "error has no rights" and as the ultimate judge of error, by virtue of its being regarded as God's representative on earth, the Roman Church maintains a dominant voice. Authoritarianism, however, is not limited to religious matters, but enters into the justification of the social structure (in providing the traditional reasons for the exclusive leadership of society by the upper class), of education (by insisting on "the given rule," and not in developing multiple hypotheses as to truth), and of

---

2 See W. Stanley Rycroft's stimulating book, *Religion and Faith in Latin America* (Philadelphia: Westminster Press, 1958).

politics (where a truly two-party government is very rare and the concept of "the loyal opposition" is denied, if not in principle, at least in fact). Authoritarianism in the intellectual field has produced some very brilliant minds, especially in the realm of history and the arts, but the same dynamic which has made men forge ahead in proof of "the given rule" has not produced, and understandably so, corresponding success in the field of science and technology. Anglo-Saxon Protestantism, on the other hand, is committed to an equalitarian concept of life, which though denied in actual practice, nevertheless becomes a significant basis for the defense of minorities, the rights of the opposition, and the freedom to question.

Passive fatalism. The passive fatalism of Latin America is a composite trait, reflecting the Iberian temperament as (1) influenced by the Moors of North Africa, whose religious theme was "submission to the will of Allah," and (2) compounded with the fatalistic concepts so dominant in many indigenous religious systems of the Americas. At the same time, the theological concept of the irrevocable sinfulness of the flesh (not because of the rebellion of the heart, but by virtue of the limitations of human nature) has cut the nerve of moral responsibility and overwhelmed men with a sense of ultimate pessimism and melancholy, so evident in Latin music, poetry, and love. This same view of life, however, helps to explain some of the incredible feats of human courage, often mixed with bravado and daring, for where human life is ultimately cheap, it can be readily risked. American Protestantism on the other hand, is impressively "action oriented" (in some respects too much so) but there is an incurable optimism in thi incessant activity and a sense of divine constraint to build, create, and improve, in order that all of life may be subjugated to the rule of God.

Division between the sacred and the secular. In the same way that the altar rail decisively separates the ordained clergy from the laity, so the traditional distinction between the sacred and secular runs throughout Latin life. Where, however, the sacred is exalted at the expense of the secular, all of life inevitably suffers, for the Biblical view is that all aspects of life must be consecrated to the service of God. Therefore the "contemplative life" has no priority over the menial and the "white collar professional" is not superior to the "shirtless" service, for we are all members of one body despite our several functions. Protestantism, though somewhat guilty of the same non-Biblical distinction, nevertheless, honors all types of work and in theory at least denies the rigid division which tends to make everyday life less noble than it must be, if all of life is to be lived unto the glory of God.

Religion as a mechanism for overcoming crises. In Roman Catholicism of Latin America, religion is not so much a matter of transfomed life as a technique for passing through or escaping life's crises. With the professional help of a specialist, the priest, one can be assured of all spiritual benefits, necessary not only for this life, but for the life hereafter. In contrast with this, Protestantism insists that Christianity is not a technique for "getting through" but a living relationship with God, which so completely transforms life that one has the spiritual strength to face up to whatever life brings. For this no special professional help is required, for we are "all the priests of God."

Personalism. A dominant theme in Latin life is expressed in the phrase *la digni-*dad de la persona* 'the dignity of the person' — one of the sublime concepts of mankind. The only difficulty is that this phrase remains ambiguous. Does it really mean *la dignidad de cada persona* 'the dignity of every person,' or does it mean *la dignidad de mi persona* 'the dignity of my person'? In other words, is this a declaration of the rights of each man or woman, or merely a person's insistence on his own rights? Here lies part of the tantalizing ambivalence in Don Quixote and Sancho Panza: the one who leads crusades for justice and the other who seeks the most effective ways of satisfying his own needs. Moreover, does *la dignidad de la persona* refer primarily to *derechos* 'rights' or to *responsabilidades* 'responsibilities'?

In some instances this orientation toward personalism in the ego-centric sense expresses itself in a man's contending that he owes it to society to give it his leadership. Even as *un indio sin patrón es como rueda sin eje* 'an Indian without a boss is like a wheel without an axle,' so society must not only be served by a man leading it, but it must also be used as a means whereby a man expresses his fullest human capacities, often at society's expense.

Protestantism also emphasizes the worth of the individual, but not primarily in terms of his *dignidad* or *honor*, but in terms of all men being individually objects of the grace of God and therefore responsible under God for the use of their divinely granted talents.

Work. The intense concern for work as divinely ordered activity is a distinctly Protestant view. In Roman Catholicism secular labor is in a sense part of the curse of mankind and must itself be redeemed by the spiritual labor of the contemplative clergy. In Protestantism work is a virtue in itself. Moreover, the man who goes about doing good, with of course certain rewards for himself, is regarded as superior to the one who seeks mystical identification with God, the highest goal in Roman Catholicism. From the Latin viewpoint, one should not work more than necessary, for work is only a means whereby one can make enough money so as to enjoy "non-work." In contrast with this viewpoint, many Protestants, and especially those in the United States, even tend to make work out of their leisure, for that too must be "activist."

The discovery of truth. The Latin orientation toward truth is that of intuitive discovery, the flash of insight, the beatific vision. In view of this basic orientation, it is little wonder that Existentialism has been received with amazing enthusiasm, for it is so congenial to Latin thought patterns. On the other hand, except for a very small minority, American Protestants have been relatively unaware of such persons as Kierkegaard, Heidegger, Sartre, Jaspers, and Tillich. They know much more of Karl Marx, but they have thought of him only in terms of a Communist bogey, not as an existential thinker, which, of course, he was. The American Protestant orientation, on the other hand, is generally framed in terms of the discovery of truth through the use of reason and discursive logic, built upon an accumulation of revelant "facts."

In the above statements of contrastive orientations between Latin and American life, it may have seemed that the judgments have been unduly critical of the Latin American "world view." This has not been intended. It must be recognized, of course, that the Protestant position, as we see it, is far more Biblical in its orientation and therefore more in accordance with God's revelation. On the other hand, Americans often deny in practice what they proclaim in theory. For example, though American life generally is nonauthoritarian, many conservative evangelicals are highly authoritarian in their religious views and exert just as exacting a censorship over the views of their "converts" as does the Church of Rome. There is no official Protestant Index, but most missions have their own ways of keeping from students the books which they regard as "inappropriate for their stage of development."

Similarly, American emphasis upon human rights is often understood in the abstract, rather than in a personal sense, so that Americans will defend the rights of people in general but have little personal interest in people as individuals. Their defense of mankind is broad, but their range of personal friendships often very narrow.

At the same time, in the matter of discovery of truth, Americans have fallen into the fatal danger of relying almost exclusively on inductive reason, arising out of so-called scientific investigations. They not infrequently spend so much time amassing the evidence that they have little time to evaluate, and hence have only a limited comprehension of its relevance. Since their study of life is so often through a screen of facts and figures, they never sense some of the living realities which only come when people see life in its closer perspective.

Paradoxes in Latin Life

The very personal and existential view of life in Latin America inevitably gives rise to certain significant paradoxes, which lend to Latin life both its charm and its vitality. On the one hand, there is the traditional religious and philosophical system of Thomas Aquinas constituting the theoretical foundation of the Latin "world view," since it has been more or less the official orientation of the Roman Church through the last few centuries. One would tend to assume that on the basis of this system, in which human reason in its neo-Platonic Aristotelianism is the foundation of truth, one would find people more enamored with the importance of reason as the gateway to reality. On the contrary, Latins generally see reality, not through the process of reason, but in the passion of feeling those intuitive perceptions of life coming in the midst of intense emotional involvement. It is this quality which prompts men to express reality through poetry, rather than in articles for scientific journals, and in drama and novels, rather than in dull sociological studies.

There is always the delightful paradox of Don Quixote and Sancho Panza, the latter who can make a skillful adjustment to the necessities of life and live with incredible endurance beneath the heavy heel of totalitarian demands, and the former who erupts in violent defense of justice and who is ready in an instant to take up arms against the heavy hand of dictatorship. On the other hand, such a hero is not usually so quick to try to overcome the very problems which have created the dictatorship in the first place. This paradox does not mean that there are two different kinds of Latins, but that most Latins combine in fascinating mixtures both the flaming idealism of Don Quixote and the patient realism of his constant companion.

Latin concern for truth expresses itself primarily in terms of ideas, not facts. Facts are generally quite uninteresting, for they are either true or false, and so what is the point of being "married" to such a concept. But with ideas everything is different, for ideas are not just faithful or unfaithful to reality, but they are mysteriously elusive, partly right and partly

wrong, never quite controllable, always responding to attention but never willing to surrender fully. Moreover, for Latins, ideas are not only like people — warm, human, and friendly — but they are almost always related to people. Men associate ideas with men, and men with ideas. This makes the Latin world of thought essentially living, vibrant, and responsive.

Latin life also involves a paradox of intense diversity within amazing unity. Students of Latin life always marvel at the similarity of viewpoints throughout the whole of Latin America, despite differences of climate, ethnic backgrounds, and individual histories. Nevertheless, beneath this unity is an amazing diversity of classes, cultures (African and indigenous American elements), and personality types. This makes Latin America not only colorful but creative, especially in the arts and music, and with far more emphasis on individualism and the development of one's own distinctive talents than is true of the United States, which has presumably been so individualistic in its cultural perspectives.

Characteristics of Latin Life Which Are Particularly Important for Communication

In order to understand more realistically some of the requirements of effective communication in Latin America, we need to treat briefly some of the factors which are primarily related to the themes and techniques of communication. For one thing, despite the general themes which are typical of Latin life, the immense cultural and personal diversity requires that literature and radio must be more selective in their audiences. The shotgun blast is almost useless in such a culturally "scattered" society.

In Latin America a dominant theme is

personal friendship, involving personal identification and often strong emotional attachment for leadership. Friendship is almost always an even more important factor than equity or justice. This means that effective communication must be built upon a sense of personal relationship and greater sensitivity to the human situation.

There is also a tendency for Latins to regard language more as an instrument for personal expression than for the conveying of information. This factor is in some measure responsible for the keen interest in poetry. In Latin America most men would like to think of themselves as poets, but in the United States a poet is only an "egg-head" of the most impractical type.

Latin Americans generally regard visual symbols, especially in religious contexts, as more important than verbal ones. Even their ideas must usually be ones for which there are perceptual models, visualizable objects in the universe which are similar. This also means that priority is given to truth as expressed in poetic figures in contrast with that which may be conveyed by completely abstract terms.

There are few places in the world where people take such delight in talking as in Latin America. Not only do Latins thoroughly enjoy conversations — even the most heated ones — but they are generally far better at expressing themselves than are North Americans.

Strength of Roman Catholicism and Pentecostalism in Terms of Communicative Techniques

Before taking up (1) the specific themes which are appropriate for evangelical communication in Latin America and (2) a series of concrete suggestions for the development of literature and radio, it seems highly desirable for us to look briefly at some of the features in Roman Catholicism

and Pentecostalism which are significant from the standpoint of communication. We are choosing these two movements because (a) Roman Catholicism is the dominant religious pattern of Latin society (though the actual active participation of the people is probably no greater proportionately than what is found among Protestants in a country such as Sweden), and (b) Pentecostalism in its many diverse forms is certainly the largest and most rapidly growing sector of Protestantism, estimated as probably equal to all the other Protestant groups put together and in a number of areas developed and carried on largely without missionary direction or support.[3]

To begin with, however, we must recognize that in all forms of religion communication is a focal element, for religion does not consist merely in a set of beliefs, but in men and women doing something about these beliefs, either by way of generally correct behavior or by worship. In worship communication is obviously central, for it is here that men communicate with God in prayer and offerings and he communicates with them in ecstatic experience the words of the Scripture, the message of the priest or prophet, and by the miracle of his presence. Moreover, in religious rites and ceremonies, man reenacts great events of communication when the mystery of Deity is revealed.

With this general background of communication as integral of religious worship, we must now look for a moment at Roman Catholicism which, despite some de-emphasis on verbal communication, has, nevertheless, a powerful communicative program. In the first place, there is the

[3] Eugene A. Nida, "The Indigenous Churches in Latin America," PRACTICAL ANTHROPOLOGY, Vol. 8, No 3 (May-June 1961), pp. 97-105, 110.

mysterious language of the mass, unintelligible but nevertheless highly "communicative" (in the expressive sense), for with deep emotional overtones it reveals as well as disguises the mystery of the eucharist. The mass itself is a communication by means of drama, but this is only one of the many rites and ceremonies by which the Church reenacts its communication.

There is also the belief in the "communication" of the very substance of Jesus Christ through the wafer and the wine. Moreover, confession constitutes a very important psychological release by way of communication to one who can assure the confessor of absolution and restoration to grace. In addition, the prayers to the saints, who seem much more personal and nearer than God, and to Mary, as the symbol of life and creativity, accompanied by candles and incense, all are designed to serve as means of communication, from God and to God. It is this sense of participating in divine communication which gives the Roman Catholic forms of worship their intense reality and emotional appeal.

Pentecostals, on the other hand, also have a highly significant system of communication. In place of the Latin which only the priests understand, Pentecostals may all receive the gift of tongues — an even more ecstatic experience than reciting the memorized phrases of a dead language. Much of Pentecostal dancing and group participation in prayer is a form of folk drama. These people do not have the miraculous wafer to offer the people, but they can offer the promise of miraculous healing, not only as the gift of God but as proof of a measure of faith and of the fact that God has answered the people's communication to him. There is great emphasis upon group participation in prayer and singing, and the sermons are generally

on the level of the people, with plenty of opportunity for men and women to respond, not only verbally but by signs of the filling of the Spirit.

In contrast with either the Roman Catholic or the Pentecostal type of service, the average evangelical meeting is so often colorless, tasteless, and boring. The sermon too often deals not with religious expression and life, but with the "grammar of religion," namely, the doctrines which are not infrequently a verbal substitute for the real life experience. Similarly the hymns are many times foreign importations, in which the words are didactic (teaching a lesson) rather than lyric (expressing a sentiment of the heart, as in Spanish and Portuguese poetry and song). The utter lack of pageantry, drama, and group participation make evangelical services seem more like a session in a lecture hall than a corporate worship of the Most High.

Despite certain excesses which may characterize some of the Pentecostal movements and despite some of the unfortunate lack of sensitivity to the needs of the human heart which predominate in certain aspects of Latin Roman Catholicism, one must, however, recognize the fact that in these two movements, people experience a sense of communication, of worship, and of the divine-human encounter.

Basic Themes for Evangelical Communication in Latin America

A careful distinction must be made between the themes which are basic to communication, of whatever kind, and the particular techniques and forms of communication. Of course, in view of the multiple and diverse character of Latin society, there are a number of themes which could be suggested, but in general these fall into three major categories: (1) emphasis upon the uniqueness of Jesus Christ, (2) Christianity as a matter of will and not of intellect, and (3) the Bible as the living account of the meeting of God and man.

In Roman Catholicism Jesus Christ has been destroyed as a symbol of Deity to which men and women can respond with living hope and vital identification, for he has been displayed almost exclusively as the dying and dead Christ.[4] Such a symbol evokes pity and sympathy, but never identification, for healthy-minded people cannot identify themselves with death. In place of the "dead Christ," the Roman Church has, in part, substituted the child Christ (as a dependent babe) in the arms of his mother (the protecting church). In addition to this, the unacceptable nature of the "dead Christ" symbol has also led to the exalting of Mary as the "Mother of God," for this female symbol, as the epitome of life, beauty, and benevolence, fits completely within the context of the female-oriented Latin society, where it is the mother of the family who represents the psychological focus of loyalty and the mediator of benefits for the children from a stern father.

In place of the weak symbol of the dependent infant or the fertility symbol of the gracious mother, evangelicals must present a vigorous symbol of a living, reigning Christ, who died but also rose and who is coming in ultimate victory "when all his enemies have been put under his feet." This is the virile symbol of the conquering hero who gained the victory over Satan on the cross, for he turns suffering into triumph and temptation into strength. Moreover, he is one who never lets his followers

down. Therefore, men who identify themselves with him can follow with steadfast assurance and supernatural power.

This must be the Christ of the open tomb and the rent veil, who broke the bonds of death and entered once and for all into the Holy of Holies to make an offering for the sins of the world. This is very God of very God, and the only mediator between God and man — the man Jesus Christ. This last word *man* is important, for in the Latin mind, Jesus is not a man, but an image; not human, but a demi-god. In all our insistence upon his Deity, we must not forget that Latin America needs to see Jesus Christ as perfect man, as well as very God. The reason for this is that in their view God has removed himself so far away (by interposing so many intermediaries of priests and saints) that he cannot be touched by man. There he stands, veiled in the mystery of ritual. But now he must be made manifest by the proclamation of his Son, for as men know him they know the Father also.

This announcement of the living Christ is integral to any relevant communication to people who relate themselves primarily to persons, rather than to abstractions, and who emotionally need to rediscover the reality of a personal God. Moreover, Jesus Christ is our only message, the only reason for our existence and the only relevant theme of our witness.

In the second place, Christianity must be presented, not as an intellectual response to a series of indisputable doctrinal formulations, but as the answer of the heart to the love of God. This means portraying Jesus Christ before men by word and life and not merely lecturing on Protestant theology. All arguments for proving God, vindicating the Bible, or defending our systematic theology must be subordinated to the meaningful proclamation

---

[4] Eugene A. Nida, "Mariology in Latin America," PRACTICAL ANTHROPOLOGY, Supplement 1960, pp. 7-15. Reprinted from Vol. 4, No. 3 (May-June 1957), pp. 69-82.

of Jesus Christ as the answer through faith to the problems of life. This does not mean that theology is irrelevant, only that if the message of the Scriptures is to be communicated to Latin Americans it needs to come to them in its truly Biblical form, as the proclamation of Good News about life, in which the theological factors are subordinated to the realistic encounter of God with men. As far as the Bible is concerned, man's difficulty is his sin, which is not an error of the mind but a rebellion of the heart. Therefore, salvation comes not by intellectual assent to correct ideas, but through the heart, which in faith says Yes to God.

In the third place, the Bible must be presented to people as a realistic account of God and man, not generalized and abstracted through our neat doctrinal formulations and topical outlines, nor robbed of its true message by undue typological and allegorical teaching (as though God delighted in hiding the truth from us), but vibrant, dramatic, and real. It should be taught in the context of struggle, testing, response, and action — the account of God who entered into history and acted to call out a people unto himself and the story of men who in response to a sovereign God have found joy through service and liberty through obedience.

The real task is not merely to teach the Bible but to teach certain people what the Bible has to say to them. In doing so, we must not be tempted by alliterative outlines or overly simple explanations, nor must we think that men will respond to arguments based on attacks upon straw men. Moreover, we must be prepared to declare the whole counsel of God in utter abandon to the Biblical viewpoint, as known from the cultural context in which this message was given to men.

The Latin soul is hungry for real spiritual nourishment, not for predigested sermon outlines. They crave realistic portrayals of the great heroes of faith: Abraham, who dared to go into an unknown land in answer to God; Moses, who faced the challenge and the danger of identification with a despised minority; Joshua, who declared himself and his family for God in the midst of mounting opposition from jealous, rebellious followers; David, who conquered a nation but fell victim to his own lust; Jeremiah, who spoke for God the truth that hurt, not only others but himself — and so it goes. The Bible is a book of life, for it comes out of the context of life and is addressed to life. It must not be disguised by our Protestant doctrinal formulations any more than the face of God should be hidden by elaborate ritual of the Roman Church.

Suggestions for Developments in Christian Literature

The following specific suggestions are designed to reflect the culturally relevant ways in which a communication of evangelical truth can best be effected. Some involve shifts of emphasis and others are perhaps new avenues of approach. There are, of course, many other phases which might be mentioned, but several seem to be the most strategic at this time.

In the first place, it is all too easy for quantitatively minded North Americans to become so engrossed in the mechanics of bigger production and wider distribution that the quality of the product, which alone is communicatively relevant and also the secret of distribution, may be inadvertently forgotten or overlooked. The emphasis should be on the creative development of really relevant communication through the printed page.

No real literary artist can be nurtured in the atmosphere of strong censorship which characterizes many evangelical publishing endeavors. Despite claims to the contrary, there is too much of the "party-line" maneuvering and too little real freedom of expression to attract young men and women with "revolutionary ideas." But if evangelical literature is going to speak to Latins, it must not say the same things which have already been said many times, and hence are by tradition stamped as "safe." It must be remembered that John Wesley was not regarded as a "safe" writer by the "defenders of the faith" in his day. The same is true of such men as William Penn, Roger Williams, John Calvin, and John Knox in former times, and in our own day many a conservative looks at C. S. Lewis and J. B. Phillips with a jaundiced eye. Nevertheless, God has used all of these men to call the church's attention to certain truths which the traditionalists of the time had failed to grasp or adequately reckon with.

Translations of English publications should be kept at an absolute minimum. Where such translations seem warranted, then they should be "adapted" (i.e. generous changes should be incorporated in order to make them speak to the Latin audience).

Concentration should be on the literary forms most appealing to the Latin constituency. This means that attention should be shifted from traditional "tract literature" (whether in four-page leaflets or in large volumes, for much of the exhortatory and expository evangelical literature in Latin America is nothing but expanded tracts), to novels, short stories, poetry, drama, and dialogue (in the Socratic sense). Such literary forms highlight the personal element and permit essential identification and emotional involvement, without which there is little chance of satisfactory response.

Advanced training for writers of promise is essential, but such training should not be restricted merely to further seminary education and in general it should be in Europe, rather than in the United States, since at the present time literary developments on the Continent are not only in many regards more creative but the ideas current in Europe are more congenial to the Latin temperament and in many regards more relevant to Latin problems. The remuneration for good manuscripts, however, must be more than a leather-bound Bible. Evangelical publishers will get just exactly what they are willing to pay for.

The formation of a writers' league for the purposes of (a) circulating challenging ideas, (b) encouraging mutual assistance, and (c) informing members as to markets for manuscripts and opportunities for study, should do much to develop better and more creative writings among evangelicals. There should also be arrangements whereby potential writers can get their manuscripts carefully evaluated free of charge.

Suggestions for Developments in Radio

In facing the almost unlimited potential in radio, it is necessary to focus one's attention on the most strategic aspects, or the results may be utterly unjustified in view of the enormous expense. Some people have even questioned whether the same amount of money spent in creative literature might not have resulted in more significant communication. But this type of question is ultimately irrelevant at this stage, for the money has been spent and more will be spent in developing radio, which is undoubtedly a highly useful tool in communication. The problem which we face now is not to rate radio against literature, but to see how the relatively large sums of money can be justifiably employed in order to obtain the most significant results.

There is always a tendency, as in the case of publishing, for American missionaries to center their attention on technical aspects, often to the neglect of significant content. Some radio stations in Latin America are very much aware of this problem, but in general the personnel responsible for programming is entirely too limited and too overworked. They simply have responsibility for too many programs if at the same time they are expected to be creative.

Missionaries have a very valid role as "catalysts" of program development, but they should be kept off of programs, and the major work, though not necessarily the kernel ideas, should be in the hands of Latins, who are far more capable of effective communication, once they have been fully "desensitized" to the North American way of doing things. In other words, Latins must have an opportunity to make creative innovations.

Too often the heavy hand of the invisible censor (in the form of the presumed supporting constituency) reduces a creative idea to a boring farce, for the problems presented over the air are not real ones, and accordingly the program does not speak to Latin life with Biblical realism, but is to all intents and purposes addressed to the United States constituency, which of course does not hear it but which would certainly approve of it if it did.

If a station is to produce programs which will really speak to people, it must employ techniques and themes which will attract attention, e.g. drama, poetry, storytelling, dialogue (but not with canned questions answered by pious platitudes), and conversations (unrehearsed but by

well-informed people who have something important to say).

In so far as possible one should try to create a Latin American hynody, excluding the ponderous Anglo-Saxon tradition and the cheap evangelical "rock-and-roll" characteristic of some Christian youth movements in the United States.

Such a program inevitably means reducing to a minimum the broadcasting of sermons. These have often been thought to be harmless "fillers," for they encourage the support of local pastors and flatter the visiting VIP. But some of these sermons are not just fillers; they are worse than nothing, for they are frequently heavy on expression and light on information. Expressive speech is not so unacceptable if the speaker is himself present, but when he is as distant as a radio receiver makes him, and even more so when he speaks in a preacherish voice, then predominantly expressive language can be intensely boring.

Such emphasis upon culturally relevant programs will result inevitably in radical changes in the way in which the Bible is taught over the air. Rather than reproduce the atmosphere of the class-room (undoubtedly the most inefficient method of vital communication yet devised by man), Bible teaching must become a varied, creative investigation of the most important message in the world, God meeting man.

Any attempt to produce programs which are fully meaningful to the Latin audience will also mean that programs sent out from the United States (which for the most part are "spiritually imperialistic" and often irrelevant in content) must be avoided. If they are merely useless, they would not be so bad, but the wrong approach can so inoculate a man against the real message that he is lost to the cause.

A survey should be made of all the creative personnel in the various evangelical radio stations in Latin America in order to ascertain the extent to which such persons might be able to take up the production of high quality programs which could be shared with other stations. These people should then be released by their societies so as to have the time for this higher quality production. Latins who demonstrate ability in writing and programming should be given special training, first under particularly competent persons in Latin American, and then later abroad.

A program of in-training improvement of broadcasting personnel (to some extent including technicians) should include instruction in technical problems of programming, culturally relevant themes and techniques of communication which must be employed if one is to present a message effectively, an analysis of creative styles of writing in Spanish and Portuguese, and methods of presenting the Bible within the scope of the most significant themes and techniques.

In order that people engaged in programming may have constant help in getting access to new ideas and creative approaches, some means should be found (probably through a form-letter) whereby notices could be given of important articles and books which might be potentially useful as leads to new ideas. This must include information on recent literary productions (dramas, novels, poetry) and current philosophical developments, as indispensable background material for those writing programs. No person who attempts to do creative work along this line can afford to read less than one new book a week.

One of the most rewarding studies which can be made of Latin American cultural themes is available in a thorough analysis of serial dramas, in terms of (a) the types of problem situations which have cultural interest, (b) the kinds of solutions which are suggested, implicitly or explicitly in the drama, and (c) the dramatic and literary styles employed. Despite the superficiality of the solutions in serial dramas, they nevertheless constitute one of the most diagnostic ways of studying basic themes and values in a modern society. Moreover, their very "broadcast form" can suggest useful ways in which more satisfactory means can be found to use this medium with greater effectiveness.

John M. Hickman

Linguistic and Sociocultural Barriers To Communication

THIS paper is about learning and teaching, and is especially concerned with the problems faced as concepts and skills are communicated across language, social, and cultural boundaries. It is a report of research and common sense experience, and many of the conclusions and solutions suggested are still being tested. Emphasis is placed on the learning problems of populations not yet well intergrated into national life, but it should be clear that the principles discussed are found in any teaching context where differences in social and cultural heritage must be overcome

Social behavior and social situation

In large part, the social situation in which the individual finds himself determines his behavior. For example, members of western-oriented societies find it quite understandable that vocabulary and actions vary for professors, preachers, prostitutes, and professional athletes. Even within a given category style and content change with situation — the preacher in church, on a fishing trip, at a political rally, or talking to small children.

John M. Hickman is Social Science Advisor to the Methodist Church in Peru (Apartado 1386, Lima, Peru. His most recent contribution to PA was a report on "The Second Andean Consultation," Vol. 13, No. 6 (Nov.-Dec., 1966), pp. 278-281.

The information and skills that an individual has available to him are shuffled and reordered continually, usually automatically and with little thinking or conflict involved. The "successful" person in a given society is the one who makes these shifts in a natural and accepted way: he knows what to say and do, and when. Language and actions are manipulated and selected to conform to the expectations of friends and strangers. All this is complicated enough within one society and culture.

Learning a second language may be nothing more than an intellectual exercise in the classroom, but the real consequences begin when one tries to live as a member of the society that produced the other language. It is relatively easy to become effectively bilingual; it is quite another matter to become bicultural. Rules of behavior must be learned that make social sense out of the new vocabulary and grammar. The newcomer has to learn table manners, gestures, and facial expressions, family customs and relationships, ideas of right and wrong, a social structure in which he has a place, and so on. In other words, the person who wishes to become bicultural as well as bilingual must learn substitutes for much of what was taught him as a child in his own home and community. He must become "successful" in a new social environment, conforming to strange behavior patterns and learning what to say and do, and when to say and do it.

A general bicultural problem

Some of the most challenging problems of communication and conversion to new ways may be found in the common situation of ethnic enclaves within national boundaries. The majority of the rural people and urban lower classes of the world do not and cannot participate fully or effectively in the national life of the larger social, economic, and political entity that is their "country". The reasons for relative isolation and low degree of integration vary, but almost always are based on old patterns of exploitation and discrimination, caste, class, and language differences.

Many nations, politely called "developing," now find themselves in the uncomfortable position of desperately trying to extend and increase the quality and quantity of the information and opportunity available to members of subordinate groups within their boundaries. Drastic measures are taken from the point of view of the historical relationships between rulers and the ruled—land reform, universal suffrage, free public education in the language of the more powerful society, economic aid and technical assistance, special protective laws and procedures. All of these activities are directed toward the rapid integration of the members of enclaves into a national, urban, and (usually) westernized way of life.

However, members of such ethnic groups tend to see urban culture and society in fragments, and not as an integrated way of life and living. They see specific advantages and luxuries that may be adopted or adapted without conflict of ideologies or loss of ethnic identity. An astounding amount of "additive" change can take place rapidly — radios, sewing machines, soap, flashlights, trucks, bicycles, clothing styles and machine-made cloth, better seed and production technology, medicines and treatment by medical doctors. There is always the possibility that a chain of such additions *may* lead to a change in basic values, but in general these "visible" changes (including learning the language of the dominant society) seldom touch the heart of ethnic identity. The borrowing of these traits from outside the traditional culture and society is a way of supplementing and often maximizing traditional life and values. The natives become less picturesque and appear to have assimilated into national life and culture, but such an impression is usually very deceiving.

Great faith is placed in national programs of formal education for the transformation of traditional values and attitudes and for eliminating customs and ways of looking at the world that do not contribute to national progress. However, formal education is usually viewed by members of traditional groups as an instrumental way of taking advantage of the dominant society, and not as a way of changing traditional life. The more an individual is able to learn about how to get along outside his ethnic group, the better he will be able to compete with members of the dominant society and perhaps "pass" into membership in that society.

For example, the general urban and western orientation of centralized government education programs helps to convince the country man that what he is seeing and hearing has its application "somewhere else." What is taught in school is seldom linked by the teacher to daily life in the traditional community, and the student is seldom motivated or able to make the connection himself. The teacher, even though he may have been born into the ethnic group he is trying to change, has been "brainwashed" by his contact with urban society, and rejects the possibility that there may be values in a rural way of life.

This strong feeling of learning something from "outside" that is not applicable in a traditional world of explanation and meaning is also found frequently in religious behavior. When Christianity, for example, is entering into a new culture and society, it is naturally defined at first as "foreign" and the property of people who are "different." This in turn encourages the continuing of many traditional beliefs and practices, since it seems obvious to the people that a way of life that comes from outside cannot take into account all the local problems that have historical solutions. To the extent that the Church becomes indigenous, such early compromises and divisions between old and new may become a part of the fabric of Christian life and thought.

This separation of what is seen and learned into isolated categories or compartments is both normal and to be expected. As long as there is no goal of really *transforming* a society and culture in terms of new concepts and skills, there need be no concern with the divided results of teaching. However, the mission of most teachers is not simply that of preparing people from traditional societies for a troubled life in urban slums. The problem is one of finding ways of implanting the new in the old, so that the traditional society may accept the new as an integral part of daily life. The goal is then to graft and not just transplant, to create and not need to destroy, to encourage the responsible development of a new way of life that is satisfying and productive for all concerned. The basic block to this ideal end point for the teaching process is psychological and social. The clues for dissolving the block are to be found in the connection between learning and practice and in the nature of bilingual and bicultural living.

Bilingual and bicultural variability

Whenever there is bilingualism there is always a degree of separation and division of knowledge and behavior. The basis for this is the social situation that is defined as being appropriate for utilizing what has been learned. The natural and expected variation of speech and behavior on the part of the same individual as he moves from one aspect of life to another within his home society, is extended to what he learns to do and say in a second society. Behavior appropriate and accepted in situations defined as "traditional" is not used while interacting with members of the second society; the same is true for what is learned in the second society when the individual returns to his home community.

Such behavior forms a barrier that keeps life less complicated when people must move back and forth between the two social systems. What gives some hope to those dedicated to the transformation of traditional ways of life is that individuals and groups vary a great deal in how rigidly they feel compelled to create and maintain such defenses against leaks from one system of thought and behavior to the other.

This variability has two extremes that have been identified.[1] At one end of the continuum is the person who keeps the two languages and two systems of behavior effectively apart and separate. This is the person who is least likely to change his traditional beliefs and practices.[2] At

[1] See especially Wallace E. Lambert, "Psychological Approaches to the Study of Language, Part II, On Second-Language Learning and Bilingualism," *The Modern Language Journal*, Vol. 47 (1963), pp. 114-121.

[2] See Edward H. Spicer, Types of Contact and Processes of Change," in *Perspectives in American Indian Culture Change*, Edward H. Spicer, ed. (Chicago: University of Chicago Press, 1961), pp. 517-544; and John M. Hickman, *The Aymara of Chinchera, Perú: Persistence and Change in a Bicultural Context*, Cornell University PhD Dissertation (Ann Arbor: University Microfilms, 1963).

the other extreme is the individual who has made the connection between old and new to the point of being able to switch back and forth easily and with little conflict. Such a person is relatively free from rigid categories of thought and action, and has the best chance of changing basic attitudes and values.

These two types represent the end points of a wide variation, with many possibilities and combinations between. The individual whose behavior and thought keep separate what he has learned and seen may be thought of as being "schizocultural," a split person from the point of view of someone observing his behavior. Such a person does his best to use one set of values in his "home" society and another when interacting with members of the second group. He is like the familiar businessman or politician who operates within only one society, but uses procedures and values in competing with rivals that he wouldn't dream of using in his relationships with family and friends.

The other extreme is more complicated. The two languages are so intermixed in the mind of the individual that he may switch from one to the other or combine them in the same sentence, without stopping his stream of thinking and expression. Differences become blurred and his deepest emotions can be communicated in either language. For members of traditional societies, the most probably social result is disappearance into the more prestigeful group, leaving behind all connection and identification with the past. Such a person has suffered through the long process of coming to understand what it means to switch societies, and has experienced the consequences. He is the relatively sophisticated end-product of learning a second language and the cultural baggage that goes with it. Like his schizocultural brother, he is well adjusted and mentally healthy. In most parts of the world, the knowledge and skills necessary to join the dominant group are not prejudiced by visual racial identification; it is the psychological hurdle of changing systems of thought and action and loyalties that must be overcome. This second type may be thought of as being "ambicultural."[3]

The vast majority of the world's population is very much like the first bicultural type, the individual who maintains effective defenses against the slipping through of values and attitudes from one thought system to the other. Relatively few people fall at the other end of the continuum where the problems of participating in two societies have been resolved either in favor of the rejection of one or the instrumental use of both.

Both groups are close to being useless in leading programs of change, either because of well-established barriers or because, if those barriers have been dissolved, the new "sophisticates" are then too far apart from their former friends and neighbors

no matter how much they might wish to help them. This leaves us with the cloudy and difficult area between, where individuals and groups are caught up in a process they do not understand—maladjusted, confused, marginal, in need of help without knowing why.

Predicting degrees of biculturalism

In order to begin to overcome the natural barriers of defense that protect traditional values and attitudes against basic change, we must be able to predict with some degree of accuracy the strength and nature of these defenses. Lambert's bilingualism studies give us clues toward this necessary goal.

The quality of an individual's learning of a second language may be understood by looking at the following variables: 1) the general aptitude and intelligence of the individual: 2) the social and cultural context in which the two languages are learned; 3) the social and cultural context in which the two languages are used; and 4) the attitudes held by the individual toward the second linguistic social group, and his motivation toward at least a partial identification with that group.

Every society, no matter how "primitive" it may seem to the outsider, includes a similar variation in intelligence and ability among its members. There are always men and women who are especially good at languages, adapting to new social situations, capable of thoughtful and philosophical dialogue in the western sense, and so on. But no matter how

[3] The descriptive terms "schizocultural" and "ambicultural" were suggested by Ellen Ross of the Commission for Aymara Literacy and Literature, in La Paz. Her help at various stages of the paper is gratefully acklowledged.

intelligent and quick to learn a person may be, The environment in which he learns the two languages will help to determine his bicultural defenses. The conditions leading to the greatest division between old and new languages (and therefore the greatest separation of content), are found when the two languages are learned in distinct social and cultural environments. The usual situation for members of subordinate groups is that there is a "home" language, the language of family, friends, and community. This language is learned during childhood and forms the basic life-orientation. The second language is almost always learned in the schoolroom (or other "outside-the-home" social context), with the teacher representing the government and pressures toward urban attitudes and values.

Besides learning the two languages in distinct social settings, the use of the two is also separated in a defined manner. The identification of "home" and "foreign" language usage maintains the division begun in the schoolroom, and helps to increase the separation in thought and practice. Generally the second language is used during school hours, to show off to friends, or to communicate with members of the second language group. However, the serious affairs of family and community are conducted in traditional terminology and thought patterns.

The fourth variable is the motivation of the individual for learning the second language. Here enter crucially the attitudes and expectations held toward the second social group by the individual, his family and friends and community. The more negative and pessimistic these attitudes, the less that will be learned and the more possibility that what is learned will be learned biculturally. The usual situation in traditional societies is that the two languages are learned and used in distinct social contexts, and that historical experience with the dominant group has left a residue of distrust and suspicion. The more intelligent boys and girls will learn a lot in school, but will have little reason or encouragement to apply what is learned to daily life in their home and community.

What kind of teacher?

A few moments reflection leads to the unsettling suspicion that most teaching and teachers fall into patterns that increase rather than decrease the barriers to communication across cultural and social lines. The teaching methods used, the content of what is taught, where and when it is taught, the motives of the teacher—often combine to encourage the general and specific separations of knowledge that prevent the real transformation of traditional society and culture. The teacher is caught in the trap of being exactly what he is: a relatively educated, sophisticated, and dedicated outsider, trying to work with people who live and think differently than he does

The transformation of a society from old to new is a group process and as such necessarily follows the rules of group decision and action Any change on a group level is the sum result of changes in individual members of that group. Therefore instruction and example on the individual level must constantly have at its base a more inclusive strategy on the group level. The branch of social science that has done the most on a practical level to help us to become effective teachers in a bicultural situation is that of community development. Experience drawn from many parts of the world gives us direction for developing a new kind of teacher and new ways of teaching.[4]

There are at least four rules to follow in becoming effective agents of change in societies and cultures that are moving toward change.[5] The first is that the teacher must explicitly understand his goals and guide his actions as a teacher. These assumptions are his points of reference for evaluating what he has done and deciding what to do next. They may be ideals that are unattainable in their pure form, but they should at least include his motivations for teaching, his way of relating to his neighbor, a clear concept of the kind of transformation he is working toward, and a realistic appraisal of the consequences of succeeding in his purpose.

The second rule is that somehow the teacher must become a part of the

process he is trying to encourage. He cannot remain an outside observer; he has to become an insider and share the problems and possibilities of the people he is serving. The degree of identification possible is finally determined by the people themselves, but the attitude of the teacher helps to expand those limits.[6] The teacher who is inside the same situation he is trying to change is in a strategic position to understand what is happening or not happening, and why things are moving as they are. The ability and willingness to analyze and evaluate is a part of the training of teachers that is generally absent.

Along with these two procedural principles, there is a corollary that is crucial to their importance and usefulness. The guiding assumptions of the teacher, his evaluation of his own behavior, and the analysis of the effects of his teaching, all must reflect and take into account the culture and society within which he is working. If the teacher continues to use exclusively the values and attitudes of his home culture, his evaluation of the reactions of the second society will be meaningless. Analysis and evaluation will be useful to the extent the teacher can put himself in the place of those he is trying to help. Communication barriers

---

[4] See George M. Foster, *Traditional Cultures: and the Impact of Technological Change* (New York: Harper and Row, 1962); Ward H. Goodenough, *Cooperation in Change* (New York: Russell Sage Foundation, 1963); and Everett M. Rogers, *Diffusion of Innovations* (New York: The Free Press, 1962).

[5] See John M. Hickman, "Vicos and Tama: Implications for Community Development and Missionary Research," PA, Vol. 12, No. 6 (Nov. - Dec. 1965), pp. 241-249, for a fuller development of these principles.

[6] A minimal requirement for a teacher in the sense we are developing here is that he be comfortable in the language of the people he is trying to help. The danger is in thinking that bilingual teaching methods automatically lead to communication and subsequent change. Glen D. Turner's article "Indian Assimilation and Bilingual Schools," PA, Vol. 11, No. 5 (Sept.-Oct. 1964), pp. 204-210, seems to come close to making this assumption.

become lower as the teacher demonstrates his ability to understand, sympathize, and express himself in terminology that is meaningful to those around him.

The third rule has already been mentioned; work for changes of behavior in the areas of the life of the people that are the most decisive for the growth of the community in a more inclusive and comprehensive sense. In other words, keep in mind that it is the group process that is being encouraged, not just the betterment of the situation of a few isolated individuals. The teacher must reach as many people as possible, and those he teaches must be motivated to multiply the teacher's efforts by in turn teaching their friends and neighbors. Such a strategy implies a priority in teaching: the development of confidence and ability on the part of the people being taught that leads logically and naturally to more and more complex ideas and skills. The teacher finds the clues he needs to capture the interest and attention of his students through his understanding of the anxieties and immediate felt needs of the people he is helping.

The conversion approach

The fourth guide to action and thought on the part of the teacher is by far the most difficult and least understood. It is also the rule that takes effective control out of the hands of the teacher and puts decision and action in the hands of the people whose change the teacher is encouraging. The term "conversion" means that the decision is a free one; there

must be no noticeable pressure toward one alternative rather than another. The decision to change must come from inside the individual and group, and it must come as a result of a process of testing and trial.

One way to say it is that the role of the teacher is to provide good alternatives. The key modification is that the alternatives be "good," and this implies that the teacher is capable of presenting alternatives based on an intimate knowledge of the areas of life to be changed. Good alternatives are those that make sense to the people in their own terms, and in terms of the problems as *they* analyze and conceptualize them. Good alternatives are those that are practical within the economic and technical resources available to the people who must make the choice. They must be alternatives that can be tested without much initial risk, and those that are clearly different in their consequences.

The further we go in developing this new kind of "teacher," the more it becomes clear that most of the teachers we are now acquainted with have little or no chance of really overcoming the bicultural barriers to communication discussed earlier in this paper. The teacher's own bicultural barriers make it next to impossible for him to identify himself convincingly with a low-prestige culture and society. He has even less chance of growing the conceptual apparatus and gaining the discipline necessary to understand and evaluate in depth the psychology, sociology, economics, technology, and religion of the society he has set about influencing toward change. But this is exactly what the bicultural situation demands that he be able to do.

Community development workers inevitably have come to the same conclusion: that the "traditional" teacher cannot be prepared for the kind of work necessary to lead to a transformation of traditional societies. They look instead for members of the traditional society to train as agents of change. They look for mature, well-integrated, and intelligent men and women, who are functioning members of their community or group. They look for men and women who are concerned about the problems of their society and who are searching for alternatives. They look for opinion leaders who may influence specific areas of life and thought, and train them to do just that. The expectation is that natural leaders, trained to present alternatives to their fellows, will form a bridge between the "outside" and the life of the community that these leaders understand and may influence. Such a bridge minimizes the problems that have loomed so large: the detailed nature of the society and culture, identification of the teacher with the people, linguistic problems of expression and explanation, and testing trial under natural conditions.

Great attention has been given to the methods and content of the training of these few leaders who are expected to influence so many. The first rule about having assumptions explicit and evaluation procedures clearly laid down also applies to the local agents of change. It has also been found that a team effort is needed, both on the part of the outsiders who are teaching the new agents of change, and on the part of the change agents themselves. The complexity of the process, and the priorities that are assigned, make it necessary to train low-level specialists in public health, agricultural technology, domestic science, formal schooling and literacy work, and in the touchy areas of religion and local political action. The emphasis is on training and re-training, loose supervision and gentle guidance.

Consequences and second thoughts

There is no doubt but that it is possible to influence and encourage whole groups of people to change their old ways of life and thought for new technology and concepts of health, religion, social structure, and so on. But at the same time it is very possible to fail to provide satisfactory alternatives and to destroy whole societies, to make mistakes that bring deep hardship and suffering in the name of Progress, Christianity, or Increased Production. It is difficult and often impossible to predict what the chain of consequences of an innovation may be, once the bicultural barriers are cut down that protected the traditional society before.[7] The

---

[7] A striking example of a chain of events following the acceptance of a simple tool is found in J. Lauriston Sharp, "Steel Axes for Stone-Age Australians," PA, Vol. 7, No. 2 (March-April, 1960), pp. 62-73 (reprinted from *Human Organization*, Vol. 11, No. 2, Summer, 1952). The substitution of steel axes for stone rapidly led to the disintegration of social structure, religion, family, and to an apathetic and dependent people where once there had been independence and vigor.

ethical and moral problems of encouraging change are terrifying, and
great caution should be exercised in
every aspect of interference with
social arrangements that have withstood the test of centuries and often
millenia.

Having said this, it must also be
said that we have no choice but to
try. The spread of urban secular behavior over the world, the explosion
of mass media and masses of people,
the obvious advantages of steel axes
and plows, the increased dependence
on a competitive money economy, and
the rise of nationalism, are pressures
that no amount of geographical isolation or traditional independence can
withstand for long. The question is
whether the change will come in a
haphazard and disruptive way, or as
a part of a planned and integrated
set of priorities and procedures that
ease the individual and his fellows
over the jumps and pitfalls of drastic
and comprehensive change. Responsible and human consideration demands the latter, and seizing this
alternative indicates clearly the challenge for applied social science and
for the teachers who need desperately
the knowledge and direction that the
social sciences are just beginning to
provide. We must learn to encourage
the conditions that minimize the bicultural barriers that remain the first-
line defense of traditional life and
thought. At the same time, we must
provide the good alternatives that will
allow the human process of conversion
to take place within individuals and
the communities to which they belong.

Jacob A. Loewen

The Question in the Communication of the Gospel

A: "ARE you looking/sitting well?"

B: "Yes, I am looking/sitting well."

A: "What of good did you bring?"

B: "We really have brought nothing."

A: "Did you ever come to this house before, older brother?"

B: "No, this is the first time we have arrived at this house."

A: "We are reading God's Word. Will you all listen with us?"

B: "Yes, we too will listen."

A: "Now, kinsman Jose, will you read again from the beginning the lesson of blind Bartimaeus begging by the roadside?"

C: (After reading) "Already it is finished!"

A: "Did your thinking catch the reading, older brother?"

B: "No, one does not catch it well."

A: "Read the story again, kinsman!" He reads.

C: (After reading) "Already it is finished!"

A: "Did your thinking catch the reading now, older brother?"

B: "No, I did not catch it well."

A: "Read it again, kinsman!"

C: (After reading) "Already it is finished!"

A: "Did you catch the reading this time, older brother?"

B: "No . . . I . . . ."

A: "You are right, older brother, you cannot catch it, for God has not yet 'cleaned up' your eyes. You are just like the blind man Bartimaeus sitting by the roadside, waiting for people to give you things because you cannot catch them with your own eyes."

"Tell me, older brother, how many people on your river are walking on 'God's road?'"

B: "None of the people on our river are walking on God's road. We do not know about God's way."

A: "Are you not the oldest one on your river, my older brother?"

B: "Yes, I am the oldest one on our river."

A: "How do you as the oldest one expect to talk to God when no one of your people is walking on God's road?"

B: "But how can we walk on God's road when we are still not knowing?"

A: "Truth you have spoken, older brother, but remember *we* are knowing and you have never yet invited us to tell you."

B: (With a voice choked with emotion) "Truth it is, your word . . . we have not asked you before, but surely you will come to our river to teach our

Jacob A. Loewen is a Translation Consultant for the Bible Societies in South America. Apdo. 5764, Lima, Peru.

649

people how to walk on God's road?"

A: "Older brother, you have spoken well! Yes, we will come. After one moon we will arrive. Then we will teach you. Then you will read God's Word, for God will clean up your eyes."

The foregoing question-and-answer exchange took place during one of the Choco services in Jaque village of Panama in 1961. Indians from the various tributaries had come to town to sell bananas. The Christian Indians were celebrating a worship service in one of the homes. Leader Aureliano had sent a child to invite some of his relatives from a different tributary to come to the service; but the child had made a mistake. It had gone to the wrong house, and had invited a group of strange Indians. Now this group of about fifteen with the old man (addressed as older brother by Aureliano) at the head, came to the meeting. When they arrived the meeting was already approaching its conclusion, but without any feeling of interruption, the leader ordered the Scripture lesson repeated for the benefit of the latecomers.

The ensuing worship service and its dramatic conclusion have already been highlighted in the question-answer exchange. In sequel it may be of interest to mention that when the proposed visit by Aureliano and a team of Christians from the El Mamey church to the river of the visitors took place, some twenty people gave "God the hand to walk on God's road" and were baptized upon the confession of their faith.

The preceding account is but one of many illustrations that could be cited concerning the use of the question in the communication of the Gospel by the Choco church. The Scriptures themselves contain many searching questions that have been very meaningful in man's experience with God. Consider the following:

"Adam, where art thou?"

"Cain, where is thy brother?"

"Whom shall I send, and who will go for us?"

"Lord, what wilt thou have me to do?"

"What wilt thou that I should do unto thee?"

The purpose of this paper is to highlight especially two functions of the question in the communication of the gospel: First, to demonstrate the use of the question as a tool in gaining an adequate understanding of the culture, so that the "good news" can be preprogrammed to meet the local need in a relevant way. Second, to illustrate the use of the question as a practical instrument in church services, especially in settings involving quite heterogeneous audiences.[1]

Ethnographic research

Systematic interviewing is really the most basic technique for the study of culture. Observation will provide many insights, but without extensive systematic

[1] The questioning scenes used to illustrate the propositions of this paper are drawn from field observations recorded during the summer programs of work with the Choco Church in Panama and from research experiences with the Lengua and Chulupi Indians in the Chaco of Paraguay. For additional information see the following papers by the author: "The Church among the Choco of Panama," PA, Vol. 10, No. 3 (May-June 1963), pp. 97-108; and "Missionaries and Anthropologist Cooperate in Research," PA, Vol. 12, No. 4 (July-August 1965), pp. 158-190.

questioning even a trained anthropologist would be hard put to understand a culture adequately within the amount of time usually allotted for field work. There is no substitute for systematic interrogation both for soliciting information about known subjects, and for identifying areas of further profitable investigation.

Consider the following experience that took place among the Chulupi Indians in the Chaco of Paraguay. The author, who did not speak the Chulupi language, the missionary serving as interpreter, and several Chulupi informants, were discussing the parts of the body during several weeks of intensive study of this Chaco culture. For each of the body parts its name, its physical function, and also metaphysical significance were discussed. Somehow in the course of the questioning, blood had been forgotten. The discussion was already revolving around a new topic when blood was finally remembered. Here follow now the questions and also the unexpected but exceedingly important new information that came out as a result:

A : " By what name do you call blood in your language ? "

B : " We call it *vatvoyey.*"

A : " Some people say that a man's soul lives in the blood. Have you ever heard your fathers say that, too ? "

B : " No, blood is just blood."

A : " Some people say that if you do certain evil things your blood will be damaged. Did your fathers ever teach like that, too ? "

B : " No, they never said anything about blood becoming damaged."

A : "Do Chulupi Indians believe that the blood can get sick ? Can it be spoiled through incest ? "

B : "No, the blood cannot get sick, nor can the blood be damaged through incest or wrong-doing. Blood is blood and that's all."

A period of silence followed during which the anthropologist was casting about for another approach to elicit more information about blood, when the informant suddenly turned to the missionary.

B : "Now I suddenly remember that my grandfather once told me that when God (Dios) made the first people he scratched himself in the arm and put some of his blood into this 'doll of mud' that he had made. That is why human beings have blood today."

A : "What was the name of this God (Dios) that gave blood to the people ?"

B : "Lhanchinish, that's what we call him."

A : "What else did Lhanchinish make?"

B : "He also made the world."

A : "What is this God doing today ?"

B : "Nothing, he has gone away into the sky-world."

A : "Did he used to live with the Indians ?"

B : "Yes, after he made the world and the people, he lived with the people for some time."

A : "Why did he go away ?"

B : "I do not know why he went away; the fathers said maybe he got angry with them. That is why he went away."

A : "How long is it since you have heard the missionaries tell about Dios ?"

B : "Probably I heard the first message when I came to F. about 'two hands' of years ago."

A : "What did you think when you first heard the missionary talk about Dios?"

B : "I thought they were talking about Lhanchinish, but they said that they were talking about Dios, so I didn't know."

The above scene shows that the questions about blood at first yielded only very meagre routine information, but suddenly a very unexpected piece of information turned up—the name for the Creator God. For twenty years the missionaries had failed to find the indigenous name for God. For twenty years they had been using the Spanish loanword *Dios* to denominate the deity whose will and word they were proclaiming. But a simple question about the blood triggered a response that led to the discovery of Lhanchinish, the Chulupi Creator God.

Locating felt need

The author had been telling the Chaco Indians who were sitting around the campfire with him about some of his early missionary experience in Colombia. He had detailed some of the errors he had made in his work while he still didn't understand the culture of the Indian people there.

A : "Have the missionaries who work here also made mistakes like this?"

B : (After a period of silence followed, broken by the Indian host.) "Yes, they also have made mistakes."

A : "Can you tell me about any mistakes they have made?"

B : "It is hard for an Indian to say such words..."

A : "True, it is hard for one to name mistakes, maybe you can name just one mistake they have made?"

B : (Again a period of silence, broken suddenly by one Indian) "It is that they often scratch where it doesn't itch."

Careful questioning and sympathetic listening are the tools par excellence for finding out "where it itches."

In another paper the author has detailed such an experience with the Chulupi Indians in the Paraguayan Chaco.[2] He had shared with them some of the struggles that he as an individual had faced in finding himself and the will of God for his life. After this period of self-exposure he abruptly turned to his Indian host.

A : "What wish do you carry deep down in your heart ? What is it that you want most of all?"

B : "One wants to become a person..."

A: (Looking around the campfire from face to face) "One wants to become a person... Are you not people today?"

B : "We are people, yes, but not *real* people like the whites."

This struggle for personal and national self-identity is one of the great "international" needs of our day. Its local shape needs to be uncovered before the missionary can expect to deliver a relevant message.

The question as a mirror

But uncovering felt need is not all. All too often this felt need is distorted by false goals and the missionary needs to serve as a mirror to "clarify" the

2 Jacob A. Loewen, "The Way to First Class : Conversion or Rebellion?" PA, Vol. 12, No. 5 (Sept. Oct. 1965), pp. 193-209.

real need and the means to meet it.

A : "So you all want to become people. Are you not people today?"

B : "No!" (The "no" was literally spat out by the individuals.) "The white settlers do not believe that we are real people."

A : "Are you already becoming people?"

B : "Yes, our church choirs all sing in harmony just like those in the church services of the white people." (The anthropologist certainly had observed this, for every Indian service he had attended, the major part of the service was spent by the choir singing songs in harmony—obviously they had been singing for his benefit to impress him that Indians were "people" equal to the whites.) "And we are also building straight walls."

A : "Ah, I guess the settlers made so much fun about your branches and grass shelters, so that now that you are building walls of adobe bricks you are making them very straight, aren't you?"

B : "Yes, we are making *mucho* straight walls today."

But their "answers" to their felt need were not real basic criteria for them to become the "first-class people" they were aspiring to be. The question was therefore used as a mirror to make them aware of some of the deficiencies, and to get them to redirect their efforts into channels which would actually lead them toward the goal that they were aspiring.

A : "Did the uprising of the 700 Chulupi Indians have something to do with their wanting to become real people?"

B : "Yes, the settlers wanted to keep them as their slaves. They didn't want them to become people, so they did not let Indians get things."

A : "Did the rebellion of the 700 help the Indians to become people?"

B : (After a period of silence one Indian spoke vehemently) "No, it didn't help. The Indians were actually put to much shame before the settlers."

A : "Most of you know already that I have been invited by the settlers to learn in what ways white people can best help the Indians to become real people. What things will you need to become real people?"

B : "We will need land, horses, plows, harnesses, cultivators."

A : "How do you expect to get these things?"

B : "We are waiting for the white settlers to give them to us."

A : "Will that make you feel like real people if the settlers give you all these things?"

B : "No, it will not make us proud of ourselves if they give us everything."

A : "Why can you not be proud when people give you things?"

B : "Because the whites always want us to say: '*Dankeschoen, Dankeschoen*' 'Thank you, thank you.'"

A : "Well, if gifts don't make you proud of yourselves, what would make you proud as real people?"

B : "Well, if we would get our own plows and horses and harnesses and then we could say to the settlers, give us land. That would make us feel very proud of ourselves."

A : "Would there be any way that you could get horses? Could you get money to buy your own horses and plows?"

B: "Yes, we could. If the settlers would keep half of our wages like in the sugar factories in Argentina and pay it in one lump sum when the work season ends, we could get a horse, a harness and a plow in one year."

Since there were many more Indians asking for land and settlement equipment than the white colonists could settle, this re-directing of the drive for the Indians to get their own equipment would provide two answers instead of only one. First, it would make it possible to help more Indians to settle with the limited funds available, and secondly, it would also help settled Indians to gain in maturity and self-respect.

To evaluate attitudes

Very often even the best programs of help are made void through hidden prejudices, unrecognized values, and malignant attitudes. In the Chaco settlement project the attitude of the Indians toward the white settlers was very crucial. Wrong attitudes and prejudices needed to be dealt with. It was part of the anthropologist's assignment to locate these "hidden spoilers." He was thus walking with a group of Lengua leaders down the central street of one of the newly settled Indian villages. In front of each farm he stopped and asked about the work and the progress of each Indian farmer. Suddenly the anthropologist—as if hit by a sudden inspiration—stopped, and then said: "Isn't it wonderful; why, now that you have land, horses, and plows, you really won't need the white settlers any more, will you?"

There was a period of silence and then the leader of the village, the host to the anthropologist, said, "You know, that's exactly what we said two years ago when we settled on this land—just give us horses and plows and land, and we won't need you white settlers any more. But now, after we have lived here for two years, we think it is better that the settlers still come and occasionally talk with us. While working for them we have learned to do many things, but very frequently we don't know when and why we should do them. We think it will be good if the settlers come and talk with us about these things."

Questions in problem solving

But not only in the beginning of a mission program are questions crucial to help identify the felt needs. Very frequently as the work progresses unexpected problems arise. Here again the question can serve first to gain insight into the nature of the problem and then also as an avenue to find a solution to it.

While visiting one of the Latin American countries, the author was invited by a mission to help them solve a very knotty problem. The local national church was faced with a large number of pregnancies among its unmarried girl members, and the leaders of the national church for some unknown reason were refusing to get involved in the matter. The missionaries had tried to talk with the leaders, but they just met with sullen silence.

The author only had two free days and that was really too short a period for solving such a problem. It was therefore agreed that he would talk to one of the important personalities of the community to see whether he could help delineate the problem. To set the stage he shared with this selected individual some of the petting problems that were developing in many Christian communities in the United States. He concluded with the question: "Do churches in your country have problems like this with young people too?"

The result was almost unexpected. The man poured forth a torrent of invective against the mission. He severely indicted the mission for alienating the children's obedience from the parents through the school system. Then he blamed the mission for the pregnancies among their girls, because they gave scholarships only to unmarried men. This meant that parents could not follow their cultural pattern of trial marriage announcements which had formerly kept the young people from promiscuity. Since parents were afraid to make these announcements for fear their boys would lose the scholarships, the young men were now becoming promiscuous and this had led to the present crisis of pregnancies among unmarried girls.

Teaching or preaching?

Western Christianity has by and large become heavily preaching-oriented. Even Sunday School, which ideally is supposed to allow for exchange between teacher and class, is often a one-man lecture. Yet great teachers have always been ones who could ask meaningful questions. Eugene Nida states the issue quite well when he says:

The sermon has become so focal a point of Protestant religious com-munication that we tend to equate the two, but it is questionable just how much communication the average sermon actually effects. In some instances the themes are so threadbare and the content so predictable that the "information" is almost nil. Too often the Sunday morning service becomes the ideal time for the second Sunday morning nap or for uninterrupted planning of the afternoon's activities or the week's work. There is a great deal of truth in the comment of the little boy who, in answer to a question about how he liked the first church service he had ever attended, said, "The music was all right, but the commercial was pretty long..."
The sermon is only one means of communication—and often not the most effective [3]

In the development of the Christian ministry among the Choco Indians in Panama, the question has been a very important item. In the summer of 1961 David Wirsche and the author went to Panama to help in the organization of the Choco church. They met with the Indians congregated in Aureliano's house for several weeks while waiting for the completion of the Indian church building.

During these days of fellowship they observed that only Aureliano and one or two of the older men had learned to pray. These few prayed long and loud. The short-term missionaries were concerned about this and began to

---

[3] Eugene A. Nida, *Message and Mission* (New York: Harper and Brothers, 1960), pp. 174-175.

wonder how they could teach all the Indians to pray. While reading several chapters of Mark every evening they came to the story of blind Bartimaeus sitting by the roadside begging.

On a sudden inspiration the missionary, who was reading the only manuscript of this Choco translation, made a local application and said, "Let us imagine that Jesus Christ is going to walk into the house this evening just like he walked by on the road beside which blind Bartimaeus was sitting. Bartimaeus wanted something very badly. All of us have needs. Let's permit Jesus to ask each one of us the question he asked Bartimaeus: 'What do you want?' Then let's each one of us answer with what we want most of all."

The author can still recall how men, women, and children uttered short sentence prayers of request concerning the things they wanted, and in this way the question, "What do you want?" became the tool to teach many people how to "talk to God."

The first Scripture and reading materials for the Choco, the booklet of Bible stories which has been described in a separate paper,[4] contained questions after each story. These questions were of two kinds, some relating to the content and others making application of the story. The first group were called, "What does the story say?" questions, and the second, "What does the story teach us?" questions. It has been interesting to observe how the Choco church has used this approach of questions and answers in the congregation

4 Jacob A. Loewen, "Bible Stories: Message and Matrix," PA, Vol, 11, No. 2 (March-April 1964), pp. 49-53.

as a type of liturgy. In this way feedback between the leader and the congregation have become an important communicative feature. In fact, as cited in the example introducing this paper, questions are an important means of involving even the unbelievers in the congregation.

The question in heterogeneous audiences

One of the most common problems in early mission work or in extension work with private home services is the heterogeneity of the audiences. There are adults and children, believers and unbelievers, avid students of the Bible, and those hearing the gospel for the first time. To serve such an audience adequately is a feat to challenge the best. The author has personally found a lot of help in a system of questions. The system has been adapted from a program of foreign-language teaching developed by Earl W. Stevick. Here is the description in Stevick's own words:

One of the best ways of developing a story, and bridging the gap between fixed text and free conversation, is through the use of questions and answers.

There are two important ways of classifying questions according to their relative difficulty and interest. The first is by the kind of answer that they call for. Easiest for the student are yes-no questions; next easiest are "alternative" questions, in which the student answers by repeating one of two answers suggested in the question. Most difficult, in general, are questions that begin with interrogative words and phrases, for in these the answer is not contained in the wording of the question.

	STAGE I	STAGE II	STAGE III
Yes-no	Did Kenneth learn to read ?	Was Kenneth intelligent ?	Do you know the word "pull" ?
Alternative	Was the word "pull" or "push" ?	Were the children angry, or happy ?	Do Japanese children learn to read at home, or at school ?
Other	What color was the box ?	Why did Kenneth pull the handle ?	When do Japanese children learn to read ?[6]

We may also classify questions according to their closeness to the subject matter of the " basic selection." Using Professor Gurrey's labels,[5] Stage I questions ask for answers that are contained within the wording of the story; Stage II requires that the answer be inferred from the story; Stage III asks about the student's own life and experiences.

Here is a chart which contains samples of these kinds of questions. Note that in general the difficulty and also the interest of these questions increases from left to right and from top to bottom.

In teaching foreign language Stevick uses questions at these three levels of content and with the three degrees of difficulty in answers to keep a class of varying abilities operating at maximum capacity. For the advanced student Stage III questions with longer answers will provide an adequate challenge, but for the weaker student this same question would be extremely discouraging—it would heighten his fear so that he would

be unable to function freely. For this reason, when the teacher finds that a student hesitates, he immediately rephrases the question in a simpler form or at a lower level. Ideally the student should always end up with a correct response.

The readers will already see the potential for missionary evangelism. The various stages and degrees of difficulty in questions can be adapted to the varying capacities of a heterogeneous audience. In fact, even the newcomer who may have gleaned only barest details of the story can be asked yes-or-no questions and "helped" until he answers correctly.

Even more effective is the development of a special series of stage III questions for newcomers. For example, if the lesson is about Peter, a question to a newcomer could be, "Have you ever known a man by name of Peter ? " If the answer is yes, one can proceed to the next stage, " Where did you meet this man Peter ? " If the person still follows with an answer one can proceed to the application level, " Would you

5 P. Gurrey, *Teaching English as a Foreign Language* (London: Longmans-Green, 1955).

6 Earl W. Stevick, *A Workbook in Language Teaching (With Special Reference to English as a Foreign Language)* (Nashville : Abingdon Press, 1963), p. 67.

want to tell us something of the Peter you knew?" or, "Was the Peter you knew like the Peter in our lesson?" Whatever the response, the teacher then uses it to clinch an application on the basis of the Bible lesson. Here now follows the suggested adaptation for missionary teaching.

Level of information	Degree of Difficulty			
	Yes-no	Alternative	Word or short phrase	Longer statement
Stated content				
Implied content				
Application				
Newcomer				

Example questions on John chapter three

In order to permit the readers to appreciate the system a little more fully, we follow through with a series of suggested questions based on the encounter between Jesus and Nicodemus described in John 3 : 1-8. The first series of questions is presented in chart form with the respective questions filling the various categories in the proposed question system. The

	Yes-no	Alternative	Word/phrase	Statement
I	Did Nicodemus come to Jesus by night?	Did Nicodemus come by day or by night?	Who came to Jesus by night?	Who was Nicodemus?
II	Did Nicodemus believe in God?	Did Nicodemus come alone or was he with someone else?	Why did Nicodemus come to Jesus by night?	Why was Nicodemus afraid?
III	Have you ever wished you could talk to Jesus?	When you are in trouble to whom would you rather talk—to Jesus or to your neighbor?	What do we usually call "talking to God"?	Can you tell us about a time when you talked to God?
III	**For a newcomer** Have you ever known a man who was afraid?	Was he afraid of people or of evil spirits?	How long ago was this? or Where did you get to know this person?	What had made this man so afraid?

rest of the example questions are presented in paragraphs organized according to the type of answer expected.

Stated content questions

Yes-no answers. Did Nicodemus call Jesus "teacher"? Did Jesus tell Nicodemus that he too must be born again? Was Nicodemus surprised when Jesus told him he must be born again? Did Jesus say "verily, verily" two times? Can "flesh" give birth to "spirit"? Can "spirit" produce "flesh"? Can people *see* the wind? Can people hear the wind?

Alternate answers. Did Nicodemus call Jesus teacher or preacher? Who said, "You must be born again," Jesus or Nicodemus? Was Nicodemus surprised or angry when Jesus said, "You must be born again"? When Jesus said, "Except a man be born of water and of Spirit he cannot enter heaven," was he emphasizing his words about being born again, or was he talking about something new? Which of the two did Jesus say first, "You must be born of water and of spirit," or "You must be born again"? What did Jesus say that flesh can produce, other flesh or spirit? What did Jesus say the spirit produces, flesh or spirit? What does Jesus compare to the wind, flesh or the spirit?

Word or phrase answers. What did Nicodemus call Jesus? From where did Nicodemus say Jesus had come? Who said, "Verily, verily, I say unto you, except a man be born again..."? Who asked, "How can a man who is old be born again"? Who can see the Kingdom of God? Who can enter the Kingdom of God? What can flesh produce? What does spirit produce? With what

does Jesus compare the spirit's way of working?

Longer statement answers. On what basis did Nicodemus say that Jesus was a teacher come from God? What did Jesus teach about being born again? With what words did Nicodemus respond to Jesus' statement on being born again? What words did Jesus use the second time he told Nicodemus that a man must change before entering heaven? Would you give in your own words what Jesus said about new birth? Would you explain in your own words what Jesus taught about the flesh and the spirit? What did Jesus say that we do not know about the wind?

Implied content questions

Yes-no answers. Was Jesus really a teacher? Had Jesus really come from God? Did Jesus do many miracles? Did Nicodemus want to go to heaven? Can a man enter his mother's womb again? Were Jesus and Nicodemus talking about the same kind of birth? Did Nicodemus understand Jesus' words about being born again? Are being born again and being born of water and of spirit the same experience? Do you agree that flesh can only produce flesh? Is it true that spirit can only produce spirit? Was Jesus right when he said, "We cannot see the wind"? Do we not know from where the wind comes nor where it goes?

Alternate answers. Who were Jesus' students, the disciples or the Pharisees? When Jesus said, "You must be born again," did he mean only Nicodemus or did he mean all people? Did Nicodemus think of spiritual or natural birth when he answered? Does spirit here mean spirit of God or a familiar spirit? Is a person who does not believe in God born of the spirit or is he only born of the flesh?

Word or phrase answers. Which miracles had Jesus already performed? Is there another word for "to be born again"? About how many kinds of birth did Jesus and Nicodemus talk? Why is being born of water and of spirit a prerequisite to entering the kingdom? Can you give another name for flesh? About which spirit is Jesus talking here? What experience must all people have before they are really children of God?

Longer statement answers. On what basis could Nicodemus say that God was with Jesus? What makes you think that Nicodemus believed in God? What makes you think Nicodemus wanted to go to heaven? Why do you think Nicodemus talked about natural birth? What does being born again really involve? What are the implications of being born of water and of spirit? Why must all men be born again? Why do you think Nicodemus was surprised at Jesus' teaching? Why is it so difficult to describe the new birth? Why does Jesus compare the working of the spirit with the wind?

Applied content questions

Yes-no answers. Does Jesus still do miracles in our day? Are there people like the Pharisees today? Can Jesus be our teacher today? Do we also need to be born again? Do you think we (whites, Indians, Negroes) also need to be born again? Must all people be born of water and of spirit? Is birth through water and spirit the only way

to be saved? Have you been born again—born of the spirit?

Alternate answers. Was Jesus a teacher only when he was on earth, or is he still our teacher? Which is more important for heaven, to be born of a mother or to born again? Can only grown men like Nicodemus be born of water and of spirit or can unmarried, young people also experience it? Concerning which birth do you as a person have a choice—your natural birth or your spiritual birth?

Word or phrase answers. Where do we find Jesus teaching us today? What must we do so that Jesus can teach us? Why should we be born again? When should we be born again? What is another name for new birth—birth of water and of spirit? Through what medium can we be born again? How can you know you are born of the spirit?

Longer statement answers. How does Jesus teach us today? What are some of the things Jesus is trying to teach us? What happens to us when we are born again? Why does Jesus call it "new birth"? Can you tell us about your own new birth? How would you expect a born-again person to behave? What does "being born of water mean"? What does "being born of the spirit mean"? Why is this new birth—birth of water and spirit—so important in our lives? Who will volunteer to share his conversion experience with us? How would you expect a born-again person to change?

Questions for newcomers

Yes-no answers. Have you ever known a teacher? Have you previously ever heard of being born again? Have you ever known a born-again person? Was the teacher you knew born again? Is the spirit of God like a familiar spirit? Have you ever felt the presence of familiar spirits? Have you ever felt the presence of the spirit of God? Would you have been surprised like Nicodemus if Jesus had told you these things? Have you known any people who were born of water and of spirit? Have you ever had any experience with wind?

Alternate answers. Was the teacher you learned to know teaching in a school or in a church? Was he an Indian or a foreigner? Who do you think is a better teacher—Jesus, or the person you knew? Was the person who told you about new birth a preacher or just a friend? Of which spirit are you afraid—the spirit of God or familiar spirits? What do you think is more important for heaven, the natural birth or the new birth? You say you know a converted person; did you know him before he was converted or only after?

Word or statement answers. What was the name of the teacher you met? In what school did he teach? Where did you first hear about "new birth"? Where/when/how did you meet this born-again person? How did you feel when the familiar spirit was near? How did you feel when the spirit of God was near? What did you think when your friend told you about new birth? How long have you known about new birth?

Longer statement answers. What did you like (not like) about this teacher you knew? Why do you think Jesus

is a better teacher? What do you think about people who talk of being born again? Can you tell us about the conversation between you and your friend? Would you tell us about your experience with the familiar spirit/spirit of God? You say you knew a born-again person—how did you know he was born again?

Conclusion

There are several conclusions which, while implicit in the paper, could be spelled out to advantage.

In order to be able to use the question effectively, the missionary will need to train himself to ask questions. This applies not only to ethnographic interviewing, but also to the effective teaching of the gospel. Asking good questions is a skill that can be developed.

Before using the question in interviewing or as a teaching tool, it will be necessary to plan in considerable detail all the basic questions one expects to use. In fact, it is often good to write out several alternate series of questions if a person anticipates that more than one approach may be necessary. Such alternate series are excellent practice to help a person make adjustments midstream in an interview.

When asking questions the interviewer-teacher needs to be constantly alert for changes in the situation which will call for changes in the questions. This may mean leaving out some prepared questions, phrasing additional questions, or merely changing the sequence. Questions can only be effectively used if the interviewer-teacher remains highly sensitive to the subtle modifications of the situation.

Experience in the use of questions will sharpen a person's sensitivity as to whether the situation is ripe for the use of questions; and if so, what kind of questions will be best to exploit potential openings.

Again, the interviewer needs to remember that under some circumstances or in some cultures specific kinds of questions must be avoided. For example, the yes-no question should be studiously avoided in some cultures because it will always cut off the information flow rather than open the door for further bidirectional exchange. As a rule, open-ended questions are better for stimulating the free flow of information, but again, the interviewer must remain sensitive to each situation and to the changing conditions of the interview or teaching setting.

Effective use of questions offers the missionary a whole "arsenal" of advantages. If he is gathering ethnographic information, pertinent questions will definitely cast him into the learner role which is a *must* for eliciting basic information. But not only for the investigator does the question bring benefits, for in the very process of eliciting pertinent information, the informant himself is brought face to face with many issues he may have never clearly analyzed before. In the case of studying some cultural problem, questions will not only detail the origins and causes, but can also precipitate the decisions to change. Again, by investigating the alternate solutions, the investigator can help the problem-involved person or persons identify their best avenue of solution. The decision thus reached will not be felt as missionary dictated. It will be considered a personal decision, and personal decisions relieve the missionary of trying to enforce the "rules he has laid down to solve a problem."

In the case of teaching, questions will open the channels for bidirectional communication. They will prevent unidirectional (and often downward slanted) propaganda preaching. Feedback from questions will permit the instructor to adjust, change, or clarify the ideas presented until the recipient has gained an adequate grasp. And what is possibly most important, the teacher will know fairly precisely just what has been understood. Where the questions place a decision before the catechumen the reaching of a "personal" conclusion will actually function as a training for the informant-catechumen to know himself (and his culture), to think constructively about his problems, and finally, to help him gain confidence that he personally can find workable solutions.

Jacob A. Loewen

Language: Vernacular, Trade, or National?

I AM writing this paper as an active member of the Mennonite Brethren Church. It is within the context of this denomination and through the help of its members and leaders that I have found a meaningful and growing faith in God, but it was also within the context of this denomination that I experienced some very serious frustrations and participated in some unfortunate language experiences.

I came to Canada from Europe as a seven-year-old, monolingual, German-speaking immigrant. I had to start school without being able to speak the language that was spoken there. In the course of my public school years I developed some rather deep-seated feelings against this symbol which made me different, if not inferior.

The Mennonite Brethren Church, as a separatist church, was tolerating the delusion that its spiritual life would suffer if the language of the church changed. The isolation from its "Jerusalem and Judea" neighbors due to this language and culture difference was often rationalized in terms of spiritual values. "People do not join our church because we are living the

separated life which God teaches in his word, and this is not popular among the people around us." One can assert that, at least in a measure, these language and cultural barriers kept the denomination from a local outreach, and that as a substitute it developed one of the largest (by ratio to church membership) foreign missions programs among North American churches. But to a large extent this was also conscience salve for the non-witness to the English-speaking neighbors of the immediate environment.

Then came the generations born in North America and addicted to the English language. The obvious result was serious tension between the generations. In the battle over what language to use in the worship services, many young people left the church (and God) in rebellion, and many older people were grieved and broken. Finally the voice of the Spirit was heeded, and the language differences were recognized to be irrelevant for the "new man of God's design"[1] who knows no racial or linguistic distinctions. But the price of the lesson in loss of witness and in human hurt was steep.

Now it seems to me that the current programs on many mission fields are

Jacob A. Loewen is Translations Consultant for the American Bible Society in South America. 315 South Wilson, Hillsboro, Kansas.

[1] Galatians 3: 10, J. B. Phillips.

in danger of developing situations that parallel the experience recounted above. The question burning in my heart is, "Can the missionary movement learn anything from a denomination's painful experience that would or could help to prevent hurt and dissension in the younger churches?" I believe it can, and this I accept as the justification for writing this paper and the preceding "confession."

Language Problems on the Field

In many of our mission fields we find a variety of tribal vernaculars spoken by preliterate minority groups. Above these diverse vernaculars is an overarching trade language, which may also be the national language. Occasionally the national language represents a third language layer above the vernacular. The vernacular will generally be identified with the sacred and best of one's own people. The trade language may be a necessity of daily and economic life, but it may also be the vehicle of unpleasant experiences with the outside world. Where this trade or national language represents the language of a conquering people, there will most likely be deeply repressed, but nonetheless potent, feelings against it by the conquered. Such emotions may often be fanned by the many active pressures of the central government, which seeks to assimilate the diverse linguistic and cultural elements into the national society.

When the missionary comes into such a multi-language situation, there is danger that he may follow exclusively one of the two possible extremes. Some decide to do all their preaching in the national or trade language, while others use only the tribal vernacular.

There are advantages to using only the national or trade language. This language will enjoy the blessing of the national government and make the latter more tolerant toward the work. It usually has a much broader application and can be the medium of communication with people from a number of tribal groups. Since it may be a language already known to the missionary, this may also be the path of least effort. The national or trade language will make possible a more profitable ecumenical experience. Church people will be able to share their experiences with a greater variety of people.

The disadvantages, however, are also many. The trade or national language may actually be a limiting factor in one's spiritual experience. Because the trade language is not the language of a man's heart and of his past religious experience, it may affect his receptivity to the message; or it may limit the depth of its penetration into the inner life. The tribal hearer may easily misunderstand the basic implications of the message because, while he may be bilingual, he will seldom be bicultural. At the same time he may get only a very superficial (if not warped) grasp of the message. Since his trade language experience will likely be limited to material concerns, his spiritual experience can likewise be limited to specific areas of his life. Thus his Christian experience may become associated with a particular type of speech.

Exclusive use of the trade or national language may also result in limiting his witness, not only because of his insufficiency in it, but also because he may be unable to convert trade language concepts into those of the vernacular; or he may restructure the message by trying to use reverse equivalents to what he understood poorly. Such limited understanding, control, or experience will hinder the spontaneous growth of the national church.[2]

In considering the second alternative, that of using only the tribal vernacular, we find an intimacy which will provide for maximun receptivity. The person's past religious experiences will be in this language, so it will not be a foreign God that is speaking; it will be "his own God." The familiarity with the conceptual world of the vernacular will also be a strong safeguard against misunderstanding or a restructuring of the message. A missionary's proficiency in the vernacular will make informal witnessing easier and more relevant, at least with his tribal neighbors, while the "hominess" of the vernacular will permit a man to find the answer to the basic needs and fears of his life and thus permit a deeper penetration of the religious experience. It will permit the resulting new church to draw heavily on the tribal leadership and thus give stability and authority to the church even while it is in its infancy.

2 Malcolm Guthrie, "Language Barriers in Evangelism," *Congo Mission News,* July 1957, pp. 5-6, contains a very worthwhile discussion of the trade language problem. The author is indebted to him for a number of the ideas expressed.

But we find that using only the vernacular can also be limiting. It can limit the message to a small minority group, and here ethnocentrism makes the language vehicle of the message a "sacred cow." This ethnocentrism can lead to suspicion of and tension with groups from other language backgrounds, even though both may be Christians. And as the tribal or national language permeates the tribal culture, the danger of tension between generations of even one and the same group will become more probable. Further, the local nature of the vernacular will limit, if not make impossible, the broader witness; and the group will tend to be a linguistic, cultural, or denominational island, which will be cut off from the blessings of a broader ecumenical fellowship.

A quick summary of the respective advantages of the two approaches reveals that the vernacular has very substantial advantages for the early witnessing experience of the convert. However, looking at the later stages of broader witnessing and ecumenicity, the trade or national language has a tremendous superiority. This leads me to the thesis of this paper that both languages have an important place. The vernacular is the best language for the initial contact with the gospel. It will aid receptivity, penetration, and easy, early witnessing. The trade or national language, if introduced early, will make possible an immediate broadening of the application of the message, permit a more ecumenical witness, and help tie the local church to the larger national, or even international, church. The following report is an account of an attempt to capitalize on these respective advantages in the mission to the Choco of Panama.

The Choco Language Scene

Choco Indian languages or dialects are today spoken by some twenty to twenty-five thousand Indians currently inhabiting an area along the Pacific Coast of northwestern South America. The area extends on the north into Panama to the Sambu River (with several small groups migrated as far north as the Chepo River); on the south, throughout the Pacific coast region of Colombia (with several interruptions in southern Colombia) into Ecuador where small groups of migrated Choco Indians have been reported on the Cayapas River; on the east, from the Pacific Ocean into the Sinú and the San Jorge River basin to a line always remaining west of the Cauca River.

Earlier research had shown that the modern Choco speech community is divided into at least two groups which call themselves the Waunana and the Epera. The Waunana language is fairly homogenous throughout the area of its extension. On the other hand, the Epera exhibits a large series of dialects, of which at least nine have been identified and studied. These nine dialects can be grouped into two clusters: Northern Epera, which includes the dialects of Sambu, Río Verde, San Jorge, and Catio; and Southern Epera, which includes the dialects of Río Sucio, Baudo, Tado, Chami, and Saixa.[3] A dialect and

intelligibility survey conducted in 1955-57 showed that the whole Choco community could be reached with three separate Bible translations: one for Waunana, one for Northern Epera, and one for Southern Epera.

Over and above the Indian languages and dialects is the Spanish, the national language of Colombia and Panama, the countries in which the Choco Indians are found. For all practical purposes Spanish is the trade language by which these Indians communicate with the hispanic world around them; and also, in the case of the most differentiated dialects, in which they communicate with each other. Though many Indians are polylingual in several of the Choco dialects, mastery of Spanish varies from area to area. In Panama Spanish is spoken quite widely and rather well by most Choco Indians. In Colombia, among the Waunana, for example, Spanish has been rather poorly mastered. There are many archaic remnants from medieval Spanish, vestiges of their early contacts with the Spanish conquerors.[4] Many of the people who do speak Spanish employ the third person singular form of the verb exclusively; that is, they use the respective subject pronoun, but the verb always remains in the third person singular form with all subjects.

Until recently the attitude of the Indians toward the Spanish language has been generally hostile. A drunken Indian, on hearing me preach in Spanish, once asked me why I wasted my time speaking about God in the

---

3 Jacob A. Loewen, "Dialectología de la Familia Lingüística Chocó," *Revista Colombiana de Antropología*, Vol. 9, pp. 9-22.

4 Jacob A. Loewen, "Spanish Loanwords in Waunana," *International Journal of American Linguistics*, Vol. 26, pp. 330-344.

language of the devils. Almost universally in Choco mythology the villain speaks Spanish. Often he is also Spanish in name, as Tío Tigre (Spanish for Uncle Tiger) or Paisa (the colloquial name for a mestizo farmer). The Choco culture hero is always engaged in struggles with these Spanish figures, and most of the crimes recounted are perpetrated in the Spanish language.

But the attitude is changing. In the paper, "A Choco Indian in Hillsboro,"[5] we reported how Indian Aureliano's view of "people" was enlarged through prayer together with Negroes, Chinese, and German-speaking people in the United States. He suddenly began to refer to his prayer companions as "Epera" or Indian people. This could be considered symptomatic of what is currently happening to the attitude of the Choco Indians in Panama toward the Spanish language. There is a widespread move in the direction of accepting the Christians of Spanish speech or of English language origin as "Epera" or people.

Both the Colombian and the Panamanian governments have made efforts to teach Spanish to the Indians. In a number of areas schools have been established.[6] Currently, only very few schools dedicated to teach Spanish to the Indians have remained. Most of those remaining are either evangelical or state church mission schools. Both in Colombia and Panama numbers of young Indians have attempted to learn the Spanish language in government day schools in competition with Spanish-speaking people; but as a result of their low level of achievement, the Indians as a whole have developed a rather defeatist attitude toward learning to read Spanish. The typical community attitude toward the Indian had come to be: "Indians are unable to learn to read Spanish; they are just too stupid." The Indians themselves had largely come to accept this attitude as a statement of fact and were repeating it of themselves.

In summary we could thus say that on the first level there are important differences even between the fairly mutually intelligible dialects of the Northern and Southern Epera clusters.[7] Next are the interlanguage differences between Waunana and the two regional Epera languages. Indians speaking only one of these languages must communicate with each other in the Spanish. Over and above the vernaculars there is the common trade language, Spanish, which is also the national language.

The Two-Language Literacy Approach

Aware of the Choco feelings against Spanish and cognizant of the failure

---

5 Jacob A. Loewen, "A Choco Indian in Hillsboro," PA, Vol. 9, No. 3 (May-June 1962), pp. 129-133.

6 Nicasio A. Vargas and Jacob A. Loewen, "Experiencia de Alfabetización con los Indios Chocoes," América Indígena, Vol. 23, pp. 121-125.

7 During the Bible translation experience in Hillsboro, Aureliano objected to some of the "adjusted" forms which became necessary to make the material applicable to four dialects. Finally, the translator asked him if he understood three of the forms in the question equally well. He did. Did the people on the river north understand them? No, they understood one, but this form was common to all. Once he understood the principle of adapting dialect differences, he was more cooperative in finding answers to such dialect conflicts.

of many Indians to learn to read Spanish in the regular government day school, David Wirsche and the author performed a literacy experiment with nine Epera Indians to see whether it would be possible to bypass the Indian psychological block, viz., that Indians were too stupid to learn to read the Spanish language. The approach proposed to teach the Indians to read their own language, which had been transcribed as far as possible with the Spanish alphabet and Spanish syllable patterns. It was based on the assumption that the Indian would feel confident when approaching his own language, especially if the sentences of the readers were taken from Indian folklore and thus geared to his own world view.[8] His confidence in his capacity to learn his own language could thus become a stepping-stone for the mastery of Spanish, toward which he had the psychological block.[9]

[8] David Wirsche, "Study of Language Universals in Teaching Reading, Applied to Sambu Dialect," an unpublished masters thesis at the University of Washington, 1963.

[9] Theodore Anderson, chairman of the Department of Romance Languages, University of Texas, Austin, in a lecture, "Do We Want Certified Teachers or Qualified Ones?" at the Kansas Modern Language Association meeting held at Kansas State Teachers College in Emporia, March 30, 1963, reported:
"A similar experiment is now being conducted in an elementary school in Texas, in which the children of Latin origin are separated from the so-called Anglos; and during their regular language session the Spanish children work at Spanish reading, writing, and literature, and the Anglo children work at their own English language. However, during the foreign-language period, the Spanish children are subjected to a study of English as a foreign language while the Anglo children are subjected to the study of Spanish as a foreign language.

The results were almost dramatic. Often in a matter of days an Indian who had never previously "read" a picture was now able to read not only his own language but also the standard elementary Spanish reading materials used in the Panamanian government schools.

The materials in the initial primers, in the folklore readers, and in the Bible stories used the Epera language exclusively. There were several reasons for the use of the native language at this stage. First of all, it was to bypass the already mentioned psychological block that prevented the Indians from learning to read Spanish. However, there was also the matter of indigenizing the message. Once the Epera achieved the facility to read the word of God, it was supposed to be their God who was speaking to them in their own language, in the vernacular in which they had their daily experiences. It was an attempt to link the values of the gospel to the values of the home language and culture of the Choco. Also on this count the results were encouraging. At Chepo, the son of a chief who had never previously heard the gospel mastered all the seven readers in two and a half days. He was given a Bible story book without comment or explanation by the missionary who then had to leave. The Indian never stopped reading until the missionary returned three hours later. His comment: "I never knew God had said

The investigators report that at about the grade six level, the efficiency in the two languages is about equal and that the children are now bilingual with about equal facility to read and write in both languages."

all these things. Things are really going to have to change on our river."

Use of Diglot Publications

All the material that has been prepared in the Indian language, since the initial readers and the first reading material in the Bible stories and folktales, has been produced in a diglot form with the Indian language on one side and the Spanish on the other. There were several reasons for this approach. First of all, this was the expressed request of the Panamanian government, which gave permission to conduct this bi-language reading experiment. Since the experiment was successful and the Indians could now read Spanish, the government graciously encouraged us to continue publishing in diglot form. It was hoped that thus the Indians would improve their facility in reading both languages, since the two-language reading experience could be mutually reinforcing.[10] From the missionary point of view, there was a concern that the Indians would immediately learn to witness to their mestizo neighbors, who speak the Spanish language. They needed to be able to convert the descriptions of their Indian experience into the language of the Spanish and vice versa. They also

needed to understand the Spanish testimonies given to them by believers from that language background and be able to translate them meaningfully for those Indians who could not understand Spanish. At the same time, a diglot translation of this nature would help them to see that God is one God. He is God not only in the Indian language but in the Spanish language as well — something their former ethnocentric view had not considered possible.

To date, the total amount of material prepared in the Indian language and published in diglot form includes the twenty-five Bible stories described in "Message and Matrix,"[11] the Gospel of Mark, the first fifteen chapters of Acts, and selected passages for different occasions translated from the letters of the New Testament. In 1962 a diglot book of hymns and choruses was added.

In 1962 a conscious effort was begun to strengthen the Spanish within the Choco church. A highly simplified Spanish version of the first fifteen chapters of Acts, already available in diglot form, was introduced. This book soon became popular, possibly even more popular than the Epera-Spanish (Valera) diglot version. The timing of the release of this book was fortunate, for when David Wirsche arrived on the field in the summer of 1962 and asked the Indians what they wanted him to do for them, they requested help in improving their facility in the Spanish language.

---

[10] During a recent trip through several Latin American republics the author was fascinated to observe that in the majority of the cases observed nationals were reading both the Spanish and the aboriginal language. Thus if the two languages were side by side, they read first one side and then the other. If the languages appeared one on the upper half of the page and the other on the lower, they just kept on reading till they got to the bottom of the page.

[11] Jacob A. Loewen, "Bible Stories: Message and Matrix," PA, Vol. 9, No. 2 (March-April 1964), pp. 49-55.

Of course, we need to recognize that there are many pressures on the Indians pushing them toward the use of Spanish. The government wants to assimilate them into national life and has already passed several laws that would make it compulsory for the Indians to send their children to Spanish schools. Then the Indians are finding that competition with the mestizos around them is increasing. This will increase even more when the Pan-American Highway works its way through their territory and more of the virgin land around them is settled by non-Indian people.

Furthermore, Spanish is the language of the officials and the educated, and therefore it does carry certain prestige advantages. Another pressure for Spanish is the fact that a number of the Indian dialects are not mutually intelligible. This makes it necessary for Indians who migrate from one part of the country to another to communicate with each other in the trade language, at least for the period of time during which the immigrant party learns the dialect of the area.

Not to be underestimated is the accessibility of simple Spanish literature. The Pan-American Union library of forty-eight books is now being distributed among the Indians and has found wide acclaim. There is also the new Spanish *Versión Popular* of the New Testament that is being produced by the American Bible Society.

Since Aureliano's visit to the United States, there has also been increasing contact between the Indians and the Criollos around them. There have been numerous occasions at which Aure-liano, an Indian, has been requested to deliver messages to the Spanish congregation in the village of Jaque. In fact, a number of these believers have been won to the Lord by the Indians and have been baptized by Aureliano. Such witnessing must all be done in Spanish, and it provides additional incentive for the Indian believers to improve their proficiency in that language.

Some Conclusions

We feel that the experiences in the Choco mission not only support the thesis proposed earlier in this paper, but also permit us to attempt some additional generalizations in regards to the Choco language scene. Since there is overlap between the support for the thesis and the subsidiary generalizations, they have been grouped together in a series of conclusions that follow.

1. The use of the vernacular in the early stages of the evangelism aided the initial reception and penetration of the message, the early witness of the church, and the strengthening of the Indians' self-image. It indigenized the message. At no point did we sense that the message was interpreted as a message from "white man's God."

It also caused a deep penetration of the message into the lives of the people and brought real change — conversion in the true sense of the word. Some changes were especially notable: the loss of the fear of the evil spirit world, which was replaced by the confidence that the more powerful God is now operating in and through their lives; the exchange of fear for each other — manifested in poisoning and social breakdown — with the restoration of group fellowship in which the people get together for several days to worship God together, or to work on each other's farms in working bees; and a new kind of self-confidence and reason-to-be that revitalized the lives of the Indians. Where they had been on the retreat, they now aggresively evangelized — not only other Indians but also their Criollo neighbors. Where, according to local law, they had formerly killed the pigs which invaded their crops, they now watched their fields and kept the pigs out so as to establish a witnessing relationship with their mestizo neighbors.

The extensive use of narrative coupled with the vernacular language in the early stages allowed all the individuals to confidently share the message with others. It was most encouraging to notice how people immediately were able to retell the Bible stories and were able to explain them to others as they were questioned in the course of teaching of reading. The reading material and the Bible stories actually provided interesting news that was good to talk about and which also was freely discussed with all with whom they came in contact.

Use of the vernacular helped bypass the psychological block that Indians could not learn to read. Indians actually learned to read their own language fluently and quickly. When Indians who had not been exposed to the reading campaign came up with the old statement that Indians are not able to learn to read, the Christian Indians immediately countered, "Yes, that may be true; but you know when you

give God the hand and walk on God's road, God cleans up your eyes and your mind in such a way that you can learn to read. And once you can learn to read you don't have to listen to other people; you can just read the message the way God said it, and you can have God speak to you directly."

2. If the vernacular is transcribed in the orthography of the trade or national language, the gain in efficiency of sizable proportions can be realized. For the Choco experiment it meant that the missionaries were able to teach reading in both languages simultaneously. The quick mastery of their own language and the ability to read the national language without much additional learning experience became a tremendous encouragement for the Indians.

3. All reading materials, except possibly the very earliest ones, are best published in diglot form. For the Choco Indians, we learned that the diglot form of the message, first of all, gave the Indians confidence that God is one for all. They realized that the messages given in the Indian language and in the Spanish are identical. The fact that both the Epera and the Spanish occurred in one book made it possible for them to read and witness from the same book to any visitor who came into their home, be he of Indian or of Spanish origin.

Since Spanish was the national language and therefore the prestige language of the country, this was an incentive for the Indians to also read the Spanish side of the book. By reading both the Indian side of the material and the Spanish side, they were mutually reinforcing their ability to read and understand both languages. And it must also be underscored that it was the emphasis on the Spanish (in terms of the diglot material and the other Spanish material that we produced) that won us warm government support. This has meant that every summer the ministry of education has extended invitations for the workers to return to Panama to continue the program.

Simplified Literature

4. The national language use can be boosted if it is introduced in its simplest form. The experiment of the summer of 1962, to introduce the simplified version of the first fifteen chapters of Acts, was a real stroke of fortune. Its simplicity permitted the Indians to read and to understand very readily some of the materials that even in their own Indian translation were somewhat difficult to follow. It capitalized on the inward and outward pressures on the Indian to gain efficiency in the use of Spanish.

This new interest in simple Spanish also led us to discover other sources of simplified literature. And we found that the Pan-American Union with its library of forty-eight booklets provides some interesting and educational materials written at a very elementary level. Several governmental agencies were willing to cooperate to provide these booklets, either free or at cost. In regard to the Scriptures, we found that the American Bible Society in its new *Versión Popular* in Spanish is actually producing the type of literature that will meet this need in the church. We feel that it has resulted in a tremendous strengthening of the ecumenical feeling between the Indian churches on the river and the Spanish church in Jaque.

5. This relates to the amount of scriptural material to be translated into the aboriginal languages.[12] While this may not apply to all societies, we feel it is certainly worthwhile to be considered for smaller tribes where the expense of extensive translation and publishing will become prohibitive in relationship to the size of the population. We have developed three criteria on which we are basing the decision for additional translation in the Choco language: (a) We will need to inject new scriptural material in the Indian language from time to time to prevent entropy. However, the amount is to be geared to the actual need. As the Indians are weaned from the native language and increase their use of the Spanish language, this need will decrease. (b) We will translate selected passages of Scripture relating to particular problems when these appear in the Indian church. It is based on the premise that the use of the vernacular will mean a more indigenous "voice of God," a greater penetration into the lives of the people, and also a greater willingness to obey the appeal of God. And (c) as the Indian church requests more material in the vernacular, we will try to provide this material. The experience of 1962, however, showed that rather than request more material in the vernacular, the request of the church was for more simple Spanish material, and this we are trying to meet.

---

12 Kenneth L. Pike of the Summer Institute of Linguistics read a preliminary draft of the paper and seriously questions this conclusion.

William J. Samarin

Language of Silence

WE have learned to expect cultures to be different from one another in innumerable and fascinating ways: in speech, burial rites, marriage practices, and eating habits. The end is hardly in sight, for each new culture studied adds in some way to our knowledge of variation in human behavior.

The stuff out of which these richly variegated cultures are made is found around man and in man — the earth, the plants, the animals, other men, and the emotions within himself. Even space is taken and utilized in particular ways. In our own society people talk to each other at a certain distance from each other, and otherwise maintain their distance so religiously that an infraction of these "rules" creates uneasiness, embarrassment, or even outright anger.[1]

None of these raw materials from which cultural elements are constructed (by selection and contrastive structuring) is more ubiquitous than silence. It is there when a stranger walks into the village and women stop pounding their grain. It is there when the guests come to sit with the sick friend or relative. But silence is not just the absence of a significant piece of behavior. It is not just emptiness. Silence can have meaning. Like the zero in mathematics, it is an absence with a function.

It is this meaningful use of silence that I call the "language of silence" (a deliberate twist of the expression for culture utilized as a book title by Edward T. Hall).[2] Not all silence carries a message. Silence is usually just a sign that some activity has ceased, that the women are no longer working. These occasions of unconscious silence are not part of man's learned behavior by which he conveys messages to others.

The most meaningful uses of silence are perhaps found in speech. As a communicative code, language consists primarily of sounds which are strung along in extremely complex but patterned ways. The units of language are phonemic, morphemic (meaningful sequences of sounds), and some others. Within this closed system whose parts must be known to "play the game" are brief episodes of hiatus which separate sounds into "words" or groups of words into "phrases," "clauses," or "sentences."[3]

---

[1] See Edward T. Hall, *The Silent Language* (Greenwich, Conn.: Fawcett Publications, 1959).

William J. Samarin is Assistant Professor of Linguistics, Hartford Seminary Foundation, 55 Elizabeth St., Hartford, Conn. A former missionary in the Central African Republic, he previously contributed "Gbeya Prescientific Ideas and Christianity" to PA. Vol. 6, No. 4 (July-Aug. 1959), pp. 179-182.

[2] Op. cit.

[3] Put into quotation marks because the terms must be defined for each language.

These "junctures" or pauses are not themselves meaningful, however. They serve only to group (along with some other features like stress, speed of utterance, pitch, etc.) the stretches of sound into units that do have meaning. One can never ask of them: What did that silence mean? We all recognize, furthermore, when the other person is tired, or when he is thinking, or when his attention has been caught by something else. Silence is often imposed on another by one's volubility! But speakers do habitually attribute explicit meaning to silence in each other's speech. They may be completely wrong in the meaning they attribute to it, but there is no denying that they can be very emphatic in its interpretation. Silence can be an evasion, an affirmation, a negation, a deception, an attempt at being coy, and so on.

Because silence can be significant man expects his interlocutor to break his silence, that is, to make it predictable and therefore not meaningful.[4]

---

[4] This is perhaps part of the mechanism for keeping down the amount of information being conveyed in face-to-face situations. (The use of "information" here is the technical one taken from information theory: the greater the unpredictability of a word or other linguistic element the more impact of information it carries. What is predictable is hence not meaningful.) There is apparently some saturation point for information beyond which comprehension is reduced, due in part to the repressive effects of anxiety. This anxiety is itself an effect of the failure to grasp all that is being said. But it is also due to concern about the style which the talk has assumed. Since speech interaction depends on some kind of harmony or understanding being established by the parties involved, anxiety can be produced by subtle changes in type of discourse, so that when a person begins to load his talk with

The universal manner of achieving this end is by uttering grunts or indeterminate sounds which vary from language to language. No conversation between people is ever free of them regardless of the verbal skill of the parties. Even the most eloquent and scintillating of conversationalists depends on his listener's "yeah," "mhm," etc. For this reason all dialogue in writing, from the most profane to the most sublime, is artificial. Writers never indicate the amount of reinforcement that each speaker gives to the other.

Cross-Cultural Differences

Once we grant that silence during periods of linguistic interaction can have meaning, we must assume that there are cross-cultural differences. We cannot expect the Gbeya of the Central African Republic, the Ata of the Philippines, or the Yupik Eskimo of Alaska to use silence in the same way we Americans do. It is the purpose of this brief study to call attention to some of the differences that we have observed, pointing out the pitfalls of ignoring them, with the hope that others might extend this investigation.

Attention to the cross-cultural differences in the use of silence was first forced upon me by my experience in

---

information — by being more articulate and precise — he runs the risk of throwing his interlocutor off balance. This is why in normal social intercourse between friends or between members of some informal in-group, there seems to be a tendency to "translate" messages into informal, redundant, even poorly structured idiom — even when one knows clearly what one wants to say. This phenomenon is extremely common at committee meetings for example.

the Central African Republic (formerly the Territory of Oubangui-Chari of French Equatorial Africa) where I had been a missionary. In this capacity I was not just an observer of the culture of the Gbeya but an unceasing participant in it. For about five years I interacted with people in the Gbeya language through experiences that ranged from the excitement, pleasure, and honor of having killed a lion to the frustration and bewilderment resulting from rejection. I came to see that the Gbeya use silence very differently from the way I was accustomed to using it.

What I say now is not based on field notes, for I did not take any on this subject. If I had done so the notes would have included information concerning the person with whom I was speaking, the topic that was being discussed, the point at which my Gbeya interlocutor became silent, what my immediate interpretation (or that of another Gbeya witness) of this silence was, and finally, how the conversation was resumed.

What struck me about Gbeya silence was how shamelessly it could be indulged in. There seemed to be no embarrassment about not continuing with the conversation when the other person left off. It seems as if the Gbeya do not feel under obligation to talk. And yet I would not consider them by any means a taciturn people. It is just that silence is looked upon as something which is as effective as speech. This attitude · is expressed to some extent in their proverbs. "Speech is an internal thing which you think about and then say." "Speech is a reedbuck. Some stay down [that is,

keep hidden] and some stand up [and are seen]." "A speech is in the white goat and the black goat does not know it." "Speech is a chicken feather [once it is out, it is scattered]." "Your internal speech does not [should not] spout out." "Speech is something internal which, when it comes out, attracts flies [like excrement]."

These proverbs reveal the protective function of silence. It is the behavioral response to one's need to be wary and cautious. If put into words the silence would mean any one of the following things: "I'm not going to get involved." "I'm not committing myself." "I don't agree but I'm not telling you so." "I'm waiting for more information." "I'm not going to say anything for fear of giving away some information."

Such ego withdrawal and anxiety reaction under certain situations are probably universal — they are certainly present in our own society — but the degree to which they are manifested by silence in various societies is different. Likewise, societies differ in the degree to which they make explicit this function of silence, either approvingly or disapprovingly. Obviously, ego-withdrawal by silence is an approved social behavior among the Gbeya. It is a kind of self-control which should be cultivated.

Less predictable is the occurrence of silence in other cultural situations. The Blackfoot Indians of the United States, for example, are said not to talk for about five minutes even when they are making social calls.[5] The

---

[5] C. F. Voegelin and Z. Harris, "Linguistics in Ethnology," *Southwestern Journal of Anthropology*, Vol. 1, p. 458 (1945).

Gbeya, for their part, are noticeably silent while eating food, especially when there are guests who are not members of the intimate family circle. The one beer-drinking "party" I witnessed was also marked by very little talk while the beer was being dished out.

For this reason I found very little pleasure of the type that I was accustomed to in entertaining Gbeya at meals. While some of the silence was probably due to the awkwardness of my guests, most of whom had never before eaten with a white man or with his paraphernalia (much simplified, to tell the truth), some of it must also be explained by the Gbeya custom of engaging in conversation after the meal, rather than during it. For me, an Occidental, the meal itself provided an opportunity for prolonged verbal interaction on a somewhat intimate level; for the Gbeya the meal is equally a sign of hospitality and good relations but much less the occasion of talk. I have asked only one Gbeya about this silence during a meal. His quick response was that if you did any talking the others would eat all the food! It should be remembered that all meals are taken from a common bowl by dipping a dough into one or two sauces which by preference contain pieces of meat.

In addition to the meal, silence is also the main feature of "sick calls." The function of this visit is to demonstrate to the family and the community that one is not happy about the person's illness, for lack of sympathy is interpreted by traditional animists as complicity in sorcery. This sympathy is expressed by assuming a lugubrious mien and sitting in silence. A minimal amount of chitchat may go on between the visitors, but it does not involve the patient. For a Westerner these comforters can be extremely disquieting as they stare into space. I have been visited on several occasions when the first pleasure of being honored by love and concern gave way to annoyance. Wracked as I was by pain, I wanted to be distracted by talk, but my Gbeya friends had not come to take my mind off my physical condition. They had come instead to remind me of their solidarity with me. This was achieved in silence.

Function of Silence in American Society

When we compare the Gbeya with our own society we must concede that there are indeed differences in the functions to which silence is put, but it also seems true that in our own society silence is less tolerated generally. Witness the image of the "ideal" high school senior or college student. He is characterized by the way he verbally manages all types of situations. In former days, and perhaps to some extent even today, conversation was considered to be the art of the cultured segment of society. Dinners and parties at the homes of certain eminent people were famous for the lively conversationalists regularly invited.

Since we believe that conversation must be maintained between individuals we can exploit the embarrassment of others in several ways, some for inane purposes. For example, we can force the other person to talk when we ourselves have nothing to say or would rather not speak until the other person's views are ascertained. Thus we almost unthinkingly ask, "What did you think of the movie?" when we are more interested in filling up silence than we are in getting information.

Certain professionals in our society are also skilled in the use of our embarrassment in silence. The livelihood of the psychologists depends on it. In our courts, on the other hand, silence on the part of a witness is not his prerogative but is held as contempt, for no matter how subtle and devious the lawyer's reasoning may be, no matter how awkward the witness's position may become, he is obligated — except for certain legal provisions — to answer.

The potential for misunderstanding and disharmony between Americans and Gbeya in the cross-cultural confrontation should be obvious. The American expects "straight talk" from the people he deals with. He does not expect honesty, perhaps; but he expects some approximation of it. The oblique approach is to him useless and fatiguing. Silence he does not understand at all! For his part, the Gbeya sees no reason why he has to commit himself to saying anything, for speech, not silence, is what gets a person into trouble.

Lois Sorensen and William A. Smalley

Planting the Church in a Disintegrating Society

I

I HAVE spent two years in southeastern Alaska doing secretarial work. The first year I worked for the territorial government and the second in a mission school. I had the opportunity of knowing and working with many of the Thlinget[1] Indian people. At the school I also had contact with students who were of Haida, Tsimpshean, and Athabaskan Indian background, as well as a few Eskimos. This paper will concern the Thlingets of southeastern Alaska only. While there I had no knowledge of anthropology, and at the same time made no attempt to study these people. Much of this paper, therefore, is written in retrospect.

During these two years, many times I asked the question, "Why aren't there more native Christians?" I worked with a native pastor who is one of the most outstanding Christians I have ever met, and there were a few other native Chris-

[1] In this paper I am using the most common spelling seen in Alaska, rather than "Tlingit" which is seen in most anthropological literature.

Miss Lois Sorensen, after a term of missionary service in Alaska, took a course in anthropology at Wheaton College. There she found the theoretical and factual basis for some of the "feelings" which she had had about the Alaskan work. Some of the problems about which she has been thinking were drawn together and described in this paper and in correspondence with friends in Alaska.

tians, but in relation to the number of churches (at least 10 in Sitka, which has a population of 3,500), their extensive work, and the length of time the church has been there (about 80 years), the number of Christians seemed very small to me. The answer I was constantly given was, "Well, the church has been here less than 100 years, and this is not very long when you consider the effect the Gospel has had in other areas." Another answer that I actually heard a couple of times from evangelical ministers was that "the Holy Spirit must have departed from Southeast Alaska!"

Conflicting Influences

The Russians occupied Alaska in the late 1700's and most of the 1800's, and organized many Russian Orthodox churches. American missionaries entered Alaska about 1870. Dr. Sheldon Jackson was among the first. He started a school for some of the boys in Sitka. The purpose of the school was to give them a Christian education which included such things as cleanliness, sanitation, and higher moral standards. To accomplish this it was necessary to separate the boys from their community life, and an American-type school was built. Dr. Jackson was the leading spirit in revolutionizing that part of Alaska in terms of the acceptance of education and in opening up the territory to Christian missionary activity. However, the consequences of his program, as it has been carried on through the years, have had their unfavorable aspects. Although it was not expressly spoken, the actions seem to imply that it would be best to destroy everything in local culture and make white men out of these students as quickly as possible. The students were forbidden to speak their native language while at the school; they therefore had to learn English.

This attitude of the necessity of turning the Indians into cultural white people as soon as possible has continued, and after 80 years of existence the school is hard at work with this problem. Dr. Jackson was also the first Education Commissioner for Alaska; the government schools were therefore all started with this same pattern. Not only has such an attitude been held by the missionaries and educators, but it has carried over also into the government departments as well. There has been little real attempt at identification with the natives, but simply a one-way communication in most cases. I realize what has been said, and will be said throughout the rest of this discussion, may seem highly critical. However, I think it will be found to be a realistic picture of the situation in this area.

White people in Alaska have not gone there to establish homes and remain for the rest of their lives, but are transient. There is a large number of service men with their families who are there, usually for two years, and then leave. The government term of service for nurses, teachers, and clerical workers is also two years. Many people who go are looking for excitement, and two years is enough for them. Life is slow in the towns because of isolation, and the ex-citement soon wears off. Other people go to Alaska to "help humanity," and often after two years feel they have done enough. Others go to escape or solve a personal problem. Alaska is often thought of as a wild place, but also as a good place to be a hermit. Many individuals live by themselves and have very little contact with others. This assortment of kinds of people is represented among staff members of the hospitals, schools, and offices. Sometimes they have not been able to get along well in the States and as a last resort have come to Alaska. Almost anyone can get a job in Alaska as the demand is so great, and the pay high, attracting many people whose feeling of security in other communities has worn thin. As a consequence, there are ill - advised adventure - seekers — often with a very minimum of training — leading the native people and setting examples by which they should live.

Not all of the people are like the former. There are *many* educated, well-adjusted, and well-trained people, but often they are in administrative positions. Even though they are the ones making decisions on policies affecting the natives, they often sit behind a desk all day and never mingle with the native people.

With the great turnover in personnel, each new group of workers that comes in is inclined to think they know how everything should be run, and immediately set about to change everything and get rid of the "old fogies" who have tested and tried many of these methods and adopted the ones that worked best. The native sees instability again and again.

Some Consequences

Even though the Thlinget language is used very little today, in the villages many still speak their native tongue. There are still a number of the older people who do not understand English. Last June a friend and I took our violin and flute and went to see a bed-ridden Thlinget friend who lives with her mother. The mother cannot speak English. After we had played a few hymns, her mother started singing in Thlinget for us. We were thrilled, as she had never done this before, and we tried to learn some of the words and sing with her. The mother, who is about 80 years of age, was literally jumping up and down with excitement, and her daughter exclaimed over and over again, "They're singing in Thlinget; they're actually singing in our language!" Yet I have been told by missionaries that it is absolutely useless to attempt to translate the Bible into this language as they know English well enough. Another friend told me of how his family made very little use of their radio until a news broadcast was started in the Thlinget language once a week. His mother, who usually retired at 9 every evening, would stay up until 10:30 just to hear that broadcast. Just listening to this once a week encouraged her to use the radio more frequently. A parallel effect might be had upon translating the Bible — the people will desire to read the Bible, and also have a greater desire for education.

The Native Social Structure

The family structure, although quite strong, is rapidly breaking down. Feelings many times continue to be strong where clan membership in matters of courtship and marriage are involved. It is no longer absolutely necessary that marriage be outside the clan, but this is still desired. One daughter remarked to her mother, "Every time I date a fellow I like, you tell me

he's related to me." They have adopted the American dating system, but still do not feel entirely free to marry anyone they please. Many of the natives feel it will advance their status if they marry white people, and there is a great deal of interracial marriage. The missionaries have told them that their matrilineal clan structure is not in accordance with the patrilineal structure of the Old Testament and they should therefore give up their matrilineal structure. The natives have probably held on to their matrilineal system more firmly, however, than many other of their cultural features. The children are confused. They are told by the white people that their parents' ideas are wrong and old-fashioned. On one hand they are drawn towards accepting the white man's way, and yet their family ties are so strong that they cannot entirely reject them.

Alcoholism

Among elders and young people, alcoholism is one of the main results of the transition process. Many of the Thlinget are confused and frustrated. They cannot live in their old way, and they cannot live in the white way either; so they turn to drink and soon become alcoholics. The police are often bribed and they pay little attention to it. It seems that almost every other door in the downtown area is a liquor store or a bar. The example of most of the white people has encouraged drinking because most of them drink. One former minister drove a cab and delivered liquor to help out in his support. The liquor business is a major business in Alaska, and since there is no law against the sale of it, the natives are often led by white example to think that there is nothing wrong with it.

Extramarital Relations

Alcohol and the presence of members of the armed services have both contributed to the presence of many illegitimate children. The parents feel badly when this happens, but do not turn their daughters away. Most of the girls refuse to marry the father of the baby because it would usually necessitate leaving home and Alaska. Of course, it is sometimes true that the father refuses to marry the girl. The Welfare Department, therefore, must support the child and its mother. When a young girl sees that she can get money for having an illegitimate child, she will often have others in order to get more money. This fact is commonly known, yet the schools and churches do very little teaching of moral principles. Most churches do not teach Christian concepts of marriage, or that one's body is a temple of the Holy Spirit.

Remnants of Old Culture

Superstition still exists, but most of it is under cover. No native would admit to a white person that he still believes in the supernatural powers remaining from the old religion, yet occasionally there will be a flare-up, or someone in close contact with the native will relate things he has observed. Such information in all probability is transmitted among people who are in church on Sunday mornings.

In earlier days the potlatch was a feast at which the host gave gifts to his guests and destroyed enormous amounts of valuable property like blankets, skins, oil, and valuable "coppers" which were symbols of wealth. This was done in order to shame the guest, and to assert the superiority of the host, or to honor someone who had recently died. A form of the potlatch still exists today; however, this too is under cover. A present-day potlatch corresponds more to our big parties where there is much eating and drinking. A very important part, also, is story-telling. The different clans represented may tell their various legends. There may be even deeper significances to the potlatch that remains in its present form which have not been obliterated nor superseded by the teaching that they have received.

Personal Suggestions

1. I believe that the native language should be used, not primarily in order to preserve the language, but as a means of teaching the older people who are the ones who rule the homes and families. It may also be used to reach the younger and middle-aged people who have been brought up in homes where the native language was spoken and native expressions and ways of thinking were learned. Many feel that this will encourage the people to go backwards. I feel that it will not do that, but will recognize the fact that the language is being used and show the people the value of their culture. The adjustment to white cultural patterns will be easier and less painful for them; and this will also give the white people a greater appreciation of the natives. Together they can then share a new if-changed world. If this, and the probable strengthening of whatever cultural integrity is left, is going "backwards," it is only if becoming a "white man" is considered "progress." The entire population of North American Indians is facing white sentiment, as well as legislation, born of this notion, that assimilation equals progress.

Recently I was talking to a young Thlinget who is studying in Chicago to be a doctor. I asked him his opinion of translating into the native language. At first he saw little value in it, but later he said, "Well, if you do that, perhaps the people will quit being the spectators and become the players, and they will see that the Gospel is really for them too, and will understand it better."

2. Potluck suppers, which have already been established, can serve as a partial substitute for the potlatch. It would be valuable to have a planned program after the supper which might be recreational, spiritual, or both. Perhaps one of the native people could tell a Thlinget legend or some of their history. (I was greatly impressed at a Sunday School picnic when the native minister told a story in Thlinget of the Raven and the Wolf, and another man translated into English.) At other times a short devotional message could be brought, preferably by a Thlinget. A greater and stronger fellowship of the Christians is possible through these potluck suppers.

3. Native leadership should be encouraged in the churches. Attempts have often been made to get native Sunday School teachers, but these have not been very successful. I think that one basic reason for the failure is that the native people do not like to be responsible to a white person. If a native were in the position of leadership, however, they would probably be more willing to help in the church. Perhaps a native could teach a small Sunday School class of adults or children in the Thlinget language. Native deacons, ushers, and choir directors have proved very effective and should be encouraged to continue.

4. The godly Thlinget pastor mentioned above is preaching to his congregation mainly in English because of the nature of the missionary methods which have prevailed. Although it has been the tradition and all of his "education" has

been against using the Thlinget language, and about half of his congregation are white and English-speaking, I believe that he should be encouraged to expand a ministry in his native language. If people will stay up an hour and a half later at night to hear the news in their language, the Gospel in their language, both in the churches and on the radio, should have far-reaching results. During the summer most of the people are out fishing and have very little opportunity for worship. Some other form of worship should be substituted, and the radio might well be a means of doing this. During the winter, when many of them are not working, they sleep late in the mornings, which means that Sunday School and morning worship are poorly attended. Many of the villages have found that it is better to have Sunday School in the afternoon and the main worship service in the evening. Many ministers, however, have felt that the morning service should be emphasized. I think that the worship service should be fitted to their schedule, as there is nothing supernatural or supercultural about holding a worship service at a certain hour in the morning or evening as it is done in the United States and Canada.

5. As much as is possible, the newcomers to Alaska should be screened and should have a good orientation and know what to expect before going. Although this is desirable, it is impossible for all personnel. But it should be imperative for missionaries. I also feel that it is impossible for a person to do a lasting job on a short-term basis (such as a 2- or 4-year term). The need is so extensive that the emphasis has often been on quantity, and not on quality, both in the church field and government work. This needs to be changed, or the results

that have already appeared will become worse, and greater problems will develop. An anthropological orientation program, I think, is vital, especially to those who expect to work with the native people.

Even if one is not working with the native people, his influence in the community will spread to the natives. This orientation needed cannot be accomplished in a 3-day training session or even a week. At least a month, plus reading of many background books would be more desirable. If someone is willing to go through all this, then chances of being accepted by the natives will be much greater because he has already shown his desire to learn and not to teach, or force (as has been the result in many cases) his knowledge on the people. Someone who is willing to go through this is probably a better adjusted person.

I found that even though I was not particularly interested in learning about the customs of the people, many times the native people would tell me about them. I think the reason for this was that I did not have a critical attitude toward them or their culture as so many white people did. I think they sensed that I was honest in wanting to help them and they did not feel that whatever they told me would be used against them. It is necessary to stay there a long time to win their confidence. The Thlinget people *will not* open up to strangers, and when someone such as a writer asks prying questions they may give him a partial answer, or say they do not know, that there is nothing unusual, or even give a wrong answer. We would react the same way if someone came prying into our personal affairs. Writers, for instance, will go to Alaska for two weeks

to two months and then go back to the States and write a book of stories on Alaska. These stories cannot possibly be altogether factual, although they have some truth in them. Above all, "the love of Christ constraineth us" is the important qualification and attitude.

6. The importance of lay workers in this area cannot be overemphasized. There are already so many churches, with just a handful of people (usually untrained) in each church. The minister is faced with being head of the Sunday school, church janitor, doing all the secretarial and bookkeeping work, making repairs, etc., plus preaching and visiting his parish. The lay worker, someone living in the community and working so that he has his own support, has an unlimited opportunity. Also, the natives can see in someone besides their minister — who gets paid for doing it — how the Christian life should be lived. There is a tremendous ministry among the white people also, both Christian and non-Christian, for the lay worker.

Unanswered Questions

So far I have said very little about how to go about developing the native church, mostly because I do not know the answer. How does one go about establishing an indigenous church in such a place where people stand between two cultures and where there is so much ambiguity in the cultural framework? Does the matrilineal system have to be replaced by the patrilineal system? Will the potlatch have to be destroyed, and if so, how? Should Alcoholics Anonymous or a similar group be sought to aid in the alcoholic problem?

Lois Sorensen

II

THE picture which you draw of Thlinget and other people of Indian background in Alaska is not as unusual as you may think. Many of the details of your description can be paralleled in one society after another around the world, places where the impact of the West upon an aboriginal culture has left a people in transition, as you say: disoriented, insecure, afraid. It has often happened that a society has been shaken to its very roots by contact with another. Its major presuppositions have been challenged. Its way of life has been changed either through force or influence. It sees a way of life which has many of the earmarks of power and the glitter of wealth — a way of life which seems materially desirable; and yet the Western alternative presented to it is too complex for it to understand. It holds tenaciously, and a little bit hysterically sometimes, to certain aspects of its past. Its insecurity, its fear, breaks out sometimes in a violent movement such as the Mau Mau and sometimes in emotional apathy and resignation. As different as the atrocities of the Mau Mau and the lethargy of many American Indian groups, seem, they are but two symptoms of the same conflict of cultures, the same breakdown of values. In your case the cultural apathy carries along with it a religious apathy, and even among those Thlinget who have become Christians the spirit of the present Thlinget world is that spirit of lethargy and deadness.

History Cannot Be Reversed

Much as you may regret it, you can never turn back the Thlinget clock. The unfortunate train of events, the unfortunate influences of the past, can never be removed. Like every other realistic missionary in the world, you have to accept people where they are and move on from there. We have outstanding precedent in this; this is the way in which God has dealt with mankind all down through Biblical history.

You might as well face the fact that by and large the Thlinget language is probably on its way out. And the truth of how long it will last probably lies somewhere between the extremes of those missionaries who feel that by teaching a few more people English they have ensured its death, and those missionaries who feel that it must be maintained at all costs. Nobody can predict without a careful ethno-linguistic survey how long the language will last as a functional part of Thlinget life. But we can be reasonably sure that eventually — in a matter of generations — it will pass on, whether we like it or not.

In the meantime, we must realize that for some of the Indians there is security and prestige in the use of English, that to some of them no doubt the use of their native language seems a mark of backwardness and inferiority. To others, as you point out, the native language is still that emotional vehicle through which they feel and to which their hearts respond.

The relationship of the church to all of this is a very serious matter. The ministry of the Gospel is to all people, including both the ones who look forward to English and those who look backward to Thlinget. It seems to me that an adequate ministry will have to provide for both. However, a missionary should not be misled by ideas about the effectiveness of Biblical translation in isolation. It is not going to be enough to translate the Scriptures and to present them to a handful of individuals who would be interested in reading them. If work is undertaken in Thlinget literature, it should be undertaken enthusiastically and fully to the point where there is some functional use for written Thlinget. This would involve reading materials both of a religious and non-religious nature. It would involve, in short, the provision of enough materials for the Thlinget reader such that he would feel that reading was worth while for him and, more than that, would provide him with these materials cast in such a way that he would not feel that it would be better to have them in English.[1]

History cannot be reversed, but a new future can sometimes be fashioned out of some of the relics of the past, and, like some other groups in the world, the Thlinget language perhaps can be an important vehicle again (along with English) if it is made functional and relevant in a way that seems worth while for the modern world (as the Thlinget looks upon it) and not simply a fossilized vestige of an unhappy past.

The Planting of the Church

Your question, "How does one go about establishing an indigenous church in such a place where people stand between two cultures and where there is so much ambiguity in the cultural framework?" is an agonizing one for many a missionary; but I think first of all we can arrive at a better understanding of its implications by foregoing the concept of "establishing" a church and speak instead of "planting" the church.[2] "Planting" essentially involves communicating. It involves the transfer of a message from one individual to another, not the concerns of organization and procedure which so occupy the thinking of many missionaries.

The task of communicating the Gospel among the Thlinget is fundamentally, of course, the same task that it is anywhere else. It is that of finding out how the message which came in the cultural garb of the Middle East hundreds of years ago, and which the missionary understands principally in the cultural garb of Western 20th century, can in turn be made to strike with impact and sharp force in the cultural garb of an Indian of Alaska. The difficulties involved are especially severe, however, because of the tensions and disintegration within the society there. There is no single unambiguous language and culture pattern for them. Instead, there is flux and insecurity, change and instability. This complicates the task but does not change its essential nature.

[1] See William D. Reyburn, "Literacy in Primitive Society," *The Bible Translator*, Vol. 9, No. 2, (Apr. 1958), pp. 76-81.

[2] See William A. Smalley, "Cultural Implications of an Indigenous Church," PRAC-TICAL ANTHROPOLOGY, Vol. 5, No. 2. (Mar.-Apr. 1958), pp. 51-65, and in this volume.

The problem remains one of speaking to the issues which the Indians see and stimulating them to put their reliance upon Jesus as Savior and Lord. It is in the determining of the issues as the Indians see them that anthropology first fits into the picture.

This is not just a matter of orienting newcomers to Alaska. Neither three days, nor three months, nor three years will do it for some people; and yet a few rare souls have such sensitivity and perceptiveness that they learn whether they are "oriented" or not. I thoroughly agree with you that all newcomers should be oriented as you suggest. But the point is that this orientation will not lead people to an effective communication of the Gospel, although it may help them to avoid many mistakes which could be a serious hindrance to the preaching of Christ.

We are going to have to be careful not to project our sense of needs completely into the Thlinget situation. When we think of religion we think of the need for morality, honesty, hard work, social consciousness, love of one's neighbor. These and a thousand other things are specific needs in our life, which the Gospel fills. Some of these needs the Thlinget will sense, and others they will not, at least not at first. I suspect that their needs would be phrased in much more highly emotional terms if they were to be phrased at all. I suspect that the need for security and protection and stability in life would rank high if the Gospel could be so presented to them. I suspect that an emotional outlet such as the Indians of the Southwest achieve through the Peyote or the Sun Dancers or which some groups of Christians achieve through highly emotional evangelistic services would rank high among Thlinget needs. It is hard to predict, but I suspect that some of the things which you have particularly mentioned like alcoholism and illegitimacy of children might not be listed at all and some things that we would never think of would be extremely important.

By this I am not saying that the needs which we see in Thlinget life are not also very real, but my point is that for the communication of the Gospel to them, the needs which they sense are those which motivate them toward Christ if they feel that He has an answer for them. After their initial contact with Him, after their conversion and that subtle transformation that occurs in culture as the result of the Holy Spirit operating through it, other needs of which they were not conscious before may well come to the surface. A new dimension of definition of needs becomes relevant to them because of the Scriptures and because of a wider outlook and understanding of God in their relationship to man.

A church springing up from such soil as this could have many forms. It might show an identification with the past, a strong sense of Thlinget solidarity, a re-expression of Thlinget moral values in a Christian setting. As such it would probably be repudiated by "progressive" elements in the Indian population. Or then it might show an identification with the West, with Western cultural forms and Western ideas. In such a case it would emphasize the use of English, the Western English Scriptures, and education in English. As such it would leave the older folks and the less Westernized people cold. Then again the new church might be a new synthesis of cultural elements such that in it and around it Thlinget of all kinds, those whose eyes are essentially on the past and those whose eyes are essentially on the West, would find a new expression, a new synthesis, a new way of life. I should hope that a church of this kind would grow out of the soil that you have described.

But for such a church to grow, what will be needed? We have already mentioned the nature of the communication that will have to take place. But I doubt if a church of this kind will really grow as a direct result of missionary activity. Usually such churches are one step removed from the missionary; they result from the work of some outstanding leader himself perhaps brought under the influence of the Gospel by a missionary, but recasting his message in terms of the aspirations and needs of his people and presenting the Gospel to them in a way that strikes home to their very souls. This is the role of the prophet, of the man who has that extra margin of vision to see beyond the horizon of his traditions, to stretch the borders of his own background, to interpret what God has for His people to them.

Should such a prophet arise and should a church be established through his work, we could almost predict that the major mission forces in Alaska will look askance at the results. The movement will most certainly be an emotional movement, and with a highly intellectual Western Christianity most of us find it hard to appreciate the Holy Spirit working through the emotions of less emotionally straitjacketed people than ourselves. A movement of this kind, even though it may not be the immediate direct product of a missionary's activity and even though it may seem strange to him in its overt expression, can still provide a tremendously significant area of work for him in his

relationship to the developing group of Christian people. If he has tact and consideration and is willing to work with the Holy Spirit and the forces of culture which are bringing the church to fruition, his ministry of translation, of teaching, of stimulation, of bringing new ideas, can be a very profound one. I know of no greater place of trust than that of a sensitive missionary in such a position as this.

I take it that a movement of this kind has not yet sprung up among the Indians of Alaska and we cannot wait for it to do so but must push ahead, seeking to understand the Indians in such a way that our feeble message as foreigners will come to them, that the Holy Spirit will supply that measure of power which will overcome our deficiency, and that God will be pleased to move in His own way and in His own time.

Some Matters of Detail

There were several specific questions of a cultural nature which were raised in your article. For example, there was that of the matrilineal system versus a patrilineal one. In the past the Thlinget people have reckoned their family systems through the mother instead of through the father and American missionaries and American administrators steeped in the traditions of the Hebrew Old Testament and the good old American way of life have felt that this is wrong. To be realistic again, we must realize that in time probably the matrilineal social structure of the Indians in Alaska will break down through the influence of the West, and its courts, and its schools. But, as I think you sense, this issue is really an irrelevant one for the church. God worked through a patrilineal society in the Hebrew people and He has worked through matrilineal societies elsewhere. There is nothing intrinsically moral or right and wrong about social structure as such. The many different social structures as found today in the world are simply many different ways of organizing group behavior into useful channels and of making life more valuable to the participants in the society. The missionary's role in relation to this as in relation to other cultural matters is to let history take its course and to concern himself with more important issues. Not that he should not understand the social structure as it exists and the tensions within it. That is very important, but it is not his place to make changes. Should the society, on the other hand, be in the process of changing, it is not his place, either, to hold tightly to the past and try to thwart the changes. It is perfectly legitimate for him to participate by pointing out difficulties or problems which he may see and possible avenues of change. He is not in a cultural vacuum and should not pretend to be so, but that is a far different matter from the deliberate and energetic attempts to promote change or resist it which have so characterized Americans, including missionaries, in their dealings with other people.

The potlatch is, of course, famous in anthropological literature. It has long fascinated me as being the symptom of a type of attitude toward one's fellow human being that also characterizes so much of American life. The potlatch was an instrument of aggression. As you well know, the Indians of the Northwest Coast destroyed or gave away property in order to shame their neighbors, in order to get the best of them. This is fantastically similar to the society of many of our big cities where people spend money so lavishly in order to best their neighbors

in the continual competition of keeping on top of the social heap. And just as the spirit which prompts these American displays of wealth can be identified as part of the American brand of worldliness, so I am sure the spirit which prompts the potlatch exhibit is likewise the Thlinget brand of that same unhealthy hold that our culture sometimes has upon us. Here again it is not the potlatch in itself as an institution, but the meaning that motivates it, that is unchristian. That same spirit that motivates it is very parallel to the spirit behind much of American life, including the life of many of the missionaries who would condemn the potlatch institution. Simply because the forms which it takes in American life seem more civilized to us, the potlatch seems a more barbaric custom, but in terms of Christian values it reflects the same agressive selfishness we show.

Again I feel that the potlatch as an institution is not really any of the missionary's business. As men are confronted with Christ in a way that makes Him seem relevant to them, a transformation takes place in their lives and it is quite possible that the spirit behind the old potlatch will be part of what is transformed into the image of God's Son.

Alcoholism likewise is a symptom. It is a symptom of the cultural tensions, the breakdown of values, the lack of moral pressures that exist. As serious as its social consequences are, no treatment of this symptom is going to have much lasting value. It is not until men have seen in Christ the fulfillment of the needs which they sense, that such problems as alcoholism will find a solution. I doubt that any such group as Alcoholics Anonymous would have much effect in Thlinget society. That particular group works on the basis of a strong desire to overcome alcoholism and upon the pressure created by the group to help each member to keep in line. An entirely new set of pressures and of values would have to be met and would have to be created in order to be based upon the needs which the Thlinget feel.

Illegitimate birth and extramarital sex behavior are again part of the frequent symptoms of this type of a cultural situation. They too will not be remedied by any direct action upon them as such, but only through a restructuring of the whole value system of the people involved. Here again the answer can ultimately only be that of the effective communication of the Gospel, to the answering of the questions which the Thlinget people unconsciously ask themselves.

I would be very cautious about functional substitutes as well. I do not think it is the missionary's place to institute functional substitutes, although it is certainly his place to suggest them at times. I think that functional substitutes are inevitable, that they must inevitably come when in the process of culture change an empty place, a vacuum, is left unmet in the needs which the society feels. Unless functional substitutes are genuinely incorporated by the people themselves, however, they are too divorced and do not really meet the need but instead simply satisfy the qualms of the missionary's conscience.

Warmth and Security of the Gospel

These brief rambling notes in reply to your article will, of course, never really come to grips with the problems that you see around you in Alaska. No one can do so from the outside. If they have any value in stimulating fruitful ideas for you or others, we will be most grateful. Let me come back once more to the basic feeling, the basic impression that I get from so many groups such as the Thlinget. It is that the church which meets their needs will be a church of warmth, of emotional activity — a church where the inhibited, the insecure, the fearful, will be able to give release to their emotions and worship their God spontaneously and freely and openly among their fellows. If I am not mistaken, Christ can be to these people a protector, an older brother, a guard, in a sense that we in our self-sufficient way will never know. There is much that we can teach the Thlinget, but I suspect that if a people's movement breaks out among them there will be aspects of their understanding of God which we have never really appreciated. If we would listen, perhaps there is much they could teach us, too.   W. A. S.

PART VIII

Cultural Processes:
Missionary Agents

William A. Smalley

Culture Shock, Language Shock, and the Shock of Self-Discovery

Culture shock has been described as that emotional disturbance which results from adjustment to new cultural environment.[1] Its cause is the loss of the familiar cues by which we interact in any society. Every culture has thousands of subtle signs of which we are usually not even conscious, by which we know our place in relation to people around us and know how to evaluate what they say and do. The loss of these cues when we enter a new culture means strain, uneasiness, and even emotional maladjustment because the props have been swept away from under us and we no longer have a familiar foundation on which to stand. Until we learn the cues of the new culture we are culturally disoriented. Language problems lie at the core of much culture shock, and the very task of language learning carries its perils. It is, however, in the shock of self-discovery that there comes the possibility of healing from culture shock.

WHEN I first went to Paris to study French, I and many other Americans like me found it difficult to know when and where to shake hands. French people seemed to us to be shaking hands all the time, and very unnecessarily so from our point of view. We felt silly shaking our hands so much, and we passed around among us the stories that we heard, such as one about how French children shake hands with their parents before going to bed every night. These stories emphasized the "queerness" of such French customs. This small and inconsequential difference of habit in shaking hands was enough to bring uneasiness, and combined with hundreds of other uncertainties brought culture shock to many.

In many parts of the Far East, where people are socially graded to a greater extent than Americans are, languages reflect social strata to the point where a speaker must know the relative position that he bears to the person with whom he is talking in order to address him properly. Members of the culture early learn the signs by which differences of status are shown, and early learn to

[1] I am indebted to Kalervo Oberg, "Cultural Shock: Adjustment to New Cultural Environments," PA, Vol. 7, No. 4 (July-August 1960), pp. 177-182, for many of the suggestions concerning cause and symptoms of culture shock which are mentioned in this paper. The examples are my own, as are the implications for the missionary language learner. Another good discussion of the phenomenon of culture shock is to be found in *The Overseas Americans*, by Harlan Cleveland, Gerard J. Mangone, and John Clarke Adams (New York: Mc-Graw-Hill Book Co., Inc., 1960) (reviewed in the last issue of PA [Vol. 10, No. 1], pp. 45-48).

reflect this knowledge in patterns of speech. For the foreigner who is learning the language these cues are not obvious. It takes him months and even years to learn them and in the meantime he may suffer the strain of never knowing quite how to speak to strangers, much as he wants to do the right thing.

Americans, furthermore, often find it very hard to adjust to the fact that they are automatically identified with a much higher class of society in many countries of Asia and Africa than they enjoyed at home. This may present problems of knowing how to behave, but most of all it leaves the missionary with a bitter tension between his Christian feeling for the importance of an identification with the down and out who comprise the great bulk of local population, and the impossibility of anyone taking such an identification seriously.

Hundreds of Americans have been caught by the difference of meaning attached to a wave of the hand in some parts of the world. My wife and I were looking out of our window in Vietnam when we saw a lady whom we had met pass by the house. My wife waved to her in friendly greeting and the lady immediately came to the door and into the house. She knew no English and we knew no Vietnamese. On both sides we stood there awkwardly grinning at each other. What we had meant as a friendly wave to her meant "Come over here." Certainly no harm was done by this friendly gesture but it was a bit uncomfortable just standing there grinning while we wondered what to do next! This uncomfortableness multiplied a thousand times may well produce culture shock.

The proper relationship to servants is a repeated cause of culture shock among missionaries. They want to be kind and Christian, and to reflect this kindness and Christianity in the equalitarian way Americans interpret Christianity for social relationships, yet this conflicts with the local understanding of the position of a servant in a house, and with what the servant finds comfortable. One missionary family in Congo suffered deeply from culture shock which centered primarily around relationships with their servants. They wanted their servants to be a part of their household in an American equalitarian sense. They wanted to bring them in as friends, to invite them to table, but this was not permitted by customs nor convention. They couldn't stand having these people in the house, and not treating them as guests. On the other hand, for many Americans with their heavily built protective wall of personal privacy, the presence of servants in the home means an invasion of privacy. They react to it emotionally as an intrusion. They feel exposed.

The problem of when to accept and when to refuse has been a frequent cause of emotional disturbance. In many societies people do not accept an offer the first time it is made, but they and the person who made the offer both judge by subtle cues of facial expression, gesture, and intonations, just how seriously the offer was intended in the first place, and just how seriously the rejection should be taken as well. In time a proper acceptance or refusal is made after the appropriate protestations. People know by the cues when this is final. A friend of mine, an American missionary studying in a language school, stopped to invite one of his teachers to ride along in his car as he was driving to school one morning. She refused and my friend rode on only to find out later that the teacher was furious that he had left her standing there at the side of the road.

The culture shock which comes to non-Caucasian overseas Americans may be particularly acute. Negroes going to Africa and people of the Mongolian race going to East Asia feel a sense of identification with the people of the area in which they are serving. They soon find, however, that their American cultural characteristics are the important fact to local people, who do not identify with them on the basis of skin color at all. One Negro missionary in Africa was offered singed caterpillars to eat as part of the meal in the home where he was visiting. When he did not eat them the lady of the house picked up the dish and carried it off muttering under her breath, "White man!" In the light of the history of Negro-White relations in the United States, you can imagine what a shock that was!

The fear of failure in participation in native life is another cause of culture shock. We know that we cannot do well in the strange moves of the Chinese version of chess prevalent in the Far East. When we try our hand at crafts or any of the occupations which take the largest share of local people's time we are slow and awkward. Our work is comparable to that of children. If we are of strongly pietistic bent, we are afraid of compromising our morals by participation, seeing dangerous religious significance in every pastime.

Symptoms of Culture Shock

One of the principal ways in which culture shock shows up is rejection. It may be rejection of the host country and its people, with the endless complaining, carping, fault-finding which is characteristic of some groups of Americans over-seas. Nothing seems to be going right, and all reactions are tinged with bitterness. Rejection of the host country leads to the development of a protective personal isolationism, and is the ground on which the "Little America" communities transplanted overseas thrive.

The rejection on the other hand may be directed against the home country. This produces the person who "goes native" in the bad sense. Now the complaint and criticism may be directed against the home country and its policies, fellow Americans abroad, and all cultural importations from the home country. In this group are the Left Bank expatriates of Paris and similar people in Latin America and Asia. Their moral restraints are broken. They live a life of imitation and emotional dependence on their host country. These people are very different from the well-adjusted Americans over-seas who adapt their lives sensibly to local patterns as far as is practical, who feel a creative sense of identification but who have not lost objectivity in the selection of the life which they are to follow. Their adaptation is not based on a pathological rejection of their past but on a wholesome selection of what is valuable from all of the cultural streams with which they come into contact.

Rejection may also be directed in a particular way against the mission board, the field executive committee, the colleagues who put the newcomer in this intolerable situation. Bitter feeling about real or imagined injustice begin to arise. Field policies are bitterly attacked. Personal failures are blamed on a lack of proper orientation, on the fact that nobody had warned him that it would be like this, that nobody had protected him from this suffering. If the person suffering from culture shock feels a sense of identification with the host country, he may lash out bitterly against the mission and his colleagues when he sees a lack of such identification in them. He projects the hostility arising out of culture shock against the symbols of authority over him.

Rejection of the mission board and of missionary colleages is often related to the shock which comes very forcibly to many missionaries when they find that with the development of "indigenized" churches no new role for the foreign missionary has yet been established. He doesn't know what he is supposed to do, or what he does does not fit his image of himself or his understanding of this calling. This can be a bitter and frustrating experience, indeed.

Or the rejection may turn against himself. The person suffering from culture shock may feel that he is a failure, that he had no business coming overseas in the first place, that he cannot possibly make good. He feels that all the money spent on him — his training, his outfit, and his transportation — has been wasted. He blames himself for every mistake and feels utterly defeated when he is not an instantaneous success in everything that he tries. His problem may be compounded by the fact that he feels guilty about feelings of rejection and hostility in any direction.

The rejection may even be focused upon God. It was God who called him into missionary work and sent him to this place. God is to blame for making such a terrible mistake.

Homesickness is often another major symptom of culture shock. It sometimes takes the first furlough to get over this homesickness and to put things back into normal perspective. The tourist bravado by which the traveler plays up the superiority of things at home is an ex-

ample of the effect of culture shock. After having observed tourists in Europe, I used to think that tourist bravado was a particularly American characteristic, until one time I was traveling on an Air France plane with a large group of French tourists returning from the United States to Europe. Their behavior was astonishingly like that of American tourists in Europe. Neither group behaves like this at home, but the displacement and the ensuing culture shock takes its toll.

Symbols of home assume enormous proportions to the person suffering from culture shock. An American flag on the tail of an airplane flying over a remote interior community may send a thrill up and down the spine of an American resident in a way that it never would in his own country, or anywhere else, if he were not identifying it with home under an extreme sense of displacement and insecurity.

One person suffered through a whole missionary term craving ice cream soda and declaring that once she returned to the States she would eat ice cream sodas every day. When she got home on furlough she didn't particularly want them. She didn't need them because she had what she was really craving, her home and familiar environment.

Soon after the war I was living in a French boarding house which did not serve very good food. At a time when I was extra low emotionally and physically because of an attack of dysentery, we received a CARE package with a chicken dinner in it. Nothing ever tasted so good to me in all of my life. The food was canned and certainly nothing exceptional, but it was familiar and symbolized the world I understood. Another important symptom of culture shock is often an excessive concern over germs and illness.

Some people become compulsive hand-washers. One missionary lady insists that everyone who comes into her house should take off his shoes and wash his feet in lysol solution before entering.

Some people refuse to eat food offered to them for fear of the germs they might ingest. Nobody can live normally in a society and refuse to eat with people in that society. A missionary cannot live by the medical books when he is out visiting in the countryside. Illness is one of the risks that are involved, a very real possibility, but the person suffering from culture shock becomes deeply disturbed over germs and illness, disturbed far beyond the actual physical danger.

Culture shock can be seen in the insistence on American doctors and American hospitals by Americans overseas. Even in Europe with its advanced medical standards, Americans will go hundreds of miles to an American hospital. Americans will sometimes put off needed dental or medical attention for months or years because the local doctor is not an American, or American-trained.

Culture shock is particularly manifest in the attitude of Americans toward their children's well-being and education. Rare is the American who will put his children in local schools. When pressure comes (as it must inevitably come in many areas) on schools for missionaries' children to accept students from the local community, missionary parents are often very frightened of the step. They see all kinds of dire consequences to the standards of the school and to the morals of their children. More than one missionary parent suffering from culture shock has moved into the "Little America" community so that his children will not have to play with "native" kids.

Shock and Recovery

Oberg mentions several stages through which many overseas Americans go. The first stage is that of fascination, where newcomers have no real contact with the country into which they have moved because friends or colleagues or hotel employees stand as buffers between them and its problems. They can communicate through their protective buffers and the world around them caters to their foreign ways.

But as they take on permanent residence and come in daily contact with local ways of doing things and run into various living problems with servants, transportation, water, telephone, and everything else that they have always taken for granted, then hostility begins to emerge. The problems which they face are to them symbols of the inferiority of the land around them. The fact that local people are indifferent to these problems is proof of this inferiority, proof of laziness, proof that such people can never get ahead. They scold everyone within hearing. Thousands of overseas Americans retreat into their "Little Americas," import instant rice to the Far East and American Nescafé to the coffee-growing countries of the world, and become utterly obnoxious to their hosts.

Eventually to some comes a beginning of a sense of humor, a lessening of a tension, and the ability to see the funny side of it all. With this of course begins healing and although many strains may remain, recovery is very likely. Once the problems begin to seem funny they are never as overwhelming.

Finally in bi-culturalism, in a degree of understanding of the new society such that the individual can begin to react in appropriate ways, real victory is obtained.

As the new cues are learned and the new signs of what is the right thing to do are assimilated, often unconsciously, and as language becomes a strong foundation for the new resident's repertoire of communication media, the bases of tension and hysteria are little by little removed.

Language Shock

Language shock is one of the basic ingredients of culture shock. Because language is the most important communication medium in any human society, it is the area where the largest number of the cues to interpersonal relationships lie. As the newcomer comes into a whole new world where he knows no language at all, he is stripped of his primary means of interacting with other people, he is subject to constant mistakes, he is placed on the level of a child again. Even after weeks of study he is unable to discuss much more than the price of a pound of potatoes. He is unable to display his education and intelligence, the symbols which gave him status and security back home. He meets intelligent and educated people but he responds to them like a child or an idiot because he is not capable of any better response.

The very exercise of language study itself gives some people acute culture shock. Many people have a mental block against practicing something they do not understand. But they can never understand a language until they have practiced it enough so that they are familiar with it. They find themselves in a vicious circle — unable to learn, unable to get along without learning. They cling to the crutch of translation and desperately try to find out how to translate the things they want to say from English into the local language, and they let this substitute for a knowledge of the language, fooling themselves into thinking that because they have learned how to make the equivalents of some English statements (even "preaching" full sermons), they know the language. Through this process they have missed whole portions of it, having cut these off by their insistence upon approaching it through English. And the portions they have missed are ever-present sources of anxiety as they miss much of what is going on around them.

The language learner has the uneasy feeling that people are laughing behind his back — and they are. His study is tiring, boring, frustrating. Nothing seems to go logically or smoothly, because logic is identified with familiar ways of talking and thinking. It is based on his language and academic tradition.

Many an overseas American who started out to learn a language has ended by rejecting it. The pattern of rejection sometimes means less and less study, the development of more and more English contacts. Sometimes it means illness, genuine physical illness. It may mean animosity against teachers, bitterness against the people who make you stick to your books. People with a little bit of linguistic background will use this as a weapon against the study program in which they are engaged. Because they do not find all of the techniques employed that they have learned to be useful, they blame their study situation for their failure to learn. Others around them are learning under the same conditions, but they blame their own failure on the antiquated study system they are following. Some people turn to errand-running and do administration, to busy work to make them feel that their time is too full to be spent in language study. Some people are constantly making trips, constantly off on one pretext or another, and never learn.

One American missionary wife not only refused to learn a language but also refused to allow it to be used in the home by her servants (who knew some English) or by her husband, who did make some attempt to use it. Whenever she had servants whose names did not sound like English she changed them to names like "Pete" and "Sue".

Shock of Self-Discovery

The shock of self-discovery is sometimes a large part of culture shock, but when it is it can be the beginning of healing. The person in culture shock who does not discover himself is less likely to be able to see other things rationally because of his suffering.

Sometimes the self-discovery comes in the frank facing of utter defeat. The high school principal, the educator so highly respected in his own home community, the minister from a large and influential church, the Ph.D., the doctor who gave up a good practice, the minister called to evangelize and sent off in a blaze of glory from his home church, all of these people may find the props taken out from under them when they arrive in another country. In language school the slip of a girl just out of Bible college without even a respectable bachelor's degree may be doing better in language study. Or worse yet the wife who always laughed at herself depreciatingly because she was so scatterbrained, and only did average work in college because she enjoyed the social life too much, finds learning the local language a lark, while her husband slogs along feeling utterly humiliated. The long habit of success is broken by failure.

For such a person the shock of self-discovery may be hard to take. There are differences in aptitude and people who have risen to high positions back home may not necessarily do well in language study. But everyone can learn. And with the shock of self-discovery can come the determination to do one's best in spite of the difficulties, to study hard, to learn well, to refuse to give in to the symptoms of culture shock but to conquer them by developing a degree of bi-lingualism and bi-culturalism as fast as possible even if the pace is slower than he would like. Sometimes the person suffering from culture shock discovers his own emotional insecurity. He finds himself behaving childishly over traffic patterns, giving vent to temper tantrums over bugs or dirt, projecting his problems upon others, and as he discovers himself he can learn to approach his problem more rationally, to attack his difficulties more systematically, and to resume a healthy outlook on his situation.

Some of the emotional bases for language and culture shock run very deep. The person who gags when trying to make certain sounds in a new language is certainly suffering from emotional disturbance which runs back into childhood and present difficulties are only triggering much more deep-seated problems. The person who strains and contorts her face in order to round her lips, puckering them for vowel articulation, and continues to do this after weeks of coaching and help, needs psychiatric help before language study can do much good.

Because some of these problems are deep-seated and because we don't like to face ourselves, some people never discover themselves in culture shock. A second generation missionary spoke Spanish fluently as a young person but "forgot" it when he returned to the States to high school. When he returned to Latin America as a missionary and entered language school again, he murdered Spanish. Once in a while when he wasn't aware of it you would hear him talking perfect Spanish and then lapsing into atrocious Spanish once more. Spanish had been rejected in his high school days because it was "queer" in an American setting. It was still being rejected and he hadn't discovered himself yet.

Signs of culture shock have been evident in students working in some of the language orientation institutes with which I have been connected in the United States. At these schools missionaries are given intensive preparation for learning a language in the field. As they come to the institute their usual props are removed. Everyone, Ph.D. and Bible college graduate, is on the same level, beginning a new and intensive study. There is very little intellectual content in the study. The work is largely a matter of drilling, a matter of learning flexibility of the speech apparatus, a habit of mimicry, a sharpness of hearing. Our educational system is geared to gaining information and not practicing skills. In this unfamiliar setting some people begin to suffer from language shock. An uneasiness settles over them at the indefiniteness of it all. There seems to be nothing that is either right or wrong, their production is either just better or worse, and somehow it always seems to be worse. Theologians

who would much rather discuss the philosophy of language find that they aren't able to articulate the vowels they are expected to make. Teachers tend to criticize the pedagogical approach taken at the institute when they find they can't move the back of their tongue the way other people can. Doctors turn upon themselves in doubt of their missionary call when they find so much trouble distinguishing one pitch from another.

For many such missionary appointees to whom the shock comes this is a time of self-discovery, a time when they learn rationally and realistically what problems they are going to face in language learning and how to attack these problems.

For many it is a time of renewed commitment to Christ. The realities of the difficulty of cross-cultural communication come upon them strongly, but in a more realistic way than ever before they are determined to continue with their task in obedience to Christ.

This, after all, is the meaning of Biblical self-denial. It involves a conversion, a discovery of one's self and a change in that self. Instead of the symptoms of rejection and insecurity comes an objective knowledge of strengths and weaknesses and with the knowledge comes a relaxed acceptance of one's self, a determination to do one's best without pretense. With it comes the basis for bilingualism and bi-culturalism without pain and without emotional suffering, although not without long hard work.

William A. Smalley

The World Is
Too Much With Us

ALICJA IWANSKA, a Polish anthropologist, in describing her observations upon an American farming community, made some generalizations which struck me as extremely pertinent as a summary of American value systems.[1] She said that for the farmers on the large Western farms which she had studied the universe was divided up into three different categories. She labeled the first category *landscape*. It included the distant mountains, the trees, the scenery, the environment of the farmers in so far as this environment was not manipulated by them. They looked at it, they enjoyed it in a disinterested sort of way. It had no high emotional content for them.

The second category of life she labeled *machinery*. To these farmers machinery was an important part of their lives. They polished their machines, they cared for them. The machines had high value to them and they rated their machines in terms of their productivity in their farming life. The livestock belonged to this machinery class of the universe. It was important according to its productivity. It was cared for and kept with much the same earnestness and much the same eye to profits that the machinery had. Real

[1] Her paper, entitled "Some American Values," was read at the annual meeting of the American Anthropological Association in Chicago, 1957.

affection and interest, and a great deal of value, was placed upon the machinery category.

Finally, the third category was that which she labeled *people*. People were neighbors, individuals who came in for a cup of coffee, folks who cooperated in times of need or emergency. People were human beings with whom one grew up and lived and died, and with whom one had constant relationships on the social and business level.

Human Beings but not People

The fascinating significance of all this, however, was that not all human beings were people. The Indians, for example, belonged to the landscape class. They were part of the scenery. On a Sunday afternoon one took a drive out to the reservation to look idly and curiously at the Indian communities as one drove by. Mexican migrant workers were machinery. Their value lay in their productivity. Their help was important to the same degree that the help of a cow or the functioning of a fuel pump was important. When their productivity was lessened they would be discarded in much the same way as an old car would be.

Human beings who were people were different in that they had value in and of themselves regardless of their productivity.

701

As I listened to her talk, I could see myself in her characterization. There have been many times when I have sensed the temptation to look on certain groups of human beings as scenery, as part of a landscape. Once, on a mission station where I was working for several months on an important language project, there were people of a colorful tribal group who passed my door daily. I found myself idly interested in them as anthropological curiosities, as part of the passing scene. Now as I visit from country to country, this temptation is always there.

The temptation to look on human beings as scenery finds one kind of expression in our romanticization of the mission field. It is reflected in the kinds of form letters which we write home to tell about color and glamor on the field — color and glamor of a *National Geographic Magazine* sort but without any real humanity in it.

And how utterly characteristic is the tendency to look on human beings as machinery! We value the preachers in the local church on the basis of the "production" of their weekly quota of sermons and pastoral calls or their converts. It is not that we do not love our machines. We like to take care of them, to keep them in good health; we like to keep them in their proper place, however, like the well-loved dog which is a member of the family so long as it sleeps on the floor. We like to have such human beings come and visit us so long as they keep their place and do not usurp the prerogatives of people, and really expect us to treat them like people.

The Need for Change

If we are going to deal with people as people in a culture that is vastly different from our own, we have to come to the fundamental realization that people are different from society to society, and to do this *we* are going to have to make the major move to change. If we are going to be persons among people, our privacy, our established patterns of what is convenient and comfortable are going to have to be drastically modified. Our sense of belonging to ourselves will have to be filed away and we will have to develop a sense of belonging to others, which characterizes so many societies in the world.

This sort of experience involves a tremendous emotional drain. It is an extremely difficult attitude to take and position to follow. It means "becoming all things to all men so that by all means we might win some" in the deepest sense, and it means a type of cultural suicide which Paul characterizes as being "crucified with Christ." On the American scene the problem is just as great. It means to count as people, and not simply as machinery, the Negro groups in our communities, so that they enter into the life of people, as people, in our church groups, in our schools, and in our neighborhoods. This requires a transformation of a major sort for the American system of values.

The deep-seated, ingrown values which have been characterized here cannot easily be peeled off. Rather, a change involves an internal restructuring. It involves being remade inside. Jesus called it being reborn. It implies an intellectual and emotional conversion on our part to the point where we can become neighbors with all human beings everywhere.

In all of the discussion about what "worldliness" means in a Biblical sense and all of the examples of various kinds of behavior which have been classified as worldly by one group or another, I think that often has been neglected the very basic fact that the spirit of this world is not easy to identify nor is it easy to shake off. Certainly it lies in the attitude and predispositions of our day more than in any particular thing we do. I believe that an important ingredient in the spirit of the American world is that we so often do not really consider human beings to be people.

William A. Smalley

The World Is Too
Much with Us—II

It seems clear that culture patterns have a strong effect on the response which people make to the preaching of the gospel, and on the effect which any conversion to Christ has in the church or in the society as a whole. That Arabs are harder to win than Vietnamese is an obvious kind of illustration, and that a church in central Africa takes on a different ethos or "flavor" from a church in southeast Asia is another.

It is also clear, I think, that Christ's requirements of total commitment are at variance, in differing amounts and in different ways, with all cultures. In saying this I mean *all* cultures, including the religious culture (the approved behavior, the ecclesiastical system) of my denomination and every other denomination or independent church. Such denominational or church groups are individual subcultures within the larger subculture of Western (and world) Christianity. Even our churches stand in the way of that relationship to God for which we were created.

Evidence of this last point can be seen in the fact that occasionally a group which has been only recently evangelized shows a response and a degree of personal loyalty to God that is rare in our own churches. To take a very specific example, the Meo culture of northern Laos seems in some areas to stand less in the way of such a relationship than does the church I attend in White Plains, New York. This is true in spite of a pagan Meo religious system which is replete with an enormous number of spirit beings who are placated, bribed, or appeased, as the situation may warrant. These spirits, beneficial or not, are equated with "demons" by the Christians and by many of their missionary teachers.

This Meo movement in the Xieng Khouang area of northern Laos has been reported in PRACTICAL ANTHROPOLOGY.[1] It is characterized by a rapid turning to Christ on the part of several thousand people, and an intense loyalty and dedication on the part of many. It is the intensity of this faith, the strength of this loyalty, which I am now contrasting with the American groups with which I am familiar.

There is a severe danger of oversimplification here. At least one other major factor enters into the picture, and that is the activity of the Holy Spirit as God works in history and in culture. I think, however, that in spite of this all-important other factor we are justified in making some generalizations on the basis of culture differences.

Some American Characteristics

If we grant that the Meo are in some ways culturally more "ready" for the

[1] G. Linwood Barney, "The Meo — An Incipient Church," PRACTICAL ANTHROPOLOGY, Vol. 4, No. 2 (Mar.-Apr. 1957), pp. 31-50, and in this volume.

704

gospel than Americans, and even American Christians, what are the peculiar *American* cultural barriers to a man's relationship to Christ? Some of these will be true of other groups as well, and some will not. Some of the cultural barriers which the Meo will have will not be true of us.

The effect of "secularism" and a mechanistic outlook on life have been cited so often as to need no discussion here. The American characteristic of looking at certain classes of people as "landscape" or "machinery," rather than as "neighbors" and fellow human beings, belongs here too.[2] The tendency to substitute theology or dogma for experiential religion is another of our temptations.

The complexity and sophistication of our life is another very strong deterrent in keeping us from Christ. Our culture shows an amazing genius for organizing our lives into ever more complicated institutions. Even the simplest of our churches are no exception unless they have reached the point of disintegration where there is no life left. Our typical response to a church problem, or to an individual need, is to organize another church group. In a typical busy American church today, if we do not participate actively in many branches of this enormous program this is a sign that we do not love God. If we do participate fully, and at the same time fulfill our obligations to the equally complex business, civic, and social life we must lead to be responsible Americans today, it is impossible to love God as we should.

2 William A. Smalley, "The World is Too Much With Us," PRACTICAL ANTHROPOLOGY, Vol. 5, Nos. 5 & 6 (Sept.-Dec. 1958), pp. 234-236, and in this volume.

The Dilemma of the Christian in Culture

At one point or another, in every culture, the sensitive Christian is brought up against the inescapable dilemma created by the conflict between culture patterns and his own relationship to God. An Abraham leaves the civilization of Ur to follow God's call into a wandering existence, a promised land, a new understanding of God, and a new course for history. An Amos burns with indignation as he sees the rich crushing the poor, the merchant with the double standards of measure, the indolence of the leisured class (cows of Bashan), and he pronounces in lyric poetry the wrath of God and the destruction of the country at the hand of its enemies. A Martha is busy getting the house and meal ready for her Lord, while a Mary sits and listens at His feet.

The dilemma of the Christian in culture is that he cannot really escape his culture, but he must transcend it, in some measure at least. The pilgrim (or missionary) who like Abraham leaves his city and his culture behind him does not really do so. He carries most of it with him. His habits of life and thought, his social relationships, his sense of values, his language, his mechanical skills, these all come along. But an Abraham is different from the people he left behind, different from the very fact that he left them behind, different from the changes necessitated by the new circumstances of his existence, different by a new developing understanding of God.

Like all prophets, an Amos is also a part of his culture and is limited by its confines — but not completely limited, because the function of the prophet is precisely one of seeing beyond the horizon his culture poses, even though it be only a little. Whether he is a prophet of God or a man with unusual vision for his time and place, he is sometimes able to speak to his culture in such a way that it listens and is changed.

In some of the stages of the history of Christianity there have been Marys who have felt that they could renounce their culture to live a contemplative life. But this, too, is at least partially an illusion. It is true that the hermit and the monk are shielded from selected details of life around them, but there is always the rest of a man's life, his background, his thoughts, his presuppositions. He carries them to the monastery or the hermit's cave. They, too, are of this world's culture.

Relation of the Christian to His Culture

What can it possibly mean to be "in the world, but not of it"? How can the Christian possibly be part of his culture and yet transcend it? There are at least two dimensions here. One is the dimension of personal ability, insight, "prophetic vision," which can be seen sometimes in non-Christians and is often not seen in Christians. In other words, there are people who by their own abilities step slightly outside the limits of their world. Some of them are Christians, though it is not this insight which makes them so.

The other dimension, one which is profoundly Christian, stems from that supercultural relationship to God which we call faith. Everyone who has that relationship to God which the New Testament speaks of in such vivid language: being brought back (redemption), making friends again (reconciliation), being rescued (salvation), has also transcended his culture. The supercultural fact of God in history, in individual life, is what really makes a Christian "not of this world."

Christians are quick to select elements of behavior from culture around them and to label these as "non-Christian" or "sinful" (like dancing or racial segregation, depending on the American denomination they belong to). In so doing they forget that the real grip of a culture lies in habits, values, and viewpoints which are not so well defined. The very complexity of our life is a case in point. It is not going to do us any good to pass denominational resolutions calling for a simpler American society. We could simplify our denominational and church structures, but I doubt that it would work. We know of no other way to operate in our complex world. The monastic escapism has been shown by history to be a false way out. It seems to me that in this tightening web of organizational activism our only hope of being in this world but not of it is to develop that independence of judgment and spiritual perception which makes it possible for us to refuse to participate when participation is required beyond the point of emotional health and spiritual wisdom.

Refusal to participate, of course, can be an escape, a way out. I am thinking of it here, however, as a creative step, a question of priorities, to make ultimately more worth-while activity possible, to foster intellectual and spiritual growth.

Frequent, and even occasional, refusal to participate in a prolifera of church activities, in a denominational survey, in a mission meeting, in an evangelistic campaign, as well as in selected secular activities ranging from PTA to a collection for the March of Dimes, will certainly be criticized in a culture which places its greatest values on prompt reports, committee attendance, and adding wheels within wheels. But in this day and age, if Martha is to sit at the feet of Jesus, even the dishes may occasionally have to stay dirty.

William A. Smalley

Proximity or Neighborliness?

MISSIONARIES talk about "going out to live among the people" (although anyone who has seen a typical mission compound will not take that cliché too literally), but how many have ever thought of being neighbors to these "people" near by?

In our western world individuals may be thrown into regular contact, even close physical proximity, over long periods of time, and not have more than the most superficial social intercourse, if any at all. This is most true in our large cities where people in adjoining apartments may never meet each other, or if they do, may have no more than a formal and polite social interchange. Even in smaller communities, however, the boss who works daily with his men may have no other contact with them (except for the annual Christmas party), and people who bow together in church may never meet during the week.

It is not until we reach the very small rural community in the United States that we find a high degree of neighborliness between people in close proximity, where everybody knows everybody else. An indication of the fact that in our culture we do not always put high value on such relationships is that we may add to the previous sentence: ... and where everybody minds everybody else's business.

Reprinted from Vol. 4, No. 3 (1957), pp. 101-104.

In our highly complex society we have built cultural devices for keeping people close by from being neighbors unless for some reason we choose to include them. These barriers provide a protection for us, keep us from having to associate with people who are not compatible, whose race or education or social status is different from ours. We can withdraw within the barriers for security from people and social patterns which conflict with our own.

Some missionaries live in large cities where this urban pattern of proximity without neighborliness may be well developed. If they bring in their insulating mechanism as part of their cultural baggage it is not particularly conspicuous, although even in the urban setting it may be an almost insurmountable barrier to effective communication on an individual level. Such missionaries have to rely on the mechanics of playing church and mass evangelism to do what has historically been most effectively done by the personal contact of one dedicated soul with his neighbor.

It is in the rural mission areas where proximity without neighborliness stands out in such painfully brutal fashion. Typically, the mission builds a compound on a hill a mile outside of the village. A cluster of huts may be built on the least desirable part of the compound for servants and hangers-on. Non-Western school teachers and preachers have their quarter, too. It is hard to imagine a more effective physical way of isolating the missionary from the people "among whom he is living."

But the psychological isolation is far more serious. As one missionary put it, "The Africans know to which missionary door they can go." A conversation which was reported to me is not an extreme case. One missionary had learned that a Bible revision committee which included both Westerners and Africans had refreshments served during the morning, and asked, "What do you do with the Africans?" When he learned that they were served, too, he asked if butter tins were brought in for the African's coffee. When he learned that they were served from cups no differently from anyone else he was horrified, considering it most unsanitary.

Some missionaries protect themselves from the people around them by a host of devices. They may never participate socially either in the local culture or through inviting people into their homes. They may not learn the language really well. They may be contemptuous of the uneducated and revolted by the unclean. They are not interested in the things which interest people. They are therefore remote, distant, and terribly cold.

On a recent trip in Africa I saw two examples of missionary neighborliness which I would like to contrast to the above. One was in the home of Dr. and Mrs. Wesley Sadler, Lutheran missionaries among the Loma people of Liberia. (In their case the "among" is not figurative.) The Sadlers' home is on the edge of a Loma village, just a few yards from the nearest Africans' houses. It is not, however, that close proximity which makes the Sadlers neighbors, it is their spirit.

During each evening while I was there, anywhere from two to five or six of the villagers, men and women, would drop in. They would come individually and stay for just a few minutes. They came naturally, without the embarrassment which marks the entrance of an African tribesman into so many missionary homes. They stopped and chatted for a few minutes and then left. They were at home. The usual barrier was not there. Equally revealing was the Sadlers' reception of their visitors. It was the reception given someone with whom you are on the very friendly relation of frequent contact. The visit was taken for granted, and it was enjoyed.

Sadlers raised their children under that thatched roof in Woozie, the little Loma village. They studied Loma life and language not just as anthropologists and linguists (Dr. Sadler's Ph.D. is in linguistics) but as interested neighbors. They liked their neighbors and wanted to know them better. I have never seen happier missionaries.

The other example of missionary neighborliness which I saw took place when I was visiting Dr. and Mrs. William Reyburn in the Camerouns. We heard drum beats one evening and went to investigate. A group of students was "playing." They had formed a circle, in which they were dancing and singing, while one person danced in the middle. The person in the center tried to perform some antic which was different from what anyone else had done. When he had finished he would point to someone in the circle who would take his place. Reyburn took a few steps so that they would not think he had come to criticize. He made everybody laugh, and then we sat down to watch.

Before long the dancer in the center pointed to Reyburn there on the bench, and he went into the circle to jump up and down. Before long I had been invited too, and we were all jumping up and down to the beat (I was at least trying) for about half an hour. Once I got over beings self-conscious, it was fun.

The next day word of the Africans' appreciation came through to the Reyburns: "It is the first time anyone [meaning missionaries] ever played with us."

William A. Smalley

Respect and Ethnocentrism

A MISSIONARY once remarked to me that the reason why his mission had an unusually splendid record for competence in the use of the language of their area of work was that they had a high degree of respect for the local culture. I think it would be possible to point to many cases where respect for local culture correlates with language competence. It would be possible certainly to point to many cases where strong disrespect for local culture correlates with abysmal language use. It may be coincidence, but the one country of the world where, in my experience, the people are most criticized by missionaries serving there is also the country which seems to have the lowest level of missionary language ability.

Our missionary's remark deserves thoughtful consideration. But if we do begin to think about it and to cite cases, we are immediately confronted with the problem of what we mean by "respect." I walked into a church of the same mission. Except for the use of the local language in the singing, preaching, and Scripture reading, what evidences of respect for local culture were there? I found none whatsoever. I did not know the language and could not understand the sermon, but the implication of the form of service was that there was nothing in the local culture worthy of its incorporation in a Christian service.

I talked with some members of the

Reprinted from Vol. 5, No. 4 (1958), pp. 191-194.

mission concerning dialects of the national language. These dialects were spoken by large percentages of the population of the country, but not by upper-class and educated people. Some missionaries showed respect for these speech differences. Others did not and felt that any use of them in the program of evangelization was a waste of time.

In contrast with this there were missionaries of other missions who concentrated on the use of the "substandard" dialects, showing a much higher degree of respect for them as media of communication with the masses of people. And whereas the first mission often showed a laudable respect for the virtues in the theological system of the religion of the country, the second group paid it little attention but showed high respect for the individual common man and his needs.

By saying this, I do not mean to imply that these attitudes are mutually exclusive in any individual or in any mission group. But they are obvious emphases, patterns of work and attitude, which reflect important differences in the values of the missionary.

Not only do we see such contrasts between missions in the same area, but we see them between the missionary traditions in various areas. Missionaries in Southeast Asia tend to learn their local languages well, while the missionaries in West Africa tend not to. On the other hand, missionaries in Africa tend to have greater respect for and use of dialect differences than do missionaries in China.

The Self-centered View of Culture

Ethnocentrism is the term used by anthropologists to represent that point of view which we all have to varying degrees, that our own culture, our own way of doing things, is best. It may lead us to assume that our own way is the only right way. It ranges from the repugnance my wife and I felt when our Khmu houseboy ate a rat we caught in a trap to the uncontrollable laughter that struck a Khmu friend when my wife cried because our pet dog died. I heard ethnocentrism in a prayer recently, when a pastor thanked God that we were privileged to live in a culture so well suited to a Christian way of life. Every missionary, no matter how keenly developed his Christology, finds some of his motivation in his ethnocentrism, and it is a major motivation in our present ideological struggle with Russia.

What we select to be ethnocentric about may vary from person to person. It certainly varies from culture to culture. It undoubtedly is somewhat different from mission to mission. I asked a missionary in Africa once if chewing Kola nut was a sin, and she replied with a twinkle in her eye that that depended on the mission station. This should not be read to imply that Christians should not make value judgments. Every human being does make them, whether he wants to or not, and every Christian is morally obligated to do so. The problem lies in the unthinking ethnocentricity of those judgments. It lies also in our imposition of our judgments on other people.

Ethnocentrism of "Respect"

A proper basis for value judgments is not the subject of this editorial, however, it is simply that we recognize the ethnocentricity of even our "respect" for other peoples. We tend to respect what we like or lean to like. If we come from a background of advanced education, of emphasis on "correctness" in our language, and on good breeding in our conduct, we tend to respect the high language and upper-class characteristics of another civilization. If we come from a lower stratum of American society, we tend to be more at home with more humble folk in a foreign culture. If we have been trained to a point of view which sees language primarily as an art, we tend to shun the less artistic, less literary forms of the language which we learn in another culture. If we see language primarily as a medium of communication, however, we want to shift our language medium according to our audience. If liturgy and art are important to us, liturgy and art we single out to enjoy in another country. If we prefer the relaxed informality of ordinary individuals, we seek them out.

Certain things which we can select to be ethnocentric about are much more detrimental to the church than others, of course. Linguistic ethnocentrism is disastrous, but so is the ethnocentrism of Methodist or Lutheran or Presbyterian or Pentecostal ritual. And so also can be the forms of education and medicine and agriculture which we employ.

Full cultural objectivity is impossible, but an awareness of the vagaries of our selective ethnocentrism is very helpful. One of the most wholesomely "respectful" of missionaries whom I ever met was a man who worked himself from dawn until bedtime with a discipline and application that very few Americans can match. He confessed that one thing he could never get used to was the African's idea of a day's work. Contrast this reluctant admission which acknowledged an awareness of ethnocentrism with the attitude of another missionary whose every conversation is punctuated with complaints of the "laziness" of people around him.

Without respect, without clear-eyed love, that identification which is essential for the missionary will never be achieved. But before we fall into the temptation of congratulating ourselves on the features which we have selected from the culture to respect, let us take stock of our attitude toward other things as well. Does our work really reflect respect for people of all classes, for the various subcultures of the community, for the church? Do we respect the church by "allowing" it to run "independently" *the way we taught it to run;* or do we respect it by watching it work out its own new society within the matrix of its daily life?

Ethnocentrism will always be with us. The value of an anthropological point of view, which sees customs and institutions in the light of the way they are worked out in many societies, is that it helps us to be aware of our ethnocentrism and to soften it. In a sense, the cross-cultural view which comes through the study of many peoples is an important aid in understanding the relationship between the cultural speck in our brother's eye as opposed to the log in our own.

William A. Smalley

Some Questions about Missionary Medicine

IN this editorial I expect to raise some questions which I cannot answer. Perhaps there are readers who will want to speak to them. In fact, I feel singularly ill-equipped to discuss missionary medicine as it is entirely outside of my experience, and I have no knowledge of its problems. Yet, as I observe it from a distance, I get the same feeling of "unrealness" from it. that I get from many missionary activities — the same lack of coming to grips with the realities of society in the less westernized parts of the world.

This uneasiness was forceably brought to my mind again by the reading of a fascinating little book, *The Edge of Tomorrow,* by Thomas A. Dooley, M.D.[1] Not that Dr. Dooley said anything about medical work in relation to Christian missions. He is the doctor who, out of his own pocket, and out of the contributions which he received from other Americans, led a medical team of Americans and Lao on a year-long venture of bringing medical relief to two isolated communities in Northern Laos in Southeast Asia. Dr. Dooley's motives were humanitarian. An Irish Catholic himself, he was driven by the desire to perform medical service to wretched people. He had become familiar with some of the problems of such medical aid through his work in the Navy in Asia, particu-

larly in the evacuation of refugees from Northern Vietnam, when Vietnam was divided at the end of its bloody civil war. The significance of Dooley's book and the work which he did lies not simply in the number of individuals who were treated or healed through his medical skill. So far as the viewpoint represented in PRACTICAL ANTHROPOLOGY is concerned, the significance lies in his attitude toward his work and its relation to the society around him.

Dr. Dooley started out to spend only one year in Laos. That year was spent in two different communities, both relatively isolated: Van Vieng and Nam Tha. He and his men plunged into their work with the facilities available, and utilized the materials at hand. Here is a description of their home in Van Vieng:

Our living quarters presented a tougher problem. Ojisan's house was a typical Lao hut perched six feet above the ground on stout poles surrounded by a "porch" and reached by a steep ladder. We climbed up, took one look inside, and came out shuddering. The place was filthy.

The boys tore out everything inside the hut including the bamboo partition between the two rooms. They swept the ceiling clear of soot, cobwebs, and rats' nests, then went to work on the walls. When this accumulation of ancient crud had been swept out, they hauled up buckets of river water, broke out

1 Published in New York by Farrar, Straus and Cudahy, 1958.

boxes of soap-powder and bleach, and swabbed the deck Navy-style.

The villagers presented us with woven bamboo mats for floor covering, and we laid out our bedrolls and hung mosquito netting. Then we installed all the packing-crate bookcases, benches and tables, and placed two cots against the wall as lounges. This would be our "living room."

Pete Kessey insisted that even the poorest white-trash back in Texas wouldn't live in such a place. Maybe so. But, at least, no one could ever say that the men of Operation Laos lived apart from the natives in an air-conditioned American compound.[2]

Their hospital was just as simple. There as no X-ray machine, no elaborate equipment. Everything was designed so that it could be carried on, when Dr. Dooley left, by the Lao individuals who were trained on the spot. Americans in the enormous Economic Aid Mission which has poured millions of dollars into Laos, with almost no grass roots service resulting from that expenditure, accused Dr. Dooley of practicing 19th-Century medicine. They are correct, said Dr. Dooley, "I did practice 19th-Century medicine, and this was just fine. Upon my departure our indigenous personnel would practice 18th-Century medicine. Good, this is progress, since most of the villagers live in the 15th Century."[3]

There lies the significance of Dr. Dooley's work. His cultural instincts are sound.

There were about four practicing mid-wives in Van Vieng when we arrived, and perhaps as many more young girls who aspired to the calling. We won them over to our side, had them help around the hospital,

and made them promise to call us for each childbirth. When we went on a call, we would take along one or two of the younger girls. And, always, we carried a bag containing the wonderful midwife's kit prepared and distributed by CARE. Each of these kits contains gowns, gloves, cord ties, basins, bowls, dressings, soaps, towels, etc. — all the essentials for the delivery of twenty-five babies.

We taught the girls the principles of modern, aseptic midwifery, and the importance of post-partum care of the mother, including removal of the placenta. Then, after each one had delivered twenty-five babies under supervision, and had proved her proficiency and dedication, she was "graduated" with appropriate ceremony, climaxed by the presentation of the CARE kit — always the bag that I personally had carried and used. (This was extremely important for "face.")

Just as in America nurses are "capped" at graduation, so we "bagged" our midwives in Van Vieng. It worked. Those wonderful young women, armed with their CARE kits and somewhat dedicated to the aseptic principles we taught them, have removed many of the old horrors from maternity in that part of Laos.[4]

Participation and Cooperation

Dr. Dooley and his men participated largely in Lao life and were part of the Lao communities in which they lived. "Participation," as always, is a relative matter. Dr. Dooley calls "lousy stuff" some of Lao food which I consider delicious! They subsisted largely on Navy C-rations. In the evening they provided entertainment for the community with movies supplied by American Information

2 Pp. 20-30.
3 P. 54.

4 Pp. 35-6.

Service, and throughout the day the community watched fascinated as they performed much of their medical work in full view. People never ceased to marvel that injections were given in the patient's "bottom" for a pain in the head!

The local "shamans," the witch doctors or medicine men, were disturbed by the Dooley mission when it came to Nam Tha. Finally they declared the hospital to be taboo by putting up the characteristic woven bamboo sign used all over Southeast Asia. No one, no matter how ill, dared come near the hospital for help. At that point Dooley did the culturally most sensible thing. He made friends and colleagues of the witch doctors.

One afternoon I returned from an emergency call in the jungle to find Pete holding an earnest professional conference with Old Joe (a medicine man.) Pete gave me the eye, and I squatted down and listened respectfully.

Old Joe had spread out before him a weird assortment of sticks, bamboo slivers, betel nuts, boiled leaves, pig grease, and cow dung, and was explaining the theory behind his *materia medica*. Most of it was fantastic. But here and there I recognized fragments of the universal folk remedies (like the use of spiderwebs in open wounds), the effectiveness of which are acknowledged by modern medicine.

"Well," said Pete, "we just belong to different schools of medicine. We use different drugs, different methods, but we are both working for the same thing — to free the people from the evils of disease and suffering. The important thing is for us to work together. We'll teach you what we know, and you will teach us." That sounded fair enough to Old Joe.

From that time on Old Joe rarely missed a sick call. We would administer a shot of penicillin, Joe would invoke the proper spirits. We would splint a fracture, then permit Old Joe to tie the indispensable red, white and black strings around the splints. If we were paid two coconuts for fee, Old Joe received one. (In America this practice is held in a bad light; they call it "fee splitting.")[5]

Expendability

Laos has only one foreign trained doctor, who is the minister of health. There are about fifteen locally trained men, many of them with little more education than would correspond to junior high school in the States. These are the doctors of the larger communities. Dooley deliberately turned his work over to these men at the end of a year's time. He wanted to return again at a later date, but he wanted to start again fresh in a new community and to begin his training work once more. He did not want to build up his own institution.

Here are the details of his final arrangements with the Lao government:

We had established the hospital at Nam Tha, and wanted to insure that after our departure it would continue to flourish. All the things we had done were so carried out that our departure would not create a void. We installed no X-ray machines, nor any large electrical plant. We had no complicated or extremely delicate instruments. We utilized ten or twelve basic antibiotics and other medicines, so that their exact usage and dosage was well understood by the local nurses. We turned over to midwives the CARE kits, making them completely self-sufficient. The

5 P. 79.

vaccination program, carried out by the locals themselves, would add a marked degree of immunity to many thousands of people in the high valley. The instructions would make them more cognizant of the relationships between dirt and disease. I did not want these accomplishments lost after our departure. I wanted to make sure that we would leave something real and substantial behind us.

I proposed three points to the Minister. I asked, first, that he give our hospital a charter. This would mean that a specific amount of money would be earmarked for the hospital based on the number of patients treated and hospitalized. This would mean that certain monies would be allotted for upkeep and care of the buildings. Instead of paint and wood being bought with my own money, the hospital would now be administered and financed by the government of Laos, and their medicines would come from the government warehouse.

Second, I asked that he send to Nam Tha two Bangkok-trained nurses to replace my men. These nurses were well trained in Thailand's school of nursing. There were only a few in the whole Kingdom of Laos, but I asked for two for Nam Tha.

Third, I asked that a *médecin indochinois* be sent to replace me. There are no other doctors by international standards in the kingdom, except the Minister himself. There are fifteen men who have had some medical training, though by our standards very little. These men could practice medicine in Laos.

If Dr. Oudom, the Minister of Health, would agree to this, I in turn would agree to leave everything that we had brought to Laos in the hospital at Nam Tha. This meant that absolutely everything would stay there, beds, mosquito nets, linens, drapes, surgical instruments, stethoscopes, house gear, and about $25,000 worth of antibiotics. All these we would turn over to the *médecin indochinois*. Then I would myself return to America.

The Minister immediately agreed, but expressed some surprise that I wanted to become expendable. I told him that in my mind America should not attempt to build a dynasty in a foreign land. We should not attempt to make a foreign land dependent on us for its maintenance.[6]

As a missionary in Laos, I have seen these local poorly trained "doctors" at work. I have seen them literally kick their patients around if those were of the mountain tribe. I know how their offices have been characterized by graft and personal gain. I can imagine what may well happen in that hospital which he left behind. But I insist that Dr. Dooley is right. Medical aid or any other kind of aid that simply results in a permanent dependency of one country upon another is in this age as bad an enslavement as the military colonialization of a past era.

Let us stop all this blather and bleat about the beatitudes of democracy. Let us get out and show, with simple spontaneity and love, our ability to work at the level of the people we aim to aid. Let us stop proclaiming ourselves as the world standard. Democracy, as championed by the United States, does not translate well into Lao. Not yet. We evolved it from 1776 to 1958. Let us be patient with the Asian. The Lao need only time, education, and stimulation.[7]

6 Pp. 192-193.
7 P. 203.

Missionary Medicine

What is the function of a medical missionary program? It is easy enough to define its humanitarian function, as thousands of the world's most miserable sick pass through the doors of mission clinics and hospitals daily. It is easy enough to define its function in terms of service to mankind as doctors leave valuable practices and excellent incomes for the reward of seeing the world's less fortunate healed of diseases which are scarcely known any longer in the West.

But what is its missionary function? And what is its function in the society within which it operates? What is its motive?

The only true motivation for missions is the extension of the church of Jesus Christ, the redemption of men. Aside from an opportunity to give a witness to a captive audience, what does the typical mission medical program contribute to that end? These are questions which missionary doctors may well be able to answer, and I would like to hear the answer. I frankly do not know what it is. It seems to me, however, that any worthwhile answer will have three ingredients at least: Christ, church, and local culture.

But, dropping the question of missionary motive, what about medical goals? Should we want to practice 20th-Century medicine everywhere? Or should we not, like Dooley, be content with 19th-Century medicine in rural areas, in the hope that some 18th-Century medical practices might be developed and used locally?

Of course 20th-Century hospitals are not out of place in the big cities of Asia, Africa, or Latin America, any more than they are in Europe or North America.

For rural areas, however, are they really functional? Would not a decentralized medical program in which a few individuals were taught some elementary skills and a degree of self-reliance and initiative in their use, be better than the full dependence of a mission medical program on a well-qualified foreign staff?

And what about practice? Is it better to take someone who is ill to an antiseptic hospital where he is terribly frightened, or to leave him in his very unantiseptic home where he feels much more secure in the face of illness and death? Many hospitals abroad, it should be noted, are much more humane than American hospitals about allowing the relatives of the ill to camp with him, cook his food, and give him the reassurance of friends about him.

And what of the medicine man? If healing were the only motive, certainly the cooperative use of the medicine man would be all-important. With the antibiotics of modern medicine and the reassurance of traditional remedies, religious and magical, the patient would get a powerful dose. Dr. Dooley gives a lot of credit for success in some of his cases to Old Joe.

Some missionary doctors shy away from such reinforcement of "superstition" and pagan religion. If it is only a matter of "superstition," I feel that they have no right to quibble. Much of their own medical lore will be classified as "superstition" two hundred years from now. If it is true that such cooperation will place a barrier between men and Christ, I would not advocate it. I suspect, however, that this again is more often a problem of the missionary's understanding than we usually think, and that lack of such cooperation may often in itself be that barrier. Here, it seems to me, is an area where some imaginative feeling for the culture could find an effective outlet.

Perhaps in medicine, as in so much of our missionary work, we think of our techniques more highly than we ought to think. Ultimately, it is the missionary doctor or nurse's reflection of Christ which will be important to His cause. Humanitarian healing work can give a splendid lens to brighten that reflection. But little reflection will take place without participation, without empathy. For a man most at home around a smoking fire in a bamboo house, participation and empathy are hard come by within whitewashed walls and bleached sheets.

Dr. Dooley, in a few months' time, succeeded in making friends on a scale which very few missionaries do. With him perhaps the Lao sensed a freedom from contempt, which is one of the most cherished of all freedoms. But what if the work he left behind disintegrates into a political plum, with the unsterile instruments, moldy medicine, and apathetic personnel so characteristics of Lao medical practice? Any answer will depend on what one's goals are, on the absolutism of one's attitudes toward the perfection of 1959 (as opposed to 1958 or 1858), medical fashion, and the realism in one's knowledge of history and of culture change.

My answer is that the type of rural medicine Dr. Dooley undertook, the respect of local culture which he showed, and his insistence on training people to do the medical tasks which they could do independently of him is more realistic for rural areas and more relevant for Christian missions than much of what we are doing. I would like to hear from the doctors on this.

Daniel N. Wambutda

An African Christian Looks at Christian Missions in Africa

The author, speaking out of sincere love and deep concern, examines very frankly some of the problems arising from the paternalism, racism, and insecurity of many missionaries in Africa.

THE introduction of the Gospel to Africa, which came at the expense of many a European missionary's life (at the least in its initial stages, until quinine was discovered in South America) will forever be venerated. We stand in deep gratitude to their unselfish services and will remind ourselves as Africans of our debt to others that have not heard of the Good News.

The Psychological Role of the Gospel

Thousands of lives have been released from the bondage of sin as

Daniel N. Wambutda is an ordained minister of the Plateau and Bauchi Church of Christ in the Sudan. After teaching at Pastors' College, Gindiri, he was called to the Editorial Committee for a new translation of the Old Testament into Hausa. He holds the Dip. Theol. from London, the B.D. from Luther Seminary, and the Th.M. from Princeton Theological Seminary. Hausa Old Testament Project, P.A. Wusasa, Zaria, North Central State, Nigeria.

they in faith confide in the Victor, Jesus Christ, the Savior and the Son to the Living God. Gone forever are their fears of the capricious gods and idols, and their hope for the better things in the afterlife is insured as Christ's Second Coming is anticipated at the consummation of the Age in which the last Utopia will fully be realised. This will be the perfect Kingdom of love where the lion will lie down with the sheep. The burden of divided loyalties to the many gods and divinities with their stringent laws has given way to a simple belief in the only One, the Triune God. There can be no doubt that the introduction of the Gospel has eased the multiplicity of psychological tensions of the African as it seeks to comfort his soul in sickness, poverty, misery, and ignorance, even though many of these ideals are virtually beyond empirical verification. To enable the African to read this vital message himself, education was necessary.

With the Gospel Came Our Education

Most of the present leaders and scholars of Africa are products at one stage or another of mission colleges and are fruits, living fruits of the missionaries themselves. It is however only fair to say that the primary aim of the missions was merely to make the African capable of reading his Bible and no more. The training of nationals in higher institutions has been forced upon missions either by the governments in power or through the need of trained personnel, and not by choice. A most familiar slogan at missionary conferences is, "Just let us preach the pure Gospel." To build institutions is a waste of money in their view. In Luther Seminary, St. Paul, U.S.A. a lady missionary on furlough from Madagascar expressed what is true of what many missionary planning committees do, when she said that usually there were long arguments to try to allocate the most money to the so-called preaching of the pure Gospel at the expense, for example, of the money needed for the erecting of a new dispensary. Even though one may argue that materialism is contextual, Africa with its low economic standards is not yet in danger of materialism.

Indeed at a stage in the history of missions on the continent of Africa, the search for a higher education was definitely hampered and is still discouraged in many parts today. An African friend of mine, now studying in Princeton Seminary, had to struggle for over two years before being allowed to leave Southern Rhodesia for further studies as the result of mission interference. Nor may the blame be laid only on the missionaries; for once the elderly African leaders themselves catch on to such ideas, they too take the opposition bench more often than not for fear of losing prestige and influence and, I am sad to say, even for plain jealousy. A missionary lady three years ago objected to my further studies in the United States because she thought not only that the London Dip. Theology that I had was enough, but that further education would make me proud. And to my amazement, she could not stand my presence any more when I came back with more than a B.D., eager and willing to serve my lowly people. Some other missionaries object to their own members who try to put the Africans on their feet. Thus it was no surprise to me when another missionary on furlough in the U.S.A. said to me, "We like Mark, but he tries to push the Africans forward when they are not ready." Then she realised she had spilt the milk and wished she had never said it. Such true missionaries (like Mark) found all over Africa, from South Africa to Zambia and from the Congo to Nigeria, usually get sent home, though not always. Their deeds shall never be forgotten. There is an undeniable and recognizable attitude of Christian missions, while initiating educational programs, to limit these programs to a low level, and not entirely without reasons.

One reason as they themselves tell me and as typified by the above-mentioned case, is to keep the African humble. What they fail to see is that a really educated man is a humble person, when he learns to know what he does not know, and that the more higher education becomes a common phenomenon the less an educated individual will esteem himself. Even if the accusation were true, it is the proud attitude that is to be attacked, not the acquisition of education *per se*. The African may see this as a clearly motivated attempt to keep him subservient and so not to jeopardize the position of authority which the missionary maintains. The missionary feels threatened.

Perhaps another reason for not wanting to educate highly the African is the fear that he may take off into the world. But it is better for the African to be allowed to develop his love for God despite the world, if his faith is to be genuine. Therefore, while a full credit may be given to the Christian missions as having initiated education in Africa, they must be held responsible for impeding the pace of our progress; the case of the former Belgian Congo illustrates the point beautifully for there was not a single indigenous medical doctor at independence.

Another reason for not bothering about the education of the African is a missions' philosophy that Paul did not preach education but the "pure Gospel." What they fail to realize is that Paul was preaching to a world which was pretty much uniform in economy and education and civilization and therefore had no need to set up schools. It is not Good News for the highly scientific Western world to come to the African condo-ning his archaic living standards. This sort of double standard, I believe, is based on the wrong understanding of "salvation" and "the Kingdom of God." It is important to point out at this juncture an answer to a question which is often asked (as was asked of me at Luther Seminary, St. Paul, Minn., U.S.A. by a missionary from the Cameroons): Why is it that *sometimes* (not always) the mission-educated indigenes turn against the missions? In broad terms, it is because of the inability of the missionaries to show concretely that they wish for the African what they wish for themselves; in other words, it is simply breaking the Golden Rule. Specifically it is because very often for higher education the indigene had to fight it out without the good will of the missions, and so is forced to acquire antagonistic attitudes toward the powers that wish to deter his efforts. What is even more irritating is the missionary's quick criticism of the indigene as uneducated and incompetent, when trained men are needed for higher posts. Let us face it, Darwin's theory of evolution has so influenced the minds of the West, missionaries included, that they have prejudged the African as innately incapable; and who can blame them when so many Africans lend themselves to such criticism by their actions. But it will suffice to say that the missions have not at the very beginning impressed upon the African minister his need for academic discipline in other fields of scholarship -- thus destroying the age-long truth that "Theology is the Queen of Sciences."

Theology and Missions

The theological or biblical discipline on our continent has been done so strictly (following the pattern of the home church) on denominational bases that disunity rather than unity of the African peoples is enhanced, especially since the work of denominations usually follows tribal lines. We have therefore thinly spread our efforts into building separately when a common front could have been presented in the face of Islam or African traditionalists, both of which are confused as to which is the true church. Neither are the *Sitz im Leben* and the customs of the Africans taken seriously in the task of theology. Therefore Christianity appears foreign to Africans since its theology is superimposed from without. Two examples will suffice. Why did missions not adopt the tribal way of marriage and baptize it into Christianity but chose rather to introduce the European way, the ceremony of which is no more biblical? Or why should there be an insistence on total abstinence where a tribe enjoys local beer at a common meal? (The Bible does not teach an imposed abstinence.) What is needed is that Christ must be allowed to be expressed in the culture of the people. This does not however mean an indiscriminate inclusion by Africans of their customs willy nilly into the Christian practices. But let us go back once again to these doctrinal differences of the missions. We need to stress in this regard that a "common-factor" theology should be developed. This means emphasis on the central things of our faith that unite

and not on the peripheral aspects of our teachings that set us apart. This is the wisdom that the world needs in order to root out bitterness among the different denominations, in other words to avoid the extremes. The whole Bible is written this way, and that is why, when Christ's divinity is stressed too much we fall into the heresy of Donatus or else into monophysitism. If we stress his manhood too much Jesus becomes a phantom, just a mere example, an ideal man. Or where do we draw the line between works and faith? Again, it is the keeping of the two in tension with each other that the Bible bequeathed to us.

Another fault in the mission-introduced theology, which may yet be corrected in future, is its failure to adopt the Old Testament festivals to correspond to some of the African feasts in which Christ may take the center. The destruction of these African customs without substituting any thing for them creates a more dangerous vacuum which may be filled with seven more wicked spirits.

Mission Style of Indoctrination

Very often the doctrines and the truth about Christ are presented in such a way that no questions are either wanted or encouraged. The missionary thinks he is overflowing with the Holy Spirit on whom he has a corner and out of the goodness of his heart bestows it on the African. The mistake is that from the very beginning Christ was not allowed to come to all of us (both missionary and African) as the Wholly Other speaking to the whole of humanity. To protect the African, certain books are banned and so our faith amounts to indoctrination. It is the stupid person that asks no questions, and the well-taught one that is a good Christian. But I am sure God is not stupid and does not appreciate people believing in him because they are ignorant of other facts. Religion in the last analysis is subjective but all the sides of issues should be known to make a responsible choice. Such style blunts the ability for creative thinking.

A Theological Blunder

One of the most unfortunate teachings that the "Red Man" (an African term for "White Man") has brought to Africa is the assumption in their preaching that Genesis 9:26-27 means that the African race is cursed from the very beginning. Once the Africans themselves caught on to this idea, its destructive psychological effect was indelible, and this belief looms high wherever African Christians are found, in Lesotho, in South Africa, the Congo, Nigeria, etc. What is worse, the Western world itself believes this widely, even though the latest scholarship would completely shatter such a view. Connected with this is the emphasis on the soul as the target for salvation and the body as less important. So that in South Africa "apartheid," racial segregation, is defended on the grounds that the true church is that which is united in the Spirit. Furthermore this type of teaching helps to kill incentive for economic growth, for all that is

of concern is the hoped for bliss of heaven to be ushered in after the surely expected death at which time the soul is freed. Oh, what a victory for Greek dualism!

The Material Outlook

There is material inequality between Christian missions and those whom they serve. This is realistic since both groups began, by the virtue of their respective situations, on different levels; what is obnoxious however is that the former group not too long ago used to drive Africans out of the Church services if shoes were worn. It is urged here again that this is to eradicate pride, but one wonders why missionaries themselves refuse to live on the same level with the nationals; and in any case their proclaimed aim to love falls into great disrepute. How could the one love the other when he fails to desire the best and nothing but the best for the other? The memories of such third class treatment are very much alive among Africans, and this sometimes explains the outburst of animosity towards the missionaries. Yet it is the same missions who would be willing to receive with strings attached, money and material from their home boards and missions. They have pitifully become victims of materialism, sacrificing their theological truths and actions which might promote unity (which is an expression of love), that they might enjoy the support of the Home Boards. Sometimes this is done at the expense of the countries' interests. It is noticed that instead of the missions encouraging the national church to pay a proper salary to the educated African (and so encourage more educated people to go into the ministry), they would rather encourage conformity to the existing low standards of living. Instead of helping the indigenes to aspire to a healthy higher standard of living the missions have bequeathed to the church the system in which the low standard and the *status quo* are to be maintained. This is actually true of religion as a phenomenon the world over. Since Africa is many miles behind the modern world, one wonders if it is not the church, with all its teaching on grace, which should help close the gap inasmuch as she is usually the best informed. Indeed in many parts where missionaries work in Africa, the influence of their teaching has made the nationals equate true Christian life with poverty, so that most stalls in the markets are owned not by Christians but by Muslims. Yet their prayer meetings are full of petitions to God to provide money to enable the church to launch the needed schemes. God is never known to have dropped dollars and pounds sterling to be picked. He only works in the hearts of those who have to give to his work.

The Decisive Factor

Before we conclude with a word on what I consider to be the remedy, let me outline what is going to be the decisive factor both for the use of Christianity to Africans and also for its spreading influence and progress on the continent of Africa. It is the racial issue which if not arrested will explode into a cosmic destruction for all of us. The plain truth is that the missionaries and the Western world at large are paternalistic, and filled with the feeling of superiority even when they don't know it. The indigenous churches are kept in the position of beggars to the parent missions, in economic and educational fields. There are still many missionaries running around not with the feeling of equality but of being little kings and expecting and even demanding that the Africans maintain their lowly position. At one point when a senior African member of staff asked that a missionary who had offended him appear with him before the leader-missionary, the head missionary said, "The time is not yet here for the African to ask for another white man to appear at the same time before me." It is all right for a missionary to go for further studies while on furlough, but is unthinkable that the African should want to build his education as high as he can. Only reluctantly have the missionaries (in some fields it took some rebuke) agreed to join the indigenous churches because, you see, the "red" missionary is too superior to be part of the lowly, incapable African *ecclesia*. They can be seen clustering together at church services. With all the racism of the Wallaces in the United States, the Enoch Powells of England, the Vorsters of South Africa and the Ian Smiths of Southern Rhodesia, which are practised even within ecclesiastical circles, the African is rightly reevaluating the true meaning and function of Christianity. Many would wish that nothing be said about such things, but we would be in the fools' paradise if we should, like the ostrich, bury our heads in the sand and feel that the whole body is safe. We should instead face the issue squarely. Shall we leave actions which rightly spring from Christian principles of the excellent, the perfect, the only way, to humanists, philanthropists, and anthropologists? The message of peace, hope, and heaven brought by the "red man" has become for many a black man disillusionment, despair, helplessness and hell. For, having converted the Africans to Christianity, the red man holds his gun over their heads telling them to be good boys as the Bible has said. So, Ian Smith can have the courage to tell the world, despite his racism as shown in a film on Africa by CBS of America,[1] that he is preaching the Gospel. What the red man does not know, except for a few like Eugene Nida and Ralph Dodge, is that for the Africans the supreme criterion for judging the value of a religion is its capability to esteem human dignity next to God. An African friend of mine said in Minneapolis, U.S.A., "I am glad I am not a Christian after seeing this racial bigotry even by Christians." When one considers the 7,000 African students in the U.S.A. and hundreds of others in England and other Western countries, most of whom show resentment of such racial practices, it is clear that Christianity has lost its meaning for them; this will certainly affect the countries to which they will later return. It is a shame to hear even Christian red

[1] Shown Sept. 10, 1967.

people argue that for example the black South African is better off than the rest of Africans on economical grounds, because they are putting at the same level human dignity and the material. An animal never becomes human no matter how much it is fed, so where human dignity is denied, no economic comfort may count for more than a morsel. In this regard South Africa may be seen by Africans, and the true Christian world as the "anti-Christ" because of what it officially stands for. But where do we go from here, and whence the remedy?

The Suggested Remedy

Christian Africans found in all the countries should open their doors wide to South Africa in fellowship and trade, not because they condone its policies but because they believe in the basic principle which brought Christianity into being which is love. Perhaps the South African government will learn. African Christians then must urge their respective governments to have diplomatic relations with South Africa.

The second pill is contained in a true understanding of the meaning of salvation being the salvation of the total man, the whole man especially when we study the meaning of yasa in the Old Testament.

The last pill is like the second, which is love. It was love that drove Christ to the cross, it was love that caused him to become man and it is not too much therefore for that race to relate to the one. If the divine can become human certainly we can relate to each other. If the Infinite stooped down to search for us the finite, is it too much that the finite should relate to another finite? The message is clear. We cannot love God and hate our brother, or isn't that black man in the image of God too? Only believers will be allowed into heaven, not races, on the basis of color. The only criterion is the love of Christ in our lives. The ability of the individual must be judged, not his race or color. It is a pity that Christianity, especially Protestantism, is the most racist religion in the world as Pastor Howard O. Jones rightly suggests in his book.[2]

[2] Howard O. Jones, *Shall We Overcome?* (Westwood, N.J.: Fleming H. Revell Co., 1966).

Our faith has made stupendous claims of being the best. As such it must speak to the *whole man*. Unless the lesson of love is learned and applied, Africa will still stand, longing, pleading with an outstreached hand and with a loud cry to the Western world saying "Is this the Christ, the Savior, or do we look for another?" It is time, let us be going, but where? W H E R E? Please tell us --- where? To Communism? Would it not be better to die for one's faith under a godless regime rather than suffer injustice at the hand of the so-called godly nations?"

Harry F. Wolcott

Too True to be Good: The Subculture of American Missionaries in Urban Africa

During a year of sabbatical leave spent in Africa, the author frequently found himself in the presence of American missionaries in urban settings. As a social scientist interested in cultural behavior, he followed his inclination to look for persistent behavior patterns that were characteristic of the missionary groups with whom he came in contact. Taking "culture" to be the shared responses to human problems, he here identifies four pan-human problem areas and describes adaptation he observed among missionaries for resolving them. Although his sample is necessarily limited both geographically and denominationally, the observations are provocative and serve as a reminder that the missionary is a product of, as well as an avowed changer of culture.

To live above, with the Saints of Love,

Oh, that will be Grace and Glory;

To live below, with the saints we know,

That is another story.

Harry F. Wolcott is Professor of Education and Anthropology and Research Associate, Center for the Advanced Study of Educational Administration, University of Oregon (1472 Kincaid, Eugene, Ore. 97403, U.S.A.). This paper began as a lecture which Dr. Wolcott presented while serving on the teaching staff of the International Institute for Christian Communication held in Salisbury, Rhodesia, May-June 1971, sponsored by Daystar Communications.

Being human is everybody's problem. Being human while trying to be an overseas missionary is a special problem. Every group develops a set of ways for coping with problems unique to its own membership as well as coping with universal problems of humanness. As these ways, or "customs," become identifiable, we come to speak of a culture, or in complex societies, of distinct subcultures. This paper describes some of the customs observed in the subculture of American missionaries, particularly those of evangelical Protestant persuasion, in contemporary urban Africa.

During a year of sabbatical study in 1970-71, I often found myself in the company of missionaries. Although most of my time was spent in southern Africa, I had opportunities for visiting or at least talking with missionaries and African churchmen from as far afield as Ethiopia, Kenya and Liberia. Through professional and academic contacts, numerous occasions presented themselves for observing their conferences and meetings, talking with or formally interviewing them, watching and listening to them in the course of their daily rounds, and, on two occasions, conducting a series of discussions on applied anthropology for them.

My purpose here is to identify some themes which seemed to manifest themselves repeatedly among the missionaries with whom I came in contact. The effort is ethnographic but not an ethnography. I am willing to have my remarks deemed to be subjective impressions if my readers are willing to entertain the possibility that they may nonetheless be true, and perhaps in some cases, too true to be good.

Although my title suggests that the account is less than an enthusiastic witness, it is not intended to be disparaging either. Missionaries are simply a fact of life to anthropologists, just as anthropologists are a fact of life to missionaries. Each group recounts tales of journeying far into the bush only to find a member of the other group (moiety?) seated at dinner opposite the chief or headman. Members of both groups have their individual tolerances for the other.

Some anthropologists have provided strong indictments of missionary actions and attitudes they have ob-

served[1], while others have documented instances in which missionaries have made outstanding contributions to ethnographic and linguistic studies.[2] Hortense Powdermaker recalled how during discussions with her fellow anthropology students missionaries were considered to be an enemy: "We talked of the need to keep the natives pure and undefiled by missionaries and civil servants,"[3] although in describing her actual confrontation during fieldwork on the African continent she noted "the high level of education and the generally liberal attitude" observed among missionaries there.[4]

Perhaps anthropologists and missionaries have contributed most to nurturing a mutual dialogue when they have acknowledged the basic differences in their assumptions about what is "best" for indigenous groups, have been charitable in recognizing integrity among members of the opposite group, and have been specific in identifying the points of contention between them. Anthropologist John Beattie provides an example in this regard. He has candidly suggested that "the uncompromising stand taken by many missionaries against such traditional institutions as polygamy, and more particularly against the traditional ritual and religious cults, not

[1] Cf. Colin M. Turnbull, *The Lonely African*, (New York: Simon and Schuster, 1962).

[2] Cf. Annette Rosensteil, "Anthropology and the Missionary," *Journal of the Royal Anthropological Institute*, Vol. 89 (1959), pp. 107-116.

[3] Hortense Powdermaker, *Stranger and Friend: The Way of an Anthropologist* (New York: W.W. Norton, 1966).

[4] *Ibid.*, p. 272.

all of which could be said to be morally objectionable by Western Christian standards . . . in some ways did more harm than good." [5] At the same time he has acknowledged the help and hospitality he has received at the hands of missionaries and native clergy and has written:

> I had, and have, nothing but admiration for the dedicated and devoted work done by missions of all denominations in Bunyoro and elsewhere, and for the many individual missionaries whom I know and respect.[6]

The present article is related less to the dialogue between anthropologists and missionaries—a dialogue for which the pages of this journal have often provided a forum—than it is intended to suggest the utility of looking at missionary behavior from an anthropological perspective. These observations are offered in the spirit of what anthropologist Clyde Kluckhohn called a "mirror for man," [7] provided so that missionaries may examine for themselves the image which they present to "outsiders." Such a behavioral mirror neither insists that the image must be improved nor suggests how changes might be brought about. Indeed, if I have succeeded in identifying core aspects of urban missionary subculture, these behaviors may not be readily amenable to change if that subculture is to remain viable. Perhaps the best purpose this article

5 John Beattie, *Understanding an African Kingdom, Bunyoro* (New York: Holt, Rinehart and Winston, 1965), p. 45.

6 *Ibid.*, p. 46.

7 Clyde Kluckhohn, *Mirror for Man* (New York: McGraw-Hill, 1949).

could serve would be to help the missionary better understand himself as a product of, as well as a producer and changer of culture.

The observations and comments are organized in terms of missionary behavior in regard to four human problems: (1) maintaining "own-group" solidarity and cohesion, (2) confronting personal inadequacy, (3) providing for basic needs, and (4) achieving status identity.

Maintaining "Own-Group" Solidarity and Cohesion—The Binds that Tie

Missionaries go forward to open up their hearts to their fellow men in the remotest corners of the world. That is their Great Commission. One might assume that in order to accomplish such difficult human business they must either have a superhuman gift of infinite tolerance for others or suspect that their tolerance for diversity along some dimensions of human behavior is gained at the cost of greatly restricting tolerance in other dimensions. My observations suggest that the second, more plausible alternative is customary: although missionaries seem magnetically drawn to major human differences such as skin color, language, and life style encountered among strangers, they also struck me as being unusually rigid in their affinity for conformity among their peers and in their rejection of others most nearly like themselves except for variations on single dimensions of behavior. They give evidence of at least *appearing* to accept the naked woman or bearded kraalhead but make little effort to hide their disapproval of latitudes in style exhibited by members of their own society. The recent fad of miniskirts probably caused many a missionary to reconsider his position on the alleged superiority of Western beliefs and practices, but missionary tolerance for differences in style and manner appear generally constricted, with the possibility of offending the indigenous group offered as the constant rationale.

Perhaps missionaries tolerate dramatic differences because, in fact, such differences offer little threat to their group solidarity. They decry the sinfulness rampant in their own society, as evidenced by different beliefs on single dimensions of social behavior like card playing, social drinking, dancing, or wearing makeup, maximizing minor differences and ignoring similarities. Even more is made of variations within subsets of the subculture. Only moments after I had introduced a missionary from the Dutch Reformed Church to an officer of the Salvation Army, the latter observed to me, "They're *so* different from us. They can smoke, and we don't allow it."

Missionaries are conspicuous in their territoriality. Their personal life space on the urban scene may lack the conspicuous boundary markings of the mission compound, but I feel safe in predicting that an analysis of the list of numbers lying beside their respective telephones would reveal that their interacting social networks have not expanded greatly. Professionally they carefully guard communities to which they have established claim. They move cautiously into unknown places,

gingerly describing their reconnaissance of a new area as an assessment of whether it is being "adequately served" when in fact they are asking, "Who is already here and how well are they doing?" In times past, missionaries were sufficiently blatant about parcelling out geographical regions among different sects that they used a special term—comity agreement—for describing their arrangements, and if such agreements are no longer prevalent, the term itself persists. When territory is being defended or invaded, references to and appreciation for the "other" groups can be considerably less than reverent.

One sees evidence of individual as well as denominational territoriality, a tendency toward in-group politicking and manipulation among the more aggressive individuals, particularly those who work inter-denominationally and beyond the borders of a single country. "Whenever a big international conference of missionaries is called," one old-timer confided, "I find myself wondering just who is doing some empire building."

At the same time that missionaries appear to provide easy access into their own closely knit in-groups among the peoples the serve, they consciously or unconsciously set up substantial barriers to such access. They simultaneously beckon and reject their would-be converts, constantly distinguishing their tiny core of true believers from an important but peripheral mass. Reporting on this phenomenon on the missionary scene in the Philippines, W.H. Scott has observed how the missionary "entertains the concept that he and his Filipino colleagues belong in some sense to two different churches... "[8] This system by which members of the established inner core are protected from inundation by the very success of their efforts at conversion works through the existence of such relatively effective obstacles as literacy exams, baptism, and catechism lessons requiring as long as three years. Permanent residence is frequently made a prerequisite, thereby systematically excluding migrant groups as well as the great proportion of semi-urban Africans whose lives are played out in the dual arenas of town and country. The ultimate prerequisite to full acceptance within the inner core of many churches is a requirement of a "personal experience of Jesus." In the crosscultural setting, where I have heard producers of materials for Christian education arguing over what color to use in a representation of Jesus' face, I am somewhat at a loss to know just what a personal experience means.

The result of establishing barriers to full acceptance serves to distinguish the core in-group from the huge coterie of "almost" Christians. Cohesion within the tight ranks of the in-group is gained at the cost of holding the secondary group in constant abeyance. The consequence, as I heard one astute missionary observer describe it, is "never a direct turning away, but a subtle realization on the part of the new converts that *they can't make it.*"

Along with references directed toward other sects, missionaries engage

in direct statements and verbal "asides" which further tend to distinguish their own elite group from the rank and file of those of us who constitute the great unwashed. Such references serve as a subtle vehicle for transmitting the superiority of the in-group and providing an ethnocentricism characteristic of and necessary (in some form) to any identifiable subculture: "*We* are the people." I recorded such comments as:

"*They* hadn't accepted Jesus Christ, *unfortunately.*"

"*Quote,* Christian, *unquote.*"

"*So-called* Christians."

Prayers are offered for "those less fortunate," or "those who haven't heard the message." I heard a reference to the "secular" man on the street who belongs to the "great unconcerned mass." "Churchgoing pagans" was the name assigned a major statistical category in one study of church growth conducted in East Africa. Referring to the fact that the husbands of two white church members whose families were being transferred from their African posts were not members of his (essentially white) urban mission church—and, heaven forbid, probably were not even Christians!—the head of one denomination's overseas headquarters conferred with his colleagues about "sanctifying the unholy" in discussing the awkward problem of including the husbands in the prayers planned for a farewell fellowship.

The unity of the subcultural system is further revealed by the fact that insiders are intuitively aware of which kinds of topics are and are not appropriate in interpersonal communication.

---

8 William H. Scott, "Some Contrasts in Missionary Patterns," *PA*, Vol. 15, No. 6 (Nov-Dec. 1968), pp. 269-276.

Every human group evolves implicit rules that guide in the selection of proper matters for public concern, setting limits about topics which should be discussed only privately or informally and identifying certain topics that can be mentioned but are never explored in depth because of their potentially disruptive nature. The latter can be discerned through the identification of a series of internalized "cut-off points" in conversation beyond which agreement is assumed or more penetrating analysis is sharply discouraged.[9] Socially sensitive topics like drinking, polygamy, adultery, lobolo payment, and even tribal dancing and singing were often alluded to but virtually never discussed in formal missionary circles, growing out of a reluctance which one inside observer refers to as the "conspiracy of silence." During a discussion of Muslims at a Christian conference, one young African man posed the question, "Should we encourage them to become good Muslims, or do we insist that they become Christians?" The response was total silence, followed eventually by a remark from the chairman, "Does anyone have anything else to say?"

Missionaries, like other viable human groups, need to be able to exert sufficient control over member to keep them in line with group norms. Naturally enough among such professionally verbal people, *verbal sanctions* are especially prevalent. Sometimes they talk directly *to* persons veering from expected behavior; more often they talk *about* them. My general impression is that missionaries are often great gossipers, and gossip is a powerful force for social control in face-to-face groups. Missionaries appear every bit as conscientious in transmitting timely Bad News among and about their close colleagues as they are about transmitting the timeless Good News to their out-group audiences. Missionaries may not readily acknowledge their proclivity for talking about others as an accepted mechanism for social control, but individuals who have felt themselves to be the subjects of such gossip are not hesitant in describing either its prevalence or its impact.

The missionary's so-called "African colleagues" are not unaware of the closed nature of white missionary groups and of the extent to which their divergent backgrounds pose a potential threat to that solidarity. Voices were lowered during one after-dinner conversation with two Africans employed in Christian work in Kenya as I turned our discussion to queries about contemporary African life, particularly to a facet in which I had become especially interested, the importance of beer in transacting sacred and secular work.[10] Both young men said that they did drink beer under circumstances appropriate to their traditional beliefs, although technically drinking was prohibited not only as a condition of employment but as a demonstration of personal commitment. "Beer drinking

---

[9] Cf. Jules Henry, "Culture, Education, and Communications Theory," in George D. Spindler, ed., *Education and Anthropology*, (Palo Alto, Calif.: Stanford University Press, 1955).

[10] Harry F. Wolcott, *The Beer Gardens of Bulawayo: Integrated Drinking in a Segregated Society*. University of Oregon. Unpublished manuscript.

and ancestor worship are two things the missionaries have never liked," my informants explained, "so we simply don't talk about such things with them." The more opportunity I had to observe and to talk with young African men employed by overseas missions, the more I was struck with what a remarkably pragmatic group they are. As one African explained, "For each missionary who comes, you have to sing his tune." If decades of missionary tutelage have in fact had a deleterious effect on the quality of indigenous African music (as I heard one music scholar insist), at least Africans seem to have become adept at singing the "new" tunes required of them. A "European" woman in Rhodesia told me about an enterprising domestic she had once employed who had succeeded in obtaining a place for each of her three children in a mission school of his avowed faith: one Lutheran, one Brethren in Christ, and one Catholic.

Overseas missionaries represent for Africans the possibility of office employment and of obtaining technical training, and jobs and training are life-blood in the fiercely competitive world of truly *white collar* jobs in their cities. Although such employment does not pay highly, at least the working conditions are pleasant and one can join the coveted ranks of the tie-wearers. Besides, there are major compensations for associating oneself with Christians from overseas. Few other jobs provide comparable opportunities for travel, for useful contacts (especially with other whites), or for further study. How many African students have been able to go to the States be-

cause of missionary help? And there are minor compensations—like meeting a constant parade of people from other countries, or appearing able to afford a white chauffeur while riding around the city. "I have to keep telling my African passengers that our opportunities for fellowship are far greater when they ride up in the front seat with me," explained an urban missionary in Uganda

Confronting Personal Inadequacy and Institutionalized Self-Doubt: Our Father and Your Father

I do not know what personality factors predominate in the selection processes for missionaries by which they come to "hear the call" for their life work. My impression is that they are people who feel a need to exert power and control over others, probably a universal quality evident in some degree among all humans. Perhaps persons drawn to missionary careers have been relatively unsuccessful in meeting or satisfying this need in their own society. I have not studied missionary careers, and I can only speculate about this possibility, but I could point out that similar conjecture has been offered about the satisfaction some anthropologists enjoy in the field: "Field-workers without high social status in their own society may have satisfaction (often unconscious) in the prestige of being a white man, a *bwana* (using the term formerly common in Africa) among black men." [11]

Hitching their wagons to the ultimate source of authority in their belief system, and advantaged by the bene-

11 Powdermaker, *op. cit.*, p. 291.

fits of American technology and wealth, the missionaries set out to find groups less advantaged whom they assume to be in need of help. Their opportunities for personal satisfaction depend on finding settings where their own idiosyncratic needs to exert power fit into a cultural framework where control as they wish to exert it does not conflict with existing forms of power already extant.

As a corollary to this seeming need to exert an influence over others, the missionaries with whom I came in contact adhered rigidly to hierarchical structure in both their personal and their professional lives. Dominance and submission are built into their every interpersonal relationship. They represent an example of a male-dominant, patriarchically organized society. If symbolically they consider themselves to be Children of God, they are considerably more active in assuming a reciprocal role as Father among Men.

I should point out that my contacts with missionaries were almost totally among married men or with husband and wife teams, and my comments here pertain to that male-dominant scene. Not until long after returning home did I learn that there are more female than male missionaries, both worldwide and in Africa. The fact that my observations were generally limited to urban settings may explain why women were not more prevalent, since so many of them render their service as teachers and nurses at mission stations. It is also possible that the particular network of churchmen and missionaries among whom I usually

moved recruits from social strata in which men customarily occupy those roles that require the overt display of authority. Further, my contacts may have included a disproportionate number of missionaries who held high ranking positions in their respective organizations, positions customarily (and perhaps exclusively) held by men.

In the families which I had an opportunity to observe, wives and children appeared simultaneously to be "priceless gifts" and a source of constant distraction and interpersonal tension in mediating between professional commitments and family ones. My impression was that wherever one found an American missionary of evangelical conviction he could expect to find the family as well. Wherever that group of missionaries congregated, I felt I could count on the presence, ritual involvement, and distraction of wives and children. The children function as impractical ornaments, but the missionary covets them on the (probably correct) assumption that his appearance as husband and father lends credence to his message of love and faith. Before leaving the subject of "missionaries' kids" the observation could be made that although they contribute little to the usual professional tasks of the missionary, they have had a profound influence on contact generations by carrying childhood diseases from the European community farther and farther into the bush.[12]

Missionary husbands seemed to me on the one hand to be quite permissive (too permissive?) with their children and on the other hand to be quite

12 Jacob Loewen, personal communication.

demanding of their wives. Rather ritualistic but nonetheless continual attention was directed toward their wives particularly in giving verbal recognition of the importance of husband and wife as a *team* and toward acknowledging the "role of the woman." Paradoxically, even if such behavior may have been born more out of deference than conviction, it contrasts sharply with traditional African attitudes. Africans who deal with urban missionaries are perplexed when missionary husbands announce that they must check with their wives before setting a date or confirming an invitation. I watched with astonishment as an experienced missionary arrived from town to attend a bush wedding and made his way directly to the "kitchen" to help the women prepare vegetables. (Do missionaries ponder how their own behaviors contribute to the overrepresentation of women and children characteristic of their African congregations?) Yet in urban settings which I observed—possibly in sharp contrast to bush settings where more business is conducted informally and at home—missionary wives were not customarily included in "high level" discussions, especially those involving only colleagues from overseas. Whatever influence the women exert is channeled through informal means in private and personal conversations or in manipulating limited resources like time, space, or transportation ("If you meet on that day, how can I get the children to the doctor?"). Intellectually the women are left by and to themselves. Wives talk to wives while the men get on

with the serious business, even if the wife member of the "team" subsequently will be expected to do most or all of the detail work of typing, bookkeeping, corresponding, hosting, or handling local arrangements.

Although restricted essentially to informal means, missionary wives exert considerable authority *within* the family; male dominance does not preclude the possibility of female domineering. There is probably no heavier personal cross to bear than a wife who cannot wait until she returns home. Further, in the frequent absences of their husbands, wives must often be left to relay messages and directions for others. Female assertiveness provides an opportunity for intercultural misunderstanding when white women from a society accustomed to such excesses as Women's Liberation give orders to African men from societies where women have never been eligible for full adult status.

Within both family and professional circles, decisions are reached and announced hierarchically. Missionary communication is generally one way: from top to bottom, and from right to wrong. The missionary himself is the customary source of authority, but he is not reticent to cite a higher authority, whether it be the unspecified "they" of the home church or the irrefutable power of personal revelation, to validate an ultimatum.

As missionaries are authoritarian fathers in their own house, so do they act among the people whom they serve. African colleagues in the ministry are often treated as para-professionals, and African peoples more generally are talked about and treated paternally as children in need of local as well as Divine guidance in the urban setting just as they have typically been dealt with when calling at the mission station. This proclivity for acting as "fathers" is explicitly reinforced in many African societies where customary deference is shown to those vested with power or authority. Africans refer to such persons respectfully as "father." This is heady stuff for dominance-seeking personalities. Once accustomed to it, missionaries appear inclined to accept such deference even while they talk a new vocabulary dealing with change, modernization, and, except in southern Africa, nationalization. One way to maintain the status of "father" is to assure that others are securely fixed into the reciprocal role of children (e.g., by delighting in the "child-like" nature of African people). A frustrated African churchman told me in this regard, "Missionaries don't pick talented Africans—they don't want the people back home to know that Africans could do the job."

Perhaps missionary authoritativeness reveals an underlying need to create order and certainty in professional and geographical domains. Certainty regarding their own future on the African Continent seemed conspicuously absent from the lives of the American missionaries I met. Collectively, missionaries form an ultra future-oriented society — their whole worldview is rooted in hope for tomorrow, sometimes to such an extent that today becomes little more than a holding operation, an endless vigil. Yet those among the urban missionaries who did seem to seek courses of positive action expressed uncertainty about their goals and appeared at a loss in finding ways to achieve them, even as they acknowledged a sense of urgency because time may be running out. Part of this sense of urgency is related, no doubt, to the characteristic technological orientation in American society in which doing things properly means doing them quickly and efficiently, an exquisite source of frustration facing the American overseas. This sense of urgency is sparked on the African scene by the fact that American missionaries have never felt themselves *individually* to be permanent residents on that continent. They are transients, without roots in African soil. Now, with the press for national identities in African states, some of them have begun to wonder if, or for how long, missionaries *collectively* will be allowed to remain on the scene.

The missionary who is successful in feeling that he can cope with or control the external vagaries of his world must also confront personal uncertainties peculiar to his role. His commitment provides ample opportunity for nurturing feelings of self-doubt. Except for a few occasions when he may report or perform in public, the work of the missionary is still conducted largely out of the view of his peers. Like a number of other professionals in service occupations, his efforts are not subject to collegial review. Who helps him to judge the quality of his interactions, the wisdom of his counsel, the sensitivity of his crosscultural communication? I came to feel, noting some jarring contrasts between what missionaries do and what they say they do, that missionaries who offered the most glowing accounts of themselves were usually (or at least charitably) regarded as successful. I could not help but wonder if others of modest inclination might perhaps be equally effective but remain unheralded simply because they failed to realize that their ranks are not as beset by humility as their tenets suggest. For those whose self-assessment is modest but who nonetheless thrive on peer approval, a successful but truly humble person could find the professional isolation and lack of peer approval of the missionary role a source of genuine frustration.

Self-doubt serves not only as a personal hazard for the evangelical missionary but is also an essential part of his professional credo. As I listened to formal and infomal conversations among missionaries I realized that a major assumption underlying their entire belief system is that man is an inherently evil creature: "A thesis which is Christian through and through: man has a sinister twist to his nature..." [13] An outsider is moved to ask if perhaps the assumption that human life is inherently evil is in itself satanical and an unfortunate premise on which to base a career or enlist enthusiastic converts. Anthropologist Colin Turnbull has written, "With the majority of missions the work of teaching had to begin with the work of destruction: the total destruction of all old beliefs, the total destruction of all old ways,

followed by the initial teaching that man is evil – particularly the black man." [14]

The social scientist is spared self-doubt on this particular issue. His "faith" does not require that he ask whether man is inherently evil *or* inherently good. He studies and accepts man as *man*, not as *sinister* man.

To cope with feelings of personal inadequacy and self-doubt, all human beings need ways to "stop the world" to regain their strength, their composure, and their perspective. We meet part of this need through the biological mechanism of daily sleep. Every culture provides additional alternatives for "copping out" when the world is too much with us and we ourselves are overcome. In a form recognized within their cultural heritage, American missionaries seemed to take extensive recourse to *sickness* as a mechanism for providing temporary respite from their incessant obligations and nagging self-doubts. Their prolonged tours overseas serve not only as a source of real and recurring maladies but also lend credence to the possible presence of other less-easily diagnosed conditions. The missionary comes from a society that institutionalizes sick leave and recognizes "not feeling well" as a culturally acceptable pattern of behavior for simultaneously evoking sympathy and escaping responsibility. My observation was that missionaries capitalize on the vagaries of personal health and manipulate it as a lever for controlling others. I was fascinated with opportunities to observe how such behavior can be subtly

---

13 Michael Green, *Runaway World* (London: Inter-Varsity Press, 1968), p. 74.

14 Turnbull, *op. cit.*, p. 98.

transmitted from missionary parents to their offspring. In African society, my impression is that needed respite is more often achieved through the reported illness of *others* and through deaths in the greatly extended networks which comprise one's "family." Americans are confronted with excuses from African constituents capable of burying a remarkable succession of "fathers" and "mothers" or looking after other members of their families; Africans are repeatedly confronted with missionary excuses relating to their own illnesses.

Public soul-searching about whether one still has "something to offer" in the overseas setting is another way in which missionaries can manipulate and control others, but urban missionaries have easy access to communications media and thus to each other, and contemporary soulsearching is probably common but less intense today than in days when contacts were infrequent. Viewing personal adequacy from the positive side, I was interested to note how often members of missionary families were armed with special talents, especially musical ones. Any evidence of talent was discussed, displayed, and sometimes rather aggressively recruited, to a far greater extent than I recall in comparable occupational groups. What other group can be characterized by a piano in every home and at least one member of the family who can play it? I found myself likening missionary families to contestants in modern beauty contests where looking good is no longer enough —one must also be able to produce visible evidence of talent.

Providing for Basic Personal Needs: Doing Good and Well

Although I have dismissed "evil," I would not want to dismiss the substance said to be its root: MONEY. Problems related to money plague and obsess many urban missionaries. They always have too much of it, and they never have enough. Their standard of living makes them seem wealthy wherever they go and results in constant conflict for them when they hold back so much of what they have for themselves. An anthropologist critical of missionaries recalled the old saw that they set out to do "good" and often end up doing "well." There are urban missionary groups so self-conscious of the standard of living they enjoy overseas that they never send back photographs of their overseas residences. Yet in terms of the resources of their own native land, missionaries work with usually meager funds not always dependable in their amount or duration.

Accountability to sponsoring churches or mission boards remains a perennial source of anxiety, raising the constant cry, "We can't seem to get them to understand us!" (Paradoxically one might ask how missionaries expect to get their message across to culturally different people overseas if they cannot make themselves understood to likeminded members of their own community back home.) Ingroup talk is sprinkled liberally with references to money, and so are the ubiquitous newsletters. I recorded comments from a number of missionaries that suggest both the preoccupation with money and something of the patterned responses for coping with its scarcity:

"There is no suggestion in Scripture that God is short of money."

"Churchmen hope to get into a position where they won't have to trust quite so much."

"We have eighteen months to set up our program, so we will have the opportunity of two 'harvest seasons.'"

"Christians don't talk about their failures very much—they're afraid it might keep people from giving for the next project."

Missionaries have evolved interesting responses to living a lifetime where their resources will probably never be adequate. They are modest to the point of frugality in spending for food and clothing. Perhaps their sense of impermanence prevents them from acquiring extensive or expensive collections of furniture, but whatever their reasons, their possessions are meager. Nor have I meant to imply that they are housed in mansions. I simply report that I met missionaries who were selfconscious about their very pleasant domiciles and who felt that they might be more adequate than what their sponsors believed they were providing —one more instance of the difficulty of maintaining a missionary image in the urban setting.

A most fascinating pattern of collective behavior in providing for mutual well-being is revealed in the existence of vast reciprocal social networks extending among other missionaries, comparable to the intricate networks of kinsmen described by anthropologists among preliterate societies. Missionaries utilize these reciprocal networks to provide entree into new settings or new communities and, far more importantly, to travel inexpensively throughout the countries and continents where they are stationed. Participating in the networks requires that an individual accommodate others just as he in turn can count on being accommodated. These reciprocal obligations extend not only to personal acquaintances but to others—including strangers—who satisfy the criterion of being "one of us." Thus someone may stay with a family whom he has never met personally, and he, in turn, may find total strangers knocking on his door confident of being received as guests. Such behavior is common in missionary life and so generally acceptable that it appears completely "natural" to them. It is certainly not restricted only to missionary subculture, but my impression is that missionaries exploit the potential of such networks of mutual obligations as fully as possible. This behavior has been explained to me as a testimony of the spirit of true fellowship which prevails among Christians. It also provides a very pragmatic test of both the extent and the dollar value of one's contacts, since the networks are almost an economic necessity in making it possible for people to move about inexpensively and securely in strange lands in spite of limited financial resources.

Some ambiguity surrounds the obligations which guests may feel toward their hosts, particularly if the purpose behind a visit is in the nature of a holiday or if the visitors include wife and children. Unless the hosts solicit a cash payment from "guests" (the practice of providing guest houses available for a modest fee is increasing in popularity in rural as well as urban settings, and in their absence I am told that missionaries living at both rural and urban crossroads stations sometimes post suggested "rates" in their guest rooms) visitors feel uncertain about whether to confront them with a gift or at least to offer one and if so, how much and of what kind. These reciprocal networks are constantly and sometimes aggressively expanded at every opportunity. Names are remembered and recorded and some individuals follow up after large conferences by sending form letters to their "new friends" as an investment in the future. Taking a clue from stories recounted to me as humorous exceptions, I imagine that these networks operate rather more exclusively than outsiders appreciate and that full household privileges are generally extended only to colleagues of closely-related sects. Hospitality limited to a meal or afternoon tea is sufficient for those outside the reciprocal network. Anthropologists operate outside the customary boundaries of these networks and have sometimes ingratiated themselves by accepting missionary hospitality and ignoring obligations. Eugene Nida has commented:

> Particularly galling to many missionaries is the polite congeniality of some anthropologists when they accept the missionary's hospitality, but their overt and often bitter hostility toward missionary activities when they are with the indigenous people.[15]

I would point out, however, that missionaries also impose upon the hospitality of reciprocating networks in which they are outsiders. I talked with rural Africans who feel they are "put upon" when urban missionaries make brief forays into the bush. I have not forgotten my first contacts with missionaries during fieldwork in a tiny Canadian Indian village on the northwest coast[16] when a constant stream of them made their way to my door.

In addition to their important economic function, interpersonal networks provide a means of checking on new acquaintances of unknown credentials. Not unlike other groups, missionaries usually tease out early in conversations with new colleagues who they know in common, or where they or mutual friends have attended seminary or Bible college or spent a term overseas. Reliance on these acquaintanceships for establishing new friends is liable to excesses. I overheard the following conversation between a White and a Black missionary meeting at a conference:

"Where are you from?"

"I'm from Nigeria."

"Oh, then you must know my friend from Canada. Hmmmm,

[15] Eugene A. Nida, "Missionaries and Anthropologists," *PA*, Vol. 13, No. 6 (Nov.-Dec. 1966), p. 273.

[16] Harry F. Wolcott, *A Kwakiutl Village and School.* (New York: Holt, Rinehart and Winston, 1967).

that's funny, I say he's my friend, and I can't even think of his name."

Missionaries look for and find aspects of their work that they find *personally* satisfying. These satisfactions, although tangential to their immediate professional tasks, are important ingredients in achieving a personal sense of accomplishment. Almost universally missionaries describe their satisfaction and reward in making new contacts. They not only collect but virtually *count* their new-made friends. They boast of invitations and privileges extended by the indigenous population, which they interpret as indices of acceptance in communities where they are newcomers.

They also know and "collect" the geographical areas in which they work. Their dwellings inevitably house personal collections indicating their appreciation for local cultures that they are otherwise hell-bent to change. In the sense of accumulating audio-visual material and traditional art forms and artifacts, they are genuine culture-vultures. Their menus often include native foods. They endeavor to establish a reputation for their interest in learning about the "old ways." They are especially sensitive to learning correct forms of greeting and respectful forms of address in the local language. They are knowledgeable guides for the stranger who seeks a thoughtful tour of an indigenous community.

Their prowess in speaking foreign languages is another source of personal satisfaction, especially when they reconvene among their English-speaking colleagues or return home. In that segment of the American community from which missionaries are selected and supported, foreign languages are an anomaly, and admiration rises remarkably for a missionary whose accomplishments include the ability to speak other languages, especially exotic ones. Missionaries are not reticent about demonstrating their linguistic skills. Perhaps they share with the anthropologists the sense that although knowing the other person's language does not guarantee communication, it at least represents tangible proof of the extent of one's effort.

Achieving Professional Status: Not-Really-A-Missionary Missionaries

At least a few urban missionaries I met adhered to what one might refer to as their own esoteric version of a "Peter Principle." Like Peter they seemed reluctant to be identified with their associates. Some who did not flatly deny their vocation at least hastened to explain that they were not missionaries in the stereotyped sense:

"Actually, my wife and I occasionally drink wine with our dinner, and we go to dances. She wears short dresses and has pretty legs, and I wear my hair long. But of course I'm supposed to be a teetotaler, and I could never let it be known that I drank. We sort of go opposite to a lot of things that most missionaries do, and we think it works better."

"Our colleagues don't like us. They think we have too wide a group of non-missionary associations."

"We're pretty threatening to most missionaries."

Presumably several factors contribute to a reluctance to identify oneself as a missionary or, more commonly, an insistence that one is such a different and special kind of missionary compared with the majority of his colleagues that he is best not thought of as a missionary at all. One such factor may be that as an occupational status wearing the missionary mantle is not sufficiently rewarding to compensate for the prevailing negative stereotype which it can evoke. Further, the position is lacking in qualities necessary to validate it as a professional one.

Outside of church circles, missionaries are not highly regarded by or in American society.[17] (Would it surprise the native populations of the world to learn how atypical and sometimes even alienated missionaries are from the majority of members in the communities they are assumed to represent?) Missionary stereotypes at home and overseas are hardly flattering; neither are they entirely lacking in accuracy. The evangelical types border on exhibitionism in their public Bible-toting, Bible reading, and praying, the more overt behaviors in a syndrome that one anthropologist has characterized as their "bitter self-righteousness." Their inattention to changing styles (due only in part to their frugality)

makes them stand out clearly, but for the wrong reasons, the characteristic hair-dos of missionary wives generally representing the epitome of other-worldliness. Curiously, the qualities that contribute most to social interaction are the very ones I found so often to be lacking among them: *joie de vivre*, humor, robustness, occasionally even genuine graciousness and tact. Their joylessness seemed especially paradoxical to me. What dour chroniclers they are to be carrying a message which they expect others to accept as one filled with joy.

By itself an unflattering stereotype probably would not distress most missionaries. However, negative aspects of the stereotype are further confounded by the fact that the missionary role itself is not well defined. The missionary occupies a position so ambiguous as to leave one wondering whether or not he possesses *any* special skills or characteristics that separate him from a non-missionary or serve within his group to separate the full professional from the beginner. The role is lacking in expertise: energy and enthusiastic witness are the requirements for entry, and longevity is the criterion of success. Where American society has been criticized for its over-attentiveness to credentials, the missionary subculture suffers because the only criterion for participation is self-proclamation.

Missionaries lack a technical and esoteric language, another dimension that ordinarily contributes to identifying professional status. They do have their own dialect, but its identifying characteristic is its ambiguity

[17] Cf. a discussion of missionary "marginality" in Jacob A. Loewen, "A Message for Missionaries from Mopass," *PA*, Vol. 17, No. 1, (Jan.-Feb. 1970), pp. 19-21.

rather than its precision–it simply is not the technical jargon of a professional group. Here are some examples of non-technical missionary language which I collected during one international gathering in East Africa dominated by American missionaries and devoted especially to using audio-visual media in communicating their message:

"Where do we in media fit into the body of Christ?" [The body of Christ was then represented on the chalkboard as a circle which the speaker subsequently divided into eight parts.]

"Audio-visual is one of God's tools." [One generation earlier, it was pointed out, films were considered to be a "tool of Satan."]

"I am grateful for the vision we have shared during the course of our time here," concluded one speaker.

Papers presented by missionaries at that conference evidenced a redundancy of topics and ideas. Missionaries are, of course, used to talking. In an occupation where being able to say something is more important than having something to say, they tend to talk a lot but to provide little information. As one of their own group warned them, "We've been willing to settle for words rather than worry about getting an understanding across." I do not mean to imply that missionary communication is unique in its emphasis on oratory rather than information; much of what I read and hear in education and the social sciences suf-

fers from the same problem. However, it may be useful to ask whether the shallownesss of content is *inherent* in the missionary situation because of its lack of a rigorous intellectual and terminological framework, while it is *incidental* (though far too prevalent) within the ranks of other professional subcultures.

Urban life can be a very unhappy setting for missionaries who suffer from status insecurity. Living in the bush, for all its hardships, may still be easier than carving out a role as missionary in a setting too familiar in terms of personal experience and totally unfamiliar in terms of professional expectation. Urban missionaries I met seemed more responsive to their urban surroundings than to their missionary calling: their dealings with their fellow men were frenetic, impersonal, and superficial–in short, more like those characteristic of urbanites, less like those I would have expected of missionaries (but strangely similar to criticisms of typical transactions at large mission stations). Referring to an urban missionary colleague toward whom he apparently felt more awe than admiration, one churchman noted, "I'd hate to know what that fellow would have been like if he *hadn't* been a Christian."

In contrast to his rural predecessors, the role of the urban missionary finds him with greatly diminished control in community programs–particularly those relating to the medical and educational services associated with mission stations. Although historically such programs have competed vigorously for missionary time and effort, they also required and allowed the missionary to develop and display the level of expertise associated with those professional fields. Urban missionaries who have been cut adrift from such obligations—and it is my impression that governmental agencies are assuming these responsibilities at ever-increasing rates—may be discovering that their freedom from programs of technical service comes with a lessened sense of professional responsibility. Perhaps this explains the heightened interest in social science methodologies and research "hardware" evident among missionaries today, an interest that one might speculate grows less out of a felt need to be scientific and efficient than out of a need to have and demonstrate some tangible kind of expertise. Quoting chapter and verse of the Bible, playing the piano, and speaking the language are no longer enough when your next door neighbor is also able to perform those feats.

The problem of identifying whether, as an urban missionary, he is a missionary at all (except for the cross-cultural setting in which he works) may well be the critical professional question of the times. In the African setting increasing use of the term "church and mission" suggests that earlier distinctions are breaking down. But just as some churchmen in Africa argue that they are not missionaries, missionaries have always regarded themselves as a special kind of overseas churchmen. So also do their sponsors. Status anxiety arises out of such conflicts between expectations and realities. Back in the States, congregations have grown used to hearing about battling the insects and boiling the water; the urban missionary is reluctant to report a contemporary range of too-familiar worries that runs the gamut from car theft to rising costs in hiring secretaries or renting space for a bookstore. So his reports emphasize the picturesque, the exotic, the "primitive," and the needy, perhaps totally ignoring the urban scene or at least ignoring the modern, prosperous side of Africa. He tells the folks back home what he believes they want to hear. And that helps perpetuate not only their subculture but his own.

William D. Reyburn

Identification in
the Missionary Task

With experience ranging from the Andes to the grasslands of West Africa,
Dr. Reyburn approaches the much-discussed subject of missionary identification with refreshing insight. Few missionaries have tried (and succeeded) in "identifying" with as many different peoples on two such
different continents as have the Reyburns. But, as Reyburn says in this
article, it is not the sheer quantity of identification that counts. Rather,
he explores the obstacles to missionary identification, as they range from
gesture to skin color, from repugnance at eating certain foods to ideological
insulation. His comments on "authority" and "liberty" are most illuminat-
ing, as is his conclusion on the Christian basis for identification.

A STEADY downpour of rain had been
falling from late afternoon until long
after dark. A small donkey followed by
a pair of men slowly made its way down
the slippery sides of the muddy descent
which wound into the sleepy town of
Baños, high in the Ecuadorean Andes.
No one appeared to pay any attention
as the two dark figures halted their burro
before a shabby Indian hostel. The taller
of the two men stepped inside the doorway where a group of men sat at a small
table drinking chicha by candle light. No
sooner had the stranger entered the room
than a voice from behind the bar called
out, "Buenas noches, meester." The man
in the rain-soaked poncho turned quickly
to see a fat-faced woman standing half
concealed behind the counter. "Buenas
noches, señora," he replied, lifting his
hat slightly. Following a short exchange
of conversation the man and barmaid
reappeared outside and led the donkey
through a small gate to a mud stable.
The two men removed their load and

carried it to a stall-like room beside the
stable where they were to spend the night.

I sat down on the straw on the floor
and began pulling off my wet clothes.
I kept hearing that word meester which
I had come to dislike intensely. Why
had that funny little woman there in
the semi-darkness of the room addressed
me as meester? I looked at my clothes.
My hat was that of the poorest cholo in
Ecuador. My pants were nothing more
than a mass of patches held together by
still more patches. On my dirty mud-
stained feet I wore a pair of rubber tire
alpargatas the same as any Indian or
cholo wore. My red poncho was not from
the high class Otavalo weavers. It was
a poor man's poncho made in Salcedo.
It had no fancy tassels and in true cholo
fashion there were bits of straw dangling
from its lower edge, showing that I was
a man who slept with his burro on the
road. But why then did she call me
meester, a term reserved for Americans
and Europeans? At least she could have

746

addressed me as *señor,* but no, it had to be *meester.* I felt as though my carefully devised disguise had been stripped from me with the mention of that word. I kept hashing it over and over in my mind. It wasn't because she detected a foreign accent, because I had not as yet opened my mouth. I turned to my Quechua Indian companion, old Carlos Bawa of Lake Colta. "Carlos, the lady knew I am a *meester.* How do you think she knew, Carlitos?"

My friend sat huddled in the corner of the room with his legs and arms tucked under his two ponchos. "I don't know, *patroncito.*" Looking up quickly at Carlos I said, "Carlos, for three days I have been asking you not to call me *patroncito.* If you call me that people will know I am not a *cholo.*" Carlos flicked a finger out from under the collar of his woolen poncho and touching his hat brim submissively replied, "I keep forgetting, *meestercito.*"

Disgusted and aching in my rain-soaked skin I felt like the fool I must have appeared. I sat quietly watching the candle flicker as Carlos dozed off to sleep in his corner. I kept seeing the faces of people along the road we had walked for the past three days. Then I would see the face of this woman in Baños who had robbed me of what seemed like a perfect disguise. I wondered then if perhaps I hadn't been taken for a European even earlier. I was hurt, disappointed, disillusioned, and to make things worse I was dreadfully hungry. Reaching into our packsack I pulled out the bag of *machica* flour my wife had prepared for us, poured in some water and stirred the brown sugar and barley mixture with my finger and gulped it down. The rain was letting up now and from a hole in the upper corner of the room I could see the clouds drifting across the sky in the light of the moon. A guitar was strumming softly out in the street and in the stall next to us a half dozen Indians had just returned from the stable and were discussing the events of their day's journey.

Blowing out the candle I leaned up against the rough plank wall and listened to their conversation, then eventually fell asleep. It was some hours later when I was startled awake by the noise of our door creaking open. I got to my feet quickly and jumped behind the opening door waiting to see what was going to happen. The door quietly closed and I heard old Carlos groan as he settled down onto his mat to sleep. Carlos was returning, having gone out to relieve himself. My companion had been warning me for several days that Indians often rob each other and I should always sleep lightly. It was quiet now, deathly silent. I had no idea what time it may have been as a watch was not suitable for my *cholo* garb. I lay on the floor thinking about the meaning of identification. I asked myself again and again what it meant to be identified with this old Quechua Indian who was so far removed from the real world in which I lived.

I was traveling the Indian markets of the Ecuadorean Andes in order to know what really lay hidden in the hearts of these Quechua Indians and Spanish-speaking *cholos.* What was the real longing in their hearts that could be touched? I wanted to know what it was that drunkenness seemed to satisfy. Was the Quechua Indian really the sullen withdrawn personality that he appeared to be before his *patrón?* Was he so adjustable to life conditions that his attitude could incorporate most any conflict without upsetting him seriously? Was he really a good Catholic, a pagan, or what kind of a combination? Why underneath was he so opposed to outward change? What was he talking about and worrying over when he settled down at night in the security of his own little group? I was after the roots that lay behind the outward symbols which could respond to the claims of Christ. The answer to questions like these would form the basis for a missionary theology, a relevant communication to these people's lives. I could see no purpose in putting the Christian proposition before a man unless it was made in such a way that it forced him to struggle with it in terms of surrender to the ultimate and most basic demand that could be placed upon him. In order to know what had to be addressed to the depths of his being I had to wade down to it through what I was convinced were only outward displays of a deeper need in his heart.

A major aspect of the missionary task is the search for what in German is called der Anknüpfungspunkt, connection or point of contact. The proclamation of the gospel aside from such a contact point is a proclamation which skirts missionary responsibility. This is simply the process in which the one who proclaims the good news must make every effort to get into touch with his listener. Man's heart is not a clean slate that the gospel comes and writes upon for the first time. It is a complex which has been scrawled upon and deeply engraved from birth to death. The making of a believer always begins with an unbeliever. Clearly this is the job of the Holy Spirit. However this does not remove man from his position of responsibility. It is man in his

rational hearing and understanding that is awakened to belief. It is the conquering of man's basic deceit that allows the Holy Spirit to lay claim to him and to make of him a new creature. A man must be aware that he stands in defiance of God's call before he can be apprehended by God's love. Before an enemy can be taken captive he must stand in the position of an enemy.

The Forms of Identification

Missionary identification may take on many different forms. It may be romantic or it may be dull. It may be convincing or it may appear as a sham. The central point is that identification is not an end in itself. It is the road to the task of gospel proclamation. Likewise the heart of the controversial matter of missionary identification is not how far one can go but rather what one does with the fruits of identification. Going native is no special virtue. Many missionaries in the humdrum of their daily routine about a school or hospital have awakened men's hearts to the claim of the gospel.

Some so-called identification is misoriented and tends to create the impression that living in a native village or learning the native tongue is automatically the open sesame of the native's heart. It is not the sheer quantity of identification that counts; it is rather the purposeful quality that comprehends man as a responsible being seeking to be in touch with his reality. The limitations for knowing what is this contacted reality are great. The practical obstacles for missionary identification are many. In the pages that follow we shall attempt to outline some of these as we have lived in them and to evaluate the effects of the lack of missionary identification and participation.

Strength of Unconscious Habit

Without doubt the nature of the obstacle to identification is the fact that one has so well learned one's own way of life that he practices it for the most part without conscious reflection. In the case described above the old Quechua Indian Carlos Bawa, the donkey and I had been traveling across the plateau of the Andes spending the days in the markets and the nights cramped into tiny quarters available to itinerant Indians and *cholos* for approximately 10 cents U.S. We had made our way from Riobamba to Baños, a three-day trek by road, and no one except an occasional dog appeared to see that all was not quite normal. It was not until stepping into the candle-lit room of the inn at Baños that I was taken for a foreigner (at least it so appeared). I suspect that it bothered me a great deal because I had created the illusion for a few days that I was finally on the inside of the Indian-*cholo* world looking about and not in the least conspicuous about it. When the innkeeper addressed me as *meester* I had the shock of being rudely dumped outside the little world where I thought I had at last gained a firm entrance.

The following morning I went to the lady innkeeper and sat down at the bar. "Now, tell me, *señora,*" I began, "how did you know I was a *meester* and not a local *señor* or a *cholo* from Riobamba?" The fat little lady's eyes sparkled as she laughed an embarrassed giggle. "I don't know for sure," she replied. I insisted she try to give me the answer, for I was thoroughly confused over it all. I went on. "Now suppose you were a detective, *señora,* and you were told to catch a European man dressed like a poor *cholo* merchant. How would you recognize him

if he came into your inn?" She scratched her head and leaned forward over the counter. "Walk outside and come back in like you did last night." I picked up my old hat, pulled it low on my head, and made for the door. Before I reached the street she called out, "Wait, *señor,* I know now what it is." I stopped and turned around. "It's the way you walk." She broke into a hearty laugh at this point and said, "I never saw anyone around here who walks like that. You Europeans swing your arms like you never carried a load on your back." I thanked the good lady for her lesson in posture and went out in the street to study how the local people walked. Sure enough the steps were short and choppy, the trunk leaning forward slightly from the hips and the arms scarcely moving under their huge ponchos.

Knowing that the squatting position with the poncho draped from ears to the hidden feet was more natural I squatted on the street corner near a group of Indians and listened to them chat. They continued with their conversation and paid no attention to my presence. Two missionaries whom I knew very well emerged from a hotel doorway nearby. I watched them as they swung their cameras about their shoulders and discussed the problem of over-exposure in the tricky Andean sunlight. A ragged *cholo* boy sitting beside me scrambled to his feet, picked up his shoe shine box and approached the pair. He was rebuffed by their nonchalant shaking of the head. As they continued to survey the brilliant market place for pictures the shoe-shine boy returned to his spot beside me. Sitting down he mumbled, "The *señores* who own shoes ought to keep them shined." I leaned toward the boy and beckoned for his ear. He bent over his shoe box as I whispered to him. The boy then jumped back to his feet and started after the pair who were crossing the street. On the other side they stopped and turned to him as he said, "The evangelicals are not respected here unless we see their shoes are shined." One man lifted a foot and rubbed his shoe on his pants cuff, while the other settled down for a toothbrush, spit and polish shine.

I arose, passed within three feet of my friends and took up a listening post in the heart of the busy market where I sat until my legs began to ache. As I got up to my feet I yawned and stretched, and as I began to walk away I noticed I had drawn the attention of those sitting about me. Again I had behaved in a way that felt so natural but in a way which was not like the local folks do. In front of me an old woman dropped a bag of salt. I unthinkingly reached down to help her, and it was only by a bit of providential intervention that I was saved from being hauled off to jail for attempting to steal.

This extremity of identification or disguise may appear as one way of overdoing a good thing. However, only a missionary among the withdrawn highland Quechuas can really appreciate how difficult it is to talk with these people in a situation of equality. I simply could not accept the Quechua's response as being valid and representing his real self as long as he was talking to the *patrón*. I wanted to hear him without a *patrón* present and I wanted to be addressed stripped of that feudal role which I was sure completely colored our relationship. I found that the submissive, sluggish Indian whom I had known in my role of *patrón* became a scheming, quick-witted person who could be extremely friendly, helpful or cruel depending upon the situation.

Limits of Identification

Perhaps the most outstanding example in which I was reminded of the limitations of identification occurred while we were living in a mud-and-thatch hut near Tabacundo, Ecuador. We had moved into a small scattered farming settlement near the Pisque river about a kilometer from the United Andean Mission for whom we were making a study. My wife and I had agreed that if we were to accomplish anything at the U.A.M. we would have to settle among the people and somehow get them to accept us or reject us. We were accepted eventually but always with reservations. We wore nothing but Indian clothes and ate nothing but Indian food. We had no furniture except a bed made of century plant stalks covered with a woven mat exactly as in all the Indian houses. In fact, because we had no agricultural equipment, weaving loom, or granary, our one-room house was by far the most empty in the vicinity. In spite of this material reduction to the zero point the men addressed me as *patroncito*. When I objected that I was not a *patrón* because I owned no land they reminded me that I wore leather shoes. I quickly exchanged these for a pair of locally made *alpargatas* which have a hemp fiber sole and a woven cotton upper. After a time had passed I noticed that merely changing my footwear had not in the least gotten rid of the appellation of *patroncito*. When I asked again the men replied that I associated with the Spanish townspeople from Tabacundo. In so doing I was obviously identifying myself with the *patrón* class. I made every effort for a period to avoid the townspeople, but the term *patroncito* seemed to be as permanently fixed as it was the day we moved into the community.

The men had been required by the local commissioner to repair an impassable road connecting the community and Tabacundo. I joined in this work with the Indians until it was completed two months later. My hands had become hard and calloused. One day I proudly showed my calloused hands to a group of men while they were finishing the last of a jar of fermented *chicha*. "Now, you can't say I don't work with you. Why do you still call me *patroncito*?" This time the truth was near the surface, forced there by uninhibited alcoholic replies. Vicente Cuzco, a leader in the group, stepped up and put his arm around my shoulder and whispered to me. "We call you *patroncito* because you weren't born of an Indian mother." I needed no further explanation.

Ownership of a Gun

Living in an African village caused us to become aware of the effect of other formative attitudes in our backgrounds. One of these in particular is the idea of personal ownership. While living in the south Cameroun village of Aloum among the Bulu in order to learn the language, we had been received from the first day with intense reception and hospitality. We were given Bulu family names; the village danced for several nights and we were loaded with gifts of a goat and all kinds of tropical foods.

We had been invited to live in Aloum and we were not fully prepared psychologically to understand how such an adoption was conceived within Bulu thinking. Slowly we came to learn that our possessions were no longer private property but were to be available for the collective use of the sub-clan where we had been adopted. We were able to adjust to this way of doing because we had about the same material status as the others in the village. Their demands upon our things were not as great as their generous hospitality with which they provided nearly all of our food.

Then one night I caught a new vision of the implication of our relation to the people of Aloum. A stranger had appeared in the village and we learned that Aloum was the home of his mother's brother. It was the case of the nephew in the town of his maternal uncle, a most interesting social relationship in the patrilineal societies in Africa. After dark when the leading men in the village had gathered in the men's club house, I drifted over and sat down among them to listen to their conversations. The fires on the floor threw shadows which appeared to dance up and down on the mud walls.

Finally silence fell over their conversations and the chief of the village arose and began to speak in very hushed tones. Several young men arose from their positions by the fires and moved outside to take up a listening post to make sure that no uninvited persons would overhear the development of these important events. The chief spoke of the welcome of his nephew into his village and guaranteed him a safe sojourn while he was there. After these introductory formalities were finished the chief began to extol his nephew as a great elephant hunter. I was still totally ignorant of how all this affected me. I listened as he eulogized his nephew's virtue as a skilled hunter. After the chief finished another elder arose and continued to cite cases in the nephew's life in which he had displayed great bravery in the face of the dangers of the jungles. One after another repeated these stories until the chief again stood to his feet. I could see the whites of his eyes which were aimed at *me*. The fire caused little shadows to run back and forth on his dark face and body. "Obam Nna," he addressed me. A broad smile exposed a gleaming set of teeth. "We are going to present our gun to my nephew now. Go get it."

I hesitated a brief moment but then arose and crossed the moonlit courtyard to our thatch-covered house where Marie and some village women sat talking. I kept hearing in my ears: "We are going to present *our* gun ... our gun ... " Almost as if it were a broken record stuck on the plural possessive pronoun it kept repeating in my ears, "*ngale jangan* ... *ngale jangan* ... " Before I reached the house I had thought of half a dozen very good reasons why I should say no. However I got the gun and some shells and started back to the club house. As I re-entered the room I caught again the sense of the world of Obam Nna. If I were to be Obam Nna I should have to cease to be William Reyburn. In order to be Obam Nna I had to crucify William Reyburn nearly every day. In the world of Obam Nna I no longer owned the gun as in the world of William Reyburn. I handed the gun to the chief and, although he didn't know it, along with it went the surrender of a very stingy idea of private ownership.

Pregnancy Taboos

I had overcome the idea that the gun was mine alone. But the greatest blow was still ahead. The man was an experienced elephant hunter. The last elephant I had seen was in the zoo in Basel, Switzerland. I did not know what was involved, but later in the evening learned that I could not participate in the hunt because Marie was pregnant. I inquired of other expecting fathers in the village and they too were forced to remain behind and they agreed that the elephant hunt was forbidden for an expecting father.

The hunt was successful and the hunters returned with only one round of ammunition expended. The trunk meat was taboo for the expecting couples. A dance was held the night of the kill. Before dawn the following day, the entire village filed out into the jungles to cut up the meat and bring it back. The expectant mothers and fathers were allowed to go this time. However, again we were told where to stand and were warned not to touch the meat. After the head had been cut off and the meat removed by the hunter, the monstrous skull was lying alone to one side. I was dying with curiosity to see how far the bullet had penetrated the skull and whether or not it had reached the tiny brain box.

I moved inconspicuously over to an axe and then when everyone was arguing over a mass of intestines as big as innertubes I quickly lifted the axe and smashed it down into the bloody skull, splitting the frontal section wide open and exposing a mass of cavernous sinus. No sooner had the axe hit the bone than everyone turned around and began to shout at me to stop and get away from the head. As I dropped the axe and moved back toward the group I felt like a school boy who had been caught with his fingers in the pie. I sat down on the grass and watched the men standing to their knees in blood and manure as they hacked away at the meat. An old toothless woman squatted beside me and said, "Obam Nna, always think of your child." I grunted a halfhearted "*ya*" and settled back to watch the gory butchering.

Conflict of Dual Roles

This elephant episode opened up many hidden vistas in the life of Aloum. It disclosed that a neighboring village where the district chief lived was at enmity with Aloum and this chief reported the elephant killing to the French administration, which soon sent a police official to pay me a visit. I was called before the government to explain the whole case. Why had I lent my gun to some Africans when the hunting permit and the gun permit were strictly private? I knew that it would be hopeless to attempt to tell a French administrator that I was really Obam Nna and not William Reyburn when I lent the gun.

A missionary dentist of the Weber Dental Clinic accompanied me on my visit to the administration office. It was, of course, quite incidental that the dentist had just fitted the official with an excellent set of false teeth. Since one of the problems about the killing of the elephant involved the disposition of the elephant's two major teeth, I thought the dentist's contribution would be invaluable. Needless to say, we were not chewed out. The matter was dropped with, "*C'est fini, monsieur.*"

Symbolic Value of Food

Another problem in village participation is the matter of food and water. However, this is not the problem most people think it is. We found while living in Paris that our French friends were often scandalized at the things which we ate. One of the most offensive of these was cheese with pie. I have seen Frenchmen grimace as if in agony upon seeing us combine these two foods.

I have stayed among the Kaka tribe on the open grasslands of the eastern Cameroun, and have made studies among them. The life of these people is quite different from the jungle Bulu of the south. Life on the savanna is more rigorous and results in a different adjustment to natural conditions. Food is much less abundant and cassava is the main staple. Unlike the Bulu who have adopted many European ways the Kaka are more under the influences of Islam which filter down from their cattle-raising Fulani neighbors to the north.

I had gone into the village of Lolo to carry out some studies relative to the translation of the book of Acts and had taken no European food, determined to find what the effects of an all-Kaka diet would be. I attempted to drink only boiled water, but often this was entirely impossible. I found that the simple mixture of cassava flour and hot water to form a mush was an excellent sustaining diet. On one occasion over a period of six weeks on this diet I lost no. weight, had no diarrhea, and suffered no other ill effects. All of this food was prepared by village women and I usually ate on the ground with the men wherever I happened to be when a woman would serve food. On several occasions when I was not in the right place at the right time it meant going to bed with an empty stomach. I carefully avoided asking any woman to prepare food especially for me, as this had a sexual connotation which I did not care to provoke.

Once I had been talking most of the afternoon with a group of Kaka men and boys about foods people eat the world over. One of the young men got his Bulu Bible and read from the 10th chapter of Acts the vision of Peter who was instructed to kill and eat "all manner of four-footed beasts of the earth, and wild beasts, and creeping things, and fowls of the air." This young Kaka who had been for a short while at a mission school said, "The Hausa people don't believe this because they won't eat pigs. Missionaries, we think, don't believe this because they don't eat some of our foods either." I quite confidently assured him that a missionary would eat anything he does.

That evening I was called to the young man's father's doorway, where the old man sat on the ground in the dirt. In front of him were two clean white enamel pans covered by lids. He looked up at me and motioned for me to sit. His wife brought a gourd of water which she poured as we washed our hands. Then flicking wet fingers in the air to dry them a bit, the old man lifted the lid from the one pan. Steam arose from a neatly rounded mass of cassava mush. Then he lifted the lid from the other pan. I caught a glimpse of its contents. Then my eyes lifted and met the unsmiling stare of the young man who had read about the vision of Peter earlier in the afternoon. The pan was filled with singed caterpillars. I swallowed hard, thinking that now I either swallowed these caterpillars, or I swallowed my words and thereby proved again that Europeans have merely adapted Christianity to fit their own selfish way of life. I waited as my host scooped his shovel-like fingers deep into the mush, then with a ball of the

stuff he pressed it gently into the caterpillar pan. As he lifted it to his open mouth I saw the burned and fuzzy creatures, some smashed into the mush and others dangling loose, enter between his teeth.

My host had proven the safety of his food by taking the first portion. This was the guarantee that he was not feeding me poison. I plunged my fingers into the mush but my eyes were fixed on the caterpillars. I wondered what the sensation in the mouth was going to be. I quickly scooped up some of the creeping things and plopped the mass into my mouth. As I bit down the soft insides burst open and to my surprise I tasted a salty meat-like flavor which seemed to give the insipid cassava mush the ingredient that was missing.

We sat silently eating. There is no time for conversation at the Kaka "table" for as soon as the owner has had his first bite male hands appear from every direction and the contents are gone. As we sat eating quickly the old man's three wives with their daughters came and stood watching us from their kitchen doorways. They held their hands up and whispered busily back and forth: "White man Kaka is eating caterpillars. He really has a black heart." The pans were emptied. Each one took a mouthful of water, rinsed his mouth and spat the water to one side, belched loudly, said "Thank you, Ndjambie" (God), arose and departed into the rays of the brilliant setting sun. My notes on that night contain this one line: "An emptied pan of caterpillars is more convincing than all the empty metaphors of love which missionaries are prone to expend on the heathen."

Ideological Insulation

There are other obstacles to missionary participation in native life which arise from background as well as local Christian traditions. It does not take a folk or primitive people long to size up the distance which separates themselves from the missionary. In some cases this distance is negligible but in others it is the separation between different worlds. Missionaries with pietistic backgrounds are prepared to suspect that everything the local people do is bad and that therefore, in order to save them, they must pull them out and set up another kind of life opposed to the original one. This process seldom if ever works, and when it does the result is the creation of a society which consists of converted souls, but no converted life. The missionary under these circumstances takes the path of least resistance, keeps himself untouched by the world and of course does not get into touch with the world in order to save it.

It is not surprising to find that American missionaries make a tradition of this mistake more than do their European colleagues. The missionary who has been brought up in a closed environment in his home town, has gone away to a church college, and proceeded then to a seminary, is usually still blissfully ignorant of the very life of his own country. He carries this wall of insulation from the world to the mission field and surreptitiously invites anyone who dares to slip inside with him. For this poor soul political questions are dangerous, sex is evil, and academic thought is suspect. This is the Christian expression which drives the man to hard work and no play, because again relaxation is an evil pulling of the world from

which he must remain isolated at all costs.

So extreme does this loss of touch with the world become that missions have been guilty of making demands on people that tend to separate them from any hope of living the Christian witness among their own people. An outstanding missionary, who spent fifteen years in the French Cameroun and was awarded the French Legion of Honor for his contribution as director of an industrial school, remarked, "When I was getting ready to go to Africa a dear old Christian woman said, 'Well, whatever you do, Mr. C., get those black people to wear shoes.' "

The children of catechists in one mission in Central Africa are required by the mission rules to wear clothes. The fact that this puts them into a special socio-economic class where they demand more and more money to buy clothes and live up to the class they have been forced into appears to the mission as a wanton materialism. In another mission in French Equatorial Africa all catechists were required recently to sign a statement that if they joined a political party they would lose their jobs. These same missionaries most likely never voted themselves in an election and now they are asking their converts to take up the same ignorant attitude toward the State which they have.

It is little wonder therefore that the French administration conceives of much of Protestant mission work in Africa as the attempt to form *un état dans l'état,* 'a state within a state.'

The closed-mind attitude toward the world can be transmitted to converts just as effectively as an open attitude which seeks to be in touch with the world. I witnessed this in particular in an inter-mission college in West Africa when I was invited to lecture to the students and to discuss problems of African culture and Christianity with the faculty members. The African members of the faculty who had been educated in the closed-mind attitude of their missionary fathers found themselves emotionally upset and unable to discuss objectively such matters as the relation of polygamy and witchcraft to Christianity because for them it was "throwing the door open," a phrase which reveals the hermetically sealed world in which they live. African teachers brought up under a different tradition found the discussions helpful and interesting and were not seized by fear in discussing the issues.

It is not surprising to find that the missionary isolation attitude produces its effects in every realm of activity when it is present. It may be seen in everything from architecture to Bible translation and language learning. One of the most conspicuous examples is the "hill top" mission station. In many areas of Africa a mission station may be located miles from the people just to be up on the top of an isolated hill where it is "healthy." The process which follows on this assumption is the creation of an artificial society the members of which depend upon some form of employment at the mission. As soon as the jobs are finished the folk move off and the station sits alone like a specter in the desert with a few hangers-on who still hope for some as yet unsatiated spiritual or material reward.

Separation from the world has been a key note in the missionary message and is a key note in the gospel. However, the way in which that separation is approached determines largely how the "separation" is effected. One of the neatest cases of literal separation which has taken place in the African churches is the matter of the African's world of the supernatural and the Christian world of the same. Because the real African thought world was often assigned by the missionary to a category that was meaningless to the African, the latter has kept his own beliefs in mysterious phenomena in one hand and Christianity in the other. That he should allow the two to confront each other again strikes him as mingling with the world, even his own world.

Linguistic Effects of Insulation

In the field of Scripture translation the attitude we are describing here has the tendency to want to "purify" the language. This purification may be in making the irregular forms to behave more regularly. This is in conformity with the closed-mind psychology which sees the world as a simple closed system which avoids serious consideration of fundamental problems. This frame of mind is happiest at being tone deaf as this eliminates another problem in learning to speak the language.

But much more serious is the fact that this way of life and thought is usually out of touch with the reality between the life of the people and the language. It is interesting in what may appear as a contradiction to this statement that in the French Cameroun the American missionaries know the languages but not the people, while the French missionaries know the people but not the languages. The reason for this is largely that the Americans learn the African languages but remain aloof from the African's social and thought world. The French are more interested in the African's thought and perception of things and can know this, even if inadequately, through the French language.

In the matter of selecting terms from pagan life, there being no other life, the closed attitude prefers to concoct a meaningless term or rehash something with an obscure meaning than to take over and convert an outright pagan term with religious nuances. In this mental posture the fear of the pagan religious term is very much justified because the translator has no plan of remaining in touch with the pagan world to grapple with it and to win over through close contact and give and take the Christian value of the pagan religious complex.

An excellent case of the retreat from the pagan complex in translation of the Bible is found in a language of the French Cameroun. The earlier translators often avoided the use of terms which might carry a pagan connotation. The substituted terms were used to educate the young. However the older people made much use of the pagan terms in their own comprehension of the Christian life and in the development of their own spiritual experiences as Christians. The missionary inventions remained foreign to the older generation and the younger ones learned to use them as words but with little meaning.

As the vernacular Scriptures among the young people are being replaced by the French, the result is a gradation of three levels all out of touch with each other. A new revision is badly needed. The older people insist on going back to former pagan expressions avoided by the missionaries. Most of these are half meaningless to the middle age group and totally meaningless to the younger generation. While the matter of translation is exceedingly technical and cannot be guided by one over-all principle, it may be seen that the avoidance of the point of contact, the retreat from the struggle with the world, can have disastrous effects even in such matters as the translation of the Scriptures.

Freedom to Witness

The Christian church sealed off from the world becomes unintelligible to the world it attempts to reach. It is like the father who can never remember how to be a child and therefore is looked upon as a foreigner by his children. Missionary participation and identification are not produced by a study of anthropology but by being freed through the Spirit of the Lord to witness to the truth of the gospel in the world.

Christianity calls men into a brotherhood in Christ, but at the same time Christians often negate that call by separating mechanisms which run the gamut from food taboos to racial fear. The Christian gospel is foreign enough to the selfcenteredness of man's view of the universe. However, before this misconception of the self can be corrected, there is a barrier that must be penetrated. In Christian terminology it is the cross which leads man from his walled-up self out into the freedom for which he was intended. There yet is another foreignness which must be overcome through sacrifice of one's own way of thinking and doing things. Christianity cannot be committed to one expression of civilization or culture. The missionary task is that of sacrifice. Not the sacrifice of leaving friends and comfortable situations at home, but the sacrifice of reexamining one's own cultural assumptions and becoming intelligible to a world where he must *not* assume that intelligibility is given.

Missionaries have often said that they were not aware of certain misinterpretations of their message because no one had made a study of it. While it is nice to make studies of things, this is a misconception of the missionary task. The responsible missionary who seeks through identification to communicate in comprehensible terms and ways of thought does so simply because for him his task is conceived as a two-way communication. He is in a search *with* the person concerned. He sees his job as becoming "converted" to the local way of things in his process to convert. The point of contact means a *seeking with* which reveals to the sensitive missionary the restructured meaning of his message.

In order that this not be construed as a sales talk for lessons in the cultures of man, it should be pointed out that science is not the motivation for such a conception of the missionary task. An understanding of cultures and peoples is not a guarantee for a proper conception of the missionary task. However, such studies are of extreme value when added to a personal sacrifice dimension as has been mentioned above.

In the areas of the world where I have seen Christian churches at work I often have the impression that Christianity is most successful where the learning of Westernization is the most complete. This situation does not in the least reflect the fact that Christianity is part and parcel of Western civilization. It exhibits rather the poverty of the Western churches in proclaiming the gospel and their self-imposed restrictions in their relationship to the freedom of the gospel. The scrip-

ture verse which places the gospel in dependence on the Spirit of God ("And where the Spirit of the Lord is, there is liberty," II Cor. 3: 17) becomes instead "and where the Christian missionary church is, there is a Western authority." The term "West" is, of course, a vague one, for in one case it means Rome and in another New York and in still another Fergass Falls, Minnesota.

Authority and Liberty

The question of authority becomes exceedingly important in the matter of the missionary task. In the closed attitude there is no room for critical questions. Often the missionizing task is carried out in the same way in which the loving parent in the tropics pushes the anti-malarial pill down the throat of the kicking child. The catechism asks the question and then proceeds to give its own answers. The would-be convert is seldom led to ask his own questions and there are often only authoritative and irrelevant answers available for his personal queries. This is particularly true in Protestantism where, due no doubt to its numerous conflicting doctrines, it seeks to make of its own doctrines a rigid form of authority. In so doing this attitude often leads its converts to the Roman Catholic faith where the confused Protestant convert can find a unified authority. This is so since the convert has been prepared to believe and accept authority.

That this attitude has been allowed to convert great numbers in Africa to Protestantism should not be misunderstood. In the past the Protestant divisions of authority were coexistent with tribal separations. People from distant tribes did not have much occasion to compare notes. Today, however, the African story passes into a new chapter. Old isolations are outmoded. People from far corners are thrown together in towns and cities, commercial and industrial centers. What has once been accepted as authority is now viewed as a relative conflict of opinion. In the cities this has resulted for some in a clinging to the tribal church if there is one available. More common is the desire to shrug off the entire matter of the conflict and to cease to have any church connection, or to resolve the conflict by placing oneself under the authoritarian wings of the Catholic church. The latter is extremely common, especially in countries of French background where the Catholic church appears to fit into the new cultural development of the country.

The essence of this problem is the *fear of freedom* on the part of Western missionary organizations and the resultant mistaken conception of authority acquired by many African churches. The general tendency of the planting of the Christian church in Africa has been to deny the freedom which belongs to the gospel, and in the African's eyes this denial has caused the African church to conceive of the Western church as totally authoritarian in nature. In many parts of Africa there is little difference between a Christian church and the law of the Old Testament. Infractions of one of the ten commandments may be written on the back of a church member's communion card, and he is then denied the holy communion for a given period of time, his sentence. It is precisely at the point where the African Christian stands in need of grace that he is denied it by the authority of the church. It is little wonder, then, that when one African church was recently granted its inde-pendent status the Africans conceived of this movement as a wrenching of authority from the hands of the mother church rather than a joy at the birth of a young church.

Missionary identification begins always with love and ends with love. One can-not be free to participate in the life of a group of primitive Africans as long as one approaches his missionary vocation as that of authority divorced from liberty. A false conception of authority and liberty prepares the missionary to fall under the spell of the superiority of his own way of thinking and doing. True Christian liberty is to be freed from oneself and placed at the disposal of God's love and call.

Identification and Taboo

An inevitable question arises in con-nection with missionary participation and identification. What about all those pagan taboos, those mistaken and evil ways of doing things? Are you not openly con-doning sin by not raising your voice and expressing your judgment on those men who forbade you to touch the ele-phant skull? The answer can only be partially given. The truth is that the African Christian often lives half under-ground because he believes in the existence of a spirit world which missionaries ascribe to foolish superstitions or the devil. It has been the naïve Western assumption that given enough education those ideas would all disappear.

Modern educated Africa witnesses to a deeper understanding of nonrational phenomena than its Western fathers. Education and labeling things as super-stitious have not succeeded in radically upsetting the African view. The Western Christian may admit certain aspects of the Africans' "other spiritual" life if it is demonstrated through rational method or argument. However, such argument is beside the point to the African. That which is a living reality needs no proof from rational explanation and theory. African thought finds no great wonder at the miracles of the New Testament. They are not a thing which needs to be explained to be able to accept. Since he is predisposed by a certain cultural orientation toward the nonrational, a senseless dimension is inserted in attempting to *explain* such things from the Western point of view. More distrust and lack of confidence have been created because of the missionaries' loss of a belief in the mysterious than in any other aspect of missionary-African relations. The result on the part of the missionary is to distrust the African as a superstitious mystic, and for the African to conceive of the missionary as a secular materialistic Christian.

The Christian African must be made to feel free to make his decisions about such things. The missionary must have sufficient faith that he is willing to run the risk of freedom in Christ. To condemn him and make authoritarian decisions for him is to rob the Spirit of the Lord the right to perform this task. Just as modern Africa must be able to dispose of its political liberty, so must African Christians be at liberty in spirit to develop a genuine spiritual orientation instead of merely chafing under an authoritarian imposition.

A missionary theology asks this question: "At what points in this man's heart does the Holy Spirit challenge him to surrender?" The missionary task is to ferret out this point of contact through identification with him. The basis of missionary identification is not to make the "native" feel more at home around a foreigner nor to ease the materialistic conscience of the missionary but to create a *communication* and a *communion* where together they seek out what Saint Paul in II Corinthians 10:5 calls the "arguments and obstacles" — "We destroy arguments and every proud obstacle to the knowledge of God, and take every thought captive to obey Christ." This is the basis for a missionary science, the Biblical foundation of a missionary theology and the *raison d'être* of the missionary calling in which one seeks, even in the face of profound limitations, to identify oneself in the creation of new creatures in a regenerate communion.

William D. Reyburn

Identification —
Symptom or Sublimation?

Two years ago, Dr. Reyburn presented an article entitled "Identification in the Missionary Task."[1] *There he described personal experiences in the field and pointed out some of the limitations encountered in identifying. That article emphasized the need for close contact between sender and receiver in the process of communication. There was a protest launched against pietism which tends to put man out of touch with the world about him.*

In his present paper Reyburn focuses upon some of the motivations for identification, particularly guilt, as experienced consciously or unconsciously by middle-class American missionaries. In so doing he is not trying to discourage missionaries from identification. Looking at the problem from another point of view does not make the first view untrue, but it is simply another perspective on complex behavior. Why do some people seem driven to identification while others shun it?

THE THESIS of this article is that missionary identification with native peoples is one of many means through which one may seek consciously or unconsciously to alleviate guilt. Discussions of identification usually conclude that it is largely a psychological matter. Is psychological identification the end product of "identification" kinds of behavior, or are not psychological forces at work deeply within us producing in some individual personalities a tendency to attach themselves to the local native community? When the question is put in this way we are free to examine the problem of identification as the result or product of some *personality variable,* and in this case it will be assumed that this is basically a conscious or unconscious feeling of guilt.

The analysis of this subject must of necessity be viewed from within the cultural values of the middle-class American, not only because the writer is best acquainted with that value system but also because the people who have been observed in identification are also from that group. An analysis of missionaries from a wider range of cultural backgrounds would contribute greatly to our understanding of this phenomenon. I have had opportunity to discuss at length these matters with German and French missionaries, but special investigations would be required in order to ascertain how general this picture is.

Guilt Feelings

When discussing guilt it should be emphasized that human beings may have deep unconscious guilt which may result from numerous repressed childhood mem-

[1] PA, Vol. 7, No. 1 (Jan.-Feb. 1960), pp. 1-15.

ories. In addition to this unconscious guilt there is also a certain amount of guilt in all of us which lies much closer to the surface of our everyday lives. The circumstances which produced the original guilt feelings may be personal as well as cultural. Probably in no event can the personal ones be separated from the cultural. If little Johnny becomes guilt-ridden for his masturbation, he shares such a feeling with untold numbers of people in his culture where a *sinful act* is assigned to masturbation. If we set down side by side Mr. Average American Missionary and Mr. Average African Villager and then examine the former's system of value, we ask what exists in the former's cultural baggage which could conceivably add to the weight of his guilt as he sits facing his peasant contemporary. Here is a suggested list:

1. He cannot disengage himself from the contradiction of the poor Christ and his own wealth.

2. He believes in a mechanical universe regulated by infallible laws of nature which are subject to divine intervention. Technology is the means for happy living.

3. He believes that generosity is a characteristic of a good person.

4. He believes in the myth of his own classless society.

5. He has renounced the major means for status seeking in his own society.

6. He has separated himself from his own friends and relatives at home.

7. He sees himself potentially separated from his own children for the sake of their acquiring some of the values which may cause him his greatest guilt. Children must be educated.

8. Where there are no visible signs of wealth, of industry, of progress and activity, he sees failure. The barefoot, half-clothed peasant is consciously or unconsciously categorized as failure.

9. He is a product of a nation which is characterized by mobility. Three million people live in trailer houses and a majority of the population is on the constant move.

10. He is in direct contact with a society which lives under the strain of the quest for space and the psychology of escape.

11. He possesses a concept of time which dominates and determines the amount and kind of contact he will be allowed with the local people.

12. He values individuality and competition as a normal relation between individuals. Interpersonal relations should be informal.

13. His ideal is that marriage should be permanent and that monogamy, if not divinely right, is at least humanistically correct.

14. He believes that all men are (or should be) equal. Egalitarianism.

15. He believes that all things should serve practical ends. Utilitarianism.

16. Segregation to him is rationalized as right or it is *sinfully* wrong.

17. He sees the reduction of the American Indian as a sin committed in American history.

18. He sees the world as a conflict of nations and power blocs edging constantly nearer the precipice.

19. He is a missionary in order to convert people to Christ and to establish a community of believers. Success tends to be counted in numbers.

20. He believes that his denominational expression of his Protestant belief is (at least for the folks at home) the correct one. He feels himself spiritually closest to outsiders who share his own eschatological theories and religious rituals. Iden-

tification with a religious body has been historically an American value and continues today in the three-way belonging value of Protestant, Catholic, Jew.[2]

Mac[3] in Action

It remains now to show that some of the cultural values and actions listed above may in certain situations contribute to or give rise to feelings of guilt. The certain situations mentioned are those face-to-face relations of our hypothetical middle-class American male missionary with his African friend. An examination of the twenty statements given above shows that they may be grouped into four major, albeit overlapping, classes. Numbers 1 to 3 are largely economic, 4 to 15 are mainly associated with social life, 16 to 18 make up a category of group conflicts, and 19 and 20 are primarily religious.

Group I, Nos. 1 to 3 (Economic). Mac finds it not a little distressing to preach and teach about the homeless Christ who had no place to lay his head when Mac slumbers sumptuously in a comfortable hilltop residence complete with fans, or even air conditioning, and other twentieth-century luxuries. He usually manages to shove such ideas into

---

[2] Will Herberg, *Protestant - Catholic - Jew, An Essay in American Religious Sociology* (New York: Anchor Books, 1960).

[3] In the paragraphs which follow there appears a hypothetical character called Mac, a middle-class American. Mac is admittedly a gross distortion, one complex personality into which are rolled more anxieties than perhaps any one human being could possibly have. No one individual, and certainly not a missionary, is represented in poor pathetic Mac. He is simply useful as a background character upon whom we may project some of the guilt situations which are possible but not necessarily characteristic or representative of any one real person.

the momentary limbo of his mind by recalling that his brother, an executive in General Electric, has two television sets, two cars, and a swimming pool. Mac's mail often comforts him, too, when he reads in the ladies' circle letter reminders that Mac is really suffering out in the dark continent. Mac knows also that it is due primarily to technology that he should live as a son of the modern era. It is technology that has provided this mechanical way of life and these time-saving devices. There is also the matter of American generosity which should not be forgotten. "For, after all, isn't America the land known for its incomparable, outflowing generosity? What other nation, what other people in history, has given away so many dollars. shiploads of wheat, tons of butter, milk, and ammunition? Settle down, Mac, and forget it, old boy. Don't let these crazy ideas get under your skin!" Mac shakes it all off with a shrug of the shoulders and hurries back to work. However, after his little conversation with himself, Mac finds he gradually develops a poor appetite and a funny pain in his stomach. None of the mission doctors can find a trace of the cause of poor Mac's complaints.

Group II, Nos. 4 to 15 (Social). Mac looks at the local society as being too stiff. There are those big chiefs that make him disgusted. The people haven't any courage or they wouldn't grovel like worms on the ground when they want to talk with the chief. They even put their hands over their mouths sometimes when they talk to Mac and he can't understand what they are saying. Mac knows you don't crawl on your stomach in America when you meet someone who is important. Be that as it may, sometimes Mac dreams about his brother. It's a real

queer dream and Mac tells it to everybody on the station. Mac sees a Jacob's
ladder all lit up with bright (General
Electric) lights. Mac stands at the bottom
of the ladder and at the top he can see
his brother laughing and waving down
to him. "It is a strange dream," laughs
Mac. "I can't get on to the steps of the
ladder and the harder I try the brighter
the lights grow and the more my brother
howls with laughter." It may be just
coincidental but Mac traveled two hundred miles recently to buy a chief's stool.[4]
He sent it to his brother for his birthday.
Mac hasn't consciously forgotten that the
opportunity for the status seeker is very
slim out in the African bush.

Mac has other dreams, too. The one
he likes to relate the most is the one he
tells to the natives. When the local folk
begin to give interpretations to dreams,
Mac always manages to moralize his and
at the same time show how they should
interpret their dreams. In Mac's dream he
sees his mother calling to him from across
a crocodile-infested river. After racing
madly up and down the river bank looking for a place to dive in, Mac finally in
fearless abandon throws himself in among
the crocodiles. Much to his chagrin he
comes up safely in the arms of his father
who cautions him to return to the bank
and forget his mother's pleas. Separation
from family and loved ones may not pass
without leaving its traces on the subconscious.

Mac and Mrs. Mac have four lovely
children. At the tender age of six each
of the children has said good-bye to
Mommy and Daddy and bravely gone
off to live in a missionary children's

school dormitory. Mrs. Mac agrees that
she has more time to give to the teaching of the local women, but her life is
empty until the children come home for
vacation. Mac has been inwardly uneasy
about the children's absence from the
home because he himself never left his
parental home until he was twenty-six.
Mrs. Mac has acquired in the children's
absence two dogs, three cats, a dozen
chickens, and a chimpanzee.

Mac is good worker. He is punctual
and expects the local teachers and catechists to be the same. He often discourses
to the natives on how high a skyscraper
ten villages could build with the man
hours that are wasted on marriage talking
in palaver houses. Everywhere he goes
he is in a rush. On several occasions
courageous natives have lectured him
on the ruinous effect his scurrying about
has on the confidence of the people. "We
can't believe that you care for us nor
that God has time for us either because
your God must be always in a hurry
to go somewhere else." This smarted for
days under Mac's thickening skin, but,
"like everything else," Mac says, "you
forget it and go on about your business."

Mac has always been strong on
competitive sports and has encouraged
them among his school boys at the station.
Says Mac, "When these boys come into
the station there is no individuality in
them. We make individuals in our school.
Every boy must learn to sink or swim
on his own." Mac's good wife eventually
pointed out to him that he was merely
coaxing the boys to transfer their dependency from their village relatives to
the mission, but the mission was unable
to shoulder the responsibility. Mac's latest
dreams have been of a huge apple tree
standing at the top of a mound. Around

---

[4] The chief's stool is a symbol of his status
and authority in many West African groups.
It is his "throne."

about beneath the tree hundreds of poorly clad children are running and clapping their hands, trying to shake down the fruit. Mac continues to deny his wife's obviously true interpretation of the dream. All Mac will grumble is, "Imagine *me* an apple tree!"

There are two counts on which Mac is deathly critical of the local people. The first is the looseness of marriage, along with the fact that polygamy is the desired form of marriage union. The second is the fact that the people enjoy talking incessantly about some local affair without apparently putting any action to their words. Mac often takes to the Sunday pulpit and harangues for an hour against the iniquitous immorality which has debased and degraded the folks. So vehement and eloquent are his tirades that the people absorb it all with rapt attention. They had never imagined that one could discourse so effectively on a subject so prosaic. Following his vindictive sermon, Mac, now drenched in perspiration and self-righteousness, walks to his house with a visiting friend and slips on his own tongue when he turns to his guest and says "Say, did you feel, I mean *see*, that woman on the front row?" With such clear evidence as this it will not be necessary to look further into Mac's naughty dreams.

Group III. Nos. 16 to 18 (Group conflicts). Mac hails from the Deep South. He has always been taught that darkies are not full-fledged human beings and should not contaminate white folks by getting too close. He has heard from his grandma that most of the colored folks have a sickness which can be had from toilet seats. It seems only natural that white men and black men should live apart. The fact is, it would simply be against the laws of nature for them to do otherwise — and the laws of nature are very fixed in Mac's little world. Mac is educated, and in his education he learned that the dark-skinned people are born to be servants and he just sort of feels that the Bible backs him up. In spite of all this Mac now finds himself in Africa where he experiences generous hospitality from black-skinned people. His very life is saved by Africans during a house fire. His children grow up playing together daily with African children and on one occasion he seriously considered adopting an African child. Young Africans come to him with newspaper accounts of the racial antagonism in America and ask him if it is true. He is caught again and again in the crossfire of contradiction which makes his sleep at times very restless.

At times Mac finds himself going far out of his way to do a kind deed for a total stranger. Once he stayed out all night in the rain waiting to cross a flood-swollen river to transport a sick baby to the hospital. As he sat out the long night in the cold and miserable forest his mind went back many times, with no apparent reason, to the novels of his childhood which depicted the massacre of Indians on the western U.S. frontier. He recalled as a boy asking his father who would be punished for killing all those Indians. His father's reply was a kind of prophetic silence. In these same still moments of quiet meditation so far removed from the struggle for power that grips the world, Mac often viewed with sympathy and admiration the tranquillity and peace that slowly pulsated in the heart of the African forest.

Group IV, Nos. 19 and 20 (Religious).
Mac is above all a missionary, and he came to Africa with a very clearly defined mission. He was to win converts to Christ and establish a church of believers. As the years slipped quickly by Mac began to see that his reports to the home board were losing contact with reality. The figures for conversions were merely last year's figures arranged in a different order. But Mac could take some consolation. He was on four more committees, a fact which he readily exploited in his form letters sent to his constituency. In desperation for converts Mac became an indefatigable organizer of evangelistic thrusts. While few of these made any dent on the natives, the activity did receive considerable credit from some fellow missionaries and provided some copy for the hungry church journals at home. In spite of all this, the result on Mac was to pray harder, longer, louder, and more often, and, when given the opportunity, to gush out cascades of verbal condemnation on the Africans for their absolute lack of conscience. In this same connection Mac often had dreams about being a salesman. He would ring the door bell and when the lady of the house came (she was always black) and refused to buy his product, Mac would throw a rock through the window and run.

Mac's home church was very exclusive. It was not only anti-ecumenical but severely castigated any of its members who married into another denomination. On the field the exclusive nature of the home church was reflected in numerous ways. For example, believers moving into Mac's area from another part of the country and coming from another church had to be re-baptized in order to enter this highly endogamous ecclesiastical circle. In the early years in Africa this never bothered Mac, but as he was forced by circumstances to rub shoulders with other missions, his own orientation became a source of disgust. Consequently, Mac finally achieved a broader concept of the Christian church, but for the sake of the home folks he continued to hew to the party line, and at the end of each six months he could push his schizoid button and eloquently and mechanically write the home church board what they wanted most to hear.

Guilt as Motivation

Having dissected Mac and found him full of contradictions and perhaps guilt, we now return to the matter which prompted this circuitous journey, identification. Let us assume now that Mac or someone like him carries a certain load of guilt which may be conscious or unconscious. We ask how this could be a cause for his identification with the local people. It should be remembered that in asking the question this way we are picking out only one of a great variety of outlets (escapes) which are available. He could turn in on himself, become involved with the mission body, seek sublimation though a variety of activities such as teaching, preaching, writing, traveling through the bush, and a host of others. The act of identification is a particularly important sublimation as it relates to his missionary vocation more overtly than does, say, making bows and arrows to send to the boys and girls at home. It is also very significant because it will vastly affect the kind of communication that goes on between Mac and the people.

It will not be necessary to trace through

the identificational potentialities contained in each of the twenty categories listed above. Let it suffice to follow up a few of them. Take, for instance, the matter of marriage. Let us suppose that Mac comes from a broken family and unhappiness. When Mac sees that local marriages are of the same kind as his own parents' failure, he may withdraw from the native situation and identify himself with the stable missionary body. But suppose that Mac himself has been divorced. He knows the sorrow of a broken family and unhappy marriage. He may react by identifying himself with the natives, since he feels a strong bond of sympathy for their problems. In so doing it may be the condemnation of the native marriages he hears from his colleagues which pushes him to associate closely with the natives. When his colleague criticizes the native marriage situation he may at the same time be condemning Mac, who consequently feels drawn to the side of the guilty.

A missionary I once knew who exhibited some paranoid tendencies became very much loved by the Africans. This man, a medical doctor, in his own paranoia associated himself very closely with Africans who in his eyes were the objects (himself) of his missionary colleague's criticism.

There is the case of the missionary who for some reason (and it is probably guilt) finds himself at odds with the rules which govern his own society. He turns and sees that these rules do not apply within the native society and so he makes an escape from his own into the other. This may be motivated from a desire to escape anything from taxes to monogamy.

I once met a man living with a native woman in the jungles of Nicaragua who said to me, "Mister, if you ever find an American down in these parts living like I am, he's either had trouble with the law or with a woman." I raised an eyebrow and looked at him questioningly, and he added, "Brother, I ain't had no trouble with the law."

It is even possible that the man who severely censures such things as extramarital sex relations, drunkenness, prostitution, and polygamy will be the one who is most closely identified with the people. What he may be condemning is his own propensity for these very things. By closely associating with the people involved he is vicariously satisfying a desire to commit these acts.

There is the case of the missionary who so earnestly believed that society should have no class distinctions that he identified very closely with the local people whom, he believed, had no such distinctions. On the other hand, a closer look at this man showed that he believed all men should be equal and himself a bit more than equal. In his own society he could not be on the top. But in this little primitive world he was king and the rest were equals, a happy solution for him. Everyone but his wife and children thought he was a true democrat.

Jockeying for position often takes place within the missionary body. Many missions consciously or otherwise have traditionally acknowledged this state of affairs and have drawn two lines forming three classes: young missionaries, old missionaries, and candidates for old missionaries. It is interesting to note how frequently those queer souls who "go native" are outside on the slippery periphery of the missionary circle. Where status seeking even in the missionary body is renounced one can often find such renouncers fancifully perched on the top of some native village hierarchy.

The guilt which arises within the breast of many American missionaries due to the segregation problem may force some to seek an abnormally attached relation to Negro people. In order to right the boat they find themselves dangerously and awkwardly leaning over backwards. No one senses this unnatural relation more than the people who are the victims of such pretentious friendship.

The missionary who dashes about the country to take "furlough pictures" just before going home typifies in a sense the psychology of the guilt report. This is a statistically loaded sheet which assures the home folks that they have not sent a dud to the mission field. Its origin is probably in guilt and in some cases its contents gives rise to new sources of guilt. There is nothing quite so good as a few weeks in the bush "to catch the atmosphere" before furlough. Also, this kind of identification may upgrade one in the missionary body since "you'd be surprised how it will improve your presentation." For the home-bound news letter it is a sure punch in an otherwise mass of monotonous trivia.

Whether identification is a symptom or a sublimation is difficult to say without knowing the circumstances in each case. However, there is sufficient reason to believe that much that goes on under the term identification can be traced back to feelings of guilt which find an escape if not a genuine sublimation in identification.

William D. Reyburn

The Helping Relationship in Missionary Work

A relationship with others which will permit us to help them at the deepest personal level of their need requires that we accept ourselves as we are. The maintenance of distance by manner of life, by a judgmental attitude, or by an impersonal, official relationship may protect our precarious self-image, but it also projects to the other our rejection of him. A helping relationship requires that we be open enough to be vulnerable which we will be unwilling to be if we unconsciously reject ourselves.

PSYCHOTHERAPISTS, particularly in the school of client-centered therapy, have gained some powerful insights which have a direct relevance to missionary work.[1] A basic concept which they employ, although it would sound very ancient to readers of the New Testament, is that the most helpful way to change a man is to accept him as he is, with "unconditional positive regard." A missionary might quite rightly object, asking: "How can I possibly accept what I know to be wrong?" Since this question tends to leap over the heads of a number of more challenging problems, and thereby avoids personal involvement, I prefer to deal with it after the content of the helping relationship has been established, for the question of how one can accept what is held to be wrong depends, at least

in part, on what we will come to understand by *acceptance* as a process in the helping relationship.

What, then, is a helping relationship? It is one I enter with another person and in which I maintain for that other an unconditional positive regard, free of self-aggrandizing goals, and with a desire to see the other made fully free to become what his and my Creator has created *us* potentially to be.

A helping relationship can never be a state of things, but a dynamic *process*, one which places me in a difficult (impossible is too strong) position, for if my goal is to free him to become what the Creator has potentially made him to become, I am in some way linked up with him

An earlier draft of this paper was read to a conference of the Evangelical Fellowship for Missionary Studies, London, January, 1969. I am indebted to Dr. Jacob Loewen for helpful discussions of its content.

[1] This view of psychotherapy is best set forth in Carl R. Rogers *On Becoming a Person, a Therapist's view of Psychotherapy* (Boston: Houghton Mifflin Co., 1961).

in *our freedom*. This is why my self-interest goals are always in conflict with the helping relationship and constantly threaten to sabotage it. The other is aware of my weakness. It communicates with his own. It suggests that I do not accept him. He knows our relationship is fragile, delicate to the point of vanishing like a handful of dust tossed into the wind. The sum total of all that threatens a human relationship is *rejection*, the opposite of acceptance.

How We Reject Others.

Every human relationship balances delicately between acceptance and rejection but rejection is accomplished with far less effort. It gives one a a false sense of freedom, at least in the sense of avoiding personal involvement with the other. Rejection simplifies (and cheapens) interpersonal relationships in that the temptation to manipulate the other for self-seeking ends is removed, or at least put off for a time. Rejection in interpersonal relations is very similar to entropy in communication. Entropy is the tendency to disorganization. The struggle against it requires the constant expenditure of energy so that information can get through. Rejection is far easier than acceptance — it can be accomplished by mere indifference — and is communicated effectively to the other with little expenditure of effort. No wonder we can all do it so wonderfully well.

How does rejection work in practical situations? There are countless ways; they operate for the most part at a symbolic level, and the rejector may or may not be concious of communicating rejection. During the Second World War Jewish prisoners were often dehumanized by their guards, probably as a defence mechanism for the guards as much as a rejection of the Jews. They called the Jews "pigs" and often to demean them they threw stones at them to get their attention, rather than calling them by their numbers. The attack of these stones upon the human dignity of the Jewish prisoners was far greater than the pain of being struck by the stones.

Missionaries have never in my experience thrown stones at native peoples. They are more likely to have stones thrown at them but sometimes missionaries do consciously or unconsciously practise rejection of the people among whom they labor. Here are some ways:

Manner of life: It may appear exaggerated to say that a mission station with its well groomed lawns, flowering hedges, and comfortable bungalows could serve as symbolic rejection. Nevertheless, a standard of life characteristic of many mission stations is a communicating environment which says something very forcefully to a people whose natural environment is a major aspect of their communication world. One need not be a disciple of McLuhan to see that the Eiffel Tower standing high over Paris communicates its distinctiveness with the rest of the buildings of that city. It is not sufficient to say, as some have claimed, that the local people are ear-oriented and, therefore, these mission station complexes are not really noticed. The ear-orientation school is unable to explain how and why the local people make adaptations in their houses of things seen on the mission station and why, when the local church becomes independent, the mission station is often the prize grab.

Most of the mission station complex as environment is impersonal: grass, houses, roads, refrigerators, etc., but the food that is prepared and eaten belongs to a more personal and even more meaningful symbolic level of rejection. This applies not only to the foreign food, but to the entire complex of ritual and etiquette employed in preparing and consuming it — much more difficult for our own children to learn acceptably well than the liturgy of the church.

There is probably no way that a missionary can express rejection more forcefully than in failure to eat native food in a native context. If it were only a matter of sampling a bite for good relations, there would be no problem. However, what counts is that the local people be convinced that the food or drink was enjoyed. This requires a great deal more energy than "having a go at a spoonful."

Language: The systematic wrenching of a language over a period of years is a stone of rejection thrown against the shrine of a people's soul. Native peoples are quick to detect the difference between missionaries who learn their language correctly and those who don't. On the other hand, I have known some missionaries who never learned the verbal system correctly and whose intonation was totally foreign to the language they spoke, but who, in spite of these shortcomings, were greatly liked by the people. At the same time there are persons gifted in language whose major effort was expended in excellent language mastery for the sheer delight of being masters over the local people. This form of rejection is seen in the missionary who is constantly correcting the grammatical errors of the native speakers. Not a few Bible translators have been guilty of this.

Rejection is frequently reflected in forms of address, personal pronouns, and/or lack of use of honorifics. African pastors have sometimes reported how they were required to use formal address when speaking to missionaries' children but were informally addressed by those children, because that's the way they heard their parents speak.

The Missionary and the Bible: Africa has witnessed the growth of nearly 7 million separatist Christians. David Barrett gives as the most fundamental of all reasons for this massive movement the translation of the Scriptures into the African vernaculars.[2] Many African separatist churches have come into existence with no missionary contact whatsoever. This is particularly true in parts of Nigeria. Nevertheless, the Africans have seen that the ideals missionaries held and what they actually did were often in sharp contrast. In addition, the life and times of Ancient Israel and the life and times of Western missionaries were

[2] David B. Barrett, *Schism and Renewal in Africa, An Analysis of Six Thousand Contemporary Religious Movements* (London: Oxford University Press, 1968).

again in contradiction at many points dear to African cultures. Missionaries have often implied that conformity to their Western manner of life was a necessary condition for becoming Christian. This has been in many instances interpreted as rejection with the result that separation from the mission church took place.

Specialization: The modern missionary movement has evolved greatly since World War II. The missionary today tends toward specialization. It may seem strange to suggest that this implies an element of rejection. Nevertheless, specialized knowledge is always the possession of a few and these few tend to be under suspicion. However, it is not so much the specialization that operates the rejection as it is the institutionalized environment where the specialist holds forth. The school, the printing plant, the hospital have the effect of limiting his contacts, of defining for him the individuals with whom he can interact. This is true anywhere, but in the institution the whole communicating environment is decreased for the specialized missionary who will have to make gigantic efforts to break out of the circle.

Time: There is nothing in the missionary's life which so effectively shuts off the helping relationship as the daily schedule. This is an element which runs through the home, the church, the individual and institutional phases of the missionary's life. The awareness of the hour and what must be done next has probably been the basis for more rejection than any other single factor.

There are many other, often far more subtle, ways in which rejection is communicated, but the foregoing should suffice to show the helping relationship is beset by many obstacles. Where a helping relationship exists some of the above have always been creatively handled; rejection has been turned into *acceptance.*

Self Acceptance

The acceptant attitude is not acquired simply by avoiding rejection situations. It is more difficult than that because acceptance involves one's relationship with oneself. If a person is defensive in his relations with the other, he becomes a threat to the other. The very presence of the other may be sufficient to cause me to throw into operation my defence mechanism. It is very much like the border patrols between unfriendly nations. As soon as enemy action is detected out comes a squadron of fighter planes "photographing" the border zone.

The acceptant attitude in the helping relationship requires first of all that I accept myself. If I don't, my failure will in a short time be detected by the other. The reasons why missionaries may not be self acceptant are basically the same as with other people. However, in the missionary situation there are some special reasons. The most common are those arising out of the rejection situations described earlier.

Once a colleague and I were about to enter a missionary lady's house when we nearly stepped on a small plastic bag lying on the floor. I picked it up and offered it to our hostess who scanned it and thrust it back.

"What is it?" she inquired.

"Native tobacco," I replied, "someone has dropped it, they will probably be looking for it."

"Heavens," the astonished missionary lady uttered. "No one who uses tobacco would come on our porch!"

This good lady was saying that anyone who uses tobacco is beyond her environment, beyond the circle of acceptance, very likely where other sinners stand in relation to her.

Is such a person self acceptant? I think not, because there is a condition laid down by her which defines her ability to be acceptant of others. She could not convincingly commucate an unconditional positive regard to a tobacco user. Her defences would reveal her rejection and at the very point where we are rejectant we are unlikely to be self acceptant.

Take the case of evangelist L., a capable and enthusiastic Kaka preacher in Cameroun. He seldom preached a sermon without a voluble tirade against polygamy. This disturbed me, for the content of his sermons, no matter how good or how bad, would drain away into these condemnations of all polygamous marriages. By developing a helping relationship with him over a period of two years, I was able to bring to light the fact that he was expressing aggressive feelings against one of his own brothers who had inherited a wife from a deceased uncle.

He had wanted the widow himself and had never accepted himself as a monogamist. His lack of self acceptance created a complex which found a partial outlet in his vitriolic attacks from the pulpit.

Role playing is a common method of avoiding self acceptance. If I can deal with people from within my role as missionary, white man, bishop, etc., I can play my part and force the other to play his. I put on whatever mask fits the situation and create a character which the other, if he is to make sense of the game, must respond to. This is a form of forced mutual rejection in which there is little real communication, for it is essentially a guessing game.

Many church sessions in Africa deal with sex offenders in just this way. Missionary N. spent a great part of his career — for careerman was the object of his missionary training — in the titillating examination of what are known in his part of Africa as "adultery palavers" or "number sevens," violations of the seventh commandment. What really underlay his preoccupation with African adultery was his own feeling of sexual inadequacy. He had believed all the exaggerated tales of African virility he had heard and compared himself with what was largely unsubstantiated rumor. His own potency could not begin to measure up to such tales of sexual fortitude and he came to reject himself as an adequate male. Through session interrogations, very unsystematic and with little basis in fact, he could participate vicariously in this more potent world. Then, when the full force of his false guilt surged, he could deal with it by disciplining the other.

Two things could have enabled him to be of help to his African congregation: he could have learned facts about their sex life by seeking to *understand*; and he could have learned to accept himself, even if such facts should prove him to be sexually weaker. He never, to my knowledge, really helped anyone.

A sense of guilt, arising from a recognition of guilt, is still another way in which missionaries sometimes fail to reach a reasonable degree of self acceptance. Here, however, it is well to distinguish with Dr. Paul Tournier[3] between true and false guilt. Guilt which arises from a sense of failure is one which I have encountered in several cases. "I just can't understand why, after all these years, I have so little to show for my work. I have preached, taught, prayed, sacrificed just about everything, and the Christians are no more mature than they were 20 years ago. Somewhere I have failed; yes, failed badly." In this case the missionary looked upon himself as a failure. He could not accept himself and it hardly needs to be said that he projected this feeling of rejection upon his converts. Unless he could accept himself, failure or not, he would not enter into a helping relationship with others. He could not even become a help to other "failures" as long as he remained self rejectant. An honest recognition of one's guilt, even of false guilt, removes the temptation to judge the other and

[3]Paul Tournier, *Vraie ou fausse culpabilité* (Génève: Delachaux et Niestlé, 1958).

opens the way to self acceptance and the capacity to accept the other. Awareness of being accepted, restored — the method varies from culture to culture — is a movement to a new environment. It is new life, a chance to start afresh.

Self acceptance is clearly necessary if one is to enter a helping relationship with another, but the thought of doing it is a threat, for when the dancer throws away the mask, there is no longer a deceptive facade. Everyone can see it is just one of the villagers after all. Self acceptance is nakedness, being transparent. When everyone else is warmly sheltered behind his defences, who in his right mind wants to step out naked into the cold light?

Furthermore, it spoils the game, for as long as we can keep the rules of the game, everyone knows how to play. A helping relationship normally develops or should develop when someone recognizes that the game of deception leads to continuous rejection.

"If I actually did what you are suggesting," a missionary once said, "I'd confuse the natives badly. You see, face saving is everything here and they would lose respect for me. After all, I am founding the native church on the local cultural pattern." This argument conceals a further defence. The missionary in this instance did not want to give up his role. He was using the local culture as a means of protecting himself and his paternalistic policies, although he was not fully concious of what he was doing.

Self acceptance and accepting the other unconditionally contains a still more subtle threat, for it means that something in me, something which I feel to be very necessary, may be lost. This feeling of loss, of some subtle destruction, may be more than just my role: it is my independence, my freedom — falsely conceived. "I will not compromise with sin" is the way in which this defence is frequently expressed.

A missionary colleague in South America wanted very much to be of help to some Quechua Indians who were dedicated drunkards. He wanted to accept them unconditionally: "But every time I get near them they offer me that sour smelling *chicha*. I'm afraid if I'd accept it once, I'd end up just like they are."

It may well be that he is being realistic with himself. However, here again the fear of the *chicha* awakened his defences, and lively defenses is what he habitually communicated to the Indians. Needless to say, he never helped them.

By learning to accept ourselves we gain a new measure of freedom, which in turn enables us to accept the other.

The Helping Relationship as Process

In my experience I find many who say, "accept him? Yes, but not his wrongdoing, his sin." Conditional acceptance, partial acceptance, always means partial rejection, and rejection is communicated in the attitude where the helping relationship struggles to take root. It is significant that psychotherapists find that the atti-

tudes of the doctor are more sensitively perceived by their patients than any instructions or other information they may offer. Furthermore, the attitudes which indicate the patient is being heard without being judged grant the patient the freedom to share his problem and consequently to find, usually for himself, the solution to his problems.

It is sometimes remarked that an unconditional positive regard for the other would lead in any cultural situation to the embracing of a fullblown cultural relativism. But cultures are abstractions. A helping relationship is two people in a specific concrete situation, dealing with specific problems. True, there are cultural differences that will enter the relationship, and these require understanding.

Cultural relativism, in the sense that one thing is as good as another and therefore there is no basis for values, is a static notion. Cultural relativists are committed to the status quo because nothing should be changed. There is no good, better or best.

A helping relationship, on the other hand, is a *process* and anyone entering it is committed to see life not in fixed static terms, but as changing, becoming something else. In fact, most meaningful relationships of this kind can't even form unless there is a recognition of a need for change; someone must have a sense of dissatisfactions and desires for change. Unfortunately, the motivations for change in a society are many and complex, resulting now and then in conversions which have little to do with what the writers of the New Testament had in mind.

Life perceived as process means that the past cannot make absolute claims on the present. True enough, the missionary and his Zulu friend come out of very different backgrounds. They may sense many aspects of life differently, but if both come to view it all as process and not a resultant state, they bend more flexibly toward each other. It is only in process living that one is willing to change. A missionary in a helping relationship is in a position to enable the other to see life from this perspective. Missionary anthropologists have always held this view. It is only since whole societies have begun to clamor for change that the professionals have even begun to consider the dynamics of cultural change as a legitimate area of study.

Conceiving the other as a state, as the fixed result of cultural forces an articial environment for the other and for ourselves. If I think of the other as a heathen, as a polymamist or a "soul to be saved" I tend, as Martin Buber says, to confirm him in that state. Perceiving by these fixed categories—probably a result of our educational process—definitely limits the potentialities of our relationships. The future is blocked. What he and I can become is limited by what we conceive ourselves to be. If at least one of us sees us as created in God's image, then the possibility of our becoming what we are potentially is vastly extended.

Withholding Judgment

Now to return to the main point. In the helping relationship the acceptant attitude, the unconditional positive regard for the other, creates the necessary condition for change: freedom. The individual who is not free to change is unable to make a meaningful change. This is, of course, the very basis of Christian conversion. God does not manipulate the individual, but grants him the freedom to revolt. Where the other exists under the threat of my evaluation of him, no helping relationship can endure.

Judgment in the sense of evalution is most natural. We could not put our shoes on in the morning without judging that it would be a good thing for our feet. Nevertheless, in the helping relationship judgment must be replaced by sympathetic understanding.

Evaluation of a harmful kind is most often expressed in the missionary situation where the local person of a different cultural history is seen as if he were operating with the missionary's cultural assumptions.

Understanding the Other's Culture

I recall my own misinterpretations best. Once while traveling with a West African pastor, we entered the house of his maternal aunt, an old grey-haired lady. To my amusement my African colleague walked across the room and sat down lightly in the old lady's lap. What struck me as a very informal gesture turned out to communicate *to them* just the contrary. He was by this act greeting her in most formal terms.

He was expressing symbolically his status in relation to her. She said, "Greetings, child," and he, a man of thirty-five years, now an ambassador to the United Nations, stood up.

There are two facts I should like to stress in relation to this problem of the missionary's understanding of the other's culture. The first I call the "anaesthesia" and the second the "warning light."

When I arrived in Africa, I was admonished by more experienced missionaries to take all the photographs I could during the first six months, "because after that you won't really see anything interesting." The idea was that the missionary becomes accustomed to his environment and familiarity produces a drabness that is of little shock value. I think what my colleagues had actually done was to draw the circle of their environment, lay down their perceptual boundaries, so that they soon found themselves thinking this was life. They had circumscribed their environment—or the institution had done it—so close in that within six months they had probably seen, felt, tasted, smelled and heard about all they would see, feel, taste, smell and hear for the next thirty years. I shook myself and determined to avoid this self-injected anaesthesia. Needless to say, such a missionary is seldom on the same wavelength with some of his colleagues when he is put on the sub-committee for termite control at the Bango-Bango station.

The second, "the warning light," refers to the automatic flashing of a red light when the engine is in trouble. Sympathetic understanding of a culture constitutes, very much like self acceptance, a genuine danger. It is always possible that I will become involved; I may change some of my cherished defences, maybe even my theology, if I go so far as to make an honest attempt to understand the other. The very thought of it starts the warning light flashing.

Understanding requires learning, and there is little learning of what lies beyond my cultural circle unless I perceive it as a problem. More, it must be a problem which I am convinced is relevant to the problems within my own limited circle. In other words, I must see the other's culture as somehow related to my own. I must recognize that we share the same basic needs for physical and emotional satisfactions. I know, at least in part, how I satisfy these. How does the other? I must see that he is motivated to actualize himself just as I am. What are the means available to him and where is he blocked in his self-actualization? Finally, the other, in his cultural setting, must be free to be himself in relation to me. If because of my strangeness, my radical otherness, he cannot be himself, he will be unable to help me to learn, to understand his culture.

A Congolese anthropologist told me recently that European anthropologists working in the Congo during colonialism probably reported fifty percent error; the Congolese people were defensive informants; they were not free to tell the truth.

Being the learner does not always

sit well with missionaries who have been commissioned and sent out to teach. But good missionaries have always been good students of the people to whom they have gone.

The Other's Perception

So far I have discussed aspects of the helping relationship largely from the missionary's side, but in all communication worthy of the name there are two, each taking his turn, now as sender, now as receiver of the message.

In the relations of counselor, psychotherapist, anthropologist or missionary the other perceives our attitudes. He tends to feel "in his skin" that I am or am not being honestly genuine. He is very likely to sense any contradictions between what I really feel inside me and what I am saying. Of course, it is possible to fool people, but not in a helping relationship which goes on for a considerable time. It has been the experience of psychiatrists that their troubled patients detect such conflicts quickly and when they do the relationship becomes defensive and unproductive.

People working with Africans, Asians and others in folk cultures have reported the same thing. It is worth pointing out some of the reasons for this. The people among whom missionaries have traditionally labored are first of all dependent upon what is *said* to determine their actions. They do not have ready access to books to check up on things. They tend to check things out by testing them on each other. Their

fellowman is not an authoritative page of script, but a proving ground for trying things out. Furthermore, anything that is new to the eye or ear is examined by the group. It is discussed for days, weeks, years, perhaps, before a feeling of acceptance may arise. Moreover, there is not often a limiting intellectual bias which tends to inhibit unconventional ways of perceiving I personally have sensed more flashes of insight revealed in an African men's club house in the discussion of such mundane things as eating with cutlery than one could possibly find in a professional lecture on the topic. This freedom from the straightjacket of categories may be, as Marshal McLuhan says, the result of Gutenberg's significant absence from our ear-oriented friends, or it may more likely be due, as others think, to a complex of factors.[4] It appears to be an overwhelming fact of life, whatever has created it, and one that has kept the perception of simpler peoples at a fine-honed edge. It is no exaggeration to say they play everything by ear.

This keen awareness on the part of the other means I must be what Carl Rogers calls "congruent" in the helping relationship. What I say to the other must match my true inner feelings.

Once when I suggested to a missionary that he go into the village and learn about a certain matter before he made a decision, one of

4Marshall McLuhan, *The Gutenberg Galaxy: the making of typographical man* (Toronto: The University of Toronto Press, 1962).

the Africans objected immediately: "It wouldn't help. We have been trying for years to tell him these things and he never listens. He hears but he doesn't listen." The rejectant attitude had been purring so smoothly for so long that understanding was, in the view of the Africans, out of the question. They knew too well that without an acceptant attitude there could be no real understanding.

Is it possible to be fully self acceptant, acceptant of others, congruent at all times and sympathetically understanding? I can confess for myself only: the answer is — no. I have failed repeatedly. Where I have failed I have seen the helping relationship damaged. The great advantage of the self acceptant orientation is that one is able to own his failures. In so doing he is able to admit his failure, to recapture a transparent relationship with the other, and to salvage what might have been a permanent loss.

I am convinced that the struggle is always worth the cost, and where good has resulted it has always been in proportion to the effort to maintain at the highest level each of the components of the helping relationship.

William D. Reyburn

Between the Embryo and the Elephant

In a previous article[1] the author referred to the incident described below as an example of the problems involved in genuine psychological identification. Now he retells the incident in fuller detail, and we publish it in PA as a graphic example of the contrary effects of different cultural presuppositions on the behavior of the different groups which hold them. It is a vivid description of contrasting points of view, and of the different behavior which results.

THE flickering fire on the dirt floor in the men's club house sent grotesque shadows leaping up and down on the mud walls of the room. On an ornate stool opposite the doorway sat a fat chief whose unsmiling speech was punctuated with animated arm-length gestures. Crouching on their haunches against the walls the elders of Baloum listened in awed silence to the words of their clan chief. As I watched their motionless faces I could discern an urgency which had not been apparent in the men's house before. The chief's voice lowered to a whisper as the elders leaned forward clinging with attention to every sound he made. The chief then pointed a stubby finger toward his nephew who had just arrived in the village that afternoon.

"This is our sister's child. And what do we know he has done? He has the power of the forest. The

---

[1] William D. Reyburn, Identification in the Missionary Task," PA, Vol. 7, No. 1 (Jan.-Feb. 1960), pp. 6-8.

elephants that walk in our forests fear him for he has killed many. Has he killed two?" Then slapping the palms of his hands together with fingers extended he replied, "No. Ten elephants have fallen before our sister's child."

The nephew waited no longer for an occasion to speak. He rose and stepped closer to the fire in the center of the room. Standing by the fire he appeared to be a giant as we looked up from the floor at him. The nephew spoke at great length with the finesse of an experienced raconteur. He retold one by one his adventures with the mighty elephants of the forest. His speech was interlaced with movements demonstrating to his attentive spectators his dexterity in the hunt. As each imaginary elephant was shot he would point a finger to his head to show the spot the bullet struck. At a proper moment the chief raised his hand toward the nephew in a sign of silence. The hunter vanished from the center of the room and was absorbed again into the shadows along the wall.

I had sat many evenings in the men's house and had listened to the stories that are told and retold, to the seemingly endless discussions of marriages, dowries, births, deaths, and intrigues. But until tonight I had always been the outsider, the foreigner who was never really involved. As I listened this night a number of questions began running through my mind. Why did the nephew come to this village to extol his prowess as a hunter? Certainly he had other uncles who had more influence than the clan chief of Baloum. Who besides myself in Baloum even had a gun? Or could it be that they were at last preparing me in some club house ritual to go on an elephant hunt? I had, it is true, spoken of my desire to shoot an elephant, but there was never any interest shown by the men of the village when I talked of it. In fact, their response had been so indifferent I had forced myself finally to forget the matter entirely.

As the eyes of the men turned again to the chief I was about to learn that I had, at last, a very important role to play in the affairs of Baloum. The chief turned and looked at me. As he spoke the dying flames of the fire illumined his large white teeth. He smiled with his mouth but his eyes remained round and business-like.

"Obam, go get *our* gun and bring it here."

Mechanically I got to my feet, crossed the club house floor and ducked my head to clear the low doorway. Once outside in the moonlight and cool air I hesitated. I could hear a low rumble of voices in the house behind me. I thought to myself, "He did say *ngale jangan* 'our gun,' didn't he? Should I go back and ask if he said 'our gun'? No, he must have said 'our gun.' There is only one gun in the village. After all, didn't they name me Obam Nna and my wife Nlemnyem? Haven't they fed us from their own gardens and never asked anything in return? Didn't they present us with a goat, their most prized gift?"

A dozen thoughts about private ownership and life in a competitive society raced through my mind. I strolled across the village compound picking my way between huddled herds of sleeping goats and sheep and recalling how we had come to be members of the little community of Baloum in Equatorial Africa.

The Village of Baloum

My wife Marie, our three-year-old daughter Anne, and I had taken up residence in the village of Baloum for the purpose of learning the Bulu language, which would be indispensable as a vehicular language in our future work. The Cameroun like certain other areas of Africa is a modern tower of Babel and one must learn at least a major tribal or trade language for the day-to-day necessities in that part of the world. Baloum had been recommended as a desirable village as the people there were known to be friendly to missionaries, and a good part of Baloum was already professing Christianity. Also important was the fact that one of the young men of the village who had become a petty official in the capital city of Yaoundé had built the only house in Baloum with a cement floor. This was a three-room adaptation of the local style rectangular houses, and like the others was covered with a raffia palm leaf roof. Baloum, unlike most of the neighboring villages, is not located on the road but lies a quarter of a mile from the road in a forest clearing and forms a quadrangle open at one end with the men's club house built squarely in the middle. From all appearances Baloum was a quiet, peaceful, jungle agricultural community.

Our arrival in Baloum was celebrated by women who danced in front of our house and who pantomimed the coming of a white family with their jeep load of the usual supplies of kerosene, soap, salt, sugar, canned milk, and, most perplexing of all, a hand-activated washing tub. This became the delight and amusement of all — except the boy commanded by the chief to push the handle back and forth.

From the time of our arrival our curiosity moved us to participate in as many local activities as were permissible. We sincerely hoped that our urban Western backgrounds would not hinder us from adapting our way of life to that of the people so that a truly harmonious rapprochement could be gained. The citizens of Baloum were likewise anxious that we abide by local customs and were not reticent to correct our behavior when we threatened to become deviant members of the community. To make us more normal residents we were given Bulu names. The second even-

ing after our arrival we were called into the men's club house and at the end of much speech-making (which was interpreted for us in French by a local school teacher) Marie officially became Nlemnyem and I was given the Baloum family name of Obam Nna.

We now had no excuse for not replying correctly to at least one Bulu question, "What is your name?" During the first few days subsequent to the naming ritual every child in Baloum took delight in asking us our names. Within a short time we were able to tell from the expression on a person's face if he or she was about to ask us our names. The reply, when correct in tone and all other points of articulation, was met with clapping of hands and often hugs. When the name was not properly uttered the inquisitor's face would fall and he would slowly shake his head as if to say, "How hopeless you are!"

Participation in Village Life

All adult male Baloumians own domestic animals. Since Obam Nna had neither a goat nor a sheep (not, in fact, even a chicken) the village fathers decided to correct this situation. They upgraded Obam Nna with the gift of a fine slick-haired black goat. It is also the mark of a man in Baloum to be able to distinguish each and every goat, sheep, and chicken which belongs to him. I have on several occasions pointed out to a group of men a goat wandering deep in the forest and asked who the owner was. No one was ever in doubt about the owner of the animal. Several times the entire village was thrown into hilarious laughter when Obam Nna was unable to distinguish his goat from other village goats. In order to avoid such a *faux pas* as this, I finally took the goat in hand and examined it in detail. I found a tiny bit of white hair on the tail. This, I thought, would be quite sufficient for me to identify my one piece of property. I discovered later, however, that any number of goats in Baloum had the same tail markings. The laughing continued.

In spite of our awkward adaptation to the Baloum way of life, the folks began to recognize that we were quite human and most of all we were trying to learn. The fact that we had one child gave credence to our being a bit normal, but one child in the African view is very, very few. Therefore, when the women of Baloum discovered Marie's pregnant condition they attached themselves to her in a way we had not witnessed before. The development of the pregnancy became a vivid topic of woman's conversation and some of the older women offered their services as midwives when Marie's time for delivery would come. The absence of regular examinations and prenatal care by a doctor does not prevent the women of Baloum from keeping close check on the developing mother and baby. Daily, Marie was questioned by the midwives of Baloum and not infrequently did they rub their hands over the front of her dress to be sure that the future Obam would have a sufficient supply of milk.

Our participation in the life of Baloum took on many forms even-

tually. One of the most pleasant of these were the night dances when under the full moon the entire village would gather in the village quadrangle and dance to the rhythm of the combination slit drums and upright skin drums. At first it seemed as though each drum rhythm was a mere repetition of the preceding one. However, the longer we were in the village the better we were able to distinguish between the different beats. Many of the pieces have their own names and most of the dancing is accompanied by singing of the women. Dancing in Baloum is not for couples but for everyone. The movement is mainly around a circle moving about a small group of women who accompany their dances with singing.

We learned also that the dance in Baloum has a therapeutic function in the monotonous routine of agricultural duties. Men and women return from the fields after a hard day's work bent over in back-breaking activity. But as the drums begin to beat it would be very rare to find any farmer of Baloum on his bed. Both men and women as well as boys and girls join into the rhythmic body movements which, as the folks of Baloum say, "make you feel relaxed as though you had never even worked that day."

It is much easier for the outsider to become a participant in the exterior forms of life in Baloum than to share in the emotions and beliefs of its people. In those exteriors, I think, we excelled. We helped break and carry stones for the construction of a building. Marie sat on the dirt floors and cooked in the women's kitchens and learned to make their dishes. She taught them also some of ours. She went with the women to their gardens, hoed their peanuts, and gathered fish from the streams. On the male side, I worked with the men in their coco gardens, ate nightly with the men in their club house, and accompanied them to their traps and hunted the birds and monkeys of the forest with them.

The one thing which caused us the most frustrations were the limitations imposed on our activities due to Marie's pregnancy. I had learned from outraged old women in Baloum that I was not allowed to go to the spring for water. We had also learned that certain activities were forbidden Marie. In spite of this, we came to feel so much a part of Baloum that these restrictions upon our activities did not bother us too much. In order not to offend our hosts we did not pursue questions if the folks of Baloum showed reluctance to give us information. Often in reply to questions which touched the deeper layers of Baloum life we were told by the village fathers, "Just sit like a child and you will learn."

Gun and Taboo

The moon was shining brightly as I crossed the village compound to get the gun. Banana leaves standing like huge flowers above and behind the raffia hut roofs reflected the light of the moon. The countless noises of the African forest at night sounded like a thousand tiny orchestras each tuning up and then abruptly silencing itself. Bats fluttered back and forth silhouetted against the whitewashed walls of the houses. I passed an open kitchen door where a mother sat on a stool nursing her child before the light of her evening cooking fire. In front of another house two old women sitting on the ground called out a muffled greeting. I returned the greeting and then in another moment reached our house. My mind was on the elephant hunt now and I was wondering if we might leave that night or before dawn. I went to the back room, removed the gun from its case, opened a box and took out a dozen rounds of steel-tipped ammunition and started to leave the house. Marie called after me, "Hunting tonight?" I replied, "Let you know when, in a few minutes."

My footsteps quickened as I hurried back to the men's house. A young man sitting outside the door called inside, "Obam has the gun." I ducked my head and entered the room with the gun tucked under my arm. The chief arose, took the gun, and passed it over to the nephew. The latter stood up and took the gun from the chief's hands. Planting himself squarely in the middle of the room he lifted the bolt handle, slid the bolt back and with an awkward trust reseated it. He then lifted the gun to his shoulder, aimed it about the roof and after some further manipulations, pulled the trigger. The hammer fell with a sounding thud. The men about the room nodded their heads in approval as the hunter lowered the gun, worked the bolt again and moved about the room. He was hunched over stalking his prey and moving about as if going through thick underbrush. Again the chief spoke and the hunter backed away to the side of the room and sat in the shadows. I had sat quietly and watched this demonstration but my curiosity was nearly out of control. I looked up at the chief and asked abruptly, "When do we leave?" My question was met with silence. I glanced across the room. No one was looking my way. There was nothing heard but the night noises of the forest outside. Slowly an old man with one eye who got about with the help of a stick stood to his feet. He leaned with one hand on his stick and the other placed flat on his hip. He turned toward me and began.

"Obam Nna, as long as the people of Baloum have hunted the elephant they have kept the pregnant women and the expecting fathers in the village. There are two great and marvelous things for a man to see. One is the baby that is born to him and the other is the slain elephant in the forest. In Baloum we say that men like you, Obam Nna, are between your baby not yet born and the elephant that walks at night in the forest. In your heart you want to go to the elephant, but in respect for what our fathers have taught, you must remain with your pregnant wife while the hunter kills the elephant."

With these words of Baloum philosophy the old man squatted again in his place and the room became silent. On the one hand I was torn by my desire to be in the hunt and on the other by my respect for the traditions of the people who had become my hosts, friends, and neighbors. I was tempted to make a plea, to remind them that their own traditions were quickly changing, to take

back my gun and stop the whole hunt. There was also the question of law — French law — in this then-mandated territory. Only the owner of the license had a right to use the gun. Yes, all this I knew and a host of arguments and reasons why I should protest flashed into my head, but I sat and said nothing. Finally, I turned to Ngambi who sat to my right. Ngambi's wife was also expecting. In a low voice I asked, "Ngambi, can you go to kill the elephant?"

His eyes stared straight ahead into the flames. "You have heard the custom from our old father."

I looked across the room to Tanye. "Tanye, do you go on the hunt?"

Tanye smiled sympathetically. "Obam, you know my Ndasa is just like your Nlemnyem."

I looked about at others whose wives were expecting and each nodded in the same way as Tanye. Turning to the chief I handed over the ammunition and said, "Here, send your sister's child to kill the elephant for us all."

The tense atmosphere of the room was immediately dispelled and solemn faces suddenly lighted up with smiles. The men's house was soon emptied and I stood with a small group and the hunter outside in the moonlight and checked out the hunter on the loading and handling of the gun. Without any further exchange the hunter and two companions disappeared across the compound in the direction of the chief's house.

Return of the Hunters

It was nearly noon the following day before the three men returned with the gun to the village. As they emerged from the forest edge and entered the compound, all activity in the village ceased. The trio, covered to their hips with dried mud, strode across the compound straight to the chief's house. The two men carried large banana leaf hundles strapped by vines to their backs. The hunter carried the gun in both hands outstretched above his head. No one called out or asked any questions. The gesture of the hunter and the packs of trunk meat were the obvious signs of a successful hunt.

The word of the hunters' return passed along the forest trails as if sent by a magic telephone system. Residents of Baloum who had moved out to their gardens for the season began to arrive in the village that night. Faces we had not seen for over a month were suddenly and mysteriously present. When I asked an old woman why she had returned to the village she looked at me as if I were joking and replied, "God loves Baloum tonight because there will be meat, as much meat as we can possibly eat."

The trunk which had been removed from the carcass and brought in was divided among those who were eligible to eat it. A great deal of secrecy surrounded the dividing and cooking of this meat. On two occasions I was abruptly prevented from entering a kitchen which I learned contained elephant trunk. By now we had learned that the elephant was taboo for us and so resigned ourselves to membership in that little group of Baloumians who were expectant parents. As I sat with Tanye by the

fire in his wife's kitchen I asked if he were angry because he would get no trunk meat to eat. He laughed and replied, "Tomorrow when the elephant is cut they will all eat."

I still was not entirely satisfied with my status of exclusion and inquired of Tanye if we expecting fathers would get to go into the forest the next day for the cutting of the meat.

"Yes," replied Tanye. "They will allow us to go but we must not touch the meat."

This was at least encouraging and so I decided to get a good night's sleep before the predawn march into the forest. While Marie and I attempted to sleep the villagers of Baloum danced the entire night in symbolic celebration of the elephant kill.

Long before dawn the voice of the chief bellowed out in the village quadrangle. In response to his call the entire village began to assemble for the trek into the forest for the cutting of the elephant. The women prepared their large garden baskets by strapping them to their backs with vines while the men sharpened knives and machetes in the light of the fire in the men's house. Finally, the last woman to emerge from her kitchen joined the end of the line and the chief with his hunter-nephew at his side holding a large flaming torch moved out. Operation butcher and palaver was under way.

I flashed my light across the compound to our house and saw Marie waving as we entered the forest. The trail was wet from recent rains. The grass and bushes along the sides of the trail were dripping with moisture. The long column of basket-bearing women slowly became visible in the dim morning light just after we had waded up to our waists across the second river.

For the first two hours the long line moved silently through the forest, but as the first warm rays of the morning sun began to penetrate through the heavy jungle foliage the chatter of voices commenced. From the chief and the hunter at the head of the file to the last woman there was a continual bantering of voices. Finally the column came to a halt. Women began slipping their baskets from their shoulders and setting them down on the trail. The air was sultry and reeked with the odors of decaying vegetation. The murmur of voices died out as if waiting for orders to proceed. Soon near the head of the column there was an exchange of words between the hunter and his two companions. I asked Tanye if he had heard it. He climbed onto a stump and cocked his ear to listen. Then he looked down at us on the trail and said, "The hunter believes we go to the right and one of the others thinks it's to the left."

We waited in silence for a minute while the hunter went on ahead. Then he called out. The column moved again. This time the march continued up and down across two hills and two more swiftly flowing streams. The trail had long ago ceased to be recognizable as such and from my position at about the middle of the column I could hear the constant swishing and hacking of machetes which were cutting the trail ahead.

About an hour later the column again came to a stop. I heard the name Obam Nna being passed back along the trail. Tanye tapped my shoulder and said, "Go up to the front. The chief has called for you."

The Elephant

I moved slowly ahead until I reached the spot where the chief stood. As I approached him he took my arm and maneuvered me to a spot a few steps to the right where I could see the hunter standing on what appeared to be a huge boulder. I wiped the perspiration from my face and pushed ahead a few yards to get a better view. Now I could see it plainly. The hunter was perched atop a massive gray mound — the slain elephant! It was to my mind unthinkable that such a monstrous creature had been alive and roaming in these forests only the day before. I looked at this spectacle of a puny human standing proudly astride the great behemoth and felt as if I had been suddenly pushed back into some prehistoric age. The elephant was swollen with gas far beyond its normal size and shape. Two legs were extended in a grotesque fashion causing me to think for a second that they had shot an innocent circus elephant in the midst of its performance. The trunk had been removed, leaving long yellowish tusks projecting from the mouth like two curved poles supporting the enormous head. In my thoughts about the carcass I had forgotten completely the restriction under which I was placed and I reached over to lift a great leaf-like ear which covered a good portion of the neck and part of the upper leg. As I put out my hand, I felt a light blow on my upper arm. I glanced up and met the cold eyes of the chief glaring at me. I recalled my obligations to Baloum traditions. The chief motioned me to one side and moved the rest of the column up to the carcass.

As the long line of basket bearers moved in on the dead elephant there was a murmur of voices. Women who had never seen such a sight clasped their hands over their naked breasts. Expecting parents slowly gravitated to a grassy spot some ten yards from the elephant. I stood close to the elephant watching the chief as he called out the names of the first butchering crew. Then I heard my name ring out from that parental corner of exclusion from which I was making every effort to dissociate myself. Again someone called, "Obam Nna, aahh Obamooo."

I played deaf and continued to be absorbed in the flurry of disorganized activity which was going on about the elephant. Suddenly the chief was standing between me and the elephant. His arm was outstretched pointing in the direction he wanted me to move. I hesitated for a moment, looked over at this defiled little group of fellow outcasts and then slowly made my way over to join the unclean. We sat and chatted with each other as the butchers began to take up positions on top of the elephant. The work of cutting off the head eventually got under way. The hunter claimed the head as his special reward and soon his arms were covered with blood up to the elbows as he cut around the neck with his knife. After a sufficiently large gash was opened

the axe was handed up to where he stood astride the head with one foot on the back and one on the great bulging bony head. Like a woodsman chopping a fallen log, the hunter hacked away at the elephant's neck. With each fall of the axe blood sprayed upward and spattered those standing on the carcass. A rusty stream of blood flowed from the neck along the ground. When the spine was cut in two the huge head slumped and a ravenous group of knife-wielding women pounced upon it. They dragged the head to one side and began to jab at the meat with a dizzying crisscross of knives and machetes.

Two old women clothed in leaf belts about their waists came up from this surgical nightmare clutching at a large chunk of meat. At the same moment they swung their knives in the air and swiped at the dripping piece of flesh. The chunk of elephant head broke in the middle and fell back against each woman's leaf belt, leaving their leaves dripping blood down the wrinkled skin of their legs. The hunter poised atop the elephant grinned with pleasure as the female vultures tore away at the meat. Finally the chief picked up a stick and struck a couple of the women over their bare backs and drove them like a pack of hungry wolves away from the head. The hunter jumped down from the elephant and began to cut with the axe into the bony structure holding the tusks. At the same time four men had begun to make long deep parallel incisions in the hide. The carcass, having lain in the forest for over 24 hours, had swollen like a balloon. As the men sliced deep into the hide an intestine was punctured and a high pitched hissing noise sounded from the hole. Then suddenly to everyone's surprise a geyser of green liquid manure spewed high into the air, falling back on to the carcass. The butchers jumped clear of the elephant but by the time the gas and manure had extinguished itself the side of the body was covered with a slippery slime which made it nearly impossible to maintain a footing on the carcass.

The operation continued as huge blocks of hide were removed and placed on the ground. Upon these slices of hide the meat was piled as it was removed. Eventually the belly was opened and gigantic intestines were exposed. I stood up to get a better view of this operation. The entrails looked more like innertubes from the tires of a tractor than like the digestive organs of an animal. Two men stood at the belly opening tugging at the intestines when all of a sudden one of the men slipped in the wet manure and fell. At this moment the massive insides gave way and slithered out covering the fallen man from his feet to his chin. The tense atmosphere which had hung over these meat-hungry Africans for the past two hours was instantly transformed into hilarious laughter. The chief, doubled over in mirth, lost his sun helmet which fell into the slime and manure. As the unfortunate butcher extracted himself from this bed of elephant intestines, voices rang out shouting, "Oh Mbandi, you are being born of an elephant!" Throughout the entire day there was laughter and ridicule of "Mbandi, the man born from an elephant's stomach."

Breach of Taboo

I maintained my association with my fellow fathers-to-be, but as I looked now at the skull stripped of meat and tusks I was seized by the desire to find how far the bullet had penetrated the bone. While all attention was focused on the men standing to their ankles in the blood of the half carcass, I inconspicuously moved over to the skull. The axe was lying beside it. As quietly as possible I turned the head so that the forehead was up and then looked about. No one had noticed. I located the bullet hole and pushed in my little finger. It was deep. I found a small stick and pushed it into the hole but it did not seem to stop against any bony wall. The only way to satisfy my curiosity was to cut the frontal section open with the axe. I realized that I would be stopped as soon as I struck it but perhaps one blow with the axe would suffice to show me what I wanted to know.

I glanced about, picked up the axe, raised it high above my head, aimed for the hole, and crash! As the axe smashed into the skull the entire front fell open and I could see just how the bullet had struck above and between the eyes piercing the solid bone, then penetrated through the cavernous sinus and reached the tiny brain box.

Shouts of disapproval filled the air and the hunter's angry voice crying, "Leave it! leave it!" caused me to drop the axe to the ground and abandon my investigations. Like a boy who had been caught with his fingers in the sugar bowl, I returned to my forbidden fellows and sat among them on the ground. A sympathetic old woman approached me and bent over to say something. She held her right hand over her mouth as· a sign of respect and mumbled, "Obam, you must not forget the life of the baby not yet born."

Controversy

I shrugged my shoulders and settled back into the grass to watch a group of women who were called out of the spectators to turn the carcass over for the second half of the dismantling of the elephant's remaining anatomy.

It was two in the afternoon before the elephant was reduced to six piles of flesh, bones, tusks, ears, hide, and feet. These piles represented the six extended family groups of Baloum. When I thought we were about to load up for the return to the village there seemed to be a terrible reluctance on the part of any family to take its share and fill the baskets. I asked why. No one seemed to want to explain. The din of voices began a gradual crescendo until it was obvious even to the most untutored outsider that killing an elephant was one thing but dividing the meat was quite another. The more I tried to inquire into the arguing and haranguing the less I learned. Then it began to rain. One might think that a drenching equatorial downpower would end all discussions, but it merely seemed to add volume to the voices. In the thick of the storm an elder of Baloum, waving a machete in his hand, climbed onto a pile of meat and brandishing his machete began an eloquent oration

exposing the reasons why the family owners of the meat on which he stood should turn it over to his family.

"You have surely not forgotten, have you, Mutaka, that the debt your father owes mine has never been paid? Is it not so that my father loaned your father five goats and ten chickens when your father married your mother? Today this debt can be paid in the eyes of all. Mutaka, do what is right and pay your father's debt with the meat under my feet."

The family of Mutaka went into a huddle for a moment, then old Mutaka, bent in age, took up a position beside a stack of meat. He lifted his hand in the air and signaled for silence. The chattering of the voices died down while Mutaka made an elaborate defense of his dead ancestors and then turned to Mbandji and accused him of turning Mutaka over to the French during World War II.

"Mbandji, you are a young man. You did not know the Germans. You never went to a German school." Mutaka interspersed his speech with half-intelligible German words. "You caused the French administrator to accuse me of cooperating with the Germans and of wanting the Germans to return. I stayed in prison because of your lying mouth, Mbandji. Now, today, before the eyes of all the families of Baloum you can make your evil way straight by giving us this pile of meat."

Each accused arose and stated his defense and in turn ended with the accusation of another. By the time all six families had been accused, made a defense and self-acquittal, the circle had been completed. Nothing resulted and no one obtained any meat from anyone else.

Return Journey

The sun, which had reappeared by the end of the speech making, was beginning to slip beneath the tops of the jungle trees in the west. The meat was plopped into the baskets and the homeward march began. A woman who was near the end of the column carried a huge garden basket strapped by vines to her shoulders with a tumpline running across her forehead. At one point along the trail she stumbled and a choice elephantine sirloin slid from the basket and plunked to the ground. Without a moment's hesitation I reached down, picked up the meat, and started to put it back into her basket.

"Leave it!" she shouted as she turned her basket away to prevent me from replacing the meat. Without giving me a chance to utter a word she wheeled away and hurried down the trail mumbling that forbidden people shouldn't be in the forest. I stood beside the path as the last three basket bearers passed. To each I offered my tender morsel and from each I got the same disdaining look with the same disgruntled remarks.

Finally I stood alone in the forest holding my mammoth steak. I looked at it and it looked back at me. Twice I started to fling it into the thickets and twice I stopped. A bond of sympathy had quickly and subtly tied this tabooed man to that defiled piece of meat. It was a natural friendship, an attachment of the disinherited.

No, the folks of Baloum never knew the end of this story. For in an African village where elephant meat was cooking on a dozen kitchen fires, who would have smelled one steak more?

Philip A. Noss

The Danger of Courtesy

The rules of behavior which make social life possible are very important; but they differ radically from society to society. The foreigner cannot ignore the code of the people among whom he is living because this would cause offense; nor can he give up his own code and totally adopt the other, because people will be suspicious of one who abandons his own code. Rather, he should learn and apply the basic tenets of the host society in appropriate situations.

EVERYMAN lives according to rules. From earliest childhood he is taught what he should do and what he should not do. He is taught what is accepted within the home and in the community, how he may act toward his own family and how he must treat a guest, he is taught table manners and playground rules. An American is raised according to Amy Vanderbilt and when he sees her admonitions and prohibitions broken, he turns to Ann Landers for advice on how to correct the situation without himself becoming guilty of violation of the code.

Upon arriving among a foreign people, the stranger is faced with a new situation. His own code is not the accepted system. He cannot depend on his own set of rules which differs from and conflicts with the rules of the new land. Several alternatives are open to him. He may try to ignore the new code completely; he may try to learn the basic tenets, at least within certain contexts; he may try to adopt the new code completely.

The first alternative is generally unacceptable because it suggests a reluctance or refusal to accept the new custom as valid, which further implies a rejection of the people to whom the system is meaningful. The third alternative is equally unacceptable because the countryman who recognizes the validity and meaning of his own customs will naturally be suspicious of the stranger who appears to totally reject his own. He comes to conclude either that the way of life from which the stranger comes is without values and mores or that the foreigner is without self-respect and self-identity. Not surprisingly,

Philip A. Noss is the son of missionaries in Cameroun. He holds the Ph. D. from the University of Wisconsin and is presently on the faculty of the Department of African Languages and Literature at the same university (Madison, Wisconsin 53706).

these conclusions are the same ones which often seem to be drawn by the visitor about the meaningless new code by which he finds himself surrounded.

The second of the above alternatives is the only acceptable possibility. It requires the recognition that everyman possesses a valid way of life, that every people has its own values and mores. This alternative compels him to accept new ways at least to the point of recognizing what they mean so that he can knowingly respond to them in the way that they were intended. This alternative further requires that he retain his own self-respect and identity.

"Anybody home?"

The differences between the codes of two peoples are perhaps most easily seen at the point of meeting. The Gbaya of Cameroun approaches the residence of the foreigner with uncertainty.[1] Normally a door is meant to be open except when it is cold, dark, or rainy, but the European prefers closed doors. The Gbaya approaches and hesitates knowing that one should not call into the house of the foreigner. He stands instead outside the door, occasionally shuffling his feel, clearing his throat, or coughing. To the European this behavior appears indirect and crude. He fails to understand that the simple knock on the door is unacceptable to the Gbaya because it signals the intruder. Only a visitor who wished to remain

[1] The Gbaya were traditionally a hunting and farming people who live now in Cameroun and the Central African Republic.

anonymous would knock. The friend would call out a greeting, inquiring whether anyone was home. The sound of his voice would both announce his arrival and identify him as a friend.

The conflict between the Gbaya and the European approach can most easily be overcome by leaving the outside door open. The visitor then knows that he is welcome and does not hesitate to make his presence known in the most appropriate manner. If the door cannot be left open, the frustrations to both the master of the house and the visitor are not easily overcome.

I lived for some months with my family in the home of an African friend in an isolated village in Cameroun. The house was his own, just completed, and he moved out of it so that we could live in it as long as we were in the village. When the door was open we found that the neighbor, the friend, or interested passerby felt free to pause for a moment to call in a greeting or to stop in for a short conversation. When the front door was closed, the visitor assumed that we were resting, eating, or otherwise busy and he left us undisturbed. Only if he needed to see us did he come around to see whether the back door might be open. If he found the back door also closed and desperately needed something, he would go to our host in the next house who would then summon us. This was the code that seemed natural -- the code that must have been very close to that surrounding the house before we moved in, and we found it very acceptable. It provided privacy when we needed it, even for an afternoon siesta, but also assured the community that it was welcome in our home.

Upon entering a house, tradition ordains that the guest shall be invited to sit down. One evening I went outside briefly to where my host was sitting in front of his house visiting with a companion. I approached to ask a question and intended to return directly to my house, but the conversation was interesting and I tarried. A few minutes later my two year old boy came and, being in tune with the prevailing code, looked all around and led me across in front of the two men to a rock where I should sit down. My host was immediately embarrassed and apologized for the breach in courtesy, and the next day the story circulated through town about the lesson in courtesy taught by the two year old child.

The cattle people, the Mbororo, had another code which neither we nor our hosts understood. They came to the house at any time, they called in or rattled tin cans whether the doors were open or closed. If the Gbaya approached to find us eating, they would discreetly withdraw until later, but the Mbororo without hesitation would enter the house and sniff the food in the frying pan or on the table to determine whether it smelled inviting. At this the Gbaya would recoil in complete disapproval. But the Mbororo code did restrain them from tasting the food. The cattle women would never request a taste of food and would rarely accept it if offered.

The differences between the manners of Gbaya and Mbororo caused friction and scorn. The Gbaya admired the nomads for their physical strength and endurance, but despised them for their lack of manners. A Mbororo might appear to be your best friend, they said, but suddenly without a word of farewell he would be gone. Some time after receiving this explanation we were able to observe the Mbororo code.

The Mbororo moved with their cattle according to the season. They were in the vicinity of our home for several months and while there they brought fresh milk and butter for sale each day. One woman was particularly conscientious, never missing a day. As the Islamic Feast of the Ram approached, she informed us that she would not be able to make the long walk from the cattle camp to our village, but that if we would send someone she would bring the milk to the nearest point along the road. When we arrived, she was already there. She said that the following day, the day of the religious observance, she would not leave camp, but that we should send someone to her so that our children would not be without milk. The messenger returned late in the afternoon bearing the milk given that day free of charge together with a gift of choice mutton. The following day it was business as usual, but in this brief interlude we were permitted to observe something of the Mbororo code of friendship.

Several weeks later the cattle woman informed us that her people would soon be leaving to return north with their herds. Should she not arrive on the following day it was because they had already left. We wondered why she could not tell us the specific day chosen for travel, but she explained that this decision rested with the leader of the camp and he would not decide until the day before departure. For several days she continued to bring milk, and then one day she did not come and we assumed that her people had moved. A few days later when traveling through a neighboring village an acquaintance stopped me to say that my friend the milk lady had left word that she and her people had moved. She asked him to bid us farewell for her and to greet us ten times. Once again the Mbororo code was evident, and the reason for the sudden departure together with the method of coping with it became clear. In that light, the cattle woman's farewell took on special meaning.

Thus, each society has its own way of welcoming and bidding farewell. Understood within their respective frameworks, each courtesy is meaningful, but frequently when interpreted within the light of one's own code, they lead to misunderstanding and suspicion.

"The Guest Does Not Take the House"

The experiences with the Gbaya and Mbororo demonstrate the deep significance attached to the guest-host relationship within traditional society.

As we prepared to go to Africa we hoped to be able to live in a village. Long before our arrival a friend heard of our plans and invited us to live

in his new house. His family had lived in it no more than several months, but when we arrived they gave it to us for as long as we would need it. Our host, his wife, and two sons moved into the older house that belonged to his brother. And his brother lived with his family in a shack out in the country by the gardens. They were the hosts, we were the the guests, and as the Ancients said, "The guest does not take the house." The house will be there after the guest leaves and only the memory will remain. The visitor must be treated well, and our host assumed full responsibility for our well-being as long as we lived with him.

Living across the road from us was a Hausa merchant. He was of a different ethnic group, his way of life was different. He was there when we arrived and stayed on after we left. When I inquired about his status I was told that he was a guest of the village. When he had first arrived, he had been given two houses for himself and his family. They would be his as long as he needed them. I questioned this kind of generosity to an outsider who had come expressly to make money off the community, but they assured me that he was their guest. Furthermore, through his connections with an outside world he provided them with outlets for their products. He also assisted them by selling the bananas, peanuts, and other produce which they left in his care while they went to the gardens to work. In addition, he was Moslem and he assumed the role of teacher for the elders who were of that faith. Thus focused on the foreign merchant two codes could be seen harmoniously functioning on the basis of mutual respect and need.

The guest–host relationship is symbolized most clearly in the breaking of bread. To invite a guest into one's home and to serve him is the greatest demonstration of respect and acceptance possible within the code of daily life. At Christmas my family and another family were invited to the home of the chief. He invited everyone, children included. Since traditionally women and children eat apart from men, we wondered how things would be arranged. We knew also that the chief was Islamic and that Christmas came that year during the Moslem fast. When we arrived we were greeted by our host and the elders. They ushered us inside to where tables were set. The chief's brother was in charge of the dinner, and once we were seated the chief himself withdrew. We were served a beautiful dinner after which we were again together with our host. Thus as our host he had welcomed us into his home and provided for us according to custom without violating his own fast.

A similar situation occurred when a Mbororo family arrived at a Gbaya home. There were obviously differences in eating habits and foods. The Gbaya therefore welcomed their guests and provided them with food which they were permitted to eat according to their own tradition.

Custom does recognize the differences that separate people. It also provides ways of bridging those differences without violation of either tradition.

To Spoil a Hunt

Specific examples of different codes can be isolated and discussed, but no element of social order functions in isolation. Each is related to another in a complex web. Something of this multidimensional network became apparent to us within the realm of the hunt.

I had gone hunting with an African hunter once before. The animals were to be found across the river and we asked the owner of the dugout tied at the crossing place if we could use his boat. Reluctantly, he consented. On our return the African hunter, who had shot several antelope, cut off a small piece of meat and bone as a gift for the owner of the boat. His home lay off the regular path and the hunter went alone to deliver it. When I questioned him about the size of the gift he said that it was big enough, we had done the rowing, not the boat owner.

Two days later a friend told me that the boat owner was very angry with me. The hunter had given him the small piece of meat and bone telling him that I had killed two antelope, but there was no gift from me. My friend cautioned him against coming to complain to me because I had in fact shot nothing.

Several weeks later a missionary friend came to visit and I wanted to take him hunting. I was told that the boat owner was in town, and I went to find him and ask if we could use his boat. He was at a drinking party and refused to come out until I personally beckoned him from the doorway.

When he had greeted me I said that I had come because I wanted to go hunting. He replied that it was not for him to deny me the right to go hunting. I explained that I wanted to beg him to let me use his boat to take my friend across the river. His refusal was immediate. He accused me of having used his boat before, of killing two antelope, and then giving him no meat, and he began to walk away. Other villagers came to my aid and begged him to listen. I had killed nothing on that hunt, they said, and the one who had accompanied us in whose care the boatman had entrusted the boat assured him that I had not even fired my gun.

He was unconvinced and began to talk. It was the villagers he was angry with, he explained, because traditional custom directs villagers to help the boatman drag his new dugout from the woods where he has felled the tree and hollowed it into a boat down to the river. In return the villagers are to be able to use the boat when they need to cross the river, but no one had been willing to help him. Four times he and his family had had to drag his boats. A village elder stood by and agreed that the village was to blame, that they should have helped him with his boats, and that what they had done was not right.

Finally, the boatman had had his say and turned to inform me that I could take my friend across and that I could use the boat whenever I wished, except if I brought along another African hunter from the city.

With that I began to turn away and noticed another elder beckoning me to come. With apologies he rebuked me. I, a foreign guest, should never have done what I did. I had given a person who was disliked by the village and considered with contempt the opportunity of refusing me and attacking me as a liar in the midst of men who had been drinking and women and children. I apologized for my error and asked what I should have done.

I should have gone to the village chief with my friend. I should have told him that I wanted to take my friend hunting and that I needed a boat to cross the river. The chief would have called the boatman and directed him to take us safely across the river and safely back again. The chief would thereby have assumed responsibility for our safety and the boatman would have been personally responsible since it was he who knew and could protect against the forces of the water. But I had gone to the drunk boatowner personally, I had been willing to talk with him and had given him a chance to abuse me in public, and now no one in the village was responsible for our safety. All in all I had done something quite wrong.

I wondered why they had chosen to scold me and not the boatman. The answer was that he had merely done what everyone would have expected of the drunk, selfish, and irritable person they knew him to be. It was I who had stepped outside myself by lowering myself to his level and allowing him to insult me. The boatman had shamed the villagers who knew what was right and they were unhappy that I should have given him the opportunity. But even more so, they scolded the two men who had taken me to the boatman. Maybe I did not know what was right, but they were villagers and it was they who were really to blame.

My friend and I returned to prepare for the hunt. A short while later one of our guides came and asked us to bring out the guns. Unless the boatman gave his blessing the hunt would not be successful after the unhappiness that had preceded our departure. When the boatman came he took a blade of grass, tied it into a knot, and spit on it. He directed us to hold it over the bow of the boat and untie it. Our hunt would be successful. If we wanted hippos, we would kill them. The guide explained that we were hunting antelope, but he said he had no power over land animals.

Armed with the knotted blade of grass we left the village. When we came to the crossing we found that the boat was moored near the opposite shore below swift rapids. For two hours we tried to cross the water, but it was impossible. The hunt seemed doomed, but the guides said the boatman had another boat downriver. We walked down and found his other boat and went downriver to where we were going to hunt. That evening we hunted and all the next morning. We found nothing except cattle.

On the way home we stopped by the boatman's home to show him that we had shot nothing. When he saw that our hunt had been "spoiled" he was distressed, and said that when he had planted his crops he would personally take us hunting where he knew there were animals.

Upon arrival at home as the story of our hunt became known, the Christian leader came and told us if he had known of the difficulties of the day before he would not have allowed us to go hunting, and certainly not to use the boat. As far as he was concerned, and as a Christian he partially apologized, the boatman's words had ruined our hunt. If there are hard words before a hunt it will be unsuccessful. Our experience was evidence again of the old truth.

I asked about future hunting trips when we might want to use the boat again. His immediate response was that we must never use the man's boats unless the owner personally came and asked to take us hunting.

A short while after the ill-fated hunt I arranged to go hunting with a young man from the village. In addition to the gun I had, we borrowed one from a village elder. As he reached to hand it to me, he laid it on the ground, and I picked it up. Tradition forbade the handing of a weapon from one man directly to another before an expedition. When the gun was in my house, the owner came and performed a small sacrifice to ensure success. The departure itself was timed for early in the morning before anyone arose because a hunting expedition should never set out in public. We did everything correctly, following the dictates of a tradition which meant little to me.

The result, or at least what happened, was a very successful hunt. Perhaps there was no relationship, but the words of the elders had proven correct. One did not go hunting following hard words. One did not take the hunt lightly. One did not violate tradition before a hunt. With a good supply of fresh meat, I was hardly in a position to refute their conclusions.

Above all, the two expeditions underlined for me the significance to a people of its tradition and custom. They also showed how at certain points I was expected to obey that code, if not for my own well being, at least so that within their own standards they would not be shamed.

Conclusion

Courtesy is the most obvious expression of the values and mores of a people. A people's code expresses the relationship that exists among persons within the society and toward outsiders. Because it is learned from earliest childhood, it becomes a part of each person, and as his expression of courtesy is misinterpreted or when he sees his code violated, he tends to withdraw and to condemn. What was intended to build a relationship leads instead toward resentment and suspicion. Living for a long time among strange codes without any apprecia-

tion for them is disastrous for the establishment of any personal relationship.

Ultimately, the code is merely an an indication of respect. To ignore a people's code is to indicate a lack of respect for them. To reject one's own code is equally dangerous because it suggests a lack of self-respect. The answer must be found somewhere between the two extremes. It lies perhaps in the guest-host relationship. Only as we permitted ourselves to be guests could our host play his role. Only as we came to depend on him and need him, could the relationship be fulfilled. Part of our need was for him to explain actions and words which were part of the code that we failed to understand. As we asked he was never unwilling to explain. He was eager to suggest what our response should be, how we should respond to his code without rejecting our own. As we learned to understand and appreciate new ways, we came increasingly to respect the people among whom we lived, and at the same time they could respect us. Perhaps error can never be totally avoided, but with the establishment of mutual respect, there is room for an occasional blunder which may even further strengthen a relationship already begun.

Donald E. Douglas

On Sharing the Wealth Philippine Style

It is paradoxical that those most highly motivated to give, with regard to their time and talents, e. g. foreign missionaries, experience such inner wrenching when it comes to sharing their personal wealth with others. Most often this tension does not occur because of blatant unwillingness to share, but simply because missionaries, particularly the newly arrived, are not aware of distinctive Philippine patterns of sharing. Fulfilling one's obligation to share, in socially acceptable ways, may help to alleviate personal tension and at the same time enhance the prospect of vital communication with individuals in the Philippines.

A common tension which seems to emerge in most newcomers to the Philippines shortly after arrival is the uncomfortable awareness of the great disparity in wealth between the new arrival and the majority of the host population. If the newcomer soon moves into a provincial situation he becomes even more aware of this divergence. The people around him appear to be depressingly poor. He looks at his personal wealth, both in terms of salary and possessions, and contrasts this with the income and life style of those about him. As a result, he is often confused and embarrassed at the role in which he is

Donald E. Douglas is Director of the Language and Orientation Department, Far Eastern Gospel Crusade, Philippines. He holds an M.A. from the University of Michigan in Far Eastern Studies (Villa Lourdes Subdivision, Lipa City, Republic of the Philippines).

cast—that of a wealthy person of upper class status. He is uncomfortable, to say the least, in this role since he does not consider himself a member of similar status in his own society. If he happens to be an American foreign missionary he may argue that he is certainly not wealthy since, in most cases, his salary is fixed at a level below the national poverty line in the United States!

It is immediately apparent in the Philippines that one's perceived status is more important than his real status. The general Filipino perception is that the American is exceedingly wealthy; far more wealthy than the Filipino ever expects to be. In addition to salary and possessions, the manner of dress, mode of transportation, quality of education and general life style of the foreigner tend to confirm this perception in the mind of most Filipinos. Attempts to recast oneself in a lower status are almost always unsuccessful.

This tension between the perceived and the real is further intensified in the case of the foreign missionary by his belief system which, among other things, maintains that he has a responsibility to share his wealth with others in order to relieve suffering and meet human need. Shortly, he may be confronted with requests for material aid, whether overt or covert, which he is unprepared to evaluate and respond to in a socially acceptable way. He may either err on the side of withholding aid altogether or, which is more common, by superfluously granting the request. In either case there is a good chance that his response will be misunderstood.

In ultimately resolving this internal conflict, one may unconsciously adopt a paternalistic attitude which is likely to become increasingly unacceptable in a nation and in a church which are determined to establish their own identities in the world and ecclesiastical order respectively. Not infrequently unwholesome generalizations about the character of a people surface which indicate that attitudes of superiority have developed in the foreigner's mind over this issue.

The purpose of this essay is not to explore the possibilities and/or perils of missionary giving in the local church. Rather, an attempt will be made to suggest ways in which foreigners in the Philippines may respond to requests which are frequently made for material aid. These requests are made not only by the citizenry in general but by those who for one reason or another consider themselves to have a special claim upon the missionary. Several different types of sharing situations may thus be distinguished in the Philippines.

Institutional Giving

In the Philippines, there are numerous associations recognized and regulated by the government for the care of the handicapped, particularly the blind. These associations send agents about the country soliciting funds for the maintenance of their work. Official receipts are presented to the donor and one may thus make a yearly donation in the same way he would contribute to the United Fund in North America. This form of institutional giving rarely causes difficulties of conscience for the foreigner since it is generally assumed that there is a good chance of one's gift being used for the genuine relief of those in need.

Professional Beggars

There is a class of people in the Philippines who may be termed professional beggars. These people usually make their appearance during the traditional periods of giving—such as the Christmas holidays or during the fiesta season. Occasionally they will carry a musical instrument with them and play a brief tune expecting, in turn, to be given a small monetary gift. These people are usually unwilling to do other forms of work.

On one occasion, during fiesta time, an itinerant beggar offered to play a tune on his clarinet for a small donation at the home of a missionary. It so happened that the missionary was at that moment involved in cutting

down a small tree in his yard. The
man proceeded to play his tune and
then made his plea for a small donation. The missionary in this case
engaged the man in conversation and
offered to pay him considerably more
than he would ordinarily give as a
gift, if the man would finish cutting
down the tree. The man immediately
refused to do this bit of physical
labor and after playing his tune and
receiving the small donation the missionary offered, continued on his way
down the road.

Seasonal Giving

Other giving situations arise on
November first during All Soul's Day
and during the Christmas season.
Children and young people usually
participate in the *pangangaluluwa* and
the *pamamasko*[1] by singing songs
from house to house in expectation
of a small monetary gift. This roughly
corresponds to the North American
practice of "begging" on Halloween
and caroling during the Christmas
season.

The Maimed

In any community there are a
certain number of individuals who
have become the unfortunate victims
of accidents or illnesses. Being indigenous to the community, they
generally make the rounds of the high
status people in the area soliciting
help. Society dictates that these
people are worthy recipients of aid.
In addition to parental directives,

---

[1] Literally, "souling" and "Christmassing."
Taken from the Tagalog roots: *kaluluwa* 'soul'
and *Pasko* 'Christmas.'

children also learn their social responsibility toward the unfortunate through
the process of their education in
elementary school.[2] It is the expectation in the Philippine setting that
those of means are in a certain
measure responsible to help those
who have suffered misfortune.

In the community in which I live,
a man who received a head injury
in an industrial accident, and is
therefore unemployable, stops by at
regular intervals for a gift. The
equivalent of from five to ten cents
is considered a satisfactory donation
in this case.

Giving in the cases cited, even for
the newcomer, usually does not create
serious tension, particularly as one
accepts his status and understands
the appropriate amount to give in these
situations. It is not expected that
seasonal gifts or gifts to the maimed
or professional beggars be large.
Furthermore, these people come at
irregular times and generally do not
prove to be a burden. One can play
his role with equanimity and little
risk of deep personal involvement
with the individual.

Sharing becomes more difficult
and tension is more sharply aroused
when a loan is requested by a person
who is near in a geographical or
emotional sense. Neighbors, members

---

[2] See the lesson entitled, "Ang Matandang
Pulubi" in the third reader for elementary
schools. Josefina L. Santos, Trinidad C. Sion
and Antonio D.G. Mariano, *Sa Bayan at sa
Nayon*, (Manila: M. E. Anatalio & Co. 1947)
pp. 22-27. In this lesson, not only are the
children reminded that they should have mercy
on the beggar, but that the one who mocks the
beggar will suffer misfortune.

of the local church and generally people who have performed some service or shown some degree of hospitality toward the newcomer are potential borrowers. The request for a loan implies a deeper, more involved relationship with an individual which the missionary may not be anxious to establish. Tension arises since he is not sure of the legitimacy of the person's need, whether or not he will be repaid and what his future relationship with the person will be depending on whether he gives or withholds the loan.

Reciprocal Relations

At this point the Philippine pattern of reciprocity comes into play. Among Filipinos, one's obligation to another is very carefully tabulated. One ingredient in this tabulation is the relative status of the individuals involved. Mary Hollnsteiner identifies two types of relationship that may exist. One is termed the "superordinate/subordinate" relationship and the other the "coordinate" relationship.[3] In both cases the borrower has incurred an *utang na loob* or debt of gratitude to the one granting the loan, but in each case different repayment is demanded. In the former case, there is a marked difference in status between the two individuals

[3] Mary R. Hollnsteiner, "Reciprocity in the Lowland Philippines," in *Four Readings on Philippine Values*, compiled by Frank Lynch, (Quezon City: Ateneo de Manila University Press, 1968), pp. 29-31. See also Charles Kaut, "*Utang na Loob*: A System of Contractual Obligation Among Tagalogs," *Southwestern Journal of Anthropology*, Vol. 17 (1961), pp. 256-272.

involved, while in the latter, the individuals are of approximately equal status. Between individuals of unequal status, repayment is not expected to equal the value of the original gift while in the second case, repayment is expected to be made with interest. Since every missionary, at least initially, enjoys upper class status, anyone of lower class status who borrows from him is not necessarily intending to make equal repayment of the initial loan. This is true even though the expression used to conclude the agreement may in fact have been the word for loan (*utang*) and not a donation or gift (*regalo*).

In the mind of the missionary the use of the term "loan" implies a contractual agreement indicating that equal repayment is due within a specified period of time. In the mind of the Filipino, however, the term "loan" does not necessarily imply the force of contract in this sense. It may rather indicate that now the borrower has incurred an *utang na loob* to the lender and this *utang* may be satisfactorily repaid in the form of goods or services as well as cash. Furthermore, the *utang* may not be strictly bound by limits of time. In sum, a loan to a Filipino is more than simply a transfer of funds. Securing a loan from an individual initiates a personal relationship which the Filipino is interested in perpetuating.

Socially Acceptable Sharing

In the light of this, how may a foreigner in the Philippines respond to requests for loans? Keeping in mind that in any society there are some opportunists who are considered poor credit risks by the community at large, and who may prey upon the newcomer, how may one fulfill the command to "give to every man that asks of you"?

A good rule of thumb is for the missionary to take his cues from those about him who enjoy the same status that he enjoys. In the case of irregular, impersonal giving the high status Filipino is ready to give the small amounts required to the singers, the beggars and the maimed. In the case of loans he is likely to be much more discerning. The most natural sources of help in time of need in the Philippine setting fall along the lines of one's alliance system.[4] One should ask himself, and perhaps the person requesting the loan, particularly since he does not belong to the individual's alliance system, why these more natural sources of aid have not been exploited.

Often, resort to a foreigner may be a last ditch effort on the part of the individual to secure a loan which, for one reason or another, has been denied him by members of his in-group or alliance. On the other hand, four possibilities for sharing suggest themselves: one is what I choose to call partial payment, another assisted payment.

---

[4] For a discussion of the alliance system see Mary R. Hollnsteiner, *The Dynamics of Power in a Philippine Municipality* (Quezon City: Community Development Research Council, University of the Philippines, 1963), pp. 63-85.

Partial Payment

Often it is impractical if not impossible to loan the full amount an individual requests. On one occasion a man approached me soliciting a loan of twenty pesos.[5] This man was the brother of a member of the local church although he himself was not a member. I had met him casually on one previous occasion during a fiesta dinner. As we discussed his need he explained that the loan was needed for personal transportation to a remote province in order to visit a son that was sick. Knowing his brother's family well and recognizing that several members of the family were wage earners, I did not feel that it would be wise or necessary to give him the total amount as a loan. After a rather lengthy discussion of the situation, I explained that I could not lend him the required amount for this trip but that I would like to make a contribution toward his need. I offered five pesos toward his transportation need and this was readily accepted. Furthermore, I explained that I did not consider this a loan, but a gift—not to be repaid.

Partial payment is suggested when the amount requested is large or when the individual is only marginally known. Since it does not constitute a refusal to grant the request, partial payment leaves the door open for further contact with the individual. Also, in this case, since the money was offered as a grant and not a

---

[5] At the time of this incident the peso was pegged to the U.S. dollar at the ratio of nearly 4:1. Today the ratio is nearer 7:1.

loan, the possibility of shame[6] arising because of inability to repay was eliminated.

Assisted Payment

Since, as I have indicated, the missionary enjoys upper class status in the Philippines he necessarily carries a certain amount of influence about with him. If he has developed contacts and friendships among other people of his perceived status, and particularly if he is in an *utang na loob* relationship with these, he may occasionally use this influence to assist individuals who approach him requesting help. For instance, a poor member of the church comes appealing for a loan in order to bring a relative into town for medical treatment. Rather than granting a cash loan, the missionary might take this occasion to approach one of his high status friends who happens to be a doctor, and thus pave the way for the individual to obtain medical services. These services usually will be performed either free or at greatly reduced rates because of the relationship previously established between the missionary and the doctor.

This type of an arrangement has two effects. First, the missionary has met his friend's need and solidified a relationship with him. Also, he has incurred an *utang na loob*, in turn, to the doctor which he must

---

[6] Shame (*hiya*) is the social sanction which reinforces conformity to the standards of reciprocity in the Philippines. Hollnsteiner, "Reciprocity," *op. cit.*, pp. 31, 41-44. See also Jaime Bulatao, "Hiya," *Philippine Studies*, Vol. 12, No. 3 (July 1964), pp. 424-438.

remember to repay at some future date. Often this type of behavior is frowned upon by North Americans since it smacks of influence peddling and involves one in entangling alliances. I would like to suggest, however, that in the Philippine setting this behavior is perfectly acceptable. Furthermore, it serves to build the kind of relationships which will ultimately aid the missionary in his primary role of communication.

Payment in Kind

Often, when people are questioned with regard to the need for the loan they are soliciting, they will indicate that a pressing physical need exists in the family for food or medical attention. Rather than simply providing cash, which may or may not be spent wisely, the missionary may accompany the individual to the market or to the drug store in order to purchase the items needed. Occasionally, the missionary may have the item on hand which the person needs to buy. In this case it would be proper to simply give the item to the individual. Of course, immediately the person will either accept, or on occasion, reject the gift. This will offer an indication as to the genuineness of the need.

Contractual Payment

On one occasion a man in the neighborhood sent his son to my home bearing a note. In quite formal English it said, in essence, that the family was in need and that the father, in this case, was ashamed to approach me to request a loan. He implored me to send a loan via his son to the family. Since I was new in the neighborhood and wanted to meet my neighbors I asked the boy to take me to his house. When I arrived the father invited me up into the house. It was obvious from the surroundings that the family was in need. This impression was reinforced by the subsequent tale of the father who was unable to find work at his trade which was housepainting. He explained that he was requesting twenty-five pesos in order to pay his daughter's tuition at the local high school. I told him that I could not lend him that much money but that I did have some painting which needed to be done around my house. He was eager for the work and I hired him. He did a very acceptable job, for which I paid him the agreed sum. As far as this person was concerned, this was a very acceptable means of meeting his need. He was happy to be employed in his trade. Our relationship was allowed to develop without the stigma of unpaid debts hanging either over his head or mine.[7]

Conclusion

Part of the missionary's purpose is to adjust to the alien society in which he finds himself in such a way as to minimize personal tensions and at the same time enhance the prospect for meaningful communication with the host population. Often, sharing one's wealth becomes a stumbling block both to personal serenity and the opportunity for effective communication on the part of many missionaries. In the Philippines, only as one accepts his place as a person of upper class status in the community as well as his role in the system of mutual obligation is he likely to experience personal tranquility and meaningful communication.

[7] It has been suggested that contractual reciprocity is actually replacing *utang na loob* reciprocity in the rural, as well as urban, Philippines. Hollnsteiner, "Reciprocity," *op. cit.*, pp. 47, 48.

O. C. *Fountain*

Religion and Economy in Mission Station-Village Relationships

IN a pioneering article[1] A. H. Cole sought to bring together economics and missionary enterprise in order to show the contribution of missionary activity to economic development in underdeveloped countries. He demonstrates how easy it is for the missionary to distort the economic "message." In a different context, that of mission station-village relationships, this article seeks to show how the economy can effect the transmission of the Christian message.

Briefly, the argument is that a large mission station makes a double impact on the village through its economic relationships and through its religious program. These tend to pull the villager in opposing directions and there is a strong possibility that economic relationships may distort his understanding of the Christian gospel.

[1] Arthur H. Cole, "The Relations of Missionary Activity to Economic Development," *Economic. Development and Cultural Change,* Vol. 9, No. 2 (Jan. 1961), pp. 120-127.

O. C. Fountain undertook M.A. thesis research in social and economic geography on a village near the mission station about which he writes. During 1964 he also taught at the school on this mission station. 7 D'Arcy St., Richmond, Nelson, New Zealand.

As a diagramatic framework for the discussion we propose a triangle, the base (AB) of which represents the mission station and the points A and B represent its economic and religious aspects respectively. The apex

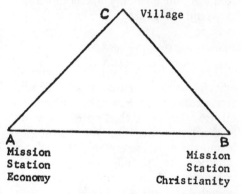

of the triangle (C), however, represents the village, where religion and economy are integrated together. The lines joining the points of the triangle are, we hope to show, lines of tension. Thus AB represents theological and practical problems between Christianity and the economy; BC indicates a tension between the mission's aim of evangelization and the religious state in the villages; and AC is the cash economy of the mission station in tension with the village subsistence economy.

The triangle envisages tension on both the intellectual and practical levels. Because these two are so interwoven, our discussion must include not only the observable facts but also the aims, attitudes and assessments of the situation by both mission and village.

The argument rests on two assumptions which must be examined. The first is that the spiritual and economic aspects of mission station life are not closely integrated, and that both mentally and in practice a distinction is made between "sacred" and "secular." The second is that this situation does not hold in the village but that there religion and economy are complementary and integrated.

Piety and Prosperity

The problem of relating economic activity to the spiritual aspects of mission station life meet the missionary on two levels, a theological one and a practical one. On the theological level, the missionary might well ask whether he should work for the prosperity of the people to whom he preaches.

In Old Testament times (as with the indigenes here and now in New Guinea) material prosperity was thought to be the mark of the blessing of God. This is clearly so in the cases of Abraham (Genesis 24:25), Jacob (Genesis 27:27-28), Joseph (Genesis 39:2), the Israelites (Deuteronomy 28:1-14), and Solomon (1 Kings 3:13), just to take a few examples. Undoubtedly the prosperity of the wicked was a cause of great mental conflict to David, as Psalm 73:12-14 shows. But the New Testament places

quite a different emphasis on the place of material prosperity. Take James 5:1-6 for example. Not that this passage should be read as a condemnation of riches as such, but rather of their abuse. Such is the frequent tenor of New Testament teaching. Even Christ seems to have emphasized the dangers of wealth rather than condemn it outright. In the parable of the rich man and Lazarus (Luke 16:19-31) the punishment of the former was not so much because he was rich but rather because he disregarded the poor.

In any case, if Christ condemned the rich, it was not that he glorified poverty. Many of his miracles were expressly to provide for physical well-being. The constant search for material things can be just as damaging spiritually as a plentiful supply. The true New Testament attitude seems to be one of neutrality to wealth. Of itself wealth is neither good nor bad. This certainly finds reflections in the Old Testament, too, as in Proverbs 30:8-9:

> Give me neither poverty nor riches;
> feed me with food that is needful for me,
> lest I be full, and deny thee,
> and say "Who is the LORD?"
> or lest I be poor, and steal,
> and profane the name of my God.

This neutrality of Scripture still leaves room for doubt as to the responsibiilty of the missionary to engage in economic projects. It may indicate the unimportance of such activity. But few would deny that in the situation of poverty a Christian has a definite responsibility to alleviate this. In New Guinea villages poverty is very much a relative thing. With ample land and food, the New Guinean is economically more prosperous than the Indian peasant. However, bases of comparison are very difficult to find between subsistence and cash economies. There is no doubt, however, that the New Guinean feels poor because he compares so badly with the resident Europeans in respect to the consumer goods he values. Should the missionary work to correct this?

On the practical level the mission station finds itself in tension between its desire to extend its spiritual influence and the natural concomitant that this means an increase in economic demands on the local population, especially where the emphasis is on institutional work. Expansion in medical and educational work means a greater demand for food, building materials, and labor. However, the point to be made here is that the average European does not consider the station trade store, the buying of food, or the running of a sawmill as part of the religious program. It is the writer's belief that these tensions on the mission station help to produce the different responses of the villagers to the economic and spiritual aspects of the mission station's work.

The Animistic View

Our second assumption is that this sacred/secular distinction does not hold for the village, but that here religious and economic activity are highly integrated. In this traditional society nearly the sum total of all religious practices were to secure economic and material well-being — to produce successful crops or to prevent sickness and death. There was little thought of securing merit or well-being in an after life. Everything was for the here and now, and economic prosperity was proof of the efficacy of the magic and rituals that surrounded the agricultural processes.

With this in mind, it is not difficult to understand the New Guinea culture's later accretion of "cargo cult" activity. It was basically an attempt to perform the religious rituals of the new religion (including such activities as the making of airstrips) in order that the material prosperity of the Europeans be provided for them. In other words, it was a direct transfer from the traditional pattern to the new influences which, by their nagging presence, demanded comprehension. The indigene naturally concluded that since the European was materially better off, his ritual practices were better. Or, at least, if one wanted European-type goods, European-type practices must be followed. That the material prosperity of the European was not directly related to the quality of his religion was quite alien to the traditional thinking, and therefore incomprehensible.

Though most of the visible evidences and anti-white aspects of militant cargo cultism have passed from this area because of government influence and instruction and demonstration by the missions, the cargo-cult/animistic pattern of thinking remains very strong. So much so that this appears to the writer to be one of the main sources of possible misunderstanding of the Christian gospel. Undoubtedly, to have a mission station in the local area is very desirable in the eyes of the indigene, not because he is interested in the message but because he believes this will bring automatic prosperity to him. An outlying village from Virnum Mission Station has a passionate desire to have a resident European because it is believed that this "ritual" will bring a heaven on earth to the village in the form of bumper crops and an end of sickness and sorrow.

Because of this view it seems important to understand the impact a sizable mission station might have as a visible representation of the Christian message. The failure on the part of the villagers to make the Western distinction between piety and prosperity may have two effects. On the one hand, it may result in a distortion of the Christian message. On the other, it may lead to frustration (and rejection of the message) because of inability to attain the higher level of living. This is most likely to occur in villages most exposed to the economic differences and may be among the chief causes for the unresponsiveness to the gospel of the village adjacent to Virnum Mission Station.[2]

Virnum Mission Station[3] is located among the southern foothills of the coastal range in the Sepik District, New Guinea. It is about ten miles from the nearest government school and about twenty-five miles from the sub-district office. To the north, the terrain is rugged with the rivers deeply incised, and to the south the hills gradually become more gentle as the

tributary rivers flow toward the Sepik. Tribal groupings are complex and fragmented. Six different language groups can be reached in two hours walk from the station. The villages, normally situated on ridge tops, have populations averaging about two hundred each.

Although the area has been under European influence for many years — Roman Catholic missionaries, labor recruiters and government patrols making irregular treks through the region — it was only in the early 1950's that the government could claim effective administrative control over it. Before this time the event of greatest significance in the minds of the people was "the war" with its lavish display of force and food, such as the indigenes had never imagined possible before. Perhaps this white man's war was the main cause of cargo cults arising so dramatically when, after the war, the white man's religion and the white man's government arrived in full force. In any case cargo cults were rife in the postwar years.

The area in the 1950's was an economic backwater. It was inaccessible except on foot or by air, and economic development was out of the question. Several schemes, including peanuts, were tried, but transport costs or market fluctuations showed them to be unworkable, and they were abandoned. This only further reinforced the villagers' consciousness of their own inability and the incomprehensibility of the outside world.

For many years the region has been subject to labor recruitment for distant coastal plantations and this may still

---

2 The lack of spiritual interest in the nearest village is repeated at a number of other mission stations in the area.

3 For obvious reasons the commonly accepted name of the mission station has not been used. Instead the name of the ground on which the station is built has been chosen.

be the main source of cash into the area. In the past, before effective administrative control, overrecruitment often left the villages seriously short of able-bodied men. However, today not more than one third of the adult male labor force should be away on plantations at any one time. The contract period is two years and it is a mark of manhood to have worked as a laborer on a plantation. There are, of course, no plantations in the subdistrict.

A marked cash-consciousness characterizes the local inhabitants. Three factors seem to be of great significance in fostering this outlook. The first, plantation labor recruitment, we have already mentioned. The second is the European, whose way of life depends on his ability to buy things rather than his blood relationships. Finally, all traditional payments have been partly or wholly substituted by cash, which has here completely ousted the traditional shell currency.

Religiously, before the arrival of the Protestant mission, the area had been nominally Roman Catholic for many years, but despite the gradually increasing influence of the Roman Catholic missionaries in the postwar years, animism and traditional ways of thought remained much more significant than the new religion. Only outwardly things had changed. A mild "yam cult" and the "tambaran houses," which embodied the secret religion of the men, had both disappeared. But sorcery and traditional practices for the invocation or appeasement of spirits were still frequent occurrences. Even today, should a person die from no obvious cause,

it is frequently suspected that somebody has "worked poison" (brought about the death by magic). During a recent epidemic the paths leading to many villages were barricaded with fronds, flowers, colorful fruits, and even bamboo crosses, to prevent the evil spirits from coming into the village. One village turned out en masse to a church service in the hope that this ritual would rid them of the sickness.

Virnum Mission Station

In this situation the Virnum Mission Station came into being in 1958. Unlike normal procedure, Virnum was selected as the site for a mission station not at the request of the local people (though they were keen about the prospect of medical and trade store facilities) or because of their religious interest, but because it seemed to be an ideal site for a hospital. The importance of this fact should not be underestimated because it has no doubt affected relationships between the station and the villages. The economic gain of having resident Europeans probably carried considerable weight in the minds of the local people. This seems even more probable to the writer because the year work commenced on the airstrip was the peak of an active cargo cult in some nearby villages.

The station's growth has been rapid and constant with an increase in both the number and size of activities. An air strip, hospital, and sawmill came into existence. A vehicular road was marked out and built, connecting the station to the subdistrict headquarters. In 1960 Virnum became the site for the annual conference of the mission, and as a result *dongas* 'small one-roomed houses' were constructed. These are used as family units during the conference week and for short visits for medical or other reasons. In addition, a missionary working as a secretary-accountant established his home here, so that in a sense Virnum became the mission's headquarters.

Although a school for children from nearby villages had been in existence for several years, the mission's Central School was started here at the beginning of 1963. With the annual intake of new pupils, the size of the school (a boarding establishment) will continue to grow in the next two or three years. Entrance to Central School is by examination at the end of Standard 2 (third year of schooling), selecting the best pupils from all the mission's schools for schooling in English.

A further addition during 1964 was the commencement of a cattle pilot project on the station property. It is manned, however, by a trained indigenous Christian from a nearby village.

Characteristic of Virnum, then, is that it has an emphasis on institutional work unmatched by the other stations of the mission. Furthermore, institutional missionary work tends to concentrate personnel and makes for a large mission station. That this is manifestly so in this case can be seen from the following figures. About a quarter of the European personnel working with the mission in New Guinea are located on this station. (There are thirteen other stations.) Virnum Mission Station has a total of one hundred and ten acres on which

are located over seventy permanent and semipermanent buildings. An average population of over two hundred during the school year means that the number of people equal to a normal village are almost totally dependent on the nearby villages for their food supply. Only supplies of meat, bread, salt, and some nonessentials flown in by plane from Wewak and a few small garden plots on the station supplement this.

Economic Relationships

It should be borne in mind that the mission has no clearly defined agricultural or economic aims as such for the betterment of the people. It is conscious of the fact that its primary work is evangelization and the planting of indigenous churches. The medical work, any agricultural interests that the missionaries may have, and to some extent even the educational program, are regarded as points of contact rather than ends in themselves. They are thus kept in this conscious perspective, even if in reality such activities consume the larger proportion of a missionary's time.

Nevertheless, the needs of the mission station combined with the demands of the people have produced a number of economic relationships which constantly impinge on the religious activities of the missionaries and villagers alike. It is at the heart of our purpose to examine the tensions thus created.

Among the more important economic activities is the mission station trade store. This is the chief source of consumer goods for the people and was largely set up as a response to local demand. (The pattern had been set by earlier established Catholic mission stations.) It is probably the commonest meeting place for people from previously unrelated and even hostile villages. Spasmodic visits may be paid to it by people from villages three or more hours' walk away. Besides the station store, however, the mission supplies goods to several village stores run by the inhabitants themselves for their own profit.

A constant economic need on the mission station is for labor. A virtually continuous building program, combined with a variety of other activities such as tree felling, saw milling, drain digging, and grass cutting, means that besides a more or less permanent labor force, there are many opportunities for casual labor. Casual labor may be drawn from a wide area, sometimes with the conscious purpose of increasing contact with an outlying village.

A more formalized relationship is the supply of food to the station. The need for a regular food supply has forced the mission station to specify on which days the various villages may bring food for sale, and also to control the amount of money to be spent each day on buying it. Seven villages bring food regularly to the station.

Even more localized in its extent is the supply of building materials like palm thatch, split logs, and bamboo for native material houses. This relationship is restricted to only three or four villages.

Finally, there are two specific relationships, the second more important than the first, with the village whose land surrounds the station. These are the supply of millable timber (beyond what is grown on the station) and the "land relationship." Residents of the immediate village, by virtue of having owned the land on which the station is located, regard the mission station as specifically theirs.

By this brief outline of the more significant economic relationships, it is clear that a series of concentric circles can be drawn around the mission station to indicate the intensity of economic involvement as indicated by the number and quality of relationships between the station and the surrounding villages.

A different schema, however, must be produced for the religious relationships emerging with the villages. Although a pattern emerges, proximity is not in direct proportion to spiritual interest. Furthermore, distortions and irregularities arise through Roman Catholic mission stations existing within the contact area.

The missionaries generally recognize the adjacent village as, by and large, apathetic and halfhearted in its response to the gospel. Several villages one to two hours' walk away show the keenest response to the gospel and contain nearly all the village Christians except for two villages on the fringe of the contact area, where the work was commenced by other mission stations. Groups from the former villages come weekly to the station for instruction classes, but no indigenous churches have been established yet.

Beyond these are a number of villages showing interest in the message and where regular church services are conducted by mission personnel in buildings erected for the purpose. Further out again are villages showing a little or growing interest but whose main contact is through regular infant welfare visits by the nursing staff of the hospital.

From a comparison of the patterning of religious and economic relationships presented here, it is suggested that intense economic involvement has a negative effect on spiritual interest.

Analysis of Tensions

Within this field of relationships two contrasting religious systems and two equally contrasting economies have been juxtaposed. This has given rise to a new dynamic social situation. The advent of the mission station has broken into what was virtually a stable equilibrium both economically and religiously, and the processes of readjustment are still in progress. A small mission station may not significantly alter the subsistence economy, but a large one provides new opportunities and makes big demands on its surrounding villages.

The coming of the mission station has provided a new source of cash for the villagers. But in the main, it has not been the traditional village leaders (usually the older men) who have been in a position to benefit from it, but rather the younger men who have been able to acquire the new skills. So in a sense the social structure of the mission station competes with that of the village in that it offers an alternative means for acquiring money and prestige. But some money earned on the mission station is used in the traditional exchange payments and so

supports the village social organization. However, a proportion of this money is spent on consumption goods at the trade store. In fact, one of the striking features of the mission station as a new factor in the economy is just this tension it has created between the traditional and the modern significance of money. It can either be used in the social exchange payments or be spent on goods. Frequently when one is told by a villager that he has no money, the truth is that it is tied up in social obligations in the village.[4]

Such a dynamic situation gives rise to a whole range of tensions. These include such adjustments as the need to fit into new patterns of work and rest; the European demand to deal with the individual rather than the group; and the new prestige of the young and able-bodied vis-a-vis the traditional village leaders. Here we are concerned with only two: tension arising out of uncertainty in the new situation, and tension arising out of economic frustration.

Especially in the first years, considerable tension arose because the new statuses which were created did not have clearly defined roles in the minds of the people and attempts to interpret the situation in terms of traditional patterns frequently ended in brawls. For example, the village X, which surrounds the mission station, regarded the mission station

---

4 This conflict in the use of money is a major obstacle to a rise in the standard of living. An estimated minimum of 3,500 pounds has been paid over by the mission station to the immediate village (for land, food, building materials, labor, etc.) in the past six years but there is scarcely any sign of a rise in living standards in the village as a result.

as its own. People from other villages were here on sufferance and according to the inhabitants of X under no circumstances should be given preference over X men in the sale of food or in work. The claim was no doubt based on land ownership, the indigenes not having grasped adequately what was involved in the legal transfer of land. The missionaries, of course, felt no such obligation to X and sought rather to spread their contact over a number of villages. It is suggested that this is another factor in the spiritual apathy of this village.

The second tension to be discussed here is the result of the failure of the mission station to fulfill the preconceived ideas of the indigenous people. Given the economic frustration that existed before the arrival of the mission station, the latter's creation presented the possibility in the minds of the villagers of providing an abundant supply of desired goods and cash. That this was not so was probably not realized at first. Take, for example, the sale of food. The station must have a regular supply of food but has only limited financial resources. Villages are allowed to bring food only on the day of the week allotted to them, but each one provides considerably more than is needed. However, a major relocation of gardens has occurred in the last two years (and the trend seems to be increasing) to positions as close as possible to the mission station. During observations of the sale of food, it was the writer's frequent experience to see far more food brought than could be bought. Frustrations and hot tempers are frequently vented at this time. Failure

to satisfy such expectations may also lead to indifference to the Christian gospel.

In what ways may the economic situation affect the spiritual work of a mission station? I suggest three.

First, there is the possibility that the mission station will support the cargo cult attitudes of the people by giving the impression that material prosperity will come automatically with conversion to Christianity. This is especially so where European missionaries have a much higher standard of living than the local people. Though the militant cargo cult attitude has passed, it has been replaced by an attitude of expecting the European to give his material benefits to the indigene. "You are our father," one is told, the inference being that one should distribute his goods to them as a father would to his children.

Second, if there is ample opportunity for obtaining cash either by labor or the sale of goods, it may deflect the villager from appraising correctly the purpose of the mission. He may feel that, with economic activities occupying such a large proportion of time, this is therefore more important in the eyes of the missionary than his spiritual work.

Third, the impossibility for the indigene to follow the European pattern of life may lead to a reticence to follow his message.

Conclusion

In this paper an attempt has been made to suggest reasons for the apathy of the nearest village to Virnum Mission Station. All of them are economic in nature and there are, no doubt, noneconomic causes, but the ones suggested seem to be of great significance. It may be felt that many of the tensions will work themselves out in a few years by the process of reeducation and the dwindling of the economic needs of the station. But certainly nothing can be gained by ignoring conflicts and confusion between the economic and religious spheres, and a lot may be gained by acknowledging it, even if it affects only the presentation of the gospel. Only too readily the writer admits that there are no easy solutions either in the particular case described or in its broader implications in the fields of religion and economy. Even if it were possible to live at the same standard of living as the indigene, one could not enter into the system of exchange relationships which is an integral part of village society. One's life would still be cash-based. Or to react by cutting economic ties because they create tensions would leave the Christian community in an unreal isolation more harmful than if it were economically overinvolved.

The principal conclusion we are led to, then — and this seems to apply to any Christian community — is that there is a need to stand back, try to see the mission station as a whole, and ask if this adequately represents Christianity. It is contended that not only the individual missionary, but the mission station too, must be a living portrayal of the gospel.

Probably in our concern with dangers, we have presented all too gloomy a picture of a mission station as it represents Christianity. Undoubtedly, medical and educational programs do portray very graphically Christ's interest in bodies and minds as well as souls. But it is suggested that if a mission station places too great an emphasis on economic activities, it does not truly reflect what Christ intended the gospel to be.

William L. Wonderly

Indian Work and Church-Mission Integration

The current trend toward "indigenization," or transferral of responsibility from the missions to the national churches and from missionaries to nationals, is represented in a number of areas today by the plan for "integration" of the mission with the national church. In this plan the mission as such is dissolved and the missionaries become "fraternal workers" under the administrative responsibility of the church in the country where they are serving. The writer of the present article discusses the danger that, for Indian work in Latin America, this integration may lead to a greater degree of paternalism toward the Indian churches, or even in some cases to curtailment of the Indian work; and suggests certain measures for the missions of the sending churches to consider as a means to offset this danger and to help the national churches develop the full potential which their Indian constituency represents. The implications of this article apply just as well to other areas where there are minority populations with different languages and cultures from the national group.[1]

The Problem

In the Latin American countries that have a significant Indian population, there are in effect two coexistent societies: the Spanish-speaking (known variously as *la-* dino, mestizo, cholo, etc.) and the Indian, with the former dominant over the latter. In a number of these countries, integration is about to take place between the missions and the national churches, and the missionaries are to be given the status of fraternal workers under the national churches. This means that, at least theoretically, the responsibility for developing the Indian churches will then be assumed largely by the national churches — which means, in terms of over-all leadership, the churches of the dominant or Spanish-speaking society. In the light of this, it is imperative that these Spanish-speaking churches and their leaders be made aware of their responsibility toward the Indian groups and of the barriers which they must overcome if they are effectively to reach them and lead them to form a functioning part of the national church as a whole.

The attitude of many of the Spanish-

[1] This article is rewritten from part of a report on a study of the Presbyterian work at the Mam Christian Center at Ostuncalco, Guatemala, made by Dr. F. G. Scovel and the author in July, 1960, by request of the Commission of Ecumenical Mission and Relations of the United Presbyterian Church in the U.S.A. Much of the information on the Mam church situation was learned in conversations with Rev. and Mrs. H. Dudley Peck and Dr. Ralph Winter, and in interviews with local Indian and Ladino members of the church. Other missionaries, as well as published materials, have provided additional information regarding the situation in neighboring districts and in the area as a whole. The present article is intended to present some of the implications of this study for Indian work in its wider scope in Latin America.

speaking people toward the Indian was effectively expressed to me years ago by Doña Ofelia, widow of a well-to-do Ladino merchant in southern Mexico whom the local Indians remember affectionately as a helper and benefactor. She said, *"El indio sin patrón es como una rueda sin eje"* ("An Indian without a *patrón* is like a wheel without an axle.") Although the social revolution in Latin America has done much to abolish the feudal system, especially in countries like Mexico, the traditional attitudes of paternalism and exploitation, together with the concept of the Indian as inferior, are still present. Unfortunately, these attitudes do not automatically disappear when people become evangelical Christians.

For example, there is the Presbyterian church in the large market town of Ostuncalco, Guatemala. This church consists of a small handful of Spanish-speaking people and some four hundred Mam-speaking Indians. Most of the latter live in outlying communities and have their own local chapels, but continue to be officially a part of the church in the market center, and a number of them attend the Sunday morning service there when they make their weekly trip to town. This lends prestige to the Indians, who have always taken pride in belonging to Ostuncalco, their political center. However, the Ladino minority fails to understand why the Sunday morning service should be in Mam (it is actually in both languages, with interpretation), since Spanish is the official language of the country and the only language which they, the people who run affairs, speak.

The elders of this church include both Ladinos and Indians; however, most of the decisions are made by the former, and the latter help to perpetuate their inferiority status by seldom speaking up to register a dissenting opinion. When the recently completed church building was constructed, the plans were made chiefly by the Ladino group but the Indians were the ones asked to contribute the major share of the cost (which they did by their harvest offerings as well as money gifts).

In a large Indian church in the Department of Huehuetenango, Guatemala, the pastor (who is a young Ladino) has repeatedly offended his Indian constituency by failing to show sufficient respect to the older men, by showing inattention during the Indian-language prayers, announcements, etc., in the church service (since he does not understand the language), and by failing to show appreciation for the Indian language in general. In this case the body of elders (all Indian) take the pastor to task periodically for this sort of thing, and he seems to have the grace to accept at least some of their counsel — but in most such churches there is not sufficient rapport for matters of this type to be discussed with such a degree of frankness.

A few years ago, in one of the presbyteries of Guatemala, a motion was actually brought to the floor which, if it had been passed, would have eliminated the use of Indian languages in the church services — even in those where most of the people who attend do not understand Spanish. The motion was made by a Ladino member of the presbytery; strangely enough, it was supported even by two of the Indian members of the presbytery. Yet this is not as strange as it may appear at first. Actually, the Indians are in the midst of a tremendous struggle to obtain the prestige which can come to them through identification with the Spanish-speaking society, and the Indian ministers, who are not exempt from this pressure, are easily tempted to bid for this prestige at the expense of an intelligible communication of their message. If we add to this the fact that their age-long heritage, both pagan and Roman Catholic, emphasizes the use of religious rites in a language unknown to the listeners, it is not surprising that insufficient importance is attached to the communication of the gospel in the mother tongue. Nothing in the historical background really calls for a relevant communication of the message to the people.

However, use of the Indian languages is not the only point at issue. The entire cultural background of the Indian groups, including their world view, their concepts of supernatural beings, their animistic beliefs of the cause and cure of illness, their value system with its concepts of sin and virtue — all these are different in greater or less degree from the ideas held by the Spanish-speaking people. But the tendency of the latter is to lump the whole Indian system of beliefs into the category of "superstitions" and largely to ignore it in the Protestant churches' ministry to the Indians. Yet it is precisely the belief system of the Indians which has provided the most effective points of contact for the gospel in those areas where Indian work has prospered.[2]

Culture Change
and Indian Values

Most Indian groups in Latin America are in the process of acculturation or cul-

ture change, under the impact of the dominant culture of the Spanish-speaking people. This change is more rapid in some groups than in others, varying with such factors as the presence of roads, schools, and movies, as well as with the less tangible factors of size and cultural vitality of the Indian group in question. But in all the groups, with the possible exception of a few small and isolated jungle tribes, this culture change is under way. This means that the older generations, with their traditional status of leadership in the society, are being threatened by the leadership of the younger generations and that the latter, although rooted in their Indian background, are beginning to learn the ways of Western civilization.

An early approach to this problem in Latin America was that of the attempt at an incorporation of the Indian into the national life which in effect would consider the Indian background as a *tabula rasa* and attempt to "give" the Indian the national culture as though he had no legitimate culture or world view of his own to start with. When in a recent consultation held by Protestant leaders in Mexico, the problems of Indian work were being discussed, one person went so far as to insist that everything Indian should, if only it were possible, be destroyed; asserting that any and all negative psychological factors such as gloominess, taciturnity, or distrustfulness which he personally, as a *mestizo,* might have in any degree were to be blamed upon the Indian side of his heritage! His opinion, offered as it was without recognition of the positive factors and contribution of the Indian, was fortunately not shared by many of those present, and might have been dismissed as irresponsible and ludicrous, were it not for the fact that it was the voice of a univer-

---

[2] For a penetrating study of this, see Eugene A. Nida, "Christo-Paganism," PRACTICAL ANTHROPOLOGY, Vol. 8, No. 1 (Jan.-Feb. 1961), pp. 1-15. For development of this in a Mayan Indian group of Mexico, see John Beekman, "Minimizing Religious Syncretism among the Chols," Vol. 6, No. 6 (Nov.-Dec. 1959), pp. 241-250, and "Cultural Extensions in the Chol Church," Vol. 7, No. 2 (Mar.-Apr. 1960), pp. 54-61.

sity-educated leader of Protestant young people, and in a country whose non-Protestant scholars and leaders have probably done more than those of any other Latin American nation to dispel this very image of the Indian and to show appreciation for his contribution to the national culture.

This approach, which fails to recognize anything of value in things Indian and seeks merely to implant a "superior" culture, has been in large measure replaced among Latin American leaders and intellectuals — but not to the desired extent in the national churches — by an approach which seeks to integrate the Indian way of life with that of the nation, establishing a society in which the values present in the Indian background are recognized and an attempt is made to relate these to the national culture. The strong sense of community responsibility of the Indian, his belief in the dignity of manual labor (compare the so-called "Protestant ethic"), and other positive characteristics are made to contribute toward community development and social betterment and, in the long run, toward the national life in its wider sense. An attempt is made to guide the change in culture in such a way as to eliminate from the Indian culture its harmful features (e.g. inadequate approach to health, nutrition, and disease) without at the same time upsetting the cultural equilibrium that must be maintained if disaster is to be avoided.

An example of the latter approach as applied to evangelical church life is to be found in the recently developed Indian church in Aguacatán, Guatemala, as told to the writer by the Rev. Harry McArthur of the Wycliffe Bible Translators. Here the Protestant church elders are actively exercising, for the Christian constituency, many of the spiritual functions that have traditionally been performed by the shaman or witch-doctor for the pagan community. These functions involve special Christian observances at the birth of a baby (for the non-Christians the shaman is paid to divine the name and future destiny of the child), special Christian functions at betrothal and marriage (paralleling the functions of the shaman), and other services performed at other life crises.

Another example of this principle may be seen in the so-called bride price that is customary among the Mam Indians, which they themselves interpret not as purchase of the woman but as a token reimbursement to her parents for her rearing and which they consider as a useful practice to enhance the value of the bride and to render separation less easy. In part of the Mam area this practice has been actively discouraged by some of the missionaries, with the result that it is now carried on surreptitiously or not at all by the evangelicals, or else substituted by token gifts of turkeys and other delicacies; while in another part of the area the practice has been allowed to continue, albeit without active encouragement by the missionaries. In both parts of the area, however, the Spanish-speaking pastors tend to discourage the practice and to suppose that it is degrading to womanhood.

An imperative need is for the development of both Spanish-speaking and Indian leaders who will be able to "look both ways," seeing in the Indian culture both its values and its defects and relating the Christian message both to the Indian background and to the national culture as it is being entered by the younger generation of Indians. To date this has, with few exceptions, not been the attitude of the national church leadership.

Some Implications of Church-Mission Integration

Protestant missions from the United States have become sensitive to the desires of the national churches for autonomy, and have come to recognize that among them there is a leadership well able to assume greater responsibilities for the ongoing work of the Kingdom of God in their countries. In a conscientious endeavor to avoid perpetuating a paternalistic approach to the churches of these lands, they are encouraging the national churches to assume greater responsibilities for the development of the church in their respective countries. In the Presbyterian work in Guatemala, for example, the date of 1962 is set for the integration of the Mission and the national Synod, which will put the responsibility for policy-making primarily upon the latter.

However, so long as the national church leadership maintains its present attitude toward the Indian and his culture, such integration with the national churches (under their leadership) may well lead to a considerably more paternalistic attitude toward the Indian work than has been held by the missions themselves. The situation becomes anomalous, in that one purpose of integration is to escape from the charge of paternalism!

An alternate possibility is that, in some cases, this integration may lead to curtailment or virtual abandonment of Indian work in favor of work among the Spanish-speaking population, inasmuch as Ladino leaders occasionally voice concern at the expenditures of money and personnel that are being made for the Indians rather than for the Spanish-speaking groups. In this case the resultant vacuum might eventually be filled by other groups, including

some of the so-called "fringe" movements, whose policies do not rule out the continued missionizing approach to the Indian areas. Some of these movements are of course doing a commendable work and should be encouraged; but in view of our Christian responsibility and of the enormous potential which the Indian groups offer for the established churches, it would not seem opportune to turn the entire Indian work over to these other movements as yet.

A Suggested Program

The alternative to these consequences would seem to be that of an intensive preparation of the leadership of the national churches, in the countries with Indian population, to recognize their responsibility toward the Indian and to develop a more adequate approach to this task. In some of the Latin American countries, especially Mexico, there have been great strides taken in *indigenismo,* or the application of social anthropology to the Indian problem. Other countries are following suit. But this approach has not yet gotten the attention of the evangelical leaders.[3]

It would therefore seem that if the missionary organizations are to turn over to the national churches the responsibility for policies of Indian work, without resulting in curtailment of the same or the development of an over-paternalistic emphasis, they must take drastic measures to insure the preparation of national leaders who will be anthropologically and linguistically oriented and conversant with the develop-

---

[3] For a fuller discussion of this development, see William L. Wonderly, "Social Anthropology, Christian Missions, and the Indians of Latin America," PRACTICAL ANTHROPOLOGY, Vol. 6, No. 2 (Mar.-Apr. 1959), pp. 55-64.

ments in *indigenismo* that are being carried on by anthropologists, including Latin Americans themselves. Such persons should be able to apply some of these concepts to Christian Indian work, and in turn to educate the national Protestant constituencies to their responsibility along these lines.

Obtaining such prepared leaders will not be easy. Few national pastors are qualified to take up a study of social anthropology on the university level, and those who are so qualified are usually too busy. Men or women with such a university background can command a higher salary than the national churches are prepared to pay. Such persons should have not only seminary preparation, but a type of university study which the national churches do not yet see the value of sponsoring. There are a few capable young people in the churches of some of these countries who have shown interest in this type of work and who have been taking some studies which would prepare them for it; but as yet there would seem to be no way in which their own churches are likely to sponsor them in such work. If the present situation continues, their talents will be used outside the church.

Because of this, it will probably be necessary for the missions of the sending churches to sponsor the preparation of such personnel, and to contribute toward their continuing support in the work as technical advisers and research people on a different level from the ordinary pastor's salary in these countries. Naturally this would be a new departure, and it would present certain new problems; but financially it may not be too different from the use of mission funds to prepare and support medical and similiar specialized personnel. If mission executives in the sending countries have not yet seen the necessity of assigning funds to this type of specialty, it is because of already existing commitments along other lines, and because until now the younger churches have not been asked to assume primary responsibility for Indian work. Now that they are being so asked, they are caught largely unprepared; and in the present transition toward integrated church-mission effort, the missions must be prepared to rethink their responsibility for helping the national churches to shoulder this specialized task.

No doubt some Latin Americans should be sent to study anthropology and linguistics in the United States in preparation for this type of leadership; but a valuable preparation in social anthropology, geared especially to the problems of these countries, is already currently available in Latin America. This is partly through the present Inter-American Program in Applied Social Sciences, sponsored by the Organization of American States,[4] which is bringing to Mexico students from all over Latin America, some on the basis of scholarships, for this very purpose. Courses are offered that are valuable not only for specialists in Indian work but for those in rural work and in the various urban social classes. Unfortunately, no Protestant organization seems to be taking advantage of this program, although the students on such scholarships do include a few who are evangelicals. On the other hand, there are some Roman Catholics who are being trained in this program for work in missions to Indians that are being conducted by this church.

Another approach is that of sponsoring local conferences on Indian work for key people in the national churches, at which

---

[4] For further information see under "Notes and News," page 216.

problems of culturally relevant communication of the gospel are discussed and to which local Latin American scholars may be invited to speak on some phase of social anthropology relevant to the interests of those present. One such conference was sponsored in Mexico by the American Bible Society in 1958, with a considerable interest shown by those attending. The annual translators' conferences in Guatemala are to some extent along this line, and in the 1960 conference a few of the Ladino church leaders were present for discussions on the effectiveness with which Christian concepts have been communicated to the Indians and to hear lectures by Guatemalan anthropologists on problems of Indian work. The holding of such conferences in strategic areas is an approach which could well be carried on by local church councils, given the needed impulse and guidance by persons with preparation in social anthropology.

A third avenue of approach is that of providing key Protestant nationals, especially those responsible in some way for Indian work, with periodic information on social anthropology in relation to the work of the church, and news of developments in the field. The writer has attempted this in Mexico on a small scale through the mailing of occasional mimeographed materials; but to be done properly this would require a regular periodical in Spanish, for which neither funds nor personnel are presently available.

A program of the type suggested in the above paragraphs should be coordinated, at least at the outset, by anthropologically oriented missionary or fraternal worker personnel from some mission or some inter-church agency. Such a person should have the means wherewith to bring to bear upon the work in various countries the developments in social anthropology that are taking place in secular circles in Mexico, Guatemala, Peru, Bolivia, and elsewhere, and should explore all possible ways to lead the Spanish-speaking churches to an awareness of their responsibility both to evangelize the Indian and to develop his potentialities for Christianity and citizenship.

This would be a new type of service offered by the sending churches to meet the new need that is arising as a result of church-mission integration and "indigenization" of the Spanish-speaking national churches. It would not be a venture into a new field, but an effort to capitalize the gains, so to speak, that have been made over the years through investment of time and money in this aspect of the work. Its goal would be the furtherance of the Indian work that has been undertaken in the past by the missions and which is now to be carried on with new leadership, but which the missions still have a responsibility to see pursued along lines at least as sound as those which Latin Americans themselves are following in their secular programs for the Indians.

Oswald C. Fountain

Some Roles of Mission Stations

The author points out that mission stations have many roles: base camp, contact, employment opportunity, evangelization, Bible teaching, medical, and educational. Some are consciously planned, some just grow. But too often the net result is to create formalized, institutional relationships between missionaries and nationals in which the former are dominant and the latter cannot respond freely; the depth of their commitment can therefore be questioned. The author advocates the view that a mission station, rather than being a closed cultural enclave dominated by the missionary, ought to serve as a cultural link with both missionaries and nationals sharing ideas and participating freely in the resulting change.

IN a previous article[1] the writer discussed the religious and economic impact of one particular mission station on its surrounding villages. It was suggested that a mission station conveys to the local people a concept of the nature of Christianity. In this article, we are attempting to generalize and expand this idea by discussing the roles of some mission stations with particular reference to Papua and New Guinea. It is hoped to show that mission stations have both conscious religious and socio-economic roles and also have clear cultural functions for both the missionaries and the indigenous people. It will be seen that mission stations are in fact agents of change within the community.

[1] O.C. Fountain, "Religion and Economy in Mission Station-Village Relationships," PA, Vol. 13, No. 2 (March-April 1966) pp. 49-58.

Growth of Mission Stations

There are probably few mission stations on which the first missionaries who acquired the land foresaw the subsequent growth and development to such an extent that the whole station as it exists today was a fully planned project from the beginning. Missionary manpower has not been sufficient nor has missionary planning been so effective! The great majority of mission stations just grew step by

Oswald C. Fountain holds a Master of Arts degree with Honours in Geography from the Victoria University of Wellington, New Zealand. He is a missionary with Christian Missions in Many Lands. This article resulted from a paper he presented at the mission's annual conference at Anguganak, August 1970. Guala Mission Station, Koroba, via Mt. Hagen, Terr. of Papua and New Guinea.

step and planning was done only if and when the need arose.

Basically, mission stations developed from the sheer need of a missionary to have somewhere to live and work out from. His desire to work with one village or a group of villages determined the location of his home. If it was the former, a mission station as such did not usually develop; if it was the latter, the central location provided the means to establish a mission station.

As the missionary set up his home, he also endeavored to make contact with the local people in various ways. He tried to meet their need for urgent medical help, literacy and education, employment and so on, while at the same time evangelizing them. Thus the initial roles of mission stations were as follows:

1. "Base camp" role. The missionary built his house there and the station became his home.

2. Contact role. The missionary saw his first task as making contact and winning the confidence of the people. He knew that he could not communicate the gospel effectively without this. Thus a number of "contact ventures" were started which helped to meet the people's felt needs and show the missionary's genuine concern for the villagers. In post-war Papua and New Guinea these contact ventures have included: trade stores, infant welfare clinics, emergency medical work, and education and/or literacy. While in the mind of the missionary, these projects were viewed as initiating contact and served as a means of bringing people onto the mission station, in the eyes of the villagers the mission station was performing the role of *supplier of goods and services.*

3. Employment opportunity role. The mission station also became the place where village people could earn a cash income. Where this was a role undertaken consciously, and in other places in the aftermath, it has been justified in various ways. The commonest of these seem to be:

(a) It was a necessity to allow the missionary to specialize in the work he came for.

(b) It was an effort to give the local people a cash income to make a contribution to their economic welfare.

(c) It was in order to give members of the local communities training in certain lines of work so that they could find employment elsewhere.

4. Evangelization role. Having made such contacts, the missionary began to proclaim the message to the people. This was done often almost concurrently with the initial contacts being made, but became more effective in time (frequently climaxing in a "breakthrough" stage).

Whether the mission stations, especially in their contact and employment opportunity roles, in fact assisted the evangelization process is difficult to tell. Alongside the argument that contact ventures and employment provided the means for effective communication must be put another. This is that these activities put the missionary in a dominant social role and thus the message he was communicating was not transmitted as amongst equals, but as superior to inferior. Receptivity was therefore sometimes more apparent than real–it paid to listen. As a further result, it seems probable that distortion and reinterpretation of the message were made more likely.

Gradually, with the arrival of more missionary personnel and the development of one or more institutions on the mission stations these initial roles became more significant. And with the expansion of the work, three more roles became distinct. These were:

5. *Bible teaching role.* Conversion in response to the message brought about the need for this. Often the missionary felt that it was more worthwhile from his point of view to have the Christians come onto the mission station for Bible teaching, rather than to go out to them. In some cases, this even developed to such an extent as to give the mission station a *church center role.*

6 and 7. *Medical and educational roles.* Most mission stations conducted increasingly large medical and educational programs.

Thus it may be seen that mission stations are truly multipurpose, performing many social, economic and spiritual roles at one time. It is probably true that all these roles (that is, 1 through 7), are found on most mission stations at present in Papua and New Guinea.

Multipurpose Mission Stations

Mission stations, as they have been described, are the product of a particular type of missionary work in a characteristically traditional social setting. In their more developed form, they appear to result from an institutional approach to missionary work which tends to concentrate the missionary force at nodal points. Although multipurpose mission stations are found in many countries, they are associated with missionary work in rural areas. Urban locations, due to pressure on the land and the density of the population, tend to prohibit such complexes developing. They are also more common in areas where cultural differences between the ways of life of the missionaries and the indigenous people are extreme. They are, for example, more common in tribal than in nontribal societies.

Many other factors have also contributed to the appearance of the mission station phenomenon. They include government legislation regarding the granting of land for mission leases, the total area and population the missionaries are trying to communicate with, and the segmentation of the society within which the missionaries are working.

Such modern multipurpose mission stations appear to be the religious equivalent of plantations in the economic realm. Both tend to function as distinct entities among communities that are at many points in striking contrast with them in social and economic patterns. Both have a wide range of integrated activities organized along "modern" lines. On both, many of the relationships are formalized and, in the case of some mission stations, structured in a hierarchical manner. Lines of command on both station and plantation are often one way, from European to indigenous.

Mission station complexes, then, tend to have the following results:

(a) They consume large chunks of missionary time in administration and coordination. The handling of station finances, supervision of employees, ordering of goods and planning and developing of the station program all fall to the lot of the missionary.

(b) They cut off the missionary from the local people by putting him in a dominant social role. On the mission station, the missionary is the employer, supervisor, trainer or teacher. He controls the timing of the daily routine of activities and he is the initiator of commands.

(c) They create a Western enclave in a local setting. It appears generally true that mission stations are organized to suit the way of life of the missionaries living there and to a large extent, they shield the newcomer from culture shock. It is the writer's experience that culture shock is more intense in the village situation than on a mission station.

It will be apparent that such results are inevitable rather than inherently bad, but they serve to emphasize the distinctiveness of mission stations within their particular social and cultural contexts. They are very much a product of a European or Western approach to life—compartmentalized, disciplined and timetabled, whereas the indigenous culture manifests cohesion, uniformity and a much more leisurely approach to life. The mission station organization encourages the view of evangelization as a work rather than a life. The jobs that need to be done easily become more important than relationships with people.

The Cultural Role of the Mission Stations

Because mission stations contrast so strongly with the surrounding social system, they have, merely by the fact of their existence, become agents for social change. Change, therefore, is inevitable, but most missionaries would probably agree that they would want to play a part in influencing the direction of change. However, the direction of change is closely related to the cultural function or role of the mission station and thus any over-all influencing of the direction of change must be approached at this deeper level.

Some of this change is a conscious process, other changes are subconscious. An example of the conscious process was experienced by the writer when he was staying in a village close to a mission station in the Sepik. During the evening he was frequently asked whether it was ten o'clock yet. When at last ten o'clock was announced, almost everybody went to their houses to sleep. The reason? Because at ten o'clock on the mission station the generator was stopped. This, therefore, must be the "right" time for people to go to sleep.

Examples could be multiplied many times. Nevertheless, both resistance to change and pressure on the missionary to adapt are common. The writer was once told by villagers that it was a bad custom to have three meals a day; two were quite sufficient.

However, whether conscious or unconscious, the direction of change is governed by the interpersonal and intergroup relationships in the particular social milieu. One aspect of this is the relationships between the mission station and its personnel with the villages and their inhabitants. Should the mission station have a dominant social role, making demands on the villagers and to a large extent interrupting the normal village social life, or deliberately not satisfying the felt needs of the people, the mission station may well encounter resistance to its stated spiritual purpose. Sometimes acceptance will be overt and the true feelings of the people hidden. If, on the other hand, there is a spirit of mutual acceptance, there is a greater likelihood of spiritual aims being realized. Such acceptance on the part of the mission station would involve a true spirit of service to the people rather than domination or control.

Another aspect is the nature of interpersonal relationships between missionaries and villagers. If missionaries are prepared to accept contact only in formal situations, formalized relationships result. Examples of such relationships are employer-employee, teacher-pupil, householder-house staff, and doctor-patient. Relationships like these win formal compliance but do not affect the deeper motivations of the subordinate. If, however, missionaries are prepared to move outside these relationships and accept the roles of friend and assistant, to swap roles occasionally and be willing to learn, then the way is open for a more mutually understanding relationship to develop.

From this it is apparent that the mission station provides for the missionary much of the framework for the formation of social relationships. It therefore performs a cultural role for both the missionaries and the village people. As for the missionaries, they can either rest content within the culturally formalized and westernized social relationships that exist on the mission station, getting out of it a feeling of security at the same time as feeling that they are doing a worthwile "work;" or they can break through such patterns, perhaps regarding them as necessary but not binding, and build significant cultural "bridges" which will foster the acceptance of change. As for the village people, they may react to the cultural setting of the mission station by accepting, through external conformity, the formal cultural situations and, while resisting the spiritual aims of the missionaries, use the station as far as possible for their own purposes; or they may by friendship (and even leadership) feel they are making a positive contribution towards the life of the mission station and thereby come to accept the spiritual aims as their own.

In this way both missionaries and villagers will find that the mission station either produces social divisions and cultural retrenchment or social cohesion and cultural progress towards a new, productive, social and spiritual life. These two alternatives require some expansion.

Cultural Enclave Mission Stations

An attempt has been made in the two diagrams that follow to clarify the extremes of the two positions just described. It needs emphasizing that these are extremes and that most mission stations would occupy a place somewhere in between.

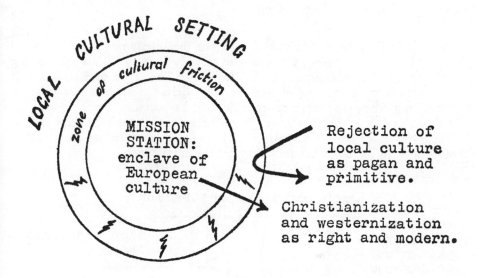

Fig. 1   The Mission Station as a Cultural Enclave

Figure 1 illustrates the situation when a mission station is regarded as a cultural enclave. In this, the missionary treats the mission station as a "home away from home." Here he finds respite and security whereas on village visitation he often feels frustration and disillusionment. The orderliness and regularity of the station program satisfy his work habits; the seeming lack of order and concern about time in the village annoy and chafe him. Furthermore, on the mission station the program runs for efficiency in the use of time and it is the missionary to whose satisfaction jobs must be done. In part, his authority in the use of time and the standards of work derives from his control over finance. He holds the purse strings. In the money economy of the mission station, money speaks because it satisfies the need for things.

Surrounding the mission station is a "zone of cultural friction." This friction has numerous manifestations.

A woman covers her breasts as she comes onto the mission station; men wear better clothes; village people become more time conscious and temporarily forsake such habits as betel nut chewing or smoking. Such behavior patterns reflect the sensitivity to the cultural contrasts and are a response to the feeling of "not belonging to us."

The friction is the result of a mutual attitude of nonacceptance. On the part of the mission personnel, local culture is thought of as pagan and primitive—and therefore worthless on both counts. It is their "backwardness" or "lack of education" that causes these people to be so often late or so frequently absent from work, or to call at such awkward times. The missionary therefore rejects the local culture in favor of his own westernized type of Christianity which, he feels, *must* be both good and right.

On the part of the villager, if he does overcome his reserve about visiting the mission station, he feels he must have a good reason for going to see the missionary who is always so terribly busy and is always looking for help. This type of missionary is rarely visited at his home by villagers just to be sociable. Furthermore, the villager probably feels he must change his behavior pattern to be accepted by the missionary.

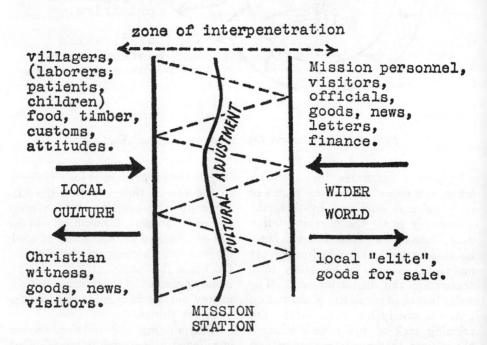

Fig. 2. The Mission Station as a Cultural Link

Cultural Link Mission Stations

Figure 2 depicts a different situation. Here the mission station performs the role of a cultural link. The missionary personnel here represent a segment of the outside world–a Christian subculture of Western society–and the mission station acts as a meeting ground of two cultures. Provided both cultures are prepared to make adjustments, the mission station itself (along with the surrounding areas during missionary village visitation) becomes a "zone of interpenetration."

What is meant by the term "interpenetration?" Firstly, it involves relationships of equality–friendship, mutual assistance, being teammates. In other words, we must create a freer situation, not bound into a highly structured formal organization. Secondly, it involves two-way communication with mutual learning. The importance of language learning (to the point of speaking like the indigenes) and of the missionary spending time off the mission station living in villages, are two obvious ways of putting the missionary into the learner category. In passing, it might be noted that tensions the missionary finds during a period of living in villages probably have their counterpart for indigenes living on the mission station! Thirdly, it involves exposing ourselves in many areas of life such as the home, the church, work and relaxation. The writer discovered a new friendliness among the local people when he accepted an invitation to join with a team playing in the local intervillage soccer competition.

Interpenetration implies the free movement of people and ideas back and forth crossculturally. Some of these are shown in the diagram. They include movements in the direction of the local culture and also into the outside world. It should be pointed out, however, that since the mission station represents only a subculture of the outside world; it acts as a filter rather than as a door and there are some aspects of the wider external culture from which its members would want to disassociate themselves.

As the diagram shows, certain cultural adjustments are necessary if the function of linkage is to be achieved. These can only be illustrated rather than defined since every local situation is different. One adjustment may be a more flexible approach to time by missionaries, to be less programmed and more approachable. Another involves indigenous participation in what are at present wholly missionary activities–in planning, in relaxation, and even in Bible study.

A particularly unfortunate aspect of mission stations which tend toward the "enclave" type is that of paternalism. This evil has many manifestations, but basically it involves a determination to retain control of the decision-making processes. The feeling may be expressed that the local people are not able to make the decisions for themselves. This is simply a lack of trust or inherent cultural pride. Paternalism demands conformity to "my way of doing things."

The attitudes that go with paternalism reflect themselves in speech.

Terms such as "natives" and "boys" (for grown men) are particularly objectionable since their clear implication is a consciousness of one's own cultural superiority. Similarly, references to the "primitive" culture of the local people deserve equal condemnation. Nevertheless, even when avoiding such terms, speech still betrays the paternalist in derogatory references or joking comments about the local culture or people.

In contrast, the absence of such attitudes and terminology is implicit in the "linkage" situation, since paternalistic terminology helps to brand the missionary as a "foreigner;" its absence encourages him to be viewed as merely an "expatriate."

Indigenous Participants in Cultural Change

In cultural change associated with mission stations, probably the most significant role is played by indigenous "middle men." These are men who are usually marginal to the local culture, that is, they are often younger than traditional leaders or not actually from the local area of the mission station. In addition, they have training or experience which gives them special qualifications for close relationship with the missionaries. Furthermore, they have leadership potential but their leadership takes a non-traditional form. Nevertheless, they are close enough in outlook to the local inhabitants for this leadership, at least in certain areas, to be accepted. Others may disagree, but it appears to the writer that those who function as "middle men" tend not to be fulltime pastors, but are engaged in practical

ministries on the mission station—teachers, carpenters, storekeepers.

Such "middle men" function in two ways. Firstly, they are transmitters of culture. They are the ones both cultures look to for communicating ideas and attitudes across from one culture to the other. Secondly, they are frequently the initiators of change. Since their point of view is often acceptable to both groups, their suggestions and proposals appear to have the widest acceptance.

However, it is important to realize that their effectiveness depends on the cultural role of the mission station, in other words, the nature of mission station-village relationships. In cultural enclave situations, the indigenous "middle man" is forced to act as a buffer between the two cultures. As a result, he will neither readily transmit information from one cultural group to the other, except in a garbled form, nor will he function easily as an initiator of change. On the other hand, if he works in a cultural linkage situation, by having a familiar relationship with members of both cultures he becomes a key man in initiating change and in producing the mutual understanding and cultural adjustments necessary.

Conclusion

The work of Christian missionaries like all Christian work, owes its effectiveness to the power of the Holy Spirit. But it does not appear to the writer that what has been said in this article is in conflict with this. The principles of openness, fellowship and love, like the other fruit of the Spirit, are the prerequisites for the Holy Spirit to be able to work through a man or a social situation to produce new life in others. What have been described are, in fact, types of human relationships and social situations on mission stations some of which help and others which hinder the growth of the church of God. The cross-cultural situation of the mission station is merely a special case with certain features and problems peculiar to itself.

PART IX

Cultural Processes: Anthropology as Culture Learning

Eugene A. Nida

The Role of Cultural Anthropology in Christian Missions

After making a survey of some of the different attitudes toward culture and the mission of the church which have stimulated the study of culture and anthropology, Nida suggests that none of them are adequate. He considers the prime service which the study of culture has to offer to be that of a valuable basis for relevant communication, whether it be in the choice of words, in the cultural relevance of the message, or the issues to which the gospel is addressed. He feels that communication based upon a perceptive understanding of a culture can stimulate some members of the culture to make vital decisions for Christ in a responsible way.

THERE have been a number of quite different concepts as to the role of cultural anthropology in Christian missions. For some the application of anthropological techniques to missions has seemed nothing less than a panacea for all ills, that is to say, the most effective means of transforming the society through newly discovered insights. Such persons have thought that if they could just understand the culture, they could easily set about changing it.[1]

Other missionaries have regarded the study of cultural anthropology as providing the data on which the missionary

might build the Christian message. As Edwin W. Smith so strongly advocated, the missionary was to find in the indigenous religious system the equivalent of the Old Testament viewpoint and background, and on this foundation he was to work out a Christian orientation. The equating of the Old Testament experience of the Jewish people with the indigenous religious traditions was thought to provide the essential contact and basis for the proclamation of the Good News.

Still a third point of view, and one not wholly dissimilar from the second, has been that the application of cultural anthropology to missionology would ease the transition from indigenous religious superstitions and practices to Christian beliefs and rites. By a carefully planned series of adjustments the people could be led progressively toward the acceptance of the gospel, with the least disruption of native cultural values. This view has been vigorously endorsed and followed

[1] Dale W. Kietzman, "Conversion and Culture Change," PRACTICAL ANTHROPOLOGY, Vol. 5, Nos. 5-6 (Sept.-Dec., 1958), pp. 203-210, has suggested those areas of personal interaction in which the application of this subject of cultural anthropology is highly relevant. Our concern is more in the direction of those procedures of acculturation which must be carried out with due concern for the culture of the people if significant or permanent changes are to be realized.

by the Jesuits in their missionary efforts,[2] and not without remarkable success, in terms of Jesuit goals.

Despite the popularity of these applications of cultural anthropology, it would seem that fundamentally none of them is satisfactory. In the first place, the knowledge of cultural anthropology is no panacea in the development of a mission program. Merely knowing how people function within their culture does not provide the answers to how certain aspects of this functioning can be changed. This does not mean that cultural anthropology cannot be highly instructive to the missionary in introducing modifications in the beliefs and practices of a people, but a mere descriptive view of a people's culture is not enough. Moreover, the methods by which the data of cultural anthropology may be effectively applied to a practical problem are not inherent within the facts of cultural study. There is much more involved — and this we shall try to explain below.

The view that the indigenous religious system, regardless of its nature, orientation, or practices, can provide a kind of "Old Testament experience" for the people is the result of a superficial understanding of either the Old Testament or the local religion. There are, of course, many similarities between religious practices recorded in the Old Testament and the so-called animistic features of primitive religions, such as ordeals, sacrifices, seers, mediums, scapegoats, taboo, etc., but there are more important matters which make the fuller religious revelation of the Old Testament unique: (1) monotheism, in contrast with henotheism (i.e. one exclusive God in place of merely one high god), (2) the relationship of moral behavior to religious holiness (i.e. the moral content of taboo), and (3) the initiative of God in loving and redeeming mankind. These three factors (and there are a number of others) set off the theology of the Old Testament from the concepts of animistic religions in such a way as to provide fundamental and basic differences, which can never be reconciled by pointing out superficial similarities and then trying to build a New Testament structure on an indigenous foundation.

Jesuit Syncretism

The Jesuit system of accommodation did not begin with the Counter Reformation, which brought the Jesuit movement into being. It actually had its start in the year 601 when Pope Gregory VII wrote to the priests attempting at that time to convert the heathen Britons:

We must refrain from destroying the temples of the idols. It is necessary only to destroy the idols, and to sprinkle holy water in these same temples, to build ourselves altars and place holy relics therein. If the construction of these temples is solid, good, and useful, they will pass from the cult of demons to the service of the true God; because it will come to pass that the nation, seeing the continued existence of its old places of devotion, will be disposed, by a sort of habit, to go there to adore the true God.

It is said that the men of this nation are accustomed to sacrificing oxen. It is necessary that this custom be converted into a Christian rite. On the day of the dedication of the temples thus changed into churches, and similarly for the festivals of the

2 Peter Duignan, "Early Jesuit Missionaries: A Suggestion for further Study," *American Anthropologist*, Vol. 6, No. 4 (August 1958), pp. 725-32.

saints, whose relics will be placed there, you should allow them, as in the past, to build structures of foliage around these same churches. They shall bring to the churches their animals and kill them, no longer as offerings to the devil, but for Christian banquets in name and honor of God, to whom, after satiating themselves, they will give thanks. Only thus, by preserving for men some of the worldly joys, will you lead them more easily to relish the joys of the spirit.[3]

In the Jesuit development of this principle (and not without opposition from many quarters of the Roman church, especially from the Franciscans and Dominicans) the technique was to assume "a thousand masks," "being all things to all men" and with "holy cunning" to accept the limitations imposed by the local situation. One must not, however, be too severe in one's criticisms of the Jesuit position, for fundamentally they recognized the fact of cultural relativism, namely, that the same practices in different cultures had quite different meanings and values. They rejected the Platonic concept of "idealistic ethics" and endorsed the Aristotelean view of Nichomachean ethics, based on a sense of cultural diversity and practical application.

Moreover, the Jesuit practices were an understandable reaction to the wanton disregard for the indigenous culture, so often practiced by other Roman Catholic orders. (For example, in Mexico the Franciscans by 1531 had pulled down 500 temples, broken 20,000 idols, burned countless manuscripts, and smashed thousands of priceless objects of art.)

Perhaps the greatest irony of the conflict between Jesuit and non-Jesuit efforts on

the part of the Roman Catholic missionaries has been the fact that both incorporated such a high degree of syncretism, whether consciously (as in the case of the Jesuits) or as forced by circumstances, that in the end the "converts" became related to a different set of practices, but with very little fundamental change in basic beliefs. What actually happened in so many cases was that Jesuits did not carry through with a total plan for adjustment, and non-Jesuits found that the shortest road to the goals established by the church necessitated adjustments, not dictated by theory, but imposed by force of circumstances.

For example, the early Franciscans destroyed the imposing temple in the ancient religious capital of Mitla, Oaxaca, Mexico. With the stones from the pagan structure they built a church in the valley, but the people continued to worship amid the ruins on the hilltop. At last, the missionaries adjusted to the pressures of the situation, had the churched pulled down, and rebuilt it on the site of the original Zapotec shrine. Of course, if the purpose of any missionary undertaking is to bring the people into the jurisdiction of the church, then a syncretistic approach is both efficient and expedient. However, if the purpose is to bring the people into a new orientation to life through a new relationship to God, as revealed in Jesus Christ, then a system of syncretism tends to cancel out any gains and the distinctiveness of Christianity becomes almost totally lost. In Orura, Bolivia, for example, during the fiesta of the Day of Temptation, not only do the devil dancers utterly fail to depict any Christian themes or motifs (despite their perfunctory blessing by ecclesiastical authorities), but the very concept of the day is perverted, for this day, which is supposed to commemorate

3 Ibid.

Christ's resistance to the wiles of the Devil, is reinterpreted by many people as a time during which people may yield to temptation without incurring penalties.

The Basis of Communication

If, however, as we have suggested, the legitimate role of cultural anthropology is not to be found in reconstructing a base for Christianity in pagan practices or easing the transition by syncretistic adaptations, what then is it? I would like to suggest that basically the study of anthropology provides a means of effective communication. In and of itself cultural anthropology does not provide the answers to how, when, and why certain approaches should be made. But it can and should resolve some of the major problems of communication which are inherent in any missionary undertaking. The implications of such a proposition are naturally very extensive, but in their simplest forms we may say that the knowledge of cultural anthropology, as it applies to the cultures involved in any missionary task (i.e. the cultures of the missionary and the people to be reached — the so-called source and target cultures), provides an orientation as to (1) the relevance of the symbols by which the Good News is communicated and (2) the means by which these symbols may be communicated in a context which is meaningful to the people of the target culture.[4]

We seem to have no difficulty in understanding the phrase "born, not of blood"

[4] It would be a mistake to assume that all the communicative symbols employed by missionaries are words (they actually include much more, e.g. gestures, acts of kindness, art forms, music, etc.), but for the sake of our limited analysis we shall restrict ourselves to verbal forms for they are indicative of the basic problems encountered in other areas of symbol utilization.

(John 1: 13) as being some reference to lineage, for we often speak of "royal blood," "a true blue-blood," and "the blood line." However, in many cultures the word "blood" has no such implications. In Apache, for example, such a phrase would be relatively meaningless, but if someone tried to attach meaning to the utterance the only significance it could have would be that a child was born without any blood in his veins or that the mother in question did not bleed at childbirth. A study of cultural anthropology can provide a missionary with a basis for recognizing the differences in the two symbolic systems, and to know that in Apache for example, the English word "blood" in this type of context must be equated with "family" or "clan."

In one area in West Africa missionaries have for years used a word for "spirit" which has quite a different meaning from the Biblical expression. In this region the word actually means "soul stuff," the basic substance which gives life to all animate existence. God Himself is regarded as possessing such a substance, and it is variously distributed throughout the universe, and quantitatively allocated in various degrees on different levels of existence, so that insects have very little, animals have more (depending upon their strength), and man most of all (with corresponding degrees of such power reflecting levels within the socio-economic structure). When in this language missionaries declare that God (whom they designate as Allah) is "soul-stuff," they are expressing nothing more or less than pantheism, and it is not without reason that these Islamicized peoples seem unimpressed, if not downright shocked, by such a heretical message.

Of course, a study of cultural anthropology will not guarantee that a message communicated to any group of people will be accepted. Far from it! Cultural anthropology only helps to guarantee that when the message is communicated, the people are more likely to understand. And it is this very fact of understanding it which may result in the people's rejecting it! But this is much better than to have them appear to accept it, when they really do not understand its significance. Once, however, the missionary has a thorough understanding of the cultural relevance of the symbols which he must employ in order to communicate, it is very much more likely that he can at least speak with meaning to the people, thus establishing the first and indispensable level for any missionary undertaking.

Basis for Cultural Relevance

Any proclamation of the Good News must, however, advance far beyond a mere recognition of the proper equivalence of word symbols. It must be so oriented that the total impact may be evident to the hearers. This means that the gospel should not be presented as one of the accoutrements of Western civilization, as a watered-down compromise with indigenous beliefs, or as merely another and more powerful technique for doing business with the supernatural. (There is no legitimate place for encouraging the view of "this Jesus-God, he strong god too.")

If the communication of the Christian message is to be culturally meaningful, in terms of the total lives of the people, certain features are essential: (1) It must use meaningful indigenous symbols wherever any concepts are crucial and (2) the implications of the message must be explained in concrete terms which are culturally applicable within a given society.

Because of the inadequacy of indigenous symbols, missionaries have often felt that they could best introduce borrowed words.

This may be quite all right for terms for *camel, phylacteries, Pharisees,* and *dragon,* for the proper understanding of these terms is not crucial; but in the case of a word for *spirit* or *God,* such borrowings are almost fatal. Certainly much of the effectiveness of the preaching of the gospel to the Navajos through the years has been hampered by the use of the English term *God,* which actually resembles in sound the Navajo term for juniper bush. In Apache, on the other hand, missionaries have employed an indigenous term meaning "by whom life comes into being," in other words the Creator, but also the Sustainer of life. This expression is culturally meaningful and has served, together with other well-chosen expressions, as part of the basis for effective communication.

Communication does not, however, consist merely of strings of utterances, meaningful as they may be within the language in question. Such words must be related to life, or they are nothing more than catechisms to be memorized (as a passport to heaven) rather than as programs for living. One must tackle real issues and in a thoroughly Christian manner. What, for example, is one to do with ritual drunkenness which occurs as a manifestation of many religious celebrations among primitive peoples? It is certainly not adequate to denounce such practices as being "naughty-naughty" or to apply to them the often unthought-out tenets of Protestant Puritanism. Such drunkenness must be treated for what it is, namely, a false kind of religious estasy,[5] a sincere but misguided attempt to find communion with God. But in its place the missionary must be able to

5 Eugene A. Nida, "Drunkenness in Indigenous Religious Rites," PRACTICAL ANTHROPOLOGY, Vol. 6, No. 1 (Jan.-Feb., 1959).

demonstrate real communion, which lifts men above the drab experiences of the secular humdrum and gives them the thrill of being the children of God.

An emphasis upon moral righteousness may lead the missionary to denounce ex' cessive "bride payment." This should not be done, however, on the basis that there is anything morally wrong in the concept of such transactions, for in their proper application they can do much to stabilize marriage and to consolidate clan relation' ships. However, in their selfish excesses such bride payments deprive many people of their moral rights, they tend to com' mercialize the sacred institution of mar' riage, and they often thwart the expres' sion of genuine love. The proclamation of the Christian way of life must involve one in just such problems, not as a despiser of all indigenous institutions, but as one who sees in all human forms the potentiality of corruption. In other words, one must take seriously "the theology of man," including a realistic evaluation of man's egocentric orientation.

Such an attempt at a realistic view of life will not prevent serious misinterpre' tations by the sending constituency as to a missionary's message or motivations. For example, he may feel his mission is not justified in refusing to grant com' munion to sincere believers who are po' lygamists and who have a high sense of moral responsibility toward obligations incurred before learning of the gospel, or to those living together in common-law arrangements which may not be resolvable because of arbitrary laws about divorce. His judgment may be based on the fact that though such refusal may preserve the sanctity of the church, it prevents the spiritual growth of men and women for whom also Christ died. In other words the spotlessness of the church may not

be so important as the spiritual nurture of human souls, who are admittedly bound for heaven because they believe in Jesus Christ but who are kept out of the fellowship of the church.

Stimulus to Radical Decisions

A study of cultural anthropology makes it possible for one to see life through the eyes of those who participate in it. Hence, the proclamation must challenge men and women where they are. The Good News for poor workers in the slum *barrios* of Lima, Peru, must not be a translation of some sermon framed for a small-town congregation in America's Bible Belt (which this writer once heard delivered). In Congo the message must deal with such matters as *gaza* rites (involving cliterectomy), equal opportunities for girls, the rightful place of education, the cor' rect employment of natural resources, such as land and game (which are being mercilessly exploited), righteous dealings between employers and employees (includ' ing everything from joining trade unions to paying decent wages to mission help), plain ordinary honesty, respect for leader' ship, abuse of power, etc. But all of these themes, which arise out of the Good News as revealed in Jesus Christ, must be related to the crucial issues of each man's life.

If the gospel is to be presented with utter abandon to the claims of God upon men, it will mean that many persons who might go along with a neutral, syncretistic, a "white-man-he-knows-better" presenta' tion of the Christian message, will reject culturally relevant proclamations. They are too hard to take — even as they were rejected by so many who listened to the Master Himself. This means, therefore, that a knowledge of cultural anthropology and the application of these data to the proclamation of the gospel may actually result in fewer responses to the Good News (at least at first). But the point is this: the relevant witness to the revelation of God in Christ will force upon men and women the necessity of making vital decisions. Such a declaration of the full claims of God upon men (for not only their souls but their lives) will make possible an ultimate acceptance of the message which will mean more than adherence to a set of ritualistic observances. It will be nothing less than a rebirth by the power of God, who alone can take this witness to the truth and communicate it to the life and heart of people.

The application of cultural anthropology thus becomes the effective instrument by which men may be pressed (by the Spirit of God) to make radical decisions about life's fundamental crises.

Jacob A. Loewen

Missionaries and Anthropologist Cooperate in Research

IN September of 1962 the Mennonite colonists[1] in the Chaco of Paraguay

[1] During 1928 and 1929 several thousand conservative Mennonites left Canada because they felt that the new government regulations on compulsory education would harm the spiritual development of their children and thus lead to apostasy in the church. After extensive searching for a new home in which they would be permitted to serve God according to the dictates of their conscience and to educate their children in the language and by the methods of their own choice, the group decided to migrate to the heart of the Paraguayan Chaco. This area was far from any civilization and the government gave them perpetual guarantees of religious and educational freedom. The group founded a colony, now known as Menno Colony. In 1930 another fifteen hundred Mennonites, refugees from Communist Russia in need of a place to establish a new home, also migrated to the Chaco of Paraguay and founded Fernheim Colony. After World War II, in 1946-47, a third colony, called Neuland, was established for Mennonites who had become DPs during the war. In summary we must say that only the first group came to the Chaco because of a religious motivation to live in isolation from the world. The second and third groups went there because they had no other place to go. While the Mennonites as a whole are a pietistic religious group of Anabaptist origin, it is only fair to say that not nearly all the colonists were Christians even by Mennonite definition. For many, the name Mennonite had come to denote more an ethnic origin rather than the type of religious faith they professed. This difference often was also reflected in the way the settlers reacted toward the Indians.

received a very severe shock, for some seven hundred Chulupi Indians rose up against them and demanded land and equipment for immediate settlement. "You came here thirty years ago, and we have worked for you all these years. Now you own good houses, fine farms, lots of cattle, and much equipment, while we still have nothing. We are still penniless and hungering. The time has now come for you to help us also to acquire land, equipment, and cattle, for we too want to become 'people.' "

At the village of Sandhorst in Neuland Colony where the fever of rebellion first broke out, the Indians began widespread stealing from their Mennonite patrons. They justified their behavior by saying that they were only taking what they had coming. They blamed the Mennonites for forcing them to use the stealing (in their own language, "taking") approach. Since their employers were not paying them a just return, the workers had no choice but to take. For several weeks at the height of an extended and very severe drought (in which food and water were very scarce), this rebellious Chulupi group actually debated through the night, "Should we or should we not dispose of some of the chief Mennonite offenders?" At first past memories and the accompanying fear of the brutal vengeance exercised by national soldiers when Chulupi Indians had killed white people delayed such action. Then opportune arrival of word (which, however, turned out to be false) that the government was giving them a land grant averted actual bloodshed.

Nevertheless, feelings ran so high that more than two hundred Sandhorst Indians bundled up their meager belongings and set out for Filadelfia, some sixty kilometers away, to wait for the arrival of confirmation on the promised land. When the rumors of official help finally proved to be erroneous, a second eruption of emotions followed, and about five hundred Chulupi Indians from Fernheim Colony, many of them from the missions and members of the church, joined the rebels and decided to strike out on their own. They would seek out a suitable camp area and claim it as their own. Should anyone try to evict them, they would take up arms. Their missionary friends and protectors pleaded with them for patience, but the irritated tribesmen completely drowned out their appeal shouting, "Our ears burn! Our ears burn!" which means, "We are tired of listening to your continual lying." When a well-meaning rancher, whose extensive property lay in the direct path of the area in which the Indians wanted to seize land, tried to dissuade them from the venture by forbidding them access to water while crossing his ranch, the mob attacked to kill, and only a quick exit with his jeep saved his life.

The story of the uprising[2] was the climax to a series of events that seriously frightened the colonists and convinced them that a thorough anthropological study of this volatile situation was imperative, both in order to try to prevent further violent eruptions and also to find the best channels for helping the Indians in their need.

This appeal from the Chaco for an anthropologist struck a favorable chord also with the North American Mennonite Central Committee,[3] which had already joined the Chaco Mennonites in forming an Indian Settlement Board whose task was to help Lengua and Chulupi Indians make the transition from hunting and gathering nomadism to sedentary agriculture. The North American committee members were conscious of the failure of the whites to help the Indians achieve a satisfactory livelyhood in agriculture in their own countries, and for this reason they felt very strongly that an anthropological study ought to be made before any major settlement efforts were launched.

Jacob A. Loewen is Translations Consultant for the American Bible Society in South America. 315 S. Wilson, Hillsboro, Kansas. Dr. Loewen is currently contributing an extensive series of articles to PA.

[2] For a fuller description of the uprising, see Jacob A. Loewen, "The Way to First Class: Rebellion or Conversion?" to be published in PA.

[3] Mennonite Central Committee is the relief and social welfare arm of all the churches of Mennonite faith. It carries on a worldwide ministry.

First, there was concern about the general feasibility of making such a drastic culture change; and secondly, the Indian Settlement Board hoped that a broader cultural analysis would provide the necessary factual data on the basis of which sound approaches — at least those approaches which would create the least amount of difficulty in adjustment for the Indians — could be chosen. Thus from July to December 1963 the author, himself a 1929 Mennonite refugee from Russia and an active member of a Mennonite church, was engaged by the Indian Settlement Board to conduct the anthropological investigation.

Approach and Purpose

The approach used in this paper is: first to discuss in detail the methods that were employed in gathering the anthropological data of this study; then to highlight a number of areas in which the results of the research were able to bring insight and understanding; and finally to present a translation of the question series that was used by the Chaco missionaries to elicit ethnographic information.

All missionary and community development programs are really programs of culture change. Sometimes these changes have been very painful and frustrating experiences, especially where the changes involved some very fundamental traits of the society. The purpose of this article is to provide some awareness of the benefits anthropological investigation can bring even to established missionary programs; to stimulate mission-

aries to consider the application of anthropological tools and insights to their own particular problems; and to demonstrate what the missionary himself can do in the area of anthropological investigation, given a minimum of specialized assistance.

Obviously the first step in the field study was the establishment of rapport and the development of channels of communication. This involved at least three major groups of people.

It involved the Mennonite colonists who were the employers of the Indians; for if the patrons of the Indians should not understand the purposes of the research, they could very readily undermine not only the investigation but also any program of culture change that might be initiated. Obviously, in this respect the Chaco situation was somewhat different from that on most mission fields, for here was a large body of European Christians who had settled beside the Chaco Indians and who had through this become the major source of authority for the aborigines.

In the second place, it involved the various groups of Indians: Lengua, Chulupi, Sanapana, Angaite, Toba, and Guarani. The Lengua and Chulupi represented the biggest concentrations, and for that reason they were also the most crucial for the investigation.

It also involved the missionaries (the majority of whom were also members of the Chaco colonies), who were really the bridge between the colonists and the tribes people. The missionaries were almost the only ones who had learned the languages of the

Indians.[4] The missionaries thus represented a very crucial group for the investigation. They already possessed many insights into the cultures. They spoke the languages of the Indians fluently. They would be able to save the investigator many steps and much trial and error by pinpointing many of the major problems, if they could be encouraged to cooperate. On the other hand, the missionaries also represented the group that would feel most keenly any exposure of error or problems which could be interpreted as representing lack of understanding or failure on their part. The anthropologist, for his part, had been warned by Chaco acquaintances that his North American origin and his professional preparation would make him suspect to both the Chaco colonists and the missionaries. Obviously missionary cooperation and the success of the research would depend on whether the approach was in the missionary's interest or whether it would put him on the defensive.

To interpret some of the ideals of such anthropological investigation to the Mennonite colonists in general, the anthropologist delivered some thirty-five lectures on culture, culture change, contact between cultures, race relations, ethnocentrism, etc. These lectures, while suggested by the anthropologist, were arranged for by the ministerial alliance of the three colonies and were held either in the

local churches or in the school-houses in communities that had no church building. Most of the lectures were delivered in the Low German vernacular (in contrast to the High German which is their official church and school language) spoken universally by Chaco Mennonites. Part of the reason for the use of this vernacular was to provide a more intimate setting while talking about a very strange, if not heretical subject.[5] It also served to prevent the lecturer from using professional anthropological terminology that would be unintelligible to his lay listeners. It initiated dialogue in the language in which the majority of the colonists were most fluent and which was probably understood best by all, even though it was not the official language.

The second group, the Indians, were of course the major concern of the research assignment. Especially in the case of the two major tribes, efforts were made to study the range of their culture, the value system, and the rate, the direction, and the possibility of further culture change. The object of such a detailed study was: (1) to identify the bases on which the culture shift from nomadic hunting-and-gathering to sedentary agriculture was now being made and could best be furthered in the future; (2) to study the areas of tensions that had already resulted from the culture change in process in an effort to seek ways and means to eliminate pressures that could lead to violent and destructive

---

[4] As a rule the Indians had been forced to learn the language of the employer, which in this case was the Low German vernacular. Of course those Indians who had previously made contact with the Paraguayans had learned either Guarani or Spanish.

[5] This was especially valuable since the vernacular is not usually used for official policy making. Thus the anthropologist was bringing information and not advocating policy.

reaction on the part of the Indians; and (3) to interpret to the Indians themselves the demands and problems entailed in such a drastic culture change as they were contemplating.

Encounter with the Missionaries

The third group with which rapport needed to be established involved the missionaries. They were crucial to the investigation because they were the actual bridge between the colonists and the Indians. They also represented the most open door through which the investigator could establish relationship with the Indians. The anthropologist had originally intended to explain to the missionaries the methods and goals of the inquiry and to solicit their help in finding appropriate bilingual informants (Low German-Indian or Spanish-Indian), so that he could at once immerse himself in the culture study without having to seek out his own informants or having to learn the several Indian languages before being able to communicate. The anthropologist had hoped that such a consultation would give the missionaries at least some participation in the investigation and by virtue of this also insure their support.

In order to provide an occasion for the anthropologist to communicate his concerns to the missionaries and at the same time to establish a confidence relationship with as many missionaries and supporting teachers and nurses as possible, an all-day meeting was called for one of the first Saturdays the anthropologist was in the Chaco. The missionaries, nurses, and teachers from the various mission organizations of the three Mennonite colonies turned out almost 100 percent.

In the first session the anthropologist, who himself had served several terms as a Mennonite missionary, shared with the assembled group some of the problems and frustrations he had experienced on the mission field. He admitted to the group that as this frustration had grown and as he had not been able to define his problems clearly, he had turned on his co-workers in an effort to find personal relief. Such behavior, however, had led to serious guilt and to mounting interpersonal tension. Obviously such an experience was not unique, for a number of the Chaco missionaries were deeply touched. A very moving period of confession followed, in which prayers of repentance for similar behavior were spoken by a number of missionaries present. The session had served as a means of facilitating meaningful spiritual identification.

During the second session the anthropologist discussed some of the problems of cross-cultural communication. Such concepts as restructuring, syncretism, propaganda, good news, preprograming, feedback, etc., were highlighted and illustrated with mission field examples. The examples "communicated" and the whole missionary group became deeply involved in the problems connected with the communication of the good news.

A third session was dedicated to considering specific problems presented by various missionaries. At this meeting the anthropologist had intended to appeal for help in the selection of appropriate bilingual informants. But before the question could actually be raised, the missionaries who had become deeply aware of how little background information they had actually gathered on the problems they were facing, asked the anthropologist for specific instructions on how they could discover the answers to some of their anthropological problems. For the researcher, this was a Godsend. If missionaries would actually do the research, there was no need to fear their opposition to findings that might not be complimentary to the program of the past. Furthermore, if they gained experience in the research at hand, they would acquire experience and facility to tackle any new problems which would arise in the work in the future.

This unexpected offer of help and request for specific research assignments on the part of the missionaries led to a sudden and complete shift in approach. The anthropologist retired to a quiet place and prepared twenty-two pages of ethnographic questions covering some of the major phases of cultural investigation. These questions were prepared in the official High German language, which was current for all the missionaries involved in the work. The questionnaires were duplicated and then mailed to each one of the missionaries with some preliminary instructions concerning the use of such questions. Accompanying the questions was the announcement that the researcher would visit each of the missionaries individually at a specified date and would demonstrate some additional

techniques of interviewing and investigation. It was suggested that the missionary look for that section in the questionnaire which most interested him and there begin to experiment with the questions, following the methods suggested. More systematic work would follow once the period of individual explanation and demonstration had been completed.

The questions covered the following areas: subsistence activities, division of labor, property, the life cycle of the individual, the rites of passage, marriage, family, sex, social relationships, social control, world view, spirit world, soul, and shamanism.[6]

During his visits with each of the cooperating missionaries the anthropologist explained and demonstrated various techniques for eliciting information. Obviously not all of them would find the same breadth of application, for some would be more applicable to specific areas of cultural investigation. Again, from this selection of techniques the individual missionary researcher could choose those methods that suited either his own personality and style or those of his informant. The following techniques were introduced and demonstrated.

**Techniques for
Gathering Information**

1. The creation of culturally relevant situations in which a given series of questions could appropriately be asked. In one demonstration, for example (to introduce the discussion on Lengua Indian values of property

---

6 See the end of this article for a translation of the questions.

and property exchange), the anthropologist highlighted his need for a horse to travel to all the different Indian camps and villages. He then confided to the informant that since his father had not been a Lengua he had not taught his son how to acquire such a horse in good Indian fashion. Would the informant be willing to teach him how? Once the informant began his instruction on the "Indian way" to the newly arrived anthropologist, it was easy to direct the discussion toward some of the specific questions contained in the prepared questionnaire. Of course, once such a discussion is moving freely, it is very easy to branch off into other areas.

2. The recounting of patterns and situations from other cultures. This technique requires some knowledge of cultures in other parts of the world. A variant of this technique involved the use of photographs and colored slides illustrating cultural practices of other South American Indian groups.[7] In the Chaco situation this technique was most profitable for the investigation of shamanism which had been under rather strong missionary condemnation and for that reason had

come to be associated with severe inhibitions. Lengthy discussions of a series of slides illustrating a Colombia Choco shaman in action effectively set the stage for a discussion of shamanism as it prevailed in the pre-Christian environment of the Chaco tribes. This discussion readily lent itself to spot questions to locate areas where the former practices had been syncretized with the newly adopted Christian patterns.

3. The use of self-exposure by means of which the investigator shared with the informant some aspects of his own culture or personal experience.[8] Like the former technique, it can provide a setting for discussing similar areas of experience in the informant's life or culture. Self-exposure can be a very useful tool for the missionary who cannot fall back on the knowledge of cultures other than his own. It is especially useful and productive for investigating the areas of sex, world view, and values, where inhibitions often prevent individuals from speaking freely and honestly.

Techniques 2 and 3 served not only as types of "pump priming" to begin discussions on the local situation, but they provided occasions for watching the informant's reactions which would indicate something of his values and attitudes. Often after the anthropologist had recounted the introductory stage setting, he would add, "That is the way we (or they) do it. What do you think about that way?" The

---

[7] Mildred Larson of the Summer Institute of Linguistics in Peru reported how a team of workers had been stymied in their attempts to elicit folktales from Indian informants of a given tribe. They just were not able to get across the idea of what they wanted. Someone suggested that they get Indians from another tribe to tell some stories in Spanish to the semi-bilingual Indians who seemingly had no stories. After listening to a few stories the informants suddenly realized what the team was after and, thus prompted, they could provide a wide selection of myths and folktales.

[8] For a fuller discussion of the principle of self-exposure, see Jacob A. Loewen, "Self-Exposure: Bridge to Fellowship," PA, Vol. 12, No. 2 (March-April 1965), pp. 49-62.

informant would then give his evaluation of the situation and often added, "No, our people do not do like that, they. ..." Then would follow his version of the situation in his culture. It was interesting to note how freely the informants often talked after the investigator had been transparent about some more delicate aspect of his own culture. It permitted the informant to speak freely about their practices without feeling that he was being investigated in an area in which it would be easy to incriminate himself. As long as the informant would talk freely, the missionary investigators were encouraged not to interrupt with questions, but to note such areas in which they needed to ask more questions later. Only when the informant seemed to hesitate was the investigator instructed to try to stimulate further flow of information through a strategic question.

4. Also related to techniques 2 and 3 was the directing of the discussion at some more distant part of the tribe, either in space or in time. For example, it was noted that the Toba informant consistently denied that dancing ever played an important part in pre-Christian Toba culture.[9] This could indicate either that the informant had developed some rather deep-seated inhibitions about dancing or that his family had been sufficiently separated from the traditional ways of the tribe so that the informant had

actually never participated in the dancing activities that had characterized his tribe in general. The anthropologist, therefore, shifted the emphasis and inquired about the dancing activities among the "less civilized" northern Toba whom the southern group calls the Pilaga. These people, though dialectically different, are more or less identical culturally. Once the attention was focused upon this distant group of people, the informant was able to supply all types of information about their dancing patterns. In fact, it was not very long before he also began to suggest that there were some people in the local area that occasionally engaged in such activities. The technique of focusing on the more distant can be used in connection with different villages, rivers, or sections of the tribe. It permits the informant to stay neutral and noncommittal while talking about areas that he fears might be self-incriminating.

As a variant of this technique, the "ancients" of the tribe can be made the focus of the discussion. Often this permits inquiry into areas that would be delicate for the present. Inquiry about the situation of the past often supplies the actual covert patterns of the present, which for some reason or other have become embarrassing.

5. A fifth technique involved conversations with a whole group of Indian people. After an appropriate introduction, individual Indians were encouraged to volunteer to report on items they had experienced or claimed to have knowledge of. Such reports were recorded on magnetic tape and then played back for the entertainment

---

9 The research on the culture of the Toba Indians of the Argentine Chaco will be presented in a separate paper, by Jacob A. Loewen, Albert Buckwalters and James Kratz, "Shamanism, Illness, and Power in Toba Church Life," to be published in PA.

of the group as a whole. After the first brave souls had broken the ice, the rest generally became eager to participate. In fact, as time went on they often vied for the opportunity to perform before the microphone. As these reports were replayed for the entertainment of the group, the missionary investigators were encouraged to write down the reactions of the listeners to the material on tape, for out of these responses valuable information about values, attitudes, and prejudices could be gleaned. Where it was possible to have two recorders, the second recorder was employed to capture some of the responses and additions that either the raconteur or the listeners provided. Later the anthropologist and the missionary investigator reviewed the contents of these accounts and formulated questions to pursue the leads that such material contained. The additional questions were generally asked in private, with only one or two informants being present. A missionary Bible school teacher used this group technique very successfully to study the Lengua spirit world with the students during some of the regularly scheduled classes. Others applied this technique to the study of individual life cycles, recent historical events, and folktales and mythology.

6. Related to the above was the delivery of public lectures to the Indians in the course of which the anthropologist explained that he had been invited by the Mennonites to help find the best ways of assisting the Indians to become "people." An appeal was then made to all individuals having knowledge of things that the anthropologist should know to draw such matters to the latter's attention. This approach was very productive in locating tension spots that were developing in the relationship between the Indian and Mennonite cultures. It was after one such lecture that a Chulupi Indian asked the anthropologist why it was that the church-going whites generally sat down one meter away from Indians, while those people who did not go to church and did not believe in God often wanted to sit down beside the Indians and drink *yerba mate* with them.

7. Another technique was assigning specific questions to individual Indians for discussion with their families or fellow villagers. This was especially valuable where the group under question was not accessible, either physically or psychologically, to the person doing the research. It was used to gather valuable information concerning the attitudes of the Indians toward given situations of past history and programs proposed for the future. Through the application of this technique, a number of areas of inter- and intracultural tensions were revealed. It also provided some insight into the attitudes of the Indians toward the Mennonites, the current program of the mission, the past settlement ventures, and the proposed settlement plans.

8. Finally, each missionary investigator was provided with magnetic tape and access to a tape recorder for recording accounts of personal experiences and observations. The prepared questions or oral questions posed by the anthropologist reviewing the information pointed out gaps in the

missionary's data. The gaps were followed up in interviews with Indian informants and some of the previously described techniques were used. Many of the missionaries found that by systematically recording some of their experiences they began to see relationships that they had not been aware of before.

Not all the missionaries actually pursued this ethnographic research to any extent, but each missionary doing research was visited several times. On such visits the anthropologist reviewed the missionary's findings and, where possible, he interpreted those situations that puzzled the missionary, asked additional questions, and pointed out further areas for investigation. At such times special questions that had arisen during the missionary's investigation were also discussed. On several occasions it was necessary for the anthropologist to use the missionary as interpreter and through this avenue to pursue some of the areas which seemed to be difficult for the missionary to penetrate. The periods of waiting while the missionary and the informant conversed in the native language provided excellent opportunities for weighing the information being gleaned and for phrasing additional questions on the data being elicited.

The Findings

It is beyond the scope of this paper to detail all the wealth of cultural information that the Chaco missionaries compiled during the months of the research. It is, however, one of the purposes of this paper to highlight several areas of significance to the missionary program in which the investigation was able to provide insight, understanding, and direction.

It is human to err, and yet everyone, including the most dedicated missionary, is sensitive about any exposure of his failures and shortcomings. It almost seems as if the more dedicated the person the more painfully he is aware of the gap between the ideal of his intentions and the actuality of his practice. The awareness of this uncomfortable gap often makes a person quite defensive. On the other hand, will the truly dedicated missionary not be very desirous to identify all that hinders God's work, so that it may progress? Well aware that the anthropological investigation could hurt and possibly even demoralize the missionaries, the anthropologist had been looking for an approach that would strengthen the missionary's self-confidence and equip him to do a better job. In this respect the volunteering of the missionaries to do the research was a most welcome though unexpected boon. Now it was not necessary for the anthropologist to convince the missionary of the problem; instead it was the missionary who discovered the problem and pointed it out to the anthropologist. Thus it was the missionary who did the research on the Lengua spirit world who was able to point out that the word for devil which was currently being used in the Bible translation referred only to a human soul gone bad and not to Satan. He pointed out also that the current word for soul did not mean a living soul but the soul of a person who had died. The reason for the latter error was not difficult to find. The Lengua seldom speak about the living soul, but they live in mortal fear of the *jangauc,* 'the soul of the dead', which always tries to drag friends and relatives with it into the world beyond. Again, another missionary discovered that one of the past tense indicators, which was currently being used in the Bible translation, actually placed the translation into myth-age hearsay and put its veracity in doubt.

Another missionary pointed out that he had discovered that the people on his station were restructuring the concept of conversion which he was preaching. Not only this, he had also analyzed his approach and was now able to point out what he had done to cause the restructuring. Here is his account:

When I began to work on this station, the medicine men were forever chanting over the sick and upsetting the people. So I decided to stop this paganism once and for all. I announced that henceforth no medicine men could operate on mission property. Whenever I heard someone performing a medicine chant, I got up — day or night — and ordered the offender either to stop or to leave the premises. After several months of struggling, the chanting finally ceased and I felt that the problem had been licked. In fact, when a group of women came to me wanting to be converted — "to change their innermost" according to the Lengua idiom — I was overjoyed at the wonderful results my firmness was producing. But when group after group came, I gradually began to wonder, "Why were so many coming?" When I asked a group of women why they wanted to change

their innermosts, they said, "Well, because you always tell us to do so." When I countered with the question, "But why do it now?" they came out with their restructured concept of conversion. "You have told the medicine men to stop singing. Well, some of them are still singing softly. Now the people are a lot more afraid of them, because if their medicine is so strong that they don't have to be afraid either of the missionary or of his God, then it is even more powerful than we used to think it was, and so we are very much afraid of the medicine men now. Thus we thought if you could help us change our innermosts, which would not get sick from the shaman's power, then we could continue with you here at the mission."

Unmasking Syncretism[10]

Like most missionaries, the Chaco missionaries had some serious concern that digging in the old "heathen" lore would lead national Christians to syncretize. There was concern that somehow the missionaries' interest would legitimatize the Indians' pre-Christian beliefs and thereby make the missionaries' task much more difficult. The author's own experience had always been the reverse, for often when such supposedly negative information was brought into view, it lost much of its potency because the Christian individual had grown or changed through his Christian experiences. As the apostle says, "If we walk in the light, as he is in the light . . . the blood of Jesus his Son

---

10 Syncretism as used in this paper emphasizes its more negative function. Actually all communication involves a certain amount of syncretism.

cleanses us from all sin."[11] This sentence from the Bible applied to the situation under question would seem to indicate that, if some of the repressed "pagan" values are brought out into the open, the convert thus opening up will often find that the value which he thought was there has actually already been largely lost for him, for in Christ his values have changed. Thus, instead of strengthening the original beliefs, it often seriously weakens them. The Chaco research provides an interesting case in point.

A former shaman of repute (now a church member) volunteered to share some of his insights and experiences as a shaman. Present at the session was another informant, a trilingual (Chulupi-Spanish-German) Indian educated by the Oblates of the Sacred Heart of Mary. This Indian converted the questions of the anthropologist and the missionary into proper cultural form for the medicine man, who turned out to be a very voluble talker. He spoke very confidently that he had known Jesus Christ long before the missionaries had come and that in those earlier times Jesus Christ had been much stronger than he was now since the missionaries talked about him. He reported that since he had become a Christian, he now prayed to *Dios* (Spanish for God) instead of talking to the familiar spirits who used to be his helpers. He explained that it was almost the same to extract disease-producing objects from patients in the name *Dios* as it had been to extract them

with the help of familiar spirits. This was syncretism at its extreme.

The missionary became very upset. Even the Catholic-trained informant, who himself was deeply involved in negative syncretism, was shocked. His evaluation was: "This man is completely lost and hopelessly mixed up." After almost two hours of listening to such syncretized "revelations," the missionary and the anthropologist retired to have a cup of tea. The missionary freely admitted that he felt sick at heart at this Christopaganism. In fact, he feared that he had done wrong by letting the man verbalize this unholy, syncretistic conglomeration. Together the anthropologist and the missionary searched for a possible point of contact to help the man into a better understanding of the Christian faith. They discussed the possibility of drawing the account of Simon the sorcerer[12] to his attention. Finally they committed the man and his problem to the Lord in prayer.

Two days later, when the anthropologist had already moved to the next area of research, the syncretizing shaman returned to the missionary and asked for an interview. At this meeting he confessed:

For six months I have felt as if I were carrying a very heavy load like stones. It weighed on me day and night, but I never knew what it really was. Now I know. When I talked to you two days ago and told you about how I healed and "sucked" in Jesus' name, I suddenly realized that it is true what the people say — that I mix shamanistic medicine with what

---

11 1 John 1: 7 RSV.

12 Acts 8: 9-24.

you teach about Jesus Christ. Today I know that this was the burden that I was carrying, and I have come to tell God that I am sorry that I have mixed everything up so much. I want you to tell the people that I am willing to pray for them and that I will no longer suck and blow on the sick like I used to when I was practicing healing with familiar spirits as a shaman.

The missionary was very wise in handling this situation. He graciously accepted the confession and said, "I will be most happy to make such an announcement for you, if you want me to. But since you were such a famous shaman, I think that, if I say it, the people may think that you are not a strong man any more and that I have persuaded you to let me say it. I wonder if the people wouldn't be more impressed if you said it yourself in some meeting. I think that, if you should make such a statement, everyone would say, 'Now there is a brave man who is willing to stand for Jesus. He must have real faith, for he is willing to trust God alone.'" The former shaman immediately saw the light and said, "That is right. I want the people to know that I am making my own decision."

One of the early questions by one of the missionaries was, "Why do Chulupi married couples facing a communion service come to confess that they have had sex relations?"[13] When going through the question on marriage and the family, the missionary himself discovered the answer. Earlier Chulupi morality required that a

---

[13] Jacob A. Loewen, "The Mennonites and Chulupi Culture Change," to appear in the *Mennonite Quarterly Review*.

mother who was nursing her baby must abstain from all sex relations. They believed that sex relations spoiled the mother's milk and spoiled milk damaged the soul. It crippled the soul, and since the soul stretched the body, the body would come out crippled, too. According to the old Chulupi pattern, after a baby had been born, the husband waited until three days before the moon in which the wife had given birth. Then he went into the forest to get some wild bee honey for his wife. Physiologically it was to give her back her appetite for meat, from which she had abstained during her bleeding period, and ritually it was his way of saying to her, "When the baby is weaned, I will return to you." He was now free to satisfy his sexual appetites with the unmarried girls who would choose him as a sex partner at the evening dances. Meanwhile, the mother dedicated herself for four to five years to the exclusive nurture and training of the infant. But now, having become Christians and having accepted the Christian morality of being faithful to one wife, the man no longer went to the unmarried but stayed with his wife. Sleeping at home, of course, led to sexual intimacies, but both husband and wife were convinced that this was immoral. They were sinning against the soul of their child. Feeling guilty, they came before every communion service to confess their "immoral" acts.

Evaluating Alternatives in Approach

One of the criticisms that had been expressed concerning the settlement program as it was being carried on by the Indian Settlement Board[14] stated that it was making "imitation Mennonites" of the Indians, for they were being settled in villages with two rows of houses, one on either side of a central street, just like the Mennonite villages. Each individual was given a private plot of property, just like the Mennonite practice. It was assumed, since the Indians had been nomadic and had shared their food products during their hunting and gathering days, that possibly the best approach to agriculture would be through communal enterprise rather than private property. However, when the matter was investigated and discussed with the Indians, it became apparent that the central street and the two rows of houses had been a very frequent Lengua and Chulupi village pattern in the past. It was only when the group was greatly afflicted by spirit fear that they built circular villages in order to be closer together.

Another interesting fact in this matter of communal versus private enterprise is that the Indians interpret the settlement implements now being added to their culture as belonging to the private property category and therefore not to be shared. In fact, several of the communal projects that had been tried, both by Roman Catholic and Protestant missions, had to be abandoned because the Indians were not interested in carrying them

on. Thus, rather than demonstrating that the approach was wrong, the research confirmed the approach as being quite adequate for the Chaco Indian situation. On the other hand, the attempt to have the Indian settlers share plows and draft animals — as the Mennonites did when they first settled and did not have enough implements and draft animals for each farmer to be independent — proved to be unworkable.

As I have said, the Indians believed in two kinds of property — shared property, which was freely used by all concerned, and private property, which was soul-linked and thus so private that no one else could use it. Horses, plows, and harnesses were private or soul-linked property and therefore it was impossible for unrelated individuals to share such equipment. Thus when the settlement officer who distributed the plows dropped off an implement at every other yard, the "innermost" of each individual linked itself with the piece of equipment. As soon as this happened, the neighbor could not use it without exposing himself to the spirit harm resulting from the "unwilling innermost" of the man who now "owned" the plow.

One settlement officer reported that when the rains came and the Indians were supposed to start plowing, nobody actually did. He became impatient and scolded them thoroughly, but still no one moved. Finally he got the horse and harness from one settler, took it to the other Indian's place and got his horse and harness, hitched the two horses together to make a team

[14] For detailed information see Jacob A. Loewen, "Research on the Question of Settling Lengua and Chulupi Indians in the Paraguayan Chaco," a mimeographed report duplicated by Mennonite Central Committee, Akron, Pennsylvania.

for the plow, and began to plow. Once
the work was in progress the administrator turned it over to the Indian, while he went on to start the
next pair of settlers. He had barely
reached the other man's place and
begun hitching up the team when
he noticed that the first man was
already unhitching. The reason: "You
wouldn't want your neighbor's angry
innermost damaging your crop and
your land, would you?" Here the
cultural research revealed that the
current settlement approach of shared
equipment not only disregarded, but
basically violated, the Indian personal
property ideals.

Culture conflict, especially where
one culture is dominated by another,
generally leads the people or the
culture under domination to repress
many of their feelings. This produces
tension, and such tension cannot go
on building up indefinitely. When
the pressure becomes too great, such
energy frequently bursts out uncon-
trolled, and such outbursts generally
lead to negative or harmful ends. In
many instances it will be possible to
identify areas where pressure is building up and to tap the pressure as a
source of steam to accomplish a meaningful end. Looking again at the
Chulupi uprising, we notice that the
Indians resented the fact that they
were being treated as inferiors. Each
added insult intensified the Indians'
drive to become first class. Finally the
pressure passed the tolerance limit
and the uprising was under way. Since
there was little direction, the rebels
became involved in many activities
of which they later were deeply
ashamed. That this was still an area

of great pressure became apparent when the anthropologist tried
to study attitudes and asked individuals to name the deepest wish they
carried in their "innermost." One of
the most frequent answers to this
question was, "I want to become a
human or a person." Currently the
criteria for measuring first class status
are some rather cheap externalities.
For example, the Mennonite settlers
— without any evil intention — had
frequently poked fun at the Indians'
irregular and crooked walls; and so
now, in building their schools and
church buildings in the newly settled
villages, the Indians made every effort
to build absolutely straight walls.
When the anthropologist visited the
building site of such a new school
building and looked at the wall to
see how straight it really was, an
Indian came close to him and asked
whether it was straight. The anthropologist's affirmative produced a second question, "Is it straight like the
Mennonites build?" When this one
was also answered in the affirmative,
the man chuckled and said to some
others, "Did you hear what he said?
He said we are building just as
straight as the Mennonites do."

Another superficial criterion that is
currently being used is the matter
of singing in harmony in church
choirs. Neither Lengua nor Chulupi
Indians would want to be caught
celebrating a worship service without
having a choir sing several special
numbers in harmony, especially if a
foreigner were present. True, Lengua
women are unable to sing alto, but
the Lengua do sing the other three
voices. A missionary nurse reported

that during her recent visit to one of the outlying villages the major part of the service was spent on songs by the choir. When the service was dismissed, people approached the nurse and asked whether the singing had been very good. When she answered in the affirmative, they wanted to know whether they were now singing almost as well as the Mennonites. Another affirmative answer evoked a murmur of satisfaction as each of them remarked to the other, "Did you hear what she said? We are singing just about as good as the Mennonites already."

Because this drive to become first class is so very potent among the Chaco Indians, it lends itself very readily as a source of steam that can be harnessed to accomplish constructive purposes. For this reason the anthropologist proposed that, rather than give the Indians all the necessary equipment (like horses, plows, and harnesses), as is currently the practice, each Indian should be required to acquire these himself. He reached this conclusion as a result of asking many Indian settlers, "Are you proud of the fact that everything is being given to you?" "No, we are not!" "Would you be happier if you had acquired your own horses and plows?" "Yes, we would!" In fact, they were able to point out two communities which had not participated in the settlement program and in which the Indians had actually acquired horses, harnesses, and plows all on their own. A common reaction was: "If the Mennonites had told us to get this equipment several years ago, we would have it today."

Progressive Enrichment of Missionary Witness

This brief experience in anthropological research has already provided the missionaries with insights into many situations which they had not understood previously, or has made them aware of others which had escaped their attention. The application of anthropological methods also led them to recognize the relationship between many individual experiences of the past, thus integrating many separate incidents into a meaningful whole. What they have learned is helping them make their current message and service more relevant. Working with the questions and the experience of collecting anthropological data has familiarized the missionaries with some of the tools for finding answers to new problems which will surely arise in the work in the future. Not only have new channels of communication between the missionary and the nationals been opened, but they have also been provided with the tools to exploit them to good ends. A side effect has also been a greater recognition of the missionary's own ethnocentric view of things. The awareness of his own ethnocentrism and the consciousness of having worked many years without asking the questions which should have been asked have led the missionaries to adopt more of a learner approach, for even though many things have been uncovered, they are painfully aware of the vast amount of data that still needs to be learned. As the missionaries take additional steps in the light of their current knowledge, their service will be progressively enriched and be made more relevant.

For the anthropologist, the cooperation with the missionaries was a very enriching experience. There was deep satisfaction in introducing one's newly found missionary friend to improved avenues of communication with the people whom the latter was trying to serve. On the other hand, in the process of sharing some of his professional tools with the missionary, the anthropologist also gained some tremendous benefits. The anthropological research was greatly accelerated because there were data gathering outposts at almost every mission station. The multiple sources provided a check on the accuracy of the material gathered because it was being collected by different individuals at different points simultaneously. The cooperation also permitted capitalizing on the missionary's rich experience in the language and the culture of the Indian people. Again, because so much of the routine anthropological data was collected by the missionaries, the anthropologist was freed to live in Indian settlements and villages and to rub shoulders with the Indian people in a much more relaxed fashion. He was not pressed to use every moment of his time to collect data on the overt culture and thus he could concentrate more on the covert attitudes, values, and reactions. For example, in the course of these relaxed visits in Indian villages he could ask such questions as, "What is the thing that you want most of all?" And the visits also became the occasion for the Indians to ask questions they had not dared to ask before.

Ethnographic Questions

The following questions were originally prepared in German for use by the missionaries in the Chaco. They have been translated into English especially for this paper. The careful reader will at once detect that these questions are slanted toward Chaco cultures. This means that anyone using them in other cultures will need to take this into account. In fact he may even have to make certain adaptations to make them applicable to the culture to be investigated. Several guidelines for making adaptations can be mentioned.[15]

It is imperative that the investigator read a survey of the culture area in which the study is to be made. For the preparation of this questionnaire the author read the Chaco section in the *Handbook of South American Indians*.[16] If no such survey volume is available, even an ethnography of a related tribe, or at least of a tribe in the general area, can often provide excellent points of reference.

The missionary investigator should consult such standard guides in ethnographic research as *Outline of Cultural Materials*[17] and *Notes and Que-*

---

[15] It is hoped that missionaries using this questionnaire will make note of the adaptations they have to make so that eventually a more detailed and more specific series of suggestions can be compiled on the basis of actual experiences.

[16] J. H. Steward, editor, *Handbook of South American Indians* (Washington: Bureau of American Ethnology, Bulletin 143, 6 vols., 1946-1950).

[17] G. P. Murdock, et al., *Outline of Cultural Materials* (New Haven: Human Relations Area Files, Inc., 1950).

ries in Anthropology.[18] Both of these volumes contain many hints and ideas on areas to be investigated and, especially the latter, suggestions on how to do it. Even for the missionary who has already worked for years with a tribe and who feels quite confident that he has learned the major cultural themes of the society, this outside reading can be extremely rewarding. It may lead him to discover emphases that have escaped his observation up to that point. Or it may suggest some radically different alignments or meanings for some of the culture traits he has observed. At any rate he will probably find items that he needs to pursue in greater detail.

Each investigator will need to take time to reflect on the cultural materials gathered. In this way he can discern patterns and phrase additional questions on areas that need checking or clarification. As a rule of thumb, one can say that the investigator will seldom ask too many questions. He will usually err on the side of not having asked enough.

One more general observation about the questionnaire in its present form needs to be made. The reader will readily notice that a number of questions are repeated in different sections of the questionnaire. This redundancy has been introduced on purpose. It is designed to emphasize the fact that culture is an interrelated whole and that the individual traits function as parts of "bundles of traits" in the various facets of culture. For this

---

[18] *Notes and Queries in Anthropology* (London: Routledge and Kegan Paul, Ltd., periodically revised).

reason it is important to follow up the same question in connection with various areas of the culture. It will make the interrelatedness more apparent and will often also reveal new dimensions in the function of various traits. Another design of the redundancy is to show that it is very easy to go from one area of the culture into another. Rather than to start "cold" in a new area of investigation, it is often wise to begin with certain questions on the area previously discussed. Once the communications flow has been established, the investigator can gently guide the investigation into the new area to be studied.

Marriage

Is there any type of engagement? What are the essential features of an engagement? What are the ideals of engagement? How is the marriage arrangement made? Today? Years ago? What kinds of festivities take place? Who initiates them? Who serves as master of ceremonies? Who makes the approach for marriage, the young man, the young woman, the parents, the uncle, or some other individual? Is marriage an agreement between the two young people or between the families? What is the goal of marriage? Is there any education for marriage? Who gives it? Which women can one marry? May one marry within the clan or group? If there are several clans, from which one may the individual choose his mate? What is one's relationship with one's in-laws? What is the relationship between the respective sets of parents? What is the status relationship between husband and wife? How do they treat their children? Who punishes the wife if she makes a mistake, the husband, the wife's father, some other individual? Is divorce possible? What is the ideal of marriage? The practice? Which acts are termed adultery? What is the literal meaning of the word for adultery? Who punishes the adulterer, the clan, the chief, the relatives? Who experiences shame in the case of adultery, the adulterer, the adulteress, the innocent party? What is the ideal goal of marriage: children, legalized sex activity, division of labor, fellowship? How many children does one want? To which clan do the offspring belong, the father's or the mother's? May one have more than one wife? How many? Are all wives of equal rank? Does the first enjoy higher status? Why? How? Do the wives live together? May one have concubines? If one may have more than one wife, is it better to marry one's wife's sister? The younger one? The older one? Or at least a relative of hers? If so, why is it better? Should the wife be a cross-cousin? A child of father's sister, or mother's brother? Does one have access to one's older brother's wives? Can a man inherit his father's wives, excluding his own mother? What about the wives of mother's brothers? Can women ever be inherited? Were wives ever killed when the husband died? Do wives occasionally bewitch their husbands? Do husbands bewitch wives? Other women? For what reasons? What must be done then? May one steal a wife from a different tribe? Will such a woman not run away? Why not? To which clan will children of a woman from another tribe belong? Must such a woman first be admitted to one of the clans of the tribe? Does the tribe practice trial marriage? If so, for how long a period? Under what conditions? Could husbands exchange wives? Under what conditions? Is it considered good or bad?

Sex Relations and Pregnancy

How does a woman become pregnant? Only through sex relations? What type of "spiritual" receptivity does a woman need to become pregnant? Can a woman prevent pregnancy? What types of contraceptives are there? Edibles? Drinkables? Magic? What is conceived, the soul or the body? Can the soul of the deceased be born another time? What may a pregnant woman do? What must she avoid? Activities? Eating? Drinking? When does the soul take possession of the body of the newly conceived child? At conception? At the first movement of the child? At birth? At some special ceremony? How many souls does a person get? How are these souls distinguished from each other? Who taught man the art of sex relations? Where may sex relations be practiced? At home? In the forest? When? How often? Who takes the initiative? The husband? The wife? How much sexual contact must a woman have for pregnancy to take place? May a pregnant woman continue to have sex relations? What about a nursing woman? What about a menstruous woman? With whom does the soul originate? With the father? With the mother? Does it come from some receptacle of souls in the environment? Or in the beyond?

What is the attitude toward abortion? If it is practiced, for what reasons is it justified? Who performs it? May a girl have sex relations before her menstruation? Who is more sex-minded, the male or the female? Why does a man become unfaithful to his wife? Is it because he has been bewitched? Does he have too strong a sex drive? Or is it because he was "stolen" by some woman? Why does a woman become unfaithful? Who ought to be punished? The man? The woman? Both? Who ought to perform the punishment? What would be a just punishment for an unfaithful husband? An unfaithful wife? Does sexual involvement leave "fire" in the body? Does the accumulation of such "fire" lead to sickness? How can one get rid of such "fire"? May a person with "fire" go to war? May he hunt? Do both men and women accumulate "fire"?

Birth

Who may be present at the delivery? What is done with the afterbirth? With what does one cut the umbilical cord? How must the navel be cared for? May evil spirits find entrance into the body through the unhealed navel? What are some of the prescriptions for the father before, during, and after the birth? Must the father be careful while the navel is not healed? Why is the top of the child's head soft at birth? Why are some children born prematurely? Why are some born in different positions? What does it mean if the feet come first? If the hand or shoulder comes first? Why is delivery occasionally fraught with difficulties? How does one get twins? Are both permitted to live? Are twins a good omen or a bad one? Or neutral? How must the body of the child be cared for? When is the danger of evil spirits greatest for the child? Why are some children born dead? If children are killed at birth, who does the killing? Mother? Grandmother? Another person? Is this considered good? Is this punishable? Who punishes the killing of infants? How? Is the deity concerned about this? With which sex (in the offspring) are parents happier, male, female? Why? Do they practice circumcision? When? What type? Clitoridectomy? Who performs it? At what age? Why? Do they pierce ear lobes? Nasal septum? At what age? Why? By whom?

Weaning and Toilet Training

How is a child weaned? At what age? Can a woman become pregnant even while she is nursing? May she have sex relations? Can mother's milk be destroyed or damaged? What effect does this have? How does the child receive toilet training? On which is more emphasis placed, defecation control or urination control? At what age does one begin? What are the means of training? Ridicule? Scolding? Bodily punishment? At what age is it expected that a child be toilet trained? If not, does one wait? Can a lecture be of any help? How must a child be treated? Taught? Punished? May one use physical violence? Under what circumstances? Who may do it? With whom does a child have the most intimate relationship, father, mother, mother's brother, grandparents? Who loves the child most?

How does this person show his love? Whom does the child love most? How does the child show his love? What ought one to do if another child is born before the first one is weaned? Should they both be permitted to live? Should they be nursed simultaneously? Should the older one be weaned immediately? Is the older punished if it cries? How? By whom?

Children

Who trains the children after weaning, mother, father, mother's brother, grandparents? How many children does one want? Who wants more children, the husband or the wife? Do they practice infanticide? When? How is the killing effected? By whom? Which sex receives preference for living, male or female? How does the child get its name? Who gives the child a name? Can the child change its name? When? How often? Can the name be used for witchcraft? Does a person have several names? Must names be kept secret? If so, who may know the intimate name of a person? What about the secret names? May several have the same name? Can power be inherited with a name? May one speak the name of a dead person? If not, for how long is it taboo? What is expected from children? Males? Females? Who is considered smarter, the youngest or the oldest? Girls or boys? How can a child be protected from illness? Who can do this? At what age is a child responsible for itself? Does one pay attention to the birthday? What is viewed as children's work? What may children know? What should children not know? In what activities may the

children participate? Who instructs a girl in the art of housekeeping? Where does a girl learn the art of child training? Other work? Who instructs the boys? In what? What special instruction is there for children before puberty?

Youth

How does a boy become a youth? At what age? When does a boy begin having sex relations? With whom? With other girls? With widows? Is masturbation permissible? How does he become recognized as a young man? What must he do? What is done to him? By whom? What instruction does he receive? By whom? Under what conditions? When does he become ready for marriage? What characteristics do women look for in a man? What is called handsome in a man? Does a young man take the first step in contacting a girl? What are the responsibilities of the youth? In the clan? At the hunt? At work? In war? In the home? Do they know anything of circumcision? At what age is it performed? Who performs it? When? Why? Is there any young men's society? What function does it fill? Do youth have sponsors among men? What is their relationship to these sponsors?

Girls and Young Women

How does a girl become a young woman and ready for marriage? Is virginity expected before marriage? When does she begin sex relations? Does one pay any attention to her first menstruation? How? Who initiates this celebration or festivity? Must such a festivity precede or follow her first menstruation? What is the intent of such a celebration? What must the girl herself do? What is done to the girl? By whom? What type of instruction does she receive? From whom? What are the qualities that one looks for in a young woman? What does the man think is ideal in a woman? What is considered beautiful? How does the courtship take place? Who takes the initiative? What type of contacts between sexes are permitted before marriage? Do parents seek to protect the girl? Is virginity a tribal ideal? If the ideal is not realized, how is it rationalized? What is done with the premarital child? The extra-marital child? Why? Who does it? Mother? Midwife? With how many young men may she sleep? May she sleep with married men? Which would be considered worse, for a girl to sleep with a married man or with an unmarried youth? Do all girls get married? Are there any "old maids"? Why did they not marry?

Grownups

What kind of class distinctions are there? How does one become a chief? A wise man? A counselor? A warrior? A hunter? A worker? A medicine man? Must one have power in order to become a man of worth? How does one earn rank? Can rank be inherited? Father to son? Grandfather to grandson? Uncle to nephew? Can one rise in status? Can one lose one's status? Is there any struggle for status? Is there any kind of election or choosing for leadership? Are there judges who will classify people? What different professions are recog-

nized? What is the division of labor between men and women? Between men and chiefs? Men and medicine men? May women also become shamans? Does the wife of a chief have more authority than an ordinary woman? Can a stranger be received into the clan? How? Can he initiate this? To which clan do the children belong if the mother comes from a different tribe? For what purposes is the clan important? Marriage? Festivity? Soul power? Status? How many different ranks are recognized? How does a person mark the transition? Does he need a sponsor from above? Does he need supernatural sponsorship? Is supernatural power available to both sexes? Do different spirits favor different sexes? Is there any struggle for power? Between all mans? Are any age groups recognized? Are there any voluntary associations? Are they graded in status? individuals? Only chiefs and sha-What is the status of widows? Widowers?

Relatives

What kind of relatives are recognized? From mother's side? From father's side? How many generations are distinguished in kinship? What is the responsibility of the mother? Of the father? Of the grandfather? Of the grandmother? Of the paternal uncle? Of the maternal uncle? Of the paternal aunt? Of the maternal aunt? Do they recognize orphans? Who is responsible for them? Are the relatives from the mother's side considered blood relatives? With whom is incest possible? May one marry the children of father's sister? Of father's brother? Of mother's brother? Of mother's sister? Which kind of marriages would be preferred? Which individuals are excluded from marriage because of blood relationship? What would be the results of incest? Who punishes incest? The clan? The spirit world? God? Does anyone know whether incest has ever occurred? When did this happen? Which relatives should one try to avoid? Mother-in-law? Father-in-law? Father's female relatives? Mother's female relatives? With whom can one joke? With men who are one's relatives? With which women may one joke? Whom must a woman avoid? With whom may she have a joking relationship? Is there any kind of child adoption? What types of rights do adopted children have? Are adopted children considered blood relatives? What is the relationship between clans? Are all clans equal? Are there any clans that show a greater relationship to each other? For what purposes? Hunting? Marriage? Festivities? Dance? War? Planting and harvesting? What are the relative or social groupings? Family? Clan? Tribe? Confederation of tribes? Enemies? Foreigners?

Old People

What is the attitude toward old age? Are old people honored? Are they killed? Are old people considered wise? Do old people have authority? Where does one seek advice? Do grandparents have responsibility for grandchildren? What are the responsibilities of the old people in the household? In child training? At festivities? Are the souls of old people

considered stronger, wiser, better, than those of the young people? Who tells the stories? All the old men? All the old women? Is there any ranking in the right to speak? Do story tellers have any special rank or recognition? Why do people get old? Does the soul also get old? Are old people dangerous to children? Do old people have special desires toward children? Why? How long into old age may a woman continue sex relations? Why do women stop menstruating? May a woman continue to live with men after her menopause? Do old people have any special organization?

Death and Burial

Do they practice mercy killing of the old? Of crippled children? How does one explain this? Do they recognize a natural death? Is death always the result of witchcraft? Due to spirit intervention? Soul loss? Or soul stealing? At what point does the soul leave the body in connection with death? Where does it go? Must the soul do certain things? Must it avoid certain things? Do souls leave the body willingly? What is the relationship of the souls of the dead to the living people? May souls of the dead do damage? How? How can one protect himself against them? How are people buried? Is there a special burial place? Must it be done soon after death? If not, how long should one wait? Must the body be burned? Does one bury the belongings? Destroy them? Why? Must the soul be trapped and penned up? Must the body be weighted down so it will not come out of the grave? In what kind of a position is the body placed in the grave? Does one use a burial urn in which to put the body? In which direction must the body face? How deep must the grave be dug? If the body is burned, for what reason? Were there different kinds of burials for different kinds of death? What is done with the bodies of chiefs? Of medicine men? Are any bodies left unburied? Why? What must the widow or widower do? May the name of the deceased be used? How long does the soul remain in the vicinity after death? To which different areas can a soul go after death? How does it travel to these places? How long does the mourning period last? What external signs of mourning does a man, a woman, a child, or other relatives have? How long must one wait before one can remarry after the death of the marriage partner? May one paint up during the mourning period? What are the results if these rules are not obeyed? May a mourner scratch himself? If not, why not? Was reburial ever practiced? For what reasons?

God[19]

How many gods are there? (If there is more than one god, the following questions should be answered for all of them.) What does the name mean? May the word be used with other meanings? What are the characteristics of this god? Is he like man? Like an animal? Of what sex? Is he beautiful? Ugly? Deformed? Is he some great spirit? Is he some great

ancestor? Where did he take his origin? Does he have a personality? Or is he just an impersonal power? In how far is he like men? Is he moral? Immoral? Amoral? How does he behave? If there is more than one god, are they ranked? Can one god fight with another? Can one god overcome another? Where do the gods live? Do they change residence? At fixed time periods? Upon invitation? Is God omnipresent? Is he a culture hero? Is he eternal? Who made him? How did he become God? Through birth? Through a victory? Through deceit? Because of his own nature? Has he made the world? Men? Animals? When? Does he work as creator even today? Who has made the non-Indians? What is his relationship to his creation? Direct? Or does he only work through the medium of the spirits? Or through human media? Is he governing the universe even today? Is he concerned about his creation and men? Is he kindly disposed toward man? How does he show this? How often does he show this? Only at special occasions? Does he also punish? Is he like a policeman who watches behavior? When is he kind? When man is good? When man obeys the taboos? Because man prays? Because man serves him? Because man offers sacrifices? Because man promises to obey? What kind of gifts can one make to him? What kind of gifts does he give? Food? Clothing? Protection? Luck in war? Luck in games? Gambling? Luck with women? Does he judge only the living? Does he also judge the dead? By what standards does he judge? Violation of taboo? Sin? Neglect of

---

19 Adapted from Eugene A. Nida, *Bible Translating* (New York: American Bible Society, 1947).

worship? How does he punish? Through sickness? Death? Loss of property? Loss of honor or respect? Are his judgments always moral? Can God be bribed? Does he often act in anger? How can one placate God's anger? Through sacrifice? Prayer? Ceremonies? Confession of sin? Repentance? Payment? Can a man communicate with God? How? Through prayer? Certain ceremonies? Dreams? Visions? Talking? Through the intermediacy of other persons or spirits? May his name be freely used? When may it not be used? Why? In what respects is God like men? Does God also forget as people do? Is God near to people? Has God ever withdrawn from men? Why? Has he ever sent a flood or a fire to punish mankind? Over which sins is he most annoyed? Why? What are his favorite punishments?

Spirit World

Is there more than one spirit? (If so, the following questions should be answered for all.) What types of spirits are there? Does a spirit have a personality? Is a spirit like people? Like an. animal? If the spirit is impersonal, how does it reveal itself? As a power? As an influence? Where do the spirits live? In special plants? Rivers? Trees? Forest? Caves? Lakes? Men? Can the spirit move around freely? Can he enter and leave bodies at will? May a spirit move about apart from a body? What kind of objects can be processed by a spirit? Do spirits have rank? Are spirits of different power? Is the spirit moral? Immoral? Wicked? Is

the spirit amoral? Can he do both good and evil? Does he play pranks on people? Does he try to scare people? Torture people? Is the spirit subservient to another spirit? Does the spirit have a special name? What does it mean? How did he get that name? With what can the spirit be compared? With a shadow? With smoke? With steam? A ghost? Fire? A dream apparition? Does the spirit have special responsibilities? Special capacities? Special strengths? How long has this spirit existed? How did he take his origin? Is he of human origin? From a dead person? Did he descend from an animal? Can he be controlled by men? What kind of men? By what means is this control exercised? Through magic? Special words? Ceremonies? Rituals? Sacrifices? Prayer? Through other spirits? Is the spirit favorable to men? Does he resist evil people? Does he ever attack people? How does such an attack take place? Does he invade man through sickness? Through death? Does he come from without through misfortune? Through other people? Other objects? How does the spirit get entrance into the human body? Which is the port of entry? Nose? Mouth? Toes? Navel? How does the spirit leave the body? Does he leave through the same place he entered? Are there special exits? Can he be made to leave the body? Can he be recalled? How does one know of the presence of a spirit in the body? Through insanity? Through speech defects? Through interpretation? Through special bodily strength? Why does a spirit do harm to man? Why does a spirit do kind things to man? How can a spirit be reconciled? Can one have spirit help to do harm? Can one catch a spirit? Can one overcome a spirit in war? If the spirit is resident in man, which is the seat of his residence? The whole body? Liver? Spleen? Intestines? Heart? Belly? What is the relationship between the indwelling spirit and man's own spirit or soul? Are certain places recognized as the habitation of the spirits? Can a human soul become a spirit? Do human souls become good spirits? Bad spirits? Why? What wanders about when man dreams, his soul or his spirit? Can one lose his soul or his spirit? How does this happen? If he has more than one, can they all be lost? What is the difference if one or another is lost? Can the soul be stolen? How? What can be done about it? Where are the souls of the dead? Do they exist under good conditions? Bad conditions? Why? Is there a special spirit world? Where is it located? At what time does the soul of the dead go there? Immediately upon death? After burial? After death but before burial? A month after burial? Can the soul of the dead be dangerous to relatives? Will the soul of the dead harm one's enemies? Can the living call upon the spirits of their dead clan members for help? Who can do this? Do spirits partake of food? What kind of shape do the souls of people have after death? Do spirits have chiefs? How does one become the chief of spirits? Are there spirit clans? Do such clans fight with each other as humans do? Can one destroy a spirit? How can this be done? What is the relationship of Christian angels to the spirit world?

The Human Soul

What are the basic parts of man? The human personality? What is the function of these individual parts? What remains after the death of the body? How is the surviving part of man related to the living person? Is the soul or spirit related to man's breath? His blood? The exuvia of the body? The semen of man? Can the soul or spirit leave the body during dreams? Visions? During sickness? In fever? Do animals have a similar nonphysical aspect about them? If human souls and animal souls are different, to what degree are they different? Does this spirit or soul live in a special part of the body? In some organ? With what does one think? Feel? Love? Hate? Desire? Are thinking and desiring related? With what does one feel homesickness? Passion? What is the seat of the emotions? The heart? Liver? Spleen? Intestines? Are certain body parts good? Are others considered bad? Does man have several natures, a higher or better nature and a lower or worse nature? Are man's soul or spirit ethical? With what does man feel it if he does wrong? Can soul and spirit be distinguished? How are these related to the brain? To the personality? Does a person have only one spirit or one soul? If more than one, what are the different names? What are the functions of the different souls? How are these souls graded in value? Are there any loose souls who like to take up residence in the human body? Do souls of ancestors ever return in the form of newborn children? Do the souls of the dead fight to possess living bodies? Or do they want other bodies or objects as places of residence? Does a tribe have a common spirit or soul? Are the souls of the members of a tribe at least related? In how far? Will relationship in life be carried on by souls after death? Can a man exchange souls during his lifetime? Can animal and human souls be interchanged? Under what conditions? Can such changes be only temporary, for a night? Are the spirits of the ancestors concerned about the living? Do the spirits of the ancestors fight for the welfare of the living members of the clan? Can the living members call dead warriors to their help as a sort of spiritual army? Are the souls of all people alike? Indians and whites? Indians and Negroes? One Indian tribe to another? How does a medicine man come into relationship with the spirit world? Must he deal with related spirits? Can one become a clan member in the spirit world? Can one feel the presence of spirits? How does one feel it? Do the spirits ever steal the soul of man? Are there also spirits that destroy the body? Do spirits also inhabit animals? Why? Can animals prevent spirits from taking residence in them? Are there some animals who are actually spirits?

Witchcraft

Who can become a shaman? Can a person choose this profession? Is a person predetermined for this position by the spirits? Does another shaman choose his successor? Can the position be inherited from one's father, uncle, or grandfather? Can women also become shamans? How early in life does one know that he is determined for this profession? Before birth? At birth? After certain signs during life? Are these signs on the person? In the environment? Does a shaman become possessed by spirits? Does he have power over the spirits? Are spirits his willing servants? Can he create his own spirits? Can anyone practice sorcery or witchcraft? What types of witchcraft are there? Can one do harm with body hair, fingernails, names, body exuvia, clothes, or any kind of personal property? Can spirits be sent to do good? To do harm? Can sent spirits be caught? Diverted? Can they be repelled through stronger spirits? Can they be misled through rituals? Singing? Dancing? Prayer? How does one know that evil spirits are in the environment? Can one cast an evil eye? Can sorcery be practiced through special rites? To be harmed, must the person come in contact with the cursed object or person? Can sorcery be practiced without any kind of contact? Can something be done to the picture of a person? His shadow? Footprint? Can one carry some type of spirit protection with him? How does one acquire it? How many spirits are subservient to a shaman? Are all shamans of equal strength? Why not? Does one pay for their service? When? Only if they accomplish the goal? What type of payments are made? Are all shamans known, or are there also secret medicine men? Is it dangerous to kill a shaman? Are shamans buried just like other human beings? Why not? What must a sorcerer do to get his strength? Must he do anything to maintain it? Can he loan his spirit power to others?

Is a sorcerer punishable if he fails to accomplish a good purpose? Who effects such punishment? Can the sorcerer find stolen or lost objects? How? Can the sorcerer determine the thief of an object or the murderer of a person? Through what ritual? Can he foretell events? What type of ceremonies does`he undergo? What objects does he use for his soothsaying? Does he drink and have visions? Does he read bones, liver, intestines of an animal or of a bird? What kind of omen must one watch for? What indicates danger, death, spirit presence?

Sin

What is good and what is bad? In how far is sin linked with the obedience to taboos? Does badness have any relationship with morality or law? Is there badness apart from morality? Can deeds be viewed as good or bad? Will good and bad deeds bring natural results in reward or judgment? For what offenses is a child punished? What crimes or wrongs does a family punish? What is punished by the clan? By the village? Does punishment have any kind of religious sanction? For what reason would the spirits punish man? For what reason would God punish men during life? After death? Are the gods or spirits concerned about morality? Do they watch over the taboos? Do they watch over the regularity of worship? Do the gods or the spirit world respect human morality? For what can man expect judgment in the world to come? From whom? How? For how long? Is there any grading of punishment? How does one know which sins are worse than others? Can one become punishable through ignorance? Will good deeds be rewarded? Which deeds get social recognition? Is there any distinction between the holy and the profane? Is there any kind of holy-evil distinction? Is there any distinction between holiness and goodness? Are members of the family, clan, or village ever avoided because of deeds? What deeds would cause such treatment? How strong is such avoidance? Must the culprits go away? Would the spirit world consider a moral transgression more serious than the disobedience of a taboo? What conception of the afterworld do the people have? What type of life or existence do they foresee? Does the place of residence after death have any relationship to behavior in life? Does life have anything to do with the condition of a person after his death? Does the soul of the dead show any relationship to the living personality? Morality during life? Obedience to taboos? The manner in which one died? Social or economic conditions? How is the life in the beyond organized? Can judgment and punishment in the beyond be prevented? Is there any kind of atonement? Can God forgive? Do the spirits ever forgive? Are there certain wrongs that cannot be forgiven? Why are they unpardonable? How many kinds of these wrongs are there? How does one determine guilt? The witness of others? Confession of the individual? A vision or declaration by a shaman? Prophet? Supernatural ordeals? How does the individual punish or avenge wrongs? What wrongs does the group punish?

How does the group do it? Are there wrongs that are against the whole society or the whole tribe?

Taboo

Taboo is distinguished from sin in that taboo is negative magic. If one disobeys a taboo, it will avenge itself. Were there any deeds considered taboo, such as relationship with strangers? Eating and drinking certain things? Leaving food uneaten? Were there taboo persons? Chiefs? Kings? Mourners? Menstruous women? Women after childbirth? Warriors returning from battle? Successful hunters, fishers, etc.? Were there any taboo objects? Sharp weapons? Blood? Sputum? Were there any taboo words or names, such as names of the dead? Special words used by the shaman? Names of God? Of other deities and spirits? What kind of taboo objects were there? Trees? Rivers? Lakes? Mountains? Ceremonial objects? Animals? Certain persons? Names? Numbers? How did they come under this taboo? By the command of God? Special use in ceremonial activities? Because an object is possessed by a god or spirit? Through some supernatural experience or vision? Through certain inherent powers that it has? Because of contact with certain taboo objects or persons? How does a taboo manifest itself? Must it not be touched? Must it not be looked at? May it not be mentioned? May it not be eaten? What is the result of the violation of a taboo? Who punishes the taboo? The gods? The spirits? The power in the taboo object? Is there any relationship between the taboo and morality?

Can one taboo object pass the taboo on to others? Is there any difference between holy things and unclean things? Can holiness or taboo be passed on through prayer? Through sprinkling? Washing? Anointing? Covering with ashes? Who has the power to make things holy or taboo? Can the power to make taboo be passed on? Is the taboo for only a limited period of time? Does it last forever? If it is temporary, how long does it last? Why does it last that long? Under which conditions must a taboo be renewed? Can a taboo become weaker? Do all strange things have a certain amount of taboo about them? Are the deeds and things belonging to God clean? Does the moral command certain respect? May one use the names of God or of certain spirits for oaths? Can they be used for swearing? For curses?

The Universe

From where does this world come? When was it made? Who made it? Have there been earlier worlds before this one? Who made them? Who made the people? Is there only one world in existence today? How does the other world look? What shape does the world have? Is it flat? Round? Circular? Global? Is there an underworld? How did it get there? Is it populated? Have people from the underworld ever visited the present world? Have people from the present world ever been able to visit the underworld? How did they get there? What happened to them when they got there? Do the people in the underworld speak the same language? How do they live there? Are the living conditions better or worse than here? Are there any higher worlds? Where are they located? How does one get there? Can living people go there? What is the entrance to this area? Is there a door? Does one need a ladder to get there? Are there any guards? What type of population does this upper world have? What are the living conditions there? Can only souls of medicine men go to these worlds? From where do the Indians of this tribe come? From where do the other tribes in the vicinity come? The white people? The Negroes? Do the clans have any relationship with special animals or birds? Do individuals have special relationships with animals or birds? Did they descend from this animal? What are the relationships with this animal today? From where do the animals come? Why are some animals enemies of man? From where do the plants come? Iron? Other minerals? The mountains? Rivers? Oceans? The sun? The moon? The stars? From where do clouds come? Where does rain come from? Hail? Fog? Frost? Wind? Tornadoes? Whirlwinds? What does the Milky Way mean? Are the sun and the moon related? How did they get there? How are the stars fixed in the heaven? Has anyone ever climbed to the sun? To the moon? Why is the Milky Way so white? What is the rainbow? How did it get there? Does it have significance? How many seasons are there? How are they distinguished from each other? How is the earth made fertile? Is there any relationship between human fertility and the fertility of the earth? If so, how did this relationship come about?

Can fertility be increased? How? Does the earth have a special spirit? Must this spirit be placated in some way? Does the earth give its products willingly? Do the people view their crops as something taken from the earth? Does it hurt the earth when the ground is plowed? Should one dig deep?

Property

Does the tribe have any common hunting land? Fishing area? Are certain areas privately owned? How did the tribe get possession of its hunting land? From God? A culture hero? Through conquering? In war? What type of property can one own? Can one own land? Can one own fruit trees? Do all people share equally in harvest? How is the product of the hunt distributed? Does one have private dwellings for the family? Are there club houses? Do they belong to the clan or to the group? To a special club group? Age group? To whom do bed clothes belong? Are clothes private property? Are names private? Are songs private property? Can everyone sing certain songs? Do people have their own private magical charms? Will the magical charm of one person work for another? How does one get private songs or private charms? Can names, magical charms, or songs be inherited? Can weapons or kitchen utensils be inherited? Is anything buried with a person? Why is it buried with him? Does he need it in the beyond? Is it dangerous to the living? If there is inheritance, along what lines does it follow? Father to son? Uncle to nephew? Mother to daughter? Can status be transmitted to the children? Can a medicine man transmit his power to his child? If there is inheritance, does it pass to the youngest or to the oldest? Do mothers pass on things to their daughters? May ceremonial objects be sold? Are ceremonial objects personal or clan property? Can private property be sold? If so, how is such an exchange effected? Who is responsible for setting the price, the seller or the buyer? Is such exchange termed "giving"? How does the original "giver" get a fair exchange? Is he responsible for getting it? Does the tribe know anything about borrowing? Can borrowing become permanent?

Food

Which fruits, roots, plants, animals, fish, and birds are considered food? What are the staples of the tribe? Who does the planting? The gathering? Is there a division of labor in planting and gathering? Must planting be done by special people? Must there be special ceremonies connected with planting? Which plants or fruits are used for making beverages? Are beverages only prepared in wine or beer, or does the tribe also distill? Is planting and harvesting also bound up with special festivities? How can one assure a harvest? How can one strengthen the fertility of the seed? Is there a god protector for the crops? Is it necessary to bring him a sacrifice of first fruits? Are the fruits and roots seasonal? Does the group move to follow the seasonally available food? What determines the rhythm of life and festivities? The availability of food? The seasons?

Are certain foods bound up with taboos? Are certain things considered man's food? Children's food? Women's food? Are certain activities in connection with crops considered men's, women's, or children's work? Do medicine men have anything to do with fertility? How? What preparations must one make for hunting? Are there taboos on women during the hunting period of the men? Which animals can be killed? Which animals should not be killed? Can one eat all types of meat? Which foods, meats, plants must be avoided by sick people? By pregnant women? By menstruous women? By mourning individuals? By children? By the aged? Are there any food taboos for warriors? For hunters themselves? How are food taboos avenged? Are there special taboos for hunters? How do these taboos avenge themselves? How are special animals and birds killed? Are some only used for feathers or hides? How are the results of the hunt distributed? Do certain parts have to be given to ranking individuals? To certain relatives? Is this considered a gift or a loan? Do such recipients ever return gifts? How does one eat his food, hot or cold? May men ever cook their food in the presence of women? How does one show that one likes the taste of food? Are there any polite gestures for eating?

Festivities

What kind of festivities does or did the tribe have? There are a number of festivities that occur frequently: (1) Fertility festivals for people, especially women, as well as for the main crops. (2) Birth or name festivals as in Bible times. (3) Puberty festivals for girls and often also for boys. (4) Engagement or wedding festivals. (5) Special ceremonies in connection with war, hunt, medicine men, or other officials. (6) Festivals of rank. If a tribe has a step system or ranking, each time a person rises a notch, it is generally celebrated with some type of festivity. (7) Mourning festivities, in connection with burial. Sometimes such festivals are celebrated a long time after the actual burial. (8) Festivals of victory after war. (9) Dedication of houses, either private or public. (10) Festivals of secret societies. (11) Clan festivals, sometimes with more than one clan together.

Where do such festivities take place? When do they take place? Who initiates them? What are the principal characteristics of the festivals? What are they to serve? Who are the principal participants? What do they do? Or what is done to them? What is the origin of the celebration? Is there any instruction bound up with the festival? Who gives the instruction? Are certain rules of the society relaxed during the festival period? How long does such a lax period last? For whom are these rules relaxed? For all? What is the purpose of this liberty? Is it honor? Special reward? What kind of special clothes, paints, masks, buildings, food, drink, dances, and experiences are connected with the festivities? What is the meaning of these events? What types of symbolism are employed? What is the ritual supposed to accomplish? If there is dancing, who participates? What does the dance represent? Animals? Birds? Experi-

ences of the ancestors? Special spirits? If there is liquor, who does the drinking? Who prepares the liquor? Is the liquor of a special kind? Does it have to be dedicated? How? By whom? Do the drinkers have to undergo any kind of dedication? Whom does the drinking honor? Man? Spirits? The ancestors? What is the attitude toward drunken behavior? Who takes care of the drunks?

Work

What is considered men's work? Women's work? Girls' work? Children's work? Young men's work? Duties of the aged? What should these various classes not do? Are there special times when one must not do certain jobs? Who is permitted to do the planting? The hunting? Going to war? Cooking? Sewing? Making of pottery? Basketry? Skinning of animals? Tanning of leathers? Gathering of roots? Making of liquor? Which types of work demand spirit empowerment? How can one get this power? For which work must one begin as an apprentice? What happens if a man does woman's work? What work restrictions does a menstruous woman have? Are there any types of uncleanness for men? What are the results if such taboos are violated? Can one hire other people to do one's work? Does one have to work in exchange, or can one give gifts or pay wages?

Hunting

Which animals are hunted? How are they hunted? For what purposes? Eating? Hides? Ceremonial usages? Are there special preparations for hunting? Does the whole tribe participate in a hunt? Are unclean individuals dangerous to a hunt? How is the product of the hunt distributed? How is the food prepared for eating? Who is permitted to keep the hide? Must the animal spirit be satisfied in some way? When? How? Who can do this? What taboos are connected with animals? Do some animals have mythological value? Do some animals have special connection with the human origin? Or with the human race? How are present animals related to mythological animals? Do animal souls survive after death like human souls?

War

Who was permitted to go to war? Men? Women? Children? When was it proper to fight? Any time of the year? Certain seasons of the moon? Was it necessary to seek an appropriate time? How could one identify the time? What preparations did the warrior make? Was he assisted by someone? Was it necessary to abstain from sex relations? Why? With whom did the tribe fight? For what reasons did they fight? Land? Women? Revenge? To extract tribute? To appropriate property? Were prisoners taken? Were prisoners killed? How were they disposed of? Were prisoners ever kept as slaves? Who was taken prisoner, only warriors? Men? Women? Children? What was considered an appropriate time for fighting? Daytime? Night? By the light of a certain moon phase? Was there any cannibalism? What parts were eaten? Why? Was it to appropriate the enemy's bravery? To feed one's spirit? Who participated in cannibal-

ism? Were captured women and children ever adopted into the tribe? What was the status of the children of kidnaped women? Was there any mechanism to receive them into the clan? Did prisoners ever try to flee? Why not? Was it a matter of honor? Was he ashamed to return to his own? Did a prisoner of war have the right to take a wife? What kind of weapons were used for war? Did the weapons have to be dedicated? Did each person make his own weapons? Were there specialists in making weapons? Could they be purchased? Bartered? Were there any deities or spirits of war? How did they get this position? Did people paint for going into war? Did they don special clothing? Was there a special war cry? Did women and children help in this respect?

Clothing and Ornamentation

Describe the clothing of daily life, festive life, dancing, and for special ceremonies. Describe the ornaments that were worn daily, for special festivals, for weddings, for war, by the chief, in honor of the dead, etc.

Who painted? When? With what? What type of patterns? Does the clan have certain patterns? How do the men wear their hair? The women? The children? May it be cut? Does the cut of the hair distinguish rank? Age?

Are the ear lobes punctured? Is the nasal septum punctured? Are men circumcised? Is there female circumcision? Is there any filing of teeth? What types of tatooing are practiced? Why? What types of scarification are practiced? What do they mean?

William A. Smalley

Making and Keeping Anthropological Field Notes

The individual who is resident among the people of another culture, even though he is not a professional anthropologist, has marvelous opportunities for observation, for casual or intensive interviewing, and for other ways of gaining extensive information about the people around him and their way of life. He often has a very real advantage over many professional anthropologists in the possibility of such contacts over a period of many years. Only a small percentage, however, of missionaries and other such residents abroad make any kind of systematic record of what they learn. This article discusses briefly the advantages of record-keeping, and makes some practical suggestions.

THE fundamental reason for making and keeping anthropological field notes is of course the need to remember. The factual details of an interview with an old shaman ("medicine man") when, in an unusually confiding mood, he tells about many of the fundamental ceremonies in his repertoire, and gives an extensive picture of their function, can quickly fade. Some of the value of the interview for an understanding of religious life will fade with it. The opportunity to compare accounts gained in other ways, or to study ceremonies actually observed in the light of the shaman's comments is dissipated. The broad, striking features of the interview may remain, but much of the detail of its content is lost forever.

The need to remember is not always fully apparent to the resident abroad. In his first weeks impressions are startlingly vivid. He learns a great deal that is new and interesting. Much of what he observes, reads, and hears is commonplace in the life around him. He may see no need to make notes on it because he knows he will see and hear many of the same things a thousand times. Note-taking may seem to be an impossibly time-consuming and voluminous task. The habit of observing more or less casually, without keeping a record, is thus quickly established and is usually not broken.

The need for a record becomes more apparent later when certain kinds of problems present themselves. In the missionary situation, for example, there may arise a realization that a certain complex of cultural values and practices needs serious study because they have a bearing on the Christian witness, the development of the church, or some other phase of the welfare of people. In the pages of PRACTICAL ANTHROPOLOGY there have been several reports on such problems.[1]

---

[1] Eunice Pike and Florence Cowan, "Mushroom Ritual versus Christianity," Vol. 6, No. 4 (July-August 1959) pp. 145-150; John C. Messenger, Jr., "The Christian Concept of Forgiveness and Anang Morality," Vol. 6,

The anthropologically curious missionary at this point may begin very serious investigation of the phenomena, in the light of everything he knows about the culture. If anything has been previously written on the culture (or this phase of it) he studies it. He starts questioning informants, and observes the problem area of cultural behavior with renewed attention. If he has been keeping notes he most certainly goes over them for the light they may shed on the problem. And whether or not he has previously kept notes, an adequate record at this point becomes imperative. Note-taking and keeping takes on new focus because it is now problem-oriented. As investigation of the problem continues he makes constant reference to earlier notes, so that an adequate overview of the accumulating information is constantly kept in mind.

Another typical situation in which the need for notes becomes very acute arises when the resident abroad wants to write something or in some way share his knowledge about the culture of his environment. Except for brief and often superficial articles, or ones based on very recent investigations of limited problems, records are indispensable. It is so very important that missionaries with cultural insight share their knowledge with their colleagues through PRACTICAL ANTHROPOLOGY and through a manual on the culture of their neighbors. It is possible, of course, to start making notes at the time when the decision to do such writing

is made. It is an enormous help, however, if a systematic record has already been kept over the full period of residence.

For the individual who is not a professional anthropologist the question of time is a major deterrent to keeping records of cultural information. In our discussion a variety of techniques will be suggested and the time factor will be taken into consideration. The student of a culture can tailor his own system to suit his needs and temperament.

Random vs. Problem-Oriented Records

A basic distinction needs to be made first of all between a system of keeping notes in which the observer keeps record of information on any phase of the culture which comes to his attention, as against one in which he has a specifically defined problem, and where he keeps records only of the information which seems · specifically to pertain directly to that problem. If a choice has to be made, the second of the two is the more valuable type of record for many reasons. When an investigator can focus on a limited set of problems he can study them much more exhaustively than he can a whole culture. He is more likely to have time to amass the necessary volume of data. The random record may be too general to · lead anywhere in particular.

In a problem-oriented record the investigator tries to keep a record which may help to provide the answers to questions which he has formulated for himself. In Haiti, for example, a missionary might well want to study the cultural phenomena related to the present rapid growth of the evangelical church. He would first of all outline some basic questions to which he needed answers.

No. 3 (May-June 1959) pp. 97-103; William D. Reyburn, "Kaka Kinship, Sex, and Adultery," Vol. 5, No. 1 (Jan.-Feb. 1958) pp. 1-21; Walter H. Sangree, "The Structure and Symbol Underlying 'Conversion' in Bantu Tiriki," Vol. 6, No. 3 (May-June 1959) pp. 132-134.

What are present attitudes of various classes of people (including both social and religious groups) toward the Roman Catholic church, "Voodoo," and the various evangelical groups? What is the attitude of the various groups toward individuals who are converted? What needs which people feel are met through conversion? What motivates people to resist conversion? What cultural imbalances are created through conversion? What adjustments are being made to compensate for them? In what ways does conversion provide a greater integration and more valuable life as people feel it? What forms of communication provide an effective witness?

Someone more familiar with the Haitian scene could better define the questions than I, but this will be indicative of the scope of one of the kinds of problems which deserves extensive investigation in every walk of Haitian life. Investigation could lead to very useful knowledge for the missionary who undertook it. This is the value of the problem-oriented study.

Unfortunately, however, the problem-oriented record is never really complete in itself. A problem can take on meaning only in relation to the major part of life. Problem-oriented studies in anthropology must be related to the culture as a whole. This poses the need for a more general record as well. Furthermore, the investigator does not always know what problems are going to interest him particularly in the future, and if a random record is not kept as well, valuable information for future problems may not be forthcoming. A problem-oriented record is not as useful for a general survey of the characteristics of the culture for newcomers, either.

Ideally, the best solution is a non-complicated way of keeping a random record which can be expanded at any point where a particularly interesting or important problem comes to the attention of the investigator. In our Haitian example above, the information on the problem defined would be filed in the religion section of a file. The file would include information on all phases of Haitian life. This particular section, however, would have much fuller notes because it was a particular focus of attention for the investigator. The techniques of note-taking and record-keeping discussed here will be applicable to random records, problem-oriented records, or a combination of both.

Chronological vs. Topical Filing Systems

The easiest way to *take* notes is in sequence, as the information comes to the investigator. "Diary" or "chronological" notes have the additional advantage of helping to reconstruct the informant situation under which information was gained when discrepancies in information turn up. Earlier investigation, likewise, is more suspect than later, because the investigator has not yet built up the necessary background and may misinterpret what he is getting. For most reference purposes, however, chronological notes are relatively useless. The investigator has to read through pages or even whole notebooks to find a certain piece of information. A topical way of *keeping* notes is therefore essential.

A combination of both systems is perfectly possible, however, with almost no extra effort. The procedure outlined here will combine the two, but individuals can select ideas which seem pertinent to their own needs if this is more than they want.

The key to making both chronological and topical records lies in the use of carbon paper. We recommend that all notes be made in triplicate. The original is for the topical file, one carbon for the chronological file, and another carbon for a second chronological file to be mailed to some other place, preferably out of the country, at weekly intervals, or as a few pages of notes accumulate. If, through some disaster, either or both of the main files are lost, it will be possible to reconstruct them from the third copy.

The notes are dated and the pages numbered in chronological order. New pages are simply added to the chronological file as they are completed. The new pages are also slipped into the proper place in the topical file. This assumes, of course, that there is only one topic on a page. Where more than one topic is included, a cross reference to the page should be made at each relevant place in the file. For each of these cross-references a reference to the chronological file will quickly find the information. If experience shows that material is repeatedly being cross-referenced, additional carbons may be added instead, and the additional copies slipped into the file at the various topics covered.

Essential to a good topical file, and one that will not need constant revision and time-consuming re-sorting, is a comprehensive basic plan. We recommend that for a general culture file the investigator use the *Outline of Culture Materials* prepared for the Human Relations Area Files by George Peter Murdock and others.[2] The *Outline* divides cultural phenomena into some seventy

primary categories (with a few additional general categories). Each of these has from six to nine subdivisions, with further subdivisions under each. The topics are also extensively cross-referenced. Not all of the thousands of topics in the *Outline* will be relevant for even the most extensive set of notes for any culture. The primary divisions, most of the first subdivisions, and some of the smallest divisions will be useful for any complete general random file.

For a starter a selection from the primary divisions is enough. File dividers or folders[3] should be prepared for each of them. It is very important that these all have the tab in the same place, preferably at the left. Subheadings can then be inserted later when needed, as a volume of information in any primary section becomes too large for convenience. The subheadings would be entered on tabs in the second position from the left. When further subdivision becomes necessary in some of the sections these tabs would be in the third position, etc. The basic structure of the file is therefore immediately apparent at all times.

In a short time, therefore, the primary divisions of a topical file can be prepared, and the investigator is in business. As he makes notes they are simply slipped behind the proper heading, regardless of chronology or of subdivision. As he needs to make reference to a section, and finds material which is quite heterogeneous, subdivision for that section becomes in order, and a few minutes with the *Outline of Culture Materials* makes it possible to restore order to that section. Two files, one expanding chronologically, and the other topically, are all that an investigator

[2] *Behavior Science Outlines*, Vol. 1, Human Relations Area Files, 333 Cedar St., New Haven, Conn. 1950. 162 pages.

[3] Questions of size and format will be discussed below.

needs, and when done in this way are not impossibly time-consuming.

Note and File Format

A basic decision which has to be made at the beginning of any note-taking is the size of paper on which it is to be done. Several considerations enter into this decision. If, for example, the primary source of information is likely to be informant sessions, where extensive, leisurely notes are possible, standard 8½ x 11 (or the European equivalent) is the most practical. If notes are taken directly on the typewriter, as is ideal in an informant situation, this presents no problem in the use of carbons, and saves inserting sheets as often as would be necessary with a smaller format. Furthermore, when it is not possible to take notes by typewriter, carbons can be inserted between the pages of a spiral notebook of these same dimensions.

The greatest problems with this format lie in filing. Folders are virtually necessary if the sheets are to be filed full size. There is a lot of waste paper on many sheets as the investigator sees a new topic emerging and puts in another sheet to make filing by topic easier. Some investigators who use this size sheet for notes cut them in half for the topical file after the page is finished. In this way the half-sheets can be filed behind file dividers, and there is not as much waste. When a topic changes during note-taking, the typewriter is simply turned up to the bottom half of the page. Alternatively, a 5 x 8 format is the most useful. Its major disadvantage is in the more frequent insertion necessary if a typewriter is used.

No matter what the size paper decided on, it should be kept uniform as much as possible. This means that the investi-

gator gets in the habit of carrying his regulation-size paper with him all the time. For those times when he does not have it, however, and has to make notes on the back of an envelope or some other paper, he may either recopy (with full complement of carbons) or simply staple the odd-size paper to a regulation one, and insert it in the topical file, without benefit of chronological file, except perhaps by cross reference.

Every sheet of notes should contain the date, place, informant, and page number (of chronological file). This can be done quickly and easily, by code. For example, 2-2-60/LP/ST/230, which would mean, February 2, 1960, at Luang Prabang (Laos) with Siang Thii as informant and page 230 of the chronological notes. Investigators differ as to whether they double-space or single-space their typewritten material. A good left-hand margin, however, is very important, as there is often need to write in observations later.[4]

Information on More than One Culture

Many residents abroad find that they are confronted with more than one culture, or at least with more than one distinct sub-culture. It is not usually necessary to have a separate file for each. Usually the investigator will concentrate primarily on one of these groupings and his file will be based on that culture. However, under each heading there may be tabs of a different color for each different culture or sub-culture. In many cases a notation may read something like this: "Rice harvesting techniques identical

---

[4] If the original is not typewritten, later comments should be written in ink of a different color from the original.

with Khmu" (in which the Khmu is the culture to which primary attention is being given). On the other hand, in certain respects the cultures will be radically different, and the second culture will require full notes if it is to be recorded.

In most cases the resident abroad will concentrate on the one culture with which he has the most contact, not making any extensive or systematic investigation of the others. As cultural information about them comes to his attention, however, he would do well to record it.

Pictures and Recordings

Photographs and line drawings have long been essential to an anthropological record. Of these, the line drawing is often more essential than the photograph, even when the investigator is as abominable an artist as this writer. That is particularly true in dealing with the technological aspects of culture.

Notes should be made when a photograph is taken, or when a line drawing is made. The notes, together with the photograph or drawing should be included in the file. This is not possible when the photograph is a color slide, but in that case there should be a cross reference to the slide file.

A newer aid to record-keeping, and one which is proving increasingly more valuable, is the tape recorder. The tape recorder is particularly valuable when it is useful to have the full text of what the informant says or of some conversation, or ceremony, or speech, etc. An important point to remember, however, is that except for music, and for some language-learning purposes, a tape recording without a written transcription is not of any ultimate usefulness.

One way of handling this problem is to take notes on tape-recorded material and to incorporate those notes in the file, with a cross reference to the recording. When this is done, record should be kept of the place on the tape where the various items occur, to facilitate finding them. When secretarial help is available, it is very valuable to have actual transcriptions of much of the tape-recorded material. If no such assistance is available, only the most important items can receive such treatment, of course.

Using Sources of Information

A word concerning the sources of information which is filed is in order, although reference has already been made to some of them. The reading of published materials on the culture gains considerably in ultimate value if some notation of the material is kept, together with exact page references. In some cases the notation may be very brief if the published material will be readily available again. For example: "Long description of the functioning of the chief's authority in the village" (with full reference to book or article and pages). Magazines or newspapers which would otherwise be thrown away may be clipped and the article stapled to a piece of paper which is standard for the topical file. Or, if this is not convenient, there may be a separate clipping file with cross reference in the topical file.

Reading, and the filing of information gained through reading, can be done even before going to the area under study. Upon arrival, observation becomes possible, even without a knowledge of the language or an interpreter. Observation of interpersonal behavior, of skills and techniques. of reactions to emergencies, of formal and ceremonial situations should all be included in the record. There may be certain occasions in which on-the-spot note-taking is impossible or impolite or otherwise inadvisable. In such cases notes should be written up as soon as possible after the event. Some investigators reserve time each evening for writing up notes on the day's events and observations.

Observation and other sources of information to be mentioned below can be considerably sharpened for the inexperienced investigator by the use of a field manual called *Notes and Queries on Anthropology*.[5] Chapters of this book include such topics as Social Structure, Social Life of the Individual, Political Organization, Economics, Ritual and Belief, etc. In these chapters profitable avenues of investigation are suggested, and important clues to look for are indicated.

Direct interviewing, either with informants regularly used for the purpose, or with friends, or with -people encountered casually in the course of everyday life is a very major source of information. Probably in most cases the largest percentage of information filed will be from such sources. Here again note-taking is not always possible or wise outside of the formal informant situation, but notes should be made immediately after the interview, and checked as well as possible. Informants should represent people of various social strata, economic and occupational differences, the various religious groups, etc.

The three preceding sources of information are more or less self-evident, but there remains a fourth. This source, sometimes more difficult, not always possible to employ, is nevertheless the most penetrating and satisfying way of gaining information. It is participation in the life of the people. There is no better way to learn how a house is built than to build a house, and at the same time one learns about the structuring of leadership in work groups, about the techniques of handling tools, about taboos and tacit assumptions that run a wide gamut of life.

Participation in some phases of life is impossible, of course. It may be unacceptable to the people themselves. It may be physically impossible to the individual brought up in another culture. It may be beyond his skill. It may be ethically, or morally, or religiously impossible for him. However, the difficulties of participation are often exaggerated by the fear of trying something new, and participation, even on a limited scale, brings insight which is otherwise very difficult, if not impossible.

For the sensitive foreigner, and especially for the missionary, participation can have another by-product, as can the greater understanding arising from systematic investigation. This by-product is that all-important ingredient in communication: emotional identification. It cannot be emphasized enough that participation is not equivalent to identification.[6] Participation may be dry and mechanical. It may be crudely imitative, insensitive to the way in which it is interpreted by bona-fide members of the culture. As an

---

[5] Written by a committee of the Royal Anthropological Institute of Great Britain and Ireland, and published by Routledge and Kegan Paul, Broadway House, 68 Carter Lane, London.

[6] See William D. Reyburn, "Identification in the Missionary Task," Vol. 7, No. 1 (Jan.-Feb. 1960) pp. 1-15.

activity of a sensitive person, on the other hand, participation may be a road to that kind of rapport and empathy which makes genuine friends out of "informants" or "potential converts" or "church members."

As the habit of note-taking and filing develops, and a routine is established, it does not need to be a burden. On the contrary, it may be a stimulus to more fruitful life, as well as a helpful avenue to insight and understanding.

E. Thomas Brewster and Elizabeth S. Brewster

Involvement as a Means of Second Culture Learning

The effectiveness of a missionary depends to a large extent on his ability to communicate in the foreign language in a culturally relevant manner. The new candidate must realize the importance of simultaneously learning the new culture and the new language. This paper discusses the involvement of missionary language learners in the target community culture as a means of learning that culture. Although a good deal is known about how to train a person to perform the duties that may be expected of him abroad, there has been little systematic information about methods by which he could be prepared to cope with the extraordinary demands of a new culture. The suggestions in this paper which are intended to help meet this need, have been presented in terms of group activities in a language school. Most of the ideas could be readily used by the motivated individual as well.

As with many complex subjects, the subject of involvement for second culture learning has various dimensions, and could profitably be studied by focusing on any one. The focus could be on the culture itself—the content to be learned; it could be on the time dimension—what subjects and activities are most suitable for the student at each stage of his development; or it could be on the activities in which learning takes place. The focus of this paper is on the activities by means of which the student is introduced to and involved in the target community culture.

E. Thomas and Elizabeth S. Brewster are the directors of the newly incorporated Evangelical Language Institutes for Missionaries (ELIM). Mr. Brewster received his Ph. D. in education administration from the University of Arizona during the summer, 1971. Mrs. Brewster is a doctoral candidate at the University of Texas with major emphasis in foreign language teaching and linguistics. Both are staff members at the Toronto Institute of Linguistics where they have taught since 1968. Their permanent address is 915 W. Jackson Street, Colorado Springs, Colorado 80907.

Definition of Terms

Target Community: The community in which the learner plans to serve, or a community which is representative of that culture.

Culture: Nelson Brooks defined culture as the "sum of all the learned and shared elements that characterize a societal group."[1] He later elaborated on that definition by saying: "Culture is the way a given people think and believe and live, with special emphasis upon the link between the individual and the total group of which he is a part."[2]

Neo-domestic: An alien who understands and is sensitive to the target culture perspective and has at least partially adapted himself to it.[3]

The Importance of Involvement

Involvement is important as a means of making language learning more effective, and as a means of preparing the missionary for his role in the community.

The Importance of Involvement for Language Learning. Various authors have stated that language learning is most effectively carried out in conjunction with involvement in the target community. One reason is that immersion makes for authenticity in language learning.

Involvement in community life is important since it is that life which

gives the language its meaning. So then, in order "to comprehend a language fully, one must share in the culture of the people who speak it. Foreign languages are not alternative codes for the familiar American reality."[4]

Eugene Nida stated that involvement not only makes language learning effective, but that it is actually what makes true learning possible:

As long as we maintain a cultural isolation, we cannot expect to learn a foreign language... Linguistic training is of great help, but it is no substitute for cultural submersion...The problem is...one of cultural isolation, of learning a great deal about the language but not learning the language... Languages can and must be learned, ...but this cannot be done outside of the total framework of the culture, of which the language in question is an integral part.[5]

Eunice Pike adds that "part of learning to talk a second language is a sociological problem. In order to learn, you must be among those whom the people of that culture select for attention; that is, you have to be in focus."[6]

[1] Nelson Brooks, *Language and Language Learning* (New York: Harcourt Brace and World, 1960), p. 83.

[2] Nelson Brooks, "Teaching Culture Abroad," *Modern Language Journal*, Vol. 53, (May 1969), p. 322.

[3] Cf. Donald N. Larson and William A. Smalley, *Becoming Bilingual*, Chapter 4.

[4] Roger Brown et al., "Developing Cultural Understanding Through Foreign Language Study," *Publications of the Modern Language Association*, Vol. 67 (December 1953), p. 1214.

[5] Eugene Nida, *Customs and Cultures*, (New York: Harper & Row, 1954), p. 325.

[6] Eunice V. Pike, "Language Learning in Relation to Focus," *Language Learning*, Vol. 19 (June 1969), p. 107.

The Importance of Involvement for the Missionary. The missionary needs to be a learner before he can serve effectively. One of the essential things he needs to learn is the culture of the country so that he can make an effective contribution. Involvement in alien ways may be the most efficient device for building a bridge from one culture to another.

George Guthrie indicated that to help another person one must become involved with him in order to grasp something of his own view of his predicament. In working with the Peace Corps he observed that "Only as the Volunteer was able to see the world approximately as the Filipino saw it, would he be able to contribute in a truly effective, efficient manner."[7]

The missionary should feel that learning and serving are interrelated goals which need to complement each other. David Szanton stated that the emphasis should be "first on learning as a means of serving more effectively; and second on serving as a means of placing oneself in an appropriate social role where deep transcultural learning can readily take place."[8]

Goals of Involvement

Various authors have raised the question of whether cultural adaptation (also called second culture learning, bi-culturation, transculturation, domestication, dealienation) can be taught. "There is a...question whether good learners of a second culture are born or made."[9] The general consensus is that cultural adaptation cannot be taught but that it can be encouraged and stimulated. "Whether empathy can be taught is questionable, but it may be that, if dormant, it can be developed."[10] One can learn *about* cultural empathy but it has to be practiced by trial and error before it comes naturally.

The following are goals which the missionary should strive to meet if he would learn in depth the target culture. Whether or not he attains these goals depends to a large degree on how willing he is to accept these goals as valid for him. Many missionaries may have no difficulty accepting the cognitive and performance goals, but some will have strong reservations about the validity of some of the affective goals. A language school can involve the learner in many activities in the life of a community, but in the final analysis it is the missionary's attitude which determines whether or not he will learn the culture and adapt to it.

Cognitive Goals. The missionary needs to acquire at least a limited

---

[7] George M. Guthrie, "Cultural Preparation for the Philippines," in Robert B. Textor (ed.), *Cultural Frontiers of the Peace Corps* (Cambridge: MIT Press, 1966), p. 24.

[8] David L. Szanton, "Cultural Confrontation in the Philippines," in Textor (ed.), *Ibid.*, p. 56.

[9] George M. Guthrie, "Preparing Americans for Participation in Another Culture," a paper presented to the Conference on Peace Corps and the Behavioral Sciences, Washington D.C., March 1963, p. 27.

[10] J.C. Catford, "Learning a Language in the Field: Problems in Linguistic Relativity," *Modern Language Journal,* Vol. 53 (May 1969), p. 316.

knowledge of the geographical, economic, and political aspects of a society, from a historical and contemporary point of view, so that he can understand the framework in which the culture functions.

He needs to know about the social institutions of the culture. This would include topics such as the religious system, the pattern of family life, the status hierarchies and the educational systems.

He needs to learn about the patterns of interpersonal relationships among the nationals, and what roles foreigners are allowed to play in the community.

He needs to learn about the value systems and reasoning processes of the members of that culture.

He needs to acquire an objective cultural framework—an understanding of the nature of culture itself.

He needs to acquire a conscious knowledge about his home culture and its value systems. He must be aware of his own values and beliefs "if he really wishes to understand what is going on in his communication with foreign peoples, or to recognize the basis on which he makes his interpretations and judgments of what he sees and experiences abroad."[11]

An understanding of one's own culture and institutions is a prerequisite to cultural empathy... The overseas American needs to study the several versions of the American dream... He may thereby learn to refrain from the quite unsporting and unproductive pastime so commonly indulged in by Americans abroad of comparing the American Dream to the foreign reality.[12]

Performance Goals. The missionary needs to be able to perform the daily social amenities such as greetings, apologies and other social forms without hesitation or self-consciousness. The skill needs to be an automatic response to the situation.

He needs to learn the acceptable techniques for handling interpersonal relationships, and especially those for handling inevitable interpersonal difficulties.

He needs to acquire the skills appropriate to the role he is to play, in order to participate as an effective member of the community. A language school cannot help each student acquire all the necessary skills, but it can help him to learn how to recognize what skills he needs and how to learn these cultural skills on his own.

Affective Goals. The missionary must develop an empathy for, and an acceptance of, individual members of the target culture. He should understand that there are differences between himself and members of the target community culture, but that those differences do not imply that

---

11 *When Americans Live Abroad*, (Foreign Service Institute, Department of State, 1965, Publication 7869), p. 6.

12 Harlan Cleveland, *et al.*, *The Overseas Americans* (New York: McGraw-Hill, 1960), p. 300.

one is better or worse than another—just different.

The missionary needs to develop an acceptance of the value systems of the target culture. "Acceptance", however, need not be equated with "agreement" or "approval."

He needs to be willing to adjust to the patterns of daily living in the target culture.

The ultimate goal is that the missionary will come to see life and circumstances as the members of the culture view them, and be willing to adjust his behavior accordingly. This does not mean that he will lose the ability or freedom to see life from his native point of view but rather that he will acquire the ability to see life through two sets of eyes and to behave in a manner consistent with the two cultures.

Methodology for Involvement

The cultural involvement activities should be an adjunct to the program of language learning and should be carried out in conjunction with that program. It is to be hoped that the two components could be well coordinated so that conversation classes could drill the structures of the language while discussing the current topic of the culture component, and so that the dialogues would reinforce the culture component.

The culture component should be planned and executed by a team consisting of members of the target culture as well as neo-domestics with skills in linguistics, education, psychology and anthropology. Together they should come to an understanding of the culture themes to be stressed and the programs necessary to accomplish these aims.

The Peace Corps training program for the Philippines found that it was: ...desirable to have nationals participate in every aspect of the program where the host country was in any way considered. They can help the trainee see how nationals perceive their own situation. The trainee will begin to see some of the nuances of the patterns of reasoning of his hosts and he will learn how to discuss with his hosts some of the troublesome and perplexing aspects of the society of which he will shortly be a part... The Filipinos could supply the anecdotal material to illustrate principles and were able to show the trainee that Filipinos were concerned in their own way with many of the matters which attracted the attention of Americans.[13]

In general, the culture component would best involve small classes of six to ten students, though sometimes two or more classes could be combined for an activity where active participation by each member was not necessary (such as listening to a preparatory lecture).

The missionary language learner is hereafter referred to as "student",

---

[13] Guthrie, *Preparing Americans... op. cit.*, p. 21.

since the new missionary candidate should devote his full creative energy to the role of student during his year of language and culture study.

Preparation of the Student for Involvement. The preparation of the student involves two phases. The first is an initial orientation which takes place during the first few days after he arrives at the school. During this time the student is introduced to the goals of the program, to some basic concepts about culture in general, and to the basic social amenities necessary for even the most casual social contacts.

To illustrate the importance of acquiring a knowledge of social practices immediately upon entering a new culture, Louise Winfield relates two anecdotes.

He needs to learn just as quickly as he can what the polite practices are in the country to which he goes so that from the beginning it will be obvious that he wants to behave respectfully in relation to the people of the new country... A woman who returned recently from a Muslim community said, "Why didn't someone tell me that it is rude to pass food or to offer gifts with the left hand?" She had been doing this for months before some one explained to her that the hand which is used to take care of personal body functions is never used, in the place where she was living, to offer things to other people.

We cannot assume that gestures, for instance, imply the same thing to people in foreign countries as they do at home. American men...frequently approach one another with a hearty slap on the back to indicate friendliness and informality. In places where the Chinese culture is dominant such an approach may have exactly the opposite effect. A turtle has a back. A turtle crawls on the ground as the lowliest of creatures. To call attention to a man's back is to imply that he is like an animal of the dust... "Why didn't somebody tell me?" a good hearted American said one day in Formosa when it finally had been brought to his attention that he was known as the "insulting American."[14]

In addition to the initial orientation, the student needs to be prepared before each involvement activity so that he knows what to focus on, and so that he understands the background of the event and how it fits in with what he has already experienced.

1. Roleplaying. In the early stages of learning, roleplaying can be used effectively to drill social amenities before going to a social event. The students need to know not only the words of the greeting formula, for example, but also the gestures which accompany it and the occasions when it is appropriate. The students can act out roles depicting various situations such

---

[14] Louise Winfield, *Living Overseas* (Washington, D.C.: Public Affairs Press, 1962).

as a formal dinner party and a casual greeting on the street, and roles depicting interaction on various levels such as greeting children and greeting superiors, so that they get a feel for the range of acceptable behaviors in the greetings,

2. *Lectures.* If the involvement activity is to be a field trip to a historic site or to some institution, a national who is an expert on the topic can be invited to lecture on the historical background of the area to be visited, and on its current importance to the community. During the early stages these lectures will likely be limited to English, but gradually lectures can be introduced in the target language.

3. *Required Reading.* In the orientation stage the student should be encouraged to read books such as *The Silent Language,*[15] *Traditional Cultures,*[16] *Becoming Bilingual,*[17] and *When Americans Live Abroad,*[18] in order to acquire a general knowledge about culture and culture adaptation.

Later, the readings should be specifically related to activity which is to follow. Sometimes each student in a class can read about a different phase of the same topic (e.g., the historical, economic, and political aspects of a current event) and then share formally or informally what he has learned.

[15] Edward T. Hall, *The Silent Language* (New York: Doubleday & Co., 1959).

[16] G.M. Foster, *Traditional Cultures and the Impact of Technological Change* (New York: Harper, 1962).

[17] Larson and Smalley, *op. cit.*

[18] *When Americans...op. cit.*

4. *Discussions.* Often an activity can best be preceded by a discussion session in which students share what they have been reading in preparation for the event, and what they have learned in other ways, and in which they can also ask questions about their role in the activity. The discussion could be led by a member of the target community or by a panel of nationals and neo-domestics.

Activities for Involvement. Nearly any activity in which the learner is in contact with members of the target community can be a means of learning about the culture. The school should encourage the learner to become as actively engaged in the culture as possible, and should be careful to allow him ample time to do so.

1. *Bringing the Community to Students.* In the early stages, it may often be desirable to bring members of the community to the school. Community members could be brought there for formal discussions, for informal conversations, or even for parties. By choosing to invite community people who are understanding of the problems of the learner and patiently tolerant of his language and social mistakes, the school can help to ensure that the students' first contact with the community is favorable.

Sometimes it might be more convenient to bring the community to the students, rather than vice versa, even at a later stage. It may be easier, for example, to bring to the school a woman to demonstrate how to make tortillas, rather than trying to fit a whole class of students into her small kitchen.

2. *Class Field Trips.* Often the whole class can arrange to take a field trip to a nearby place of interest such as a museum, a historical site, a religious shrine, archeological ruins, an art exhibit, a folk dance, a business office, an institution, a police station, etc. The number of places which can be visited is limited only by the interest of the group, the amount of time available for field trips, and the imagination of the planners.

Sometimes the field trips could involve an overnight or week-end trip to another town. (Such class trips might be optional, while the shorter trips would be part of the regular required activities.) Such a trip might involve acquainting the students with a local mode of transportation, as well as focusing on a particular activity at the destination. Students should be encouraged to use their own automobiles at little as possible during their time of study since a car tends to isolate the occupants from their surroundings.

3. *Assigned Activities for Individuals.* Not all students will share the same interests, and for this reason it is a good idea to allow time for activities of individual interest. This is especially true toward the end of the program of study, when students might want to specialize on topics which would be directly applicable to their role in the community. Thus, for example, a nurse might want to study the role and activity of the public health nurses

in the community and could be encouraged to join them in their rounds on a Saturday and discuss with them the needs and problems of nursing in the community. On the other hand, a music teacher might be more interested in attending the local symphony productions and talking with local musicians, and learning about folk music of the area.

The individual activities should be chosen by the student, but would not be optional. They should be considered by the student to be a part of his learning activities.

4. *Activities of Daily Living.* Daily contact with members of the culture is the most effective way to come to an understanding of the patterns of family living and of interpersonal relationships acceptable to the culture.

Students should be encouraged (or perhaps even required) to live in the home of a member of the community as a guest for a period of time. The time might be most convenient near the middle of the program of study, at a point where the student had acquired enough fluency in the language to feel comfortable in informal situations, and before he began his period of specialization, so that he could be most free to participate in the normal family activities. A family home stay could be the most rewarding involvement activity. It should be continued beyond the point where the host family feels it has to be unnaturally polite to a short-term visitor.

In addition to living with a national family, the student should be encouraged to spend as much free time as possible with members of the community on a friend-to-friend basis. Often it is especially rewarding to spend time around families with young children. Children usually have the time and inclination to talk to an adult who wants to chat, and they are often more frank in pointing out his mistakes than an adult would be. Also, the student can learn from the corrections which the parents make of their children's grammar and manners. Thus, for example, a parent might be very explicit in showing a young child the proper way to use his eating utensils, and the learner can take that as an opportunity to unobtrusively learn the culturally appropriate eating habits.

The student should be encouraged to seek maximal cultural exposure and participation in his activities of daily living. For example, he can be encouraged to shop in the local market. When he goes for a walk he can use the opportunity to practice receiving directions from strangers (during the beginning stages of language study he should concentrate on asking directions to places he is already familiar with so that he can concentrate on listening without being nervous about getting lost) — as soon as one stranger is out of sight he can ask another person the same question, until he feels comfortable with the polite formulas for asking and receiving information.

Skill in cultural activities, like skill in language, requires practice and drill, and the more imaginative the student is in finding ways to practice what he is learning the more efficient and enjoyable his learning will be.

5. *Extracurricular Activities.* The school should encourage the student to take advantage of all opportunities to learn about the culture and participate in the life of the community. In order to do this, the school needs to be aware of the events in which he can participate (on an optional basis) if he is interested. There should be a bulletin board where there can be posted schedules and announcements of concerts of various musical groups (classical to popular), of fairs, public lectures given by nationals on topics of interest to the students (given a large enough student body, almost any topic will be of interest to at least one person), special holiday celebrations, religious observances, parades, etc.

Follow-up of Involvement Activities. Almost every scheduled activity, and many extracurricular activities should be concluded with some form of follow-up activity so that the student has an opportunity for synthesis and understanding, and for tying up any loose ends.

Generalizations can be helpful at this point, whether generalizations formed by the students or given by a discussion leader; but the generalizations should be carefully stated so that they are not overgeneralizations.

I think it is a point of agreement among humanists as well as social scientists that we should demand the verifiable sort of generalizations wherever the nature of the data permits. A verifiable statement about a small part of a foreign population, such as that people of the middle class within given regions at a given period of time, behave thus and so, is far more valuable than the unverifiable, sweeping generalizations one usually hears. It is necessary therefore to recognize regional and socioeconomic subcultures and also age levels and religious or ethnic groups within a culture. These we need to keep in mind in order not to overgeneralize.[19]

Another form of synthesis would be to seek for a functional explanation of the aspect of culture being studied: What function does this custom serve? What needs does it meet in relation to the target culture? How does this custom establish new needs and affect other customs? The search for a rationale can make the student's observations meaningful and useful.

1. Discussions. One of the more effective activities for follow-up might be an informal discussion in which the students can describe what they experienced and see if their interpretation of the event conforms to the way in which it was interpreted by members of the culture.

We know from a good many experiments in psychology that an individual tends to impose meaning on almost anything he sees. In doing so he calls on his previous experience. Faced by a different culture, he is likely to impose meaning on his observations rather than to feel that he does not understand... The presence and participation of host country nationals (in discussions) enables the volunteers to see how these aspects of the nation are seen by those most intimately involved.[20]

Sometimes it might be helpful to have an enculturated neo-domestic lead a discussion in order to help the students see how to adjust to a stressful situation, or to help the students see an event in the target culture in relation to some familiar custom from his own culture which might be superficially similar but fundamentally very dissimilar.

Discussion time can also be an occasion for the students to inquire about the proper social formula to use in an unfamiliar situation which was encountered in the activity.

2. Written and Oral Reports. When there have been assigned activities for individuals, it is a good idea to have them report in some way what they have learned. This allows them to analyze their experience and to share their newfound knowledge with the other class members. The focus, however, should not be on the report as an end in itself, but rather on the experiences which are being reported.

19 Howard L. Nostrand, "Describing and Teaching the Sociocultural Context of a Foreign Language and Literature," in Albert Valdman (ed.), *Trends in Language Teaching* (New York: McGraw-Hill, 1966), p. 15.

20 Guthrie, *Preparing Americans .... op. cit.,* pp. 19, 21.

3. Roleplaying. After an activity involving interpersonal relationships with members of the community it may often be helpful during the early stage of study to engage in roleplaying on the situations which students found stressful or awkward in the activity, or in which a student committed a *faux pas.* This roleplaying could be both follow-up of the previous activity and preparatory to a similar activity to be carried out in the near future.

If, for example, the leader noticed that one of the students had committed a social error in the activity and then didn't know how to apologize, the leader might show the class one or more accepted apology formulas and direct roleplaying situations in which these should be used. In Spanish there are two apology forms—"con su permiso" and "perdóname" – which foreigners often have trouble knowing when to use. The former is generally used before an act such as walking in front of someone, while the latter is used to ask for pardon for an act already committed. Roleplaying could be used to help the students learn to make the correct automatic response.

In summary, follow-up activities help to avoid the two major errors which aliens make when confronted with a new cultural event:

1) concentrating on the quaint, alien surface patterns of a foreign culture (decidedly viewed from the outside). This we might call the *corrida de torros* or "tourist" attitude; 2) refusing altogether (and this refusal may be just below the threshold of consciousness) to comprehend the alien structures, resorting to a process of learning disconnected or erroneously integrated facts. (The amount of such learning is irrelevant.) This is the "Soviet Studies" attitude.[21]

Building on the Foundation. The student should be made aware of the fact that, no matter how long his training program, the school cannot teach him all there is to know about the target culture–it can only lay a foundation on which the student can build as he serves in the community after he graduates. The various involvement activities engaged in, as well as their preparation and follow-up, are tools which the learner can continue to use in culture exploration after graduation. In addition, he can heed the following suggestions given by Virginia Allen:

> Try to establish contact with people in different age groups... preferably people from small towns,
>
> Get to know people who are considered conservative by their own fellow citizens...,
>
> From these people find out what games children and others play, songs most people know, legends, stories and rhymes children grow up with, books everyone can remember having read, proverbs most people recall,

---

21 Michel Beaujour, "Teaching 'Culture' in NDEA Foreign Language Institutes," *Modern Language Journal*, Vol. 46 (November 1962), p. 309.

Learn from these people what forms of behavior are approved and disapproved of; learn the forms of reward and punishment that are meted out; discover how to write socially approved invitations, letters of sympathy, etc., and

Read and discuss with adults various pieces of contemporary fiction, samples of humor, editorials in newspapers...

Also, on your own,

Read books on child care that parents in your host country read,

Read history books designed for elementary school pupils...,

Read etiquette books intended for adolescents,

Follow soap operas on radio and TV, and

Attend church services, school ceremonies, sporting events.[22]

Guthrie suggested that each person, even after his formal training, consider himself a learner and choose a particular aspect of the culture to study actively after training.

It was our prediction that the adoption of a learner's role would enhance the Peace Corps Volunteer's acceptance by Filipinos and give added meaning to his experience which would sustain him when other sources of satisfaction had failed. We encouraged each volunteer to...

take steps to utilize it for a program of observation and note taking which would contribute to his long-range goals. We urged each volunteer to select some phase of the Philippines, the music,...child rearing practices, almost anything for his own area of concentration. We were convinced that gathering information on and being well informed about some phase of the Philippines would serve as a sort of knothole through which one could observe much of the society. From their letters we gather that at least a few of the volunteers have found this to be the case.[23]

The missionary will study the religious aspect of the culture in order to perform the basic requirements of his work. However, he will find many doors open to him if he is able to converse intelligently with nationals about local politics, geography, history, or any of numerous other aspects of the culture.

Problems in Involvement

Such close relationships between the foreign students and the community are bound to cause friction. Both the students and the community will feel the tension created by the conflict between the two cultures. The school needs to be sensitive to the problems and to seek to act as a "shock absorber" as much as possible.

22 Virginia Allen, "Understanding the Cultural Context," *Modern Language Journal*, Vol. 53 (May 1969), p. 326,

23 Guthrie, "Preparing Americans..." *op. cit.*, p. 18.

The Problems of Culture Shock and Culture Fatigue. Culture shock is a "somewhat psychotic state that people get into when they are in a cultural situation whose cues are misleading because they have learned either responses that are wrong for the cues or no responses at all."[24] It has been described as a "kind of vertigo such as one has never experienced before. One blames one's glasses. What is really changing are the glasses through which one's mind has looked at the world."[25]

While culture shock seems to be an experience common to nearly all people who become involved in a foreign culture, it is well to note that there are degrees of shock:

> We should note that a shock may be gentle, or harsh, or lethal. In the same way, cultural shock may amuse, enlighten, overwhelm, and even destroy... (It) is a function of the "self vs. life" encounter. It is a circumstance in which life demands a conformity that the self cannot supply without a jolt and a loss of poise that leads to bewilderment and even injury.[26]

1. Common Symptoms of Culture Shock. One of the principal symptoms is rejection of the target community, coupled with a protective isolation from that community into a "Little America." "They would band together, going impressive distances to meet with their own kind on weekends. Here they would swap experiences and reactions and withdraw from the African reality to the remembrance of a near Utopian America."[27]

Others go to the opposite extreme and reject their home country, and try to "go native." Cleveland calls them the "snugglers";

> Those Americans who feel that the way to overcome culture shock is to forget America and melt into a new, adopted nationality and culture... In India there are Americans who profess an exaggerated admiration for everything Indian;... Their homes take on a native air, they lose no occasion to compare American culture unfavorably with the Indian... The snugglers want, quite simply, to belong. They are prepared to pay what they think is the price of belonging–the rejection of their own background as Americans. When they find that they cannot "pass" as Japanese, Indians or Arabs, when they realize they will always be outside looking in, the snugglers may neurotically turn their wrath and resentment on the foreigners who won't permit an American to escape his Americanness.[28]

Some missionaries reject the sending agency who "got them into this·

24 Nostrand, *op. cit.,* p. 6.

25 Carmen J. Nine, "Experiences in Culture Shock," *Modern Language Journal,* Vol. 51 (Feb. 1967), p. 89.

26 Brooks, "Teaching Culture Abroad...." *op. cit.,* p. 321.

27 Textor, *op. cit.,* p. 183.

28 Cleveland *et al., op. cit.,* pp. 28,29.

mess," or their colleagues. Those who "go native" tend to reject their colleagues who haven't done so, and those who refrain from going native tend to reject their colleagues who have done so.

Another common symptom of culture shock seen in students under the combined strain of cultural adjustment and language learning is the tendency to reject or at least lash out at the language school and its program which "forces" them to study and to participate in stressful target community involvement activities.

Some people respond to culture shock by rejecting themselves. The person feels that he is a failure and "blames himself for every mistake and feels utterly defeated when he is not an instaneous success in everything that he tries. His problem may be compounded by the fact that he feels guilty about feelings of rejection and hostility in any direction."[29]

Another symptom of culture shock is a homesickness which attaches excessive significance to symbols relating to the life left behind. For example, Americans commonly glamorize symbols such as the American flag, a "good ole hamburger," ice cream cones, apple pie, or a baseball game.

One symptom that is especially common among women is an excessive concern over germs and illnesses, coupled with an insistence on European or American trained doctors whenever an illness does take place. "Despite

the dysentery, the gastronomic risks, and the dilemmas of diplomacy, the general experience overseas is that very little time is lost through illness. What bothers the overseas wife is less the reality than the threat of health trouble, the dread of 'what would happen if...' "[30]

Another symptom which affects women quite commonly is an excessive concern for their children's well-being, and a desire that the children not play with the target community children.

2. *Culture Fatigue.* Culture shock, intense as it may be for a time, is rarely the major problem, for "shock passes quickly, even culture shock. But stress lingers, gnawing and sapping one's strength and often going unnoticed from one day to the next."[31] This stress, called culture fatigue or culture stress, is the "physical and emotional exhaustion that almost invariably results from the infinite series of minute adjustments required for long-term survival in an alien culture"[32]

Frustration leads to symptoms of culture shock. When such frustration is delayed, and endures over a longer period, it leads to culture fatigue. "The cumulative effect of many anomalies and stresses produces not a sense of shock but of emotional fatigue."[33]

Culture stress develops not only as a response to frustration, but also be-

29 William A. Smalley, ''Culture Shock, Language Shock, and the Shock of Self-Discovery,'' PA, Vol. 10 (March-April 1963), p. 52.

30 Cleveland, *et al.*, *op. cit.*, p. 51.

31 Larson and Smalley, *op. cit.*, p. 5.

32 Szanton, *op. cit.*, p. 43.

33 Lawrence H. Fuchs, *Those Peculiar Americans* (New York: Meredith Press, 1967), p. 111.

cause of a feeling of aloneness. In his own culture and society the missionary belonged to many different groups (family, work, social, church, civic) which he expressed as "we" in his daily conversation. But when he moves to another culture and society, he "lives as an 'I' in a community of 'they's' for a length of time." If this isolation is prolonged, culture fatigue occurs.[34]

Fuchs describes the major factor in culture fatigue as being "loneliness in the face of pervasive cultural differences".[35]

The symptoms of culture stress include those of culture shock as well as a feeling of physical and emotional fatigue. "The various symptoms which may follow are as varied and as insidious as those one might develop at home under conditions of chronic stress."[36]

It has been hypothesized that the degree of culture shock which an individual might experience is directly related to the degree of difference between his home culture and the target culture, while the degree of cultural stress might be inversely related to that same difference.[37] A person going into a radically different culture is bombarded immediately with a sense of the strangeness of everything and with his own disorientation to the situation, and is, therefore, apt to experience a great degree of culture shock; but as he learns the appropriate responses and finds the people to be predictable within their own system, the shock lessens and he is able to cope with life in the community. On the other hand, a person who enters a country where the culture is very westernized (and perhaps the language is English) may not experience very much culture shock at all—he thinks that he can interpret life there as he did at home. But gradually he finds that his interpretations of the interpersonal cues and value systems are not the same as those of the target community, and this conflict causes stress, especially if that person is not able to recognize the overt differences between the cultures, and insists on treating other people in the target community as he would treat his fellow country men. Guthrie found that Americans developed more severe manifestations of culture fatigue in the Philippines, where the language and culture are at least superficially similar to those of America, than they did in other Asian countries such as Japan or Thailand where the cultural differences were more consciously recognized from the beginning.[38]

3. *Therapy for Culture Shock and Fatigue.* William Smalley stated that one of the important steps in getting over culture shock and stress lies in discovering oneself.

---

[34] Donald N. Larson, lecture presented at the Toronto Institute of Linguistics, June 1969.

[35] Fuchs, *op. cit.*, p. 111.

[36] George M. Guthrie, "Psychological Preparation for Service in the Philippines," Mimeographed paper, p. 2.

[37] Cf. Textor. *op. cit.*, p. 306; Guthrie, "Preparing Americans...." *op. cit.*, p. 15.

[38] Guthrie, *Ibid.*, p. 15.

The shock of self-discovery is sometimes a large part of culture shock, but when it is, it can be the beginning of healing... Sometimes the person suffering from culture shock discovers his own emotional insecurity. He finds himself behaving childishly over traffic patterns, giving vent to temper tantrums over bugs or dirt, projecting his problems upon others, and as he discovers himself he can learn to approach his problem more rationally, to attack his difficulties more systematically, and to resume a healthy outlook on his situation.[39]

No training program can keep a student from experiencing culture shock or culture fatigue, but it can help him to develop the tools and attitudes necessary for cultural and self-understanding which will help him overcome the stress. A training program can also help the student become aware of the mechanisms operating in culture fatigue so that he can understand what is happening to himself and to his peers when the experience comes.

Problems in Community-School Relationships. In order for the students to be involved in the life of the community there has to be a certain amount of openness and acceptance on the part of the community toward the school and toward the students in particular. Developing and conserving this openness in the community is a vital task of the school staff.

[39] Smalley, *op. cit.*, p. 55.

1. Problems Associated with "Ugly Americans." One of the activities indulged in by many people who are experiencing culture shock or fatigue is that of criticizing the target culture and community. The school needs to keep a good relationship with the community so that if a student becomes aggressively critical, the community will recognize that these attitudes are individual ones, and are not representative of the feelings of the school personnel. When a student is experiencing culture shock the school personnel need to be especially sensitive to his needs, but at the same time they need to be able to steer him into activities where he has contact with only the more tolerant members of the community and where he will not have intensive contact with community people who might be more easily offended by his attitudes and his lack of cultural sensitivity. The school also should encourage the student to learn how to withhold strong negative criticism (especially that directed toward members of the target community) for a time until he is able to see things in perspective.

The Peace Corps experienced this difficulty when volunteers

Openly expressed their negative, fatigued feelings to Filipinos, perhaps as the result of advice received from some of the Representatives that they ought to "act naturally—be yourself"... All in all, it seems likely that many Filipinos must have suffered considerably at the hands of Volunteers. Fortunately, however, most of them understood that the PCVs were in the throes of an "adjustment problem," and were therefore patient. Another factor that sometimes protected the feelings of the Filipinos was the simple fact that they, lacking familiarity with American cultural and linguistic cues, frequently missed the full import of the Americans'comments, especially when expressed as sarcasm.[40]

While the community may be able to sense that a person is having an "adjustment problem" this does not necessarily mean that it will continue to respond tolerantly toward him. "If you are frustrated and have aggressive attitudes to the people of the host country, they will sense this hostility and in many cases respond in either a hostile manner or try to avoid you. In other words, their response moves from a preliminary phase of ingratiation to aggressive ridicule and on to avoidance."[41]

2. *Problems Associated with "Provincialism."* Sometimes it is the community which rejects the students (and all other foreigners) because of a natural shyness toward outsiders or even because the community is experiencing a form of culture shock because of the presence of these members of an alien culture (even though the aliens have been acceptant of them).

One way to help open the community to the students is to invite members of the community to the school for various community activities, rather than emphasizing the involvement of the student in the active life of the community, until the community opens of its own accord. As individuals from the community become acquainted with individual students, the community people will soon begin inviting students to community activities and thus gradually the door will open for all the students.[42]

On other occasions, the opening of the community to the students might be accomplished by the exemplary actions of those students who are living in homes of community members. Robert Mead found that the American teachers who lived in Mexican homes during a summer NDEA Institute were instrumental in opening the community toward Americans in general.

Time after time I was...gratified to observe how even families, some of whose members were hostile to the U.S., gradually came round to a more favorable view of us after several weeks of life with two of our high school Spanish teachers as guests in their homes. In fact, this improvement in their image of us was the leit-motiv of the majority of my conversations with the families who housed our teachers, in my talks with local officials who came in con-

---

[40] Szanton, *op. cit.*, p. 51.

[41] Kalavero Oberg, "Culture Shock, Adjustment to New Cultural Environments," *PA*, Vol. 7 (July 1960), p. 180.

[42] Eugene Savaiano, "Wichita State University's Involvement in the NDEA Instituted Program," *Hispania*, Vol. 52 (Sept. 1969), p. 379.

tact with the institute, and with local university students who served as informants, group leaders, etc., for the institute.[43]

Conclusion

Second culture learning is not something which can be accomplished in a school. It is an on-going process which is never totally complete. The school should emphasize that it is seeking to give the student the tools which he can use to help him adapt to and learn the target culture. This learning begins in school, but should continue throughout the time that the individual lives in that culture.

The new missionary who would learn a second culture must cast himself in the role of the learner and be willing to accept the inevitability of mistakess, and be willing to learn from these mistakes. "What appears to be needed is humility about one's own social competence and enough self-confidence to keep trying."[44]

At this point, it would appear that training in this domain can help a person develop an attitude of curiosity about the

society, suggest some technique by which the curiosity can be satisfied, and offer some principles which may help the Volunteer make sense of what he encounters.[45]

Finally, this is a struggle that is never won.

Learning must continue throughout one's stay abroad. An inquiring attitude, constantly seeking the meaning of the unfamiliar, an attitude which also looks inward is probably the best defense against the withdrawal or the irritation which follows unsuccessful contact with the new society. It is in the emotional domain in which lie some of the greatest hazards of living in another society, and it is there also that one can discover its greatest rewards.[46]

A constant attitude of cultural sensitivity is an important basis for an effective and rewarding ministry. The ideas for cultural involvement presented in this paper should be helpful for the missionary, not only during his time of language study, but also throughout his years of living in the target culture.

---

43 Robert Mead, "Second-Level Spanish Institutes in Latin America under the NDEA," *Hispania*, Vol. 46 (March 1963), p. 107.

44 Guthrie, "Psychological Preparation..." *op. cit.*, p. 6.

45 *Ibid.*, p. 13.

46 *Ibid.*, p. 15.

William L. Wonderly

Social Anthropology, Christian Missions, and the Indians of Latin America

Mexico has been in the vanguard, among the nations of the American continent, with respect to the application of the principles of social anthropology in the secular fields to the problems of indigenous or Indian groups. The present article attempts to summarize for English readers some of the major bases of this movement as it is being carried forward by Mexican social anthropologists of today. It then points out certain of the principles of the movement which are of special significance for the work of Christian missions among the Indian groups of Latin America, and certain points at which the movement, due to its commitment to a secular approach, needs to be supplemented by the development of a parallel Christian movement by groups who can come to closer grips with the specifically religious anxieties of the Indian peoples.

ONE of the outstanding names among the indigenistas[1] of Mexico is that of Dr. Alfonso Caso, director since 1949 of the Instituto Nacional Indigenista and a distinguished scholar in Middle American archaeology, anthropology, and other fields. His recent book (in Spanish) entitled Indigenismo[2] is a collection of

twenty articles and lectures, mostly published elsewhere, which have the purpose that is stated on the back cover: that of "explaining, in the simplest possible terms, the theory upon which the indigenista action in Mexico is based and the results which have been obtained from it."[3]

In the first chapter of the book,[4] Caso attempts to define who and what are to be considered as Indian. He uses a com-

[1] The Spanish term indigenismo is frequently translated as "Indianism" and indigenista as "Indianist" or "Indian." These translations, however, seem to be quite inept, inasmuch as the English words are not normally used in the same sense as the Spanish terms. Dr. Gonzalo Aguirre Beltrán, in his significant treatment of "Indigenismo y mestizaje" (Cuadernos Americanos 15.4, July-August 1956, pp. 35-51), uses indigenismo in contrast with indianismo, which further complicates the translational difficulties. In the present article we shall regretfully use the terms indigenismo and indigenista in their Spanish form, without attempting an English equivalent.

[2] Alfonso Caso, Indigenismo. Instituto Nacional Indigenista, México, D. F., 1958. Pp. 159; 19 plates. 12.00 Pesos Mex.

[3] All quotations from Caso's book in this article are our own translation. A number in parentheses following the quotation will identify the page in the original.

[4] The book itself, consisting as it does of separate materials published elsewhere, has a great deal of repetition; many of the chapters or articles develop in brief and interesting fashion an overall view of indigenismo or of certain of its aspects, but the progression from chapter to chapter is not worked out as it would be if the book had been written as a unit. Hence our presentation will not follow the order of the book's contents, but will attempt to give the materials in a somewhat rearranged form for the sake of continuity.

bination of four criteria: biological, cultural, linguistic, and psychological. The first three are objective and accessible to the outsider; the fourth, the sense of belonging to an Indian community, is subjective and less amenable to outside investigation, but is the most important from the Indian's own point of view. Caso's primary definition is therefore a definition of the INDIAN COMMUNITY; his definition of the individual Indian is in relation to that community. We give the following translation of his definition:

An Indian is a person who feels that he belongs to an Indian community; and an Indian community is one in which non-European somatic elements predominate, which speaks and prefers an Indian language, which has a large proportion of Indian elements in its material and spiritual culture and, lastly, which possesses a social feeling of being an isolated community among the other communities that surround it, resulting in its considering itself as different from both white and mestizo[5] peoples (pp. 15-16).

Caso insists that the Indian problem be recognized for what it is, and reminds us of the cultural isolation of the Indian groups, especially those who are monolingual:

The Indian problem is for Mexico a fundamental one, since 1 inhabitant out of 5 is Indian as to his culture and way of life, 3 out of 20 speak Indian languages, and 1 out of 13 speaks only an Indian language[6] and

therefore lives outside the culture of Mexico and the Mexican community (21).

The orientation with respect to the Indian community as a whole rather than the individual alone is an important principle, which is discussed again and again in the book. But just as the individual is not to be considered apart from his community, so the Indian community needs to be treated as part of a larger context, the INDIAN REGION, which includes both the Indian communities and the mestizo town or city with which these are in a symbiotic relationship.

...We now speak not merely of Indian communities, but of INDIAN REGIONS; that is, of more or less extensive regions that are characterized by being made up of numerous Indian or Indian-mestizo communities which depend economically, culturally, socially and politically upon a mestizo city, which we call the METROPOLIS of the Indian region in question.

This is the case, for example, with Tlaxiaco, in relation to the surrounding region of the High Mixteco, in the State of Oaxaca; and with San Cristóbal Las Casas and the Tzeltal-Tzotzil region in the State of Chiapas. . . .

On the other hand, the Indian communities themselves have a decided influence upon the METROPOLIS, giving it a character which distinguishes it from other mestizo cities of the country. Thus there is an interaction from every point of view. We may say that the METROPOLIS of a region would be unable to live without its surrounding communities, from which it gets raw materials for its sustenance, for its commerce, and for its local industries (usually carried on by small artisans); and

---

5 Since the Spanish word *mestizo* has already crept into our English language and dictionaries, we use it. It should be kept in mind that it means "mixed," and is used to refer to the mixture of Indian and Spanish in both the biological and the cultural sense.

6 On page 52 he says that 1 out of 20 speaks an Indian language only.

that the Indian communities themselves would be unable to live without the METROPOLIS, where they must go to exchange their surplus domestic produce for objects which they do not themselves produce but which they consume ... (76-77).

The character of the metropolis, or mestizo center of an Indian region, is thus influenced by its long and intimate contact with the Indian communities, who have contributed to the mestizo population many aspects of their world view, religious outlook, folk medicine, and so on; and whom the mestizos have at the same time looked upon as an inferior group that is to be exploited for their benefit. Hence any valid approach to the Indian community must also take the mestizo center into active consideration.

Cultural Equilibrium and Acculturation

In a chapter on "Culture and Acculturation," Caso defines culture in the anthropological sense, discusses the various categories of material and spiritual culture, explains acculturation as meaning the transformation of a backward community through contact with the dominant cultural group. He points out that in this transformation the social anthropologist should be called upon to help plan and direct the acculturation process so as to avoid the disorganization of the weaker community and its exploitation by the stronger community.

He insists upon the INTEGRAL CHARACTER and the EQUILIBRIUM of the Indian culture, and the importance of an overall approach to the guidance of the acculturation process.

We consider it to be impossible to transform a community if only one of the aspects of its life is changed; for we believe that the Indian communities have their own culture, and that every culture is an equilibrium in which one cannot change a given aspect without the other, unchanged, aspects of culture feeling the effect of the action on the one hand, and on the other hand acting as a brake to retard the proposed change. One cannot, for example, change the economy of a community without taking into account its taboos, its ideas of social prestige, and the ways by which it incorporates its children into the community. For this reason the policy which the Instituto Nacional Indigenista has chosen to follow is what may be called an INTEGRAL POLICY — that is, we study and modify the economic aspect and the social organization, and endeavor to accelerate, through public health, education and road construction, the incorporation of the community into the political and cultural life of the nation (65-66).

As we shall discuss below, however, one of the most important of the aspects which serve to integrate an Indian culture is the religious aspect; and it is difficult for us to agree that any approach to acculturation can, in the full sense of the word, be termed an "integral" policy so long as it concerns itself with the transformation of communities "in their economic, hygienic, educational, and political aspects" (35) but does not squarely face the full religious implications of these aspects of the culture change. This statement is not intended as a negative criticism of the indigenista movement, but rather as an indication of wherein lie some of its limitations.

Protection and Help, not Charity

On the matter of official Indian policy, Caso emphasizes time and again the need and justification for protective laws for the benefit of the Indian, rather than simply considering him as having equal rights with others and as being capable of defending these rights. Just as minors, women, and the physically handicapped are possessed of certain biological limitations which prevent them from holding their own as equals with the rest of the population, so the Indian is socially handicapped and needs the protection of special laws. He is the equal of any other member of the human family as far as his racial heritage goes, but is in a position of real inferiority socially, culturally, and economically; therefore to make him the object of supposedly equal treatment for all men is to take an unrealistic attitude toward him and to actually make him the victim of discrimination. Hence the need for protection and aid, not merely for theoretical equality before the law.

But Caso insists that such protective laws, and Indian policies in general, should not be such as to keep the Indian in a perpetual state of inferiority, but that "the Indian communities should be given all the hygienic and cultural elements necessary to speed up their transformation and to bring them into step with the progress of the rest of the communities in the country" (40). In other words, the Indian communities are not to be helped or protected as if they were indigent groups in need of charity, but are to be given such technical aid as will enable them to become true participants in the culture of the nation.

The Indian is to be helped by giving him education as to hygiene, medicine, agricultural techniques, etc.; he is to be given means of communication so as to market his products; he is to be given opportunity, through radio, moving pictures, and other media, to realize that

he is part of a larger world and is no longer isolated. But all this must be done in a way that will avoid such a conflict between the Indian culture and modern culture as would disrupt the Indian culture.

For these reasons, any government action undertaken to better the condition of the Indians of our countries should be based on recommendations made by anthropologists; inasmuch as it is impossible to change one aspect of a culture without at the same time producing an impact upon all other aspects. One cannot, for example, change the economy of a community without at the same time affecting the family and social organization, the attitude of the individual toward his family and his community, and even his concept of life itself (54).

Among the positive values of the Indian culture that are to be conserved wherever possible, special mention is made of the Indian's sense of community solidarity and of responsibility for mutual help within his group, which is a feature that can be a valuable contribution to the national life as the Indian communities become interrelated with it. Emphasis is also placed upon the artistic sense of many of the Indian groups, and the popular art that is produced by them and which should be encouraged. Four chapters of the book are devoted to various aspects of popular art in Mexico, with special reference to the Indian's contribution to it and to ways of protecting and encouraging it.

The Indigenista Movement in Mexico

In one of the chapters, Caso points out that the "social transformation that is taking place in Mexico today, ... starting with the Revolution which began in 1910, has manifested itself in every sphere: economic, political, social and cultural" (85). He then relates to this historical development the "experiment in social anthropology" (85) that is being conducted by the Instituto Nacional Indigenista, which was established in 1948 and which has been carrying out extensive pilot projects in five regions (the Tzeltal-Tzotzil, Mazateco, Tarahumara, and two Mixteco regions). In these projects, three basic policies are observed (90): use of demonstration rather than compulsion; enlistment of the cooperation of at least part of the community prior to carrying out any action; and the use of bilingual Indians as employees and PROMOTERS to carry the action to the people and to promote cultural change.

The projects of the Institute include the promotion of economic change through securing of land, teaching of new agricultural techniques, use of better seed, crop rotation, forest conservation and use, establishment of cooperative stores, etc. They include work in public health and hygiene, and in literacy and the teaching of Spanish. With reference to religion, the approach is definitely secular; Caso indicates the policy toward religion when that it is preferable

... not to persecute the individual who makes offerings to the gods of the mountains or to the saints so that it may rain and so he may cultivate his maize, but to construct dams and irrigation ditches which will make constant watering possible, as a better way than that of prayers and offerings (81).

These various activities are directed toward the region as a whole and the culture as a whole:

The mission undertaken by the Institute is regional and integral. It is regional because it attacks not just the problems of one community, but extends to the problems of an entire region that shares a language and other cultural features, and includes in its radius of action the mestizo city as well, which we call the METROPOLIS of the region. ... Our action is integral because it has to do with all the aspects of the culture of the community (90).

... The clear and definite purpose that we have undertaken is that of accelerating the development of the Indian community so as to integrate it as early as possible with the economic, cultural and political life of Mexico, but without producing disorganization in the community itself. That is, our purpose is to speed up the change, which is inevitable anyway, that will lead to the transformation of the Indian community into a Mexican peasant community, and of the Indian region into a Mexican region with all the characteristics of the other regions of the country. Of course this does not mean an attempt to destroy the positive aspects that remain in the Indian cultures, such as the solidarity of the Indian with respect to his community, the use of certain regional costumes, the production of artistic objects, etc.; ... but it is useless to conserve outmoded ideas regarding the causes of natural phenomena and the means of utilizing the forces of nature; it is both useless and injurious to conserve the old ideas of the causes and cures of sickness, or to perpetuate backward and unscientific techniques of exploiting land and forest resources, of animal husbandry, etc. (77-78).

Use of Indian Languages in Education

With reference to the use of the Indian languages in the program of the Institute, Caso writes, without much elaboration:

In matters of education, our Indian promoters teach the children to read in their own language, as a step toward teaching them to speak, read, and write in Spanish (92).

This of course follows the pedagogical principle of beginning with the known before proceeding to the unknown; i.e. the learner is taught to read in a language that he already knows, and then his knowledge of reading helps him to go on to the learning of Spanish.

However, in the program of most *indigenistas* the teaching to read in the Indian language appears to be thought of as almost solely for this purpose of bridging the gap to Spanish. Very little basic education seems to be carried on in the Indian languages; as soon as the pupil learns to read his own language and then to read Spanish, he is expected to acquire the rest of his education in Spanish. This of course appears in keeping with the overall goal of bringing the Indian into effective contact with the cultural life of the nation, whose chief linguistic vehicle is Spanish. Yet there are two major difficulties which we may mention here, that are not discussed by Caso. (1) The Indian who learns to read Spanish at this early stage is unable to read it with comprehension unless he is already highly bilingual; reading in Spanish therefore becomes a feat whereby the Indian acquires a bit of added prestige, but does not become a tool whereby he can acquire significant information. (2) Even for the bilingual Indian who does learn to read with comprehension, reading materials in the type of Spanish with which he is familiar are sadly lacking. Very few Indians who are literate in Spanish continue as readers after they leave school.

Without belittling the importance of the use of Spanish, it would seem that somewhat more of the basic education program should be carried on in the Indian language, as soon as the initial hurdle of learning to read in the language is passed. By so doing, reading can immediately become a means of acquiring information, thus making it an activity which is satisfying and relevant to life. And the basic information thus acquired should lead to an earlier participation of the Indian in at least certain aspects of the national culture. In terms of the work of Christian missions, it is of course especially important that the message be communicated in a form that will be intelligible to individuals within their linguistic background as well as their cultural background.

Significance of Indigenismo for Christian Missions

Many aspects of the *indigenista* movement are highly significant in relation to the development of evangelical Christianity among the Indians of Latin America. In a country where there exists this movement to effectively relate the Indian communities to the life of the nation, an obvious corollary is the responsibility for the churches and missions to relate the evangelical Indian congregations to the life of the evangelical church in its national character. If this is not done, the Indian may upon conversion end up as culturally isolated both from his community and from the nation. But just as in all other aspects of the culture the integration process needs to be carried forward, as Caso emphasizes, without disruption of the existing cultural pattern and loss of the positive values in the Indian cultures, so also in the church this integration needs to be accomplished without the cultural disorganization that will result if the Indian congregations are forced into the Procrustean mold of outward conformity to mestizo church patterns.

A significant experiment in integration is now being conducted among the Chol Indian churches of the National Presbyterian Church of Mexico, in which the Chiapas Presbytery has formed a "Chol Institute of Coordination," whereby the elders of the organized Chol churches compose a body authorized to discuss and decide on problems of local nature which do not involve the Presbytery as a whole. For example, cases have arisen regarding marriage of two people who although unrelated have the same surname — a matter that would hardly even be recognized as a problem if brought before the mestizo Presbytery, but which is a very real problem for Indians who carry this prohibition over from an earlier practice of clan exogamy. The Indian coordinating group may also handle problems of how to dispose of the maize received in the harvest offerings, or of how to carry on Christmas and Easter celebrations in a way which, while Christian, will still meet the cultural needs formerly met by semi-pagan *fiestas*. Although it is still too early to evaluate the success of this experiment, this kind of an attempt, within the organizational structure of a national church organization, to provide a way for Indian groups to work out their own special problems would seem to be highly significant.

Caso's concept of the Indian region as a whole, with its mestizo center, has implications that are of great importance for the development of the church in such regions. The writer of the present article spent a number of years in the mestizo-Indian town which serves as a center for part of the Zoque region in Chiapas. He now feels, in retrospect, that one basic reason why no effective evangelical witness resulted from his work there, either among Indians or mestizos, is that almost all his efforts were directed toward the Indian people in isolation. He failed to realize the importance of the interrelationship between the Indian and mestizo people, to whom the former look for much of their leadership and who are the ones through whom the Indians expect cultural innovations to enter the region. (In support of this thesis, it may be said that during the same period the Seventh Day Adventists were successfully developing a work which did include the region as a whole, beginning with Spanish-speaking nuclei and embracing both mestizos and Indians indiscriminately).

The recognition of the Indian community as forming part of the larger mestizo-Indian region has a significant bearing upon the missionary's concept of the indigenous church. Most Indian groups are at some stage or other in the process of becoming peasant groups — i.e. they are no longer primitives living in complete cultural isolation, but are people who, although they conserve basically their own way of life, exist against a background of the mestizo culture and the urban way of life that they know exists "out there." They recognize the outside culture as having certain values to which either they or their children should aspire, and they seek to find points of contact between their own group and the mestizo group. To the degree to which this is true for a given community, the indigenous church goal should not be an isolated Indian church. If the church in an Indian community is to be really indigenous (that is, if it is to truly "belong" in the community), it should in such cases function against a background of the evangelical church in its national character to a degree comparable to that in which the community in general functions against the background of the national scene as a whole. This of course does not mean absorption of the Indian church by the national church to the point that the former loses its identity; but it does mean that the Indian church should be so organized as to be constructively related to the national church. To effect such a relationship will not always be the easiest way of organizing a church; it may involve tensions and problems of leadership personnel and of organizational patterns. But it is important that such problems be faced realistically and not with what Caso terms an "erroneous attitude [of] a false and romantic *indigenismo* [which] considers that it is best to leave the Indians alone and isolated" (100).

A further significance of Caso's concept of the Indian region with its mestizo center is that the evangelical church in the center needs an educational program that will help its own constituency to understand the problems of the Indian churches in the region. The church in the center needs to cease thinking of Indians as second-class brethren and learn to appreciate the Indian culture and the positive .values it can bring to the church as a whole. It then needs to seek ways in which it can help in integrating the Indian churches with the national church life, while at the same time maintaining the cultural integrity of the Indian groups and giving them the effective content of the gospel message by using, wherever necessary, the native language for the proclamation and teaching of the Christian message. No project of Christian work among an Indian group can be

said to have been adequately undertaken until these aspects of the problems are squarely faced.

There also exists a need for communicating these concepts to the wider protestant constituency in Latin America, and especially to the leaders of the evangelical movement who are responsible for guiding the development of the national churches in their relationships with the Indian groups. Caso's book itself sets an instructive example of a scholar's endeavors, through lectures and journal and magazine articles, to "sell" the generally educated public on the importance of an anthropological approach and to communicate to them something of its basic principles. Similar efforts need to be made to communicate, to the general protestant constituency, the basic principles of social anthropology as applied from a Christian standpoint to the problems of the Indian groups.

Need for a Christian Indigenismo

As mentioned earlier, *indigenismo* as it is being developed at present in Mexico is committed to a secular approach. This is in part due to the ideologies of the men who are developing it, and is justifiable on the official level because the organizations concerned are connected with a government which, under its national constitution, does not and cannot maintain any connection with religious organizations or movements. But whatever may be the reasons and justification for a secular approach, the fact remains that the Indian outlook on life is not secular but religious. Agriculture, medicine, social organization — all are permeated with religious attitudes; and any attempt to guide acculturation without taking these into consideration is seriously hampered from the outset. It is hardly accurate to say that such an effort "has to do with all the aspects of the culture of the community" (90).

Furthermore, religion is one of the major stabilizing factors in the maintenance of a cultural equilibrium and of the integral quality of an Indian culture. Granted that our western culture, toward which acculturation is directed, is highly secularized; but the Mexican peasant way of life toward which the Indian groups are actually moving is much less secularized than is our urban culture. The Indian in process of culture change needs, perhaps more than ever before, a faith which will enable him to meet the changing situation and around which he can build his new way of life without the moral chaos and social disintegration that can result if he loses faith in his old beliefs but remains unable to cope with the new anxieties that accompany what we call civilization.

Of course we are not hereby suggesting that the government-sponsored agencies, which in Mexico and some other Latin-American countries, even as in the U.S.A., are committed to separation of church and state, try to direct the religious acculturation of the Indian communities. What we are trying to say is (1) that there does exist a process of religious acculturation which, due to the very cultural equilibrium that Caso mentions, inevitably accompanies the changes that take place in other aspects of the culture; (2) that if left unattended this process may lead to loss of confidence in the old values and failure to discover new ones; and (3) that in order to avoid this creation of a moral and religious vacuum it is important that other agencies, which are specifically committed to a religious approach, develop an *indigenismo* that can supplement in a positive way what is

being done in the secular field. Such a Christian *indigenismo* need not be in competition with the secular agencies, nor should it get involved politically. Its purpose should be to make the Biblical message relevant in terms of the changing Indian culture, and thereby to give a spiritual basis to the new way of life that the older religion, geared as it is to the older technologies and forms of social organization, is incapable of giving.[7]

A Christian *indigenismo* will seek to discover those aspects of the Biblical message which most directly relate to the anxieties of the Indian group and to the tensions that are created by the process of change. It will endeavor to find the most effective ways of communicating this message, whether by the use of the Indian language or by the cultivation of Christian practices to replace pagan ones; and in either case it will be concerned to put into the message such content as will be meaningful in terms of the cultural situation.

This orientation in Christian work will

[7] Manning Nash (*Machine Age Maya: The Industrialization of a Guatemalan Community; American Anthropologist Memoir* 87, 1958) found that in the industrialization of a Quiché Indian community the people have compartmentalized their thinking, maintaining their older religious practices (with some modification) with respect to their agriculture and family life but not effectively relating their religion to their factory experiences or their labor union organizations. He suggests that the basic religious attitudes have been left unchanged by the advent of the textile factory, but thinks the lack of change may be at least partly because the factory is institutionalized and beyond the immediate control of the Indian, who works as an employee but bears no responsibility for the management of the industry. Hence the situation described by Nash is not entirely parallel to the introduction of modern technologies into the average Indian community.

also give due recognition to the fact that, in many of the Indian groups, the younger generation's ambitions and outlook upon life are no longer limited to the horizons known to their elders. The recognition of this fact will call for the preparation of Christian Indian leaders who not only are oriented toward the Indian cultural background but who are also equipped to face those aspects of the modern world that are even now affecting the life of the young people in their churches. This ability of the Christian leaders to face both ways, as it were, is an especially important qualification in situations where a church has become established and the children of the originally converted group are growing up as "second-generation Christians."

Although there is still much to be desired and much left to accomplish, we believe Caso to be correct when he affirms that "Mexico can be justly cited as the country that has made the greatest effort to solve its Indian problem" (21). But the very fact that this is true in the secular sphere makes it incumbent upon the churches of Mexico to bring their own country's progress to bear upon the problems of the Indian groups for whose spiritual welfare they are responsible, and thereby to help in the establishment of patterns for church development among Indians elsewhere in Latin America as well. In other Latin American countries there is also progress in *indigenismo,* and in each situation the churches and missionary organizations should recognize their responsibility (1) to relate these developments to the growth of the Indian churches and the meaningful proclamation of the Biblical message and (2) to help the Indian groups maintain, in the face of cultural change, a sense of direction and spiritual stability which is necessarily outside the domain of the secular *indigenista* movement, due to the very nature of the latter.[8]

8 Since this paper was written, there has come to the writer's attention a brief but informative report in English on the work of the Instituto Nacional Indigenista, in the following two articles: Alfonso Caso, "Ideals of an Action Program," *Human Organization* 17, Spring 1958, pp. 27-29; and Julio de la Fuente, "Results of an Action Program," ibid., pp. 30-33.

ABOUT THE EDITOR

William A. Smalley is at present a research consultant for the United Bible Societies, studying problems of translation, the linguistic structure of discourse, and related questions. For many years he was a translation consultant in Southeast Asia, and still undertakes some responsibilities for training translators in Asia from time to time. Dr. Smalley is the author of several books and articles, and has edited several volumes, largely in the fields of linguistics, translation, and cultural anthropology as applied to the communication of the Christian faith. For several years he was editor of *Practical Anthropology,* a periodical designed to make the insights of the social sciences of use to people involved in cross-cultural communication.

BOOKS BY THE
WILLIAM CAREY LIBRARY

GENERAL

American Missions in Bicentennial Perspective edited by R. Pierce Beaver, $8.95 paper, 448 pp.

The Birth of Missions in America by Charles L. Chaney, $7.95 paper, 352 pp.

Education of Missionaries' Children: The Neglected Dimension of World Mission by D. Bruce Lockerbie, $1.95 paper, 76 pp.

Evangelicals Face the Future edited by Donald E. Hoke, $6.95 paper, 184 pp.

The Holdeman People: The Church in Christ, Mennonite, 1859-1969 by Clarence Hiebert, $17.95 cloth, 688 pp.

On the Move with the Master: A Daily Devotional Guide on World Mission by Duain W. Vierow, $4.95 paper, 176 pp.

The Radical Nature of Christianity: Church Growth Eyes Look at the Supernatural Mission of the Christian and the Church by Waldo J. Werning (Mandate Press), $5.85 paper, 224 pp.

Social Action vs. Evangelism: An Essay on the Contemporary Crisis by William J. Richardson, $1.95x paper, 64 pp.

STRATEGY OF MISSION

Church Growth and Christian Mission by Donald A. McGavran, $4.95x paper, 256 pp.

Church Growth and Group Conversion by Donald A. McGavran et al., $2.45 paper, 128 pp.

Committed Communities: Fresh Streams for World Missions by Charles J. Mellis, $3.95 paper, 160 pp.

The Conciliar-Evangelical Debate: The Crucial Documents, 1964-1976 edited by Donald McGavran, $8.95 paper, 400 pp.

Crucial Dimensions in World Evangelization edited by Arthur F. Glasser et al., $7.95x paper, 480 pp.

Evangelical Missions Tomorrow edited by Wade T. Coggins and Edwin L. Frizen, Jr., $5.95 paper, 208 pp.

Everything You Need to Grow a Messianic Synagogue by Phillip E. Goble, $2.45 paper, 176 pp.

Here's How: Health Education by Extension by Ronald and Edith Seaton, $3.45 paper, 144 pp.

The Indigenous Church and the Missionary by Melvin L. Hodges, $2.95 paper, 108 pp.

A Manual for Church Growth Surveys by Ebbie C. Smith, $3.95 paper, 144 pp.

Mission: A Practical Approach to Church-Sponsored Mission Work by Daniel C. Hardin, $4.95x paper, 264 pp.

Readings in Third World Missions: A Collection of Essential Documents edited by Marlin L. Nelson, $6.95x paper, 304 pp.

AREA AND CASE STUDIES

Aspects of Pacific Ethnohistory by Alan R. Tippett, $3.95 paper, 216 pp.

A Century of Growth: The Kachin Baptist Church of Burma by Herman Tegenfeldt, $9.95 cloth, 540 pp.

Christian Mission to Muslims - The Record: Anglican and Reformed Approaches in India and the Near East, 1800-1938 by Lyle L. Vander Werff, $8.95 paper, 384 pp.

Church Growth in Burundi by Donald Hohensee, $4.95 paper, 160 pp.

Church Growth in Japan by Tetsunao Yamamori, $4.95 paper, 184 pp.

Church Planting in Uganda: A Comparative Study by Gailyn Van Rheenen, $4.95 paper, 192 pp.

Circle of Harmony: A Case Study in Popular Japanese Buddhism by Kenneth J. Dale, $4.95 paper, 238 pp.

The Deep-Sea Canoe: The Story of Third World Missionaries in the South Pacific by Alan R. Tippett, $3.45x paper, 144 pp.

Frontier Peoples of Central Nigeria and a Strategy for Outreach by Gerald O. Swank, $5.95 paper, 192 pp.

The Growth Crisis in the American Church: A Presbyterian Case Study by Foster H. Shannon, $4.95 paper, 176 pp.

The How and Why of Third World Missions: An Asian Case Study by Marlin L. Nelson, $6.95 paper, 256 pp.

I Will Build My Church: Ten Case Studies of Church Growth in Taiwan edited by Allen J. Swanson, $4.95 paper, 177 pp.

Indonesian Revival: Why Two Million Came to Christ by Avery T. Willis, Jr., $5.95-paper, 288 pp.

Industrialization: Brazil's Catalyst for Church Growth by C.W. Gates, $1.95 paper, 96 pp.

The Navajos Are Coming to Jesus by Thomas Dolaghan and David Scates, $5.95 paper, 192 pp.

New Move Forward in Europe: Growth Patterns of German-Speaking Baptists by William L. Wagner, $8.95 paper, 368 pp.

People Movements in the Punjab by Margaret and Frederick Stock, $8.95 paper, 388 pp.

Profile for Victory: New Proposals for Missions in Zambia by Max Ward Randall, $3.95 cloth, 224 pp.

The Protestant Movement in Bolivia by C. Peter Wagner, $3.95 paper, 264 pp.

Protestants in Modern Spain: The Struggle for Religious Pluralism by Dale G. Vought, $3.45 paper, 168 pp.

The Religious Dimension in Hispanic Los Angeles by Clifton L. Holland, $9.95 paper, 550 pp.

The Role of the Faith Mission: A Brazilian Case Study by Fred Edwards, $3.45 paper, 176 pp.

La Serpiente y la Paloma (La Iglesia Apostolica de la Fe en Jesuchristo de Mexico) by Manual J. Gaxiola, $2.95 paper, 194 pp.

Solomon Islands Christianity: A Study in Growth and Obstruction by Alan R. Tippett, $5.95x paper, 432 pp.

Taiwan: Mainline Versus Independent Church Growth by Allen J. Swanson, $3.95 paper, 300 pp.

Tonga Christianity by Stanford Shewmaker, $3.45 paper, 164 pp.

Toward Continuous Mission: Strategizing for the Evangelization of Bolivia by W. Douglas Smith, $4.95 paper, 208 pp.

Treasure Island: Church Growth Among Taiwan's Urban Minnan Chinese by Robert J. Bolton, $6.95 paper, 416 pp.

Understanding Latin Americans by Eugene A. Nida, $3.95 paper, 176 pp.

A Yankee Reformer in Chile: The Life and Works of David Trumbull by Irven Paul, $3.95 paper, 172 pp.

APPLIED ANTHROPOLOGY

Becoming Bilingual: A Guide to Language Learning by Donald Larson and William A. Smalley, $5.95x paper, 426 pp.

Christopaganism or Indigenous Christianity? edited by Tetsunao Yamamori and Charles R. Taber, $5.95 paper, 242 pp.

The Church and Cultures: Applied Anthropology for the Religious Worker by Louis J. Luzbetak, $5.95x paper, 448 pp.

Culture and Human Values: Christian Intervention in Anthropological Perspective (writings of Jacob Loewen) edited by William A. Smalley, $5.95x paper, 466 pp.

Customs and Cultures: Anthropology for Christian Missions by Eugene A. Nida, $3.95 paper, 322 pp.

Manual of Articulatory Phonetics by William A. Smalley, $5.95x paper, 522 pp.

Message and Mission: The Communication of the Christian Faith by Eugene A. Nida, $3.95x paper, 254 pp.

Tips on Taping: Language Recording in the Social Sciences by Wayne and Lonna Dickerson, $4.95x paper, 208 pp.

THEOLOGICAL EDUCATION BY EXTENSION

Principios del Crecimiento de la Iglesia by Wayne C. Weld and Donald A. McGavran, $3.95 paper, 448 pp.

The World Directory of Theological Education by Extension by Wayne C. Weld, $5.95x paper, 416 pp., *1976 Supplement only*, $1.95x, 64 pp.

Writing for Theological Education by Extension by Lois McKinney, $1.45x paper, 64 pp.

REFERENCE

An American Directory of Schools and Colleges Offering Missionary Courses edited by Glenn Schwartz, $5.95x paper, 266 pp.

Bibliography for Cross-Cultural Workers, edited by Alan R. Tippett, $4.95 paper, 256 pp.

Church Growth Bulletin, Second Consolidated Volume (Sept. 1969-July 1975) edited by Donald McGavran, $7.95x paper, 512 pp.

Evangelical Missions Quarterly Vols. 7-9, $8.95x cloth, 330 pp.

The Means of World Evangelization: Missiological Education at the Fuller School of World Mission edited by Alvin Martin, $9.95 paper, 544 pp.

Protestantism in Latin America: A Bibliographical Guide edited by John H. Sinclair, $8.95x paper, 448 pp.

The World Directory of Mission-Related Educational Institutions edited by Ted Ward and Raymond Buker, Sr., $19.95x cloth, 906 pp.

POPULARIZING MISSION

Defeat of the Bird God by C. Peter Wagner, $4.95 paper, 256 pp.

The Night Cometh: Two Wealthy Evangelicals Face the Nation by Rebecca J. Winter, $2.95 paper, 96 pp.

The Task Before Us (audiovisual) by the Navigators, $29.95, 137 slides

The 25 Unbelievable Years: 1945-1969 by Ralph D. Winter, $2.95 paper, 128 pp.

The Word-Carrying Giant: The Growth of the American Bible Society by Creighton Lacy, $5.95 paper, 320 pp.

BOOKLETS

The Grounds for a New Thrust in World Mission by Ralph D. Winter, $.75 booklet, 32 pp.

The New Macedonia: A Revolutionary New Era in Missions Begins (Lausanne paper and address) by Ralph D. Winter, $ .75 booklet, 32 pp.

1980 and That Certain Elite by Ralph D. Winter, $ .35x booklet, 16 pp.

Penetrating the Last Frontiers by Ralph D. Winter, $1.00 booklet, 32 pp.

The Two Structures of God's Redemptive Mission by Ralph D. Winter, $ .35 booklet, 16 pp.

The World Christian Movement: 1950-1975 by Ralph D. Winter, $ .75 booklet, 32 pp.

HOW TO ORDER

Send orders directly to William Carey Library, 1705 N. Sierra Bonita Avenue, Pasadena, California 91104 (USA). Please allow four to six weeks for delivery in the U.S.

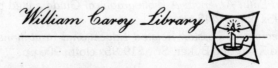